Biological Anthropology

The Natural History of Humankind

SECOND EDITION

Craig Stanford
University of Southern California

John S. Allen
University of Southern California

Susan C. Antón
New York University

Upper Saddle River, New Jersey 07458

Library of Congress Cataloging-in-Publication Data

Stanford, Craig B. (Craig Britton), 1956–
  Biological anthropology : the natural history of humankind / Craig Stanford, John S. Allen,
Susan C. Antón. — 2nd ed.
    p. cm.
  ISBN 978-0-13-601160-6 (alk. paper)
  1. Physical anthropology—Textbooks. I. Allen, John S. (John Scott), 1961– II. Antón, Susan C.
III. Title.
  GN25.S73 2009
  599.9—dc22

                                                            2007052429

Editorial Director: Leah Jewell
Director of Marketing: Brandy Dawson
AVP, Publisher: Nancy Roberts
AVP, Editor-in-Chief of Development: Rochelle Diogenes
Development Editor: Carolyn Viola-John
Senior Operations Supervisor: Sherry Lewis
Operations Specialist: Ben Smith
Marketing Manager: Lindsey Prudhomme
Full-Service Project Management: Sandra Reinhard
    and Katrina Ostler, Black Dot Group
Production Liaison: Cheryl Keenan
Editorial Assistant: Lee Peterson
Marketing Assistant: Jessica Muraviov
Senior Art Director: Nancy Wells
Art Director/Interior and Cover Design: Ilze Lemesis

Line Art Illustrations: Maria Piper
Scientific Illustrations: Precision Graphics
Director, Image Resource Center: Melinda Patelli
Manager, Rights and Permissions: Zina Arabia
Manager, Visual Research: Beth Brenzel
Manager, Cover Visual Research and Permissions:
    Karen Sanatar
Image Permission Coordinator: Debbie Latronica
Photo Researcher: David A. Tietz
Front Cover Art: Anup Shah/Nature Picture Library
Back Cover Art: Craig Stanford
Director, Media and Assessment: Shannon Gattens
Supplements Editor and Pegasus Progam Manager:
    Mayda Bosco

This book was set in 10.5/12 Sabon by Black Dot Group and was printed and bound
by Courier Kendallville. The cover was printed by Phoenix Color Corp.

For permission to use copyrighted material, grateful acknowledgment is made to the copyright
holders listed on page 587, which is considered an extension of this copyright page.

Pearson Education LTD.
Pearson Education Singapore, Pte. Ltd
Pearson Education, Canada, Ltd
Pearson Education–Japan
Pearson Education Australia PTY, Limited

Pearson Education North Asia Ltd
Pearson Educación de Mexico, S.A. de C.V
Pearson Education Malaysia, Pte. Ltd
Pearson Education, Upper Saddle River, New Jersey

10 9 8 7 6 5 4 3 2 1

ISBN-13: 978-0-13-601160-6

ISBN-10: 0-13-601160-8

*We dedicate this book
to the memory of
F. Clark Howell
(1925–2007)
who fostered an
interdisciplinary and
integrative vision of
Biological Anthropology*

BRIEF CONTENTS

CONTENTS

PART I   Mechanisms of Evolution

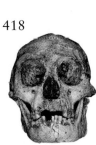
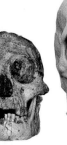

PART V New Frontiers in Biological Anthropology

CHAPTER 15
Evolution of the Brain and Language   436

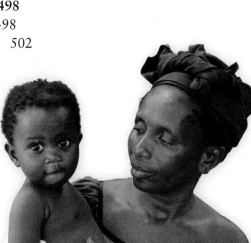

We are proud to introduce you to the second edition of *Biological Anthropology: the Natural History of Humankind*. After teaching biological anthropology for nearly 20 years, we felt there was a great need for a new textbook that introduced students to the evolutionary biology of humankind. Decades ago the field of physical anthropology was mainly about human anatomy, human fossils, and the study of racial variation. Over the past 30 years, the field has evolved from physical anthropology into biological anthropology. Now biological anthropology is an integrative combination of information from the fossil record and the human skeleton, the genetics of individuals and populations, our primate relatives, human adaptation, and human behavior, among other topics. The first edition of our text, published in 2005, was very well received, and the fast pace of change in biological anthropology has led to this new, updated edition. The second edition combines updated, comprehensive coverage of the material that any traditional biological anthropology text explains, with a modern biological approach that includes fields that have become major areas of research by biological anthropologists. Though comprehensive, the book is written as accessibly as possible to be useful to students from community college to research-oriented university levels. We authors conduct our research in three of the main areas of biological anthropology: the human fossil record (Susan Antón), primate behavior and ecology (Craig Stanford), and human biology and the brain (John Allen). This has allowed us to provide a specialist approach to each of the broad areas of biological anthropology that the text covers.

Undergraduate enrollment in introductory biological anthropology courses has increased sharply as biological anthropology has become one way to fulfill the basic natural science requirement at many colleges and universities. We believe the changing field and the new audience have created a need for a text such as this one, integrating traditional physical anthropology with a modern Darwinian framework.

We authors are anthropologists with extensive backgrounds in both biological and social sciences who both teach and conduct research. In a field changing as rapidly as human evolutionary science is today, we feel it is critical for active researchers to produce textbooks that portray recent advances in the field and serve the needs of students. In addition to the strong biological orientation of the book, we try to frame questions about humankind in light of our understanding of culture and the ways in which culture interacts with biology to create the template for human nature.

In a field famous for intellectual disagreements over the meaning of fossils or interpretations of Darwinian theory, we feel it is essential to provide students with well-rounded views of the evidence. There are places where, because of the introductory nature of the text, we have not delved deeply into the details of some debates, but we have nevertheless tried to balance multiple views of ongoing unresolved questions.

Foundation: Organization of the Text

The book is organized in much the same way that we three authors have taught introductory courses in biological anthropology. Although we have different backgrounds within the discipline, we share the common intellectual thread that is also the heart and soul of biological anthropology: the theory of evolution by natural selection. This is the unifying aspect of each chapter, and indeed for the entire discipline. The new Introduction and Part I, Mechanisms of Evolution (Chapters 1 through 5) reflect this. The text begins with an overview of the field of biological anthropology in the larger context of the social and life sciences, including a brief history of the field. Chapter 1 reviews the roots of evolutionary thinking and how it became central to biological anthropology. Chapters 2 through 5 review at length the mechanisms of evolution and describe the applications of modern genetic research techniques to unraveling some of the mysteries of human evolution. Chapters

2 and 3 review cellular, molecular, and population genetics. Chapter 4 takes the discussion of genetics into modern evolutionary theory: the formation of species and the central topics of natural selection and adaptation. Chapter 5 surveys the field of human adaptation and the ways in which evolutionary forces mold human populations.

Part II, Primates (Chapters 6 and 7) presents the living nonhuman primates. We review their classification, their anatomical and behavioral adaptations, and their social life. We delve into new areas of research such as primate culture and tool use. We cautiously use the behavior of living monkeys and apes to understand what their ancestors, and therefore ours, may have been like.

Part III, Paleontology and Primate Evolution (Chapters 8, 9, and 10) introduces the foundation for understanding primate and human evolution. In the most complete synthesis of its kind in a biological anthropology text, we explain how scientists interpret the environmental context and geological age of fossils, and we review the periods of Earth's history during which primates arose (Chapter 8). We present the fossil evidence for primate evolution starting 65 million years ago (Chapter 9), and we discuss the anatomical transition from an ape to human ancestor (Chapter 10), a change that set off a cascade of effects that we feel to the present day.

Part IV, The Human Fossil Record (Chapters 11 through 14) presents the direct physical evidence for human origins. Chapter 11 describes the most up-to-date information on the earliest known hominids in Africa such as *Ardipithecus* and *Australopithecus*. Chapter 12 introduces the genus *Homo*, including *H. habilis* and *H. erectus*, and the causes and consequences of dispersal from Africa. Chapters 13 and 14 cover the more recent hominid fossils, including Neandertals, and the origins of our own species. We have provided up-to-the-minute information on the discovery of new human fossils including new text and figures of the Dikika child from Ethiopia, new research on the Flores remains, and the latest fossils of early *Homo* from Kenya.

Part V, New Frontiers in Biological Anthropology (Chapters 15 through 18) is about the biology of modern people. We include coverage of the human brain and the evolution of language (Chapter 15), and biomedical anthropology (Chapter 16). Chapter 17 discusses biocultural aspects of the evolution of human behavior, including the lives of traditional foraging peoples, aspects of human sexual behavior, and how behavioral disease can be understood in an evolutionary context. The book concludes with the new chapter on Bioarchaeology and Forensic Anthropology (Chapter 18).

The appendices offer reference material on the brain (Appendix A), the primate skeleton (Appendix B), the Hardy–Weinberg equilibrium (Appendix C), and metric to imperial conversion factors (Appendix D).

Student-oriented pedagogy has been maintained in each chapter. We begin each chapter with a short **vignette** depicting the main topic of the chapter. Some of these are quotes taken from famous works by biological anthropologists, such as Dian Fossey describing a day with mountain gorillas at the beginning of Chapter 7. For other chapters, one of the authors has written a short description of how someone studying human fossils, for example, might experience a day in the field. The vignettes should be used as a way to get a feel for the chapter topics and as an enjoyable and informative reflection on the text material.

Other features include a margin **glossary** to define new terms as students encounter them and a complete glossary at the back of the book. Each chapter is summarized by a list of questions and answers and each chapter ends with several **critical thinking questions** intended to stimulate discussion as well as explore a topic. We have listed a few **suggested readings** with each chapter, with an emphasis on books that are highly readable, nontechnical accounts that an introductory student may want to peruse. And at the end of the book the **bibliography** contains all the references used and cited in the text.

Innovation: Changes to the Second Edition

We tried in the first edition of *Biological Anthropology* to include topics not covered in many of the existing texts while preserving a comprehensive coverage of traditional topics. In this new edition, we have relied on instructor and student feedback as well as new events in the field to make further changes.

By popular demand, the first edition's appendix on forensic anthropology (a topic not traditionally covered in introductory biological anthropology texts) has been expanded to a full chapter (18) on bioarcheology and forensic anthropology. Field recovery methods, identification techniques, and applications of both bioarchaeology and forensic anthropology are described in a way that will appeal to students.

Biomedical anthropology is still featured in its own chapter, and a large part of Chapter 17 discusses the behavior and biology of modern people, from the study of foragers (hunter–gatherers) to approaches to understanding the human psyche (evolutionary psychology). We also include the most extensive discussion in any biological anthropology textbook of the geological background necessary for understanding human evolution (Chapter 8).

We have presented some text material in the *Insights and Advances* boxes in each chapter. These insets expand on text material or call your attention to current events connected to our field, to emerging debates, or sometimes just to fascinating side stories.

Introduction:	A Paradigm Split in Anthropology?
Chapter 1:	Darwin versus Wallace?
	What Is Intelligent Design?
Chapter 2:	Cloning Controversies
	Biochemical Individuality
Chapter 3:	Popular Mendelism and the Shadow of Eugenics
Chapter 4:	What's in a Name? Species Concepts, Genetics, and Conservation
Chapter 5:	Technology and Extreme Environments
Chapter 6:	The Rarest of the Rare
	The Impending Extinction of the Great Apes?
Chapter 7:	The Infanticide Wars
	Are Chimpanzees from Mars and Bonobos from Venus?
Chapter 8:	The Piltdown Hoax
	Dating Controversies
Chapter 9:	Subfossil Lemurs of Madagascar
Chapter 10:	Overheated Radiator?
Chapter 11:	A Rose by Any Other Name: Hominids versus Hominins
	Treasures of the Afar Triangle
Chapter 12:	Understanding the Meat-Eating Past through the Present
	What's Size Got to Do with It?
Chapter 13:	Neandertal Image Makeovers
Chapter 14:	The Little People of Flores
	The "Vitamin D Line"
Chapter 15:	The Ten-Percent Myth: Evolution and Energy
	Ape Language Studics
Chapter 16:	Kuru, Cannibalism, and Prion Diseases
Chapter 17:	Reading, Writing, and Evolution
Chapter 18:	Ancestry Genetics
	The Genghis Khan Effect

New double-page features called *Innovations* have been added in select chapters. *Innovations* provide an intense visual presentation of new, burgeoning areas of research in our field. These include The Wide World of RNA (Chapter 2), Culture in Nonhuman Primates (Chapter 7), Time in a Bottle (dating fossil sites, Chapter 8), Dikika and Development (studying development in fossils, Chapter 11), Neandertal Genes (Chapter 13), and Music, the Brain, and Evolution (Chapter 15).

New marginal comments call students' attention to key topics or provide interesting observations about the topics within each chapter.

Illustrations

Illustrations play a major role in any textbook, and they are crucial learning tools in introductory science texts. The publisher and authors have worked together to provide you with the best possible photos and drawings of every topic covered in the book. Most of the photographs of living primates, fossils, and fossil sites, were taken by one of the authors or were contributed by other biological anthropologists. Prentice Hall has worked hard to produce some of the finest images of everything from molecular genetics to stone tools that have ever been published in a biological anthropology textbook. The maps have been specifically created for this book by Dorling Kindersley, a leading publisher of atlases for both the educational and consumer markets. These maps describe the geography of everything from the distribution of living primates in the world today to the locations of the continents in the distant past. We authors worked with Prentice Hall to be sure everything in this second edition is depicted accurately and clearly, and we hope you will gain a better understanding of the science by studying the visual material as well.

Along with the new *Innovations* features, additional special two-page figures appear in a number of chapters, especially in Part IV, and provide a snapshot of evolutionary development through time. These special figures provide a concise way for the reader to easily grasp the evolutionary changes through a vast sweep of time that are presented in greater detail in the text.

A NOTE ABOUT LANGUAGE

Authors must make decisions about language and terminology, and textbook authors make those choices with the knowledge that they may be influencing the mindset of a generation of young scholars. Some of these choices are modest. For instance, we use the modern American spelling *Neandertal* instead of the more traditional European spelling *Neanderthal*. Other language choices are more central to the subject matter. Perhaps the most significant choice we have made is with regard to primate classification. Although the primate order historically has been subdivided into anthropoids (the apes and monkeys, including us) and prosimians (the "lower" primates, including lemurs, galagos, lorises, and tarsiers), this dichotomy does not reflect the molecular relationships among groups of primates as well as a subdivision into haplorhines and strepsirhines. Haplorhines include all anthropoids and tarsiers, and strepsirhines include all prosimians except tarsiers. We discuss this distinction in some depth in Chapter 6 and use the terms *strepsirhine* and *haplorhine* rather than *prosimian* and *anthropoid*. In another case, we have opted to use the more traditional family-level designation *hominid* to refer to humans and our ancestors rather than the alternative tribal-level *hominin*, which is less broadly used in the research literature. We discuss this classification in Chapter 11.

A NOTE REGARDING ABBREVIATIONS AND TIME

Because of the plethora of sometimes conflicting abbreviations used to refer to time throughout the text, we have attempted to spell out time ranges (e.g., "millions of years ago" or "thousands of years ago"). Where this is not feasible, such as in tables, we use the abbreviations most common to anthropology textbooks (*mya* for "millions of years ago" and *kya* for "thousands of years ago"). However, students should note that the standard usage in geology and paleontology is *Ma* (mega-annum) and *ka* (kilo-annum).

Supplemental Resources

The ancillary materials that accompany *Biological Anthropology, Second Edition* are part of a complete teaching and learning package and have been carefully created to enhance the topics discussed in the text.

INSTRUCTOR SUPPLEMENTS

Instructor's Resource Manual with Tests (0-13-601161-6) For each chapter in the text, this valuable resource provides a detailed outline, list of objectives, discussion questions, and classroom activities. In addition, test questions in multiple-choice, true-false, and short answer formats are available for each chapter; the answers to all questions are page referenced to the text.

TestGEN-EQ (0-13-601199-3) This software allows instructors to create their own personalized exams, to edit the existing test questions, and to add new questions. Other special features of this program include random generation of test questions, creation of alternative versions of the same test, question sequence scrambling, and test preview before printing.

Strategies in Teaching Anthropology, Fifth Edition: (0-13-603466-7) Unique in focus and content, this book focuses on the "how" of teaching Anthropology across all of its subfields: Cultural, Social, Biological, Archaeology, and Linguistics to provide a wide array of associated learning outcomes and student activities. It is a valuable single-source compendium of strategies and teaching "tricks of the trade" from a group of seasoned teaching anthropologists who work in a variety of teaching settings and share their pedagogical techniques, knowledge, and observations. Please see your local Pearson sales representative for more information.

Faculty Resources on CD-ROM (0-13-601163-2) This interactive CD pulls together all the print and media assets available to instructors. In addition, instructors can insert media—PowerPoint® slides, graphs, charts, and maps—into their interactive classroom presentations.

STUDENT SUPPLEMENTS

Method & Practice in Biological Anthropology: A Workbook and Laboratory Manual for Introductory Courses (0-13-225006-3) Designed to complement a wide variety of introductory level laboratory courses in biological anthropology, this new manual written by Samantha Hens of California State University, Sacramento provides optimum flexibility to suit almost all laboratory environments. The manual is divided into four sections, reflecting the typical design of introductory courses in biological anthropology: genetics and evolution, the human skeleton, the nonhuman primates, and our fossil ancestors. Each chapter has similar pedagogical elements, beginning with a list of chapter objectives, an array of topical lab exercises to choose from, and a set of pre- and post-lab questions. For more information, please contact your local Pearson sales representative.

MyAnthropologyKit: MyAnthroKit is an online resource that contains book-specific practice tests, chapter summaries, learning objectives, flashcards, weblinks, Research Navigator, and media-rich activities that enhance topics covered in your textbook. For more information, please contact your local Pearson sales representative.

Dorling Kindersley/Prentice Hall Atlas of Anthropology (0-13-191879-6) Beautifully illustrated by Dorling Kindersley, with narrative by leading archaeological author Brian M. Fagan, this striking atlas features 30 full-color maps, timelines, and illustrations to offer a highly visual, but explanatory geographical overview of topics from all four fields of anthropology. This atlas can be ordered in a package with a new copy of *Biological Anthropology, Second Edition.*

Research Navigator™ can help students to complete research assignments efficiently and with confidence by providing three exclusive databases of high-quality scholarly and popular articles accessed by easy-to-use search engines.

EBSCO's ContentSelect™ Academic Journal Database, organized by subject, contains 50–100 of the leading academic journals for anthropology. Instructors and students can search the online journals by keyword, topic, or multiple topics. Articles include abstract and citation information and can be cut, pasted, e-mailed, or saved for later use.

The New York Times **Search-by-Subject™ Archive** provides articles specific to anthropology and is searchable by keyword or multiple keywords. Instructors and students can view full-text articles from the world's leading journalists writing for *The New York Times*.

Link Library offers editorially selected "best of the web" sites for anthropology. Link Libraries are continually scanned and kept up to date, providing the most relevant and accurate links for research assignments.

Gain access to **Research Navigator** by using the access code found in the front of the brief guide called *The Prentice Hall Guide to Research Navigator™* (0-13-600863-1). The access code for Research Navigator is included with every guide and can be packaged for no extra charge with *Biological Anthropology, Second Edition*. Please contact your Pearson representative for more information.

Acknowledgments

Textbooks require the collaboration of many people with many areas of expertise, and this book made good use of all of those involved. The process begins with each author compiling his or her notes from years of teaching biological anthropology and thinking about how the course could be more effectively taught. Over the years the students in our courses have helped us to assess what did and did not work in conveying the information and excitement of biological anthropology, and for this we are extremely grateful. For her vision and steady guidance over the past five years we are most grateful to Nancy Roberts, publisher of anthropology at Prentice Hall. We also thank Nancy's assistant, Lee Peterson, for keeping the chapters flowing, and media editor Mayda Bosco for the media that accompanies this text. We owe a debt of gratitude to our development editor, Carolyn Viola-John, for her tireless and careful editing and for her patience and diplomacy in dealing with the logistics of working with three different authors. The outstanding efforts of Ilze Lemesis in coordinating and creating all design elements resulted in this beautiful text. Cheryl Keenan, production liaison at Prentice Hall, and Sandra Reinhard and Katrina Ostler at Black Dot Group did a remarkable job of coordinating the entire production process. Maria Piper was tireless in coordinating the extensive art program that accompanies this book. We appreciate the diligence of copyeditor Marne Evans and the creativity of photo researcher David Tietz. Thanks also to marketing manager Lindsey Prudhomme for directing the marketing campaign.

For contributing photos and published or unpublished material to help in writing the text, we thank Brad Adams, Takeru Akazawa, Christopher Boehm, David Brill, Peter Brown, Joel Bruss, Christian Crowder, Hanna Damasio, Chris Dean, Anna Delaney, Eric Delson, Todd Disotell, Craig Feibel, Ken Garrett, John Krigbaum, David Lordkipanidze, Laura MacClatchy, Lisa Matisoo-Smith, Melanie McCollum, William McComas, Monte McCrossin, Salvador Moya-Sola, Jackson Njau, The National Museum of Kenya, Amy Parish, Briana Pobiner, Allysha Powanda, Tim Ryan, Paul Sledzik, Josh Snodgrass, Fred Spoor, Carl Swisher, Judy Suchey, Ian Tattersall, Brent Turrin, Alan Walker, Randy White, Tatiana White, Andrea Wiley, and Milford Wolpoff.

All three of us cut our teeth teaching introductory biological anthropology as graduate students apprenticing as teaching assistants at the University of California. Our fellow TAs shared their ideas and our tasks, for which we are thankful. We are most grateful to the triumvirate of faculty with whom we apprenticed and from whom we learned much about the subject matter, how to teach it, and how an introductory course can be made a rewarding, enriching experience for undergraduates. Our heartfelt thanks go to Katharine Milton, Vincent Sarich, and Tim White.

Graduate teaching assistants in our own courses at the University of Southern California, the University of Auckland, the University of Florida, Rutgers University, and New York University brought new enthusiasm and ideas, and we are grateful to them all.

This revision grew out of the comments of reviewers who helped to create the brief version of this text, *Exploring Biological Anthropology*, as well as those who read the first edition of this book. For their help and guidance, we thank the anonymous reviewers and:

Wendy A. Birky, California State University, Northridge
Erin Browder, Southwestern College
Helen Cho, Davidson College
Denise Couch, Southwestern College
Darna L. Dufour, University of Colorado
Steven Gaulin, University of California, Santa Barbara
Mary Glenn, Humboldt State University
Nicholas V. Kilzer, Northeastern Illinois University
Kenneth E. Lewis, Michigan State University
Lindsay Magnuson, Humboldt State University
Frances Purifoy, University of Louisville
John J. Schultz, University of Central Florida
Roger J. Sullivan, California State University, Sacramento
Nancy E. Tatarek, Ohio University
Natalie Vasey, Portland State University
Daniel J. Wescott, University of Missouri

In addition, we would like to thank the reviewers of the original manuscript; we wouldn't have reached this point without their comments and questions:

Robert L. Anemone, Western Michigan University; *John R. Baker*, Moorpark College; *Art Barbeau*, West Liberty State College; *Anna Bellisari*, Wright State University; *David W. Frayer*, University of Kansas; *Sarah A. C. Keller*, Eastern Washington University; *Andrew Kramer*, University of Tennessee; *John R. Lukacs*, University of Oregon; *Peer H. Moore-Jansen*, Wichita State University; *Leanne T. Nash*, Arizona State University; *Robert R. Paine*, Texas Tech University; *Jill D. Pruetz*, Iowa State University; *J. Richard Shenkel*, University of New Orleans; *Lynnette Leidy Sievert*, University of Massachusetts-Amherst; *Larissa Swedell*, Queens College–CUNY; *Trudy R. Turner*, University of Wisconsin-Milwaukee; *Daniel J. Wescott*, University of Missouri-Columbia; *Bruce P. Wheatley*, University of Alabama-Birmingham; *Linda D. Wolfe*, East Carolina University.

We've made a great effort to produce a comprehensive and fully accurate text, correcting minor errors from the first edition. We would be grateful for comments or corrections from students and instructors using *Biological Anthropology, Second Edition*, as we know that, inevitably, some errors may remain. And we hope you find this account of human evolution as fascinating and compelling as we do.

Craig Stanford

John S. Allen

Susan C. Antón

Craig Stanford is a professor of anthropology and biological sciences at the University of Southern California, where he also directs the Jane Goodall Research Center. He has conducted field research on primate behavior in south Asia, Latin America, and East Africa. He is well known for his long-term studies of meat-eating among wild chimpanzees in Gombe, Tanzania, and of the relationship between mountain gorillas and chimpanzees in the Impenetrable Forest of Uganda. He has authored or coauthored more than 120 scientific publications. Craig has received USC's highest teaching awards for his introductory biological anthropology course. In addition, he has published eleven books on primate behavior and human origins, including *Significant Others* (2001), *Upright* (2003) and *Beautiful Minds* (2008). He and his wife, Erin Moore, a cultural anthropologist at USC, live in South Pasadena, California, and have three children.

John Allen is a research scientist in the Dornsife Cognitive Neuroscience Imaging Center and the Brain and Creativity Institute at the University of Southern California, where he is also an adjunct research associate professor in the Department of Anthropology. Previously, he was a neuroscience researcher at the University of Iowa College of Medicine and a faculty member in the Department of Anthropology at the University of Auckland, New Zealand, for several years. His primary research interests are the evolution of the human brain and behavior, and behavioral disease. He also has research experience in molecular genetics, nutritional anthropology, and the history of anthropology. He has conducted fieldwork in Japan, New Zealand, Papua New Guinea, and Palau. He has received university awards for teaching introductory courses in biological anthropology both as a graduate student instructor at the University of California and as a faculty member at the University of Auckland. John and his wife, Stephanie Sheffield, have two sons, Reid and Perry.

Susan Antón is an associate professor in the Center for the Study of Human Origins, Department of Anthropology at New York University, where she also directs the M.A. program in Human Skeletal Biology. She is joint editor of the *Journal of Human Evolution*. Her field research concerns the evolution of genus *Homo* in Indonesia and human impact on island ecosystems in the South Pacific. She is best known for her work on *H. erectus* in Kenya and Indonesia. She received awards for teaching as a graduate student instructor of introductory physical anthropology and anatomy at the University of California and was Teacher of the Year while at the University of Florida. She has been twice elected to *Who's Who Among America's Teachers*. Susan and her husband, Carl Swisher, a geochronologist, raise Anatolian shepherd dogs.

Biological Anthropology

INTRODUCTION:
What Is Biological Anthropology?

2

On a sunny morning in east Africa, with the temperature already climbing past 90 degrees, a scientist stands in a shallow pit, carefully examining the dusty ground. All around her are the tools of her trade: shovels, dental picks, whisk brooms, surveying equipment. Something glinting in the morning light catches her eye. She bends over to examine a tiny fragment of whitish bone, then another and another. Realizing that her week of hard, sweaty work has just paid off, she beckons her assistants to see the prize, then carefully begins to map the spot for the work that now begins: unearthing the fossilized skeleton of an ancient primate, perhaps the forerunner of all modern apes. Weeks later, returning to the capital city and its museum, the scientist compares the new fossils with previously collected specimens. She finds that a few of the pieces her team has excavated fit together with the long-neglected bones of a fossil ape discovered at the site in the 1930s. The scientist devotes long hours to studying every detail of the skeleton. A new picture emerges: This ancient ape may have been the first to come down from the trees and venture forth on the ground below.

A FEW HUNDRED MILES AWAY, ANOTHER SCIENTIST sits in the tall grass of a high mountain meadow. All around him are massive, shaggy-haired mountain gorillas, happily munching on wild celery. A bright-eyed baby gorilla ambles up to the scientist and toys with the laces of his boot, then runs quickly back to its mother. Two silverbacks, majestic 400-pound males wearing saddles of gray hair across their backs, sit like enormous statues a few yards away. The scientist uses the tools of his trade: a notebook and checklist to record behavior, plus a handheld global positioning system unit to map the animals' travels. As the gorilla group finishes its lunch, the silverbacks get up and head off into the forest, bulldozing a trail that the females, babies, and scientist obediently follow.

AT THE SAME TIME, HALF A WORLD AWAY, a third scientist is sitting in a laboratory intently studying a computer monitor. He looks at a three-dimensional, high-resolution image of a human brain. Millimeter by millimeter, he examines the frontal lobe, a region of the brain thought to be of key importance in the evolution of modern people. By moving the screen cursor slightly, he can study the brain's surface from every possible angle, making virtual slices through it to study its internal organization. Unlike skulls, brains do not become preserved as fossils, so the scientist uses images of the brains of living humans and other primates to reconstruct the way in which the brains of long-dead ancestors may have been organized.

What do these three scientists—one studying ancient fossils, another observing primate behavior, and the third studying the evolution of the human brain—all have in common? They are biological anthropologists, engaged in the scientific study of humankind (from *anthropos,* meaning "human," and -*ology,* "the study of"). Despite our exalted intellect, our mind-boggling technology, and our intricately complex social behavior, we are nonetheless biological creatures. Humans are **primates** and share a recent ancestry with the living great apes. Like the apes, we are the products of millions of years of **evolution** by natural selection.

The famed geneticist Theodosius Dobzhansky once said, "Nothing in biology makes sense except in the light of evolution." Biological anthropologists spend their careers trying to understand the details of the evolutionary process and the ways in which it has shaped who we are today. They use a central, unifying set of biological principles in their work, first set down by Charles Darwin nearly 150 years ago. The frequency of a particular trait and the genes that control it can change from one generation to the next; this is evolution. This elegantly simple idea forms the heart and soul of **biological anthropology.**

The evolutionary process usually is slow and inefficient, but over many generations it can mold animals and plants into a bewildering variety of forms. Our ancestry includes many animals that little resemble us today. Biological anthropology is particularly concerned with the evolutionary transformations that occurred over the past 6 million years, as an apelike primate began to walk on two legs and became something different: a **hominid.** From the perspective of evolutionary theory, humans are like all other biological species, the product of the same long process of **adaptation.**

The Scope of Biological Anthropology

The scope of biological anthropology is vastly wider than the study of primates, fossils, and brain evolution. Any scientist studying evolution as it relates to the human species, directly or indirectly, could be called a biological anthropologist. This includes a number of related disciplines (Figure 0.1).

PALEOANTHROPOLOGY

When an exciting new fossil of an extinct form of human is found, paleoanthropologists usually are responsible (Figure 0.2). **Paleoanthropology** is the study of the fossil record for humankind, and fossilized remains are the most direct physical evidence of human ancestry that we have to understand our origins. The discovery of skeletal evidence of new ancestral species, or additional specimens of existing species, revises our view of the human family tree. Discoveries of hominid fossils—some as famous as Peking Man or Lucy (Figure 0.3) but many less known—have profoundly changed the way we view our place in nature. Paleoanthropology also includes the study of the fossil record of the other primates—apes, monkeys, and prosimians—dating back at least 65 million years. These early fossils give us key clues about how, where, and why hominids evolved millions of years later. There are fossil sites producing important fossils all over the world, and with more and more students and researchers searching, our fossil history grows richer every year. In fact, although the first half of the twentieth century witnessed discoveries of new human fossils every decade or so, the pace of discovery of new species of fossil humans has accelerated rapidly in recent years. This is because more students and researchers are searching for fossils and because global and regional political changes have allowed researchers into areas that were long off limits because of civil war or political unrest.

Paleoanthropological research begins in the field, where researchers search the landscape for new discoveries. Much of the scholarly work then takes place in museums and university laboratories around the world, where the specimens are archived and preserved for detailed study. Because we can safely assume that the evolutionary process taking place in the present also took place in the past, the study of the meaning of human and nonhuman primate fossils proceeds from comparisons between extinct and living forms. For example, the presence of large canine teeth in the male specimens of a fossil monkey species implies that in life, the species lived in multiple male groups in which males competed for mates. This

primate Member of the mammalian order Primates, including prosimians, monkeys, apes, and humans, defined by a suite of anatomical and behavioral traits.

evolution A change in the frequency of a gene or a trait in a population over multiple generations.

biological anthropology The study of humans as biological organisms, considered in an evolutionary framework; sometimes called physical anthropology.

hominid A member of the primate family Hominidae, distinguished by bipedal posture and, in more recently evolved species, a large brain.

adaptation A trait that increases the reproductive success of an organism, produced by natural selection in the context of a particular environment.

paleoanthropology The study of the fossil record of ancestral humans and their primate kin.

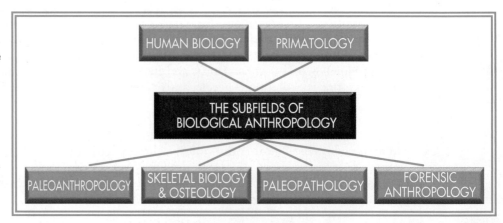

FIGURE 0.1 Subfields of biological anthropology.

conclusion was reached because major differences in male and female canine tooth size indicate mate competition in living monkeys.

As the fossil record has grown, we have begun to see that the evolutionary history of our species is extremely complicated; most lineages are now extinct, but many thrived for millions of years. The ladder of progress notion—an older, more linear view of our ancestry in which each species evolved into more complex forms—has been replaced by a family tree with many branches.

FIGURE 0.2   Paleoanthropologist Jane Moore maps sites at Kanapoi, Kenya.

SKELETAL BIOLOGY AND HUMAN OSTEOLOGY

Osteology is the study of the skeleton. The first order of business when a fossil is discovered is to figure out what sort of animal the fossil—often a tiny fragment—may have been in life. Osteologists must possess extraordinary skills of identification and a keen spatial sense of how the pieces of a jigsaw puzzle—or an array of bone chips—fit together when they are trying to understand the meaning of fossils they have found.

Among the first generation of biological anthropologists (Figure 0.4) were the *anthropometrists*, who made detailed measurements of the human body in all its forms, and their work is still important today. Understanding the relationship between genetics, human growth and stature, and geographic variation in human anatomy is vital to identifying the origins and patterns of human migration across the globe during prehistory. For example, when a 9,000-year-old skeleton was discovered some years ago on the banks of the Columbia River in the Pacific Northwest, osteologists with expertise in human variation in body form were among those who sought to identify its ethnic affinities.

Skeletal biology, like osteology, is the study of the human skeleton, but because the bones of the body develop in concert with other tissues, such as muscles and tendons, a skeletal biologist must know the patterns and processes of human growth, physiology, and development, not just human anatomy.

The famous Kennewick Man skeleton was found in a riverbank in Washington State: its ethnic relationships and anatomy are still being studied.

osteology   The study of the skeleton.

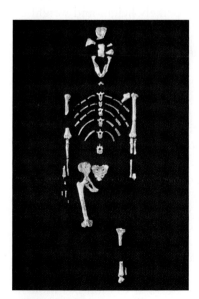

FIGURE 0.3   Lucy, a partial hominid skeleton.

FIGURE 0.4   An osteologist at work.

FIGURE 0.5 Forensic anthropologists use skeletal remains to identify victims of war in Bosnia.

paleopathology The study of diseases in ancestral human populations.

forensic anthropology The study of human remains applied to a legal context.

primatology The study of the nonhuman primates and their anatomy, genetics, behavior, and ecology.

FIGURE 0.6 Recovery team at work at the World Trade Center Ground Zero following the September 11, 2001 attack.

PALEOPATHOLOGY

Hand in hand with skeletal biology is **paleopathology**: the study of disease in ancient human populations, as evidenced by telltale signs on the skeleton. When the Neandertal fossils first appeared in the mid-nineteenth century, there was much scientific debate about whether they represented a true species or "race," or whether they were simply modern individuals who had suffered from some pathological condition. It took nearly 30 years and the discovery of several additional specimens to resolve the issue. Today, paleopathologists would help resolve such a debate much more quickly.

Paleopathologists also work with archaeologists excavating ancient humans to study the effects of trauma, epidemics, nutritional deficiencies, and infectious diseases. If archaeologists find evidence that an ancient civilization crashed precipitously, a paleopathologist will study the remains of the bodies for signs of anything from outbreaks of sexually transmitted disease to poor nutrition.

FORENSIC ANTHROPOLOGY

Although biological anthropology is concerned primarily with basic research into human origins, biological anthropologists also play roles in our daily lives. **Forensic anthropology**, the study of the identification of skeletal remains and of the means by which the individual died, is a contemporary application of biological anthropology. Forensic anthropologists take their knowledge of osteology and paleopathology and apply it to both historical and criminal investigations (Figure 0.5). During the war crime investigations into mass graves in Bosnia, forensic anthropologists were called in to attempt to identify victims, as they also were after the terrorist attacks in New York, Washington, and Pennsylvania on September 11, 2001 (Figure 0.6). When police were investigating the murder of the wife of football star O. J. Simpson, forensic scientists used the footprints in blood left at the murder scene to try to reconstruct the height and weight of the murderer. This is not so different from what paleoanthropologists did when they discovered a set of tiny human-like footprints imbedded in fossilized ash at Laetoli in northern Tanzania. They used forensic skills to try to reconstruct the likely height and weight of the creatures that had left those prints nearly 4 million years ago.

PRIMATOLOGY

Primatology is the branch of biological anthropology that is best known to the public through the highly publicized work of renowned primatologists Jane Goodall and Dian Fossey. Primatologists study the anatomy, physiology, behavior, and genetics of both living and extinct monkeys, apes, and prosimians. Behavioral studies of nonhuman primates in their natural environments gained prominence in the 1960s and 1970s, when the pioneering work of Jane Goodall was publicized widely in the United States and elsewhere. In the early days of primate behavior study, the researchers were mainly psychologists. By the late 1960s, however, biological anthropology had become the domain of primate behavior study, especially in North America.

Primatologists study nonhuman primates for a variety of reasons, including the desire to learn more about their intrinsically fascinating patterns of behavior (Figure 0.7). Within an anthropological framework, primatologists study the nonhuman primates for the lessons they can provide on how evolution has molded the human species. For example, male baboons fight among themselves for the chance to mate with females. They are also much larger and more aggressive than females. Do larger, more macho males father more offspring than their smaller and gentler brothers? If so, these traits appear to have emerged slowly through generations of evolutionary change, and the size difference between males and females is the result of selection for large body size. Then, what about the body-size difference between men and women of our own species? Is it the result of competition between men in prehistory, or perhaps a preference by women in prehistory for tall men? The clues that we derive about human nature from the behavior and anatomy of living primates must be interpreted cautiously but can be vitally important in understanding who we are and where we came from.

FIGURE 0.7 Jane Goodall is a pioneering primatologist whose studies of wild chimpanzees changed our view of human nature.

Biological anthropologists trained as primatologists find careers not only in universities but also in museums, zoos, and conservation agencies. Many important wildlife conservation projects seeking to protect endangered primate species are being carried out around the world by biological anthropologists.

HUMAN BIOLOGY

In addition to paleoanthropology and primatology, biological anthropologists span a wide range of interests that are often labeled **human biology**. Some work in the area of *human adaptation*, learning how people adjust physiologically to the extremes of Earth's physical environments. For instance, how does environment affect children's development if they grow up high in the Andes mountain range of South America at elevations over 14,000 feet (4,270 m)? Other human biologists work as *nutritional anthropologists*, studying the interrelationship of diet, culture, and evolution. Biological anthropologists interested in demography examine the biological and cultural forces that shape the composition of human populations. Other biological anthropologists are particularly interested in how various hormones in the human body influence human behavior and how, in turn, the environment affects the expression of these hormones. The study of *human variation* deals with the many ways in which people differ in their anatomy throughout the world.

At an earlier time in history, the scholarly study of physical traits such as height, skull shape, and especially, skin color was tainted with the possibility that the researcher had some racially biased preconceptions. Today, biological anthropologists are interested in human variation, both anatomical and genetic, simply because it offers clues about the peopling of the world by the migrations of early humans. Understanding when, where, and how people left Africa and began to colonize Europe, Asia, and eventually the New World can tell us a great deal about the roots of modern languages, diseases, population genetics, and other topics of great relevance in the world today.

Many contemporary biological anthropologists are interested in research problems that require an understanding of both biological and cultural factors. Biological anthropologists with these interests sometimes are called *biocultural anthropologists*. One area in which a biocultural perspective is vitally important is *biomedical anthropology* (Figure 0.8). Biomedical anthropologists might study how human cultural practices influence the spread of infectious disease and how the effects of pollution or toxins in the environment affect human growth. Biomedical

human biology Subfield of biological anthropology dealing with human growth and development, adaptation to environmental extremes, and human genetics.

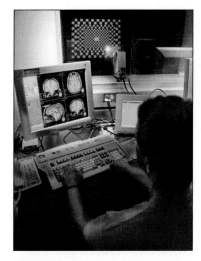

FIGURE 0.8 Biomedical anthropologists study, among other things, the human brain.

FIGURE 0.9 Vincent Sarich and Allan Wilson helped pioneer the molecular anthropological approach to studying primate and human evolution.

anthropologists are particularly interested in studying the human health effects that arise when an urbanized (and Western) lifestyle is adopted by people who have previously lived under more traditional, non-Western conditions. The expression of many human diseases is influenced by genetic factors, and biomedical anthropologists often look at the long-term evolutionary consequences of disease on human populations. Finally, an increasing number of biological anthropologists work in the field of genetics (Figure 0.9). *Molecular anthropology* is a genetic approach to human evolutionary science that seeks to understand the differences in the genome between humans and their closest relatives, the nonhuman primates. Because genetic inheritance is the basis for evolutionary change, a geneticist is in a perfect position to address some of the fundamental questions about human nature and human evolution. We know that the human DNA sequence is extremely similar to that of an ape, but what exactly does this mean? At which points do the differences result in some key shift, such as in the use of language? These are some of the questions that may be answerable in the very near future with the help of anthropological geneticists.

The Roots of Modern Biological Anthropology

In 1856, the fossil of an ancient human ("Neandertal Man") was discovered in Germany (Schaaffhausen, 1858). In England in 1859, Charles Darwin published *On the Origin of Species*. Darwin's work had a greater immediate impact than the Neandertal's appearance because it was some time before scientists agreed that the Neandertal was an ancient human rather than just an odd-looking modern one. Darwin's introduction of an evolutionary perspective made many of the old debates about human origins irrelevant. After Darwin, scientists no longer needed to debate whether humans originated via a single creation or if the different races were created separately (*monogenism* versus *polygenism*); the study of the natural history of humans became centered on the evolutionary history of our species. Human variation was the product of the interaction between the biological organism and the environment. Apes and monkeys—the nonhuman primates—became our "cousins" almost overnight.

The field known in North America as **physical anthropology** was established as an academic discipline in the second half of the nineteenth century (Spencer, 1997). In France, Germany, and England it was called simply *anthropology*. Most early physical anthropologists were physicians who taught anatomy in medical schools and had an interest in human variation or evolution. In the first half of the twentieth century, much of physical anthropology was devoted to measuring bodies and skulls (*anthropometry* and *craniometry*), with particular attention paid to the biological definition of human races. Physical anthropologists also studied the comparative anatomy of nonhuman primates and the limited fossil record of humans and other primates.

By the mid-twentieth century a new physical anthropology emerged, led by a generation of scholars who were trained as anthropologists, first and foremost, and who in turn trained hundreds of graduate students who benefited from the expansion of higher education fueled by the Baby Boom generation. The new physical anthropology, whose main architect was Sherwood Washburn of the University of Chicago and later of the University of California, Berkeley, embraced the dynamic view of evolution promoted by the adherents of the neo-Darwinian synthesis. This synthesis of genetics, anatomy, ecology, and behavior with evolutionary theory emerged in the biological sciences in the 1930s and 1940s. In the new physical anthropology, primates were not simply shot and dissected; their behavior

Collecting and measuring human skulls and bones was a popular hobby among nineteenth-century physicians, some of whom were the first physical anthropologists.

physical anthropology
The study of humans as biological organisms, considered in an evolutionary framework.

and ecology were studied in the natural environment as well as in the laboratory (Goodall, 1963). The study of human races as pigeonholed categories gave way to the study of evolving populations, with a particular emphasis on how human populations adapt to environmental conditions. The field of paleoanthropology was revolutionized by the introduction of new dating techniques and the adoption of a multidisciplinary approach to understanding ancient environments. Molecular genetics research in anthropology gave us a whole new way to reconstruct the biological histories of human populations and of primate species as a whole (Goodman, 1962; Sarich & Wilson, 1967).

Today, biological anthropology embraces a wide variety of approaches with the goal of answering a few basic questions: What does it mean to be human? How did we become who we are today? How does our biological past influence our lives in the environments of the present? What is the place of human beings in nature?

Anthropology and its Subfields

Anthropology is the study of humankind in all its forms. But of course, this definition does not distinguish it from other disciplines that study the human condition, such as psychology, history, and sociology. The critical aspect that sets anthropology apart from the other social sciences is its cross-cultural, holistic nature. That is, anthropologists try to understand the inner workings of a group of people who hold different worldviews, values, and traditions than they do. The unusual thing about the human animal is that we have **culture**. Although it often seems that anthropologists spend their careers arguing about how to define culture, we can say simply that culture is the sum total of learned traditions of a group of people. Language is culture (although the ability to use language is biological), as is religion, as are the way people dress and the foods they eat. These human behaviors vary greatly from one culture to the next. But what about the universal taboo on incestuous relations with one's siblings? Or the observation that across many human societies, women tend to marry older men? Are these common threads of human cultures the result of learned traditions, passed down across the generations, or is there a biological influence at work? As we will see, the interplay between biology and culture provides many of the most intriguing and perplexing clues about the roots of our humanity. It also creates many of the most intense debates; for decades scholars have debated whether genes or the environment have played the more important role in molding intelligence and other human qualities.

The dichotomy between biological and cultural influences on humankind is a false one, as we examine in detail later in the book. In earliest humans, biological evolution produced the capacity for culture: Intelligence had to evolve before learned traditions such as tool using could flourish, as we see in wild apes today. Our biology produced culture, but culture can also influence biology. We study these patterns under the rubric of **biocultural anthropology**.

Anthropology is divided into four subfields: biological anthropology, cultural anthropology, linguistic anthropology, and archaeology (Figure 0.10). Some

Although all academic disciplines consist of subfield specialties, those in anthropology are particularly diverse.

anthropology The study of humankind in a cross-cultural context. Anthropology includes the subfields cultural anthropology, linguistic anthropology, archaeology, and biological anthropology.

culture The sum total of learned traditions, values, and beliefs that groups of people, and a few species of highly intelligent animals, possess.

biocultural anthropology The study of the interaction between biology and culture, which plays a role in most human traits.

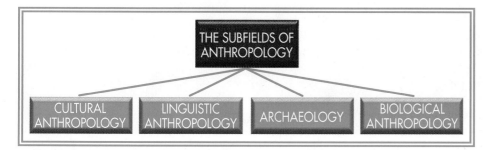

FIGURE 0.10 The subfields of anthropology.

anthropologists consider linguistics and archaeology as subfields within cultural anthropology. In addition, applied anthropology—a method more than a discipline—is sometimes considered a fifth subfield. The majority of practicing anthropologists in the United States are cultural anthropologists, who typically make up more than half of the faculty of anthropology departments in universities, as well as others who find employment in a variety of nonacademic settings, as you will see in the following section.

CULTURAL ANTHROPOLOGY

Cultural anthropology is the study of human societies in a cross-cultural perspective. The amazing variety of ways in which people lead their daily lives is at the heart of the field. Recent trends in cultural anthropology that have tended to deemphasize quantitative data about other cultures in favor of interpretive, subjective accounts have moved some anthropologists further away from science and toward the humanities. This trend has stretched the spectrum of anthropology, as faculty members in the same academic department may run the gamut from molecular biochemists to political philosophers (Insights and Advances: A Paradigm Split in Anthropology?).

    Ethnology, one of the subfields of cultural anthropology, is the study of human societies and of the behavior of people within those societies. It might include everything from the way marriages and funerals are arranged, to the economic system, to the kinship system. The practice of ethnology is called **ethnography** (literally, the describing of culture). The study of the way in which foraging people track down their prey is ethnography. As is a written account of the initiation rituals of Los Angeles street gangs or the study of how parents in Boston care for their children relative to parenting among the Sherpas of highland Nepal. The common thread that runs through all these studies is that they are structured to bring an understanding of the workings of another culture by comparing it with the culture of the investigator (Figure 0.11). Although sociologists could also say they study culture, ethnologists immerse themselves in the hour-to-hour process of human lives in a way that is different from other academic fields, both in the degree of immersion and the emphasis on cross-cultural differences.

cultural anthropology
The study of human societies, especially in a cross-cultural context; the subdivision of anthropology that includes ethnology, archaeology, and linguistics.

ethnology The study of human societies, their traditions, rituals, beliefs, and the differences in these traits between societies.

ethnography The practice of cultural anthropology. Ethnographers study the minute-to-minute workings of human societies, especially non-Western societies.

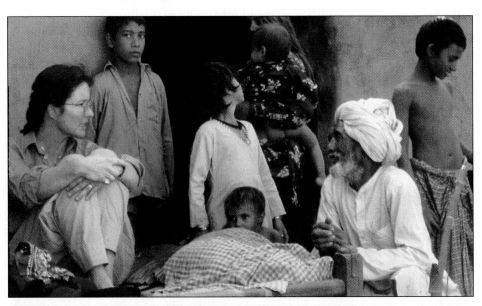

FIGURE 0.11 Cultural anthropologist Erin Moore interviews a family in a village in Rajasthan, India. Ethnographers immerse themselves in local cultures to better understand them.

A Paradigm Split in Anthropology?

A *paradigm* is a conceptual framework that allows scholars to make sense of existing information. It is the rules and methods by which a scientist works. Newtonian physics is a paradigm; so is Freudian psychology. Darwin's theory of evolution is the paradigm anthropologists have used for a century and a half to make sense of the natural world. But in the first decade of the twenty-first century, the field of anthropology is experiencing sharp growing pains. Many cultural anthropologists have come to reject biological influences on human behavior, and a debate over paradigms has ensued. During most of the twentieth century, all anthropologists shared a common mindset: that we can study human societies scientifically by gathering information about them and testing ideas in much the same way that scientists in other fields work. In the 1960s, a cultural anthropologist might have gone off to rural Africa to spend a year studying the religious practices and beliefs of a tribal culture there; she made an educated guess about the reasons that a given religious ritual was performed and then collected data to test her hypothesis or idea. She would then come home and write a book that would become the authoritative work on the subject, partly because the culture she studied would not have had literate scholars of its own.

In the past decade, there has been a movement to reconsider the role that the anthropologist plays in describing a culture. A White male anthropologist from an urban background will have a very different perspective on the culture under study than will a Black female anthropologist from a rural background. If these two anthropologists, both highly trained in the practice of ethnography, see the same culture differently, what does this say about the notion of objective science? The view that scholarly study is subject to the biases inherent in the background and philosophy of the researcher is part of a worldview called *postmodernism,* in which a new age of scholars seek to "deconstruct" the conclusions of an earlier generation of anthropologists. The benefit of this approach is the open acknowledgement that an observer brings his or her own background into a scientific question. We are never fully objective observers of events around us: Postmodernists reflect on their own role in these events and in how they tend to interpret them. This movement has swept the humanities and social sciences in recent years and is having a profound impact on how cultural anthropology and the other subfields of anthropology are practiced today in America

and abroad. It has meant that some of the new generation's cultural scholars regard the time-honored ethnographies of the past with skepticism. One healthy result has been an increase in the recognized importance of ethnographies written by scholars of color, especially those who are from the culture they study.

The result of this paradigm shift is that many anthropology departments in American universities are split between cultural and biological approaches to their research. Biological anthropologists are universally empirical, testing hypotheses within an objective scientific framework. Many cultural anthropologists now reject this framework, preferring to interpret what they see in other cultures in light of issues of power, gender, and ethnicity. Many biological anthropologists consider the interpretive approach to be so subjective that little information of long-term merit can come from it.

Although some see this split as a natural outgrowth of the fields, most anthropologists savor the cross-fertilization of ideas that occurs when cultural and biological perspectives are present in the same academic program. Whether this trend toward separation of the disciplines will continue and result in a breakup of the field or is simply a temporary fissure, only time will tell.

ARCHAEOLOGY

Archaeology is the study of how people used to live, based on the materials, or **artifacts**, they left behind. These artifacts, art, implements, and other objects of **material culture** form the basis for the analysis and interpretation of everything from what an ancient culture ate to how its people imagined the afterlife. Because archeological studies have such a broad scope, it is understandable that archaeologists come in many different stripes (Figure 0.12 on page 12).

Prehistoric archaeologists work closely with biological anthropologists. They study cultures that did not leave any recorded written history, from the early hominids to the preliterate antecedents of modern cultures from Hawaii to Africa.

archaeology   The study of the material culture of past peoples.

artifacts   The objects, from tools to art, left by earlier generations of people.

material culture   The objects or artifacts of past human societies.

FIGURE 0.12 Archaeologists doing fieldwork.

linguistic anthropology
The study of language, its origins, and use; also called anthropological linguistics.

When a biological anthropologist excavates a 2-million-year-old fossil site in East Africa, a prehistoric archaeologist often works with the team to document the discovery, map the site, and analyze the primitive stone tools that may be found alongside the fossilized bones. The bones are the direct physical evidence of humanity, and the stone tools are the material cultural evidence. From the study of such stone tools, a prehistoric archaeologist may be able to reconstruct whether the maker of the tool was a hunter or a scavenger, and left- or right-handed.

Archaeologists work at sites all over world, studying time periods from the advent of stone tools 2.5 million years ago to the much more recent past. There are Iron and Bronze Age archaeologists working at sites across Europe and New World archaeologists studying pre-Columbian civilization in Latin America. The history and pattern of settlement of the New World and subsequent migrations of early Native Americans are also studied by archaeologists. What kinds of insight can we gain from the things left behind? Archaeologists in the American Southwest have been embroiled in a fierce debate in recent years about whether the Native Americans we call Anasazis were peaceful farmers or violent warriors. The rapid abandonment of their elaborate stone dwellings in the Southwest by Anasazi people about 800 years ago traditionally was linked to drought and food shortages (Figure 0.13). The Anasazi then scattered across the Southwest, where their descendents live today. But studies of that drought by archaeologists (who studied tree rings to understand how severe the drought may have been, as recorded in patterns of tree growth) led some archaeologists to argue that drought was not enough to move the Anasazi (LeBlanc & Register, 2003). This new view holds that social factors, specifically, intertribal warfare and even internal warfare, were the driving causes that sent the Anasazi from their traditional home.

LINGUISTIC ANTHROPOLOGY

Language is perhaps the only uniquely human social behavior. Whereas other animals have communication systems based on a variety of sounds and calls that you might consider a language—chimpanzees use pant-hoots, pant-grunts, and several dozen other sounds to communicate, for example—only humans have a richly *symbolic* language. Linguists often study language structure: the grammar and sentence structure that are the mechanisms of speaking and writing. They also study the function and development of human speech and language.

FIGURE 0.13 Archaeologists were able to understand why the Anasazi disappeared by studying their material culture.

Linguistic anthropology is the study of the form, function, and social context of language. Linguistic anthropologists usually are more interested in language use and the role that language plays in shaping culture than they are in the technical aspects of language structure. For instance, an anthropological linguist might study the aspects of Black English that set it apart from mainstream English—its word choice and usage—and be interested in the roots of Black English on slave plantations and in West Africa. People tend to use language to conform with their cultural, environmental, and social needs. In India, for instance, Hindi and Bengali speakers have specific labels for a far wider variety of kinship categories (such as a wife's older brother) than English speakers use.

SUMMARY

1. **How is anthropology different from other disciplines that involve the study of humankind?**

   Anthropology is the study of humankind in a cross-cultural perspective. Anthropologists study cultures in far-flung places, and they also study subcultures in our own society, typically immersing themselves in other cultures in ways scholars in other disciplines do not.

2. **What exactly is *culture*, and why do anthropologists care so much about it?**

   Culture is a set of learned behavior traditions. Every human group has its own distinctive culture, which includes its collective values and beliefs. Our capacity for culture itself is biological, and the evolution of intelligence in humans that allowed us to learn much of our behavior is a defining feature of our humanity.

3. **How does biological anthropology differ from the other subfields of anthropology?**

   Biological anthropology is the study of humans as biological creatures. It is the study of where we came from, our evolution, and how our biology interacts with our culture today. Biological anthropology is one of anthropology's four subfields, along with archaeology, cultural anthropology, and linguistic anthropology.

4. **What is the central unifying theory of biological anthropology?**

   Evolution by natural selection is the principle by which biological anthropologists understand the place of humans in the natural world.

CRITICAL THINKING QUESTIONS

1. For centuries, people have argued about whether biology or culture is the more important influence on human behavior, intelligence, and a wide range of other human qualities. This has sometimes been called the genes–environment debate or the nature–nurture debate. Why is the dichotomy between biology and culture a false one? Considering any human trait, from aggression to intelligence to courtship, how might human biology and culture interact with one another?

2. How might a forensic anthropologist be useful to a paleoanthropologist? Can you think of other special training, apart from that described in this chapter, which someone studying the human fossil record might want to have to more fully understand what he or she is studying?

KEY TERMS

primate	osteology	anthropology	ethnography
evolution	paleopathology	culture	archaeology
biological anthropology	forensic anthropology	biocultural	artifacts
hominid	primatology	anthropology	material culture
adaptation	human biology	cultural anthropology	linguistic
paleoanthropology	physical anthropology	ethnology	anthropology

SUGGESTED READING

Darwin, Charles. (1859). *On the Origin of Species by Means of Natural Selection; or, The Preservation of Favoured Races in the Struggle for Life.* Murray, London.

Mead, Margaret. (1972). *Blackberry Winter: My Earlier Years.* William Morrow & Company, New York.

Spencer, Frank. (1997). *A History of Physical Anthropology: An Encyclopedia.* New York: Garland.

CHAPTER

1 | Origins of Evolutionary Thought

CHAPTER OUTLINE

n a courtroom in Pennsylvania, a battle was fought in 2005 over science and religion. A newly elected school board in the town of Dover had passed a policy introducing the teaching of creationist beliefs for the origins of life. The board claimed that, in mandating that intelligent design creationism be taught in high school science classes, they were simply trying to present students with an alternative scientific theory to evolution. Several dismayed parents sued the school board, and the case ended up in a federal court. After a six-week trial that featured impassioned pleas from parents, scientists, and educators, the judge ruled that there was overwhelming evidence that intelligent design is a religious view, a mere relabeling of creationism, and "presents students with a religious alternative masquerading as a scientific theory."

Although some members of the school board said they would appeal the ruling, the next round of local elections saw those members swept from office, and replaced by a school board that favored the teaching of evolution. The battle over evolution was hardly over, however: Other such legal battles over the separation of church and state loomed in Georgia and Kansas.

THE DOVER CASE WAS ONLY ONE OF THE MORE RECENT HIGHLY PUBLICIZED battles between evolution and creationism that have occurred in the United States in the past century. The best-known case was the "Scopes Monkey Trial," which pitted two famous lawyers against each other and focused national attention on the issue in 1925 (Figure 1.1 on page 16). The 1920s was a decade of rapid social change, and conservative Christians, in an effort to preserve traditional values, wanted to ban the teaching of evolution in public schools. The state of Tennessee passed such a ban in 1925.

In the summer of that year, in the small town of Dayton, famed trial attorney Clarence Darrow defended John Scopes, a young schoolteacher charged with illegally teaching evolution. The legendary William Jennings Bryan, a former U.S. secretary of state, represented the state of Tennessee and argued that Scopes should be fired for espousing views that ran counter to literal acceptance of the age of the earth and of humankind as described in the Old Testament. On the witness stand, Darrow forced Bryan to acknowledge that the six-day creation of the Book of Genesis, along with the idea that the earth was very young, were powerful myths not meant to be taken literally. In the end, Scopes was found guilty, was fined $100, and lost his job.

It took decades and numerous court battles before all the states dropped laws banning the teaching of evolution from their books. In each case contested before a federal court, the judge has ruled in favor of the separation of church and state, meaning that religious views should not be taught in a public school classroom. The courts have also stated that evolution is the unifying principle of the life sciences, without valid competition in a science curriculum from theological explanations.

For centuries, people considered the earth to be young and life to be unchanging. Perhaps this is because the reality of evolutionary change is inconceivable to some people. You can't see it, touch it, or sense it happening in any way, unlike more easily perceived physical laws such as gravity. The 80-year human life span is far too short to watch evolution, a process that typically happens on a scale of

FIGURE 1.1 The Scopes Trial: William Jennings Bryan (right) represented the state of Tennessee, and Clarence Darrow (left) represented John Scopes.

thousands of years. The enormous time scale of evolution is one reason that religious fundamentalists in the United States can continue to argue that "evolution is only a theory" and therefore campaign for equal time in public schools for biblical explanations for the origins of life and of humankind. As we shall see in this chapter, evolution is a theoretical framework that is the only way to make sense of a tremendous amount of evidence in support of the theory that is all around us. Fossilized dinosaur bones and ancient hominid skulls are evidence of evolution. But so are disease resistance to antibiotics and the need to develop new pesticides in order to cope with the evolution of resistance in insect pests.

In this chapter we will examine the history of ideas about how life came to be and the proponents and opponents of evolutionary theory and fact. We will also consider the issue of creationist opposition to evolutionary science. Biological anthropologists, as human evolutionary scientists, often find themselves on the front line of the debate over science and creation. First, we need to consider what science is and how it works.

What Is Science?

Science is a process, not a result. The process involves **observation** of a natural phenomenon with some **deduction** about its cause. This leads the researcher to pose a **hypothesis**—a preliminary explanation. Armed with this hypothesis, the scientist tests it (**experimentation**) by collecting of evidence (**data**) that either supports or refutes the hypothesis. This is the **scientific method** (Figure 1.2). It is the way scientists proceed when they have a question that needs answering or a possible explanation for a natural phenomenon that needs testing. Suppose a scientist proposes that the reason that humans walk upright and apes do not is that walking upright uses less energy (in the form of calories burned) per mile of walking, thereby giving early humans who stood up to walk an advantage over their ape ancestors (Rodman & McHenry, 1980). This is the hypothesis. The scientist would then gather evidence—the data—to test this hypothesis. He might compare the caloric output of two-legged and four-legged walking by having a human and a chimpanzee walk on a treadmill while measuring the oxygen consumption of each. If chimpanzees were discovered to be less efficient walkers than humans, then the hypothesis would be supported. Of course, there are always alternative hypotheses; perhaps another researcher would argue that chimpanzees are *more* efficient walkers than other four-legged animals, in which case a whole new study that measures walking efficiency of many other animals will be needed before the first researcher can truly stake his claim.

Science is an *empirical* process that relies on evidence and experiment. Science is not perfect, because data can be subject to differences in interpretation. But

observation   The gathering of scientific information by watching a phenomenon.

deduction   A conclusion that follows logically from a set of observations.

hypothesis   A preliminary explanation of a phenomenon. Hypothesis formation is the first step of the scientific method.

experimentation   The testing of a hypothesis.

data   The scientific evidence produced by an experiment or by observation, from which scientific conclusions are made.

scientific method   Standard scientific research procedure in which a hypothesis is stated, data are collected to test it, and the hypothesis is either supported or refuted.

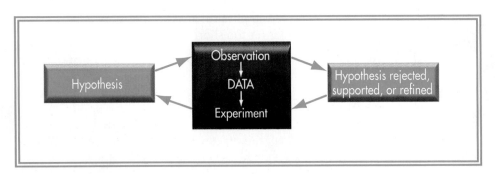

FIGURE 1.2 The scientific method.

science has the essential property of being *self-correcting*. If one scientist claims to have found evidence that the earth is flat but others claim it is round, this question can be resolved by examining all the data, which can be published for the scientific world to scrutinize. If the data supporting the flat-Earth hypothesis are weak, and the weight of scientific evidence indicates that the earth is round, the flat-Earth research will be ignored or overturned. In other words, the hypothesis that the earth is flat is **falsifiable**. Such falsifiability is a defining trait of science. It means that rarely does a scientist claim to have "proven" anything. Instead, results are presented, and a hypothesis is either supported or rejected. Falsifiability is also a primary reason why science is such a powerful way to understand the world around us: The opportunity always exists for others to come along and correct earlier mistakes. This can be a long, slow process. Once a **paradigm**—an intellectual framework for understanding a given set of information—is in place, it may take a great deal of conflicting evidence and debate between scientists before that paradigm is overturned and replaced by a new one. In the next section we examine the great intellects whose ideas changed the paradigm of how we see the natural world.

FIGURE 1.3   Aristotle

The Early Thinkers

Although Darwin is the central intellectual figure in biology and in biological anthropology, his ideas did not reach the public until the publication of his first great book, *On the Origin of Species,* in 1859. For hundreds of years before this event, scholars had been thinking about the nature of life and of humanity. The ancient Greeks often are credited with the first written efforts to understand the natural world and our place in it. In the fourth century B.C., Aristotle (Figure 1.3) described the animal and plant life of the Mediterranean region; he believed that each living form possessed an absolutely fixed essence that could not be altered (**immutability** of species) and that all life was arranged in an orderly, hierarchical ladder, with humans at the very top. Ironically, both Aristotle and Plato considered experimental science to be a crude endeavor compared with the innate beauty and elegance of mathematical theory (White, 2001). Although we often think of these natural philosophers as the first real scientists, they did not see themselves this way.

THE ROOTS OF MODERN SCIENCE

The idea of the fixity of species was the spiritual, legal, and political norm during the Middle Ages. The church set doctrine that could be opposed only under penalty of imprisonment, or worse. Part of this doctrine was that the natural world had always existed in the same form as it exists today. Aristotle's Great Chain of Being, the idea that all organisms existed on a hierarchical ladder of sorts, with people at the top rung, was very much in place as both a natural philosophy and a legal code. Under this mindset, it is easy to see why science barely progressed.

During the Renaissance (fourteenth through sixteenth centuries), three critical developments laid the foundation for the establishment of an academic discipline devoted to a scientific understanding of the human condition (Hodgen, 1964; Rowe, 1965). First, Renaissance scholars saw themselves as "rediscovering" the knowledge of the ancient Greeks and Romans. From our perspective, what they discovered was not as important as their approach to science, which was "modern." Renaissance scholars developed a strong sense of time, their own past, and the process whereby that past is reconstructed. They also developed a sense of cultural variation as they came to realize that the people of antiquity were not like them. Indeed, science became modern when it overturned the old notions of fixity and hierarchy, which were reinforced by the powerful religious doctrine that held sway in the Middle Ages.

Second, great artists of the Renaissance, such as the Italian Leonardo da Vinci (1452–1519) and the Belgian Andreas Vesalius (1514–1564), raised the scientific study

falsifiable   Able to be shown to be false.

paradigm   A conceptual framework useful for understanding a body of evidence.

immutability (or fixity)   Stasis, lack of change.

FIGURE 1.4 Vesalius's *De Humani Corporis Fabrica* was an important early work on the human species.

Contrary to popular notions, the Renaissance was not a time when science was in vogue, although the culture in which it eventually flourished did begin. Instead, mathematics and the arts were held in the highest esteem.

polygenism   Ancient belief that people are derived from multiple creations.

monogenism   Ancient belief that all people are derived from a single creation.

of human anatomy to new heights. Leonardo was perhaps the first true scientist in the modern sense. Representations of the human body in medical texts of the Middle Ages were simplistic and inaccurate, and the anatomical works of the classical physician Galen were still taken to be definitive into the Renaissance period. However, by combining scientific curiosity—culminating in the systematic dissection of the human body—and consummate artistic skill, Renaissance artist–scientists literally changed the way scholars looked at the human body. Vesalius's *De Humani Corporis Fabrica* (*On the Structure of the Human Body,* 1543) became a standard medical text replacing Galen's works (Figure 1.4). Vesalius even demonstrated that Galen's descriptions of human anatomy had been based on the dissection of animals.

Finally, the Renaissance coincided with the first circumnavigation of the globe and the European discovery and exploration of the New World. European naturalists got their first look at thousands of exotic plant and animal species at about the same time that they were trying to be more systematic and accurate in describing the natural world around them. Europeans were exposed to a greater range of human variation, both biological and cultural, than they ever knew existed. Although it was clear that the peoples of the New World were not the monsters of medieval travelers' tales, questions were raised as to their basic humanity. Were they fully human? Did they possess souls? Could their origins be traced to Adam and Eve and the Garden of Eden? Could they be converted to Christianity? The church was definitive on this issue: By proclamation of Pope Paul III in 1537, the Indians of the New World were declared to be, in the eyes of the church, "truly men," sharing a common creation with all other men. This was used as the rationale for converting them to Christianity. This edict was strongly enforced. Sixteenth- and seventeenth-century scholars who argued for multiple origins of humanity—**polygenism**—as opposed to a single, divine origin—**monogenism**—were imprisoned or even burned at the stake. Unfortunately, the declaration that the indigenous people of the New World were indeed people did not prevent their enslavement or exploitation by Christian colonizers.

As classification took precedence in the seventeenth and eighteenth centuries, the issue of the ultimate biological origins of humans was pushed aside. Monogenism, the biblical orthodoxy that all humans were derived from a single creation, held sway in both Protestant and Catholic countries. At the turn of the nineteenth century, natural historians who wrote about people, such as the American Samuel Stanhope Smith (1750–1819) and the German Johann Friedrich Blumenbach (1752–1840), indicated their strong support for the basic unity of humankind via monogenesis. However, in the first half of the nineteenth century, an increasing number of scholars supported polygenism or multiple origins (see Chapter 5).

Most natural historians and philosophers before the nineteenth century believed that there was a single creation event. Anglican archbishop James Ussher (1581–1656) calculated the date of the creation of Earth using the only evidence of the age of Earth available to him: the Old Testament of the Bible. By counting backward using the ages of the main characters as given in the books of the Old Testament, Ussher arrived at 4004 B.C. as the year of the creation. Although it sounds a bit silly today, Ussher had no other chronological evidence available to him. He knew that Adam had lived to a ripe old age and begat Cain and Abel; the cumulative ages of these founders and all their descendants added up to about a 5,500-year history of the world. Ussher's date provided the time frame for understanding the natural history of Earth for more than two centuries and to this day is accepted by fundamentalist Christian creationists as a reasonably accurate estimate for the age of Earth.

During this period of European history, the church exerted enormous influence over scientific thinking. Speaking out against church doctrine was a crime punishable by death. When Italian mathematician Galileo Galilei (1564–1642) turned his homemade telescope to the night sky in 1609 and saw that the giant planet

Jupiter had four large moons orbiting it, he immediately realized that he had proof of Copernicus's sun-centered theory of a century earlier. The universe was not, as church doctrine held, Earth-centered and stationary; the planets of the solar system obviously were in orbit around our sun. But this was heresy, and Galileo spent years under house arrest by order of the pope for publishing his findings in a famous little book called *The Starry Messenger,* published in 1610. The law of the church was simple and steadfast: God created Earth and everything on it, and life as we know it today remains unchanged since the moment of the creation.

Over time, with the advent of more powerful telescopes and with the work on motion and gravity by German mathematician and astronomer Johnannes Kepler (1571–1630) and English physicist Isaac Newton (1642–1727), it became impossible for the church to argue against the burgeoning evidence of a sun-centered solar system constantly in orbital motion. But the official church doctrine, stating that humans were the center of the creation and that all current forms of life remain unchanged from their original forms, stayed firmly entrenched.

LINNAEUS AND THE NATURAL SCHEME OF LIFE

In the seventeenth and eighteenth centuries, naturalists became more concerned with developing classification schemes for naming and organizing plants and animals. Nevertheless, they did not part company with the theological view of a static, unchanging world. The classification scheme we use in the biological sciences today (now called the *Linnaean system*) dates from this period.

Anglican minister John Ray (1627–1705) was the first naturalist to use the terms *genus* and *species* to designate types of animals and plants. Later, Carolus Linnaeus (1707–1778), an eminent Swedish botanist and the author of the *Systema Naturae,* built on Ray's writings to create the most comprehensive classification of the plant world compiled at the time (Figure 1.5). In addition to his work on plants, Linnaeus studied the diversity of animal life, often based on specimens shipped to his laboratory from far-flung corners of the world. He used the physical characteristics of plants and animals to assign them to a scheme of classification. The science of classifying and naming living things that Linnaeus invented is called **taxonomy**. Sorting organisms into categories was a vital way to make sense of their patterns of relationship, so he applied a hierarchy of names to the categories of similarity, which today we call the Linnaean hierarchy.

The two-level genus–species labels, or **binomial nomenclature**, were at the heart of taxonomy; a **taxon** is any unit of this formal hierarchy. Linnaeus followed the naming pattern of the ancient Greeks by using Greek and Latin languages for his scheme. But Linnaeus was intellectually hidebound by his theology. He believed firmly in the immutability of species—that each species existed as a completely separate entity from every other species and that these separations were fixed by God. Influenced further by his belief that apes and humans could not be closely related by common descent, Linnaeus assigned people to the family Hominidae and great apes to the family Pongidae. This separation stands to this day although, as we shall see, it may not be justifiable on biological grounds.

An obvious example of how Linnaean categorizing could have helped to make sense of human nature is the taxonomic comparison of apes and humans. One of the earliest anatomical descriptions of an ape—a young, female chimpanzee—was published in 1699 by Edward Tyson. In his description, the chimpanzee is referred to variously as a "pygmie" and an "orang-outang." Tyson wrote, "Now notwithstanding our *Pygmie* does so much resemble a *Man* in many of its parts, more than any of the *Ape-kind,* or any other *Animal* in the World I know of" (McCown & Kennedy, 1971, p. 43).

Tyson considered this African ape to be very similar to humans and to the Asian ape (the orangutan). He saw it as different from both humans and monkeys but sharing many features with each. Nonetheless, Tyson was certain that the ape was a species

FIGURE 1.5 Carolus Linnaeus

taxonomy The science of biological classification.

binomial nomenclature Linnaean naming system for all organisms, consisting of a genus and species label.

taxon A group of organisms assigned to a particular category.

FIGURE 1.6   Comte de Buffon

FIGURE 1.7   Georges Cuvier

catastrophism   Theory that there have been multiple creations interspersed by great natural disasters such as Noah's flood.

theory of inheritance of acquired characteristics   Discredited theory of evolutionary change proposing that changes that occur during the lifetime of an individual, through use or disuse, can be passed on to the next generation.

of animal and not a mixture of species. Not until Linnaeus, however, did anyone undertake a truly systematic study of anatomical comparisons among the primates.

The Road to the Darwinian Revolution

In the eighteenth and early nineteenth centuries, a number of European natural historians made their mark in explaining the nature of the diversity of flora and fauna on Earth. Some of these directly influenced Darwin's thinking decades later; most were also following in Linnaeus's taxonomic footsteps. Prominent among these were three eminent French natural historians.

Comte de Buffon   Georges-Louis Leclerc, Comte de Buffon (1707–1788), accepted the general notion of biological change. Buffon (Figure 1.6) observed that animals that migrate to new climates often change in response to new environments, although like others of his day, he had no idea about the mechanism of change. He famously claimed that the animals of the New World were weaker and smaller than their counterparts in the Old World, a result of a generally less healthy and less productive environment. This claim was vigorously refuted by Thomas Jefferson in his *Notes on the State of Virginia* (1787).

Georges Cuvier   By the turn of the nineteenth century, discoveries of dinosaur bones across western Europe had made it difficult for biblically driven scholars to continue to deny the importance of change to the history of Earth. Georges Cuvier (born Jean-Léopold Cuvier; 1769–1832) rose rapidly in the ranks of the world's foremost natural scientists at the Natural History Museum of Paris, where he spent his entire career. Cuvier (Figure 1.7) was a steadfast opponent of the modern concept of evolutionary change. The existence of extinct creatures such as dinosaurs was a large problem for Cuvier and other creationist scientists of the day because their bones presented compelling evidence of a past world very different from that of the present day. Cuvier and his supporters sought to explain away these fossils by embracing the concept of extinction and change, but with a biblical twist. They advocated a theory now known as **catastrophism**, in which cataclysmic disasters were believed to have wiped out earlier forms of life on Earth. One such natural disaster that Cuvier had in mind was Noah's flood. After such an event, Cuvier argued, more advanced animals from other regions of world moved in to repopulate the flooded area. These replacement populations were thought to be more advanced than the originals.

Geoffroy Saint-Hilaire   Cuvier's contemporary Geoffroy Saint-Hilaire (1772–1844) was an anatomist and a strong advocate of evolutionary change. He engaged in acrimonious public debate with Cuvier on the subject after he corrected Cuvier on identification of a crocodile skeleton as a fossil species, which Cuvier had believed to be an unknown modern species. Saint-Hilaire's work led him to support his senior colleague Jean-Baptiste Lamarck, who had proposed a system to explain the process of evolution.

Jean-Baptiste Lamarck   In 1809, Lamarck (1744–1829) proposed his **theory of inheritance of acquired characteristics**, which is today often called simply *Lamarckianism*. Lamarck (Figure 1.8) argued that all organisms make adjustments to their environment during their lifetime that could be passed on to their offspring, making those offspring better adapted to their environment. It relied on the concept of *need and use*. For example, if an animal that lived by the seashore spent much of its time swimming in the ocean, its offspring, according to Lamarck, would be better swimmers than their parents had been. In postulating this sort of evolutionary process, Lamarck made one laudable breakthrough and one major error. The breakthrough was seeing the crucial relationship between the organism and its environment. But the fundamental error was thinking that evolutionary change could occur during the lifetime of an individual. This error is easily recognized by taking Lamarck's theory to its logical extension: If a mouse loses its tail to a cat, does the mouse later give birth to babies lacking tails? Likewise, no amount of bodybuilding will enable you to give birth to muscular children.

Larmarck's idea is often ridiculed today, but it was a brilliant notion in light of the evidence of evolutionary change available in the eighteenth century. Lamarck knew nothing about the mode of inheritance—genes—and his theory of the inheritance of acquired characteristics served as a natural antecedent to Darwin's theories (Figure 1.9).

The so-called **Lysenkoism** incident in the twentieth century illustrated the failure of Lamarck's theory in a dramatic way. Trofim Lysenko, although never formally educated in biology, was one of the top-ranking botanists in the Soviet Union from the 1930s to 1960s. He argued that Darwinian thinking was inherently capitalist in its focus on the individual struggle for existence. He also rejected the "capitalist" model of population growth and ensuing fierce competition for scarce resources described by British social theorist Thomas Malthus (1766–1834). Malthus had observed that if left unchecked, human populations would grow rapidly, outstripping their resources and ultimately crashing because of famine.

Lysenko campaigned successfully for a Lamarckian (he called it Stalinist–Marxist) model of evolution to be applied to Soviet agricultural production. He took the environmental focus of Larmarck's work to an illogical extreme. For years

FIGURE 1.8 Jean-Baptiste Lamarck

Lysenkoism Soviet-era research program that tried to apply Lamarckian thinking to agricultural production.

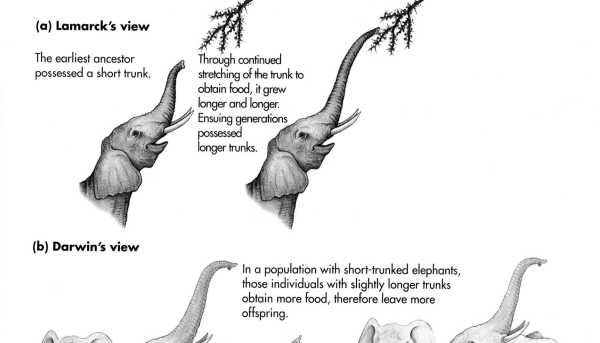

(a) Lamarck's view

The earliest ancestor possessed a short trunk.

Through continued stretching of the trunk to obtain food, it grew longer and longer. Ensuing generations possessed longer trunks.

(b) Darwin's view

In a population with short-trunked elephants, those individuals with slightly longer trunks obtain more food, therefore leave more offspring.

Many generations later, natural selection has changed the species to an elephant that possesses a long trunk.

FIGURE 1.9 Lamarckian and Darwinian views of evolution.

FIGURE 1.10   Charles Lyell

Soviet scientists stored winter wheat grain at low temperatures, on the theory that such exposure during the seeds' lifetime would create a new generation of wheat that was cold tolerant, thereby turning the colder parts of the Soviet Union into a new breadbasket. Of course, the experiment was an embarrassing and tragic failure. Soviet biology was set back decades (many of their best genetic scientists were exiled to concentration camps, never to be seen again). Lysenkoism is a good example of why political ideology should never drive scientific practice.

THE UNIFORMITARIANS: HUTTON AND LYELL

At about the same time that Lamarck's ideas were being debated, a key piece of the evolution puzzle fell into place. Along the rocky Scottish seacoast, James Hutton (1726–1797) spent his career studying, among other things, layering of rock formations. One of the fathers of modern geology, Hutton saw clear evidence of past worlds in the upthrusting of the earth. A devout Christian, Hutton attempted to shoehorn his observations into a biblical framework. However, he did assert a central principle that stands to this day: **uniformitarianism**. Hutton asserted that the geological processes that drive the natural world today are the same as those that prevailed in the past. Hutton was not prepared to extend this theory to the living world; that was left for Charles Darwin many years later. But his views of the changing Earth strongly influenced a generation of geologists.

Charles Lyell (1797–1875), another British geologist, was a strong proponent of uniformitarianism, arguing that slow, gradual change was the way of the physical world and that if one looked in older and older rock sediments, one would find increasingly primitive forms of life. Although an ardent creationist, Lyell (Figure 1.10) became the leading geologist of his day; through his research and his prominence in the social hierarchy of nineteenth-century London, Lyell exerted an enormous influence over his academic peers. His acquaintance with Darwin certainly was a strong influence on the latter's evolutionary ideas. His book *Principles of Geology*, published in three volumes beginning in 1830, was a work that Darwin carried and read time and again during his voyage of discovery on the sailing ship HMS *Beagle*. Lyell played a key role in convincing both the scientific world and the public that the earth's history could be understood only in the context of deep, ancient changes in geology, which necessarily cast creationist explanations for life in a different, more dubious light.

uniformitarianism   Theory that the same gradual geological process we observe today was operating in the past.

The Darwinian Revolution

Charles Darwin (1809–1882) was one of six children born into a life of affluence. His father was a prominent physician, his maternal grandfather was famed pottery maker Josiah Wedgwood, and his paternal grandfather was Erasmus Darwin (1731–1802), an eminent naturalist and philosopher. Darwin's mother died when he was 8 years old. An ardent naturalist from an early age, Darwin wandered the English countryside in search of animals and plants to study. However, he was a lackluster student. When Darwin was 16, his father sent him to study medicine at the University of Edinburgh. Uninterested in his studies and appalled at the sight of surgery, young Darwin did not fare well academically. He did, however, make his initial contacts with evolutionary theory, in the form of Lamarck's ideas about evolutionary change.

Darwin subsequently left Edinburgh and headed to Cambridge University, where he studied for the ministry in the Church of England (Figure 1.11). Two key events in Darwin's career took place there. One of his professors at Cambridge was John Henslow, a botanist and eminent naturalist who deeply influenced Darwin's scientific thinking. Second, Darwin read, and was greatly inspired by, the travel and natural history accounts of the renowned German explorer and scientist Baron Friedrich Heinrich Alexander von Humboldt. Darwin received his divinity degree in 1831;

FIGURE 1.11   Charles Darwin

however, his university studies in the natural sciences had left him more eager for adventure and natural history study than for a vocation in the ministry.

In the summer of 1831, while Darwin was on a natural history field trip in Wales, Henslow was meeting with Captain Robert Fitzroy (1805–1865). Fitzroy, an officer in the Royal Navy and himself a keen amateur naturalist, was planning a voyage to map the coastlines of the continents, particularly South America, on the sailing ship HMS *Beagle*. He had invited Henslow to accompany him, but he turned down the offer, as did Henslow's first-choice alternate, his brother-in-law. Henslow then put Darwin's name forward, and Fitzroy accepted. Charles Darwin thus departed in December 1831 as the "gentleman" amateur naturalist aboard the *Beagle*, a trip that changed not only Darwin but also modern science. It also changed Captain Fitzroy, whose deep Christian beliefs eventually led him to regret his decision to take Darwin along on the voyage.

> *Robert Fitzroy later married an evangelical Christian woman, deepening his own faith and intensifying his dislike of Darwin's ideas. He battled Darwin for the remainder of his life.*

THE GALÁPAGOS

It's hard for us to appreciate today what a rare gift a trip around the world was for a naturalist in the early nineteenth century. The 22-year-old Darwin, who had left the Britain Isles only once before his voyage on the *Beagle,* spent 5 years of his life exploring the seacoasts of South America, Australia, and Africa, with many stops along the way (Figure 1.12). From 1831 to 1836, unburdened by other distractions, he was able to devote most of his waking hours to observing myriad plants and animals in their natural environment.

Contrary to the popular image of Darwin spending 5 years at sea, most of his time was spent on land expeditions or in seaside ports in South America. He rode horses in Patagonia, trekked in the Andes, and explored oceanic islands in the Atlantic and Pacific Oceans. Of these oceanic island stops, one had a profound influence on Darwin: the Galápagos Islands.

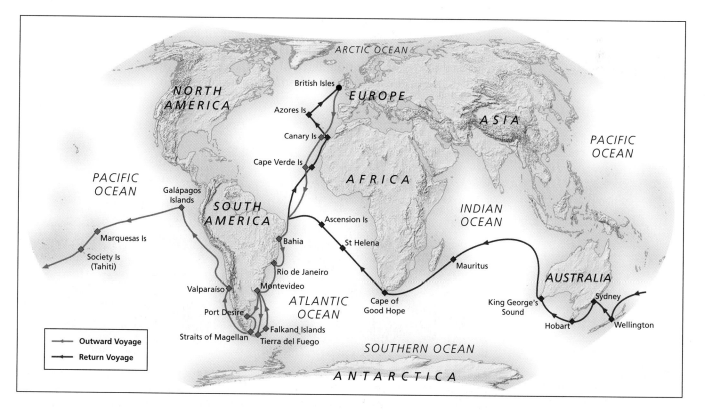

FIGURE 1.12   Map of Darwin's voyage on the HMS *Beagle.*

FIGURE 1.13   Darwin was deeply influenced by his stop in the Galápagos Islands, isolated volcanic rocks off the coast of Ecuador.

The *Beagle* dropped anchor amid a cluster of rocky islands 600 miles off the coast of Ecuador on September 15, 1835. The two dozen Galápagos Islands, most of them tiny lumps of rock, are of recent volcanic origin (Figure 1.13). Most of the islands are rather barren, possessing only a few species of large animals, most notably reptiles and birds. Darwin was amazed by the bizarre and oddly approachable animal life of the islands, including iguana-like lizards that dived into the sea to forage for seaweeds and enormous tortoises that weighed more than 400 pounds shown in Figures 1.14 and 1.15 (Darwin, 1839).

Each of the Galápagos Islands had its own varieties of animals. There was a distinctive variety of giant tortoise on each, many of which still survive today. It was the birds, however, that provided Darwin with the key piece of evidence for his eventual theory of evolution. Each of the islands had its own species of finch. Some lived on the arid rocky islets, and others on lusher parts of the island group. There

FIGURE 1.14   Darwin observed that tortoises on islands that are arid tend to have saddle-shaped shells, allowing them to reach into trees to browse.

FIGURE 1.15   But tortoises on lusher islands where grass is plentiful and the need to reach into trees not so frequent, have dome-shaped shells.

were finches with rather generic-looking beaks; finches with long, slender beaks; and finches with remarkably large, strong beaks. Altogether, Darwin collected at least thirteen different varieties of small, brownish or black finches in the islands, skinning them and packing them into crates to carry back to London's British Museum.

There are many myths about the influence the Galápagos had on Darwin. He certainly did not immediately formulate the theory of natural selection upon spending a month there. In fact, Darwin left the Galápagos an uneasy creationist, his heretical ideas taking shape only months and years later (Larson, 2001). And although history often records Darwin as immediately recognizing something of evolutionary importance when he began to see the variations among finch species, this was not the case. Darwin collected hundreds of the little birds but never saw the importance of their small differences in appearance. In fact, he never even labeled the specimens as to the specific island on which he had collected them. It was ornithologist John Gould in London who studied the expedition's collection of finches, now stuffed, and realized that they could be sorted into an array of different species according to island. In his published journal of voyage of the *Beagle*, written the year after he returned home, Darwin said,

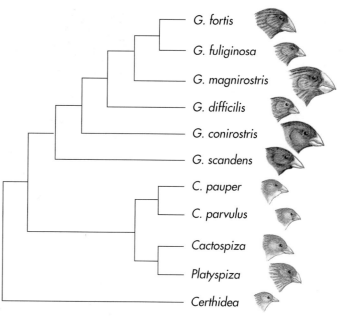

FIGURE 1.16 Darwin's finches: Adaptive radiation of bill types.

> Seeing this gradation and diversity of structure in one small, intimately related group of birds, one might really fancy that from an original paucity of birds in this archipelago, one species had been taken and modified for different ends. (Darwin, 1839)

In light of Gould's discovery of bill differences, Darwin realized the importance of the finches for his budding theory. He surmised that the various animal varieties of the Galápagos, from giant tortoises to mockingbirds, probably were descended from a very small number of creatures that had reached the islands (presumably from the South American mainland) long ago and had then diversified in response to the different island habitats they found there (Figure 1.16). Darwin referred to this process of many species emerging from one or few ancient ones, like the spokes of wheel emerging from the hub, as **adaptive radiation**. The process of biological change in a species by which such a radiation occurs, Darwin referred to as **natural selection**. In fact, the Galápagos were the perfect setting for Darwin to see evolution in action. Because they are islands, isolated from the mainland, and because they are relatively young, they are biologically simple. Only a few species had managed to reach the islands. Perhaps the ancestors of the finches had been blown off course while flying in a storm and ended up there; ocean currents probably had carried the tortoises and iguanas there as they floated or clung to pieces of driftwood. Finding rocky islets that had food and shelter but few competitors, the species flourished, and eventually their descendants had radiated into the available space in the archipelago.

In setting out his theory of evolution, Darwin used what he had learned from the Galápagos in three ways. First, he observed that isolated oceanic islands seem to hold many species found nowhere else, many of them closely related. Second, isolated islands often lack whole groups of animals found on the mainland; for example, the Galápagos Islands lack any large mammals. Darwin therefore suggested that because only a few tenacious species reach such islands, others fill the place of missing species. In the Galápagos, the place of land mammals may be taken by gigantic tortoises and oversized iguanas. Third, the distinctive animals and plants of isolated islands tend to resemble close relatives on the mainland, even when the environment of the island differs greatly from that of the mainland.

adaptive radiation The diversification of one founding species into multiple species and niches.

natural selection Differential reproductive success over multiple generations.

FIGURE 1.17   Darwin spent most of his life after the voyage of the *Beagle* at Down House in the village of Downe, south of London.

REFINING THE THEORY OF EVOLUTION BY NATURAL SELECTION

Home in England, Darwin took up a life of nature study, contemplation, and writing. He married his cousin Emma Wedgwood and purchased a manor house in the village of Downe, some 15 miles south of London (Figure 1.17). Beset by a variety of health problems, he rarely left Downe and was bedridden for long periods. But he spent years developing his theory of natural selection, drawing extensively on the parallel process of artificial selection. When animal breeders try to develop new strains of livestock, they select the traits they want to enhance and allow only those individuals to breed. For example, a farmer who tries to boost milk production in Guernsey cows must allow only the best milk producers to breed, and over many generations, milk production will indeed increase. Darwin developed friendships with some of the local breeders of fancy pigeons and drew on their work to elaborate on his theory of natural selection. Pigeons, horses, cows, dogs: All are fine examples of what selective breeding can achieve in a few generations. What artificial breeders do in captivity, natural selection does in the wild—with one key exception. The animal breeder chooses certain traits, such as floppy ears or a long tail, and pushes the evolution of the breed in that direction generation after generation (Figure 1.18). He or she has a goal in mind with respect to animal form or function. Natural selection has no such foresight. Instead, it molds each generation in response to current environmental conditions.

Darwin's theory was really composed of two separate ideas. First, he argued that life on Earth had arisen by evolution rather than by separate creation (although in his early publications he used the term *descent with modification* instead of *evolution*). Whereas separate creation advocates believed modern animals and plants each had their own separate origin (having been created by God), Darwin proposed that all life forms descended from common ancestors. The second, and really groundbreaking part of Darwin's theory, was the mechanism behind the evolutionary process: natural selection.

(a)

(b)

(c)

(d)

FIGURE 1.18 Species of horses: (a) zebra, (b) Przewalski's horse, (c) Tibetan kiang, and (d) thoroughbred race horse.

As Darwin worked his theories into publishable form, he had frequent discussions with his two closest colleagues. One of these was Joseph Hooker, Henslow's brother-in-law and a well-known botanist. The other was T. H. Huxley (Figure 1.19), an ally whose support Darwin relied on time and again during his life after the publication of *On the Origin of Species,* and who remained a loyal advocate of Darwinian theory long after the author's death. Darwin was content to ruminate on his ideas, reworking them over and over and publishing only short sketches of the theory in the 1840s, even as his friends pushed him to go public. For years Darwin demurred, fearing the public reaction to his controversial idea.

Alfred Russel Wallace   In 1858 an event occurred that galvanized Darwin into action. He received a letter and manuscript from Alfred Russel Wallace (1823–1913), another field biologist then collecting plant and animal specimens in Indonesia (Figure A in Insights and Advances: Darwin versus Wallace? on page 28). Wallace's life paralleled Darwin's only in his citizenship and lifelong fascination with nature. Otherwise, in the class-conscious society of nineteenth-century England, the

FIGURE 1.19   Thomas H. Huxley

INSIGHTS AND ADVANCES

Darwin versus Wallace?

Imagine you are a prominent scientist who has been working day and night for 20 years on a groundbreaking theory that you are certain will revolutionize the life sciences. Then one day you receive a thin parcel in the mail, sent by a colleague who has innocently enclosed a manuscript detailing exactly the same theory. Furthermore, the letter asks your help in improving the theory and your advice on how best to publicize it to the world.

This is the situation in which Charles Darwin found himself on a day in June 1858. The mail delivery to his home in England included a package sent by steamship from the remote reaches of the Indonesian islands. The parcel from Alfred Russel Wallace had been 2 months in transit. Darwin and Wallace had corresponded for several years since the publication of a short paper Wallace had written on his early ideas about evolutionary change in animal populations.

Wallace's cover letter described a handwritten manuscript he had enclosed that detailed a theory he had been working on for many years. Wallace titled the manuscript "On the Tendency of Varieties to Depart Indefinitely from the Original Type." We can picture the mailing envelope opening and that cover page sliding before Darwin's eyes. As he no doubt immediately saw, the manuscript proposed a slight variant of the theory of evolution by natural selection. Beginning with a rejection of Lamarckian notions of change, Wallace outlined the way in which some variations in nature are favorable and others unfavorable, and the tendency for such variation to produce new forms better suited to their environments. He even paralleled Darwinian thinking in his use of Thomas Malthus's work on populations. Wallace's idea differed in two important ways from Darwin's. Wallace rejected artificial selection—selective breeding—as analogous to natural selection, while Darwin felt animal breeders were essentially mimicking the lengthy process of

natural selection. Wallace also placed more emphasis on the replacement of groups and species by other groups and species than did Darwin, who focused on individuals (in this Wallace was certainly wrong).

Although the exact date that Darwin replied to Wallace's letter and manuscript is not known, journals and letters written by the two men suggest that Darwin waited for several weeks, during which he chronicled his worries about receiving proper credit for the theory in his journal. He characterized the similarities between Wallace's theory and his own:

> I never saw a more striking coincidence, if Wallace had my m.s. [manuscript] sketch written out in 1842 he could not have made a better abstract. (Browne, 2002)

Darwin finally wrote back to Wallace, responding politely but with a note of territoriality. He reminded Wallace that "this summer marks the twentieth year since I opened my first notebook on the question how and in what way do species and varieties differ from each other." (Browne, 2002). He apparently spent weeks fretting that his own work had been rendered unoriginal by Wallace. But Darwin's allies Lyell and Hooker would have

FIGURE A   Alfred Russel Wallace

none of this. They insisted that Darwin had priority of place and that he should assert his primacy in responding to Wallace and presenting their ideas before the British scientific community.

Darwin and his ally Hooker proposed in separate letters to Wallace that Darwin be allowed to present a jointly authored paper with an introduction by Lyell and Hooker at a meeting of the Linnean Society of London, announcing both theories simultaneously. Wallace was delighted that his work would receive such prominent attention in the scientific world and that his ideas would be linked to those of such eminent thinkers. Several months later, Wallace received another letter from Hooker, informing him that the joint Darwin–Wallace presentation had taken place and that the two papers had been read: first Darwin's, then Wallace's. The paper was then published as one paper in the proceedings of the event, with Darwin as first author and Wallace listed second. The title of Wallace's original manuscript had been altered, however: The term *natural selection,* which Darwin had coined, had been inserted into it.

Three factors may have guaranteed Darwin's fame as the founder of the theory of natural selection. First, Wallace recognized that Darwin had been thinking and writing about his ideas for 20 years and had published a sketch of his theory as early as 1845 (in a revised version of his journal of the voyage of the *Beagle*). Second, Wallace granted enormous respect to Darwin, who was a member of the upper class and had powerful scientific allies. Third, Wallace was living in the jungles of Malaysia and so was unable to argue his own case or present his own paper to the Linnean Society. Had Wallace been in London at the time, and had he been a bit less respectful of his senior colleague, the theory of the origin of species might have emerged quite differently.

two men were from different worlds. Whereas Darwin was from wealthy landed gentry, Wallace grew up in a working-class family, leaving school at an early age. His employment as a specimen collector for wealthy patrons took him on far-flung adventures and set the stage for him to gain many of the same insights that Darwin had gained on the *Beagle*. Wallace had come up with his own version of the theory of evolution by natural selection and was writing to Darwin for advice as to whether the idea was sound and worthy of publication (Insights and Advances: Darwin versus Wallace?). With prodding from Hooker and Huxley, Darwin wrote up his own theory and readied it for presentation before the Royal Linnaean Society and for publication.

Twelve hundred copies of *On the Origin of Species* were published on November 24, 1859, and quickly sold out of every bookshop in London. Alongside the expected best sellers that autumn—Charles Dickens's *Tale of Two Cities* and Alfred Lord Tennyson's *Idylls of the King*—it was a surprise hit. Darwin wrote, as did many scientific authors of his day, with both a scientific audience and the reading public in mind. He was immediately besieged by letters and requests for personal appearances. Darwin was suddenly one of the most famous men in the world.

In presenting his theory of evolution by natural selection as laid out in *On the Origin of Species,* Darwin explained his three observations and two deductions:

Observation 1. All organisms have the potential for explosive population growth that would outstrip their food supply. Darwin took this idea directly from Malthus, who had been concerned with human population growth. A female bullfrog may lay 100,000 eggs every spring, but we don't see bullfrogs hopping everywhere. Even humans, with their very low reproductive potential compared with most animals, can undergo exponential population growth, as evidenced by the global population explosion.

Observation 2. But when we look at nature, we see populations that are roughly stable.

Deduction 1. Therefore, there must be a struggle for existence. That is, the bullfrog's 100,000 eggs may yield no more than a handful, or even just one, adult frog. This, Darwin labeled *natural selection* to parallel the term *artificial selection* in use by animal breeders of the period.

Observation 3. Nature is full of variation. Even in one animal group, every individual is slightly different from every other individual. If you look closely enough, even a basketful of uniform-looking bullfrogs will resolve into myriad small differences in size, shape, color, and other features.

Deduction 3. Therefore, some of these variations must be favored, and others must be disfavored, in a process we can call natural selection.

This elegantly simple set of ideas is the heart of evolutionary theory. Famed biologist Julian Huxley, the grandson of Darwin's ally T. H. Huxley, referred to the idea as bringing about "the greatest of all revolutions in human thought, greater than Einstein's or Freud's or even Newton's." Far from the eternally static cubbyholes that most earlier thinkers had conceived, species were dynamic units, constantly in flux in response to changing environments and the unceasing pressure of competitors (Figure 1.20 on page 30). Natural selection was a filtering process in which unfavorable traits lost the race with more favorable traits. As Darwin saw it, natural selection is all about reproductive success. The time-honored definition of natural selection as "survival of the fittest," a phrase coined by social theorist Herbert Spencer, is misleading. It is much more about the number of offspring an organism leaves in the next generation, who themselves survive to reproductive age, a measure we call **fitness,** a biological measure of reproductive success (not a reference to physical fitness). This can be measured, and the qualities that contribute to reproductive success can often be determined. Natural selection can therefore be defined as differential reproductive success across multiple generations and among the individuals of a given population of animals or plants.

*The term "evolution" became common after Darwin used it in later editions of **The Origins of the Species**. It is nearly absent from the first edition.*

fitness   Reproductive success.

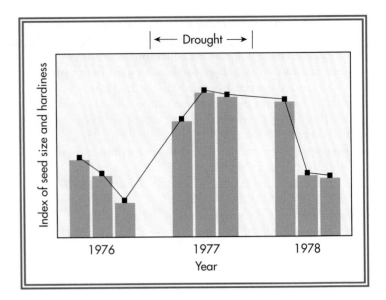

FIGURE 1.20 Index of seed size and hardiness prior to, during, and after drought.

For natural selection to work, three preconditions must be met (Figure 1.21):

1. *The trait in question must be inherited.* For example, if you incubate the eggs of some animals, such as reptiles, at temperatures that are too high or too low, the resulting baby will have odd color patterns. These are not genetic and so are not under the control of natural selection.

2. *The trait in question must show variation between individuals.* Natural selection cannot distinguish good from bad traits if all individuals are genetically identical clones. This is rarely the case in nature, where variants abound, and is the key difference between organisms that reproduce by asexual splitting, such as amoebas, and higher animals that reproduce sexually. Higher animals are all genetically unique, so their traits can be selected or not selected.

3. *The filter between the organism and its genetic makeup is the environment, which must exert some pressure in order for natural selection to act.* Many scholars believe that humans evolved rapidly in part because the environment in which our ancestors lived underwent many dramatic fluctuations caused by world climate swings.

Evolution is about change. Although in common English usage *evolution* sometimes is used to describe the changes an individual goes through in the course of a lifetime ("in my evolution as an artist …"), in biology this is never the case. It is a change in a **population** (a breeding group of organisms of the same kind) in the frequency of a trait or a gene from one generation to the next. The currency of change is the genetic material, in which alterations in the DNA sequence provide the raw source of variation—**mutation**—on which natural selection can act. Whereas

population An interbreeding group of organisms.

mutation An alteration in the DNA, which may or may not alter the function of a cell. If it occurs in a gamete, it may be passed from one generation to the next.

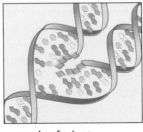

(a) Mode of inheritance

(b) Variation among individuals

(c) Environmental pressure

FIGURE 1.21 The prerequisites needed for natural selection to occur.

evolution happens at the level of the population, natural selection occurs at the level of the individual organism. As we will see, this has important implications for understanding how the evolutionary process produces the myriad forms we see in nature.

The Response to Darwin

Although many people think that Darwin's (and Wallace's) theory of evolution by natural selection was a dramatically new view that replaced the old view of immutability, this is only partly true. Scholars had held evolutionary views for generations; recall Lamarck and his many advocates right up to the time of Darwin. Darwin simply offered a mechanism, one so elegantly simple and effective that many scholars were surprised that they had not themselves seen it.

But the response to Darwin by some scholars was not immediate acceptance. The church and many religious people were offended and outraged by the implication that there was no meaning to existence other than the random sorting of traits by natural processes. Even in the scientific community there were many holdouts who continued to argue for other forms of evolutionary change into the midtwentieth century. For instance, Louis Agassiz of Harvard University was one of America's most prominent naturalists around the time of the publication of *On the Origin of Species*. Darwin's book rendered Agassiz's work on animal classification instantly obsolete.

Agassiz not only repudiated natural selection but also set out to refute it (Larson, 2001). He offered his own view, based on Cuvier's theory of catastrophism and multiple new creations, to explain the appearance of fossil animals that no longer existed. Agassiz fought Darwin tooth and nail, motivated by both professional jealousy and a deeply held belief that natural selection's failure to invoke the power of a divine creator made it fatally flawed. He mounted expeditions to the Galápagos and elsewhere to seek evidence that natural selection was wrong. He seized on Darwin's prediction that the creatures of the Galápagos, ridiculously tame and approachable in the 1830s, would evolve a fear of humans once they had been hunted for generations. Agassiz tried to demonstrate that the creatures' continued tameness in the 1860s showed that Darwinian theory must be flawed. Most other naturalists chastised Agassiz for this futile attempt to refute natural selection since intense hunting of the Galápagos animals had begun only a century earlier. Agassiz's death after his return from the 1873 expedition silenced his voice of opposition.

Failure to accept natural selection came from other scientific quarters as well. Neo-Lamarckian views surfaced in the decades after the publication of the *Origin* and persisted well into the twentieth century. Darwin himself, challenged repeatedly by critics and hampered by the general lack of understanding of genetic transmission, acknowledged that Lamarckian mechanisms might have some role in evolutionary change. Not until the so-called neo-Darwinian modern synthesis of the 1940s and 1950s, when Ernst Mayr and other biologists integrated ecology with Darwinian theory, genetics, anatomy, and other fields, did the full weight and influence of Darwin pervade the biological sciences and, by extension, the field of biological anthropology.

Science and Creationism

Ever since the publication of *On the Origin of Species*, a small but vocal minority in the United States (and other countries) have argued against the teaching of the principles of evolution. They argue instead for a biblical, creationist view of the origin of species and of humanity. But what exactly is a *creationist*? A scientist who studies the origins of the known universe but who believes that the universe may have been created 14 billion years ago by a single supernatural force is a creationist. So is a fundamentalist who believes the earth and every living thing on it

Although scientists reject the idea of a six-day creation, many scientists reconcile their own faith and their science by believing in some force in the universe that goes beyond what science currently can explain.

FIGURE 1.22 A student protesting the teaching of creationism.

were created in 6 days, that dinosaurs and other extinct animals never existed, and that we are all descendants of Adam and Eve. Creationism is simply a belief in a single creative force in the universe.

The ongoing conflict between evolution and creationism lies in the claim by some fundamentalist religious groups that the creation story in the Book of Genesis is a viable alternative to science as the explanation for how humans came to be. These groups argue that evolution is a theory that has no more scientific validity than biblical explanations for the origins of life and of people. The intellectual centerpiece of their thinking is that the earth is very young (i.e., it is approximately the age calculated by Ussher) and that the sedimentary layers of the earth that provide scientists with evidence of antiquity, and also yield most of our fossils, were really the product of Noah's flood and are of very recent origin. They consider the species found alive today and in the most recent fossil beds to be the species that could swim well enough to escape the rising flood waters. This belief can be easily overturned by an examination of the fossil record and by the study of radiometric dating of the age of the earth's layers.

A religious belief in a divine creation relies entirely on faith. The sole evidence of this faith in Judaeo–Christianity is the Book of Genesis in the Old Testament of the Bible. Although the Bible is a profoundly important book, its contents are not testable evidence. Nowhere in the evaluation of the truth of the Old Testament does the scientific method come into play; either you accept the reality of the Old Testament or you don't. A literal interpretation of Genesis would mean accepting a six-day creation. However, many Christians accept the Old Testament as a powerful and important work that is not intended to be taken literally. The problem that most scientists have with teaching religion in public schools therefore is not due to lack of respect for religion—some are quite religious themselves—but rather that science classes are intended to teach children how to think like scientists.

The political agenda of some American antievolution fundamentalist groups belies their stated belief in offering diverse approaches to human origins. Religious fundamentalists often support the teaching of the Judeo–Christian creation story as fact but do not want to allow other creation stories to be taught alongside them in classrooms. Christianity, Judaism, and Islam are creationist faiths: They identify a single creator. Other major religions of the world, such as Hinduism, do not accept a single creator. Fundamentalists fight politically for the right to teach the Judeo–Christian belief system in public schools, but generally do not support and sometimes even oppose teaching other religious points of view.

Repeated state court and Supreme Court decisions have ruled that creationism should not be taught alongside science in public schools. For example, the U.S. Supreme Court ruled that a Louisiana law requiring public school teachers to read a disclaimer about evolution (saying it did not address the validity of biblical accounts of the creation) to their students was unconstitutional. Nevertheless, creationists continue to fight. Many teachers themselves support offering religious views of life in science classes. A local public school board in the suburbs of Atlanta recently approved the teaching of "alternatives to evolution" in science classes only to back down after national and regional condemnation from many quarters (Figure 1.22).

All the pieces of evidence for evolution, from fossils to DNA, are facts that add up to a body of evidence for a scientific theory without viable competitors. In recent years, however, challenges have come to evolution in the form of new incarnations of creationism. **Creation science** is one approach taken by fundamentalists. Recognizing that the Old Testament is not scientific evidence for life's origins, many creationists have argued in the negative, trying to refute the voluminous evidence for evolution. They ask why there are gaps in the fossil record; where, they ask, are the intermediate forms that ought to exist between *Homo erectus* and modern humans? Don't these gaps support the notion of a divine power molding our species? The fossil record is fragmentary, and always will be because of the low odds of fossils being formed, preserved, and then found millions of years later. Creationists seize on these

INSIGHTS AND ADVANCES

What Is Intelligent Design?

Intelligent design is a recent attempt to repackage creationist ideas in a way that might be more palatable for society and the scientific community. Instead of arguing outright for a biblical or divine basis for life, intelligent design advocates claim they have evidence that evolution by natural selection cannot fully explain the diversity of form and function that exists in nature. This school of thought is fond of using the argument of "irreducible complexity": There are aspects of the design of some organisms that are so complex that gradual, successive small modifications of earlier forms (evolution) could not have produced them. Advocates of intelligent design claim that if removal of one part of an organism's adaptive complex of traits causes the entire complex to cease functioning, then a supernatural force must have been its actual creator. The example of a mousetrap is often cited. Without each essential feature of a mousetrap—the wooden platform, the spring mechanism, and the latch holding it—the device fails to function at all. Intelligent design advocates say that unless the trap were assembled all at once, it would be useless and therefore could not be created by natural selection. Michael Behe, a biologist and an influential advocate of intelligent design who seeks to reconcile evolution with religious faith, has claimed that there are examples of irreducible complexity in biology that make natural selection an inadequate mechanism for all change. For instance, Behe claims that the working of cells at the biochemical level, in which cellular function can occur only after numerous working integrated parts are in place, might be an example of irreducible complexity (Behe, 1996).

Unfortunately for adherents of intelligent design, their few examples of irreducible complexity have been met with refutations in the scientific literature. Behe himself acknowledges that whereas gradual, Darwinian change by natural selection can be studied and tested using the scientific method, intelligent design cannot. By definition, if the original design is supernatural, understanding this design must be beyond the reach of science or rational explanation. In other words, the intelligent design movement asks us to accept on blind faith that supernatural forces are at work in designing life. Rather than offering rational explanations for features that might challenge Darwinian theory, advocates of intelligent design offer criticisms that cannot be addressed by further research. The whole belief system of intelligent design therefore stands well out-

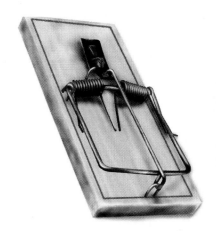

side of science—in the realm of faith—rather than offering a scientific alternative to evolution by natural selection.

As the latest addition to the beliefs of the creationist movement, intelligent design is unlikely to go away any time soon. Indeed, because it is an intellectual, if not scientific, approach to evolutionary change, it is held by some academics, including university-level science instructors. Because instructors in universities can cite the legal right of academic freedom, the teaching of intelligent design creationism in classrooms is hard to prevent.

gaps, arguing that they indicate that God must have stepped in and guided the process. As we shall see in later chapters, the fossil record for human ancestry is in fact quite rich, with a progression of brain size and anatomical changes bridging the apes, early hominids, and modern humans. Creation science is a denial of science rather than science itself and has not been any more successful in the U.S. court system than were earlier approaches by creationists. In recent years other attempts have been made to resurrect creationism in American education. **Intelligent design** is one such school of thought (Insights and Advances: What Is Intelligent Design?).

The relationship between the church and the teaching of evolution remains an uneasy one even in the twenty-first century. The late Pope John Paul II stated publicly that the Roman Catholic Church accepts the reality of evolution, even though the essence of humanity is still maintained to be a divine product.

intelligent design A creation school of thought that proposes th natural selection cannot account f the diversity and complexity of fo and function seen in nature.

Most biological scientists have deep respect for all religious beliefs. Scientists want only that creationist thinking be excluded from science curriculum in government-supported schools because that is the place where children are being trained to think like scientists. In addition, the U.S. Constitution mandates a separation of church and state in our society, so that the rights of those of all religious faiths, or those without religious faith, can be fully respected. A public school course in comparative world religions would be an entirely appropriate format in which to consider Judeo–Christian creation beliefs alongside those held by many other cultures.

SUMMARY

1. **What are the key features that distinguish the scientific from the religious view of the origins of life?**

   Science is a form of inquiry based on hypothesis testing via evidence collection. It is falsifiable and self-correcting. Religious ideology is based on faith; it cannot be tested in an empirical way.

2. **Before Darwin, why was the notion of evolutionary change forbidden?**

   The church had decreed that the world was created by God and had existed in its original form until the present; to contradict that was heresy punishable by imprisonment or worse.

3. **What is catastrophism, and can you think of a modern idea that is similar to it?**

   Catastrophism is the eighteenth-century theory that natural disasters had wiped out life on parts of the earth multiple times, and each time new forms of life moved in from other regions. This would explain the occurrence of past life forms that no longer exist without invoking evolutionary change.

4. **How did the false view of evolution expressed in Lamarckian theory differ from Darwinian theory?**

   Lamarck proposed that the use of a trait could influence an offspring's phenotype in the next generation; Darwin showed that change could occur across generations based only on the selective retention of some traits and the filtering out of others.

5. **Why does Alfred Russel Wallace deserve a great deal of credit for formulating the theory of evolution by natural selection?**

   Wallace independently developed the theory of natural selection at the same time as Darwin did. He corresponded with Darwin, who agreed to a joint presentation of their ideas to the scientific world.

6. **How was Darwin's *On the Origin of Species* influenced by his association with geologist Charles Lyell?**

   In addition to being the most influential geologist of his time, Lyell was Darwin's close friend and trusted advisor. When Darwin learned of Wallace's manuscript on evolution, it was Lyell, along with botanist Joseph Hooker, who persuaded their friend to put his theory of evolution by natural selection into writing. Eventually, Darwin's and Wallace's papers were jointly presented to the scientific community.

7. **What are the three conditions necessary for natural selection to work?**

   Natural selection can occur only if a trait can be inherited, if there is variation within a population, and if there is pressure from the environment.

CRITICAL THINKING QUESTIONS

1. Was it really so absurd for Bishop James Ussher to come up with a date of 4004 B.C. as the moment of creation? If you had only your own intuition and observation to guide you, how could you prove to others that the world is round or that the earth is ancient? This leads to the question, What exactly is a fact?

2. How would you handle the science versus creationism issue?

3. Despite Linnaeus's contribution to the study of animal and plant life through the invention of the classification scheme we call taxonomy, his approach hampers us today in understanding what a species is. Why do you think this is true?

KEY TERMS

observation
deduction
hypothesis
experimentation
data
scientific method
falsifiable

paradigm
immutability (or fixity)
polygenism
monogenism
taxonomy
binomial nomenclature
taxon

catastrophism
theory of the inheritance
   of acquired
   characteristics
Lysenkoism
uniformitarianism
adaptive radiation

natural selection
fitness
population
mutation
creation science
intelligent design

SUGGESTED READING

Brooks, J. L. (1984). *Just before the Origin*. Columbia University Press, New York.

Browne, Janet. (1995). *Charles Darwin: Voyaging*. Alfred A. Knopf, New York.

Browne, Janet. (2002). *Charles Darwin: The Power of Place*. Alfred A. Knopf, New York.

Ridley, M. (2005). *How to Read Darwin*. W. W. Norton and Co., New York.

Shermer, M. (2006). *Why Darwin Matters*. Henry Holt and Co., New York.

Weiner, J. (1994). *The Beak of the Finch*. Vintage Books, New York.

Cells and Molecules

CHAPTER OUTLINE

The package the molecular anthropologist had been waiting for finally arrived. Taking it to an isolated part of her laboratory, she opened it carefully. Wrapped inside was a vial containing a very small piece of bone. The bone looked unremarkable, but it was not. It came from the remains of an extinct member of the human family: a Neandertal. The anthropologist's job was to extract the genetic material of life—DNA—from the fossil sample. The remains had been in relatively cold and dry conditions since the individual died some 40,000 years ago, so it was reasonable to expect that the DNA it contained could be recovered and its genetic message read, at least in part. Neandertals appeared in Europe and western Asia about 140,000 years ago, and the information carried by the DNA from the bone fragment might provide vital clues about the course of human evolution.

As she stared at the vials, lost in deep thought, her technician walked up behind her and asked, "Is that the Neandertal bone sample?"

"Yes," she said, "it finally arrived."

"When you consider how old that bone is," the technician said, "how it dates back to the dawn of humanity—all I can say is, we'd better not screw it up."

Compared to the DNA recovered from a living person, the "ancient DNA" in the fossil sample they were working with was not in very good condition. Over time, even under ideal preservation conditions, the DNA molecules break down or become chemically damaged. Nonetheless, using very clever techniques to make millions of copies of the fragmented DNA segments that are left in the sample, molecular anthropologists can recover enough of the DNA to get a sense of the genetic makeup of the long-dead individual. By comparing these fragments to the complete genomes of modern humans and chimpanzees, they can painstakingly start the process of reassembling the Neandertal genome. Their work will not lead to the resurrection of the Neandertal, but to a better understanding of the place of Neandertals on the human evolutionary tree.

ONE OF THE MOST STRIKING examples of the power of modern genetic science is the ability to recover DNA from a wide range of biological tissues, including hair, feces, saliva, and even the fossilized remains of long-dead organisms. Although the revival of extinct animals (as in the movie *Jurassic Park*) remains in the realm of science fiction, we should nonetheless be impressed—even in the case of Neandertal DNA, where recovery is limited to small portions of the total DNA present in life—that such a delicate aspect of the living organism can be observed after tens of thousands of years.

Some argue that our current age is almost too focused on genetics and on what genetic science might someday do for us, but a concern with genetics and its applications is nothing new. Ideas about heredity can be found in all human cultures. There is no more basic observation of nature than "like begets like"; it applies to plants, animals, and people. Without some understanding of heredity, the domestication of plants and animals, which began at least 10,000 years ago, would not have been possible. Over the past hundred years, the modern science of *genetics* has developed to give us a much better understanding of the biological processes underlying heredity. We need to understand genetics if we are to understand how evolution happens, because genetic variation provides the raw material for evolutionary change.

In this chapter, we will begin our exploration of genetics, which will continue in Chapter 3, with an overview of genetic science today. First we will look at the basic building block of life, the cell, and consider its structure and function. Then we will discuss DNA, the genetic material itself, and how it carries out the important functions of replication and protein synthesis. We will also learn how DNA is packaged into structures called chromosomes, which become visible during the two kinds of cell division, meiosis and mitosis. The chapter will conclude with a discussion of the molecular methods biological anthropologists use to study human and primate evolution.

Genetics

The first decade of the twentieth century was an exciting time in the history of genetics, with researchers inspired by the rediscovery in 1900 of the groundbreaking research and theories of Austrian monk Gregor Mendel (see Chapter 3). The term *gene* was coined in the early 1900s by a Danish botanist named Wilhelm Johannsen (1857–1927). Neither Johannsen nor any of his colleagues at that time knew exactly what a gene was in a biochemical sense, but Johannsen thought it was a good little word to describe the "something"—the particulate unit of inheritance—that was being passed on from generation to generation. Ironically for Johannsen, although the word *gene* continues to be used, his own theories about the relationship between genes and evolution have largely been forgotten. The twentieth century saw a steady increase in our understanding of how heredity works, with the gene evolving from a theoretical unit to a well-described biochemical entity.

THE STUDY OF GENETICS

If a scientist says that she works on the genetics of an organism, her words can be interpreted in several different ways. Biological organisms differ greatly from one another, ranging from the very simple (such as a bacterium) to the very complex (a mammal). In complex animals, genetics can be approached from several different levels, depending on what aspect of the organism is of interest. These include the following:

- *Cellular and molecular genetics.* Cellular and molecular genetics involves the study of genetics at the level of the basic building blocks of bodies (cells) and at the most fundamental level of genetic transmission (the DNA molecule). We often hear about exciting advances in molecular genetics in the news as scientists attempt to devise genetic therapies for disease or determine the precise makeup of our DNA and that of other animals.

- *Classical or Mendelian genetics.* Classical genetics, such as that done by Mendel or Johannsen, involves looking at pedigrees of related individuals (plant or animal) and tracking how various traits are passed from one generation to the next. Although pedigree studies go back to the beginning of genetic science, they are still essential in the age of molecular genetics. After all, we are usually not interested in the variation of the molecules per se but in the observable traits they influence. These traits must first be identified as genetic features using pedigree analysis or a related technique.

- *Population genetics.* Biological species usually are divided into populations composed of groups of individuals who associate more with one another than with members of another population. Different populations within species almost always vary at the genetic level. By examining the genetic variation within and between populations (at both the molecular level and at the level of observable traits), we can gain insights into the evolutionary history of those populations and of the species as a whole.

- *Phylogenetics.* This field is concerned with determining evolutionary relationships between species, usually by constructing treelike diagrams that visually indicate how closely or distantly species are related to one another. Although traditionally this has been done by comparing observable traits, over the last 30 years the methods of molecular genetics have come to the forefront of phylogenetic analysis.

- *Behavioral genetics.* When one honeybee transmits information to another honeybee about the location of a flower, the behavior of both honeybees is under strong genetic control. When we look at other animals, especially those who engage in more complex forms of behavior that may involve learning, the role of genetics is more difficult to ascertain. Behavioral genetics involves trying to understand how the behavior of animals, including humans, is influenced by genetics. Behavioral genetics is a controversial field, especially in regard to human behavior, because human behavior is especially complex and the product of multiple, interacting influences.

Biological anthropology is concerned with the evolution of the human species in all its aspects. Because genetic variation underlies all evolutionary processes, each of the different approaches to the study of genetics listed here is relevant to understanding human evolution. The field of biological anthropology is also concerned with human biological variability, which arises from both genetic and environmental influences. Biological anthropologists often work at the intersection of biological (genetic) and environmental (cultural) sciences as they try to understand human variation and its evolution.

GENETIC METAPHORS: BLUEPRINTS, RECIPES, OR WHAT?

Even the most hardened scientists resort to the use of metaphor to explain the "big picture" of how genes somehow become bodies. So before getting to the actual biological mechanisms of heredity, let us consider how we might characterize the role of genetics in producing an individual organism. Do genes provide the "blueprint" for an individual, as is sometimes claimed? Not really. The idea of a blueprint is reminiscent of medieval notions that a tiny version of a fully formed individual, a *homunculus,* is what is passed between generations (Figure 2.1). The blueprint metaphor also implies construction—a builder—and the potential for deconstruction. You cannot "unbuild" a body by breaking it down into its original component parts. Throughout the course of biological development, a body maintains a unity that is quite different from the process of constructing a building by starting with the foundations, and then the walls, and so on. Scientists have identified a class of genes— *homeotic (Hox) genes*—that underlies the development of basic body structure in both invertebrates and vertebrates (Carroll, 2005). The expression of this set of genes has been modified by evolution to produce the extraordinary range of animal bodies we observe today. The existence of Hox genes demonstrates that bodies grow under the influence of genes in a way very different from how humans build buildings.

Some scientists have suggested that our genes, in their totality, are much more akin to a recipe than to a blueprint. A recipe includes two things: a list of ingredients and the instructions for what to do with those ingredients. To some extent, the genetic material is a recipe for converting energy and a host of essential components into a body, an organism that cannot in any sense be "unmade." However, the main difference between our genes and a recipe is that in cooking, the environment specified by the recipe can be controlled and modified as needed to produce a final product. In contrast, the environments in which genes exist cannot be controlled. However, humans have a biologically unprecedented ability to modify their own environments, making them more hospitable for the genes they carry.

More recently, as befits the Information Age, there has been a tendency to consider genetic material to be a form of information storage. There can be no doubt that our genes carry information about the bodies they make and that they contain information for the growth and development of those bodies. The problem with seeing genetic material principally as an information storage device is that it is so much more than that. As you read this, genes in your body are doing at least a thousand tasks. Some are being turned on while others are being turned off. Genes are not just information but are part of the essential machinery of the living body. In the fossil remains of an extinct species, of course, genetic material is more like

FIGURE 2.1 An old concept of genetic transmission—a homunculus in a sperm cell. The drawing was done by Nicolas Harsoeker, in his *Essai de dioptrique*, 1694.

"Heredity is nothing but stored environment."— Luther Burbank (1849–1926), American horticulturalist

prokaryotes   Single-celled organisms, such as bacteria, in which the genetic material is not separated from the rest of the cell by a nucleus.

eukaryotes   A cell that possesses a well-organized nucleus.

nucleus   In eukaryotic cells, the part of the cell in which the genetic material is separated from the rest of the cell (cytoplasm) by a plasma membrane.

cytoplasm   In a eukaryotic cell, the region within the cell membrane that surrounds the nucleus; it contains organelles, which carry out the essential functions of the cell, such as energy production, metabolism, and protein synthesis.

somatic cells   The cells of the body that are not sex cells.

gametes   The sex cells: sperm in males and eggs (or ova) in females.

stem cells   Undifferentiated cells found in the developing embryo that can be induced to differentiate into a wide variety of cell types or tissues. Also found in adults, although adult stem cells are not as totipotent as embryonic stem cells.

pure information, to be used by molecular anthropologists to reconstruct evolutionary relationships between species, including humans.

The genetic system underlying the development of life on Earth is a unique and truly extraordinary thing. No simple metaphor can encompass all of its properties and functions. Although our discussion will now turn to the somewhat unromantic realm of cell structure and function, we should not cease to wonder at the exquisite machinery of heredity, which has been shaped by nearly 4 billion years of evolution.

The Cell

The basic building block of life is the cell. A cell is a microscopic organic entity in which genetic material and other structures are separated from the surrounding environment by a semipermeable membrane. Some organisms, such as bacteria or protozoans, are made up of only a single cell. Others, including humans and every other form of life that can be seen with the naked eye, are *multicellular* organisms. Complex multicellular life forms are made up of hundreds of billions of cells, although less complex forms have considerably fewer cells. The marine sea slug (*Aplysia californica*) has long been the object of scientific study in part because its central nervous system consists of a manageable 20,000 cells (Kandel et al., 2000). In contrast, the human brain, which has approximately 10 billion nerve cells, is complicated.

The basic division of life on Earth is not between single-celled and multicellular creatures but between **prokaryotes** and **eukaryotes**. The prokaryotes, which include bacteria and blue-green algae, are all single-celled organisms with no major compartments within the cell to separate the genetic material from all other components of the cell. The eukaryotes, which include all other forms of life, are characterized by a cellular anatomy that separates the genetic material from the rest of the cell in a structure known as the **nucleus**. The outer boundary of the cell is defined by a *plasma membrane*, which regulates the transport of material into and out of the cell and governs communication and coordinated activity between cells. The fluid-filled space within the cell and surrounding the nucleus is known as the **cytoplasm**. The cytoplasm contains a number of structures, known collectively as *organelles,* which help maintain the cell and carry out its functions. Fossil prokaryotes appear in the fossil record about 3.4 billion years ago, whereas eukaryotes do not appear until about 1.5 billion years ago. Eukaryotes that more closely resemble those found today evolved around 850 million years ago, and multicellular organisms (such as plants and animals) made their first appearance only 600 million years ago (Kostianovsky, 2000). Thus single-celled creatures have dominated most of the history of life on Earth (Figure 2.2).

Complex organisms have a variety of different somatic cell types. **Somatic cells** are simply the cells of the body that are not **gametes**, or sex cells; gametes are the germ cells that are directly involved in propagation or reproduction. Humans have around 200 different types of tissues, each of which is composed of a characteristic somatic cell type (Klug & Cummings, 2003). We have nerve cells (neurons), muscle cells, skin cells, bone cells, cells that secrete hormones, and so on. At the earliest stages of its development, the human embryo contains a population of cells known as **stem cells**. These cells are *totipotent*, which means they can differentiate into any of the somatic cell types found in the fetus or adult. Stem

FIGURE 2.2 Stromatolite fossil cut away to reveal the internal concentric banding. Stromatolites are large, stony, cushion-like masses, composed of numerous layers of cyanobacteria (blue-green algae) which have been preserved due to their ability to secrete calcium carbonate. They are among the oldest organic remains to have been found, the oldest structures dating from over 3,000 million years ago. Stromatolite formation reached a peak during the late Precambrian period, but is still occurring today. Present-day formations can be seen in the Everglades, Florida, USA, and in Shark Bay, Australia.

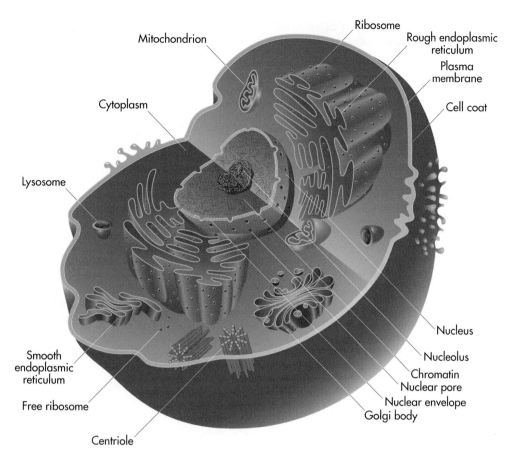

Mitochondrion

Ribosome

Rough endoplasmic reticulum

Plasma membrane

Cytoplasm

Cell coat

Lysosome

Smooth endoplasmic reticulum

Free ribosome

Centriole

Golgi body

Nuclear envelope

Nuclear pore

Chromatin

Nucleolus

Nucleus

FIGURE 2.3   A typical eukaryotic cell.

cells are also found in adults, but adult stem cells can differentiate into a more limited variety of cell types (Stewart & Pryzborski, 2002).

Stem cell research has become an important and controversial topic in recent years. Given their totipotent capacity, embryonic stem cells may be useful for treating diseases that are characterized by the loss of specific types of cells. An example of this is *Parkinson disease* (PD), a nervous system disorder characterized by movement problems, which is caused by the loss of a certain population of cells in the brain. It is hoped that embryonic stem cells may be able to replace (i.e., take on their form and function) the specific cells lost in Parkinson disease. At this time, stem cell scientists have had only limited success converting stem cells into the kind of cells that are lost in Parkinson disease, although progress is being made on this front (Taylor & Minger, 2005). Even after the proper cells can be made in sufficient numbers, there is still the issue of how well they maintain their function once they are transplanted into the brains of Parkinson disease sufferers. The controversy surrounding embryonic stem cell research lies in the fact that human embryos (produced in the laboratory through in vitro fertilization) are our only source of totipotent stem cells; after the stem cells are removed, the embryos are no longer viable (Insights and Advances: Cloning Controversies on page 42). Research is also being done on adult stem cells to see whether they can be coaxed into forming a greater variety of cell types than they would under more natural conditions.

CELL ANATOMY

Different types of cells have different anatomies, which serve the functional or structural needs of a particular tissue. Nonetheless, almost all somatic cells share some basic characteristics. Although gametes share some of the characteristics of somatic cells, there are also some fundamental differences, which we'll discuss separately.

In most eukaryotic cells (Figure 2.3), the most prominent structure in the cytoplasm is the nucleus. The nucleus is bounded by its own membrane or envelope,

INSIGHTS AND ADVANCES

Cloning Controversies

On July 5, 1996, a sheep was born at the Roslin Institute in Edinburgh, Scotland. This sheep, named Dolly, was as unremarkable as any other sheep with the exception of one fact: She was a clone, an exact genetic copy of another sheep (Figure A). Dolly was the first mammal ever cloned, and her birth raised many questions about the nature, and even the moral status, of cloning. If a sheep could be cloned, why not a human?

The process of cloning is straightforward but not easy (Solter, 2000). First, the nucleus of a somatic cell (which contains a copy of all of the genetic material of an individual) is carefully removed. The cell often comes not directly from the body but from a cell line that has been established in the laboratory. At the same time, the nucleus of an egg (or *oocyte*) is carefully removed, preserving the cell membrane and the cytoplasm as much as possible. The nucleus from the somatic cell is then transferred to the oocyte either mechanically via microinjection or by using an inactivated virus as a vector. Once the new nucleus is introduced to the egg, the egg is *activated,* which initiates the development of the embryo. In normal fertilization, the introduction of the sperm to the egg causes activation. In cloning, an electrical current applied to the egg (with the new nucleus) activates the egg. Once the embryo begins to develop, the egg can be implanted into a surrogate mother and the pregnancy proceeds in the usual way.

Sheep, cows, mice, and pigs have all been cloned. For each group, the success rate of growing a clone (egg with a new nucleus) to adulthood is about 1%. The live-birth rate is perhaps twice as high as this, but a number of cloned newborns have problems and die before adulthood. It is likely that one barrier to successful cloning arises in the reprogramming stage after activation (Fairburn et al., 2002).

Another problem that arises with cloned individuals is that even if they survive to adulthood, they do not live as long. In a study of cloned mice, it was found that only two of twelve cloned mice lived as long as 800 days, compared with ten of thirteen control mice (Ogonuki et al., 2002). The famous cloned sheep Dolly lived less than 7 years, whereas sheep usually live to be 11 to 12 years (Coghlan, 2003). One possible cause of the short life span of cloned individuals involves structures called *telomeres.* Telomeres are pieces of DNA that cap the ends of chromosomes. As an individual ages and cells divide, the telomeres shorten. Shortening telomere lengths are a sign of aging in cells. If cloning is done with the genome of an adult, then the short telomeres may be passed on directly to the cloned individual, resulting in accelerated aging or the development of diseases early in life that are associated with aging.

Why do we need cloning? Agricultural scientists are working on cloning in order to develop methods for efficiently propagating animals who have desired characteristics. Sexual reproduction leads to an inefficient genetic mixing (recombination or crossing over) every generation.

Other scientists see cloning as a potential tool to save endangered or even extinct species, such as the giant panda or the extinct Tasmanian wolf (Mazurek, 1999). The largest wild populations of our closest relatives, the chimpanzee and gorilla, declined by one-half between 1983 and 2000 (Walsh et al., 2003), and the development of efficient cloning techniques may someday help save these very threatened species.

Arguments in favor of human reproductive cloning are harder to come by. The poor survival rate of cloned individuals from other mammal species is reason enough to

FIGURE A   Dolly, the cloned sheep.

consider human reproductive cloning to be an unethical undertaking. On the other hand, many consider therapeutic cloning to be a different matter. Imagine a patient who has a disease that may be curable by the introduction of a working cell type to replace cells that are nonfunctional or have been destroyed. Somatic cells from that patient could be used to make cloned embryos. At a very early stage of development (the blastocyst stage), embryonic stem cells could be recovered and then coerced in the lab into growing into the cell type the patient needs. Once a population of these cells has grown, they would be transferred to the patient. Because the patient would be the original cell source, immunological rejection would not be a worry. It is clear that even if some countries ban therapeutic cloning, other countries will work hard to develop this technique.

which separates its contents from the rest of the cytoplasm. Within the nucleus, the hereditary material, **deoxyribonucleic acid (DNA)**, is found. DNA is a double-stranded complex molecule, and the elucidation of its structure by James Watson and Francis Crick in 1953 launched the modern era in molecular genetics. Two of the primary functions of DNA are making **proteins** for the body, or **protein synthesis**, and cellular replication. Another complex molecule, **ribonucleic acid (RNA)**, which is similar structurally to DNA but is single stranded, is also found in large quantities in the nucleus and in the cytoplasm, as well. RNA is essential for carrying out the protein synthesis function of DNA.

Several other important structures or organelles float in the cytoplasm of the cell (Figure 2.3). These structures are like the organs of the body, and they are responsible for functions such as metabolizing nutrients and eliminating waste, energy synthesis, and protein synthesis. The **mitochondria** (sing., *mitochondrion*) are capsule-shaped organelles that number in the hundreds or thousands in each cell. A series of metabolic reactions take place in the mitochondria, resulting in the production of an energy-rich molecule, adenosine triphosphate (ATP), which fuels the activities of the cell. Known as the "powerhouse" of the cell, mitochondria have their own DNA, which is not contained in a nucleus and is different from the DNA found in the nucleus of the cell. It is likely that the mitochondria (and their plant analogs, chloroplasts) had their origins as a prokaryotic cell that evolved in symbiosis with a nucleated cell to produce the eukaryotic cell. As we will see later in the chapter, *mitochondrial DNA* (mtDNA) has proved to be an important tool in evolutionary and anthropological research.

The **endoplasmic reticulum (ER)**, another organelle found in the cytoplasm, is a complex structure, with a folded-sheet appearance. It provides increased surface area within the cell for metabolic reactions to take place. Some of the endoplasmic reticulum has a knobby appearance; this is known as *rough endoplasmic reticulum.* The knobs are **ribosomes**, the site in the cell where proteins are synthesized. Molecules of ribosomal RNA (rRNA) form a large component of ribosomes. The synthesis of ribosomes begins in the nucleus but can be completed only in the cytoplasm. Because completed ribosomes cannot pass through the nuclear membrane, protein synthesis always occurs in the cytoplasm.

DNA Structure and Function

Hereditary material—DNA—has to be able to do three things. First, it must be able to make copies of itself, or *replicate,* so that it can be passed from generation to generation. Second, it has to be able to make proteins, which are the most important components of cells. Third, it must coordinate the activity of proteins to produce bodies, or have some way to translate the information it carries about making bodies into growing actual bodies (i.e., development). As it turns out, the chemical structure of DNA lends itself to self-replication and to carrying the information necessary for making proteins; we will discuss these two DNA functions in detail. However, the third function—directing development—is much more complex and is beyond the scope of this text.

DNA STRUCTURE I: THE MOLECULAR LEVEL

The structure of the DNA molecule is a double helix, resembling a ladder twisted around its central axis. The basic unit of DNA (and RNA) is a molecule called a **nucleotide** (Figure 2.4 on page 44). A nucleotide consists of three parts: a sugar (deoxyribose in DNA and ribose in RNA), a phosphate group, and a nitrogenous **base**, a molecule that includes one or two rings composed of carbon and nitrogen atoms. The DNA molecule is assembled from four different nucleotide units, which vary according to the base they carry. There are two classes of bases: the *purines* and the *pyrimidines*. The purines are *adenine* (A) and *guanine* (G); the

deoxyribonucleic acid (DNA) A double-stranded molecule that is the carrier of genetic information. Each strand is composed of a linear sequence of nucleotides; the two strands are held together by hydrogen bonds that form between complementary bases.

proteins Complex molecules formed from chains of amino acids (polypeptide) or from a complex of polypeptides. They function as structural molecules, transport molecules, antibodies, enzymes, and hormones.

protein synthesis The assembly of proteins from amino acids, which occurs at ribosomes in the cytoplasm and is based on information carried by mRNA.

ribonucleic acid (RNA) Single-stranded nucleic acid that performs critical functions during protein synthesis and comes in three forms: messenger RNA, transfer RNA, and ribosomal RNA.

mitochondria Organelles in the cytoplasm of the cell where energy production for the cell takes place. Contains its own DNA.

endoplasmic reticulum (ER) An organelle in the cytoplasm consisting of a folded membrane.

The structure of DNA is an example of how the complexity and diversity of life is generated from a relatively simple set of basic building blocks.

ribosomes Structures composed primarily of RNA, which are found on the endoplasmic reticulum. They are the site of protein synthesis.

nucleotide Molecular building block of nucleic acids DNA and RNA; consists of a phosphate, sugar, and base.

base Variable component of the nucleotides that form the nucleic acids DNA and RNA. In DNA, the bases are adenine, guanine, thymine, and cytosine. In RNA, uracil replaces thymine.

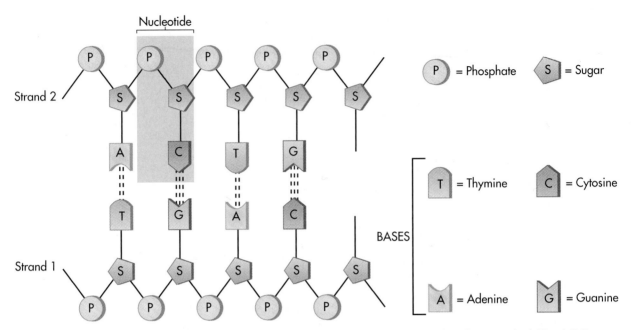

FIGURE 2.4   The nucleotide structure of DNA. The dashed lines between the A-T and C-G pairings indicate hydrogen bonds.

pyrimidines are *cytosine* (C) and *thymine* (T). DNA consists of two separate strands, corresponding to the two sides of the ladder, each of which is made up of a chain of nucleotides (Figure 2.5). The sugar of one nucleotide bonds to the phosphate group of the next one; thus, each side of the DNA ladder is composed of alternating sugar and phosphate molecules. The bases point toward the center of the ladder and form its rungs. The rungs are formed by two bases, one projecting from each side of the ladder.

In the late 1940s and early 1950s, biochemist Erwin Chargaff and his colleagues found a curious pattern in the distribution of nucleotides in DNA: The amount of A present in the sample was always about the same as the amount of T, and the amount of C equaled the amount of G. This information, along with an X-ray crystallograph of the DNA molecule provided by physical chemists Rosalind Franklin and Maurice Wilkins, helped Watson and Crick formulate their model of DNA structure (Figure 2.6). As they surmised, the rungs of the DNA ladder are composed of two bases, and the base combinations are always A-T or C-G. For example, if there is a sequence of nucleotides on one side of the DNA that goes ATCGATCG, then on the other side of the ladder, the sequence will be TAGC-TAGC. The two sides of the DNA double helix complement each other (sometimes the two strands are nicknamed "Watson" and "Crick"). A purine (A or G) is always opposite a pyrimidine (C or T) because purines are larger molecules than pyrimidines, and the purine–pyrimidine combination is necessary for the two sides of the ladder to maintain a constant distance from each other. The more specific A-T and C-G pairings occur because these combinations form hydrogen bonds (three for G-C and two for A-T), which hold the two sides of the ladder together. Such hydrogen bonding cannot occur between A and C or G and T. Hydrogen bonds are quite weak (compared with the chemical bonds that form between the sugars and phosphates, for example), but in a DNA molecule, thousands of nucleotides line up against thousands of other nucleotides, thus giving strength to the entire molecule.

RNA is very similar to DNA except that it is a single-stranded molecule, and ribose replaces deoxyribose as the sugar in the nucleotide. In addition, thymine is not found in RNA but is replaced by another pyrimidine base, *uracil* (U), which also bonds to adenine.

enzyme   A complex protein that is a catalyst for chemical processes in the body.

DNA FUNCTION I: REPLICATION

A complete copy of the DNA is found in the nucleus of almost every cell of the body. When a mother cell divides into two daughter cells, other cell components can be split between the cells, but a faithful copy of the genetic material must be deposited in each daughter cell. After all, once the two cells have split from each other, they no longer have access to the genetic material of the other cell.

The very structure of the DNA molecule suggests a mechanism for its replication (Figure 2.7 on page 46). Watson and Crick immediately recognized this after they determined the structure of the molecule. In simple terms, DNA replication occurs in the following manner. The DNA molecule, or a portion of it, divides into two separate strands. The two strands can be separated when the weak hydrogen bonds between the base pairs are broken. After separation, each of the strands serves as a template for the assembly, nucleotide by nucleotide, of a new complementary strand of DNA. When the process is completed, there are two copies of the mother DNA molecule, each of which is made up of one original side and one newly synthesized side.

Each step of DNA replication, from the uncoiling of the DNA double helix to "proofreading" and correcting the occasional errors that occur in the process, is mediated by a particular **enzyme**. An enzyme is a complex protein molecule in the body that mediates a chemical or biochemical reaction. One of the first enzymes associated with DNA replication to be discovered is called *DNA polymerase I* (Kornberg, 1960). If you place a single-stranded template strand of DNA in a test tube with all four nucleotide bases (A, T, C, and G) and add DNA polymerase I, you will get synthesis of double-stranded DNA. The observation of its action in the test tube led to the discovery of other DNA polymerases more critical to DNA replication (as it turned out, DNA polymerase I was more critical for proofreading DNA in prokaryotes than for DNA replication).

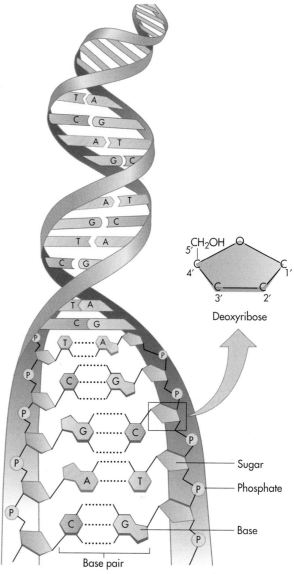

FIGURE 2.5 The double-helix structure of DNA.

FIGURE 2.6 (a) The 1962 Nobel Prize winners. Francis Crick is at far left, Maurice Wilkins is next to Crick, and James Watson is third from the right. At his right is John Steinbeck. (b) Rosalind Franklin made an essential contribution to the discovery of DNA structure, but died four years before these Nobel Prizes were awarded.

(a)

(b)

We will see in this chapter that the proofreading and repair of DNA are critically important because errors in DNA replication can have important consequences for the survival of an organism. If these errors in DNA replication are not corrected, they can lead to permanent changes, or mutations, in the DNA of cell. Mutations can alter cell function in many different ways. For example, a mutation can transform a cell, causing it to replicate at an accelerated rate; such uncontrolled cell growth is the basis of cancer. Mutations that occur in gametes can be passed from one generation to the next and may have profound effects on the biology of offspring.

DNA FUNCTION II: PROTEIN SYNTHESIS

Proteins are the workhorse molecules of biological organisms and the most common large molecules found in cells. Structural tissues, such as bone and muscle, are composed primarily of protein. Proteins such as **hemoglobin**, a protein molecule in red blood cells, bind to oxygen and transport it throughout the body, and other

= Adenine   = Thymine

= Guanine   = Cytosine

FIGURE 2.7   DNA replication.

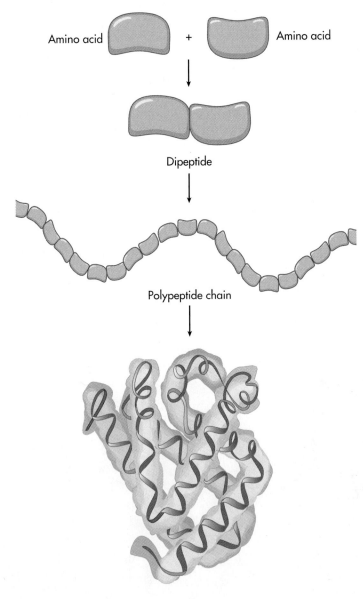

FIGURE 2.8   Schematic representation of protein structure.

hemoglobin   Protein found in red blood cells that transports oxygen.

transport proteins facilitate the movement of molecules across cell membranes. Some proteins function as **hormones** and hormone receptors and regulate many bodily functions. Antibodies or immunoglobulins are proteins of the immune system, which our bodies use to fight disease or any biochemical invader. Enzymes, such as DNA polymerase I, are the largest class of proteins in the body. These proteins lower the activation energy of (*catalyze*) countless biochemical reactions in cells. So enzymes are essential for life.

Proteins are complex molecules made up of smaller molecules known as **amino acids** (Figure 2.8). Amino acids share a common chemical structure that allows them to bond to one another in long chains. There are twenty different amino acids that function as building blocks for proteins (Table 2.1). Of these twenty, nine are essential amino acids (Laidlaw & Kopple, 1987). This means they cannot be synthesized by the body and must be obtained from protein in the diet. The nonessential amino acids can be synthesized from the essential amino acids.

A typical protein may be made up of a chain of 200 amino acids; such a chain can also be called a **polypeptide**. Any combination of the twenty different amino acids may go into this chain. Thus the number of possible 200–amino acid proteins that may be generated from the twenty kinds of amino acids is immense (20^{200}). At a primary level, proteins differ from each other by length and by the sequence of amino acids in the polypeptide chain. Protein structures generally are much more complex than a simple linear chain, however. The sequence of amino acids in a polypeptide governs

hormone A natural substance (often a protein) produced by specialized cells in one location of the body that influences the activity or physiology of cells in a different location.

amino acids Molecules that form the basic building blocks of protein.

polypeptide A molecule made up of a chain of amino acids.

TABLE 2.1   The Genetic Code

	Amino Acid				
		DNA triplets	mRNA codons		
Alanine		**Glycine**		**Proline**	
CGA, CGG, CGT, CGC	GCU, GCC, GCA, GCG	CCA, CCG, CCT, CCC	GGU, GGC, GGA, GGG	GGA, GGG, GGT, GGC	CCU, CCC, CCA, CCG
Arginine		**Histidine***		**Serine**	
GCA, GCG, GCT, GCC, TCT, TCC	CGU, CGC, CGA, CGG, AGA, AGG	GTA, GTG	CAU, CAC	AGA, AGG, AGT, AGC, TCA, TCG	UCU, UCC, UCA, UCG, AGU, AGC
Asparagine		**Isoleucine***		**Threonine***	
TTA, TTG	AAU, AAC	TAA, TAG, TAT	AUU, AUC, AUA	TGA, TGG, TGT, TGC	ACU, ACC, ACA, ACG
Aspartic Acid		**Leucine***		**Tryptophan***	
CTA, CTG	GAU, GAC	AAT, AAC, GAA, GAG, GAT, GAC	UUA, UUG, CUU, CUC, CUA, CUG	ACC	UGG
Cysteine		**Lysine***		**Tyrosine**	
ACA, ACG	UGU, UGC	TTT, TTC	AAA, AAG	ATA, ATG	UAU, UAC
Glutamine		**Methionine* (initiation codon)**		**Valine***	
GTT, GTC	CAA, CAG	TAC	AUG	CAA, CAG, CAT, CAC	GUU, GUC, GUA, GUG
Glutamic Acid		**Phenylalanine***		**Termination Codons**	
CTT, CTC	GAA, GAG	AAA, AAG	UUU, UUC	ATT, ATC, ACT	UAA, UAG, UGA

*Essential amino acids

Source: Laidlaw & Kopple (1987).

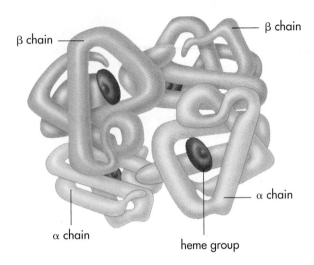

β chain

β chain

α chain

α chain

heme group

FIGURE 2.9 The complex structure of the hemoglobin protein, which comprises four polypeptide chains in association with iron-based heme groups that are essential for oxygen binding and transport.

genetic code   The system whereby the nucleotide triplets in DNA and RNA contain the information for synthesizing proteins from the twenty amino acids.

codon   A triplet of nucleotide bases in mRNA that specifies an amino acid or the initiation or termination of a polypeptide sequence.

gene   The fundamental unit of heredity. Consists of a sequence of DNA bases that carries the information for synthesizing a protein (or polypeptide) and occupies a specific chromosomal locus.

how the chain may be folded in space or how it may associate with other polypeptide chains to form a larger, complex protein. For example, the protein hemoglobin is composed of four separate polypeptide chains, which in conjunction assume a complex three-dimensional form. The three-dimensional form a protein takes is directly related to its function (Figure 2.9).

As we saw earlier, proteins are made of chains of amino acids. The structure and therefore the function of proteins are determined by the sequence of amino acids in their polypeptide chains. The structure of DNA, in which different bases are lined up in sequence, is ideal for carrying other kinds of sequential information, such as the sequence of amino acids in a protein. The system that has evolved to represent protein amino acid sequences in the base pair sequence of DNA is known as the **genetic code** (Table 2.1). The basic structure of the genetic code was worked out by Francis Crick and his colleagues in 1961.

There are twenty different amino acids in proteins, but there are only four different bases in DNA. Obviously, there are not enough types of bases to represent each amino acid. If two bases in sequence were used to represent an amino acid, there would still be only sixteen possible combinations (4^2), which is not enough to represent the twenty amino acids. However, three bases in sequence produce sixty-four (4^3) unique triplet combinations—more than enough to have a unique triplet sequence of bases represent each of the twenty amino acids. The genetic code therefore consists of three-base sequences, called **codons**, each of which represents a single amino acid. There is *redundancy* in the code: Given that there are sixty-four possible codons and only twenty amino acids, most of the amino acids are represented by more than one codon. Three of the codons (termination codons) do not code for any amino acid but instead signal that the protein chain has come to an end. Another codon (TAC) represents the amino acid methionine and also typically serves as an initiation codon, signaling the beginning of a polypeptide chain.

The information to make proteins is represented, via the genetic code, in the sequence of bases in a portion of a DNA molecule. The part of a DNA molecule that contains the information for one protein (or for one polypeptide chain that makes up part of a protein) is called a **gene**. One DNA molecule can have many genes arrayed along its length. Given the triplet codons of the genetic code, a protein with 300 amino acids would need 900 bases to represent it (not including initiation or termination signals) in a gene. If the first twelve bases of that gene were TGA CCA CTA CGA, the first four amino acids of the protein would be threonine, glycine, aspartic acid, and alanine. A single gene can consist of hundreds of thousands of bases. Current estimates are that human beings have no more than 25,000 genes in total, although some estimates run higher (http://www.ornl.gov/sci/techresources/Human_Genome/faq/genenumber.shtml). This figure surprised many scientists because it is not that many more than the 20,000 genes a simple roundworm (*C. elegans*) has, and previous estimates had placed the total number of human genes as greater than 100,000.

So how does the information to make a protein, encoded in the DNA, actually become a protein? It involves two steps, *transcription* and *translation,* along with the participation of RNA molecules with specialized functions. Transcription occurs in the nucleus of the cell, while translation (protein synthesis) occurs in the cytoplasm. Each step is mediated by specialized enzymes (Figure 2.10).

Transcription begins when the two DNA strands split apart in a region where a gene is represented on one of the strands. The whole molecule does not split apart because only the region where the gene is located must be read. When the DNA molecule separates, the strand corresponding to the gene can serve as a template for the synthesis of a single-stranded RNA molecule. As mentioned previously, RNA is a nucleic acid, like DNA, composed of nucleotide bases (C, G, A, and U, instead of T). At the site of the gene, a complementary RNA molecule is synthesized: In effect, the information of the gene is transcribed from the language of DNA to the related language of RNA. When an RNA molecule has been synthesized that corresponds to the entire gene, it separates from the DNA and exists as a free-floating, single-stranded molecule. The two strands of the DNA reattach to each other, returning the DNA to its intact double helix structure. The free RNA molecule is called **messenger RNA (mRNA)**, because it carries the information of the gene from the nucleus of the cell to the cytoplasm, which is where protein synthesis or translation takes place.

Protein synthesis occurs at ribosomes, thousands of which are found in the cytoplasm of every cell. At the ribosome, the information the mRNA carries is translated into a protein molecule. The mRNA is read at the ribosome, from beginning to end, two codons at a time. At this point in the process, another critical

messenger RNA (mRNA) Strand of RNA synthesized in the nucleus as a complement to a specific gene (transcription). It carries the information for the sequence of amino acids to make a specific protein into the cytoplasm, where it is read at a ribosome and a protein molecule is synthesized (translation).

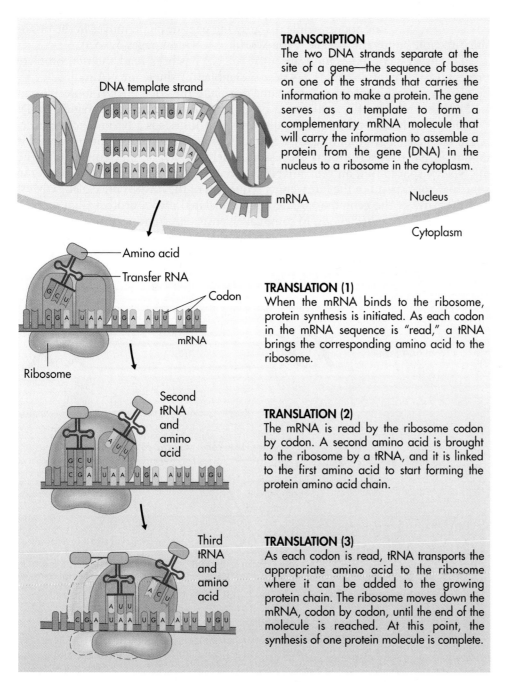

TRANSCRIPTION
The two DNA strands separate at the site of a gene—the sequence of bases on one of the strands that carries the information to make a protein. The gene serves as a template to form a complementary mRNA molecule that will carry the information to assemble a protein from the gene (DNA) in the nucleus to a ribosome in the cytoplasm.

TRANSLATION (1)
When the mRNA binds to the ribosome, protein synthesis is initiated. As each codon in the mRNA sequence is "read," a tRNA brings the corresponding amino acid to the ribosome.

TRANSLATION (2)
The mRNA is read by the ribosome codon by codon. A second amino acid is brought to the ribosome by a tRNA, and it is linked to the first amino acid to start forming the protein amino acid chain.

TRANSLATION (3)
As each codon is read, tRNA transports the appropriate amino acid to the ribosome where it can be added to the growing protein chain. The ribosome moves down the mRNA, codon by codon, until the end of the molecule is reached. At this point, the synthesis of one protein molecule is complete.

FIGURE 2.10 Protein synthesis. Transcription occurs within the nucleus, while translation takes place in the cytoplasm.

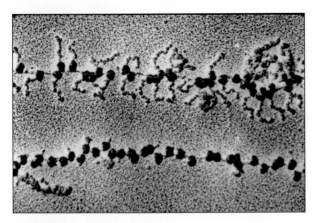

FIGURE 2.11 Electron microscope photo of an mRNA molecule being read by ribosomes (the dark, round structures) with growing polypeptide (protein) chains forming at the ribosomes as the mRNA is read.

transfer RNA (tRNA) RNA molecules that bind to specific amino acids and transport them to ribosomes to be used during protein synthesis.

molecule enters the picture: **transfer RNA (tRNA),** which carries a single, specific amino acid to the ribosome, so that it can be attached to the growing protein chain. The tRNA has a three-base region called the *anticodon* that is complementary to the codon on the mRNA. When an mRNA codon (ACU, for example, which corresponds to the DNA triplet TGA) is read at the ribosome, a tRNA with the anticodon UGA temporarily aligns to the mRNA and brings the amino acid threonine into position. Then the next codon on the mRNA is read, and a second tRNA brings the appropriate amino acid into position next to the first amino acid. Once the two amino acids are next to each other, a chemical reaction requiring energy occurs, and a bond is formed between the two amino acids. The ribosome then moves down one codon, while the growing peptide chain moves in the opposite direction (Innovations: The Wide World of RNA on pages 52–53).

This process continues until the entire mRNA has been read and the complete protein (or polypeptide chain) has been assembled. A single mRNA molecule can be read by several ribosomes at the same time, and thus one mRNA molecule can lead to the synthesis of several copies of the same protein molecule (Figure 2.11).

Of course in the real world of cells, protein synthesis is a bit more complicated. In most cases, after an mRNA is formed but before it reaches the ribosome, it undergoes posttranscriptional processing whereby intervening sequences in the mRNA are spliced out, and the mRNA molecule is reassembled. The parts of the gene that correspond to the intervening sequences of the mRNA are called *introns*, and the parts of the gene that are actually translated into a protein (that is, they are expressed) are called *exons*. In some cases, posttranscriptional processing means that a single gene can produce different (but related) protein products depending on which intervening sequences are processed out (Figure 2.12).

Post-Transcriptional Processing

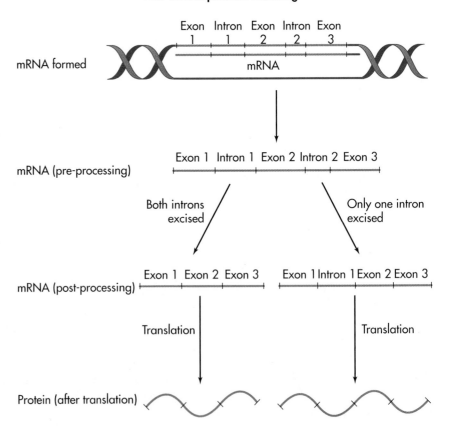

FIGURE 2.12 Processing of an mRNA molecule after transcription.

The second complicating factor is that most of our DNA does not code for anything; in other words, it is not made up of exons. According to recent results from the attempts to elucidate the complete human DNA structure, only about 1.1% of the bases are expressed (Venter et al., 2001). Another 24% are introns; they are transcribed into mRNA but are not translated into protein. From the organism's perspective, the rest of the DNA does not do anything but replicate. As we will see later, this noncoding DNA has important ramifications for a variety of genetic processes.

chromatin   The diffuse form of DNA as it exists during the interphase of the cell cycle.

mitosis   Somatic cell division in which a single cell divides to produce two identical daughter cells.

meiosis   Cell division that occurs in the testes and ovaries that leads to the formation of sperm and ova (gametes).

chromosomes   Discrete structures composed of condensed DNA and supporting proteins.

DNA STRUCTURE II: CHROMOSOMES AND CELL DIVISION

We have 2 to 3 meters (6–9 ft) of DNA in the nucleus of each somatic cell. Most of the time, the DNA in these cells exists in dispersed, uncoiled strands, supported by proteins. DNA in this state is called **chromatin**. However, during **mitosis** and **meiosis**, the two processes of cell division or replication, the chromatin condenses and coils into larger, tightly wound, discrete structures called **chromosomes** (which, like chromatin, are composed of DNA and supporting proteins) (Figure 2.13). Each

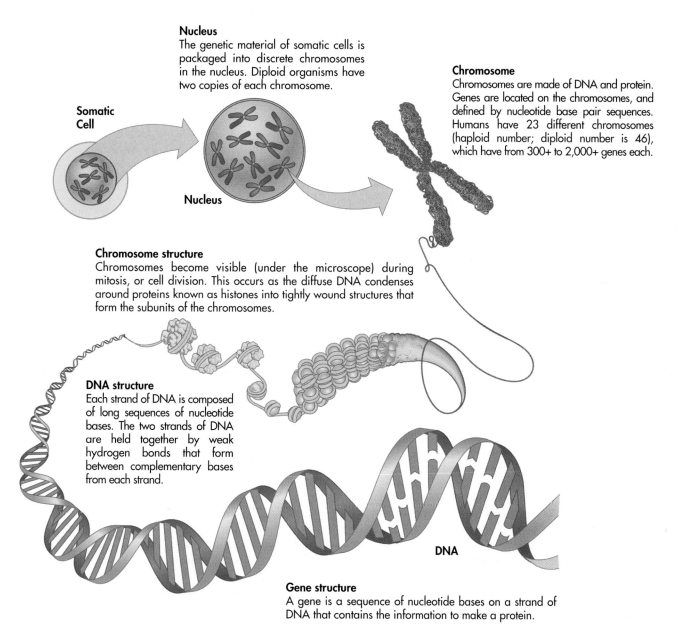

Nucleus
The genetic material of somatic cells is packaged into discrete chromosomes in the nucleus. Diploid organisms have two copies of each chromosome.

Somatic Cell

Nucleus

Chromosome
Chromosomes are made of DNA and protein. Genes are located on the chromosomes, and defined by nucleotide base pair sequences. Humans have 23 different chromosomes (haploid number; diploid number is 46), which have from 300+ to 2,000+ genes each.

Chromosome structure
Chromosomes become visible (under the microscope) during mitosis, or cell division. This occurs as the diffuse DNA condenses around proteins known as histones into tightly wound structures that form the subunits of the chromosomes.

DNA structure
Each strand of DNA is composed of long sequences of nucleotide bases. The two strands of DNA are held together by weak hydrogen bonds that form between complementary bases from each strand.

DNA

Gene structure
A gene is a sequence of nucleotide bases on a strand of DNA that contains the information to make a protein.

FIGURE 2.13   Chromosome structure.

The Wide World of RNA

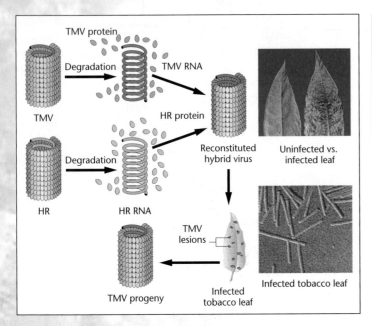

Some viruses, such as the tobacco mosaic virus, use RNA as their genetic material

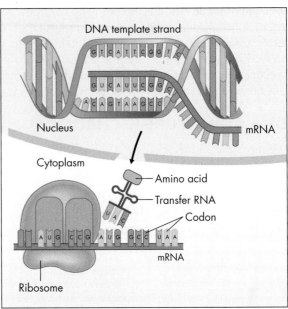

Messenger RNA (mRNA) carries genetic information from the nucleus to the cytoplasm for protein synthesis

If RNA could talk, probably the first thing it would say is "Why all the fuss about DNA?" Almost everyone knows that DNA is the chemical of life, of genetic transmission. Although it has long been known that there are some viruses that depend on RNA for genetic transmission, these were thought to be a relatively minor exception to the general rule. But as we have seen in our discussion of protein synthesis, forms of RNA play a critical role in this essential function of the cell. Messenger RNA (mRNA) carries the message of the gene from the nucleus to the cytoplasm, while transfer RNA brings the amino acids to the ribosome to be assembled into protein chains. The ribosome itself is composed of RNA molecules as well (rRNA).

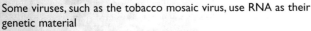

Transfer RNAs (tRNA) carry amino acids to the ribosome to be synthesized into proteins

In general, RNA was thought to play a more limited role in cell function than DNA or proteins due to the fact that it is an inherently less stable molecule (Cohen, 2004). It is now quite clear that there are forms of RNA that can catalyze chemical reactions in the cell—in other words there are RNAs that can function as enzymes. For example, small nuclear RNAs (snRNA) are active in the posttrascriptional processing of some mRNAs, working with proteins to splice out introns. In some simple species, the introns in messenger RNAs that ultimately form ribosomal RNAs actually contain the information to splice themselves out of the molecule. In this sense RNA is said to be "autocatalytic." When this discovery was made in the early 1980s, it was again thought to be an exception that proved the rule—the retention of a primitive biochemical mechanism that was no longer generally used.

Another class of RNA molecules—microRNA (miRNA)—may play an even larger and much more widespread role in cell function (Kloosterman & Plasterk, 2006). MiRNAs affect gene expression by destabilizing mRNAs or otherwise interfering with translation. Although research on miRNA is still in the early stages, studies indicate that they may play an important role in tissue growth and development, some genetic disorders, and may even be associated with some forms of cancer. The ability of miRNAs to regulate gene expression has not gone unnoticed by the pharmaceutical industry, where *RNA interference* (RNAi) is one of the hottest areas of research and development. One way that therapeutic RNAi may work is by the introduction of short strands of RNA that function in the same way as the natural miRNAs. Recent studies indicate that under certain circumstances RNAi may be used to turn genes on rather than off, which would broaden the therapeutic horizons considerably. RNA interference has not been observed in bacteria, suggesting that it is a later evolutionary development and not a primitive retention. Unlike single-stranded messenger RNA, miRNAs fold back on themselves to form a short double-stranded molecule. The therapeutic use of RNAi will depend on the introduction to the body of short (20+ base pairs) double-stranded RNA molecules, targeted to influence specific mRNAs.

Several other classes of RNA have been shown to be active in gene regulation. Researchers of RNA feel that they are at the beginning of a new era in which the critical role RNA plays in the most basic aspects of gene expression is finally being recognized. The 2006 Nobel Prize in Medicine was awarded to Andrew Fire and Craig Mello for their work on RNA interference.

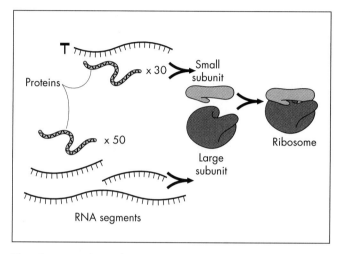

The ribosomes themselves are composed of RNA strands

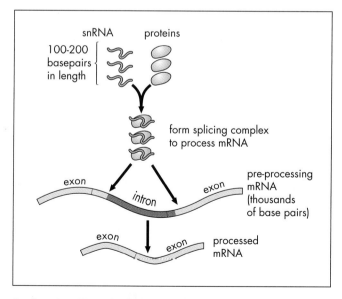

Small nuclear RNAs (snRNA), 100-200 bp in length, form part of the splicing mechanisms to process mRNAs

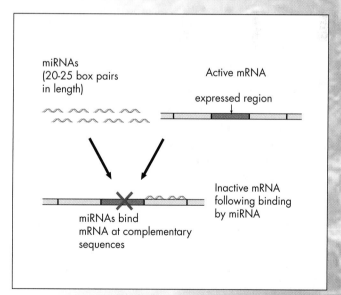

Micro RNAs (miRNA), 20-25 bp in length, can inactivate mRNAs

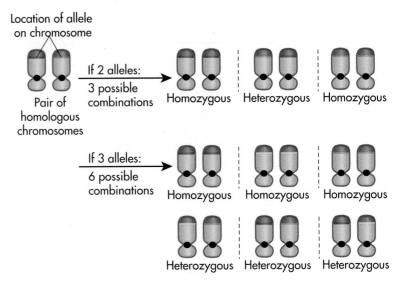

FIGURE 2.14 Homozygosity and heterozygosity.

centromere   Condensed and constricted region of a chromosome. During mitosis and meiosis, location where sister chromatids attach to one another.

diploid number   Full complement of paired chromosomes in a somatic cell. In humans, the diploid number is 46 (23 pairs of different chromosomes).

haploid number   The number of chromosomes found in a gamete, representing one from each pair found in a diploid somatic cell. In humans, the haploid number is 23.

homologous chromosomes   Members of the same pair of chromosomes (or autosomes). Homologous chromosomes undergo crossing over during meiosis.

locus   The location of a gene on a chromosome. The locus for a gene is identified by the number of the chromosome on which it is found and its position on the chromosome.

alleles   Alternative versions of a gene. Alleles are distinguished from one another by their differing effects on the phenotypic expression of the same gene.

homozygous   Having the same allele at the loci for a gene on both members of a pair of homologous chromosomes (or autosomes).

heterozygous   Having two different alleles at the loci for a gene on a pair of homologous chromosomes (or autosomes).

chromosome has a distinctive size and shape, which are observable under the light microscope. The shape is determined in part by the position of the **centromere**, a condensed and constricted region of chromosomes that is of critical importance during cell replication. The size is determined by the size (in numbers of base pairs) of the DNA molecule that makes up the chromosome.

Except for the gametes, or sex cells, each somatic cell in an individual's body has the same number of chromosomes. In fact, chromosome number is a constant across entire species. Most organisms have two copies of each chromosome in each cell; in each of these pairs of chromosomes, one is from the mother and the other from the father. The total number of chromosomes in each somatic cell is called the **diploid number**. Sex cells have only half as many chromosomes as somatic cells (one copy of each chromosome), so the total number of chromosomes in a sex cell is known as the **haploid number**. In a diploid cell, the members of each pair of chromosomes are known as **homologous chromosomes**.

The genes are distributed across the chromosomes, and the locations of specific genes can be mapped to specific chromosomes (Figure 2.14). Sometimes the term **locus** (pl., *loci*) is used interchangeably with the term *gene*. More specifically, we can think of the locus as the location of a gene on a chromosome. Because somatic cells have two copies of each chromosome, they also have two copies of each gene, one at each locus. Genes come in different versions, called **alleles**. For example, there might be a gene for eye color, but it could have two alleles, one for brown and one for blue; the locus of this gene could be mapped to a specific chromosome. A real example involves the ABO blood type system (which is discussed in more detail in Chapter 5). At that locus (which is on chromosome 9), there are three possible alleles, called A, B, and O, which determine blood type. When an individual has the same allele for a gene at each locus on each chromosome, this individual is called **homozygous** for that gene. If the individual has different alleles of the gene at each locus, then he or she is **heterozygous** for that gene. When we consider that each individual has thousands of genes, each of which may be represented by several alleles, it is easy to see that the number of possible different combinations of alleles is enormous (Insights and Advances: Biochemical Individuality on page 56).

Mitosis   Mitosis, the process whereby a somatic cell replicates, leads to the formation of two identical daughter cells. Mitosis is the basis of all cell proliferation,

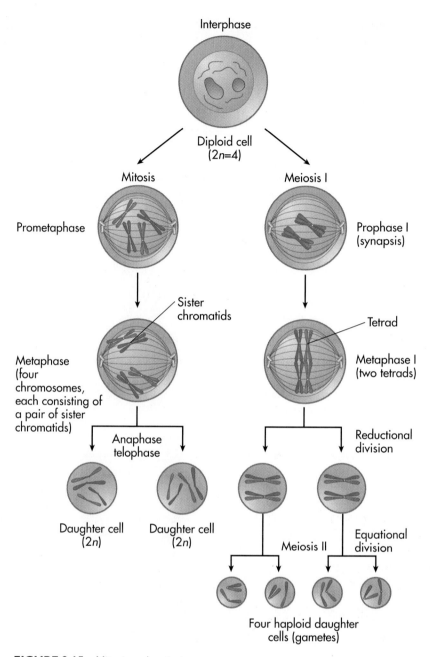

FIGURE 2.15   Mitosis and meiosis.

which can occur when an organism grows, during healing, or during any physiological process in which new cells are needed to replace the loss of cells (Figure 2.15).

The ongoing process of cell division and nondivision sometimes is known as the *cell cycle*. The cell cycle can be divided into several stages. The *interphase* is the stage of a cell's life when it is not involved in mitosis; instead, most of its energies are devoted to metabolism and growth. Although the interphase is not part of mitosis, an important premitotic activity occurs toward the end of interphase: The DNA is replicated in preparation for mitosis. During interphase, DNA is packaged into chromatin, and discrete chromosomes are not visible.

INSIGHTS AND ADVANCES

Biochemical Individuality

Individual human beings differ from one another in physical appearance. Even identical twins have subtle physical differences that allow others to tell them apart. But individuality extends to the biochemical and genetic levels as well. We are as much unique individuals at the biochemical level as at the anatomical level.

In the 1950s, biochemist Roger Williams wrote a monograph called *Bio-chemical Individuality* in which he argued, based on innumerable biochemical measures, that everyone deviated from the norm in some way. In other words, at the biochemical level, everyone was an individual. For example, Williams measured amino acid secretion in saliva. He found that every individual secreted a different combination of amino acids and in different amounts. There were amino acids that were secreted by a small percentage of the people, and others that were more commonly secreted. Williams pointed out that people varied from each other in levels of enzymatic activity, nutritional metabolism, and many other phenotypic expressions of biochemical processes.

Williams's work anticipated later developments in genetics that made it possible to develop unique biochemical profiles for every individual. These methods have come to be used in a variety of forensic settings, especially in the analysis of blood (*forensic serology*). The ability of investigators to identify different alleles of proteins provides a valuable tool for individual identification.

Blood types, such as the ABO system, represent one such allelic system, but several other proteins that can be isolated from blood samples also show allelic variation. These proteins allow individual identification because it is very unlikely that two individuals will share exactly the same combination of alleles from a number of variable proteins. For example, if we examine ten blood proteins, each with two alleles that are represented in the population at a frequency of 0.5, the chance that any two individuals from that population will have the same combination of ten alleles is 0.5^{10}, or about 0.00098. If you add some more proteins or if the individual has some alleles that are very rare in the population, you can develop an allelic profile that is unique among the entire human population. It is important to keep in mind that the allele frequencies used to make these calculations must be derived from the individual's own biological population because allele frequencies vary from population to population.

Over the last 20 years, a technique known as *DNA fingerprinting* has been developed to further refine the ability of investigators to make individual genetic identifications (Jeffreys et al., 1985). DNA fingerprinting is based on the fact that there are segments of DNA (called *minisatellites*) dispersed throughout the genome at different loci, which are composed of different numbers of repeated base pair sequences. These sequences do not code for anything and are highly variable. When the DNA from an individual is digested using an enzyme called a *restriction endonuclease,* a unique pattern of DNA fragments derived from these minisatellites will emerge for each individual (Figure A). They are truly as unique as fingerprints.

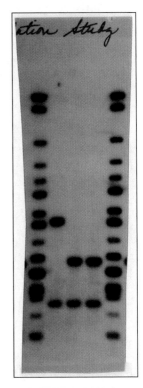

FIGURE A   DNA fingerprint.

The first stage of mitosis is the *prophase*. Three important things happen during the prophase:

1. The nuclear envelope breaks down and disappears.

2. The diffuse chromatin fibers condense and begin to form dense chromosomes. The individual chromosomes actually are doubled chromosomes, composed of two identical sister *chromatids*.

3. The polar orientation of the cell for the division into two daughter cells is established. The prophase often takes up at least half of the process of mitosis.

After prophase, the chromosomes migrate to the equatorial center of the cell, where they line up in an orderly fashion. When they have reached this position, the cell is in the *metaphase*. The *anaphase* follows the metaphase as the sister chromatids split apart and migrate to opposite ends of the cell. This is usually the shortest part of mitosis. Once the anaphase is completed, there will be a complete diploid complement of *daughter chromosomes* at each end of the cell.

The final stage of mitosis is the *telophase*. During this period, the cytoplasm is split into two, resulting in the complete separation of the two daughter cells, each with its daughter chromosomes. Once the separation is complete, the chromosomes uncoil into chromatin, and the nucleus of the cell forms around the genetic material. The new cell then enters interphase, restarting the cell cycle.

Meiosis   The process of meiosis (Figure 2.15) leads to the formation of the gametes (sperm in males and eggs in females), which are cells that have the haploid number of chromosomes (that is, one copy of each chromosome as opposed to the two copies of each found in diploid somatic cells). Meiosis occurs only in the testes of males and the ovaries of females. Like mitosis, meiosis begins with diploid cells, but through an additional cell division, haploid gametes eventually result. The sex cells must be haploid because when the sperm and egg unite to form the **zygote** (fertilized egg), the resulting zygote should reestablish the diploid number of chromosomes.

The first meiotic prophase is similar in some ways to prophase in mitosis but with some critical differences. It is similar in that the replicated DNA condenses into chromosomes, and sister chromatids form. However, unlike in mitosis, in meiosis the double-stranded homologous chromosomes pair up, forming units that are in effect made up of four chromatids (that is, two pairs of sister chromatids); this unit is known as a *tetrad*. At this stage, an important process called **crossing over** occurs. Crossing over is the process whereby genetic material is exchanged between pairs of homologous chromosomes. This process results in a **recombination** of alleles on the chromosomes.

Crossing over is extremely important because it enables new genetic combinations (although not new genes) to be assembled along each chromosome. Crossing over increases the available genetic variability in a population, thereby increasing the amount of variability available for natural selection to act on. The rate of evolution in sexually reproducing species therefore is much faster than in asexually reproducing species. Without sexual reproduction, it is likely that the complexity of plant and animal life on Earth could never have been achieved. Only mutation can provide wholly novel new variants in a population, but the new combinations of genes that arise from sexual reproduction are of critical importance in evolution by natural selection. One advantage of nonsexual reproduction is that it is possible to make sure that an exact copy of a parent is created. Although this would not be an advantageous long-term evolutionary strategy, some people today think that there may be commercial and other reasons to develop artificial cloning techniques.

After crossing over occurs in the first meiotic prophase, a metaphase follows and tetrads align along the equator of the cell. During the *first meiotic division* (also known as the *reduction division*), the chromatid tetrads split, and a double-stranded chromosome is sorted into each daughter cell. This is very different from what happens in mitosis. In mitosis, the doubled-chromosomes separate so that each daughter cell winds up with one paternally derived chromosome and one maternally derived chromosome, just as the mother cell had. In the first meiotic division, one daughter cell has two copies of the maternal chromosome and the other has two copies of the paternal chromosome (although after crossing over, of course, they are no longer identical to the parental chromosomes).

Once the first cell division is complete and after another round of prophase and metaphase, the *second meiotic cell division* occurs. During this division, the paired

zygote   A fertilized egg.

crossing over   Exchange of genetic material between homologous chromosomes during the first prophase of meiosis; mechanism for genetic recombination.

recombination   The rearrangement of genes on homologous chromosomes that occurs during crossing over in meiosis. The source of variation arising out of sexual reproduction; important for increasing rates of natural selection.

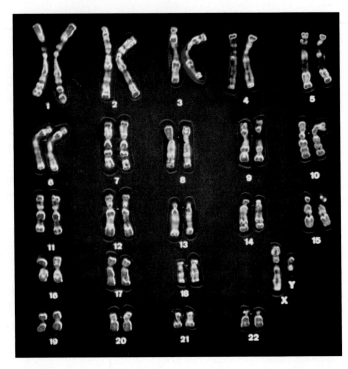

FIGURE 2.16 A human karyotype.

chromatids split—as they do in mitosis—resulting in a total of four haploid gametes (two from each of the two daughter cells of the first meiotic division) with only one copy of each chromosome.

Different Kinds and Numbers of Chromosomes   As mentioned previously, chromosomes come in different sizes and shapes, and different species have different numbers of chromosomes. During mitosis, when the chromosomes become visible, it is possible to study the chromosomes by taking a photograph of them through a microscope. From such a photograph, a **karyotype** of an individual can be made (Figure 2.16). A karyotype shows all the chromosomes in a single somatic cell. Humans have twenty-three different chromosomes (haploid number) and a diploid number of forty-six. Of the forty-six chromosomes in humans, forty-four can be distributed into twenty-two homologous pairs. These are called **autosomes**. The **sex chromosomes** are the twenty-third pair. In mammals, the sex chromosomes are labeled X and Y, and the autosomes are numbered (in humans, from 1 to 22). Mammalian males have one X chromosome and one Y chromosome, whereas females have two X chromosomes. Because females have only X chromosomes, it is the sex cells of the male, who can produce gametes with one X and one Y chromosome, that determine the sex of the offspring.

Even closely related species can have different numbers of chromosomes. In chimpanzees, our closest living biological relatives, the haploid number is twenty-four chromosomes, and the diploid number is forty-eight. At some point since humans and chimpanzees last shared a common ancestor, the packaging of DNA into chromosomes changed. As it turns out, the other great apes, the gorilla and orangutan, to whom we are also closely related, have the same number of chromosomes as a chimpanzee. Thus, along our unique evolutionary lineage, humans had a fusion of two chromosomes, resulting in the loss of one chromosome. Note that this does not mean a loss of DNA because chromosomes are indicative only of the

karyotype   The complete chromosomal complement of an individual; usually based on a photograph of the chromosomes visualized under the microscope.

autosomes   Any of the chromosomes other than the sex chromosomes.

sex chromosomes   In mammals, chromosomes X and Y, with XX producing females and XY producing males.

packaging, but not the amount, of DNA. We do not know whether the fusion of these two chromosomes was a critical event in human evolutionary history.

Chromosomal Abnormalities   In humans, individuals with abnormalities in chromosome number usually suffer from a range of medical and developmental problems; chromosomal abnormalities probably are also a common cause of miscarriages. **Nondisjunction errors** that occur during meiosis result in the misdistribution of chromosomes to the sex cells (that is, one receives both copies of the chromosomes and the sister cell receives none). If fertilization occurs with either of these sex cells, this leads to an inappropriate number of chromosomes in the fertilized egg, or zygote. Two common kinds of nondisjunction errors are *monosomy,* which occurs when one chromosome in a pair is absent, or *trisomy,* which occurs when there is an extra chromosome, resulting in three copies of the chromosomes rather than a pair. An example of monosomy is *Turner syndrome.* Females with Turner syndrome have only a single X sex chromosome (represented as XO) rather than XX or XY. The absence of the second X chromosome leads to a delay or absence of sexual maturation, small physical stature, delayed mental maturation, and other physical abnormalities.

An example of trisomy, *Down syndrome,* or *trisomy 21,* occurs when an individual has three rather than two copies of chromosome 21. Individuals with Down syndrome share a constellation of features, including a common facial anatomy and head shape, short stature, a furrowed tongue, and short, broad hands with characteristic palm and fingerprint patterns. People with Down syndrome also show retarded physical and mental development, and they are also prone to heart disease and leukemia. Another striking feature of Down syndrome is that as they age, people with the condition almost always develop *Alzheimer disease,* the most common form of age-related dementia. Alzheimer disease is characterized by the development of microscopic plaques in the brain (which cause the death of neurons); a primary component of these plaques is a protein called *beta-amyloid.* As it turns out, the gene for beta-amyloid is on chromosome 21. The susceptibility of people with Down syndrome to Alzheimer disease probably is a result of the overexpression of this gene caused by the fact that three copies are present rather than two.

It is important to keep in mind that for most chromosomes, monosomy or trisomy is incompatible with life. Down syndrome and Turner syndrome are the exceptions rather than the rule. The rate for Down syndrome is only 0.05% in pregnancies in 20-year-old women but rises to 3% in women over 45. When you consider that all of the chromosomes are vulnerable to trisomy, it is easy to see why it is so difficult for older women to produce a viable zygote (Figure 2.17 on page 60). Studies show that about 2% of all recognized pregnancies (including those that result in miscarriage) in women 25 years or younger are trisomic for some chromosome; this compares with 35% in pregnancies in women over 40 years (Hassold & Hunt, 2001). Nondisjunction errors obviously are more common with increasing maternal age; evidence of an effect of increasing paternal age is not strong.

Molecular Tools for Bioanthropological Research

Understanding genetics is critical to understanding evolutionary phenomena such as adaptation and the biological histories of populations and species. Over the years, biological anthropologists have used a variety of molecular genetics techniques to study the natural history of people and other primate species. The application of these techniques to anthropological problems and issues will be considered in later chapters.

Prenatal testing for chromosomal abnormalities and other genetic disorders is much more common in wealthier rather than poorer groups in the United States and other countries.

nondisjunction error   The failure of homologous chromosomes (chromatids) to separate properly during cell division. When it occurs during meiosis, it may lead to the formation of gametes that are missing a chromosome or have an extra copy of a chromosome.

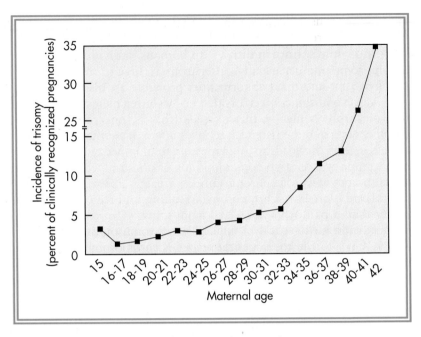

FIGURE 2.17   Increased risk of trisomy with maternal age.

INDIRECT VERSUS DIRECT RESEARCH METHODS

The ultimate indirect method to study genetics is to look at the anatomy and physiology of an organism. But as we will discuss in more detail in Chapter 3, individual organisms are a result of complex interactions between genes and the environment. Molecular structures provide a more straightforward way to compare populations or species because they are not strongly influenced by environmental variables.

The problem with molecules is that they are very small and difficult to see. Clever techniques have been developed to visualize molecular structures. The visual representation did not have to be an exact replication of the molecule, but it had to provide enough information so that inferences about structure could be made. In anthropology, the concern was to find techniques that would provide information about *variation* in molecular structures without necessarily worrying about the exact structure of the molecules. In the 1960s and 1970s, biological anthropologists made extensive use of *indirect* molecular techniques to study evolutionary relationships. Indirect techniques, such as *protein immunology* or *DNA hybridization*, allowed protein or DNA structures from different species to be compared without actually determining amino acid (for proteins) or base pair (for DNA) sequences. Although these techniques were crude by contemporary standards, they revolutionized how evolutionary relationships both within and between species, including humans, are studied (Goodman, 1963; Sarich & Wilson, 1967; Sibley & Ahlquist, 1984).

The most commonly used indirect method for uncovering protein variation (that is, allelic variation) is *protein electrophoresis*. Proteins vary not only by size but by electrical charge, which is determined by the amino acid composition of the protein. If you place small amounts of a protein in a thin sheet of agarose gel and run an electric current through it, the proteins will migrate across the gel, driven by the current. The protein can be visualized on the gel by using a variety of dyes. This technique is useful for detecting protein and allelic variation because different versions of a protein migrate at different speeds across the gel, depending on their amino acid composition. For example, an individual who is heterozygous at some locus may produce two different bands on a gel, reflecting the two slightly different versions of the same protein that his body produces. For many years, protein electrophoresis was the primary tool for looking at variation between populations within a species.

In recent years, advances in molecular genetics techniques have allowed the direct sequencing of proteins and DNA. Although *protein sequencing* has been used for evolutionary research, *DNA sequencing*—determining the actual base sequence of a gene or stretch of DNA—is by far the most widely used tool in molecular anthropology today (Figure 2.18). DNA sequencing provides the most direct kind of evidence about the genetic makeup of individuals and species, and it can yield insights about both coding and noncoding regions of the **genome**—the sum total of all the genes carried by an individual. The development of these methods in the 1970s and 1980s made possible much of the "molecular revolution" of the end of the twentieth century.

One of the most spectacular achievements of the molecular revolution has been the sequencing of the entire human genome (International Human Genome Sequencing Consortium 2001). The Human Genome Project was initiated in the late 1980s with the then-outlandish goal of determining the sequence of all the bases in a single human genome. With increasingly sophisticated and cost-effective DNA-sequencing technology becoming available, the goal of sequencing the human genome—and the genomes of many other organisms—is now achievable. The Human Genome Project has been a massive undertaking, involving thousands of researchers, working in dozens of dedicated research centers throughout the world. But the payoff in scientific terms is potentially immense, for the study of development, physiology, medicine, and evolution. The recent sequencing of the chimpanzee genome (Chimpanzee Sequencing and Analysis Consortium 2005)

genome The sum total of all the genes carried by an individual.

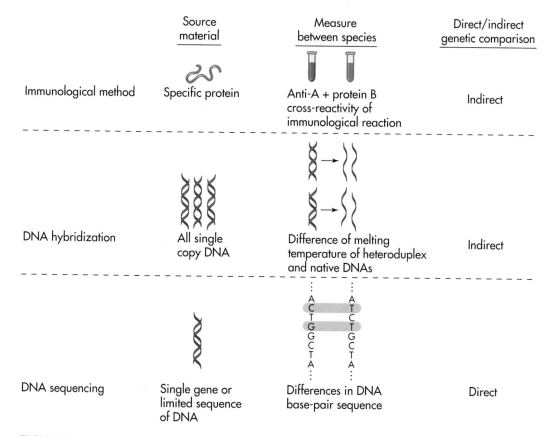

	Source material	Measure between species	Direct/indirect genetic comparison
Immunological method	Specific protein	Anti-A + protein B cross-reactivity of immunological reaction	Indirect
DNA hybridization	All single copy DNA	Difference of melting temperature of heteroduplex and native DNAs	Indirect
DNA sequencing	Single gene or limited sequence of DNA	Differences in DNA base-pair sequence	Direct

FIGURE 2.18 Indirect and direct methods for molecular genetic analysis.

demonstrates the potenial value of these genomic undertakings for evolutionary studies. We now know that since humans and chimpanzees last shared a common ancestor (5–7 million years ago), over 40 million genetic differences have accumulated between the species. This may sound like a lot, but this number should be considered in the context of the billions of base pairs that make up the human or chimpanzee genomes.

PCR, MITOCHONDRIAL DNA, AND ANCIENT DNA

In addition to automated DNA sequencing, the other essential tool of the molecular revolution is a technique known as the **polymerase chain reaction (PCR)** (Mullis, 1990). The key feature of PCR is that an extraordinarily small amount of DNA can be used to make millions or even billions of copies of a specific DNA segment. The technique depends on a specialized enzyme, called *Taq polymerase,* which causes the extension of a single strand of DNA (if free nucleotide base pairs are available). Once the *target sequence,* the specific region of DNA that is to be amplified, has been identified, two *primers* must be designed, one for each end of the sequence. These primers are short segments of DNA (about fifteen to twenty base pairs long), which are necessary for the Taq polymerase to begin extension of the two DNA strands. They attach to the DNA at each end of the target sequence because they are designed to complement the DNA sequence in that region.

Here's how the process works (Figure 2.19). DNA containing the target sequence, base pair nucleotides (A,T,C, and G), the two primers, and Taq polymerase are placed in a test tube that is then heated to the point where the DNA strands separate—about 95°C. After this, the solution is cooled to about 55°C. This allows the primers to attach to the single DNA strands at the positions flanking the DNA segment of interest. The temperature is then raised to somewhere around 75°C. At this temperature, the Taq polymerase works to extend the target segment's DNA strands starting at each of the primer positions. Copies of the target DNA are being made during this step in the process. This heating-cooling-heating cycle is then repeated twenty-five or thirty times. Every newly synthesized strand of DNA becomes a target for copying in each new cycle, which results in an exponential increase in the number of target DNA sequences in the reaction tube.

PCR allows the recovery of DNA sequences from miniscule samples, such as a single hair or dried saliva on an envelope obtained at a crime scene. In biological anthropology, PCR often is used to study evolutionary patterns in mitochondrial DNA and nuclear DNA recovered from bone, or *ancient DNA.*

Mitochondrial DNA   The mitochondria are the organelles found in cells in which energy metabolism occurs, but they have their own DNA, as well. **Mitochondrial DNA (mtDNA)** is a circular structure of about 16,600 base pairs (Figure 2.20 on page 64). Each mitochondrion may have several copies of its DNA, and each cell can have hundreds or thousands of mitochondria, thus each cell also has hundreds or thousands of mtDNA copies. Although there are several genes in the mtDNA genome, there are also regions that do not code for anything. These regions (such as one called the D-loop) tend to evolve quickly, so they are highly variable. They are very useful for looking at evolutionary patterns between closely related species, or even between populations within a single species. These regions are so variable that families may have mutations or sequences specific to them. Sequences of these highly variable mtDNA regions therefore are very important in forensic investigation because they allow otherwise unidentifiable pieces of tissue or bodily fluids to be linked to a known individual (provided an appropriate DNA sample from the individual or a relative is available for comparison).

There are two important things to keep in mind about mtDNA. First, unlike nuclear DNA, mtDNA has no exchange (crossing over) between maternal and

polymerase chain reaction (PCR)   Method for amplifying DNA sequences using the Taq polymerase enzyme. Can potentially produce millions or billions of copies of a DNA segment starting from a very small number of target DNA.

mitochondrial DNA (mtDNA)   Small loop of DNA found in the mitochondria. It is clonally and maternally inherited.

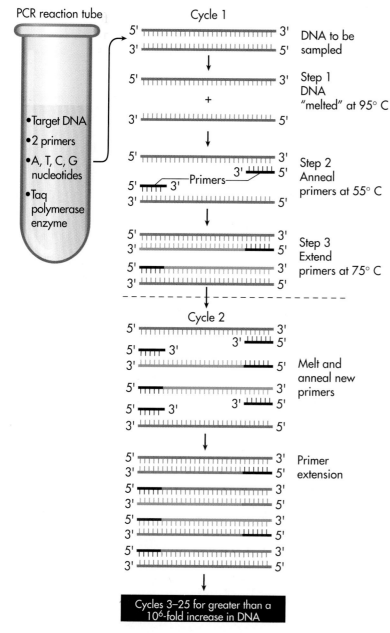

PCR reaction tube

• Target DNA
• 2 primers
• A, T, C, G
  nucleotides
• Taq
  polymerase
  enzyme

Cycle 1

5' 3' DNA to be
3' 5' sampled

5' 3' Step 1
        DNA
   +   "melted" at 95° C
3' 5'

5' 3' Step 2
3' 5'   Anneal
5' 3'   primers at 55° C
  Primers
3' 5'

5' 3' Step 3
3' 5' Extend
5' 3' primers at 75° C
3' 5'

Cycle 2

5' 3'
5' 3' 3' 5'
3' 5' Melt and
5' 3' anneal new
        primers
5' 3' 3' 5'
3' 5'

5' 3' Primer
3' 5' extension
5' 3'
3' 5'
5' 3'
3' 5'
5' 3'
3' 5'

Cycles 3–25 for greater than a
10^6-fold increase in DNA

FIGURE 2.19   The polymerase chain reaction (PCR).

paternal DNA as it is passed down through the generations. Instead, mtDNA is passed on clonally from generation to generation. Second, mtDNA is passed on only through the mother because an offspring's mtDNA comes from the mitochondria floating in the cytoplasm of the egg. The mitochondria of the sperm are concentrated in the tail region of the cell and are not injected into the egg with the nuclear DNA at fertilization. All of your mtDNA came from your mother, and if you are a male, you are an mtDNA evolutionary dead end. The Y chromosome acts as the male version of the mtDNA: It undergoes minimal recombination and is passed on only through males. It is also being used in evolutionary studies of populations.

Ancient DNA   Bones as old as 100,000 years can yield DNA. PCR is essential for recovering ancient DNA sequences, as the DNA in bone is often fragmentary or degraded. In general, it is easier to amplify mtDNA rather than nuclear DNA. There are thousands of copies of mtDNA per cell, thus there are potentially many

Although we may only be able to recover DNA from fossils less than 100,000 years old, recent studies have shown that protein sequence information can be recovered from dinosaur bones 68 million years old.

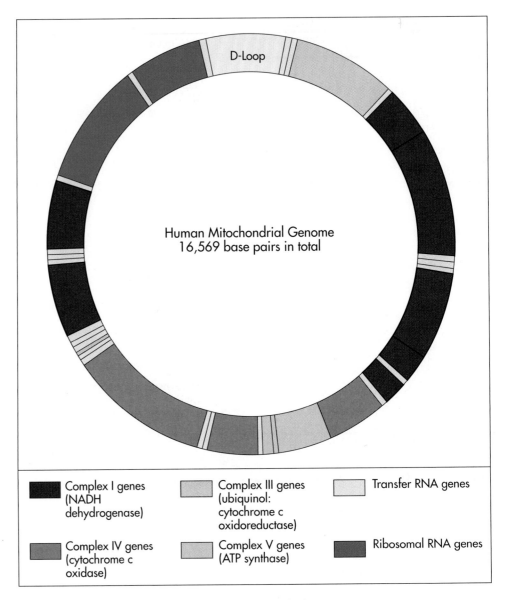

FIGURE 2.20   Schematic map of the human mitochondrial genome.

more individual copies of mtDNA than nuclear DNA in bony remains, which may be used as a target for amplification (Figure 2.21). However, recent advances in molecular techniques make it possible to recover not only mtDNA but nuclear DNA sequences as well. For example, in looking at the ancient DNA of fossil relatives of humans, the sequencing of the entire human genome provides a comparative database with which to identify relatively intact and evolutionarily meaningful fragments of nuclear DNA from extinct forms (Green et al., 2006).

The recovery of DNA in bone often involves pushing the PCR technique to its limits, and contamination is a major worry. If the PCR primers find complementary DNA sequences to attach to, amplification (i.e., making many copies) of DNA will occur, even if it is not the target sequence. This is especially a concern if one is examining human bones—because the experimenters themselves become the source of contamination: The primers designed to work on the ancient sample might also work on the researcher's DNA. Given the sensitivity of PCR, even a single molecule of contamination can distort the results of an experiment.

1) Excavation of bone

(Clean and dry conditions)

2) Selection of sample

Tooth

Intact bone fragment

0.5–1.0 grams of sample sufficient

3) Clean and grind sample:
removal of surface or drill into bone

4) Chemicals and enzymes applied to
extract fragmentary DNA

5) PCR-primers selected to amplify relatively short
(<1000 BP) DNA section

Target
in intact
DNA

DNA fragments
from ancient DNA

6) Sequencing of amplified DNA

Compare

Ancient

Contemporary

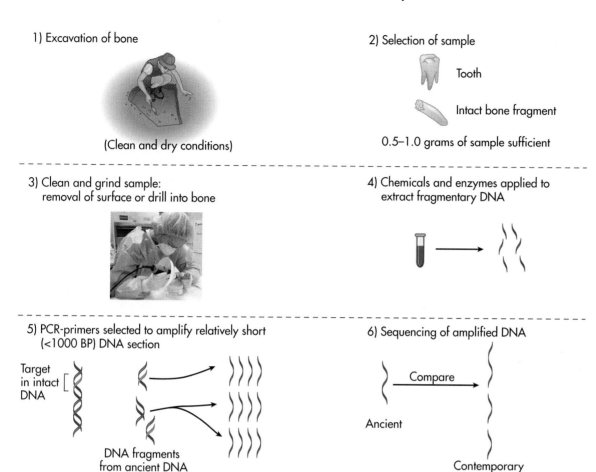

FIGURE 2.21   Recovery process of ancient DNA.

This is particularly important when looking at the ancient DNA of a form as closely related to us as Neandertals. Recent ancient DNA studies of the Neandertal genome indicate that their base pair sequences are about 99.5% identical to our own (Green et al., 2006; Noonan et al., 2006). We will discuss Neandertal DNA in more detail in Chapter 14. Some molecular archaeologists specialize in looking at the ancient DNA from domestic animals, such as cows, and commensal animals, such as rats, which inevitably share living spaces with humans in many parts of the world (Matisoo-Smith et al., 1998). This tends to limit the possibility of contamination, at least from the excavators or the laboratory workers.

In this chapter, we have reviewed some of the most fundamental aspects of life on Earth: DNA, cells, proteins, and the basics of cell growth and organismal reproduction. Although humans may in some ways be unique among our planet's life forms, molecular genetics reaffirms the evolutionary continuity between us and other organisms, ranging from bacteria to plants to all other animals.

SUMMARY

1. **What are the different levels at which scientists study genetic phenomena?**

   Genetics can be studied at the cellular and molecular, individual, population, and species levels. The genetic bases of physical and behavioral traits of an organism can also be studied. The ultimate goal of genetic science is to understand how genes interact with each other and with the environment to produce complex organisms. This requires understanding genetic expression at each level.

2. **Why is the cell called the fundamental building block of life?**

   All of the different tissues and structures of the body are composed of cells. Although the cells from different tissues become specialized and differ substantially in appearance, all cells have a similar basic design. Even single-celled organisms have the same basic structure as cells from more complex, multicellular life forms.

3. **What is the difference between prokaryotes and eukaryotes?**

   Prokaryotes, such as bacteria, are single-celled life forms in which the genetic material is not contained within a nucleus in the cytoplasm. In eukaryotes, the genetic material is contained within a structure in the cytoplasm known as the nucleus. Eukaryotes include single-celled and multicelled life forms, including all complex plants and animals.

4. **What are DNA and RNA? What functions do they serve in the cell?**

   In both prokaryotes and eukaryotes, the genetic material is composed of DNA. DNA is a double-stranded nucleic acid made up of a sequence of bases. The sequence of bases is used to carry the information (in genes) to synthesize proteins and to direct growth and development via cellular replication. RNA is a single-stranded nucleic acid. Different kinds of RNA (e.g., messenger RNA, transfer RNA, and ribosomal RNA) have specific roles in protein synthesis. More recent research indicates that some forms of RNA are directly involved with gene expression through the posttranscriptional modification of mRNA molecules.

5. **What are proteins, and what functions do they serve in living organisms? How are proteins synthesized?**

   Proteins are large molecules composed of amino acids. An amino acid chain is also known as a polypeptide; a protein may be formed from several polypeptide chains. Protein synthesis occurs via a two-step process occurring in the nucleus and cytoplasm. Transcription occurs in the nucleus and involves the synthesis of an mRNA molecule that is complementary to the base sequence of a gene. The mRNA molecule carries the genetic information to make a protein from the nucleus to the cytoplasm. At ribosomes located in the cytoplasm, translation occurs, a process in which the information carried by the mRNA is read and a polypeptide or protein is assembled. The language of protein synthesis that allows the conversion of DNA base pair sequences into protein amino acid sequences is known as the genetic code.

6. **How are mitosis and meiosis different from one another? How does crossing over during meiosis increase genetic variability?**

   Mitosis is the process of somatic cell replication in which the diploid chromosome number is maintained in each of the daughter cells after a cell divides. Meiosis is the process of cellular replication that results in the production of sex cells, or gametes. Meiosis has one more step of cell division than mitosis, which results in four daughter cells with the haploid number of chromosomes. Crossing over during meiosis leads to new combinations of genes on chromosomes, which in turn provides new variants on which natural selection can work.

7. **Why is mitochondrial DNA important in the recovery of ancient DNA?**

   DNA in bony remains degrades over time and becomes fragmented. In order for DNA to be recovered from bone, the PCR method is used to amplify target sequences. Because there are thousands of copies of mtDNA per somatic cell, target sequences from mtDNA are more likely to be present and intact than would target sequences from nuclear DNA (for which only one or two copies would be present per cell).

CRITICAL THINKING QUESTIONS

1. What is a gene? Compare physical and theoretical definitions. How do you think laypeople conceive of the gene and how it works?

2. What do you think about the ethics of cloning and stem cell research? Should they be allowed to continue or be restricted by society and the government?

KEY TERMS

prokaryotes
eukaryotes
nucleus
cytoplasm
somatic cells
gametes
stem cells
deoxyribonucleic acid
　(DNA)
proteins
protein synthesis
ribonucleic acid
　(RNA)
mitochondria

endoplasmic reticulum
　(ER)
ribosomes
nucleotide
base
enzyme
hemoglobin
hormone
amino acids
polypeptide
genetic code
codon
gene
messenger RNA (mRNA)

transfer RNA (tRNA)
chromatin
mitosis
meiosis
chromosomes
centromere
diploid number
haploid number
homologous
　chromosomes
locus
alleles
homozygous
heterozygous

zygote
crossing over
recombination
karyotype
autosomes
sex chromosomes
nondisjunction
　error
genome
polymerase
　chain reaction
　(PCR)
mitochondrial DNA
　(mtDNA)

SUGGESTED READING

Maddox, Brenda. (2003). *Rosalind Franklin: The Dark Lady of DNA.* Perennial, New York.

Ridley, Matt. (2000). *Genome.* HarperCollins, New York.

Watson, James D. (2001). *The Double Helix: A Personal Account of the Discovery of the Structure of DNA.* Touchstone Books, New York.

On a spring day in 1900, a scientist from Cambridge named William Bateson was riding on a train to London. Although relatively young, Bateson was widely recognized among scientists interested in heredity and evolution. He had conducted field and experimental research on both plants and animals and had been involved in theoretical debates about the nature of evolutionary change. Bateson was heading to London to give a talk to the Royal Horticultural Society. In his talk to the society in the previous year, Bateson had forthrightly argued that if the mechanisms of heredity were ever to be worked out, it would only be through the careful breeding of plants or animals, with precise recording of the expression of characters in parent and offspring generations. The expression of these characters would have to be statistically analyzed to make sense of the patterns of hereditary transmission.

As he rode on the train, Bateson read a scientific paper that he had recently seen mentioned in a new publication by a Dutch botanist named Hugo de Vries. The paper, in an obscure Austrian journal, was not hot off the presses; in fact, it had been published 35 years before. Bateson was not familiar with the author, Gregor Mendel, whom he realized had probably been dead for some time.

As he read, one word came to Bateson: *remarkable*. Mendel had conducted a long series of painstaking breeding experiments using the common garden pea. Bateson was impressed by the scale of the experiments, his description of them, and, most particularly, the analysis of the results Mendel provided. Bateson immediately recognized that the research program he had so boldly advocated the year before had already been implemented by Mendel—more than four decades earlier!

Bateson had prepared his talk to the Royal Horticultural Society before leaving Cambridge, but after arriving in London he hurriedly added a long section to the end discussing and lauding Mendel's work. During his presentation, he admitted some puzzlement as to how research as significant as Mendel's could be all but forgotten or unnoticed for so many years. He proclaimed that Mendel's ideas would "play a conspicuous part in all future discussions of evolutionary problems." Bateson was confident that the "laws of heredity" were finally within reach.

Bateson returned to Cambridge a self-avowed "Mendelian," and, within two years, published a book-length defense of "Mendelism." He devoted the rest of his career to the promotion of Mendel's ideas and to explaining what Mendelism meant to understanding evolutionary change (taking time out to father a son, Gregory, born in 1904, who grew up to be one of the most famous cultural anthropologists of the twentieth century). Strictly speaking, Bateson did not rediscover Mendel. Rather, he did something that was even more important: He recognized the significance of the rediscovery of Mendel and that a whole new science—*genetics* (a term Bateson coined in 1908)—was at hand.

IN CHAPTER 2, WE DISCUSSED the cellular and molecular bases of heredity. William Bateson (1861–1926) and other scientists had a concept of the gene long before anyone knew what DNA was or how it played its role in heredity. In this chapter, we explore in greater detail the observable effects of genes on the structures of plants and on the bodies and behavior of animals, including humans. As we will see, the relationship between gene and structure sometimes is very simple and straightforward and at other times is much more complex.

structural genes Genes that contain the information to make a protein.

regulatory genes Guide the expression of structural genes, without coding for a protein themselves.

genotype The genetic makeup of an individual. *Genotype* can refer to the entire genetic complement or more narrowly to the alleles present at a specific locus on two homologous chromosomes.

phenotype An observable or measurable feature of an organism. Phenotypes can be anatomical, biochemical, or behavioral.

Human genetics encompasses a wide range of phenomena. Genetics is vitally important for understanding human evolution, and it has a key role in many contemporary medical and cultural issues. As we cover these diverse topics in this chapter, it is useful to keep in mind the universality of the system of inheritance shared by all forms of life. After all, modern human genetics has its beginnings in research conducted on the common garden pea, a species with whom humans last shared a common ancestor hundreds of millions of years ago.

From Genotype to Phenotype

Little-known Austrian scientist Gregor Mendel (1822–1884), who was "rediscovered" by Bateson and his contemporaries, had a sense of how genes worked almost 90 years before Watson and Crick figured out the structure and function of DNA. This was a striking achievement when you consider that Mendel and his followers could not explore the laws of heredity by looking at the genes themselves. Instead, they had to make inferences about how genes worked based on observations of how specific traits of plants and animals were passed from generation to generation. Such research was painstaking and took years to complete.

How do we make the connection between genes and the physical traits we can observe? As we learned in Chapter 2, DNA functions include replication and protein synthesis. But DNA must do more than this: The genetic information of the DNA must somehow be translated into the physical reality of working bodies. Even today, with all the great advances in molecular biology, understanding of this process is still at an early stage (Carroll, 2005). A simple framework we can use to approach this topic is to recognize there are basically two kinds of genes. Genes that contain information to make proteins are called **structural genes**. Structural genes are surrounded by *regulatory regions,* sequences of bases that are important in initiating, promoting, or terminating transcription. If these regulatory regions are altered or missing, the expression of the gene can be affected. Beyond these regulatory regions, however, there must also be **regulatory genes** that further guide the expression of structural genes.

Structural genes may be quite similar across different (but related) species, so regulatory genes probably are critical in determining the form an organism, or species, takes. For example, two species may have several differences in the structural gene for some protein. Given the redundancy of the genetic code and the fact that the function of a protein may not change even with one or more amino acid substitutions, the structural protein may function in the same way in both species despite the changes at the structural gene level. However, a single change in a regulatory gene could result in the synthesis of the protein being shut down in one species while it is maintained in the other. This could lead to major differences between the two species in anatomy, physiology, or behavior. Recent estimates indicate that DNA base sequences in humans and chimpanzees are 95–96% identical (including coding and noncoding regions) (Britten, 2002; Cheng et al., 2005). The small number of base pair differences between human and chimpanzee DNA indicates that the physical and behavioral differences between the species result primarily from regulatory rather than structural genes (Figure 3.1).

When Wilhelm Johannsen introduced the term *gene* in the early twentieth century (see Chapter 2), he introduced two other terms that remain in use today: **genotype** and **phenotype**. The genotype is the set of specific genes (or alleles) an organism carries; it is the genetic constitution of that organism. The phenotype is the observable physical feature of an organism that is under some form of genetic control or influence. In some cases, the relationship between genotype and phenotype is direct: The observed phenotype is a direct product of the

FIGURE 3.1 Genetically closely related species can have profound anatomical differences, as this movie still from the 1938 film *Her Jungle Love,* featuring Dorothy Lamour and one of her chimpanzee co-stars, indicates.

underlying alleles. In other situations, the genotype interacts with factors in the environment to produce a phenotype. In phenotypes that are the result of complex gene–environment interactions, it can be difficult to figure out the contributions each makes to the variation we observe. Two contrasting examples of the relationship between genotype and phenotype in humans are the ABO blood type system and obesity.

THE ABO BLOOD TYPE SYSTEM

The **ABO blood type system** illustrates a straightforward relationship between genotype and phenotype. The ABO system (important in typing for blood transfusions) refers to a protein found on the surface of red blood cells, which is coded for by a gene located on chromosome 9. This gene has three alleles: A, B, and O. A and B stand for two different versions of the protein, and O stands for the absence of the protein (more precisely, A and B represent versions of the protein modified by enzymes from a common precursor, whereas O has only the precursor version of the protein). Because we are diploid organisms, we have two copies of each gene, one on each chromosome. As we discussed in Chapter 2, if an individual has the same allele of the gene on each chromosome, he or she is said to be homozygous for that gene; if the alleles are different, then the individual is heterozygous. In many cases, the phenotypic expression of the alleles for a gene depends on whether the genotype is heterozygous or homozygous.

An allele that must be present on both chromosomes to be expressed (that is, homozygous) is called a **recessive** allele (or gene). In the ABO system, O is a recessive allele: In order for it to be expressed, you must be homozygous for O (that is, have two copies of it). An allele that must be present at only one chromosomal locus to be expressed is called a **dominant** allele (or gene). Both A and B are dominant to O and **co-dominant** with each other: Only one copy is needed. As you can see in Table 3.1, there are six possible genotypes and four possible phenotypes. Even though this example illustrates a direct relationship between genotype and phenotype, knowing an ABO blood type does not necessarily tell you what the underlying genotype is if you are type A or B. The phenotype is a direct product of the genotype; no amount of environmental intervention will change your blood type.

OBESITY: A COMPLEX INTERACTION

Obesity provides a more complex example of the interaction between genes, environments, and phenotypes (Ulijaszek & Lofink, 2006). Studies have shown that some people with an obese phenotype, defined as some percentage of body weight greater than population norms or ideals, are in some way genetically predisposed

> *The ABO system is one of several blood protein polymorphisms that exhibit Mendelian inheritance.*

ABO blood type system   Refers to the genetic system for one of the proteins found on the surface of red blood cells. Consists of one gene with three alleles: A, B, and O.

recessive   In a diploid organism, refers to an allele that must be present in two copies (homozygous) in order to be expressed.

dominant   In a diploid organism, an allele that is expressed when present on only one of a pair of homologous chromosomes.

co-dominant   In a diploid organism, two different alleles of a gene that are both expressed in a heterozygous individual.

TABLE 3.1 ABO Blood Type System Genotypes and Phenotypes		
	Genotype	**Phenotype**
Homozygous	AA	Type A
	BB	Type B
	OO	Type O
Heterozygous	AO	Type A
	BO	Type B
	AB	Type AB

to such a condition. Recent research in both lab animals and humans indicates that there are specific genes that are critical to regulating appetite, which would be an important factor in overall body development. Some individuals have alleles for these genes that make it difficult for them to regulate their appetites (Figure 3.2); these individuals tend to become morbidly obese at a young age. Genes that regulate fat storage, metabolism, and so on, would also be critical in the development of an obese phenotype. If we could look at all the genes underlying the development of body size and shape, we might be able to come up with combinations of alleles that might indicate that an individual is prone to developing obesity. This will be no easy task, however, as literally hundreds of genes and chromosomal regions have been found to be associated with obesity in humans (Perusse et al., 2005).

Of course, the development of obesity depends on the availability of food in the environment (Figure 3.3). Before 10,000 years ago, obesity was probably unknown, but with the development of agriculture and economically stratified societies, obese individuals became more common (Ulijaszek & Lofink, 2006). No one becomes obese, even those in possession of alleles predisposing them to obesity, if there is not enough food to maintain an adequate body weight. Over the past 60 years in developed nations, the availability of food (especially in high-calorie, high-fat form), combined with the decline in activity levels, has led to the creation of truly *obesogenic* environments. In these environments, the potential for obesity in the majority of people is unleashed, and obesity develops in far more individuals than just the small number who may be exceptionally prone to developing the condition. This "epidemic of obesity"—which is associated with increased rates of heart disease and diabetes, among other medical conditions—probably is a clear example of the mismatch between the environment in which humans evolved and the environment in which people in developed countries now live. People in general are genetically adapted for an environment where food is not so plentiful and where simply accomplishing everyday tasks uses a substantial amount of energy. The obesity phenotype is the product of genes and the environment even in people who do not have an "obesity genotype."

Despite the very different biological levels at which they are expressed, both ABO blood types and obesity are phenotypes. They are both measurable traits that are under a greater or lesser degree of genetic control. However, in neither case does the observation of the phenotype necessarily provide an unequivocal understanding of the underlying genotype.

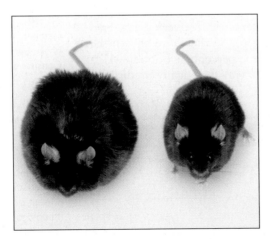

FIGURE 3.2 Laboratory mice demonstrate that genetic differences can have profound effects on the propensity to gain weight.

FIGURE 3.3 Obesity is becoming an epidemic in the United States and other developed countries due in part to a mismatch between genes and the environment.

Mendelian Genetics

Many of the basic mechanisms of heredity seem obvious once you know something about DNA structure, chromosomes, meiosis, and mitosis. However, what is now obvious was once quite mysterious. In the nineteenth and early twentieth centuries, scientists embraced ideas about heredity that were ill-conceived or were later proved to be simply wrong.

One such nineteenth-century notion (supported by Charles Darwin, among others) was **blending inheritance**. Blending inheritance was based on two assumptions: Each parent contributes equally to the offspring, and these contributions are halved at each successive generation. The first assumption is valid. The second assumption only *appears* to be valid, based on selected observations. Blending inheritance was commonly used in the late nineteenth century as an argument against evolution by natural selection because it was thought that it would be virtually impossible to select for any trait if it were being "blended out" with each passing generation (Figure 3.4). The logic for this argument went as follows: Suppose a trait appeared in a population that greatly enhanced the fitness of the individual who possessed it. With blending inheritance, it would be expected that if this individual mated with an individual who did not possess that advantageous trait, their offspring would represent some intermediate form between the phenotypes of the parent. As such, the offspring would not have the fitness advantage possessed by the parent with the new trait. With each passing generation, the advantageous trait would be diminished, blended out of existence. It was very difficult to see how natural selection could work under such circumstances.

Gregor Mendel's careful experimental work demonstrated the nonblending, particulate (that is, genetic) nature of heredity, or **particulate inheritance**. Unfortunately for Mendel, his research was so far ahead of its time—a time when ideas about blending inheritance held sway—that his work was not discovered until 16 years after his death and 35 years after he published it.

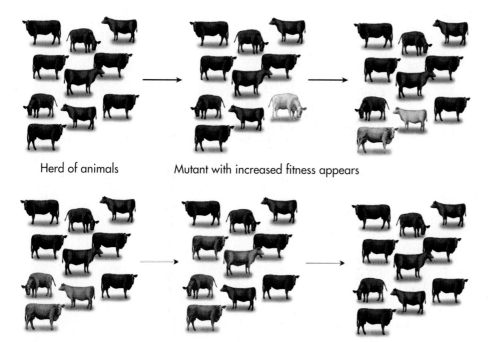

Herd of animals   Mutant with increased fitness appears

With each passing generation, the advantageous feature is "blended out"

FIGURE 3.4 Blending inheritance formed the basis of nineteenth-century critiques of evolution by natural selection.

blending inheritance Discredited nineteenth-century idea that genetic factors from the parents averaged-out or blended together when they were passed on to offspring.

particulate inheritance The concept of heredity based on the transmission of genes (alleles) according to Mendelian principles.

FIGURE 3.5   Gregor Mendel

Mendel was an Austrian monk who, between about 1856 and 1868, conducted plant breeding experiments in the garden of the abbey in which he lived and taught (Figure 3.5). These experiments were conducted on different varieties of the common garden pea (genus *Pisum*) and involved a series of hybridizations or crosses in which Mendel carefully recorded the transmission of several characters across generations. As it turned out, the garden pea was an ideal organism for demonstrating the particulate nature of genetic transmission. Its best feature is that it displays two alternative phenotypes, or *dichotomous variation,* for several different and independent traits: They appear in one distinct form or the other with no apparent blending.

In his breeding experiments, Mendel focused on the following seven features of the pea: seed coat (round or wrinkled), seed color (green or yellow), pod shape (full or constricted), pod color (green or yellow), flower color (violet or white), stem form (axial or terminal), and stem size (tall or dwarf) (Figure 3.6). In his simplest experiments, Mendel looked at the expression of just one trait at a time in the first generation (the F_1 generation) when he crossed two lines that were true-breeding (e.g., wrinkled seeds × smooth seeds, green seeds × yellow seeds, and so on); a true-breeding line is one that reliably produces the same phenotype

CHARACTER	CONTRASTING TRAITS		F_1 RESULTS	F_2 RATIO
SEEDS	round/wrinkled		all round	3 round:1 wrinkled
	yellow/green		all yellow	3 yellow:1 green
PODS	full/constricted	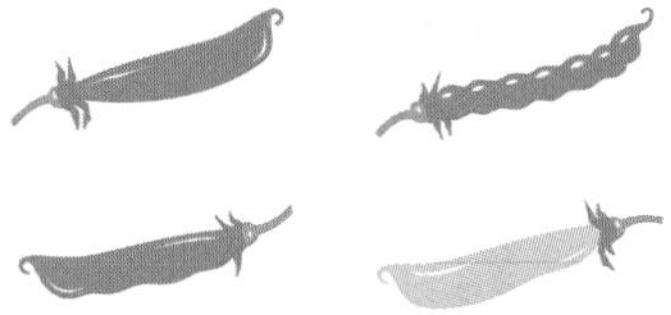	all full	3 full:1 constricted
	green/yellow		all green	3 green:1 yellow
FLOWERS	violet/white		all violet	3 violet:1 white
STEM	axial/terminal		all axial	3 axial:1 terminal
	tall/dwarf		all tall	3 tall:1 dwarf

FIGURE 3.6   The traits Mendel used in his experiments, and the results of the F_1 and F_2 generation crosses.

generation after generation. In the next stage of the experiment, he bred the F_1 generation plants with themselves ($F_1 \times F_1$), and looked at the distribution of characters in the second generation (F_2). He obtained similar results for each feature he examined:

1. Although the F_1 generation plants were the result of crosses between different true-breeding lines, only one of the parental generation traits was expressed. For example, when he crossed full pea pod plants with constricted pea pod plants, the F_1 generation consisted entirely of full pea pod plants. For none of the seven traits he examined did Mendel find evidence of blending inheritance.

2. In the F_2 generation, the version of the trait that had disappeared in the F_1 generation returned, but was found in only one-quarter of the offspring plants. The other three-quarters of the plants were the same as those in the F_1 generation. In other words, there was a 3:1 ratio in the expression of the original parental lines. For example, in the cross involving seed color, in which yellow is dominant to green, Mendel counted 6,022 plants with yellow seeds and 2,001 with green, for a ratio of 3.01:1. Similar results were obtained for the other six traits. Mendel called the version of the trait that appeared in the F_1 generation dominant, while the trait that reappeared (as one-quarter of the total) in the F_2 generation was called recessive.

From these basic observations, Mendel developed a series of postulates (laws or principles) that anticipated the work of later generations of geneticists.

MENDEL'S POSTULATES

In the postulates listed (Klug & Cummings, 2003), the Mendelian insight is in italics while the modern interpretation of his insight is discussed below it.

1. *Hereditary characteristics are controlled by particulate unit factors that exist in pairs in individual organisms.*

The unit factors are genes, and they exist in pairs because in diploid organisms, chromosomes come in pairs. Each individual receives one copy of each chromosome from each parent, thus he or she receives one of his or her pair of unit factors from each parent. Different versions of the unit factors (alleles) may exist. An individual may have two that are the same (homozygous) or two that are different (heterozygous).

2. *When an individual has two different unit factors responsible for a characteristic, only one is expressed and is said to be dominant to the other, which is said to be recessive.*

In heterozygous individuals, those who have different versions of a gene on each chromosome, the allele that is expressed is dominant to the allele that is not expressed. Thus in Mendel's experiments, round seed form was dominant to wrinkled seed form, yellow seed color was dominant to green, and so on. Mendel did not examine a co-dominant character, such as AB in the ABO blood type system.

3. *During the formation of gametes, the paired unit factors separate, or segregate, randomly so that each sex cell receives one or the other with equal likelihood.*

This is known as **Mendel's law of segregation,** and it reflects the fact that in diploid organisms, the chromosomes in a pair segregate randomly into sex cells during meiosis. Mendel formulated this law based on his interpretation of the phenotypes expressed in the F_1 (100% of which had the dominant phenotype) and F_2 generations (dominant:recessive phenotype ratio of 3:1). It is easy to understand Mendel's insight if we use a kind of illustration known as a *Punnett square,* named after British geneticist R. C. Punnett (1875–1967).

The Punnett square allows us to illustrate parental genetic contributions to offspring and the possible genotypes of the offspring (Figure 3.7). For example, in

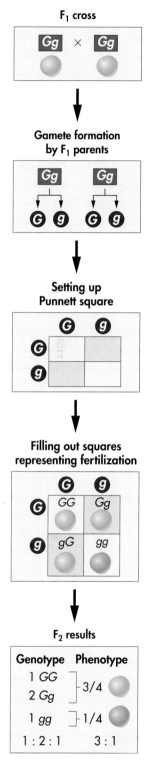

FIGURE 3.7 The Punnett square demonstrates how the F_2 ratio arises from an $F_1 \times F_1$ cross.

Mendel's law of segregation
The two alleles of a gene found on each of a pair of chromosomes segregate independently of one another into sex cells.

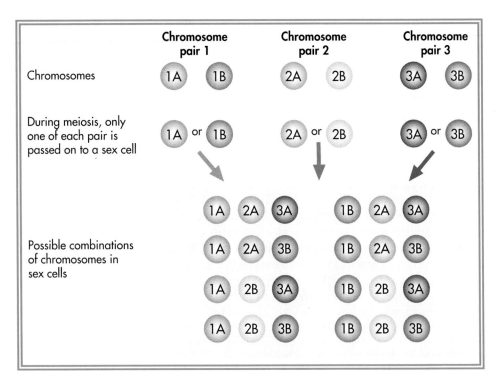

FIGURE 3.8 Mendel's law of independent assortment. Each sex cell receives one chromosome (either A or B) from each of the three paired chromosomes. The assortment of one pair of chromosomes is not influenced by either of the other chromosome pairs, hence "independent assortment." There are eight possible combinations of chromosomes in the resulting sex cells.

the cross between green peas and yellow peas, yellow is dominant to green. Let us call the alleles G and g, for the dominant yellow seed and recessive green seed, respectively. The yellow seed parent can contribute only the G allele and the green seed parent can contribute only the g allele to the offspring. In the Punnett square, you can see that all of the offspring will be heterozygous Gg. Because G is dominant to g, all of the offspring have yellow seeds. Now, if we cross the heterozygous offspring (Gg) of the F_1 generation with each other, we get three possible genotypes: GG (25%), gg (25%), and Gg (50%). As we can see from the Punnett square, 75% of the offspring will produce yellow seeds and 25% of them will have green seeds. Thus the 3:1 phenotypic ratio of Mendel's F_2 generation is obtained. Punnett squares are quite handy and can be used to illustrate the parental contributions to offspring for any gene.

4. *During gamete formation, segregating pairs of unit factors assort independently of each other.*

This is known as **Mendel's law of independent assortment** (Figure 3.8). Mendel did a series of more complex pea breeding experiments known as *dihybrid crosses* that looked at the simultaneous transmission of two of the seven genetic characters of peas. For example, Mendel looked at how both seed color and seed shape might be transmitted across generations. What he found was that the unit factors (alleles) for different characters were transmitted independently of each other. In other words, the segregation of one pair of chromosomes into two sex cells does not influence the segregation of another pair of chromosomes into the same sex cells. Mendel explored the transmission of seed color (yellow dominant to green) and seed shape (round dominant to wrinkled) in a dihybrid cross experiment (Figure 3.9). He started by crossing yellow–round with green–wrinkled and yellow–wrinkled with green–round. In both crosses, he obtained peas that expressed the dominant characters of both traits (yellow and round) but were heterozygous for both as

Mendel's law of independent assortment   Genes found on different chromosomes are sorted into sex cells independently of one another.

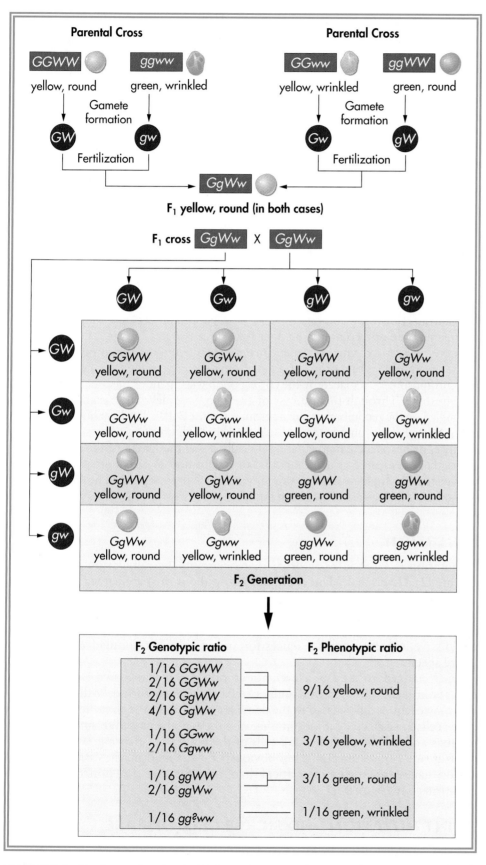

FIGURE 3.9 The Punnett square of a dihybrid cross demonstrates Mendel's law of independent assortment. The F_1 heterozygous plants are self-fertilized to produce an F_2 generation. Mendel was able to infer the genotypic ratios from observing the phenotypic ratios.

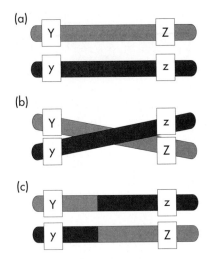

FIGURE 3.10 Crossing over during meiosis leads to allele combinations in sex cells that are not present in the parent chromosomes. (a) A pair of homologous chromosomes is represented, carrying alleles YZ and yz, respectively. (b) Crossing over occurs during meiosis. The more distant from each other two genes are on a chromosome, the more likely they are to be separated during meiosis. (c) Two recombinant chromosomes, with allele combinations of Yz and yZ, may now be passed into sex cells.

linkage   Genes that are found on the same chromosome are said to be linked. The closer together two genes are on a chromosome, the greater the linkage and the less likely they are to be separated during crossing over.

point mutation   A change in the base sequence of a gene that results from the change of a single base to a different base.

sickle cell disease   An autosomal recessive disease caused by a point mutation in an allele that codes for one of the polypeptide chains of the hemoglobin protein.

well. So the genotype of these plants (the F$_1$ generation) was GgWw. He then crossed the F$_1$ generation (GgWw × GgWw) with itself. There are sixteen possible genotypes resulting from this cross, with four possible phenotypes (yellow–round, yellow–wrinkled, green–round, green–wrinkled). Mendel found that approximately 9/16 were yellow–round, 3/16 were yellow–wrinkled, 3/16 were green–round, and 1/16 were green–wrinkled. This 9:3:3:1 ratio is what would be expected if the two characters are transmitted independently of each other. Hence, we can say that they are independently (and randomly) assorted during meiosis.

LINKAGE AND CROSSING OVER

The law of independent assortment applies only to genes that are on different chromosomes. Because the chromosome is the unit of transmission in meiosis, genes that are on the same chromosome should segregate together and find themselves in the same sex cells. This is known as **linkage**. A chromosome may have thousands of genes, and these genes are linked together during meiosis by virtue of being on the same chromosome.

However, decades of genetic research on fruit flies and other organisms have shown that independent assortment of genes on the same chromosome is not only possible but relatively common. How does this happen? It occurs through the process of crossing over, or recombination, which we discussed in Chapter 2. During meiosis there is a physical exchange of genetic material between nonsister chromosomes (that is, the chromosomes that originally came from different parents), so that a portion of one chromosome is replaced by the corresponding segment of the other homologous chromosome. Through this process of crossing over, new allele combinations are assembled on the recombinant chromosomes (Figure 3.10). The likelihood of any two genes on a chromosome being redistributed through crossing over is a function of distance, or how far apart they are physically along the length of the chromosome. Genes that are located near one another on a chromosome are more strongly linked than genes that are far apart and thus are less likely to be separated or "independently assorted" during meiosis through crossing over.

Mutation

A mutation is essentially an error that occurs in the replication of DNA (see Chapter 2). Given that Mendel did not know about the biochemical mechanisms of heredity, he was not too concerned with mutations as we know them. However, Mendel and his contemporaries were acutely aware that the spontaneous appearance of new variants in a species, or "sports" as Darwin called them, could have important consequences for an individual, a population, or even an entire species.

Getting back to the DNA level, a mutation is any change in a DNA sequence that becomes established in a daughter cell. Any time somatic cells divide, a mutation may occur and be passed to the daughter cells. However, mutations that occur in sex cells are especially important because they can be passed to subsequent generations and will be present in all cells of the bodies of offspring. Mutations can occur in any part of the DNA, but obviously those that occur in structural or regulatory genes are much more critical than those that occur in noncoding regions or introns (see Chapter 2).

POINT MUTATION AND SICKLE CELL DISEASE

There are several different kinds of mutations. A **point mutation** occurs when a single base in a gene is changed. A number of diseases can be attributed to specific point mutations in the gene for a protein. One of the most well-known and anthropologically important is the mutation that results in **sickle cell disease**.

Sickle cell disease is caused by an abnormal form of the protein hemoglobin, which is the protein that transports oxygen throughout the body in red blood cells (it makes up 95% of the protein found in a red blood cell). Hemoglobin molecules normally exist separately in the red blood cell, each binding to a molecule of oxygen. In sickle cell disease, the hemoglobin molecules are separate from each other when they bind oxygen, but upon the release of oxygen, the abnormal hemoglobin molecules stick together, forming a complex structure with a helical shape. These long helical fiber bundles deform the red blood cells from their normal, platelike shape to something resembling a sickle, hence the name of the disease (Figure 3.11).

Red blood cells, which lose their nucleus not long after they are formed, are remarkably flexible and malleable in order to squeeze through tiny blood vessels. In contrast, sickled red blood cells lose this flexibility. They clump together in small blood vessels and impair circulation in capillaries; they also collect in the spleen, causing damage to that organ. The sickling also damages the red blood cells themselves. If a sickled red blood cell can make it back to the lungs and become reoxygenated, then the cell returns to its normal shape and can be used to transport oxygen. But repeated sickling shortens the life span of the red blood cells, contributing to the development of anemia. In addition, abnormal complexes of hemoglobin cause the body's immune system to make antibodies against these cells, further exacerbating the anemia. In periods of oxygen stress, such as during exercise, oxygen uptake and release increases, boosting the formation of sickle cells. Sickle cell disease is characterized by chronic anemia, but the secondary effects of the circulation of sickled cells can also be deadly during a crisis.

Hemoglobin (Hb) is a protein that consists of four polypeptide chains (two *alpha* chains and two *beta* chains) (see Chapter 2). The *beta* chains consist of 146 amino acids. The normal, adult hemoglobin is called HbA. In the *beta* chain, the sickle cell hemoglobin, or HbS, is one amino acid different from HbA: The sixth amino acid in HbA is glutamic acid, whereas in HbS it is valine (Figure 3.12 on page 80). This amino acid substitution is caused by a mutation in the codon from CTC to CAC. Out of 438 bases, this is the only change. A striking feature of the mutation in sickle cell is that it does not directly affect the ability of the hemoglobin to carry oxygen but rather causes the hemoglobin molecules to stick together, leading to the deformed cell shape. Of course, a mutation that rendered a red blood cell totally incapable of carrying oxygen probably would be directly fatal.

Sickle cell disease appears in people who are homozygous (have two copies) for the HbS allele. A disease of this kind that is caused by being homozygous for a recessive, disease-causing allele is known as an **autosomal recessive disease**. People who are heterozygous HbA HbS produce enough normal hemoglobin to avoid the complications of sickle cell disease under most circumstances, but they are *carriers* of the disease: They do not suffer from the disease but can pass on the allele that causes the disease. If a carrier mates with another individual who is a heterozygous carrier, then following Mendelian laws, there is a 25% chance that the offspring will be a homozygous sufferer of the disease. We will discuss the biological anthropology of sickle cell disease in greater detail in Chapter 5.

TRINUCLEOTIDE REPEAT DISEASES

In addition to point mutations, another common kind of mutation involves the **insertion mutation** or **deletion mutation** of several bases in sequence. In the last decade, at least sixteen genetic diseases have been found to be caused by a specific kind of insertion mutation, which involves the multiple, repeated insertion of trinucleotide (three-base) repeat sequences (Fischbeck, 2001). The best-known of **trinucleotide repeat diseases** may be *Huntington disease* (which claimed the life of

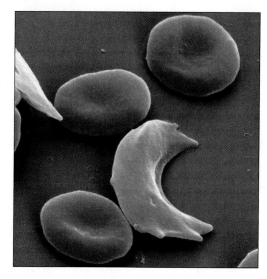

FIGURE 3.11 Comparison of normal and sickle cell red blood cells.

autosomal recessive disease A disease caused by a recessive allele; one copy of the allele must be inherited from each parent for the disease to develop.

insertion mutation A change in the base sequence of a gene that results from the addition of one or more base pairs in the DNA.

deletion mutation A change in the base sequence of a gene that results from the loss of one or more base pairs in the DNA.

trinucleotide repeat diseases A family of autosomal dominant diseases that is caused by the insertion of multiple copies of a three-base pair sequence (CAG) that codes for the amino acid glutamine. Typically, the more copies inserted into the gene, the more serious the disease.

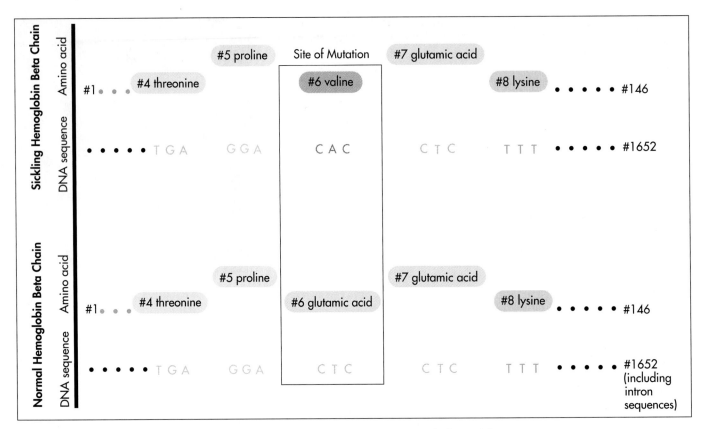

FIGURE 3.12   A single base substitution leading to a single amino acid substitution in the hemoglobin *beta* chain is the cause of sickle cell disease.

folksinger Woody Guthrie), a degenerative neurological disorder that is caused by a dominant allele: It is an **autosomal dominant disease.**

The gene that causes Huntington disease (which produces a protein called *huntingtin*) is located on chromosome 4. In normal individuals, a trinucleotide sequence, CAG, which codes for the amino acid glutamine, usually is repeated 10–35 times. In contrast, people who have Huntington disease have 40–120 CAG repeats. Huntington disease usually is thought of as a disease that strikes people in middle age, with a gradual onset of symptoms, including loss of motor control and ultimately dementia. However, there is variability in the age of onset, and it is directly related to the number of CAG repeats a person is carrying. If someone has more than 80 repeats, the age of onset could be in the teenage years, whereas someone with 40 repeats may not show signs of illness until he or she reaches 60 years of age (Figure 3.13). In addition, the more repeats, the more severe the disease. About half of the known trinucleotide repeat diseases are characterized by CAG repeats; they are also known as *polyglutamine expansion* diseases. Another major class of trinucleotide repeat diseases is the *polyalanine expansion disorders*, which cause syndromes typically associated with multiple congenital malformations (Albrecht & Mundlos, 2005).

MUTATIONS: BAD, NEUTRAL, AND GOOD

The idea that mutations are bad pervades our popular culture. After all, you would probably not consider it a compliment if someone called you a mutant. However, although several diseases arise as a result of mutations in normal genes, it is important to keep in mind that the vast majority of mutations probably are neutral.

Mutations that occur in noncoding regions are by definition neutral because they make no contribution to the phenotype. Mutations that occur in a gene but

autosomal dominant disease   A disease that is caused by a dominant allele: Only one copy needs to be inherited from either parent for the disease to develop.

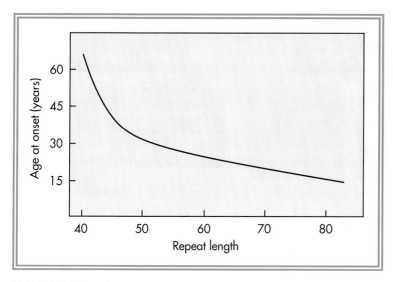

FIGURE 3.13   Relationship between the number of CAG repeats in a gene and the age of onset of Huntington disease.

do not alter the amino acid in a protein also have no phenotypic effect. These kinds of mutations are common because of the redundancy in the genetic code. For example, if a codon changes from CGA to CGG, alanine is still placed in the corresponding position in the polypeptide chain. On top of that, proteins can endure amino acid substitutions without changes in function. There are usually some parts of a protein that are more critical to function than other parts. Amino acid substitutions in noncritical parts of a protein may not affect the function of the protein at all. In fact, protein variation within a species or population is extensive, and in many cases it does not appear to have any functional consequence. If protein function is not affected, then there is likely to be no change to the physiology or anatomy of the organism.

Finally, a mutation may affect the anatomy or physiology of an organism and still have no direct affect on the fitness of an individual. A famous example of such a trait is the *Habsburg face,* which is composed of a characteristic combination of facial features, including a prominent lower lip (hence the name *Habsburg jaw,* by which it is also known). This trait is found in many European noble families, and its transmission has been traced over twenty-three generations (Wolff et al., 1993). Because these European nobles were painted and sculpted with some regularity, there are many accurate historical representations of people with this condition, which is caused by an autosomal dominant allele (Figure 3.14).

Can mutations be good? Absolutely. Mutations are the ultimate source of variation, and variation is the raw material on which evolution acts. Without mutation, there could be no natural selection. Although chromosomal processes such as crossing over create new allele combinations and thereby increase phenotypic variability, mutation is the only source for new alleles that can be combined in novel ways. "Good" mutations—those that increase an organism's chance of surviving and reproducing—do not have to be common. The process of natural selection makes their spread throughout a population possible. Once this happens, they are no longer considered to be mutations but are the normal or wild type (Figure 3.15 on page 82).

If we focus on any given gene, we will find that mutations are not very common. However, if we consider the genome as a whole, then mutations are not so hard to find. The calculation of mutation rate is very complicated. It is made even more complicated by the fact that the mutation rate varies between species, and within species, different genes appear to undergo spontaneous mutation at different rates (Eyre-Walker & Keightley, 1999). Many autosomal dominant disorders

FIGURE 3.14   King Charles V, Holy Roman Emperor and ruler of Spain from 1516–1556, possessed the distinctive Habsburg jaw.
Source: Barent (Bernard) van Orley (c. 1492–1542), "Portrait of Charles V as a boy". Oil on Wood. Herve Lewandowski/Musee Louvre, Paris. RMN Reunion des Nationaux/Art Resource, NY.

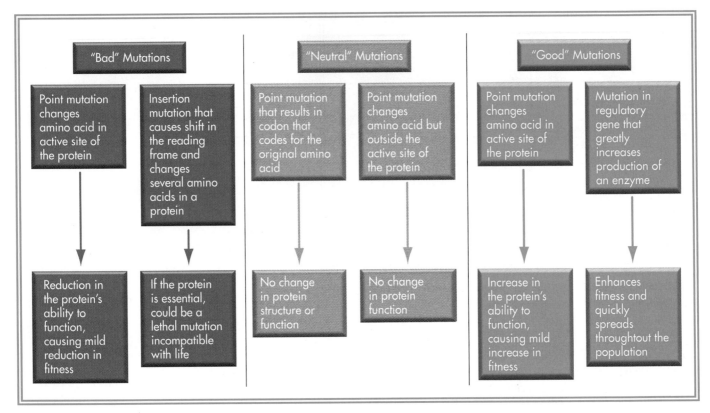

FIGURE 3.15 "Bad," "neutral," and "good" mutations.

(such as *achondroplasia,* a disorder characterized by dwarfism caused by impaired long bone growth) occur at rates on the order of 1 in 10,000 births, and they result almost entirely from new mutations. Let us suppose that the mutation rate in humans for any given gene averages about 1 in 10,000 per generation (a very rough estimate). That might not seem very high, but when we consider that humans have two copies each of 25,000+ genes, then it is likely that every individual carries a mutation in some gene. And if we search in a population of individuals, the chance of finding mutations in more than one gene is very high indeed.

X-LINKED DISORDERS

We discussed chromosomal mutations or abnormalities in an earlier section. However, there is one class of gene mutations that is directly related to chromosome structure. These are the **X-linked disorders.** As discussed in Chapter 2, the sex chromosomes in human males are XY, and in human females they are XX (technically speaking, males are the *heterogametic* sex and females are the *homogametic* sex). The Y chromosome is very small compared with other chromosomes and contains a small number of genes. In contrast, the X chromosome contains a large number of genes.

Because human males have only one copy of the X chromosome, they are susceptible to a host of diseases that are caused by mutations in X chromosome genes. These diseases are much less common in females because they are essentially autosomal recessive disorders and will appear in a female only when they are present in two copies. Female children of affected males are all carriers of the condition because one of their X chromosomes is a copy of their father's (only) X chromosome. **Pedigrees** of families affected by X-linked disorders show a typical pattern whereby the disorders appear to skip a generation. If a male has an X-linked disorder, he cannot pass it on to his sons because he does not pass an X chromosome to them. His daughters will not have the disease but will be car-

X-linked disorders provide a rationale for the folk observation that some heriditary conditions "skip" a generation.

X-linked disorders Genetic conditions that result from mutations to genes on the X chromosome. They are almost always expressed in males, who have only one copy of the X chromosome; in females, the second X chromosome containing the normally functioning allele protects them from developing X-linked disorders.

pedigree A diagram used in the study of human genetics that shows the transmission of a genetic trait over several generations of a family.

riers. Their sons then have a 50% chance of getting the disorder because they have a 50% chance of receiving the affected X chromosome.

X-linked disorders that cause death before reproductive age, such as *Lesch–Nyhan syndrome,* which is characterized by mental and motor retardation, self-mutilation, and early death, and some severe forms of muscular dystrophy, are never seen in females because they are on X chromosomes that are never transmitted to the next generation. A female can develop an X-linked disorder if her father has one of the disorders and her mother is a carrier (or via an extremely unlikely combination of family genetics and a new mutation).

Hemophilia, a disease characterized by the absence of one of the clotting factor proteins in blood, is perhaps the most well-known X-linked disorder. Boys and men with this condition are very vulnerable to hemorrhage and severe joint damage. With advances in the treatment of hemophilia, males with the condition are able to live long and productive lives. Several of the male descendants of Queen Victoria suffered from this condition (Figure 3.16). *Red color blindness* and *green color blindness* are both also X-linked disorders and therefore are much more common in men than in women. In European-derived populations, the frequency in men is about 7% and in women about 0.4%. The genes affecting red and green color vision are located next to each other at one end of the X chromosome (Vollrath et al., 1988). The high frequency of color blindness may reflect the absence of selective pressure against the condition. In addition, studies of the alleles of color-blind individuals indicate that those alleles have all arisen via recombination events. Recombination rates often are higher at the end of a chromosome, which is where the genes for red and green color vision are located.

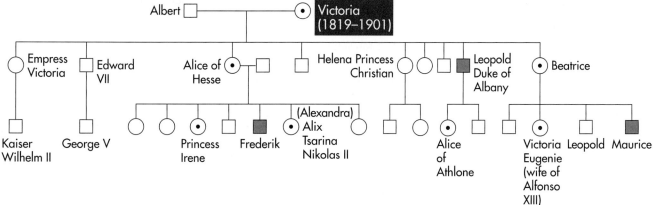

FIGURE 3.16   Queen Victoria and her family and a pedigree showing the transmission of hemophilia in the British royal family.

TABLE 3.2   Mendelian Inheritance in Humans

Disorders	Descriptions
AUTOSOMAL RECESSIVE DISORDERS	
Cystic fibrosis	Causes abnormal mucous secretions, which affect several organs, especially in the respiratory system. In European and European-derived populations has a frequency of about 50/100,000 births.
Sickle cell disease	Abnormal hemoglobin molecule causes sickling of red blood cells, impairing oxygen transport in the body. Particularly common in some African and African-derived populations.
Tay–Sachs disease	Most common in Ashkenazi (European) Jews, caused by an abnormal form of an enzyme that breaks down a fatty substance known as ganglioside GM2. When this substance builds up, it is toxic to nerve cells, and death usually occurs before 5 years of age.
Phenylketonuria (PKU)	Defects in the enzyme phenylalanine hydroxylase cause a buildup of the amino acid phenylalanine, which results in mental retardation and physical abnormalities if phenylalanine is not removed from the diet.
AUTOSOMAL DOMINANT DISORDERS	
Huntington disease	Polyglutamine expansion disease that causes uncontrolled movements, mental and emotional problems, and progressive loss of thinking ability (cognition).
Neurofibromatosis type I	Causes the growth of noncancerous tumors along nerves called neurofibromas, usually in the skin but also in the brain and other parts of the body. Causes mental retardation in about 10% of cases, and about half of afflicted individuals have learning disabilities.
Myotonic dystrophy	Most common form of muscular dystrophy in adults. Causes a progressive wasting of the muscles, particularly in the lower legs, hands, neck, and face.
Achondroplasia	Form of dwarfism caused by a failure to convert cartilage to bone, especially in long bones. Individuals have a slightly enlarged head, with prominent forehead, and other physical anomalies in addition to short stature.
X-LINKED DISORDERS	
Fragile X syndrome	Causes mild to severe mental retardation. Result of the insertion of hundreds of copies of the triplet CGG into a gene on the X chromosome (normal is about 40 repeats).
Hemophilia	Absence of one of the clotting factors in the blood leads to uncontrolled bleeding upon even mild injury. In severe cases, spontaneous bleeding can occur in joints and muscles.
Lesch–Nyhan syndrome	Caused by the overproduction of uric acid, leading to the development of goutlike joint problems, kidney and bladder stones, and involuntary flexing and jerking movements. Self-injury through biting and head banging is common.

MENDELIAN GENETICS IN HUMANS

Over the past century, hundreds of human disorders and diseases have been cataloged, which can be explained in terms of Mendelian genetic transmission (Table 3.2). Besides those discussed previously, there are traits such as earlobe form (free-hanging is dominant to the recessive attached form) or the ability to taste the chemical phenylthiocarbamide (PTC; tasting is dominant to nontasting) that appear to conform to simple Mendelian rules of transmission. The Online Mendelian Inheritance in Man (OMIM) Web site (http://www3.ncbi.nlm.nih.gov/Omim/) provides an extraordinary database on genetic conditions in humans, from the most innocuous to the most lethal. An examination of this database conveys a sense of the complexity inherent in studying even the simplest genetic conditions. Even such classic examples as earlobe form and the ability to taste PTC are not necessarily as clear-cut as they have appeared to be.

Genetics beyond Mendel

Mendelian genetics provided a beginning for our understanding of the biological mechanisms of heredity and evolution. By studying the genetics of phenotypes that are determined by a single gene, which have a small number of alleles, scientists have gained a significant understanding of many other more complex biological phenomena. However, it is important to keep in mind that a single-gene, dominant–recessive model of heredity cannot explain much of the biological world we see around us. As Kenneth Weiss (2002, page 44) has pointed out, although Mendelian genetics provides a foundation for understanding heredity, "a misleading, oversimplified, and overdeterministic view of life is one of the possible consequences." Not long after the rediscovery of Mendel, the overly enthusiastic application of Mendelian principles to human affairs, in combination with certain political and nationalistic movements, had a number of important consequences (see Insights and Advances: Popular Mendelism and the Shadow of Eugenics on page 86).

Mendelian genetics is most useful in examining traits for which there are different and nonoverlapping phenotypic variants. This is called **qualitative variation**. An example of qualitative variation in humans (in addition to some of the Mendelian conditions discussed earlier) is *albinism*, which is the absence of pigmentation in the skin, hair, and iris of the eyes. Although this may be caused by different genes, in each case it is inherited in an autosomal recessive fashion. Seed color in peas (green or yellow) or the different phenotypes in the ABO blood system are examples of qualitative variation. In contrast, **quantitative variation** refers to continuous variation for some trait, which emerges after we measure a character in a population of individuals. It is not possible to divide the population into discrete groups reflecting one variant or another because the variation is overlapping. For many characters, if we measure enough individuals, we find that there is a normal (or bell-shaped) distribution in the individual expression of the character. Individuals who have extremely high or low measurements are most rare, and those who have measurements near the population mean, or average, are most common. Stature in humans is a classic example (Figure 3.17). Very short and very tall people are much less common than are people of average height. Stature is influenced

qualitative variation Phenotypic variation that can be characterized as belonging to discrete, observable categories.

quantitative variation Phenotypic variation that is characterized by the distribution of continuous variation (expressed using a numerical measure) within a population (for example, in a bell curve).

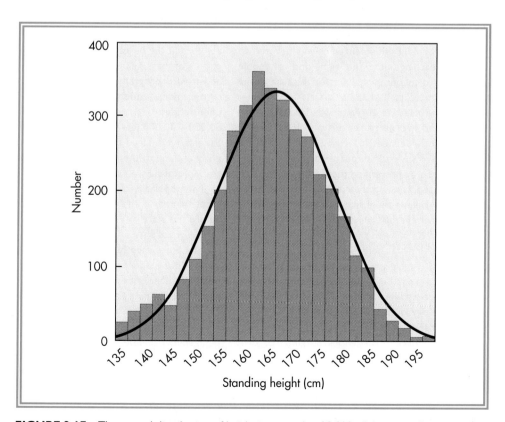

FIGURE 3.17 The normal distribution of height in a sample of 3,808 adult men and women. Mean is 165.2 cm (standard deviation 11.3). (NOTE: Data taken from the National Health and Nutrition Survey 2001–2002, National Center for Health Statistics.)

INSIGHTS AND ADVANCES

Popular Mendelism and the Shadow of Eugenics

In the 1920s, if one attended a state fair or similar public gathering, it would not have been unusual to see a display explaining the finer points of Mendelian inheritance. These displays were not simply meant to be educational; rather, they served as a warning to the dangers and costs of "bad heredity." One might learn that the cross between a "pure" and "abnormal" parent would result in the production of "normal but tainted" children and some "abnormal" grandchildren. A cross between a "tainted" individual and another "tainted" individual would produce the Mendelian F_2 ratio of one "abnormal," one "pure normal," and two "tainted" offspring (Kevles, 1985). Such a display would certainly make a person think twice about the genetic quality of a prospective mate, which was exactly the point of the display.

The popular enthusiasm for Mendelism was directly linked to a broader social and intellectual movement known as *eugenics*. The term was coined in 1883 by Francis Galton (1822–1911), cousin of Charles Darwin and a pioneer in the application of statistical methods to biological phenomena. *Eugenics* was derived from a Greek root meaning "good in birth" or "noble in heredity." In the view of Galton and his followers, eugenics was fundamentally about "the future betterment of the human race." Of course, not everyone can agree on what direction the human race should take.

Eugenics had a remarkably widespread appeal (Figure A). In the first decades of the twentieth century, eugenics societies were founded in countries throughout the world, and the ideals of eugenics could be shaped to serve any number of causes. Women often were active in eugenics societies, and the increasing control of women over their reproductive lives may be one of the ultimate outcomes of the eugenics

movement (Kevles, 1985). In Western countries, eugenics tended to be more enthusiastically embraced by middle- and upper-class people, many of whom worried about the decline in the quality of their compatriots caused by the unchecked population growth of lower-class people and other "undesirables."

The eugenics movement called for deliberate intervention in the "natural" evolutionary processes that were ongoing in human populations. This intervention could take either positive or negative forms. In many countries, significant numbers of upper-class people believed that there was a disturbing trend for the better-educated, more intelligent, and sensitive young people to marry later and to have fewer children than the less-educated, coarser, and less intelligent lower classes. Positive eugenics was devoted to reaching out to the "right kind" of people and encouraging them, for the sake of the "race," to have more babies.

Negative eugenics was far less benign and had more serious and longstanding consequences. It focused on removing the "wrong kind" of people from the population by preventing them from having children, banning their entry into a country, expelling them from a country, or killing them. In the United States, legislation in the 1920s allowed the involuntary sterilization of "mental defectives" and the exclusion of immigrants from certain (that is, non–northern European) countries; both actions were strongly influenced by an ideology of negative eugenics. In Nazi Germany, the implementation of the "final solution"—the genocidal killings of Jews,

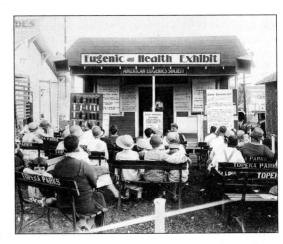

FIGURE A   Eugenics display at the Kansas Free Fair in the 1920s.

Gypsies, Eastern Europeans, and others whom the Nazis considered undesirable—was the most horrifying form of negative eugenics. Although these killings may represent the culmination of various historical trends, historian Robert Jay Lifton (1986) argues that the bureaucratic and practical origins of mass killings in Nazi Germany began with programs to "euthanize" all chronic mental patients and other medical undesirables. It is estimated that 80,000–100,000 chronically mentally ill patients were killed by Nazi doctors as a grisly prelude to the millions killed during the Holocaust.

The popularity of the eugenics movement waned in the United States even before the start of World War II, but the term *eugenics* often arises, usually from critics, any time when human genetics intersects with broader social issues. One can only hope that critics who use "eugenics" as a contemporary pejorative do not have as simplistic and deterministic a view of history as the eugenicists did of human biology, genetics, and behavior.

by genes, but except for rare kinds of dwarfism, the phenotypic distribution of stature in humans does not lend itself to a simple Mendelian explanation.

Stature and other complex phenotypes, such as the timing of puberty, skin color, and body composition, are **polygenic traits**. Their expression depends on the action of multiple genes, each of which may have more than one allele. The more genes and alleles that contribute to a polygenic trait, the more genotypes—and phenotypes—are possible. Thus when continuous variation for a trait is observed in a population (whether or not it is normally distributed), it is much more likely to be caused by polygenic inheritance rather than a single gene effect.

Single genes that produce qualitative variants often are referred to as though they produced the whole trait, when in fact the trait in question results from the combined effects of several genes. For example, Mendel focused on a specific gene and two alleles that influenced the height of pea plants, such that he was able to dichotomize the phenotypes as short and tall. However, stem height in peas is really under the control of several genes, some of which have several alleles (Weiss, 2002). Similarly, we often hear that the gene for some disease in humans has been discovered, but that does not mean that the single gene is responsible for the organ system in question. For example, the most common form of short-limbed dwarfism in humans, achondroplasia, is caused by a single dominant gene (Figure 3.18). Although this gene certainly influences stature in a fundamental way, the development of stature in humans is nonetheless a polygenic trait.

Just as one trait can be the result of the interaction of more than one gene, one gene can have multiple phenotypic effects (Figure 3.19 on page 88). This is called **pleiotropy**. For example, the gene that causes achondroplasia—the fibroblast growth factor receptor–3 gene—has the paradoxical effect of shortening limb length while leading to larger than average head size (megalencephaly). Artificial breeding for docility in foxes leads to the development of coat colors not found in wild foxes; this is undoubtedly a pleiotropic effect of whatever genes underlie that behavioral pattern. As we will discuss in Chapter 16, aging patterns in humans may best be explained as resulting from the pleiotropic effects of genes selected for their effectiveness during the reproductive phase of life.

FIGURE 3.18 Achondroplastic dwarf represented in a carved pipe made by Adena Indians who inhabited the central and southern regions of Ohio in the first millennium B.C.

POLYGENIC TRAITS, THE PHENOTYPE, AND THE ENVIRONMENT

On its own, polygenic inheritance may produce a bell-curve distribution for the expression of a trait. However, the expression of many traits is a result not only of multiple genes, but of an interaction between those genes and the environment in which the individual was raised. Such *complex phenotypes* pose a problem for human geneticists in that it can be difficult to determine if the observed variation in the trait is due to genetic or environmental factors, or some combination of the two.

When scientists investigate the relative contributions of genes and environment to the production of the phenotype, they often use a statistical concept called **heritability**. If we look at variation for some trait in a population, we can be certain that the total variation we observe is caused by some combination of environmental and genetic factors. Heritability is a measure of the proportion of the total variation observed in a population that can be attributed to genetics rather than to the environment:

$$\frac{\text{Variability caused by genetics}}{\text{Variability caused by genetics} + \text{Variability caused by the environment}}$$

Heritability can range from 0 to 1. A heritability of 0 would mean that all of the observed variation is due to environmental factors, while a score of 1 would

polygenic traits   Phenotypic traits that result from the combined action of more than one gene; most complex traits are polygenic.

pleiotropy   The phenomenon of a single gene having multiple phenotypic effects.

heritability   The proportion of total phenotypic variability observed for a given trait that can be ascribed to genetic factors.

(a) Polygenic trait: many genes contribute to a single effect.

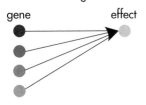

gene   effect

(b) Pleiotropy: one gene has multiple effects.

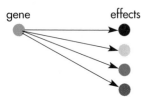

gene   effects

FIGURE 3.19 Contrasting (a) polygenic and (b) pleiotropic effects.

Twins separated at birth and raised separately are also studied in genetic research, but such cases are extremely rare.

twin method A method for estimating the heritability of a phenotypic trait by comparing the concordance rates of identical and fraternal twins.

mean that it is all due to genetic factors. It is easy to measure heritability if you can control all the critical factors in the environment, as a scientist working on a short-lived experimental animal might be able to do in the laboratory. In humans, heritability is much more difficult to measure because we obviously cannot use humans in breeding experiments or control the environmental variables under which people grow up.

Geneticists have come up with several strategies to estimate heritability in human populations. Simply looking to see if a feature "runs in the family" can be a good place to start, but since families typically share genes and environments, it is not a method that will usually produce a very reliable estimate of heritability. *Adoption studies* in which children adopted out of families are compared to members of their adoptive and biological families can provide better estimates of heritability. These kinds of studies require access to good adoption records and stable populations over generations, so there are a limited number of situations in which they can be used.

Perhaps the most commonly used strategy is the **twin method** (Figure 3.20). As is well known, there are two kinds of twins: *identical* or *monozygotic (MZ) twins* and *fraternal* or *dizygotic (DZ) twins*. Monozygotic twins are genetically identical to each other, and they are the result of the fertilization of a single egg that splits into two embryos very early in development. Dizygotic twins result from the separate fertilization of two eggs during the same ovulatory cycle. They are no more alike than any other full siblings, and they share, on average, half of their genes.

If two twins share a common phenotype or if both get a certain disease, we say that they are *concordant* for that trait; if the twins are dissimilar, then they are *discordant*. Twins raised together typically share a very similar environment. If we compare the MZ and DZ concordance for a trait, a significantly higher concordance rate in the MZ twins indicates that genetic factors may be important in the expression of that trait. Both MZ and DZ twins share a common environment (some critics have argued that MZ twins may share a more similar environment than DZ twins, which may be true, but how much this may contribute to similarities or differences must be assessed for each condition examined), but MZ twins share a much stronger genetic link than DZ twins. For example, concordance for ABO blood type is 100% in MZ twins and 66% in DZ twins. This indicates that the

FIGURE 3.20 The twin method can be used to investigate genetic and environmental influences on the development of phenotypes.

variability in blood type is due entirely to genetics. Allergy patterns have a concordance rate of 59% in MZ twins and 18% in DZ twins. This indicates that genetics plays an important role in developing allergies. However, the fact that the concordance rate is not 100% in MZ twins indicates that the environment plays a substantial role as well. Many complex diseases such as schizophrenia and heart disease have MZ and DZ concordance rates that indicate that both genetic and environmental factors play a role in their expression.

Although concordance rates cannot be directly used to compute heritability values, they can be incorporated into mathematical models for estimating heritability. In addition, they indicate the possible roles of genetic and environmental factors in the expression of a complex phenotype or disease, providing useful directions for future research or intervention.

Heritability is an extremely important tool in trying to understand genetic influences on complex phenotypes. However, the discovery of significant heritability for a trait does not provide information about which or even how many genes are responsible for a phenotype. Heritability is a population statistic and provides no direct insight into individual genetic mechanisms. Also, heritability does not provide an absolute measure of the genetic contribution to the development of a phenotype. It is a relative statistic that measures the influence of genetics in a specific environment. If that environment is highly variable and most of the variation results from environmental factors, then the heritability will be low. On the other hand, if the environment is uniform and all members of the population are affected equally by environmental factors, then heritability will be high. As variation caused by environmental factors decreases, any remaining variation we observe can result only from genetic factors.

HERITABILITY AND IQ TEST SCORE PERFORMANCE

Perhaps the most well-known and controversial use of heritability statistics has been in the study of variation in IQ test score performance (Mackintosh, 1998). IQ test scores exhibit continuous variation in human populations, with a normal distribution. Innumerable studies of the heritability of IQ test score in industrial societies have been conducted over the years, and they almost all agree that genetics is an important factor in producing the variation observed within populations (heritability ranges from 0.3 to 0.75). Most scientists, although not all, interested in IQ test score would agree that in a population with an absolutely uniform environment, you would still observe variation for IQ test score performance, which would result from genetic factors.

Most people would not argue with the idea that genetics and environment both play some role in IQ test score performance. But what does heritability tell us about an issue of potential anthropological importance: ethnic differences in IQ test score performance? There is much empirical evidence to demonstrate that American Whites score on average about 100 (the designed mean for the test) on IQ tests, with American Blacks scoring substantially lower (7–12 points less), and Asian Americans somewhat higher (about 5 points higher, with most of the difference on the nonverbal portions of the test). Do the heritability studies of IQ test score performance indicate that the ethnic differences we observe result from genetic differences? No. Heritability scores apply only *within* a population or environment, not *between* populations. Heritability may give us some insight into the production of variation within each ethnic group, but it cannot be used to address issues of population variation between groups. The variation between groups could result from genetics, the environment, or both, but heritability scores, whether high or low, do not directly inform us about between-group differences.

In fact, it is theoretically possible that you could observe low within-population heritabilities for some trait, whereas the between-population differences could result entirely from genetic factors. For example, imagine that we have two distinct

IQ tests were originally designed to be a tool for the early identification of children with learning problems or disabilities.

populations, one with a substantially greater mean stature than the other one. Let's say that this difference in stature reflects the presence of "tall" alleles in one population that are absent in the other. If in both populations access to food while growing up is highly variable, then within each population the distribution of stature would result primarily from environmental factors (that is, food availability). This would mean that heritability measured separately in both populations would be low. There would still be a difference in mean stature between the populations, caused entirely by genetics. Thus low within-population heritability does not mean that between-population differences cannot be caused by genetic differences, and vice versa.

Phenylketonuria: Illustrating Mendelian and Post-Mendelian Concepts

Before the advent of universal neonatal screening for the condition (Lindee, 2000), **phenylketonuria (PKU)** was one of the most common causes of mental retardation. Pedigree studies have shown that the transmission of PKU appears to follow classic Mendelian rules. It is caused by a recessive allele and therefore is seen only in people who are homozygous for this allele. People who have just one copy of the allele are heterozygous carriers of the condition.

Individuals with PKU accumulate large quantities of the amino acid phenylalanine in the blood (up to forty times the normal amount) (Scriver et al., 1985). In newborns and infants, a high level of phenylalanine is toxic to the developing nervous system. The most prominent feature of the PKU phenotype is mental retardation, which is a direct result of the neurotoxic effects of high levels of phenylalanine. However, people with PKU also tend to have light skin and hair and abnormal gait, stance, and sitting posture, among other characteristic features. It is quite clear that the allele for PKU has pleiotropic effects.

At a biochemical level, PKU is the result of a deficiency of an enzyme, *phenylalanine hydroxylase,* which converts phenylalanine to another amino acid, tyrosine. Phenylalanine builds up in the bloodstream because the PKU phenylalanine hydroxylase either is inactive or has much lower than normal activity. Because the phenylalanine is not converted to tyrosine, people with PKU also tend to have less tyrosine available for metabolic reactions. Tyrosine is the starting point for the body's synthesis of melanin, which is one of the most important components of skin pigment. This explains one of the pleiotropic effects of the PKU allele: Light skin and hair is a result of low tyrosine levels and low production of melanin.

Over the past 20 years, there have been many advances in our understanding of the molecular genetics of PKU. The gene for phenylalanine hydroxylase has been localized to chromosome 12, and hundreds of different point mutations in the gene have been identified. The effects of these mutations on phenylalanine hydroxylase activity vary tremendously, with some of them rendering the enzyme inactive, whereas others show no effect or only a mild depression in activity (Benit et al., 1999). The variability in the alleles of the phenylalanine hydroxylase gene explains why PKU exhibits a good deal of phenotypic variability. Remember that PKU is an autosomal recessive disorder: Individuals who have one normal phenylalanine hydroxylase allele are phenotypically normal.

Screening for PKU in newborns is done by assessing phenylalanine levels in the blood not long after birth. Profoundly elevated levels of phenylalanine indicate the presence of PKU and the need for dietary intervention. This intervention takes the form of drastically reducing the amount of phenylalanine in the diet. This is easier said than done because phenylalanine is an important component of proteins found in meat, fish, eggs, cheese and other milk products, legumes, and some cereals. Babies with PKU must take special formula that provides calories and essential nutrients, and children with the condition must adhere to a very limited diet.

phenylketonuria (PKU) Autosomal recessive condition that leads to the accumulation of large quantities of the amino acid phenylalanine, which causes mental retardation and other phenotypic abnormalities.

FIGURE 3.21   Two sisters with PKU. The younger sister (left) was diagnosed at birth and followed a strict phenylalanine-limited diet. The older sister (right) was not diagnosed until she was 1 year of age. She is symptomatic of PKU.

They must also learn to be wary of dietary additives such as the artificial sweetener aspartame, which is a dipeptide composed of phenylalanine and aspartic acid. The good news is that when they become adults, most PKU sufferers can adopt a normal diet because their nervous system is no longer developing. However, if a woman with PKU wants to become pregnant, she must resume the restricted diet, or the elevated levels of phenylalanine in her blood will damage the developing nervous system of her developing child.

PKU provides a striking example of the relationships between genotype, phenotype, and the environment. People with PKU are different from other people because they have two copies of an abnormal allele for a single enzyme. If they grow up in a typical dietary environment, their nervous systems will not develop normally and they will have a seriously dysfunctional phenotype. On the other hand, if we place children with PKU in a different, highly artificial nutritional environment, they will develop normally. Figure 3.21 depicts two sisters with PKU. The older sister was born before there was routine screening of newborns and intervention for PKU, and she suffers from the disease. The younger sister was identified as having PKU immediately after birth, avoided phenylalanine while growing up, developed normally, and later had a healthy child. The sisters have the same PKU genotype, but their divergent phenotypes were shaped by different nutritional environments.

Genes and Environments

When we hear the word *environment* we usually think about the world around us—such as the air and water, trees and other plants, and all the other critters with whom we share the world. But from a gene's perspective, the environment is made up mainly of other genes. Concepts such as pleiotropy and polygenic inheritance emphasize that the genetic environment is just as critical to the production of phenotypes as any other kind of environment.

Mendelian concepts such as independent assortment and segregation were useful in establishing the activities of genes in isolation from one another. This was essential for doing away with concepts such as blending inheritance. But it is clear that the challenge of genetics in the twenty-first century will be to determine how genes work together, not separately, to produce complex phenotypes in the context of complex environments.

SUMMARY

1. **What is the difference between structural genes and regulatory genes?**

   Structural genes carry the information to make proteins. Regulatory genes guide the expression of structural genes. Given that the DNA of humans and chimpanzees is so similar—their DNAs are about 95% identical—many scientists believe that changes in regulatory genes have been critical in producing the profound physical and behavioral differences between the species.

2. **What are genotypes and phenotypes?**

   The genotype consists of the specific genes (or alleles) an organism carries; it is the genetic constitution of an individual. The phenotype is an observable or measurable feature of an organism. Phenotypes can be anatomical, biochemical, or behavioral. If we look at the expression of a phenotype among a group of organisms in a population, we will probably see some variation. This variation could be caused by genetic factors; individuals may have different genotypes that influence the expression of the phenotype differently. It could also be caused by environmental factors if the expression of the phenotype changes with changes in the environment. In many cases, the observed phenotypic variation is caused by a combination of genetic and environmental factors.

3. **What is heritability?**

   Heritability is a measure of the proportion of the total phenotypic variation that is caused by genetics. It can range from 0 to 1. For example, in a population where all organisms have exactly the same environment, all observed variability would have to be caused by genetic factors, and the heritability would be 1.

4. **What did Mendel's experiments on the garden pea show us about the nature of genetic transmission?**

   Mendel's work demonstrated first and foremost the particulate nature of genetic inheritance: There was no "blending" of the basic genetic factors (that is, genes) during sexual reproduction. Mendel showed that genes for a single phenotypic trait come in pairs and that these are passed to the next generation independently of each other (law of segregation). He also showed that the pairs of genes for one trait are passed on independently of the pairs of genes for other traits (law of independent assortment).

5. **What are X-linked disorders?**

   X-linked disorders are diseases or conditions that are almost always seen in males and appear in pedigrees to skip a generation after their appearance in a male sufferer. An X-linked disorder is caused by a mutation in a gene on the X chromosome. If a woman carries this mutated allele on one of her X chromosomes, she does not develop the disease because she also has a normal allele on the other X chromosome. However, if her son receives a copy of the mutant allele from his mother, he will develop the disease because he has only the single copy of the X chromosome (along with the Y chromosome). Because he can pass on an X chromosome only to his daughters, they will be carriers of the condition but not suffer from it, and they can later pass it on to their sons. Therefore, it appears to skip a generation. Hemophilia is the best-known X-linked condition.

6. **Compare and contrast polygenic traits and pleiotropy.**

   Polygenic traits are those that are the product of the action of more than one gene, each of which may have more than one allele. Observed quantitative variation in a polygenic trait often follows a bell-curve distribution because of the many possible genotypes that may underlie the expression of a single phenotype. Pleiotropy is the converse: A single gene can influence more than one phenotypic trait. This is seen in the condition known as achondroplasia, in which several changes in the phenotype result from a change in a single allele.

CRITICAL THINKING QUESTIONS

1. What is the role of genetic knowledge in our day-to-day lives? Should information about the alleles we carry be available to employers or health insurance providers? Would you want to know if you are carrying an allele that might cause you to have a fatal illness 20 years from now?

2. Mendel often is said to have been "ahead of his time." Why? Do you think such a delay between the discovery and the recognition of the discovery could happen today?

KEY TERMS

structural genes	blending inheritance	sickle cell disease	X-linked disorders
regulatory genes	particulate inheritance	autosomal recessive	pedigree
genotype	Mendel's law of	disease	qualitative variation
phenotype	segregation	insertion mutation	quantitative variation
ABO blood type	Mendel's law of	deletion mutation	polygenic traits
system	independent	trinucleotide repeat	pleiotropy
recessive	assortment	diseases	heritability
dominant	linkage	autosomal dominant	twin method
co-dominant	point mutation	disease	phenylketonuria (PKU)

SUGGESTED READING

Dawkins, R. (1989). *The Selfish Gene* (new edition). Oxford University Press, Oxford.

Shell, E. R. (2002). *The Hungry Gene. The Science of Fat and the Future of Thin*. Atlantic Monthly Press, New York.

Mendel, G. (1866). Versuche über Plflanzenhybriden (Experiments in plant hybridization). *Verhandlugen des naturforschenden Vereines in Brünn, Bd. IV für das Jahr 1865*, 3–47. (English translation available at www.esp.org/foundations/genetics/classical/gm-65.pdf.)

Provine, W. B. (1971). *The Origins of Theoretical Population Genetics*. University of Chicago Press, Chicago.

The Forces of Evolution and the Formation of Species

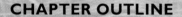

CHAPTER OUTLINE

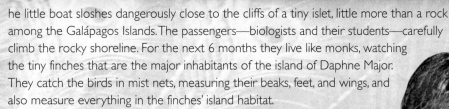

The little boat sloshes dangerously close to the cliffs of a tiny islet, little more than a rock among the Galápagos Islands. The passengers—biologists and their students—carefully climb the rocky shoreline. For the next 6 months they live like monks, watching the tiny finches that are the major inhabitants of the island of Daphne Major. They catch the birds in mist nets, measuring their beaks, feet, and wings, and also measure everything in the finches' island habitat.

The scientists come and go for 30 years, spanning about thirty generations of finches and a large portion of their own life spans. The island is subjected to a terrible drought. The drought is followed by several years of plentiful rainfall, turning the island green and lush. Throughout these periods of plenty and famine, the scientists dutifully collect their birds and record their measurements.

Then one day they notice that something astounding is happening. The dimensions of the beaks of the finches have changed in direct relationship to the periods of drought and plenty. When food is scarce, the major available seeds are thick-shelled and very tough to crack. The birds that hatched with minutely larger, stronger beaks survive better and leave more baby finches than their smaller-beaked neighbors. When the rains come again and food is plentiful, the trend reverses. The evidence is indisputable: The species is evolving. In the span of just a few years, climate and food conditions have changed the appearance of the tiny finches because finches with stronger beaks are better able to crack open hard-shelled seeds and therefore produce more offspring than their smaller-beaked neighbors.

DEMONSTRATING NATURAL SELECTION in the wild is not easy. It takes many generations and a great deal of tedious field research. However, the results show the truth of Darwin's ideas. The now-famous field study just described, conducted by biologists Peter and Rosemary Grant, is one of the best demonstrations of evolution by natural selection under natural conditions. In this chapter we will examine the principles of the evolutionary process. These include but are not limited to Darwinian natural selection. We will consider where variation in nature comes from and how the forces of evolution act on this variation to mold the form and function of animals and plants. We also examine another important question: What is a species?

How Evolution Works

The forces of evolution are those factors occurring in natural populations that cause changes in gene frequencies over multiple generations. These include both adaptive and nonadaptive causes. Natural selection is the most cited cause of evolution, and much evidence suggests that it is the most important force. As we will see, however, several other causes of evolutionary change exist as well. Moreover, evolution can only occur in the presence of a source of variation, which is mutation.

WHERE DOES VARIATION COME FROM?

In Chapter 2, we saw that alterations occur in the DNA sequence during the course of replication, changing the allelic expression at a given locus. A change in a base on the DNA molecule is a *point mutation*. Larger-scale errors during replication can result in *chromosomal mutations,* when entire chunks of chromosomes are transposed with one another. Such changes in the genetic material, whether large or small, are the stuff from which new variation springs. Mutations of great significance occur very rarely. Many mutations are neutral and have no effect on the offspring's viability, survival, and reproduction. Only through the accumulation of mutations do new traits enter a population, allowing natural selection and other evolutionary forces to filter out undesirable traits and perpetuate favorable ones.

HOW NATURAL SELECTION WORKS

Natural selection takes the package of traits each animal or plant inherits from the previous generation and then alters it in response to the current environment. Natural selection is not simply about genes and traits. The environment is the filter through which traits—and the genes that control their expression—are selected for or against. As we saw in Chapter 3, each organism's genetic makeup, or genotype, is fixed from conception. Natural selection acts on the organism's phenotype, the actual expression of the alleles present in the genotype. The environment can play a critical role in how the genotype is expressed, even when basic Mendelian principles are operating at single gene loci. Such environmental effects include sunlight, nutrition, and exposure to toxins, all of which can have profound biological effect on one's phenotype without affecting the genotype. If you spend years sunbathing to acquire a deep tan, your phenotype—skin color in this case—has changed while your genotype stayed the same. However, skin cancer from ultraviolet rays in sunlight is a biological effect on which natural selection can act by removing afflicted individuals from the breeding population. *Natural selection operates on the phenotype of an individual organism.* As individuals with the greatest genetic susceptibility to skin cancer—perhaps those with the palest skin—are removed from the breeding population, the frequency of genes influencing skin color will change too. This is evolution, so cultural practices such as sunbathing can potentially have evolutionary effects.

Populations evolve as the frequency of certain genes changes; individual organisms don't evolve. The result is that the frequency at which a gene or a trait governed by genes occurs in a population changes over time. This change generally happens very slowly, although it can be seen easily when researchers study animals with very short generation lengths, such as fruit flies or mice, or when animal breeders take selection into their own hands and choose which animals will breed and which will not. In this latter case, selection is not necessarily based on survival and reproductive value of traits. For instance, cattle breeders may select cows for milk production, or they may select them for purely aesthetic reasons such as body size, temperament, or color. This artificial selection is analogous to natural selection, as Darwin himself understood.

The case of natural selection pushing the size of finch beaks larger and stronger when food is scarce and pushing it back the other way when food is plentiful is an example of **directional selection** (Figure 4.1). Of course, it could also be the case that selection is intense for certain beak dimensions when times are lean, and this pressure is diminished when the rains come again. A relaxation of selection pressure in a population might be difficult to distinguish in nature from selection in the opposite direction from earlier generations.

If natural selection can drive gene frequencies in a certain direction by elaborating or eliminating a certain trait, can it also be responsible for keeping populations uniform? It can, by a process known as **stabilizing selection**. The first demonstration of stabilizing selection was an early study of natural selection in the wild. In the winter of 1898, 136 house sparrows were found lying on the icy

Darwin himself used selective breeding of pigeons and other domestic fowl to understand how artificial selection is analogous to natural selection.

directional selection   Natural selection that drives evolutionary change by selecting for greater or lesser frequency of a given trait in a population.

stabilizing selection   Selection that maintains a certain phenotype by selecting against deviations from it.

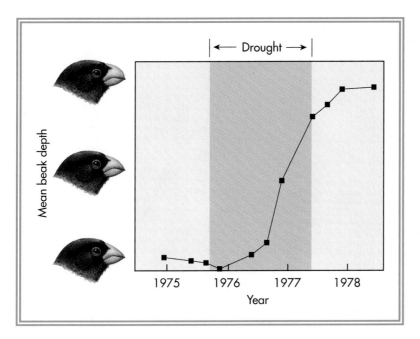

FIGURE 4.1 Directional selection pushes a phenotype one way or another.

ground the morning after a severe snowstorm in Providence, Rhode Island. They were taken to biologist Herman Bumpus at nearby Brown University. Seventy-two of the birds recovered; the other 64 died of exposure to the frigid conditions. Bumpus (1899) then measured nine traits of the birds to see whether there were anatomical differences between the sparrows that survived the storm and those that died. He found that there were anatomical differences between survivors and nonsurvivors. Surviving birds were smaller-bodied and had shorter wings than those that died, and they were more similar to the average size of birds in the local population. In other words, natural selection favored certain *phenotypes* in an environmental crunch. We don't know the exact mechanism—why smaller-bodied birds survived the storm better—but we can say that birds that deviated greatly from certain sizes and shapes were not favored by natural selection.

There are many such examples of natural selection in populations of wild animals. Showing natural selection at work in a human population is far more difficult: People reproduce slowly, and the genetic code for specific human traits is rarely known. One well-documented case of natural selection in human populations is birth weight. Producing a healthy baby is a critical precondition for reproductive success (Figure 4.2). Studies have shown that birth weight of newborns is a key factor influencing the probability of their survival. In one study of nearly 6,000 births in a New York City hospital, researchers found that male and female babies had optimal birth weights of 7.96 pounds (3.62 kg) and 8.5 pounds (3.84 kg), respectively (Van Valen & Mellin, 1967) (Figure 4.3 on page 98). The likelihood of infant mortality was directly related to deviation from the optimal birth weight even when factors that influence birth weight, such as length of the pregnancy and ethnic background, were controlled for. Natural selection favored survival of infants who were within a certain optimal range of birth weights. Over human history, birth weights that deviated far from the mean were selected against, producing a normal distribution of birth weights with a well-defined optimum.

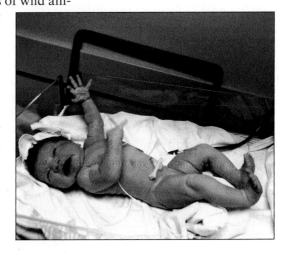

FIGURE 4.2 Human infants are like all other placental mammals, except they are born at a less developed state.

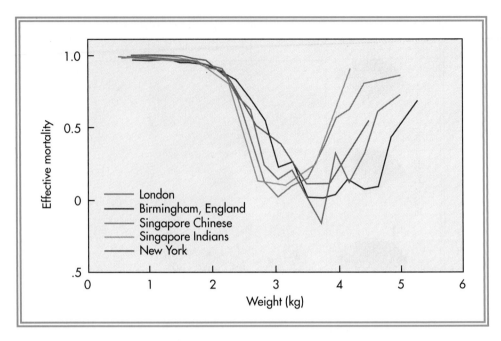

FIGURE 4.3 The birth weight of human infants is tightly constrained by natural selection. Note the high mortality of newborns of very high or low body weight based on hospital records.

OTHER WAYS BY WHICH EVOLUTION HAPPENS

The power of natural selection remains a topic of debate. Some scholars argue that natural selection alone cannot account for the rapid evolution of wholesale changes in anatomy that we sometimes observe. These critics are not creationists; they simply question whether natural selection can or should be expected to have produced all the myriad traits we see in nature. There are at least two other important natural processes that produce evolutionary change in populations that are unrelated to natural selection: gene flow and genetic drift.

Gene Flow   When humans or other animals migrate from one place to another, or when wind carries airborne seeds hundreds of miles from where the parent tree stands, **gene flow** has occurred. *Migration* refers to animals on the move; *gene flow* refers to the genetic material they carry with them in their genotypes. The exchange of genes between populations in different geographic locations can produce evolutionary change, as can stopping the exchange of genes between two areas. Movements, both permanent and temporary, of people to new locales have characterized human history. These migrations have become widespread and rapid as regional and global transportation has improved in recent centuries. When migrants produce offspring in new populations, whether they remain in the population long term or not, their genes enter the new gene pool and provide biological diversity and new traits that may eventually change the evolutionary character of the population. An excellent example of how gene flow can change a population occurred in 1789, when the crew of the British sailing ship HMS *Bounty* mutinied against Captain William Bligh. Surviving crew members ended up on Pitcairn Island in the South Pacific, and after much battling among the crew (primarily over Tahitian women they brought to the island), one sailor named Adams ended up as a permanent resident. Over the ensuing years, Adams fathered many children, and his genes, including those for his blue eyes, became widespread in the population of Pitcairn.

The end of gene flow can be as important an evolutionary force as gene flow itself. If a population receives genetic contributions (*admixture*) from other

Even today, Adams' descendants make up the majority of the Pitcairn Islanders.

gene flow   Movement of genes between populations.

nearby populations for a long period of time, it may create one large gene pool spread across two areas through extensive interbreeding. Suppose that interbreeding stops because of changes in social behavior (two neighboring tribes go to war, and all exchange between them is halted for centuries) or changes in geography (a flood creates a wide river barrier between the two populations). In either case the lack of gene flow means that random mutations that were formerly passed back and forth are now confined to only one population. As they accumulate, the two populations will diverge genetically and perhaps anatomically as well.

Studies of the genetics of human and other populations have generally concluded that despite our long-standing belief that **inbreeding**, or reproduction between close kin, is always bad for the health of a population, very limited amounts of gene flow can eliminate the harmful effects of inbreeding. A study of rhesus macaque monkeys conducted in the mountains of Pakistan showed only limited migration between breeding groups. Nonetheless, very limited gene flow from males who immigrated to the valley where the study was conducted was enough to maintain high levels of genetic diversity (Melnick & Hoelzer, 1996). Studies such as this do not imply that inbreeding is normal and healthy, only that a low level of immigration apparently can offset its harmful effects in a population.

Genetic Drift　Despite the importance of selection pressure on animal phenotypes, evolution can also result from nothing more than chance. **Genetic drift** is a change in the frequency of a gene in a population over time caused entirely by random factors. The odds that genetic drift will have great importance in changing the frequency of a trait are greatest in very small populations. Consider this analogy: Someone wagers you that if you flip a coin ten times, it will land heads-up nine times. You take the bet, knowing that the odds of a heads-up coin flip are 50% on each flip, and ten flips should produce about five heads-ups. But in fact the coin lands heads-up nine times in ten flips. Do you accuse the person making the wager with you of cheating? You do not, because we all know that although each flip has a random chance of landing either heads or tails, ten coin flips sometimes produce very skewed results. But suppose the person now wagers that if you flip the same coin a million times, it will land heads-up 900,000 times. This is extremely unlikely to happen, simply because of the very low statistical probability of having the coin lands heads-up so many consecutive times.

The comparison between small and large samples of coin flips and small and large populations is apt in the case of genetic drift. Each flip of the coin is analogous to the likelihood that a given allele for a gene is passed to the next generation during reproduction. Although on average, each cross of two people who are heterozygous for a trait should produce half heterozygous children, one-quarter homozygous dominant, and one-quarter homozygous recessive (recall Mendelian crosses from Chapter 3), this does not always occur. At a population level, genetic drift brings about evolutionary change through the same principle of alleles appearing or disappearing by random chance. This is important mainly in small populations, where an allele can easily disappear entirely or become prevalent in all individuals (going to *fixation*, in genetic terms). The smaller the population, the larger the potential effect of genetic drift on gene frequencies. Distinguishing drift from the effects of natural selection is not always easily done because selection in a small population would have similar visible results to the gene pool.

There are many examples of genetic drift in human and other mammalian populations, most often caused by another aspect of genetic drift, called **founder effect**. When a small subset of a much larger population becomes isolated or cut off from genetic contact with its parent gene pool, its gene pool consists only of the genotypes of the individuals in the new, small subpopulation. Only through a long and slow accumulation of mutations can the genetic diversity of the subset increase. If you and a boatload of fellow travelers were stranded permanently on a desert

inbreeding　Mating between close relatives.

genetic drift　Random changes in gene frequency in a population.

founder effect　A component of genetic drift theory, stating that new populations that become isolated from the parent population carry only the genetic variation of the founders.

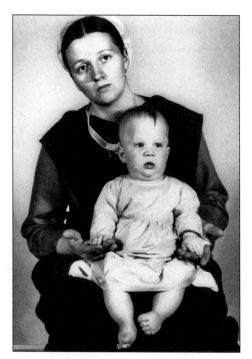

FIGURE 4.4   A child with Ellis–van Creveld (EVC) syndrome.

island, the genetic makeup of the new human population of that island would consist only of the combined genotypes of all the passengers. Founder effect and gene flow often are linked, as in the case of the Pitcairn Islanders receiving new residents in the form of the *Bounty* mutineers. The combination of immigration and very small population size of the island enabled the genes of one British mutineer to become widespread in a short period of time.

Some immigrant groups to the United States who have chosen to live in closed societies experience the effects of genetic drift. The Amish, a well-known religious sect, immigrated to the United States from Germany and the Netherlands in the 1800s (Figure 4.4). They practice farming with nineteenth-century technology, avoiding contact with the larger American culture around them; until recently very few Amish married outside the Amish community. As a consequence, some genetic diseases that were rare in the parent population in western Europe are common among the Amish in America. *Ellis–van Creveld (EVC) syndrome,* a genetic disease common among the Amish, is a form of dwarfism, and its victims always possess an extra finger on each hand and sometimes extra toes on the feet, a condition known as *polydactyly.* Not only is the EVC gene more common among the Amish than in the larger American gene pool, but it is restricted mainly to the Amish settlements in Lancaster County, Pennsylvania, and is extremely rare elsewhere. It appears that one or a few Amish individuals carried the gene with them from Europe to Lancaster County and, by virtue of their high reproductive rate (the Amish often have ten or more children), spread the gene rapidly through the very small founding population of other Amish (McKusick et al., 1964).

A phenomenon associated with the founder effect that can bring about evolutionary change is a **genetic bottleneck**. A bottleneck occurs when a large, genetically diverse population undergoes a rapid reduction in size and then increases again (Figure 4.5). When the population size declines, a large percentage of the alleles present may be lost, and after the bottleneck, only the accumulation of mutations will rebuild genetic diversity. For example, Native Americans, Russians, and then Americans hunted the southern elephant seal, a minivan-sized marine mammal, nearly to extinction from the eighteenth to twentieth centuries. By the time complete protection was enacted, there were only a few dozen southern elephant seals left in the wild. But elephant seals breed rapidly, and over the past several

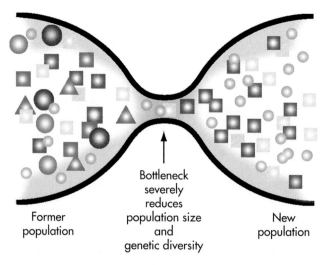

Former population

Bottleneck severely reduces population size and genetic diversity

New population

genetic bottleneck Temporary dramatic reduction in size of a population or species.

FIGURE 4.5   A genetic bottleneck reduces a population temporarily to very low levels, removing much of its genetic diversity.

decades their numbers have grown exponentially. They are returning to former breeding beaches up and down the California coast (including a few bathing beaches, to the shock of human sunbathers). However, the new elephant seal population has a potential problem. It possesses only the genetic diversity present in the new postbottleneck population. Should a disease strike the seals, it could well be that a gene for disease resistance that existed in the population before the bottleneck is gone, and the disease could devastate the remaining seals. Hundreds of generations will have to pass before mutations can begin to restore this diversity.

Natural selection is not the only mechanism by which evolution can occur, although it is considered by most researchers to be the predominant way the variation present in nature is molded into new forms.

FIGURE 4.6 A male peacock displays his genetic worth for a female.

Sexual Selection: Darwin's Other Great Idea Although Darwin's *Origin of Species* in 1859 laid the groundwork for all research on evolution by natural selection that followed, he made another contribution in a later book, the importance of which is less appreciated. In his 1871 book *The Descent of Man,* Darwin extended his evolutionary principles directly to humankind. In it, he explained another major evolutionary force: nonrandom mating brought about by **sexual selection**. Social animals don't mate and bear offspring simply because they bump into each other like balls on a pool table. Females choose particular males as their mates, and they make their choices based on natural variations in male traits (Figure 4.6).

Just as the struggle for existence defined natural selection, Darwin identified two components to sexual selection: the struggle between males to gain access to mates and the struggle by a female to choose the right mate. Sexual selection can be defined as differential reproductive success among the members of the same sex within a given species. Female choice of particular genetically based male traits, such as antlers or large muscles or bright colors, leads to the evolution of males that exhibit those traits because these males enjoy greater reproductive success. Many animal traits that we once believed had evolved to allow males to defend themselves and their group against predators, such as horns and antlers, are now believed to be the products of sexual selection.

Although Darwin considered sexual selection to be an aspect of natural selection, the two forces can operate independently and even in opposition. Although early research on the topic tended to focus on competition between males for mates and assumed that male competition was the driving force behind sexual selection, scientists today recognize that the opposite is more likely. Females of many animal species drive evolutionary change through their selection of certain male phenotypes. For example, female choice has been shown to drive the appearance of long tail feathers in male birds (Andersson, 1992), bright colors in male guppies (Endler, 1983, 1986), and male mating calls in frogs (Ryan, 1990). Increased male body size is a common outcome of sexual selection; in a few primate species, males are nearly twice as large as females. This results from female choice for larger body sizes, and implies competition between males for access to females. **Sexual dimorphism**, a difference in size, shape, or color between the sexes, usually is brought about by evolutionary changes in male appearance caused by female mate preferences.

But why should females prefer males with large antlers, outlandish tail feathers, or brilliant colors? Females are thought to be under selection pressure to choose a male that offers her a direct benefit, such as help in offspring rearing or protection against predators. She may use physical features of the male to judge his quality in these areas (Kirkpatrick, M., 1982). If the capacity for judging males on this basis evolves in females, then males are expected to evolve more and more elaborate features to impress females. Or females may choose males by selecting for

sexual selection   Differential reproductive success within one sex of any species.

sexual dimorphism   Difference in size, shape, or color between the sexes.

"What's the matter? Not puffy enough for you?"

FIGURE 4.7
©The New Yorker Collection 2004 Carolita Johnson from cartoon-bank.com. All Rights Reserved.

indirect benefits. In species where males offer nothing to a female except their genes at conception, we expect a female to choose a mate based on his genetic quality. To judge a potential mate's genetic quality, a female may use a male's ornamental features as clues (Figure 4.7). Brightly colored feathers may indicate a male's underlying genetic health. Elaborate male ornaments, such as a peacock's enormous tail feathers, may be the result of what famous geneticist R. A. Fisher (1958) called *runaway sexual selection*. In this process, female preference for a trait and male evolution of that trait to compete for females reinforce each other endlessly. A more recent theory to account for elaborate male traits is *costly signaling*, which derived from the *handicap principle* posed by Israeli biologist Amo Zahavi. Males may display outlandish ornaments in order to state to a female just how vigorous they must be to survive the appendage or brilliant color they bear. Peacocks must escape from tigers and leopards despite their heavy tails; a male who has a large tail may be signaling his genetic quality to females (Zahavi, 1975).

Why is it that males compete for females, and females choose male traits, rather than the other way around? The theory of sexual selection, as developed by more recent generations of evolutionary biologists, proposes that the sex with the more limited **reproductive potential** should be competed over by the sex with the greater reproductive potential. For nearly all higher animals, this means that females are competed over by males because females are the limited commodity that males need to achieve reproductive success. Whereas a male mammal's fitness often is limited only by access to females, a female must bear most of the costs of reproduction: gestation, lactating, and nurturing. Her level of *parental investment* is far greater than that of males.

The difference in reproductive potential in males and females can be as dramatic in a slow-reproducing animal such as humans as in any other organism. Consider the maximum number of children you've ever heard of a woman giving birth to. The *Guinness Book of World Records* cites a woman in Taiwan with twenty-four children born in 33 years as the largest number of offspring of any woman alive (an eighteenth-century Russian woman is alleged to have had sixty-nine children). By contrast, the same source confirms the maximum recorded children for a man to be 888, by the Moroccan ruler Ismail the Bloodthirsty. In addition to the disparity in reproductive potential, males and females often differ greatly in their **reproductive variance**, the degree of variation from the mean of a population in the reproductive potential of one sex compared with the other. One consequence of a

reproductive potential   The possible output of offspring by one sex.

reproductive variance   A measure of variation from the mean of a population in the reproductive potential of one sex compared with the other.

female's lower reproductive potential—she can be fertilized only once in each breeding season—is that whereas nearly all the females find mates, many males fail to find females. This reproductive asymmetry between males and females holds major consequences for how males and females behave toward one another during courtship, as we will see in Chapter 7.

We can test whether certain male ornaments evolved to display quality to females as a mating strategy by considering animal species with sex role reversal. In a few bird species, such as the small sandpiper-like phalaropes, males rather than females invest the most time and energy in offspring care. In those species, females compete over males, females are larger than males, and females are more brightly colored than males. Phalaropes and a few other sex role–reversed species appear to be the exceptions that prove the sexual selection rule. Sexual selection is currently a hot research area for evolutionary biologists, and new discoveries are being made all the time. For example, only recently have evolutionary biologists begun to appreciate that the loss of male ornaments, caused by loss of female preference for them, may be as common in the animal kingdom as the evolution of those traits in the first place (Wiens, 2001).

Classification and Evolution

In order to understand the natural world, we categorize plants and animals according to the similarities of their features. The science of taxonomy that Linnaeus devised forms the basis for the study of biological classification today. But as we saw in Chapter 1, Linnaeus's scheme did not incorporate modern notions of evolutionary change. Instead of considering species as dynamic entities that are formed from combination and recombination of gene pools, he saw them as immutable cases of God's handiwork.

TAXONOMY AND SPECIATION

Linnaeus classified species in much the same way that we all classify things in our everyday lives, lumping types together based on physical characteristics that were readily apparent to the eye. Presented with an assortment of glasses of wine at a wine tasting, you could quickly sort them into two general "taxa": reds and whites. You could then sort the reds into a wide variety of lower-level categories: merlot, cabernet sauvignon, pinot noir, and so on. Each of these could in turn be subdivided based on other descriptive features such as taste (dry or fruity), geographic origin (France or California), vintage (2002 or 1902), and other qualities.

Unfortunately, sorting species is not exactly like sorting wines. Wines are made to human-desired specifications, and so a finite number of varieties exist. Animal or plant species are dynamic units, always changing in ways that may be too small or slow for us to see in comparing any two or three generations. Furthermore, species themselves don't care whether we can identify them; animals themselves determine the boundaries of species units by their willingness to mate or not with animals from other similar species. Our natural tendency to treat species as distinct, separate categories even when this does not reflect biological reality has contributed to great confusion about species and their formation.

Linnaeus established a hierarchy of categories to classify all living things (Table 4.1 on page 104). Each of these levels of the hierarchy is like a set of nested Russian dolls. As one descends the categories, the distinctions between related forms become increasingly small. The only "natural" category is the species. All others are a taxonomist's way of making sense of the evolutionary past of clusters of related species. Notice that humans and chimpanzees are classified in the same taxonomic categories until the level of the family, and if Linnaeus had not been so driven by theology he would have placed us in the same family. Tortoises, on the other hand, are separated from humans and chimpanzees at the level of the class. To Linnaeus,

TABLE 4.1 The Linnaean Hierarchy			
Linnaean Category	**Human**	**Chimpanzee**	**Tortoise**
Kingdom	Animalia	Animalia	Animalia
Phylum	Chordata	Chordata	Chordata
Class	Mammalia	Mammalia	Reptilia
Order	Primates	Primates	Testudines
Family	Hominidae	Pongidae	Testudinidae
Genus	*Homo*	*Pan*	*Manouria*
Species	*Homo sapiens*	*Pan troglodytes*	*Manouria emys*

this indicated that tortoises had been created in a different image than primates in God's plan. Today, we recognize that the class-level distinction indicates distant evolutionary relatedness.

Evolutionary biologists use a variety of methods to determine relationships between related evolutionary groups. Today the study of taxonomy usually is called **systematics**. Systematists rely on the principle of **homology**, the notion that similar features in two related organisms look alike because of a shared evolutionary history. The bones of your arm have homologous counterparts in the flukes of a whale; despite the whale's aquatic lifestyle, its evolution as a land animal is revealed in the bones it shares with all other land animals. On the other hand, some features are similar because of similar patterns of use rather than shared ancestry. The wings of a bird and the wings of a bat are both used for powered flight, but they evolved independently (Figure 4.8). Although both are warm-blooded vertebrates, bats and birds have not had a common ancestor for tens of millions of years. Bird and bat wings are **analogous** and have evolved through **convergent** (or parallel) **evolution**. The problem of convergence has vexed systematists because natural selection can produce stunningly similar adaptations in distantly related creatures that happen to live in similar environments. Animals with placentas and marsupials that reproduce without a placenta are two distantly related groups of mammals that nevertheless have members that bear striking resemblances to one another. There are marsupial mice in Australia that look so much like placental mice in North America that a biologist would have to dissect them to tell the difference.

We use anatomical *characters*, meaning physical features, to categorize organisms. Two principles are commonly used. First, all organisms are composed of many *ancestral* characters, inherited from ancestors they share with living relatives. Second, organisms also possess *derived* characters: features they alone possess that distinguish them from all related species. By identifying the derived characters, systematists can begin to establish a family tree, or *phylogeny*, of the degree of evolutionary relatedness of one form to another. Phylogenies are the evolutionary histories of groups of related organisms, illustrated in a way that the relationship and the time scale of splitting between ancestors and descendants are shown.

Another brand of evolutionary classification has emerged more recently. This new school of thought is called **cladistics** (from the Greek word *clados*, meaning "branch"), a science of classification in which certain traits are considered more evolutionarily important and informative than others. After establishing which traits are ancestral and which are derived, cladists then analyze the uniquely derived characters. If a cladist is trying to build a taxonomy of all monkeys, he will study the anatomies of enough known species to identify which traits are shared by all and which are possessed by only a few species. If a cluster of species displays a trait that no other group displays, then this *clade*, or cluster of species linked by a set of unique traits, can be studied further to distinguish which traits of the cluster are

systematics   Branch of biology that describes patterns of organismal variation.

homology   Similarity of traits resulting from shared ancestry.

analogous   Having similar traits due to similar use, not due to shared ancestry.

convergent evolution   Similar form or function brought about by natural selection under similar environments rather than shared ancestry.

cladistics   Method of classification using ancestral and derived traits to distinguish patterns of evolution within lineages.

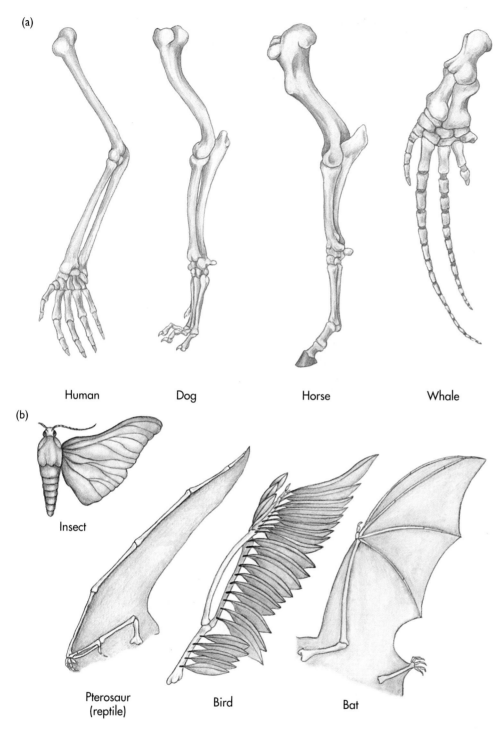

FIGURE 4.8   (a) Homologous traits are similar due to shared ancestry. (b) Analogous traits (bats', birds', and flies' wings) evolved independently but serve a similar purpose.

ancestral and which are derived. The cladist might identify monkeys that possess a grasping tail as a clade and then try to determine the evolutionary path by which grasping tails evolved, studying the presence or absence of other traits in the same clade in which the grasping tail appears. The result of this analysis is a **cladogram**, or branching order of the origins of the lineage of monkeys (Figure 4.9 on page 106). A cladogram does not depict the distance in time between the clades, only the relative degree of anatomical and evolutionary difference.

cladogram   Branching diagram showing evolved relationships among members of a lineage.

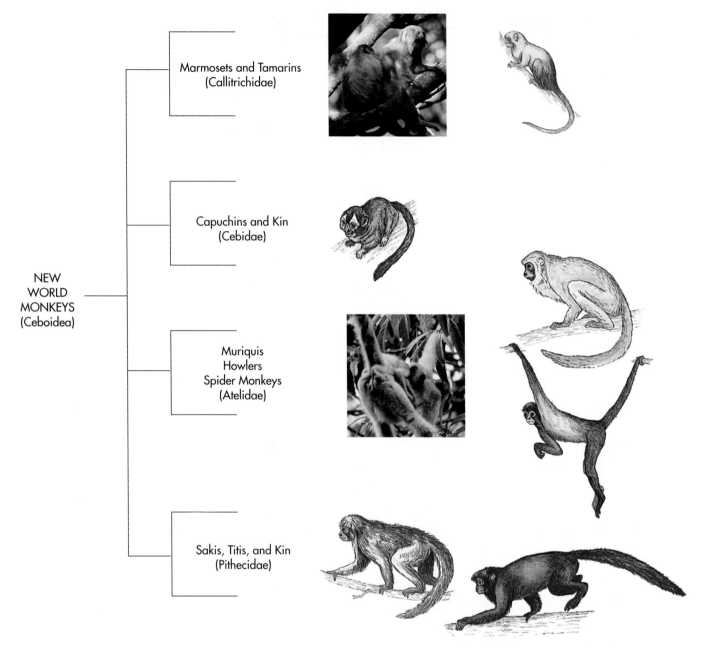

FIGURE 4.9 Example of a cladogram, or branching order, of the New World monkey Superfamily Ceboidea. A cladogram is a family tree but does not show evolutionary time scales.

You may see that there is at least one potential problem with this approach. What about the possibility that the trait in question, a monkey's prehensile tail, evolved twice? The separate, convergent evolution of very similar traits is a confounding factor in cladistic analyses. One way around this problem is to make a very reasonable assumption: A given feature is unlikely to have evolved twice independently in the same lineage or to have disappeared and then re-evolved later in the same lineage. This is called the *law of parsimony,* nicknamed *Occam's razor* after medieval English philosopher William of Ockham (1285–1349). Ockham often used his "principle of unnecessary plurality" in his writings, arguing that one should always seek the simplest explanation for a natural phenomenon.

A second approach to systematics is called *phenetics,* or numerical taxonomy. This perspective is used less than cladistics in anthropology. Pheneticists use all traits that link two organisms, not worrying whether they are similar because of homology or analogy. Phenetics relies solely on numerically describing degrees of similarity and difference between organisms, without biases created by knowing some groups are more closely related than others. Unrelated animals sometimes are lumped in the evolutionary group under this scheme. Taxonomies created by phenetics often differ in important ways from those assembled by cladists or other systematists. Phenetics is now out of fashion, and most scholars studying nonhuman primate and human evolution use the principles and language of cladistics in their work.

WHAT IS A SPECIES?

There is no issue more confusing to both students and scientists of evolution than the question "What is a **species**?" It is really two questions. First, what does the word *species* mean? Second, how should we identify species in nature? You might think these are easy questions because we all believe we can distinguish a lion from a tiger or a horse from a donkey. In Linnaeus's time the answer was easy: Species were fixed pigeonholes without evolutionary pasts or connections to other species in the present. But ever since Darwin, we recognize that species are dynamic, ever-changing entities, and finding a consensus on concepts of species has proved vexing. The formation of new species, or **speciation**, is a fundamental evolutionary process.

Species are difficult to define because of the amount of variation found in nature. What we call species tend to be overlapping categories, rather than completely distinct units. So taxonomists who apply names to species are superimposing their labeling scheme onto natural variation, and the result can be contrived and subjective. And as a result of the artificial nature of labeling species, there are many concepts and definitions of how species are formed. Whereas earlier generations of scientists had only outward appearance to go by to identify species, modern evolutionary biologists can use DNA analysis and studies of physiology, ecology, and behavior. Yet the problem of unambiguously answering the question "What is a species?" remains.

A GUIDE TO SPECIES CONCEPTS

Evolutionary biologists have a wide variety of species concepts from which to choose. The most widely used definition of species is the **biological species concept**, first proposed by biologist Ernst Mayr (1942, 1963). Scientists who argue for their own new concept of species must first show why the biological species concept is inadequate. Mayr (1942) defined species as "groups of actually or potentially interbreeding natural populations which are reproductively isolated from other such groups." This definition has two key phrases. *Reproductive isolation* is at the heart of this concept. If two types of related animals can be distinguished absolutely, then they must have been reproductively isolated for some period of time. But the phrase *actually or potentially* indicates that populations of animals that could cross-breed to create hybrid offspring in nature—but don't—should be considered separate species. Therefore, Mayr's definition referred to *natural populations* only.

Consider lions and tigers. They seem to be two obviously distinct species, the lion with its mane and tawny body, the tiger with its bold black stripes and orange fur. But these differences are only skin deep. The two species are closely related, and if housed together in the same zoo exhibit, a male lion and female tiger will produce a hybrid cub called a liger. Ligers are much larger than either lions or tigers. Female ligers are fertile and can mate with either lions or tigers and produce their own offspring (male ligers are sterile). In the one natural habitat the two species share (the Gir Forest in western India), lions and tigers do not hybridize.

species An interbreeding group of animals or plants that are reproductively isolated through anatomy, ecology, behavior, or geographic distribution from all other such groups.

speciation Formation of one or more new species via reproductive isolation.

biological species concept Defines species as interbreeding populations reproductively isolated from other such populations.

It's common for hybrids of two species to exhibit traits not present in either parent, such as large body sizes in ligers.

So are lions and tigers considered separate species according to the biological species concept? The answer is yes, because in nature the species are reproductively isolated: There is no overlap between the two species' phenotypes and no evidence of them interbreeding naturally. They also differ ecologically, the lion preferring more open country and the tiger preferring dense thickets. There are many such examples of animals that do not ever meet in nature, because they live thousands of miles apart or occupy different niches in the same habitat, but hybridize readily if placed in the same cage or pond. Nevertheless, these have been traditionally considered separate species.

There are many alternatives to the biological species concept; no fewer than twenty-five definitions of *species* have been proposed in the scientific literature. The **evolutionary species concept** is used by many scientists who study the fossil record and therefore cannot directly observe the reproductive isolating mechanisms on which the biological species concept relies. Proponents of the evolutionary species concept consider the enormous geologic time needed to establish the evolutionary history of a species to be an important criterion of a species. Its proponents say that a species not only should be phenotypically distinct from all other species but also should have its own evolutionary identity. As paleontologist George Gaylord Simpson (1961) put it, a species should be a lineage evolving separately from other lineages, having its own evolutionary tendencies. The **ecological species concept**, proposed by Leigh Van Valen (1976), says that a species should occupy its own unique ecological niche, or role, that distinguishes it clearly from all other species. The **recognition species concept** (Paterson, H. E. H., 1986) states that species have their own unique systems for recognizing mates, which may be a widespread basis for reproductive isolation. For example, galagoes (bush babies) are small nocturnal primates who use calls to recognize one another in dark tropical forests. Each species has a unique set of calls that apparently prevents accidental matings between members of different galago species. Studying these calls with an emphasis on how galagoes of one species find each other for mating uses the principle of the recognition species concept.

The difficulties raised by applying multiple species concepts create problems for anthropologists trying to understand the human fossil record. Just as species in the present day are best seen as dynamic entities that overlap genetically in many cases, drawing the line in history where one species has evolved into another species often is problematic. We will see in Chapters 9 through 13 that some early human species can be considered one species or four depending on which taxonomist one listens to and which species concept that taxonomist uses.

In addition to confusion over species concepts, interpreting fossils is complicated by individual variation. If we identify a species in the fossil record, some individuals will look more alike than others because of random variation of the kind that makes one person taller or thinner than another today. Moreover, individuals can harbor diseases or other physical conditions that make them look somewhat different from other members of their species. And often whole populations, the breeding subunits of each species, look a bit different from other populations of the same species (Insights and Advances: What's in a Name? Species Concepts, Genetics, and Conservation on page 110). Such subunits often—but not always—are the embryonic stages of formation of new species.

REPRODUCTIVE ISOLATING MECHANISMS

If species are reproductively isolated from other species, then what factors keep species apart? Such mechanisms can be sorted into two categories: premating isolating mechanisms and postmating isolating mechanisms (Table 4.2). Such **reproductive isolating mechanisms (RIMs)** have been built into the phenotypes of animals to prevent them from accidentally mating with members of another, similar species. Such a mistaken hybrid mating in most cases would be a wasted repro-

evolutionary species concept
Defines species as evolutionary lineages with their own unique identity.

ecological species concept Defines species based on the uniqueness of their ecological niche.

recognition species concept
Defines species based on unique traits or behaviors that allow members of one species to identify each other for mating.

reproductive isolating mechanisms (RIMs) Any factor—behavioral, ecological, or anatomical—that prevents a male and female of two different species from hybridizing.

TABLE 4.2	**Reproductive Isolating Mechanisms (RIMs)**
PREMATING ISOLATING MECHANISMS	
1. Habitat isolation	Species A and B occupy different habitats, such as tree limbs versus the ground beneath the tree.
2. Temporal isolation	Species A and B breed in different seasons or in different months, or are active in day versus at night.
3. Behavioral isolation	Courtship or other behavior or calls by male of species A do not elicit mating response by female of species B.
4. Mechanical incompatibility	Species A and B cannot mate successfully because of anatomical difference, especially in the reproductive organs.
POSTMATING ISOLATING MECHANISMS	
1. Sperm–egg incompatibility	Mating occurs, but sperm of species A is unable to penetrate or fertilize egg of species B because of biochemical incompatibility.
2. Zygote inviability	Species A and B produce fertilized egg, but it dies at early stage of embryonic development.
3. Embryonic or fetal inviability	Offspring of hybrid mating dies before birth.
4. Offspring inviability	Hybrid offspring is carried to term but dies after birth.
5. Offspring sterility	Hybrid offspring is healthy but reproductively sterile, as in mules born from horse–donkey matings.

ductive effort, and natural selection promotes mechanisms to prevent such matings. Although premating and postmating barriers to accidental cross-species breeding have evolved, premating barriers are prevalent because they prevent lost mating efforts and prevent wasting of sperm and eggs.

THE ORIGIN OF SPECIES: HOW SPECIES ARE FORMED

The process of speciation can occur in a variety of ways. One species can evolve into another over time, a process known as **anagenesis**. In this mode of change, species 1 would slowly become species 2, and species 1 would no longer exist or be identifiable in the fossil record (Figure 4.10). The question then becomes when taxonomists should stop referring to the species as 1 and begin calling it species 2.

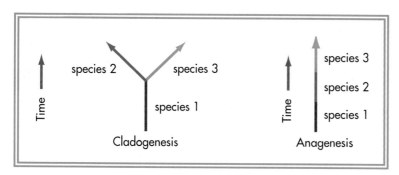

FIGURE 4.10 Two modes of evolutionary change. (a) In cladogenesis, one species branches into multiple new species. (b) In anagenesis, one species evolves into another new species over time.

anagenesis Evolution of a trait or a species into another over a period of time.

INSIGHTS AND ADVANCES

What's in a Name? Species Concepts, Genetics, and Conservation

With many of the world's primate species in danger of extinction, scientists are trying to determine the population size of each remaining species. One factor complicating this effort is confusion about species concepts. Whether one species of primate with a population of 3,000 remaining individuals should be split taxonomically into three with only 1,000 each has critical consequences for conservation efforts. Scientists studying these issues have a new arsenal of genetic research tools at their disposal. But these new tools of an evolutionary biologist's trade have not necessarily resolved species identity problems.

Recent fieldwork has identified numerous populations of great apes across Africa that had not previously been described. With the advances in DNA technologies, it is now possible to collect fecal material from these little-known populations and conduct genetic analysis to tell us how closely related new populations are to other, known ape populations. In some cases the combination of new genetic data and traditional studies of the skeletal anatomy of apes and other primates has led researchers to claim that multiple species exist in places where we previously believed there was one.

Recent genetic studies of gorillas (*Gorilla gorilla*) have revealed an amazing amount of genetic diversity (Gagneux et al., 1996; Jensen-Seaman & Kidd, 2001) and demonstrate how misleading the outward appearance of the animals can be for understanding evolutionary relationships. In eastern Africa, mountain gorillas occur in two populations—the Virungas Volcanoes and in the nearby Bwindi Impenetrable National Park (Figure A). Separated by only 25 miles (40 kilometers), these two populations are genetically indistinguishable. They are similar in appearance but can be distinguished by subtle differences in hair color and length

FIGURE A   Only 650 mountain gorillas remain in two tiny forests in East Africa.

(Virungas gorillas are jet black, with longer, shaggier coats). Their behavior differs, too: The Bwindi gorillas climb trees routinely, whereas their Virungas counterparts rarely climb. But despite their geographic separation and differences in appearance and behavior, no one would advocate considering the two variants of mountain gorillas to be separate species.

Meanwhile, lowland gorillas in western Africa also exist in multiple separate populations (Figure B). Unlike their mountain cousins, lowland gorilla populations show a startling degree of genetic divergence. In fact, some western lowland gorilla populations are as different from one another genetically as gorillas are from chimpanzees. Their genetic diversity has prompted some scientists to propose splitting lowland gorillas into at least two species, although this remains controversial. This implies a very long history of separation among the populations. However, despite this genetic divergence, western

lowland gorillas all look very much alike; in other words, their phenotypes have remained the same.

The lesson vividly illustrated by lowland gorillas is that the genetic distance between two species does not necessarily correspond to the formation of new species. So, learning that two species have been on separate phylogenetic paths for a million years does not necessarily mean that they will look less similar than two other species that have been on separate paths for 100,000 years. This complicates an already thorny conservation question. If gorillas, long considered to be one species across Africa, are really three or more species, how should this change the way we try to protect their future? Splitting one species into three means we would have two additional, even more critically endangered populations. It might also discourage future generations of conservationists from introducing animals to new populations as a means of increasing genetic diversity. On the other hand, creating new gorilla species may help focus world attention on the plight of endangered populations. So when it comes to gorillas, the question "What is a species?" is far from academic.

FIGURE B   Most of the world's remaining gorillas are western lowland gorillas.

Species 1 might also branch into two or more new species, a process called **cladogenesis**. In cladogenesis, species 1 might or might not still exist as one of the new array of species.

Beyond these two general modes of evolutionary change, there are specific processes by which new species are formed. One of these is **allopatric speciation** (Mayr, 1942). In allopatric speciation, the trigger to the emergence of new species is geographic separation between two populations of the same species (Figure 4.11). For example, a river that cuts into its banks grows wider and wider over eons. Eventually the river's course becomes a canyon that separates the populations of animals that live on one side from those on the other side. If the animals are small and unable to cross the chasm, gene flow is interrupted. Over thousands of generations, random mutations accumulate in each population until each is different enough that they can be considered separate species. Such circumstances of isolation and divergence happen frequently in nature; islands and river-course changes both create fragmented animal habitats that lead to allopatric speciation all the time. In fact, one squirrel species is believed to have speciated into two because of the formation of the Grand Canyon in Arizona; as the chasm grew deeper and wider, what had been one species was fragmented into two. Today, the north and south rims of the canyon support separate, closely related squirrel species.

Darwin's finches, speciating in isolation on the many islands of the Galápagos, are another good example of allopatric speciation. Scientists studying the great apes believe the closely related chimpanzee and bonobo may have been formed when the great Congo River split and isolated two populations of an ape species that was their common ancestor (Figure 4.12 on page 112). Apes do not swim, and with a lack of gene flow over thousands of generations, two apes with differing anatomies and behavior emerged where there had been one.

But what happens if the individuals from the two now-separated species contact each other again? Do the species merge again, or are they forever split? If ocean levels drop and islands become reconnected to the mainland, many species that had been isolated for thousands of generations may be exposed to potential

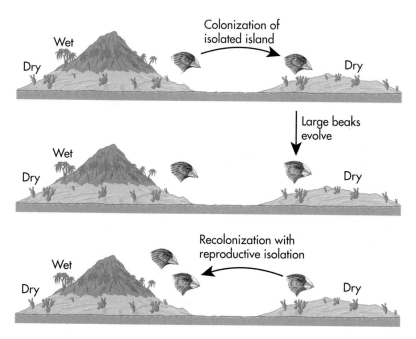

FIGURE 4.11   How allopatric speciation works.

cladogenesis Evolution through the branching of a species or a lineage.

allopatric speciation Speciation occurring via geographic isolation.

(a)

(b)

FIGURE 4.12 (a) Chimpanzees and (b) bonobos likely diverged from a common ancestor due to allopatric speciation in central Africa.

Despite recent claims that sympatric speciation is an important mode of species formation, it remains controversial.

parapatric speciation Speciation occurring when two populations have continuous distributions and some phenotypes in that distribution are more favorable than others.

sympatric speciation Speciation occurring in the same geographic location.

mates from what are now distinct but closely related species. The differences between the two new species can be reinforced through secondary contact. In a process called *reinforcement*, random mating between the two species is discouraged by natural selection because the hybrid would be less genetically fit than the offspring of two mates of the same species. Because natural selection favors premating reproductive isolating mechanisms, new points of difference between the two species often evolve (perhaps courtship behavior or structure of the reproductive anatomy) that make hybrid mating unlikely.

A second process of species formation is **parapatric speciation**. When two populations occur adjacent to one another, with continuous gene flow back and forth between them, speciation of one from the other is possible, especially if one or both species occur over a very large geographic area. This can make one part of a population remote enough from another that new traits can appear, and over time parts of the original populations diverge more than others. Often, a zone of overlap remains where the new populations, now two species, continue to interbreed. Such hybrid zones are confusing to evolutionary biologists because they can remain stable, without disappearing or growing, over many years. In northeastern Africa, a hybrid zone exists between savanna and hamadryas baboons. In the strip of arid land that is the hybrid zone, but nowhere outside of it, baboons exist that share a mosaic of traits between the two species. These traits are not only morphological ones such as hair color or body size; they include aspects of mating behaviors in hybrids that resemble a mixture of the behavior of both species. Such hybrids therefore allow primatologists to better understand the degree of genetic influence over particular traits.

Another mode of speciation is **sympatric speciation**, which occurs when ecological factors create more than one phenotype in a single population. No spatial separation of the parent species is needed. Each subpopulation diverges genetically from the other, perhaps due to limited resources, until two species have formed in the place of the original one. There have been relatively few demonstrations of sympatric speciation in animals, although it is well documented in plants, in which a single mistake made during reproduction produces large-scale chromosomal mutation. The mutation isolates a whole new form of plant reproductively from its neighbors, thereby creating a new species, which can lead to very rapid speciation because of its dramatic genetic effects.

THE TEMPO OF SPECIATION

When Darwin considered evolution by natural selection, he considered mainly one kind of change. Lineages of animal and plant species evolve slowly, gradually evolving into new species over vast periods of Earth's history. This is known as **gradualism** and is widely accepted as the most important and prevalent type of biological evolution. Although Darwin knew about the occurrence of "sports," as he called mutations that differed radically in color or shape from their parents, he considered these extremely rare aberrations. Darwin and most biologists since have accepted gradualism based on the occurrence of so many intermediate forms in the fossil record and the intricate relationships between an organism's adaptations, which imply small incremental evolutionary changes because rapid major changes would disrupt the way an organism functions.

Given this evidence of gradual evolution, how do we explain the presence of gaps in the fossil record? Creationists point to these gaps as evidence that a divine power has created at least some species, and therefore they lack an evolutionary history. Scientists point out that the fossil record is fragmentary, and if complete it would reveal all the gradual changes that evolution has produced.

An alternative explanation for gaps in the fossil record is **macroevolution**, meaning rapid, large-scale evolutionary changes. The most commonly cited mode of macroevolution is **punctuated equilibrium** (Eldredge & Gould, 1972). The theory of punctuated equilibrium holds that most species' phenotypes remain static, changing very little over long periods of time. These long periods of stasis are punctuated by bursts of evolutionary change that happen rapidly (Figure 4.13). Such a process would produce gaps in the fossil record because intermediate forms would occur only in brief windows in time. The theory's advocates claim that this may explain large gaps in the fossil record for the most ancient invertebrates, in which wholesale changes in the phenotypes of lineages appear suddenly and without evidence of immediate ancestors.

Punctuated equilibrium is a radical variation on the traditional Darwinian theory of gradual evolutionary change. Most scientists studying the fossil record of more recent animal life are skeptical of punctuated evolution, for at least two reasons. First, the fossil record is extremely fragmentary, and in cases where abundant fossils are discovered for a lineage of animals, evidence of gradual change exists. Second, there is much evidence that species change slightly over time without evolving into new species, as opposed to the claim of punctuated equilibrium theorists that species remain static for long periods.

However, scientists who study the deep history of life on Earth have a very different view of punctuated equilibrium. The fossil record of very primitive life forms living hundreds of millions of years ago provides strong evidence that punctuated equilibrium might have been an important mode of speciation. Most evidence of punctuation events comes from patterns of wholesale changes in communities of ancient marine animals, in which large-scale change can be seen in short periods of time. Punctuated equilibrium is a good example of how scientists' views differ widely depending on their perspective of nature. Those looking at only recent evolution on Earth see little evidence of punctuation events, whereas those studying enormously long time scales and more complete fossil records see ample evidence.

An even more extreme version of punctuation theory, called *saltation* (literally, evolution by leaps), argues that macroevolutionary changes were so sudden and

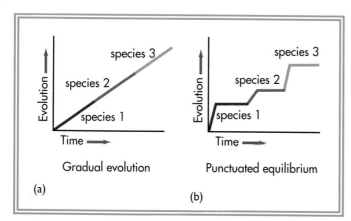

FIGURE 4.13 The tempo of evolution: (a) Gradual evolution involves small, steady changes over a long period; (b) punctuated equilibrium involves long periods of stasis punctuated by bursts of change.

gradualism Darwinian view of slow, incremental evolutionary change.

macroevolution Evolution of major phenotypic changes over relatively short time periods.

punctuated equilibrium Model of evolution characterized by rapid bursts of change, followed by long periods of stasis.

FIGURE 4.14   A feathered dinosaur.

so large in effect that intermediate forms did not exist at all. Unlike punctuated equilibrium, which is a Darwinian theory working on large time scales, saltation is a departure from Darwinian explanations for the evolution of life.

As we saw earlier and will examine in detail in the next section, adaptation is a fundamental aspect of evolution by natural selection. Many scientists question whether punctuated equilibrium can account for the ever-present force of adaptation in nature.

ADAPTATION

Adaptations are evolved phenotypic traits that increase an organism's reproductive success. The eye is an obvious adaptation, and the ways in which eyes differ (nocturnal animals possess very different eye adaptations from other animals) are further examples of adaptations. The concept of adaptation is central to modern biology, but it is also much debated. Some evolutionary biologists consider any well-designed trait an organism possesses to be an adaptation. Others use a stricter definition; they consider an adaptation to be a trait that evolved for a purpose and is still serving that purpose. A trait that evolved for a purpose other than what it does today would not be considered an adaptation.

For instance, we can be sure that the wings of birds did not evolve for powered flight. We know this because natural selection sorts among the available adaptive advantages an organism possesses *in each generation*. There would have been no selective advantage to an ancient bird in having wings that were just slightly adapted for flight. Instead, wings must have evolved for another function entirely and then were co-opted for flight. Some evolutionary theorists think that feathered wings were initially adaptive as organs that absorbed solar radiation, allowing a proto-bird to bask in the sun and warm up more effectively (as some birds do today). As feathered wings evolved, they became useful for gliding and then eventually were modified for powered flight (Figure 4.14). As in other cases of explaining retrospectively the origin of an adaptation, finding intermediate stages of its evolution during which it would have been adaptive is the key.

IS EVERYTHING ADAPTIVE?

If you were asked to develop a hypothesis in the next 5 minutes to describe the evolutionary origin of the human chin, you probably could think of something plausible. The chin, you might argue, evolved to aid our ancestors in the days when they ran across the savanna, protecting their eyes by jutting out from the face to absorb the first shock if they tripped and fell. Or perhaps the chin evolved to provide a place to catch soup as it dribbled out of the mouth. Such scenarios, though silly, are hard to disprove. As we saw in Chapter 2, evolutionary science works by posing a reasonable hypothesis to explain a feature or behavior and then figuring out the sort of data one needs to collect to test that hypothesis. In practice, this means that assuming that a trait may be adaptive at the outset of a study is the way to proceed. The premise of your hypothesis would be that the human chin is an adaptation, evolved for a purpose related to reproduction and survival.

It would be naive to think that all evolution is adaptive; we saw that genetic drift and its components are notable exceptions. Some scientists tend toward **adaptationism**, accepting that every aspect of an organism is the product of natural selection or sexual selection. Others, including members of one school we can call *holism,* are skeptical that natural selection is all-powerful and consider many apparent adaptations to be merely the by-product of other evolutionary changes. Holists would point out that the chin is only the meeting point of the two halves

adaptationism   A premise that all aspects of an organism have been molded by natural selection to a form optimal for enhancing reproductive success.

of the lower jaw, which do not fuse until infancy in human development. The chin exists because of the position of the teeth, not because the chin has any adaptive role of its own.

These two schools of thought represent very different ways of understanding how evolution works. Adaptationists tend toward **reductionism**, trying to understand the function of each component of an organism in order to understand the organism as a whole. They make the working assumption that each part of the organism is adaptive. Holists claim that reductionists oversimplify the nature of adaptation and see natural selection in places where it had not occurred. In a well-known 1979 article, biologists Steven Jay Gould and Richard Lewontin argued that adaptationists overlook or ignore many nonadaptive means by which evolution may occur. They analogized evolution to the arches of a cathedral. As a graceful architectural feature, the spaces between the archways (spandrels) appear to have been created for aesthetic reasons. In fact, spandrels are merely the by-product of building an arch (Mayr, 1983; Gould & Lewontin, 1979).

Adaptationists respond that assuming that traits are adaptive is the only rational starting point for using the scientific method to test their hypotheses. Just as there are both evolved and immediate causes in biology, there are both adaptive and nonadaptive explanations for what an organism looks like. Using an adaptive, reductionist framework as the way to begin investigating those traits is the best, and perhaps the only, way to conduct scientific research into human evolutionary biology. The holistic approach cautions us against assuming that all features of an organism are adaptive. But in practice, biological anthropologists tend to begin with adaptive hypotheses and test them until they appear to be poor explanations for a phenomenon, and then turn to other possible explanations.

FIGURE 4.15   G. H. Hardy

HARDY–WEINBERG EQUILIBRIUM

What would populations be like if evolutionary change never occurred? Although this is not possible in nature, it can be studied in a mathematician's laboratory, and the experiment is extremely useful for understanding the **null hypothesis**, that natural selection and other evolutionary forces have no effect on a population. In 1908, English mathematician G. H. Hardy (Figure 4.15) published a short article in the journal *Science,* which contained a point of math so elementary that he apologized for having to point it out to biologists. But Hardy's paper played a vital role in the reconciliation of Mendelian and Darwinian views of nature. It also laid the foundations for the modern field of population genetics and other mathematical approaches to understanding evolution.

Before 1908, geneticists struggled with concepts of equilibrium in biological populations. At what point would genetic stability be reached in these dynamic populations? Looking at it from the simplest perspective of one gene with two alleles (one dominant and one recessive), Yule (1902) argued that equilibrium would be reached in a population when there was a 3:1 ratio of the dominant to the recessive phenotype. Most geneticists with practical experience, such as R. C. Punnett, knew this was wrong but did not know how to prove it was wrong. This is where Hardy stepped in.

Suppose we have a population of diploid, sexually reproducing organisms. Assume that this population is not subject to any evolutionary forces that might lead to changes in allele frequencies: no mutation, no natural selection, no migration. Assume that it is infinitely large (that is, no genetic drift) and that mating is random (that is, allele frequencies cannot be influenced by assortive or disassortive mating practices). This is obviously an "ideal" population, but that is not a problem, as we will see. Let us take the case of a single gene A with two alleles, A_1 and

reductionism   Paradigm that an organism is the sum of many evolved parts and that organisms can best be understood through an adaptationist approach.

null hypothesis   The starting assumption for scientific inquiry, that one's research results occur by random chance. One's hypothesis must challenge this initial assumption.

A_2. The frequencies of these alleles in the population can be represented by p and q, respectively (see also Appendix C). By definition, $p + q = 1$.

Hardy showed that after one generation, the genotype frequencies in the population can be represented by a simple quadratic equation:

$$(p + q)^2 = p^2 + 2pq + q^2 = 1$$

This means that the frequencies of the homozygous genotypes A_1A_1 and A_2A_2 are p^2 and q^2, respectively, and the frequency of the heterozygote A_1A_2 is $2pq$. No matter what values p and q have, if the assumptions of no evolution, infinitely large population, and random mating hold, these allele (and genotype) frequencies will not change over generations of breeding. The population is in equilibrium, at least for this single gene or locus.

Despite the fact that ideal populations rarely exist in nature, Hardy's equation, which later became known as the **Hardy–Weinberg equilibrium,** has proved to be valuable in many ways. It can be mathematically expanded to model the distribution of more complex genetic systems, including polygenic traits and those for which more than two alleles exist. One can also use it to calculate approximate allele frequencies based on knowledge of the phenotypic frequency of a homozygous recessive trait. For example, there is a chemical called phenylthiocarbamide (PTC), which can be tasted by about 75% of the European population but cannot be tasted by the other 25%. It is known that this is controlled by a single gene with two alleles, where "tasting" is dominant to "nontasting." Thus the allele frequency of nontasting (homozygous recessive) equals the square root of 0.25, or 0.5 (see also Chapter 3).

Finally, although ideal populations rarely exist, the allele distributions of many genes often are found to be in equilibrium. Of course, when we find an allele distribution that is not in equilibrium—that can be the most exciting finding of all: It may mean that an evolutionary force is at work in the population, waiting to be uncovered by a curious investigator.

Hardy's article put to rest any ideas of "blending" inheritance. He demonstrated not only that in the absence of evolution allele frequencies are in equilibrium but also that phenotype frequencies are in equilibrium. There would be no averaging out of beneficial traits, which for many years was the standard argument against Darwinian evolution by natural selection.

And who is Weinberg? Hardy did not know Wilhelm Weinberg, a German physician, who in 1908—and some months before Hardy—presented an equilibrium model of allele frequency stability identical to Hardy's. Wilhelm published several articles on population genetics in 1909, many of which anticipated later developments in the field. They were all ignored and therefore had no influence on the development of population genetics. It was many years later, after the rediscovery of Weinberg's work, that the Hardy equilibrium became universally known as the Hardy–Weinberg equilibrium.

Hardy–Weinberg equilibrium   The theoretical distribution of alleles in a given population in the absence of evolution, expressed as a mathematical equation.

group selection   Notion, largely discredited by the rise of Darwinian theory, proposing that animals act for the good of their social group or of their species.

Levels of Selection

A final consideration about the nature of selection and evolution is the level at which evolution by natural selection occurs. Darwin considered an individual's lifetime reproductive success as the bottom line for natural selection. Challenges to this idea have consistently been shown to be in error. Biologist V. C. Wynne-Edwards (1962) attempted to show that natural selection could sometimes occur for the good of a whole group of animals, which he called **group selection.** He claimed that when animals are overcrowded, they regulate their reproduction rather than overpopulate their range and outstrip their food resources. But biologist George C. Williams (1966) showed clearly that in such a situation, the individual that is concerned only with itself always prospers evolutionarily. Consider a herd of 100 antelope that are beginning to run out of food because of overpopulation. Ninety-nine antelope stop bearing offspring for 1 year because natural selection has a mechanism that is intended to prevent overpopulation, but one antelope continues having babies. That one selfish antelope would eat heartily and pass its genes for selfish behavior to the next generation, whereas its altruistic neighbors did not. In time, *altruism* would be extinguished in favor of selfish behavior. Williams showed succinctly that in the face of selfish behavior, there are few scenarios in which self-sacrifice in the animal kingdom could proliferate.

INCLUSIVE FITNESS

More recent evolutionary thinkers argue that selection may operate at other levels as well. Individual selection leads us to believe that all behavior should be selfish; altruism should be very rare. But social animals such as primates behave in ways that benefit their close relatives, often to the detriment of their nonrelatives. Such behavior, called **kin selection**, first framed by biologist William D. Hamilton (1964), is part of a larger concept known as **inclusive fitness**. Instead of considering only an animal's own reproductive success, evolutionary biologists realized that the reproductive success of one's kin also matters because it can contribute indirectly to the animal's fitness by helping its offspring survive and reproduce. Inclusive fitness predicts that social animals should behave less competitively toward close kin because of their shared genes. For example, a female baboon has a variety of routes to achieve reproductive success; she can produce and nurture her own sons and daughters, but she can also help her nieces, nephews, and grandoffspring grow up by treating them favorably relative to unrelated baboons.

The evolutionary concepts of inclusive fitness and kin selection are an important part of modern *behavioral ecology*. The majority of scientists who study animal social behavior in the wild today use an evolutionary framework to understand why animals behave as they do. Because full siblings share more of their genetic material than distant cousins, we can make predictions about how animals will behave in nature. These predictions lead to testable hypotheses, and have brought the study of the evolution of social behavior into the mainstream of the behavioral sciences. Kin selection has wide applications. For example, food-sharing between chimpanzees is far more likely to occur between close relatives than between nonrelatives. While we would naturally expect that mothers are more likely to share with their children than with others, kin selection provides a framework for asking exactly why this would be true. The answer is: A mother favors her offspring over other individuals because she shares about half of her genotype with each of her offspring.

Kin selection also allows us to test apparent paradoxes in nature. Ground squirrels sitting near their burrows give piercing alarm calls when hawks or coyotes appear. Isn't this altruistic behavior hard to explain in Darwinian terms because the call attracts attention to the caller, making him more likely to be eaten than his neighbor? Researchers found that alarm calls are given mainly when the nearest neighbor is a close relative; when a squirrel is sitting near nonrelatives, he is the first animal to flee into the burrow when danger approaches (Figure 4.16) (Sherman, 1977). The calling ground squirrel is behaving exactly as kin selection would predict; favoring its kin over nonkin.

Kin selection operates based on a *coefficient of relatedness*, expressed as $rb > c$, or Hamilton's rule, where r is the degree of kinship between two animals, b is the benefit of altruism to the recipient, and c is the cost of altruism to the altruist (the alarm caller, for instance). The closer the degree of kinship, the more likely

kin selection   Principle that animals behave preferentially toward their genetic kin; formulated by William Hamilton.

inclusive fitness   Reproductive success of an organism plus the fitness of its close kin.

FIGURE 4.16 Ground squirrel predator warnings illustrate how kin selection may work.

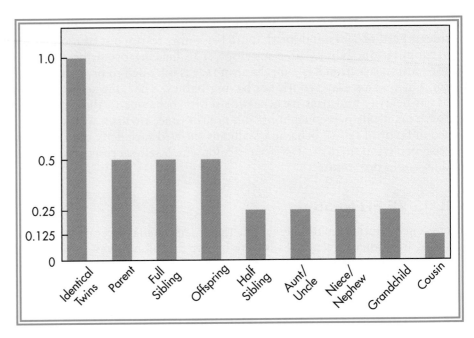

FIGURE 4.17   Coefficients of relatedness: How kin selection works.

altruistic behavior becomes, and the more likely an animal is to engage in dangerous behavior to help its kin (Figure 4.17). This principle guides much of the modern-day research into the social behavior of our closest relatives. We will return to the subject of kin selection when we consider the relevance of natural and sexual selection to primate social behavior in more detail in Chapter 7.

SUMMARY

1. **How does natural selection work to mold adaptations?**

   Natural selection filters genetically inherited traits by favoring some phenotypes in a given environment and disfavoring others. The process perpetuates and enhances mutations that have positive effects on an organism's survival and reproduction. The same process can remove harmful or nonadaptive traits from a population.

2. **What is the goal of taxonomic analysis?**

   Taxonomists attempt to categorize organisms based on their phenotypes. Cladists use ancestral and derived traits to separate lineages and to sort members of a single lineage.

3. **What is the difference between Linnaeus's way of classifying species and our modern notion of species?**

   Linnaeus used a typological pigeonholing scheme for sorting species by similarities to other species. Modern evolutionary biologists recognize that species are dynamic entities that are in flux.

4. **Are there nonadaptive modes of evolution?**

   Genetic drift, including the founder effect, is an example of evolution without adaptation.

5. **How does population size affect the impact of random forces such as genetic drift?**

   Genetic drift and other random factors are much more powerful in very small populations because traits can become fixed (100% occurrence) or lost more easily.

6. **Does sexual selection ever work against the effect of natural selection? How?**

   Sexual selection promotes the elaboration of male traits that enhance reproductive success but not necessarily phenotypic traits that enhance survival. In some cases sexual selection appears to favor traits that adversely affect survival.

7. **What is the reproductive asymmetry between males and females?**

   Males typically have a far greater potential for reproductive success than do females, and also a far greater variance in mating and reproductive success.

8. **How can we resolve the paradox of animals behaving altruistically toward each other, when Darwin predicted that all behavior should enhance one's own reproductive success?**

   Through kin selection, animals act in ways that enhance their own fitness. When an animal shares genes with another through kinship, altruistic or cooperative behavior helps the giver as well as the recipient of the cooperation.

9. **Is every aspect of an organism adaptive?**

   As an initial working hypothesis, we can presume that a trait evolved to enhance an organism's fitness; this is the reductionist approach. We attempt to understand adaptations by considering each element of an organism's phenotype as the product of natural selection.

CRITICAL THINKING QUESTIONS

1. How can sexual selection sometimes work against natural selection? How can we decide whether sexual selection is a part of or acts in opposition to natural selection?

2. How should we choose which species concept to apply? Is it acceptable to use different species concepts in different circumstances? Shouldn't a species be unambiguously identifiable in all cases?

3. Can behavior be a phenotype? What conditions must be met for natural selection to mold a given behavior?

KEY TERMS

directional selection
stabilizing selection
gene flow
inbreeding
genetic drift
founder effect
genetic bottleneck
sexual selection
sexual dimorphism
reproductive potential
reproductive variance
systematics

homology
analogous
convergent evolution
cladistics
cladogram
species
speciation
biological species
    concept
evolutionary species
    concept

ecological species
    concept
recognition species
    concept
reproductive isolating
    mechanisms (RIMs)
anagenesis
cladogenesis
allopatric speciation
parapatric speciation
sympatric speciation
gradualism

macroevolution
punctuated equilibrium
adaptationism
reductionism
null hypothesis
Hardy–Weinberg
    equilibrium
group selection
kin selection
inclusive fitness

SUGGESTED READING

Endler, J. (1986). *Natural Selection in the Wild*. Princeton University Press, Princeton, NJ.

Hey, J. (2001). The mind of the species problem. *Trends in Ecology and Evolution* 16: 326–329.

Mayr, Ernst. (2001). *What Evolution Is*. Basic Books, New York.

Weiner, Jonathan. (1994). *The Beak of the Finch*. Vintage Books, New York.

Williams, G. C. (1966). *Adaptation and Natural Selection*. Princeton University Press, Princeton, NJ.

CHAPTER OUTLINE

**Human Variation
at the Individual
and Group Level**

**Historical
Perspectives on
Human Variation**

Population Genetics

**Polymorphisms and
Natural Selection in
Human Populations**

**Adaptation
and Adaptability**

My dear Gray

It is a horrid shame to trouble you, busy as you always are, but there is one point on which I am very anxious to gain information & possibly it may be gained in the S[outh]. of your country & I can think of no one to apply to but you. Old writers often insist on differences of constitution going with complexion; & I want *much* to know whether there is any truth in this. It has occurred to me that liability to such a disease as yellow-fever would answer my question in the best possible way. Do you know anyone of a scientific mind to whom to apply to ask whether any observations have ever been made or *published* , whether Europeans (without of course any *cross with negro-blood*) of dark complexion & black hair are more liable or less liable to be attacked with yellow-fever (or any *remittent Fever*), than persons of light complexion. If you could aid me in this it would be of much value to me. But do not trouble yourself to write merely to acknowledge this.—

I have just published a little notice in Gardeners Ch. on the fertilisation of Leguminous plants, which rather bears on our Fumariaceous discussion.

I sincerely hope that you are well & not working yourself to death

Pray believe me | My dear Gray | Yours most sincerely | C. Darwin

A sort of vague feeling comes over me that I have asked you all this before; if I have, I beg very many apologies.— I know I once wrote several letters to various parts of world for similar information.

(letter source: The Darwin Correspondence Project letter 2364, www.darwinproject.ac.uk)

IN NOVEMBER 1858, CHARLES DARWIN wrote this letter to his American colleague, Asa Gray (1810–1888), professor of natural history at Harvard University. Gray would eventually become known as America's foremost Darwinist, although before the publication of *Origin of Species*, Gray's main service to Darwin was in answering questions from him concerning a wide range of biological topics. In this letter, Darwin asks about the possible adaptive value of darker skin color; he wants to know why people with darker skin—whatever their geographical origins—might be favored in warmer climates compared to people with lighter skin. What is interesting about this letter is that it reveals Darwin's attempt to understand this trait outside of a racial context. He is not simply taking skin color as an indelible hallmark of race, but as a feature subject to the effects of natural selection.

The origins of biological anthropology go back to the first half of the nineteenth century, an era when evolution had yet to be accepted by most natural historians and fossils representing human ancestors were all but unknown. At that time, biological anthropology was essentially the study of human variation, examined in the context of the short history of biblical creation. Like Charles Darwin, who once he completed his voyage on the *Beagle* never went to the field again, most of the earliest anthropologists did not go into the field to meet their research subjects. Instead, they relied on others' accounts of exotic peoples from faraway places and waited in their universities, hospitals, and museums for specimens, such as skeletal remains, to be sent to them.

Today, we study human variation using the evolutionary approach pioneered by Darwin. The field covers a wide range of topics, encompassing population genetics and the evolutionary history of human populations, how natural selection influences human biology, and how humans biologically and culturally adapt to environmental stress. However, before considering how biological anthropologists now approach the topic of human variation, it is important to examine past approaches, many of which were centered on the concept of race and the goal of racial classification.

Human Variation at the Individual and Group Level

It is obvious that modern humans show substantial *individual variation*, but biological anthropologists are generally interested in variation at the *group* or *population level*. Humans have long noticed that people from different populations (or "races," as they were sometimes called) may look different from one another. They also noticed that they may behave differently. The science of anthropology developed in order to systematically examine biological and cultural differences observed between different human populations. Population variation is widespread and can be measured both morphologically (characteristics of the body) and genetically. As anthropology has developed over the years, methods for disentangling genetic, cultural, and environmental factors responsible for producing population variation have become more refined. It is important to remember, however, that there are many other dimensions of human variation, other than that associated with being part of a specific population. People vary by age or sex, for example, and in their own particular combination of alleles they possess (Figure 5.1).

WHAT IS A POPULATION?

The word *population* is a very flexible term although it is typically used to describe a group or community of animals that is identifiable within a species. As we discussed in Chapter 4, the members of a biological population constitute a potentially interbreeding group of individuals. An individual organism will find its reproductive mates from among the other members of its population. Many other terms have also been suggested for groups below the species level. Population geneticists have used several that emphasize that populations are assemblages of genes as well as individuals: *gene pool, local Mendelian population,* and *panmictic unit* (a local population in which mating is completely random) (Mettler et al., 1988). In general, geneticists use the term **deme** to refer to populations that are being defined in terms of their genetic composition (such as allele frequencies). All of these terms are meant to suggest that although these groups are in some way stable and identifiable, they are by no means genetically impermeable. After all, we study gene flow *between* populations.

deme   Local, interbreeding population that is defined in terms of its genetic composition (for example, allele frequencies).

FIGURE 5.1   Humans vary according to age, sex, and population of origin.

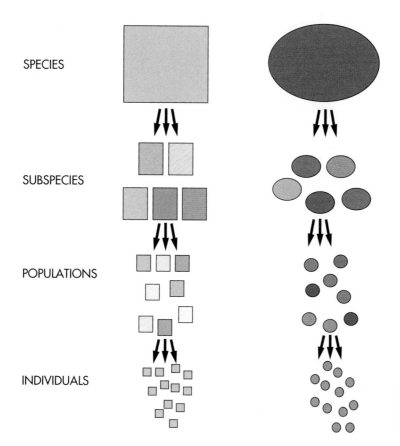

SPECIES

SUBSPECIES

POPULATIONS

INDIVIDUALS

FIGURE 5.2 Species, subspecies, populations, and individuals. Species are reproductively isolated from one another, but all members of a species can interbreed.

Subspecies is another term some biologists use to describe variation below the species level. A subspecies is defined as a group of local populations that share part of the geographic range of a species and can be differentiated from other subspecies based on one or more phenotypic traits (in rare cases, a subspecies could consist of a single local population). Theoretically the identification of a subspecies is done somewhat more formally than the identification of a population. In the biological sciences, the term **race** has been used interchangeably with *subspecies*. As we will see in this chapter, however, the historical use of the race concept in anthropology has not been a simple matter of identifying biological subspecies. Anthropologists have generally subscribed to the idea that human races, like biological subspecies, correspond to groups of populations that are found in or derived from a particular geographic area (Figure 5.2). *Homo sapiens* can be called a **polytypic species**, one that is divided into local populations that differ by one or more phenotypic traits.

All terms used to describe groups of individuals or populations within species share some basic shortcomings. There can be no objective way to decide how much variation (genetic or anatomical) is enough to consider two groups worthy of separate identification, nor is it possible to declare that all individuals in a geographic area are by definition members of a single population. Modern bioanthropological, medical, and genetic researchers also seem to use the term *population* in a pragmatic way. For example, investigations of diseases in the United States often are conducted by measuring the rates in different groups that have biological, historical, and cultural relevance in this setting, such as "American Black" and "American White." An anthropologist investigating the evolution of modern humans as a species might not find these categories useful, nor would a geneticist who is looking at gene flow between Africa and different North and South American populations. However, the issues being examined and the groups accessible for research influence how populations are identified.

subspecies Group of local populations that share part of the geographic range of a species, and can be differentiated from other subspecies based on one or more phenotypic traits.

race In biological taxonomy, same thing as a subspecies; when applied to humans, sometimes incorporates both cultural and biological factors.

polytypic species Species that consist of a number of separate breeding populations, each varying in some genetic trait.

One problem that has arisen repeatedly in the investigation of variation within our species is that in the past the pragmatic concerns of some people were centered on identifying inferior and superior races, and in using "racial science" to reinforce and justify the prevailing social order. The science of anthropology was born in the nineteenth century, when there were incendiary debates about the moral and scientific correctness of slavery. Was it the natural right of a "superior race" to enslave the members of an "inferior race"? In the twentieth century, Nazi Germany used "racial science" to justify the genocide of Jews and Gypsies. Increasingly, *race* is viewed as a strictly cultural or sociological term, denoting group membership by an inconsistently applied range of criteria. Most biological anthropologists thus avoid using the term altogether, for both scientific and historical reasons.

Historical Perspectives on Human Variation

The most basic and universal classification of human variation at the group level is "us" and "them." The field of **ethnobiology** is dedicated to understanding the different systems that cultures have developed to classify the objects and organisms in the world around us (Berlin, 1992; Atran, 1998). One thing that ethnobiology makes clear is that human beings are masters at making up categories and classifications in which to place things. It comes as no surprise that humans have made efforts to classify people as well.

RECORDING HUMAN VARIATION IN PAST CIVILIZATIONS

In the nineteenth century, archaeologists discovered that the ancient Egyptians depicted human variation in some of the hieroglyphic records they left behind (Stanton, 1960). The Egyptians had extensive contact with peoples to their north and south and were well aware of the physical differences between them. As the great antiquity of the Egyptian civilization began to be appreciated, Egyptology figured strongly in two major nineteenth-century racial debates. One involved the origins of races themselves. Did evidence of human variation (and races clearly recognizable to nineteenth-century scientists) in ancient Egypt, which existed not long after the biblical creation (4004 B.C.), indicate that races were created by God and were therefore immutable (see Chapter 1)? The other debate focused on the physical constitution of the Egyptians themselves: Were they "African Negroes" or a more typically Middle Eastern people? Because the Egyptian civilization was viewed as one of the first great Western civilizations, this was considered to be an issue of some importance.

The ancient Greeks also knew of dark-skinned Africans, whom they called *Ethiopians*, a term meaning "scorched ones" in Greek (Brues, 1977). The poet Homer and the historian Herodotus also make reference to Africans in their work. In his *Histories,* Herodotus also made note of nomads from the north, the "Scythians," who had light skin and red or light hair, in obvious contrast to the darker skin and hair of the Greeks themselves, and he was aware of darker-skinned peoples from India. The ancient Romans had at least as extensive knowledge as the Greeks of the variety of peoples that could be found in the western part of Eurasia and north Africa; they even had limited contact with Han Chinese traders who had ventured as far west as Turkestan (Brues, 1977). However, in general the Romans made very little of the biological differences among its subject peoples.

After the collapse of the (western) Roman Empire in the fifth century A.D., the peoples of Europe entered the Dark Ages (as the early Middle Ages were characterized), and their knowledge of the world and peoples beyond their local borders diminished along with many other aspects of learning. It was during this period that tales of monsters and other fantastic beasts took center stage (de Waal Malefijt, 1968). Greek and Roman writers had reported the existence of monstrous sorts of people, with greater and lesser degrees of skepticism. There were tales of cyclops,

ethnobiology   The study of how traditional cultures classify objects and organisms in the natural world.

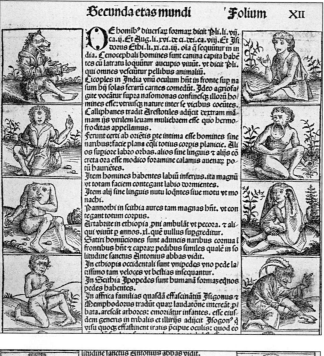

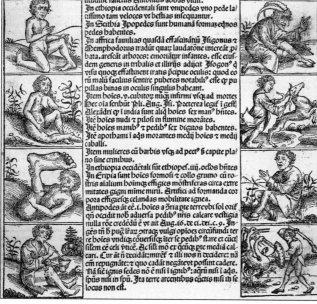

FIGURE 5.3 Monstrous people from distant lands depicted in a fifteenth-century European woodcut.

headless people, and people who hibernated or transformed themselves into wolves during the summer (Figure 5.3). These views persisted until the Renaissance (14th–17th centuries), when slowly, a more rational and evidence-based view of the natural world started to develop. Ancient Greek and Roman scholars were rediscovered during this period, broadening the Renaissance scholars' perspectives on people through time and space.

When the European age of discovery began in 1492, Europeans came into contact with many peoples who were new to them, but the basic question was, Were these actually people? Shakespeare's depiction of the strange and brutish Caliban (an anagram of *cannibal*) in *The Tempest* illustrates a common European view of people from the New World. In 1537, when Pope Paul III declared that American Indians were humans, he established a policy that became church orthodoxy for centuries: that all people, of all races, were the product of a single creation. In later scientific debates, this position became known as *monogenism* (see Chapter 1).

THE MONOGENISM–POLYGENISM DEBATE

During the eighteenth century, Linnaeus introduced a biological classification system that formed the basis of the one we use today (see Chapter 1). In the tenth edition of *Systema Naturae* (1758), Linnaeus provided a new name for our species, *Homo sapiens,* and with it he identified five subspecies or races:

Homo sapiens afer (Africans)

Homo sapiens americanus (American Indians)

Homo sapiens asiaticus (Asians)

Homo sapiens europaeus (Europeans)

Homo sapiens ferus (Wild Men)

Linnaeus also identified a second species, *Homo monstrosus,* which included a variety of human- and apelike forms.

German anatomist Johann Friedrich Blumenbach (1752–1840), in many ways the father of physical anthropology, established one of the first large collections of biological anthropological material, including a large number of skulls, for which he carefully noted their place of origin in order to better understand the biological diversity of the human species. Like Linnaeus, Blumenbach was also a monogenist, and he fully recognized the pitfalls of naming races:

> There is but one species of the genus Man; and all people of every time and climate with which are acquainted, may have originated from one common stock. All national differences in the form and colour of the human body are not more remarkable nor more inconceivable than those by which the varieties of so many other organized bodies, and particularly of domestic animals, arise, as it were, under our eyes. All these differences too, run so insensibly, by so many shades and transitions one into the other, that it is impossible to separate them by any but very arbitrary limits (Blumenbach 1779, 1780, in McCown & Kennedy, 1972).

Despite the fact that he knew the limits were arbitrary, Blumenbach identified five races for the sake of convenience:

Caucasian

Mongolian

Ethiopian

American

Malayan

Blumenbach was the first to use the term *Caucasian* to describe the people of western and southern Eurasia because he believed that a likely source of these peoples was to be found somewhere in the Caucasus region in present-day Georgia (Keith, 1940).

A basic problem for the monogenists was how to explain where the different races came from if they all had a recent common origin. Many believed in a very strong form of **environmentalism**, which held that the human body was biologically quite plastic and that the environment had great power to shape our anatomy. The Reverend Samuel Stanhope Smith (1751–1819), a president of Princeton University and one of the first American writers to address the natural history of human beings, provided an example of the power of the environment to shape anatomy; Smith (1965[1810]) looked to the "blacks in the southern states." Smith claimed that the

environmentalism The view that the environment has great powers to directly shape the anatomy of individual organisms.

field slaves were darker and retained more of their "African" features, both physical and behavioral, than the domestic slaves, who were more "refined" in appearance, with lighter skin and elegant manners. He argued that the effects of civilization on the domestic slaves shaped their anatomy to make them more like their "civilized" masters (of course, Smith did not acknowledge that the domestic slaves might resemble their masters because they were related to them, or that they were chosen because of their "refined" appearance). By the standards of his day, Smith was not a racist; he believed that exposure to European-based civilization would cause people (African or Indians) to take on a European appearance.

In the early nineteenth century, as more information on the diversity of humanity became available, many scientists found it harder to believe that all of the racial diversity they observed could have arisen within the biblical time frame. Samuel George Morton (1799–1851), a Quaker anatomist and physician from Philadelphia, was one of the most prominent advocates of polygenism, or multiple creations or origins (Stanton, 1960). He argued that given only 6,000 years of Earth history and the fact that different races were represented in ancient Egyptian monuments, there was not enough time for the differentiation to occur. The polygenists rejected the idea that the environment had almost unlimited powers to reshape the human body. By the mid-nineteenth century, the polygenist position became increasingly accepted by serious scientists.

The issue of slavery often was associated with debates about racial origins, although not in a consistent way (Figure 5.4). In England, early anthropological societies were split on the basis of their adherence to monogenesis or polygenesis, a split that also reflected differing views on the equality of races and the legitimacy of slavery (Stocking, 1987). In the United States, before the Civil War (1861–1865), although the origin of races became an issue in the abolition debates, advocates of polygenism and monogenism did not consistently line up on one side of the debate or the other (Haller, 1970).

After the publication of Darwin's *On the Origin of Species* in 1859, the polygenism–monogenism debate subsided. To some extent, the evolutionary viewpoint could be made to accommodate aspects of both positions. Clearly, all humans were members of one species that shared a common evolutionary history, a viewpoint that was consistent with monogenism. On the other hand, the different races could be viewed in terms of their own evolutionary histories, and it was not difficult to construct hypothetical evolutionary scenarios that underscored racial differences and the "evolution" of racial inequality.

FIGURE 5.4 This watercolor depicts the miserable conditions Africans endured as they made the passage across the Atlantic and into slavery in the New World. In the mid-nineteenth century, debates about the abolition of slavery were often focused on concepts of racial origins.

RACE AND RACISM IN THE TWENTIETH CENTURY

Throughout the twentieth century, the scientific study of human population variation was shaped by political and cultural forces. Of course, this has always been the case, but an increased recognition of the impact of these factors on "objective" science has developed, especially since the end of World War II (1939–1945). There has also been an increasing awareness of **racism**, scientific and otherwise. At one level, racism is simply prejudice against a person based on his or her racial heritage. The basis of such prejudice is the idea that important qualities of an individual (such as intellect, physical ability, and temperament) are biologically determined by his or her membership in a racial group. *Stereotyping,* in which the qualities of an individual are projected onto a larger group or vice versa, is also an important component of racism, especially of the more "everyday" variety.

racism A prejudicial belief that members of one ethnic group are superior in some way to those of another.

Racial issues were of critical importance, in different ways, in three of the principal nations involved in World War II: Germany, Japan, and the United States. In Depression-era Germany, the Nazi party rose to power on the basis of an ideology that was centered on a celebration of *Aryanism*, a form of racism that was, in effect, a mythical rendering of the racial history of northern Europeans. The Aryan myth celebrated the "true" German as being the member of a "superior race" and was used to justify the subjugation and ultimately the extermination of "inferior races," such as Jews and Gypsies (Roma). Nazi ideology tapped into and amplified racial prejudices that had long existed, and the Nazis themselves acted on these impulses on an unprecedented scale. In prewar Japan, the imperial government and military also fostered an ideology of racial superiority, focused on the godlike status of the emperor (Bix, 2000). Some Japanese leaders were particularly attuned to racial issues in conflicts between Japan and Western powers, arguing that they were fueled in part by Western concepts of Japanese racial inferiority. Japanese imperialists justified their invasions of the Chinese province of Manchuria and other Asian nations as being in part a war of liberation from non-Asian colonizers, while asserting their superiority over their subject peoples.

The United States in the first half of the twentieth century was a fundamentally racist country. The conquest of the Native Americans was complete, and their demise was celebrated in the literature and films of the time. Blacks and Whites lived separate and unequal lives; the second-class status of African Americans was reinforced legally by Jim Crow laws and extralegally by lynchings and other violent means of coercion. Immigration laws restricted the entry of "undesirables", such as Asians and southern, central, and eastern Europeans. During World War II, Japanese Americans and Japanese nationals living in the continental United States were interned in "relocation" camps for the duration of the war. After the war, advocates of civil rights and racial equality recognized how ironic it was that the United States had helped to defeat two racist regimes while maintaining racist policies and cultural attitudes at home.

CHANGING ATTITUDES TOWARD RACE IN ANTHROPOLOGY

Anthropologist Franz Boas and his followers instigated a reappraisal of the race concept early in the twentieth century. Boas was a general anthropologist who conducted research in the cultural, biological, and linguistic realms. Although he did not reject the race concept, he took great pains to emphasize that biology, culture, psychology, and language needed to be carefully studied in any group so that they may be understood in local terms. In *The Mind of Primitive Man* (1911/1938) Boas argued that there was little evidence of a strong relationship between racial biology and cultural achievement. Boas's biological work focused on craniometry and **anthropometry**, the measurement of different aspects of the body, such as stature or skin, and culminated in his large-scale study comparing head and body form in immigrants to the United States and their U.S.-born children (Boas, 1912/1940; Allen, 1989). The differences he observed between parents and offspring led Boas to emphasize that there was a good deal of biological plasticity within "racial" types. Boas had a much softer view of race than many of his contemporaries. Although the validity of Boas's work on bodily form changes in immigrants continues to be debated (Sparks & Jantz, 2002; Gravlee et al., 2003), and his own particular type of cultural anthropology goes in and out of fashion, there can be no doubt that the critique of race and racism that Boas initiated was one of the greatest scientific achievements of the twentieth century.

A tireless opponent of the use of the term *race* was anthropologist and writer Ashley Montagu (1905–1999). Montagu was the principal author of the United Nations Statement on Race (1950), a far-reaching and influential document in which a powerful argument was made that the "racial science" of the Nazis—and

anthropometry The measurement of different aspects of the body, such as stature or skin color.

even the term *race*—had no scientific validity. Although he did not invent it, Montagu was a proponent of the term *ethnic group* to describe human populations (Montagu, 1974). Ethnic groups are separated from one another primarily by social barriers, which may lead to biological differentiation or be a marker of biological difference. Although the term has come into widespread usage, in many cases as a replacement for *race*, it is far from ideal for use in biologically oriented research because it explicitly incorporates sociocultural factors in group identification.

Today, biological anthropologists do not typically use the term *race*, preferring almost always to use the term *population*. But if biological anthropologists do not use the term *race*, does that mean that races do not exist? In a formal sense, the answer is yes, but the word *race* is commonly used every day, by all sorts of people, in all kinds of contexts. These people are talking about something, and other people understand what they are referring to, so in that sense races must exist. Take "racial profiling" in law enforcement, for example. Say that a police force has a policy of pulling over young African American men when they drive through certain neighborhoods in a community. We can be fairly certain that the police force is not pulling over young men who are predominantly of Scandinavian origin. It *is* possible to sort Scandinavians from Africans or, for that matter, to sort Chinese from Cherokees or Lapplanders from Inuit people. Population-level biological differences do exist and in some cases are quite significant.

> *The American Anthropological Association believes its Statement on "Race" reflects the perspective of the majority of anthropologists. It can be read at http://www.aaanet.org/stmts/racepp.htm.*

DECONSTRUCTING RACIAL FEATURES

A few key traits have loomed large in how both scientists and laypeople have defined different racial groups. Even if the race concept itself is not considered valid in biological anthropology, what about the features people have been focusing on for so many years (Figures 5.5 and 5.6)? What is their biological relevance or irrelevance?

ethnic group   A human group defined in terms of sociological, cultural, and linguistic traits.

FIGURE 5.5 An 1827 portrait by George Catlin of Eeh-Nis-Kin (Crystal Stone), a Blackfoot woman.
Source: George Catlin (1796–1872), Eeh-nis-kim, Crystal Stone, Wife of the Chief. 1832. Oil on Canvas. 29″ × 24″. Smithsonian American Art Museum, Washington, DC/Art Resource, NY.

FIGURE 5.6 A nineteenth-century Japanese portrait of Commodore Matthew Perry, who "opened up" Japan in 1854.

Skin Color   Skin color is perhaps the most important morphological feature in cultural racial categories. Variation in human skin color is of no small biological significance. Because humans do not have fur, our skin is more directly exposed to the environment, and skin color probably is influenced by natural selection, as we will discuss later in this chapter. On a global scale, however, skin color is not a particularly good indicator of geographic origins. Populations from different parts of the world may have similar skin colors because they share a common environmental feature, namely the intensity of sunlight exposure. Very dark-skinned populations can be found in Africa, India, and Melanesia, but these populations do not share a recent common ancestry compared with other populations. The amount of variation in skin color of people classified as "White Americans" is substantial and reflects the diverse population origins (in terms of sunlight exposure, among other things) of this "race," which ranges from the Middle East and Mediterranean regions to the far north of Europe.

Eye Form   North and East Asians, as well as some of their descendant populations in the New World, have a high frequency of a morphological feature known as an *epicanthic fold*. This is the classic racial marker of "Oriental" or "Mongoloid" populations, although it can appear in individuals from other parts of the world. The epicanthic fold is a small flap of skin extending from the eyelid to the bridge of the nose. It has no known biological function. Alice Brues (1977) suggests that it is a secondary anatomical feature that results from a combination of a fatty eyelid and a low nasal bridge, both of which, she argues, may reflect adaptations to cold. She points out that epicanthic folds are more common in women than men in some Native American populations and in children rather than adults in European populations; both patterns may be a function of the relative development of the nasal bridge.

Hair Color and Form   Human populations vary significantly in the color and form of the hair. There are no generally accepted functional explanations for why hair color, form, or thickness varies. It is clearly a polygenically inherited trait. Hair color is determined in part by the same substance as skin color (melanin), so it is no surprise that the two are correlated. However, some dark-skinned Australian aborigine populations have a large number of individuals with blond hair, especially when they are children. This may indicate that a different set of alleles may be governing hair color in these populations than in others (Molnar, 2002). Hair form varies from straight to tightly spiraled or woolly. Again, although there may be differences in the insulation properties of straight and spiraled hair, arguments can be made that this would be an advantage in either warm or cold climates. African and Melanesian populations both have woolly hair, but at a microscopic level their hair forms are quite different, indicating separate genetic origins.

Head Shape   In the 1840s, Swedish anatomist Anders Retzius (1796–1860) introduced a statistic, the cranial or cephalic index (CI), to characterize the shape of the human skull. The CI is simply the width of the skull divided by the length multiplied by 100. Skulls that are narrow, or *dolichocephalic*, have CIs in the 70s, whereas those that are rounder, with CIs in the 80s, are called *brachycephalic*. Despite the fact that the CI was used to categorize skulls (and people) as "longheaded" or "rounded-headed," all normal skulls are longer than they are wide. Retzius's work introduced cranial shape as a widely used marker of racial affiliation. Some racist scientists of the late nineteenth and early twentieth centuries seemed to put an inordinate amount of emphasis on the shape of the skull as a key racial feature. One reason for this may have been that the CI was something that was not immediately obvious and required scientific measurement to be obtained, which was important as precise measurements were incorporated into essentially folk racial typologies. Although racial schemes based (in part) on cranial shape are not considered valid today, it remains true that human populations show substantial variation in cranial shape and other cranial measures. In an analysis of a large number of skulls from populations around the world, Kenneth Beals and colleagues (1984) found that there is a relationship between skull shape and climate, with skull breadth increasing in colder climates. From a volume-to-surface ratio perspective, this makes sense in terms of the conservation of heat in a cold climate, which will be discussed later in the chapter.

Population Genetics

The field of **population genetics** is concerned with uncovering genetic variation within and between populations of organisms. In Chapter 4 we discussed several evolutionary processes, such as natural selection, gene flow, and genetic drift, which are all studied by population geneticists. Studying the dynamic distribution of alleles across populations can require complex mathematical tools (Cavalli-Sforza et al., 1994), many of which are derived from the Hardy–Weinberg equilibrium (see Chapter 4 and Appendix C). Although discussing these tools in detail is beyond the scope of this text, we will consider some of the results they have produced.

Population genetics is concerned primarily with **microevolution**, or evolutionary processes that occur within a species (in contrast to *macroevolution*; see Chapter 4). With increasingly sophisticated molecular biological techniques now available, the line between microevolutionary and macroevolutionary studies is becoming less clear-cut.

POLYMORPHISMS: ABO AND OTHER BLOOD TYPE SYSTEMS

If we look at a population and find that there are at least two alleles present for a given gene, and the alleles are both present at a frequency greater than 1%, then we can say that the population is **polymorphic** for that gene. The term is also used to describe variation at the more observable phenotypic level (see Chapter 4). For example, in a population where both blue- and brown-eyed people live, we can say that it is polymorphic for eye color, assuming that it is a genetic feature and that both phenotypes are present at a frequency of at least 1%. Many protein polymorphisms have no phenotypic effect other than the fact that they are slightly different versions of the same protein. The 1% figure is used as a cutoff because it is substantially above the level you would expect if a rare allele or phenotype were present simply because of the occurrence of mutations.

In Chapter 3 we discussed the ABO blood type system, which is a classic example of a polymorphic genetic system. Although Karl Landsteiner discovered the ABO system in 1901 (for which he received the 1930 Nobel Prize in Medicine), it was not until 1919 that Polish physicians Ludwik and Hanka Hirszfeld published the first report on "racial" variation in the ABO system. They did this study at the end of World War I, on the Macedonian battlefront, where soldiers from Europe, the Middle East, Africa, and southern Asia could be tested. It is interesting to note that ABO distribution initially was of little interest to many anthropologists because it did not correlate particularly well with traditional notions of racial classification (W. C. Boyd, 1950), a fact pointed out by the Hirszfelds themselves. In *clinal* maps of the distribution of the ABO alleles throughout the world's populations are presented. A **cline** represents the distribution of a genotypic or a phenotypic characteristic(s) across geographical space.

The clinal maps in Figure 5.7 on page 132 clearly illustrate that the ABO system is highly polymorphic across the species but that some populations are essentially monomorphic for type O, including several South American Indian groups. The allele frequencies for A and B never exceed 50% and typically are much lower than this. High A frequencies are found in some European populations, in some North American Indian groups, in Inuit living in arctic North America and Greenland, and in

population genetics   The study of genetic variation within and between groups of organisms.

microevolution   The study of evolutionary phenomena that occur within a species.

polymorphic   Two or more distinct phenotypes (at the genetic or anatomical levels) that exist within a population.

cline   The distribution of a trait or allele across geographical space.

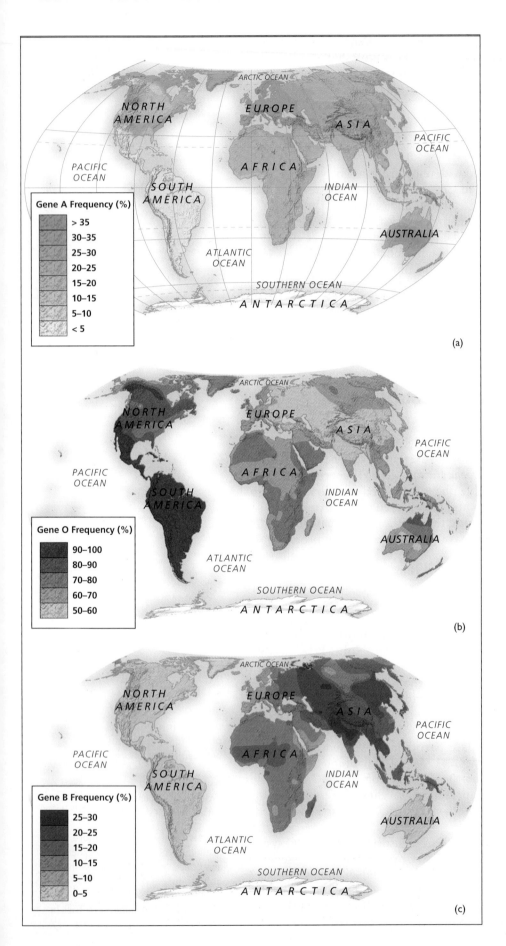

FIGURE 5.7 Clinal maps of ABO allele distributions in the indigenous populations of the world. (a) Frequency distribution of the A allele. (b) Frequency distribution of the O allele. (c) Frequency distribution of the B allele.
Source: Adapted from Mourant et al. (1976). *The Distribution of Human Blood Groups (2nd Edition).* Oxford University Press, London.

some Australian aborigine tribes. High B frequencies are found in central Asia, especially in the Himalayan region, declining gradually as one moves away from this high-frequency zone. There are also pockets of high B frequency in sub-Saharan Africa. The B allele is almost entirely absent from the Americas or Australia. One worldwide estimate for the frequencies of the three alleles is 62.5% O, 21.5% A, and 16.0% B (MacArthur & Penrose in Harrison et al., 1988).

The distribution of ABO alleles in populations raises some interesting evolutionary issues. Why are the polymorphisms maintained in different populations? Why do we not see more alleles at fixation in different populations because of the effects of genetic drift or bottlenecks? Why are the A and B allele frequencies always less than 50%? Recent research on A and B antigens strongly suggests that natural selection has influenced their population distribution in some way (Koda et al., 2001). Over the years, several investigators have suggested that infectious disease plays a key role in the distribution of ABO alleles in different populations. Robert Seymour and his colleagues (2004) recently suggested that a balance between A and B alleles is maintained in populations with a heavy load of bacterial disease, whereas O would be expected to predominate in populations that are more vulnerable to viral disease. Their mathematical genetic models suggest that the relative frequencies of A, B, and O alleles are maintained by the relative impact of bacterial and viral diseases in a population.

Maternal–Fetal Incompatibility   Another factor that influences the distribution of ABO alleles in a population arises out of the immune response of a pregnant woman and how it influences the health of her fetus. **Maternal–fetal incompatibility** occurs when a mother has type O blood and her infant has type A, B, or AB or when a woman has type A and the infant has type B and vice versa. In the case of a type O mother and a type B infant (the father must carry a B allele), because the mother does not possess the B antigen on her red blood cells, she will make anti-B antibodies upon exposure to the fetus's blood. For much of the pregnancy, the maternal and fetal blood do not mix; however, at birth the mother is almost always exposed to fetal blood through ruptures in tissues caused by the delivery or separation of the placenta from the uterine wall. Upon exposure to the B antigen, the mother's immune system is primed to produce anti-B antibodies. In subsequent pregnancies, the red blood cells of fetuses that carry the B allele are subject to attack by the maternal anti-B antibodies, which can cross the placental barrier. When the infant is born, he or she can be anemic (usually mildly so) because of the reduction in the number of oxygen-carrying red blood cells. This is known as *hemolytic anemia*. There is some evidence that ABO incompatibilities can have a damaging affect early in pregnancy, resulting in a higher rate of spontaneous abortion (Bottini et al., 2001).

The **rhesus (Rh) system**, another blood group, was originally identified by using antibodies made against rhesus macaque red blood cells. It is of particular clinical importance because maternal–fetal incompatibility in this system leads to the development of a much more severe form of anemia in the newborn, resulting in a disease called *erythroblastosis fetalis,* than does ABO incompatibility (one reason for this is that unlike the Rh factor, the A and B antigens are expressed in tissues other than the red blood cells, so there are fewer maternal antibodies available to attack the fetal red blood cells). The genetics of the Rh system are complex and involve three major genes with at least two alleles apiece (Cavalli-Sforza et al., 1994). For our purposes we can concentrate on one of these loci, which has two alleles, D and d. Individuals who are homozygous DD or heterozygous Dd are called *Rh-positive*, and those who are homozygous dd are *Rh-negative* (Figure 5.8 on page 134). Similar to cases in which the mother is type O and the infant is type A, B, or AB, maternal–fetal incompatibility arises when the mother is Rh-negative and the infant is Rh-positive. The first pregnancy usually is fine, but subsequent incompatible pregnancies can lead to the development of severe

maternal–fetal incompatibility   Occurs when the mother produces antibodies against an antigen (for example, a red blood cell surface protein) expressed in the fetus that she does not possess.

rhesus (Rh) system   Blood type system that can cause hemolytic anemia of the newborn through maternal–fetal incompatibility if the mother is Rh-negative and the child is Rh-positive.

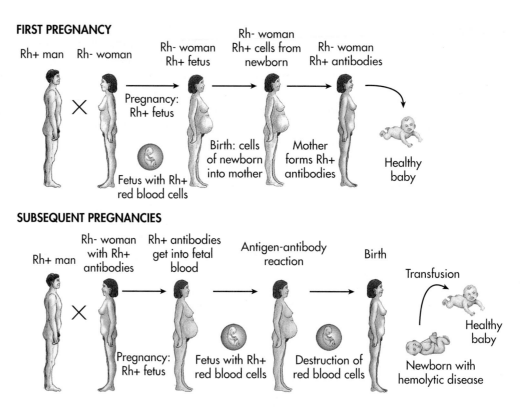

FIGURE 5.8   Maternal–fetal incompatibility in the Rh system.

hemolytic anemia in the newborn, which may necessitate blood transfusions. It has been found that giving the mother anti-D antibodies early in pregnancy can suppress her immunological response: The anti-D antibodies "intercept" the fetal red blood cells before the mother's immune system is exposed to them. This prevents development of anemia in the at-risk newborn.

Maternal–fetal incompatibility in both the ABO and Rh systems influences the distribution of their alleles in populations. For example, in the Rh system, only heterozygous offspring of an Rh-negative mother and an Rh-positive father are at risk of developing anemia. In a traditional culture, these infants would be at great risk of dying without reproducing. Simple genetic models indicate that in a population that has a D allele frequency of 50% or more, the d allele eventually will be lost. The opposite case is also true if the d allele frequency reaches 50% (assuming that no selection or other evolutionary factors are at play) (Cavalli-Sforza & Bodmer, 1971/1999). Because of factors such as genetic drift, founder effect, and genetic bottlenecks, high rates of Rh-negative or Rh-positive individuals could evolve. However, only one population has a majority of Rh-negative individuals: the Basques of southern France and northern Spain. The Basque population was historically isolated and is well known for having a language unrelated to any other in Europe. Although one might predict that Rh-negative alleles should go to fixation, there is enough admixture with the predominantly Rh-positive surrounding populations that this may be unlikely.

The Human Leukocyte Antigen (HLA) System   Besides the ABO and Rh systems, several other blood systems are used in population genetic studies. These include the Diego, Duffy, Kell, Kidd, Lewis, Lutheran, and MNS systems. A different class of blood group markers is formed by the **human leukocyte antigen (HLA) system**. These antigens are proteins found on the surface of white rather than red blood cells. There are many classes of white blood cells, all of which are critical in the immune response (an elevated white blood cell count indicates that the

human leukocyte antigen (HLA) system   Class of blood group markers formed by proteins expressed on the surface of white blood cells (leukocytes).

body is fighting an infection). As most people know, the ABO antigens are critical for determining who can donate blood to whom. The HLA system is critical in matching donors and hosts for organ and skin transplants. Some HLA alleles are associated with protection from a variety of infectious diseases, including malaria, HIV, hepatitis B, and bacterial diseases (Cooke & Hill, 2001). The high degree of variability within the HLA system is evidence in itself that natural selection and other nonrandom evolutionary forces have been critical in shaping the distribution of its alleles (Meyer & Thomson, 2001).

GENE FLOW AND PROTEIN POLYMORPHISMS

Because allele frequencies for countless proteins vary from population to population, genetic polymorphisms can be used to look at patterns of gene flow and migration from one population to another. For example, because the A and B alleles are so rare in indigenous South American populations, the ABO system can be used to measure gene flow or admixture with European or African populations that have migrated to the region since 1500 A.D. This is despite the fact that on a worldwide basis, there is much overlap in the distribution of ABO alleles in different populations.

The history of the human species has been characterized by events involving migration and gene flow. Even when there are cultural prohibitions against mating with others outside the group, there is ample evidence that such matings occur. Official written records do not always indicate the scope of admixture between distinct cultural groups living in the same area.

Gene Flow in Contemporary Populations   Countless gene flow studies have been done on populations throughout the world. For example, the complex origins of the Hungarian people, who live in central Europe at the crossroads between Asia and Europe, have recently been examined using a variety of classic (protein) markers (Guglielmino et al., 2000). One Hungarian ethnic group, the Örség, was found to be particularly closely related to populations from the Ural Mountains in Central Asia. Hungarian is a non–Indo-European language of Uralic origin, and these results confirmed oral histories and traditions that linked the Örség to populations that had migrated from the Ural region in the ninth century.

Numerous studies have also been done to trace the complex genetic history of Jewish populations in western Eurasia and Africa. The migrational history of Jews is complex, dating back to the *diaspora* or dispersal of the Jews from ancient Palestine to Babylonian exile in 586 B.C. The diaspora became a permanent feature of Jewish life and included events such as the expulsion of Jews from Spain in 1492. Gene flow studies have produced conflicting results, some indicating substantial admixture between Jewish and other populations located in an area and others indicating much less gene flow. More recently, Y-chromosome markers have provided new insights into the histories of some Jewish populations. The Lemba, or "Black Jews," of southern Africa have a long oral tradition of Jewish ancestry (a claim that has been regarded with more than a little skepticism). Consistent with this tradition, genetic studies indicate that about half of the Y-chromosomes in the Lemba population are of Semitic origin (Figure 5.9 on page 136) (Spurdle & Jenkins, 1996). Michael Hammer and colleagues (2000) looked at Y-chromosome **haplotypes** in Jewish and non-Jewish men from populations throughout Europe, Africa (including a Lemba sample), and the Middle East. Haplotypes are combinations of alleles (or, at the sequence level, of mutations) that are found together in an individual. In many cases, combinations of alleles or mutations are more informative than alleles or mutations considered singly. Hammer and colleagues found that the Jewish populations closely resembled non-Jewish Middle Eastern populations, with whom they are presumed to share a common ancestry, in the distribution of Y-chromosome haplotypes, more so than non-Jewish populations near which they may currently be living. Thus Jewish populations, despite numerous migrations

Some HLA alleles are associated with increased risk of developing autoimmune disorders, such insulin-dependent diabetes and lupus.

haplotypes   Combinations of alleles (or at the sequence level, mutations) that are found together in an individual.

FIGURE 5.9 Members of the Lemba ethnic group from southern Africa.

Duffy blood group   Red blood cell system useful for studying admixture between African- and European-derived populations.

across a broad geographic area, appear to be more similar to one another and to non-Jewish Middle Eastern populations than to other populations, at least in terms of the Y-chromosome.

Several gene flow studies have been done in African American populations to assess the contribution of European alleles in the composition of their genetic structures. Although for much of U.S. history admixture between African and European Americans has been strongly proscribed, gene flow studies indicate that it was not an unusual occurrence. A classic genetic study using a **Duffy blood group** allele that is largely absent in Africa but common in European populations showed that European admixture in five African American populations ranged from 4% in Charleston, South Carolina, to 26% in Detroit (Reed, 1969). In a more recent study using autosomal DNA markers, mtDNA haplotypes, and Y-chromosome polymorphisms, Esteban Parra and colleagues (1998) confirmed these high rates of admixture. Looking at nine communities, they found admixture rates ranging from 11.6% in Charleston to 22.5% in New Orleans (Table 5.1). A sample from a Jamaican population showed a European proportion of only 6.8%, indicating a substantial difference between Afro-Caribbean and African American communities. The mtDNA (maternally inherited) and the Y-chromosome (paternally inherited) data indicated that gene flow from European to African American populations was strongly sex-biased, with men making a substantially greater contribution than women. This comes as no surprise, given that sexual contacts between male slave owners and female slaves were not uncommon.

Morphological Features and Gene Flow   Morphological features (such as eye or hair color) are rarely used today to study gene flow between populations. There are several reasons for this: Many morphological features have complex genetics, thus making patterns of inheritance difficult to discern; their expression in an individual may be highly subject to environmental factors during development; and more so than genetic markers, morphological markers may be subject to the forces of natural selection, leading, for example, to convergent evolution. Of course,

TABLE 5.1	European Genetic Contribution to African American and Jamaican Populations
Location	**Percentage**
Detroit	16.3
Maywood, Illinois	18.8
New York	19.8
Philadelphia	13.0
Pittsburgh	20.2
Baltimore	15.5
Charleston, South Carolina	11.6
New Orleans	22.5
Houston	16.9
Jamaica	6.8

Source: Parra et al. (1998).

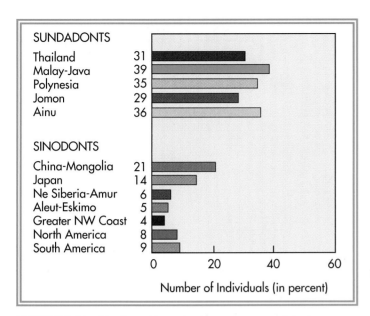

FIGURE 5.10 Number of lower molar cusps is one of the features used to distinguish sundadonts from sinodonts. Graph shows that four-cusped molars are more common in sundadont populations rather than sinodont populations.

even with our ability to recover ancient DNA, morphological features may be all we have to study gene flow in past populations.

One set of morphological features, dental traits, has been extensively used to study gene flow in skeletal populations. Some discrete dental traits appear to be transmitted in a simple genetic fashion, are resistant to environmental factors (except wear), and can be easily examined in large numbers of skeletal specimens. Christy Turner (1989, 1990) has argued that a constellation of dental features, known collectively as *sinodonty,* links northern Asian populations with the populations of the New World. Not all North American populations have high frequencies of sinodonty, but because it is absent elsewhere, it provides evidence of a migrational link or gene flow between the northern Asian and Native American populations. Southeast Asian, Australian aborigine, and Ainu (aboriginal Japanese) populations exhibit a different dental pattern, which Turner calls *sundadonty.* Turner used eight dental features to distinguish sinodonts from sundadonts. For example, shovel-shaped incisors are more common among sinodonts than sundadonts, and four-cusped lower molars (cusps are the bumps on the chewing surfaces of molars; five is the typical number) are significantly more common in sundadonts than sinodonts (Figure 5.10). Turner places the origins of sinodonty at 18,000 years ago or earlier in northern China.

POLYMORPHISMS AND PHYLOGENETIC STUDIES

Allele frequencies, haplotype frequencies, and DNA and protein sequence information can all be used to construct an evolutionary tree, or **phylogeny**, relating populations (if frequency data are used) or individuals from different populations (if sequence data are used). The statistical mathematics underlying the construction of these trees is beyond the scope of this text, but the basic principles are not.

Constructing a Phylogenetic Tree   Any phylogenetic tree aims to cluster closely related populations together compared to less closely related populations (Figure 5.11 on page 138). Closely related populations share a *branch:* a lineage or a clade (see Chapter 4). Branching points, or *nodes,* in the tree represent the separation or division of any pair (or groups) of populations. For example, a particular genetic

phylogeny An evolutionary tree indicating relatedness and divergence of taxonomic groups.

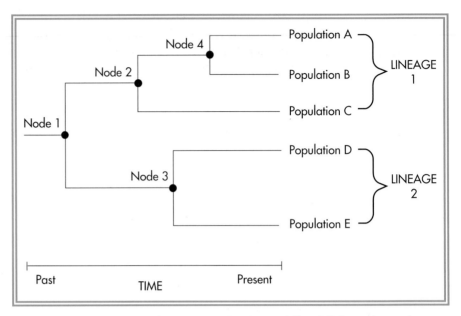

FIGURE 5.11   A generic phylogenetic tree. Populations A, B, and C share a lineage (or clade) and are more closely related to each other than populations D and E of lineage 2. Populations A and B share a more recent common ancestor (at node 4) with each other than they do with population C. The last time all five populations shared a common ancestor was at node 1.

Unlike Lamarck, Darwin recognized that evolution implied that widely divergent organisms shared a common ancestry. Darwin drew tree-like diagrams in his earliest private notebooks to illustrate phylogenetic relationships.

mutation may be found in some populations but not others; possessing that particular mutation could serve as the basis for putting those populations together on one branch of the tree separate from the others. The node in the tree where that branch begins represents when the ancestral population possessing the mutation split off from the other populations. Longer branches and deeper nodes indicate that more change has occurred along the evolving lineages, and thus that more time has elapsed since the separation of the two populations (assuming the rate of genetic change is relatively constant). A phylogenetic tree produced from a genetic dataset should incorporate the fewest number of evolutionary steps or events; in other words, the tree should be constructed parsimoniously (see Occam's razor in Chapter 4).

Making a phylogenetic tree that incorporates a large amount of genetic information from several different populations can be quite a complex task. Phylogenetic trees are not precise reconstructions of evolutionary events. They are hypotheses about the way evolution happened, inferred from genetic or other kinds of data collected from extant or extinct populations. Even a tree that is statistically rigorous may be subject to different kinds of interpretation.

A Genetic Tree of the World's Populations   Geneticist Luigi Luca Cavalli-Sforza and colleagues (1994) provided an extensive analysis of the distribution of 120 alleles (29 of which come from the HLA system) in forty-two populations throughout the world. The selection of these forty-two populations was based on several criteria, not least important of which was the availability of genetic data for inclusion in the analysis. They provide a good sample of the world's populations as they were distributed at the arbitrary cutoff date of 1492 A.D. The phylogenetic tree of these forty-two populations divides into nine major clusters: Africans (sub-Saharan), Caucasoids (Europeans), Caucasoids (non-Europeans), northern Mongoloids (excluding arctic populations), northeast Asian arctic populations, southern Mongoloids (mainland and island Southeast Asia) (Figure 5.12), New Guineans and Australians, inhabitants of the minor Pacific islands, and Americans.

Although slightly different trees result depending on the method used and how the populations are constructed, some basic conclusions are possible. First, the deep separation of the African populations from others is an indication that this reflects the earliest genetic event in human history. This event could have happened outside Africa, although paleontological evidence indicates that modern humans evolved first in Africa, followed by migration to other parts of the world (see Chapter 14). A northern Eurasian cluster clearly includes both Caucasoid and northeast Asian (including arctic and American) populations. The relationships between Australians, New Guineans, and Southeast Asians are less clear-cut. One tree groups the Southeast Asians with the Australians and New Guineans, and another places them as an early split from the northern Eurasian cluster. Given the complex patterns of population movements throughout Southeast Asia and Melanesia into Polynesia and Micronesia, it is not surprising that unambiguous clusters are not always possible.

Polymorphisms and Natural Selection in Human Populations

Many polymorphisms in human populations have come about as a result of genetic drift or gene flow, but it is also clear that some have been shaped by natural selection. An obvious example of negative selection can be seen in maternal–fetal incompatibility, which has led to polymorphisms in the ABO and Rh blood type systems. But positive selection for new genetic variants has also shaped the distribution of some human polymorphisms. One example of this involves the ability of some people to digest milk. Although many of us take this for granted and entirely "natural," many people around the world do not find drinking milk to be a particularly healthy or enjoyable experience. Positive natural selection has shaped this polymorphism, which has arisen only in the past few thousand years.

THE EVOLUTION OF LACTOSE TOLERANCE

One of the main characteristics of mammals is that newborns and young animals suckle milk from their mothers. After weaning, young mammals are no longer directly dependent on their mothers for food, and they never drink milk again. The main carbohydrate in mammal milk is a sugar called *lactose*. Lactose is actually a *disaccharide*—or a sugar made up of two smaller sugars—composed of

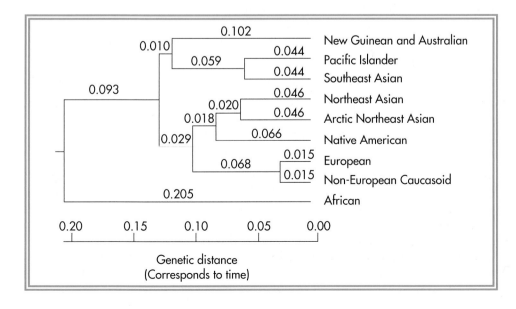

FIGURE 5.12 Phylogenetic tree based on the distribution of 120 alleles in 42 populations from around the world, clustered into 9 major groups. *Source:* Cavalli-Sforza et al. (1994).

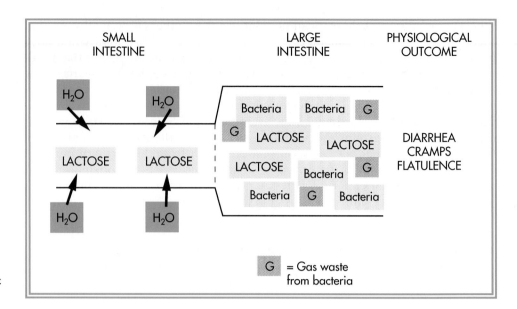

FIGURE 5.13 Physiological effects of the accumulation of lactose in the intestines of a lactose-intolerant individual.

Perception of symptoms associated with lactose intolerance vary considerably among individuals who are lactose malabsorbers.

the monosaccharides glucose and galactose. In order for lactose to be metabolized, it must first be split into glucose and galactose; this is done by an enzyme called *lactase,* which is present in the small intestine of most young mammals. As mammals get older, their bodies shut down production of lactase, so older mammals cannot digest lactose. As adults, they are *lactose malabsorbers.* Indeed, many older mammals suffer gastric distress if they consume milk, with symptoms such as abdominal distention, flatulence, cramps, acidic stools, and diarrhea. These digestive problems are caused by the accumulation of lactose in the small intestine, which changes the osmotic activity in that part of the gut, leading to an influx of fluid (that is, diarrhea), and excess lactose in the large intestine, which is fermented by bacteria in the colon (that is, gas production). An individual who has these symptoms after consuming milk products is **lactose intolerant** (Figure 5.13).

It was once thought that humans were unique among mammals in the continued production of lactase through adulthood, which allows humans to digest lactose (milk products) as adults. However, research in the 1960s on European and African Americans demonstrated that only *some* humans were lactose tolerant as adults (Cuatrecasas et al., 1965). Indeed, as more research was done, it was discovered that most people in the world are lactose intolerant as adults and that lactase production is a highly polymorphic trait across the human species (Allen & Cheer, 1996). Table 5.2 presents lactose absorption rates for populations throughout the world. High-absorber populations are concentrated in Europe or in populations with a high degree of European admixture (such as Polynesian populations in New Zealand). In addition, some African ethnic groups, such as the Tussi, Fulani, and Hima, also have high rates of lactose tolerance (the African figures in the table are for countries, not ethnic groups). Other populations, such as many in Asia, some African, and many Native American groups, have very low frequencies of lactose absorbers.

The Genetics of Lactase Production   The genetics of lactase production is reasonably well understood. The lactase gene is located on chromosome 2. Continued lactase production in adulthood is caused by a dominant allele (called the *lactase persistence allele,* or *LCT*P*), so heterozygous and homozygous individuals with this allele can produce lactase. The lactase enzymes produced by lactose tolerant and lactose intolerant adults are identical in structure and function, although there are many "silent mutations" in the base pair sequence that can be

lactose intolerant   The inability to digest lactose, the sugar found in milk; most adult mammals (including humans) are lactose intolerant as adults.

used for phylogenetic studies of this locus (Hollox et al., 2001). Variants found in regions several thousand base pairs from the lactase gene differentiate lactase persistent from lactase nonpersistent individuals (Enattah et al., 2002). These regions clearly have a regulatory function (as yet undetermined) in the timing of lactase synthesis.

Explanations for the Lactase Polymorphism   Lactose tolerant individuals are found at high frequency in populations with a long history of dairying and using milk products (Simoons, 1970; McCracken, 1971; Durham, 1991). There has been strong selection for LCT*P in these populations. In nondairying populations, the distribution of haplotypes associated with lactase nonpersistence are consistent with evolution primarily by genetic drift (Hollox et al., 2001). The *cultural historical hypothesis,* suggested by Simoons and McCracken independently, proposes that in populations where animals were domesticated and milk products used (dating back to about 9000 B.C. in the Middle East), there has been strong selection for lactose-tolerant individuals. Milk is a valuable food providing both carbohydrates and proteins, and in an environment where other nutritional resources might be scarce, individuals who could digest milk as adults would have a substantial

TABLE 5.2 Lactose Absorption Rates in Different Populations	
Population	**Percentage Lactose Absorbers**
AFRICA	
Bantu (West Africa)	4
Watutsi (East Africa)	83
Nilotic (Sudan)	39
South Africa	17
ASIA	
South India	33
Japan	0
Thailand	2
Taiwan Chinese	0
EUROPE	
Britain	94
Germany	85
Sweden	100
Italy	25–50
NORTH AMERICA	
European American	80–94
African American	25–30
Apache	0
Chippewa	30
PACIFIC	
Fiji	0
New Zealand Maori	36
Australian Aborigines	16
Papua New Guinea	11
Sources: Allen & Cheer (1996), Molnar (2002).	

survival advantage. Modest selective advantages (relative increases in fitness) of 5–10% could account for the high frequencies of lactose tolerance found in northern European populations over a period of about 6,000 years (Aoki, 1986; Feldman & Cavalli-Sforza, 1989). A recent ancient DNA study of the remains of several individuals dating from the European Mesolithic and Neolithic (up to 8,000 years old) showed that none of them possessed an allele that is closely associated with the LCT*P allele (Burger et al., 2007). According to the authors of this study, these results are consistent with the strong natural selection model of the cultural historical hypothesis: There is no evidence that there was by chance a widespread distribution of LCT*P allele in European pre-dairying populations that made them pre-adapted for the use of dairy products.

There are populations in which dairying is present but lactose tolerance frequencies are low, such as those in central and southern Asia. In many of these populations, milk is not drunk raw but is processed into yogurt or cheese. In the making of yogurt and cheese, bacteria are used to convert lactose to lactic acid. Thus the ability to digest lactose is not critical in obtaining the nutrients from these products, and lactose tolerant individuals historically have had no selection advantage in these populations.

The evolution of lactose tolerance is a clear-cut example of the interaction of biological and cultural factors in shaping biological variation within our species.

BALANCED POLYMORPHISMS: SICKLE-CELL AND OTHER CONDITIONS

In any population, the polymorphism for lactose digestion ability in adulthood can be explained in terms of cultural practices, natural selection, gene flow, and genetic drift. However, when we look at other genetic systems and populations, it appears that there are polymorphisms that are quite stable and are not the result of obvious historical factors. Something is preventing alleles from going to fixation or being lost. This is called a **balanced polymorphism**. A fascinating aspect of microevolution is the attempt to explain mechanisms underlying balanced polymorphisms.

The large number of variants present in the HLA system may be evidence of a balanced polymorphism in this genetic system. If HLA variants are useful for conferring resistance to infectious diseases, then some HLA polymorphisms may be maintained as a **frequency-dependent balanced polymorphism** (Cooke & Hill, 2001). In this situation, an allele (or trait) has an advantage in a population relative to other alleles until it reaches a certain frequency in the population. If it becomes more common than this frequency, it loses its advantage, and the balanced polymorphism is maintained. In the HLA system, an HLA variant may confer resistance to a specific infectious disease. While it is rare in the population, it will have an advantage because the infectious agent itself has not evolved to overcome whatever defense it confers. However, as the resistant variant becomes more common in the population, there will be selection on the infectious agent to adjust to it. Eventually, a frequency will be reached at which the disease-resistant variant loses its advantage. A high degree of polymorphism in a population may result as this process is repeated for multiple alleles, and the resulting polymorphism is stable or balanced.

Heterozygous Advantage   It has been noted that genetic diversity in breeding plants and animals often results in improved yields; this is called hybrid vigor or *heterosis*. It is assumed that this may result from a high frequency of heterozygosity at many loci underlying a complex genetic trait. However, **heterozygous advantage** has been observed in much simpler genetic contexts. In a one-gene, two-allele situation, a balanced polymorphism will be maintained if

balanced polymorphism   A stable polymorphism in a population in which natural selection prevents any of the alternative phenotypes (or underlying alleles) from becoming fixed or being lost.

frequency-dependent balanced polymorphism   Balanced polymorphism that is maintained because one (or more) of the alternative phenotypes has a selective advantage over the other phenotypes only when it is present in the population below a certain frequency.

heterozygous advantage   With reference to a particular genetic system, the situation in which heterozygotes have a selective advantage over homozygotes (for example, sickle-cell disease); a mechanism for maintaining a balanced polymorphism.

the heterozygotes have a selective advantage over both of the homozygotes. This is just the opposite of what happens in cases of maternal–fetal incompatibility, which actually works against the maintenance of a polymorphism.

The classic example of a balanced polymorphism maintained by heterozygous advantage is the high frequency of the *sickle-cell trait* in some populations with endemic *malaria*. In Chapter 3 we discussed the molecular and cellular genetics of sickle-cell disease, which is caused by an abnormal hemoglobin protein, HbS (as opposed to the normal HbA), that impairs the ability of red blood cells to deliver oxygen to the tissues of the body. It is an autosomal recessive disease, and people who are heterozygotes are carriers of the condition. In a nonmalarial environment, the carriers show few signs of illness, although they may be slightly at risk in low-oxygen environments.

Malaria may have killed more people—especially children—than any other infectious disease. According to the World Health Organization, more than 40% of the world's population lives in malarial regions, it affects 300–500 million people per year, and it kills a million children per year under the age of 6 in Africa alone. In addition, chronic malaria has incalculable negative economic, social, and political effects. There is no doubt that malaria has exerted a strong selection pressure on human populations for many thousands of years.

Malaria is caused by protozoa from the genus *Plasmodium*. Of the 120 species in this genus, 4 cause malaria: *P. malariae*, *P. vivax*, *P. falciparum*, and *P. ovale*. The symptoms of malaria include fever, anemia, inflammation of the spleen, and headache. Cerebral malaria is especially serious and may lead to insanity, unconsciousness, and death. Humans are infected with the *Plasmodium* parasite via the bite of a female *Anopheles* mosquito, which is an essential carrier or *vector* of the disease. The *Plasmodium* life cycle requires both human and mosquito hosts. Because malaria depends on the mosquito for its spread from human host to host, the ability of the mosquito to survive and breed is a critical factor in local patterns of malarial expression. For example, in regions that have a pronounced dry season, mosquito breeding is highly seasonal, and malaria does not become a stable and constant aspect of life. In contrast, malaria is endemic in wet, equatorial climates in Africa and Southeast Asia, where mosquito breeding continues year-round.

Although human intervention has worked to limit the range of malaria, human cultural practices have also helped to increase its impact on human populations. The development of slash-and-burn agriculture in Africa led to clearing of tropical forests; an increase in the amount of standing, stagnant water; and higher human population densities (Figure 5.14) (Livingstone, 1958). All of

FIGURE 5.14 Slash-and-burn agriculture in Africa.

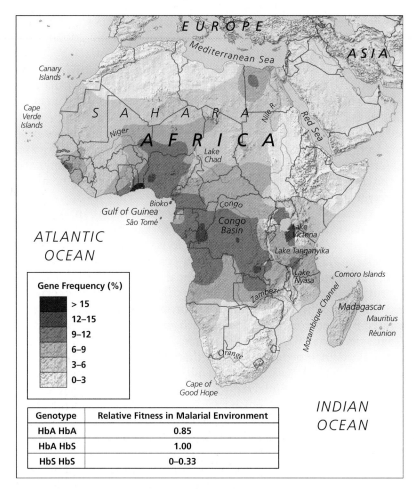

Genotype	Relative Fitness in Malarial Environment
HbA HbA	0.85
HbA HbS	1.00
HbS HbS	0–0.33

FIGURE 5.15 Clinal map of the distribution of HbS in Africa.

these worked to increase the disease's spread. In addition, the disrupted tropical forest conditions favored breeding of a particular species of mosquito, *A. gambiae*, which is the vector for *P. falciparum*, which in turn causes the most lethal form of malaria. This was the context for the evolution of high frequencies of the HbS allele (Allison, 1954).

In malarial environments, individuals who are heterozygous HbS HbA have higher reproductive fitness than either HbA HbA or HbS HbS homozygotes (Figure 5.15). Individuals who are homozygous HbS HbS have sickle-cell anemia, a disease that, in traditional settings, drastically shortens the life span, precluding reproduction. However, heterozygous individuals with sickle-cell trait are more resistant to developing malaria than homozygous HbA HbA individuals. This is because the presence of abnormal hemoglobin in the red blood cells of heterozygous individuals seriously affects the life cycle of the *P. falciparum* parasite, though not enough to affect human physiology in any meaningful way. In these malarial regions, heterozygote individuals are overrepresented in populations over age 45, indicating their enhanced survival. The HbS allele cannot go to fixation because the homozygotes are seriously impaired. Thus the HbA–HbS polymorphism is maintained by heterozygous advantage.

Sickle-cell carrier frequencies are almost 40% in some African populations. High HbS frequencies are also found in Mediterranean, Middle Eastern, and Indian populations, reflecting former and present malarial loads in these regions. African Americans also have a high frequency of HbS, which reflects their ancestral populations. However, without malaria in the environment, heterozygotes are no longer at an advantage, and the frequency of HbS is declining because of the reduced fitness of HbS homozygotes.

Several other alleles that directly or indirectly affect red blood cell physiology (such as the thalassemias, which directly affect the structure of hemoglobin, and G6PD polymorphisms, which affect key metabolic pathways) are also found in high frequency in malarial areas. These conditions, along with sickle-cell trait, are compelling evidence of the importance of malaria as a selective force in human evolution.

Other Possible Disease-Associated Balanced Polymorphisms   The sickle-cell polymorphism is the best example we have of a balanced polymorphism maintained by heterozygous advantage. The high frequencies in some populations of alleles responsible for two other autosomal recessive diseases—*Tay–Sachs disease* and *cystic fibrosis*—have led some to suggest that a similar mechanism may be underlying their polymorphisms (M. T. Smith, 1998). For both of these genetic diseases, the hypothesized selective agent in the environment was *tuberculosis*, a bacterial disease that was once one of the main causes of death in urban populations in Europe and the United States.

Tay–Sachs disease (TS) causes the accumulation of a fatty substance in the nerve cells of the brain. There is no treatment for the disease. Although a child with TS is normal for the first few months of life, as the disease takes hold there is a progressive loss of mental and physical function, resulting in death within a few years. Tay–Sachs is found at high frequency in Ashkenazi (European) Jewish populations and occurs at a rate of about 0.2–0.4 in 1,000, which makes it about 100 times more common in these populations than in others. A rate of 0.4 in 1,000 would indicate a TS allele frequency of 2% and a heterozygote carrier frequency of 3.9% (0.98 * 0.02 * 2) in Ashkenazi populations. Several geneticists have argued that given the ancient origins of the TS allele in Palestine, some selection advantage—specifically resistance of the heterozygotes to tuberculosis or typhoid (Myrianthopoulos & Aronson, 1966; Chakravarti & Chakraborty, 1978)—must be working to maintain its presence in the historically isolated and diverse Ashkenazi populations.

Cystic fibrosis (CF) is the most common autosomal genetic disorder in northern European–derived populations (Ratjen & Döring, 2003). Although it is found in other populations, the rates are much higher in populations with European ancestry. Cystic fibrosis is a disease of the mucus- and sweat-producing glands, characterized by symptoms such as excessive sweating (leading to mineral imbalances in the blood, which can in turn lead to heart problems) and the accumulation of thick mucus in the lungs and intestine. Lung disease is the most common cause of death in CF; today, with medical treatment, the average life span of a CF sufferer is about 30 years (although it can be significantly longer than this with aggressive treatment). In European populations, the rate of cystic fibrosis is about 0.5 in 1,000 births. As with Tay–Sachs, given the obvious reduction in fertility of the homozygous sufferers, several investigators have suggested that the heterozygote CF carriers may be more resistant than normal homozygotes to developing disease. Meindl (1987) argued specifically that CF carriers have a greater ability to resist damage caused by pulmonary (lung) tuberculosis and that there has been selection for the CF allele in European populations since tuberculosis first became a public health problem in the sixteenth century. Other investigators have suggested that the CF allele may confer a resistance to intestinal bacteria that are known to induce diarrhea, which can pose a serious health risk, especially to children (Hansson, 1988).

Although intriguing and plausible cases can be made for heterozygous advantage in CF and TS, it is important to keep things in perspective: HbS carrier frequencies approach 40% in some malarial populations, compared with 3–5% for CF and TS carriers in their high-frequency populations. The HbS heterozygous advantage may simply be that much greater, or its allele frequencies may have had more time to evolve. It seems likely that heterozygous advantage is an important factor in determining CF and TS allele frequencies, but we do not know whether sickle-cell disease is a particularly accurate model for the maintenance of these other polymorphisms.

Adaptation and Adaptability

A variant that can be demonstrated to increase fitness in a specific environment (such as the ability to digest lactose as an adult) is an adaptation in the classic evolutionary sense. However, adaptation is a more general phenomenon. All organisms exhibit some degree of *biological plasticity*: an ability on the part of individuals to physiologically respond to changes in the environment. This is obvious in poor environments; for example, if there is not enough food, an animal will become thinner. When the phenotype of an organism reflects *positive* changes that arise in the context of short- or long-term exposure to a set of environmental conditions, this is called **adaptability**. Differences in environments can thus lead to population-level differences, as individuals within the populations biologically adapt to local conditions. Because of biological plasticity and adaptability, populations may phenotypically differentiate from one another without any underlying changes to the genotypes. Adaptation and adaptability are not always separate and distinct issues. The ability of a phenotype to respond differently to different environments an organism may encounter in a lifetime may in itself be an adaptation.

LEVELS OF ADAPTABILITY

The process of very short-term changes in physiology that occur in response to changes in environmental conditions is called **acclimatization**. We are all familiar with acclimatization. When people from sea level move to high altitude, they have to cope with a reduction in the amount of oxygen available in the atmosphere. Initially, the body physiologically adapts by breathing more quickly and increasing heart rate. Over time, more profound changes in the body occur, such as an increase in red blood cell production, which allows the individual to cope with a lower-oxygen environment. Tanning is another example of acclimatization, which will be discussed later in this chapter.

In contrast to acclimatization, adaptability refers to the physiological changes that arise in individuals who have lived their entire lives under a certain set of environmental conditions (Figure 5.16). Thus their bodies reflect the influence of the environment on development as they were growing up and the long-term effects of continued exposure to such an environment.

Again, acclimatization, adaptability, and genetic adaptation are all interacting forces in the production of individual phenotypes. They reflect different mechanisms that organisms possess to adapt to the environments in which they live. Humans also use cultural adaptations to cope with the environment (see Insights and Advances: Technology and Extreme Environments on page 148). These cultural adaptations can interact with biological adaptations to shape patterns of human variation.

adaptability   The ability of an individual organism to make positive anatomical or physiological changes after short- or long-term exposure to stressful environmental conditions.

acclimatization   Short-term changes in physiology that occur in an organism in response to changes in environmental conditions.

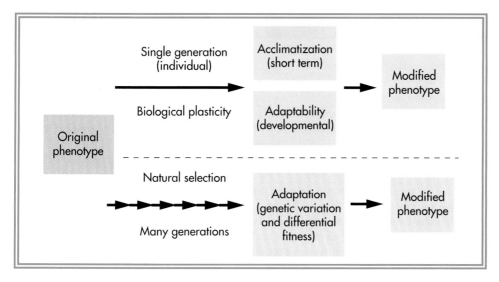

FIGURE 5.16   Adaptability and adaptation.

HEAT AND COLD

From the arctic to the desert, humans live in a vast array of thermal environments, some of them with marked seasonality (see Insights and Advances on page 148). One way we cope with changes in ambient temperature is through the cultural adaptation of wearing more or less clothing. But in addition to clothing, humans display a variety of physiological adaptations to heat and cold, some of which reflect adaptations of a genetic kind, whereas others are better described in terms of acclimatization and adaptability (Moran, 2000; Beall & Steegman, 2000; A. T. Steegman 2007).

When people get too hot, the body responds through a process of *vasodilation* and sweat. Vasodilation (which appears as flushing in lighter-skinned people) increases blood flow to the surface of the body, which allows heat from the core of the body to be dissipated into the environment. The primary mechanism for dissipating heat at the surface of the body is sweating. The human body is unusual (although not unique) among mammals in having more than a million specialized sweat glands distributed over the skin. Despite the great range of thermal environments in which people live, there is almost no population variation in the number of sweat glands per person. This may reflect the fact that we are ultimately of tropical origin and that our bodies are well adapted to this kind of environment.

The evaporation of 1 liter of sweat removes 560 kcal of heat from the body, and people can sweat up to 4 liters/hour (Beall & Steegman, 2000). Heat stroke—when the core temperature of the body reaches 41°C (105.8°F)—is a serious condition, with the depletion of fluid from the body unleashing a cascade of events that ultimately leads to the coagulation of blood and the death of brain tissue. Even today, heat waves in urban environments kill hundreds or even thousands of people. Heat is a strong selective force.

Cold is also a strong selective force in environments where temperatures go significantly below freezing. Death from hypothermia is likely to result if the body's core temperature falls to 31–32°C (88–90°F). Because the body's reaction to cold is to decrease blood flow to the periphery—*vasoconstriction*—in order to maintain core temperature, frostbite, resulting in serious damage to the appendages and face, is another serious consequence of prolonged exposure to cold. Another basic acclimatization mechanism to cold is shivering. A decline of the body's core temperature by 2–3°C brings on the shivering response, which generates heat.

Human populations show significant variation in response to cold. In the Korean War, U.S. soldiers of African ancestry suffered higher rates of frostbite

INSIGHTS AND ADVANCES

Technology and Extreme Environments

Human beings have had thousands of years to adapt to certain kinds of natural environments. However, our technological prowess allows us both to exploit and to create new environments. These new environments require a physiological response from our bodies if we are to survive within them.

A *zero-gravity* or *microgravity* environment is one of the most exotic to which any human being would have to adapt (Figure A) (D. R. Williams, 2003). Since the advent of extended (weeks and months) stays in space, with the Skylab and Mir programs and the development of the International Space Station, dozens of people have had to deal with how their bodies react to an

environment essentially free of the effects of gravity. Over time, people in a microgravity environment have muscle atrophy and loss of muscle strength. There are also cardiovascular changes, which can affect the ability to maintain blood pressure after one returns to Earth. The most critical change may be the loss of calcium in bone. In certain bones, prolonged microgravity exposure causes calcium levels to drop two standard deviations below normal levels. Although this loss is mostly reversible when one returns to gravity, it is not known what the effects would be after a very long-range flight, such as would be needed for a manned mission to Mars. Another medical issue that arises with prolonged microgravity exposure involves how the symptoms of various diseases might be influenced by bodily changes. For example, physicians recognize appendicitis by the presence of pain in a certain part of a patient's abdomen (although it varies widely). In space, the effects of microgravity on both the structure and function of the gastrointestinal tract could totally change how appendicitis presents to physicians (Williams, 2003).

In contrast to the small numbers of people affected by the space environment, billions of people around the world are subject to the effects of industrial pollution in the environment. Lawrence Schell and Elaine Hills (2002) argue that polluted environments, as much as high altitude or

hot or cold climates, should be considered extreme environments to which humans must adapt. Industrial pollution has been a problem for some human populations for more than 150 years, and even as some parts of the developed world clean up their air and water, people living in developing countries are increasingly being exposed to toxic substances in their environments. Air pollutants, such as carbon monoxide, sulfur dioxide, and ozone, contribute to increased mortality rates and may also affect prenatal and postnatal growth. Exposure to lead, mercury, and other substances may also affect growth and have cognitive effects. Schell and Hills point out that people with the highest exposure to one pollutant are also likely to have high exposure to others. These people also tend to be the poorest in a society, thus the human biology of pollution exposure interacts with social issues such as access to food, health care, and adequate housing.

Human technological achievements can be characterized as triumphant, as in the "conquest of space," or tragic, as in the "poisoning of the environment" by pollution. In either case, technology places individual human bodies into new environments to which they are not well adapted. It will be interesting to see what the long-term effects of exposure to these environments will be.

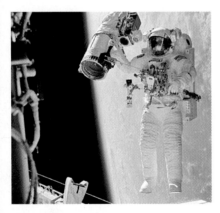

FIGURE A   A human in a microgravity environment.

than those of European ancestry (Schuman, 1953). However, there is no particular evidence that European-derived populations are particularly cold-adapted; the difference between European American and African American soldiers in frostbite susceptibility may have resulted from the fact that African Americans in general show a more acute sympathetic nervous response to stress, which may lead to a more pronounced vasoconstriction response to cold (Beall & Steegman, 2000).

Humans can cope with temperatures in the freezing range via a combination of shivering and vasoconstriction. Subcutaneous fat also helps insulate the core of the body from the external cold. Populations vary in how these mechanisms are used to deal with cold. Arctic Inuit populations, who must deal with extreme cold, use cultural adaptations such as clothing, combined with biological adaptations, such as subcutaneous fat storage and vasoconstriction, to cope with cold on an ongoing basis. In addition, research involving hand immersion in a cold water bath indicates that Inuit maintain higher hand temperatures than do European or African Americans after prolonged exposure to cold (Meehan, 1955). At the other extreme, desert-dwelling Australian aborigines must cope with a great range of temperatures on a daily and seasonal basis. In winter, they sleep in near-freezing temperatures uncovered and without shelter. They cope with the cold by using an extreme vaso-constriction response, which causes the skin surface temperature to fall 2.5°C. Given that the temperatures they must cope with are not severely cold, frostbite does not occur, and they conserve energy while maintaining adequate core body temperatures. It is assumed that the adaptive responses seen in these populations are a result of both genetic adaptation and the process of developmental adaptability.

BODY SIZE AND SHAPE

In the nineteenth century, two biologists, Carl Bergmann (1814–1865) and Joel Asaph Allen (1838–1921), looked at the relationship between body size and climate in a wide range of mammals. They found that within polytypic species, there were predictable relationships between body form and proportions and temperature. **Bergmann's rule** (1847) focuses on body size. He found that the colder the climate, the larger the body. This makes geometric sense in that as volume increases, surface area decreases as a proportion of the volume. This would decrease the rate of heat dissipation through the surface, which helps to maintain a higher core temperature. **Allen's rule** (1877) focuses on the appendages of the body. For example, limbs should be longer relative to body size in warmer climates because that would help to dissipate heat, whereas shorter limbs in colder climates would conserve body heat. An example of Bergman's and Allen's rules can be found in comparing snowshoe and desert hares (Figure 5.17). The ears of the desert hare are much longer than those of the arctic hare and the body much leaner and rangier; both are features that dissipate heat.

Do Allen's and Bergmann's rules hold for human populations? Body forms of peoples living in some extreme environments are consistent with the rules. If we

Bergmann's rule Stipulates that body size is larger in colder climates to conserve body temperature.

Allen's rule Stipulates that in warmer climates, the limbs of the body are longer relative to body size to dissipate body heat.

(a)

(b)

FIGURE 5.17 Bergmann's and Allen's rules expressed in two rabbit species. (a) A snowshoe hare. (b) A desert-living black-tailed jack rabbit.

(a)

(b)

FIGURE 5.18 Bergmann's and Allen's rules expressed in two human populations. (a) Sudanese tribesmen have body types adapted to warm climates. (b) Inuit people have body types adapted to cold climates.

look at the Inuit in the Arctic and Nilotic peoples from East Africa, we see that the stocky, short-limbed Inuit body seems to be structured to conserve heat, whereas the long-limbed Nilotic body is designed to dissipate heat (Figure 5.18). Looking at a broad range of populations, there is a general trend among humans for larger body size and greater sitting height (that is, body length) to be associated with colder climates, whereas relative span (fingertip to fingertip length divided by height) tends to be greater in warmer temperatures (that is, longer appendages relative to body size) (Roberts, 1978).

Because it seems unlikely that an Inuit person raised in East Africa would grow up with drastically modified limb and body proportions, should we assume that the associations between body form and climate in humans always result from genetic differences? The evidence that body-size proportions reflect developmental adaptability is not particularly strong. The results of a classic study conducted in the 1950s on U.S. soldiers showed a relationship between state of origin (that is, warmer or colder) and body proportions (Newman & Munroe, 1955) and was interpreted to represent an example of adaptability or acclimatization rather than adaptation. However, a recent analysis of updated Army data shows that if one takes into account whether the soldiers are of African or European ancestry, the climate association disappears (Steegman, 2003). American Whites have shorter legs and longer trunks than do Blacks, and warmer (that is, southern) states may have a greater representation of Blacks than do colder states.

One study shows that climate change may affect primate phenotypes in accordance with Allen's and Bergmann's rules (Paterson, 1996). In the 1960s, two troops of Japanese macaques (*Macaca fuscata*) were transferred from one location in Japan to an Oregon primate center. Subsequently, one of the troops was moved to a facility in Texas. Analysis of long-term records (more than 20 years) on body size and proportions in the troops showed that by the 1990s, the Oregon monkeys were significantly larger than their Texas cousins, whereas the Texas monkeys had significantly longer limbs. The Oregon monkeys lived at latitude 45° N, whereas the Texas troop was at 28° N; the Texas site was substantially warmer. Thus the results were in accordance with predictions based on Allen's and Bergmann's rules. Although natural selection could have been responsible for the body changes, it would be surprising to see such effects after only two generations and in the absence of any obvious differences in fertility.

LIVING AT HIGH ALTITUDE

Humans originally evolved in a warm, humid climate, which was at low altitude. But millions of people today live at very high altitudes of 3,500–4,000 m (11,600–13,200 ft), in environments that are typically dry and cold (Figure 5.19). Another major difference between high- and low-altitude environments is that atmospheric pressure is much less at high altitude. Although oxygen makes up the same proportion of the air at high and low altitude (21%), the lower pressure means that hemoglobin molecules in red blood cells take in fewer oxygen molecules with each breath—about one-third less at 4,000 m than at sea level (Harrison et al., 1988; Beall, 2001). The effects of altitude on oxygen availability start to become an issue at around 2,500 m.

Any person accustomed to breathing at sea level who goes to one of these high-altitude locations is at risk of *hypoxia,* or "oxygen starvation." Immediate acclimatization to hypoxia involves increasing heart and breathing rates in order to increase circulation of oxygen. This is only a temporary solution, and the long-term effects of increased lung ventilation include headaches, tunnel vision, and fainting. Hemoglobin concentrations are increased by initially reducing the volume of blood plasma, followed by an increase in the production of red blood cells. Over time, the maximal oxygen consumption capacity reduces, which is an adaptation to the reduction in oxygen available. There are few indications that high altitude alone poses any particular long-term health problems. Growth is slower in children, but the total growth period is prolonged, so overall size is not decreased (Frisancho & Baker, 1970). High altitude has been no barrier to the development of large-scale, well-populated civilizations.

The inhabitants of three high-altitude populations have been extensively studied to determine the mechanisms underlying adaptation to hypoxia. These include Andean populations in South America, Tibetans in South Asia, and Ethiopians in Africa (Beall, 2001; Beall et al., 2002). A striking result of these studies is that there does not appear to be a single way in which humans adapt to high altitude: A variety of mechanisms or combinations of mechanisms are

The highest Inca archaeological site discovered is at the summit of Llullaillaco, a volcano in northwest Argentina that is 6,739 m tall (22,110 ft).

FIGURE 5.19 Anthropologist Andrea Wiley (left) investigates the effects of high-altitude living on reproductive health in Ladakh, India.

observed. For example, the increase in ventilation induced by hypoxia, the *hypoxic ventilatory response* (HVR), is initially quite elevated in lowland people who go to high altitude, although it reduces significantly over time as they acclimatize. Andean and Tibetan populations show significant differences in HVR. The Andean populations show a marked blunting in HVR, resembling the acclimatization response of lowlanders at high altitude. In contrast, Tibetan populations maintain a higher ventilation response, which is close to those observed in sea level populations and twice that of Andean populations.

We mentioned that hemoglobin concentrations increase in low-altitude individuals going to high altitude. Another difference between Andean and Tibetan populations is that whereas increased hemoglobin concentration is seen in Andean individuals, it is not seen in Tibetans. Cynthia Beall's (2001) analysis of several studies shows that at a mean elevation of 3,859 m, the hemoglobin concentration for acclimatized lowlanders was 18.2 g/dL, for Andean men it was 18.1 g/dL, and for Tibetan men it was only 16.9 g/dL. Ethiopian males have a concentration of 15.9 g/dL, which is within 2% of the U.S. male sea level value of 15.3 g/dL (Beall et al., 2002). Ethiopians living at only 2,400 m have similar hemoglobin concentrations to those living at about 3,500 m, indicating that there is no increase of hemoglobin with altitude in this population. Although Ethiopian and Tibetan populations have similarly low (for high altitude) levels of hemoglobin, they differ in the extent of oxygen saturation in arterial blood. Tibetans have low oxygen saturation compared with sea level populations, which is not surprising because they do not produce more hemoglobin to deal with the reduced atmospheric pressure. However, the Ethiopians have oxygen saturation percentages similar to those seen in sea level populations. Basically, the Ethiopian population at high altitude has a blood oxygen profile that resembles most other populations at sea level.

SKIN COLOR

The skin is one of the largest and most complex organs of the body (Robins, 1991; Molnar, 2002). It has two main components: the thick *dermis* and the much thinner *epidermis,* which covers it (Figure 5.20). The dermis is a connective tissue layer consisting of collagen and other fibers, sweat and sebaceous glands, hair follicles,

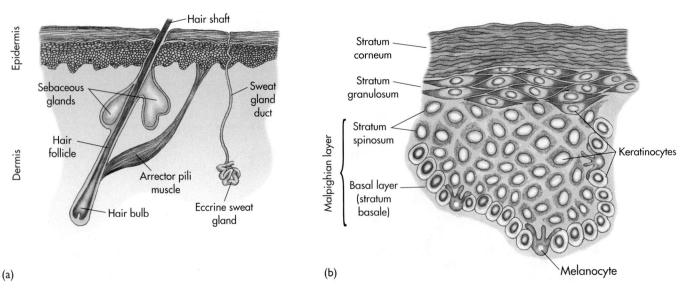

(a)   (b)

FIGURE 5.20   The structure of skin (a) and epidermis (b) at the microscopic level.

and hair. The epidermis is a thin layer of tissue consisting 95% of epithelial cells called *keratinocytes,* with 5% pigment cells, or **melanocytes**. Keratinocytes are synthesized at the base of the epidermis and migrate over the course of 4 to 6 weeks to the surface, where they are shed. Thus the epidermis is a continually renewing tissue layer.

Skin has several important functions. It is a fluid barrier, keeping the body protected from most chemicals in the environment. It is extremely important in thermoregulation (maintaining body temperature in the normal range) thanks to blood vessels located in the dermis and the cooling effects of the evaporation of sweat on the surface of the body. Skin also plays a critical function in the metabolism of various vitamins. This function may be critical to our understanding of the evolution of skin color in human populations.

Skin color is produced primarily by two substances. *Oxidized hemoglobin* in red blood cells contributes red, and its contribution can be seen in heavily vascularized structures, such as the nipples. By far the most important component of skin color is **melanin**, a dark pigment produced by the melanocytes of the epidermis. Like neurons, with which they share a common embryonic origin, melanocytes are cells that consist of a cell body and long projections known as dendrites. The melanin in melanocytes is packaged into an organelle in the cytoplasm known as the *melanosome.* Through its dendrites, the melanocyte deposits mature melanosome in the keratinocytes surrounding it. Skin color is produced by a combination of melanosome size, the density of melanosomes within each keratinocyte, and the distribution of keratinocytes (Robins, 1991). People with darker skin have more melanin in their epidermis than people with lighter skin.

The distribution of skin color in the populations of the world follows a fairly orderly pattern, especially in the Old World (Africa and Eurasia). People with the darkest skin live at the equator or in the tropics (Figure 5.21 on page 154). As you go north or south to higher latitudes, skin color becomes progressively lighter. In the New World, skin color does not follow such an orderly distribution, probably because of the recent migration (less than 15,000 years ago) of peoples to the New World from temperate Asia. Migration patterns over the past few hundred years have further disrupted this orderly picture, with people from higher latitudes moving to places with an abundance of sun (for example, people of northern European ancestry living in Australia) and people from equatorial regions moving to places where there is not so much sun (for example, people of west African ancestry living in the northeast United States). Such migrations and mixings are nothing new. For example, Khoisan peoples have lived in the temperate climate of south Africa for thousands of years and have substantially lighter skin color than Bantu-speaking Zulu people, who came to the area from equatorial Africa only 1,000 years ago (Jablonski & Chaplin, 2002).

Reconstructing the evolution of skin color depends on explaining the advantages of dark skin in more abundant sunlight and of light skin in less abundant sunlight. Many attempts to explain this pattern have been based on diseases or conditions associated with having the "wrong" skin color for the environment.

Advantages and Disadvantages of Light and Dark Skin Color   Electromagnetic energy from the sun comes to the earth not only in the form of visible light but also in the form of *ultraviolet radiation* (UVR), which is below the wavelength for visible light. Although much of the UVR is absorbed by the ozone layer, enough reaches the earth to profoundly affect the biology of many organisms, including human beings.

In humans, the two most visible effects of UVR are *sunburn* and *skin cancer.* Sunburn causes congestion of subcutaneous capillaries, destruction of skin cells, and edema (collection of fluids under the skin), and it can permanently damage skin. Besides being uncomfortable, sunburn can be very serious because it may interfere

melanocytes   Cells in the epidermis that produce melanin.

melanin   A dark pigment produced by the melanocytes of the epidermis, which is the most important component of skin color.

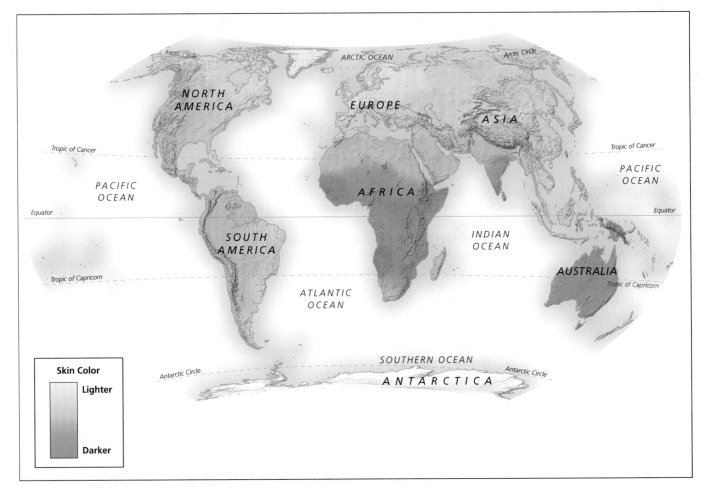

FIGURE 5.21   World map of the distribution of skin color. Note that darker skin colors are found near the equator, especially in the Old World.

with the body's ability to cool itself and lead to the development of wounds that are highly vulnerable to infection. Ultraviolet radiation also damages DNA, which in turn leads to the development of skin cancer. Most skin cancers, though unsightly, are benign. However, cancer of the melanocytes, *malignant melanoma,* spreads easily throughout the body and must be treated early.

Melanin blocks or filters out incoming UV waves. Thus people with more melanin or the ability to temporarily produce more melanin in response to light (that is, *tanning*) are less susceptible to the effects of UVR than people who have less melanin. As most of us know, very light-skinned people who cannot tan are very susceptible to sunburn. They are also more susceptible to skin cancer. People from the British Isles who have migrated to sunnier climates provide an example of the effects of increased UVR on light skin. In Britain, the skin cancer rate is 28 per 100,000 in males and 15 per 100,000 in females. In Queensland, Australia, much of which is tropical, the rates are 265 and 156 per 100,000. Despite the health risks of skin cancer in light-skinned peoples today, for most of human history, when most people did not enjoy long lives, it was probably protection against sunburn that provided the greater fitness benefit because cancer typically takes its toll later in life.

Another important factor that may influence the evolution of skin color is *vitamin D synthesis*. Vitamin D is an essential compound in calcium metabolism and is necessary for the normal development of bones and teeth. Dietary sources of vitamin D are not common, although it is present in large quantities in some fish oils and to a much lesser degree in eggs and butter. Most people get their vitamin D from the sun, or, more accurately, UVR in the sun causes a photochemical reaction in the epidermis, converting *7-dehydrocholesterol* (7-DHC) into a precursor of vitamin D, which is transformed in the kidney into vitamin D over a period of 2 to 3 days. Vitamin D deficiency leads to the development of a serious medical condition known as *rickets*. Because calcium metabolism is disrupted, children with rickets have bones that are severely weakened. The bones can become deformed or are prone to breakage. Rickets can range from very mild to quite severe and can even result in death. On the other side of the coin, vitamin D toxicity can also have important health consequences, but it is almost impossible to get enough vitamin D via exposure to sunlight to cause toxicity (Robins, 1991).

Because melanin blocks the effects of UVR, people with darker skin cannot synthesize vitamin D as efficiently as people with lighter skin. Dark skin takes six times longer to make vitamin D as light skin (Holick et al., 1981). In the tropics, this is not an issue because intense sunlight is readily available and seasonality is minimal. At the higher latitudes, the sunlight is less intense, and seasonality means that during certain times of the year, access to sunlight is nearly cut off. Cold weather necessitates covering the skin, further limiting the skin's exposure to direct sunlight. Vitamin D synthesis in the skin is very efficient, however, so even the exposure of a limited amount of skin (as little as 20 cm^2) to sunlight can provide sufficient vitamin D.

Rickets was first recognized to be a major health problem in the industrialized cities of northern Europe and North America at the beginning of the twentieth century. The cities' northern location and smoky pollution limited exposure to sunlight, and it was very dark in the dingy, overcrowded tenements where factory workers and their children lived. Up to 90% of children in these cities suffered from some degree of rickets (Robins, 1991). In the 1920s, rates for rickets in African American children in the United States were two to three times higher than for European American children. The epidemiology of rickets led to the development of the *vitamin D hypothesis* for the evolution of skin color (Murray, 1934; Loomis, 1967). In a nutshell, this hypothesis proposes that the evolution of lighter skin color—starting from darker-skinned ancestry—occurred in areas with less sunlight as a direct result of selection for more efficient vitamin D synthesis. Impaired movement or childbearing ability (if the pelvis is affected) in rickets would provide the negative consequences of vitamin D deficiency that would drive the selection for light skin color.

Skin color also influences the metabolism of *folate* (folic acid). Folate is a B vitamin essential for DNA synthesis and cell replication, and exposure to UVR in the dermis causes the breakdown of folate in the bloodstream. This effect is particularly pronounced in people with light skin, who do not filter out UVR as efficiently as people with dark skin (Branda & Eaton, 1978). Deficiencies in folate during pregnancy can cause neural tube birth defects in the developing embryo. Jablonski & Chaplin (2000, 2002) propose that retention of folate may be a critical factor in the evolution of dark skin color in places with strong sunlight.

Evolutionary Synthesis   Diseases associated with skin and skin color provide several potential insights into the evolution of skin color. Jablonski and Chaplin (2000, 2002) have mapped out the distribution of UVR on the earth and used it to create a map of the predicted distribution of skin color. They found that the skin color prediction was very accurate for the Old World. Indigenous peoples of the New World tropics do not have skin as dark as predicted. However, as we discussed

FIGURE 5.22   Moken children can see small objects under water.

previously, they are recent arrivals to that region, and thus we can explain the mismatch between skin color and UVR exposure by historical factors. Jablonski and Chaplin suggest that the distribution of skin color in human populations is maintained by a balance between the contrasting effects of UVR on vitamin D synthesis and on folate degradation. Jablonski and Chaplin focus on the role of vitamin metabolism, but factors such as resistance to sunburn may have also contributed to the evolution of the distribution of skin color. Although there may have been some primary driving force in the evolution of skin color, the different evolutionary models are not mutually exclusive.

ADAPTABILITY TO WATER

There are no human populations that live under water. However, there are populations whose inhabitants traditionally have made a living on what they can harvest from the sea. Tribal groups in Southeast Asia known as "sea gypsies" have long been known for their diving and swimming ability, which they use to collect shells, clams, and sea cucumbers (Gislén et al., 2003, Ivanoff, 2005). The Moken are one such group living in coastal areas of Burma and Thailand. Moken children are expert divers and are noted for their ability to locate objects under water without the benefit of diving goggles or masks (Figure 5.22).

Being terrestrial animals, humans are not well adapted to seeing under water. We lose about two-thirds of our focusing power under water, which explains why everything appears blurry to us and it is almost impossible to pick out small objects. Given this limitation, the ability of Moken children to pick out small objects under water is remarkable. In a study comparing a group of Moken children with a group of European children, Anna Gislén and her colleagues (2003) found that both groups of children had equivalent vision out of the water. The underwater visual acuity of the Moken children, however, was twice as good as that of the European children.

How do they see under water? The eye focuses through a process known as accommodation, which involves, among other things, constricting the pupil. Gislén and colleagues found that unlike European children, Moken children accommodate under water by constricting their pupils. Underwater environments typically are darker than open-air environments, so the natural response of the pupil is to expand under water, not constrict. Somehow, accommodation in Moken children takes precedence over pupil expansion to compensate for the reduction in light. Furthermore, underwater pupil constriction and accommodation in the Moken children are at the known limits of human performance for children their age.

As in other examples of coping with extreme environments, it is not clear whether the Moken ability to see under water results from a genetic adaptation or is an example of human adaptability or acclimatization. People can be taught to voluntarily accommodate to some extent, so this may simply represent an extreme version of that kind of learning. However, there is no evidence that Moken children are trained to accommodate except by diving under water. On the other hand, given their traditional lifestyle, the ability to accommodate under water may have been strongly selected for.

Human variation is a truly multifaceted topic. It goes right to the heart of what it is to be a human being. Although in the past some scientists looked at human variation as a means of dividing our species into competing groups, contemporary views emphasize differences without resorting to division. Human diversity is a beautiful thing, and that diversity reflects our extraordinary ability to adapt to different environments and our penchant for migrating across great swaths of the planet. Our individual biologies reflect where we came from, in both a genetic and environmental sense. We are all products of a dual heritage.

SUMMARY

1. **Why do we say that *Homo sapiens* is a polytypic species?**

   A polytypic species is one that can be divided into local populations that differ from each other by more than one phenotypic trait. Human populations exhibit substantial population-level diversity, which can be observed both genetically and anatomically.

2. **How do the biological and genetic definitions of *population* differ?**

   The classic biological definition of *population* focuses on the organism: A population is a potentially interbreeding group of individuals. A genetic population—sometimes called a deme—is defined in terms of that genetic composition of a group of animals, expressed, for example, in terms of allele frequencies. Both viewpoints agree that populations defined within a species are fluid and that gene flow or migration can occur between populations.

3. **Compare and contrast the terms *race* and *subspecies*.**

   A subspecies is defined as a group of local populations within a species that share a geographic range and can be distinguished from other subspecies based on one or more phenotypic traits. In biology, a subspecies is the same thing as race. Historically, however, many classifications of human races, both formal and informal, have incorporated behavioral, cultural, and sociological factors that have extended the definition of human race beyond that of a biological subspecies.

4. **What is maternal–fetal incompatibility, and how does it influence allele frequencies in a population?**

   Maternal–fetal incompatibility arises in the context of the ABO blood type system and, more critically (from a medical point of view), in the Rh system. It occurs when the mother does not possess a red blood cell surface protein, while the fetus does (inherited from the father). In the case of an Rh-negative mother, the Rh-positive fetus causes her to create antibodies against the Rh-positive blood cells. Although the first incompatible pregnancy usually is normal, in subsequent incompatible pregnancies, her immune system will produce antibodies that attack the red blood cells of the infant, resulting in severe anemia of the newborn.

5. **Why did lactose tolerance evolve in some human populations?**

   Mammals typically lose the ability to digest lactose, the sugar found in milk, after weaning. Most humans share this mammalian characteristic. However, in human populations that have a long history of dairying, a high frequency of individuals continue to produce the enzyme lactase through adulthood, and they can therefore digest lactose as adults. In these populations it is likely that lactose tolerance is an adaptation that has been selected for in an environment where raw milk products are available and consumed.

6. **What do sickle-cell anemia, Tay–Sachs disease, and cystic fibrosis have in common?**

   All three are autosomal recessive diseases whose disease-causing alleles are found in higher than expected frequency (given the low fitness of homozygous individuals who have the diseases) in certain populations. It has been suggested that the alleles underlying these diseases are maintained in these populations as balanced polymorphisms by heterozygous advantage. Sickle-cell carriers are more resistant to developing malaria than are unaffected homozygotes. Similarly, it has been suggested that Tay–Sachs and cystic fibrosis carriers may have increased resistance to tuberculosis.

7. **What role does temperature play in influencing the distribution of body size and shape in the human species?**

   In cold climates, body heat must be conserved, whereas in hot climates, it is necessary to dissipate heat. Bergmann's rule states that animals in colder climates should have larger bodies because the greater the volume, the smaller the relative surface area and the less loss of heat through the body's surface. Allen's rule states that in hotter climates, appendages should be longer compared with the size of the body because that will increase surface area and promote heat dissipation. These rules are expressed in human populations adapted to extreme temperatures, such as in the arctic Inuit and Nilotic tribes of Africa.

8. **Why are high-altitude environments considered to be stressful?**

   Humans originally evolved in warm and humid environments at low altitude. High-altitude environments tend to be dry and cold. In addition, the decrease in atmospheric pressure at higher altitudes reduces the ability of hemoglobin molecules to carry oxygen. This becomes an issue at altitudes greater than 2,500 m. Individuals from different high-altitude populations (Andes, Tibet, and Ethiopia) have different physiological adaptations to high-altitude conditions.

9. **What are some of the selection pressures influencing the distribution of skin color around the world?**

   The main selection pressure is exposure to UVR. However, there are several ways in which exposure to UVR can influence the evolution of skin color. In areas of high UVR (high sunlight), selection for dark skin as a protection from sunburn and skin cancer may have occurred; dark skin color may also prevent the breakdown of folic acid. In northern latitudes with less direct sunlight exposure, light skin color may have been selected in order to facilitate vitamin D synthesis. Low vitamin D levels can cause the disease known as rickets.

CRITICAL THINKING QUESTIONS

1. How is the concept of race currently being used in your community? Are you comfortable with its usage? Is it consistent with what we know about human biological variation?

2. How can the modern evolutionary approach to human variation be used to combat racism?

3. In what ways is natural selection acting on human populations today? Is it possible to identify these selective forces now, or can it be done only retrospectively after their effects are more apparent?

KEY TERMS

deme
subspecies
race
polytypic species
ethnobiology
environmentalism
racism
anthropometry
ethnic group

population genetics
microevolution
polymorphic
cline
maternal–fetal
 incompatibility
rhesus (Rh) system
human leukocyte antigen
 (HLA) system

haplotypes
Duffy blood group
phylogeny
lactose intolerant
balanced polymorphism
frequency-dependent
 balanced
 polymorphism
heterozygous advantage

adaptability
acclimatization
Bergmann's rule
Allen's rule
melanocytes
melanin

SUGGESTED READING

Cavalli-Sforza, L. L. and Cavalli-Sforza, F. (1996). *The Great Human Diasporas: The History of Diversity and Evolution*. Perseus, Reading, MA.

Jablonski, N. G. (2006). *Skin: A Natural History*. University of California Press, Berkeley, CA.

Molnar, S. (2002). *Human Variation: Races, Types, and Ethnic Groups* (5th ed.). Prentice Hall, Upper Saddle River, NJ.

Montagu, A. (1974). *Man's Most Dangerous Myth: The Fallacy of Race* (5th ed.). Oxford University Press, London.

CHAPTER

6 The Primates

CHAPTER OUTLINE

- The Primate Radiation
- A Guide to the Nonhuman Primates
- Primate Ecology
- Primate Communities

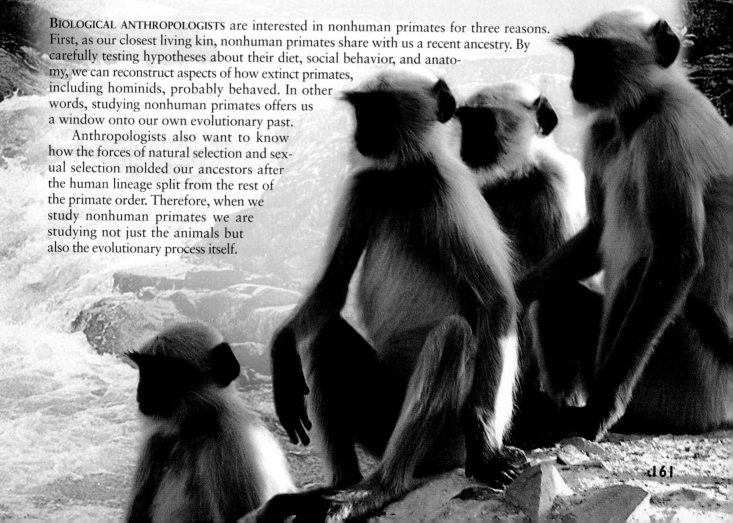

Ranomafana National Park in Madagascar is a range of rugged, rain-soaked hills and rushing streams, and is home to some of the world's most unusual, beautiful, and endangered primates. We've come here to spend a few days looking for them.

Unlike monkeys and apes, which are active in the daytime and sleep all night, many of the most interesting primates in Madagascar are nocturnal. Finding them means hiring a guide, who can lead us with his headlamp along muddy trails in the rainy dark. We have high hopes of seeing some of the forest's more exotic residents, such as aye-ayes, dwarf lemurs, and avahis. For several hours we follow in our guide's footsteps as the beam of his light falls across prehistoric-looking chameleons clinging to tree limbs along our path.

Around midnight we cross our umpteenth muddy ravine, and I am cold and tired and beginning to privately curse my guide for leading me on this wild primate chase. Just then he stops and points at the tree branches overhead. Looking up, I see movement in the foliage and spot several small rat-sized creatures bounding about. We stare at them, and one stares back. It's a mouse lemur, one of the world's smallest primates, weighing in at only a few ounces.

If I were not in Madagascar, I would assume it was a rodent. But due to Madagascar's isolation, natural selection took the primate path in an idiosyncratic direction, and primates evolved along some bizarre lines. I reflect on the difference between a mountain gorilla, with a close genetic kinship to me, and this little creature that seems more rat than primate. But the mouse lemur is just as much a primate as the gorilla is; the two species share an ancestor that lived over 60 million years ago before they and the monkeys and apes went separate evolutionary ways. If we look back far enough into Earth's past, this tiny mammal's ancestor and my ancestor are the same.

The mouse lemur takes a last look at us, its eyes glowing in the beam of our headlamps, then turns and bounces off into the rainy night.

Craig Stanford, Madagascar

BIOLOGICAL ANTHROPOLOGISTS are interested in nonhuman primates for three reasons. First, as our closest living kin, nonhuman primates share with us a recent ancestry. By carefully testing hypotheses about their diet, social behavior, and anatomy, we can reconstruct aspects of how extinct primates, including hominids, probably behaved. In other words, studying nonhuman primates offers us a window onto our own evolutionary past.

Anthropologists also want to know how the forces of natural selection and sexual selection molded our ancestors after the human lineage split from the rest of the primate order. Therefore, when we study nonhuman primates we are studying not just the animals but also the evolutionary process itself.

FIGURE 6.1 Kangaroos and other marsupials lack a placenta; they give birth to poorly developed offspring that grow and develop in a pouch.

FIGURE 6.2 Most modern mammals are placentals.

metatheria Mammals that reproduce without a placenta, including the marsupials.

prototheria Mammals that reproduce by egg-laying, then nurse young from nipples. The Australian platypus and echidna are the only living monotremes.

Finally, biological anthropologists study nonhuman primates simply because they are intrinsically fascinating animals. Most living nonhuman primate species are under threat of extinction because human activities are destroying their habitat and the animals themselves. To develop strategies for primate conservation, we must first have detailed information about their habitat needs and behavioral biology. Only with this knowledge can we hope to ensure their survival.

This chapter introduces the nonhuman primates, their habitat, and their anatomical and ecological adaptations. After considering the place of the order Primates among the mammalian orders, we examine the suite of traits that characterizes the order. We then survey primate taxonomy and general traits of the major primate groups. In the latter part of the chapter, we turn to the topic of primate ecology—the role of nonhuman primates in tropical ecosystems—and look at the ecological factors that have molded primate behavior.

The Primate Radiation

About 5 to 10 million species of animals and plants inhabit Earth today. Only a tiny fraction of these, about 4,000 species, are mammals. Taxonomists divide the mammals into three groups:

1. The **metatheria**, or marsupials, reproduce without use of a placenta. Instead, their offspring are born in an almost embryonic state. They leave the mother's reproductive tract and crawl into her pouch, where they attach themselves to a nipple. After a further period of development, the offspring leave the pouch at a well-developed stage. Metatheria include the kangaroos (Figure 6.1), koalas, opossums, and a wide variety of other mammals, most of which are confined to Australia and nearby islands. Recent evidence suggests that marsupials and placental mammals have occurred together in Australia for long periods. This may mean that a long-held notion that marsupials diversified only because they did not face competition from placentals in Australia is not accurate. You should not consider marsupials "primitive" and other mammals "advanced"; marsupials possess a number of adaptations to their habitat that other mammals lack. For instance, many marsupials can undergo diapause, in which females are able to stop the development of an embryo when food is scarce and continue the embryo's development months later when environmental conditions improve.

2. The **prototheria** are the monotremes, a small and unusual taxonomic group that includes only the Australian platypus and echidna. These species reproduce by egg-laying, but they nurse their young with milk in the manner of other mammals. Paleontologists believe that monotremes were more diverse and numerous in the past than they are today.

TABLE 6.1 Some Mammalian Orders and the Number of Species in Each	
Order	**Number of species**
Chiroptera (bats)	>1,000
Rodentia (rodents)	1,700
Insectivora (hedgehogs, tree shrews, and kin)	380
Carnivora (dogs, cats, weasels, raccoons, and kin)	240
Marsupials	270
Nonhuman primates (strepsirhines, monkeys, and apes)	250
Source: Adapted from Nowak & Paradiso (1983).	

3. The **eutheria**, or placental mammals, include some two dozen orders, one of which is the order Primates. Primates and other placental mammals reproduce by means of internal fertilization, followed by implantation of the fertilized zygote on the wall of the uterus. The developing embryo is nourished via thickened tissue that connects the circulatory system of the mother with that of her offspring. The pattern of reproduction, length of gestation, and degree of development of the newborn offspring vary widely among placental forms (Figure 6.2 on page 162).

THE EXTRAORDINARY DIVERSITY OF NONHUMAN PRIMATES

Some 250 species of nonhuman primates are currently recognized (Table 6.1), but including all the minor taxonomic variations of these species, there are more than 350 varieties, or *taxa* (Groves, 2001). This is a small percentage of overall mammalian diversity, but nonhuman primates nonetheless exhibit an amazing variety of size and form. Adult body weights range from less than 2 ounces (40 g) in mouse lemurs to more than 450 pounds (200 kg) in

FIGURE 6.3   Primate body size and shape vary widely from the 440-lb. (200-kg) gorilla to the 2-oz. (40-g) mouse lemur.

gorillas (Figure 6.3). Body shapes range from the graceful arm-swinging gibbon to the bizarre aye-aye.

WHAT EXACTLY IS A PRIMATE?

Primates are mammals with grasping hands, large brains, a high degree of learned rather than innate behavior, and a suite of other traits. However, the primates are a diverse group, and not all species share the same set of traits. The order Primates is divided into two suborders: the **Strepsirhini**, or **strepsirhine** primates (lemurs and lorises), and the **Haplorhini**, or **haplorhine** primates (tarsiers, monkeys, apes, and humans) (Figure 6.4). We should not consider strepsirhines more primitive than haplorhines; both groups have been evolving on their own paths for more than 60 million years. But many of their adaptations are clear holdovers from the early days of the Primate order (Figure 6.5 on pages 164–165). The strepsirhine–haplorhine classification system reflects genetic relationships and was developed by St. Hilaire in the late eighteenth century, long after Linnaeus's earlier primate taxonomy. Many taxonomists use another traditional naming system, which is based on aspects of anatomy, for the major primate groups: the **prosimian** and **anthropoid** suborders. We'll see how the strepsirhine–haplorhine classification differs from the prosimian–anthropoid classification later in the chapter.

eutheria   Mammals that reproduce with a placenta and uterus.

strepsirhine (Strepsirhini) Suborder of the order Primates that includes the prosimians, excluding the tarsier.

haplorhine (Haplorhini) Suborder of the order Primates that includes the anthropoids and the tarsier.

prosimian   Member of the primate suborder Prosimii that includes the lemurs, lorises, galagos, and tarsiers.

anthropoid   Members of the primate suborder Anthropoidea that includes the monkeys, apes, and hominids.

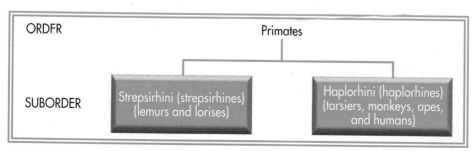

FIGURE 6.4   The major groupings of living primates.

(a) Skeleton of a vertical clinger and leaper

Indri

(b) Skeleton of a brachiator

Gibbon

FIGURE 6.5   The Primate order displays a diversity of ways of moving around.

ANATOMICAL TRAITS

We distinguish primates from other mammals by a set of traits that all primates share.

Generalized Body Plan   The primate body plan is generalized, not specialized. Many mammals have extremely specialized body designs; consider a giraffe's neck, a seal's flippers, or an elephant's trunk. Primates typically lack such specializa-

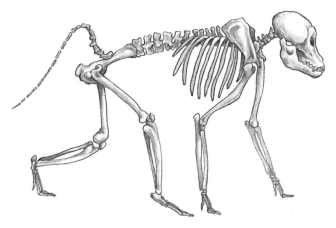

(c) Skeleton of a terrestrial quadruped

Baboon

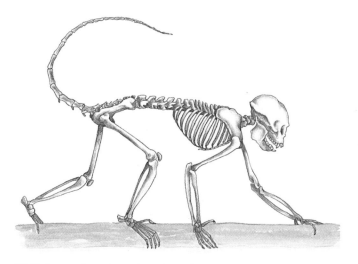

(d) Skeleton of an arboreal quadruped

FIGURE 6.5   (*Continued*)

Uakari

tions. Their generalized body plan gives them versatility; most primate species engage in a wide variety of modes of travel, for instance, from arm-swinging (in apes) to running, leaping, and walking (Figure 6.5).

All nonhuman primates are quadrupeds, designed for moving about using all four limbs, but there is great variation in the way they use their limbs. Many strepsirhines move by *vertical clinging and leaping* (VCL, Figure 6.5a). Their hind limbs are longer than their front legs. This allows them to sit upright against a tree trunk or bamboo stalk, then launch themselves from a vertical posture through the air, turning as they leap and landing upright against a nearby upright support. For instance, sifakas bound from tree trunk to tree trunk at high speed using this locomotor technique.

Contrary to the commonly depicted image of them swinging through treetops, monkeys actually walk and run (on the ground and in trees) in much the same way that dogs, cats, and other four-legged mammals do (Figure 6.5d). Rather than arm-swing, monkeys run and leap along branches, their arms and legs moving in a limited plane of motion. The palms of the hands and feet make contact with the surface they are walking on. The skeleton of a monkey such as a baboon, which lives both on the ground and in trees, shows this clearly (Figure 6.5c). The running motion of any four-legged animal, whether a dog or a monkey, features a limited range of motion of the limbs, which are adapted for fast forward running, not

Notice how much the body of the baboon looks like that of a dog or cat.

three-dimensional climbing. The shoulder blade, or scapula, is oriented vertically across the upper arm and shoulder, allowing the arms to swing back and forth in a rapid pendulum motion but not to rotate. Although a few monkey species use their arms in what appears to be a semi–arm-swinging motion, this is by no means a widespread or well-developed adaptation in monkeys.

By contrast, an ape's arm has a full range of motion (Figure 6.5b). As we shall see, this is an adaptation to arm-hanging for feeding. Arm-hangers need a scapula that is oriented across the back rather than on the sides of the upper arms to allow this freedom of motion. Apes also possess a cone-shaped rib cage and torso; long, curved digit bones; small thumbs; and long arms to aid in arm-swinging.

Grasping Hands with Opposable Thumbs or Big Toes   The grasping hand with opposable thumb is believed to be the fundamental primate adaptation, although some prosimians don't fully exhibit this trait. Like most other mammals, primates typically have five digits per hand or foot. Having a thumb and big toe that are anatomically opposed to the other four digits allows primates to grasp objects with greater precision than other mammals. In some primates, such as colobine monkeys, gibbons, and spider monkeys, the four fingers are so elongated or the thumb is so reduced that the digits do not meet, rendering them less useful for gripping. Nonhuman primates also have an opposable hallux (the big toe).

For example, an ape uses its feet in much the same way that we use our hands. Humans have instead evolved a foot in which all the toes line up in the same plane, at the cost of a loss of dexterity of the foot.

Flattened Nails   The primate grasping hand has flattened nails at the ends of the digits instead of claws. This is the case for all primates except one group, the marmosets and tamarins. In addition, many strepsirhines have a combination of nails and a single clawed digit on their hands and feet.

Forward-Facing Eyes with Stereoscopic Vision   Consider the way you see the world and compare it with the view of most other mammals (Figure 6.6). For example, a horse has eye sockets mounted on either side of its head. It has a field of vision that extends nearly 360 degrees, except for a blind spot directly behind. However, the horse's forward vision is not very good because the fields of vision of its two eyes don't fully overlap in front. Now consider your own vision. Like those of nonhuman primates, your eyes are mounted flush on the front of your head; your peripheral vision to the sides and behind you is

Animals that evolved as prey species, like the ancestors of horses, needed a full field of vision to watch for predators stalking them from behind.

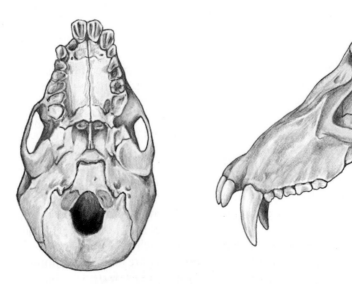

FIGURE 6.6   The primate skull is generalized compared to many other mammals.

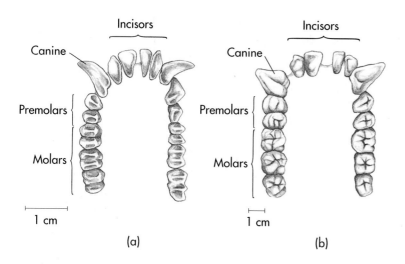

FIGURE 6.7 The primate dental formula illustrated for (a) the lower dentition of an Old World monkey and (b) the upper dentition of a gorilla.

severely constrained by this anatomy. But your forward field of vision is covered by both eyes. This stereoscopic view enables you to have excellent *depth perception* because the overlapping fields of vision provide a three-dimensional view of the world.

Stereoscopic vision, grasping hands, opposable thumbs, and nails rather than claws seem like an obvious suite of adaptations to life in the trees. This was the thinking of Frederic Wood-Jones and George Elliot-Smith, two British anatomists who proposed the idea in the 1920s. Their **arboreal hypothesis** was widely accepted and stood unchallenged for a half-century. But in the 1970s Matthew Cartmill, a young primate anatomy student, pointed out some key flaws in that model. Squirrels, he noted, lack the primate stereoscopic vision and grasping hand with nails, yet they scamper up and down trees with great agility. To understand primate origins, Cartmill argued, we should consider how the very earliest primates and their close kin lived. The fossil record shows that early on, primates were anatomically very much like modern insectivores. Today, such small creatures live in the tangled thickets that grow around the base of tropical forest trees, where they live by stalking and capturing insects and other fast-moving prey. Cartmill hypothesized that these creatures are a useful analog for early primates; his **visual predation hypothesis** proposed that forward-facing eyes, depth-perceptive vision, and grasping hands for catching their prey, not for climbing in trees, were the key adaptations of ancient primates (Cartmill, 1974). Many predators have forward-facing eyes—eagles, owls, and cats, for instance—which are thought to aid them in precisely homing in on their prey.

The arboreal hypothesis and the visual predation hypothesis are not mutually exclusive; at some point ancient nonhuman primates did indeed live in the trees. Variants of these two theories have been put forward by scholars such as Robert Sussman (1991), who proposed that excellent stereoscopic vision and grasping hands were essential for foraging for flowering plants, which arose during the same geologic period in which early primates emerged.

Generalized Teeth   Teeth are an extraordinarily important part of a nonhuman primate from an anthropologist's perspective. Their shape tells us a great deal about everything from a species' diet to its mating system (Figure 6.7). Fossilized teeth also allow us to cautiously infer patterns of behavior and diet in extinct primates we study. Most nonhuman primates eat a diet that is some combination of leaves, fruit, and other plant products, with occasional animal protein in the form of insects, small mammals, or other animals. Only one, the tarsier, eats mainly animal protein.

arboreal hypothesis   Hypothesis for the origin of primate adaptation that focuses on the value of grasping hands and stereoscopic vision for life in the trees.

visual predation hypothesis   Hypothesis for the origin of primate adaptation that focuses on the value of grasping hands and stereoscopic vision for catching small prey.

Nonhuman primates do not possess enormous canine teeth for tearing food, as carnivores do, nor do they have the heavy grinding molars that grazing animals have. Scientists believe that nonhuman primates have undergone an evolutionary reduction in the degree of specialization of the teeth, evident in the small canines and incisors and the rounded molars of most of them. If we consider the **dental arcade**, the arc of teeth along either the bottom or top of the mouth, beginning at the midline of the mouth there are four types of teeth arranged in the following dental formula: two incisors, one canine, two premolars (what your dentist calls bicuspids), and three molars. The exceptions to this pattern are most of the New World monkeys, which have a third premolar, and the strepsirhines, which have varying dental formulas.

Petrosal Bulla   The petrosal bulla is the tiny bit of the skeleton that covers and protects parts of the inner ear. Its importance to primate taxonomists is that this is the single bony trait that is shared by all primates, living or extinct, which occurs in no other mammalian group. When a fossil of questionable status is uncovered, researchers examine the ear portion carefully in search of the petrosal bulla.

Enclosed Bony Eye Orbits in the Skull   Primates also have an apparent anatomical adaptation to the importance of vision: enclosed (or partially enclosed) bony eye orbits in the skull, which may protect the eye more effectively than the open orbit of lower mammals (Figure 6.6). This orbital closure is more complete in haplorhines than it is in strepsirhines.

LIFE HISTORY TRAITS

The life history of mammals—their trajectory from conception to death—varies widely. In general, mammals that reproduce slowly, live long lives, and acquire information about their world through learning and not their genes, have delayed maturation and drawn-out life histories. Primates take this trend to an extreme.

Single Offspring   Nearly all primates give birth to single offspring. Many mammals, especially smaller species, give birth to litters or twins. The only exception among nonhuman primates is the marmosets and tamarins, which give birth to twins. Single births, combined with the long maturation period and the amount of time and energy mothers invest in their offspring, represent a strategy in which investment of time and energy in a few babies has replaced the more primitive mammalian pattern of litters of offspring that receive less intensive care.

Large Brains   Primates have large brains. They possess a high degree of *encephalization,* or evolved increase in the volume of the **neocortex** of the brain, which is involved in higher cognitive processes. This is more obvious in the brains of haplorhine primates than in strepsirhines, and we see it in the greater number of convolutions that compose the ridges and fissures (sulci and gyri) of the brain's surface. These convolutions increase the effective surface area of the brain and are believed to contribute to higher cognitive function.

There is much debate among scientists about the reasons for the evolutionary expansion of brain volume in primates and for the survival value of a big brain itself. The primate brain is such a large, metabolically expensive organ to grow and maintain that it must have important survival and reproductive benefits. We will consider these in Chapter 7.

Extended Ontogeny   Primates live by learned behaviors as much as they do on hardwired instinct. For example, many primates live in social groups, so a baby monkey or ape must learn how to be a member of a social group if it intends to successfully court a mate and rear offspring itself; these are largely learned behaviors. Thus it is important for primates to be socialized within their communities, a process that can take up a large proportion of their infancy and maturation.

dental arcade   The parabolic arc that forms the upper or lower row of teeth.

neocortex   The part of the brain that controls higher cognitive function; the cerebrum.

Many animals live much longer life spans than primates do. Giant tortoises may live 150 years, and even among mammals some whale species may live more than 100 years. But primates are notable for the extended length of each stage, from infancy to adulthood, of their life cycle. The life cycle is also called **ontogeny** (Figure 6.8). The gorilla life span is about 20 times longer than that of a mouse, but the time it takes from gestation to sexual maturity is almost 80 times longer (about 15 years, compared with 10 weeks). Why?

Consider the sort of information a growing primate must learn in order to survive in the world. In addition to learning how to find food and water, the primate must learn how to live in a social group. The process of learning to live in

ontogeny The life cycle of an organism from conception to death.

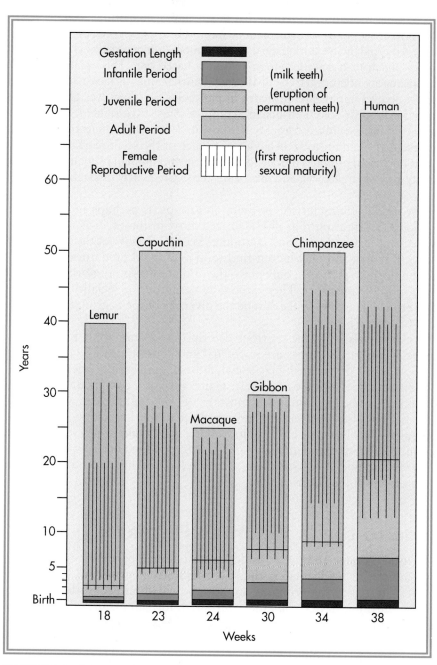

FIGURE 6.8 Primates exhibit prolonged life histories, spending more time in each stage of life than most other mammals do.

a group is a long one, and the behaviors involved tend not to be purely instinctual. An infant monkey or ape reared in isolation will end up severely deficient in the social skills it needs to be part of a social group. Parental investment in the infant is dramatically greater in primates than it is in rodents or most other mammals because social skills require years of maturation and practice.

BEHAVIORAL TRAITS: ACTIVITY AND SOCIALITY

Activity Patterns   Most primate species are active during daylight hours, possess color vision, and have limited olfactory senses. Many mammal species are nocturnal and rely on their sense of smell to negotiate their physical and social environment. Consider a cat, rat, or wolf, all of which are primarily nocturnal and have a sense of smell thousands of times more powerful than that of any haplorhine primate. Many strepsirhines are **nocturnal** (active at night), but all haplorhines except one, the night monkey *Aotus,* are **diurnal** (active during the daylight hours). Primates made a fundamental shift from an olfactory-based lifestyle to a visually based one. This entailed shifting from being primarily nocturnal to being diurnal. Diurnal animals have a greater need for color vision, and haplorhine primates in particular use their eyes to find plant foods, including brightly colored fruits, in a complex forest environment. At the same time, diurnal primates evolved complex patterns of visual communication, such as bright colors and communicative behaviors, in place of the scent-marking communication that nocturnal primates use. In addition, some nonhuman primate species are active mainly at dusk and dawn, and others are active irregularly throughout the day and night.

Sociality, or the characteristic of living in groups, is perhaps the most fundamental social adaptation that characterizes most primates. It is the adaptation by which a primate survives and reproduces because it provides the animal with ready access to mates and may help it find food and avoid predators.

Of the haplorhine primates, only one—the orangutan—is not normally found in a social group of some sort. There are many variations in sociality among the nonhuman primates, and we will examine the diversity of social grouping patterns in detail in Chapter 7.

All the characteristics in the previous descriptions do not apply to every primate species. Many strepsirhines are nocturnal and some are solitary, navigating by olfaction, whereas others are highly social, diurnal, and visually oriented. Strepsirhines often possess a mixture of primate traits, such as a combination of claws and nails on the hands. Don't make the mistake of thinking that lemurs and their kin are necessarily "less evolved" or more primitive than monkeys. The simple fact is that, as we will examine in detail in Chapter 10, monkeys and strepsirhines share a common ancestor, and after the split between the two lineages, each group evolved in separate lines. Natural selection favored diurnality and sociality more in monkeys than it did in strepsirhines.

A Guide to the Nonhuman Primates

As we discussed on page 163, we consider the nonhuman primates as two major groups within the order Primates: the suborders Strepsirhini and Haplorhini (Figure 6.9). Alternately the primates can be subdivided into suborders Prosimii and Anthropoidea. Recall that the Linnaean system for naming includes not only order, family, genus, and species but also higher and lesser categories (see Chapter 4). So primate families that are anatomically similar are lumped in the same superfamily, and subgroups of families are called subfamilies. Not all taxonomists agree on how to classify the primates, and one nonhuman primate, the tarsier, straddles the two suborders. The geographic distribution of nonhuman primates is presented in Figure 6.10 on pages 172–173.

nocturnal   Active at night.

diurnal   Active during daylight hours.

sociality   Group living, a fundamental trait of haplorhine primates.

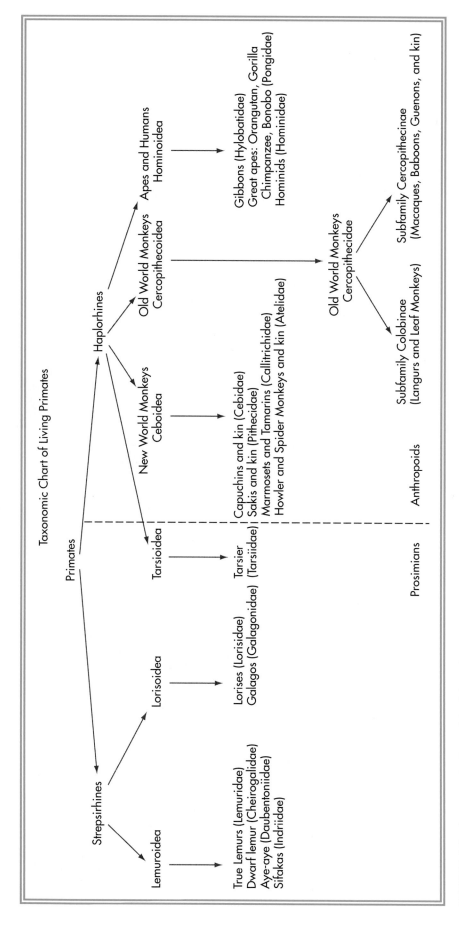

FIGURE 6.9 A taxonomic chart of the living primates.

A World Map of Living Nonhuman Primates

NORTH AND SOUTH AMERICA

Figure 6.10 Primates in the New World tend to be small-bodied compared to those elsewhere. All species are primarily arboreal, and some have grasping tails to aid in tree-top feeding. New World primates are found from central Mexico to Argentina, and in some equatorial forests numerous species can be found sharing the same habitat.

UAKARI Native to seasonally flooded rain forests

MURIQUI Highly endangered, the largest new world monkey

GOLDEN LION TAMARIN One of Brazil's endangered primates

EUROPE AND ASIA

Nonhuman primates are found across tropical Asia, occurring as far north as central Japan (the Japanese macaque). They occur in only the tiniest bit of Europe, on the island of Gibraltar (where they may have been introduced by people). Asia is the home of gibbons and orangutans, many species of Old World Monkeys (the langurs, leaf monkeys and macaques) plus numerous strepsirhines.

DeBrazza's Guenon A diverse group found in African forests

Galago Live in many African forests; Also called Bushbabies

Golden Snub-Nosed Monkey One of China's beautiful and endangered primates

Savanna Baboon Baboons are found across subsaharan Africa

Chimpanzee Found in suitable habitat across equatorial Africa

Hanuman Langurs Found all across the Indian Subcontinent

Lar Gibbon Found in forests from India through South East Asia

Lorises The only Strepsirhine primates in Africa and mainland Asia

Tarsier The only entirely carnivorous primate, found in Southeast Asia rain forests

Gorillas Live in both lowland and mountain forests

Red-Bellied Lemur Found only on Madagascar

Lion-Tailed Macaque One of the world's most threatened primates, found in hilly forests of Southern India

Orangutan Live only on the Islands of Sumatra and Borneo in Indonesia

AFRICA

Primates are found across subSaharan Africa and also in small areas of northwestern Africa and in the Arabian peninsula. Primate biodiversity peaks in the central African Congo Basin, where more than fifteen species can be found in the same tropical rain forest habitat. Africa provides primate habitat ranging from rain forest to savanna to high mountain meadows, across a vast area. Moreover, since humans evolved in Africa, we can study African primates with a eye toward learning something about the environment of the human past.

FIGURE 6.11 Lemurs are found only in Madagascar.

FIGURE 6.12 The lemurs rediated into a variety of forms, including the sifaka.

THE STREPSIRHINES

The primates of the suborder Strepsirhini include the lemurs of Madagascar and the lorises and galagos of mainland Africa and tropical Asia. Linnaeus originally subdivided the primates into two major groups—the prosimians (sometimes called the lower primates) and the anthropoids (higher primates)—based on a number of anatomical features. *Strepsirhine* and *prosimian* are not completely synonymous; one prosimian primate, the tarsier, is a haplorhine, not a strepsirhine. But all strepsirhines and prosimians share some common anatomical features: a reliance on olfaction, nocturnality, and a lack of complex social behavior patterns. Their incisor teeth protrude from the front of the mouth to form a comblike surface, known as the *tooth comb*, used for grooming. Many also have specialized clawed toes that serve as grooming tools. Long believed to be largely solitary, even the nocturnal strepsirhines such as lorises and dwarf lemurs live in a wide array of societies, ranging from pairs and social clusters to a few solitary species. Some lemurs violate these general traits, however, as we shall see next.

The Lemurs   The superfamily Lemuroidea is found only on Madagascar and consists of the families Lemuridae (true lemurs), Cheirogaleidae (dwarf lemurs), Indriidae (the sifakas and indri), and Daubentoniidae (the aye-aye). The fourth largest island on Earth, Madagascar is home to perhaps the best example of an adaptive radiation we know of among living nonhuman primates (Figure 6.11). Madagascar broke away from the eastern coast of the continental mainland of Africa, through the process of continental drift, beginning some 100 million years ago. By the time the separation was complete, the earliest members of the primate order had evolved in Africa. As Madagascar drifted slowly out of contact with the rest of Africa, the primitive primates stranded on its land mass began to evolve without gene flow from other primates. Some researchers believe that lemurs may have other, more ancient origins as well, but the bulk of evidence indicates an African ancestry, and that all modern lemurs are descended from a single origin of Madagascar primates.

Over time, these animals developed a wide range of adaptations to exploit the many available habitats and niches on Madagascar (Figure 6.12). In the absence of large predators (there are no big carnivores or large eagles on the entire island), a diverse array of forms radiated from the ancestral colonizing forms. Sadly, many of those species are now extinct, presumably because of hunting by people, who arrived on the island beginning 1,500 to 2,000 years ago. We know about the extinct forms through the skeletal remains we have found; we call these remains *subfossils* because they are found as bones, rather than fossils, due to the recent date of the animals' disappearance (in about the past 1,000 years).

FIGURE 6.13   A subfossil lemur, *Megaladapis.*

There was once an adaptive radiation on Madagascar of large-bodied, slow-moving lemurs, both arboreal and terrestrial. Many of the extinct species were quite large; *Archaeoindris* and *Megaladapis* ambled along the ground like large bears (Figure 6.13). One entire subfamily, the Paleopropithecines, were sloth lemurs; some of these species apparently hung upside down from tree limbs, as New World sloths do. Lacking natural predators, they would have been plentiful prey for the human colonizers. The species still alive today may be those that were simply too small or too elusive for human colonizers to bother hunting (Insights and Advances: The Rarest of the Rare on pages 178–179).

New subfossil lemur species are still being discovered in remote caves and other sites in Madagascar.

The four families of lemurs alive today range in size from the 2-ounce (40-g) mouse lemur to the 20-pound (8-kg) indri. The families are quite distinct from one another. The dwarf lemurs are small, nocturnal, dull-colored insect- and fruit-eaters. Once thought to be solitary, they live in diverse social systems consisting of small clusters or loosely associated pairs. True lemurs tend to be diurnal and social, living in social groups like those of many haplorhine primates. The well-studied ring-tailed lemur (Figure 6.14) lives in groups of up to 25 in which, as among many true lemurs (Figures 6.15 and 6.16), females are dominant to males (Ganzhorn & Kappeler, 1993). The indri and several sifaka species are the largest living prosimians. The indri is noted for its monogamous social system; its loud,

FIGURE 6.14   The ring-tailed lemur is the best-known of the Madagascar primates.

FIGURE 6.15   This red-bellied lemur shows clearly the traits that characterize strepsirhine primates.

FIGURE 6.16   The endangered ruffed lemur.

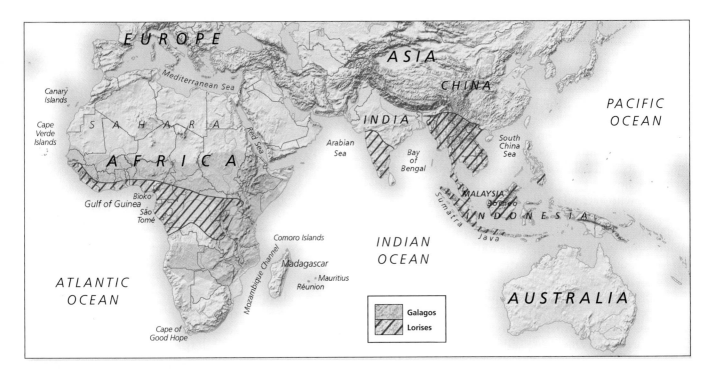

FIGURE 6.17   The distribution of lorises and galagos.

FIGURE 6.18   A loris.

FIGURE 6.19   A galago, or bush baby.

haunting call; and its diet of leaves. The aye-aye is nocturnal and largely solitary. It feeds on bird eggs, fruit, and insect larvae that it locates by tapping fallen tree trunks with its long middle finger. Grubs respond to the tapping by wriggling, and the aye-aye then digs under the bark to find its meal.

The Lorises   The lorises are a diverse group of strepsirhines in tropical Africa and Asia (Figure 6.17). They include the various species of galago, or bush baby, which occur only on Africa and are now considered to be in their own family, the Galagonidae. Recent behavioral and genetic studies have warranted the splitting of many new species from this group (Bearder et al., 1995; Groves, 2001).

Lorises (Figure 6.18) and galagos (Figure 6.19) probably resemble the primitive ancestors of modern haplorhines. They communicate both vocally and olfactorily, by scent-marking objects in their environment. They are nocturnal and spend their nights feeding on fruits and hunting for insects and other small animals. In a classic study, Pierre Charles-Dominique (1977) found that in West African forests, multiple species of lorises and galagos shared their habitat by dividing up the available food items and by foraging at different heights within the forest canopy and understory. During the daylight hours, many lorises and galago species stay curled up in a nest in a tree cavity, and some species also park their offspring in such nests when they are out searching for food.

Lorises include the slender and slow loris of Asia and the potto and angwantibo of tropical Africa. All are slow-moving, deliberate stalkers, capturing small prey. Galagos are active, leaping animals (using VCL) that range in size from a housecat to a rat and generally are more insectivorous than the lorises.

Although lorises and galagoes were long thought to be exclusively solitary, recent research has shown that many species are in fact social at certain times and in certain circumstances (Radespiel, 2006). Our notion that these strepsirhines as not very social may well be revised in coming years.

FIGURE 6.20   The tarsier is a haplorhine, and may represent an evolutionary bridge between lower and higher primates.

FIGURE 6.21   The distribution of the tarsier.

THE HAPLORHINES

The nonhuman primates of the suborder Haplorhini include the tarsier, New World monkeys, Old World monkeys, apes, and hominids. The tarsier is a haplorhine but also a prosimian. It is closely related to the anthropoids but occupies an evolutionary status intermediate between the lower and higher primates. All the other haplorhines can also be called anthropoid primates. Haplorhines possess the full suite of adaptations that characterize the living primates. Without exception haplorhines are guided more by vision than by olfaction. This emphasis on vision is reflected in the full closure of the back of their eye orbits, providing bony protection for the eye that strepsirhines and most other mammals lack. Living haplorhines also possess a lower jaw that is fused at the midline in adulthood; in prosimians and most other mammals the jaw is two pieces joined in the middle with cartilage.

With few exceptions (the owl monkey and tarsier), haplorhines are diurnal. And with one exception (the orangutan), they live in social groups. The ratio of brain to body size in haplorhines is higher than in strepsirhines; cognition is part of the haplorhine suite of adaptations. Cognition also is related to the degree of social complexity we observe among haplorhines, greater than what we usually see among the strepsirhines. The haplorhines include all extinct forms of hominids, as well as humans.

The Tarsiers   Tarsiers are haplorhine primates that are thought to occupy an evolutionary position between the prosimian and anthropoid primates. Tarsiers possess a mixture of traits of anthropoid and prosimian primates, but they are generally considered to be closer to anthropoids (Figure 6.20). Frederick Szalay and Eric Delson (1979) tried to resolve the status of tarsiers by classifying them as both prosimians and haplorhines to indicate their mixed evolutionary bridge. That is, they are haplorhines but have anatomical links to the strepsirhines.

The several species of tarsier recognized today live in Indonesia and nearby island groups (Figure 6.21). They occupy an owl-like ecological role as nocturnal predators on small vertebrates and are the most highly carnivorous of all nonhuman

INSIGHTS AND ADVANCES

The Rarest of the Rare

Although extinction has always been a natural event in the history of life on Earth, humans have dramatically increased the odds of extinction for many species. Of the 250 living nonhuman primate species, the majority are threatened with extinction. For perhaps half of these, the new century may bring an end to their existence on Earth.

At least 50 species are critically endangered. Many of these endangered species live in one of several hotspots of biodiversity, geographic regions known for a unique assortment of highly diverse animals and plants (Mittermeier et al., 2002). Not surprisingly, these areas are centered in equatorial regions, where large tracts of forests in the Amazon Basin of South America and the Congo Basin of central Africa remain. In these strongholds it is still possible to find 15 or more nonhuman primate species in a single tract of forest. Other areas, such as Madagascar, harbor whole ecosystems full of primates that exist nowhere else on Earth.

These vanishing treasures include the following:

- *Golden bamboo lemur* Discovered only in the late 1980s, this beautiful 5-pound (2-kg) prosimian (*Hapalemur aureus*) lives in Ranomafana National Park, a densely forested preserve of lemur biodiversity in eastern Madagascar (Figure A). It feeds on bamboo, which it shares with two other species of bamboo lemur in the same forest. The golden bamboo lemur eats the inside of the stem of the bamboo, whereas the other two species eat the leaves. The pith contains high levels of cyanide; every day the lemur consumes enough cyanide to kill a horse (Meier et al., 1987; Glander et al., 1989). An estimated 300 to 400 of the animals exist in

FIGURE A   The golden bamboo lemur.

the only remaining forest habitat left to this species.

- *Zanzibar red colobus* Zanzibar, a palm-covered tropical island just off the coast of the East African nation of Tanzania, is home to a small and dwindling population of red colobus monkeys (*Procolobus badius kirkii*) (Figure B). They are gorgeous animals, with a crimson back and black face fringed with white tufts of hair. A remnant population lives in tiny patches of forest amid villages and palm groves on both Zanzibar and neighboring islands. Their long-term prospects are bleak in the face of land development and human population increase.

- *Golden snub-nosed monkey* Snub-nosed monkeys are still little known to Western science because their several species live in China and Vietnam, which until recently were closed to foreign scientists. The golden snub-nosed monkey (*Rhinopithecus roxellanae*) has the largest population, about 20,000, centered in the high mountain ranges of Sichuan and Hubei

FIGURE B   The beautiful Zanzibar red colobus.

Provinces in central China (Figure C). A male can weigh nearly 50 pounds (22 kg) and possess a thick mane of golden-

FIGURE C   The golden snub-nosed monkey.

FIGURE D   The lion-tailed macaque.

orange hair that drapes across its back. This, combined with a pale blue face, gives the species a dramatic appearance. In Shennongjia Nature Reserve, it lives in pine and fir forest not unlike the Rocky Mountains of the United States, and it survives the snowy winters eating pine needles and lichens. Two close relatives, *Rhinopithecus bieti* and *R. brelichi,* are more critically endangered, with populations of only a few hundred each.

• *Lion-tailed macaque* The western Ghat mountains of southern India are home to a number of rare primates. Among these is the lion-tailed macaque (*Macaca silenus*), so named for its long tail ending in a tuft and its mane of white hair (Figure D). The species has never been common, and its limited habitat of lush mountain valleys is threatened by construction of a controversial hydroelectric project by the Indian government, which will flood part of the macaque's range.

• *Muriqui* The largest nonhuman primate in the Western Hemisphere is also one of the rarest (Figure E). The muriqui, or woolly spider monkey, lives in forest fragments in the Atlantic coastal forest of Brazil, where ranching has eaten up almost all its remaining habitat. Conservation efforts have focused on preserving existing habitat on private lands; fewer than 1,000 animals may remain.

• *Golden lion tamarin* This flame-colored, 1-pound (0.4-kg) monkey lives in the same region as the muriqui and is also critically endangered because of habitat loss (Figure F). A novel project has reestablished golden lion tamarins in forests in which they had gone extinct by releasing monkeys that have been reared in zoos and then "rehabilitated" to survive in the wild. After years of shaky progress, this project has restored healthy populations of golden lion tamarins to some former habitats and shows how sound knowledge of a species' needs in nature can be essential for its long-term conservation.

The current approach to nonhuman primate conservation is to try to protect hotspots of nonhuman primate diversity that are home to species such as these and to prevent people from exploiting the forest resources at unsustainable levels. The threat is clear: If we do not act now, a large proportion of the diversity of nonhuman primates will be gone within a generation.

FIGURE F   The golden lion tamarin.

Nearly all threatened nonhuman primate species live in developing countries. The challenge is to help these countries develop without casting aside regard for the health of the environment.

In the whole of the twentieth century, not one primate taxon went extinct. It seems very unlikely we will be able to make the same statement about the twenty-first century. Indeed, in the few years since the new century opened, one species, Miss Waldron's red colobus, has already been reported to be on the brink of extinction in West Africa.

FIGURE E   The muriqui.

primates, eating small prey such as lizards, frogs, and insects. They live in monogamous pairs, are exclusively nocturnal, and park their young in tree nests while out foraging (Gursky, 1994, 1995).

THE NEW WORLD MONKEYS

The New World monkeys are classified in the infraorder **Platyrrhini** (referring to the flat shape of the nose) and are all in the superfamily Ceboidea. They live in the tropical and subtropical forests of the Western Hemisphere, from Argentina northward to within a few hundred miles of the U.S. border in the state of Veracruz, Mexico (Figure 6.22). All the New World monkeys share three features:

- *Small body size.* The largest New World monkey, the muriqui (Figure 6.23), weighs only about 25 pounds (12 kg). The smallest, the marmosets and tamarins, range from 1.5 pounds (0.6 kg) down to just a few ounces.

- *Three premolar teeth.* Whereas all other haplorhine primates have two premolars (bicuspids) and three molars in each quadrant of the mouth, New World monkeys have three. (The ceboid monkeys possess three molars and the Callitrichidae only two.)

- *Arboreality.* There are no primarily terrestrial New World nonhuman primates, even though there are large stretches of grassland in parts of South America (as opposed to Africa, where baboons and other nonhuman primates make use of open country). In addition, some New World monkeys have grasping

Platyrrhini Infraorder of the order Primates that is synonymous with the New World monkeys, or ceboids.

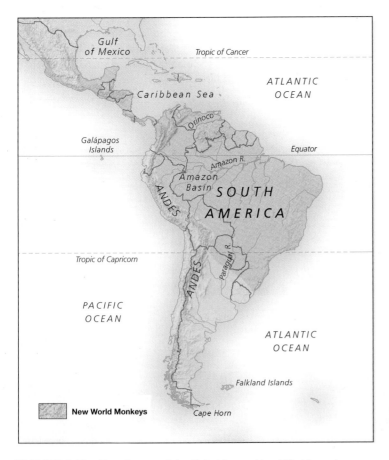

FIGURE 6.22 Distribution of the Ceboidea, or New World monkeys.

FIGURE 6.23 The muriqui of Brazil, the largest New World monkey.

FIGURE 6.24   A prehensile tail is an adaptation to grasping branches for support while feeding.

FIGURE 6.25   The red-faced uakari, a bizarre-looking New World monkey.

prehensile tails; this trait occurs in some members of the families Cebidae and Atelidae (Figure 6.24). The prehensile tail is an adaptation to feeding, allowing a monkey to hang beneath slender branches to reach food.

The Ceboidea are currently classified as four families: Cebidae (capuchins), Pithecidae (sakis and related species; Figure 6.25), Atelidae (howlers, spider monkeys, and muriquis), and Callitrichidae (marmosets and tamarins; Figure 6.26). A few taxonomists (Fleagle, 1999; Groves, 2001) consider the Callitrichidae to be so closely allied with the Cebidae that it should be a subfamily within it. The callitrichids are unique among primates for their suite of traits that resemble those of lower mammals: small body size, claws instead of nails, and the routine birthing of twins rather than a single offspring. In some species a **polyandrous** mating system, in which one female has more than one male mate, is characteristic. The evolutionary reasons behind these traits are complex; we will discuss them further when we consider the diversity of nonhuman primate mating systems.

THE OLD WORLD MONKEYS

The Old World monkeys, along with the apes and humans, are in the infraorder **Catarrhini** (or primates with downward-facing nostrils). Old World monkeys occur in many parts of Africa and Asia and also in small areas of the Middle East

prehensile tail   Grasping tail possessed by some species of the primate families Cebidae and Atelidae.

polyandrous   Mating system in which one female mates with multiple males.

Catarrhini   Infraorder of the order Primates that includes the Old World monkeys, apes, and hominids.

FIGURE 6.26   The rare golden lion tamarin is the largest callitrichid monkey.

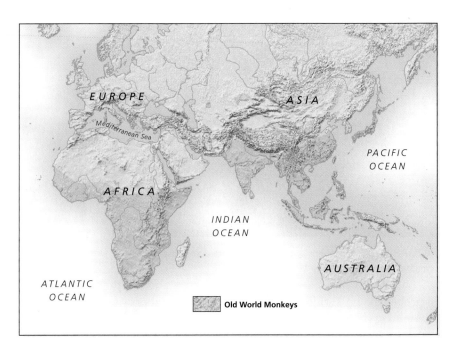

FIGURE 6.27   Distribution of the Old World monkeys.

(Figure 6.27). They are in the superfamily Cercopithecoidea, which contains the single family Cercopithecidae. Old World monkeys have exploited a wider variety of habitats than their New World counterparts, occupying every ecological setting from tropical rain forest to savanna to desert.

As a family, the Old World monkeys share *ischial callosities:* thickened calluses on the rump that presumably make sitting on rough surfaces more comfortable. They also possess double-ridged molar teeth. These *bilophodont molars* are believed to be an evolutionary advance for biting through fibrous plant material. Old World monkeys display a greater size range than New World monkeys, from 2-pound (0.8-kg) talapoins (*Miopithecus talapoin*) to 70-pound (32-kg) baboons (*Papio* ssp.). Some groups also display a greater degree of sexual dimorphism than we see in any New World monkey species.

Two subfamilies within the Cercopithecidae merit special attention. Colobines are the so-called leaf-monkeys, langurs, and odd-nosed monkeys of Asia (Figure 6.28)

Their ability to digest high fiber leaves also allows colobines to live in very dry areas where water and tender leaves are scarce.

FIGURE 6.28   The Hanuman langur, a widely distributed Asian colobine.

FIGURE 6.29   The black-and-white colobus is an African colobine.

and the colobus of Africa (Figure 6.29). They have evolved a semichambered stomach that resembles that of a cow and can digest tough, cellulose-laden foods in an organ called a foregut, using a community of microbes that break down the cellulose compounds in their food for them. This adaptation enables colobines to live at high population densities in forests where they would otherwise be hard-pressed to find edible foods. The gruesome but intriguing behavior of infanticide also occurs more widely among colobines than any other monkey taxonomic group (See Insights and Advances: The Infanticide Wars, Chapter 7, pages 218–219).

The cercopithecines include the macaques of Asia and the baboons, guenons, drills, mangabeys, and patas monkeys of Africa (Figures 6.30 and 6.31). They share the presence of cheek pouches for food storage. Females of some Old World monkey species undergo a regular period of sexual receptivity, or **estrus**, during which skin around the genital area inflates with fluid and serves as a billboard of her fertility. Sexual dimorphism is generally more pronounced in cercopithecines than in colobines. Some of the cercopithecines—the baboons of Africa and the rhesus macaque in Asia—are among the most studied species of all primates.

FIGURE 6.30   Baboons are African cercopithecines.

FIGURE 6.31   De Brazza's monkey and its fellow guenons are in the subfamily Cercopithecinae.

FIGURE 6.32 All living apes possess rotating, suspensory shoulders, as do humans.

THE HOMINOIDS

The apes and humans, past and present, are classified in the superfamily Hominoidea. This includes the ape families **hylobatid (Hylobatidae)** and **pongid (Pongidae)** and the human family **hominid (Hominidae)**. As we saw earlier, had Linnaeus not been so bound by his theology, humans and apes probably would have been placed in the same family, based on their many shared anatomical traits.

The hominoids extend many haplorhine traits: increased brain volume and intelligence, extended ontogeny, increased complexity of social interactions, and large body size. The hylobatids, or gibbons, often are called the lesser apes, based on minor anatomical differences from the four pongids, or great apes: the chimpanzee, bonobo, gorilla, and orangutan.

Apes and humans share several key postcranial anatomical traits. Foremost among these is the suspensory, rotating shoulder apparatus that allows for arm-hanging and arm-swinging, or **brachiation**. The anatomy that allows a quarterback to throw a football or a gymnast to perform on the high bar is the same as that which allowed fossil apes to hang from branches in the canopy of ancient forests (Figure 6.32), although it probably did not evolve for that purpose. Instead, researchers believe that arm-hanging initially was adaptive for suspending a large-bodied ape underneath a tree limb from which ripe fruit was growing. A branch that could not support the weight of an ape walking on top of it could support the same weight hung beneath it. In this way, the rotating shoulder of the ape may have an evolved function similar to that of the prehensile tail of many New World monkeys. The four great apes move about by a modified form of quadrupedalism called knuckle-walking (Figure 6.33) or, in the case of the orangutan, fist-walking. Apes also lack tails.

The social complexity of the hominoids does not apply to all taxa. We see it to its greatest extent in chimpanzees, bonobos, and human societies. Anthropologists study ape behavior because, in addition to being intrinsically fascinating, apes are among the most intelligent animals with which we share the planet. Only in great apes do we see tool technologies that resemble simple versions of human tool industries; lethal aggression between communities that resembles human warfare; and cognitive development, including language acquisition, which parallels that of children.

Gibbons   Gibbons are fourteen species of closely related apes, all currently classified in the genus *Hylobates* (although some taxonomists divide the genus into three or four genera). Gibbons live in Asian tropical and subtropical forests from easternmost India and Bangladesh through mainland Southeast Asia and the Indonesian archipelago (Figure 6.34). They range in size from the 10-pound (4-kg) Kloss's gibbon of the Mentawai Islands to the 25-pound (12-kg) siamang of peninsular Malaysia.

hylobatid (Hylobatidae)   Member of the gibbon, or lesser ape, family.

pongid (Pongidae)   One of the four great apes species: gorilla, chimpanzee, bonobo, or orangutan.

hominid (Hominidae)   Member of our own human family, past or present.

brachiation   Mode of arm-hanging and arm-swinging that uses a rotating shoulder to suspend the body of an ape or hominid beneath a branch or to travel between branches.

FIGURE 6.33 Great apes knuckle-walk when traveling on the ground.

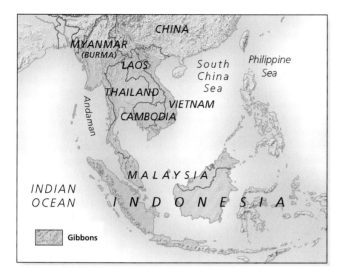

FIGURE 6.34 Distribution of the gibbons.

FIGURE 6.35 Gibbons are lesser apes, and live in the forests of south and Southeast Asia.

Gibbons are rain forest canopy inhabitants, their bodies well adapted for a highly arboreal existence of brachiating among and hanging beneath tree limbs (Figure 6.35). They possess long arms, extremely elongated fingers, shortened thumbs, and a suspensory shoulder designed for treetop life. Most gibbon species are highly **frugivorous,** or fruit-eating, using their high-energy diet to engage in a high-energy lifestyle of brachiating and singing. They are among the most vocal of all nonhuman primates; their whooping songs are given from morning until night and serve as declarations of territorial boundaries for other members of their species. Mated pairs also sing duets that reinforce the bond between male and female.

Gibbons have long been considered the most monogamous of the higher primates, living in pair bonds that last many years (Brockelman et al., 1998). However, recent field studies have shown that secretive matings outside the pair bond are not uncommon (Palombit, 1994). Gibbons are best considered to be socially monogamous but not necessarily reproductively monogamous. Whereas early gibbon researchers believed that monogamy among gibbons benefited the females, with the male providing protection against predators and other gibbons, modern researchers believe much the opposite. A female tolerates a male because he provides an essential service, helping to defend the patch of forest on which she must find food to nourish herself and her offspring (Sommer & Reichard, 2000).

Orangutans   Orangutans (*Pongo pygmaeus*) are the most enigmatic of all the hominoid primates. These red apes are among our closest living kin and among the largest-brained animals on Earth. But compared with other apes, they are largely solitary. Found in the rapidly disappearing rain forests of the Indonesian islands of Sumatra and Borneo (Figure 6.36 on page 186), orangutans are large-bodied and extremely sexually dimorphic. Males may weigh 200 pounds (78 kg), more than twice the size and weight of adult females (36 kg) (Figure 6.37 on page 186).

Orangutans are highly arboreal, traveling slowly through the forest canopy in search of fruit. Adult females and their dependent offspring occupy territories

frugivorous   An animal that eats a diet composed mainly of fruit.

FIGURE 6.36 Orangutans are limited to the islands of Sumatra and Borneo, where their numbers are rapidly declining.

FIGURE 6.37 Orangutan males are twice the size and weight of females.

Because orangutans are solitary much of their lives, it has taken primatologists far longer to learn the details of their social lives.

that they defend from other adult females. Adult males attempt to maintain control over a number of female territories, moving over a much larger area to attempt to monopolize them for mating purposes. Surplus males that cannot obtain access to their own females live as transients, attempting to approach females without being detected by the resident adult male. Resident adult males use resonating, loud calls to warn transients away. Birute Galdikas (1985), who did pioneering field research on Bornean orangutans in the 1960s, first observed transient males trying to forcibly mate with females, sometimes successfully. It became clear only recently that these transient males, long assumed to be adolescents because of their small size and lack of adult male physical features, often are adult males that have retained adolescent features. In fact, these "pseudo-adolescents" possess the physical features of immature males but produce male sex hormones and sperm (Maggioncalda et al., 1999). This appears to be a case of sexual selection for *bimaturism*, in which adults can take two different forms, allowing males to approach females by "posing" as adolescents without arousing the ire of resident adult males.

Orangutan reproduction is strongly influenced by the food supply. Cheryl Knott (1998) has documented that *mast-fruiting*, the unpredictable ripening of many fruit trees at the same time in Indonesian rain forests, triggers ovulation among female orangutans. At times of fruit abundance, orangutans form temporary associations of several individuals, presumably for mating purposes.

When times are lean, orangutans cope with the lack of fruit by feeding on whatever foods are available, including tree bark. They possess thickened molar enamel, unlike that of the African apes, which may be an adaptation to eating seeds and unripe fruits (Leighton, 1993).

Orangutans share the extended ontogeny of the other great apes; females reach sexual maturity at age 11 to 15 and males not until 15. The interval between successive births is longer in orangutans than in any other primate, nearly 8 years (Galdikas & Wood, 1990). When females mature, they disperse from their mother's territory to a nearby area to establish themselves as breeding adults. Males disperse more widely and often are alone for long periods (Delgado & van Schaik, 2000).

Sumatran and Bornean orangutans are quite different morphologically, and many researchers advocate considering them separate species (Delgado & van Schaik, 2000).

FIGURE 6.38   Distribution of the African great apes.

FIGURE 6.39   Gorillas are the largest living primates.

Bornean males have enormous flanges of flesh around the face and long, pendulous throat sacs (probably used to produce their resonating long calls).

Gorillas   The largest primates, weighing more than 400 pounds (200 kg) in the wild, gorillas today have a severely fragmented geographic distribution (Figures 6.38 and 6.39). Most of the estimated 80,000 gorillas in equatorial Africa are lowland gorillas and live in forests across central and western Africa. Lowland gorillas are extraordinarily diverse genetically, and some isolated populations are being elevated to full species status on the basis of the degree of their divergence from other gorillas (Gagneux et al., 1996). In eastern Africa, mountain gorillas also live in a highly fragmented distribution, but their overall numbers are far lower. Only 600 remain in the wild in two mountain ranges, the Virunga Volcanoes and the Bwindi Impenetrable Forest, along the border of Uganda, Rwanda, and the Democratic Republic of the Congo (Insights and Advances: The Impending Extinction of the Great Apes? on page 188). The two populations are nearly identical genetically and were separated by forest clearing only in the last several hundred years (Garner & Ryder, 1996; Stanford, 2001). Between the ranges of western lowland and mountain gorillas live eastern lowland gorillas, which occur across a wide elevational range in eastern Congo. Only a few thousand eastern lowland gorillas are believed to remain in the wild.

Gorillas are extremely sexually dimorphic, with males outweighing females by more than 50%. In their mid-teen years, males reach sexual maturity and acquire a gray saddle of hair on their backs, hence the label *silverback* for an adult male gorilla and *blackback* for an adolescent male. Females give birth about every 4 years. At or after sexual maturity, females tend to migrate to other groups, often in the company of sisters or close female kin (Figure 6.40). Life can be difficult for a female if she migrates with offspring; infanticide by silverbacks is a leading cause of mortality among mountain gorillas (Watts, 1989).

FIGURE 6.40   Gorillas live in one-male or multimale groups, from which females emigrate at sexual maturity.

INSIGHTS AND ADVANCES

The Impending Extinction of the Great Apes?

For more than 20 million years, apes have flourished in the tropical forests of the Old World. But today, throughout their geographic distribution in equatorial Africa and Southeast Asia, the great apes are in grave peril of extinction. For the most critically endangered, the orangutan and bonobo, this could mean extinction in the wild within your lifetime. Can this be prevented? Conservation efforts must begin with an understanding of the threats to the endangered species. These threats exist in several key areas:

• *Habitat destruction* The loss of tropical forest habitat is the single greatest factor causing the decline in nonhuman primate populations worldwide (Figure A). From Congo to Indonesia, forest clearing is accelerating, and with it comes the loss of thousands of animal and plant species. Forests are cut by local farmers so they can plant crops, but forests are also cut by government-sanctioned logging companies in many regions.

Recent estimates on the Indonesian island of Sumatra place the loss of orangutan habitat at 80% in the past two decades, and the population declined 45% just from 1993 to 1999 (van Schaik et al., 2001). At current rates of habitat loss, the 20,000

FIGURE A The destruction of tropical forests, the habitat of living great apes, continues at an alarming rate.

orangutans remaining in the wild face extinction within 15 years.

• *Bushmeat* A major cause of population decline among apes in central and western Africa is the bushmeat trade. Bushmeat is simply the meat of any wild animal that is eaten by people.

In Africa, the smoked flesh of gorillas, chimpanzees, and bonobos is highly valued. People have been hunting and eating apes for thousands of years, but recently the pattern has changed. No longer is ape hunting practiced only by local villagers trying to put some protein in their children's stomachs. As international logging companies from Europe cut logging roads deep into pristine rain forests, they create a pipeline by which ape carcasses can be easily transported from remote areas. Businessmen in towns and cities pay hunters to send them as many apes as they can kill, the meat of which is sold on the black market, and sometimes in the open market, for several times the price of beef. In Africa, government officials and wealthy people exhibit their affluence by serving ape meat to visitors, including stunned foreigners.

Apes have withstood low levels of hunting for millennia, but the recent intense pressure, combined with the very slow reproductive rate of the great apes (perhaps one baby every 4 years), has resulted in dramatic population decline even in forests that have seen little human use. Stopping the bushmeat trade entails not only law enforcement but also a change in cultural values so that Africans do not consider the eating of apes to be a status symbol.

• *International zoo, laboratory, and pet trade* Despite increased public awareness of the evils of taking apes from the wild, poaching for the live animal trade still occurs. Hundreds of baby orangutans are caught every year to be sold illegally as pets in Southeast Asia.

Some years ago, conservationists estimated that there were more baby orangutans being kept as household pets on the island of Taiwan than were being born in all of

Borneo each year. For every baby entering the pet trade alive, many others die before reaching the market.

Poaching has been outlawed, but the practice continues. Although most labs in Europe and the United States now use captive-bred apes, gorillas and chimpanzees sometimes are poached for their value as laboratory animals in other countries and for sale to unscrupulous zoos.

• *Disease* Emerging viruses, including Ebola and anthrax, have recently been discovered in wild ape populations and pose a great threat.

What can we do? The first step is habitat protection. Many conservation organizations work in Africa to preserve ape populations. This goal can be achieved only by providing local people with an economic incentive to protect the animals and other forest resources. Because apes are valued as tourist attractions, ecotourism sometimes provides that incentive.

In Bwindi Impenetrable National Park in southwestern Uganda, tourists pay up to $400 per hour to view wild mountain gorillas. A percentage of this fee goes to local villages, for building and staffing clinics and funding other entrepreneurial endeavors. Ecotourism does not work everywhere, however, and is highly vulnerable to the political instability that plagues much of Africa. In addition, close contact between tourists and apes increases the risk of disease transmission from us to them. Most wild ape populations have no immunity to flus, colds, and other human diseases that, because of their genetic kinship with us, they can easily catch.

Conservationists must provide a simple economic rationale for local people and governments: How will protecting the forest and its inhabitants, rather than destroying them, help people living near great apes? The answer to nonhuman primate protection lies in improving the living conditions of people. Scientists from wealthier countries help to train students to become conservation leaders themselves in countries where apes live. In this way, we hope to help people in Asia and Africa preserve their natural heritage for future generations.

Gorillas live in highly cohesive groups, ranging in size from several animals to several dozen. Males have two reproductive options. They can remain in their birth group, waiting to join the ranking silverback as a breeding adult male someday (or wait for him to die or be driven out). Alternatively, they can emigrate and attempt to find mates elsewhere. Young silverbacks often spend months or years on their own or live in bachelor groups of other silverbacks. Such bachelors wait for opportunities either to take over a male–female group by driving out the resident silverback or to steal a female or two away from an established group. Female gorillas are prone to emigrate just after encounters between groups occur; they may be sizing up the males in the new group to assess whether the time is right to leave with them (Harcourt, 1978). Contrary to the image of a "harem" of females led by a single silverback male, many gorilla groups have two or more silverbacks.

Our view of gorillas as slow-moving, terrestrial leaf-eaters living in one-male harems was shaped by the pioneering study of mountain gorillas begun by Dian Fossey in the Virunga Volcanoes. Following early work by George Schaller, Dian Fossey gave up her training as an occupational therapist to begin the first long-term study of wild gorillas. She established a research camp in the mountains of Rwanda and began to document the daily lives of her study subjects. Fossey's mountain gorillas ate a diet that was nearly 100% high-fiber, poor-quality plants, for which they foraged slowly, almost exclusively on the ground (Fossey, 1983).

As more recent studies of gorillas elsewhere in Africa have been carried out, it has become clear that most wild gorillas do not behave much like those in the Virungas. At Bai Hokou in the Central African Republic, Melissa Remis found that lowland gorillas ate a highly varied diet containing many fruit species. At the same site, Michele Goldsmith found that gorillas walked nearly 2 miles (3 km) per day in search of food (Remis, 1997b; Goldsmith, 1999). It appears that gorillas all over Africa prefer to eat fruit but can fall back on fibrous leaves as a staple when fruit is not widely available. Contrary to their terrestrial image in the Virungas, gorillas in other forests, including mountain gorillas in the Bwindi Impenetrable Forest (Uganda), climb trees readily and often are seen feeding on fruits more than 100 feet (30 m) from the ground. Socially, lowland gorillas appear to forage in a more dispersed way than do mountain gorillas and may live in less cohesive groups (Remis, 1997a). In some sites in central Africa, lowland gorilla groups use open swampy clearings to gather and feed, even wading into water in search of aquatic plants to eat. Researchers have recently observed simple forms of tool use among some lowland gorilla populations (Breuer et al., 2005).

Chimpanzees Along with bonobos, chimpanzees (*Pan troglodytes*) are our closest living relatives (Figure 6.41). The genetic similarity between a chimpanzee and us is greater than the chimpanzee's evolutionary affinity to a gorilla. The most abundant of the three living African apes, with a total wild population estimated at 150,000 to 200,000, chimpanzees are extraordinarily adaptable animals, found across equatorial Africa from lowland rain forest to nearly open grasslands. Males may weigh up to 150 pounds (68 kg) and are 10–15% larger and heavier than females.

Unlike most nonhuman primates, chimpanzees do not live in cohesive, stable social groups but rather in a multimale, multifemale community called a **fission–fusion** mating system. A community may number 20 to 120 individuals, in which the only stable unit is a mother–offspring pair. Its members come together in unpredictable social groupings to form foraging subgroups, the size and composition of which seem to be determined by a combination of fruit distribution and the presence of fertile females (Figure 6.42 on page 190). The community occupies a territory, which is defended by its males with great ferocity. Males band together to patrol the territorial boundaries on a regular basis and may attack and attempt to kill any chimpanzee, male or female, that is found encroaching on their land. The only exception occurs when male patrols encounter sexually receptive females from other

fission–fusion Form of mating system seen in chimpanzees, bonobos, and a few other primates in which there are temporary subgroups but no stable, cohesive groups.

FIGURE 6.41 Chimpanzees and humans share a very close genetic and evolutionary kinship.

FIGURE 6.42 Chimpanzees live in complex kin groups in which lifelong bonds and individual personalities play key roles, as in human societies.

communities, in which case the female may be coercively brought back to the home community (Goodall, 1986).

Within the community, males and females have very different social behavior patterns. Males tend to be highly social with one another, forming strong, long-lasting coalitions that they use to try to control females, patrol, and hunt. These alliances are not necessarily based on genetic relatedness among the males (Goldberg & Wrangham, 1997). Females travel more independently, apparently in order to avoid feeding competition from other adults. After an 8-month pregnancy, a 4-year infancy, and a prolonged juvenile period, a female chimpanzee reaches sexual maturity at about age 12. After this time, most females begin to visit neighboring communities, eventually settling there as breeding adults. The result is that adult females tend to be unrelated immigrants with few bonds in the new community (Goodall, 1986). Males remain in their birth community their entire lives, reaching maturity at 15 years of age. In the wild, chimpanzees live to a maximum age of 45; in captivity some have been known to reach 60 years of age.

Chimpanzees eat a highly diverse diet that is composed mainly of ripe fruit. In addition, they eat leaves and other plant products, plus insects such as termites and ants, which they extract from termite mounds using hand-fashioned tools (Figure 6.43) Some West African chimpanzee populations use stones and clubs collected from the forest floor to crack open hard-shelled nuts. Researchers recently observed one

FIGURE 6.43 Wild chimpanzees make and use simple tools to obtain food, learning tool making from one another.

chimpanzee population extracting galagos from tree cavities using sharp sticks (Pruetz & Bertolani, 2007). The pattern of tool use varies across Africa and is a prime example of another aspect of chimpanzee sophistication: culture. More than any animal other than humans, chimpanzees live by learned traditions and pass these traditions on to their offspring. Tool use is not genetic, although the intellectual capacity to understand how a tool is used certainly is.

Chimpanzees also relish meat, in the form of monkeys, wild pigs, young antelope, and other small animals. In some forests, chimpanzees kill and eat hundreds of animals every year (Stanford, 1998a). Meat-eating patterns vary from site to site and seem to be subject to the same learned traditions that characterize tool use and other behaviors. Anthropologists find chimpanzee hunting behavior intriguing as a model for how early hominids may have behaved. Jane Goodall's pioneering research on chimpanzees, followed by research by Toshisada Nishida (1990), set the stage for much modern primate research.

Bonobos   Bonobos (*Pan paniscus*), sometimes called pygmy chimpanzees because of their slightly more slender build, are close relatives of chimpanzees and are classified in the same genus (Figure 6.44). They exhibit more modest sexual dimorphism than the other great apes. Males and females have similar body sizes but males have larger skulls and canine teeth. They occur only in a limited region south of the Congo River in the Democratic Republic of the Congo (DRC; formerly Zaire), mainly in lowland rain forest habitat. Their total population is estimated at only about 25,000 (Insights and Advances: The Impending Extinction of the Great Apes? on page 188). Far less is known about bonobos than about chimpanzees; the first detailed field studies were conducted only in the 1980s, and political turmoil in Congo has repeatedly disrupted long-term research (Susman, 1984).

Bonobos eat a largely fruit diet but rely more on leafy plant material from the forest floor than chimpanzees do. Their more consistently available food supply may allow bonobos to live in larger parties than do chimpanzees (Malenky et al., 1994). Although they hunt and kill other mammals, bonobos do not necessarily eat them. At Lilungu, DRC, bonobos have been observed to capture young monkeys and use them as playthings, releasing them unharmed after they became bored with their prey (Sabater-Pi et al., 1993). At other sites, however, bonobos catch and eat small antelopes (Hohmann & Fruth, 1993).

Like chimpanzees, bonobos live in large, fluid social groupings we call communities. Males remain in the community of their birth, whereas females migrate between communities after sexual maturity. Males engage in border clashes with males from neighboring communities (Kano, 1992). But there are some striking differences between bonobo and chimpanzee societies. Unlike female chimpanzees,

The first bonobo specimen to be sent from the congo to Europe arrived in the late 1920s, making it one of the last large mammals whose existence was known by western scientists.

FIGURE 6.44 Bonobos are close relatives of chimpanzees and of humans.

ecology   The study of the interrelationships of plants, animals, and the physical environment in which they live.

female bonobos forge strong bonds and use female coalitions to prevent males from dominating them. Females engage in *genitalgenital (or GG) rubbing*, a sociosexual behavior that reduces tensions between individuals. Immigrant females ally themselves with individual resident females and slowly extend their social network (Furuichi, 1987). Females achieve dominance status in bonobo communities far beyond that of female chimpanzees (Parish, 1996).

Bonobos have become well known to the public because of reports of their hypersexuality. The contrast between their behavior and that of chimpanzees has led to a debate over which species is the better model for how early humans may have behaved. Bonobos are said to be closer in sexual behavior and biology to humans than any other animal. Whether this is fully accurate has been questioned by a number of researchers (Insights and Advances: Are Chimpanzees from Mars and Bonobos from Venus?, Chapter 7, page 222).

In addition to their interesting behavior patterns in the wild, bonobos have been the subjects of exciting research on the origins of human language. Kanzi, a male bonobo at Georgia State University, understands several hundred words in spoken English and communicates using a symbol board (Savage-Rumbaugh & Lewin, 1994).

Primate Ecology

It's important to remember that despite their interesting social behavior, primates are first and foremost parts of ecosystems. A revolution has taken place in the way we see primates and other animals in their natural habitat, as a result of advances in the field of ecology. **Ecology** is the study of the interrelationships of animals, plants, and their physical environment. The environment provides the template on which natural selection molds behavior. At the same time, primates influence the ecology of many tropical forests, as dispersers of seeds and even as pollinators of flowering plants. Primate behavior evolved in direct response to environmental pressures, and we can understand most aspects of primate behavior only in the context of the natural environment in which the primate evolved.

Several key ecological factors have shaped the evolution of nonhuman primates and continue to shape them today. Finding and eating food is a constant, chronic concern that occupies much of the day for nonhuman primates. They are bound by the same equation that faces all other wild animals: The energy that is expended to find food (calories burned) must be balanced by the quantity (calories consumed) and quality (nutrients such as fats, proteins, and carbohydrates) of the food eaten. This need is even greater for females because of the physical cost of reproduction. To understand how nonhuman primates live, we must therefore understand something about the nature and distribution of their favorite foods and how that affects aspects of their behavior. In this section we consider primate ecology, which will allow us, in Chapter 7, to understand how primate social systems may be adapted to the environment.

Most primates are *herbivores*, living largely on a plant food diet (Figure 6.45). Exceptions to this pattern are many of the lower primates, which eat insects as a substantial portion of the diet, and a few higher primates (including humans) that also eat meat. Only one primate group is entirely carnivorous: the tarsier of Southeast Asia, which subsists on insects, lizards, frogs, and other small animals. For the rest, much of the diet is composed of two items: fruits and leaves.

We tend to think of the natural world in a very human-centric way. But for a moment, consider a tropical forest from the point of view of a tree. As a tree, you produce several products that are highly valued by the animals you share the forest with: fruit, leaves, flowers, seeds, and so forth. All around you there are birds, monkeys, and small mammals that hunger after the fruit you produce. There are also millions of leaf-eating insects,

FIGURE 6.45   Like all animals, primates must balance their calories expended searching for food with calories, protein, fat, and other nutrients obtained.

monkeys, and other animals that eat your leafy foliage. But fruit and leaves have very different values to the potential herbivore. Leaves are the factories of a tropical tree; they take in sunlight and synthesize energy for the tree by the process of photosynthesis. For this reason, if a horde of insects or leaf-eating monkeys comes along and eats all its leaves, the tree will be unable to produce energy or obtain the nutrients it needs. At best it will have to endure a difficult period until new leaves can be grown, and at worst it could die. So ecologists predict that natural selection should endow trees with the means to protect their leaves.

Fruits have a very different value. They are the vessels that hold the seeds, which are the reproductive opportunities for the tree—its embryos for the next generation. Therefore, a tree "wants" its fruit to be eaten by animals, carried away somewhere, and then excreted out so that its seeds can germinate on the forest floor some distance away from their parents. Whereas trees and leaf-eaters, or **folivores**, are in a constant evolutionary battle, trees and fruit-eaters, called *frugivores*, are in a long-running symbiosis. So ecologists predict that natural selection should build traits into fruit that encourage frugivores to seek out the fruit crop and eat it.

There is abundant evidence that this is exactly what has happened. Consider how you choose a peach in the market that is ripe and ready to eat. First you look at it; is it orange and red, or still green? Then you touch it; is it soft, or still rock hard? Finally, you may smell it; does it have a pleasant, sweet smell? Wild primates use exactly the same criteria for choosing their fruits in tropical forests. And all these qualities—bright color, soft texture, and a good smell—were built into fruits by natural selection to convince frugivorous animals that they are delicious, nutritious, and ready to be eaten. These signals show a foraging primate that the fruit contains high levels of carbohydrate in the form of sugars, providing a caloric boost for an active day of foraging. Certainly brightly colored fruit did not evolve solely in response to primates; many birds eat fruit too, and their ancestors predate those of modern primates. But like birds, many primates are color-visioned fruit foragers. A primate must be able to efficiently locate fruits and then compete successfully for access to them as fruit availability is far less predictable than leaf availability.

Fruit-eating primates reap the benefit of a carbohydrate-rich diet, but at a cost. Fruits are temporary tree products that ripen and rot quickly, so fruit availability is far less predictable than leaf availability. And fruit is sought after by a wide range of animals because of its high caloric content (fruits tend to be high in carbohydrates and low in proteins). A primate must be able to efficiently locate fruits and then compete successfully for access to them. Fruits also tend to be patchily distributed on the tree.

Leaves are an entirely different story when it comes to foraging. Leaves are found everywhere in a tropical forest, so you might think all a monkey has to do is reach out and pluck its breakfast. But a tropical forest is not the cornucopia of food that it might appear. Leaves tend to be poor sources of nutrients and calories compared with fruits, but they can contain large amounts of protein. Because leaves are such a valuable and dependable resource, trees protect them against folivores in a variety ways. First, many leaves are coated with bristles, spines, or hairs that make them difficult or painful to ingest. A primate must also have a digestive system designed to cope with *fiber*. Fiber is a barrier to digestion, as anyone who eats raw corn or other high-fiber vegetables knows. Young tender leaves contain minimal fiber because the cell walls in each leaf have not yet built up layers of cellulose and hemicellulose that later become the structural support of the plant (Figure 6.46 on page 194). Mature leaves are tougher and highly fibrous.

In addition to physical barriers, folivorous primates must cope with chemical defenses that plants put into their leaves. Leaves often contain an array of chemicals, called **secondary compounds** (because they are the by-products of plant metabolism), which are toxic or at least indigestible to a primate. We're all familiar with secondary compounds; the reason tea becomes bitter when brewed too long is the presence of *tannins* in the tea leaves. Alkaloids and phenols are other secondary

folivores Animals who eat a diet composed mainly of leaves, or foliage.

secondary compounds Toxic chemical compounds found in the leaves of many plants which the plants use as a defense against leaf-eating animals.

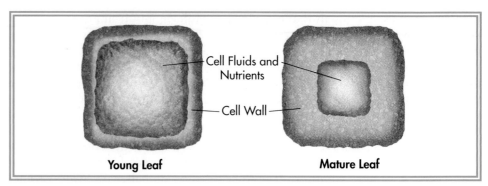

FIGURE 6.46 Comparison of a tender and mature leaf. As leaves mature, they become fiber-filled and harder to digest.

compounds commonly found in tropical forest foliage. The presence of secondary compounds is greatest in mature trees growing in poor soil, apparently because the tree needs to protect its leaves most in circumstances where nutrients for new growth are most limited.

THE CYCLES OF A TROPICAL FOREST

Tropical trees do not influence primate behavior only by the nutritional content of their food products. The distribution of foods is also profoundly important. In a temperate forest in the northern United States, an acre of forest might contain 500 trees of several species: oaks, maples, pines, and so forth. In an acre of tropical rain forest the diversity of species would be dramatically higher; 400 different species might be represented among the 500 trees. The cycle of a forest's trees producing new leaves, fruit, and flowers is its **phenology**. However, many tropical forest trees have *asynchronous cycles*, meaning that while one individual tree is laden with ripe fruit, the other trees of the same species standing nearby have no fruit at all. This is apparently an evolved strategy to protect trees by preventing predators ranging from insects to monkeys from homing in on a whole stand of trees and devouring all of their fruits in one swoop.

The staggering level of species diversity and the existence of asynchronous cycles in the tropics mean that wild primates must know their habitat intimately in order to find food. In Bwindi Impenetrable National Park, Uganda, chimpanzees travel from ripe fig tree to ripe fig tree. But even researchers cannot predict when a given tree will next produce ripe fruit (fruiting may happen once a year or every third year) or whether any of the fig trees will have fruit at a particular time.

Climate seasonality is another very important dietary factor to primates because they must locate tender new leaves and ripening fruit before other animals in the forest find it. In a northern climate, seasons are obvious: Autumn arrives and all the leaves fall. In the tropics, seasons exist, contrary to widespread belief, but they are staggered and asynchronous. While one species is dropping its leaves, another species standing nearby may be growing new ones.

In addition to leaves and fruit, most primates eat at least small quantities of other foods. Many species eat insects and other small invertebrates such as spiders, grubs, scorpions, and (for those leaving near water) crayfish and crabs. Many strepsirhine species rely heavily on small, living prey. And a few species, primarily the marmosets and tamarins, rely on another source: the resin that flows from tree trunks. These monkeys use well-shaped front teeth to scrape away the uppermost layer of bark from trees in their home range, causing sap to flow. They then return to the spot over and over to eat the gummy resin. Like people tapping maple trees to obtain syrup, marmosets reap a bounty of carbohydrates from such behavior.

The stunning diversity of life in tropical forests is the reason why there are many secrets, from undiscovered medicines to new species, remaining to be found.

phenology   The leafing and fruiting cycles of a forest.

A final source of nutrition for wild primates is the meat of other mammals. Chimpanzees are the most avid hunters of mammalian prey, but many other species hunt as well. In some Brazilian forests, capuchin monkeys hunt the endangered golden lion tamarin. The highest daily meat consumption ever recorded among nonhuman primates was by savanna baboons at Gilgil, Kenya, in a field study by Shirley Strum. Strum's baboon group ate nearly one mammal, usually a rabbit or baby antelope, per day (Strum, 1981).

YOU ARE WHAT YOU EAT: DIETARY AND DIGESTIVE STRATEGIES

For most primates, finding a suitable diet means foraging in the right place at the right time, and then selecting the most edible and nutritious plant foods available. But as we saw earlier, the best foods often are fiercely competed for. So many primates have evolved dietary or digestive specializations that allow them to coexist with other species by carving out their own ecological niche. For example, colobine monkeys of Africa and Asia possess a specialized digestive tract that allows them to consume large amounts of high-fiber, low-quality leaves and derive maximum nutrients from them. They can do this because all colobines possess a digestive system somewhat similar to that of a cow, with a semichambered stomach and the clear division of a *foregut* from the main gut. In the foregut, symbiotic bacteria break down dietary cellulose fiber in much the same way that microbes in a termite's gut break down wood. There is also evidence that this specialized gut can partially detoxify leaves that are high in some secondary compounds. This adaptation has allowed colobines to invade habitats in which other monkeys do not thrive and to live at higher densities than other monkeys where several species are sympatric.

In general, the largest-bodied primates rely least on insect prey, although a few primates, such as chimpanzees and capuchin monkeys, forage for insects very intensively and at times consume large numbers of them. Gorillas don't eat many insects, and very small-bodied primates rarely eat large quantities of leafy matter. This is because of the time and energy needed to make a living on these diets in relation to the time and energy needed to properly digest leaves, fruits, and live prey. The very largest primates tend to be folivorous, although there are exceptions. So gorillas are able to subsist on a diet of high-fiber plants, which they slowly pass through a very long digestive tract that provides the space for maximal breakdown of food before excretion. The smallest primate that is highly folivorous is a species of dwarf lemur (*Lepilemur mustelinus*).

DIET AND FEEDING COMPETITION

In nature, there are only so many hours of daylight during which a diurnal primate can make its living. A primate's **activity budget** allows it to compensate for calories expended with calories consumed. Diurnal primates forage during the day, nocturnal primates come out of hiding at night, and *crepuscular* primates forage at dawn and dusk. *Cathemeral* primates have irregular active periods during both the day and night. Each activity period has its share of foods available and predators lurking to catch unwary prey.

Activity budgets are tightly linked to dietary quality. Primates that live on high-fiber, low-calorie diets also tend to be more sedentary than those living on a high-fruit diet; compare the fission–fusion social system of the chimpanzee or spider monkey with the slowly moving cohesive groups in which howlers or mountain gorillas live. Gibbons brachiate acrobatically through Asian forests, eating fruit as their dietary staple. Muriquis of the Atlantic coastal forest of Brazil wake up late, go to sleep early, and in between forage slowly through their treetop habitat for a diet that consists largely of leaves. Mountain gorillas in

activity budget The pattern of waking, eating, moving, socializing, and sleeping that all nonhuman primates engage in each day.

Rwanda move at a glacial pace, walking as little as a few hundred yards in a day. Their high-mountain habitat contains practically no fruit trees, so their diet is mainly wild celery and other highly fibrous plants. But lowland gorillas a few hundred miles to the west live in tropical forests with a high diversity of fruiting trees, and they eat a great deal of fruit. Lowland gorillas travel up to 2 miles (3 km) per day. They travel such distances to find widely scattered fruit trees, and the energy they burn in their travels is replaced by the high carbohydrate value of their fruity diet.

Katharine Milton (1980) conducted a field study of howler and spider monkeys that illustrates the contrasts between frugivore and folivore activity patterns and what they may mean for primate evolution. On Barro Colorado Island in Panama, Milton observed howlers eating a diet high in leaves. The howlers carefully selected the most tender, young growing parts, but their diet contained little other than fiber. They were also very sedentary, moving very slowly through the forest canopy in a cohesive group. Meanwhile, spider monkeys ate a diet high in ripe fruit and traveled many times farther per day than howlers. Milton (1981) further considered the relative brain sizes of the two species; spider monkeys have larger brain–body size ratio than do howlers. She hypothesized that the evolutionary pressure of finding and remembering the changing locations of ripe fruit trees had placed a premium on cognition in spider monkeys, leading to brain-size increase in this primate but not in the related howlers.

Primates live in communities with a host of other animals, both primates and nonprimates. In many tropical forests, when a large tree bears ripe fruit it becomes an arboreal banquet table for a wide variety of animals, both mammals and birds, day and night. The problem for the primate is that it competes for the bounty of energy-rich food with numerous other species. Primatologists have debated for years over which is the more important influence on the evolution of primate social systems: competition between the members of a group, called *intragroup feeding competition,* or competition between two groups, or *intergroup feeding competition.*

When animals feed together in social groups, feeding competition is likely to occur. Such competition is more intense when the quality of the food is high, and especially when the food is distributed in small, scattered parcels that concentrate feeding at a few spots. When a group of monkeys enters a fruit tree, they all want to eat the ripest fruit. But inevitably, higher-ranking animals, older animals, and males tend to control and monopolize the food at the expense of smaller, weaker, lower-ranking animals and females. This direct squabbling over food is called *contest feeding competition* and is very common among frugivorous group-living primates. Although contest competition usually is considered an aspect of intragroup competition, it can also occur between groups.

When feeding competition occurs but enough food exists so that every animal nevertheless gets some food, *scramble feeding competition* has occurred. Folivorous primates often are scramble competitors: Leaves are everywhere, and everybody will find some, even if some animals find more than others. Primate species that practice scramble competition often lack rigid dominance hierarchies, perhaps because there is less pressure to compete intensely when food is evenly distributed. Scramble competition often characterizes intragroup competition in folivorous primate groups.

The effects of feeding competition are cumulative: Over time, if you can't get quite enough good food to eat, you will be stressed, and such stress may lead to poor health, lower dominance rank, and lowered fertility. There is ample evidence of the negative effects of feeding competition in nature. For example, Charles Janson showed that for a population of cebus monkeys in Manu National Park, Peru, the amount of food eaten by each monkey was limited by aggressive competition with other monkeys in the same group (Janson, 1985). In some primates, competition is lessened when males and females have slightly different diets, as

Natalie Vasey demonstrated for two lemur species on the Masoala Peninsula of Madagascar. Vasey (1996) found that among red ruffed lemurs, females ate a lower-fiber, higher-protein diet than males, and this difference was even more pronounced during the breeding season.

Sue Boinski studied two squirrel monkey species in forests in Central and South America and found that despite similar feeding patterns and similar levels of predation, the two species differed in the degree of intragroup feeding competition. Females of the Costa Rican species, in which feeding competition was intense, formed rigid dominance hierarchies, whereas the Peruvian species, in which feeding competition was lower, did not exhibit such rigid hierarchies (Boinski, 1994).

Natural food shortages have a severe effect on wild primate populations. A long-term study of ring-tailed lemurs in Beza Mahafaly Reserve, Madagascar, by Michelle Sauther and colleagues (1999) showed that nearly one-third of all adult females died during a particularly harsh drought in the 1990s, during which infant mortality reached 80%. Some primate ecologists believe that feeding competition matters mainly when the environment takes a turn for the worse. In such ecological crunch times, food may become severely limited, and natural selection may favor the individuals that are the best foragers and food competitors. Evidence that lean times, droughts, and famines increase feeding competition have been reported for primates as diverse as mouse dwarf lemurs (Hladik, 1975), howlers (Milton, 1982), and vervet monkeys (Cheney et al., 1988).

TERRITORIES AND RANGES

All mammals, including nonhuman primates, live in defined places called **home ranges** (Figure 6.47). This area can be very limited—smaller than a football field in the case of some nocturnal strepsirhines—or many square kilometers in the case of some apes and monkeys. The range must contain all the resources needed by a nonhuman primate or a social group: water, food, shelter, and mates. Home ranges often overlap, either slightly or entirely. Parts of the home range that are used most intensively are called the **core area**. In some species,

home range The spatial area used by a primate group.

core area The part of a home range that is most intensively used.

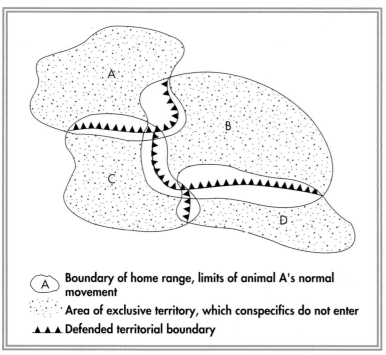

Ⓐ Boundary of home range, limits of animal A's normal movement

⋯⋯ Area of exclusive territory, which conspecifics do not enter

▲▲▲ Defended territorial boundary

FIGURE 6.47 Primates use their space in a variety of ways: home ranges, core areas, and territories.

territory The part of a home range that is defended against other members of the same species.

such as gorillas, home ranges overlap greatly, and groups encounter one another often. In other species, such as chimpanzee, community ranges overlap only slightly, and aggressive encounters occur in the overlap zone. In some species, the home range is defended against other members of the same species, in which case we call it a **territory**. The defended portion of the home range usually is the part in which critical resources are located.

Territorial defense can take the form of vocalizing, such as the songs of gibbons. By setting up loudspeakers within, at the border of, and outside the territorial boundaries of gibbon pairs, John Mitani (1985) showed that gibbons use their songs as territorial markers. As Mitani predicted, gibbons that heard the calls of strange gibbons coming (via loudspeakers) from within their territory responded most vigorously, calling and approaching the site of the call in obvious territorial defensiveness. Territorial defense can also result from visual encounters along territorial borders, in which males, females, or both (depending on the species) intimidate and chase the potential intruders. Among many Old World monkeys, females rather than males engage in territorial disputes. In some species, territorial disputes may be settled through physical contact, including lethal contact in rare cases, such as with chimpanzees.

Why be territorial? Primatologists have spent years trying to understand the key resources nonhuman primate groups are willing to protect. Males seek to obtain and control females. In some mammals (ungulates, for instance), males try to hold territories because females are on those territories, and females may judge a male's quality by the size and quality of the territory he commands (Jarman, 1974). This is less true among nonhuman primates. We believe that nonhuman primates defend their home ranges when food resources are worth defending because of their high nutritional value or when males can control females through their defense of territory. But territories typically are defended only when it is energetically possible and worthwhile to do so. A slow-moving colobus monkey may not defend a patch of forest containing its favored leaves because the folivore may not be able to effectively monopolize its range, and the leaves may not be nutritious enough to warrant defending anyway.

Mate-defense territoriality is a different equation. Females in many nonhuman primate species use their habitat to maximize their intake of food for themselves and their offspring. As we saw in Chapter 4, males are concerned mainly with where females are. So what might appear to be male defense of a territory for the sake of protecting a relished fruit tree may in fact be territorial defense aimed at keeping males from other groups away from the male's females. This is dramatically the case in chimpanzees, in which male patrols capture young, fertile females near territorial boundaries, and males attack intruders who may be intent on doing the same in the residents' community.

PREDATION

Nonhuman primates in the wild face the difficult challenge of finding food while avoiding attacks by predators. Failing to find food on a given afternoon will leave a monkey hungry the next day, but failing to avoid an attack by an eagle or leopard will leave it dead or injured. So we should expect that nonhuman primates have evolved behavioral defenses against predators. But actually observing predation is difficult because the predators are stealthy and usually nocturnal and solitary (Figure 6.48). Most often a member of a nonhuman primate group being studied disappears one day, and the researcher has no idea whether disease, accidental death, or a predator was responsible.

Despite a lack of field observations, we can make a few generalizations about predation. First, small-bodied nonhuman primates are more vulnerable to predation than are larger species. In Madagascar, owls have been reported to kill up to one-quarter of the mouse lemur population each year (Goodman, Connor, and Langrand, 1993). Even a much lower predation rate could be a major source of mortality in a

FIGURE 6.48 Primates face a wide variety of predators in the wild, including birds of prey.

population of monkeys. Second, many nonhuman primate species exhibit behaviors that appear to have evolved in response to the threat of predation. Alarm calls are often given when a predator approaches, and experimental studies using loudspeakers to play the calls of leopards and eagles have shown that monkeys respond in a variety of ways. Vervet monkeys studied in Amboseli National Park, Kenya, by Dorothy Cheney and Robert Seyfarth (1991) give alarm calls that vary depending on the type of predator spotted; different calls are given for eagles, leopards, and pythons. Red colobus monkeys studied by Ronald Noë and colleagues in the Taï Forest of Ivory Coast responded to the calls of wild chimpanzees by moving toward other monkey species nearby; the chimpanzee calls seemed to be acting as early warning systems that the colobus could capitalize on (Bshary & Noë, 1997).

One of the few cases in which we can directly observe predation on nonhuman primates is in African forests in which chimpanzees prey on other nonhuman primates. We saw earlier that chimpanzees are avid meat eaters, and red colobus monkeys are their most frequent prey. Where chimpanzees are accustomed to being watched by human observers, both their hunting behavior and its impact on red colobus can be studied in detail. In Gombe National Park, Tanzania, chimpanzees kill 18% of the red colobus population living in their home range in some years (in other years predation is much lighter; Stanford, 1998a). Red colobus living in larger groups have a lower individual risk of being captured by a chimpanzee, and red colobus groups containing many adult males are at less risk than groups with only a few males. This is the case because adult male colobus mount a fierce counterattack when chimpanzees attack them. The counterattack is more likely to succeed in driving off the chimpanzees when there are five or more male colobus defending.

Finally, studies have shown that the pattern of predation on the colobus depended very much on where the colobus lived relative to the border of the territory of the chimpanzee community. In the chimpanzees' core area, predation on colobus monkeys was intense, and as a consequence groups were small and had few immature members (Gombe chimpanzees kill mainly young colobus monkeys). Toward the periphery of the chimpanzees' community territory, hunting was much less common. Chimpanzee predation was overall such a major source of colobus mortality that the colobus population would have been in serious decline at Gombe were it not for the fact that in some years predation was infrequent.

Primate Communities

If you were to walk through some tropical forests, you would see not one but many species of primates. In the Congo Basin of central Africa or the Amazon Basin of Peru, it's possible to see more than a dozen primate species in a single acre of forest. If you were to take a walk through the same forest at night, you would see a different, nocturnal community of primates. With so many closely related and often morphologically similar primates sharing the same forest, why isn't there more intense competition between them for food and other resources? The answer is that there is or was competition in the evolutionary past of the species. Ecological theory predicts that when two or more organisms with very similar needs are sympatric, sharing the same space, they will diverge from one another in some critical aspect of their *niche*, or ecological role. For example, two monkeys that seem to eat the same foods will be found to eat different diets when food is scarce. One species might forage high in trees, whereas the other finds its food on the ground. Without such *niche separation*, species would drive each other into extinction far more often than they are observed to.

For example, in a study of two lemur species in Beza Mahafaly Reserve in Madagascar, Nayuta Yamashita found that Verreaux's sifakas ate a more folivorous diet than sympatric ring-tailed lemurs did in the same habitat. The sifakas have dental adaptations to a tough, fibrous diet, which may allow them to coexist with more frugivorous species such as the ring-tailed lemurs (Yamashita, 2002). In Ranomafana

FIGURE 6.49 Ranomafana National Park, Madagascar, home to multiple species of lemurs that divide up the forest resources.

National Park, also in Madagascar, Chia Tan found that three closely related bamboo lemurs (of the genus *Hapalemur*) shared the same forest space, and all ate bamboo (which accounted for at least 88% of the annual diet of all three) (Figure 6.49). Given what we said earlier about the impossibility of multiple species living on the same diet, how could these three lemurs coexist without driving each other into extinction? Tan found that one species ate mainly the tender young shoots of the bamboo, whereas the other two species ate different bamboo species during some seasons. In this way the three species partitioned their food resources (Tan, 1999).

Niche separation occurs among all primates that are sympatric, and such divergence often is evident only during ecological crunch times. What's more, it can be very difficult to demonstrate feeding competition in the wild—simply overlapping strongly with another species' ecology is not evidence that the two species compete—so field studies more often record the nature of ecological overlap than the occurrence of ecological competition. Gorillas and chimpanzees share forests across central Africa, and both species prefer a diet heavy in ripe fruit. But during lean seasons, gorillas fall back on fibrous plants as their staple, while chimpanzees continue to forage widely for fruit. Although the diets of the two ape species overlap extensively, direct contest competition over food is rare (Stanford & Nkurunungi, 2003).

Some primates form *polyspecific groups*, made up of two, three, or more species that travel and feed together for part or all of each day. These have been studied both in the Old World tropics and also the New World (Terborgh, 1983). The antipredator benefits of foraging in such a group are obvious; more eyes on the lookout mean safer and better foraging. Feeding competition is lessened by the fact that the participating species usually have key differences in some aspect of their diet or feeding strategies. African guenons, for example, have a strong tendency to form such associations (Gautier-Hion & Gautier, 1983).

Marina Cords studied blue monkeys and red-tailed monkeys, two closely related guenons, in Kakamega forest of western Kenya. She found that neither blue nor red-tailed species seemed to benefit greatly or suffer feeding competition when feeding in the same tree (Cords, 1990). In West Africa, however, another guenon, the diana monkey, often is joined by red colobus. The latter appears to use the former as a sentinel, fleeing from predators when they hear the diana monkeys give alarm calls (Bshary & Noë, 1997). In Gombe National Park, Tanzania, the relationship between guenons and red colobus is the opposite: Red-tailed and blue monkeys use colobus as sentinels to warn them of approaching danger (Stanford, 1998a). The interactions between primate species can be as diverse as the primate species themselves, depending once again on the habitat and its ecology.

As you can see, primates are a highly diverse group of mammals that are subject to many of the same evolutionary and ecological principles that guide the lives of other mammals. However, nonhuman primates have two adaptations—sociality and large brains—that set them apart from nearly all other animals. In the next chapter, we will examine nonhuman primate social behavior and cognition to see what they tell us about human evolution.

SUMMARY

1. What characteristics distinguish nonhuman primates from other mammals?

Primates share a suite of characteristics: grasping hand and opposable thumb, stereoscopic vision, single births, sociality, large brain–body size ratio, extended ontogeny, visually oriented daytime activity, nails instead of claws, and an enclosed bony eye orbit.

2. What are the main hypotheses that account for the origin of the primates?

The arboreal hypothesis was the first theory put forward to explain primate origins. This centered on the role of stereo vision and the grasping hand adapted for life in the trees. The leading alternative theory is the visual predation hypothesis, which Cartmill proposed based on the likely predatory behavior of the earliest nonhuman primates.

3. **Why is the diversity of lemurs on Madagascar today only a shadow of lemur diversity in the past?**

The largest lemur species went extinct not long after human arrival on Madagascar about 1,500 to 2,000 years ago. The species found there today are mainly the smaller species, presumably less desirable as food, and so, less hunted.

4. **What is the taxonomic position of the tarsier?**

The tarsier is a haplorhine, linking it to the anthropoid primates, but it retains many prosimian characters, such as a combination of nails and claws on its feet. Therefore, it may represent an evolutionary bridge between the prosimian and anthropoid primates.

5. **What is an ape?**

An ape is an anthropoid primate with a suspensory shoulder anatomy that allows brachiation. Apes also lack tails, have large brains, and exhibit a highly elaborated degree of social complexity.

6. **Why is it a mistake to think of a tropical rain forest as a cornucopia of food available for wild nonhuman primates?**

Plant foods in tropical forests are protected by a variety of adaptations, from high-fiber content to bristles to chemical defenses. In addition, tropical forest trees often produce leaves and fruit at different times, making it difficult for nonhuman primates to predict when they can harvest the trees' products.

7. **What is the difference between a home range and a territory?**

A home range is the area that a nonhuman primate or nonhuman primate group uses over a long period of time. A territory is the part of the home range that is defended against members of other groups of the same species. All, part, or none of the home range may be defended as a territory.

8. **Why would primates of different species associate together despite increased feeding competition?**

Primates of different species may capitalize on the food-finding and predator-detection abilities of other species, which may outweigh the disadvantages of being in a larger group.

CRITICAL THINKING QUESTIONS

1. We say that primates are the mostly highly social animals on Earth. But many animals, from fish to birds to hoofed mammals, live in enormous herds, flocks, or schools that are far larger than any primate group. What is difference between those sorts of groups and those in which nonhuman primates live?

2. Chimpanzees and bonobos are very similar anatomically but quite different behaviorally. Based on what you learned about species concepts in Chapter 4, should they be considered separate species or merely variants on a single species? Why?

3. Why should we consider the primate body plan to be a series of evolutionary compromises?

KEY TERMS

metatheria	visual predation	prehensile tail	fission–fusion
prototheria	hypothesis	polyandrous	ecology
eutheria	dental arcade	Catarrhini	folivores
strepsirhine	neocortex	estrus	secondary compounds
(Strepsirhini)	ontogeny	hylobatid (Hylobatidae)	phenology
haplorhine (Haplorhini)	nocturnal	pongid (Pongidae)	activity budget
prosimian	diurnal	hominid (Hominidac)	home range
anthropoid	sociality	brachiation	core area
arboreal hypothesis	Playtrrhini	frugivorous	territory

SUGGESTED READING

Cheney, Dorothy, and Robert M. Seyfarth. (1991). *How Monkeys See the World*. University of Chicago Press, Chicago.

Goodall, Jane. (1986). *Chimpanzees of Gombe*. Harvard University Press, Cambridge, MA.

Stanford, Craig. (2001). *Significant Others*. Basic Books, New York.

Strier, Karen (2003). *Primate Behavioral Ecology*. (2nd ed.). Allyn & Bacon, Boston.

CHAPTER

7 Primate Behavior

The Following day I Tracked Group 8 [a group of gorillas] into the saddle area west of Visoke and contacted them from a distance of about sixty feet. They gave me the calmest reception I had ever received from an unhabituated group. The first individual to acknowledge my presence was the young silverback, who strutted onto a rock and stared with compressed lips before going off to feed. I named him Pugnacious, Pug for short. He was followed by the extremely attractive blackback, who nipped off a leaf to fold between his lips for a few seconds before spitting it out, a common displacement activity known as symbolic feeding and indicative of mild unease. After whacking at some vegetation, the magnificent male swaggered out of sight into dense foliage, seemingly quite pleased with himself. I named him Samson. Next, the two young adults scampered into view and impishly flipped over on to their backs to stare at me from upside-down positions, giving the impression they were wearing lopsided grins. In time they were named Geezer and Peanuts. When the elderly female came into view, she gazed briefly at me in a totally uninterested manner before sitting down next to Peanuts and maneuvering her patchy rump almost into his face for grooming. I named her Coco because of her somewhat light chocolate-colored hair. Lastly, the old silverback came forward. In all my years of research I never met a silverback so dignified and commanding of respect. His silvering extended from the sides of his cheekbones, along neck and shoulders, enveloped his back and barrel, and continued down the sides of both thighs. Having little to go by in comparison, except for zoo gorillas, I estimated his age as approximately fifty years, possibly more. The nobility of his character compelled me to seek a name for him immediately. In Swahili, *rafiki* means "friend." Because friendship implies mutual respect and trust, the regal silverback became known as Rafiki.

Dian Fossey, *Gorillas in the Mist* (1983)

WATCHING NONHUMAN PRIMATES IS ONE THING; understanding their behavior is another. But observation of behavior is at the heart of the subfield of biological anthropology known as *primatology,* as pioneering researcher Dian Fossey understood.

Primates are intrinsically fascinating animals that serve as illustrations of evolutionary principles of natural selection, adaptive radiation, convergent evolution, and sexual selection. They also inform us about human evolution, offering a window onto how early humans may have behaved. In this chapter we will consider how biological anthropologists study nonhuman primates and their social evolution. We will see that evolutionary principles that you learned in Chapter 4, such as natural selection and sexual selection, play key roles in shaping primate behavior. You'll also examine the diversity of societies in which nonhuman primates may live and explore the reasons these societies evolved the way they did. And you will read about some of the current controversies over the form and function of primate social behavior.

Studying Primates

As we saw in Chapter 6, *sociality* is the most fundamental primate behavioral adaptation (Figure 7.1 on page 204). It is the hallmark of nearly all the haplorhine primates, and its study is an essential component of nearly all nonhuman primate behavior research. Primatologists want to learn why nonhuman primates are social. To do this they study the costs and benefits of group living and examine how the same evolutionary processes that promoted sociality in nonhuman primates may have promoted the emergence of humankind.

FIGURE 7.1 Sociality is the most fundamental behavioral adaptation of the primates.

FIGURE 7.2 Jane Goodall pioneered the modern approach to studying primates in the wild, involving close-up observation of known individuals over many months.

The modern approach to the study of nonhuman primate behavior occurred when we began to study the animals systematically. The earliest field researchers spent only a few days or weeks watching nonhuman primates in the wild. Jane Goodall (1968) was the first researcher to immerse herself in the lives of the animals, following her subjects year after year and learning intimate details of their lives (Figure 7.2). What Goodall did in the early 1960s is now the norm for primatologists; graduate students typically spend 1 to 2 years living in the habitat of the primates for a doctoral thesis project. Many field studies of more than 10 years' duration have been carried out. In extended studies, multiple primate generations can be followed and individuals' lives more fully understood. Studies of nonhuman primate demography have revealed aspects of the evolution of life histories and the ways in which long-term patterns of mating success are related to reproductive success. Primatologists have also added new research tools to their arsenal: paternity tests using DNA from hair follicles, feces, or urine; studies of endocrine influences on behavior using hormones extracted from feces or urine; and studies of communication using sophisticated sound recording equipment (Figure 7.3).

We can study nonhuman primates in several different settings, each of which strongly influences the sort of research that is possible. A **captive study** allows us to closely observe nonhuman primates up-close and personal, since they won't hide in dense trees for hours on end. We often study captive populations over many generations and know their family histories in great detail. We can also manipulate the study group; the researcher might move a new male into the social group in order to observe the effect on the rest of the group. This opportunity makes behavioral experiments possible that we cannot usually achieve in the field. The downside of studying nonhuman primates in captivity is obvious: The animals are kept in highly unnatural settings rather than the forests in which their behaviors evolved, and so we cannot expect to see natural patterns of behavior. Enforced proximity leads to higher levels of aggression, sex, and affiliation than we would see in the same animals in the wild. The artificial food supply also means we cannot conduct ecological studies. A valuable use of captive studies is to confirm and refine the results of studies done in the wild.

Some nonhuman primate studies are conducted in a more spacious **semi–free-ranging** environment. Very large enclosures, or even small islands, sometimes have nonhuman primate populations. Cayo Santiago, an islet off the coast of Puerto Rico onto which rhesus macaques from India were introduced in the 1930s, is one example. The animals in a semi–free-ranging setting can establish territories, form their own groups, and forage for food, even though they are in captivity. Because they

captive study Primate behavior study conducted in a zoo, laboratory, or other enclosed setting.

semi–free-ranging Primate behavior study conducted in a large area that is enclosed or isolated in some way so the population is captive.

FIGURE 7.3 Modern primate study sometimes involves high-tech methods. This golden lion tamarin is having a battery changed in its radio transmitter collar.

are confined (though in a large area), we can easily study kinship and follow many generations of the animals. This setting is a compromise between the confines of captivity and an entirely natural field study. Semi-free-ranging primates exhibit a more natural pattern of behaviors than they would in zoo, but not so natural as in the wild.

A modern study of primate behavior called **field study** is conducted in the habitat in which the species evolved. Only in the field can researchers see patterns of behavior that evolved in response to environmental variables (Figure 7.4). As we saw earlier, the interplay between genes and behavior depends on a third critical variable: the physical environment. Studies of nonhuman primates in the wild focus on various aspects of ecology, such as diet and its influence on grouping patterns and social behavior; *positional behavior*, the relationship between locomotor morphology and the physical environment; and social interactions within and between primate groups.

There are significant difficulties in studying nonhuman primates in the wild. First, the primatologist must accustom the animals to his or her presence. This is a slow process that can take months or even years. Only once habituated can the primates be identified as individuals and observed closely. However, habituation may also allow other people, including poachers intending to kill the animals, to approach. Therefore, habituation can be undertaken only in areas where the animals' lives will not be placed in danger should the scientists pack up their project and go home. And even well-habituated primates are difficult to watch because so much of their behavior takes place behind dense foliage and rocks or in tall trees. Some nonhuman primates have huge home ranges, and just locating the group every day can be a challenge. A year spent in the wild watching monkeys may produce a small fraction of the observation hours that a scientist could obtain in a zoo in one month. Manipulations of the social and physical environment that can be done easily in captivity, such as changing the diet or taking DNA samples, are rarely possible in the wild.

FIGURE 7.4 Field research on free-living primates allows primatologists to study patterns of behavior in the setting where the behavior evolved.

The Evolution of Primate Social Behavior

We can understand and study behavior at different levels. All behaviors we see in the wild have immediate causes: hunger, fear, sexual urges, and the like. The immediate, or *proximate*, causes involve the hormonal, physiological reasons for the animal to act. At the same time, behaviors reflect deeper, evolved tendencies that have been shaped over millions of years of natural and sexual selection to promote reproductive success. A baboon mates because of immediate impulses that are both hormonal and social. But ultimately, the urge to mate reflects deeper, evolved strategies that arise through natural selection to enhance the baboon's odds of reproduction. In Chapter 4 you saw how these evolutionary forces work on an organism's phenotype. In this chapter you will examine how the same forces shape primate behavior as a phenotype.

The value of an evolutionary approach to nonhuman primate behavior and ecology is that it allows us to test hypotheses. Using an evolutionary framework, we can study mating as one of many behaviors that has fitness consequences. The pattern of mating may be related to everything from dominance relationships and coalitionary networks to female physiology, which may in turn reveal something important about the evolution of the social system. In other words, behavior can be seen as an adaptation, one aspect of the primate's phenotype. Although the genetic basis for a specific trait remains largely unknown, we can study the consequences of the behavior. For example, if being aggressive promotes reproductive success for a baboon compared with less aggressive baboons in the group, we may infer that aggression is subject to evolutionary forces.

field study Primate behavior study conducted in the habitat in which the primate naturally occurs.

(a)   (b)

FIGURE 7.5   (a) Savanna baboons live in female-philopatric groups, among which males migrate.
(b) Chimpanzees live in male-philopatric communities, among which females migrate.

SOCIAL BEHAVIOR AND REPRODUCTIVE ASYMMETRY

The reproductive asymmetry between males and females plays a key role in our understanding of the evolution of nonhuman primate social strategies. Females have a lower reproductive potential and lower variance in reproductive output than do males. Females invest far more energy and time in offspring, during both gestation and offspring-rearing, than males do. In accordance with Darwinian sexual selection theory, females tend to be competed for by males, rather than the other way around. As a result, we expect females of all social mammals to prioritize obtaining adequate food supplies for themselves and their offspring. Females do not need to be very concerned about finding a male; because of their lower reproductive potential, they will always be the sought-out sex, and males will find them. Because the availability of females is the single factor that most limits a male's opportunity to achieve reproductive success, we expect that males will go where females go and will map themselves onto the landscape in accordance with the distribution of females.

The form the social system takes therefore depends on the way females distribute themselves. The social system of nonhuman primate species in which females form the core of the group is called **female philopatry**. This means that females do not migrate at maturity; they stay in the group of their birth to reproduce and rear offspring. In such groups, males typically migrate. Females in female-philopatric groups often form tight bonds, based partly on the likelihood of their kinship. Such matrilines of mother, daughters, grandmother, and so on can form the core of the group. In **male philopatry**, males remain in their natal home range throughout life, and females migrate. The two types of social systems are closely connected to other important aspects of behavior, so each bears closer examination.

When female kin live together, they share a strong incentive to cooperate or at least to limit their competition over food resources. Studies have shown that in female-philopatric groups, territorial defense is done mainly by females, and the degree of affiliation among females is far greater than among females in male-philopatric species. For instance, in Gombe National Park, Tanzania, female baboons, which are female philopatric, spend much time sitting together and grooming one another. In the same forest, female chimpanzees, which are male philopatric, rarely engage in social grooming or contact (Figure 7.5). Competition among females can be fierce, with nutrients and calories for bearing and rearing offspring at stake. But on the whole, females in female philopatric societies—such as most macaques,

This pattern of cooperation among related females in female-philopatric societies is true not only among primates, but for many other mammalian species as well.

female philopatry   Primate social system in which females remain and breed in the group of their birth, whereas males emigrate.

male philopatry   Primate social system in which males remain and breed in the group of their birth, whereas females emigrate.

baboons, and numerous other Old World monkey taxa—socialize in ways that females in male-philopatric species do not.

When females feed on widely scattered resources, as species exhibiting the fission–fusion social system seem to, males may not be able to maintain access to them. In such a situation, male bonds may be the most effective way of controlling females. This may explain the fact that chimpanzees, bonobos, some spider monkeys, and a few other species are male-bonded. These bonds are based partly on male kinship because remaining in the natal group means that a male ends up living next to his cousins, brothers, and other male kin. Closely allied males, whether relatives or not, can coerce females for mating purposes, and control access to fruit trees that other male cohorts might want to enter. So, male-bonded primate societies offer some major nutritional and reproductive benefits to males and uncertain benefits to females. The benefits to males are believed to be sufficient to keep males on their natal home range. Females tend to be the sex that emigrates (because one sex or the other presumably must emigrate to avoid inbreeding problems).

Females in male-philopatric societies, on the other hand, may not show a high degree of affiliation, perhaps because of their lack of kinship (Figure 7.6). In chimpanzee society, females rarely groom one another, and they often engage in competitive aggression, including infanticidal aggression in which a female may attempt to kill the offspring of another female. Bonobos are an exception to this pattern in that immigrant females in a community, though unrelated, establish close bonds with one another. These bonds are used to protect females from harassment by males.

The form of the social system cannot be entirely explained by the behavior of females, however. Some researchers have linked the number of males in a primate group to other factors, such as the intensity of the risk of predation. In separate studies, Carel van Schaik and Marc Hörstermann (1994) and John Mitani and colleagues (1996) hypothesized that the number of males in a primate group, though subject to multiple factors, depends most strongly on the number of females and also on the presence of predators in the species' habitat.

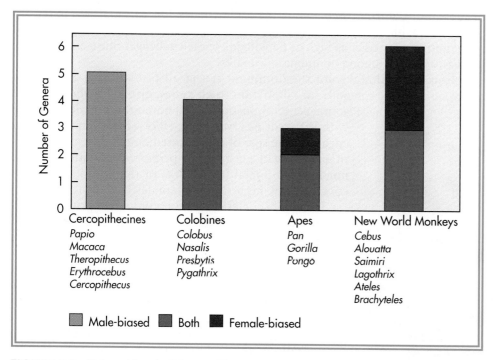

FIGURE 7.6 Male and female philopatry. The internal dynamics of primate societies differ greatly depending on which sex emigrates from the group at sexual maturity.

MALE REPRODUCTIVE STRATEGIES

Within a primate society, both males and females seek the same goal: reproductive success, or fitness. The ways each sex tries to enhance its fitness differ dramatically, however. A male baboon should be expected to fight with other male baboons over females if fighting improves his opportunities to place his genes into the next generation. If fighting and aggression were counterproductive, we should expect to see male baboons achieving mating success some other way. In practice, however, strategies for achieving reproductive success are much more complex than just being aggressive or nonaggressive. Males rarely engage in paternal care, and in most species their relationship with offspring is neutral or even harmful. Their direct contribution to their offspring's health and welfare often is only their genes. In the few species in which males provide parental caregiving, such as marmosets and tamarins, the selection pressures on males may be very different from those on, say, a male baboon. The degree of parental investment is a key factor in shaping the evolution of the social system.

Dominance   One important way males and females achieve reproductive success is by establishing dominance relationships with other members of the same sex. Once he enters a new group, a male must compete directly with the resident males over the group's females. Although this is sometimes done by fighting, competition often is settled through the establishment of dominance hierarchies, in which high-ranking and low-ranking males sort out their relationship through a series of contests that leaves the lower-ranking animal unlikely to challenge the more dominant one.

Dominance relationships among males are established early in life, as males play together and some assert themselves over others. Of course, males that later emigrate from their home group cannot assume high rank in a new group, at least initially. Males growing up in male-philopatric groups may face a different dilemma. To achieve high rank they must demonstrate to males that they have grown up and that they are now a force to be reckoned with. In chimpanzee society, all the adult males in the community are dominant to all the females. An adolescent male climbs the dominance hierarchy by first taking on and dominating (fighting with or supplanting at fruit trees) each of the adult females. Once he has risen to the top of the female hierarchy, he will begin to challenge the lowest-ranking males, and so on until he has risen as high as he will go. These challenges illustrate the political nature of life among nonhuman primates.

However, males are not the dominant sex in all primate species. Among many lemur species, females are dominant to all males, displacing them at food sources and choosing newly immigrated males to mate with (Erhardt & Overdorff, 1998). Male lemurs do not engage in the sort of complicated dominance interactions that we see in anthropoid primates, perhaps because much of the social intercourse of the group is strongly controlled by high-ranking females.

Dominance relationships in nonhuman primate males are far more complicated than the image you may have of a pecking order. In fact, rarely do the males of a polygynous group sort themselves into a neatly linear hierarchy (Figure 7.7). Far more commonly, dominance relationships take a flexible, multifaceted form in which Monkey A is dominant to Monkey B, except when Monkey B is in the company of Monkey C, in which case B and C are dominant to Monkey A. In a classic study of a captive chimpanzee colony at the Arnhem Zoo in the Netherlands, Frans de Waal (1982) described the triangular nature of many chimpanzee dominance interactions, in which Chimp C was able to assert himself while Chimp A was

FIGURE 7.7 Dominance relationships among individuals play an important role in many primate societies.

busy dealing with Chimp B. These sorts of fast-paced, often subtle interactions in nonhuman primate groups are challenging for primate researchers to observe but crucial in explaining the role that cognition and social complexity play in nonhuman primate societies.

Why males should strive to become dominant has always been perplexing. The long-standing assumption was that high-ranking males were able to obtain a higher proportion of matings with females, so dominance was part of the overall male reproductive strategy. But field studies have returned mixed results with respect to the correlation between dominance and reproductive success. For example, in the 1970s Glenn Hausfater (1975) reported that dominant male savanna baboons (*Papio anubis*) had greater mating success than lower-ranking animals, which they achieved by monopolizing females during their peak ovulatory periods. But studying the same species, primatologist Barbara Smuts (1985) found no such correlation. In fact, low-ranking males enjoyed greater mating success than the alpha. And we know that high-ranking males often have higher levels of cortisol, the hormone that is associated with stress-related diseases in many primates including humans, which may be necessary to keep them continuously primed to function as the most powerful male in the group. So the benefit to a male of achieving high rank is presumed to be reproductive, but the evidence is ambiguous.

FEMALE REPRODUCTIVE STRATEGIES

Females invest much more time and energy in reproduction than males do, and their reproductive strategies reflect this. Instead of competing for males, female nonhuman primates typically are competed over. But females do not mate with whichever male is the winner of the competition. Sexual selection theory predicts that females should choose their mates carefully because a given mating may result in years of investment in gestation, lactation, and offspring-rearing (Figure 7.8). A nonhuman primate must undergo years of socialization to learn how to behave successfully as an adult, and this socialization is closely connected to the development and growth of its brain. During the socialization period the maturing offspring is utterly dependent, physically and psychologically, on its mother. And we know from Jeanne Altmann's (1980) long-term study of mother and infant baboons that when they are carrying fetuses or young infants, females suffer high mortality rates, presumably because they are less able to escape predators and more likely to suffer nutritional stress, leading to disease.

As we have seen, female choice of mates drives the appearance and behavior of the males of many social animals. However, what we call female choice is a bit unclear. Meredith Small (1989) has pointed out that female primates are clearly choosy about their mates. Depending on the species, they prefer males based on body size, color, aggressive behavior, nonaggressive (caregiving) behavior, and familiarity. But choosiness is not the same thing as evolved mate choice. Is there evidence of mate choice in nonhuman primates? One example of such evidence is that male savanna baboons that were observed as being the most protective and nurturing allies of females received the most matings (Smuts, 1985).

Role of Dominance   Although dominance rank usually is not as important to female primates as it is to males, dominance may nonetheless have important consequences for female reproductive success. A study of the relationship between dominance and reproductive success among Gombe chimpanzees showed that there was a small but significant influence of

FIGURE 7.8 Despite the traditional focus on males, females actively choose mates and are the driving force in the reproductive process.

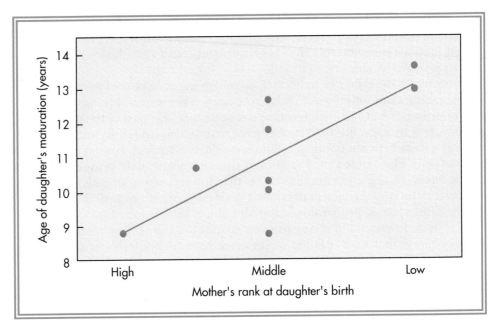

FIGURE 7.9 In some species, dominant females have more surviving offspring that mature earlier indicating an adaptive value for high social status.

sexual receptivity Willingness and ability of a female to mate, also defined as fertility.

rank on the number of surviving offspring a mother bore (Figure 7.9). The daughters of high-ranking females also matured slightly more rapidly than did those of low-ranking females (Pusey et al., 1997). And as we have seen, females form matrilineal kin groups in Old World monkeys such as baboons, macaques, and langurs, within which a female's status may influence her reproductive success.

Primatologists think females choose dominant males more often than low-ranking males because dominant animals are so often in better health, with priority of access to food. The offspring of dominant animals also tend to grow up to be high-ranking; we can't say whether this reflects a genetic predisposition to become dominant or is the proximate result of having a mother who is dominant herself and whose alliance network and socialization perpetuate high status.

Sexual Receptivity Signals Female primates use sexual signals to promote their reproductive success. These signals can be behavioral, anatomical, or physiological. Such signals are intended to advertise a female's **sexual receptivity**, or willingness to mate. They also make a female more attractive to males. Some nonhuman primates use body posture to indicate receptivity; female Hanuman langurs arch their tails over their backs and shake their heads side to side to indicate willingness to mate. Females of many other species simply move in front of a male and present their rumps as a solicitation for mating. As we saw in Chapter 6, behaviors associated with such a willingness to mate constitute *estrus*.

Nearly all female mammals are fertile during only a restricted part of each reproductive cycle. The time around ovulation often produces changes in female appearance and behavior that incite males to compete to mate with them. Only during this time are females likely to conceive, and only then are they willing to mate. Around the time of ovulation, the rump of a female primate may change color, produce a fluid-filled swelling, or emit odors, any of which will signal males in the vicinity that she is ready and willing to mate (Figure 7.10). Although it was long thought that such female features existed for the convenience of males, we now realize that females evolved these traits to aid their own reproductive strategy. Because females choose their mates, using vivid sexual signals to excite males is a

FIGURE 7.10 Sexual swellings are one way for females to advertise their mating availability, thereby inducing male competition for them.

good way to persuade them to compete with one another. This competition may allow a female to assess the quality of her potential mates.

Sexual swellings have evolved independently at least three times in the primate order, always in species living in multimale polygynous groups. Female baboons possess enormous fluid-filled swellings during a brief portion of their monthly cycle, and some colobine monkeys exhibit subtle versions of swellings too. Among the great apes, female chimpanzees and bonobos exhibit swellings for about one-quarter of their monthly cycles. In chimpanzees, a female swells for approximately 10 days of a 37-day menstrual cycle, and ovulation occurs near the end of the swelling period, after which the swelling rapidly deflates. The swelling doesn't always signal ovulation, however; even females that are pregnant or nursing babies swell, although less regularly. Males may be able to distinguish "real" swellings from nonovulatory ones by sight or smell.

The adaptive function of sexual swellings and other such signals of fertility lies in the information it conveys to males. They may confuse paternity, in that many males are attracted to the swollen female, who mates with as many males as possible during this brief period. This leaves each male in the group with a chance of being the father of the ensuing offspring and may discourage them all from being aggressive toward the infant or its mother. Alternatively, the swelling may increase the investment a male makes in the female and her offspring by establishing paternity. This would work best if the female mates only with one male during her peak period of ovulation (Hrdy & Whitten, 1987).

We know little about how males determine a female's sexual receptivity in the wild, because it is difficult to study the role of smell versus sight in a forest setting.

Why Are Nonhuman Primates Social?

Primatologists choose their study subjects according to the evolutionary principles they intend to investigate. Sociality is one of the most fundamental primate adaptations, and primatologists study the evolution of the types of primate societies that exist. A primatologist wanting to understand how monogamy works in nonhuman primates, with an eye toward understanding the origins of monogamy in human societies, might study a monogamous primate such as the gibbon. The gibbon certainly is an animal of great intrinsic beauty and interest, but to a primatologist it is also an illustration of how natural and sexual selection operate in the wild.

We are limited in our ability to extrapolate likely patterns of behavior in ancient primates, including hominids, by the small number of nonhuman primate species living. By contrast, biologists seeking to understand the evolution of bird social behavior have more than 9,000 species from which to draw examples of how adaptation and natural selection work. Nevertheless, we have made much progress in recent years in understanding the evolutionary and ecological influences on sociality.

THE PARADOX OF SOCIALITY

Nonhuman primates, like all other social mammals, tend to behave in ways that maximize their individual fitness. But this creates a paradox: Why would any animal live in a group if its evolutionary goal is individual mating success? Group living is an evolved primate adaptation, which improves access to mates, food, and protection from predators (see Innovations: Culture in Nonhuman Primates on pages 212–213). Each of these benefits has, however, a significant downside.

Access to Mates   Access to multiple potential mates is an obvious benefit of living in a group. Nonhuman primates exhibit a variety of grouping patterns, but in each mating system male and female goals are the same: enhancing their reproductive success. The behavioral strategies employed by each sex are, however, quite different.

Group life may provide access to mates, but it also means that males must compete for mating. Among nonhuman primates that live in large social groups,

Culture in Nonhuman Primates

One of the one most important discoveries about the behavior of higher primates made in the past decade has been the importance of cultural variation. We have known for decades that unlike many lower animals whose behavior patterns are largely innate, primates must learn many of the skills they need to survive and reproduce. Only in the past few years, however, have we gathered enough long-term information on many primate societies to reveal the importance of culture. Chimpanzee behavior, for example, differs from one forest to another in many ways that are the product of innovation and learning, not genetics.

On these two pages you can see several examples of cultural traditions in apes and other nonhuman primates. Primatologists believe these behaviors originated in the same way that human behaviors often do—they were invented long ago and then spread through observational learning to other group members.

A chimpanzee in Tanzania uses a "wand" to dip for safari ants. These ants have a painful bite. The chimpanzee suspends herself over the ant nest with an arm and two legs to avoid the bites, while putting a stick into the nest with an arm, which is swarmed over by the soldier ants. She will withdraw the wand and quickly eat the ants from it.

a

b

Nonhuman primates groom one another for social bonding as well as parasite removal. Chimpanzees in the Gombe National Park, Tanzania groom each other by holding an overhead branch with one hand and grooming a partner with the other (a). Chimpanzees in nearby Mahale National Park practice a different grooming style: they clasp hands while grooming (b). Such local differences in traditions are analogous to people in two different cultures having slight differences in body language.

Perhaps the first documented example of culture in a wild nonhuman primate was Imo. In the late 1940s, Japanese scientists began studying Japanese macaques on the island of Koshima. They put sweet potatoes on the beach to lure the monkeys within easy observation distance. A few years into the study, a young female named Imo began carrying her sweet potatoes to the water's edge to rinse it in seawater. The tradition spread, and within a decade most of the monkeys washed their potatoes before eating them.

Although chimpanzees are the best known tool users among nonhuman primates, they are by no means the only ones. The capuchins of the New World are also highly adept tool users. Studies in Brazil have shown that they use stones, sometimes as large as they are, to crack open palm nuts in much the same way that chimpanzees in some populations do.

In 2007, primatologists studying chimpanzees in Senegal reported something amazing; chimpanzees were using sticks to catch bushbabies. The chimpanzees stripped the tip of the stick to taper it to a point, then jabbed it into holes in trees in which bushbabies were hiding. When successful, the result was a mortally injured bushbaby, which was then extracted by hand and eaten by the chimpanzee. Although chimpanzee have often been observed to use sticks to extract food from tree holes, this was the first observation of systematic use of a "weapon" to catch prey.

Although most observations of chimpanzee tool use involve sticks or stones, other natural materials are used as well. Jane Goodall first observed Gombe chimpanzees chewing leaves, then dipping the chewed-up "wadge" into tree cavities containing rain water. The wadges acted like sponges, soaking up drinking water, which the chimpanzee would not have been able to reach otherwise.

(a)   (b)

FIGURE 7.11   (a) Male competition can be fierce. (b) This male baboon has bite wounds suffered in competition with other males.

enormous energy and time are consumed in the quest for mating success, and many males lose out. When access to a female is at stake, male baboons are more willing to engage in highly aggressive behavior toward one another, inflicting injury (Figure 7.11). Males also form alliances when females are ovulating and sexually receptive; if a male is not in an alliance his ability to obtain matings may suffer.

The intensity of male–male competition, and the importance of female choice of male traits, is also reflected in the level of sexual dimorphism we see among primates. Species in which males compete aggressively for females tend to feature high degrees of sexual dimorphism because male size and strength help to determine mating success. Species exhibiting sexual dimorphism in body size also tend to live in **polygynous** groups, which have multiple females living with either one or multiple males. Monogamous and solitary species tend to be less dimorphic. In baboons, for instance, males compete fiercely with other males for mating opportunities and are about 30% larger and heavier than females. Gibbons, on the other hand, live in monogamous pair bonds and are not dimorphic with respect to body size (Figure 7.12). There are exceptions to this pattern, however, such as the highly dimorphic but largely solitary orangutan.

Food   One benefit of living in a group is exploiting the food-finding abilities of others. But the feeding and foraging benefits of living in a social group are offset by the need to compete for food once food is found. If a monkey is led to a bonanza of fruit by others in the group, it must then compete with its group mates. Much evidence supports the notion that feeding competition strongly affects group life in nonhuman primates, lowering the nutrition and survival of animals who don't compete successfully. Females are particularly dependent on the availability of food resources in their habitat because they must nourish themselves adequately to bear the costs of reproduction. When females live in large groups, they often form **matrilineal** clusters in which mothers, daughters, and other female relatives socialize with each other more than they do with nonrelatives.

Avoiding Predators   As we saw in Chapter 6, many species of predatory animals hunt nonhuman primates. In tropical forests, attacks by birds of prey, big cats, large snakes, and humans are all potential causes of mortality. Predation can have a major impact on nonhuman primate populations, even when it occurs rarely. We should therefore expect evolved responses to predation in any nonhuman primate species prone to being hunted. However, little direct evidence of predation exists because of the difficulty of observing predation. Predators themselves tend to be silent, stealthy, and often nocturnal, so a primatologist records only the sudden disappearance of one of his study subjects from its

polygynous   Mating system in which one man is allowed to take more than one wife.

matrilineal   Pattern of female kinship in a primate social group.

group. Whether the disappearance resulted from disease, migration, infanticide, or predation often is unclear.

There is abundant indirect evidence, however, that group living helps nonhuman primates avoid predators. In larger groups, there are more eyes to act as sentinels, warning group members about danger approaching. For example, Michelle Sauther studied the response to predation risk by small and large groups of ring-tailed lemurs in Beza Mahafaly Reserve in southern Madagascar. She found that lemurs in small groups avoided foraging on the ground in areas where predator pressure was intense. Therefore, those animals found less food. On the other hand, small groups tended to associate with other lemur species when feeding and during the birth season, when highly vulnerable infants were present. Sauther reasoned that small ring-tailed lemur groups compensate for their lack of numbers by combining with other species. Larger groups entered new and unknown areas of the forest and therefore encountered predators more often than smaller groups did and reaped more food. Sauther (2002) showed that lemurs face tradeoffs between predation risk and food intake that vary according to social factors such as group size.

In some nonhuman primate species, social groups actually mob predators, counterattacking in the hope of persuading the predator that hunting them is not worth the trouble or risk of injury. Terrence Gleason and Marilyn Norconk (2002) found that among the small South American white-faced saki, smaller predators (small hawks, cats, and snakes) evoked a mobbing response. Faced with larger, more dangerous predators such as eagles, the monkeys retreated quickly into dense thickets and froze to avoid detection. Simply being in a large group means that if a predator strikes, one's individual chances of being the victim are lowered. Although being in a large group may be an effective way to detect predators, it may also make the group itself more easily detected because large groups are noisy and visible.

Most nonhuman primate species have an alarm call of some sort that they use to warn group members of approaching danger. This suggests that predation is a strong evolutionary pressure molding their behavior. Nonhuman primates also tend to be very vigilant, scanning the ground and trees around them continually while feeding. Many studies of primates and other mammals have shown that animals of many species spend less time scanning their surroundings when they live in larger groups, which suggests a greater margin of safety when more eyes are present to look for danger.

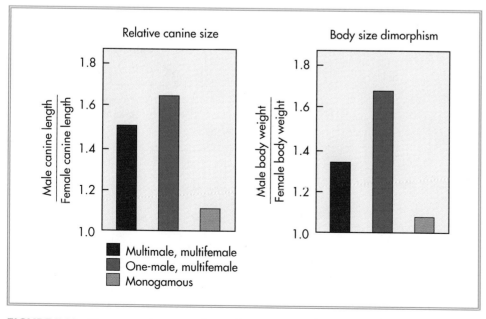

FIGURE 7.12 The most polygynous primates live in groups with many more females than males. In such species the degree of sexual dimorphism tends to be pronounced.

TYPES OF NONHUMAN PRIMATE SOCIETIES

social system The grouping pattern in which a primate species lives, including its size and composition evolved in response to natural and sexual selection pressures.

monogamy A mating bond; primates can be socially monogamous but still mate occasionally outside the pair bond.

Nonhuman primates number only 250 species but exhibit great diversity in grouping patterns. We call the type of group in which nonhuman primates live their **social system**. Earlier generations of primatologists viewed social groups as male-centered; they believed that females wanted to live with or near males, and so males determined the form that social systems took. However, the consensus today is that females have evolved strategies, behavioral and ecological, to cope with the need to balance limited food supplies while avoiding predators with the demands of mating and rearing offspring. Males then use their habitats in such a way as to maximize their access to females. This section outlines the types of nonhuman primate social systems.

Solitary Some strepsirhines live in a social system similar to that of the earliest primates. They are solitary; females occupy individual territories along with their dependent offspring, which they defend by scent-marking objects (Figure 7.13). Of course, no mammal is truly solitary; it must locate mates during the breeding season. Males occupy territories that overlap a number of female territories; they attempt to maintain exclusive mating access to all these females and keep transient males away. Males use scent-marking and a variety of calls to communicate with one another and to warn intruders to stay out. This social system characterizes many of the strepsirhines, especially the nocturnal galagos and lorises.

When females live solitary lives, males must choose whether to try to defend them from all other males or to share access to them with other males. Most solitary nonhuman primate species feature males that attempt to maintain exclusive access, as is the case in monogamy.

Monogamy The social system in which a male and female live in a pair bond for an extended period of time, perhaps years, is called **monogamy** (Figure 7.13). Recent studies have shown that our notion of monogamy needs some adjusting because members of pair bonds sometimes mate secretly outside the pair bond as well. In some cases, a pair of gibbons may live as a socially monogamous pair bond, but both the male and female secretively mate with other gibbons. Social monogamy thus is not necessarily strict reproductive monogamy.

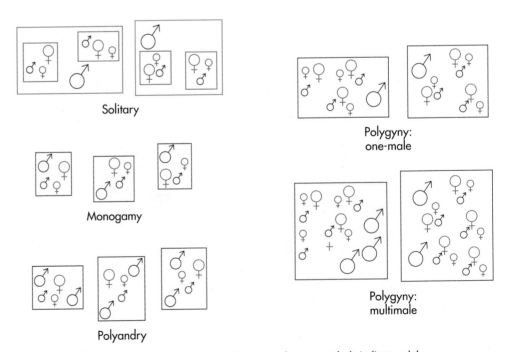

FIGURE 7.13 A taxonomy of primate social systems. Larger symbols indicate adults.

Monogamy is best understood as a female reproductive strategy. Monogamous female primates establish and hold territories, and on each territory a single male attaches himself to the resident female. The female therefore tolerates the presence of a male. The male may provide some essential services to the female, such as aiding in territorial and food defense or protecting the female's offspring from infanticide by marauding males. In a few species, males actually aid in the rearing of infants by carrying young and shielding them from harm. In exchange for this service, they receive a high degree of certainty that they fathered the offspring (though not absolute certainty, as females are prone to sneaking off to mate with other males).

Because males in monogamous pairs don't appear to compete as directly with other males as those in social groups need to, we expect that sexually selected aspects of male competition, such as large canines or big body size, would be deemphasized. And we find this to be the case. For instance, gibbons exhibit little sexual dimorphism except in hair color.

Polygyny   The majority of haplorhine nonhuman primate species live in groups composed of one or more males and more than one female, a social system called **polygny** (Figure 7.13). Groups composed of multiple males and multiple females often are called **polygynandrous** (literally, "many males and many females"). Of course, many animals, from geese to deer, live in large social groups comprising both males and females. What characterizes nonhuman primate polygyny is the complexity of social interactions. In a few species, sociality has accompanied the evolution of brains capable of remembering a long history of interactions with group mates—the debts and favors an animal owes and is owed by others—and of strategizing accordingly.

The complexity of social interactions in nonhuman primate groups is influenced by the social system. A male in a multiple-male group must by necessity use a far more complex set of tactics to obtain mates than does a male living in a group in which he is the only male or living monogamously with just one female.

One-Male Polygyny   *One-male polygynous groups* are what primatologists used to call harems. One male lives with as many females as he can monopolize (Figure 7.14). The term *harem* implies male control over females and is obsolete because it dates from a time when primatologists did not appreciate the role that females play in the mating system. In some cases one-male groups are driven by choices made by females, not males. For example, Robin Dunbar showed that in the multitiered social system of the gelada baboon, females bond to one another, and the male, despite all appearances of being the central hub of the social system, is simply hoping to be accepted by "his" females (Dunbar, 1983). Among mountain gorillas, half of all groups are one-male. But females often transfer between groups, and resident silverbacks appear to regard other males with fear and anxiety mainly because of the risk that their own females may emigrate for a new silverback in a different group.

When one-male polygynous groups exist, males who are not able to obtain females usually live as extragroup males—either alone or in all-male "bachelor" groups. In some species, these all-male groups attack one-male groups and attempt to evict the resident male from his females (Insights and Advances: The Infanticide Wars on pages 218–219 and Figure 7.15 on page 220).

In some one-male group species, there are occasional influxes of males from outside the group, particularly if the species has a well-defined breeding season. The resident male then finds it impossible to restrict access to the group's females, and the females may have an active interest in seeking matings with the extragroup males. Such influxes occur seasonally in blue monkeys (Rowell, 1988), Hanuman langurs (Boories et al., 1999), ring-tailed lemurs (Sussman, 1992), and sifakas (Richard, 1992). These events may contribute to the formation of multimale groups.

polygyny   Mating system consisting of at least one male and more than one female.

polygynandrous   Primate social system consisting of multiple males and multiple females.

FIGURE 7.14   A group of capped langurs.

INSIGHTS AND ADVANCES

The Infanticide Wars

Infanticide is the killing of infants. Scientists have observed infanticide in many different animal species, from birds to monkeys to humans. Most of the debate among scientists has centered on infants that are killed by a male other than the biological father.

Scientists once believed that the ultimate goal of animals living in a social group was the attainment of group harmony. Events that disrupt the harmony, such as fights or sexual jealousy, were thought to disrupt the balance of the group in a negative way. But the rise of Darwinian theory to explain social behavior changed that. Scientists recognized that individuals seek to reproduce themselves, often at the expense of other, unrelated individuals.

In the early 1970s Sarah Blaffer Hrdy was planning a doctoral thesis on Hanuman langur monkeys, a large and graceful monkey ubiquitous across the Indian subcontinent (Figure A). Hrdy had heard re-

FIGURE A Infanticide in nonhuman primates has been best-documented in Hanuman langurs.

ports from the arid western regions of India that langurs living at high population density committed infanticide. She set off to investigate, settling in Mount Abu, a town nestled among the red hills of southernmost Rajasthan.

At Abu and elsewhere, langurs live in two types of social groups: one-male and multimale. One-male groups predominate at Abu, and in this social setting the lone resident male becomes a target for attack by bands of males that lack a group of females of their own. As it turned out, some of the Abu langurs were killing infants, and they did not seem to be acting pathologically. Instead, Hrdy observed bands of males invading established social groups, ousting the resident male, and in some cases killing infants sired by him. She observed four infanticides and strongly suspected numerous others over a 5-year period.

Hrdy viewed the killings in a Darwinian light. Instead of pathological reactions to overcrowding or stress, Hrdy saw infanticide as a reproductive strategy by otherwise bachelor males. By ousting a resident male and then fending off other competitors, a marauding male langur reaped a sudden windfall of mating opportunities with the group's females, except that some or all of the females were preoccupied, reproductively speaking, because they were pregnant by the previous resident male or were nursing his infants. In either case, the females would not be cycling, rendering them unavailable for a new male eager to sire his own progeny. Hrdy reasoned that if the tendency toward infanticide were inherited, males who engaged in the behavior would have greater reproductive success

than other, noninfanticidal ones. This suggested that infant killing was an adaptive strategy evolved through sexual selection to promote a male's genes, at the expense of other males. Female langurs who preferred noninfanticidal males as mates lost in the evolutionary arms race because by failing to kill rivals' offspring, their sons would leave fewer descendants.

The results of Hrdy's long-term field research at Abu appeared in her 1977 book *The Langurs of Abu: Female and Male Strategies of Reproduction.* The reaction from the scientific community was swift and angry. Many primatologists initially denied that the infanticides she reported had occurred at all. When it became clear that the infant killing had occurred in this and other populations of langurs, the critics argued against its evolutionary relevance. The critics noted that most reported cases of infanticide were only circumstantial; the prime evidence often was an infant found dead with bite wounds shortly after a group takeover. Critics charged that the explanation for langur infanticide at Abu was social pathology, not reproductive strategy (Curtin & Dolhinow, 1978). Perhaps the high langur population density and level of human disturbance in and around Abu had made it impossible for males to take over new groups in a gradual, nonaggressive fashion (Figure B). Instead, in the melee of male–male encounters, aggression directed at other males and at females sometimes injured or killed infants accidentally.

The debate over langur infanticide continued to rage as other researchers produced field data supporting the reproductive strategy theory. Primatologist Volker Sommer

FIGURE B   Some scientists believed that langur infanticide was influenced by human disturbance.

FIGURE C   Primatologist Volker Sommer and his colleagues showed that langur infanticide had adaptive value and is likely an evolved reproductive strategy.

studied langurs living in the arid scrubland of Jodhpur, Rajasthan, in collaboration with an Indian team led by S. M. Mohnot (Figure C). Between 1969 and 1985 they documented fourteen cases of infanticide, plus twenty other suspected killings and fourteen non-fatal attacks on infants. They also showed that the pattern of aggression was consistent with the sexual selection hypothesis. Females whose babies were killed by incoming males began to cycle again significantly sooner than those whose infants survived, thus rewarding a marauding male with procreative opportunities months earlier than he would have gotten by waiting for the infants to mature (Sommer, 1994).

Elsewhere in India, zoologist Paul Newton documented infanticide in a pristine forested region in Kanha National Park. In Kanha, langurs live in a natural state, preyed upon by tiger and leopard while foraging among Kanha's rich wildlife diversity. Newton demonstrated that infanticide and heightened male aggression were not correlated with either langur or human population density, refuting the idea that infant killing was the outcome of monkeys living at high density in human-disturbed environments (Newton, 1987). More recently, a team of researchers led by primatologist Carola Borries and colleagues (1999) conducted paternity analysis using DNA from langur feces on a population of the monkeys from southern Nepal. They showed that in all cases, the infanticidal males were not the fathers of the infants they killed.

Meanwhile, reports of infanticide mounted for a wide range of species. David Watts (1989) showed that among the mountain gorillas of the Virunga Volcanoes, infanticide by silverback males is a leading cause of infant mortality. In species as different as marmosets and macaques, the killing of infants was witnessed, often in scenarios that were consistent with the Darwinian model.

For the past two decades, researchers have produced increasingly strong evidence that infanticide among social animals often is carried out strategically in accordance with Darwinian predictions. Opponents of the adaptationist approach argue that unless a gene or complex of genes can be found that causes infanticidal behavior, we should not speak of infant killing as an evolved trait.

Although there are a few examples of direct gene–behavior relationships (some captive-bred strains of mice commit infanticide whereas other strains do not), higher social animals are too complex genetically and behaviorally for simple gene–behavior links to be made. No doubt infanticide occurs in a variety of scenarios and for a variety of reasons, and not all episodes of infanticide can be linked to reproductive benefits to the infant killer. However, the weight of current evidence lends support to the reproductive strategy theory.

FIGURE 7.15   In one-male group species, extra males typically reside in all-male "bachelor" groups. These are Hanuman langurs.

Multimale Polygyny   A male nonhuman primate would like to have as many females to himself as he can monopolize. The downside of this is that he may have to constantly fend off intruding males who want to mate with his females. As the number of females in a one-male group increases, it becomes impossible for a male to prevent other males from joining the group. A better option for him may be to allow other males to enter the group but continue to obtain the majority of matings with the females by being socially dominant. So in many species, we see multimale, multifemale polygynous groups.

Instead of competing for sole access to females, males in multimale groups may compete for priority of access. Priority often takes the form of a **dominance hierarchy**, in which a top-ranking, *alpha male* allows other males access to the females in the group but may attempt to exclude his rivals when females are in estrus and may conceive. In this way he strikes a balance between the goal of maximizing mating success and the burden of spending all his time and energy fending off other males. In species living in multimale groups, females are not typically all in estrus at the same time. When one female enters estrus, she becomes a focus of competition among the group males. That such competition is far more intense than among monogamous primates is reflected in polygynous primates' canine-tooth size and body-size sexual dimorphism, both of which contribute to male success in mate competition. Mating competition might also be indicated by the size of the males' testes, which may allow him to produce more sperm than other males to impregnate a female.

In some multimale groups, intense mating competition occurs when the species breeds seasonally. This is because the high-ranking males are unable to restrict access to all the females at the same time. In squirrel monkeys (*Saimiri* spp.), for example, males undergo dramatic physiological changes during the mating season, bulking up in order to compete successfully with other males in the group. The largest male tends to be the most dominant for that mating season and also has the highest reproductive success (Boinski, 1987).

Some nonhuman primate species maintain both one-male and multimale groups in the same population. Hanuman langur monkeys live across the Indian subcontinent in populations that can be mainly one-male or multimale. Why this variation occurs is unclear. Primatologists have tried to explain it as a response to the local physical environment, local demographic trends, or the number of

dominance hierarchy   Ranking of individual primates in a group that reflects their ability to displace, intimidate, or defeat group mates in contests.

females and the overall population density (Newton, 1987; Sommer, 1994). In any case, populations featuring a preponderance of one-male groups also tend to exhibit higher levels of intergroup aggression and especially a tendency for strange males to attempt group takeovers of existing groups, with accompanying **infanticide** of the group's infants (see Insights and Advances: The Infanticide Wars on pages 218–219).

A few polygynous species organize themselves in multitiered social systems. In northeastern Africa, both hamadryas baboons and gelada baboons live in small one-male groups. But these one-male units join other one-male units to form larger bands, and these bands sometimes merge to form troops. In both species, enormous herds sometimes form, especially at sleeping sites in the evening, made up of many one-male groups (Kummer, 1968; Dunbar, 1983). This unusual social system probably results in part from phylogeny—inherited patterns of social behavior—and in part from local ecology (sleeping in large groups may help protect individuals from attacks by predators such as leopards). A parallel to this social system may be found among the Asian snub-nosed monkeys (genus *Rhinopithecus*). Chinese golden snub-nosed monkeys forage in groups of up to 300 animals, but within this group there are well-defined smaller units, each controlled by only one or a few males (Kirkpatrick, R. C., 1998). The groups forage in pine forests and on the ground, feeding heavily on lichens and mosses, which are abundant and evenly distributed. Such a widespread resource may enable the formation of such enormous groups, within which individual males compete for access to smaller numbers of females.

Fission–Fusion Polygyny   One additional form of polygyny is perhaps the most complex social system found in nonhuman primates. A few species do not live in cohesive groups; instead, temporary associations of individuals come together and split up repeatedly (Figure 7.13). This is called **fission–fusion polygyny**, and it is seen in species as different as chimpanzees, bonobos, and spider monkeys. Instead of forming a well-defined stable group, populations divide into communities. These communities have distinct home ranges and community membership, within which the community members join and part with one another unpredictably in temporary foraging units called parties. The same chimpanzee may be in a party of two at dawn, of ten an hour later, and of thirty later in the day. The only stable unit in the social system is a female and her young offspring. Males often travel together, forming coalitions among themselves (see Insights and Advances: Are Chimpanzees from Mars and Bonobos from Venus? on pages 222–223).

Fission–fusion polygyny is believed to be an evolved response to reliance on ripe fruit in the diet. Because of the patchy and seasonal distribution of fruits in a tropical forest and the daily variation in fruit availability, foraging for food in large cohesive groups would incite intense competition for resources. Females forage on their own to optimize their access to fruit, and males attempt to control access to females by forming bonds with one another.

Polyandry   When one female lives in a reproductive or social unit with multiple males, we say the social system is polyandrous (Figure 7.13). **Polyandry** is quite rare in nonhuman primates; it is better known in birds, where it has demonstrated key rules of sexual selection. Among nonhuman primates, only a few species of marmosets and tamarins in New World tropical forests exhibit this social system, and it remains poorly understood. In some species of these monkeys, males bond together and help females to rear offspring. This is probably a reproductive strategy by males. Marmosets and tamarins are very small (<1 kg) monkeys and are vulnerable to a wide range of predators. Females boost their reproductive output by producing twins, but these twins weigh an extraordinary 20% of the mother's

infanticide   The killing of infants, either by members of the infant's group or by a member of a rival group.

Fission-fusion is such a complex form of social system that it was more than ten years after researchers began studying chimpanzees that they began to understand how this type of primate society works.

fission–fusion (polygyny)   Type of primate polygyny in which animals travel in foraging parties of varying sizes instead of a cohesive group.

polyandry   Mating system in which one female mates with multiple males.

Are Chimpanzees from Mars and Bonobos from Venus?

Jane Goodall shocked the scientific world in 1961 when she reported that chimpanzees relish meat and hunt other mammals eagerly; they are not the vegetarian pacifists they had always been thought to be. As observations in the wild accumulated, it became clear that there is a brutal side to chimpanzees (Figure A).

Males strive to ascend a rigid dominance hierarchy, and upon reaching high rank they wield their political power with Machiavellian cunning. They patrol the perimeter of their territory, attacking and sometimes killing their unwary neighbors (Goodall, 1986).

Chimpanzees are also efficient predators, consuming hundreds of prey animals including monkeys, antelope, and wild pigs

FIGURE B   Bonobo females form close alliances, maintained through sex, but these alliances are lacking in chimpanzees.

FIGURE A   Chimpanzees are studied more than bonobos.

at some study sites. Colobus monkeys are attacked by hunting parties of chimpanzees, and the male colobus defend their groups by courageously counterattacking the ape marauders. Nearly all kills are made by males, and after a successful hunt the meat is controlled by the high-ranking males in the hunting party.

Only since the mid-1980s has the closely related bonobo become well known to science (Figure B). Studies of bonobo behavior have revealed a society contrasting sharply with the hierarchical nature of chimpanzee society. Bonobo social life is marked by female cooperation, sex as social communication, and alliance formation rather than aggression. Female bonobos band together in coalitions to dominate males, avoiding the sort of domination and sexual coercion that male chimpanzees routinely inflict on females. Such coalitions among females are nearly unknown in chimpanzees (Parish, 1996).

Bonobos often are said to be the "make love, not war" ape. They mate in more positions, seemingly for recreation as much as procreation, than any mammal other than humans. They engage in same-sex pairings, in which two females rub their genital swellings together ("GG rubbing"). This behavior eases tensions between individuals and may allow them to feed near one another without undue stress. This female bonding is absent in chimpanzee society.

An even more striking difference between female chimpanzees and female bonobos exists in reproduction. Females of nearly all mammalian species are reproductively active only during a constricted time period surrounding ovulation. This estrus period characterizes all the higher primates except humans (Chapter 6). Females of our species, though more likely to conceive around the time of ovulation, are free of the bonds of a strictly defined period of "heat." As a result, sex serves not only for procreation but also as a mechanism of social communication and reinforcement of long-term pair bonds. This release from the constraints of estrus means that the timing of ovulation is no longer advertised to males and is thought to have been a pivotal event in the evolution of early human society.

Bonobo females often are said to be the only mammals other than humans to be released from the bonds of estrus (de Waal & Lanting, 1997). They maintain their sexual swellings for a much longer portion of their menstrual cycles than chimpanzees do and therefore mate nearly throughout the cycle, as humans do. Being released from estrus, bonobos have come to use sex as much for communicating with males as for conceiving offspring, as in our own species.

In conflict, as in mating, bonobos and chimpanzees appear to be strikingly different. Bonobo researcher Takayoshi Kano (1992) observed that when two bonobo communities meet at a range boundary, not only is there no lethal aggression, but there may be socializing and even sex between females and the enemy community's males.

In hunting and meat-eating, which chimpanzees so relish, we see another apparent contrast between the two apes. Bonobos capture baby monkeys and then use them as dolls or playthings for hours, only to release the monkey unharmed (though worse for the wear) without eating them, as a chimpanzee would (Sabater-Pi et al., 1993).

The close genetic kinship between these apes and humans and the behavioral differences between them have led anthropologists to debate which species is the better model for understanding the evolution of human behavior. Were our ancestors violent, meat-eating male-dominated creatures or more gentle, female-bonded vegetarians?

While this debate rages, some researchers have pointed out that the differences between chimpanzees and bonobos may not be as rigid as they are usually depicted. Many stark behavioral contrasts reported between chimps and bonobos have been based on comparisons between wild chimpanzees and captive bonobos (Stanford, 1998b). Animals in captive settings are well known for their tendency to display greater frequencies of the whole gamut of social behavior, from fighting to sex, than do their wild counterparts. Therefore, their behavior patterns do not necessarily reflect those that evolved for living in an African forest.

Although wild bonobos are far less studied than chimps, we know about naturalistic patterns of bonobo behavior from two long-term study sites in the Democratic Republic of the Congo: Wamba, the site directed by Takayoshi Kano, and Lomako, which has been occupied by two separate research teams including scientists from the United States and Germany. Field data show that in two important respects, female bonobos are not more sexual than their chimpanzee counterparts. First, the frequency of copulating, in which captive bonobos show a markedly higher rate than wild chimpanzees, is no different between wild bonobos and wild chimpanzees (Stanford, 1998b). Second, the idea that bonobo females are released from estrus is derived from data on the duration of sexual swelling taken mainly from bonobos in captivity. In captivity, female bonobos maintain their sexual swelling for up to 23 days, nearly half of their 49-day (captive) cycle. This dwarfs the receptive period of wild female chimpanzees, who swell for about 10 days of their 37-day cycle. However, this comparison changes completely if we consider wild bonobos rather than captive specimens, whose excellent nutrition may enhance the reproductive system. Wild bonobos from Wamba are swollen for only 13 days of a 33-day cycle, numbers that are much closer to those of wild chimpanzees than they are to captives of their own species. A report of captive bonobos in Belgium shows that even in captivity bonobos do not necessarily have longer swelling durations than chimpanzees (Vervaecke et al., 1999).

Meat-eating, though certainly less common than among chimpanzees, may be quite common among bonobos as well, but it has been underrated because little field research has been done on this ape. German researchers Gottfried Hohmann and Barbara Fruth (1993) have observed extensive meat-eating and meat-sharing by bonobos at Lomako, but most chimpologists still call the bonobo the "vegetarian" great ape.

Finally, the idea that bonobos are somehow more closely linked to humans has been based on the claim that they walk upright more often than chimpanzees do (Kano, 1992). But this may also be a myth: In a recent study that compared bipedal walking captive bonobos and captive chimpanzees, Elaine Videan and William McGrew (2001) found that bonobos were no more bipedal than chimpanzees.

Before we tar ourselves with the legacy of the male-chauvinist, carnivorous, warring chimpanzees or congratulate ourselves for leaning toward the sisterhood-is-powerful bonobos, we would do well to consider how our depiction of primate societies sometimes becomes intertwined with our own political views.

body weight. Males assist in infant caregiving by carrying babies and may help in antipredator defense as well. Males may opt to assist a female for the opportunity to achieve reproductive success; if two males mate with the same female, each has a 50% chance of being the father of the twins.

Primatologist Paul Garber has shown that the presence of multiple males increases a female's overall reproductive success as well, a compelling argument for males to engage in this sort of cooperative breeding (Garber, 1997). However, another field study by Leslie Digby has shown that among the two or more males in a marmoset group, one tends to be socially dominant and to sire most of the infants (Digby, 1995). In other words, marmosets and tamarins are perhaps best considered to be socially polyandrous but reproductively monogamous.

Reconstructing the Evolution of Primate Societies

In the early years of modern nonhuman primate behavior study, many primatologists believed the form a primate social system took followed fairly simple ecological rules. They created taxonomies of social systems in relation to the species' natural habitat. For instance, because a number of distantly related primate species ate a fruit diet and lived in polygynous groups, it was thought that frugivory and polygyny were linked. Monogamy was also thought to be linked to fruit-eating and territoriality because gibbons exhibit both. But as more and more nonhuman primate field studies were carried out, it became clear that such pigeonholes were simplistic.

Today, primatologists use increasingly quantitative models and large numbers of field studies of nonhuman primates and their ecology to understand the workings of primate social systems. However, primate social systems are molded by the evolutionary history of each species. This makes interpreting the effect of natural selection difficult because for many primates the environment that molded their evolution may not be the one they currently occupy. Anthony Di Fiore and Drew Rendall (1994) used statistical models of primate family trees to show that the evolutionary history of a primate lineage plays a major role in determining what the social system looks like today. Unfortunately, in most cases we can only guess about the way in which this evolution happened.

Primate ecologists differ on which influences—feeding competition, mate competition, or predation—are the most important in shaping primate societies. In the 1980s, several theorists attempted to explain primate societies based on the importance of intragroup and intergroup competition. Carel van Schaik surveyed a range of primate societies and found that female reproductive success was lower in larger groups suggesting that intragroup feeding competition was important. This implied that group living was overall a negative influence on sociality and led him and his colleagues to devise a number of innovative tests for other possible influences on why nonhuman primates should be social. They concluded that depending on the taxon, predation and infanticide were extremely important influences that molded sociality in nonhuman primates (van Schaik & van Hooff, 1983; van Schaik & Hörstermann, 1994).

Meanwhile, Richard Wrangham proposed a model for why primates formed male-philopatric or female-philopatric groups. He pointed out that, as we saw in discussing sexual selection, females are the ecological sex in that their reproductive success is so closely tied to their ability to find and defend food. He proposed that the key to solving the paradox of female sociality—that female primates live with group mates that limit their food intake—was the kinship patterns in female-philopatric groups. Where females live together, they tend to be relatives, and this

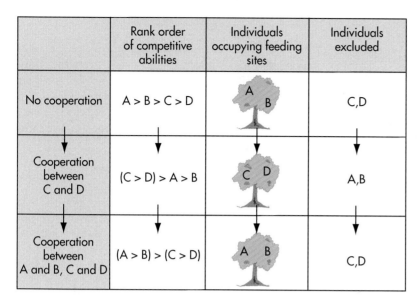

	Rank order of competitive abilities	Individuals occupying feeding sites	Individuals excluded
No cooperation	A > B > C > D		C,D
Cooperation between C and D	(C > D) > A > B		A,B
Cooperation between A and B, C and D	(A > B) > (C > D)		C,D

FIGURE 7.16 Richard Wrangham's "female-bonded" theory of intergroup competition was highly influential in our understanding of the evolution of primate societies.

kinship mitigates the high cost of intragroup feeding competition. Wrangham (1980) proposed that kin groups of females may jointly defend key feeding trees (Figure 7.16). Because larger groups could successfully control more fruit in bigger trees, there would be a strong benefit for females to live together in large groups.

As mentioned earlier, feeding competition, mate competition, and predation often are interrelated. We can see their relationship clearly in a study by Charles Janson and Michele Goldsmith. They analyzed the relationship between group size and ranging among diverse primate species and found that larger groups tend to travel farther. Janson & Goldsmith (1995) argued that this occurs because each group member must travel a bit farther to find food when surrounded by more competitors. In an earlier study, Janson (1985) had shown that capuchin monkeys vie for a position near the center of a foraging group, probably to be able to obtain the best food while avoiding the most predators. In the group center there are more eyes to detect the approach of a predator. Craig Stanford (1998a) found that red colobus monkeys living in larger groups were less vulnerable to predators, even though larger groups were more often detected by predators. This was true probably because in a larger group, the odds of an individual monkey being killed are lower. But feeding competition was higher in larger groups too. So there were survival advantages and disadvantages in both large and small groups for both obtaining food and avoiding predators. As in many other primate examples, group life is all about costs and benefits and tradeoffs between different behavior options.

In Chapters 6 and 7, you have seen how the lives of nonhuman primates inform us about ourselves and our ancestry. In this chapter we examined social behavior, but social behavior and ecology cannot be fully separated from each other. Primate social behavior has been molded by natural selection, with the environment as the filter. These same natural forces shaped human ancestry, human anatomy, and perhaps aspects of human behavior. Now that you have seen the context for the roots of human evolution, it's time to turn in Chapter 8 to the fossil record and what it tells us about the context of primate evolution.

SUMMARY

1. **What do we mean by the *reproductive asymmetry* between males and females?**

   Females have a lower reproductive potential than males, which makes them the object of male competition in most species. Because females invest so much more time and energy in reproduction, they tend to be more discriminating in choosing a mate.

2. **What are the three major influences on the evolution of nonhuman primate sociality?**

   All wild primates must find mates, find food, and avoid predators in order to survive and reproduce.

3. **Why are social systems and mating systems not always the same?**

   A primate may live in a particular grouping pattern but mate outside that pattern. For instance, a gibbon may live in a socially monogamous pair bond but mate secretly with gibbons other than his or her mate.

4. **Do dominant males always enjoy high mating success?**

   Dominance and mating success often are associated, but the equation is complicated. Dominant males may have high social status but low mating success, or vice versa. Low-ranking or adolescent males may compensate for their low dominance rank by mating covertly with females.

5. **What is the basis of female mate choice in nonhuman primates?**

   We know that female primates are choosy when it comes to selecting a mate. We believe that aspects of this choice are under evolutionary pressure. Females may choose males on the basis of size, strength, or aggressiveness. But they may also choose males for their caregiving behavior and their lack of aggression toward them. We believe females seek genetic quality in a mate; how they discover this in potential mates is an area of intense research.

6. **What is the likely function of sexual swellings during estrus?**

   Sexual swellings are female reproductive adaptations. They may allow a female to confuse a mate as to paternity of her offspring by attracting many males to mate with her. This may discourage males from later aggression toward her infant.

7. **What are the major types of nonhuman primate grouping patterns?**

   Nonhuman primates may live solitarily, monogamously, or in polygynous groups that can be one-male, multimale, or fission–fusion, or they can be polyandrous.

8. **What key ecological factor affecting sociality do the van Schaik and Wrangham models have in common?**

   Both van Schaik and Wrangham theorize that feeding competition is the key ecological influence on sociality, although van Schaik emphasizes competition within the group, whereas Wrangham emphasizes competition between groups.

CRITICAL THINKING QUESTIONS

1. If primate behavior tells us much about human origins because primates are big-brained and socially complex, then what other animals unrelated to primates might be informative about the origins of human social behavior?

2. Why would male primates spend their lives striving to rise in dominance rank if being high-ranking does not guarantee high mating success?

3. Nonhuman primates are but one type of animal living in tropical forests. Do you think that they have had a major impact on the evolution of tropical forests? Why or why not?

KEY TERMS

captive study	male philopatry	social system	dominance hierarchy
semi–free-ranging	sexual receptivity	monogamy	infanticide
field study	polygynous	polygyny	fission–fusion polygyny
female philopatry	matrilineal	polygynandrous	polyandry

SUGGESTED READING

de Waal, Frans B. M. (1982). *Chimpanzee Politics*. Johns Hopkins University Press, Baltimore.

Hrdy, Sarah B. (1999). *Mother Nature*. Pantheon Books, New York.

McGrew, W. C., Marchant, Linda F., and Nishida, Toshisada (Editors). 1996. *Great Ape Societies*. Cambridge University Press, Cambridge, UK.

Wrangham, Richard, and Peterson, Dale. (1996). *Demonic Males*. Boston: Houghton Mifflin.

Carbon 14
Unstable (radioactive)

As the sun drops toward the horizon over a remote African badland, a sunburnt geologist sets down his rock hammer, takes a swig of lukewarm water from his canteen, and mops the sweat from his forehead with a bandanna. He has just finished collecting chunks of volcanic ash from layers above and below the place where fossils of a primitive human ancestor had been recovered earlier that field season. He carefully seals the bags and records his location. With the samples stowed safely in his backpack, the scientist scrambles down the slope and makes the long hike back to base camp.

Back in his laboratory a few weeks later, portions of each rock sample are broken up with a mortar and pestle. The scientist peers through a microscope, picking through the sample of volcanic ash with steel forceps, carefully selecting fresh feldspar crystals. He cleans the crystals in an acid solution and then places each into the recess of a sample chamber. The chamber is sealed and sent to a nuclear reactor for irradiation, and the scientist moves on to other projects. A month or so later, the chamber returns marked with a radioactive warning label. After a cooling off period it will be placed in the way of a laser beam, and each crystal in turn will vaporize slightly, then bubble and melt. A key piece of equipment, a mass spectrometer, begins to analyze the isotopes in the gas released from the melting crystal. After several months of experiments and calculations, checking and rechecking, the scientist has an age estimate—sometimes, the results can be quite surprising.

Techniques developed over the last 50 years allow scientists such as this geochronologist to provide a more accurate context for understanding our evolutionary past. **Paleontology**, a field that takes its name from the Greek words for "old" (*paleos*) and "existence" (*ontos*), is devoted to gleaning all the information that can be extracted from **fossils**, the preserved remnants of once-living things. This information includes how ancient the fossil is; what kind of organism it represents; and the ecological adaptations of the organism, such as its diet and locomotion. We must also know about how that fossil came to be preserved where it was, and how the preservation process affected the fossil. A fossil without its context is almost useless because we have no way of assessing how old it is, what kind of environment it lived in, or what other animals it might have lived and competed with.

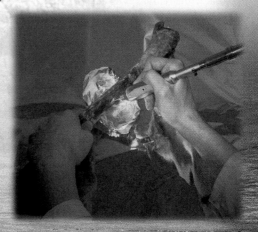

In this chapter we will set the stage for answering these questions by looking closely at the field of **geology**, the study of the earth, to understand the preservation, age, and environment in which primate fossils are found. Because the evolutionary history of humans and our primate relatives is a story that unfolds through time, geological principles are fundamentally important to the study of human evolution. We will see how materials fossilize and look at what we can learn from both the fossils themselves and the surroundings in which they

are found. We'll introduce and compare some of the most important dating methods in use today and the context in which each is most valuable. Finally, we'll explore conditions on Earth during the Cenozoic Era, the time period in which primates evolved.

How to Become a Fossil

You might think that fossils are abundant. After all, every organism eventually dies, and natural history museums are filled with fossils of dinosaurs and other prehistoric creatures. In reality, very few living things become fossils and only an exceedingly small proportion of these fossils are discovered, collected, and studied. Thus, the fossil record preserves some organisms in abundance, whereas others are seldom preserved.

Taphonomy, the study of what happens to remains from death to discovery, reveals some of the factors that determine whether an organism becomes a fossil (Shipman, 1981). These include both biological and geological processes. Death might come to a human ancestor or any other animal in a number of ways, such as injury, disease, or predation (Figure 8.1). In many instances, the agent of death may leave marks on the skeleton, such as the bite marks of a predator. After death, the carcass begins to decompose and numerous microbes, such as bacteria and mold, and insects, accelerate this process. While this is happening, scavengers may ravage the carcass, consuming its soft tissues and perhaps even chomping on its bones. Eventually, only the most durable tissues remain, especially the densely constructed middle parts of the limb bones, the jaws, and the teeth (Brain, 1981). Even these durable remains can disappear through various means including erosion and trampling.

To become a fossil, part of the organism must be preserved by burial, a natural process in which the carcass or part of it is covered with sediment. Burial interrupts the biological phase of decomposition, protecting the skeleton from further ravaging and trampling by biological organisms. Because sediments such as sand, silt, mud, and gravel usually are carried by water, burial often occurs in the floodplains of rivers, along the shores of lakes, and in swamps where uplift, erosion, and sedimen-

paleontology   The study of extinct organisms, based on their fossilized remains.

fossils   The preserved remnants of once-living things, often buried in the ground.

geology   The study of Earth systems.

taphonomy   The study of what happens to the remains of an animal from the time of death to the time of discovery.

FIGURE 8.1   Fossils are formed after an animal dies, decomposes, and is covered in sediment. Minerals in ground water replace bone mineral, turning bone into stone that may later be discovered if the surrounding rock erodes away.

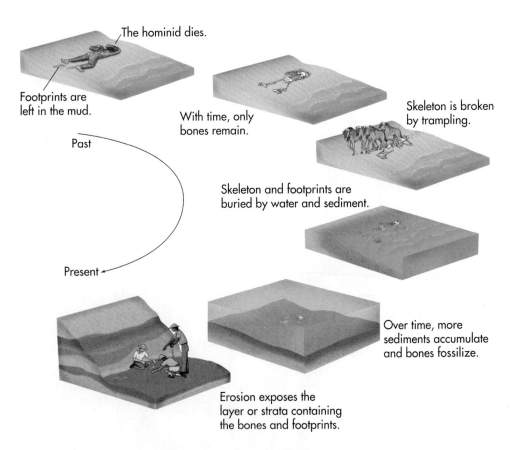

The hominid dies.

Footprints are left in the mud.

Past

With time, only bones remain.

Skeleton is broken by trampling.

Skeleton and footprints are buried by water and sediment.

Present

Over time, more sediments accumulate and bones fossilize.

Erosion exposes the layer or strata containing the bones and footprints.

tation are occurring. In other circumstances, sediment such as dust and volcanic ash carried by the wind sweeps over the remains. Once buried, skeletal remains may absorb minerals from the surrounding soil or ground water, which eventually replace the organism's original inorganic tissues. The result is *petrifaction* the process of being turned to stone. In the past, scientists were puzzled by the problem of how a solid (a fossil) could end up in another solid (the rock), and fossils were thought to be of perhaps supernatural origin. In 1669, Danish geologist Nicolas Steno (1638–1686) explained in his *Forerunner to a Dissertation on a Solid Naturally Occurring in Another Solid* how this could occur naturally through burial and fossilization. This book was one of the turning points in our understanding of paleontology and geology.

Although most fossilized remains are of hard (skeletal) parts, on occasion soft parts such as skin, hair, or plant parts may be preserved (Figure 8.2). In very exceptional circumstances, the original tissues of an organism are preserved largely intact, as when animals' bodies are frozen, such as the well-known mammoths of Siberia, or when ancient people are naturally mummified. Finally, *trace fossils* such as the tracks left by animals may provide impressions of their activities, and *coprolites*, or fossilized feces, also tell us about the presence of past animals.

The Importance of Context

A fossil without its context is useless, except perhaps as a pretty object on the mantelpiece, because we cannot assess its age, or the environment in which it lived. In this section we review the important principles used in geology to understand the position of a fossil in its rock layers and of different fossil sites relative to each other.

STRATIGRAPHY

Imagine driving through a road cut where you see what looks like layers or bands of rock. These are **strata**, literally "layers" in Latin. In some road cuts these layers are basically horizontal, but in others they may be more vertical or even quite deformed (Figure 8.3). **Stratigraphy** is the study of the

(a)

(b)

FIGURE 8.2 Past life is preserved in many forms. (a) Soft tissues or plant parts may be preserved in rock. (b) Whole skeletons or their parts may be fossilized in rock. From these various clues paleontologists piece together the evolutionary history of the animals preserved.

strata   Layers of rock.

stratigraphy   The study of the order of rock layers and the sequence of events they reflect.

(a)

(b)

FIGURE 8.3 Rock layers (strata) usually look like the layers in a cake (a), but geological processes such as earthquakes and mountain building can deform these once horizontal layers. (b) The paleoanthropologist must understand these deformations in order to figure out which strata a fossil comes from and how old it is.
Source: a: © Carr Clifton.

distribution of these layers. In 1830, Charles Lyell, whose work influenced Darwin (see Chapter 1), synthesized a number of accepted geological principles including the principles of stratigraphy. The principles of geology rely in large part on the concept of *uniformitarianism,* originally developed by James Hutton, a Scottish geologist, in 1785 and further promoted in Lyell's book. Uniformitarianism suggests that processes operating today are also those that operated in the past and thus they can explain the fossil and geological record. The principles of stratigraphy include four that are critical to an understanding of the context of a fossil: original horizontality, superposition, cross-cutting relationships, and faunal succession.

The *principle of original horizontality,* formulated by Nicolas Steno, says that layers of rock (strata) are laid down parallel to the earth's gravitational field and thus horizontal to the earth's surface, at least originally (Figure 8.4). All the deformations and upendings that you see in road cuts are caused by later activity such as earthquakes and volcanic eruptions.

Building on the principle of original horizontality is the principle of superposition, also proposed by Steno. The *principle of superposition* (Figure 8.4) states that, with all other factors equal, older layers are laid down first and then covered by younger (overlying) layers. Thus older sediments are on the bottom, and the fossils found in them are older than those found above. However, stratigraphy is not always so straightforward, and in the late 1700s James Hutton added the *principle of cross-cutting relationships,* which says simply that a geological feature must exist before another feature can cut across or through it and that the thing that is cut is older than the thing cutting through it (Figure 8.4), just as the layers of a cake must exist before you can stick a candle into them.

Finally, the *principle of faunal succession,* first proposed in 1815 by William Smith (whose nickname was "Strata" because of his passion for stratigraphy), addresses the changes or succession of fauna (animals) through layers. Smith

FIGURE 8.4 (a) The principles of stratigraphy help us understand the relative age of rock layers. (b) Layers are deposited parallel to Earth's surface (horizontality). Younger layers are deposited on top of older layers (superposition). A layer that cuts across others is younger than those it cuts (cross-cutting relationships).

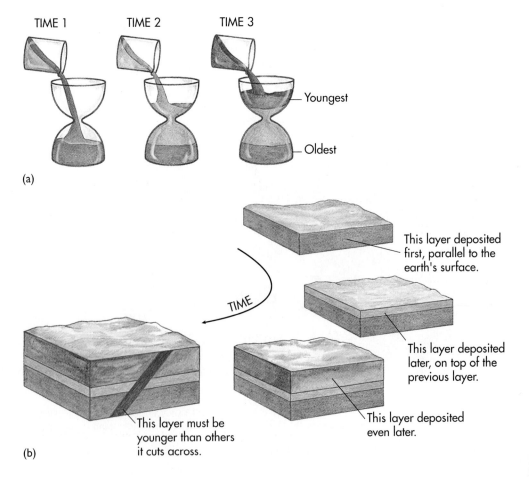

TIME 1   TIME 2   TIME 3

Youngest

Oldest

(a)

TIME

This layer deposited first, parallel to the earth's surface.

This layer deposited later, on top of the previous layer.

This layer must be younger than others it cuts across.

This layer deposited even later.

(b)

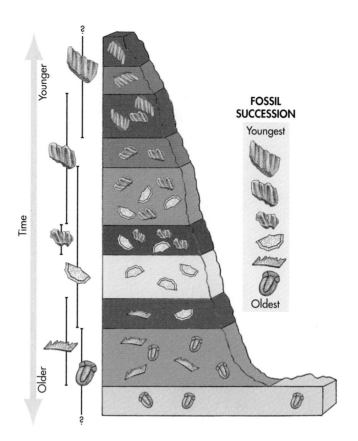

recognized not only that deeper fauna is older but also that there are predictable sequences of fauna through strata, that successive layers contain certain types of faunal communities and types of fossils that follow one another in predictable patterns through the strata (Figure 8.5). Certain of these animals that typify a layer are called index fossils. Furthermore, Smith noted that once a type of fossil leaves a section, it does not reappear higher in the section. With the benefit of Darwin's work, we know this is because once a type of animal goes extinct, it cannot reappear later (and so cannot be fossilized in younger sediments). Smith's observations were made on invertebrates but apply equally well to vertebrates.

Using the principles of stratigraphy, as we shall see when we discuss dating techniques, we can determine which strata are older and younger. Comparisons between sites can provide a sequence of rocks from older to younger for both areas. By comparing the stratigraphy of sites from around the world, especially for marine sediments that are very continuous, geologists have assembled a great geological column from the very oldest to the very youngest rocks on Earth. This geological column, with age estimates provided by dating techniques discussed later in this chapter, is called the geologic time scale.

The laws of stratigraphy are critical for understanding the relative age and context of fossils.

THE GEOLOGIC TIME SCALE

The **geologic time scale (GTS)** is divided into nested sets of time. From most inclusive to least inclusive these are eons, eras, periods, and epochs (Figure 8.6 on page 234). The earth itself is approximately 4.5 billion years old, and the GTS covers this entire time, although human and primate evolution occurs only in the Cenozoic Era, or about the last 65 million years.

The scale is divided into two eons, the Precambrian and Phanerozoic. The Precambrian dates from 4.5 billion to 543 million years ago and is divided into three eras: the Hadean, Archean, and Proterozoic. The Phanerozoic Eon dates

geologic time scale (GTS)
The categories of time into which Earth's history is usually divided by geologists and paleontologists: eras, periods, epochs.

FIGURE 8.6 Earth's history is divided into nested sets of time—eons, eras, periods, and epochs—and is called the geologic time scale.

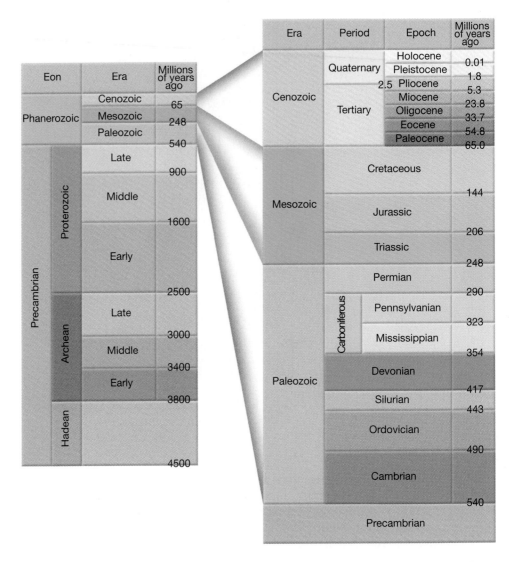

from 543 million years ago to the present and is divided into three eras; from oldest to youngest they are the Paleozoic, Mesozoic, and Cenozoic. "Zoic" in each of these names refers to the presence of animals.

Although we will spend the next several chapters discussing the fossil record of only the last 65 million years (the Cenozoic Era), take a moment to consider the enormity of time represented by the entire history of the earth, 4.5 billion years (Figure 8.6). Primates are present for a little less than 1.5% of that tremendous span, and humans and our closest ancestors are present for only about 0.1% of that time. To put this in perspective, think about your 7-day spring break and the time you allot to different activities. On this scale, the Primates have existed for about 2.4 hours, and the human lineage has existed for about 11 minutes and 20 seconds. Hopefully that's less time than you allot to your least favorite spring break activities like homework!

Mammals arose in the Mesozoic Era; *Mesozoic* literally means "middle age of animals," but the era is often called the "age of reptiles" because of the abundance of dinosaurs (Figure 8.7 on pages 236–237). The Mesozoic spans 248–65 million years ago and has three periods: the Triassic, Jurassic, and Cretaceous. The Cenozoic, or recent age of animals, spans from 65 million years ago to present and has two periods: the Tertiary and Quaternary. The Tertiary Period, from 65 to 2.5 million years ago spans parts of five epochs: the Paleocene (65–54.8 million years ago), Eocene (54.8–33.7 million years ago), Oligocene (33.7–23.8 million years ago), Miocene (23.8–5.3 million years ago), and the first part of the Pliocene (5.3–2.5 million years ago). The Quaternary period from 2.5 million years ago to present, spans parts of three epochs: the remainder of the Pliocene (2.5–1.8 million years ago), the Pleistocene (1.8 million years ago to 10,000 years ago), and Holocene (10,000 years ago to present). We live in the Holocene Epoch of the Quaternary Period of the Cenozoic Era of the Phanerozoic Eon.

The lengths of epochs, periods, and eras are not standard in the GTS. Boundaries are placed at points in the time scale where large shifts are evident in the geological column or the fossils contained within it. For example, the boundary between the Cretaceous Period of the Mesozoic and the Tertiary Period of the Cenozoic Era (or the Cretaceous/Tertiary [K–T] boundary) records a great change in animal taxa: the drastic decrease of dinosaur species and increasing number of mammals. The boundary between the Tertiary and Quaternary periods signals the onset of glacial events in the Northern Hemisphere, and was recently moved from 1.8 to 2.5 million years ago to reflect evidence for glaciations becoming severe at that time.

How Old Is It?

How do we determine where in the geologic time scale a site and the fossils within it fall? A vital first step in determining the antiquity of fossil remains is learning their **provenience**, the precise location from which the fossils come. After we have established provenience, we can apply a wide variety of techniques to estimating the age of fossil remains. These techniques fall into three main categories depending on the underlying method used. Relative dating techniques use concepts of stratigraphy to establish relative ages between localities and fossils found in these localities. Calibrated relative dating techniques compare a relative technique to an absolute time scale. Chronometric (or "absolute") dating techniques use an absolute clock, such as radioactivity, to produce an age estimate in years before present. Collectively, the field of geology devoted to studying time in the fossil record is *geochronology*. We review some of the major methods of this field in the next section.

RELATIVE DATING TECHNIQUES

Relative dating techniques tell us how old something is in relation to something else without applying an actual chronological age. If you say you have an older brother, we know your relative ages even though we do not know whether the two of you are 6 and 16 years old, 19 and 25, or 60 and 65. Almost all relative dating techniques rely on the geological principles of stratigraphy discussed earlier. These techniques include lithostratigraphy, biostratigraphy, tephrostratigraphy, and chemical methods.

Lithostratigraphy   Using the characteristics of the rock layers themselves to correlate across regions is called **lithostratigraphy** (*litho* refers to rock). For example, if millions of years ago a layer of limestone was formed by an inland sea that extended over a large area of West Virginia, across Pennsylvania, and into New York, then we would expect to see the limestone layer in all these areas even if they exhibit different sequences of rock layers above and below the limestone. Therefore, the limestone layer allows us to correlate the widely separated sequences of rock layers (Figure 8.8 on page 238).

Tephrostratigraphy   An increasingly important variant of lithostratigraphy is **tephrostratigraphy**, the identification of a volcanic ash by its chemical fingerprint of major, minor, and trace elements (Feibel, 1999). Chemical similarities allow us to correlate volcanic ashes (*tephra*) with each other, demonstrating time equivalence even in widely separated sites. This technique has been used with great success in the Turkana Basin of northern Kenya and southern Ethiopia, where researchers have made many important discoveries of ancestral human fossils.

Biostratigraphy   Using Smith's principle of faunal succession (Figure 8.5), we can use the biological organisms found in rocks to correlate age between sites and across regions and thus to provide age estimates for fossils found at those sites. Making correlations based on biological organisms is called **biostratigraphy**. Organisms that are

provenience   The origin or original source (as of a fossil).

relative dating techniques   Dating techniques that establish the age of a fossil only in comparison to other materials found above and below it.

lithostratigraphy   The study of geologic deposits and their formation, stratigraphic relationships, and relative time relationships based on their lithologic (rock) properties.

tephrostratigraphy   A form of lithostratigraphy in which the chemical fingerprint of a volcanic ash is used to correlate across regions.

biostratigraphy   Relative dating technique using comparison of fossils from different stratigraphic sequences to estimate which layers are older and which are younger.

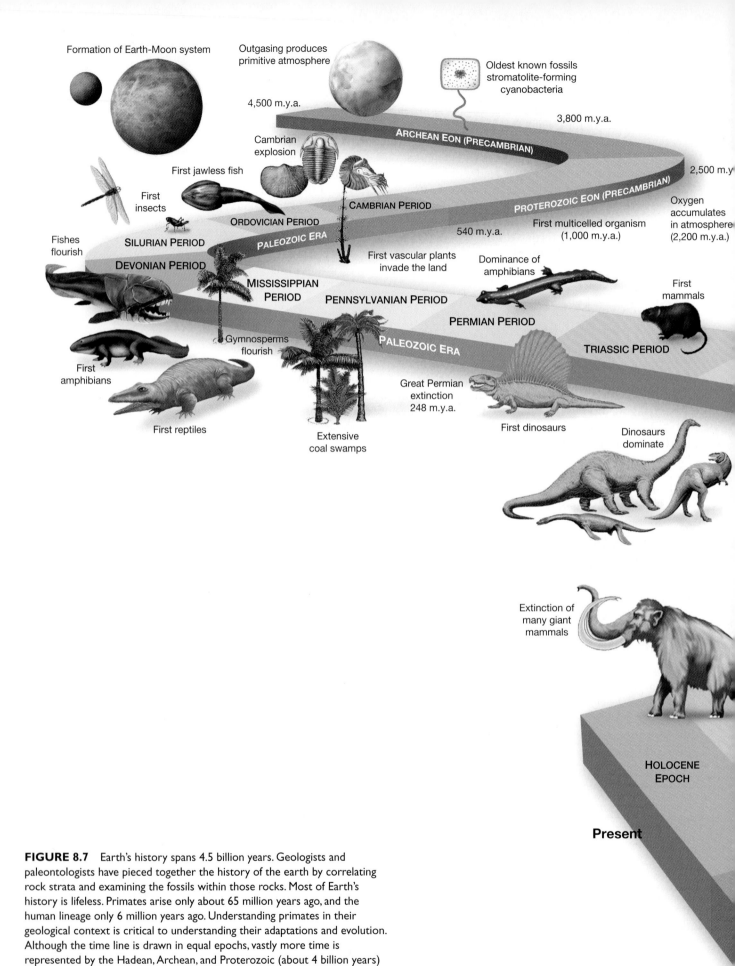

FIGURE 8.7 Earth's history spans 4.5 billion years. Geologists and paleontologists have pieced together the history of the earth by correlating rock strata and examining the fossils within those rocks. Most of Earth's history is lifeless. Primates arise only about 65 million years ago, and the human lineage only 6 million years ago. Understanding primates in their geological context is critical to understanding their adaptations and evolution. Although the time line is drawn in equal epochs, vastly more time is represented by the Hadean, Archean, and Proterozoic (about 4 billion years) than by all of the later periods, which span only the last 540 million years.

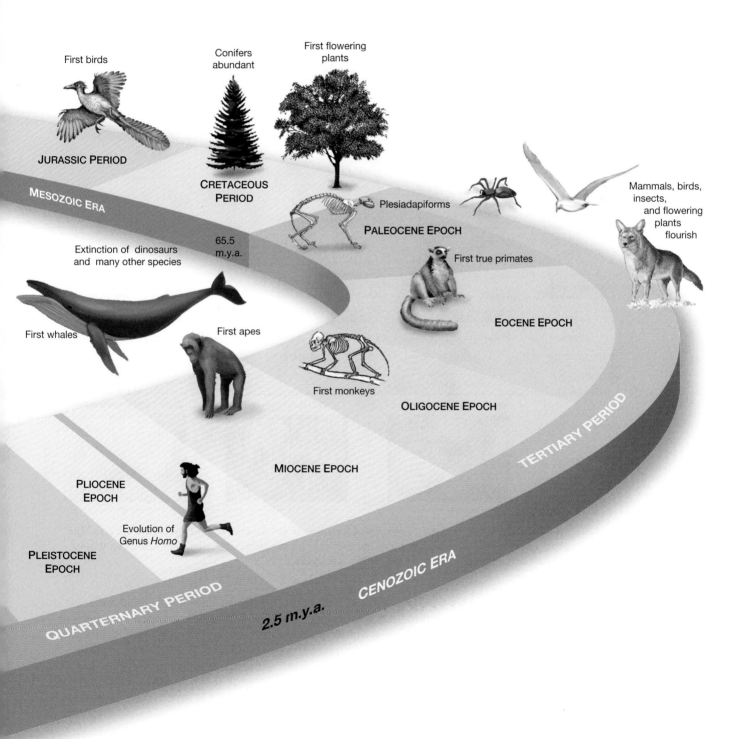

First birds

JURASSIC PERIOD

Conifers abundant

CRETACEOUS PERIOD

First flowering plants

MESOZOIC ERA

Extinction of dinosaurs and many other species

65.5 m.y.a.

Plesiadapiforms

PALEOCENE EPOCH

Mammals, birds, insects, and flowering plants flourish

First true primates

EOCENE EPOCH

First whales

First apes

First monkeys

OLIGOCENE EPOCH

TERTIARY PERIOD

MIOCENE EPOCH

PLIOCENE EPOCH

Evolution of Genus *Homo*

PLEISTOCENE EPOCH

QUARTERNARY PERIOD

CENOZOIC ERA

2.5 m.y.a.

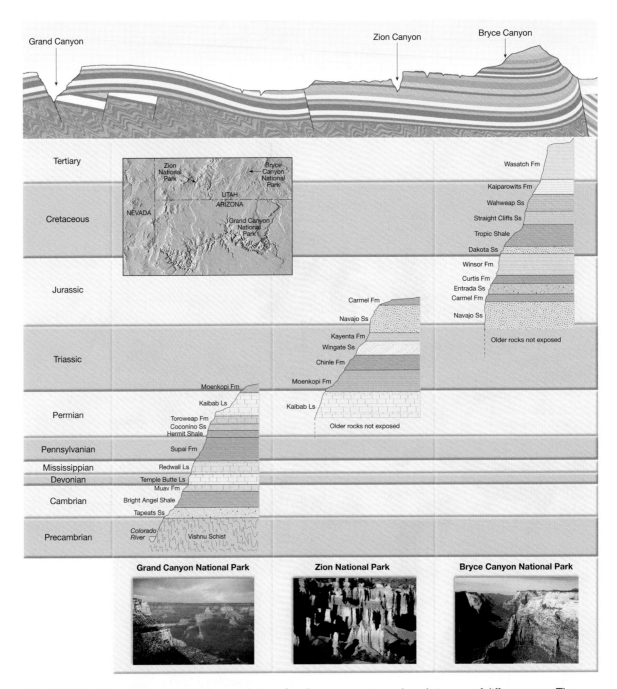

FIGURE 8.8 Lithostratigraphy uses the correlation of rock units to estimate the relative age of different areas. The overlapping rock units for U.S. parks show that the Grand Canyon contains strata that are mostly older than those at Zion National Park, and that Bryce Canyon National Park is the youngest.

geographically widespread and vary anatomically through short time periods are the best biostratigraphic markers. Biostratigraphic markers that appear and disappear (go extinct) at roughly the same chronological time in all regions are most useful.

Rodents often are good biostratigraphic indicators of age. For example, the presence of certain rodent taxa that went extinct in the early Pleistocene has been used to estimate the age of Dmanisi, in the Republic of Georgia, the site of some of the earliest hominids outside Africa (see Chapter 12). In East Africa during the Plio-Pleistocene, the changes in pig taxa are systematic enough to also be good indicators of relative age. The presence of certain taxa, such as pigs or rodents, tells you only how old the site is relative to other sites with similar or different animals.

An absolute age (that is, an age in years, such as 1.6 million years old) can be assigned only because at other sites with these index fossils there are also associated chronometric ages. So in the case of the Dmanisi site the age must be older than 1.6 million years ago because, based on sites with absolute ages in Europe, the rodents present at Dmanisi are known to have gone extinct by that time.

Chemical Techniques within Sites   A few chemical techniques are useful for identifying the relative age of different fossils from the same site. These techniques include the analysis of the fluorine, uranium, and nitrogen content of the fossils themselves. Such techniques become important when the association between different fossils or between the fossils and their sediments is in question, as in the Piltdown hoax, in which chemical techniques proved that the human fossils were fakes (see Insights and Advances: The Piltdown Hoax on pages 240–241). As bones and teeth lie buried in sediment, they take up fluorine and other elements from the soil, roughly in proportion to the amount of time they have been buried (Oakley, 1963). How much of these elements is available is dependent on the local environment, so the techniques are not useful between sites. However, two bones buried in the same sediments for the same amount of time should have similar chemical signatures. Thus these methods test associations within sites.

CALIBRATED RELATIVE DATING TECHNIQUES

Calibrated relative dating techniques include regular or somewhat regular processes that can be calibrated to a chronological scale if certain conditions are known. Such techniques include obsidian hydration, amino acid racemization, and paleomagnetism. Given the time scale of interest, we discuss only the latter in this section.

Geomagnetic Polarity   Although we take for granted the current position of Earth's north and south magnetic poles, the polarity of the magnetic field has alternated through geologic time (Brown, 1992). Currents in the earth's outer core create this magnetism, and as they change, the polarity may flip. At times in the past, magnetic north has been the opposite or reverse of today, that is, in the South Pole. Such reversals occur quickly, perhaps over thousands of years, and do not last for set periods of time. As rocks are formed, their magnetic minerals orient themselves toward magnetic north. Rocks laid down today would have a polarity, or orientation, similar to today's magnetic field. Such polarities are called *normal*. Rocks formed under a reversed field have a *reversed polarity*. Geologists use these facts to assist in the dating of stratigraphic units.

Paleomagnetists have assembled a **geomagnetic polarity time scale (GPTS)** that records the orientation of sediments from different intervals (Figure 8.9). The time scale is based on a sequence of changes in the magnetism of ancient layers, or **paleomagnetism** that has been pieced together, mainly from sediments that have spread outward from midoceanic ridges at the bottom of the sea (Cande & Kent, 1995). The GPTS is divided into long intervals of similar polarity (normal or reversed) called chrons. Within these chrons there are often short periods of opposite polarity called subchrons. The GPTS extends back into the Jurassic Period, but here we are most concerned with the last four chrons, the Gauss (reversed, 4.2–3.5 million years ago), Gilbert (normal, 2.6–3.5 million years ago), Matuyama (reversed, 2.6 million years ago–780,000), and Brunhes (normal, 780,000–present), and some of their subchrons. The present-day interval is the Brunhes Chron, which began about 780,000 years ago.

Paleomagnetists can use the polarity of sediments to assess site ages. First, they collect multiple samples from the site, being sure to indicate the direction of present-day north (Figure 8.10 on page 242), and measure the rock's polarity in the laboratory. Their analyses must carefully consider whether secondary overprints of polarity exist in the sample. Certain conditions such as weathering, heating, or

calibrated relative dating techniques   Techniques that use regular or somewhat regular processes that can be correlated to an absolute chronology to estimate the age of a site.

geomagnetic polarity time scale (GPTS)   Time scale composed of the sequence of paleomagnetic orientations of strata through time.

paleomagnetism   The magnetic polarity recorded in ancient sediments. Reversed or normal direction is used to correlate with the geomagnetic polarity time scale to infer an age for a site.

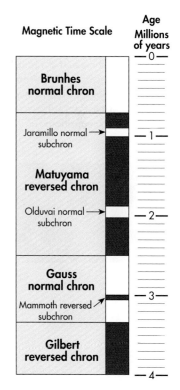

FIGURE 8.9 The geomagnetic polarity time scale shows how Earth's magnetic pole has changed through geologic time. Red bands indicate periods of reversed polarity and white bands indicate normal polarity.

INSIGHTS AND **ADVANCES**

The Piltdown Hoax

The most vivid example of how relative dating techniques revealed a hoax is the case of Piltdown Man (Figure A). From 1908 to 1913,

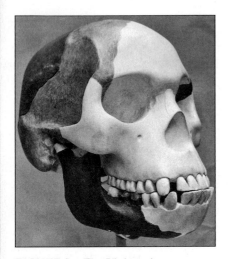

FIGURE A   The Piltdown hoax was exposed by fluorine analysis, a relative dating technique that can test whether two bones have come from the same paleontological site. The mandible and skull fragment were shown to have different fluorine compositions.

a number of fossil fragments were uncovered in a gravel pit at Piltdown Common, near the village of Uckfield in southern England. These finds appeared to show that the cradle of humankind was in the United Kingdom. The hoax would eventually be revealed by a relative dating method—fluorine analysis.

In 1908, a laborer who was quarrying gravel at the site struck a human skull fragment. He turned his discovery over to Charles Dawson, a local attorney and amateur geologist, who launched an intensive three-year search at the site for more fossils. In 1911, Dawson teamed up with Arthur Smith Woodward of the Natural History Museum in London (Figure B) to lead excavations that would retrieve more primitive human fossils and fossils of an assortment of long-extinct mammals. The key finds were the original skull, with a brainsize smaller than that of a Neandertal but in other respects quite modern looking, and a large mandible with apelike teeth (Spencer, 1990).

Because he fit the preconceived notions of how human evolution occurred, when Piltdown Man was announced to the world in 1912 he was accepted as the first Euro-

pean. At the same prehistory conference two far better-documented fossil humans, Neandertal and Java Man (*Homo erectus*), were disputed and even dropped from the human family tree by some prominent scientists, because few could imagine our ancestors as being other than large-brained Europeans. This notion, along with the abundant other fossil mammals with which the Piltdown remains were found, contributed to the acceptance of Piltdown as the first European, something of which the British scientific establishment was quite proud. Yet as new human fossil finds began to accumulate in the 1920s and 1930s, all presented a view of human prehistory different from that offered by Piltdown's advocates. Instead of a large braincase and apelike jaw, most of the new fossils had small brains.

Beginning in 1950, British scientists conducted chemical relative dating tests on the fossil. These tests revealed that the level of fluorine in the Piltdown skull did not match that of the mandible or the fauna; Piltdown was indeed a fraud. Piltdown Man was really a modern human brain case, artfully stained to appear ancient,

lightning strikes can cause either the formation of new minerals with new polarities or the resetting of the polarity of existing minerals to reflect the polarity at the time the condition occurred, not the polarity at the origin of the rock. Often these overprints can be removed, but if they are not considered they can lead to an erroneous conclusion regarding polarity and ultimately age (see Insights and Advances: Dating Controversies on page 243).

After overprint removal, paleomagnetists observe the sequence of polarities and compare it with the GPTS. Because paleontological localities do not often contain long stratigraphic sequences and can be only either reversed or normal, there is likely to be more than one match between the GPTS and the site polarity. This means that we must use other means, usually either chronometric ages or index fossils, to constrain or calibrate the possible ages provided by the GPTS. However, paleomagnetic analyses can be critical tests of absolute chronologies because the GPTS provides an

FIGURE B　Anatomists disagreed on the importance of the find.

with an associated orangutan mandible whose teeth had been filed down to appear more human (the file's scratches were clearly visible under a microscope). The mandible's connecting points with the skull had been carefully broken off to disguise the fact that the two did not belong together.

Who did it? All eyes turned initially to Dawson himself; who better to discover a new "fossil" than the person who planted it in the soil? However, as an amateur, Dawson seems unlikely to have planted a fake fossil if his passion was for finding real ones. Professional scientists such as Teilhard de Chardin, an avid archaeologist who was religiously passionate enough to be a skeptic about human fossils, Arthur Keith, or his colleague Grafton Elliot Smith all have been suspected at times because of the attention a fossil such as Piltdown could bring to their careers. Even Sir Arthur Conan Doyle, author of the Sherlock Holmes mysteries, has been suggested as perhaps having set out to embarrass the scientific community, whose respect he craved, with an ingenious practical joke.

The mystery remained unsolved until a cleaning of the attic of the Natural History Museum in London in the 1980s revealed a trunk with the initials of a former museum clerk, Martin Hinton, filled with an assortment of hippo and elephant teeth, all stained to the exact color of the Piltdown fossils. It also included human teeth that had been stained in different ways, as though by someone practicing the best way to fake an ancient appearance.

Hinton had a financial dispute with one of the curators of the museum and may have wanted to embarrass the museum officials by luring them into boastful claims about a fake ancestor (Gardiner, 2003). In addition, he was also an avowed anti-Darwinian, preferring Lamarck's debunked views.

It is not clear how Hinton would have planted the fossils in the quarry unless Dawson (who had a history of "discovering" historical artifacts that turned out to be frauds) was a co-conspirator. It appears that Hinton and Dawson were the likely perpetrators of one of science's greatest hoaxes.

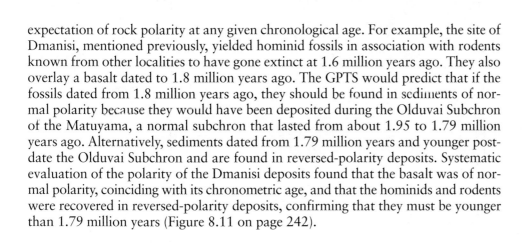

expectation of rock polarity at any given chronological age. For example, the site of Dmanisi, mentioned previously, yielded hominid fossils in association with rodents known from other localities to have gone extinct at 1.6 million years ago. They also overlay a basalt dated to 1.8 million years ago. The GPTS would predict that if the fossils dated from 1.8 million years ago, they should be found in sediments of normal polarity because they would have been deposited during the Olduvai Subchron of the Matuyama, a normal subchron that lasted from about 1.95 to 1.79 million years ago. Alternatively, sediments dated from 1.79 million years and younger postdate the Olduvai Subchron and are found in reversed-polarity deposits. Systematic evaluation of the polarity of the Dmanisi deposits found that the basalt was of normal polarity, coinciding with its chronometric age, and that the hominids and rodents were recovered in reversed-polarity deposits, confirming that they must be younger than 1.79 million years (Figure 8.11 on page 242).

(a)   (b)

FIGURE 8.10   (a) At Sangiran, Java, scientists collect rock samples to measure the polarity of the sediments around the time *Homo erectus* fossils were deposited. (b) In the field the scientists use a compass to record the direction of present-day magnetic north, which is marked directly on the rock. The polarity of the minerals in the rock itself will be measured later in the lab.

CHRONOMETRIC DATING TECHNIQUES

chronometric dating techniques   Techniques that estimate the age of an object in absolute terms through the use of a natural clock such as radioactive decay or tree ring growth.

Unlike relative dating methods, **chronometric dating techniques** provide a chronological age estimate of the antiquity of an object in years before the present (see Innovations on pages 250–251). These methods rely on having a clock of some sort to measure time. Such clocks include annual growth rings on trees and the recording of annual cycles of glacial retreat, which date very recent events. Radioactive clocks date more distant events, depending on the isotope used. The most famous of the radioactive decay clocks is Carbon-14 (^{14}C, or radiocarbon).

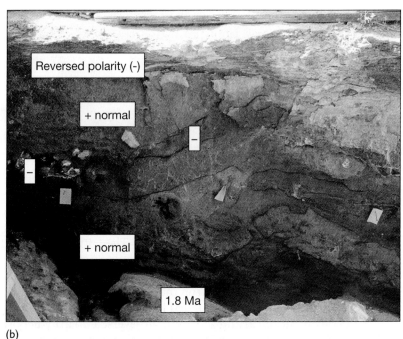

Reversed polarity (-)

+ normal

−

−

+ normal

1.8 Ma

(a)   (b)

FIGURE 8.11   (a) The site of Dmanisi, in the Republic of Georgia, has produced some of the earliest *H. erectus* outside of Africa. (b) The basalt below the hominids is dated to 1.8 million years ago using argon–argon techniques, and the geomagnetic polarity of the sediments is recorded by pluses and minuses on the wall of the excavation. The fossils come from reversed polarity sediments.

INSIGHTS AND **ADVANCES**

Dating Controversies

Although modern radiometric dating techniques provide some of the most rigorously scientific data available to biological anthropologists, the resulting age estimations often are highly controversial. A number of variables introduce uncertainty into our attempts to estimate the age of fossils. One vexing problem is the absence of material suitable for chronometric dating. A number of chronometric dating techniques (including potassium–argon, argon/argon, uranium series, and fission track) date the geological context and not the fossils themselves. Consequently, an age determination for a fossil is doubtful unless there is a secure understanding of the relationship between the fossil and its geological context. Biostratigraphic and tephrostratigraphic correlation provide an important means of testing the validity of chronometric age estimations and have pointed out simple errors in radiometric dates on a number of occasions.

An example of one such instance, which comes from Pliocene deposits of Ethiopia, illustrates this point and shows how all available dating information ultimately yields resolution of the ages of a fossil locality. The Hadar Formation in the Afar Triangle of Ethiopia provides the most complete paleontological evidence currently available for human ancestors between 3 and 4 million years ago. Geochronologists using the argon/argon technique estimated an age of 3.8 million years before present on a basalt in the Hadar sequence, suggesting that many of the Hadar hominids were more ancient than the same species from the 3.5- to 3.7-million-year-old site of Laetoli in Tanzania (Walter & Aronson, 1982). In contrast, tephrostratigraphic correlation between Hadar in Ethiopia and the Turkana Basin in Kenya indicated that these same Hadar hominids should be younger than 3.4 million years old (Brown, 1983). Detailed biostratigraphic comparisons concurred, revealing that the assortment of fossil mammals from Hadar is most comparable to those from

deposits dating from approximately 3.4–3.0 million years ago in the Lower Omo River Valley of Ethiopia (White et al., 1984) (Figure A). The radiometric and other age estimates differed by 400,000 to perhaps 800,000 years. This discrepancy led to a closer inspection of all of the age indicators. Ultimately, it was discovered that simple arithmetic errors had contributed to the 3.8-million-year age estimate for the Hadar basalt. The corrected age more nearly matched the other estimates; scientists concluded that the important sample of early human ancestors from Hadar dated to the 3.0- to 3.4-million-year time period rather than to 3.8 million years before present as once claimed.

Without the use of several lines of evidence, the true age of the locality might not have been resolved.

Dating controversies will continue to exist, but securely establishing provenience and applying multiple methods of age estimation should almost always lead us to the correct determination of antiquity.

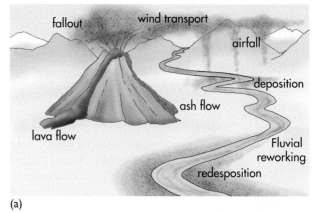

(a)

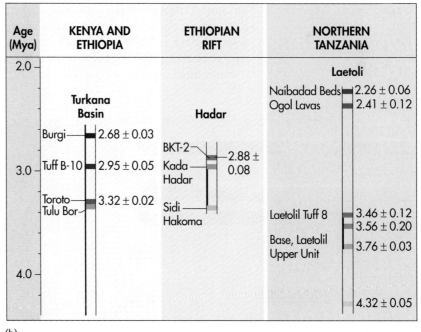

(b)

FIGURE A (a) Scientists use the chemical signature of sediments from volcanic eruptions to correlate across large areas. (b) Correlations among East African hominid sites. The absolute ages are provided by argon/argon or potassium–argon techniques.

Other chronometric methods measure not the amount of radioactivity lost since formation but the amount gained from the environment since deposition. These include the electron trap techniques of electron spin resonance (ESR), optically stimulated luminescence (OSL), and thermoluminescence (TL). Because we are concerned primarily with providing age estimates over the past 65 million years to perhaps as recently as 100,000 or 50,000 years ago, we focus here on the clocks appropriate for this time scale. Figure 8.12 illustrates the relative age ranges of the different chronometric techniques discussed in this chapter, and Table 8.1 compares the materials dated. The more prominent techniques are compared in Innovations: Time in a Bottle on page 250.

radiometric dating   Chronometric techniques that use radioactive decay of isotopes to estimate age.

isotopes   Variant forms of an element that differ based on their atomic weights and numbers of neutrons in the nucleus. Both stable and unstable (radioactive) isotopes exist in nature.

half-life   The time it takes for half of the original amount of an unstable isotope of an element to decay into more stable forms.

parent isotope   The original radioactive isotope in a sample.

daughter isotope (product)   The isotope that is produced as the result of radioactive decay of the parent isotope.

Radiometric Dating   **Radiometric dating** relies on the natural, clocklike decay of unstable isotopes of an element to more stable forms. *Elements* are chemically irreducible categories of matter such as carbon (C), hydrogen (H), and oxygen (O) that form the building blocks of all other matter, such as molecules of water (H_2O) and carbon monoxide (CO). Elements often occur in nature in more than one form, differing slightly on the basis of their atomic weights, which reflect the number of neutrons and protons in the nucleus. These different forms are called **isotopes.** For example, there are three isotopes of carbon, ^{12}C, ^{13}C, and ^{14}C, each with six protons (positively charged) but with six, seven, and eight neutrons (neutral particles), respectively (Figure 8.13). Although ^{12}C and ^{13}C are stable (they do not naturally decay), the extra neutron of ^{14}C makes it unstable or prone to decay. The rate at which this radioactive decay takes place is constant, and the **half-life** of the isotope is the amount of time it takes for one-half of the original amount to decay. To determine the age of a sample we measure the amount of **parent isotope,** the original radioactive isotope the sample started with, and the amount of **daughter isotope (product)** in the sample, which is the isotope formed by radioactive decay of the parent isotope (Figure 8.12b). The total of these two is the amount of total parent that existed before radioactive decay started. The amount of daughter as a percentage of total parent tells you the number of half-lives expended. Knowing the length of the half-life yields an age (number of half-lives × length of half-life = age estimate) (Figure 8.12a). For example, the half-life of ^{14}C is about 5,730 years; if we know that two half-lives have passed in our sample, then we know that the sample is 11,460 years old. In this section we

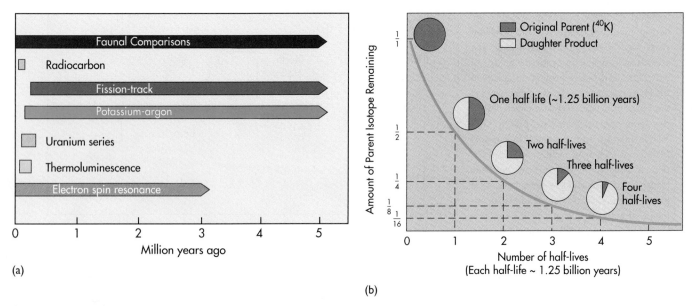

(a)

(b)

FIGURE 8.12   (a) The relative age ranges of different dating techniques depend upon the half-life of the system used. (b) For example, potassium–argon can date very old events because of its long half-life.

TABLE 8.1	Comparison of Chronometric Techniques	
Technique	**Age Range**	**Materials Dated**
K–Ar	10,000–4.5 billion years	K-bearing minerals and glass
$^{40}Ar/^{39}Ar$	Same as for K–Ar	K-bearing minerals (can date single grains)
Fission track	Tens of millions of years	Uranium-bearing, noncrystalline minerals, zircon, apatite, and glasses
Uranium series	Thousands to 500,000 years	Uranium-bearing minerals, $CaCo_3$, flowstones, corals, shells, teeth
Radiocarbon	<40,000 years	Organic materials such as wood, bone, shell
TL	100–500,000 years depending on material	Quartz, feldspars, pottery, stone tools
OSL	1,000–400,000 years	As above
ESR	Typically to 500,000 years and possibly to a few million years depending on material	Uranium-bearing materials and either closed or open systems in which uranium has been taken up from external sources

review the radiometric techniques most commonly used in paleoanthropology, beginning with those that measure samples of the oldest geological age.

Potassium–argon (K–Ar) dating was first developed as a dating technique in the 1960s (Evernden & Curtis, 1965). The system measures the decay of the isotope ^{40}K (potassium) to ^{40}Ar (argon) and requires potassium-bearing minerals, such as feldspars, to work. Unlike the short half-life of ^{14}C, the decay from potassium to argon has a half-life of 1.25 billion years, making its effective range quite extensive (Deino et al., 1998). This decay series has been used to date some of the oldest rocks on Earth and has also dated events as recent as the eruption of Mt. Vesuvius in Italy in A.D. 79. K–Ar dating is useful in dating the timing of the eruption of volcanic sediments because heating during the eruption drives off all argon gases, and at the time the volcanic material cools, the clock is effectively set to zero (there is no argon and only potassium in the system). We call this time of formation T_0.

Thus the method dates the timing of the formation of the volcanic rocks. Fortunately, there are many situations in which fossil hominids are in sediments sandwiched between volcanic sediments, so we can estimate the fossil ages by their association with the age of the volcanics (Figure 8.14 on page 246).

However, K–Ar as a technique has some limitations. Potassium exists as a solid, and argon is a noble gas. So, measuring the relative amounts of these entails

potassium–argon (K–Ar) dating Radiometric technique using the decay of ^{40}K to ^{40}Ar in potassium-bearing rocks; estimates the age of sediments in which fossils are found.

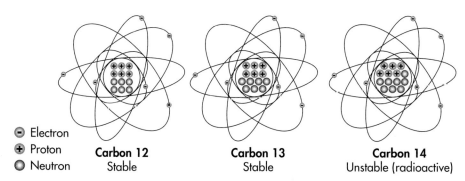

- ⊖ Electron
- ⊕ Proton
- ◯ Neutron

| **Carbon 12** | **Carbon 13** | **Carbon 14** |
| Stable | Stable | Unstable (radioactive) |

FIGURE 8.13 Isotopes may be stable or radioactive depending on the arrangement and number of neutrons in the nucleus. ^{14}C is heavier than ^{12}C or ^{13}C because it has more neutrons, and it is radioactive (or unstable) for the same reason.

FIGURE 8.14 The argon–argon method is useful for dating volcanic sediments such as those at the Sangiran Dome region of Java that has yielded many *Homo erectus* fossils. Geologists have used lithostratigraphy to define the stratigraphy of the region. Argon/argon on tuffs in the section provide ages for the fossils and magnetic polarity provides confirmation.

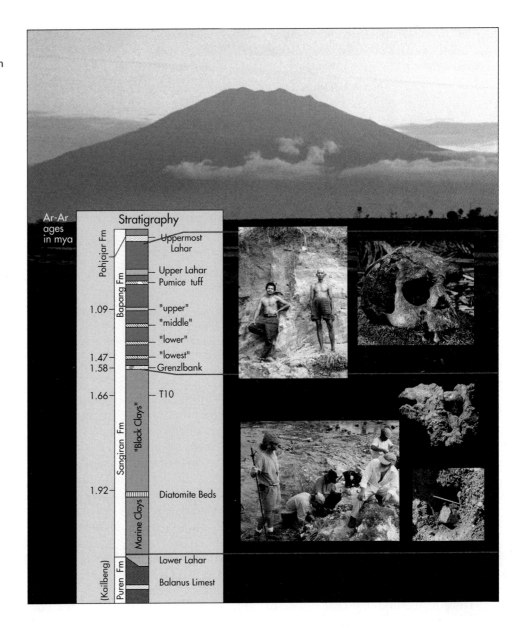

argon/argon ($^{40}Ar/^{39}Ar$) dating Radiometric technique modified from K–Ar that measures ^{40}K by proxy using ^{39}Ar. Allows measurement of smaller samples with less error.

using two different samples of the same rock, measuring potassium as a solid in one sample and argon as a gas from the other. This assumes that all parts of a rock are homogeneous and that each sample is measured without error, assumptions that are often incorrect. Furthermore, it entails the use of whole rock samples, which increases the risk of contamination from trapped argon or argon loss. Extra argon not produced by decay of potassium makes a rock appear too old because the amount of daughter product is artificially large, whereas losing argon artificially lowers the amount of daughter product, making the rock appear too young.

Argon/argon ($^{40}Ar/^{39}Ar$) dating is a refinement of the K–Ar method that allows the use of smaller samples, sometimes even a single crystal, and greater control over the measurements and possible sources of sample error. $^{40}Ar/^{39}Ar$ uses a trick to measure ^{40}K by a proxy gas, ^{39}Ar, thus allowing measurement of both parent and daughter in a single sample. So in the $^{40}Ar/^{39}Ar$ method both isotopes of argon are measured as gases, eliminating the limitations we saw in K–Ar. The ratio of ^{40}Ar to ^{39}Ar is the percentage of parent that has decayed (^{40}Ar = the amount of daughter product, ^{39}Ar = proxy for the amount of total parent originally in the system), and with this and the known half-life an age can be calculated.

An advantage of measuring both parent and daughter products as gases is that we can use smaller samples. This means that crystals can be picked for freshness, making less likely the possibility of argon loss caused by weathering. And it is possible to measure many different crystals from a rock instead of averaging them all for a whole rock sample. This means that you can be sure whether your crystals represent a single age population or whether they include older, reworked crystals (thus yielding too old an age). Thus our confidence in the age increases.

K–Ar and the $^{40}Ar/^{39}Ar$ methods have been widely used in paleoanthropology for dating volcanic sediments associated with hominids in Africa, the Republic of Georgia, and Indonesia. In the late 1960s early K–Ar dates suggested that hominids had left Africa and migrated to Indonesia by about 1.9 million years ago, a remarkably early age given the conventional wisdom of the time. Because most of the volcanic rocks in Indonesia are very low in potassium, it was not until 1994 and the application of the more accurate $^{40}Ar/^{39}Ar$ method that these early ages were confirmed and expanded upon, and it is now generally accepted that *Homo erectus* dispersed to Indonesia by at least 1.6 million years ago (see Chapter 12).

Fission track dating provides age estimates for volcanic glasses, tektites (glasses formed by meteoritic impacts on the earth), and zircons that contain uranium. Only these noncrystalline materials can be dated with fission track techniques because the method relies on counting the small tracks produced each time an atom of ^{238}U decays by fission (hence its name). The technique involves etching the surface and counting the tracks (a proxy for the daughter product) of the sample, then irradiating the sample and measuring the number of additional tracks made by the fission of the nonradioactive ^{235}U. Because the ratio of ^{238}U to ^{235}U is known, the tracks from ^{235}U are a proxy for the original amount of parent isotope. Fission track dating provides a viable age range from about 100 years to the oldest rocks on Earth, although it is not as reliable for very young (<100,000 years) or very old samples. The low density of tracks makes it difficult to date very young samples, and old samples have too many tracks to count accurately. In addition, a number of processes can cause undercounts (and artificially young ages), so, particularly in glasses, fission track ages should always be considered minimum ages. In fact, fission track often is used as an ancillary technique to other chronometric methods.

Recently, the fission track method has been used to date tektites in the Nihewan Basin in China that were found in association with early evidence of stone tool manufacture. Thus the age of these tools, as established by fission track dating, makes them among the earliest stone tools in China.

Uranium series (U-series) techniques use the decay chain of ^{238}U, ^{235}U, and ^{232}Th, all of which decay to stable lead isotopes, to provide age estimates for calcium carbonates, such as flowstones precipitated in caves, shells of invertebrates, and sometimes teeth. Intermediate steps in the decay chain produce isotopes with very different half-lives, and the technique takes advantage of disequilibrium between the ratios of the various parent and daughter products to estimate an age (Figure 8.15 on page 248) rather than relying on the single parent-to-daughter decay of a system such as K–Ar. Because uranium is soluble in water but its daughter products (thorium, protactinium, and lead) are not, at the time of formation of the shell or flowstone (T_0), no daughter products are present. Once formed, the daughter products produced by the radioactive decay of each step in the decay chain are trapped in the crystal lattice of the flowstone (or shell) and can be measured to provide an age estimate. Uranium series techniques usually date strata associated with a fossil, not the fossil itself. Associations therefore are critical to providing the correct age estimate for a fossil, and because cave stratigraphy often is complex, these associations may not be accurate.

It may be possible to date a fossil directly with uranium series techniques, but the method is more complicated. Uranium does not naturally occur in either tooth or bone but is introduced to the system when these structures are buried in sediments. Remember that uranium is soluble in water, so uranium from groundwater can migrate into the crystal lattice of, say, a tooth and from there begin its production of

Argon/argon and K–Ar techniques date volcanic sediments associated with fossil hominids.

fission track dating
Radiometric technique for dating noncrystalline materials using the decay of ^{238}Ur and counting the tracks that are produced by this fission. Estimates the age of sediments in which fossils are found.

uranium series (U-series) techniques Radiometric techniques using the decay of uranium to estimate an age for calcium carbonates including flowstones, shells, and teeth.

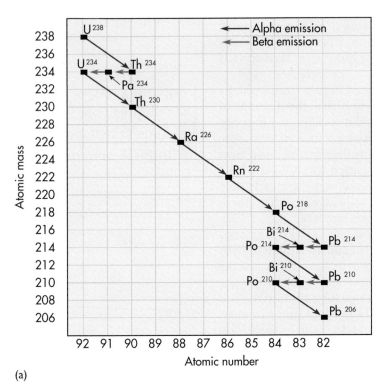

(a)   (b)

FIGURE 8.15 (a) Uranium series dating uses the decay chain of radioactive uranium (^{238}U) to stable lead (^{206}Pb). The daughter products, such as those of thorium (^{234}Th and ^{230}Th), each have half-lives of different lengths that can be used to estimate age. (b) Stalactites, stalagmites, and flowstones are often dated via uranium series methods.

radiocarbon dating Radiometric technique that uses the decay of ^{14}C in organic remains such as wood and bone to estimate the time since death of the organism.

decay products. However, we can't always tell how quickly in-migration of uranium occurs, and modeling this uptake is critical to age assessment. Out-migration of parent or daughter may also occur; tooth and bone are not closed systems, making age difficult to determine. In general, tooth enamel is considered preferable for dating because of its tighter crystal lattice and, presumably, its lower susceptibility to migration of uranium. Despite these pitfalls, uranium series techniques have been critical for estimating ages for hominid sites, particularly those outside the range of radiocarbon and those in areas lacking volcanic rocks, such as China. Uranium series techniques on both flowstones and teeth at Chinese hominid sites have established ages for the famous Peking Man *Homo erectus* site that suggest a time range between about 250,000 and 600,000 years ago (see Chapter 12).

Radiocarbon dating is the primary technique for estimating the antiquity of organic items from the latest Pleistocene through the present, including primate and human fossils as well as artifacts from archaeological sites. All living organisms are composed of molecules that contain carbon. Recall that three isotopes of carbon, ^{12}C, ^{13}C, and ^{14}C, exist in the atmosphere, only one of which, ^{14}C, is radioactive. As plants photosynthesize carbon dioxide they take up these isotopes at atmospheric levels. Animals that eat plants then take up carbon, as do animals that eat other animals. Uptake of carbon ceases at the death of the organism. At this point (T_0), the atoms of ^{14}C begin to decay and are not replenished by additional ^{14}C from the atmosphere. We estimate age in the usual way by comparing the amount of daughter product (in this case ^{14}N) with the amount of original parent in the material and then multiplying this percentage by the half-life.

The decay rate of ^{14}C is well understood, with a half-life of 5,730 years (Taylor, 2000). Because this half-life is so short, the radiocarbon technique is useful for organic remains from the last 30,000 to 40,000 years. So little of the original ^{14}C remains after this time (less than 1%) that counting errors preclude age estimates beyond that range. In some cases, we can improve precision by measuring samples using accelerator mass spectrometry, but even then objects older than 40,000 years are beyond the reach of this technique. The limited age range of the ^{14}C technique limits its paleoanthropological applications to the latest part of the Neandertal lineage and their overlap with anatomically modern humans.

Electron Trap Techniques   Up to this point we have been discussing techniques that measure the decay of radioactive isotopes within a specimen. **Electron trap techniques**, however, measure the effect that exposure to radioactivity has on the specimen. Only crystalline materials can be dated with these methods. When materials are exposed to naturally occurring radiation, some of their electrons become excited and separate from the parent atom. In a crystal lattice, these excited electrons may become trapped in defects or open spaces of the lattice rather than returning to their original location around the parent atom. If the *dose rate*, that is, the amount of radiation to which an object is exposed over a given period of time, is constant, then the number of trapped electrons will be proportional to the age of the material (age = total dose/annual dose rate, or the length of time since the electron traps were all empty). The main techniques are thermoluminescence, optically stimuated luminescence, and electron spin resonance.

   Thermoluminescence (TL) measures the number of trapped electrons by measuring the amount of light given off when they are released. TL is useful on materials that had their traps emptied by being heated some time in the past. It is particularly useful in dating pottery that was fired or stone tools that were heated in a campfire. As these items lie buried they begin to trap new electrons. In the lab we measure these newly trapped electrons by reheating the object and measuring the amount of light it emits. TL can date things over hundreds of thousands of years but is most typically used in the range of the past 100,000 years, which is older than ^{14}C can measure. TL on burnt flints has been important in establishing that the Near Eastern Neandertal sites of Amud and Kebara are younger (about 45,000–60,000 years) than those of modern humans in the same region (about 100,000 years), whereas the Neandertals at Tabūn, Israel, are older (about 100,000–150,000 years) (Figure 8.16). These dates suggest that Neandertals and modern humans alternated their use of the region over time, perhaps in response to changing climate (see Chapter 13).

electron trap techniques   Radiometric techniques that measure the accumulation of electrons in traps in the crystal lattice of a specimen.

thermoluminescence (TL)   Electron trap technique that uses heat to measure the amount of radioactivity accumulated by a specimen such as a stone tool since its last heating.

FIGURE 8.16   In the caves of the Mt. Carmel region of Israel, electronic spin resonance, uranium series techniques, and thermoluminescence have shown that modern humans and Neandertals alternated their use of the region.

K-Ar and Ar/Ar

Some radiometric or "absolute" dating methods use the accumulation of a daughter product from the radioactive decay of a parent element to estimate age. For example, the Potassium-Argon (K-Ar) and Argon/Argon ($^{40}Ar/^{39}Ar$) methods use the amount of ^{40}Ar accumulated from the decay of ^{40}K to estimate age. To make this estimate we must know that the system starts with no ^{40}Ar gas and that all the accumulated argon has occurred since the formation of the rock. An ideal situation for this is when a volcano erupts; the molten lava releases all its argon gas and effectively sets the clock to zero age (or time zero, T_0).

We can estimate the age since the time of eruption by considering how much argon has accumulated after T_0. As the molten lava solidifies into rock, any newly formed ^{40}Ar will be trapped inside the rock. Estimating the age then relies on measuring the ^{40}Ar and the remaining ^{40}K, and calculating how much of a half life has passed since the rock formed.

$^{40}K \rightarrow {}^{40}Ar$

Ash

The longer the time since the lava or ash cooled to rock, the greater the amount of ^{40}Ar, the less ^{40}K present, and the greater the age.

Ash

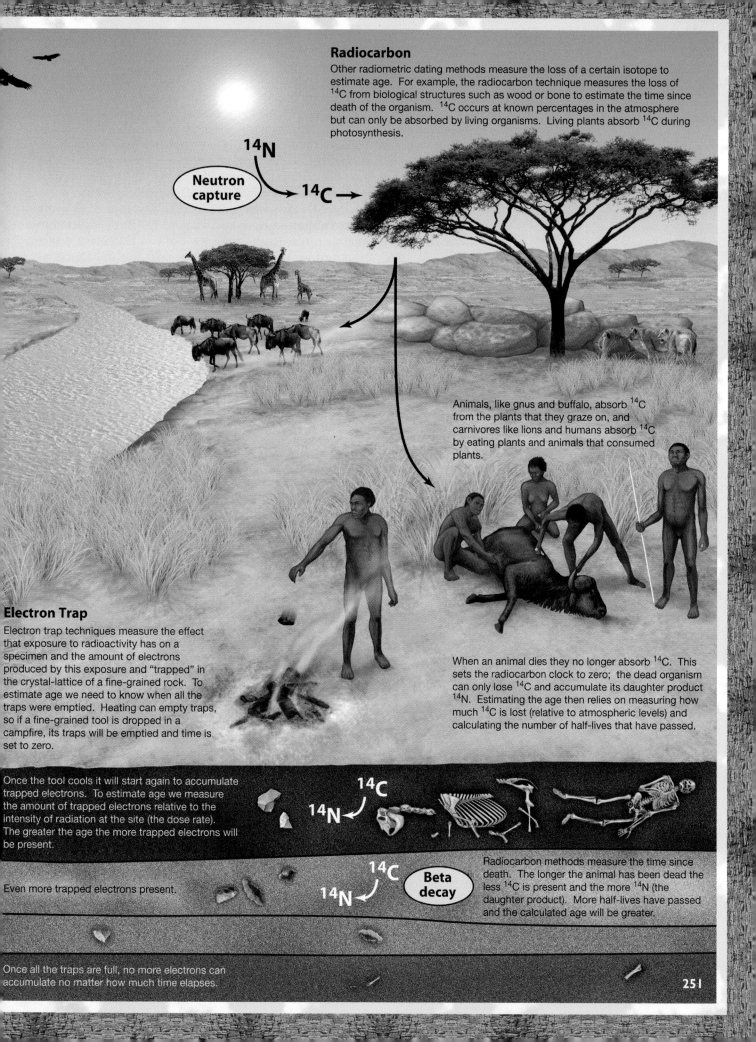

Radiocarbon

Other radiometric dating methods measure the loss of a certain isotope to estimate age. For example, the radiocarbon technique measures the loss of ^{14}C from biological structures such as wood or bone to estimate the time since death of the organism. ^{14}C occurs at known percentages in the atmosphere but can only be absorbed by living organisms. Living plants absorb ^{14}C during photosynthesis.

^{14}N

Neutron capture → ^{14}C →

Animals, like gnus and buffalo, absorb ^{14}C from the plants that they graze on, and carnivores like lions and humans absorb ^{14}C by eating plants and animals that consumed plants.

Electron Trap

Electron trap techniques measure the effect that exposure to radioactivity has on a specimen and the amount of electrons produced by this exposure and "trapped" in the crystal-lattice of a fine-grained rock. To estimate age we need to know when all the traps were emptied. Heating can empty traps, so if a fine-grained tool is dropped in a campfire, its traps will be emptied and time is set to zero.

When an animal dies they no longer absorb ^{14}C. This sets the radiocarbon clock to zero; the dead organism can only lose ^{14}C and accumulate its daughter product ^{14}N. Estimating the age then relies on measuring how much ^{14}C is lost (relative to atmospheric levels) and calculating the number of half-lives that have passed.

Once the tool cools it will start again to accumulate trapped electrons. To estimate age we measure the amount of trapped electrons relative to the intensity of radiation at the site (the dose rate). The greater the age the more trapped electrons will be present.

^{14}C
^{14}N

Even more trapped electrons present.

^{14}C
^{14}N Beta decay

Radiocarbon methods measure the time since death. The longer the animal has been dead the less ^{14}C is present and the more ^{14}N (the daughter product). More half-lives have passed and the calculated age will be greater.

Once all the traps are full, no more electrons can accumulate no matter how much time elapses.

Optically stimulated luminescence (OSL) dates materials whose traps were emptied by bleaching from sunlight. Thus OSL dates the time at which an item was buried. We reexpose the materials to light of a known wavelength and measure the resulting luminescence, hence the name of the technique. Many measures from a sample are needed, and caution is necessary because incomplete emptying of traps yields ages far too old. The age range that OSL can measure is similar to that of TL. The method has been used successfully to investigate the initial colonization of Australia.

Electron spin resonance (ESR) has been most successfully applied to tooth enamel. The tooth is powdered and exposed to microwaves. The trapped electrons resonate as they absorb the microwaves, and the extent of this resonance is proportional to the total amount of trapped electrons. However, not only must we measure the number of trapped electrons, but we must model the way uranium is introduced into the tooth in the first place. Hydroxyapatite, the mineral of tooth enamel, accumulates all of its radioactivity after burial, so we must adjust the age for the way in which radioactive uranium is taken up by the tooth. The early uptake (EU) model assumes that all of the uranium uptake occurs soon after burial. The linear uptake (LU) model assumes uranium uptake occurs continuously through time. The choice of model can greatly affect the age estimates. The age range of ESR is about the same as that for the uranium series techniques, and the two are often used together if U-series is being conducted on tooth rather than on flowstone. For example, ESR analyses have been critical in corroborating the early age of the Tabūn Neandertals (about 100,000–150,000 years) and of the Skhūl and Qafzeh modern human sites (about 100,000 years) in the Near East (Stringer et al., 1989; Grün et al., 1991). In conjunction with uranium series and TL analyses, these data suggest that modern humans occupied the Near East early but that the region was occupied by Neandertals both earlier and later in time (see Chapters 13 and 14).

The Earth in the Cenozoic

Having established the various ways we might assess the age of a paleontological site and the fossils within it, we now turn to other issues of understanding the context in which fossil primates are found. Most importantly, we will look at the position of the major land masses during the Cenozoic, which has implications for how animals moved from one place to another, and then we consider the various methods scientists use to reconstruct the habitat that animals once lived in.

CONTINENTS AND LAND MASSES

As you may be aware, the continents have not always been in their current locations. Approximately 200 million years ago the earth was divided into two major land masses that we now call Laurasia and Gondwanaland. Laurasia was composed of most of present-day North America and Asia, and Gondwanaland included Africa and South America (Figure 8.17). By 50 million years ago North America and Asia were beginning to spread apart, and both South America and Africa had separated from one another and from the other continents. Africa eventually became connected to Asia via the Near East, North America and Asia were separated by a chain of islands (but remained connected during low sea levels), and South America was an island continent until well into the Pliocene (~3.5 million years ago), when the Central American land bridge connected it to North America. As we will see in Chapter 9, these movements are critical for understanding early primate evolution, particularly the distribution of the Eocene primates and the conundrum of the origin of the South American primates (which appeared while that continent was still an island). Once the continents were in their present positions, the onset of severe glacial events in the late Pliocene and Pleistocene periodically lowered sea levels, exposing additional land and sometimes resulting, as is the case between continental Asia and Indonesia, in land bridges between otherwise isolated areas (see Chapter 12).

optically stimulated luminescence (OSL) Electron trap technique that uses light to measure the amount of radioactivity accumulated by crystals in sediments (such as sand grains) since burial.

electron spin resonance (ESR) Electron trap technique that measures the total amount of radioactivity accumulated by a specimen such as tooth or bone since burial.

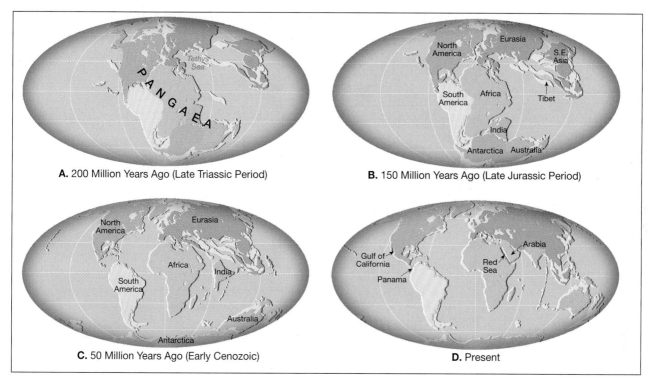

A. 200 Million Years Ago (Late Triassic Period)

B. 150 Million Years Ago (Late Jurassic Period)

C. 50 Million Years Ago (Early Cenozoic)

D. Present

FIGURE 8.17   The continents were not always in their present positions. The position of the continents is important for understanding movements of primates in the past.

THE ENVIRONMENT IN THE CENOZOIC

As we saw in Chapter 1, conditions in the environment naturally select individuals most suited to them, and because of their favored traits, these individuals reproduce more than others in the population. Understanding past environmental conditions is critical to understanding the selective pressures affecting the survival and extinction of animals at a site. We can reconstruct environmental conditions from several kinds of geological and biological evidence.

Oxygen Isotopes, Temperature, and Sea Level   Perhaps the best-known climate proxies are oxygen isotope curves that rely on the past ratio of stable oxygen isotopes as a proxy for global temperature and sea level. The process works like this. Two stable isotopes of oxygen, ^{16}O and ^{18}O, differ in weight, with ^{18}O being the heavier of the two. These isotopes exist as oxygen in water molecules and other compounds. In water they are incorporated into the shells of marine invertebrates that are composed of calcium carbonates. Water molecules formed of the lighter isotope tend to float nearer the ocean surface, whereas water molecules formed of the heavier isotope tend to sink; therefore, the lighter isotope of oxygen tends to evaporate from ocean surfaces sooner than does ^{18}O. During cold periods when ^{16}O evaporates from the ocean, it is not returned to the world's water reserves via rain but is locked up in ice at the poles and northern latitudes. Consequently, sea levels are lower during cold periods and contain a greater percentage of ^{18}O than during warmer periods. Therefore, the $^{18}O/^{16}O$ ratio increases in sea water during cold periods and in the shells of the marine animals formed in them at that time.

Geologists studying marine cores measure the $^{18}O/^{16}O$ ratio of these marine shells through time to develop the oxygen isotope curves. Higher ratios indicate colder climates and lower sea levels, whereas lower ratios indicate warmer climates and higher sea levels. We can also use the oxygen isotope ratios in lake sediments to infer local climate, and some scientists have even measured these ratios in human teeth to estimate the temperatures those humans lived in.

FIGURE 8.18 The oxygen isotope curve illustrates the ratio between ^{16}O and ^{18}O. More of the heavy isotope indicates colder periods (even-numbered stages); more of the lighter indicates warmer periods (interglacials, odd-numbered stages; After Klein, 1999).

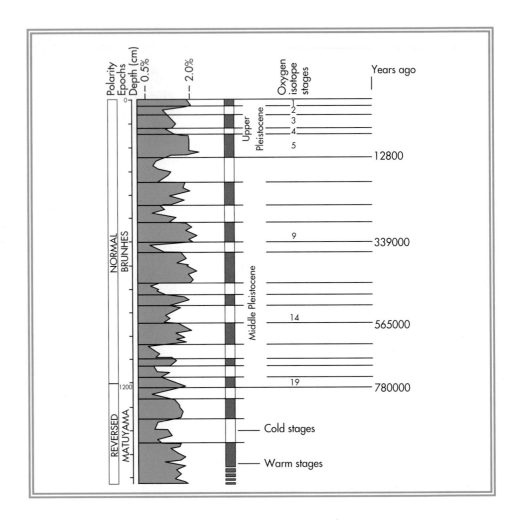

The Plio-Pleistocene is characterized by oscillations in temperature from colder (glacial) to milder (interglacial) periods (Figure 8.18). Oxygen isotope curves have been important for reconstructing climate patterns in the mid- and late Pleistocene and correlating the movements of Neandertals and modern humans in relation to climate change (see Chapter 13). Microclimates still exist within these patterns—for example, think of the differences in climate between the beach and the mountains—but global climatic proxies can help us understand what kinds of conditions animals lived in during the past.

Paleosols and Loess   Soil structure reflects conditions in the environment at the time the soil was formed. For this reason we can use **paleosols,** or ancient soils, to understand past environmental conditions. For example, different kinds of paleosols form in more temperate humid conditions than in dryer colder conditions. Paleosols can also correlate strata between sites. In addition to paleosols, we can also use windblown sediments, such as loess, in both stratigraphy and paleoclimate reconstruction. Asian loess (windblown silt) indicates drier conditions than other loess in the world and is often interstratified with paleosols that provide additional paleoclimatic and environmental information (Lowe & Walker, 1997).

Vegetation   Plant macrofossils (or other traces such as root casts) may be preserved at some sites. Local plants often are preserved in bog or peat environments, but plants and plant imprints may also fossilize in very fine-grained sediments. The sediments that yield the winged dinosaurs of Liaoning, China, for example, also preserve early examples of flowering plants (angiosperms). And leaves from Eocene fossil floras share features in common with leaves from tropical and subtropical trees today.

paleosol   Ancient soil.

Evidence of the vegetation at paleontological sites can be used to compare the environments that animals once lived in with those of today. For example, using fossilized sediments and vegetation data from ancient riverside habitats, Jeanne Sept compared the plant diversity in modern East African *gallery forests*, those that grow alongside streams, with that in the Pliocene (Sept, 2001). She was able to make a vegetation map of the "edible landscape" available to early human ancestors called australopithecines (see Chapter 11) and to conclude that, based on available resources, closely related hominids could have coexisted mainly if one species was an omnivore. Sandi Copeland (2007) made such a vegetation map for Olduvai Gorge, an important fossil site for australopithecines and early *Homo* (see Chapter 12), and concluded that even though resource diversity was low in any one environment, the close proximity of many types of habitats meant that our early ancestors had access to a variety of important food resources.

The recovery of fossil pollens can also tell us about the presence of certain kinds of plants in an area. The Neandertal site of Shanidar has been purported to show a burial ritual with a Neandertal interred on a blanket of flowers (based on the plentiful pollen around the skeleton; see Chapter 13). But it is possible that modern pollens were introduced to the site, either as the archaeologists excavated or as the wind blew over local plants.

Another direct means of assessing plant resources is the presence of **phytoliths**, opaline silica bodies secreted by some plants, especially grasses, whose shape is often characteristic of that plant. The presence of phytoliths has been important in the reconstruction of available plants and diet of the Miocene ape *Sivapithecus* (see Chapter 9) and has been used to interpret the uses of some stone tools.

Stable Carbon Isotope Ratios   *Stable carbon isotope ratios* are also used to reconstruct the types of vegetation in a region. We can use carbon isotopes to differentiate between plants using different photosynthetic pathways. Plants use three basic means to photosynthesize. Trees and shrubs are mostly C_3 plants, so called because these plants make a three-carbon compound during the first stage of photosynthesis, as do most of the world's plants. Tropical grasses are almost all C_4 plants, so called because they make a four-carbon compound during photosynthesis. Fewer than 1% of the earth's plants are C_4 plants. Finally, CAM (Crassulacean acid metabolism) plants exist in areas where preventing water loss is critical. CAM plants use a C_4 pathway at night, and as a result of their more complicated pathway they tend to lose less carbon during photosynthesis. About 4% of the world's plants are CAM plants, including cacti and agave (the plant from which tequila is made). Because of their different pathways for photosynthesis, different types of plants retain different amounts of the carbon isotopes. Plants categorized as C_3 tend to have less ^{13}C and hence lower $^{13}C/^{12}C$ ratios. C_4 plants have more ^{13}C. By evaluating these ratios we can tell whether there was an abundance of C_3, C_4, or CAM plants. Fortuitously, $^{13}C/^{12}C$ ratios are produced during analyses for ^{14}C dating.

By looking at these ratios of stable carbon isotopes in the teeth of fossil animals, we can infer the type of vegetation the animals ate and the type of vegetation present in the area. By looking at these ratios in various animal taxa in an area or through time, we can begin to build a vegetation map. For example, fossil horse teeth have been used to look at the distribution of grass types throughout the world during the Pleistocene (McFadden et al., 1999). This work suggests that Pleistocene vegetation gradients varied by latitude, as they do today.

We can also look at the stable carbon isotope ratios in paleosols because the organic carbon found in soils comes from local plants. Analyzing paleosols in this way has been important in reconstructing environments in Africa during hominid evolution, particularly because the abundance of C_3 and C_4 grasses varies between open (savanna) environments and shaded or wooded environments (Figure 8.19 on page 256). Knowing the kind of environment hominids originated in is critical to many explanations for how and why bipedality evolved. We used

Ratios of stable carbon isotopes in an animal's teeth and bones provide clues about its diet.

phytoliths Silica bodies produced by some plants, especially grasses, that can be used to indicate the presence of certain types of vegetation at a fossil site.

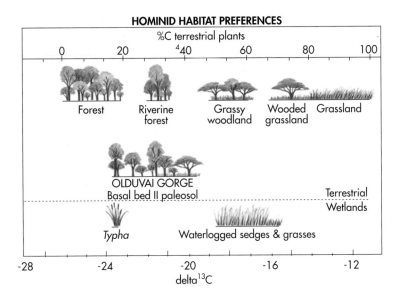

HOMINID HABITAT PREFERENCES

FIGURE 8.19 Habitat reconstruction is possible based on the kinds of plants present at past sites. The kinds of plants present are reflected in the ratios of stable carbon isotopes in soils, fossils, and fossil carbonates.

to think bipedality arose in an open savanna environment, perhaps implicating heat stress or other selective factors in its origin. However, we are learning that many of the early hominid environments were more wooded, suggesting that another selective factor was at work; perhaps bipedality was an efficient means of crossing short distances between food patches while also carrying food.

Animal Communities   Although some types of animals seem to be able to live just about anywhere, most have preferred types of habitats. Hippos and crocodiles live near water sources, and the presence of monkeys usually indicates wooded areas (Figure 8.20). Animals that are adapted to running long distances over open terrain tend to have longer, slighter limbs; those adapted to life in forested areas often tend to have shorter limbs. Based on comparisons with the adaptations in living animals of known habitat preference, paleontologists infer the climatic and environmental preferences of past animals. When hominids are found with these fossil animals we can then infer the kinds of environments in which the hominids lived.

These types of analyses focus on all the animals found at a particular site during a particular time interval, not just on a single species. This is important because the relative abundance of animals can tell you more about an environment than can the presence of a single species. This work focuses on trying to reconstruct the community of animals that lived at the site and their dietary and locomotor adaptations. Using the skeleton, paleontologists try to understand whether the animal in question was terrestrial, arboreal, a combination of the two, aquatic, or a burrower or digger. And they infer whether the animal ate leaves or grasses, fruit or meat, and in combination with what other foods. Combining this information from all the animals within a site gives a good impression of the kind of habitat (trees, water, open areas, and so on) and food (grasses, trees, insects, and so on) that was available. This gives a pretty clear idea of what kind of habitat hominids were living in.

For example, Kaye Reed looked at the skeletal adaptations of different species of fossil antelopes found in early hominid sites. Using the adaptations of the antelopes as a guide, Reed found that early australopithecines likely lived in wooded regions interspersed with lakes and rivers. Later in the fossil record, again

FIGURE 8.20 Different species have specific habitat preferences. Hippos indicate a nearby water source. Wildebeest prefer more open areas, other species prefer more wooded areas. Identifying the kinds of fossils at hominid sites suggests the kind of environments Hominids may have lived in during the past.

using antelope species as markers, the robust australopithecines appeared to prefer habitats that included swamps and marshes (Reed, 1997). These kinds of reconstructions of animal communities have been critical for reconstructing paleoenvironments of the Plio-Pleistocene hominids in Africa and elsewhere (see Chapters 11–14).

OVERVIEW OF CLIMATIC CHANGES DURING THE CENOZOIC

Based on the kinds of studies just described, scientists have drawn a general picture of the climate during the evolution of the Primate order. Climate and environment are the source of important selective pressures that influence the evolution of all animal groups. Figure 8.21 provides a graphic overview of temperature changes throughout the Cenozoic.

Climate and environment are among the most important natural selective pressures that mold the evolution and adaptation of organisms.

Paleocene to Miocene Climate   The story of Cenozoic climate change is generally one of cooling and drying. The Cenozoic began much, much warmer than it is today. Furthermore, there was less difference between temperatures at the equator and the North and South poles than we currently experience. Thus, when primates first arose, not only were they equatorial and subequatorial animals, as they largely are today, but they existed fairly far north and south. Although it was warmer than today, there was some climatic fluctuation during each epoch. As the era proceeded, the climate cooled and dried but still fluctuated somewhat.

The Paleocene and early Eocene were by far the warmest epochs of the Cenozoic. During the Eocene there was a precipitous drop in global temperature until finally, at about the Eocene/Oligocene boundary (around 36 million years ago), there was a decided cold snap that resulted in large-scale extinction and replacement of many species. This "turnover" is often called the *Grande Coupure* (or big cut) because of the large number of taxa that went extinct. The early Oligocene continued to see decreases in temperature, and then late in the Oligocene temperature rose a bit, returning to the levels at the beginning of the epoch (so it was still quite cold compared with most of the Eocene but warm by modern standards). It is likely that the lowest temperatures in the Oligocene (at the start, and then again around 31 million and 24 million years ago) were associated with short glacial periods. These temperature changes may have been caused by the movement of continents and the resulting changes in ocean and wind currents that alter climate patterns.

From the end of the Oligocene to about the middle of the Miocene temperature rose again gradually, although it remained well below levels of the Eocene.

FIGURE 8.21   Climate has cooled substantially during primate evolution.

About the middle of the Miocene, perhaps 15 million years ago, another abrupt cooling and drying trend occurred, this time driving temperatures well below any previously experienced in the Cenozoic. This severe cooling probably was related to the appearance of a permanent Antarctic ice sheet at the South Pole. The evolution of the Antarctic ice sheet removed a lot of water from the oceans, resulting in the so-called Messinian event or crisis in which the Mediterranean ran dry, leaving a great salt lake. As we will see in Chapter 9, these changes in climate often are correlated with the origin, extinction, or diversification of primate groups.

Pliocene to Early Pleistocene Climate   During the early Pliocene temperatures increased and the Mediterranean Sea refilled, but shortly thereafter cooling began again. Ice sheets at both poles became permanent features throughout the Pliocene. Cyclic glaciation set in only about 3 million years ago but did not become more intense until 2.5 million years ago and then became even more intense in the Pleistocene.

Many workers have argued that these climatic fluctuations were critical to the origins of our lineage, the hominids, in Africa. For example, Elisabeth Vrba has proposed that quick changes, or pulses, in climate resulted in "turnovers," or extinctions in animal communities. Her turnover–pulse hypothesis suggests that during some of these pulses we also see the origin and extinction of some hominid groups. René Bobe and Anna Behrensmeyer also see changes in abundance of mammalian species in response to climate, especially between 4 and 2 million years ago. They suggest that the origin of our genus, *Homo*, coincided with the periods of greatest climatic variability.

Early to Late Pleistocene Climate   Starting around 1.8 million years ago, glacial cycles intensified. (We know the extent of the glaciation based on the oxygen-isotope curves). The glaciation was so severe that it lowered sea levels enough to connect island Southeast Asia to mainland Asia for the first time. This connection was important because animals and hominids (who left Africa around this time) could walk back and forth between Asia and island Southeast Asia at times and were isolated from one another at other times (see Chapter 12).

Another result of this increasing cold and glacial cycling is that latitudinal variation in climate became quite significant (remember that temperature varied little from north to south early in primate evolution). As hominids began to move out of Africa around 1.8 million years ago and into western Asia and ultimately the northerly latitudes of Europe (~800,000), climatic conditions in some instances were quite harsh. This harsh climate appears to have kept hominids from moving too far north permanently until they had sufficient cultural means of mitigating the conditions. Not until Neandertals and their ancestors was there permanent settlement in Europe (see Chapters 13 and 14).

Understanding the context in which fossils are formed and found is critical to identifying their age and the natural selective factors that influence their evolution. Here we have set the foundation for understanding the geological age and environmental context of fossil primates. In Chapter 9 we embark on the evolutionary journey of the Primates as written in the fossil record.

SUMMARY

1. **Why is the fossil record so fragmentary?**

   The fossil record is fragmentary because only a tiny fraction of Earth's creatures die in a circumstance in which they may be fossilized, and then only a tiny fraction of those are ever found by paleontologists.

2. **What is taphonomy?**

   Taphonomy is the study of what happens to remains from the death of the organism until the discovery of the fossils.

3. **What is the difference between *relative* and *chronometric* dating techniques?**

   Chronometric dating techniques provide a fairly precise date for a fossil, based on measurement of some natural clock, often the radioactive decay of an element such as potassium (K) or carbon (C) in either the rock in which the fossil is found or in the fossil itself. Relative dating techniques provide only an estimate of whether a fossil is older or younger than other materials found above and below it at the same site or in sediments at other sites.

4. **Why does ^{14}C usually date younger sites than K–Ar?**

Because of the short half-life of radiocarbon, too little of the radioactive isotope remains after about 30,000 to 40,000 years to be accurately measured. K has a longer half-life and thus can estimate age over longer time periods. In special circumstances we can also use it to determine the age of younger fossils.

5. **How do oxygen isotopes tell us about past climate?**

Two stable isotopes of oxygen, ^{16}O and ^{18}O, differ in weight, with ^{18}O the heavier of the two. In water they are incorporated into the shells of marine invertebrates that are composed of calcium carbonates. During cold periods, when ^{16}O evaporates from the ocean, it is not returned to the world's water reserves via rain but is instead locked up in ice at the poles and northern latitudes. Consequently, sea levels are lower and contain a greater percentage of ^{18}O than is normal. The ^{18}O$/^{16}$O ratio increases. Higher ratios indicate colder climates and lower sea levels, whereas lower ratios indicate warmer climates and higher sea levels.

6. **How do scientists think climate changed from the Paleocene to present, and on what do they base their evidence?**

Past climate reconstructions are based on geological and biological data including oxygen isotope curves, fossil soils, fossil animals, fossil plants, and pollens. These reconstructions suggest that temperatures were warmer and moister in the past and have cooled and dried over the Cenozoic. There were marked cooling events at the Eocene/Oligocene boundary and the onset of severe glaciation in the late Pliocene and Pleistocene.

CRITICAL THINKING QUESTIONS

1. Given how few of Earth's creatures end up as fossils, do you think we will continue finding new and important fossils, or have we already found most of those fossils that exist?

2. Given the different techniques used to reconstruct climate and environment, if you were leading a paleontological project, how would design your research program to figure out the context in which the fossils from your site came?

3. Imagine that you find a fossil hominid with some animal bones. How would you go about determining whether the animals and the hominids were deposited at the same time (were the same age)? Do you think that you could be mistaken, and what factors might make determining the age of the fossils difficult?

KEY TERMS

paleontology
fossils
geology
taphonomy
strata
stratigraphy
geologic time scale (GTS)
provenience
relative dating
    techniques
lithostratigraphy

tephrostratigraphy
biostratigraphy
calibrated relative dating
    techniques
geomagnetic polarity
    time scale (GPTS)
paleomagnetism
chronometric dating
    techniques
radiometric dating
isotopes

half-life
parent isotope
daughter isotope
    (product)
potassium–argon (K–Ar)
    dating
argon–argon (^{40}Ar/^{39}Ar)
    dating
fission track dating
uranium series (U-series)
    techniques

radiocarbon dating
electron trap techniques
thermoluminescence
    (TL)
optically stimulated
    luminescence (OSL)
electron spin resonance
    (ESR)
paleosol
phytoliths

SUGGESTED READING

Cutler, Alan. (2003). *The Seashell on the Mountaintop*. Plume, Penguin Group, New York.

Lowe, John J., and Walker, Mike J. C. (1997). *Reconstructing Quaternary Environments*. (2nd ed.). Prentice Hall, Englewood Cliffs, NJ.

Repcheck, Jack. (2003). *The Man who Found Time: James Hutton and the Discovery of the Earth's Antiquity*. Perseus Publishing, New York.

Shipman, Pat. (1981). *Life History of a Fossil*. Harvard University Press, Cambridge, MA.

Tarbuck, Edward J., and Lutgens, Frederick K. (2004). *Earth: An Introduction to Physical Geology*. (8th ed.) Prentice Hall, Englewood Cliffs, NJ.

Taylor, R. E., and Aitken, M. J. (1998). *Chronometric Dating in Archaeology*. Kluwer, Dordrecht, the Netherlands.

9 Origin of Primates

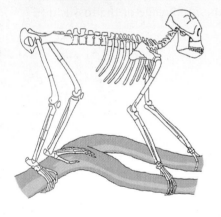

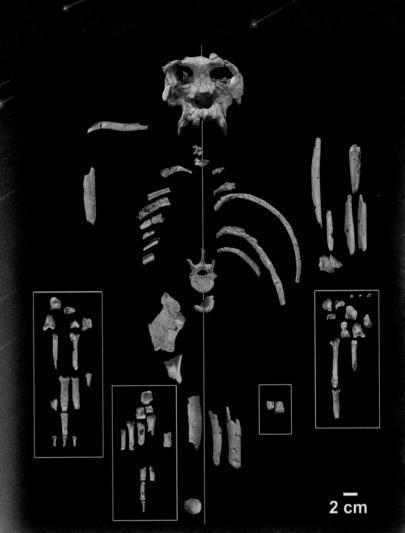

2 cm

"oom was coming out of the sky in the form of an enormous comet or asteroid—we are still not sure which it was. Probably 10 km across, traveling tens of kilometers a second, its energy of motion had the destructive capability of a hundred million hydrogen bombs" (p. 5).

"It is worth pondering the realization that each of us is descended from unknown ancestors who were alive on that day when the fatal rock fell from the sky. They survived and the dinosaurs did not, and that is the reason why we are here now—as individuals and as a species. That one terrible day undid the benefits which 150 million years of natural selection had conferred upon the dinosaurs, making them ever fitter to be the large land animals of Earth. Evolution had not equipped them to survive the environmental disasters inflicted by a huge impact and when the holocaust was over, they were gone.

Evolution had not provided impact resistance for the mammals either, but somehow they did survive. No one knows why, but it must have helped that they were smaller and therefore much more numerous than the dinosaurs, so that there was a better statistical chance that some would live.

When the environmental disruptions from the impact had waned and the mammal survivors emerged into a new world they must have faced great dangers and great opportunities"—W. Alvarez, *T. rex and the Crater of Doom* (1997:130)

AS THE VIGNETTE SUGGESTS, geological forces have a critical impact in developing new opportunities for mammalian evolution, including primate evolution. In Chapter 8 we set the foundation for understanding the context in which animals evolved, based on the geological clues gathered from paleontological sites. We now turn to the primate fossil record itself. Throughout this chapter, keep in mind that living primates evolved from fossil primates. Our task is to try to figure out what kind of primate each fossil group represents and then, by looking at the context in which the fossils are found and the characters they exhibit, to consider what kinds of selective pressures led to their evolution. By doing this we will understand more of the process by which living primates came to be, and we will move well on our way toward understanding our own origins.

To help in this task you will want to refer to the family tree of living primates in Chapter 6 (Figure 6.9) and review the bony characteristics that allow us to recognize animals at different levels of that tree. You will also want to refer back to the geological time scale in Chapter 8 (Figure 8.6). As we examine the primate fossil record, compare the skeletal characters of the fossils with the characters that differentiate primates from other mammals and groups of primates from one another. On the basis of these anatomical characters, decide where on the tree you think the fossils fit and think about what the characters tell you about the selective pressures that might have molded these species. You may find it useful to make yourself a large primate chart of living taxa along with a small card for each fossil group that lists its anatomical characters. Tack your chart on a bulletin board or your fridge and then attach the fossil cards at the appropriate place on the living hierarchy.

In this chapter we review what we know about the origin of the Primate order and the major nonhuman primate groups from the Paleocene through the Miocene epochs. We begin with fossils that are only questionably associated with primates and consider the strepsirhine–haplorhine split, the origin of Old World and New World monkeys, and finally the origin of the apes. In each case we focus on the anatomical characters of the fossils and the ecological circumstances in which they evolved, and we discuss possible scenarios for what this evidence tells us about the natural selective factors that favored the origin of each group. The chapter concludes with a review of what the molecular data tell us about the timing of primate evolution and the genetic changes that led to the origin of the human lineage, setting the stage for the next section of the book in which we review the human fossil record.

The Mesozoic and Beyond

The origin of primates is tied first to the origin of mammals, which began in the Mesozoic Era (225–65 million years ago), an age dominated by dinosaurs. During this era critical ecological changes provided opportunities for small, insect-eating mammals from which primates evolved.

DAWN OF THE AGE OF MAMMALS

The mammals of the Mesozoic Era were small, secretive creatures, overshadowed both in our imaginations and in reality by their contemporaries, the dinosaurs. The mammals that first appeared during the late Triassic Period most closely resembled the living monotremes, such as the echidna and platypus. In the Jurassic Period the first marsupial and placental mammals appeared, and both diversified greatly during the final period of the Mesozoic, the Cretaceous.

Diversification of the mammals in the middle to late Cretaceous was almost certainly a result of profound diversification of *angiosperms,* or flowering plants, at the end of the Mesozoic that heralded the beginning of one of the most important ecological interactions in modern ecosystems: pollination of flowering plants by insects. To disperse their pollen, flowering plants evolved showy blossoms and sweet nectar to entice insects. The presence of abundant insects buzzing around flowers probably attracted vertebrates, including birds and mammals. As we saw in Chapter 6, flowering plants also lure birds and mammals into dispersing their seeds by producing sweet and colorful fruit. Early primate ancestors also ate these insects.

THE CRATER OF DOOM: WHAT HAPPENED AT THE K–T BOUNDARY?

At the end of the Mesozoic, drastic environmental changes, probably arising from an asteroid or comet crashing into the surface of the earth, caused or contributed to the extinction of the dinosaurs and generated opportunities for mammals (Alvarez et al., 1980). These wide scale faunal changes occurred between the end of the Cretaceous Period and the beginning of the Tertiary Period; a time frame called the K–T Boundary. Evidence of such an impact comes from a giant crater called Chicxulub in the Yucatán Peninsula.

The impact probably caused an all-consuming firestorm and a number of tidal waves, followed by abrupt global cooling. It is thought that this combination of fire and cold killed off much of the terrestrial plant life at that time, which caused the extinction of herbivorous dinosaurs and then also of the carnivorous dinosaurs that preyed on them.

The ensuing environmental and ecological circumstances, including the absence of large prey animals, favored small, insect-eating mammals over the larger dinosaurs. Some of the primitive mammals of the Mesozoic, such as *multituberculates,* persisted into the Paleocene, the earliest Cenozoic epoch, but for the most part there is a comprehensive replacement of mammals at the K–T boundary. Many of these new mammals are archaic forms that are not traceable to living groups. Such is the case with the possible ancestors of the primates.

Changes in the Paleocene: The Origin of Primates?

During the Paleocene Epoch, many archaic groups of mammals arose that are not precisely like any living group. Among these groups are the ancestors of living mammalian orders, including primates. Among the new arrivals at the beginning of the Paleocene are primate-like mammals, the **plesiadapiforms** (Figure 9.1), either a separate order of mammals or a suborder of the primates, on equal footing with strepsirhines and haplorhines (see Chapter 6). Known mainly from North America, the plesiadapiforms have also been discovered in Europe and in China and range from the late Cretaceous/early Paleocene to the late Eocene.

Much controversy has swirled around whether the plesiadapiforms were true primates (Szalay, 1975) or representatives of another closely related order of mammals such as the Scandentia (tree shrews), Dermoptera (colugos or "flying lemurs"), or Chiroptera (bats). In recent years, there has been a tendency to exclude some or all of the plesiadapiforms from the order Primates (Rasmussen, 2002), but new fossil evidence indicates that at least some of these archaic forms were true primates that diverged before the last common ancestor of living species (Bloch & Silcox, 2001). And, as we shall see at the end of this chapter, genetic evidence suggests that at about the time of *Purgatorius* (63 million years ago) the primate lineage arose.

Paleontologists use the form of teeth and bones to decide to which group a fossil belongs; so to be identified as primates, fossils must show the primate trends in anatomy. The controversy with the plesiadapiforms arises because in many ways they were more primitive than any living primate. They had small brains, a **prognathic face** that projected well in front of their braincase, and small eye sockets positioned on the sides rather than on the front of their face. They lacked a **postorbital bar,** a bony ring encircling the eye, a key feature of primates that indicates the importance of vision to the order. Many plesiadapiforms possessed large, rodent-like lower incisors

plesiadapiforms Mammalian order or suborder of mammals that may be ancestral to later Primates, characterized by some but not all of the primate trends.

prognathic face Projection of the face well in front of the braincase.

postorbital bar A bony ring encircling the lateral side of the eye but not forming a complete cup around the eye globe.

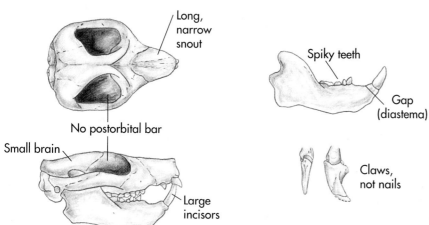

FIGURE 9.1 The plesiadapiforms may have been primates but they lacked certain features, such as a postorbital bar and nails, common to living primates. Note also their small brain and long nose.

It is often difficult to discern the earliest members of a lineage in the fossil record because the closer you are to the origin of a group, the more the anatomy differs from living members and approaches that of the last common ancestor.

that were separated from the premolars by a large **diastema**, or gap between their anterior teeth. Some had claws (rather than nails) and lacked an opposable big toe. In all these ways plesiadapiforms do not look like primates.

Only jaws and teeth are known for the earliest representative of the plesiadapiforms, *Purgatorius*, so named for its type locality in Purgatory Hills, Montana (Buckley, 1997). Compared with other mammals from the very earliest Cenozoic, the molar teeth of *Purgatorius* are less specialized; they have somewhat less spiky cusps, suggesting a diet of both insects (the spikes help break into the insect shell) and fruit. The dental formula (see Chapter 6) of *Purgatorius* is 3:1:4:3, meaning that the genus is generalized enough to have given rise to the first clear primates that appear in the fossil record of the Eocene.

From an ancestor such as *Purgatorius*, an *adaptive radiation* (see Chapter 1) of plesiadapiforms evolved, ranging from the very tiny, mouse-sized forms (approximately 0.70 lb [20 g]) to creatures that are about the size of a small monkey (11 lb [5 kg]). These include the genus *Plesiadapis*, a rodent-like animal from the early Paleocene and Eocene of Europe and North America that seems to have moved slowly along tree branches and perhaps traveled on the ground. Another family of plesiadapiforms, the paromomyidae, lived from the middle Paleocene until the late Eocene of Europe and North America, and may have fed on sap and gum gouged from tree bark.

The plesiadapiform radiation shows that very early primates (or primate-like mammals) were anatomically more primitive than living primates in almost all respects, although some families were also quite specialized. Some of the more generalized forms may have been ancestors of the primates alone or of primates and other closely related mammals (such as tree shrews, colugos, and bats). The more specialized forms probably were side branches that went extinct without issue. Although some plesiadapiforms persisted into the Eocene, they failed to compete with two new kinds of mammals that made their appearance at the beginning of the Eocene: rodents and the first "primates of modern aspect."

WHY PRIMATES?

As we saw in previous chapters, environmental conditions shape the characteristics of a group by favoring individuals who exhibit certain traits and selecting against individuals without those traits (see Chapter 1). So what environmental change or problem favored the origin of the primate trends? The Paleocene was warmer than today and was a period of recovery from the giant impact described earlier (see Chapter 8). In the Paleocene flowering plants evolved, insects increased in number and diversity as pollinators for these plants, and the plants evolved visual cues to lure these insects. The plesiadapiform fossils suggest that primate ancestors took advantage of these changing resources by eating insects (remember the spiky teeth of the plesiadapids that are good for crunching the hard bodies of insects) and possibly fruit from new plants (remember also that the teeth of *Purgatorius* are slightly less spiky than rodents of the Cretaceous, better for mashing fruit). We know that living primates emphasize vision over olfaction and have tactile pads on their fingers, not hard pads and claws (see Chapter 6).

In the past, scientists thought that primates evolved these features in response to life in the trees rather than on the ground. However, the fossil record of early proto-primates such as the plesiadapiforms has helped us to understand that early primate forebears probably were *visual predators* dependent on sighting and catching insects to survive rather than clambering on branches for fruit (see Chapter 6 for a review of the visual predation hypothesis). As we move into the Eocene, we will see the first true primates and the many ways in which they expand on this early primate adaptation.

diastema   Gap between anterior teeth.

Early Primates of the Eocene

Climate warmed significantly at the beginning of the Eocene, around 54 million years ago (see Figure 8.21 on page 257), resulting in the replacement of the archaic mammals of the Paleocene by the first representatives of a number of modern orders of mammals, including Rodentia (mice, squirrels, beavers, and so on), Artiodactyla (even-toed ungulates or hooved animals such as deer, camels, antelopes, hippopotami, and pigs), Perissodactyla (odd-toed ungulates such as horses, rhinoceros, and tapirs), and of course Primates.

The fossil record of the Eocene reveals the first true primates, those that possess the bony characters by which we identify living primates (Figure 9.2). We also see the origin of the strepsirhine–haplorhine split during this epoch. The two main superfamilies of Eocene primates, the Adapoidea and Omomyoidea, appeared at the beginning of the Eocene. They flourished during the Eocene of Europe, North America, North Africa, the Middle East, and Asia but declined during the Oligocene (Covert, 2002).

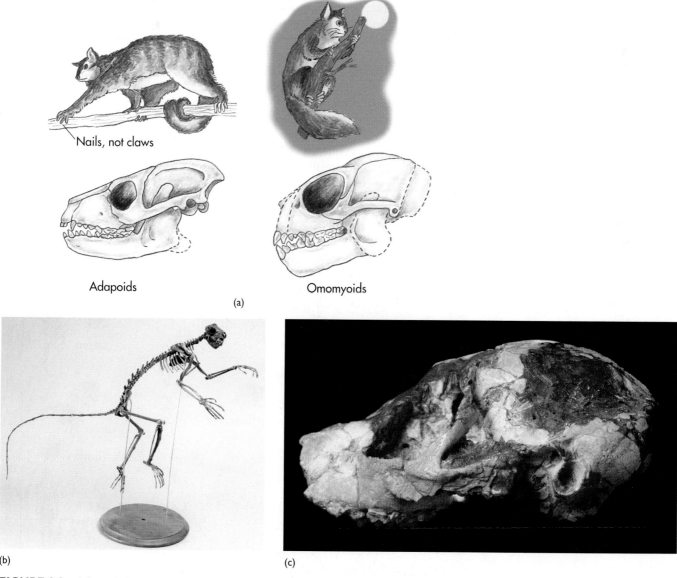

Nails, not claws

Adapoids

Omomyoids

(a)

(b)

(c)

FIGURE 9.2 Adapoids (a, b) and omomyoids (a, c) had longer snouts and are the first "true" primates. Both have a postorbital bar. Omomyoids have shorter snouts and include *Necrolemur antiquus*.

We recognize these fossils as true primates because, unlike the plesiadapiforms, they possess the full suite of primate trends. In particular, they possess slightly larger brains than plesiadapiforms, eye sockets positioned on the front of the face (allowing stereoscopic vision and depth perception), a complete postorbital bar for greater protection of the eye, an opposable big toe, and nails (rather than claws) at the ends of their fingers and toes. At the same time, the reduction of their snouts and whiskers suggests that smell was less important for locating food than was sight (Figure 9.2). Based on other anatomical evidence discussed in this chapter, we think the adapoids and omomyoids gave rise to the lineages that became the living strepsirhines (lemurs and lorises) and haplorhines (tarsiers, monkeys, and apes), respectively. Although other scholars think that adapoids might be ancestral to anthropoids.

ADAPOIDS (STREPSIRHINE ANCESTORS)

The **adapoids** were mostly small- to medium-sized and weighed approximately 3.5 oz to 15 lb (100 g to 6.9 kg). They were slow-moving arboreal quadrupeds that were active by day and probably ate fruit and leaves (Figure 9.2).

The highly successful superfamily Adapoidea is usually divided into three families: the Notharctidae, Adapidae, and Sivaladapidae (Fleagle, 1998). They occur in both North America and Europe, which were connected to one another at the time these primates lived, but are most abundant in the Old World. And some adapids may also have lived in Asia. Fossils of genera such as *Notharctus* and *Adapis* show long broad snouts with teeth that suggest some may have eaten a fibrous diet. Their eyes indicate some were probably nocturnal, others diurnal. Their postcrania suggest a diverse range of locomotion from leaping to quadrupedal climbing.

Adapoids resemble modern strepsirhines mainly in primitive ways, and most lack the features of modern strepsirhines such as the tooth comb. Therefore, the adapoids are best considered the most primitive known group of early modern primates. The adapoids probably gave rise to strepsirhines before the evolutionary divergence of lemurs and lorises (Figure 9.3). This interpretation is consistent with

adapoids   Family of mostly Eocene primates, probably ancestral to all strepsirhines.

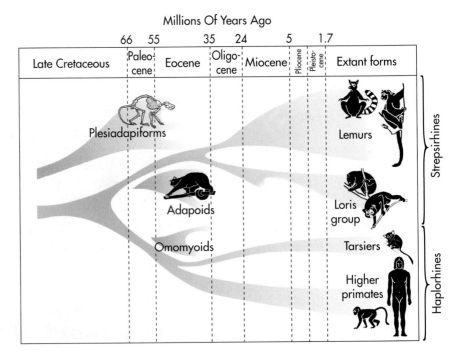

FIGURE 9.3   Possible relationships between fossil and living primates: Plesiadapiforms may or may not be primates. Adapoids are probably ancestral to living strepsirhines, and omomyoids to living haplorhines.

the molecular evidence that suggests lemurs and lorises diverged around 45 million years ago (later than the first appearance of the adapoids) but that strepsirhines and haplorhines had already split by about 58 million years ago, and it is consistent with much of the anatomical evidence (Kay et al., 1995). Some adapoids share characteristics with anthropoids, and some scholars therefore see these early primates as ancestral to anthropoids. However, the close affinities between tarsiers and anthropoids and tarsiers and omomyoids (see Omomyoids section) would mean that substantial amounts of parallel evolution would have to have occurred if adapoids were ancestral to anthropoids but omomyoids were ancestral to tarsiers. For all these reasons it seems more likely that adapoids were ancestral to strepsirhines not to haplorhines or anthropoids.

Although some of the adapoids are likely to be ancestral to living strepsirhines (lemurs and lorises), and early representatives of the lorises and galagos have been discovered in Eocene deposits of North and East Africa (Le Gros Clark & Thomas, 1952; Seiffert et al., 2003), the fossil record of true lemurs is confined to the Holocene of Madagascar. This record of lemur diversity before human occupation of the islands provides a good example of an adaptive radiation and devastating documentation of the calamitous impact that humans can have on ecosystems (see Insights and Advances: Subfossil Lemurs of Madagascar on page 268).

OMOMYOIDS (HAPLORHINE ANCESTORS)

The **omomyoids** were even more diverse than the adapoids. Omomyoids were smaller-bodied primates weighing 1 oz to 5 lbs (30 g to 2.2 kg) that ate diets of insects and fruit and had larger orbits, probably for a nocturnal lifestyle. Their limb bones probably were evolved for active arboreal quadrupedalism and leaping, like those of living mouse lemurs and galagos (Godinot & Dagosto, 1983). Although they occur in both Eurasia and North America, the first possible omomyoid occurs in the Paleocene (about 60 million years ago) of Africa as *Altiatlasius koulchii*. This earliest omomyoid is very fragmentary and later omomyoids are more abundant in North America. The best known genus of the Omomyidae is the tiny *Necrolemur* (Figure 9.2) whose skull clearly shows the short face and large eye sockets typical of nocturnal and insectivorous strepsirhines, such as galagos and mouse lemurs. A galago-like mode of vertical clinging and leaping locomotion is indicated by the anatomy of omomyid hind limb and ankle bones.

These similarities to lorises led some experts to suggest that omomyids were ancestral strepsirhines; others have thought that the omomyoids were ancestors only of tarsiers. However, although both cranial and postcranial evidence point to a link between omomyoids and haplorhines (the suborder that allies tarsiers with anthropoids), omomyoids differ from tarsiers. Omomyoid eye sockets are not nearly as large as those of tarsiers, and their ankles do not possess the unique tarsier features for exceptional leaping. These differences suggest that omomyoids may have been ancestral to all haplorhines rather than only to tarsiers.

Omomyoids are probably best regarded as Eocene primates that had recently diverged from the adapoids and may have given rise to the common ancestor of both tarsiers and anthropoids (Figure 9.3). This view is consistent with the anatomical evidence and with the molecular evidence that suggests that the strepsirhine–haplorhine split occurred around 58 million years ago.

CONTINENTAL DRIFT AND EOCENE PRIMATES

The geographic distribution of the adapoids and omomyoids in North America and Europe reflects the position of the continents between 54 and 34 million years ago. Europe and North America were joined by a broad band of land, and there

When inferring relationships among fossils and living groups, the paleontologist must consider the anatomy of the groups as well as what is known of the molecular relationships of living groups and their age of divergence.

omomyoids Family of mostly Eocene primates probably ancestral to all haplorhines.

INSIGHTS AND ADVANCES

Subfossil Lemurs of Madagascar

Among living strepsirhines there are more families, genera, and species of lemurs from Madagascar than there are lorises and galagos from Africa and Asia combined. And, unlike the entirely arboreal, nocturnal, and solitary lifestyles of the lorises and galagos, the lemurs include one species that is semiterrestrial, a few species that are diurnal, and some that live in social groups composed of several individuals.

But the diversity of living lemurs is only a shadow of their actual radiation (Figure A). Cave deposits from the late Pleistocene and Holocene of Madagascar have yielded skeletons of a bewildering array of giant lemurs (Godfrey & Jungers, 2002). There were at least sixteen species of these subfossil lemurs (their remains are so recent that the bones have not yet fossilized). A 22-lb (10-kg) subfossil aye-aye, *Daubentonia robusta*, is about five times larger than the living aye-aye.

However, the most astonishing subfossil lemurs are members of the Lepilemuridae, the family that includes the living sportive lemurs, and ten species of the Indriidae, including the living sifaka and indri. The living lepilemurids are an anomaly; they eat leaves but are much smaller than all other folivorous primates. Mature leaves often include toxins and structural carbohydrates that are difficult to digest, and animals that eat leaves tend to be large and have large guts to assist in their digestion (see Chapter 6). Weighing in at only 17 oz (500 g), *Lepilemur* (the living sportive lemur) is so small that its gut has difficulty digesting leaves. Occasionally the sportive lemurs even eat their own feces to give their digestive systems a second chance to break down the leaves. But just a few thousand years ago, the sportive lemurs were much larger creatures called koala lemurs (Godfrey & Jungers, 2002). Another subfossil lepilemurid was the huge *Megaladapis* that weighed 165 lb (75 kg), about as much as a female orangutan. *Megaladapis* also ate leaves. The postcranial skeleton of *Megaladapis,* especially its enormous hands and feet, indicates that it was mainly a slow, tree-climber that moved along vertical branches as it foraged for leaves. And a few thousand years ago one group of subfossil indriids, known as the monkey lemurs (Godfrey & Jungers, 2002), came down from the trees and adopted a macaque- or baboon-like lifestyle, foraging for food on the ground. The most specialized monkey lemur is *Hadropithecus,* a 55- to 65-lb (25- to 30-kg) form with a short, robustly built face that appears to have evolved for processing grass and seeds. Another group, the sloth lemurs, used their enormous hooklike hands and feet to suspend themselves beneath horizontal tree limbs and move slowly through the forests of Madagascar, munching on leaves in much the same way as the living sloths of South America. One sloth lemur, *Archaeoindris,* is estimated to have weighed about 440 lb (200 kg), the same as a male gorilla!

The subfossil lemurs reveal a great many things about how competition and predation limit strepsirhine diversity. In continental Africa and tropical Asia, most strepsirhines are small, cryptic creatures that are nocturnal and arboreal. On Madagascar, there was no competition from monkeys and apes or from many other herbivorous mammals, such as antelopes and pigs, and there were fewer predators. Unfettered by competition and predation, the Madagascar lemurs exploited lifestyles that we don't normally associate with strepsirhines: diurnal activity patterns, suspensory and terrestrial locomotion, specialized leaf eating, and very large body size.

Although Madagascar is currently home to more than 55 species of lemurs (and new species probably remain to be discovered), the fossil record suggests past diversity was far greater. Without the fossil record we would have no idea of the devastating role humans played in the demise of the lemurs. Most extinct lemurs appear to have perished about 2,000 years ago. Radiocarbon dates and anecdotal reports suggest that some subfossil lemurs persisted until just a few hundred years ago. Larger species seem to have been particularly acutely affected. The extinction of the subfossil lemurs seems to be related in large part to the activities of people, including predation and deforestation.

FIGURE A   The subfossil lemurs of Madagascar filled a variety of niches occupied elsewhere by monkeys, as shown in this artist's rendition.

was little difference in climate from north to south or east to west (see Figure 8.21 on page 257). Thus the distribution of primates from North America to Europe makes sense given that they could have freely walked (or leaped or scampered) between the two.

SELECTIVE PRESSURES FAVORING THE STREPSIRHINE–HAPLORHINE SPLIT

Adapoids and omomyoids seem to represent the origin of the split between strepsirhines and haplorhines, with adapoids probably giving rise to the former and omomyoids to the latter. Again we may ask what aspects of the environment might have driven their evolution. In the Eocene in particular, what selective pressures may have favored the divergence of strepsirhine and haplorhine lineages? We know from molecular data that the groups diverged around 58 million years ago, but anatomically they are similar in some aspects throughout the Eocene epoch. Clues from anatomy such as relative snout length and the shape of their teeth suggest that adapoids and omomyoids (that is early strepsirhines and haplorhines) divided up the available food resources, thus avoiding competition. Adapoids ate leaves and relied more on their sense of smell (remember their longer snouts). Omomyoids focused on fruit and insects and had a shorter snout. From these original differences, the haplorhines eventually diverged quite far from the original primate niche.

Evolution of Higher Primates

Representatives of the higher primates (monkeys and apes, including humans) first appeared in the late Eocene and early Oligocene epochs, after the strepsirhine–haplorhine split. The earliest higher primates are generalized monkeys that probably gave rise to all later higher primates. Early apes appeared in the Miocene and were also more generalized than their living descendants and more diverse. The initially diverse apes decreased in abundance through time, while the monkeys became more abundant.

THE FIRST MONKEYS?

The molecular evidence tells us that the first monkeys occurred between 58 and 40 million years ago, after the split between tarsiers and anthropoids and before New World and Old World monkeys diverged. The marked cooling and drying of the climate at the end of the Eocene resulted in a large-scale faunal turnover called the Grande Coupure (see Chapter 8). Like all large-scale climatic changes, the Grande Coupure created both challenges and opportunities for the animal populations alive at the time. In response, the adapoids and omomyoids nearly vanished from North America and Eurasia, as did many other mammalian taxa. Likewise, animals that we recognize as monkeys first appeared in the Oligocene. Remember from Chapter 6 that all higher primates (monkeys, apes, and humans) share certain anatomical characters, including greater enclosure of the orbits, smaller snouts, fewer teeth, a fused frontal bone and a fused mandible, and larger body size (Figure 9.4 on page 270). These anatomical changes signal changes in the foraging habits of these primates, probably catalyzed by the changing environmental conditions.

The fossil record provides two windows into the origin of anthropoids. One is in the Eocene of China, the other in North Africa and the Middle East. Purported anthropoids from Asia, such as *Pondaungia*, are more likely to be late surviving adapids that have slightly changed their diet and converged on some anthropoid dental characters. However, a strong candidate for ancestor of the earliest anthropoids was recently found at Shanghuang in Jiangsu Province, China, and dated to the middle Eocene (Beard et al., 1994). This tarsier-sized (~3.5 oz, 100 g) animal was named *Eosimias* and placed in its own family, the Eosimiidae. Several genera exist from about 45 million years ago in China to about 32 million years ago in Pakistan. Some details of the anatomy of the jaws, teeth, and ankle bones suggest that the Eosimiidae are at the very base of the anthropoid radiation, before its diversification into platyrrhines (New World monkeys) and catarrhines (Old World monkeys, apes, and humans), and that the African anthropoids are descended from those in Asia (Seiffert et al., 2005). However, the relationships between early African and Asian forms are hotly contested.

Much of what we know about the evolution of higher primates in the late Eocene and early Oligocene comes from the research of Elwyn Simons' team at the Fayum depression in Egypt. During the Eocene and Oligocene the Fayum was a lushly forested area surrounding a large river system that supported a great diversity of tropical fauna and flora (Figure 9.5). Scientists have found several genera of small (approximately 17-oz to 2.2-lb or 500- to 1,000-g) early anthropoids in these deposits. As with the Eosimiidae of China, these early forms from the Fayum combine primitive (in this case adapoid) features and anthropoid-like features.

At the end of the Eocene and the early Oligocene we find at least three families of early anthropoids at the Fayum: the Parapithecidae, the Oligopithecidae, and the Propliopithecidae. Like living monkeys, these early anthropoids possessed advanced features of the skull and jaws, including a fused frontal bone, a fused lower jaw, and postorbital closure, that distinguish them from strepsirhines (Figures 9.4 and 9.5). In the (lower) earlier part of the Fayum sediments, the anthropoids are fairly small (most weigh less than 1 kg). The later Fayum anthropoids are somewhat larger in size, but none exceeds the size of a medium-sized monkey today.

The Parapithecidae is a diverse group of early anthropoids that includes the genus *Apidium* (Figure 9.6 on page 272). In life, *Apidium* probably resembled the South American squirrel monkey, weighing approximately 2.2 lb (1 kg), leaping and running among tree branches on all fours, and eating mainly fruit and some insects (Fleagle & Kay, 1987; Kirk & Simons, 2001). Like living New World monkeys, *Apidium* possessed three premolars in each quadrant of its jaws, suggesting that

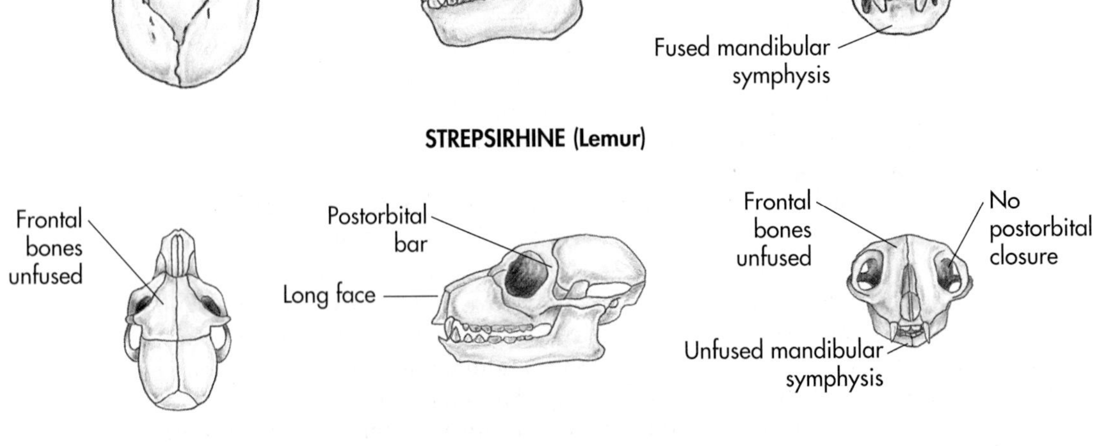

HAPLORHINE (Cebus Monkey)

Frontal bone fused

Fully enclosed orbit

Shortened face

Enlarged brain

Frontal bone fused

Postorbital closure

Fused mandibular symphysis

STREPSIRHINE (Lemur)

Frontal bones unfused

Postorbital bar

Long face

Frontal bones unfused

No postorbital closure

Unfused mandibular symphysis

FIGURE 9.4 The skulls of living haplorhines differ from those of strepsirhines by having enlarged brains, an enclosed orbit, and a fused frontal and mandible.

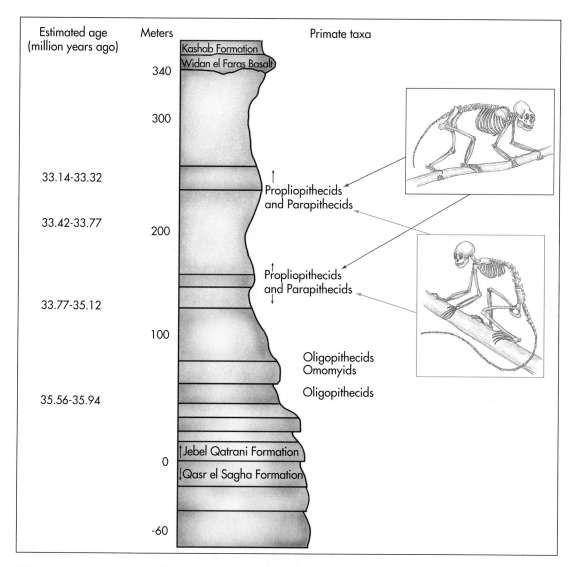

FIGURE 9.5 Stratigraphic section of the Fayum shows the relative age of early anthropoid fossils. The primates include the potential ancestor for all anthropoids (*Apidium*, a parapithecid) and the potential ancestor for all Old World monkeys and apes (*Aegyptopithecus*, a propliopithecid).

it predated the split between New World monkeys (with three premolars) and Old World monkeys (with two premolars).

The Oligopithecidae, including *Oligopithecus* and *Catopithecus,* weighed only 1.8 to 3.3 lb (800–1,500 g). They were quadrupedal monkeys that lived in the trees and probably ate mostly fruit and some leaves (Simons, 1995; Kirk & Simons, 2003). This group combined primitive, strepsirhine-like molars with the earliest known record of more advanced features such as a fused frontal bone and postorbital closure.

The Propliopithecidae (Figure 9.7 on page 272) were the largest of the Fayum primates weighing 13 to 15 lb (6–7 kg). These most advanced of the early anthropoids from the Fayum are exemplified by the genus *Aegyptopithecus* (Simons, 1987). In life, *Aegyptopithecus* may have looked something like the living howler monkey of South America, slowly moving from branch to branch in search of fruit and leaves. Unlike the parapithecids, both the oligopithecids and the propliopithecids had the 2:1:2:3 dental formula of living Old World higher primates.

The Fayum also was home to a diversity of strepsirhine primates. These were all small fruit, insect, and perhaps gum eaters. And they became less diverse with time just as the anthropoids became more diverse.

FIGURE 9.6 *Apidium* may be ancestral to all later higher primates and is reconstructed as looking like a small-bodied monkey. The genus has the skeleton of an arboreal quadruped and a 2:1:3:3 dental formula.

FIGURE 9.7 *Aegyptopithecus* may be ancestral to catarrhines and has full postorbital closure and two premolars. *Aegyptopithecus* has the skeleton of an arboreal quadruped.

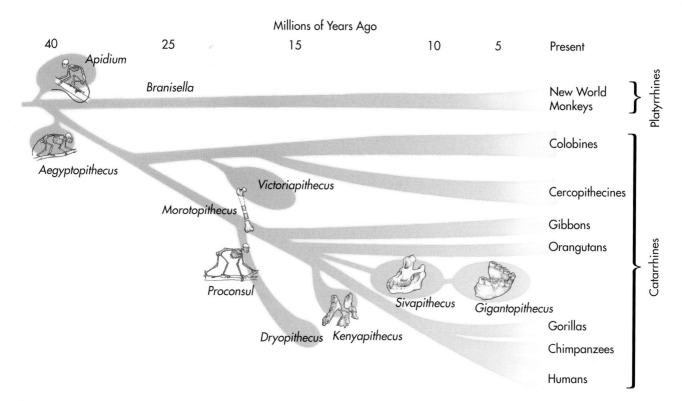

FIGURE 9.8 Proposed relationships between living and fossil platyrrhines and catarrhines.

The early anthropoids of the Fayum reveal a radiation of early monkeys. Some of them (*Apidium*) may have been ancestral to all later anthropoids, but others (*Aegyptopithecus*) may have been early representatives of the Old World higher primates, before the divergence of Old World monkeys, apes, and humans (Figure 9.8).

NEW WORLD MONKEYS

The molecular evidence suggests that New World and Old World monkeys diverged around 40 million years ago, but the earliest fossil record of monkeys in South America comes later from the late Oligocene (about 25–30 million years ago). During this period, Bolivia was home to the enigmatic genus *Branisella* (Fleagle & Tejedor, 2002). How monkeys got to South America is still something of a mystery. South America was an island continent during the early part of the Cenozoic; the connection to Central and North America, via the Panamanian Isthmus, was established less than 5 million years ago by sea level changes (see Figure 8.17 on page 253).

New World monkeys could have originated from Eocene adapoids or omomyoids in North America or from the most primitive anthropoids of Africa. Perhaps New World monkeys are descended from North American Eocene primates that migrated south across open waterways between islands. If this is true, New World monkeys would have evolved in parallel with Old World monkeys and not have shared an ancestor with them since around 50 million years ago, or more. However, the molecular evidence argues that New World and Old World monkeys split relatively recently, about 40 million years ago. Also, New World monkeys have three premolars rather than the two seen in all catarrhines, linking them to *Apidium*, a fossil monkey from Fayum, Egypt. Because of these anatomical and molecular links, most scientists currently support a model that supposes an *Apidium*-like ancestor "rafting over" from Africa to South America during the late Eocene or early Oligocene (Hartwig, 1994). The Atlantic Ocean was not as wide as it is today,

FIGURE 9.9 Monkeys may have reached South America by floating on natural mats as is known to happen occasionally to mammals, including humans, after tremendous floods.

and we know that during floods animals, including humans, get isolated on floating mats of vegetation and are carried to sea (Figure 9.9). Perhaps early monkeys reached the New World in this way.

However they got there, in the early and middle Miocene we see an increasingly rich fossil record of New World monkeys. This record shows diversification into the five major subfamilies of living New World monkeys: Cebinae, Aotinae, Pitheciinae, Atelinae, and Callitrichinae (Rosenberger, 2002).

OLD WORLD MONKEYS

According to DNA comparisons, Old World monkeys and apes shared a common ancestor about 25 million years ago. The fossil record tells us that ancestor had anatomical features shared by both monkeys and apes, such as a bony ear tube and presence of two rather than three premolars, but lacked characters unique to each group, such as the bilophodont molars characteristic of modern Old World monkeys and the suspensory shoulder characteristic of modern apes.

The earliest fossil evidence of a lineage leading just to Old World monkeys comes from the 19-million-year-old site of Napak in Uganda. This monkey represents an early radiation of the family Victoriapithecidae that predates the split between the subfamilies of the modern leaf-eating Colobinae and fruit-eating Cercopithecinae and may be a good candidate for the common ancestor of all later Old World monkeys (Benefit, 1999). The Victoriapithecidae lived in the early to middle Miocene of eastern and northern Africa, but they are best known from thousands of specimens of the species *Victoriapithecus macinessi* from 15-million-year-old deposits at Maboko Island in Kenya (Benefit & McCrossin, 2002).

Victoriapithecus weighed between 6.6 and 11 lb (3–5 kg) and was one of the oldest and smallest anthropoid primates to make the shift to life on the ground. Its snout was moderately long, like a macaque's, but its braincase was longer and lower than in modern monkeys, and it possessed a strong sagittal crest not seen in living forms (Figure 9.10). Its low molar cusps and broad upper incisors suggest that *Victoriapithecus* probably ate hard fruits and seeds. Victoriapithecid's ability to eat hard foods on the ground and in the trees appears to have been a very successful adaptation for these Miocene monkeys.

The molecular evidence suggests that the cercopithecine and colobine lineages of Old World monkeys split between about 14 and 16 million years ago. The first true cercopithecines (*Macaca* sp.) appear in the fossil record of North Africa about 11 million years ago (Delson, 1980), and the first true colobines appear in Kenya at about the same time. Soon after they appear, colobine monkeys expanded their ranges in Eurasia. Although cercopithecines may have delayed their migration into Eurasia, they are represented by numerous Pleistocene Asian macaques.

The Plio-Pleistocene radiation of African Old World monkeys is documented by fossils collected at numerous sites that are more famous for their hominid remains, such as Koobi Fora, Kenya (see Chapters 11 and 12). These monkeys were more diverse in terms of their body size, locomotion, and dietary habits than monkeys are today. They also appear to have formed distinct communities in eastern and southern areas of Africa. For example, there were many medium- and large-sized colobine species in the Plio-Pleistocene of eastern Africa, where some were adapted for life in the trees and others apparently lived on the ground. Eastern Africa was dominated by a variety of *Theropithecus* baboons that shared a dentition similar to that of the modern gelada baboon, presumably for eating grasses, but otherwise differed significantly from their modern counterparts in their postcranial anatomy and size.

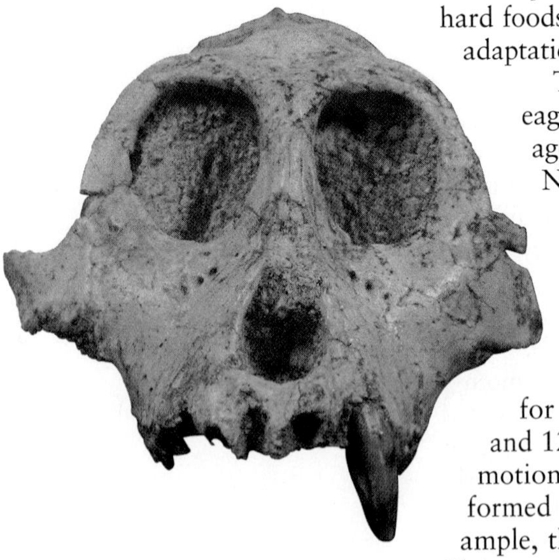

FIGURE 9.10 The most complete *Victoriapithecus* skull from Maboko Island, Kenya, is a likely ancestor for Old World monkeys. *Victoriapithecus* had complete postorbital closure, and partially bilophodont molars.

WHAT FAVORED THE ORIGIN OF ANTHROPOIDS?

What selective pressures influenced the origin and diversification of true anthropoids during the Oligocene? What conditions drove their evolution? Global temperatures continued to cool during the Oligocene opening up new niches and probably causing the decline of adapoids and omomyoids. Early anthropoids and tarsiers are small bodied, and unlike most adapoids and omomyoids, diurnal. We know from the fossil evidence that some of the early monkeys, such as *Victoriapithecus*, were eating tough objects and that their bodies were growing bigger. Their skulls were also changing, the mandible becoming a single bony unit, as did the frontal bone, and the orbits becoming completely enclosed by bone. This evidence seems to suggest that the early monkeys were successful because they were able to chew a tougher diet and better protect their eyes.

Although these may seem like unrelated abilities, it turns out that they are not. A fused mandible transfers force from one side of the jaw to the other more effectively than an unfused mandible. Perhaps chewing on a harder diet favored animals with fused or partially fused mandibles. Greater chewing efficiency might have allowed them to eat more, leading eventually to larger body size. Orbital closure may also be related to chewing, although this is more debatable. One of the main chewing muscles, the temporalis muscle, is located just behind the eye on the side of the skull. If you place your finger on your temple and clench your teeth you will feel your temporalis muscle contract. Your eye is protected from that contraction (and expansion) of the muscle by the bone plate that sits between the muscle and your eyeball. In strepsirhines, however, that muscle can bulge into the orbital area, deforming the globe of the eye and causing vision to blur momentarily. If vision were critical to survival, an anthropoid might be favored if it had a bone cup around its eye. On the other hand, some scientists argue that the postorbital closure of anthropoids arose as a consequence of the greater orbital frontality seen in anthropoids, and that their origin, like the extinction of many adapoids and omomyoids in North America and Europe, was related to global climate change. Both hypotheses recognize the increasing importance of stereoscopic vision to anthropoid survival. The Old World monkeys took this initial adaptation and enhanced it with adaptations to a more leaf-based (folivorous) diet.

Changes in climate and diet favored the origin of anthropoids.

THE EARLIEST APES

Living ape species are few in number and limited to just four genera: *Hylobates* (the gibbons and Siamangs), *Pongo* (the orangutan), *Gorilla* (the gorilla), and *Pan* (the bonobo and the common chimpanzee). However, the fossil record of hominoid primates reveals a surprisingly diverse succession of adaptive radiations. This ape fossil record is characterized first by the appearance of **dental apes**, animals with apelike teeth but monkey-like postcranial skeletons.

Molecular evidence suggests that the monkey and ape lineages diverged about 25 million years ago. Fossil apes first appeared during the early Miocene, approximately 23 to 16 million years ago. At that time, hominoids were almost totally restricted to Africa, where they are well known from sites in Kenya, Uganda, Ethiopia, and Namibia (Figure 9.11 on page 276). Unlike today, the early Miocene of Africa probably was covered by uninterrupted expanses of forest and moist woodland. The uplifting and rifting that dominate eastern Africa today had not yet occurred, nor had the climatic divisions of arid and wet zones.

On this forested continent lived dozens of genera of early apes with very monkey-like postcranial skeletons. In fact, we might call them *dental apes* to show that we recognize them as apes based mostly on their dental anatomy. You'll remember from Chapter 6 that Old World monkeys possess specialized, high-crested bilophodont

dental apes Early apes exhibiting Y-5 molar patterns but monkey-like postcranial skeletons.

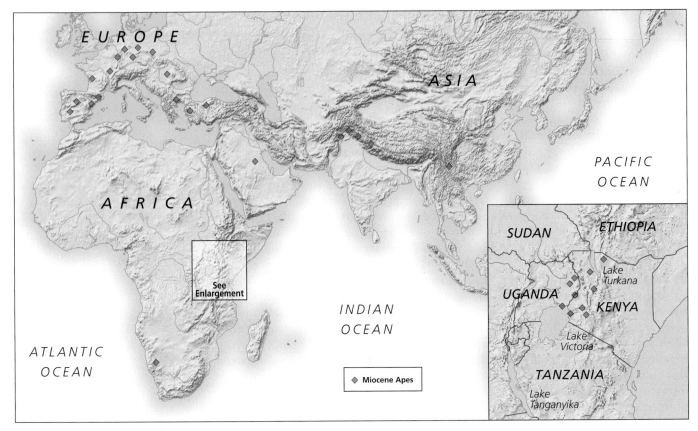

FIGURE 9.11   Miocene apes were found throughout Europe, continental Asia, and Africa. Important eastern Africa localities are plotted on the inset map.

lars for shearing leaves, but all apes possess molars with five rounded cusps, connected by a pattern of Y-shaped fissures or grooves (Figure 9.12). This "Y-5" molar pattern is seen in even the most primitive apes. The dental apes were small-bodied compared with modern apes, they lacked a suspensory shoulder for brachiating, and they walked in plantigrade fashion, that is, on the soles of their feet rather than on their knuckles.

The best known of the early dental apes is the genus *Proconsul* (Figure 9.13), which lived in Africa about 18 to 20 million years ago. There are at least three *Proconsul* species, ranging in size from approximately 33 to 110 lb (15–50 kg) (Walker & Teaford, 1989). *Proconsul* was discovered in the 1920s in East Africa

FIGURE 9.12   The Y-5 molar pattern (left) characterizes the ape, whereas bilophodont molars (right) characterize the Old World monkey. Both have a 2:1:2:3 dental formula.

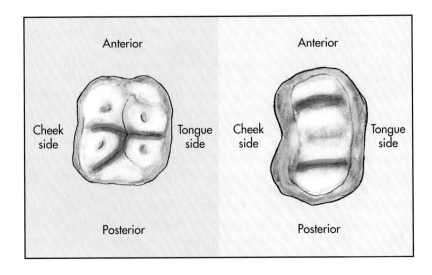

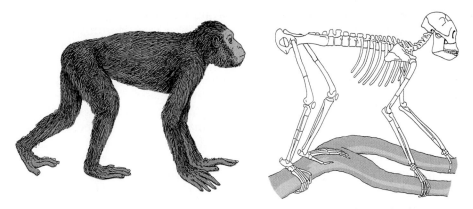

FIGURE 9.13   The dental ape *Proconsul* has an apelike dentition but monkey-like skeleton.

and was named Consul, after performing chimpanzees of that era. *Proconsul* teeth are apelike, with a Y-5 molar pattern, and aspects of the limb skeleton show a more monkey-like locomotor adaptation for running. In addition, *Proconsul* appears to have possessed a long and flexible torso, like that of quadrupedal monkeys, rather than the short and stable back of living suspensory apes, and perhaps a tail (Ward, 1997). Although the adaptations vary between different groups, a number of other African ape genera, including *Nacholopithecus, Equatorius,* and *Afropithecus,* share some derived features of the skull and teeth with living apes but lack the suspensory postcranial adaptations seen in living apes.

Until recently, *Proconsul* was thought to be the last common ancestor of great apes and hominids, but *Morotopithecus bishopi* may be a better candidate (Figure 9.14). In 1997, paleoanthropologists Daniel Gebo and Laura MacLatchy named a new species of Miocene ape, *Morotopithecus bishopi,* from the 20.6-million-year-old site of Moroto in Uganda, based on fossils that had been collected in the 1960s and 1990s. *Morotopithecus* exhibits primitive conditions of the upper jaws that indicate a basal position within the hominoid radiation, but portions of the backbone and the shoulder girdle suggest that, unlike *Proconsul, Morotopithecus*

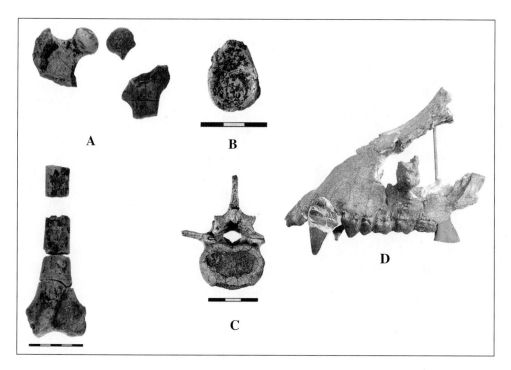

FIGURE 9.14   *Morotopithecus* is the earliest fossil ape to show postcranial adaptations similar to those of living apes.

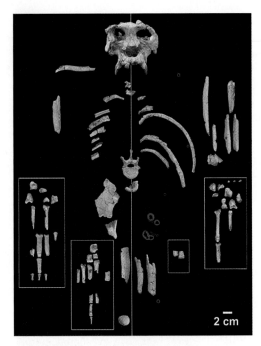

FIGURE 9.15 *Pierolapithecus catalunicus* may be an ancestor of great apes and humans. Its postcranial skeleton shows adaptations for suspensory locomotion, and its skull shows some features of living apes.

possessed the short and stiff back of living apes and a suspensory shoulder anatomy unlike monkeys (MacLatchy et al., 2000). *Morotopithecus* was one of the earliest and largest hominoids from this time period (Gebo et al., 1997).

Around 17 million years ago there appeared the first evidence of a land connection between Africa and Eurasia, created mainly by the northern movement of the plate on which Africa rests. This connection allowed hominoid primates to migrate outside Africa for the first time, and small, gibbon-like forms appeared in China (Harrison & Gu, 1999).

Sweeping environmental changes transformed the world during the middle Miocene, and the diversity of fossil apes eventually declined. Previously, Africa had been moist and forested, but fauna and flora from middle Miocene sites such as Maboko Island and Fort Ternan in Kenya indicate that these areas were dry and the vegetation was open, with dry woodland and even grassland emerging as the dominant environment. The molecular evidence suggests that around this time (14 million years ago) the African great ape and human lineage diverged from the Asian great ape lineage (the orangutans). In Africa these apes include genera like *Kenyapithecus*.

During the middle and late Miocene (approximately 15 to 5 million years ago), large-bodied hominoids dispersed into Europe and Asia. Some of these apes, like *Sivapithecus*, are related to later Asian apes, but others are probably extinct side branches of the ape lineage (*Dryopithecus, Lufengpithecus, Oreopithecus*). One, *Ouranopithecus*, may be related to gorillas. And the most recent discovery, *Pierolapithecus*, from Spain (12.5–13 million years ago) may be ancestral to great apes and humans (Figure 9.15) (Moyà-Solà et al., 2004).

Sivapithecus, named after the Hindu figure Siva, is found in the late Miocene sediments of the Himalayan foothills of northern India and Pakistan. Cranial and dental remains of *Sivapithecus* exhibit several similarities to the orangutan. The eye orbits are long and oval and separated from each other by a tall and narrow septum. Also, in side view the face is strongly "dished," or concave, except for the portion of the upper jaw that holds the incisors, which is convex (Figure 9.16). Taken together, these features indicate an evolutionary relationship between *Sivapithecus* and modern orangutans (Pilbeam, 1982). In other ways, however, *Sivapithecus* is distinct from the orangutan; the chewing surfaces of its molar teeth, although possessing a thick coat of enamel, are smooth and differ from the strongly *crenulated* (wrinkled) enamel of the orangutan, and the postcranial remains of *Sivapithecus* indicate arboreal quadrupedalism rather than the quadrumanous ("four-handed")

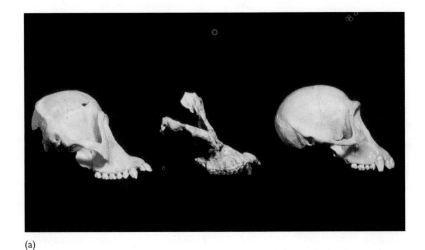
(a)

(b)

FIGURE 9.16 (a) *Sivapithecus* is a Miocene ape (middle) with anatomical similarities to orangutans (left) rather than chimpanzees (right). (b) Siwaliks, Pakistan, where *Sivapithecus* was found.

clambering seen in orangutans. Therefore, *Sivapithecus* is a relative of the modern orangutan but not its unique ancestor.

At about the same time that *Sivapithecus* lived, a huge new ape arose in the same geographic region. In the 1930s, German paleontologist Ralph von Koenigswald searched for fossils in drugstores as well as the field because fossil bones and teeth often are used in traditional East Asian medicine. In 1935, in drugstores in Hong Kong and the Philippines, he found enormous primate molars. He named the previously unknown creature to whom they belonged *Gigantopithecus* (von Koenigswald, 1952). Although an early form of this genus occurred in the late Miocene, it is better known from the early and middle Pleistocene of China and Vietnam, where it grew to an enormous size, perhaps as large as 660 lb (330 kg), and coexisted with *Homo erectus* (Figure 9.17). *Gigantopithecus* was thus the largest primate that ever lived. Some scholars speculate that legends of the sasquatch in North America and the yeti in Asia may have begun long ago when *Gigantopithecus* walked the earth. Most authorities view *Gigantopithecus* as a distant relative of *Sivapithecus*. Based on its large size and molar anatomy, *Gigantopithecus* probably ate a tough, fibrous diet, perhaps even bamboo.

Ouranopithecus was a very large 242-lb (110-kg) hominoid from the late Miocene (10 million years ago) of Greece (deBonis & Koufos, 1993). Unlike *Sivapithecus* and orangutans, *Ouranopithecus* possessed a massive browridge and a wide space between the eye sockets, thus resembling a gorilla. Some researchers have argued that *Ouranopithecus* is an ancestor of both African great apes and hominids. However, details of its face, jaws, and teeth may indicate that *Ouranopithecus* lacks aspects of cranial anatomy that are shared, derived features of both African great apes and humans (Benefit & McCrossin, 1995).

Another late Miocene ape from Europe is *Dryopithecus*, long known from isolated jaws, teeth, and an upper arm bone. Recent discoveries of a skull and skeleton at Can Llobateres in Spain have greatly improved our understanding of this 8- to 12-million-year-old form. Although it was large bodied, weighing between 44 and 77 lb (20–35 kg), *Dryopithecus* does not share derived features with either Asian or African great apes. Instead, *Dryopithecus* possesses a primitive anatomy reminiscent of both *Proconsul* and gibbons. Additional fossils from Rudabánya in Hungary reinforce the interpretation that *Dryopithecus* is a late-surviving, primitive Miocene ape.

In many ways the most peculiar and vexing of the European hominoids is *Oreopithecus*, from the late Miocene of Italy. An almost complete but very flattened skeleton of *Oreopithecus*, a primate that weighed about 66 lb (33 kg), was found in coal deposits that had developed in a swampy environment between 7 and 8 million years ago. Paleontologists Meike Köhler and Salvador Moyà-Solà consider *Oreopithecus* to have been a biped, based on their reconstruction of the creature's feet and ankles, but not a biped like us. They argue that its feet were shaped almost like tripods in life, with a divergent big toe and four other toes that were aligned in nearly the opposite direction. The researchers do not argue that *Oreopithecus* was a direct hominid ancestor; instead, they think the species evolved in the isolated habitat of a Mediterranean island that lacked predators, leading to adoption of a strange and awkward way of walking. Other researchers argue that a more accurate reconstruction of *Oreopithecus* indicates monkey-like quadrupedalism. The teeth of *Oreopithecus* are also distinctive, featuring unique molar cusps and crests. These features suggest that *Oreopithecus* ate leaves. Overall, therefore, *Oreopithecus* appears to have been a unique lineage in the ape and human family tree, and one that left no living descendants.

Although we have identified many ape taxa from the Miocene, we have little or no fossil evidence for the lineages that led directly to gorillas, chimpanzees, and bonobos. One possible exception is *Samburupithecus*, a poorly known fossil ape from the late Miocene (approximately 8–9 million years ago) of Kenya (Ishida & Pickford, 1997) whose upper molars are like those of a gorilla, and

(a)

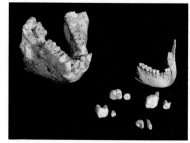

(b)

FIGURE 9.17   (a) Reconstruction of *Gigantopithecus*, a fossil ape, towers over artist Bill Munns. (b) The enormous mandible of *Gigantopithecus* dwarfs a modern human mandible.

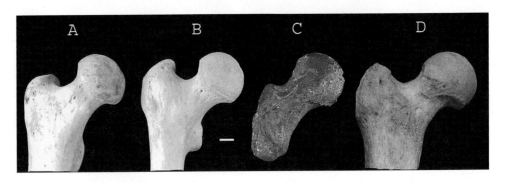

FIGURE 9.18 The fossil record of chimpanzees is sparse. The femur from Kikongo, Uganda (c) may represent a late Pleistocene chimpanzee rather than a human (d). The other femora are (a) gorilla and (b) chimpanzee.

possibly *Ouranopithecus*. More recently, a late Miocene orangutan from Thailand, *Khoratpithecus piriyai*, has been discovered (Chaimanie et al., 2004). It is similar to living *Pongo* in most dental dimensions, which suggests that it also had a similar diet (Taylor, 2006), The first fossil chimpanzees are reported from the middle Pleistocene of Kenya (545–284 thousand years ago; McBrearty & Jablonski, 2005) and possibly from the late Pleistocene of Uganda (DaSilva et al., 2006) (Figure 9.18). However, the late dates of these remains mean they can tell us little about the early evolution of the separate ape lineages. The dearth of fossils is related in part to the tropical forests in which apes live, moist places where biological processes often lead to the complete destruction of the skeleton.

The Miocene hominoids provide a picture of the ape and human family tree before it was so drastically pruned to just the few branches that exist today (Figure 9.8 on page 273). Some genera, such as *Proconsul*, were early representatives of the superfamily that diversified before the common ancestor of living forms. One Miocene hominoid, *Sivapithecus*, appears to be allied to the modern Asian great ape lineage, the orangutan. Other late Miocene Eurasian hominoids, such as *Dryopithecus* and *Oreopithecus*, now appear to be side branches that left no modern descendants. Finally, a few genera, perhaps including *Pieralopithecus*, appear to be members of the African ape and human clade that diversified before the last common ancestor of gorillas, chimpanzees, and humans. However, the relationships of Miocene hominoids are hotly debated. What is certain is that after their early diversification, the number of ape genera and species declined while Old World monkeys diversified.

SELECTION PRESSURES AND THE DIVERGENCE OF MONKEYS AND APES

Monkeys and apes differ in specific anatomical ways related to their form of locomotion, so the origin of hominoids probably is related in part to this shift in locomotor pattern. Monkeys have bodies shaped more or less like your dog or cat: The thorax is narrow from side to side but deep from back to front. Apes are the opposite, having wide but not very deep thoraxes. This change may be related to the origin of a particular kind of suspensory locomotion called *brachiation* that is used by living gibbons and siamangs and probably by the common ancestor of all apes. Because a brachiator with an arm positioned far from its midline has a locomotor advantage, through time apes evolved a wide thorax (and longer clavicles, or collarbones). During suspension and brachiation the arm is often over the animal's head, so a brachiator with a rounded joint surface on the top of the humerus (humeral head) and a scapula rotated onto its back would also be favored (Figure 9.19).

The apes appear to have evolved their specialized locomotor capacity in the early middle Miocene (remember *Morotopithecus*), when forests were widespread.

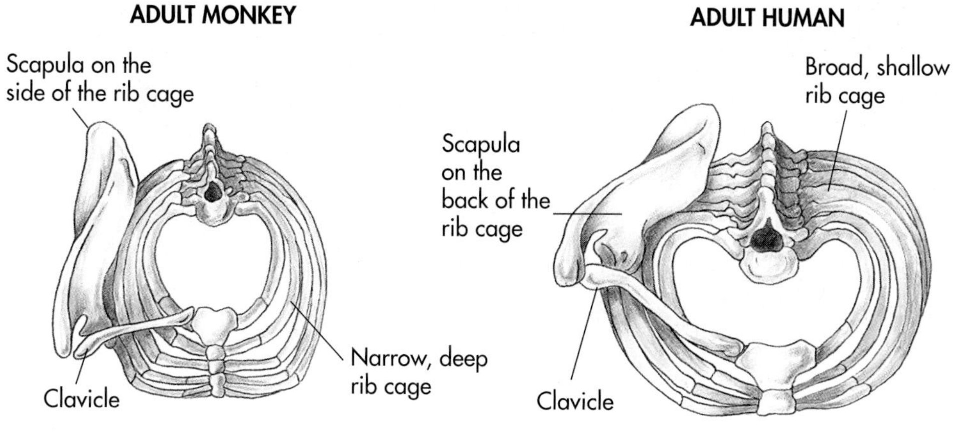

ADULT MONKEY

Scapula on the
side of the rib cage

Clavicle

Narrow, deep
rib cage

ADULT HUMAN

Broad, shallow
rib cage

Scapula
on the
back of the
rib cage

Clavicle

FIGURE 9.19 The thorax of apes, including humans, is broad but shallow in contrast to the narrower, deeper chest of the monkey.

Later the African apes modified this brachiating anatomy for knuckle-walking so that in the middle Miocene, when body size increased and apes became more terrestrial, we see evidence of knuckle-walking anatomy. Orangutans, after *Sivapithecus*, eventually become quadrumanous.

So, part of the origin of the living hominoid pattern is related to shifts in climate and the relative abundance of forested and unforested areas. However, you will recall that the first distinctive evidence of apes in the fossil record is from the dentition and the groups we called dental apes. The shape of these dentitions suggests that the initial change in the ape lineage was a dietary shift, probably to eating more fruits. During the Miocene we see global drying and cooling and the breaking up of habitats into smaller wooded areas and patchy grasslands. And in this changing environment the monkey and ape lineages differentiated, with monkeys focusing increasingly on more leafy diets and early apes focusing more on fruits. Some later apes, such as the gorilla, return to a fibrous diet, modifying the original ape niche.

THE MONKEY'S TALE: WHAT HAPPENED TO PRIMATE DIVERSITY IN THE MIOCENE?

From the beginning to about the middle of the Miocene, fossil apes were abundant and monkeys fairly rare. But after the mid-Miocene it is a monkey's world, with apes decreasing in both diversity and number of taxa. Why this shift?

Recall the climatic changes of the Miocene, when the world got drier and colder (see Chapter 8). Forests dried up, grasslands and wooded grasslands became more abundant, new niches became available. Animals that once lived in the forest had a few possible routes to survive: Stick with the same old pattern but reduce numbers of individuals (after all, the forested areas were smaller) or strike out into a new area with new resources necessitating new adaptations. Animals that reproduce more quickly, that is, those that are **r-selected**, could colonize areas faster and rebound from population declines more quickly and thoroughly. Although monkeys reproduce more slowly than many nonprimates, they reproduce more quickly than apes and so had an advantage in colonizing new areas. Apes are strongly **k-selected**, exhibiting the opposite reproductive characteristics of r-selected animals. In addition, the shape of the monkey thorax and limbs is more conducive to evolution of quick terrestrial locomotion. These attributes seem to have favored the monkeys over the apes during the late Miocene. In contrast, the apes seem to have stuck with their shrinking, forested homes. Their numbers decreased along with their habitat and continue to do so today. Only one group of apes seems to have overcome the issues of locomotion and reproduction to move into new, more open habitats. This lineage eventually evolved into humans (Figure 9.20 on pages 282–283).

r-selected Reproductive strategy in which females have many offspring, interbirth intervals are short, and maternal investment per offspring is low.

k-selected Reproductive strategy in which fewer offspring are produced per female, interbirth intervals are long, and maternal investment is high.

Primate Evolution

Figure 9.20 Primates or primate ancestors appear around 63 million years ago and diversify into niches created by the extinction of the dinosaurs but do not show most of the anatomical characters of living primates. Strepsirhine and haplorhine lineages appear in the early Eocene. The first monkeys with postorbital closure appear in the Oligocene. Apes diversify in the Miocene but are rare by the Pliocene.

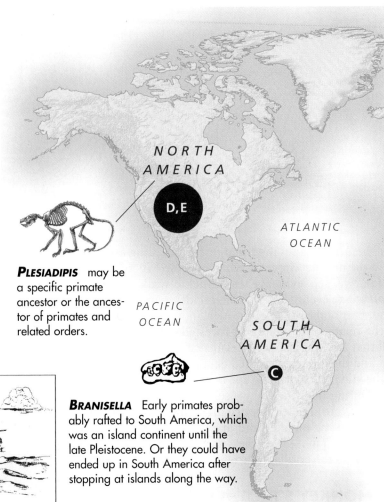

PLESIADIPIS may be a specific primate ancestor or the ancestor of primates and related orders.

BRANISELLA Early primates probably rafted to South America, which was an island continent until the late Pleistocene. Or they could have ended up in South America after stopping at islands along the way.

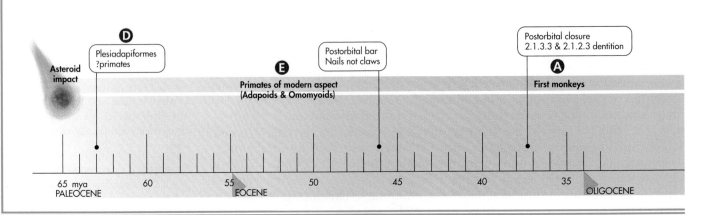

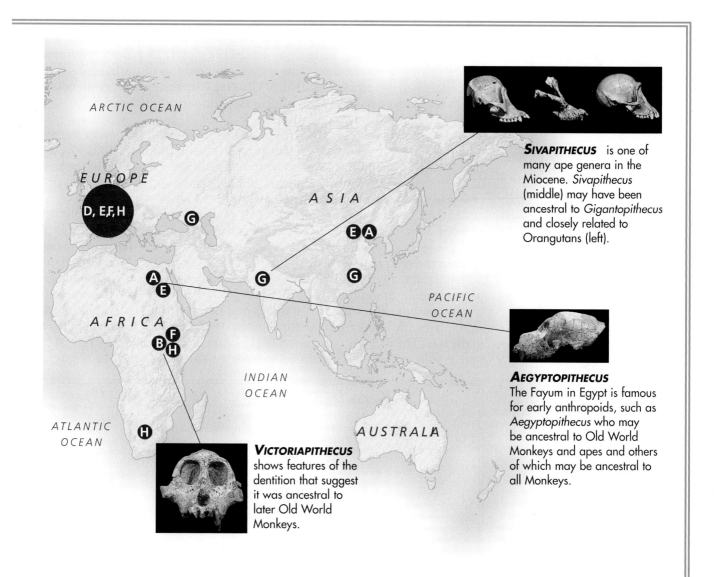

SIVAPITHECUS is one of many ape genera in the Miocene. *Sivapithecus* (middle) may have been ancestral to *Gigantopithecus* and closely related to Orangutans (left).

AEGYPTOPITHECUS
The Fayum in Egypt is famous for early anthropoids, such as *Aegyptopithecus* who may be ancestral to Old World Monkeys and apes and others of which may be ancestral to all Monkeys.

VICTORIAPITHECUS shows features of the dentition that suggest it was ancestral to later Old World Monkeys.

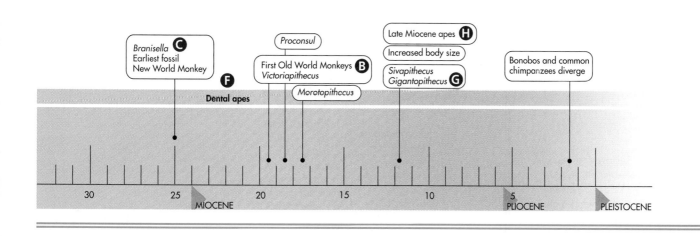

Molecular Evolution in Primates

Throughout the chapter we have presented the picture of primate evolution that can be drawn from fossil remains and augmented it with estimated divergence times based on molecular evidence. In Chapter 2 we discussed several methods by which molecules can be used to inform evolutionary studies—to figure out phylogenetic relationships among species.

A *molecular phylogeny* is a tree of relatedness among species, or larger taxonomic groupings, based on a gene or protein (such a tree can also be constructed by pooling information from more than one gene [see Chapter 5]). The structure of the tree provides a visual summary of how similar or dissimilar a given molecule is in any two or more of the taxa represented on the tree.

In 1967, a key advance in molecular phylogenetics occurred when anthropologist Vincent Sarich and biochemist Allan Wilson demonstrated that it was possible to use molecular relationships between species to determine divergence dates in the past; in other words, there existed a **molecular clock**, or a systematic accumulation of genetic differences through time that, if measured, could be used to estimate the amount of time since two groups shared a last common ancestor.

A molecular clock needs two things in order to work. First, the clock must be *calibrated* with a date from the fossil record that corresponds to one of the nodes in the tree. The date for this one node can be used to determine the rate of change in the molecule, which then allows us to date each node in the tree (Figure 9.21).

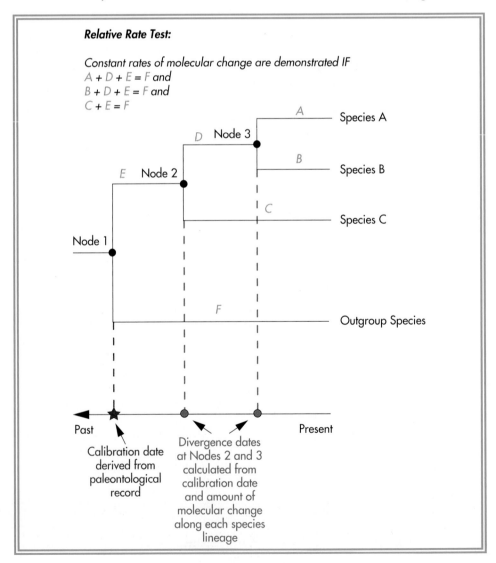

FIGURE 9.21 Relative rate test, calibrating the molecular clock, and calculating divergence dates. Letters *A–F* correspond to amounts of molecular change or molecular distance along each lineage.

Second, there must be a demonstration of *rate constancy* in the molecule that is used to make the tree: A molecular clock can work only if the molecule is changing at a similar rate in each branch or lineage represented in a phylogeny. Sarich and Wilson proposed a way to demonstrate rate constancy for any protein or gene. A **relative rate test,** or a comparison of the amount of genetic difference between each primate species of interest and a member of an *outgroup,* such as a dog. If the DNA of each primate is equally different from a dog's DNA, then there must be rate constancy within primates; if there had been a slowdown in the rate of change on one lineage, then that lineage would have shown fewer differences from the outgroup DNA than the others did. Relative rate tests can be used to account for variability in the rates of change of genes in different lineages, if they are present.

Not all genetic systems can be used as molecular clocks because some systems are influenced by natural selection, lineage-specific rate changes, and other factors that make them inappropriate for timing evolutionary events. However, several different proteins, genes, and noncoding regions of DNA have proven to be useful as molecular clocks. Molecular phylogenies sometimes have been controversial, especially when they do not agree with phylogenies determined by traditional anatomical and paleontological methods. However, only one history is being reconstructed and ultimately molecular and paleontological phylogenies must agree with each other.

Not all genetic systems are good molecular clocks. Many systems are influenced by natural selection or lineage-specific mutation rates.

A PRIMATE MOLECULAR PHYLOGENY

In 1998, Morris Goodman, a pioneer of molecular anthropology, published a comprehensive phylogeny of primates based primarily on evolution in the *beta-globin* gene cluster on chromosome 11 (in humans) (Goodman et al., 1998; Goodman, 1999). Beta-globin is one of the polypeptide chains that make up hemoglobin. Goodman's phylogeny is based on gene sequences from more than 60 primate species, calibrated with several dates from the fossil record (Figure 9.22 on page 286). In terms of the largest branches and major nodes, this molecular phylogeny, which relies on multiple calibrations from the fossil record, fairly accurately represents current ideas about the major phylogenetic events in primate evolution. However, controversy still remains regarding the synthesis of fossil and molecular data in determining primate phylogenetics of closely related groups of primate species (Stewart & Disotell, 1998).

We have referred to these divergence time estimates in earlier sections and bring them together here as an overview of the timing of primate evolution. Goodman's phylogeny places the *last common ancestor* (LCA) of all primates at 63 million years ago. It is at this point that we get the deepest split within primates, that between the strepsirhines and the haplorhines. Within the strepsirhines, there was a split between the lemurs and lorises 45 million years ago. Within the haplorhines the tarsiers branched off from the anthropoid lineage at 58 million years ago, and the major split within the anthropoids, that between the platyrhines and the catarrhines, occurred 40 million years ago. Within the catarrhines, the division between the cercopithecoids and the apes occurred 25 million years ago, just at the beginning of the Miocene. Within the Old World monkeys, cercopithecines and colobines split about 16 million years ago. Within the apes, lesser apes (gibbons and siamangs) split about 17 million years ago from the great apes. African and Asian great apes split around 14 million years ago, gorillas split from the chimp–human clade about 8 million years ago, and human and chimp lineages split about 6 million years ago. Chimps and bonobos split about 2.2 million years ago.

MOLECULAR PHYLOGENY AND HUMAN ORIGINS

Molecular phylogenies have instigated two major shifts in thinking about human origins. In 1967, the first molecular phylogeny by Sarich & Wilson showed that

molecular clock A systematic accumulation of genetic change that can be used to estimate the time of divergence between two groups if relative rates are constant and a calibration point from the fossil record is available.

relative rate test A means of determining whether molecular evolution has been occurring at a constant rate in two lineages by comparing whether these lineages are equidistant from an outgroup.

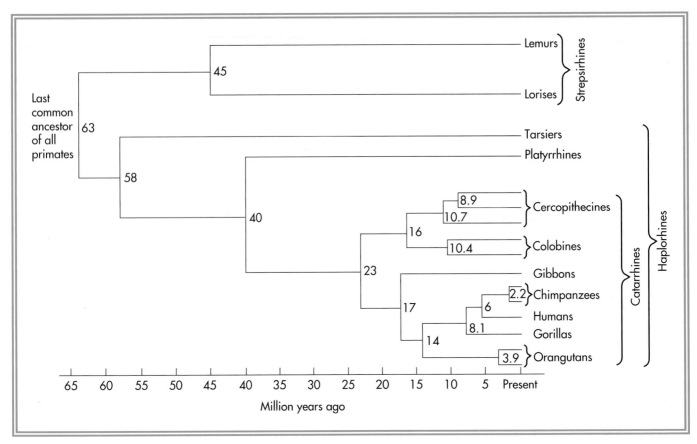

FIGURE 9.22   Relationships and dates of divergence of living primate groups based on molecular and DNA comparisons (Data from Goodman, M., 1999).

the origin of hominids was more recent than the prevailing view at the time. They showed that hominids arose around 5 million years ago, but the 15-million-year-old *Ramapithecus* (now *Sivapithecus*) was considered the earliest hominid in the fossil record, an assignment based entirely on characteristics of the teeth and jaws. This first molecular phylogeny caused a re-evaluation of the fossil evidence and has been confirmed by additional fossil discoveries.

In 1997, Maryellen Ruvolo performed a combined analysis of DNA sequence data from fourteen different loci that had been analyzed in humans, chimpanzees, and gorillas. She concluded that chimpanzees and humans are more closely related to each other than either is to gorillas despite strong anatomical similarities between chimps and gorillas. This division is also favored in the Goodman phylogeny. Given the molecular consensus on this issue and the current understanding of the hominid fossil record, it is safe to say that any claims for a hominid ancestor older than about 6 million years will be regarded with a healthy amount of skepticism by both molecular geneticists and paleontologists.

The fossil record of primate evolution provides a full view of the history of primate relationships, adaptations, and ecology. In addition to documenting the evolutionary history of nonhuman primates, this record sets the stage for the emergence of the lineage that ultimately led to humans. In the next section we explore the fossil record for hominid evolution and the selective pressures that shaped the evolution of our ancestors.

SUMMARY

1. **Were plesiadapids the first primates?**

   This depends on which authority you ask. After their discovery, plesiadapids were considered to be primates. This view faded after many researchers noted their lack of modern primate anatomical traits. They occur about the right time, according to molecular data to be primate ancestors, but they may be just primate-like mammals. In recent years, however, researchers have begun to reconsider the role of plesiadapiforms in primate evolution.

2. **How are adapoids and omomyoids similar, and how do they differ?**

   Both existed in Europe and North America, although adapoids were more prevalent in Europe and omomyoids in North America. Adapoids had longer snouts and smaller eyes and probably ate leaves. They are the likely ancestors of strepsirhines. Omomyoids had shorter snouts and larger eyes and probably ate fruit and insects. They are the likely ancestors of haplorhines.

3. **What is the significance of *Apidium* for reconstructing the primate phylogeny?**

   The significance of *Apidium* is its dental formula: 2:1:3:3. This is the same as that of New World monkeys and is the primary link between Old and New World fossil monkeys. *Apidium* supports the hypothesis that New World monkeys are descendants of fossil Old World monkeys that rafted across the then-smaller Atlantic Ocean in the late Eocene.

4. **Why were the earliest apes not easily identified as such?**

   The earliest apes did not possess the anatomical features of living apes such as a suspensory shoulder and knuckle-walking hands. They can be identified as apes based on their molar teeth, which feature the same Y-5 configuration of cusps and fissures as those of all living apes. For this reason we call these primitive hominoids the dental apes.

5. **How do molecular phylogenies help us to understand primate evolution?**

   Molecular phylogenies provide an estimate of the relationships and dates of divergence of living primate taxa that we can use to augment information from the fossil record. However, divergence dates are calibrated by the fossil record.

CRITICAL THINKING QUESTIONS

1. How would the rise of rodents in the Eocene have contributed to the demise of the plesiadapids? What evolutionary principles can be applied here?

2. When we had only anatomical comparisons to rely on, we could not learn whether New World monkeys were descended from Old World monkeys or from early Eocene primates in North America. Now, with the rise of genetic dating, the answer is still unclear. What do you think this tells us about the limitations of genetic techniques for resolving problems of primate phylogenetics?

3. Discuss the possible selective pressures involved in the origin of primates, strepsirhines, and anthropoids. Can you think of other possible scenarios for the origins of these groups?

KEY TERMS

plesiadapiforms	diastema	dental apes	molecular clock
prognathic face	adapoids	r-selected	relative rate test
postorbital bar	omomyoids	k-selected	

SUGGESTED READING

Alvarez, Walter (1997). *T. rex and the Crater of Doom.* Princeton University Press, Princeton, NJ.

Beard, Christopher K. (2004). *The Hunt for the Dawn Monkey: Unearthing the Origins of Monkeys, Apes, and Humans.* University of California Press, San Francisco.

Fleagle, John G. (1998). *Primate Adaptation and Evolution.* (2nd ed.) Academic Press, San Diego, CA.

BECOMING HUMAN:
The Ape–Hominid Transition

CHAPTER OUTLINE

Becoming a Biped

The Transition to Human Behavior

A chimpanzee in Tanzania pauses in her daily journeys to pluck a twig from a bush. She strips the leaves from the twig, then inserts it between her lips and walks on. A hundred meters ahead she arrives at an enormous termite mound, standing 2 meters high and extending an equal distance underground. Inside, millions of the small insects live in a colony, using tunnels that extend to the surface. The chimp scratches the dirt away from the entrance to one of the tunnels and extends her probe inside. Soldier termites rush to defend their nest, grabbing the twig with their mandibles. Smaller worker termites also swarm onto the stick. The chimpanzee delicately draws the probe from the tunnel and runs it between her lips, crunching the meaty soldiers along with hundreds of workers. In 30 minutes, she eats thousands of termites. Two thousand miles west, in Côte d'Ivoire, another chimpanzee carefully places a nut into a shallow depression between the roots of a huge tree. She then wields a rock in her fist, pounding the nut time and again, replacing it in her makeshift anvil when it pops out. After several whacks, the nut breaks open, and she reaps a meal rich in protein and fat.

SIX MILLION YEARS AGO, WE SHARED A common ancestor with these tool-making chimpanzees, and by studying their anatomy and behavior we can start to reconstruct the likeliest path from an ape ancestor to a hominid. We will never know exactly how the earliest humans looked or behaved. But biological anthropologists have a number of intellectual tools that help them reconstruct ancient lifeways. Anatomically inclined anthropologists analyze the functional shifts involved in changing a four-legged ape into a two-legged human. Indeed, the fossil record is the only direct physical evidence of our ancestry that we will ever have. Behavior experts attempt to extrapolate the likely range of behaviors that might have been present in the last common ancestor of apes and humans from comparative studies of living nonhuman primates. And genetic studies have helped unravel the mystery of our divergence from the apes and have become increasingly central to our understanding of our own relationship to extinct species in our lineage. One thing our tool-making relatives make clear is that intelligence was an important ingredient of our common ancestor.

Recall from Chapter 6 the adaptations that characterize living African apes, our closest relatives. These adaptations include a large brain-to-body size ratio and extended growth periods compared with monkeys, traits related to knuckle-walking, and traits related to a brachiator ancestor (including thorax shape, a highly mobile shoulder, and the absence of a tail). In a remarkable adaptive shift at the end of the Miocene, this combination of traits gave way to a new suite of traits in a new family, the Hominidae. (Hominids include humans and our extinct ancestors after the split from the last common ancestor with chimps.)

Initially, the most noticeable anatomical development in the early hominid lineage is a suite of traits related to bipedality, along with slightly smaller canine teeth. The dramatic expansion of the brain that characterizes living humans came millions of years later. The appearance of cultural traditions such as stone tool use also came later, although early hominids, like living apes, probably made and used organic tools. Because the fundamental adaptation was the shift to upright postures, this is where we begin to try to understand how and why one lineage of Miocene apes evolved into the earliest hominids.

FIGURE 10.1 Habitual bipedality is a relatively rare occurance and the striding bipedalism of hominids required particular anatomical adaptations not found in quadrupeds.

In this chapter we review the basic anatomical changes that natural selection produced in the bipedal skeleton. Once we understand how anatomy changed, we explore scenarios for why a bipedal primate might have evolved. Many of the time-honored assumptions about human origins have been questioned or challenged in recent years, and we review some of the controversy. Then we examine the behavioral changes that mark the transition from an apelike ancestor to a human lineage, specifically those related to the evolution of the brain and intelligence.

Becoming a Biped

Walking upright is an extremely rare way to move about (Figure 10.1). In the entire history of life on Earth, truly bipedal posture and walking have appeared in just a few lineages. Of some 4,000 living mammals, only humans are habitual striding bipeds today. A number of other primates, from sifakas to chimpanzees, stand upright occasionally while walking or feeding (Figure 10.2). However, only hominids possess extensive morphological adaptations to bipedality.

ANATOMICAL CHANGES

An animal walking on two legs has to solve several problems not encountered by our four-legged friends. Critical among these is the issue of balancing the body's weight over two limbs (while standing) and often over one limb (while walking) (Figure 10.3). Think of the quadruped as a four-legged table: The center of gravity falls in the area between the four legs, and the body weight is distributed equally over all four limbs (while standing). Remove one leg and it is still possible to balance the table's weight by shifting it to the area between the three legs. But take away two legs and the task becomes extremely difficult. When an animal that evolved to walk on four legs walks on its two hind limbs instead, it compensates for this lack of support by constantly moving its weight between the remaining limbs. Imagine your dog dancing on its hind limbs for a treat, constantly in motion forward and backward (trying to move under that center of gravity) and standing only briefly, tiring quickly from the constant muscular work. But when you stand, your body weight falls naturally between your two feet—no dancing required (although you can if you like). And when you walk, your foot naturally falls directly under your center of gravity. This greater efficiency means that while standing at rest, you burn only a few more calories than you would when lying down. The reasons for these differences are found in the structural changes in our skeleton that directly affect the skull, spine, pelvis, leg, and foot.

FIGURE 10.2 Some nonhuman primates can walk bipedally for short periods of time but lack key bipedal adaptations.

(a)   **(b)**   **(c)**   **(d)**

FIGURE 10.3   Becoming a biped changes the way an animal balances. The quadruped's center of gravity goes right through its back to the ground, balancing its weight over four legs (a). If the quadruped stands on two legs it either must bend its knees (b) or fall forward (c). A habitual biped has structural changes in the skeleton so that the center of gravity falls between the two feet when standing with legs extended (d). (After Wolpoff, 1999)

The Vertebral Column and Skull   The spine, or **vertebral column**, is made up of a series of bones in the neck (**cervical vertebrae**), thorax (**thoracic vertebrae**), lower back (**lumbar vertebrae**), and pelvic (**sacrum** and **coccyx**) regions (Figure 10.4; Appendix B). The quadruped has a gently C-shaped curve that makes the thoracic region of the spine slightly convex. The biped has an S-shaped spine made by adding two secondary and opposing curvatures (in the cervical and lumbar regions) to the C-shaped curvature of the quadruped. If you stand a quadruped up on its back legs, the C-shape of its spine tends to put the center of gravity in front of its feet, causing the animal to fall forward (or dance to avoid falling). The secondary curvatures in the bipedal spine compensate for that C-curve and bring the center of gravity back closer to the hips, ultimately resting over the biped's two feet.

The weight of the biped is borne down the spine to the sacrum, where it passes to the hips, and from there through the two legs. The amount of weight increases as you go down the spine, which is reflected in the size of the vertebrae of a biped. Vertebrae get bigger toward the lumbar region. In contrast, weight-bearing doesn't increase along the quadruped's spine, and the vertebral bodies are of nearly equal

vertebral column   The column of bones, and cartilaginous disks, that houses the spinal cord and provides structural support and flexibility to the body.

cervical vertebrae   The seven neck vertebrae.

thoracic vertebrae   The twelve vertebrae of the thorax that hold the ribs.

lumbar vertebrae   The five vertebrae of the lower back.

sacrum   The fused vertebrae that form the back of the pelvis.

coccyx   The fused tail vertebrae that are very small in humans and apes.

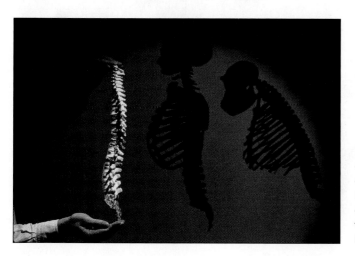

FIGURE 10.4   The spine of a biped has two additional curves in it at the neck and lower back to move the center of gravity over two feet. The ape (quadruped) has a C-shaped spine.

size in different regions of the spine. These differences can have adverse effects on the biped's body. Lower back problems, especially among pregnant women, are among the most common medical ailments today; these problems are a side effect of the changes naturally selected for in our ancestors for efficient bipedalism.

The vertebral column is also oriented differently to the head of the biped, coming out from the bottom rather than the back of the skull. So the junction of the spinal cord and the brain, which occurs through a hole called the **foramen magnum** in the occipital bone, is positioned underneath the skull in bipeds but toward the back of the skull in quadrupeds (Figure 10.5 and Appendix B, page 550). In addition to the foramen magnum, another indicator of the angle at which an animal holds its body in life is the form of the **nuchal plane**, the flattened bony area of the occipital to the rear of the foramen magnum that provides surface area for the attachment of neck muscles. In modern humans the nuchal plane is a horizontally flat region on the bottom of the skull, facing directly downward. In a quadruped, however, the nuchal plane faces rearward. In apes the nuchal plane's angle is somewhere between the human and quadruped condition. So the occipital bone is a clue for paleoanthropologists about the way in which a fossil may have stood and walked.

The Pelvis and Birth Canal   When you walk, you spend a significant amount of time on one leg. To do this you must keep your center of gravity over that one leg and not fall off to the unsupported side. Quadrupeds such as chimps accomplish this by throwing their weight over the supporting limb when they walk bipedally. As they walk they must rock from side to side, which wastes a lot of energy. The skeleton of habitual bipeds such as hominids evolved changes that automatically facilitate this balancing and save the biped energy. Many of these changes occur in the pelvis. The bony pelvis consists of two **innominate bones (os coxae)**, each composed of three other bones (the **ischium**, **ilium**, and **pubis**) that fuse during adolescence, and the sacrum, part of the vertebral column (Figure 10.6 and Appendix B on page 550). The ischium is the bone you sit on. The ilium is the bone you feel when you put your hands on your hips. And the pubis is the bony portion of the pelvis in the pubic region.

foramen magnum   Hole in the occipital bone through which the spinal cord connects to the brain.

nuchal plane   Flattened bony area of the occipital posterior to the foramen magnum, to which neck muscles attach.

innominate bones (os coxae)   The pair of bones that compose the lateral parts of the pelvis; each innominate is made up of three bones that fuse during adolescence.

ischium   Portion of the innominate bone that forms the bony underpinning of the rump.

ilium   The blade of the innominate to which gluteal muscles attach.

pubis   Portion of the innominate that forms the anterior part of the birth canal.

FIGURE 10.5   (a) The spine meets the skull from below in a biped, so the foramen magnum, in blue, is directly beneath the skull and the neck muscles run down from the skull. (b) In the ape the spine meets the skull from the back so the foramen magnum is positioned posteriorly and the neck muscles also run posteriorly from the skull.

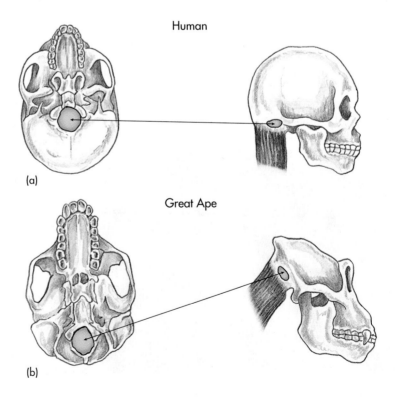

Human

(a)

Great Ape

(b)

Human   Great ape

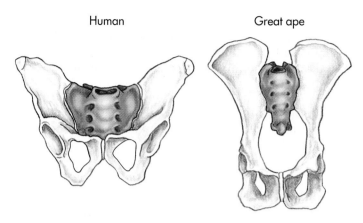

FIGURE 10.6   To maintain balance the bipedal pelvis has a foreshortened ilium and is broader and bowl-shaped. The quadrupedal pelvis has a long ilium positioned on the back, not the side, of the animal.

The pelvis of a biped is basin-shaped with a short, broad ilium that runs from the posterior to the anterior of the animal. The quadruped ilium is long and flat and situated on the back of the animal. The basin shape supports abdominal organs that tend to be pulled downward by gravity, and it places important locomotor and postural muscles in a better mechanical position. Most important are the anterior **gluteal muscles** (gluteus minimus and medius), which attach to the ilium and are rotated around to the side of the biped. In this position they connect the ilium to the top of the femur (thigh bone), and when you stand on one limb they contract, pulling the ilium (and your center of gravity) over the foot you are standing on. The gluteus maximus runs from the back of the ilium to the back of the femur, and when it contracts it keeps your pelvis (and you) from tipping forward in front of your feet (Figure 10.7 and Figure 10.3). The shortening and broadening of the ilium also places the hip joint (**acetabulum**) closer to the joint between the sacrum and ilium. This is good for balance but narrows the birth canal, a problem with which later hominids including ourselves have to contend.

Efficient bipedalism requires a narrow pelvis, but that need must be balanced against the need for a birth canal wide enough for the large shoulders of an ape-sized infant. Early in hominid history selection for birth canal size probably widened the pelvis from side to side by widening the sacrum. Later, as brain size increased, the baby was also required to rotate during delivery (see Chapter 16). Chimpanzee or gorilla babies emerge from the mother's body face up, but human babies emerge face down. We do not know exactly when this shift occurred, but its evolution was crucial to successful birthing in later, larger-brained hominids. The evolutionary

gluteal muscles   Gluteus maximus, medius, and minimus, the muscles of walking, which have undergone radical realignment in habitual bipeds.

acetabulum   The cup-shaped joint formed by the ilium, ischium, and pubis at which the head of the femur attaches to the pelvis.

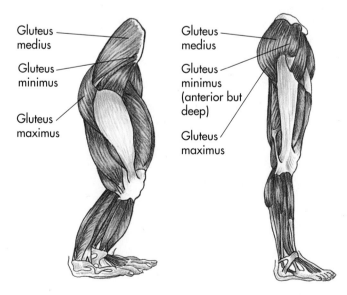

Gluteus medius
Gluteus minimus
Gluteus maximus

Gluteus medius
Gluteus minimus (anterior but deep)
Gluteus maximus

FIGURE 10.7   The gluteal muscles are repositioned in the biped and aid in support. (After Wolpoff, 1999)

drawback of this new anatomy was that it left the mother unable to assist in the birth of her own child. Karen Rosenberg and Wenda Trevathan (1996) see the constraints of bipedalism as an evolutionary incentive for the development of socially assisted birthing, in which females aid one another in achieving successful births.

The Leg   The broad pelvis places the top of the femur far to the side of the biped. However, when you walk your foot must fall directly below your center of gravity. A straight femur, such as that seen in a quadruped, would place the foot far to the side of the center of gravity. Natural selection favored bipeds with a femur that was angled from the hip into the knee because the angle places the foot below the center of gravity, which saves energy while walking (Figure 10.8 and Figure 10.3). However, an angled femur creates problems at the knee because the musculature attached to the femur must also act at an angle. When the animal flexes its muscles on the front of the femur in an effort to extend the knee, the muscles pull both superiorly (up) and laterally (out). The patella (knee cap) sits in the tendon of this muscle and moves outward as the muscle contracts. To avoid dislocating the patella, the groove on the femur that the patella sits in is deep, and the outside edge or lip is enlarged in a biped. In addition, to help support the excess body weight going through each limb, the bottom of the femur (**femoral condyles**) is enlarged as is the top of the tibia or shin bone to which the femur attaches.

Although relatively short in early hominids, the leg lengthened relative to trunk length during human evolution. A longer limb is favored because it increases stride length and efficiency in walking. Imagine a Great Dane and a Chihuahua walking side by side and the greater number of steps the shorter-legged dog takes compared with the longer strides of the Great Dane. Our relatively long legs and shorter trunk had evolved by the time of *Homo erectus*.

The Foot   At the end of this elongated leg, the foot of a biped is also radically modified from that of a quadruped. The foot skeleton is composed of three types of bones: **tarsals**, which form the heel and ankle region; **metatarsals**; and **phalanges** (the toes) (Figure 10.9). In bipedal walking, the heel strikes first, followed by the rest of the foot. The main propulsive force comes at toe-off, when the big toe pushes off from the ground and the toes bend strongly backward (dorsiflex). To accommodate toe-off and dorsiflexion, the big toe moves in line with the other toes and becomes much, much larger than the other toes, and all the phalanges shorten and change joint orientation. Imagine the advantage to the biped of shorter toes; it is rather like the difference between walking in floppy clown shoes and wearing shoes with regular-sized toes.

A biped's foot is stouter and has arches that accommodate the great weight put on the two feet. The tarsal bones and big toe are robust and bound tightly together by ligaments, providing stability but decreasing overall flexibility of the foot. The foot has two arches that act as shock absorbers: a transverse arch running from medial

femoral condyles   The enlarged inferior end of the femur that forms the top of the knee joint.

tarsals   Foot bones that form the ankle and arches of the foot.

metatarsals   Five foot bones that join the tarsals to the toes and form a portion of the longitudinal arch of the foot.

phalanges   Bones that form the fingers and toes.

FIGURE 10.8   To keep the foot under the center of gravity, the biped's femur is angled from hip to knee. The quadruped femur is not.

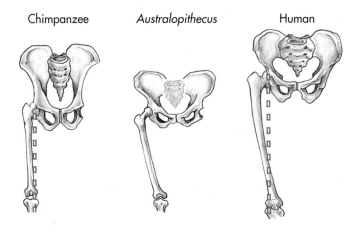

Chimpanzee   *Australopithecus*   Human

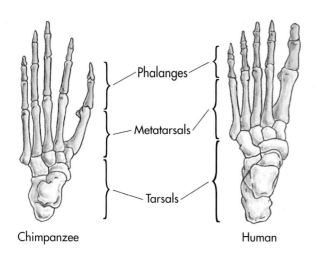

Chimpanzee   Human

FIGURE 10.9 The biped's foot bears more weight than the quadruped's and so the bones are stouter. The big toe is especially big and in line with the others, and the phalanges are shorter and less curved.

to lateral that is formed by the wedge-shaped tarsals, much like a stone architectural arch, and a longitudinal arch running the length of the foot and formed by the metatarsals and tarsals. The arches store and return some of the energy during walking, and help to reduce the incidence of fatigue fractures to the biped's lower leg.

The Arm   One advantage of walking on two legs is that it frees the arms to do other things. Carrying objects and tool making are two activities often associated with the hominid lineage (although they are not exclusive associations). Because bipeds do not use their arms for walking, the arm and hand skeleton have changed throughout human evolution. Early hominids started with relatively long arms, a holdover from the suspensory ancestor. With time, body proportions changed: The hominid leg gets longer and the arm relatively shorter. The arms also become less robust since they no longer bear weight during walking. And as fine manipulations became more critical for stone tool making, the thumb became opposable and the phalanges shortened. The arm assumed modern human proportions around the time of the origin of *Homo erectus,* and some australopithecines and all *Homo* species have changes to the thumb that suggest fine motor skills.

CONSTRUCTING THE BIPEDAL BODY PLAN

It is easy to make the mistake of thinking that once the shift from quadrupedalism to bipedalism began, it was somehow preordained that an efficient biped would result. But remember that such master plans do not exist in evolution: All the anatomical changes we've discussed occurred like the construction of a mosaic, with interlocking pieces driven by natural selection in every generation. Natural selection drove the evolution of bipedalism because in each subsequent generation once the shift began, each transitional stage conferred survival and reproductive benefits on individuals. The mental image of a shuffling prehominid that was neither an efficient quadruped nor biped is certainly wrong. Instead, in each generation the emerging biped must have been very good at surviving and reproducing, or else natural selection would not have pushed the process further. This strongly suggests that bipedalism arose in a variety of forms and functions, some of which may have died out while others succeeded. Ultimately, one lineage of bipeds—our own—succeeded, and we are the product of that lengthy process.

Master plans do not exist in evolution. In order for bipedality to evolve, in each generation the emerging biped must have a good chance of surviving and reproducing.

LOCOMOTION OF THE LAST COMMON ANCESTOR

Because African apes and humans differ so dramatically in their anatomical adaptations to locomotion, identifying our ancestors in the fossil record is easy. We just

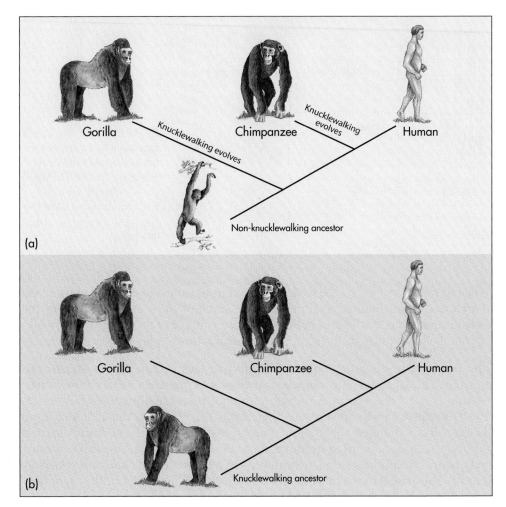

FIGURE 10.10 (a) If the last common ancestor of gorillas, chimpanzees, and humans was not a knucklewalker, then knucklewalking would have evolved independently in both the chimpanzee and gorilla lineages and the ancestral condition for humans is not knuckle-walking. (b) Alternatively, if the last common ancestor of gorillas, chimpanzees, and humans was a knuckle-walker, then the ancestral condition for humans (and the other African apes) is knuckle-walking.

look for the anatomical adaptations to bipedalism. However, scientists disagree as to the most logical precursor of bipedalism. Did the last common ancestor (LCA) of African apes and humans knuckle-walk? Or were they adapted to life in the trees? Sir Arthur Keith (1923) raised the possibility that humans were descended from arboreal apes, not knuckle-walkers (Figure 10.10a). Orangutans walk upright when on slender branches and use their arms to grab branches overhead for balance. New work suggests that such behavior in an early common ancestor would have been an appropriate precursor for bipedality as well as the knuckle-walking and fist-walking practiced by the great apes (Thorpe et al., 2007). Alternatively, although a deeper arboreal ancestor is accepted, other researchers argue that the LCA of chimps and humans was a knuckle-walker (Gebo, 1996; Figure 10.10b).

WHY BIPEDS?

Bipedalism is the basic adaptation of the hominid line, and by now you are probably wondering why bipedalism evolved. What was it about bipedalism that helped our distant ancestors to survive? Were they more energy efficient? Could they get more food? Were they more attractive to mates? Many scenarios have been proposed for what selective pressures favored the origin of bipedalism (Figure 10.11). For purposes of explanation, we can categorize these scenarios as those related to energetics, ecology, diet, and sexual selection. Some of the scenarios overlap.

Energetic Efficiency and Bipedalism   Bipedal walking is a more efficient way of traveling than walking on all fours, at least if we compare human and

Carrying tools, food, or infants

Ecological influences: traveling between trees
or seeing over tall grass

Preadaptation from a change in feeding postures

Provisioning family

Energy efficiency

FIGURE 10.11   Several scenarios for what led to the origin of habitual bipedalism.

chimpanzee walking. Peter Rodman and Henry McHenry (1980) pointed out that although humans do not necessarily walk more efficiently than all quadrupeds, they certainly walk more efficiently than knuckle-walking apes. In other words, if hominids evolved from a knuckle-walking ancestor, then the shift to upright posture would have made perfect energetic sense. Although there is still some argument about the relative efficiency of early hominid walking (see Chapter 11), most studies suggest that bipedal walking (but not running) is a more efficient means of locomotion than knuckle-walking (Leonard & Robertson, 1997).

A second way in which the body plan of a biped may have been more efficient than its ape ancestor is in its ability to dissipate heat. Overheating poses a greater risk to the brain than to other parts of the body. Dean Falk and Glenn Conroy (1983, 1990) suggest that successful hominids in open (unforested) areas had a means of draining blood (the vertebral plexus) that also cooled the brain. In addition, Pete Wheeler (1991) has shown that bipeds dissipate heat faster than quadrupeds because they stand slightly taller above the ground, and when exposed to midday sun they present less surface area to be heated. We discuss these provocative models of bipedal origins in Insights and Advances: Overheated Radiator? on page 299. However, although hominids may have been better at dissipating heat from their bodies and brains than was the LCA, it seems as likely that hominids benefited from these qualities once bipedalism arose for other reasons as it does that bipedalism arose as a solution to overheating.

Ecological Influences and Bipedalism   Ecological models for the origin of bipedalism focus on the role of the changing environment of East Africa between 5 and 8 million years ago that may have placed a premium on the ability to walk upright. In the late Miocene of Africa, grasslands expanded and forests decreased in a response to global cooling and drying. This trend culminated in the widespread savannas we find in East Africa today. More grassland meant greater distances between the food trees protohominids needed for their meals, so they had to forage over longer distances across more open country. With increased travel across open country, natural selection may have driven the evolution of a more energy-efficient mode of transport, namely bipedalism.

Many researchers have observed that standing upright would have offered greater ability to see over tall grass or to scan for potential predators. Gaining a better view of one's surroundings by walking upright has long been advocated as the selective advantage necessary to drive the evolution of bipedalism. But other researchers ask why the enormous changes to the anatomy that allow habitual bipedalism would have taken place, when a brief look over tall grass now and then might have been just as effective without these fundamental anatomical changes.

Dietary Influences on Bipedalism   There may also have been dietary rewards to bipedalism. Perhaps a lineage of fossil apes became bipedal because of the value of standing upright for feeding in fruit trees. In the 1970s and 1980s, Russell Tuttle (1981) developed the idea that the earliest stages of bipedalism may have taken place in the trees, based on his observations of gibbons walking bipedally on tree limbs. About the same time, Clifford Jolly (1970) proposed models of the evolution of upright walking based on observations of the upright posture and short-distance shuffling that some baboons do while feeding on seeds scattered in African grasslands. He argued that such posture might have been a preadaptation to upright stance. In the 1990s, Kevin Hunt proposed that the value of standing upright, both on the forest floor and on tree limbs, was that it made the plucking of small fruits such as figs more efficient. Craig Stanford (2002) also observed chimpanzee bipedal feeding, which occurred mainly on the largest limbs of large fruit trees. The chimpanzees stood on two legs for only a few seconds at a time and for only a few minutes a day. Although differing in detail, these researchers all envision a protohominid that became increasingly bipedal for the feeding advantages that this posture offered, eventually becoming a habitual biped. It is important to note that these scenarios propose that certain feeding postures are important preadaptations for bipedality, but they do not propose that early hominids ate particular food items, such as seeds, only that they took up certain kinds of postures probably while feeding. Whether such feeding benefits would have made the conversion to full-time bipedalism likely is a question that remains unanswered.

Others have argued that bipedality, group size, and body size increased in response to not only the greater patchiness of food resources and the need to walk across open areas to access food but also to the greater risk of being eaten while crossing those areas. In this case, safety in numbers applies to animals crossing savannas, so Lynn Isbell and Truman Young (1996) suggested that one possible response to the increasing patchiness of forests was to increase group size and body size. In such a scenario, the most efficient bipeds are likely to be the ones that survive and reproduce. Isbell and Young saw this as the route taken by early hominids. An alternative route is to stay in forested areas and keep group size small when foraging but to merge groups for mating and other behaviors. Isbell and Young suggested this was the route taken by the chimpanzee lineage, leading to their fusion–fission group form (see Chapter 6).

INSIGHTS AND **ADVANCES**

Overheated Radiator?

Dogs pant when they're hot, slobbering all over your carpet. We sweat, sometimes profusely. A baseball pitcher can lose 10 pounds of body fluid while putting in nine innings on a hot July afternoon. People who lose the ability to sweat (New York Yankee great Whitey Ford had this medical problem late in his career) are in grave danger of lethal overheating. When early humans began to walk upright, their walking no doubt took them out of the forest and into blazing tropical sunshine. Like any other warm-blooded animal, they must have had a way of cooling themselves.

A four-legged animal walking in the hot equatorial sun exposes the expanse of its broad back to the sun, a sure recipe for hyperthermia without some adaptation for rapid, effective heat loss. Many mammals use a complex system of transferring heat from the blood of the arteries being pumped from the heart to the cooler blood of the veins as it returns to the heart. Humans don't possess this system. But, as Pete Wheeler noted, two-legged walkers are in a better position, literally: The sun strikes only the top of their head and shoulders (Figure A). Even the slight height difference between a quadruped's head and that of a biped puts us in significantly cooler air because wind speed is higher and the temperature is cooler than near the ground. Being naked rather than hairy helps too, because hair traps heat.

But standing tall created a new heating problem: the need to get blood up to the head, counter to the force of gravity. Most animals that constantly shift from horizontal to vertical orientations have evolved circulatory system features that combat the pull of gravity. When snakes climb upward, the pattern of blood flow to the head is radically altered by circulatory adaptations, including a forward-positioned heart, designed to keep blood flowing. When a giraffe leans its elegant neck down to a waterhole and then raises it again, special valves, tissue wraps, and pumps prevent blood from pooling in the lower body and boost it up to the head.

When you lie down, blood flowing to the heart drains away from your skull through your neck's jugular veins. But when you stand up, the blood seeks a different escape route through a vast network of veins surrounding the spinal cord. Called the vertebral plexus, this network extends from the skull down to the base of your spine. It diverts blood into the smallest vessels, boosting the blood's flow rate and its capacity to move about the body.

FIGURE A   At midday, the sun only strikes the head and shoulders of this Masai.

Anthropologists Dean Falk and Glenn Conroy applied this knowledge to the human fossil record and found two different methods of draining blood in different fossil lineages. They reasoned that the routing of the circulatory system provides keys to the lives and habitats of earliest humans. When the shift to bipedalism happened, it must have been accompanied by a change in the way blood was moved up and down the now-vertical column of the body.

Falk (1990) suggested that the vertebral plexus evolved to cool down a rapidly expanding brain as emerging humans moved out onto the open, sun-soaked grassland. The idea is provocative: the circulatory system as a radiator designed to keep a growing brain cool, enabling more and more brain expansion in one lineage but not in another. If Falk is right, there were two ways to drain blood from the human skull in prehistory. One option was taken by the early hominids that were direct forerunners of modern people. Another was used by other lineages that went extinct without any descendants. It can thus be used as a test of which species of our ancestors were our direct forbears.

The hypothesis is not without detractors. Both ways of draining the blood can be found in modern people, suggesting that variation between individuals in prehistory may be more important than species-wide differences. And the correlation between species with "radiator" skulls and open-country habitats is not perfect. But as a prime mover hypothesis, the idea has generated a great deal of valuable discussion. (Adapted from Stanford, 2003)

Sexual Selection and Mating Strategies   Lovejoy and other researchers have proposed that bipedalism arose because it conferred mating benefits on protohominids that walked upright. Nina Jablonski and George Chaplin (1993) argued that bipedalism would have been beneficial to males engaging in social displays. Male chimpanzees often stand upright briefly when they assert their dominance over other males during charging displays; upright posture presumably makes a charging male look more impressive. If habitually walking upright made males look more imposing perhaps it also resulted in more mating opportunities. But it is unclear why this benefit would lead to habitual bipedalism and all the accompanying anatomical alterations rather than just a temporary behavioral tactic. In the 1980s, C. Owen Lovejoy proposed a model that tied together information about ancient climate, anatomy, and reproductive physiology to explain the evolution of bipedalism. He argued that the slow reproductive rate of the hominid lineage, like that of many of the fossil ape lineages, would have led to our extinction if we had not found some means of increasing reproduction. He also argued that the evolution of the monogamous mating system offered a way to increase the likelihood of infant survival, and he saw male provisioning of females and their young as critical to this system. However, males needed to ensure their paternity and females needed to ensure continual male support. As forests contracted, males had to walk farther to find food to carry back to the females they were guarding from the attentions of other males. Bipedality raised the energy efficiency of walking and enabled the male to carry food in his arms. Female protohominids did not "announce" they were ovulating through swellings on their rears (as living chimpanzees do) and these females had an advantage in this system because the provisioning male would need to remain in the near vicinity or return constantly to increase his chances of mating when the female was fertile. The female's physiology, thus fortified by the extra nutrition she received from her now-attentive mate, could produce more offspring. The interval between births shortened, and the emerging hominids not only staved off extinction but also invaded a new grassland niche.

A number of faults might be found with Lovejoy's model; for example, bipedality arose millions of years before hominids moved into the grassland niche and the earliest hominids may not have had monogamous mating systems as they were probably highly sexually dimorphic (see Chapter 6). Despite these issues, it is important to emphasize, however, that a complex evolutionary change like bipedality is more likely to be brought about by a web of factors, such as those proposed by Lovejoy, than by a single cause.

A web of natural selective factors was likely to be involved in the origin of bipedality.

The Transition to Human Behavior

How did the behavior of emerging hominids change as they developed more upright posture and a new form of locomotion? Although the behavior of extinct primates is not preserved in their fossilized remains, we can make strong inferences about how they behaved because we have every reason to assume that primates living in the past followed the same guiding principles of natural selection and sexual selection that primates follow today. These inferences allow us to reconstruct diets, modes of locomotion, and other aspects of primate lives that inform us about the ways extinct hominids behaved. Because of the evolutionary relationship between humans and nonhuman primates, we look to the higher primates first when we want to reconstruct aspects of the behavior of our ancestors. In so doing we are using the principle of homology, as discussed in Chapter 4, that shared ancestry allows us to infer how we once used to be. One critical ingredient to the origin of apes and hominids seems to have been brain size increase and, presumably, intelligence. Because brains are so physiologically costly to grow, to understand human evolution we must understand what selected for brain size increase.

PRIMATE INTELLIGENCE: WHY ARE HUMAN BRAINS BIG?

Although many large mammals, such as elephants and whales, have brains larger in absolute size, no mammalian group rivals the higher primates for the ratio of brain to body size. Because brains require a lot of energy to grow, we can be sure there were benefits to the evolution of intelligence that drove brain size and reorganization forward in each successive generation. Exactly how big brains facilitated survival is still unknown.

Scholars have long disagreed about how to define intelligence. The term "intelligent" has very little precise meaning when we speak of animal behavior in particular; does it refer to learning, memory, or some other cognitive factor? Psychologist Richard Byrne (1995), one of the leading researchers in the area of primate intelligence, considers problem-solving capacity to be a measure of intelligence. Problem solving allows primates to respond effectively to novel situations. Throughout history, primates have had to navigate physical and social environments that tested their ability to survive and reproduce. Primate intelligence, Byrne and others argue, is the way natural selection promoted those survival skills. We will consider three competing schools of thought for the origins and evolution of primate intelligence: technical, ecological, and social.

Technical Intelligence and Tool Use   The ability of some nonhuman primates to use tools to extract food and other resources from their natural environment is called **technical intelligence**. Because durable technology is a major hallmark in human evolution, tool use by other primates may offer intriguing clues about the evolution of human intelligence and of culture. As we will see in Chapter 12, human stone tool use dates back at least 2.5 million years. Before that time, however, our most primitive ancestors no doubt fashioned and used tools in much the same way that some great apes do today (Figure 10.12). Early hominids probably made and used biodegradable tools much as the chimpanzees described in the chapter-opening vignette do.

Chimpanzee tools fall into four broad categories: probes to extract insects and other food items, hammers to crack open nuts, sponges to soak up liquids, and branches wielded as weapons against prey or other chimpanzees. Tool use varies

technical intelligence   Hominid intelligence and brain size increase is seen as the result of tool use and extractive foraging.

widely between different chimpanzee populations across Africa. In general, stick probe tools are more commonly found in eastern Africa, and stone hammers are more commonly found in western Africa. However, there is a great deal of variation in the distribution of tool cultures.

Bill McGrew (1992) has done extensive research on patterns of tool use by wild chimpanzees and what they may mean for the advent of human culture. Defining culture as the learned traditions of a group, McGrew considered whether the differences in tool cultures across Africa are the result of genetic differences among chimpanzee populations, environmental differences among the sites, or cultural traditions that differ between sites. He concluded that cultural traditions best explained the diversity of tool cultures. Although there has been genetic differentiation

FIGURE 10.12 Technical intelligence, tool use, and culture may have spurred our intellectual development and favored the ape origin of our large brains.

among African chimpanzee populations, there is no reason to expect that individual tool-using behaviors would be under genetic control, just as cultural traits particular to individual human cultures have no basis in genes. The environmental explanation fails because in many cases the same resources are available in different forests, yet chimpanzee cultures differ across those forests. For example, Gombe National Park is a rock-strewn landscape, yet Gombe chimpanzees do not use rocks as tools. By contrast, the lowland rain forests of western Africa, where chimpanzees use stone tools, have few rocks, and the apes must search for the tools they need. There are also sex differences in chimpanzee tool use. Females at Gombe are more avid termite foragers throughout the year, whereas males tend to fish for termites seasonally (McGrew, 1992). This contrasts with the effort put into acquiring the meat of other mammals, in which males predominate.

Nonhuman primates make and use tools, some of which are fashioned from biodegradable materials that would leave no trace in the archeological record.

Tools are an obvious element of cultural variation among chimpanzees, but they are not the only examples of culture. In a study of the diversity of chimpanzee cultural traditions across several long-term study sites, Whiten and colleagues documented thirty-eight cultural features—not only tool use but also styles of grooming and other behaviors—that occurred consistently across populations and appeared not to be environmentally determined (Whiten et al., 1999).

Not all tool-using primates make their own tools. Indeed, chimpanzees are the most technological of all nonhuman primates by a wide margin. Other primates use simple tools. For example, capuchin monkeys in Central and South America use sticks to gain access to insects and other food items hidden within plants and to break open nuts. Orangutans use simple sticks as probes in tree cavities in much the same way that chimpanzees fish for termites.

The ability to use tools entails some sophisticated cognitive skills. One must be able to use foresight, plan, and be flexible enough to apply the tool to a variety of similar contexts. The invention of the tool may have been the work of a distant ancestor, but in each generation offspring must observe the style and technique of tool use in order to master it. Juvenile capuchins play at breaking open nuts with tools, but adults are far more efficient at accessing this resource, which suggests that this skill takes years to learn. Many scientists think that tool use, production, and transmission over generations indicate a level of sophisticated cognitive skill in primates. However, other scientists disagree.

As important as the use of tools would have been for early humans, there is at least one good reason that technical intelligence probably was not the impetus for hominid origins. The earliest bipeds arose between 5 and 6 million years ago or possibly earlier, but the first stone tools did not appear in the fossil record until 2.5 million years ago. Tool use, beyond the level exhibited by living apes, therefore is unlikely to have played a major role in the origins of bipedal locomotion. And brain size, which Darwin thought was in a feedback loop with bipedalism and tool use, did not expand dramatically until about 300,000 years ago. Until that time, brain expansion was incremental, and it may have been scaled to gradual evolutionary increases in body size (see Chapter 15).

Ecological Intelligence   Models of **ecological intelligence** suggest that the key impetus for the expansion of the brain was the selective advantage of being able to navigate and find food in a highly complex environment. A tropical forest, with its patchy and temporary availability and distribution of fruit, placed a premium on the evolution of large brains, especially in frugivorous species, which had to remember food locations and be able to navigate between them. Although many animals forage in ways that optimize their chances of stumbling onto good food patches—hummingbirds and bumblebees fly optimized routes in fields of wildflowers, for example—primates possess mental maps of the landscape they live in.

ecological intelligence   Hominid intelligence and brain size increase is thought to be a result of benefits of navigating and foraging in a complex tropical forest ecosystem.

Highly frugivorous anthropoid primates may have larger brain-to-body size ratios than folivorous species (Milton, 1981). In African forests, chimpanzees travel from tree to tree, feeding all day long. Many fruit species, such as figs, ripen unpredictably, but a party of chimpanzees usually will be at the tree as soon as ripe fruits appear. This suggests that the apes are monitoring the fruiting status of trees as they forage and remember which trees are worth waiting for (Figure 10.13). Paul Garber (1989) studied callitrichid monkey food-finding abilities in South American rain forests and found that even these little monkeys have the ability to recall the locations of hundreds of potential food trees. We know that nonhuman primates can hold fairly sophisticated information about food items in their heads. Marc Hauser and colleagues (2001) showed that rhesus macaques can count up to three food items, a skill that might be useful when foraging. Charles Menzel (1991) found that monkeys appear to locate food by using a cognitive map that keys on familiar food items.

FIGURE 10.13 The complexity of a tropical forest may have favored the evolution of primate intelligence.

If environmental complexity accounted for the increase in brain size that began with the emergence of the hominids, then the expansion of savanna that occurred in the late Miocene might have been the driving force. As forests became more fragmented, the patchiness of the habitat increased, and emerging hominids with the capacity to navigate through it would have had a selective advantage. However, some scholars have pointed out that many very small-brained animals successfully navigate and forage in the same highly complex environment in which primates were thought to benefit from their large brains. There is no evidence that small mammals such as squirrels are less efficient foragers than primates. In addition, the premise of the ecological complexity argument for hominization, that hominids arose in fragmented forest with patches of open grass, has been questioned in recent years. As we shall see in the coming chapters, some of the earliest discoveries of fossil humans have come from sites that appear to have been forest, not savanna, in the late Miocene and Pliocene.

Social Intelligence   The prevailing view among scientists today is that the brain size increase that occurred in great apes and was extended into hominids resulted from the premium that natural selection placed on individuals that were socially clever. This theory, often called **social intelligence** or Machiavellian intelligence, argues that the primary evolutionary benefit of large brain size was that it allowed apes and hominids to cope with and even exploit increasingly complex social relations. In large social groups, each individual must remember the network of alliances, rivalries, debts, and credits that exist among group members. This is not so different from the politics of our own day-to-day lives. Frans deWaal (1982) has observed that chimpanzees seem to engage in a "service economy" in which they barter alliances and other forms of support with one another.

The individuals best able to exploit this web of social relationships would have reaped more mating success than their group mates. Richard Byrne and Andrew Whiten (1988a, b) point out that the ability to subtly manipulate others is a fundamental aspect of group life. Robin Dunbar (1992) argues that increases in average group size selected for individuals with a larger cerebrum, or neocortex, of the brain as they were better able to handle the additional input of social information. Dunbar observes that small-brained primates, such as strepsirhines, typically live alone or in smaller groups than do most monkeys and apes.

Increasingly complex social relationships may explain the evolutionary advantage of large brains in primates.

social intelligence   Hominid intelligence and brain size increase theorized as a result of benefits of being politically or socially clever when living with others; sometimes called Machiavellian intelligence.

Richard Byrne and Andrew Whiten (1988b) collected examples of potential lying or tactical deception in nonhuman primates and concluded that this behavior was more widespread in higher primates. Great apes seem to be skilled at deceiving one another, whereas lemurs rarely if ever engage in tactical deception. Cheney and Seyfarth observed that vervet monkeys sometimes give a predator alarm call as their group feeds in a desired fruit tree. As other group members flee from the "predator," the call-giver capitalizes on its lie by feeding aggressively. Great apes sometimes use deception to get what they want. Craig Stanford once watched a low-ranking Gombe male chimpanzee named Beethoven use tactical deception to mate with a female, despite the presence of the alpha male, Wilkie. As a party of chimpanzees sat in a forest clearing, Beethoven did a charging display through the middle of the group. Because Beethoven was a low-ranking male, this was taken by the alpha Wilkie as an act of insubordination. As Beethoven charged past Wilkie and into dense thickets, Wilkie pursued and launched into his own display. With Wilkie absorbed in his display of dominance, Beethoven furtively made his way back to the clearing and mated with an eagerly awaiting female.

Why do primate researchers think that deception is at the heart of understanding the roots of human cognition? The reason lies in the nature of intentional deception. In order to lie to someone, you must possess a **theory of mind**. That is, you must be able to place yourself in the mind of another, to understand the other's mental states. The ability to lie, to imitate, and to teach all rely on the assumption that the object of your actions thinks as you do. Whether nonhuman primates possess a human-like theory of mind is a subject of intense debate. Small children develop a theory of mind as they grow up, but not until they are past the age of about 2 years. Of course, to some extent the ability to impute mental states to others around you is a fundamental prerequisite to living in a complex social group. Among primates social dynamics are complex enough that a theory of mind becomes a critical issue.

Here's an example of why it is difficult to determine whether primates have a theory of mind. Michael Tomasello and colleagues set out to determine whether a chimpanzee could imitate the way a person performs a task requiring forethought and planning. He set up an experiment in which one could reach a ball at the end of a table only by inserting a rake through a grate from the opposite end and using the rake to drag the ball (Figure 10.14). When a small child observed this, it took the child only one trial to learn how to get the ball using the rake, and the child perfectly imitated the researcher's demonstration. The chimpanzee also was able to get the ball after watching a single trial. However, the chimp devised its own method of using the rake to obtain the ball, not the style the researcher had demonstrated. Tomasello concluded from this that the chimpanzee failed to imitate the process—even though it could achieve the same result—because it lacked a theory of mind that is necessary for true imitation. Tomasello labeled what the chimpanzee did *emulation*: achieving the goal without understanding the importance of imitating the process. Tomasello and a number of other researchers doubt that chimpanzees possess a theory of mind. But their critics point out that the rake–ball test is conducted in a context highly familiar to many children and utterly unnatural to any chimpanzee. This is a persistent problem for laboratory studies of great apes, primates that evolved cognitive abilities in response to the ecological and social pressures of tropical forest environments, not captive settings. Most laboratories provide severely impoverished social learning environments for their study subjects relative to what children growing up in families experience.

The problem with the social intelligence model as an explanation for the evolution of intelligence among apes and humans is twofold. First, if increasing social

theory of mind Ability to place oneself into the mind of others; necessary for possessing an awareness of the knowledge or cognitive ability of others and for imitating or teaching others.

FIGURE 10.14 Both humans and apes readily engage in learned imitative behavior.

complexity went hand in hand with increasing brain size, then why is the brain-to-body size ratio of early hominids only modestly larger than that of great apes? Second, other animals with much more modest brain size, such as wolves, nevertheless exhibit social dynamics as complex as those seen in nearly all nonhuman primates. At the same time, one of the biggest-brained primates, the orangutan, does not live in large complex groups. In fact, orangutans don't live in groups at all, casting doubt on the ability of the social intelligence school to fully explain the rise of hominid intelligence.

WHAT MADE HUMANS HUMAN?

Although there is no single explanation for the behavioral shift from apes to humans, we can be sure of a few facts. First, the anatomical shift from quadrupedalism came after a behavioral shift began. Whether for feeding or carrying or any other reason, natural selection favored individuals possessing slight anatomical differences that made them better bipeds.

Second, the transition to bipedality happened only because at every stage of the process, natural selection favored the form the evolving protohominid took. At each intermediate stage in our evolution the emerging hominid had to be very good at what it did or bipedalism and increasing brain size would not have been the result. We can be sure that the earliest hominids were agile, powerful creatures, combining elements of ape and human behavior and morphology. Even if they were not as efficient at walking upright as modern people are, they were, without doubt, highly effective foragers.

Third, although we have focused on both bipedalism and intelligence in this chapter, at the earliest stages of hominid evolution brain size and intelligence were quite apelike. Paleoanthropologists debate exactly when hominids became more like people than like apes, but certainly the very earliest hominids (and also the australopithecines we will discuss in Chapter 11) retained ape-sized brains. Terry Deacon (1990) points out that the notion of linear progression in brain size from the most primitive to the brainiest primates is largely a fiction. Deacon's research on primate brains showed that a good deal of the variation in brain-to-body size ratio in the Primate order results from body size differences between taxa, with the brain being scaled in size accordingly, rather than from natural selection operating directly on brain size itself. The bigger-is-naturally-better notion may be the product of outdated thinking about the evolution of intelligence. Natural selection will select for a bigger brain only if other, less costly solutions are not available. Only in the hominid lineage, and only relatively late in time, does this happen.

We have now examined several models that seek to explain why primates are intelligent. Earlier in the chapter we considered some models to explain the origin of bipedalism. From this foundation we turn, in Part IV, to the hard evidence for human evolution, the fossils themselves.

SUMMARY

1. **What effect did the shift to bipedal posture have on human birth?**

   The requirements of habitual bipedal posture select for a narrow pelvis, but this need must be balanced by the need to accommodate wide shoulders and eventually large human brain sizes. The shape of the human pelvis reflects this balance, as does the rotational means of giving birth, in which the baby rotates in the birth canal.

2. **How does the foot skeleton differ between a biped and a knuckle-walker?**

   The foot of a biped has more robust bones for greater weight bearing, which are more tightly bound together by ligaments (less flexible). The big toe is enlarged and in line with the other toes, all of which are shortened. The tarsals form two arches that serve as shock absorbers.

3. **What is the "radiator" model?**

   This model suggests that hominids evolved a special blood drainage system that facilitated cooling of their enlarged brains as they walked on the savanna.

4. **What is *ecological intelligence*?**

   Ecological intelligence models suggest that the key impetus for the expansion of the hominid brain was the selective advantage of being able to navigate and find food in a highly complex environment.

5. **What is a *theory of mind*?**

   To have a theory of mind is to have the ability to place yourself in the mind of another, to be able to understand the other's mental states. The ability to lie, to imitate, and to teach relies on the assumption that the object of your actions thinks as you do.

CRITICAL THINKING QUESTIONS

1. Evolution by natural selection is all about tradeoffs: One trait is enhanced, but another connected trait is compromised as a result. What were some of the tradeoffs that accompanied the evolution of bipedal posture?

2. Many scenarios have been put forward to explain the origin of bipedalism. Which one do you favor and why? Are there elements to a successful model, apart from the factual evidence, that may explain why it is accepted and others are not?

3. You've read about the three leading schools of thought to explain the rise of intelligence: technical, ecological, and social. But are these mutually exclusive? Explain why or why not.

4. Do you think human cognitive abilities are an extension of those of nonhuman primates? Or have humans made an evolutionary break from our primate past in some way? If so, in what way?

KEY TERMS

vertebral column	foramen magnum	pubis	phalanges
cervical vertebrae	nuchal plane	gluteal muscles	technical intelligence
thoracic vertebrae	innominate bones	acetabulum	ecological intelligence
lumbar vertebrae	(os coxae)	femoral condyles	social intelligence
sacrum	ischium	tarsals	theory of mind
coccyx	ilium	metatarsals	

SUGGESTED READING

Byrne, Richard W. (1995). *The Thinking Ape.* Oxford University Press, Oxford, UK.

Meldrum, Jeff E., and Hilton, Charles E. (2004). *From Biped to Strider: The Emergence of Modern Human Walking, Running, and Resource Transport.* Kluwer, Dordrecht, the Netherlands.

Savage-Rumbaugh, Sue, and Lewin, Roger. (1996). *Kanzi: The Ape at the Brink of the Human Mind.* Wiley-Liss, New York.

Stanford, Craig B. (2003). *Upright.* Houghton Mifflin, Boston.

The sky was hazy as the sun began to lower in the distance. The small hominids coughed slightly as they breathed the dusty air, the result of a burping volcanic eruption earlier in the day. They looked around furtively for a stand of trees and began moving toward them. Night would fall sooner than usual given the volcanic haze, and predators were sure to be on the move. A light rain began falling, dampening the ash layer that covered the ground like a dusting of snow. Two hominids walking side by side were followed by a third as they moved toward the relative safety of the trees. Other animals moved about as well, disturbing the pristine ash fall. Gazing back over her shoulder briefly a young hominid watched the tracks they made, tracks similar to those you and I would make on a wet sand beach. She worried slightly that this strange new trail would give them away. Little did she know how permanent the trail would be, with the ash drying to a hard cement and future explosions soon covering the lot and immortalizing her journey.

Millions of years later in the 1970s, a team of paleontologists led by Mary Leakey was unwinding by tossing a "Frisbee" at Laetoli in northern Tanzania, not far from Olduvai Gorge. There, Paul Abell, a geochemist with the group, found the first evidence of the fossilized footprint trail that would ultimately yield the long-buried prints of those early hominids, probably *Australopithecus afarensis*. The tracks were well preserved and dated to about 3.6 to 3.7 million years ago. They told of a small but capable biped weighing 77 to 88 pounds walking toward something.

THE FOOTPRINT TRAIL MADE BY THIS SMALL GROUP of hominids in the early Pliocene provides scientists with clues about the anatomy and behavior of our earliest ancestors. In this chapter we examine the fossil record for early hominids, beginning around 7 million years ago. We explore the adaptations of the very earliest hominids and how we recognize their fossils as such. Then we explore the radiation of the genus *Australopithecus,* whose species exhibit a diverse array of dietary adaptations and favored habitats. One species of the genus is likely to have given rise to our genus, *Homo.* At the end of the chapter we consider who the likely candidates are for the last common ancestor of *Homo* and set the stage for Chapters 12 through 14, in which we explore the evolution of our own genus.

Will You Know a Hominid When You See One?

Hominids are the family of primates that includes humans and our ancestors since diverging from the last common ancestor with chimpanzees, about 6 million years ago. (Currently, there is a debate over the best name for this group; the traditional classification we use calls them *hominids*, but classifications based on molecular evidence call them *hominins* [Insights and Advances: A Rose by Any other Name: Hominids versus Hominins]). Recognizing a hominid in the fossil record isn't always easy because all we have to work with are fossilized skeletal remains. Early in the hominid record we look for evidence of the fundamental adaptation of the lineage. In Chapter 10 we discussed the anatomical characters that distinguish bipeds (humans) from quadrupeds (apes), and we can use these features to recognize the fossilized remains of bipeds, and hence, hominids.

In addition to skeletal differences due to bipedality, features of the skull and dentition also differ between humans and apes. We infer that a fossil possessing the human condition of these traits, or an intermediate condition tending toward the human

INSIGHTS AND ADVANCES

A Rose by Any Other Name: Hominids versus Hominins

The traditional classification system of the hominoids—hominids, the great apes, and the lesser apes—is based on morphological characteristics. The superfamily Hominoidea contains three families: the Hominidae, Pongidae, and Hylobatidae (Figure A Part (a)). In this system the Hominidae, or hominids, are humans and our extinct ancestors; the Pongidae includes the great apes; and the Hylobatidae are the lesser apes. This system reflects how startlingly different we bipeds are from our closest quadrupedal relatives. However, genetic distances suggest a slightly different classification system. Recall from Chapter 9 that genetically, humans and chimpanzees are more closely related to one another than either is to gorillas. Therefore, humans and chimps should be grouped together, despite their morphological differences. And both African apes are more closely related to humans than either is to orangutans.

A new classification system that reflects these genetic distances is growing in scientific popularity (Figure B Part (b)). In this grouping the superfamily Hominoidea includes two families: Hominidae and Hylobatidae. The Hominidae includes humans and our extinct ancestors as well as great apes and their ancestors. Within the family Hominidae are two subfamilies that separate the African apes including ourselves (Homininae) from the orangutans (Ponginae) because of our genetic differences. And within the subfamily Homininae humans and our ancestors are in the tribe hominini, or hominins for short. In this book we use the more traditional classification system and call humans and our exclusive ancestors hominids because this is the way that most of the current literature is constructed. But you should be aware that the use of *hominins* is on the rise.

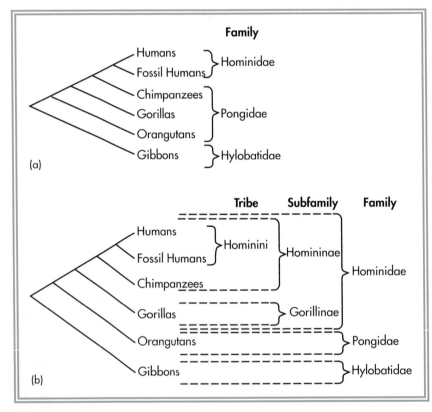

FIGURE A   Taxonomic classification of hominins versus hominids. (a) A traditional classification system recognizes only humans and our fossil ancestors in the family Hominidae, which we refer to as hominids. (b) A classification system that reflects molecular relationships groups African great apes and humans together at the subfamily level in the Homininae and humans and our ancestors in the tribe hominini or hominins.

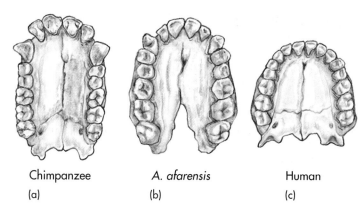

Chimpanzee
(a)

A. afarensis
(b)

Human
(c)

FIGURE 11.1   (a) Chimpanzees and other great apes have large incisors and projecting canines, a diastema, and U-shaped dental arcades caused by parallel rows of cheek teeth. (b) Early hominids like *A. afarensis* have relatively smaller canines, little or no diastema, and a less U-shaped arcade with a still-shallow palate. (c) Modern humans have very small canines, no diastema, and a parabolic dental arcade.

homodont   Having teeth that are uniform in form, shape, and function.

heterodont   Tooth array in which different teeth have different forms and functions.

CP₃ (sectorial premolar complex)   Combination of canine and first premolar teeth that forms a self-sharpening apparatus.

australopithecines   The common name for members of the genus *Australopithecus*.

condition, is a hominid. For example, the modern human dental arcade is shaped differently than an ape's. The human tooth row forms a rounded, parabolic arch reflecting the smaller anterior teeth (canines and incisors) and posterior teeth (premolars and molars). The dental arcade of a primate with large canines, such as an ape or baboon, is broader in front (Figure 11.1) and U-shaped, with the teeth behind the canines forming two parallel rows. Early hominids tend to have somewhat smaller anterior teeth than such primates, but the arcade remains relatively U-shaped. In addition to changing the shape of the dental arcade, large anterior teeth also contribute to greater *facial prognathism*, the degree to which the face projects in front of the braincase. Like that of apes, the face of most early hominids is relatively prognathic.

The sizes and shapes of the teeth also differ between apes and humans. Lower vertebrates such as lizards and fish tend to have a **homodont** dentition, teeth that all look alike and serve essentially the same purpose: grabbing and bolting down food. Mammals are distinct in possessing a **heterodont** dentition; they have an array of different types of teeth in the mouth, each with a different function. The typical pattern in living primates is two incisors, one canine, two or three premolars, and three molars in each quadrant. As we saw in Chapter 6, the form and function of these four types of teeth differ depending on the primate group.

One aspect of the dental pattern that paleoanthropologists use to differentiate fossil apes from fossil hominids is the **CP₃**, or **sectorial premolar complex** (Figure 11.2). In a monkey or ape, the enormous canines of the upper jaw (the maxilla) must fit into a space or *diastema* in the tooth row of the lower jaw (the mandible) where they slide past the third premolar, hence the name *CP₃* for the area. (This premolar is called P₃, even though in an ape it is the first premolar in the tooth row, because the first and second premolars were lost during evolution.) The back of the upper canine is sharpened, or honed, by the bladelike or sectorial P₃. As canines shorten during evolution, the blade on P₃ disappears and the tooth changes from having one cusp to having two. The very earliest **australopithecines** show some reduction of the canine, the absence or reduction of a diastema, and at least partial loss of the CP₃ honing complex, often including the presence of a two-cusped P₃.

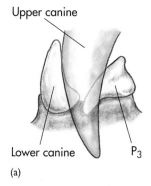

Upper canine

Lower canine   P₃

(a)

(b)

FIGURE 11.2   (a) A canine/premolar or CP₃ honing complex consists of a large, projecting upper canine passing across the bladelike edge of the lower premolar. Hominids lose this complex as the anterior teeth decrease in size. (b) Monkeys and apes such as this chimpanzee can be recognized in the fossil record by the anatomy of their teeth.

Another aspect of the teeth that differs between humans and apes is the thickness of the enamel, the white outer coating of our teeth. African apes have thin enamel, but our enamel is thick. All but the earliest hominids have somewhat thicker enamel than do apes, and this character has often been used to identify hominids. However, thicker enamel probably arose several different times during primate evolution as an adaptation to the kinds of foods a group was eating, so the presence of thick enamel alone does not guarantee that we are looking at a hominid tooth.

Apes and humans also differ in brain size, cranial proportions, and cranial cresting. Although early hominids possessed essentially ape-sized brains, throughout hominid evolution brain size increases while facial size decreases. This change in proportions reflects both a de-emphasis of the masticatory (chewing) system and an emphasis on brain size and probably intelligence (see Chapter 15). In early hominids this de-emphasis results in the loss of **cranial crests** in one lineage and, as a result, a more rounded braincase. The decrease in facial size also reflects the change in the size and shape of the teeth described previously.

So fossil hominids, including human ancestors since the split from the chimpanzee lineage, can be recognized by anatomical characters related to bipedalism and by reduction of the canine teeth and CP_3 complex and changes in palate shape. The very earliest of the hominids show these features to only a very slight degree and therefore are often difficult to differentiate from fossil apes. Other changes that we associate with humans, such as our very large brain and extremely small face and jaws, appear later in human evolution.

The First Hominids?

The majority of the fossil evidence of the earliest hominids has come from the Great Rift Valley of East Africa, a broad expanse that runs north to south from the Horn of Africa at the Red Sea southward to Zambia (Figure 11.3). The valley contains a series of ancient volcanoes and a string of lakes—Lake Victoria, Lake Turkana, Lake Tanganyika, and Lake Malawi, among others—that are often called the Great Lakes of Africa. The Rift Valley's tectonic history resulted in the creation and disappearance of lakes and streams during hominid evolution. These waterways provided likely habitats for species of early hominids, and the volcanic sediments allow radiometric assessment of fossil ages.

During the later Miocene (10–5.5 million years ago) and early Pliocene (5.5–4 million years ago) at least one lineage of apes made the adaptive shift to a terrestrial niche and became increasingly bipedal. The shift to bipedality came about partly in response to major climatic changes that were occurring in equatorial Africa in the late Miocene. This shift was accompanied by anatomical changes to the pelvis, spinal column, and other body systems of hominids.

Molecular evidence suggests that the first signs of hominization should appear in lineages of late Miocene apes. Unfortunately, between 10 and 6 million years ago, the fossil record for the roots of the Hominidae is poorly represented. Between 7 and 4.4 million years ago, we have several candidates for the site of the earliest

cranial crests Bony ridges on the skull to which muscles attach.

TABLE 11.1	Candidates for the Earliest Hominid (all could be fossil apes)	
Site	**MYA***	**Species**
Toros-Menalla, Chad	7.0–5.2	*Sahelanthropus tchadensis*
Tugen Hills, Kenya	6.0	*Orrorin tugenensis*
Middle Awash, Ethiopia	5.8–5.2	*Ardipithecus kadabba*
Lothagam, Kenya	5.8	??
Tabarin, Kenya	5.0	??
Aramis, Ethiopia	4.4	*Ardipithecus ramidus*

*MYA = millions of years ago

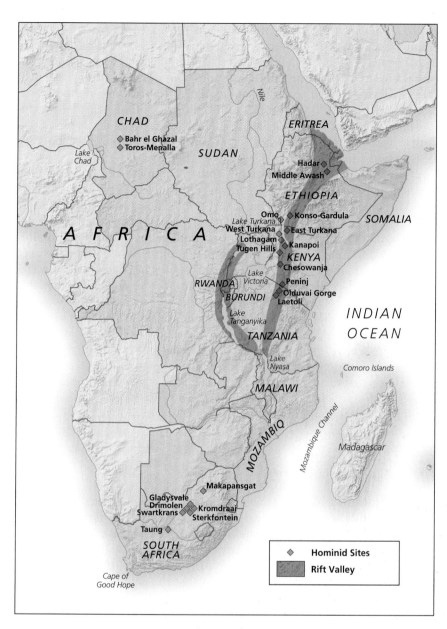

FIGURE 11.3 Geographic distribution of early hominids. Hominids are limited to the continent of Africa until about 1.7 million years ago. Some of the important sites for australopithecine and other early hominid fossils are located on the map. Although most known sites are in eastern and southern Africa, *Australopithecus* likely inhabited most of the African continent.

hominid remains, but all or some of them may represent fossil apes rather than hominids. Some of these sites (Lothagam, Tabarin, Djurab, and Tugen Hills) have produced evidence too fragmentary for an unambiguous answer. The others (Aramis and several Middle Awash sites) have produced a plethora of remains, but the analysis of the material is still in progress (Table 11.1). Two recently discovered fossils from 7 to 6 million years ago may be the very earliest hominid remains known. However, both have generated much debate, and whether they are primitive hominids or fossil apes remains to be determined.

SAHELANTHROPUS TCHADENSIS (7.0–6.0 MYA)

A French expedition led by Michel Brunet discovered a fossilized skull, which the team nicknamed Toumai ("hope of life"), in the sands of the Djurab Desert in northern Chad in 2001 (Brunet et al., 2002) (Figure 11.4 on page 314). Formally named *Sahelanthropus tchadensis* ("the Sahara hominid from Chad"), the fossil was

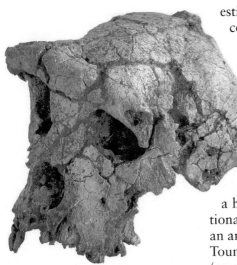

FIGURE 11.4 The skull of *Sahelanthropus tchadensis* is argued to be the earliest of the hominids and one of only two species known from western Africa. The significance of the specimen is still hotly debated.

estimated to be between 5.2 and 7 million years old based on biostratigraphic correlations with East African sites, with 6–7 million years considered most likely by Brunet. This age would make it the oldest member of the Hominidae. Toumai would also be the oldest hominid found west of the Great Rift Valley of East Africa; a jaw fragment assigned to *Australopithecus bahrelghazali*, also found by Brunet, dates to about 3 million years ago and is the only other hominid from Chad. The site where Toumai was found was a dry, lightly forested area near a lakeshore in the late Miocene, when *S. tchadensis* lived.

The Toumai fossil consists of a fairly complete skull, mandibular fragments, and isolated teeth. Surprisingly, the face is less prognathic than expected for an early hominid. Other characters that argue for Toumai being a hominid are a large browridge, somewhat smaller canine teeth, a non-functional CP_3 honing complex, no diastema, a horizontal nuchal plane, and possibly an anteriorly placed foramen magnum, which may indicate bipedality. However, Toumai also exhibits a number of apelike characters, including small brain size (cranial capacity is 320–380 cc), a U-shaped dental arcade, and somewhat thin enamel (but intermediate between chimps and *Australopithecus*). Milford Wolpoff, Brigitte Senut, and Martin Pickford (2002) argue that Toumai is nothing more than a fossil ape that was deformed after burial. They point out that large female apes (such as gorillas) can have small canine teeth. Alternatively, some of those who accept Toumai as a hominid prefer to place it in the genus *Ardipithecus*, thus making it closely related to the somewhat later hominids from Ethiopia. In either case, Toumai is profoundly important because it fills key gaps in the fossil record of 6 to 7 million years ago and may push the distribution of fossil hominids far to the west of the Rift Valley.

ORRORIN TUGENENSIS (6.0 MYA)

In 2001, Martin Pickford and Brigitte Senut announced the discovery of "Millennium Man" (Pickford & Senut, 2001), so named because the discovery was made in the year 2000. The approximately 6-million-year-old fossils were found in the Lukeino formation of the Tugen Hills of Kenya and consist of fragmentary cranial and postcranial remains, most importantly multiple femoral (thigh bone) fragments (Figure 11.5). Pickford and Senut thought that the new fossils were so different from other known hominids that they chose a new genus name, *Orrorin tugenensis* ("hominid from the Tugen Hills"). They argue that *Orrorin* is a hominid because of a suite of postcranial characters that indicate it was a biped, but the anatomy of the femur and the arm are not conclusive indicators of bipedality. The remains do indeed indicate a larger body size than expected for a late Miocene ape and internal femur anatomy may support bipedality (Galik et al., 2004). Also linking *Orrorin* to the hominids is the fact that its small teeth possess thick enamel. However, the upper canine is large and a bit more apelike. Because we typically define hominids based on anatomy related to bipedality, more fossilized remains will be needed before we can make a final determination about the place of *Orrorin tugenensis* in the hominoid family tree.

ARDIPITHECUS RAMIDUS (4.4 MYA) AND ARDIPITHECUS KADABBA (5.8–5.2 MYA)

In 1994, an international team led by Tim White, Berhane Asfaw, and Gen Suwa, announced the discovery of fossilized remains of a very primitive hominid in the northeastern part of Ethiopia near the Red Sea (Figure 11.6). In the Middle Awash region of an ancient river delta called the Afar Triangle the group collected fossils at a site called Aramis (see Insights and Advances: Treasures of the Afar Triangle

The earliest hominids may be difficult to recognize because they are close in both time and anatomy to our last common ancestor with chimpanzees.

FIGURE 11.5 Brigitte Senut exhibits a femur of *Orrorin tugenensis*. Discovered in 2000, "Millenium Man" may be among the oldest of the hominids, although its taxonomic position is still debated.

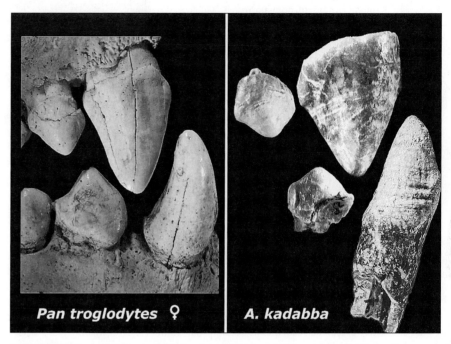

Pan troglodytes ♀   *A. kadabba*

FIGURE 11.6 *Ardipithecus kadabba* has large canine teeth that are only slightly smaller than those of living apes. The oldest of the Ethiopian hominids at 5.7 million years old, *A. kadabba* was ancestral to the 4.4 million-year-old *A. ramidus* and perhaps the rest of the hominid lineage.

on page 316). In the late Miocene and early Pliocene, Aramis had been a dense forest inhabited by ancestors of modern colobine monkeys and forest antelopes. This is very interesting because we expected to find the earliest hominids living in open savanna habitat, not closed forests similar to those in which apes live today (see Chapter 10).

Ardipithecus ramidus ("ground-living root hominid") is a primitive hominid. The presence of more primitive traits than *Australopithecus*, including thinner enamel and less postcanine enlargement or **megadontia**, led the Middle Awash team to assign the fossils to a new genus, *Ardipithecus*. The Middle Awash group argued that *Ardipithecus* was a hominid on the basis of its somewhat smaller canine and the anterior position of its foramen magnum, which may indicate it was bipedal. The researchers noted that the arm bears similarities to both bipeds and quadrupeds, and they could not definitively say how *Ardipithecus* had walked. In addition, the molars are apelike in size and have intermediate enamel thickness between apes and humans. The bipedal nature and hominid status of *A. ramidus* are still questioned by some scientists. There seems to be more certainty that *A. ramidus* was a biped and therefore a more likely candidate for the stem hominid than either *Orrorin* or *Sahelanthropus*, but the possibility remains that *A. ramidus* may not be directly ancestral to later hominids.

In 2004, the same team that discovered *A. ramidus* announced new specimens they considered minor (subspecific) variants of *A. ramidus* that had lived much earlier, around 5.7 to 5.8 million years ago. On the basis of the species' more apelike

megadontia Enlarged teeth.

Treasures of the Afar Triangle

The Afar Triangle of northeastern Ethiopia (Figure A) is among the most famous of hominid fossil-bearing regions. It is not unique in the sheer quantity of fossils it has produced; the Gobi Desert of Mongolia has far more dinosaurs and early mammals, for example. But the Afar has produced the most extensive record of human evolution, including examples from the earliest days of the Hominidae until the dawn of modern people.

Today the Afar is a dry, dusty badlands that features baking hot days, chilly nights, and a stark, otherworldly landscape. But between 6 and 2 million years ago, the Afar was a fertile valley, the delta of a great river called the Awash, which flowed through the region en route to the sea. It is in and around the Awash that the most exciting finds have been made.

In 1972, Maurice Taieb led Donald Johanson to an unexplored site in the Afar called Hadar (from *Ahda'ar,* or "treaty stream" in the local Afar language). This 20-km² region holds an exquisitely preserved record of hominid evolution. In late 1973 Johanson made the first major discovery, the fossil knee of an unknown primitive hominid that was later dated to 3.0 million years ago. In late 1974, during a follow-up expedition his team discovered more fossils, including the now-famous Lucy. Then in 1975, Johanson's team unearthed the "First Family," a group of at least 13 individuals of Lucy's species, *Australopithecus afarensis.* In the three decades since, *A. afarensis* has become the best known of the early hominids and in 2006 the spectacular partial skeleton of an *A. afarensis* child was discovered from the

FIGURE A Location of the Afar triangle.

nearby Dikika region (Innovations: Dikika and Development on page 322).

Not far from Hadar, the international Middle Awash team including Tim White, Berhane Asfaw, Giday WoldeGabriel, and Gen Suwa discovered new hominids in the early 1990s and 2000s. *Ardipithecus ramidus* and *A. kadabba* lived in the then forested Afar some 1.5 to 3 million years before *Australopithecus afarensis* roamed there.

More recent hominids and their artifacts have also been found in the Afar. In the late 1990s, the Middle Awash team found the earliest evidence of hominid meat-eating and butchery at Bouri, only 40 miles from Hadar. The fossilized remains of a 2.5-million-year-old hominid, named *Australopithecus garhi,* were found just a short distance from butchered antelope remains.

In 2000–2001, Ethiopian paleoanthropologist Sileshi Semaw's team found the oldest known stone tools at Gona, dated to about

2.6 million years ago (see Chapter 12). The team also found a nearly complete cranium of a 1.5 to 2.0-million-year-old hominid of the genus *Homo,* and numerous other hominid remains. More recently, a nearby site, Dana Aoule, has yielded stone tools that may be even older than those from Gona. From younger levels of the geological strata have come hand axes and remains of *Homo erectus* from 1.5 to 1.0 million years ago, as well as the famous Bodo specimen of a hominid that appears transitional between *Homo erectus* and more modern *Homo sapiens* (see Chapters 12 and 13).

The Afar was also home to some of the very earliest members of our species, *Homo sapiens.* In 1997, the Middle Awash team discovered 160,000-year-old specimens of early modern humans, from Herto (see Chapter 14). The skulls from Herto form the recent end of an amazing spectrum of human use of the Afar region extending from the dawn of humankind to the near present.

dentition, the researchers have proposed elevating the former variant of *A. ramidus* called *A. r. kadabba* to its own species, *Ardipithecus kadabba.* These finds by Yohannes Haile-Selassie and colleagues have expanded our understanding of the range of variation in *A. ramidus,* and their anatomy and age suggest to some that the genera *Orrorin* and *Sahelanthropus* should be lumped into the genus

Ardipithecus (Haile-Selassie et al., 2004a). All early hominids would be defined by absence of a functional CP_3 honing complex.

Australopithecus and Kin

Recognizing the very earliest members of a group in the fossil record is difficult because the record is fragmentary and incomplete. Also the more ancient the ancestor, the less it will look like its living descendants. So it will be very hard to differentiate an early hominid from an ape, for example. The first hominids discussed previously fall into this nebulous category.

However, most of the early members of the Hominidae do not suffer from this ambiguity and are assigned to the genus *Australopithecus*. The name *Australopithecus*, meaning "southern ape," was coined by Raymond Dart in the 1920s for the very first specimen of the genus ever discovered. Since that time, discoveries of australopithecines have revealed an adaptive radiation of early hominids that filled a variety of habitat types in eastern, southern, and central Africa and are now known to have lived from 4.2 to about 1.0 million years ago. The genus *Australopithecus* includes species of bipedal apes that are small bodied (64–100 pounds) and small brained (340–500 cc), had moderately prognathic faces, and a mosaic of primitive and derived craniodental anatomy (Figure 11.7).

Scientists disagree a bit over the composition of the genus; the newly described genus *Kenyanthropus* has been proposed for one species that other scientists include in *Australopithecus*, and many researchers assign *A. robustus* and *A. boisei* to the genus *Paranthropus*.

As we discover new specimens and new taxa, we will no doubt expand both the geographic distribution and the time span for this group and raise additional questions about their origins and descendants (Figure 11.8 on page 318).

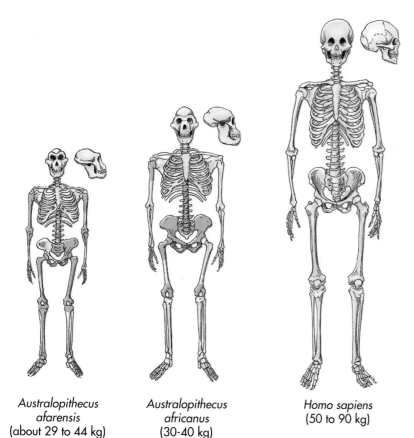

Australopithecus afarensis (about 29 to 44 kg)

Australopithecus africanus (30-40 kg)

Homo sapiens (50 to 90 kg)

FIGURE 11.7 Comparison of hominid skeletons. The australopithecines (left) were short bipedal primates most with relatively long arms and short legs. Compared to modern humans (right) the australopithecine torso was broad and funnel shaped.

Early Hominid Evolution

FIGURE 11.8   The earliest hominids appeared around 6 million years ago in western and eastern Africa. About 4 million years ago *Australopithecus*, a bipedal genus characterized by small brains, large jaws, and small body size arose. *Australopithecus* is probably the first stone tool maker, and one species is likely to have given rise to *Homo*.

Several species of the genus overlapped with one another in time and space, probably avoiding competition by relying on slightly different food resources. In one lineage, the robust australopithecines (*A. aethiopicus, A. robustus* and *A. boisei*), several species evolved massive jaws, molar teeth, and cranial skeletons optimized for producing large chewing forces. These hominids probably relied on hard to open food items during times of nutritional stress.

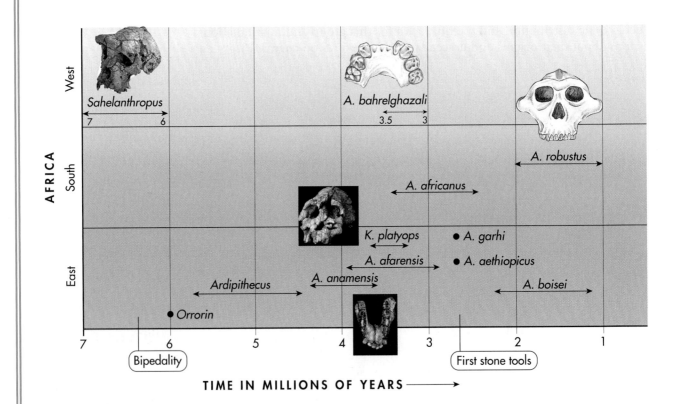

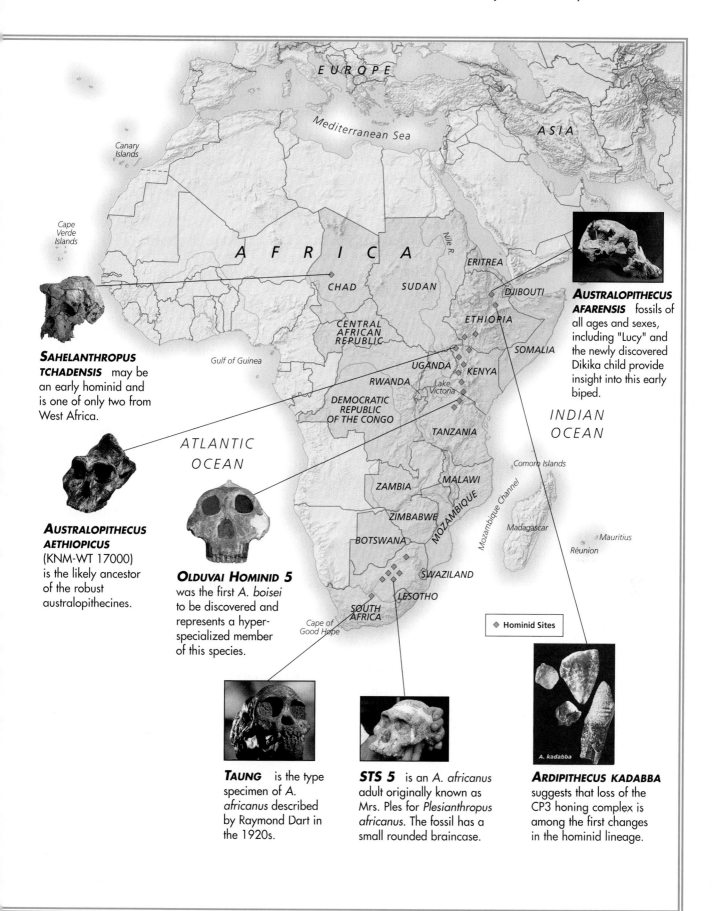

SAHELANTHROPUS TCHADENSIS may be an early hominid and is one of only two from West Africa.

AUSTRALOPITHECUS AETHIOPICUS (KNM-WT 17000) is the likely ancestor of the robust australopithecines.

OLDUVAI HOMINID 5 was the first *A. boisei* to be discovered and represents a hyper-specialized member of this species.

AUSTRALOPITHECUS AFARENSIS fossils of all ages and sexes, including "Lucy" and the newly discovered Dikika child provide insight into this early biped.

◆ Hominid Sites

TAUNG is the type specimen of *A. africanus* described by Raymond Dart in the 1920s.

STS 5 is an *A. africanus* adult originally known as Mrs. Ples for *Plesianthropus africanus*. The fossil has a small rounded braincase.

ARDIPITHECUS KADABBA suggests that loss of the CP3 honing complex is among the first changes in the hominid lineage.

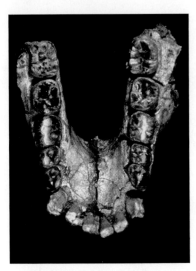

FIGURE 11.9   The remains of *Australopithecus anamensis* from Kenya date to about 3.9 to 4.2 million years old.

AUSTRALOPITHECUS ANAMENSIS (4.2–3.9 MYA)

Around 4 million years ago several similar forms appeared roughly simultaneously. The oldest and most primitive of these is *Australopithecus anamensis* (Figure 11.9). Announced in 1995, *A. anamensis* ("southern ape of the lake") was discovered by a team led by Meave Leakey. At separate sites near Lake Turkana, Kanapoi, and Allia Bay, Leakey's team uncovered dozens of cranial and postcranial bone fragments, dating to 4.2 to 3.9 million years ago.

Other remains, discovered in 1965 by a Harvard University excavation, have also been assigned to this species. Associated fossils of fish and aquatic animals indicate that both Allia Bay and Kanapoi were streamside forests in the early Pliocene, when *A. anamensis* roamed the area.

Australopithecus anamensis provides the earliest incontrovertible evidence of bipedality. In particular, its tibia has thickened bone at its proximal and distal ends, where bipeds place stress on their lower legs. Furthermore, the tibial plateau, where the tibia meets the femur, is enlarged as the result of the greater weight bearing experienced by the bipedal lower limb.

The *A. anamensis* teeth and jaws are more primitive than those of later hominids but more derived than those of early hominids such as *Ardipithecus*. The dental arcade is U-shaped, with parallel sides and large anterior teeth, and the palate is shallow, all features that are more apelike than human. Although the canine is smaller than in *Ardipithecus*, the root of the canine is longer and more robust in *A. anamensis* than in *Australopithecus afarensis*, and there is a distinct CP_3 complex, but the molars of *A. anamensis* are shorter and broader. As in later australopithecines, the molar enamel of *A. anamensis* is distinctly thicker than in the more primitive *Ardipithecus ramidus*, all characters that make *A. anamensis* a hominid.

In many respects, the fossils of *A. anamensis* strongly resemble those of *A. afarensis*, and some researchers think the two species should be considered one and the same. However, *A. anamensis* is more primitive than *A. afarensis*, especially in aspects of the mandible and dentition, and this led Leakey's team to assign the fossils to a new hominid species. These two species seem to be good examples of an ancestral-descendant lineage (Alemseged et al., 2006).

AUSTRALOPITHECUS AFARENSIS (3.9–2.9 MYA)

In 1974 Donald Johanson and his team discovered Lucy, the famed skeleton of *Australopithecus afarensis*, at Hadar in the Awash Valley of the Afar Triangle of Ethiopia (see Insights and Advances: Treasures of the Afar Triangle on page 316). The discovery of the diminutive A.L. 288-1 (Lucy's museum catalog number) was extraordinary for two reasons. First, her anatomy is more primitive than that of any hominid discovered up to that time, and it includes a clear mosaic of human-like and apelike features. She stood a little over a meter tall and possessed a cranial vault suggesting a modest brain size about equal to that of an adult chimpanzee.

Second, her skeleton is more complete than that of nearly any other fossil human. Although more primitive hominids have been discovered since, none is nearly so well studied, and *A. afarensis* has remained the benchmark by which the anatomy of all other early hominids is interpreted. In addition to Lucy, thousands of finds of *A. afarensis* have been made in the Afar and other East African localities in the past 30 years, including the 2006 discovery of a child's partial skeleton near Dikika in the Afar (see Innovations: Dikika and Development on pages 322–323). In fact, the **type specimen** of the species, the specimen that according to the laws of zoological nomenclature serves as the original anatomical reference for the species, is the LH 4 mandible from Laetoli, Tanzania.

type specimen   According to the laws of zoological nomenclature, the anatomical reference specimen for the species definition.

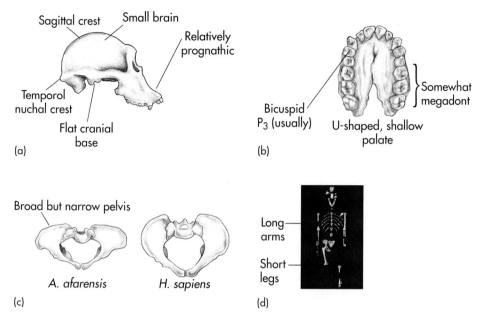

(a)
Sagittal crest
Small brain
Relatively prognathic
Temporol nuchal crest
Flat cranial base

(b)
Bicuspid P3 (usually)
U-shaped, shallow palate
Somewhat megadont

(c)
Broad but narrow pelvis
A. afarensis
H. sapiens

(d)
Long arms
Short legs

FIGURE 11.10 Key features of *Australopithecus afarensis* include (a) a small cranial capacity, and cranial crests (b) a shallow, U-shaped palate with reduced canines and (c, d) features of the postcranial skeleton that indicate habitual bipedality.

There are several key anatomical features of *A. afarensis* (Figure 11.10), some of which are shared with *A. anamensis* suggesting the two species form a lineage. The cranium and teeth of *A. afarensis* are intermediate in appearance between those of a living ape and a modern human. The cranial capacity is small but slightly larger than that of earlier hominids and living apes (range 350–500 cc).

A complete skull recovered by Bill Kimbel and Don Johanson shows that the *A. afarensis* face was prognatic, but not as much as that of the living apes, and the cranial base was relatively flat, similar to that of living apes (Kimbel et al. 2004) (Figure 11.11). Cranial crests, flanges of bone on the braincase for muscle attachment, are present, including both a **sagittal crest** (for the temporalis muscle) and a **compound temporonuchal crest** (formed where the neck muscles approach the temporalis muscles). These crests tell us that *A. afarensis* still placed a premium on chewing. The dental arcade is U-shaped, with large anterior teeth, parallel rows of cheek teeth, and a shallow palate, all primitive, apelike traits. But as expected of a hominid, the canine teeth are much smaller than those of a chimpanzee or of the earlier hominids *Ardipithecus* and *A. anamensis* but larger than those of more recent hominids or other *Australopithecus* species. With smaller canine teeth, no CP3 honing complex is present in *A. afarensis*, and many specimens have premolars with two cusps. The molar and premolar teeth are modest compared with those of later *Australopithecus* but much larger than those of the earliest hominids and *A. anamensis*.

In its postcranial skeleton, *A. afarensis* is clearly an accomplished biped. *A. afarensis* possesses a pelvis with short, broad iliac blades that curve around the side of the animal, forming the attachment area for the gluteal muscles, which aid in bipedal walking (see Chapter 10). The femur is angled in toward the knee, which keeps the foot under the animal's center of gravity; the condyles on the lower end of the femur are enlarged; and the groove for the patella is deepened. The tibia is modified to bear more weight, and the big toe is in line with the other toes. Indirect evidence of bipedal walking in *A. afarensis* comes from the Laetoli footprint track pictured at the start of this chapter that, on the basis of its age and location,

sagittal crest Bony crest running lengthwise down the center of the cranium on the parietal bones; for the attachment of the temporalis muscles.

compound temporonuchal crest Bony crest at the back of the skull formed when an enlarged temporalis muscle approaches enlarged neck (nuchal) muscles, present in apes and *A. afarensis*.

FIGURE 11.11 A complete cranium of *A. afarensis* from Hadar, Ethiopia, shows a prognatic face and small braincase.

Dikika and Development

Evolution often proceeds by modifying the pattern of development. Slight modifications during growth can lead to large anatomical differences between adults. Such modifications might alter the rate and timing of growth, or they might alter processes; for example depositing bone at a certain spot in one species while resorbing bone in that same spot in another species. New technologies such as X-rays, scanning electron microscopy, computed tomography (CT), and microCT are being used to understand growth in fossil hominids. First, however, fossil children must be discovered.

In 2006, Zeresenay Alemseged and his team announced a spectacular discovery of an infant skeleton of *Australopithecus afarensis* from Dikika in Ethiopia dated to about 3.3 million-years-old. This child's bones were retrieved over several field seasons in three different years. The work included the careful survey of an entire slope and the screening of excavated sediments. Most of the skull and part of the postcranial skeleton, especially the arm, was recovered, but many of the bones were cemented together by sediment. The analyses would include CT scanning to determine which bones and teeth were present and how old the child was. Although you would suppose that children's remains are rarely preserved in the fossil record, almost every fossil hominid species has at least one, fairly well-preserved subadult specimen. Indeed, the first australopithecine ever discovered was the Taung Child from South Africa.

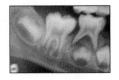

The first step in understanding development of any fossil specimen is to evaluate its developmental age. If the fossil has teeth, dental development is the best means for assessing age (see also Chapter 18). Radiographs, X-rays like the ones your dentist takes, and CT scans can be used to visualize the relative development of the tooth crown and its roots (Dean 2007). Using comparative standards for apes and humans a developmental age can be assigned. In the case of Dikika, only baby teeth were visible externally, but adult teeth could be seen developing in the jaw. An ape developmental standard suggests the child was about 3 years old when she died. The same techniques can be applied to other species. For example, the 3-dimensional CT scan of King Tut reveals his third molars (wisdom teeth) were unerupted, which is consistent with his reported age of 19 years at the time he died.

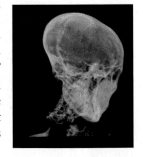

More detailed information about growth rate and timing is revealed by examination of the microstructure of tooth crowns and roots. Tooth enamel is laid down in daily increments with darker bands accumulating about once a week. By counting these bands and the

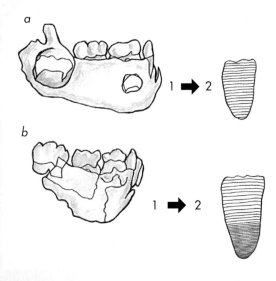

space between them, relative rate of growth can be assessed. Beynon and Dean (1986) used crown development to show that robust australoithecines developed their incisors more quickly than did non robust species like Dikika. And both groups erupt their teeth at earlier ages than do living humans.

Robust and non-robust australopithecines of similar dental ages also show different patterns of facial growth. Using scanning electron microscopy (SEM) scientists can see whether bone in a particular region of the skeleton was being deposited or resorbed (Bromage 1987).

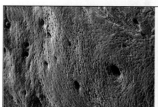

Melanie McCollum (2007) has analyzed growth in the face of an extensive sample of recent chimpanzees and human children, and compared this with patterns in fossil subadults, including non robust species such as the Taung Child (*A. africanus*) and the Hadar Baby (A.L. 333-105, *A. afarensis*), the same species as the

Dikika 3-year-old, and *A. robustus* (SK-66). Robust australopithecines show bone resorption on their anterior maxilla, while non-robusts of the same age do not. This response is in some small way responsible for the facial differences in these species.

The most recent technology to be applied to understanding growth is microCT—or Computed Tomography able to visualize structures of very, very small scale. Using this technology Tim Ryan and Gail Krovitz (2006) have established how the spongy bone in the top of the femur changes in density and organization during growth. They looked at the changes in humans from fetal to about 9-years-old to understand how becoming bipedal might influence bone structure. Around two or three years of age, the three-dimen-

sional structure of the top of the femur reorganized in ways that were consistent with changes in loading caused by unassisted walking as opposed to crawling.

Their work establishes a baseline for understanding how changes in behavior influence structure—an understanding that one day may help us understand fossil specimens such as the Dikika 3-year-old.

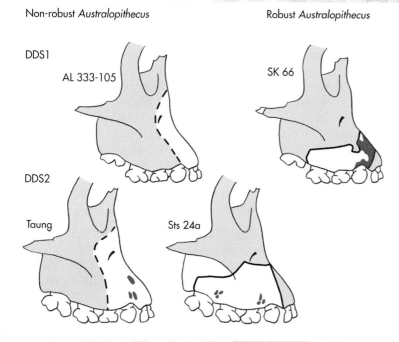

Non-robust *Australopithecus*

Robust *Australopithecus*

DDS1

AL 333-105

SK 66

DDS2

Taung

Sts 24a

TABLE 11.2	Comparisons of *A. afarensis*, Great Ape, and Modern Humans	
	Cranial Capacity (cc)	**Sexual Dimorphism (Males X Percent Heavier)**
A. afarensis	450	56%
Chimpanzee	400	15%
Gorilla	500	50%
Orangutan	400	Nearly 100%
Early genus *Homo*	600	63%
Modern human	1,400	15%

is thought to have been made by *A. afarensis*. All these characters tell us that *A. afarensis* was a striding biped and clearly, therefore, a hominid.

The postcranial skeleton also differs from that of modern humans, however (see Figure 11.7). The thorax is more funnel shaped, similar to an ape's, perhaps indicating that *A. afarensis* had a large gut and a largely vegetal diet. *A. afarensis* arms are somewhat longer relative to leg length than in modern humans but their anatomy is unlike that of modern apes who use their arms for walking. *A. afarensis* also has more curved phalanges of both the toes and fingers; smaller, perhaps more flexible tarsal bones; and aspects of the shoulder and hip joints that may indicate some level of arboreality.

This mosaic pattern of postcranial anatomy indicating a successful biped that probably spent time in the trees as well has stirred debate about the type of bipedalism practiced by *A. afarensis*. Perhaps the pelvic and lower limb anatomy of *A. afarensis* indicate that the species walked nearly as efficiently and gracefully as we do today (Johanson et al., 1982; Lovejoy, 1978, 1988). But anatomical aspects of the feet, toes, and lower limbs all seem to suggest some degree of adaptation to arboreality (Stern & Susman, 1983; Susman et al., 1984). Although it seems clear that on the ground *A. afarensis* moved about on two legs, they may have retreated to the trees to escape from predators, to forage for fruits and leaves during the day, and to sleep at night. Habitat reconstructions based on antelope remains found at *A. afarensis* sites suggest the hominids were living in woodlands rather than on open savannas (see Chapter 8; Reed, 1997), which supports the idea that trees could have served as a refuge from predators or as sleeping areas for these small hominids.

It is likely that *A. afarensis* lived in groups, and because they were very sexually dimorphic, they probably were not monogamous. The largest adults from Hadar are, in some measures, nearly twice the size of the smallest *A. afarensis* (Lucy is one of the very smallest). This extensive range of variation has led some experts to suggest that *A. afarensis* is actually two species, not two sexes. However, the prevailing opinion is that *A. afarensis* shows an extreme level of sexual dimorphism similar to that of modern orangutans (McHenry, 1991) (Table 11.2). From this we infer that *A. afarensis* had a polygynous mating strategy because in living primates great sexual dimorphism usually is associated with multiple mates (see Chapter 6).

AUSTRALOPITHECUS BAHRELGHAZALI (3.5–3.0 MYA)

As we have seen, most early fossil hominids have come from eastern Africa, with two exceptions: the early hominid *Sahelanthropus tchadensis* and the later-living *Australopithecus bahrelghazali*. In 1995, Michel Brunet announced the discovery of the first hominid from West Africa, *A. bahrelghazali* ("the hominid from Antelope Creek"). The species is known from a single fossil: the front of a mandible with seven teeth (Figure 11.12). Most researchers think that *A. bahrelghazali* is in fact

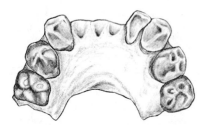

FIGURE 11.12 The mandible of *A. bahrelghazali*. The first hominid found in western Africa, *A. bahrelghazali* dates to about 3.5 million years ago.

a member of *A. afarensis* or at least that it is too fragmentary to form the basis of a new species. Until additional fossils are known, the major importance of this find is its confirmation that hominids lived over much of the African continent, not only in East Africa.

KENYANTHROPUS *PLATYOPS* (3.5 MYA)

Working on the arid western shore of Lake Turkana in northern Kenya, a place made famous by many other fossil finds, Meave Leakey and her team discovered an early hominid dated to 3.5 million years ago (Leakey et al., 2001). Leakey and Fred Spoor thought the specimens, particularly a nearly complete but crushed cranium, were sufficiently different from members of the genus *Australopithecus* that they should be given a new genus name (Figure 11.13). The researchers based their argument on the specimen's surprisingly flat face, a derived trait of later hominids rather than of *A. afarensis* and its kin, and its small molar teeth, a condition more primitive than the other australopithecines. They proposed the name *Kenyanthropus platyops* ("the flat-faced hominid from Kenya"). Some researchers think *Kenyanthropus* should be considered just another species of *Australopithecus* or even a member of *A. afarensis*, although it differs from *A. afarensis* not only in facial morphology but also in having other, more primitive cranial characters. Tim White suggests that the specimen was so deformed during fossilization that interpretation of *Kenyanthropus*' relationships to other hominids may be in error. Given the recency of the find, this question remains a point of contention.

Whether a distinct genus or a separate species, at 3.5 million years old, *Kenyanthropus* lived at the same time as *A. afarensis*. The presence of multiple taxa, or an adaptive radiation based on dietary differences, as Leakey's group suggests, means that one of these taxa is not a direct ancestor of modern people. It is not possible at this time to determine which is more closely linked to later hominids. But we now must acknowledge that the early days of the bipedal hominid radiation were more complex, and perhaps less linear, than we had realized.

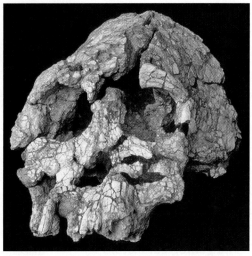

FIGURE 11.13 The cranium of *Kenyanthropus platyops* dates to about 3.5 million years ago in Kenya. The species takes its name from the very flat face.

AUSTRALOPITHECUS *GARHI* (2.5 MYA)

Another recent discovery of an australopithecine species has yielded possible information about how these creatures lived. The Middle Awash team discovered the skull fragments and other pieces of a previously unknown hominid at Bouri, not far from other hominid discoveries in the Middle Awash Valley in the Afar region of Ethiopia (Asfaw et al., 1999). These fossils date to approximately 2.5 million years ago. *Australopithecus garhi* ("the unexpected southern ape from the Afar") had a small brain (450 cc), a prominent prognathic face, large canines, and a sagittal crest (Figure 11.14). In most respects *A. garhi* is quite primitive anatomically, even for an australopithecine. Some workers argue that *A. garhi* may be better interpreted as a late surviving member of *A. afarensis*; remember that that species existed until about 2.9 million years ago in the same geographic area. Besides its age, *A. garhi* differs from *A. afarensis* only in a few anatomical characters, including having larger cheek teeth (molars and premolars) that diverge from one another near the back of the palate and a slightly larger canine. If the postcrania from a nearby site belong to this species, then, surprisingly, *A. garhi* has more human-like proportions between its arms and legs (because of a long femur) but apelike proportions between its upper arm (humerus) and forearm (radius and ulna). These proportions seem to differ from those of *A. afarensis*, which has a shorter lower limb.

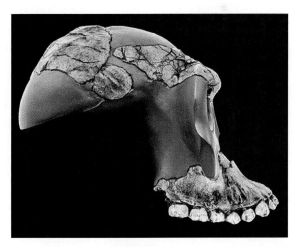

FIGURE 11.14 *Australopithecus garhi* dates to about 2.5 million years ago in Ethiopia and was found in the same beds as early stone tools. It is slightly younger than *A. afarensis* and its cheek teeth are more robust.

Regardless of its taxonomic attribution, the proximity of *A. garhi* fossils to the earliest known stone tools is significant. At Bouri, and also at nearby Gona, archeologists found stone tools in association with the fossilized remains of antelope and other likely prey species. These animal bones show cut marks and percussion marks, unmistakable evidence that early hominids had been using stone tools to butcher carcasses. We cannot say whether *A. garhi* was the butcher, but no other early hominid fossils have been found in the same strata. If supported by further finds, this would be the earliest evidence of tool use by an australopithecine.

AUSTRALOPITHECUS AFRICANUS (3.5–<2.0 MYA)

We have thus far examined only hominids that occurred in West and East Africa. But southern Africa also saw a major radiation of hominid species during the Pliocene. In fact, the first australopithecine ever discovered, the Taung Child, was discovered in southern Africa, which is why the genus is called *Australopithecus*, or "southern ape-man."

There are a few key differences between the study of fossils in southern and eastern Africa. Unlike the open-air sites of East Africa, most South African fossil sites are in cave and cliff deposits. Hominids and other animal remains are found in a mixture of ancient marine limestone and bone cemented into a **breccia**. The hominids did not live in the caves in which they were found, although the caves could easily be misinterpreted this way because natural processes can produce fossil deposits that look very much like they were created by humans. Careful taphonomic study of the caves and their included fossils reveals instead that the skeletal remains probably fell into the South African caves, which themselves are the result of dissolution of the bedrock by groundwater (see Chapter 8). South African caves often appear as sinkholes in the ground, similar to those seen in parts of Florida, and often have trees growing along their rims (Figure 11.15). Animals are thought to have fallen into these caves by accident or in some cases to have been introduced after having been killed by carnivores, such as leopards, which cache their kills in the branches of trees overhanging the sinks to protect them from larger carnivores (Brain, 1981) (Figure 11.16 on page 328).

There is another key difference between the East and South African fossil record. Volcanic ash that forms the matrix in which many East African fossils are embedded can be dated quite precisely using the ^{40}Ar/^{39}Ar techniques you read about in Chapter 8. However, South African deposits cannot be dated using these techniques. Some uranium series dates have been attempted, but mostly paleontologists must rely on geomagnetic polarity data and relative dating methods. They compare the fauna (biostratigraphy) and geology (lithostratigraphy) of rock strata containing human fossils with strata in other regions such as East Africa that contain similar fossil sequences but can be more precisely dated. This provides an estimate of the age of the deposits. However, the stratigraphy of the South African caves is complex, so establishing the sequence of which fossil species lived contemporaneously with others sometimes is not possible.

In 1924, Raymond Dart, a young professor of anatomy in Johannesburg, South Africa, received a shipment of crates loaded with fossils collected from the Taung limestone quarry. One of the crates held a tiny partial skull, of a primitive hominid, and a baby at that (Figure 11.17 on page 328). The face and teeth were attached to a fossilized impression of the interior of the braincase as well, a so-called natural **endocast**. After carefully extracting the specimen from the limestone matrix, Dart realized that this endocast revealed the general appearance and size of the brain of the creature.

"The Taung Child" appeared to be a very young, apelike hominid who retained some baby teeth, which suggested an age of 5 or 6 years, based on modern

The geological history of eastern Africa, including abundant volcanic activity, allows radiometric dating of many hominid sites in Ethiopia, Kenya, and Tanzania. Southern African sites lack volcanic deposits and are usually dated via biostratigraphy.

breccia   Cement-like matrix of fossilized rock and bone. Many important South African early humans have been found in breccias.

endocast   A replica (or cast) of the internal surface of the braincase that reflects the impressions made by the brain on the skull walls. Natural endocasts are formed by the filling of the braincase by sediments.

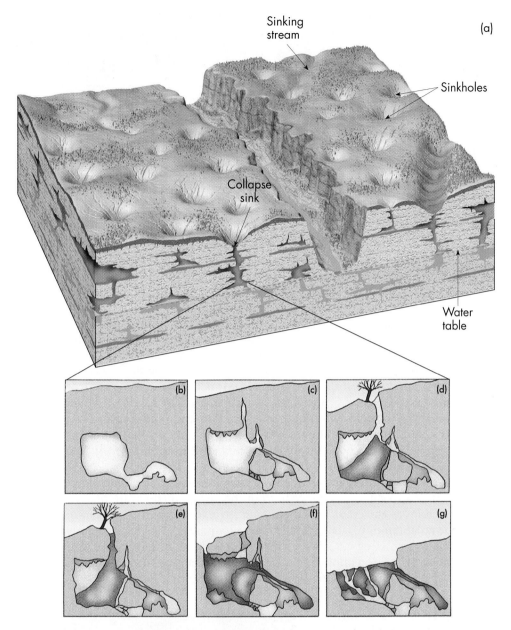

FIGURE 11.15 South African cave sites were formed by the dissolution and collapse of (a) bedrock that later trapped sediments and animals, including hominids. (b) Initially, bedrock is dissolved by groundwater. (c) When the water table lowers, there may be roof collapse into the chamber and sta-lagmite/stalactite formation. (d) With time, the chamber may erode further, eventually connecting to the surface. (e) Vegetation and trees often grow near these wet openings and sediments and animals may fall into the chambers. (f) Over time other openings to the surface may form introducing new sediments and bones. (g) Erosion of the surface exposes the stratigraphy of these sediments, the relative ages of which are difficult to interpret because of their complex history.

human growth rates. This estimate of Taung's age at death has long been in debate because we can't be sure whether early hominids grew up along the same trajectory as modern people or as the great apes. Recent research suggests australopithecines followed a developmental rate similar to an ape and that the Taung Child was about 2 or 3 years old at the time it died.

In an article for the British science journal *Nature*, Dart (1925) argued that Taung was a hominid, based on the position of the foramen magnum, which was on the underside of the cranium, as it would be in a biped (see Chapter 10).

FIGURE 11.16 Some fossil remains of early hominids show evidence of carnivore bite marks similar to those made by lions, cheetahs, and other carnivores, suggesting that our early ancestors may have been hunted.

An authority on the brain, Dart devoted much space in the article to describing the features of the brain's surface that could be detected from the endocast, features that supported his contention that Taung was a direct link between the small-brained apes and larger-brained humans. Dart derided the place accorded to Piltdown man (see Chapter 8: Insights and Advances: The Piltdown Hoax on page 240), which he thought had too apelike a jaw to be human, and also the *Homo erectus* skull dubbed Java Man (see Chapter 12). He concluded his paper by acknowledging Darwin's long-ago assertion that Africa, not Europe or Asia, was the birthplace of humanity.

The response of the British scientific establishment was predictable; it still accepted Piltdown Man as evidence both of the big-brained nature of early humans and of Britain as the cradle of humankind. In a series of letters to *Nature*, nearly all of the great minds of early twentieth-century paleoanthropology rejected the significance of the Taung discovery. The majority thought that Taung was merely a new variety of ape and implied that Dart (who had a reputation as a grandstander) had sought attention for himself in his bold assertions about the fossil.

FIGURE 11.17 The Taung child, the first of the australopithecines to be discovered, is the type specimen for *Australopithecus africanus*.

FIGURE 11.18 The site of Gladysvale in South Africa is excavated for *Australopithecus* remains.

Because of the controversy surrounding Taung and the entrenched view about Piltdown, it was not until nearly 1950 that *Australopithecus* was given its rightful place as a southern African forerunner of modern humans. Meanwhile, many other discoveries of fossils of the same species as Taung were being made. Most of these fossils have been dated to between 3.5 and 2.4 million years ago, with the possibility that some of the material may be much younger, possibly little more than 1 million years old.

The oldest *Australopithecus africanus* fossils come from Sterkfontein, Taung, Gladysvale, and Makapansgat (Figure 11.18). Dart's colleague Robert Broom, a Scottish-born doctor and amateur paleontologist, followed up on Dart's early claims for hominids in South Africa starting in the 1930s. In 1947, Broom discovered a partial skull of a presumed female *A. africanus* from Sterkfontein, a limestone quarry near Johannesburg. Broom called the fossil "Mrs. Ples," short for the genus name *Plesianthropus* that he assigned to it (Figure 11.19). This discovery has been estimated to date to 2.6 million years ago and made it impossible for skeptics of Taung to insist that *A. africanus* might have only been an ape because the adult Mrs. Ples

FIGURE 11.19 Francis Thackeray holding Sterkfontein 5 (STS 5), a presumed female *Australopithecus africanus*, that shows the rounded vault and moderate facial prognathism of that species.

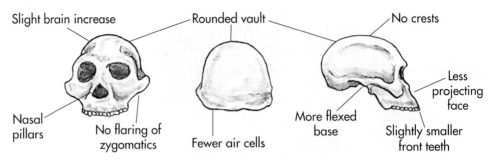

FIGURE 11.20 Key features of *Australopithecus africanus* include a rounded vault without cranial crests, a slightly flexed cranial base, and moderate facial prognathism.

was clearly bipedal (Broom, 1947). Later, Phillip Tobias made important contributions in this area as well, and hundreds of *A. africanus* specimens of various ages and probably both sexes have been found since Broom's initial work. A nearly complete skeleton of *A. africanus* is being extracted from the deposits at Sterkfontein.

Australopithecus africanus is more derived than *A. afarensis* in several aspects of its cranial skeleton (Figure 11.20). Compared with *A. afarensis*, *A. africanus* has a larger braincase (about 450–550 cc, still quite small by modern standards), a rounded vault that lacks cranial crests and has fewer air cells in it, a less prognathic face, and a more flexed cranial base. The teeth of *A. africanus* are generalized and the molars more modestly proportioned than in later, more specialized australopithecines such as *A. robustus* and *A. boisei*. This has led to a classification into gracile australopithecines, including *A. africanus*, and robust australopithecines for *A. robustus*, *A. boisei*, and *A. aethiopicus*. *Australopithecus africanus* has small anterior teeth, especially canines, compared with earlier hominids such as *A. afarensis* but larger anterior teeth than most of the later robust australopithecines. However, the molars of *A. africanus*, although clearly larger than in earlier forms, are smaller than the enormous molars of the robust australopithecines.

Australopithecus africanus was a small-bodied biped that possessed the broad and short iliac blade of the pelvis and structural adaptations in the spine, leg, and foot that characterize habitual bipeds (see Chapter 10). Based on an extensive collection of postcranial remains, body size has been estimated at about 65–90 pounds for *A. africanus* (which is slightly smaller than the later robusts). *Australopithecus africanus* has the same general body plan as *A. afarensis*, with a more funnel-shaped thorax than in humans, although *A. africanus'* arms may be shorter (Figure 11.7).

The other animals found at sites with *A. africanus* suggest that these hominids, like those in eastern Africa, were living in woodland and open woodland environments (Reed, 1997). These wooded areas may have provided some protection from predators. There are currently no earlier hominids in South Africa than *A. africanus*, but it is generally assumed that *A. africanus* evolved from a population of East African hominid, probably *A. afarensis*, that migrated to the south.

THE ROBUST AUSTRALOPITHECINES (OR PARANTHROPINES)

The robust australopithecines are a group of early hominids that appears to have been an evolutionary dead end because of their extreme anatomical specializations. The first robust was found in 1938 in South Africa by Robert Broom, and the East African species was first found by Mary Leakey at Olduvai Gorge, Tanzania, in 1959 (Figure 11.21).

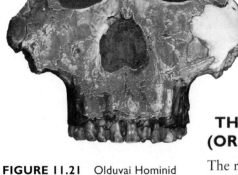

FIGURE 11.21 Olduvai Hominid 5 (OH 5) is a hyper-robust member of *Australopithecus boisei* discovered in Tanzania by Mary Leakey.

The robust australopithecines are united by a suite of cranial features related to their feeding adaptation that made them extremely efficient at producing a lot of force at their molars (Figure 11.22). These cranial features often are thought of as an adaptation to **hard object feeding**, chewing tough food items such as hard-shelled nuts or fibrous vegetation. In fact, early fossils were nicknamed "nutcracker man" for this reason. To produce large bite forces, the **muscles of mastication** that produce chewing force are maximized in size and placement for mechanical efficiency. The robust australopithecine skull reflects these changes. One of these muscles, the temporalis, which sits on the side of the braincase, lifts the mandible. (You can feel your own temporalis doing the work of chewing if you touch your temples while closing your jaw.) In the robusts, the temporalis is enlarged and moved forward, which is reflected in the presence of an anterior sagittal crest for its attachment, the presence of extreme **postorbital constriction** to accommodate its large size, and the flaring of the **zygomatic arches** laterally to accommodate the bigger muscle (Figure 11.23). Another muscle, the masseter, sits on the outside of the jaw and also raises the mandible. (You can feel your masseter work if you

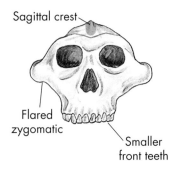

Sagittal crest

Flared zygomatic

Smaller front teeth

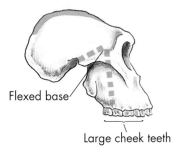

Flexed base

Large cheek teeth

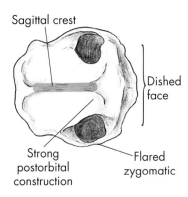

Sagittal crest

Dished face

Strong postorbital construction

Flared zygomatic

FIGURE 11.22 Key features of robust australopithecines include adaptations to heavy chewing such as a large sagittal crest and flaring zygomatics, a dished face, and strongly flexed cranial base.

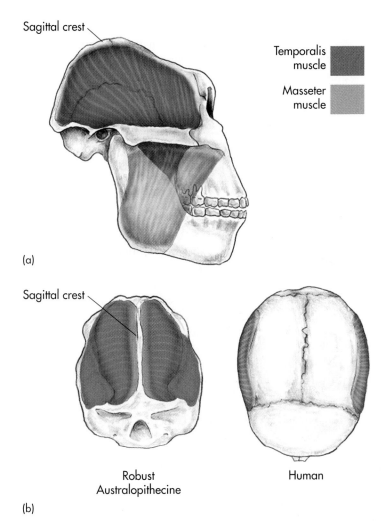

Sagittal crest

Temporalis muscle

Masseter muscle

(a)

Sagittal crest

Robust Australopithecine

Human

(b)

FIGURE 11.23 Muscles of mastication in robust australopithecines. (a) The temporalis muscle (red) attaches to the sagittal crest and the mandible, and the masseter muscle (pink) attaches to the zygomatic bone, which is moved directly over the molar teeth. (b) From above we can see that robust australopithecines had much greater muscle attachment area on their skulls than do modern humans (right).

hard object feeding   Chewing tough, hard-to-break food items such as nuts or fibrous vegetation.

muscles of mastication   The chewing muscles: masseter, temporalis, medial and lateral pterygoids.

postorbital constriction   The pinching-in of the cranium just behind the orbits where the temporalis muscle sits. Little constriction indicates a large brain and small muscle; great constriction indicates a large muscle.

zygomatic arch   The bony arch formed by the zygomatic (cheek) bone and the temporal bone of the skull.

put your fingers on the outside and rear of your lower jaw and clench your teeth.) The masseter is moved forward over the teeth in robusts by placement of the zygomatic (cheek) bones to which the muscle attaches in a more forward position. This results in a dished face in which the cheeks extend further forward than does the nose. Flexing the cranial base brings the face (and the teeth) up under the vault and chewing muscles, including the masseter. The mandible is large and deep, and the face is tall to counter these muscle forces. The molars and premolars are enormous, further indicating that at least at some times of the year these hominids relied on a diet that included tough objects. The premolars are like small molars and are referred to as molarized. In contrast, the anterior teeth are tiny, indicating what little importance they had in the dietary habits of the robusts.

Scientists think that these adaptations allowed robust australopithecines to survive during times when not much food existed because they were specialized for eating a kind of food that other hominids could not eat. Most of the time robusts probably ate a lot of different things, but when food was scarce they relied on their "fallback food." Isotopic research on South African robusts shows that they were omnivores, probably eating some kind of animal protein (perhaps termites) at some times of the year. There is also evidence that they may have used bone tools to access this food, and they have been found with stone tools, as well, suggesting that they were fairly intelligent creatures. However, their reliance on tough foods during times of resource scarcity seems to become more specialized through time. Eventually, this overspecialization would lead to their demise when food resources changed too dramatically and their fallback foods disappeared.

Habitat reconstructions based on the other animals found at robust australopithecine sites suggest that these hominids, like *A. africanus* and those in eastern Africa, were living in woodland and open woodland environments (Reed, 1997). However, some robusts seem also to have lived in slightly more open habitats but always to be associated with streams or waterways.

Paranthropus *is a genus name used by some scientists for the robust australopithecines. Using* **Paranthropus** *implies that these species shared a recent common ancestor and are more closely related to one another than to any of the other australopithecines.*

Some scientists think that the robust australopithecines are so different from other australopithecines that they should be placed in their own genus, *Paranthropus*. The decision to define a new genus for a set of closely related species requires evidence that these species, in this case the robusts, share an adaptive plateau that separates them from other related species. Proponents of the use of *Paranthropus* argue that the specialized chewing apparatus of the robusts is evidence of such an adaptive plateau. By using this separate genus name these scientists also are accepting that all the robust species are more closely related to one another than they are to species outside of *Paranthropus* and thus that they descend from a recent common ancestor who also shared some part of this adaptation. As we shall see, other scientists disagree as to how closely related the robust species are to one another, so in this book we take a conservative approach and include them in *Australopithecus*.

Australopithecus (P.) aethiopicus (2.7–2.5 mya)   There is no evidence that the robust australopithecines left any descendants, but there is some tantalizing evidence about their origin. In 1985, Alan Walker and Richard Leakey found the skull of a very primitive robust australopithecine that is a good candidate for the ancestor of both later robust species, *A. (P.) boisei* and *A. (P.) robustus*, and also shows some links to other early hominids (Walker et al., 1986). The fossil was discovered on the western shore of Lake Turkana, an area famous for many other fossil hominid finds. The fossil had been stained black by minerals in the sediment in which it was buried and therefore was dubbed "the Black Skull" when it was unearthed. (Figure 11.24). Walker and Leakey assigned the fossil, also known by its museum number as KNM-WT 17000, to *A. boisei* because it retains key traits derived in *A. (P.) boisei.*

FIGURE 11.24 *Australopithecus aethiopicus*, called the "Black Skull" because of its manganese staining, is an early robust form dating to about 2.5 million years ago in Kenya.

Because it retains primitive characters not found in *A. (P.) boisei*, some scientists prefer to call it *A. (P.) aethiopicus*.

Australopithecus (P.) aethiopicus shares the suite of masticatory (chewing) characters described for the robust australopithecines but with some modifications and some more primitive characters as well. *A. (P.) aethiopicus* has a sagittal crest, dished face, flared zygomatics, and huge molars that both *A. (P.) boisei* and *A. (P.) robustus* possess, although the sagittal crest is positioned more posteriorly in *A. (P.) aethiopicus* (Figure 11.24). But *A. (P.) aethiopicus* also retains primitive traits from an earlier hominid, *A. afarensis*. *Australopithecus (P.) aethiopicus* differs from other robusts and is more similar to *A. afarensis* by being small brained (about 400 cc), with a prognathic face, flat base, and large anterior teeth. There are no known postcranial remains of *A.(P.) aethiopicus*. At 2.5 million years old, *A. (P.) aethiopicus* is also slightly older than *A. (P.) boisei* but younger than *A. afarensis*. Many paleoanthropologists think that *A. (P.) aethiopicus* is primitive enough to be the evolutionary link between the early trunk of the hominid family tree and the specialized branch that led to the robust australopithecines (Figure 11.25). However, because *A. (P.) aethiopicus* and *A. (P.) boisei* uniquely share features (such as a heart-shaped foramen magnum) that differentiate them from *A. africanus* and *A. (P.) robustus*, some scholars still consider it possible that the East and South African robusts could represent two more distantly related lineages that have converged on a shared anatomy based on a similar dietary adaptation to hard object feeding, at least during fallback periods.

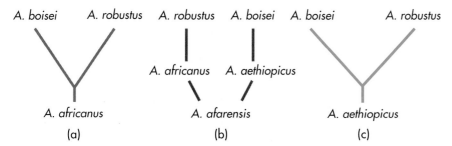

FIGURE 11.25 Some possible phylogenies for the robust australopithecines.
(a) *A. africanus* may give rise to both *A. robustus* and *A. boisei*. (b) *A. afarensis* may give rise to two separate lineages, one of East African robusts the other of South African robusts. (c) Or *A. aethiopicus* may give rise to both *A. robustus* and *A. boisei*.

FIGURE 11.26 *Australopithecus robustus* is a South African robust australopithecine first discovered in 1938.

Australopithecus (P.) boisei (2.3–1.2 mya) The culmination of the lineage that started with *A. (P.) aethiopicus* is *A. (P.) boisei* (Figure 11.21). In 1959, the skull that Mary Leakey found while working alone one day at Olduvai became the type specimen for a new genus and species, *Zinjanthropus boisei* ("hominid from Zinj; after a benefactor named Boise"). It was later renamed *Australopithecus boisei* (Leakey, 1959).

Since 1959, East African sites in Kenya, Tanzania, and Ethiopia have yielded a plethora of *A. (P.) boisei* remains, both cranial and postcranial. Although the Leakeys did not know it at the time, Zinj represented the most specialized end of this East African species of robusts. The species spans the time period from about 2.3 to about 1.2 million years ago, based mostly on radiometric ages. The brain size is about the same as that of the robusts from South Africa, and the postcranial skeleton is large, with an estimated body size between 75 and 110 pounds (McHenry, 1992, 1994).

The cranial skeleton of *A. (P.) boisei* reflects the suite of masticatory adaptations discussed previously and some features shared with *A. (P.) aethiopicus* but not shared with the South African forms; these include the shape of the nasal bones and browridge, and the absence of nasal pillars. However, an important fossil find from Konso, Ethiopia, shares the South African condition of some of these features, muddying the distinctions.

Australopithecus (P.) robustus (2.0–1.5 MYA) When Robert Broom discovered the first robust australopithecine in 1938 at Kromdraai in South Africa, most of the scientific community still doubted the presence of early hominids in Africa. However, Broom recognized that the forward location of the foramen magnum indicated a biped and thus a hominid rather than a robust ape skull (Figure 11.26). This was also a species quite different from the more gracile australopithecine fossil from Taung. The characters that led Broom to his conclusion are the suite of masticatory characters discussed previously. These characters led Broom to name the genus *Paranthropus* ("next to man"), and the species *robustus*. Later the Swartkrans remains were reassigned to genus *Australopithecus*.

Australopithecus (P.) robustus is known principally from Kromdraai, Swartkrans, and Drimolen; and based on biostratigraphy it dates to about 2.0–1.5 million years ago. Its cranial capacity is between 500 and 550 cc, and the postcranial skeleton indicates a body size of about 70–90 pounds (McHenry, 1993, 1994). *Australopithecus (P.) robustus* differ from their East African counterparts in several minor characters, including the shape of the nasals and browridge and the presence of bony pillars next to the nose.

In addition to hard-shelled, tough foods, isotopic studies suggest that *A (P.) robustus* also ate substantial quantities of animal protein. (see Chapter 8 to read about the method). Andrew Sillen (1988) found that the ratio of isotopes of strontium and calcium in *A. (P.) robustus* fossils was consistent with what we would expect in a grassland inhabitant whose diet was composed at least partly of animal protein; *Australopithecus africanus* does not have such values. Julia Lee-Thorp and her colleagues (1994) suggested on the basis of carbon isotopic values that *A (P.) robustus* probably ate grass-eating insects such as termites. Supporting this idea are the wear patterns found on the ends of animal bones probably used by *A. (P.) robustus* as digging sticks (d'Errico et al., 2001). The researchers think that, unlike chimpanzees who improvise termite-collecting tools from blades of grass and twigs (see Chapter 7 and 10), the robust australopithecines used a more powerful bone tool to open up the massive mounds of hardened soil in which termites live.

Understanding the Australopithecine Radiation

Just as the Miocene period was a time of great diversification of the apes, the Pliocene was a time of adaptive radiation and diversification of the early hominids. We still do not know how large this radiation was, but frequent new discoveries suggest that many more species of australopithecines and other hominids remain to be found. Some of the increase in diversity in the Pliocene results from the "naming game," the splitting of previously named species or genera into two or more new taxa. But most of the recently named new species are based on new fossil discoveries.

COHABITATION

It is difficult for us to imagine today that at various times in the past, two or even three hominid species lived in the same regions of the African continent (Table 11.3). In some of these cases, two species occurred at the same time and in the same habitat. When two or more species with similar diets and behaviors coexist in the same place, scientists predict that some key aspects of their biology will diverge as a result of competition. If this does not occur, then one species or the other probably should become rare or extinct in the face of direct competition with the other. The australopithecine species that appear to have shared the same habitat at the same time show striking morphological differences. This suggests that natural selection molded them to avoid feeding competition.

In the past it was common for two or more hominid species to coexist at the same time and in the same environments.

One good way to understand the likely ecological relationship between sympatric early hominids is to look at how living great apes share a habitat. In Africa, there are many forests in which chimpanzees and gorillas coexist. Both apes travel on the ground to find food, but chimpanzees spend far more time feeding in trees than gorillas do. Both build nests each night, but gorilla nests usually are on the ground, and chimpanzee nests normally are high in trees. And although both species prefer fruit to all other forest foods, gorillas fall back on high-fiber leafy foods in lean seasons, whereas chimpanzees forage far and wide to continue eating fruits. In other words, although these two large-bodied apes are similar in many respects, there are key differences that probably are the result of their ancestors evolving together in African forests and that today allow them to coexist (Tutin, 1996; Stanford & Nkurunungi, 2003).

In addition to *A.(P.) africanus* and *A. (P.) robustus* in southern Africa, potential cases of sympatry in the hominid fossil record include *A. (P.) boisei* (robust) and early genus *Homo* (gracile) in eastern Africa, *A. garhi* and *A. (P.) aethiopicus* in eastern Africa, and *A. afarensis* and *K. platyops* in eastern Africa. In all these cases it has been argued that anatomical differences between taxa reflect differences in dietary adaptations that suggest the hominids were partitioning the available resources, which allowed them to coexist.

TABLE 11.3	**Examples of Potentially Contemporaneous Hominids by Region**		
Age (MYA)*	**West Africa**	**East Africa**	**South Africa**
~6	Sahelanthropus tchadensis	Orrorin tugenensis	
3.9		Australopithecus afarensis, A. anamensis	
3.5	A. bahrelghazali	A. afarensis, Kenyanthropus platyops	A. africanus
2.5		A. garhi, A. aethiopicus	A. africanus
2.5–2		A. boisei, A. garhi	A. africanus, A. robustus
2–1.5		A. boisei, Homo sp.	Homo sp., A. robustus
*MYA = millions of years ago			

TOOLS AND INTELLIGENCE

We used to think that only members of our own genus *Homo* were clever enough to make tools. Australopithecines were considered dim-witted in comparison and without tools. However, until the 1960s tool making was also unknown in the living great apes. Although no nonhuman primates make stone tools, making tools from other materials is common in the great apes and even in some monkeys. Chimpanzees make and use probes to extract insects and other food items, make sponges to soak up liquids, use hammers to crack open nuts, and wield branches as weapons against prey and other chimpanzees (see Chapter 6). Other apes and even capuchin monkeys use organic tools, although they may not make them (see Chapter 7, Innovations: Cultured Apes on page 212). We might expect, then, that early hominids such as australopithecines fashioned tools, perhaps out of organic materials, but did not necessarily make durable tools.

In the 1950s, Dart interpreted the animal remains from early hominid sites as evidence of what he called the **osteodontokeratic culture** in which he envisioned australopithecines using the bones, teeth, and horns of animals as tools (hence the name he gave the culture). Dart also considered the australopithecines to be bloodthirsty hominids. Recent research suggests that the accumulated remains found in South African cave sites probably represent natural accumulations of bone rather than australopithecine tool kits. Although his evidence has not held up under more recent scrutiny, Dart may have been right in thinking that australopithecines made and used tools.

There is tantalizing evidence that australopithecines were smarter than we might think. The earliest evidence of tool use in the genus is the possible association between *A. garhi* and the butchered remains of animals about 2.5 million years ago in Ethiopia. At other sites in East and South Africa stone tools are found in the same beds and even at the same localities as the remains of robust australopithecines. No other hominid genera are known from these particular contexts, so this may indicate the production and use of stone tools by australopithecines. And as we saw earlier, *A. robustus* may have used animal bones as digging sticks.

Hand anatomy also gives us a small clue that the robust australopithecines may have been capable of tool production. The robusts share thumb anatomy that is similar to that of tool-making hominids such as ourselves and other members of the genus *Homo*, but earlier species of *Australopithecus* such as *A. afarensis* lack this anatomy. This may indicate that the robusts could make stone tools, although it does not tell us whether they did.

If tool production requires sophisticated cognitive skills, as argued in Chapter 10, then the australopithecines were at least as sophisticated as living great apes. However, it is not until around 2.5 million years ago, well into the australopithecine radiation, that we see the first use of stone tools. Thus the additional access to resources that these tools provide could not have been among the primary reasons that the genus arose. Indeed, as we discussed in Chapter 10, the benefits of bipedality as a foraging strategy appear to be the primary advantage that early hominids had over their quadrupedal relatives.

ANCESTORS AND DESCENDANTS

There are several ways to envision the relationships among the early hominid species we have examined in this chapter (Figure 11.27). Based on anatomy, many scientists derive *A. afarensis* from the more primitive *A. anamensis* and then see *A. afarensis* as the base of the radiation of *A. africanus*, *A. garhi*, and *A. aethiopicus,* and possibly the *Homo* lineage. Each of these lineages takes the *A. afarensis* anatomy in a slightly different direction depending on the environmental conditions in which it lived and by which individuals were selected for or against. Many see *A. (P.) aethiopicus* giving rise to the robust radiation of *A. (P.) boisei* and *A. (P.) robustus*, whereas others derive the East African robusts from *A. (P.) aethiopicus* but the South African robusts from *A. africanus*. This splitting into South and East African lineages means that these

osteodontokeratic culture
A bone, tooth, and horn tool kit envisioned by Raymond Dart as made by *Australopithecus*.

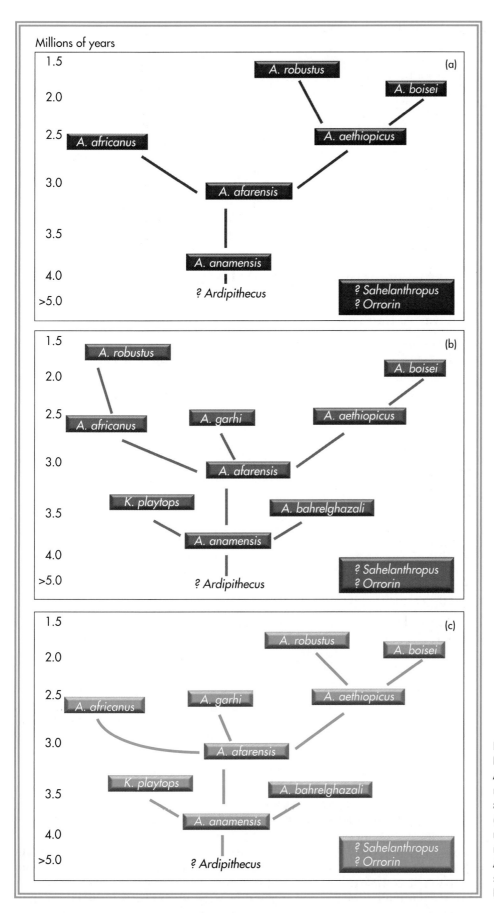

FIGURE 11.27 Three possible phylogenies for the australopithecines with *A. anamensis* as the stem ancestor and recognizing a small number of species and close relationships between (a) *A. robustus* and *A. boisei*, (b) a larger number of species and only distant relationship between *A. robustus* and *A. boisei*, or (c) a large number of species and a close relationship between *A. robustus* and *A. boisei*.

scientists don't think the robusts shared a last common ancestor exclusive of other australopithecines and therefore are not part of a separate genus, *Paranthropus*. *Australopithecus africanus*, *A. afarensis*, and *A. garhi* have all been implicated as possible ancestors for the genus *Homo*; however, one thing that almost all scientists agree on is the idea that the robust australopithecines are too specialized to be ancestral to genus *Homo*. The key to a good potential ancestor is that it exists early enough to give rise to the later groups, is not more derived than those groups, and has characters that look as if they could give rise to later groups.

Because the fossil record is sparse, each new fossil discovery throws the tree into brief disarray, after which paleoanthropologists try to sort out the most likely phylogeny suggested by the sum of the evidence. This may seem as though scientists cannot agree, but disagreement is a healthy feature of evolutionary science. Each new find tests previous hypotheses and produces new interpretations, new research, and new results that push the state of our understanding of human ancestry forward.

Questions for Future Paleoanthropologists

Despite all we have learned about the earliest hominids through the eight decades since Raymond Dart's time, the questions still far outnumber the answers.

How Many Species Were There? First and foremost, we don't know how extensive or diverse the early hominid radiation really was. In all likelihood there are more species, perhaps many more, waiting to be found. The rate of discovery of new hominid fossil taxa has increased in recent years; today a new species is described nearly every year.

How Large Was Their Geographic Distribution? So far the fossil record suggests that the earliest divergence of the australopithecines from ancient ape stock occurred in eastern Africa, probably in the Great Rift Valley. But the discovery of *Sahelanthropus* and *A. bahrelghazali* in Chad reminds us that very early hominids, or very hominid-like apes, also lived far outside East Africa. Conditions ideal for bone preservation, fossilization, and later discovery of ancient hominids are present in East Africa. Less ideal conditions and less intensive prospecting have limited the fossil yield from West Africa to date.

But we must remember the old adage that absence of evidence is not evidence of absence. The African continent is enormous, and there is no reason to think that early hominids did not inhabit most of it. If early hominids radiated geographically across the warmer regions from east to west, as chimpanzees do today, there are vast areas and diverse habitats into which they may have radiated. If even a few of the australopithecine taxa were as versatile ecologically as chimpanzees, most of the African continent may have once been populated by early hominids. Their remains are yet to be discovered. However, there is currently no evidence that early hominids ever occurred outside the African continent.

Did Only One Lineage Emerge from the Ancestral Ape Stock? There are two ways to interpret the earliest stages of hominid evolution. The first is the traditional view that between 5 and 7 million years ago, a single lineage of primitive apelike anthropoids evolved into hominids, and some species of this lineage eventually evolved into *Homo sapiens*. The alternative view is that early in hominid evolution, natural selection experimented with bipedal posture and locomotion and increased brain size, and there were multiple lineages of apelike hominids in Africa. In this latter view, bipedalism was not the defining hallmark of hominids; more than one bipedal lineage arose, but only one eventually survived to become our direct ancestor. The defining characteristic of the hominids would thus remain unidentified but might include dental changes such as absence of a functional CP_3 honing complex. The degree of taxonomic diversity in the Pliocene will remain an intriguing and important question in decades to come as more and more fossils reinforce some views of the hominid phylogeny and contradict others.

SUMMARY

1. **Why are the earliest hominids difficult to identify?**

   As you get closer to the last common ancestor (LCA), hominid features appear more like the LCA making it difficult to distinguish early hominids from other apes.

2. **What are the several traits that define the australopithecines? Include both cranial and postcranial traits.**

   The genus *Australopithecus* is defined by being bipedal but of small body size, with a funnel-shaped thorax, small canines but postcanine megadontia, and small brains.

3. **What key anatomical traits define *A. afarensis***

   A. afarensis is characterized by a mosaic of primitive and derived characters, including bipedality, reduced canine size, loss of the CP_3 complex, and postcanine megadontia (derived), and small brain size, compound temporonuchal crest, flat cranial base, shallow, U-shaped palate, large anterior teeth, long arms, and curved phalanges (primitive).

4. **Why do we have precise dates on the ages of East African early hominid discoveries and only rough estimates of those in South Africa?**

   East African sites more often have volcanic rocks associated with them that can be dated using radiometric techniques such as argon–argon and potassium–argon. South African sites rely mainly on biostratigraphic age correlations.

5. **What key anatomical traits define the robust australopithecines?**

   The robust australopithecines share a suite of anatomical characters related to mastication. These include enormous postcanine megadontia and increased jaw size, enlarged chewing muscles (as reflected in a large sagittal crest, strong postorbital constriction, and flaring zygomatics), and a dished face and flexed cranial base.

CRITICAL THINKING QUESTIONS

1. How many australopithecine species do you think are waiting to be discovered? How would you go about estimating how many more might exist?

2. If we discover an early hominid that exhibits great sexual dimorphism, such as the Hadar fossils, what are some of the inferences we can make about the social behavior of those creatures in life?

3. If gracile and robust australopithecines share the same habitat, why don't we see evidence of their hybridizing?

4. As recently as the late 1990s, we thought *A. afarensis* was the stem of the hominid family. What happened to cast doubt on that view, and what does it tell us about the human family tree?

KEY TERMS

homodont
heterodont
CP_3 (sectorial
   premolar)
   complex
australopithecines

cranial crests
megadontia
type specimen
sagittal crest
compound
   temporonuchal crest

breccia
endocast
hard object feeding
muscles of mastication
postorbital
   constriction

zygomatic arch
osteodontokeratic
   culture

SUGGESTED READING

Johanson, Donald, and Edey, Maitland. (1981). *Lucy: The Beginnings of Humankind*. Simon & Schuster, New York.

Morell, Virginia. (1995). *Ancestral Passions: The Leakey Family and the Quest for Humankind's Beginnings*. Simon & Schuster, New York.

"For the following few weeks, the excavating brought nearly nonstop excitement, but there was some meticulous scientific work behind the celebrations ... The bones kept coming, right up to the last moment, so we knew we would have to come back. Nearly everything we found was part of our skeleton ... When we closed down the site for the season, on September 21, 1984, we had found more of *Homo erectus*—the classic missing link—than anyone had ever seen. The next four field seasons laboring in the pit, as we came to call the enormous excavation, would see 1,500 cubic yards of rock and earth moved by hand. Our schoolboys, who worked with us faithfully year after year, grew from adolescents to young men while the Nariokotome boy, as we took to calling the specimen, grew from a fragment of skull to the most complete early hominid skeleton ever found."

—from *The Wisdom of the Bones,* by A. Walker and P. Shipman

THE DISCOVERY OF THE SKELETON OF THE NARIOKOTOME boy, the remains of a *Homo erectus* youth, dramatically changed our understanding of early *Homo*. His lanky build suggests that the transition from the apelike body proportions of *Australopithecus* to modern human proportions occurred in the short time interval between 2.3 and 1.7 million years ago. What we know about the transition from *Australopithecus* to earliest *Homo* rests ultimately on the fossil record. And what we know of the fossil record, including the discovery of the Nariokotome boy, rests in equal parts on skill, perseverance, planning, and sheer luck. In fact, the early fossil record of genus *Homo* is remarkably sketchy in comparison to the australopithecine record, making the task of understanding the origin of the genus that much more difficult.

In this chapter we examine the early radiation of the genus *Homo*, from its beginnings in apelike hominids to the first migrations out of Africa and into other parts of the Old World. We discuss the definition of the genus and the appearance of *Homo erectus*, whose larger brain and body size may signal a shift in diet, who makes increasingly sophisticated tools, and who may use fire. Then we examine early tool technologies and subsistence. And finally we consider the debate over later stages of *H. erectus*.

Defining the Genus *Homo*

Recall that a genus name implies a certain adaptive strategy, so the switch from *Australopithecus* to *Homo* should tell you to expect to see a suite of adaptive differences between species in the two genera. In general, genus *Homo* differs from australopithecines by having a larger braincase; a smaller, less projecting face; smaller teeth; and eventually a larger body and more efficient striding bipedalism. These features may be related to an adaptation that includes a shift to a more animal-based diet, greater ranging, and greater food processing through tool use. However, early members of the genus *Homo* differ less strongly from australopithecines than do later members and therefore are harder to distinguish from them. In fact, the first species of *Homo* are not all that different from some australopithecines.

There is much taxonomic debate over the application of species names to fossil *Homo*. Depending on the scientist, earliest *Homo* is conceived of either as a single, variable species (*H. habilis*) or as multiple, less variable species (usually *H. habilis, H. rudolfensis, or H. sp. nov.,* referring to an unnamed new species of *Homo*). Similarly, *H. erectus* is seen as either a single species or two species, *H. ergaster* and *H. erectus,* and the presence of any of these taxa in Europe and the transition to modern humans is hotly debated. All this disagreement results in part from the paucity of the fossil record, differences in species concepts (lumpers versus splitters), and the inherent difficulty of applying a static classification system to the dynamic process of evolution.

Some scientists think that the variability that we see in these species is partly related to the climate in which they evolved—specifically climate fluctuations—and that these fluctuations favored behavioral flexibility. During the Pliocene, cyclic glaciation began about 3 million years ago and these cycles became increasingly intense throughout the Pleistocene (1.8 million to 10,000 years ago). The first appearance of fossils of the genus *Homo* around 2.5 million years ago coincides with a period when we see many changes in the occurrence of different species of mammals and the appearance of early stone tools. During a later period of fluctuation, a bit more than a million years ago, australopithecine taxa went extinct. It may be that our genus adapted to periods of climatic instability and that our intelligence and adaptability were honed as a result of it (Potts, 1996). This difference in behavior and adaptability between *Homo* and *Australopithecus* was recognized by Louis Leakey when he found the earliest fossil member of our genus, *Homo habilis,* and suggested that they were the sole makers of stone tools.

Earliest Genus *Homo*

In the 1960s Louis and Mary Leakey discovered a nearly 2-million-year-old juvenile partial skull at Olduvai Gorge in Tanzania. Olduvai Hominid 7 (OH 7) possessed

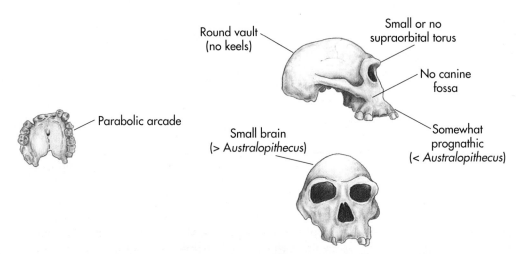

FIGURE 12.1 Key anatomical features of *Homo habilis* include reduced facial size, a parabolic palate, and some brain enlargement.

a brain larger than any known australopithecine and differed markedly from *Zinjanthropus boisei* (see Chapter 11). Louis Leakey, Philip Tobias, and John Napier used the fossil to name the new species *Homo habilis*. The name, meaning "the skilled human or handyman" refers to the use and manufacture of stone tools, which the anthropologists thought was an important adaptive strategy linking this new species to us (Figure 12.1). Their announcement was met with initial skepticism; however, additional fossils from Olduvai and elsewhere have confirmed the initial diagnosis.

In the early 1970s at Koobi Fora on the eastern shore of Lake Turkana, Richard Leakey's team discovered a more intact skull of *H. habilis*, known by its National Museums of Kenya catalog number KNM-ER 1470 and dated to approximately 1.8 million years old (Figure 12.2). KNM-ER 1470 has a large cranial capacity of 775 cc. Additional finds of *H. habilis* from Koobi Fora,

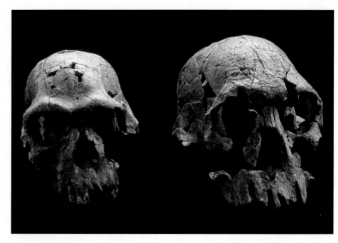

FIGURE 12.2 Crania of KNM-ER 1813 and 1470 differ enough that some scientists include them in two different species.

TABLE 12.1 Cranial Differences between Key Early *Homo* Fossils		
	KNM-ER 1813	**KNM-ER 1470**
Cranial capacity	510 cc	775 cc
Browridges	Moderate to small	None
Face	Small	Large
Posterior tooth size	Small	Large

which range in geological age from about 1.4 to 1.9 million years old, vary greatly in size (Figure 12.2). The earliest fossil *Homo,* dating to some older than 2.3 million years, are fragmentary remains from Hadar in Ethiopia, Uraha in Malawi, and possibly the Chemeron Formation in Kenya.

Many scholars think that differences between the largest (1470) and smallest early *Homo* crania are too great to be encompassed by the variation of a single species (Table 12.1). The smallest has a brain almost one-third smaller (only 510 cc) than the largest specimens, smaller teeth, and a differently proportioned face. To further complicate things, the smaller postcranial remains have longer upper limbs (a primitive trait) than do the larger specimens. Most who separate these fossils into two species place Olduvai Hominid 7, the type specimen and name-bearer of the species, with other small-brained crania, calling this *H. habilis,* while 1470 becomes the type specimen for *H. rudolfensis.* Other researchers think the larger and smaller individuals were a male and female, respectively, of the same hominid species.

Splitting early *Homo* into two species would mean that there were sympatric members of the genus living in East Africa between 1.5 and 2.0 million years ago along with sympatric australopithecines. It would be unclear which of the two species of early *Homo, H. habilis* or *H. rudolfensis,* gave rise to the later species *H. erectus* and *H. sapiens.* Is the larger brain of 1470 a link to *H. erectus*? Or are dental and facial similarities a link between the smaller specimens of early *Homo* and *H. erectus*?

Although some of these specimens are bigger-brained than others, none show the extensive cranial and postcranial enlargement or adaptation for long stride length seen in *H. erectus.* Bernard Wood and Marc Collard (1999) suggested that the smallest-brained early *Homo* resembles larger-brained australopithecines and should be relegated to *Australopithecus* because of similarities that suggest they shared similar patterns of behavior and ecology. Wood and Collard particularly

The variation in brain size and other anatomical characters may indicate that early **Homo** *fossils represent two species,* **H. habilis** *and* **H. rudolfensis.** *Or the fossils may be males and females of the same species.*

focus on differences in the postcranial skeleton between *H. erectus* and *H. habilis.* In this book we use *H. habilis* rather than *Australopithecus habilis,* but Wood and Collard have given important food for thought to researchers studying the emergence of the genus *Homo.* Whatever you call these fossils, there is clear evidence that they made and used stone tools.

Early Tool Use

Whoever the first toolmaker was, stone tools are found in the record starting about 2.5 million years ago. The earliest tools are known as the **Oldowan** industry, so named for their first discovery at Olduvai Gorge in Tanzania (Figure 12.3). We refer to stone tools made in a particular way or tradition as a **tool industry.** Oldowan tools consist mainly of **cores,** lumps of stone, often river cobbles modified from the original rock by the removal of pieces from it, and **flakes,** the small fragments taken from the core. Archaeologists used to think the core itself was the tool, but experimental evidence suggests the flakes were used as cutting and scraping tools. The cores probably were used to produce flakes until they became too small and were discarded (Schick & Toth, 1993). Flakes can be extremely sharp and are effective at cutting through tough animal hides and removing meat from bones. Other Oldowan tools called **hammerstones** were used to crack open the bones of large animals to extract marrow and to remove flakes from cores. Oldowan tools are deceptively simple in appearance; if you held one you might not be able to distinguish it from a naturally broken piece of rock. However, archaeologists, some of whom are proficient stone toolmakers themselves, use various clues to distinguish stone tools from naturally broken stone.

Tool making was first and foremost an adaptation to the environment of the late Pliocene. Through the use of tools hominids could cut open animal carcasses and break into the fat stored in their bones. These animal foods became an increasingly important adaptive strategy for early humans. It seems that early *Homo* probably carried tools with them rather than constantly discarding or continually making them anew. If early humans carried their tools around it must be because those tools were an important part of their daily routine. Just think about the things you choose to put in your backpack each day—like your cell phone and wallet—and what that means about their importance in your routine.

Oldowan The tool industry characterized by simple, usually unifacial core and flake tools.

tool industry A particular style or tradition of making stone tools.

core The raw material source (a river cobble or a large flake) from which flakes are removed.

flake The stone fragment struck from a core, thought to have been the primary tools of the Oldowan.

hammerstone A stone used for striking cores to produce flakes or bones to expose marrow.

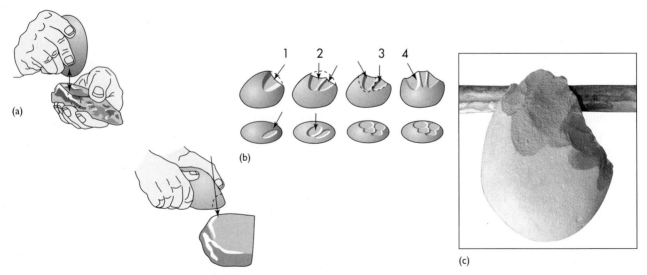

FIGURE 12.3 Oldowan tools are simple flake tools struck from a core using (a) a hammerstone or an anvil technique. The flakes are often removed from only one side of the core (b), and are useful for cutting through hides, muscle, and plant material. (c) An experimentally made Oldowan type core.

Archaeologists specializing in the study of stone tools have categorized the patterns of tool use at various Oldowan sites in East Africa. Some of these are thought to have been **butchering sites:** A variety of mammal bones, some bearing cut and percussion marks made by stone tools, have been found with such tools. A site at Olduvai Gorge contains the remains of a hippo with cut marks on its bones along with scores of flakes, suggesting the hippo had been butchered by early hominids. Stone implements are found in great abundance at **quarrying sites,** where hominids went to obtain the raw material for the tools. A third type of site is what the archaeologist Glynn Isaac (1978) called a **home base.** Isaac hypothesized that hominids repeatedly brought butchered carcasses back to a more comfortable central place, perhaps near a shade tree or a water hole, where they slept and ate in greater safety than at the site where the animal was killed. At such a site, the hominids would have been manufacturing or refining tools as well. Other archaeologists are skeptical of this idea, arguing that natural processes such as movement of remains by water, wind, and animals may account for what look like human-created bases of activity. Still others think that the accumulations may represent caches of material made by hominids for their later use rather than campsites.

We don't know for certain which early hominid made which tools because we don't find hominid fossils actually holding the tools. We can only infer tool use by the association between tools and hominid remains in the same excavations. Even this is dangerous, because antelope are the most abundant fossils found in association with stone tools, and we are quite sure the antelope are not the toolmakers! The first indisputable evidence of tool use is from cut marks on fossilized bones of antelope about 2.5 million years ago. The tools and marks were probably made by earliest genus *Homo* but perhaps also by *A. garhi*. Before this time, if emerging humans were making and using tools, they were using materials such as wood or unmodified bone that did not accumulate or preserve in the fossil record. And if they were eating meat or marrow without the assistance of stone tools, we have no visible archaeological record of it.

Despite the enormous amount of evidence of meat eating, in the form of butchered bones, the debate about the role of meat in the early human diet has a long and tumultuous history. We don't know how often a group of early *Homo* might have actually eaten meat or how important meat (or marrow) was in their diet. Did a group of *H. habilis* butcher and consume one large mammal per week? Per month? Per year? Did all members of the group participate in this butchering activity and in the feast? How much did the incorporation of stone tool manufacture and annual consumption affect other aspects of early hominid behavior, ecology, physiology, and biology? It seems that after 2.5 million years ago, meat eating took on increasing importance, but whether that also included hunting is a point of some contention.

Hunting and Scavenging

We would like to know whether our own lineage arose with the help of a hunting or scavenging because each of these entails a different set of behavioral adaptations. There are currently three main models for how early hominids acquired carcasses. Did bands of early humans courageously attack and slaughter large and dangerous game (hunting)? Did they fight off large predators such as saber-toothed cats to gain access to significant amounts of meat (confrontational scavenging)? Or did they creep nervously up to decomposing, nearly stripped carcasses to glean a few scraps of meat and fat (passive scavenging)? Mostly, however, discussion focuses on general differences between hunting and scavenging.

In 1966 a perspective on human evolution known as "Man the Hunter" was articulated in which men played the important role of obtaining the highest-quality nutrients and the calories that their households would use. The original proposal

butchering site A place where there is archaeological evidence of the butchering of carcasses by hominids. The evidence usually consists of tool cut marks on fossilized animal bones or the presence of the stone tools themselves.

quarrying site An archaeological site at which there is evidence that early hominids were obtaining the raw material to make stone tools.

home base Archaeological term for an area to which early hominids may have brought tools and carcasses and around which their activities were centered.

was put forward by Sherwood Washburn and Chet Lancaster. They explained the 3.5-fold increase in human brain size and complexity as "evolutionary products of the success of the hunting adaptation." According to Washburn and Lancaster, "men hunt while women gather." This scenario also implied that men had a natural right to occupy the glamour role of clever-minded forager, meat provider, and conqueror in human societies because hunting selected for intelligence. Ever since, many scenarios of human evolution have focused on male activities rather than female ones as the core human adaptations.

Many anthropologists took issue with the "Man the Hunter" perspective, because in some of the traditional societies that are most vaunted for the man's role in hunting, up to 85% of the protein obtained by a household came not from men but from women gathering foods such as nuts, tubers, and small animals (Tanner & Zihlman, 1976). Eventually, the reaction to "Man the Hunter" had the effect of swinging scientific research toward examining the possibility that *H. habilis* and kin were scavengers, not hunters, and that they were not necessarily the sole accumulators of fossil bone (Brain, 1981). Some fossilized carcasses even seem to have been chewed on by carnivores first and butchered later. When anthropologists Rick Potts and Pat Shipman studied the bones of animals from Oldowan sites, they found cut marks made by ancient, sharp-edged tools as well as tooth marks made by the gnawing of contemporaneous lions, hyenas, and leopards (Figure 12.4). When they examined these more closely, they saw that on some of the bones, the human-made cut marks were on top of the carnivore tooth marks, evidence that humans were cutting flesh from the bones *after* they had already been chewed by a predator. The implication was clear: On at least some occasions, hominids were scavengers rather than hunters.

To be a scavenger rather than a hunter affects every aspect of daily life. Instead of depending on an ability to chase down and kill elusive prey, a scavenger relies on finding the kills made by other animals and then somehow usurping some of the meat. Many scavengers, such as vultures and jackals, are tolerated by larger carnivores at a kill; would early hominids have been? Through the 1980s, archaeologists adopted new experimental approaches to understanding the role that the hominids may have played in those ecosystems (see Insights and Advances: Understanding the Meat Eating Past through the Present). These studies suggested that ample scavenging opportunities existed for hominids 2 million years ago. By the 1990s, field studies of meat eating by wild chimpanzees showed that even without tools, apes can capture and consume large quantities of small mammals (Boesch & Boesch, 1989; Stanford, 1998). John Yellen (1991) showed that modern hunter–gatherers consume large amounts of meat in the form of small mammals, none of which would leave any archaeological evidence had early hominids done the same. Archaeologists began to reinterpret the models for hominid scavenging behavior, arguing that aggressive, active carcass piracy was far more likely than passively locating dead animals that were already mostly consumed by primary predators (Bunn & Ezzo, 1993).

FIGURE 12.4 Carnivores such as these wild dogs have skeletal adaptations for eating meat. In contrast, early *Homo* used stone tools to obtain meat and marrow.

INSIGHTS AND ADVANCES

Understanding the Meat-Eating Past through the Present

In the 1970s and 1980s Glynn Isaac, an innovative experimental archaeologist who thought the past could be better understood through direct analogies with the present, mentored a series of students who turned to the behavior and ecology of living carnivores to understand how early hominids might have used animal resources. In many modern ecosystems, even after a predator is done eating, the carcass provides rich sources of fat and protein in the form of bone marrow and brain that support a community of scavengers, a community that might have once included early hominids.

Robert Blumenschine (1987) conducted field studies of lions, hyenas, and other African carnivores on the Serengeti. He found that early hominids would have had an ample supply of resources from carcasses left over after kills by lions and leopards, especially in woodlands located near streams where scavengers like hyenas are often delayed in finding the kills (Figure A). Blumenschine (1986) also found that predators and scavengers follow a customary sequence in which they rapidly devour the hindquarters, then the ribs and forelegs, followed by the bone marrow, and finally the contents of the head. This sequence can be used to identify hunting and scavenging in the fossil record. Because scavengers eat the remains of what hunters leave behind, they should eat a disproportionate quantity of the last body parts with edible meat. Blumenschine and his students have expanded these actualistic studies for understanding hominid access to kills and interpreting what kinds of predators were involved based on the tooth marks left on bones. Tanzanian archaeologist Jackson Njau has identified crocodiles as important predators (Njau & Blumenschine, 2006), and Briana Pobiner is using tooth marks to distinguish between different-sized carnivores (Figure B).

Another of Isaac's students, archaeologist Curtis Marean (1989) thinks that early *Homo* could have occupied a scavenging niche simply by cleaning up after saber-toothed cats. Saber-tooths were among the top predators in many East African habitats 2 million years ago. Some were powerful, solitary hunters that could kill animals with much more meat than they themselves could hope to eat or store, leaving a potential niche for a scavenging hominid to fill.

And Isaac's students Nicholas Toth and Kathy Schick used actualistic studies to understand how sites formed at archaeological localities such as Koobi Fora, Kenya (Schick & Toth, 1993). Toth learned to make stone tools and using these replicas a group of archeologists butchered the carcass of an elephant (which had died of natural causes in a zoo and was donated as a research subject). They showed that using only the simple core and flake tools of the Oldowan industry, early humans could have sliced through the thick hide of large animals.

Because it is unlikely that *H. habilis* and kin would have had the means to kill such large and dangerous animals, their work supports the possibility that early humans could have made a good living simply by scavenging already dead animals with the help of tools.

(a)

FIGURE A Hyenas and other scavengers may have competed with early hominids for access to carcasses.

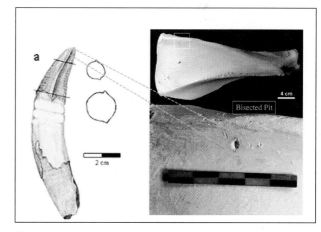

(b)

FIGURE B Crocodiles leave distinctive bite marks that reflect the shape of their teeth, as shown by this work by Njau and Blumenschine (2006).

Early views of the hunting and scavenging debate tended to emphasize a black or white approach, which is rarely the way that living creatures behave. Instead perhaps *H. habilis* acquired animal resources in any form they could, through both hunting for small animals and scavenging carcasses. Modern foragers do the same. Cultural diversity in modern chimpanzee populations (see Chapter 10) suggests that some populations of early genus *Homo* could have hunted, whereas others may have preferred scavenging, and both strategies probably were included in a flexible behavioral repertoire. Regardless of whether meat was obtained by hunting or scavenging, the archaeological record shows that hominid stone tool–assisted consumption of large animals began about 2.5 million years ago and gradually increased through time. The two innovations of stone tool manufacture and animal resource exploitation undoubtedly shaped much of subsequent human evolutionary history.

Who Was *Homo Erectus?*

Sometime around the Plio-Pleistocene boundary, about 1.8 million years ago, hominids underwent a major adaptive shift. This is reflected in the fossil record by body size increases and changes in body proportions, such as lengthening of the femur, which indicate a more efficient gait, similar to that of modern humans. These changes may have been this group's response to environmental and climatic changes during that time period. Remember, however, that while the early *Homo*

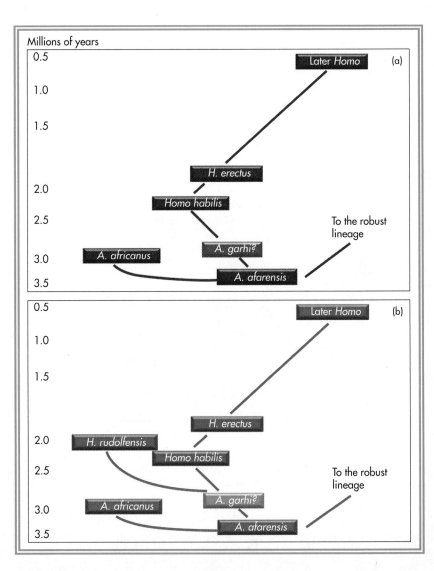

FIGURE 12.5 Possible phylogenies for early *Homo*.

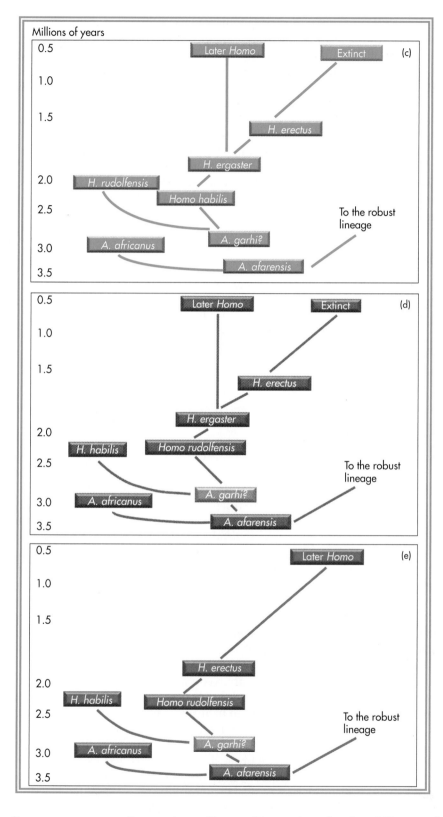

FIGURE 12.5   (*Continued*)

lineage was responding to these climate changes by adaptive shifts, another—the robust australopithecines—responded not by changing but by intensifying its previous adaptation to hard object feeding.

H. erectus appeared in Africa about 1.8 million years ago and was the first hominid to leave the continent, probably around 1.7 or 1.8 million years ago (Figure 12.5). Until just a few years ago, the fossil evidence suggested that

H. erectus did not leave until about 1.0 million years ago. However, increasing evidence shows that our ancestors began migrating to other parts of the Old World much earlier, at about 1.8 million years ago. Some paleoanthropologists call these earliest *H. erectus* by another name, *Homo ergaster* (see Figure 12.5) (Wood & Collard, 1999). Whatever you call them, these hominids quickly left Africa. But just why they left when they did is a source of debate. What is certain is that dispersal probably was the result of multiple movements of small groups of hominids into new territories.

The last members of the species exist more than 1.5 million years later, being found in the late Pleistocene of Indonesia. These hominids overlap in time with hominids from other parts of the world, such as Europe and Africa, which seem to be transitional between *H. erectus* and either Neandertals or modern humans (see Chapter 13).

ANATOMICAL FEATURES

H. erectus had a somewhat larger body and brain and a uniquely shaped skull compared with earlier *Homo*. In its postcranial features *H. erectus* shows the beginnings of a modern human body plan with legs that are much longer than its arms and a less funnel-shaped thorax than earlier hominids and living apes.

The Skull and Teeth   *H. erectus* crania are easily identified by their shape (Figure 12.6). The skull is thick-boned and robust, much longer than it is wide, relatively low and angular from the side, and pentagonal in rear view. The angularity of the skull is enhanced by a series of cranial superstructures, regional thickenings of bone along certain sutures and across certain bones. These include thickenings such as the prominent **supraorbital torus** or browridge on the frontal; a thickened **angular torus** on the back of the parietal; and the **occipital torus**, a ridge of bone that runs horizontally across the occipital. In addition, the forehead has a low, sloping or receding appearance and is often separated from the supraorbital torus by a gully or furrow. The pentagonal rear view is formed by other thickenings including those along sutures such as the **sagittal keel** along the sagittal suture that joins the two parietals and the **metopic keel** along the midline frontal at the site once occupied by the metopic suture of the infant. The pentagon is widest at its base; the sides slant inward from there to the lateral part of the parietal and then turn in to meet at the tip of the pentagon, which is formed by the sagittal keel. Although it is easy to see these anatomical features, it is not so clear why they exist. Unlike the cranial crests of earlier hominids and apes, these thickenings are not related to muscle attachments. Instead they may just be a way to strengthen the braincase as brain size increases.

Homo erectus brain size ranges from approximately 700 cc to 1,200 cc, averaging about 900 cc (Figure 12.7 on 352). Partly as a result of this expansion, the degree of *postorbital constriction* is less than in australopithecines but still marked compared with later forms. Of course, key factors in determining the cognitive ability of a species lie not only in sheer brain volume but also with the organization of the brain. Certainly in absolute brain size, *H. erectus* was less cognitively endowed than modern humans. However, the brain size of *H. erectus* also shows regional and evolutionary variation (Table 12.2), indicating progressive but slow increase in the lineage through time (Antón & Swisher, 2001; Leigh, 1992). Brain size increases by about 160 cc per million years in *H. erectus* but by about 800 cc per million years from archaic *H. sapiens* to modern humans (Figure 12.8 on page 352). Early brain size increases in *H. erectus* may occur simply in proportion to body size increases in the species and real (that is, disproportionately large) brain

supraorbital torus   Thickened ridge of bone above the eye orbits of the skull; a browridge.

angular torus   A thickened ridge of bone at the posterior inferior angle of the parietal bone.

occipital torus   A thickened horizontal ridge of bone on the occipital bone at the rear of the cranium.

sagittal keel   Longitudinal ridge or thickening of bone on the sagittal suture not associated with any muscle attachment.

metopic keel   Longitudinal ridge or thickening of bone along the midline of the frontal bone.

LATERAL VIEW

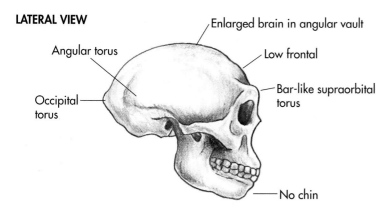

Angular torus

Occipital torus

Enlarged brain in angular vault

Low frontal

Bar-like supraorbital torus

No chin

FRONTAL VIEW

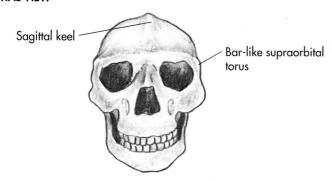

Sagittal keel

Bar-like supraorbital torus

PENTAGONAL REAR VIEW

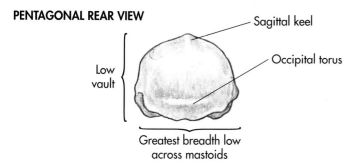

Sagittal keel

Occipital torus

Low vault

Greatest breadth low across mastoids

TABLE 12.2 Cranial Capacities for *Homo erectus*	
Region	**Range (cc)**
Africa	690–1,067
Indonesia	800–1,250
China	855–1,225

FIGURE 12.6 Major features of *Homo erectus* include increased brain size, an angular vault, and cranial superstructures (such as tori and keels).

size evolution may not occur until archaic *H. sapiens,* just a few hundred thousand years ago. Because there are so few associated skeletons, it is difficult to know whether the increased brain size of *H. erectus* was a unique adaptation or simply a result of their larger body size.

The jaw of *H. erectus* was as robust and powerfully built as the rest of the cranial complex. The proportions of the mandible contrast with the small teeth in some of the earlier *H. erectus* specimens from Africa (Wolpoff, 1999). The lingual (tongue) sides of the incisors are concave, with ridges along their edges forming the

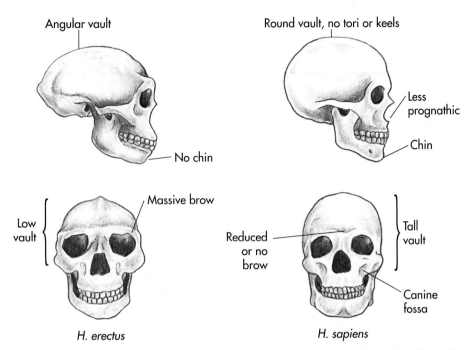

Angular vault

Round vault, no tori or keels

Less prognathic

Chin

No chin

Massive brow

Low vault

Tall vault

Reduced or no brow

Canine fossa

H. erectus

H. sapiens

FIGURE 12.7   Compared with modern humans, *Homo erectus* has a larger face, lacks a chin and canine fossa, and has a more angular vault and smaller brain.

shovel-shaped incisors   Anterior teeth which on their lingual (tongue) surface are concave with two raised edges that make them look like tiny shovels.

shape of a tiny shovel; referred to as **shovel-shaped incisors.** This shape likely prevents damage when the front teeth are exposed to heavy wear from food or other uses. Some researchers have attempted to link ancient Asian *H. erectus* populations with modern Asian people, based on this apparent continuity of incisor shape (see Chapter 14). However, because most *H. erectus* specimens from all regions possess this trait, as do Neandertals, it seems more likely that it is a primitive

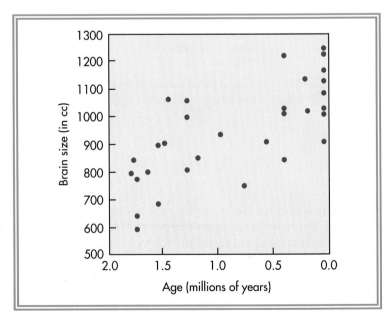

FIGURE 12.8   Although average brain size increases gradually through time in *H. erectus*, individuals with small brains are present even late in time. Dots represent individual fossils.

trait for the genus that may or may not suggest a link between modern and ancient Asian populations.

Body Size and Shape   Despite the large numbers of *H. erectus* skulls and teeth that have been found over the past century, what we know of the postcranial skeleton comes from just three partial skeletons and some isolated bones, mostly from East Africa. The most important of these is the remarkably complete KNM-WT 15000 skeleton—the Nariokotome boy whose discovery is described at the beginning of this chapter (Figure 12.9). These specimens suggest not only that *H. erectus* was robustly proportioned but also that some individuals were quite tall as adults, between five and a half and six feet (Walker, 1993; McHenry & Coffing, 2000). The long bones of the arms and legs are thick; the femur is **platymeric**, which means it is flattened from front to back, and the tibia is **platycnemic**, flattened from side to side. These features are distinctive to *H. erectus* but not *H. sapiens* and do not differentiate *H. erectus* from later Neandertals or archaic *H. sapiens*.

In addition to being taller on average, *H. erectus* in Africa may also have been narrow hipped, at least based on reconstructions of pelvis shape in KNM-WT 15000 by Chris Ruff (Figure 12.10). These body proportions—long and linear—seem to follow the latitudinal gradient seen in modern humans adapted to tropical environments (see Chapter 5). If the reconstructions are correct, and there is some argument about this, then they suggest that *H. erectus* was dissipating heat in much the same way that we do, that is, by sweating. This ability to dissipate heat may have allowed *H. erectus* to be more active during midday.

HOMO ERECTUS VERSUS HOMO ERGASTER

As was the case with *H. habilis*, opinions differ about whether *H. erectus* constitutes one widely dispersed, variable species or two (or more) distinct species, *H. erectus* and *H. ergaster*. The argument focuses mainly around the early African and Georgian forms of *H. erectus* that some researchers recognize as *H. ergaster*, using the mandible KNM-ER 992 as the type specimen. The main differences

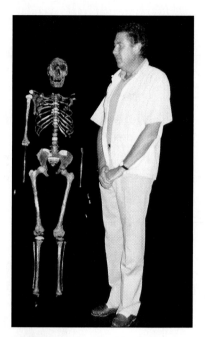

FIGURE 12.9   Dr. Alan Walker stands next to the skeleton of the Nariokotome *H. erectus* boy.

platymeric   A bone that is flattened from front to back.

platycnemic   A bone that is flattened from side to side.

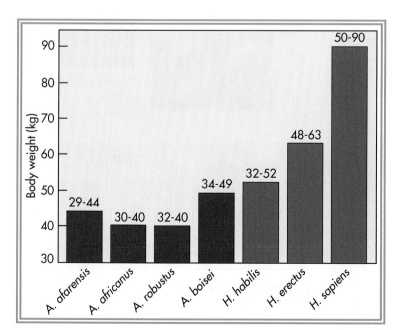

FIGURE 12.10   Body weight estimates from fossil remains show that *H. erectus* had a larger body than earlier hominids did.

The Genus *Homo* Through Time

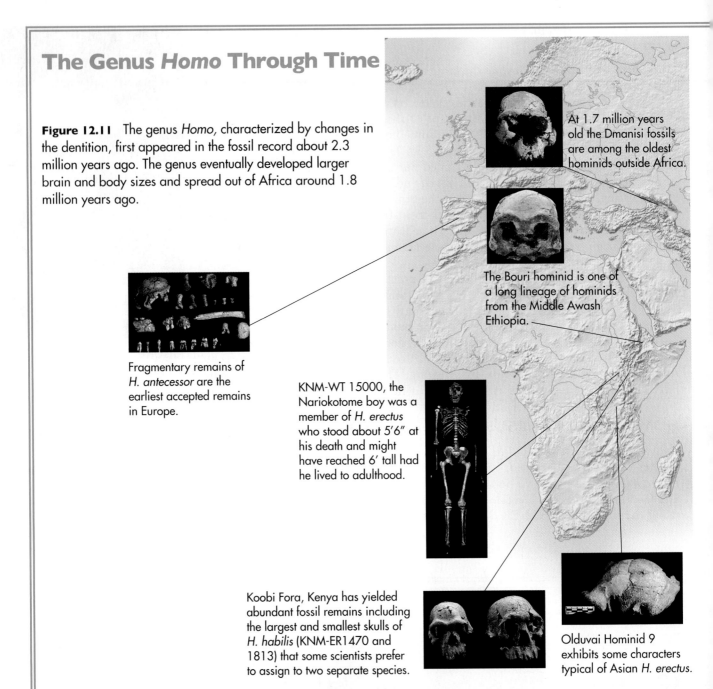

Figure 12.11 The genus *Homo,* characterized by changes in the dentition, first appeared in the fossil record about 2.3 million years ago. The genus eventually developed larger brain and body sizes and spread out of Africa around 1.8 million years ago.

At 1.7 million years old the Dmanisi fossils are among the oldest hominids outside Africa.

The Bouri hominid is one of a long lineage of hominids from the Middle Awash Ethiopia.

Fragmentary remains of *H. antecessor* are the earliest accepted remains in Europe.

KNM-WT 15000, the Nariokotome boy was a member of *H. erectus* who stood about 5'6" at his death and might have reached 6' tall had he lived to adulthood.

Koobi Fora, Kenya has yielded abundant fossil remains including the largest and smallest skulls of *H. habilis* (KNM-ER1470 and 1813) that some scientists prefer to assign to two separate species.

Olduvai Hominid 9 exhibits some characters typical of Asian *H. erectus.*

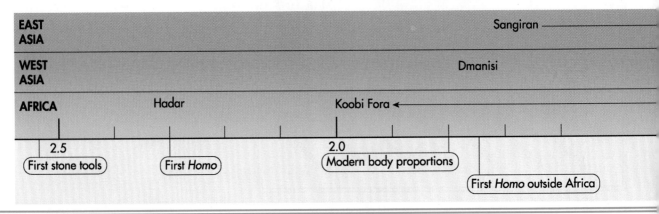

EAST ASIA		Sangiran
WEST ASIA		Dmanisi
AFRICA	Hadar	Koobi Fora ←

2.5   2.0

First stone tools   First *Homo*   Modern body proportions   First *Homo* outside Africa

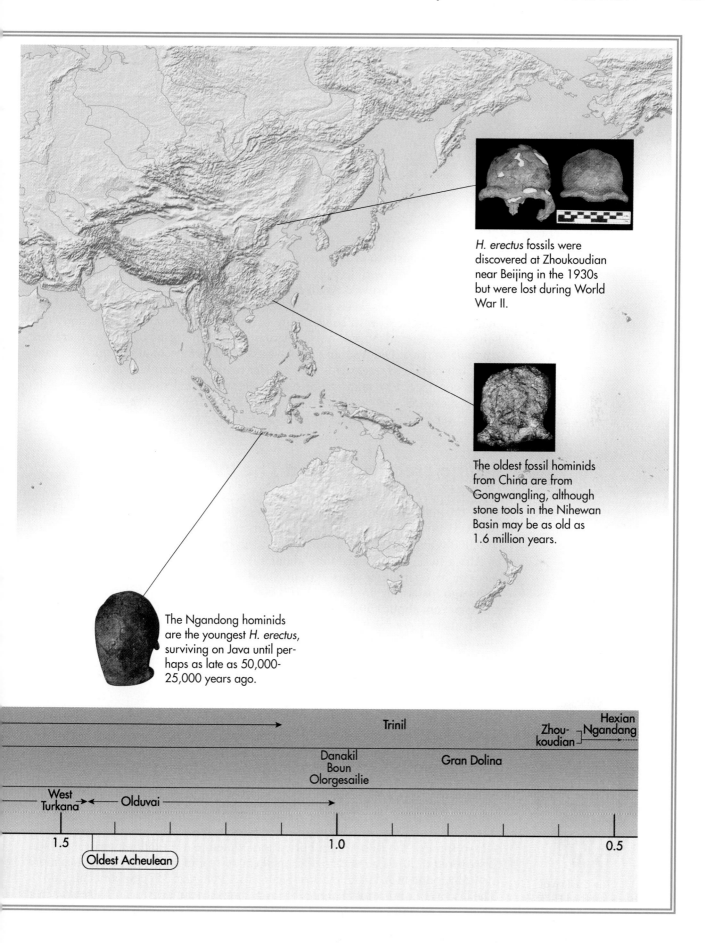

H. erectus fossils were discovered at Zhoukoudian near Beijing in the 1930s but were lost during World War II.

The oldest fossil hominids from China are from Gongwangling, although stone tools in the Nihewan Basin may be as old as 1.6 million years.

The Ngandong hominids are the youngest *H. erectus*, surviving on Java until perhaps as late as 50,000–25,000 years ago.

Trinil

Zhou-koudian

Hexian
Ngandang

Danakil
Boun
Olorgesailie

Gran Dolina

West
Turkana

Olduvai

1.5

1.0

0.5

Oldest Acheulean

TABLE 12.3   Comparison of *Homo ergaster* and Classic *Homo erectus*

	Region	Skeleton	Date (MYA)
H. ergaster	E. Africa	Thinner cranial bones	1.8–1.0
	Rep. Georgia	Less pronounced browridges	
H. erectus	Asia	Thicker cranial bones	1.8–0.05
		More pronounced browridges	

* MYA = millions of years ago

between *H. ergaster* and *H. erectus* are summarized in Table 12.3 and include more gracile crania with less pronounced browridges in African forms and more robust and thicker-browed Asian forms, with larger teeth and more pronounced cranial superstructures (keels and tori, discussed previously). There are also archaeological differences, with some of the African forms found in association with somewhat more advanced tools, whereas even later forms of Asian *H. erectus* continue to make Oldowan-like tools, (see "The Lifeways of *H. erectus*" on page 364). In practice, *H. ergaster* is used to refer to early African *H. erectus* specimens and is considered by many to be only a slight regional variant of the pan–Old World species *H. erectus* (Rightmire, 1993; Antón, 2003). Here we will consider *H. ergaster* a regional variant or subspecies of *H. erectus*.

Homo *Erectus* around The World

If we accept *H. erectus* as a single, widely dispersed species, then it represents more than 1.5 million years of time and a broad geographic range (Figure 12.11 on pages 354–355). *H. erectus* sites range in age from about 1.8 million years to 100,000 years (and perhaps much younger in Indonesia). *H. erectus* is found first in Africa (where it persisted until about 1.0 million years ago), in the Republic of Georgia at 1.7 million years ago, in island Southeast Asia by about 1.8 million years ago (persisting until at least 100,000 years ago), and only later in continental Asia from about 800,000 to about 200,000 years ago. There is controversy as to whether *H. erectus* is found in western Europe, with many researchers arguing that the fossils that appear there from about 800,000 until 200,000 years ago belong to a different lineage than *H. erectus* (see later in this chapter and Chapter 13).

AFRICAN ORIGINS

The earliest fossil evidence for *H. erectus* comes from Koobi Fora in Kenya 1.8 million years ago. The oldest remains are a largely complete cranium, KNM-ER 3733, dated at 1.78 million years old and with a cranial capacity of only about 850 cc (Figure 12.12). Slightly older remains from Koobi Fora of 1.89 and 1.95 million years ago may also be *H. erectus* but are too fragmentary or are parts of the postcranial skeleton that cannot be identified to species with certainty. Many other fossils from East Turkana exhibit similar anatomy and range in age from about 1.5 to 1.78 million years (or older). Recently a partial cranium from Ileret, Kenya (part of the Koobi Fora Formation), dated to 1.55 million years ago, was discovered that has a very small cranial capacity and some characteristics more typically found in Asian *H. erectus* (Figure 12.13 on page 357) (Spoor et al., 2007). The discovery of this fossil argues for including African and Asian *H. erectus* in a single species and tells us important things about size variation in *H. erectus*.

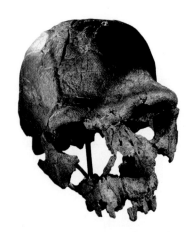

FIGURE 12.12 The cranium of early African *H. erectus* KNM-ER 3733 is nearly 1.8 million years old.

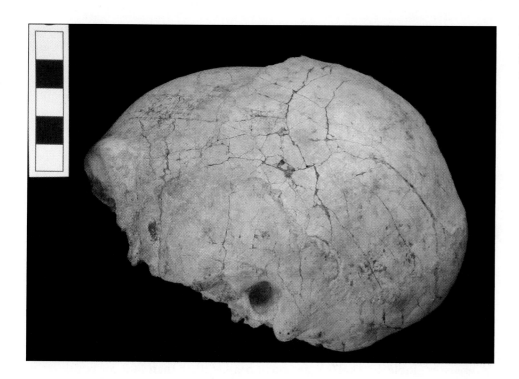

FIGURE 12.13 The recently discovered Ileret calvaria from Kenya is the smallest *H. erectus* and shares many traits with Asian *H. erectus*.

Important African *H. erectus* fossils also come from the western side of Lake Turkana and Olduvai Gorge. The Nariokotome skeleton from West Turkana described in the vignette is important for understanding growth and body proportions (see "*Homo erectus* Life History" on page 367). The largest-brained African *H. erectus*, OH 9, is from Olduvai Gorge. With a cranial capacity of a little more than 1,000 cc, OH 9 dates to about 1.47 million years ago. However, some of the latest *H. erectus* in Africa are also the smallest, including OH 12, from Olduvai, dated to perhaps as little as 780,000 years ago, with a capacity of only 727 cc, and the recently discovered Olorgesailie hominid at about 900,000 years old (Figure 12.14) (Potts et al 2004).

H. erectus from the Bouri Formation of the Middle Awash, Ethiopia (Asfaw et al., 2002) and the Danakil Depression in Eritrea are around 1 million years

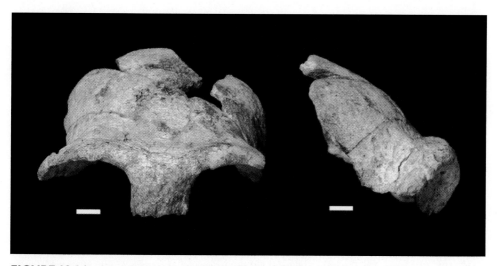

FIGURE 12.14 A small adult *H. erectus* from Olorgesailie, Kenya, is also one of the youngest in Africa at about 900,000 years old.

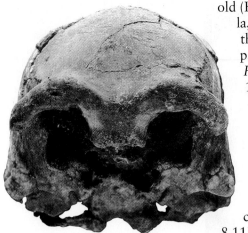

FIGURE 12.15 *Homo erectus* from Bouri Formation of the Middle Awash, Ethiopia, is about 1 million years old.

old (Figure 12.15) (Abbate et al. 1998). Another Ethiopian site, Konso-Gardula, has very ancient (1.8 million years old) fragmentary *H. erectus* fossils and the oldest known *H. erectus*–associated stone tools. The Bouri lineage in particular will prove significant for understanding the evolution of genus *Homo* because it also contains fossils of the earliest *H. sapiens* (see Chapter 14).

THE FIRST AFRICAN DIASPORA: REPUBLIC OF GEORGIA

About 50 miles southwest of Tbilisi, the capital city of the Republic of Georgia, lies the village of Dmanisi. Nearby, beneath a medieval village built at the confluence of two rivers, a stunning series of finds in the 1990s changed our understanding of when humans left the cradle of Africa (Figure 8.11). Excavations by an international Georgian and German team headed by Leo Gabunia and David Lordkipanidze discovered evidence of early *H. erectus*–like hominids outside Africa at approximately 1.7 million years ago and associated with Oldowan-like stone tools. Since 1991, at least five crania and some postcranial remains have been found in a small area (16 m²) beneath the medieval village (Figure 12.16).

The Dmanisi hominids are very similar to early African *H. erectus*, or so-called *H. ergaster* (Table 12.4). They are small brained (less than 800 cc) but differ in anatomy from the more primitive *H. habilis*. The Dmanisi hominids are linked to *H. erectus* by their premolar and molar tooth structure, the development of browridges, and the shape of their braincase. They are markedly more similar to the early African *H. erectus* fossils than they are to early Asian *H. erectus* (Gabunia et al., 2000). But compared with early African *H. erectus*, the Dmanisi hominids are small (Rightmire et al., 2006). They are also interesting because a number of individuals show health problems not usually seen in fossil crania: one is entirely toothless, which poses questions about how he/she prepared his food and whether he could survive on his own or needed assistance from others in the group (Figure 12.16b). Other individuals show abnormalities of the teeth often seen in closely related individuals, perhaps indicating that this was a closely related group.

The Dmanisi skulls show conclusively that early humans had migrated out of Africa at nearly the same time that *H. erectus* first appears in Africa. Thus, shortly after the emergence of *H. erectus* in Africa, the species moved out of the African continent and into other regions and other ecosystems.

(a)

(b)

FIGURE 12.16 (a) The Dmanisi cranium (right) shows similarities to early African *H. erectus* including the Nariokotome boy (left). (b) One individual from Dmanisi lost all his teeth before he died.

TABLE 12.4   Dmanisi Hominids Compared with Other Early Hominids

Taxon	Brain Size (cc)	Body Height (in.)	Body Weight (lb)
Dmanisi	650–780	57–63	90–110
H. sapiens	x̄350	60–75	100–200
African *H. erectus*	690–1,067	63–71	120–145
Asian *H. erectus*	800–1,250	55–67	90–120
Earliest *Homo*	500–750	39–63	70–130
A. africanus	448	45–54	66–90

Source: Gabunia (2001), Lordkipanidze et al. (2007), and Antón et al. (2007)

DISPERSAL INTO EAST ASIA

The oldest Asian *H. erectus* are from island Southeast Asia, particularly the island of Java, and date to about 1.6–1.8 million years ago. The sea level was substantially lower 1.8 million years ago than it is today, and Java and nearby islands were connected to mainland Asia by landbridges (Figure 12.17). So colonizing the far reaches of Asia meant only walking a long distance, not crossing water. Although travel through continental Asia is necessary to reach Southeast Asia, so far the

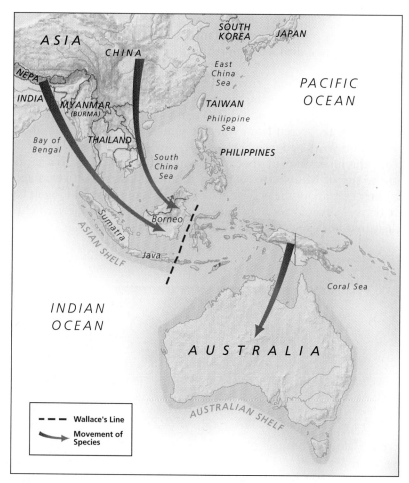

FIGURE 12.17   Landbridge connections between continental Asia and Indonesia during glacial periods (and low sea level) extend as far as Wallace's line.

earliest evidence of *H. erectus* on the eastern part of the continent is only about 1.6 million years old in China.

Indonesia   The very first *H. erectus* fossil ever found, and thus the type specimen for the species, was discovered in 1891 in Indonesia (Figure 12.18). A few years earlier, a young doctor named Eugene Dubois left Amsterdam by steam ship in search of human fossils in the Dutch East Indies (now called Indonesia). Following Darwin's lead, Dubois considered the tropics a likely cradle of humankind. But he also thought that Asia was a more likely spot for the origin of humans than Africa because African apes, with their primitive appearance and robust facial features, seemed to him unlikely human antecedents, whereas the slender-bodied, monogamous Asian gibbons and modern humans seemed more similar (Shipman, 2001). Dubois went to Indonesia to find the missing link between the two.

In October 1891, in the banks of the Solo River near the village of Trinil, Java, Dubois's team unearthed the **calotte** or skullcap of an early human. Although only the top of the skull was found, Dubois could see that it was hominid and that in life it possessed a large brain, in a robust braincase more primitive than that of any hominid known at that time. He named the species *Pithecanthropus erectus* ("the upright ape-man"), and this specimen, Trinil 2, also nicknamed Java Man, became the type specimen for the species. The team later found a fossilized femur that Dubois believed to be of the same individual, thereby proving to him that the creature was fully bipedal.

However, Dubois' claims were met with much skepticism in part because of preconceived ideas about evolution and which characters had appeared first in our evolutionary history (Insights and Advances: the Piltdown Hoax in Chapter 8 page 240). Although by the 1940s *P. erectus* was classified in our own genus as *H. erectus* and recognized as a primitive hominid intermediate between the apes and modern people, Dubois himself died well before this, embittered about his treatment by the scientific community.

The volcanic sediments of Java provide the ideal context for estimating the radiometric age of fossil hominids using the argon–argon technique (Chapter 8). The Trinil site has been dated to about 900,000 years old. A series of fossils from the Sangiran Dome were recovered from volcanic sediments ranging from about 1.7 to about 1.0 million years ago (see Figure 8.14) (Swisher et al., 1994; Larick et al., 2001). And the most ancient specimen from Java, a child's **calvaria,** or braincase, from the site of Mojokerto, is dated to about 1.8 million years ago. There is some controversy about the precise geological ages of individual fossils because many have been discovered not by scientists but by farmers making rice fields; however, it is clear that both sites are far older than 1.0 million years.

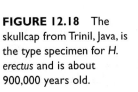

The type specimen for H. erectus *was discovered on the island of Java in 1891.*

calotte   The skullcap, or the bones of the cranium exclusive of the face and the base of the cranium.

calvaria   The braincase; includes the bones of the calotte and those that form the base of the cranium but excludes the bones of the face.

FIGURE 12.18   The skullcap from Trinil, Java, is the type specimen for *H. erectus* and is about 900,000 years old.

FIGURE 12.19   The site of Sambungmacan, Java, as it looks today.

The latest surviving *H. erectus* are also from Java and represent the youngest *H. erectus* anywhere in the world. A series of partial crania and other fossilized remains were excavated in the 1930s at the site of Ngandong in eastern Java. Using uranium series and electron spin resonance (ESR) methods (see Chapter 8), Carl Swisher and colleagues redated the fauna associated with the Ngandong hominids and those from nearby Sambungmacan (Figure 12.19) to a remarkably recent 27,000 to 53,000 years ago (Swisher et al., 1996). More recently, a different radiometric technique has suggested similar ages for one of some of the Ngandong hominids (Figure 12.20). Previously thought to have been present at least 250,000 to 500,000 years ago, *H. erectus* may have survived in this island refuge even while going extinct in other parts of the world. Recent finds on the island of Flores dating to 18,000 years may also support a young age for late surviving *H. erectus* (see Insights and Advances: The Little People of Flores in Chapter 14 on page 418).

FIGURE 12.20   Ngandong calottes from Java are the youngest *H. erectus* fossils at perhaps 27,000–50,000 years old.

Since Indonesia achieved independence in 1945, a series of other fossils have been recovered by Indonesian scientists Teuku Jacob, Fachroel Aziz, and Sartono. As a group, these Indonesian *H. erectus* have cranial capacities that vary between about 800 and 1,250 cc. These finds have helped us to understand the anatomy and evolution of *H. erectus*, but tools are almost entirely lacking in Indonesia. Tools of an Oldowan-like technology have been found, but they are few, and none were found in association with fossil hominids.

China   Perhaps the most famous of the *H. erectus* remains are the so-called "Peking Man" fossils from China. Discovered in the 1930s, they are now dated to between about 600,000 and 200,000 years ago, much younger than those in Africa or earliest Indonesia. However, *H. erectus* almost certainly occupied China as early as they did Indonesia. Although the oldest Chinese fossil hominids, fragmentary, and crushed remains from Gongwangling, are only about 1.2 million years old, sites with stone tools in the Nihewan Basin are about 1.6 million years old (Zhu et al., 2004).

The story of the famed Peking Man fossils is one of discovery and loss. Chinese paleontologist Pei Wenshong discovered the original skull in December 1929 at a quarry site, Chou Kou Tien (now transliterated as Zhoukoudian), not far from modern Beijing (Figure 12.21). Along with Davidson Black, a Canadian anatomist, he described and initially named the fossil *Sinanthropus pekinensis* ("Chinese human from Peking"). After Black's untimely death, Franz Weidenreich, a Jewish anatomist who had fled his native Germany during the Nazi era, took over anatomical work on Zhoukoudian.

In the mid-1930s, Japan invaded China before the American entry into World War II, and work at Zhoukoudian stopped. Fear spread that the Zhoukoudian *H. erectus* fossils, objects of great cultural and historical value, would be confiscated, destroyed, or taken as gifts to the Japanese emperor, a noted naturalist. So Weidenreich made extensive measurements, drawings, and plaster casts of the Zhoukoudian remains. The fossils were then placed in the care of the United States Marines, who guarded them on a train from Beijing to the coast, where they were to be put on a ship for San Francisco. The train arrived at the Chinese coast on December 7, 1941, the day of the Japanese attack on Pearl Harbor. The Marines were taken prisoner, and the crates of fossils have never been found (Shipman, 2001).

Because of Weidenreich's careful molding and measuring of the Zhoukoudian fossils, at least we have replicas of the Peking Man fossils, comprising more than

(a)

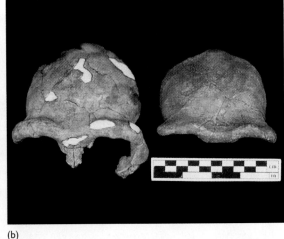

(b)

FIGURE 12.21   (a) The site of Zhoukoudian outside of Beijing, China, spans several hundred thousand years and (b) yielded numerous *H. erectus* fossils.

a dozen calvaria and hundreds of associated teeth and bone fragments (Weidenreich, 1943). They represent as many as forty individuals who lived nearby Zhoukoudian between 600,000 and 200,000 years ago. Although it was originally described as a cave where *H. erectus* lived, used fire, and cooked meals, more recent archaeological work at the site has found that it is a series of sediment-filled cracks in the rock not a habitation site (Goldberg, et al., 2001). In addition to the Zhoukoudian material, other Chinese *H. erectus* have been discovered including the more recently discovered Nanjing and Hexian crania, which are morphologically very similar to the Zhoukoudian finds (Wu, X. and Poirier, 1994). In most ways, *H. erectus* from China looks like other Asian *H. erectus*.

Despite their similarities, Chinese *H. erectus* also show some regional differences from the Indonesian *H. erectus* in their frontal and occipital regions (Antón, 2003). These differences may reflect the intermittent isolation of these two groups from each other during the Pleistocene. Each time sea level rose in the Pleistocene, continental and island Southeast Asia, and the hominids and land mammals living on them, were isolated from each other. These periods of separation might last 10,000 to 50,000 years—that is many, many generations of fossil hominids. Such isolation could have led to some genetic (and morphological) differences between the populations over time.

Unlike island Southeast Asia, China lacks Pleistocene volcanic sediments, posing a problem for the radiometric dating of hominid sites there. Earlier volcanics provide good age control of Jurassic and Cretaceous sites such as those in which the feathered dinosaurs of Liaoning are found. But younger volcanics are missing. Thus Chinese hominid ages are established by relative methods such as biostratigraphy or lithostratigraphy, loess stratigraphy, or, more recently, uranium series or ESR ages (see Chapter 8). At Zhoukoudian, for example, U-series and ESR age estimates on fauna suggest that the multiple layers at the site were occupied over a time span of several hundred thousand years. The earliest ages associated with hominids are nearly 600,000 years, and the youngest a bit more than 200,000 years (Grün et al., 1997). These dates suggest that the site represents a long time period, although it may be even older than previous estimates, with the youngest hominid layers being perhaps 400,000 years old (Shen & Wang, 2000).

THE STATUS OF *HOMO ERECTUS* IN EUROPE

Early humans that somewhat resembled *H. erectus* occupied Europe during the same time period that *H. erectus* occurred in Asia. However, most of the fossils discovered so far differ from the typical *H. erectus* seen in Africa, Asia, or Southeast Asia. Many of the European fossils resemble *H. sapiens* as well as *H. erectus* and Neandertals, and they may well be transitional, or archaic, forms of *H. sapiens*. The later middle Pleistocene European fossils, those dated between 500,000 and 200,000 years ago, are likely to be ancestral only to Neandertals and are discussed in Chapter 13.

The oldest of the European hominid fossils are those recovered from Gran Dolina in the Sierra de Atapuerca region of Spain and dated to nearly 800,000 years ago, more than 200,000 years older than any other known hominids in western Europe (Figure 12.22 on page 364). Although there are older stone tool sites, they lack fossil remains. The Gran Dolina fossils were found by a team led by J. M. Bermudez de Castro, E. Carbonel, and J. L. Arsuaga (1997) in the oldest of a series of deposits in the Sierra de Atapuerca that were exposed when a roadcut was made for a now abandoned rail line. Younger deposits from the same region are discussed in Chapter 13. The fossils recovered so far consist of young individuals, between 3 and 18 years of age at the time they died that exhibit a mix of characteristics, some of which appear to foreshadow Neandertals, others of which seem to link the fossils to modern humans. In particular, the presence of a **canine fossa** (an indentation on the maxilla above the canine root) has been used to argue

Although archaic hominids reached Europe by about 800,000 years ago, **H. erectus** *seems never to have lived there.*

canine fossa An indentation on the maxilla above the root of the canine, an anatomical feature usually associated with modern humans that may be present in some archaic *Homo* species in Europe.

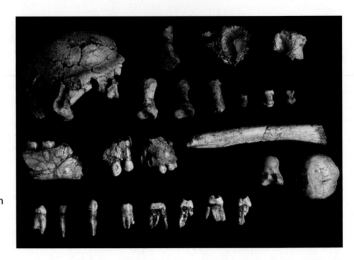

FIGURE 12.22 The Gran Dolina locality in Spain has yielded the oldest fossil hominids in Europe.

that the Gran Dolina fossils represent a previously unknown hominid species, *Homo antecessor,* which may have been the common ancestor of both Neandertals and modern *H. sapiens* (Arsuaga et al., 1999). However, many researchers are skeptical of this new classification, because the species *H. antecessor* was based largely on characters exhibited in a child's partial crania, characters the child might have lost as it aged. Another adult calvaria, Ceprano, from Italy, is said to be 800,000 years old and a member of *H. antecessor,* but it lacks the critical facial bones that define that species. It also differs anatomically from typical *H. erectus* and, more importantly, may not be nearly as old as is claimed. Only the discovery of more complete adult fossils will settle the question of the identity of *H. antecessor.* Regardless of whether *H. antecessor* is a valid taxon or part of *H. heidelbergensis* or archaic *H. sapiens* (see Chapter 13), anatomically they cannot be classified as *H. erectus,* suggesting that this species may never have made it into Europe.

The Lifeways of *Homo Erectus*

How did *Homo erectus* live? The fossils themselves are evidence of the physical adaptations of the species, and the stone tools are a window into their activities and their minds. *H. erectus* is associated with two different tool technologies that reflect advanced cognitive skills. *H. erectus* appears to have undergone a dietary shift to a more heavily meat-based diet than its predecessors, and this shift seems to have fueled both its dispersal from Africa and a different pattern of growth.

HOMO ERECTUS AND THE EARLY STONE AGE

Acheulean Stone tool industry of the early and middle Pleistocene characterized by the presence of bifacial hand axes and cleavers. This industry is made by a number of *Homo* species, including *H. erectus* and early *H. sapiens.*

Early Stone Age (or Lower Paleolithic) The earliest stone tool industries including the Oldowan and Acheulean industries, called the ESA in Africa and the Lower Paleolithic outside Africa.

bifaces Stone tools that have been flaked on two faces or opposing sides, forming a cutting edge between the two flake scars.

From 1.8 to about 1.5 million years ago in Africa, only Oldowan tools are found with *H. erectus.* The earliest tools found outside Africa at Dmanisi in the Republic of Georgia are also Oldowan-like assemblages (Gabunia et al., 2001). However, starting about a million and a half years ago in Africa some *H. erectus* are found with a different tool technology called the **Acheulean** tradition. This tradition persists until about 250,000 years ago and is made by a number of different species of the genus *Homo.* Together, the Oldowan and Acheulean are known as the **Early Stone Age** or **Lower Paleolithic.**

Acheulean assemblages are characterized by specifically shaped tools called hand axes and cleavers that are worked on two sides. Both are thus **bifaces,** tools whose cutting edge is formed by the removal of flakes from opposing sides of the piece. The scars left by the removal of these flakes meet to form the sharp edge. A **hand axe** is a bifacially worked, symmetrical, teardrop-shaped tool (Figure 12.23). A **cleaver** has a broader working end where the point of the teardrop would have been in a hand axe.

For the first time in human prehistory we see hominids making standardized tools that clearly indicate they had a plan or mental template in mind. Hand axes and cleavers were highly uniform in appearance. They were made from stone cobbles or larger flakes that had been carefully selected for size and weight. The toolmaker roughed out the axe first, and then refined the product with more subtle flaking to achieve a particular shape.

Indeed, one of the most extraordinary aspects of the Acheulean industry is its persistence and uniformity over great spans of time and space. We first see hand axes at about 1.4 million years ago, and they persist almost unchanged until about 250,000 years ago. In comparison, how many of our tools do you think will still be in use 1.2 million years from now and in nearly the same form they have today? This conservatism is also found across vast geographic areas. Hand axes appear in western and northern Europe, in East and North Africa, and in the Near East. (However, as we saw, they are very rare, or absent, in the East Asian *H. erectus* sites.) The uniformity of hand axe appearance suggests that they were used for specific purposes and in standard ways.

The advantages of the hand axe and cleaver over the simple flake are their ability to hold a sharp edge for a long period of time, the greater length of their working edge, and their generally convenient size, which allows them to be used for holding and cutting without fatigue. Nick Toth and Kathy Schick think that hand axes and cleavers are best seen as tools specifically developed for the butchery of large animals (see Insights and Advances: Understanding the Meat-Eating Past through the Present). The circular pattern of flaking around the perimeter of the axe leads some scholars to consider them primitive versions of a circular saw in which more flaking was done as earlier edges became worn and dull. But other hypotheses for the use of hand axes cannot be discounted. A recent study found evidence of fossilized *phytoliths*, microscopic mineral particles from plants (see Chapter 8), on the cutting edge of some hand axes. Their presence suggests that the tool was used to scrape plant material. This could have meant the users of the tools were sharpening a wooden spear, or perhaps stripping bark from wood for building or eating. Alternatively, hand axes might also have been used as digging implements or as projectiles, thrown at prey animals or even at hominid enemies. Although it seems unlikely, it is also possible that hand axes were simply raw material, the cores from which flake tools were struck. *H. erectus* might have simply carried hand axes around and struck flakes off them until the axe core was exhausted.

Whatever their use, the Acheulean industry presents an innovative technology that extended over much, but not all, of *H. erectus's* Old World range. As mentioned, Asian sites yield Oldowan-like tools but no true hand axes, at least not until late in time. The division between hand axe–bearing areas and those without hand

hand axe Type of Acheulean bifacial tool, usually teardrop-shaped, with a long cutting edge.

cleaver Type of Acheulean bifacial tool, usually oblong with a broad cutting edge on one end.

FIGURE 12.23 The Acheulean industry is typified by hand axes and cleavers.

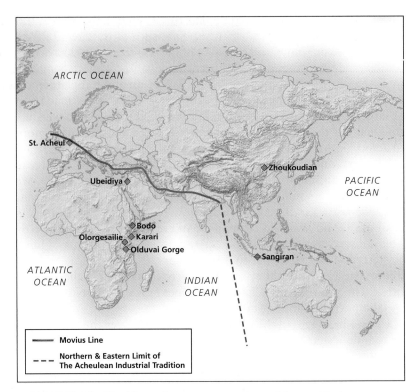

FIGURE 12.24 The Movius line separates regions of the world where Acheulean hand axes were made from regions where they were not.

axes is called the **Movius line**, after Hallam Movius, an early archaeologist who first recognized this puzzling distribution (Figure 12.24). There are two not necessarily mutually exclusive hypotheses for the Movius line. The first suggests that the absence of hand axes reflects a loss of hand axe technology in Asia caused by differences in selective pressures and raw materials between Asia and Africa. In particular, organic materials such as bamboo are inferred to have been used by the hominids. In this view, African *H. erectus* left the continent with Acheulean technology but reverted to Oldowan technology in their new environment. Alternatively, other scientists suggest that the hominids that inhabit Asia left Africa before Acheulean tools were developed, so their absence is not so much a loss of technology as a difference in the technological paths taken in Asia and Africa. This difference may result from differences in available resources and selective pressures as well.

However, it is important to recognize that there is no one-to-one correlation between a species and a technology. Oldowan tools are used by both *H. habilis* and *H. erectus* (and perhaps any number of australopithecines), and different groups of *H. erectus* use Oldowan or Acheulean tools, or both. *H. erectus* continued to make and use Oldowan industry tools in Africa and elsewhere even after Acheulean tools came into widespread use, and later hominids used Acheulean tools in Africa and Europe.

A HIGHER-QUALITY DIET: *HOMO ERECTUS* SUBSISTENCE

We assume that *H. erectus*, like modern foraging peoples, ate mostly plant foods, but there is no mistaking the archaeological evidence that *H. erectus* also ate meat. About 1.8 million years ago, an important biological shift apparently occurred in the hominid lineage, in which the human form became much more modern, taller,

Movius line The separation between areas of the Old World in which Acheulean technology occurs and those in which it does not; named by archaeologist Hallam Movius.

more linear, and with a larger brain. Shortly after this time hominids left Africa and began their worldwide geographic expansion. Both these things tell us that the shift probably was associated with a major increase in the quality of the diet, which was needed to maintain a larger body and brain (see Insights and Advances: What's Size Got to Do with It? on page 368; Leonard and Robertson, 1997; Antón et al., 2002).

Many scientists think the adaptive shift occurred when hominids became predators (Shipman & Walker, 1989). As they became carnivores, their small intestine would have lengthened while the large intestine shortened because meat takes less time in the large intestine for processing. The amount of leisure time would have increased as the time needed to forage for plants decreased. Population density would have been low because predators sit atop the food chain and must exist at low densities to avoid outstripping their prey supply. But the ability to disperse may have increased as hominids became less dependent on specific plant resources and more dependent on animal resources. Migrating herds might have led hominids to follow them, and in new areas meat is fairly safe, regardless of species, but new plants might be poisonous or inedible.

Most scientists argue that the adaptive shift happened with the emergence of *H. erectus* about 1.8 million years ago and that *H. erectus* was the first truly predatory human species. They base their assertion on the increasingly sophisticated tools associated with *H. erectus,* which may have been used for butchering prey, and on evidence that as *H. erectus* spread its range across the Old World, they lived at low population densities in the manner of a hunting species. Alan Walker and colleagues (1982) found one *Homo erectus* individual who may have died from too much vitamin A, a condition which is known to occur in modern people that eat too much internal organ meat, such as the liver, from prey animals. In addition, it seems that human-specific tapeworms share a history with tapeworms that live in hyenas but diverged from them about 1.8 million years ago. This suggests that ancient hyenas and humans were eating the same infected animals about 1.8 million years ago, further suggesting that humans had made the shift from a largely vegetarian to a more heavily meat diet.

Once meat was obtained, there is only equivocal evidence that *H. erectus* was the first hominid to prepare it for consumption by cooking it. Archaeologists working in East Africa at Koobi Fora and Chesowanja have found hominid and animal fossils associated with burnt earth that suggests the possible use of fire as early as 1.6 million years ago (Bellomo, 1994). However, it is unclear whether this was hominid-controlled fire, perhaps collected from a natural fire, or hominid-made fire, or even just a natural fire. To date, most researchers think this may be evidence of brush fires that were not human made. The best unequivocal evidence of hominid-controlled fire comes much later in time during the middle Pleistocene. Although the evidence of *H. erectus* controlling fire is questionable, some researchers hypothesize that the advent of cooking created whole new adaptive niches for *H. erectus.* They suggest that eating potato-like tubers rather than meat could have provided the higher-quality diet necessary for expansion of the human brain (Wrangham et al., 1999). Wrangham and colleagues suggest that lightning-set fires on the African savanna created an opportunity for early humans to see the effects of fire on the charred underground tubers that survive wildfires (Wrangham et al., 1999). Nonetheless, during this time period, evidence of meat eating is overwhelming, whereas the evidence of tuber cooking is scanty at best.

*The dispersal of **H. erectus** from Africa may have been aided by a shift to a higher quality diet consisting of animal meat and marrow.*

HOMO ERECTUS LIFE HISTORY

As adults, modern humans and *H. erectus* look remarkably different, but are they more similar as children? The discovery of the Nariokotome boy (KNM-WT 15000), the remarkably complete *H. erectus* youth discussed earlier, highlighted how little we know about growth in fossil hominids (see Chapter 11 Innovations: Dikika and

INSIGHTS AND ADVANCES

What's Size Got to Do with It?

Homo erectus were bigger, in some cases much bigger, than *H. habilis.* On average, they had bigger brains and bigger bodies, an increase perhaps due to their ability to access a higher-quality diet. However, there was also a lot of size variation in *H. erectus,* and a number of new fossils suggest that some *H. erectus* individuals were no bigger than some of the larger members of *H. habilis.*

The smallest of the new fossils is a recently discovered calvaria from Ileret, Kenya, that at 1.5 million years old is about the same geological age as the largest of the African *H. erectus,* OH 9 (Figure A) from Olduvai Gorge, Tanzania (Spoor et al., 2007). The Ileret specimen, discovered by Meave and Louise Leakey's Koobi Fora Research Project has a cranial capacity of just 690 cc, and external vault dimensions that are even smaller than those of the Dmanisi fossils (Figure 12.16). Yet, the specimen has all the cranial characters typical of *H. erectus:* cra-

nial superstructures, an angulated vault, and so on. In fact, the Ileret specimen is more similar to some Asian *H. erectus* than are other Koobi Fora specimens. And this makes a good argument for Asian and African specimens belonging to a single species.

The Ileret and Dmanisi specimen are examples of small, early *H. erectus,* and there appear to have been small *H. erectus* individuals through the entire time range of the species. At the younger end of the *H. erectus* range in Africa lived the relatively small individuals at Olduvai and those recently discovered at Olorgesailie, which are both larger than the Ileret specimens. With all these specimens, we see that some cranial characters become more exaggerated at larger sizes. Cranial thickness is greater in larger-brained *H. erectus,* and their browridges are larger as well. But other characters, such as some cranial superstructures and dental proportions, do not

vary with overall size, and these also differentiate even small *H. erectus* individuals like Ileret from *H. habilis.*

Taken as a group, the amount of variation in African *H. erectus* is larger than that seen in living humans or chimpanzees, but smaller than that seen in gorillas today and in earlier hominids like *A. afarensis.* Because we can't tell which fossils are males and which are females, we do not know if these size differences are related to sexual dimorphism. If they are, they might give us clues about a non-monogamous mating system in *H. erectus* (see Chapter 6). Or they could be related to individual differences in genetic background, diet, and other factors. For example, humans in industrial societies have undergone an increase in height related to changes in nutrition (see Chapter 16). Perhaps the size differences in the Dmanisi group tell us about local resource scarcity in the early Pleistocene rather than sexual dimorphism.

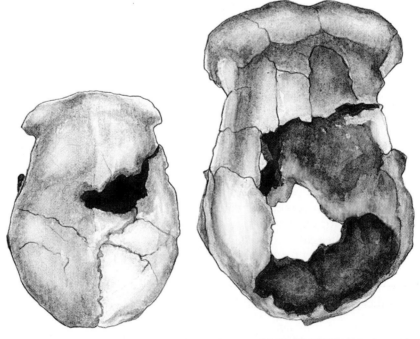

FIGURE A   Crania of the smallest African *H. erectus* (KNM-ER 42700) and of one of the largest (OH 9) illustrate the substantial size range that existed in this species at around 1.5 million years ago.

Development). At first this may seem unimportant, but in small ways and in larger ways, modifications of the developmental process produce the differences we see in adult forms. So understanding the developmental pattern is critical to understanding hominid evolution.

As you saw in Chapter 5 and we will explore further in Chapter 16, because of our large brain, humans grow slowly and mature late compared with nonhuman primates, even chimps. This makes us extremely k-selected, even compared with the other great apes. During this long development, human maturation is characterized by two growth spurts. The first occurs in the middle of childhood, around the age of 5, and the second is the adolescent growth spurt that occurs in humans in the teenage years (see Chapter 16 and Figures 16.8 and 16.9). Neither exists to the same degree in chimpanzees, posing the question of when during hominid evolution they arose and what their behavioral implications are.

Teeth have been the most informative structures from which we learn about development because their internal structure forms by layers deposited in cyclical patterns in daily increments during dental development. As the crown develops, a number of bands are formed, and by looking at these bands we can glean something about the age and rate of development. Work on dental microstructure by Chris Dean and colleagues suggests that early development in *H. erectus* was fast. Based on these data, this group concluded that the Nariokotome boy would have been no more than about 8 years old at the time of death even though a modern human of similar development would be more like 11 or 12 years old. And *H. erectus* probably reached adulthood earlier than we do, perhaps around the age of 15 years. Despite this rapid maturation, *H. erectus* were certainly as k-selected as the great apes and had a relatively large brain at birth.

HOMO ERECTUS LEAVES AFRICA

The most important adaptive shift *H. erectus* made was the first migration out of Africa (Figure 12.25). This emigration meant moving across a variety of ecosystems, climates, and ecological settings. Each of these would have presented *H. erectus* with new challenges never encountered by a hominid. Most important was the move from tropical and subtropical Africa into the more seasonally cold regions of the

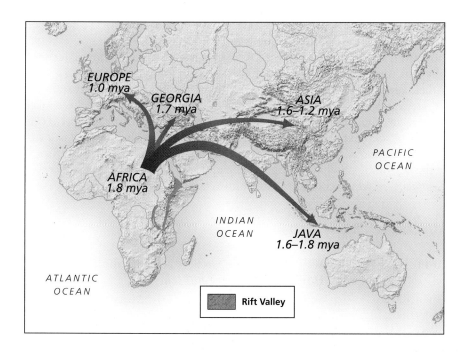

FIGURE 12.25 *H. erectus* migrated out of Africa beginning about 1.8 million years ago and is first known from Georgia and Java.

Northern Hemisphere in Eurasia and the Far East. This change alone demonstrates the remarkable adaptability and behavioral flexibility our lineage had evolved by just under 2 million years ago. The ability to adapt to a wide range of novel environments is a hallmark of the human species.

One question remains: Why did hominids remain in Africa for more than 3 million years, only to disperse rapidly after the origin of *H. erectus?* Some of the likely causes we have suggested in this chapter form a web of ecological and morphological advantages that facilitated *H. erectus* dispersal. World climate was beginning to undergo some severe fluctuations slightly before the rise of *H. erectus* (see Chapter 8). The African area was cooling and drying around 2 million years ago, leading to diminished forests with larger grasslands between them. The rise of grasslands saw the increase in the quantities of grass-eating animals like antelope and the evolution of a new niche for animals (including hominids) that could eat them.

H. erectus seems to have taken advantage of these opportunities by using Oldowan tools to access animal foods it was not physically adapted to acquire. The higher-quality animal diet that resulted allowed the growth of larger bodies, and their more linear body shape probably allowed greater midday activity because they coped better with the heat. Larger bodies and different limb proportions allowed greater ranging (home range, the area an animal traverses over a year, is positively correlated to body size in mammals and bipedal ranging efficiency relates to a relatively long leg compared to body size). As animals such as antelope migrated, hominids may have followed.

In the late Pliocene, at about the time that we see other African fauna migrating into the Near East and western Asia, we also see *H. erectus* migrating. Were they following this food resource? Earlier hominids had not migrated during earlier faunal migrations out of Africa. Perhaps they remained in place because of their greater reliance on plant foods. It does seem that at this point *H. erectus* was able to do something that earlier hominids were not capable of doing. It seems reasonable to assume that tool use and the access to previously inaccessible resources it allowed were fundamental to the ability to migrate. However, a complex web of factors must have been involved in dispersal.

There is unlikely to have been a single directional dispersal event from Africa to Asia. Rather, random movements of multiple hominid groups over time probably led to the eventual dispersal of the species across the Old World, and some back migrations probably also occurred. Even though the entire dispersal seems a long one, consider that an average change in home range of just 1 km a year (less than a mile), over a period of 10,000 or 15,000 years, would have led to a slow dispersal, yet it would look geologically instantaneous.

Having moved into many parts of the Old World using a combination of technology and physical adaptation, and having made a shift in foraging strategy to a higher-quality diet, early *H. erectus* was poised to begin the brain size expansion and intellectual development characteristic of the genus. Through time, *H. erectus* continued a gradual development of physical and cultural evolution. However, more recent species of genus *Homo* exhibited even more dramatic changes. Intelligence is a survival strategy of enormous evolutionary importance to the human lineage. In *H. erectus,* we see the beginning of what intelligence meant for the hominid lineage. Now we turn to *H. sapiens,* in which cognition and culture take on far more importance.

SUMMARY

1. **How do we define the earliest members of the genus *Homo?***

   Genus *Homo* is defined by brain size greater than 500 cc, a smaller and less prognathic face, and smaller teeth than australopithecines possess.

2. **Why do some researchers consider the earliest genus *Homo* to be *Australopithecus?***

   Some researchers think that the earliest known *Homo* species, such as *Homo habilis,* are so apelike they should be lumped with *Australopithecus* and that genus *Homo* should be reserved for the larger-brained, longer-limbed *H. erectus* and kin that appeared later.

3. **When and where did *H. erectus* appear?**

The earliest *H. erectus* are often called *H. ergaster* because of their small brain and body size. They appeared in East Africa and also outside Africa in the Republic of Georgia about 1.8 million years ago.

4. **What are the differences between Asian and African *H. erectus*?**

Asian *H. erectus* are different from African *H. erectus* in having thicker-walled crania, more robust facial features, larger teeth, and more cranial superstructures.

5. **What sort of stone tools did *H. erectus* use?**

H. erectus used both Oldowan and Acheulean tools but may have been the hominid that invented Acheulean tools.

6. **Why do we think that *H. erectus* was the first hominid that ate substantial quantities of meat?**

H. erectus made stone tools and there is archaeological evidence that these tools were used to butcher large animals, suggesting substantial meat consumption. In addition, its larger body and brain size and its greater range (across the Old World) suggest that *H. erectus* must have had a higher-quality diet than earlier *Homo* in order to meet its higher energetic needs.

CRITICAL THINKING QUESTIONS

1. What possible reasons might there be for the long duration of use of Acheulean hand axes and what might this mean about the culture and mind of *H. erectus*?

2. How might we interpret the fact that the earliest *H. erectus* fossils come from East Africa, but that there are other very *H. erectus*–like fossils from outside Africa at about the same time?

3. What was the main survival value of larger brain size to *H. erectus*? What could they do that earlier hominids could not that allowed them to expand the human range beyond Africa?

KEY TERMS

Oldowan
tool industry
core
flake
hammerstone
butchering site
quarrying site

home base
supraoribital torus
angular torus
occipital torus
sagittal keel
metopic keel
shovel-shaped incisors

platymeric
platycnemic
calotte
calvaria
canine fossa
Acheulean

Early Stone Age (or
    Lower Paleolithic)
bifaces
hand axe
cleaver
Movius line

SUGGESTED READING

Lewin, Roger. (1997). *Bones of Contention*. (2nd ed.). University of Chicago Press, Chicago.

Schick, Kathy, and Toth, Nicholas. (1993). *Making Silent Stones Speak: Human Evolution and the Dawn of Technology*. Simon & Schuster, New York.

Shipman, Pat. (2001). *The Man Who Found the Missing Link*. Harvard University Press, Cambridge, MA.

Walker, Alan, and Shipman, Pat. (1996). *The Wisdom of the Bones*. Vintage Books, New York.

Wolpoff, Milford. (1999). *Paleoanthropology*. (2nd ed.). McGraw-Hill, New York.

Archaic *Homo sapiens*
and Neandertals

n an open coal pit in Schoeningen, Germany, a huge mechanical shovel grinds away at the earth, stripping away not only vast amounts of coal but also Holocene and Pleistocene deposits. Over the years, archaeologists have identified a number of Lower Paleolithic sites in the pit. The sites are several meters below ground and date to about 400,000 years ago: the Middle Pleistocene. The material found includes flint tools and flakes, combined with the remains of extinct elephants, bovids, deer, and horses. No hominid remains are found, which is unfortunate given the scarcity of fossils from this critical period in human evolution. But after several years of excavation, archaeologist Hartmut Thieme discovered something that was even more scarce, and perhaps more significant, than additional fossil remains: four large wooden spears.

The spears are impressive: Two of them measure more than 2.25 m (7 ft) in length. Three of them are sharpened at one end. They are carefully shaped and their weight is distributed to make them aerodynamically efficient when thrown. It is also possible that they could have been used as lances and thrust at prey. The fourth, perhaps a throwing stick or small thrusting spear, is smaller (less than 1 m long) and sharpened at both ends. Three smaller wooden implements, made from the branches of trees, were also found. Although the function of these implements is not clear, they each had a groove cut into one end that could have been used to hold flints, perhaps creating a composite cutting or chopping tool.

These wooden tools show us how hominids of the Middle Pleistocene made use of organic materials in their lives and provide us with a window to the past that is typically shuttered. They remind us that hominid behavior may have been much more sophisticated during this period than we may sometimes think.

Today, one species of hominid, *Homo sapiens*, occupies the globe. As a species, we share a common origin that should be traceable back to a population that existed at a certain time and place: but which time and place? Hominids definitely have an African origin. We do not find hominids outside Africa until after 2 million years ago. But because *Homo erectus*, the presumed ancestor of all later hominid species, lived throughout the Old World in regions that were later occupied by modern humans, it is not immediately clear which *H. erectus* populations, if any, are directly ancestral to us. In addition, the tools these populations made and the behaviors they record become more complicated throughout the Pleistocene. The discovery of tools made from organic material, such as the wooden spears at Schoeningen, reminds us just how much information is missing from the archaeological record of early humans. To understand the evolution of our genus during the Pleistocene, we need to consider both the anatomical and behavioral traits of our ancestors.

In this chapter, we look at the anatomy and behavior of the hominids of the Middle to Late Pleistocene. Hominid fossils from this evolutionarily dynamic period have been found throughout much of the Old World, but taxonomic assignments for the fossil specimens remain controversial. How many hominid species were present? What constitutes enough variation to differentiate them from one another? Are the famous Neandertals simply another type of human or something more distinct? How did they behave and what does that tell us about the selective pressures and evolutionary changes that led to the origin of our own species?

Hominid Evolution in the Middle to Late Pleistocene

As we saw in Chapter 8, the Pleistocene dates from 1.8 million years ago to 10,000 years ago. In about the middle of this epoch we begin to find fossils that exhibit features often interpreted as being more "advanced" or derived in the direction of *H. sapiens* than was *H. erectus*. These specimens often are informally labeled "archaic *Homo sapiens*" or "advanced *H. erectus*," designations that distinguish them from anatomically modern *H. sapiens* and classic *H. erectus*. Such informal labels indicate the transitional nature of these fossils between *H. erectus* and *H. sapiens* and the difficulty of elucidating their relationships to other hominids. In addition to archaic *H. sapiens*, classic *H. erectus* survived in China and Indonesia until at least 100,000 years ago and maybe later (see Chapter 12). The earliest representatives of the Neandertals make their first appearance in Europe, and it is possible that the earliest modern humans may also have made their first appearance in Africa at the very end of the Middle Pleistocene (see Chapter 14).

DEFINING ANATOMICALLY MODERN *HOMO* SAPIENS

Archaic *H. sapiens* are intermediate between classic *H. erectus* and anatomically modern *H. sapiens*. To understand what this means, let us consider the features that distinguish modern humans from other hominids (Clark, 1975).

Compared with other members of genus *Homo*, the skull of anatomically modern *H. sapiens* is large (average capacity 1,350 cc) and gracile (Figure 13.1). Muscular ridges on the cranium are not strongly marked. Supraorbital (brow) ridges are not well developed or are absent altogether. The occipital region of the cranium is rounded, lacking development of an occipital torus and usually without an **occipital bun** (a backward-projecting bulge on of the occipital part of the skull). The forehead is rounded and more vertical than in other groups of *Homo*. Seen from behind, the maximum breadth of the skull is high (in the *parietal* region), and the vault is parallel-sided in rear view. The **mastoid process**, a protrusion from the temporal bone of the skull located behind and below the ear, is large and pyramidal in shape. The jaws and teeth are small. The third molars (wisdom teeth) sometimes are poorly developed or even absent. Following jaw size, the face is smaller and retracted under the braincase to a greater degree than in previous hominids because the cranial base is more flexed. A *canine fossa* (a depression in the maxilla above the root of the upper canines) also develops. There is marked development of a chin. The limb bones are straight and slightly built, with the lower limb much longer than the upper.

Archaic *H. sapiens* tend to exhibit a mosaic of *H. erectus* (see Chapter 12) and *H. sapiens* features, in many cases retaining the robustness of classic *H. erectus* but with a larger cranial capacity and a shape more similar to anatomically modern *H. sapiens*. This intermediate or transitional nature of archaic *H. sapiens* poses problems for classifying these fossils.

occipital bun A backward-projecting bulge of the occipital part of the skull.

mastoid process A protrusion from the temporal bone of the skull located behind the ear.

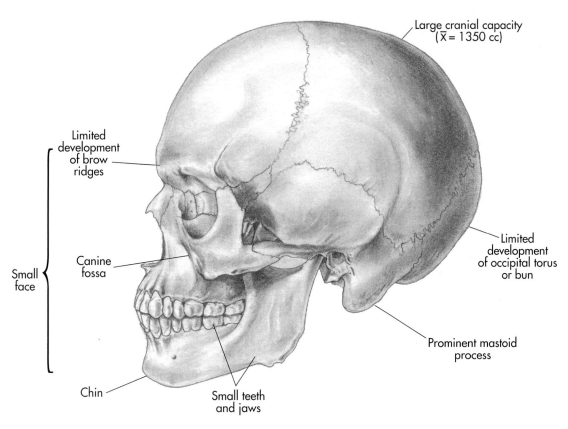

Large cranial capacity
($\bar{x}$ = 1350 cc)

Limited
development
of brow
ridges

Canine
fossa

Small
face

Chin

Small teeth
and jaws

Limited
development
of occipital torus
or bun

Prominent mastoid
process

FIGURE 13.1   Features of the skull of anatomically modern *Homo sapiens*.

Archaic *Homo sapiens*

Archaic *H. sapiens* fossils reflect an important transitional period during human evolution. As we review the individual fossils, keep in mind that although we may call them archaic *H. sapiens*, that does not mean we consider them ancestral to later anatomically modern *H. sapiens* (although that may be a reasonable hypothesis), nor do they necessarily all represent the same species, although many scientists argue that they do. Anatomically the group is diverse, but it seems to differ consistently from *H. erectus* by having larger brains (1,000–1,400 cc), more parallel-sided, taller, and less angular cranial vaults, robust but arching rather than straight supraorbital tori, and in some instances, wide nasal apertures (Figure 13.2 on page 376). Archaic *H. sapiens* differ from modern humans by retaining robust supraorbital tori, large faces, and thicker-walled, lower cranial vaults.

EUROPEAN ARCHAIC *HOMO* SAPIENS

The first archaic *H. sapiens* to be discovered in Europe was a mandible found in 1907 in a sandpit in the village of Mauer, near Heidelberg, Germany (Figure 13.3 on page 376) (Schoetensack, 1908). Based on faunal and stratigraphic dating (no absolute dating is possible at the site), the mandible was assigned an age of 400,000 to 500,000 years. Because the Mauer mandible is clearly not modern—it is quite robust and lacks a chin—it was correctly identified in 1908 as a hominid species distinct from our own. Because *Homo* (*Pithecanthropus*) *erectus* was not a generally accepted taxon at that time, the Mauer mandible was given the name *Homo heidelbergensis*.

After *H. erectus* became more accepted, some researchers argued that the Mauer mandible should be placed in that species. However, others argue that the mandible

Archaic *Homo sapiens*

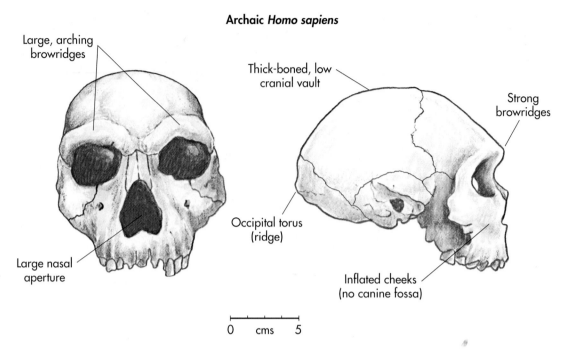

FIGURE 13.2   Features of the skull of archaic *Homo sapiens*.

differs from classic *H. erectus* in both its bony anatomy and its dentition and resembles several more complete specimens that were discovered later and are often called archaic *H. sapiens*. However, mandibles are notoriously hard to classify during this time period, and so the debate continues. For the many researchers who think that the informal label "archaic *H. sapiens*" should be replaced with a formal species designation, the name *H. heidelbergensis* would have priority because the Mauer mandible was the first of this group to be discovered and named.

More complete fossils provide a more detailed picture of European hominids in the Middle Pleistocene (Figure 13.4). These include the Petralona cranium from Greece (150,000–300,000 years ago), the Steinheim cranium from Germany (200,000–250,000 years ago), the Arago 21 partial cranium from France (300,000–600,000 years ago), and the back of a cranium from Swanscombe, England (200,000–250,000 years ago). Less complete remains of archaic *H. sapiens* are known from several other sites in Europe, such as Bilzingsleben and Véretesszöllös in Hungary. The greatest number and the oldest of the archaic *H. sapiens* fossils recovered from a single locality come from a younger part of the same cave system in which *H. antecessor* was discovered, the Sierra de Atapuerca, Spain (Arsuaga et al., 1997; Arsuaga, 2002) (Figure 13.5). This cave (or pit) known as *Sima de los Huesos* (literally, the "bone pit"), is about 500,000 to 600,000 years old based on U-series dating (Bischoff et al., 2007). The pit yielded at least 28 individuals ranging in age from 4 to 35 years. The extensive postcranial remains from Sima de los Huesos and the 500,000-year-old tibia from Boxgrove in southern England, suggest that like other premodern *Homo*, archaic *Homo sapiens* were robust with strong muscle markings and thick cortical bone, large joint surface areas, and strongly buttressed, broad pelves (Stringer et al., 1998; Arsuaga et al., 1997; Arsuaga, 2002).

All these archaic *H. sapiens* specimens resemble *H. erectus* in having thick cranial bones and less round cranial vaults and similar postcranial skeletons, but they differ from classic *H. erectus* in vault shape and size, browridge conformation, and facial morphology.

FIGURE 13.3   The Mauer mandible, discovered in Germany in 1907.

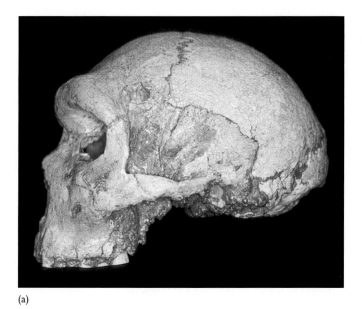

(a)   (b)

FIGURE 13.4   (a) The Petralona cranium from Greece. (b) The Steinheim cranium from Germany.

Their cranial capacities range between 1,100 and 1,390 cc, making them larger brained than typical *H. erectus* specimens. They have taller vaults with the greatest cranial breadth higher on the parietal than in *H. erectus,* yet their braincase is lower than ours.

These Middle Pleistocene European hominids are too primitive to be considered Neandertals, but those from the Sima de los Huesos exhibit several cranial features that are very Neandertal-like. Facial features that are the most Neandertal-like include a double-arched supraorbital torus and **midfacial prognathism,** the forward

midfacial prognathism   The forward projection of the middle facial region, including the nose.

FIGURE 13.5   Skeletal remains from the Sima de los Huesos, Sierra de Atapuerca, Spain.

FIGURE 13.6 The Kabwe cranium (left) and the Bodo cranium (right) from Ethiopia, which shows signs of having been defleshed with stone tools.

projection of the middle facial region, including the nose. The nasal bones actually form a shelf projecting from the face, and the cheek bones gradually recede from these rather than being perpendicular to the nose, as in our face. The nasal aperture is also quite wide. These features suggest that the Sima de los Huesos hominids and other European archaic *H. sapiens* may be directly ancestral to the later Neandertals. We will discuss this phylogenetic model and others later.

AFRICAN ARCHAIC *HOMO* SAPIENS

The African continent has yielded at least four crania that are generally regarded as archaic *H. sapiens* because of their large cranial capacities, massive but more arching, non-barlike supraorbital tori, and less angular vaults, with their greatest width higher on the cranium. Two are perhaps large males (Figure 13.6). The oldest of these is the partial cranium from Bodo, Ethiopia, which preserves the face and anterior braincase and dates to as much as 600,000 years ago. The Bodo cranium has a capacity of about 1,300 cc (Conroy et al., 1978). Its most extraordinary features are cut marks on the face that appear to be made by stone tools that may reflect a burial or ritual practice (White, T. D., 1986). The Kabwe cranium and several postcranial elements, discovered in northern Rhodesia (present-day Zambia) at the Broken Hill limestone mine in 1921, are more complete but slightly smaller (1,280 cc) than the Bodo cranium. The Kabwe remains are also known as Rhodesian Man or Broken Hill for their find spot. Dating of the site is uncertain, although an age of 125,000 years is suggested based on biostratigraphy. Both Kabwe and Bodo have large nasal apertures and somewhat prognathic midfaces with massive, arched brows. The previous classification of Broken Hill as an African Neandertal, although now discarded, may indicate an ultimate ancestry to the Neandertal lineage.

Two smaller archaic *H. sapiens* crania also exist in Africa. The Ndutu partial cranium from Lake Ndutu near Olduvai Gorge in Tanzania has a cranial capacity of about 1,100 cc (Rightmire, 1990). Dates for the Ndutu cranium range from between 200,000 to 400,000 years ago. The Salé partial cranium from Morocco has a smaller cranial capacity (900 cc), and dates to about 200,000–250,000 years ago (Hublin, 1985). Like the Steinheim cranium from Germany, these crania may be from small females, with similarly small cranial capacities. Although not particularly large, Ndutu and Salé share features of the cranial vault with other archaic *H. sapiens*, including a high maximum cranial breadth and rounder vaults.

The European and African archaic *H. sapiens* specimens share many features and have a similar overall appearance. However, so far no African archaic *H. sapiens* possess the specific derived features that the Sima de los Huesos hominids and other European fossils are claimed to share with later Neandertals.

ASIAN ARCHAIC *HOMO* SAPIENS

Archaic *H. sapiens* from Asia differ from *H. erectus* in vault size and shape and supraorbital toral shape. Reasonably complete crania from the sites of Dali, Maba, and Jinniushan, China, range in age from 130,000 to 200,000 years old (Figure 13.7). The finds from Jinniushan also include some postcrania. Two other crania from Yunxian probably also represent archaic *H. sapiens* based on the shape of the browridge. However, both are heavily distorted and difficult to interpret (Li & Etler, 1992). The oldest hominid remains on the Indian continent come from the Narmada Valley, where a partial calvaria dates to perhaps 125,000 to 150,000 years ago. The Narmada cranium was initially classified as belonging to *H. erectus*; however, later analyses established its transitional character, indicating that it was more similar to archaic *H. sapiens* (Kennedy et al., 1991). It has an estimated cranial capacity of 1,150 to 1,400 cc, more vertically sided vault walls, and an arched browridge.

Although dating is a problem for the Chinese and Indian archaic *H. sapiens,* evidence indicates that archaic *H. sapiens* probably were present in Asia by 200,000 years ago. Given some of the late dates for classic *H. erectus* in Asia (see Chapter 12), if you accept that archaic *H. sapiens* is a different species than *H. erectus,* then two distinct hominid species were present in Asia at this time.

Behavior of Archaic *Homo sapiens*

Reconstructing the behavior of archaic *Homo sapiens* poses a somewhat different problem from reconstructing the behavior of earlier hominids. Given their large brain size and probable close relationship to modern humans, we are compelled to consider archaic *H. sapiens* behavior from the perspective of what we know about the behavior of contemporary humans. Unfortunately, the material culture of archaic *H. sapiens* doesn't provide a comprehensive rendering of their behavior. Nonetheless, archaeological excavations at many sites in the Old World dating from 150,000 to 500,000 years ago indicate this was a period of evolutionary, although perhaps not revolutionary, change in behavior.

STONE TOOLS

Stone tool types and distributions that characterized the Early Pleistocene were still present in the Middle Pleistocene. In Africa and Europe, where the Acheulean was well represented, Acheulean traditions—including production of bifaces (hand axes)—continued until about 150,000 years ago. In China, where hand axes were never associated with *H. erectus,* archaic *H. sapiens* are found in association with simple flake tools and cores. Together the Oldowan and Acheulean industries are known as the *Lower Paleolithic* in Europe or the *Early Stone Age* in Africa.

Middle Paleolithic (Middle Stone Age) industries that used *prepared core* technologies originated in the Middle Pleistocene (Figure 13.8 on page 380). Prepared core technologies require that the toolmaker modify the original core by a number of flake removal steps in order to prepare it to produce a flake of a prescribed size and shape. Although wasteful of raw material in one sense, prepared core technology allows great control of production of a main tool type, the so-called *Mousterian*

Middle Paleolithic (Middle Stone Age) Stone tool industries that used prepared core technologies.

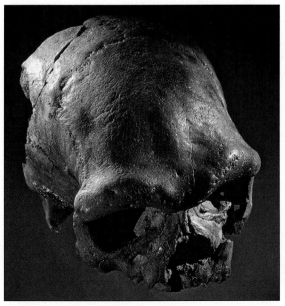

FIGURE 13.7 Dali, a Chinese archaic *Homo sapiens.*

THE LEVALLOIS TECHNIQUE

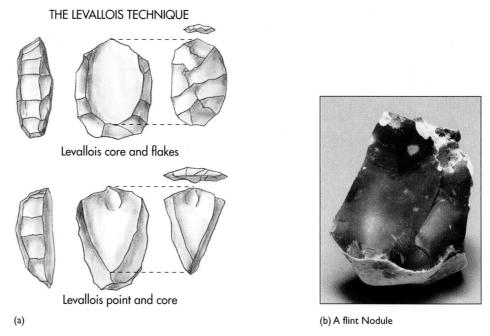

Levallois core and flakes

Levallois point and core

(a)

(b) A flint Nodule

FIGURE 13.8   (a) The Levallois technique for making uniform flakes from a prepared core. (b) Flint and other fine-grained rocks are used for making stone tools.

point. Such preparation in pursuit of a particular flake indicates increasing forethought and abstract thinking. Prepared core techniques include the **Levallois technique** that was developed in Africa between 200,000 and 300,000 years ago. In addition to prepared cores, Middle Paleolithic industries also used other flaking methods, characterized by a greater prevalence of soft hammer techniques (in which materials such as bone, antler, or soft stone were used to remove flakes), more retouched tools, and a larger variety of possibly stylized tool shapes. Tools include a number of different kinds of scrapers, made from flakes, and the previously mentioned points. The advantage of Middle Paleolithic industries, beyond the predictability of flake size and shape, is that from a given amount of raw material they produce more cutting surface than Early Paleolithic techniques. Once these tool types appeared in the late Middle Pleistocene, no new tool types were introduced until the Late Pleistocene.

BIODEGRADABLE TOOLS

Based on the behavior of living nonhuman primates and humans, we assume that hominids also used tools made from organic materials that would rarely be preserved in the archaeological record. Chimpanzees fashion tools from twigs and leaves, and it is likely that early hominids did as well. Although we have seen evidence of bone tool use by the robust australopithecines (see Chapter 11), modified bone or antler tools are missing from the archaeological record of archaic *H. sapiens*. There is, however, indirect evidence, from flake scars on stone, that bone and antler were used as soft hammers to produce stone tools (Stringer et al., 1998).

In addition, the wooden spears, throwing stick, and worked branches from Schoeningen, Germany, described at the beginning of the chapter, provide important evidence of the use of wood. The implements are dated to 400,000 years ago. The three worked branches may be as significant as the spears, since they may have been the handles of stone–wood composite tools, a technologically advanced technique. Because the tools were found in close association with numerous animal remains, they could be evidence of large game hunting. Regardless of their use, the well-crafted wooden implements suggest that wood was a common medium, at least for this archaic *H. sapiens* population in Germany.

Levallois technique   A Middle Paleolithic technique that made use of prepared cores to produce uniform flakes.

BIG GAME HUNTING

There is little doubt that big game hunting would have been advantageous for some archaic *H. sapiens* (or *H. erectus*) occupying northern latitudes in Europe or Asia. In those locations, there probably would have been a seasonal dependence on animal food, and the ability to hunt big game would have made it easier to expand into colder areas, even if scavenging were still done. In the 1960s and 1980s Clark Howell and Les Freeman excavated at the Spanish sites of Ambrona and Torralba, dated between 200,000 and 400,000 years ago, and found the remains of large game in association with Acheulean artifacts (Howell, 1966; Howell et al., 1991) (Figure 13.9). Critics point out that associations such as this do not constitute proof of hunting because they could have resulted from the activity of other animals or other nonhominid depositional forces. Perhaps the Ambrona and Torralba animals were scavenged not hunted; the sites were in a swamp, and some investigators think the animals could have died while stuck in the mud and then have been scavenged (Shipman & Rose, 1983). Others argue that finding both large animals and artifacts at watering spots simply means that water was important for both hominids and other animals and does not indicate a reliance on big game by either hunting or scavenging (Klein & Edgar, 2002).

However, excavations at two sites in the 1990s provide increasing evidence in support of the hypothesis that hominids hunted big game by the Middle Pleistocene. The Schoeningen spears were found in direct association with the butchered remains of ten horses and flake tools that could be used to deflesh the carcasses. Although it is impossible to be certain that the spears were used to bring down the horses, it seems reasonable to conclude they were made to be thrown at large, living animals. Excavations at the Boxgrove site in England (Figure 13.10 on page 382) provide further evidence of big game hunting (Stringer et al., 1998; Roberts & Parfitt, 1999). In addition to a few hominid remains, numerous remains of small and large animals in association with stone tools, mostly hand axes, have been meticulously excavated at Boxgrove. Mark Roberts and his colleagues argue that big game hunting rather than scavenging explains how these animals and tools came to be deposited together: Taphonomic analysis indicates that hominids defleshed the remains before carnivores or scavenging animals; stone tool cut marks always underlay carnivore teeth marks, and butchering marks indicate that eyes and tongues were removed by hominids ahead of bird scavengers. Furthermore, butchered rhinoceroses at the site were all healthy midlife adults with no apparent disease or defect, and a horse scapula (shoulder blade) recovered from the site has a projectile wound, a hole about 50 mm (2 in) in

By the Middle Pleistocene, hominids appear to have been accomplished big game hunters.

FIGURE 13.9 Excavations of elephant remains at Torralba, Spain.

FIGURE 13.10 Evidence for big game hunting by archaic *H. sapiens* is suggested by the association of hand axes and red deer bones at the Box-grove site, England.

diameter; just the kind of wound you would expect from spears like those found at Schoeningen.

Thus, evidence seems to be mounting that archaic *H. sapiens* were capable of bringing down large game and that they did so in a cooperative manner, using Acheulean technology. At this point, however, it seems that these Middle Pleistocene hominids did not have a great impact on the populations of large game animals they hunted. We do not, for example, see any evidence of animals driven to extinction by archaic *H. sapiens,* as we would see in some regions of the world in the Late Pleistocene when modern *H. sapiens* overhunted their large game species. This may indicate that big game hunting occupied a less important role in the subsistence strategies of archaic *H. sapiens* than it did for anatomically modern *H. sapiens.* It may also speak to differences in population size between the hominids.

FIRE, CAMPSITES, AND HOME SITES

Evidence of the use of fire and campsites by archaic *H. sapiens* is rare. No proper hearths have been discovered, but ash deposits and charred bones recovered from a number of sites indicate that fire may have been used by archaic *H. sapiens.* Archaic *H. sapiens* did not make a particularly strong impact on the landscape. Although it is reasonable to assume that they had campsites and home bases, there are few signs of them in the archaeological record. No postholes or storage pits have been found, for example. The use of caves as shelter was also limited. Evidence of Acheulean "beach huts" at the site of Terra Amata in the South of France has been claimed. However, disruption of the "living floor" of the site and the somewhat random scatter of bone and stone remains make this interpretation difficult to accept (Stringer & Gamble, 1993).

The Neandertals

Compared with the little we know of archaic *H. sapiens* we know much more about the anatomy and behavior of the Late Pleistocene hominids informally known as Neandertals. The complete or partial remains of several hundred Neandertal individuals have been discovered from sites dating between 27,000 and 150,000 years ago in Europe, the Near and Middle East, and western Asia (Figure 13.11 on pages 384–385) (Stringer & Gamble, 1993; Trinkaus, 1995). As you will recall from Chapter 8, this time period is one of extreme oscillations in temperature caused by strong glacial and interglacial cycles (see Figure 8.18). One of the results is that latitudinal variation in climate became quite significant (remember that temperature varied little from north to south early in primate evolution). Thus climate is a particularly important variable for understanding the origin and evolution of Neandertals who lived fairly far north (Howell, 1964). At the end of their existence Neandertals and anatomically modern *H. sapiens* overlap in time and space. How they share the landscape, and indeed the relationships between them, are points of some debate.

Scientists disagree as to whether Neandertals should be considered a species within the genus *Homo* (*H. neanderthalensis*) or a subspecies within *H. sapiens* (*H. s. neanderthalensis*). As was the case for archaic *H. sapiens*, choosing a taxonomic name for the Neandertals depends on how we define a species and on the phylogenetic model for the emergence of anatomically modern *H. sapiens* to which we subscribe. There is little disagreement that "classic Neandertals" are an anatomically distinct group of hominids that lived during a short period of time and occupied a circumscribed portion of the Old World. However, there is much disagreement as to whether or not these anatomical differences mean that Neandertals are a separate species or simply a geographic variant of modern humans.

GEOGRAPHIC AND TEMPORAL DISTRIBUTION

Neandertals occupied a circumscribed portion of the old world (Figure 13.12 on page 386). The largest number of Neandertal sites, including the oldest (about 150,000 years ago) and the youngest (about 27,000–30,000 years ago), are located in Western Europe. Fossil-bearing sites are plentiful in Germany (Neandertal, Ehringsdorf), Belgium (Spy, Engis), Spain (Zafarraya, Gibraltar), Italy (Guattari), and France (La Quina, La Ferrassie, St. Cesaire, La Chapelle). However, the Neandertal range extends into central Asia at the site of Teshik Tash in Uzbekistan, into the Near East (Kebara, Amud, and Tabun, Israel; Dedirayah, Syria), into the Middle East (Shanidar, Iraq) and DNA evidence suggests even into Siberia at Okladnikov. In addition to fossil-bearing localities, archaeological sites of the same ages span the entire region, telling us about site distribution and Neandertal movements relative to time and climate.

Most Neandertal fossils are found in caves, indicating extensive use of these areas as living sites. However, most Middle Paleolithic archaeological sites are open air localities. Cave use results in better preservation of remains and thus the better fossil record for Neandertals than for earlier hominids.

Neandertals lived around the Mediterranean basin with sites extending into Uzbekistan and, according to DNA analyses, into Siberia. Many of these are cave sites, which ensure good preservation of bone.

HISTORY OF NEANDERTAL DISCOVERY

From the mid-1800s until the 1930s, when *H. erectus* became a more widely accepted taxon and the South African australopithecines started to come to light, Neandertals were the core of the hominid fossil record. In the popular imagination, "Neandertal" and "caveman" became synonyms. But as the best-known representative of our evolutionary past, Neandertals also became the focus of negative portrayals and feelings (see Insights and Advances: Neandertal Image Makeover on page 388). Ideas about progress along with anxiety about our animal origins cast the Neandertal in the loser's role in the evolutionary game.

The significance of the first Neandertal finds was not fully appreciated at the time of their discovery. The first Neandertal discovered, the cranium of a small child aged 2 to 3 years, was found in 1830 at the Engis cave site in Belgium. Even

Hominid Evolution in the Mid-To-Late Pleistocene

Figure 13.11 Beginning about 600,000 years ago in Africa, hominids who were somewhat larger-brained than classic *H. erectus* but still cranially robust appeared in Africa, and then later in Europe and Asia. This group is usually referred to as archaic *Homo sapiens* (or by some as *H. heidelbergensis*). In Europe and western Asia, a distinct type of hominid, the Neandertals, appeared about 140,000 years ago.

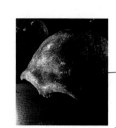

BOXGROVE Evidence of big game hunting by archaic *H. sapiens* is hinted by hand axes and deer bones at the Boxgrove site, England.

NEANDERTALS Neandertal specimens are numerous enough that we can begin to understand developmental changes across their lifespan.

ATAPUERCA Remains of more than 30 archaic *H. sapiens* individuals have been found in the *Sima de los Huesos* at Sierra de Atapuerca, Spain.

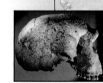

STEINHEIM is a possible contemporary of Petralona.

Map labels: ARCTIC OCEAN, ATLANTIC OCEAN, Neader Valley, Swanscombe, Schöningen, Boxgrove, Mauer, Steinheim, Atapuerca, Arago, Ambrona/Torralba, Salé, ATLANTIC OCEAN

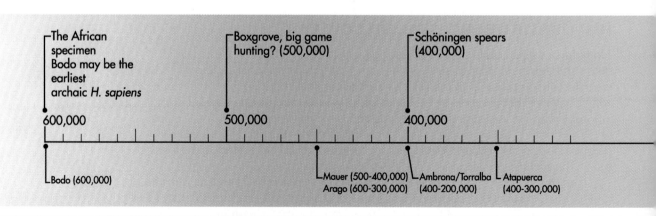

- The African specimen Bodo may be the earliest archaic *H. sapiens*
- Boxgrove, big game hunting? (500,000)
- Schöningen spears (400,000)

600,000　　500,000　　400,000

- Bodo (600,000)
- Mauer (500-400,000) Arago (600-300,000)
- Ambrona/Torralba (400-200,000)
- Atapuerca (400-300,000)

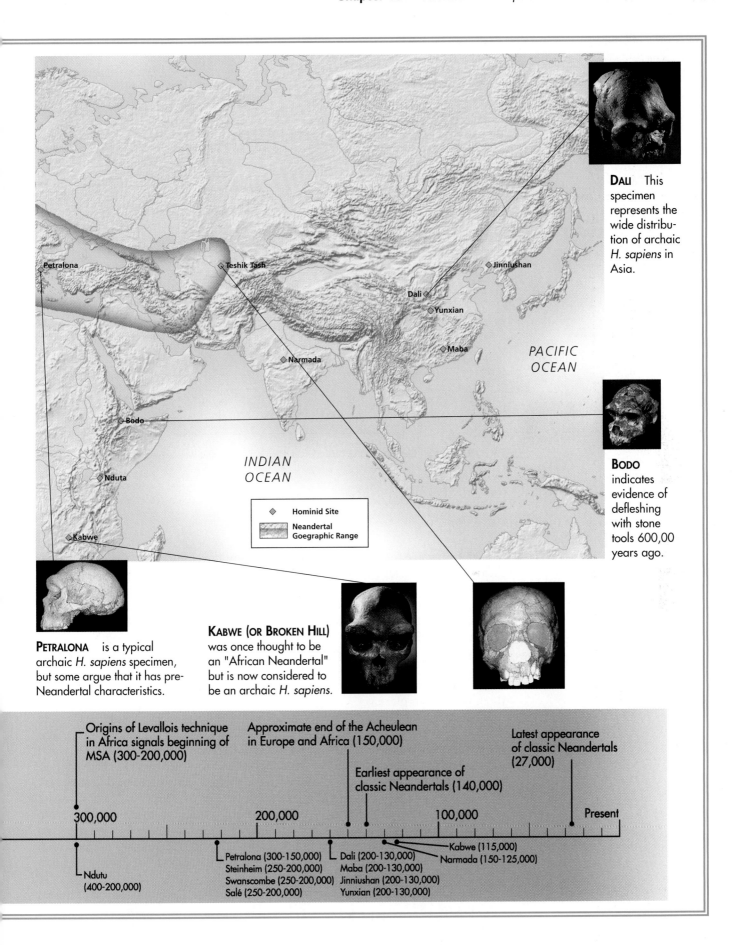

DALI This specimen represents the wide distribution of archaic *H. sapiens* in Asia.

BODO indicates evidence of defleshing with stone tools 600,00 years ago.

PETRALONA is a typical archaic *H. sapiens* specimen, but some argue that it has pre-Neandertal characteristics.

KABWE (OR BROKEN HILL) was once thought to be an "African Neandertal" but is now considered to be an archaic *H. sapiens*.

Hominid Site
Neandertal Goegraphic Range

Origins of Levallois technique in Africa signals beginning of MSA (300-200,000)

Approximate end of the Acheulean in Europe and Africa (150,000)

Latest appearance of classic Neandertals (27,000)

Earliest appearance of classic Neandertals (140,000)

300,000   200,000   100,000   Present

Ndutu (400-200,000)

Petralona (300-150,000)
Steinheim (250-200,000)
Swanscombe (250-200,000)
Salé (250-200,000)

Dali (200-130,000)
Maba (200-130,000)
Jinniushan (200-130,000)
Yunxian (200-130,000)

Kabwe (115,000)
Narmada (150-125,000)

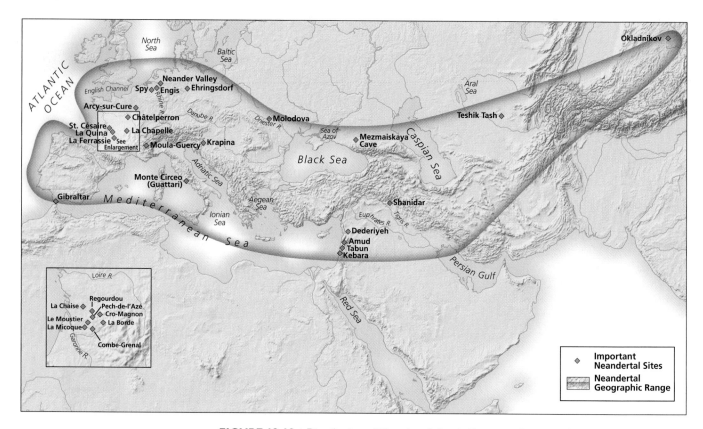

FIGURE 13.12   Distribution of Neandertal sites in Europe and western Asia.

at that young age the Engis child shows incipient development of a double-arched Neandertal browridge. The second Neandertal discovery, in 1848, was a nearly complete cranium from the British colony of Gibraltar on the southern coast of Spain. It took nearly 20 years for the Gibraltar cranium to be recognized as a Neandertal; although considered from the time of its discovery to be an ancient specimen, the Engis child was not "rediscovered" to be a very young Neandertal for more than a century. Perhaps they were not appreciated because both were discovered well before Darwin published his theory of evolution by means of natural selection in 1859, and thus the framework necessary for understanding them was not in place.

The original Neandertal specimen (for which the group was named) was found in 1856 in a limestone quarry in the Neander Valley (in German, the word for valley is *tal*) near Düsseldorf. The quarry was dotted with caves filled with clay and debris that had to be removed before the limestone could be mined. The Neandertal remains, including a skullcap and partial skeleton, were discovered in such clay deposits that had been thrown 20 m (60 ft) down a hill (Figure 13.13). The owner of the quarry saw large bones in the deposit and, thinking that they were from cave bears, contacted a local schoolteacher and natural historian, Johann Carl Fuhlrott. Fuhlrott identified the bones as human and, recognizing the potential significance of the find, he contacted noted anatomist Professor Herman Schaafhausen, who led the scientific analysis.

Professor Schaafhausen presented his initial analyses of the Neandertal remains in 1857, a full 2 years before Darwin published *On the Origin of Species*. Schaafhausen noted the long and low shape of the skullcap, the large browridges, and the development of an occipital bun. All these features distinguished this specimen from modern humans. Furthermore, the postcranial bones were very robust and marked with strong ridges for the attachment of large muscles; the ribs were rounded, indicating a barrel-chested individual. One of the bones of the lower left arm (the ulna) had clearly been broken and healed awkwardly; it is likely that the arm was not usable in life, and it showed some signs of atrophy due to disuse. Schaafhausen concluded, however, that the left arm was the only pathological aspect of a skeleton that otherwise reflected the normal development of a race of men (or perhaps a species) who lived in Europe long before the Romans or Celts. Critics argued the remains were simply those of an odd or pathological human: perhaps a Cossack who had died during the Russian invasion of Germany in 1814, or possibly an unfortunate individual who suffered from a variety of pathological conditions, thus explaining his obviously injured left arm.

Thomas Henry Huxley, who was known as "Darwin's bulldog" for his vociferous defense of natural selection (see Chapter 1), provided one of the first evolutionary analyses of the Neandertal specimen, in 1864. Although Huxley was impressed with the "pithecoid" (apelike) nature of some aspects of the skull, such as the thickness of the bones and the browridges, he concluded that the Neandertal was no ape-man or "missing link." The cranial capacity clearly exceeded that of any ape and was in the human range, and the postcranial skeleton, though robust, was essentially human. Huxley placed the Neandertal at an extreme end of variation seen in modern humans. While Huxley was presenting his analyses, British anatomist George Busk recalled the odd-looking skull from Gibraltar he had seen years before. In 1864, he presented the Gibraltar cranium as the second Neandertal specimen.

Arguments that the Neandertal specimen represented only a diseased modern human rather than a distinct fossil ancestor would not be disproven until more fossils were discovered. By 1915, Neandertals were known from sites in Germany, Spain, Belgium, Croatia, and France. In the 1920s and 1930s, they were discovered in sites in the Middle East and as far as Uzbekistan in central Asia. We now have the remains of hundreds of Neandertal individuals recovered from dozens of sites.

Although the original cave was destroyed by commercial quarrying, the deposits removed from the cave were recently rediscovered through study of the archives of the mining company (Schmitz et al., 2002). More than 140 years after the initial find, additional bones and artifacts from the Neander Valley indicate that there were at least three individuals in the cave. Almost unbelievably,

FIGURE 13.13 The original Neandertal remains from the Neander Valley, Germany.

INSIGHTS AND ADVANCES

Neandertal Image Makeovers

It is definitely not a compliment to be called a Neandertal, and most of us are familiar with the stereotype of the brutish caveman. Although the origins of the stereotype have their roots in early negative portrayals of Neandertals presented by scientists, it is safe to say that the scientific appraisal of Neandertals over the past several decades has been far more positive than negative, despite debates about their status vis-à-vis anatomically modern *H. sapiens* (Figure A). So why does the negative connotation of Neandertals remain in the popular culture?

Erik Trinkaus and Pat Shipman (1992, pp. 406–407) chronicled the ambivalence of popular and scientific images over the years writing "They [historical Neandertal images] testify to an ongoing struggle between our willingness to accept Neandertals as close relatives and yet our abhorrence at having anything so potentially inhuman so close at hand. It is the age-old struggle between the god-like and the bestial in humans restated." According to Trinkaus and Shipman the oldest illustration of a Neandertal was from a popular

FIGURE A   A scientific reconstruction of a Neandertal family.

magazine article published in 1873. This picture of a Neandertal couple and their dogs has an almost romantic quality. The Neandertal male is portrayed as a kind of "noble savage," ready to meet head-on anything that might appear at the mouth of their cave to challenge them. The woman's portrayal, on the other hand, constitutes a

stereotype of Victorian notions of female passivity. Clearly, this view of Neandertals is not wholly negative or bestial, although it reflects Victorian mores.

However, later reconstructions seesawed between beast and gentleman. The discovery of the French La Chapelle-aux-Saints Neandertal led to reconstructions

additional remains of the original Neandertal specimen were discovered. This re-excavation allowed dating of the finds for the first time, giving them an age of 40,000 years.

Besides modern humans, Neandertals are by far the most thoroughly represented hominids in the fossil record. Given the large number of Neandertal remains available, it is possible to study aspects of their growth and development and demography, population-level variables that are impossible to realistically examine in earlier hominids. It is likely that compared with earlier hominids, the cultural behavior of Neandertals was more complex, so it is more difficult to interpret in the context of the archaeological record.

FIGURE B Historical reconstruction of a Neandertal.

of Neandertals in the popular press that were clearly not of the noble savage type. Instead, an image from a popular French publication (1909) reveals a feral and beastly Neandertal who is very unlike a modern human (Figure B). Not long after this, scientist Marcellin Boule depicted Neandertals as stooped and hulking. Their brawn was emphasized over their brains.

By the 1930s, anthropologist Carleton Coon produced a drawing of a Neandertal dressed in modern clothing, making the point that a Neandertal could ride on the New York subway with little notice if he were dressed correctly and given a good shave. And yet a 1950s horror movie, *The Neanderthal Man,* indicates that the more beastly view was easier to sell to the moviegoing public.

Popular views of Neandertals reflect not only deep-seated tensions about the conflict between humanity and bestiality, as Trinkaus and Shipman suggest, but also feelings about racial inferiority and superiority. After all, humans have a long history of considering those who do not come from their own particular group as being something less than human, even when they most obviously are. In his novel *Dance of the Tiger,* which dramatizes the demise of the Neandertals in northern Europe some 40,000 years ago, noted paleontologist Björn Kurten makes a point of depicting the Neandertals as light-skinned and destined to be replaced by darker-skinned modern humans from the south. Although these skin color assignments are justifiable based on scientific grounds, from a literary standpoint Kurten was also using race as a

device to make an ancient species-level conflict more poignant for twentieth-century readers.

Recently, a series of car insurance commercials have played on this ambivalence about Neandertals, promoting their product as "so easy a caveman could do it," but then showing the astute and sensitive caveman as traumatized by this stereotyping (Figure C).

FIGURE C A current popular rendition of a "caveman."

NEANDERTAL ANATOMY AND DNA

Neandertals possess some derived features that are not present in either anatomically modern humans or archaic *H. sapiens* such as *H. heidelbergensis* (Figure 13.14 and Figure 13.15 on page 390). Therefore, many scientists think that they represent a unique evolutionary trajectory. Some of their derived features seem to be anticipated by the anatomy of some archaic *H. sapiens*, especially those from Sima de los Huesos, perhaps suggesting that Neandertals descended from these populations.

Although the Neandertal vault is long and low, its size and shape are quite different from that of *H. erectus*. The Neandertal cranium is much larger than

NEANDERTAL

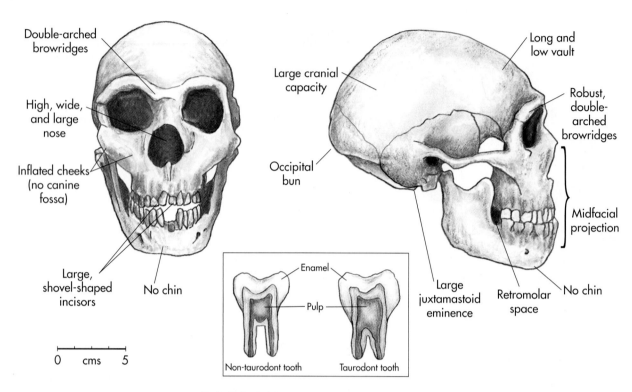

Double-arched browridges

High, wide, and large nose

Inflated cheeks (no canine fossa)

Large, shovel-shaped incisors

No chin

0   cms   5

Large cranial capacity

Occipital bun

Enamel

Pulp

Non-taurodont tooth

Taurodont tooth

Long and low vault

Robust, double-arched browridges

Midfacial projection

Large juxtamastoid eminence

Retromolar space

No chin

FIGURE 13.14 The Neandertal skull and teeth. Neandertals have taurodont molars.

that of *H. erectus* or *H. sapiens;* presumed females have an average cranial capacity of 1,300 cc and presumed males an average of 1,600 cc. Research on Neandertal brains (as studied from endocasts) suggests they were fully modern in their organization and that the large size of the brain was a function of large body size and adaptation to the cold environments in which they evolved (Holloway, 1984).

In addition to these size differences, vault shape differs in important ways. The maximum cranial breadth in Neandertals tends to be in the middle of the cranium,

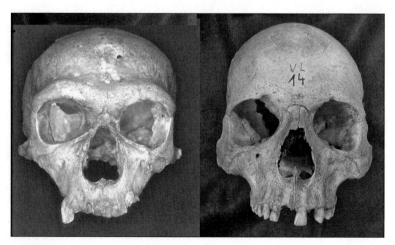

FIGURE 13.15 The faces of Neandertal (left) and anatomically modern *H. sapiens* (right) display anatomical differences including a double-arched brow and absence of a canine fossa in Neandertals.

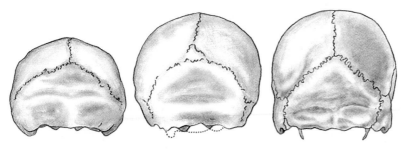

FIGURE 13.16   Posterior views of *H. erectus*, Neandertal, and modern *H. sapiens* show differences in vault shape.

giving it an oval appearance when viewed from the rear. In contrast, in humans, the maximum cranial breadth is higher on the skull, and the side walls are parallel. In *H. erectus* maximum breadth is low on the vault, and the side walls slope inward, forming a pentagon in rear view (Figure 13.16). At the back of the Neandertal cranium, the occipital bone bulges posteriorly, forming the occipital bun. The mastoid process in Neandertals is smaller than in modern humans, but a ridge of bone just next to it, the **juxtamastoid eminence**, is larger than the mastoid process.

The face of the Neandertals also differs from those of *H. erectus* and modern humans. Among the most important of the derived characters of the Neandertals is their midfacial prognathism (Figure 13.15). The middle part of the face, around the nose, projects strongly anteriorly, and the cheek region is placed far posteriorly, with an even grade between the two. It is almost as if someone has grabbed the Neandertal nose and pulled it away from the cheeks, forming a smooth transition from cheek to nose. Therefore, the cheeks of Neandertals are often described as "swept back." The face as a whole is also quite tall. Probably related to the anterior position of the midface (and upper dentition) is the presence on the rear of the mandible of a *retromolar space* between the third molar and the ascending ramus. Like earlier hominids, Neandertals show no development of a chin.

There are also important differences between the inner ear anatomy of Neandertals and that of modern humans and *H. erectus*. The semicircular canals of the inner ear assist in maintaining balance, but there is variation in their structure even between closely related species. Although modern humans and *H. erectus* do not differ in inner ear anatomy, work by Fred Spoor and his colleagues using three-dimensional imaging shows that Neandertals have a different and probably derived inner ear anatomy (Fig. 13.17 on page 392); (Spoor et al., 2003). The differences are so clear that they have been used to definitively identify the infant temporal bone from Arcy-sur-Cure, France, as a Neandertal, an important identification for this site that had otherwise nondiagnostic fossil remains (Hublin et al., 1996). More recent detailed analyses of the teeth from the site also support a Neandertal affinity for the remains (Bailey & Hublin, 2006). Arcy-sur-Cure is one of only two sites in which Neandertals are associated with an Upper Paleolithic (blade-based) technology known as the Châtelperronian and may also show association with symbolic remains. These clear-cut differences in ear anatomy also support the idea that the Neandertals may be a species separate from modern humans.

Several prominent features characterize Neandertal teeth: The upper incisors of Neandertals were more curved than those of modern humans and had built-up ridges of enamel on the side nearest the tongue (lingual surface), giving the tooth a *shovel-shaped* appearance. Shovel-shaped incisors generally are considered to provide greater resistance to wear. Lower fourth premolars are perhaps the most distinctive difference between Neandertals and modern humans; Neandertals have

juxtamastoid eminence   A ridge of bone next to the mastoid process; in Neandertals, it is larger than the mastoid process itself.

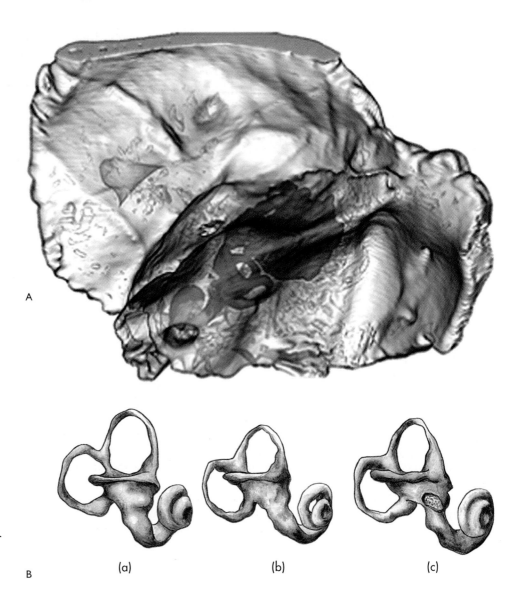

FIGURE 13.17 Neandertal inner ear anatomy is distinctive from modern humans. The inner ear is figured in blue in this temporal bone from Engis images by Antoine Balzeau (a). The size and shape of the canals differ between the Neandertal ear (on the right) and the modern human ear on the left (b).

extra subcusps that modern humans lack and are very asymmetric. Neandertal molars also tended to have extra cusps more frequently than modern humans, and the molars had expanded pulp cavities and fused roots, a feature known as **taurodontism** (Figure 13.14). Taurodont teeth can sustain more wear than nontaurodont teeth because they maintain a broader base for wear after the enamel of the crown has been worn away. Both taurodont molars and shovel-shaped incisors are found in modern human populations at various frequencies. Finally, Neandertal anterior teeth show an unusual amount of wear that is much greater than that on the molars and is greater than among modern human populations, even those who use their anterior teeth extensively.

Many have speculated about why Neandertals had such prognathic faces, large noses, and heavily worn teeth. A popular idea is that the nose warmed cold air before it reached the respiratory system and brain. Among modern humans, however, cold-dwelling populations tend to have long and narrow noses to restrict cold airflow to the brain, whereas broad noses are found in more tropically adapted humans and facilitate heat dissipation (Stringer & Gamble, 1993). Others argue that the prognathic midface (and the large nose associated with it) helps dissipate heavy bite loads on the anterior dentition. However, in animals and hominids that produce large bite forces, the face typically is retracted, not prognathic (remember

taurodontism   Molar teeth with expanded pulp cavities and fused roots.

the adaptive suite of the robust australopithecines, for example), and Neandertal muscle forces may not have been much greater than in modern human fossils with very different facial morphologies (Antón, 1996; O'Connor et al., 2004). No convincing argument for an adaptive function for the large Neandertal face and nose has yet to be generally accepted, and it may be that Neandertal facial morphology results from a variety of phylogenetic trends or evolutionary forces. In particular, genetic isolation in glacial environments may have produced the Neandertal face via genetic drift from an already prognathic ancestor as Clark Howell proposed many years ago. Although these features are striking compared with modern humans, Erik Trinkaus (2003) points out that the large faces of Neandertals reflect continuation of a trend seen in archaic *H. sapiens;* thus, modern humans should be thought of as having small faces. Similarly, large nose size and other features in the nasal region of the Neandertals also reflect well-established evolutionary trends observed in a wide range of Middle and Late Pleistocene hominids (Franciscus, 1999, 2003).

The postcranial skeleton of the Neandertals was massive compared with that of modern humans, although Neandertals were shorter on average than we are (Figure 13.18, on the left). Neandertal males are estimated to have stood about 169 cm (5 ft 6.5 in) tall, with a weight of 65 kg (143 lb), whereas females were 160 cm (5 ft 3 in) and 50 kg (110 lb) (Stringer & Gamble, 1993).The chest was barrel-shaped and the limbs, especially the forearm and shin, were short. These characteristics are consistent with a body designed to conserve heat in a cold climate (see Bergman's and Allen's rules in Chapter 5), and Neandertals have been described as having "hyper-polar" bodies (Holliday, 1995).

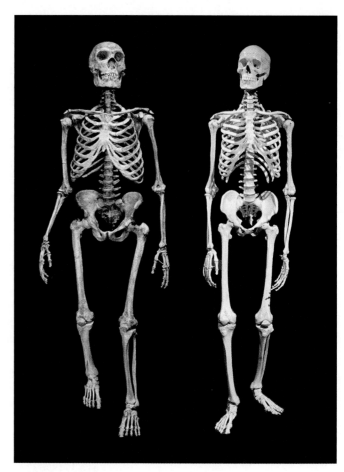

FIGURE 13.18   These articulated skeletons suggest that Neandertals were much more heavily built than anatomically modern humans.

The long bones and major joints were all larger and more robust than those found in modern humans, features that Neandertals may have shared with earlier hominids and that indicate a physically demanding lifestyle.

The Neandertal skeleton shows evidence of having had very large, powerful muscles. Erik Trinkaus suggests that this powerful build indicated high levels and possibly even long hours of physically difficult activity. The energetic costs of such activity have been estimated by Mark Sorenson and Bill Leonard (2001), who suggest that Neandertals would have had daily energy needs much higher than those of modern human hunter–gatherers and more similar to those of trained athletes and subsistence farmers.

Neandertal and modern human postcranial skeletons differ in several other respects. One of the most striking differences appears in the anatomy of the *pubic bone,* which forms the front part of the pelvis. The upper, anterior part of the pelvis, formed by the *superior pubic ramus,* was longer and more gracile in Neandertals than in modern humans. This is in direct opposition to the pattern established by the rest of the skeleton. Much speculation about the function of the Neandertal pubis has been offered. However, the complete Neandertal pelvis discovered at Kebara, Israel, shows that the lengthened pubis does not result in a larger pelvic outlet (Figure 13.19 on page 394). This suggests that pubis size is not related to either increased birth efficiency or increased gestation time, as has been previously argued. The broader pelvis may simply have been the Neandertal way of establishing greater body breadth (and greater volume relative to surface area) to aid in heat retention.

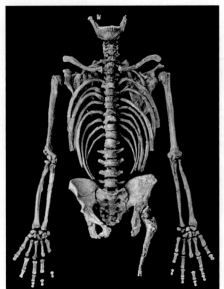

FIGURE 13.19 The Kebara remains from Israel had a complete innominate that shows that the birth canal was no larger in Neandertals than in modern humans.

In the late 1990s, the original Neandertal remains again came to the attention of the scientific world when it was announced that DNA from this specimen had been successfully extracted, amplified, and sequenced (see Innovations: Neandertal Genes on page 396; Krings et al., 1997). DNA from the recently discovered Mezmaiskaya subadult and a number of other individuals has also been extracted and analyzed (Schmitz et al., 2002). Attempts to extract DNA from fossils this old (hominids or other animals) often are unsuccessful, but the cold climate the Neandertals lived in may have helped to preserve their DNA. Initially scientists had only small snippets of Neandertal mitochondrial DNA that is quite different from that of living peoples. Recently two groups of scientists have isolated nuclear DNA as well (Noonan et al., 2006; Green et al., 2006). A collaboration is now underway to attempt the sequencing of the entire Neandertal genome. The phylogenetic implications of this difference will be discussed in Chapter 14.

GROWTH AND DEVELOPMENT

Neandertals are the only fossil group to be reasonably well represented by children's remains. In Belgium, the first Neandertal ever discovered was the 2- to 3-year-old Engis child, and the site of Spy also yielded deciduous (baby) teeth. In France, at La Ferrassie, remains of six children ranging in age from not much older than newborn to about 12 years of age were found, and at another French site, La Quina, an important cranium of an 8-year-old child was discovered. Devil's Quarry on the island of Gibraltar yielded a 2- to 5-year-old child's cranium. And of the thousands of bone fragments at Krapina in Croatia, many of the twenty-five individuals were subadults. In the northern Caucasus, northeast of the Black Sea, a partial skeleton of a Neandertal neonate or fetus (estimates of age range from 7 months gestational age to 2 months neonatal age) was recovered from Mezmaiskaya Cave. This infant, estimated to have lived about 29,000 years ago, may have been a member of one of the last surviving Neandertal populations (Ovchinnikov et al., 2000). The easternmost Neandertal, Teshik Tash from Uzbekistan, is also a child, the skeleton of a 9-year-old (Figure 13.20). In the Near East, several

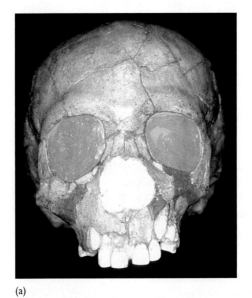

(a)

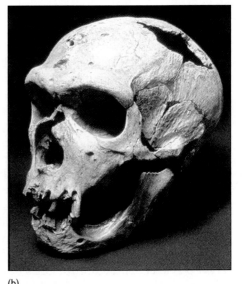

(b)

FIGURE 13.20 Neandertal development and aging. (a) Remains of a child from Teshik Tash. (b) The "Old Man" from La Chapelle.

infants have been found at Amud Cave, including a 10-month-old who clearly bears Neandertal features in its cranial anatomy (Rak et al., 1994). And excavations under the direction of Takeru Akazawa at the cave of Dederiyeh in Syria have yielded partial remains of two toddlers who died about 50,000 years ago. The more complete, Dederiyeh 1, (Figure 13.21) is a nearly complete skeleton (Kondo et al., 2000; Akazawa and Muhesun, 2002). Both toddlers were about 17 to 19 months of age when they died—based on dental microstructure. Although they are similar in age, the more complete skeleton is also more robust than the more fragmentary one. Despite their young ages, the Dediriyeh children and the other fossils discussed are clearly identifiable as Neandertals rather than modern humans.

In the 1950s Clark Howell argued that understanding the ontogenetic pattern of Neandertals was critical for understanding their relationships to one another and to living humans. He proposed that the Neandertals from Europe and the Near East/Asia presented different populations with different trends in growth. While the details of the argument may no longer apply given changes in our understanding of the geological ages of particular Neandertals, the concept of understanding growth patterns to illuminate the meaning of adult morphology, as well as considering the importance of local adaptation in particular subgroups of fossil hominids, is an important organizing principle in fossil studies.

With a relative abundance of subadult remains, the Neandertals are the only fossil hominid group for which most developmental stages are known and for which detailed studies of growth can be made. Recall the work by Chris Dean (see Chapter 12) that indicated *H. erectus* had a faster dental developmental rate than modern humans; this same study found Neandertals had a dental developmental rate more similar to humans. More recent studies suggest that some Neandertals may have grown even more quickly. Studies of mandibular growth, including the Dederiyeh toddlers, indicate that early in development Neandertal children may have grown faster than modern human children but that growth rates are generally similar between the two (Kondo et al., 2002). Likewise, growth in the postcranial skeleton of the Dederiyeh toddlers suggests similar processes as in modern humans, albeit some may occur earlier in Neandertals than in modern humans (Sawada et al., 2004). Neandertals thus seem to show, for the first time in hominid evolution, growth patterns similar to our own.

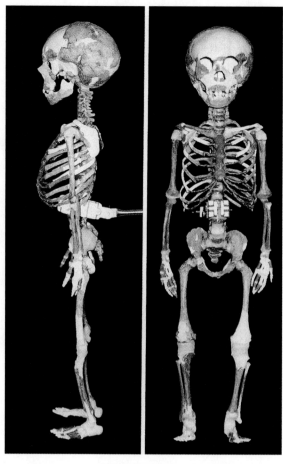

FIGURE 13.21 The Dederiyeh 1 infant from Syria preserves nearly the entire skeleton of a 17- to 19-month old Neandertal. Another, more fragmentary, toddler of the same age was also found at the site.

HEALTH AND DISEASE

The history of Neandertal research has been strongly influenced by the recognition and interpretation of pathological conditions in bone. Recall that the type specimen from the Neander Valley, Germany, was at the center of an argument over whether it was a pathological human or a distinct species or subspecies. For many years the common perception of Neandertals as primitive creatures came from reconstructions produced by Marcellin Boule from a Neandertal skeleton from La Chapelle, France. The "Old Man" of La Chapelle-aux-Saints was found buried in a small cave in the Dordogne region of France and dates to about 40,000 years ago. The skeleton is clearly that of an older male, although in this context *old* means about 40 years of age. He suffered from numerous pathological conditions: a deformation in the pelvis, a crushed toe, severe arthritis in several of the vertebrae, and a broken rib sustained not long before death. He was missing many teeth, and the mandible and maxilla showed a significant amount of bone loss (Figure 13.20b).

Neandertal Genes

Ancient DNA (aDNA) recovered from fossils provides a direct window into the genetics of past populations. Unfortunately, only a small percentage of fossils actually preserve any DNA. Several factors influence whether DNA will be preserved. Age is a critical factor. Although in the early days of ancient DNA research (the late 1980s and early 1990s) many claims were made for the recovery of DNA from samples more than 1 million years old, subsequent studies indicate that recovering usable DNA from fossils older than 100,000 years is extremely unlikely (Wayne et al., 1999). Temperature and humidity are also critical to whether DNA will be preserved: Cold and dry is better than warm and wet. For example, Late Pleistocene mammoths preserved in arctic permafrost and Östi the ~5,000 year old 'Tyrolean Iceman' discovered in the Alps preserve DNA quite well (Rollo et al., 2006). In terms of hominid fossils, this suggests those from northern Europe and northern Asia are the most likely to provide intact DNA, whereas hominids in the tropics such as portions of Africa and Southeast Asia are least likely.

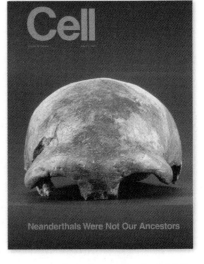

Ancient DNA from several Neandertals and modern humans has been recovered and analyzed. Ancient samples from archaic *H. sapiens* specimens have not yet been obtained. The Neandertal samples include two from the Feldhofer Cave, Germany, the original site of the Neandertal's discovery (Krings et al., 1997; Schmitz et al., 2002), three from the Vindija Cave in Croatia (Krings et al., 2000; Serre et al., 2004), and one each from Mezmaiskaya Cave in the northern Caucasus (Ovchinnikov et al., 2000), the sites of Engis and Scladina in Belgium (Serre et al., 2004; Orlando et al., 2006), El Sidrón in Spain (Lalueza-Fox et al., 2005), Monte Lessini in Italy (Caramelli et al., 2006), Rochers de Villeneuve and La Chapelle-aux-Saints in France (Serre et al., 2004; Beauval et al., 2005), and Okladnikov in Siberia (Krause et al., 2007). These samples cover much of the Neandertal geographic and temporal range including some of the last surviving Neandertals (the Mezmaiskaya infant dating to about 29,000 years ago) and some of the older Neandertals (the Scladina site is the oldest sampled with an age of about 100,000 years ago). The modern human samples include two from Mladec in Czechoslovakia, one each from Cro-Magnon, Abri Pataud, and La Madeleine in France (Serre et al., 2004), and two from Italy (Caramelli et al., 2003). More than twenty-five Neandertals and forty fossil humans were sampled to achieve these few results.

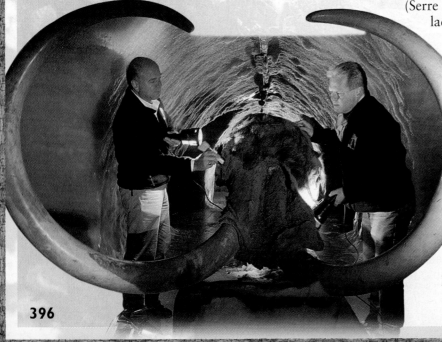

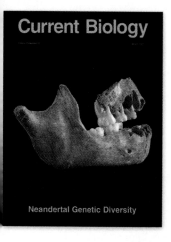

Current Biology

Neandertal Genetic Diversity

Most of the DNA extracted from Neandertals is ancient mitochondrial DNA, some of it from the hypervariable region 1. Remember that mtDNA is passed down only through the maternal lineage, and represents a fairly small part of the whole genome (see Chapter 2 for a review). The snippets of mtDNA recovered from Neandertals are all fairly similar to one another. They cluster together as a group to the exclusion of DNA from ancient *H. sapiens* and from living humans. Like living humans, Neandertals have relatively little diversity in their mtDNA. The amount of variation between Neandertals and ancient *H. sapiens* is greater than amongst living humans, but it is much less than the variation seen among chimpanzees and gorillas. This difference in diversity is probably related to a rapid population expansion in the human lineage before *H. sapiens* and Neandertals diverged.

Recent ancient DNA studies have yielded some surprising results. DNA analyses have extended the easternmost range of Neandertals into Siberia at a site called Okladnikov. And ancient DNA from Neandertals at El Sidrón in Spain has suggested that, like living humans, some Neandertals had pale skin and red hair (Lalueza-Fox, 2007). This suggests that adaptations to low UV radiation, including skin depigmentation, occured in Neandertals.

The date for the most recent common ancestor (MRCA) of *H. sapiens* and Neandertals is between 365,000 and 853,000 years ago. Using mitochondrial DNA, an MRCA date for the western (Feldhofer and Vindija) and eastern (Mezmaiskaya) Neandertal samples has been estimated to be between 151,000 and 352,000 years ago.

Recently nuclear DNA has been sequenced as well (Green et al., 2006; Noonan et al., 2006). So far, nuclear DNA has come from just a single fossil from Vindija and has been sequenced using two different techniques that yield similar results (Noonan et al., 2006; Green et al, 2006). DNA was also isolated from cave bear fossils from the same site and compared to modern carnivores to test the technique. Nuclear DNA suggests a similar date for the split between Neandertals and *H. sapiens* of between 460,000 and 700,000 years, with an inferred population split of around 370,000

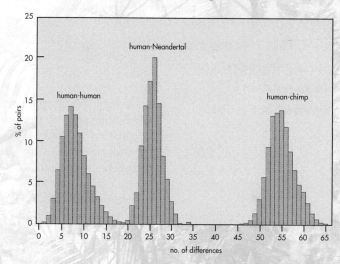

years ago. The nuclear DNA results indicate that about 30% of derived alleles are in the Neandertal lineage. This high frequency may suggest some gene flow between modern humans and Neandertal populations (Green et al., 2006).

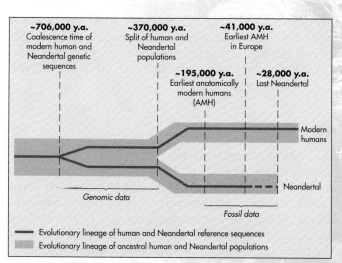

Boule reconstructed the Old Man as having a stooped posture and a shuffling gait, far from the upright stride of modern humans. In part, Boule may have been misled by the numerous pathological conditions in the skeleton, but recent investigators who have examined the skeleton and Boule's work also believe that his interpretation of the skeleton was biased by his preconceptions about the "primitive" Neandertals (to be fair to Boule, the excavators of the Spy Neandertals also interpreted the skeletons as having a stooped posture). Nonetheless, Boule's appraisal and interpretation of the Old Man of La Chapelle-aux-Saints was very influential, and it formed the "scientific" basis for the negative image of Neandertals for decades (Insights and Advances: Neandertal Image Makeovers on page 388).

Other Neandertal skeletons provide abundant evidence of traumatic injuries. Nearly all the Shanidar remains from Iraq, dated to about 40,000 to 50,000 years ago, provide evidence of the hard lives that Neandertal individuals led (Trinkaus, 1983). Shanidar 1, a male between 30 and 45 years old, had a healed fracture of his left eye socket, and he may have been blind in that eye. The right side of his body had suffered even more extensive trauma: The lower right arm and hand were missing (the skeleton was otherwise intact and well preserved), probably because of an extensive injury that led to atrophy of the upper right arm and shoulder; he also showed signs of injury in the right leg and foot. It is possible that this individual could not have survived such injuries without help from other Neandertals, although drawing such a conclusion based on paleopathology alone is problematic (Dettwyler, 1991).

In fact, so many Neandertals exhibit healed fractures that their cause has been sought. Some scientists think the fractures, especially the high incidence of head and neck fractures, indicate that Neandertals were routinely getting close to dangerous prey while hunting (Berger & Trinkaus, 1995). But the spears from Schoeningen suggest that Neandertals should have been able to hunt from a distance. Other scientists suggest that fracture rates may vary by geographic region according to the ruggedness of the terrain.

Many Neandertals have healed fractures suggesting that they participated in rugged or dangerous activities.

Neandertal Behavior

When we reconstruct past human behavior based on the archaeological record, we make inferences based on direct observation of living humans. We can be fairly certain that modern humans do not provide a perfect model for Neandertal behavior, but we do not know how bad the fit is. Take something as fundamental to human behavior as language. It is not unreasonable to assume that the Neandertals possessed some fairly sophisticated form of communication, but how did it compare to language in its ability to transmit ideas and information (see Chapter 15)? The Neandertals' large brains indicate that they were among the most cognitively sophisticated species that have ever lived, but what exactly did they do with these abilities?

MATERIAL CULTURE

Most Neandertal fossils have been found in association with the Middle Paleolithic tools. This tool industry builds on earlier tool cultures such as the Acheulean by using some similar tools, like bifaces, and adding prepared core technologies. There is a greater reliance on small flaked tools and systematic variation in tool complexity in the Middle Paleolithic industries. For example, the late Neandertals of Mezmaiskaya Cave possessed a Middle Paleolithic technology that made extensive use of bifaces, a feature more commonly associated with the Acheulean. Likewise, all early Neandertals and contemporaneous anatomically modern humans (such as those from Skhūl and Qafzeh in Israel) are associated with Mousterian tools. This indicates that there is no reason to expect that stone tool traditions will correlate with anatomical differences between hominids.

All later anatomically modern humans and a few later Neandertals are found with the **Upper Paleolithic (Later Stone Age)**, which we discuss in more detail in Chapter 14 (Figure 13.22). The Saint-Césaire and Arcy-sur-Cure Neandertals from France are associated not with the Middle Paleolithic but rather with tools from an Upper Paleolithic industry, the **Châtelperronian** (Hublin et al., 1996). Upper Paleolithic industries are characterized by the development of blade-based technology. **Blades** are flakes that are twice as long as they are wide. In addition, Upper Paleolithic technologies use more refined flaking techniques, and an increase in the variety of flaked tools. Saint-Césaire and Arcy-sur-Cure demonstrate that Neandertals were capable of producing Upper Paleolithic technology. At some archaeological sites without hominids we find Châtelperronian and another Upper Paleolithic industry, the *Aurignacian* (which is associated with modern humans), interstratified through time in the site as if the groups were taking turns using the area. Given that most Neandertals produced Middle Paleolithic tools and only a few, late Neandertals produced Upper Paleolithic tools it is possible that this technology may have been adopted from anatomically modern groups.

Middle Paleolithic assemblages have few bone or antler tools. Although there have been no wood tool discoveries directly associated with Neandertal remains, a wooden spear dated to 130,000 years old from Lehringen, Germany suggests that Neandertals, like earlier archaic *H. sapiens,* must have made extensive use of wood. Additionally, many smaller Mousterian points probably were hafted to wooden shafts to form spears or lances.

The anterior teeth of the Neandertals may be their most unusual tool. As mentioned earlier, the anterior teeth of Neandertals are large and heavily worn compared with their back teeth, indicating that they were used in a viselike manner. Wear patterns on the teeth indicate that both animal and vegetable matter were held in the front teeth. This may indicate that Neandertals used these teeth to hold objects. Cut marks on the teeth further indicate that Neandertals held objects with their front teeth while cutting what they held, perhaps hide or pieces of meat, with stone tools. It is possible to imagine—but difficult to prove—any number of tasks that the Neandertals might have accomplished using their front teeth. All we can say for certain is that most Neandertals regularly used their front teeth as tools.

COPING WITH COLD

Neandertal bodies are typical of cold-adapted populations, and their archaeological sites also give indications of behavioral adaptations to cold. Charcoal deposits and ashy dump spots are commonly found in Middle Paleolithic sites, indicating that Neandertals used fire as a way to cope with cold. True hearths are rare, but they have been identified in a 60,000-year-old Middle Paleolithic site in Portugal. It is also very likely that Neandertals used animal skins and hides to protect themselves from the cold. No sewing tools, such as awls or bone needles, have been found in the Middle Paleolithic; so if they did use hides there is no evidence that they were sewn. In Molodova in the Ukraine, a Middle Paleolithic site has yielded a ring of mammoth bones, approximately 5 × 8 m (15 × 24 ft) in size, which encloses a dense concentration of artifacts, bones, and ash. Although it could be a natural deposition, many scientists think that this site represents a living space of some kind, a wind-sheltering structure, or perhaps even a tent. If this is the case, the walls of structure probably were constructed from animal hides. As yet, there is no evidence of more substantial Neandertal structures.

FIGURE 13.22 Upper Paleolithic stone tools include blade-based tools as seen here being produced from a blade core.

Upper Paleolithic (Later Stone Age) Stone tool industries that are characterized by the development of blade-based technology.

Châtelperronian An Upper Paleolithic tool industry that has been found in association with later Neandertals.

blades Flakes that are twice as long as they are wide.

Another way to cope with cold is to avoid it, either by seasonally migrating over long distances or by moving as overall conditions get colder (or warmer) during all parts of the year. Middle Paleolithic archaeological deposits indicate that Neandertals were a mobile people seasonally occupying sites for short periods of time. In general, their sites served as temporary spots for camping, hunting, or food processing, but their mobility seems to have been limited. Most of the raw materials they used for stone tools came from within 5 km (3 miles) of where they were found, with a maximum distance of 80 km (Stringer & Gamble, 1993). Thus Neandertals did not move over a large enough area to avoid seasonal cold altogether, but rather probably moved locally to exploit scarce resources within a small area. The distribution of Neandertal sites through time indicates that they did migrate in and out of areas over longer periods of time depending on whether glacial or interglacial conditions persisted. For example, across the eastern Russian plain Neandertal sites are found far north only during interglacial periods and are located farther south during glacial periods, as if the Neandertals were retreating in the face of the harsh glacial climate. Neandertals probably never, even during interglacials, lived as far north as anatomically modern humans eventually would.

Similarly, Neandertals appeared to move south into the Near East during glacial times, and modern humans occupied the region during warmer interglacials. Five prominent cave sites located on Mount Carmel in Israel have been the focus of much attention over the years (excavations in this area began in the late 1920s) because they possess either Neandertal or anatomically modern human fossils. Three of these sites have produced classic Neandertals: Tabūn (dating to about 110,000 years ago), Kebara (60,000 years ago), and Amud (35,000–40,000 years ago). And two, Skhūl and Qafzeh, have yielded anatomically modern human fossils dated to about 90,000 to 110,000 years ago. All these hominids, Neandertal and modern human, were found in association with Mousterian (Middle Paleolithic) stone tools, which are more typically found in association with Neandertals.

Scientists long thought that the anatomically more modern-looking Skhūl and Qafzeh specimens were younger than the Neandertals, but electron spin resonance and U-series dates turned that idea on its head. Neandertals clearly occupied the region for a long time, but the current evidence for occupation by modern-looking humans is more limited. If you accept Neandertals as a separate species, then it is likely that Neandertals and modern humans were alternatively using the region during varying climatic times: Neandertals during cold spells, modern humans during warmer spells. Others argue that Neandertals and modern humans could be representatives of a single, highly variable species. The Middle Eastern hominids as a group would be considered a variant on the classic Neandertal form, and the more modern features seen in some of the specimens would simply reflect local population variation. In a crossroads region (at the intersection of Africa, Europe, and Asia), it might not be surprising that this population would vary more than isolated populations.

HUNTING AND SUBSISTENCE

Stable isotope ratios of carbon and nitrogen indicate that Neandertals ate a lot of meat (Richards et al., 2000). They undoubtedly used all the hunting strategies known by archaic *H. sapiens* and earlier hominids. Different Neandertal sites indicate that they used a variety of subsistence strategies depending on local conditions and the game available in a given area. Although they may have scavenged meat opportunistically, there is little evidence that Neandertals engaged in scavenging on a broad scale (Marean & Assefa, 1999).

An in-depth study of Neandertal subsistence has been undertaken at the site of Kebara in Israel. John Speth and Eitan Tchernov (2001) looked at faunal remains found in Middle Paleolithic deposits dating from 48,000 to 60,000 years ago, concentrating on a collection of 21,000 ungulate bones. Most of these bones came from two species, the mountain gazelle and the Persian fallow deer, but other kinds of deer, wild boar, and aurochs (the precursor to domestic cattle) were also hunted. Speth and Tchernov found little evidence in the processing of the bones to indicate that they were scavenged rather than hunted. In fact, a high percentage of the animals were healthy adults, indicating that the Kebara Neandertals were very capable hunters. A consistent distribution of burned bones indicates that they were cooked rather than accidentally burned after consumption. Speth and Tchernov found evidence of a *midden* located along one wall of the cave, indicating that the Neandertals cleared waste and debris from the area in a consistent way. In general, these studies support the conclusion that Neandertals were competent hunters and in some cases large game hunters.

CANNIBALISM

Many human cultures have engaged in cannibalism, although it is generally thought to have been undertaken mostly in a political or ritualistic context. Because there is little evidence of ritual behavior in Neandertals, cannibalism is perhaps better classified as a kind of specialized subsistence strategy. Early claims for Neandertal cannibalism came from Italy based on a cranium (known as Guattari 1) discovered in 1939 at the cave of Monte Circeo near Rome and dated to about 60,000 years ago. The cranium is reasonably complete, but there is a large hole in its base. Early researchers thought that it was likely that the hole in the base of the cranium had been deliberately made to facilitate access to the brain during some sort of cannibalistic rite, which was indicated by the supposed placement of the skull in a circle of stones. However, the base of the cranium is a weak part of the skull, often broken by natural forces; thus its absence is not direct evidence of cannibalism.

More substantial evidence of cannibalism can be found in the fragmentary remains from Krapina, Croatia, dated to about 130,000 years ago (Figure 13.23). D. Gorjanović-Kramberger, who excavated the site in the early twentieth century, pointed out that among the thousands of fragmentary hominid bones almost no intact long bones were present, a sign that the bones may have been split open to access the marrow within. He also thought that the bias toward juveniles at the site was an indication of cannibalism. Furthermore, many of the bones showed signs of burning. More recent research has established that some of the bones show cut marks as well, although this is not in itself evidence of cannibalism (Russell, 1987).

The recently excavated Mousterian cave site of Moula-Guercy in France, dating to about 100,000 years ago, provides an even better case for Neandertal

FIGURE 13.23 The Krapina remains may provide evidence of cannibalism by some Neandertals.

cannibalism (Defleur et al., 1999). Seventy-eight hominid bone fragments are mixed in with several hundred animal bone fragments (mostly from red deer). Diagnostic Neandertal anatomy is apparent in several of the fragments. The hominid remains from Moula-Guercy display numerous cut marks; these are consistent with expected defleshing and butchering patterns. All crania and long bones have been broken, presumably to gain access to the brain and marrow. A key piece of evidence indicates that these remains were processed for access to meat rather than for some other purpose: The deer and other animals from the site were treated in the same manner as the hominid remains. Because it is unlikely that the game species were being treated to some sort of mortuary processing that did not involve being eaten, Alban Defleur and his colleagues conclude that the Neandertals were also being eaten by other Neandertals.

BURIALS

The notion that some Neandertals may have buried their dead goes back to the discovery of the Spy skeletons in Belgium in the 1880s (Stringer et al., 1984). Unlike the earlier discoveries from Gibraltar and Neanderthal, the Spy remains were carefully excavated. The two Spy adult skeletons were found complete and fully articulated, suggesting that they may have been intentionally buried in the cave. Since that time, numerous Neandertals have been found in caves; most scientists interpret these remains as deliberate burials. Often these Neandertal skeletons have been recovered in situ and fully articulated, and many were in a flexed position. Although the sites may be littered with disarticulated animal bones, only the Neandertal bones remain in anatomical position, protected from the effects of geology or scavengers. For example, evidence of Neandertal burials came from the site of La Ferrassie in southern France (excavated in the early 1900s), where several adults and subadults, perhaps forming a burial complex, were found at a single cave site. Many researchers think that the assemblage of individuals at the site was not an accidental grouping but indicates deliberate burial or internment. In 1938, the skeleton of a 9-year-old child found in the small cave of Teshik Tash in Uzbekistan was claimed to have been interred surrounded by six pairs of upright goat horns, reflecting some sort of ritualistic activity. Although there is no doubt that the goat horns were found near the child, researchers today are skeptical that they were distributed in a "meaningful" way.

In the 1950s the idea of burial and compassionate Neandertals was further supported by the remains from the 40,000- to 50,000-year-old Iraqi site, Shanidar, excavated by Ralph Solecki (1971). The Shanidar 4 individual may have been buried on, or perhaps covered by, a bed of wildflowers (Figure 13.24). The claims were based on the position of the skeleton and a large quantity of wildflower pollen associated with this individual. There is no certainty, however, that wildflowers were placed there deliberately by Neandertal mourners. The same pollen exists in the region today and could have been blown into the cave. Nonetheless, both the "flower burial" and the obvious survival of badly injured individuals at Shanidar led to a softer and more humanized perspective of Neandertals in the 1960s and 1970s.

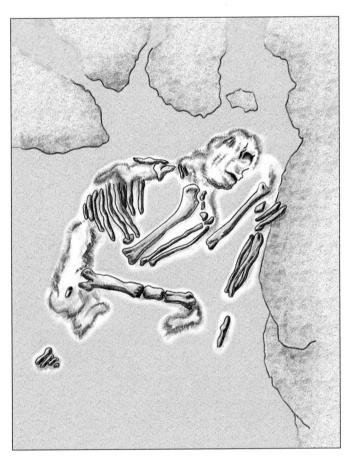

FIGURE 13.24 The Shanidar 4 skeleton has been argued to represent a purposeful burial on a bed of wildflowers.

However, some investigators argue that it is possible to account for the deposition of articulated Neandertal skeletons in caves by natural forces (Gargett, 1989, 1999). One criticism is that many Neandertal sites were excavated decades ago, before the development of modern excavation techniques or accurate recordkeeping. Without a clear rendering of the excavation context, it is difficult to assess the status of a claim of deliberate burial. Recent excavators of Neandertal sites, mindful of the need to provide evidence for burial rather than simply assume it, have gone to some effort to prove what was once considered obvious. Recently excavated Neandertal infants from Amud (Hovers et al., 2000), Mezmaiskaya Cave (Golovanova et al., 1999), and Dediriyeh (Akazawa and Muhesun, 2002) are all argued to be from deliberate burials, and the context of these discoveries strongly indicates that such small and delicate remains probably were preserved because they were shielded from damage by deliberate burial (Figure 13.25).

FIGURE 13.25 The Dederiyeh infant burial from Syria. The cave in which this infant was buried is pictured in the chapter opener.

Neandertal burials would represent a novel behavioral development of the Middle Paleolithic. Before that time we may have evidence of mortuary practices in the defleshing of the Bodo cranium and the possibly deliberate deposition of remains in the bone pit of Sima de los Huesos at Atapuerca. There is no evidence of deliberate burial of archaic *H. sapiens* remains, but Neandertal burials are significantly different from Upper Paleolithic burials of anatomically modern *H. sapiens* that begin to appear around 40,000 years ago. Neandertals have not been found to be interred with grave goods, objects placed with the corpse at the time of burials. On occasion a stray animal bone or horn has been found in association with a Neandertal burial, but it is very difficult to demonstrate that they were placed there deliberately. In contrast, grave goods often are found in Upper Paleolithic burials, sometimes in great abundance. Another difference between Neandertal and Upper Paleolithic burials is that the Neandertal burials always occur in cave sites, whereas burials at open air sites are common in the late Upper Paleolithic. Because it is presumed that Neandertals lived and died in open areas as well as in caves, they must not have buried their dead in those regions or, if they did, they did not do so in a way that prevented the disruption of the corpse by other forces.

Extrapolating from the cultural behavior of modern humans, it is easy to assume that Neandertal burial indicates some kind of ritualistic belief or significance, but the context of Neandertal burials is equally indicative of "corpse disposal" as it is of ritualized internment (Stringer & Gamble, 1993). It is clear, however, that some Neandertals dedicated a significant amount of time and energy to the burial of the dead, selecting an appropriate site, placing the body in a certain position, and covering the body with a large stone. Furthermore, chimpanzees and other mammals can show attachments to the remains of deceased infants or individuals with whom they have had a long-term relationship, even though they ultimately abandon the body. Elephants have been reported to stand vigil over dead relatives and to revisit the site of the death and handle their skeletal remains (Poole, 1996). And Jane Goodall reported instances of chimpanzee mothers carrying their infants with them long after they had died. Thus even if it is impossible to know whether there was a ritual or symbolic content to the burial of the dead in Neandertals, it is reasonable to assume that when they chose to dispose of a corpse in this manner, it was both an emotional and a pragmatic decision.

Unlike modern human sites, Neandertal sites have little evidence of ritual or symbolic behaviors.

RITUAL AND SYMBOLIC BEHAVIOR

If burials cannot be seen as evidence of ritualistic or symbolic behavior, then there is very little else in the Neandertal archaeological record to indicate such behaviors. A small number of incised bones have been recovered from Mousterian sites, but what these scratches might mean is beyond the scope of scientific inquiry. If Neandertals possessed something like human language, then obviously they were capable of symbolic behavior because language is reliant on symbolic representation. But there is no direct evidence of this in the archaeological record. The strongest evidence of symbolism comes from items of personal adornment. Pierced animal teeth from Arcy-sur-Cure in France may be pendants. Other engraved or incised items include a plaque or incised plate of a mammoth tooth, from the site of Tata, and an incised flint from Quinetra in the Golan Heights (Marshack, 1996; White, 2001). All of these occur late in Neandertal times, with the most secure—those from Arcy-sur-Cure and Quneitra—being 55,000 years old or younger. Even if we accept these few finds as symbolic behavior by Neandertals, they are qualitatively different from the systematic evidence of such behavior, including extensive personal adornment, in Upper Paleolithic sites associated with modern humans (Chapter 14).

Phylogenetic and Taxonomic Issues: An Overview

Our interpretations of taxonomic and phylogenetic relationships between Middle and Late Pleistocene hominids depend largely on how we view the origins of anatomically modern *H. sapiens*. However, we can have a preliminary discussion based on the archaic *H. sapiens* and Neandertal fossil records.

The labels "archaic *H. sapiens*" and "Neandertal" are not taxonomically formal designations. We use informal labels because there is no consensus as to what the formal labels should be. Archaic *H. sapiens* include a widely distributed group of hominids who lived from about 150,000 to 800,000 years ago (Figure 13.11 on page 384). Neandertal refers to a predominantly European and western Asian group of hominids who lived about 30,000 to 130,000 years ago. Both these groups possess features that clearly distinguish them from *H. erectus* and anatomically modern *H. sapiens*. Yet many researchers argue either that the differences are not profound enough to warrant species designations or that using such designations would arbitrarily impose separations on a continuous evolutionary lineage and thus be highly misleading (Figure 13.26).

From the "lumper's perspective," the informal, subspecific labels for these groups of hominids provide an acceptable solution to the problem. In this view, archaic *H. sapiens* and Neandertals were all part of one potentially interbreeding species. Obviously, there was regional variation within the species, and variation across time as well, but lumpers see all the larger-brained hominids of the last half of the Pleistocene as part of a *single evolving species*.

The "splitter's perspective" begins with recognizing the Neandertals as a separate species: *H. neanderthalensis*. They argue that the distinctive anatomy and limited distribution of the Neandertals indicate a specialized hominid taxon fundamentally different from anatomically modern *H. sapiens*. The species designation means that Neandertals and modern humans did not or could not interbreed or did so very infrequently; it suggests that Neandertals represent an extinct type of hominid, which was ultimately replaced across its entire range by modern humans.

In the splitter's view, archaic *H. sapiens* also gets a species designation: *H. heidelbergensis*. *H. heidelbergensis* is considered a species distinct from *H. erectus*,

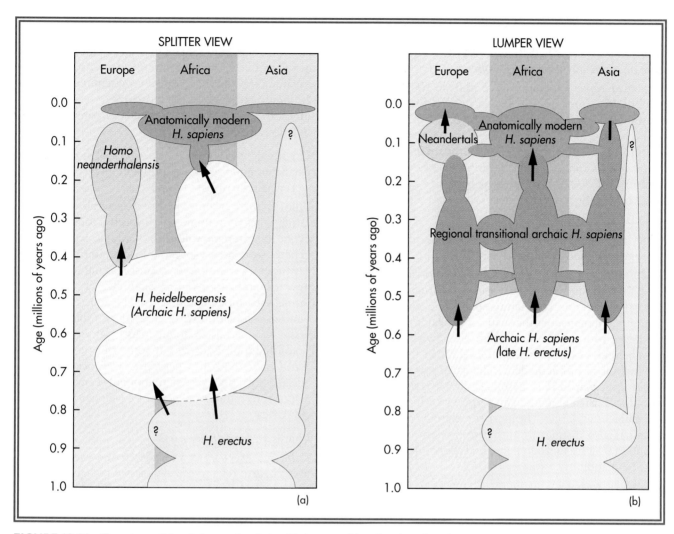

FIGURE 13.26   Two views of the phylogenetic relationship between Neandertals and modern *H. sapiens*. (a) The splitter view; (b) the lumper view.

based on the anatomical features we discussed earlier. In effect, *H. heidelbergensis* becomes the stem species for both Neandertals and anatomically modern *H. sapiens*. In Europe, *H. heidelbergensis* specimens such as Petralona and those from Sima de los Huesos are seen to be proto-Neandertals, extending the Neandertal lineage back hundreds of thousands of years. In Africa, *H. heidelbergensis* specimens such as Bodo and Kabwe are thought to be early representatives of a population from which anatomically modern *H. sapiens* evolved.

At the same time that Neandertals were living in Europe and western Asia, hominid evolutionary developments were also taking place in other parts of the world, most significantly the evolution of anatomically modern *H. sapiens*. In Chapter 14 we will more fully explore the evolutionary connections between our own species and these earlier forms. As we will see, the debate about the origins of modern humans involves not only paleontological and archaeological data but also genetic information derived from contemporary humans and a few fossil specimens.

SUMMARY

1. **What cranial features distinguish archaic *H. sapiens* from anatomically modern *H. sapiens*?**

   Archaic *H. sapiens* are much more cranially robust than modern *H. sapiens*, with thicker cranial bones and substantial development of browridges (supraorbital tori). The face, including the jaws and the nasal aperture, tends to be larger in archaic *H. sapiens* than in modern *H. sapiens*. Cranial capacities in archaic *H. sapiens* range from 1,000 to 1,400 cc, which places them in the lower half of the modern human range, and the cranial vault is lower and longer.

2. **What cranial features distinguish Neandertals from anatomically modern *H. sapiens*?**

   Neandertal crania have double-arched browridges, an occipital bun, and substantial midfacial prognathism. Cranial capacity in Neandertals equals or exceeds that of modern humans, but the shape of the vault is longer and lower, with a maximum cranial width (when viewed from behind) at the midcranium level rather than high on the skull, as it is in modern humans. In rear view the vault is oval shaped. The mastoid eminence is smaller in Neandertals than in modern humans, but the juxtamastoid eminence is larger. The inner ear anatomy of Neandertals is also distinct from that of modern humans. Neandertals were taurodont and had retromolar spaces on their mandibles.

3. **What is the collective significance of the Near Eastern sites of Tabūn, Kebara, Amud, Skhūl, and Qafzeh?**

   These five sites, all located near one another on Mount Carmel in Israel, provide evidence that modern humans and Neandertals lived in the same area but at different times, with the earliest site, Tabūn (100,000 years ago), occupied by Neandertals; then Skhūl and Jebel Qafzeh (90,000–110,000 years ago), occupied by modern humans; followed by another, later Neandertal occupation indicated by fossils from Kebara (60,000 years ago) and Amud (35,000–40,000 years ago). It is possible that Neandertals lived in this area during colder periods, as they were driven southward by glaciers during ice ages, and that anatomically modern humans moved in during warmer interglacials. An alternative explanation is that they are all representatives of a single, highly variable species, located in a region that was subject to a large amount of population movement and gene flow.

4. **Why should we be wary of equating tool industries with specific hominid species or populations, especially during the Middle to Late Pleistocene?**

   Although there is some validity to generalizations associating types of hominids with specific tool industries, several counterexamples are available from specific archeological sites, especially in the later parts of the Pleistocene, to caution us against making too much of these generalizations. For example, at the Mount Carmel sites, modern humans and Neandertals are both found in association with Mousterian tools, and later classic Neandertals are found in association with Upper Paleolithic tool industries at some sites in Europe (at Saint-Césaire and Arcy-sur-Cure in France). Archaeological associations of Asian hominids cannot be easily fit into tool industry sequences developed for Europe and Africa.

5. **What is *H. heidelbergensis*?**

   H. heidelbergensis is a species name used by some researchers to refer to the majority of archaic *H. sapiens* specimens found in Europe and Africa. The type specimen for this species is the Mauer mandible found in Germany in 1907. Many researchers who accept *H. heidelbergensis* as a species also think that Neandertals are a species distinct from anatomically modern humans: *H. neanderthalensis*. *Homo heidelbergensis* is seen as the ancestral species to both modern humans (in Africa) and Neandertals (in Europe). Other researchers argue that the archaic *H. sapiens*, Neandertals, and modern humans are all part of a single polytypic species, which shows evolutionary change over the course of the later Pleistocene. Thus they do not accept *H. heidelbergensis* or *H. neanderthalensis* as valid taxa.

CRITICAL THINKING QUESTIONS

1. Besides most wood implements, what other sorts of things do you think are missing in the archaeological record of Middle to Late Pleistocene hominids?

2. Is the label "archaic *H. sapiens*" useful or confusing?

3. What do you think of the "humanity" of Neandertals? In a broader primate context, should they be regarded as just a slightly different kind of human being?

KEY TERMS

occipital bun
mastoid process
midfacial prognathism

Middle Paleolithic
   (Middle Stone Age)
Levallois technique
juxtamastoid eminence

taurodontism
Upper Paleolithic (Later
   Stone Age)

blades
Châtelperronian

SUGGESTED READING

Stringer, Christopher, and Gamble, Clive. (1993). *In Search of the Neanderthals*. Thames & Hudson, New York.

Trinkaus, Erik, and Shipman, Pat. (1992). *The Neandertals*. Vintage Press, New York.

Wolpoff, Milford, and Caspari, Rachel. (1997). *Race and Human Evolution*. Westview Press, Boulder, CO.

The Emergence and Dispersal of *Homo sapiens*

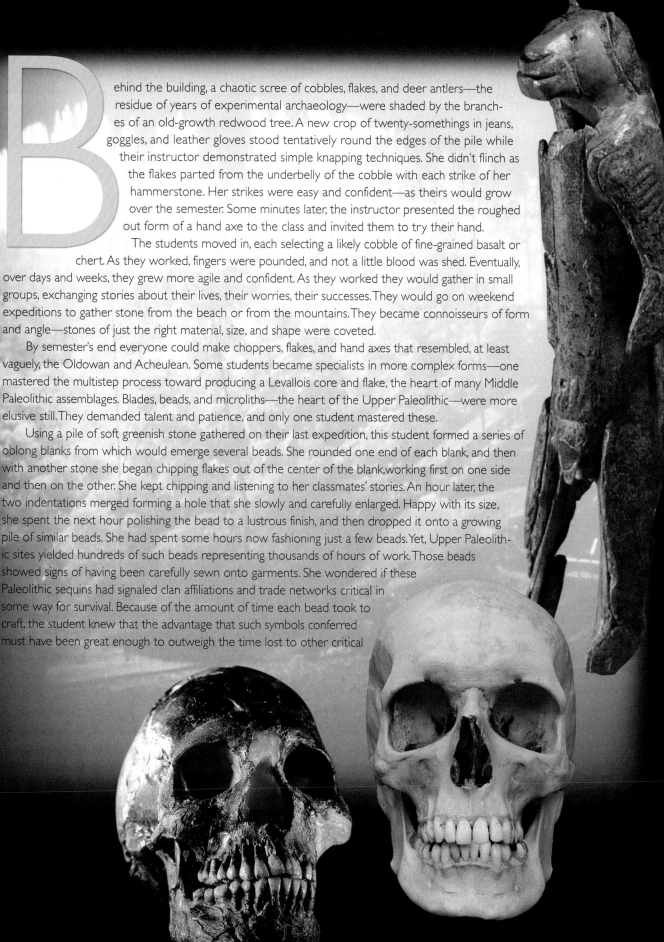

Behind the building, a chaotic scree of cobbles, flakes, and deer antlers—the residue of years of experimental archaeology—were shaded by the branches of an old-growth redwood tree. A new crop of twenty-somethings in jeans, goggles, and leather gloves stood tentatively round the edges of the pile while their instructor demonstrated simple knapping techniques. She didn't flinch as the flakes parted from the underbelly of the cobble with each strike of her hammerstone. Her strikes were easy and confident—as theirs would grow over the semester. Some minutes later, the instructor presented the roughed out form of a hand axe to the class and invited them to try their hand.

The students moved in, each selecting a likely cobble of fine-grained basalt or chert. As they worked, fingers were pounded, and not a little blood was shed. Eventually, over days and weeks, they grew more agile and confident. As they worked they would gather in small groups, exchanging stories about their lives, their worries, their successes. They would go on weekend expeditions to gather stone from the beach or from the mountains. They became connoisseurs of form and angle—stones of just the right material, size, and shape were coveted.

By semester's end everyone could make choppers, flakes, and hand axes that resembled, at least vaguely, the Oldowan and Acheulean. Some students became specialists in more complex forms—one mastered the multistep process toward producing a Levallois core and flake, the heart of many Middle Paleolithic assemblages. Blades, beads, and microliths—the heart of the Upper Paleolithic—were more elusive still. They demanded talent and patience, and only one student mastered these.

Using a pile of soft greenish stone gathered on their last expedition, this student formed a series of oblong blanks from which would emerge several beads. She rounded one end of each blank, and then with another stone she began chipping flakes out of the center of the blank, working first on one side and then on the other. She kept chipping and listening to her classmates' stories. An hour later, the two indentations merged forming a hole that she slowly and carefully enlarged. Happy with its size, she spent the next hour polishing the bead to a lustrous finish, and then dropped it onto a growing pile of similar beads. She had spent some hours now fashioning just a few beads. Yet, Upper Paleolithic sites yielded hundreds of such beads representing thousands of hours of work. Those beads showed signs of having been carefully sewn onto garments. She wondered if these Paleolithic sequins had signaled clan affiliations and trade networks critical in some way for survival. Because of the amount of time each bead took to craft, the student knew that the advantage that such symbols conferred must have been great enough to outweigh the time lost to other critical pursuits such as foraging or hunting. She didn't have to choose between making a bead and eating a meal, but for her Paleolithic counterparts she knew the benefit of the bead must have outweighed its cost in some important way.

MODERN HUMAN ORIGINS ARE NOT SIMPLY A MATTER of anatomy but also of behavior. No matter how cognitively sophisticated our close cousins the Neandertals or archaic *Homo sapiens* were or how close the size of their brains was to our own, they did not attain the same level of technological achievement. The bead described in the vignette is not much of an artifact; it is not even a tool. But it provides material evidence of personal decoration and symbolic representation. Such evidence is abundant in the archaeological record of modern humans and all but absent from the records of Neandertals and archaic *H. sapiens*.

In this chapter, we review the three distinct sources of evidence used to reconstruct the critical events surrounding the emergence of modern people. Paleontological and geological data chart the distribution in time and space of anatomically modern *H. sapiens*. Archaeological data shed light on the changes in behavior that allowed modern humans to exploit the natural world in a way that would ultimately make us the dominant species on the planet. Genetic data provide information on the web of biological relationships between us and our closest relatives. By synthesizing data from these interrelated realms, biological anthropologists attempt to address the fundamental question of our field: How did human beings evolve?

The Emergence of Modern Humans

The emergence of modern humans can be seen anatomically in a combination of cranial features that distinguish us from archaic *H. sapiens* and Neandertals (see Chapter 13). These features include a gracile skull and postcranial anatomy; limited development of browridges or other cranial superstructures; a rounded cranium with its maximum breadth high on the vault, and parallel sides in rear view; a prominent mastoid process; a retracted face with a canine fossa; small teeth and jaws; and development of an obvious chin (Figure 14.1). However, large brain size does not set us apart from archaic *H. sapiens* or Neandertals. Many Middle and Late Pleistocene hominid fossils have cranial capacities that are easily within the modern human range (whose average is about 1,350 cc), and a number of them exceed the human mean by a substantial amount.

Despite the fact that there is no significant difference in absolute brain size, when we look at the archaeological record associated with modern humans—the Upper Paleolithic or Later Stone Age—we find evidence of substantial behavioral differences between our close relatives and us. The rapid pace of change and the

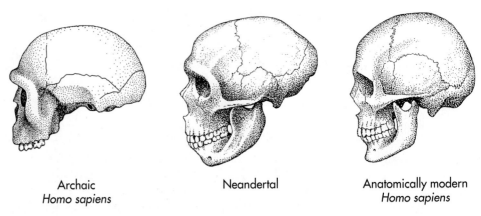

Archaic
Homo sapiens

Neandertal

Anatomically modern
Homo sapiens

FIGURE 14.1   Variations on a theme: archaic *Homo sapiens*, Neandertal, and anatomically modern *Homo sapiens* skulls.

appearance of symbolic behavior are two of the hallmarks of the Upper Paleolithic revolution, which some scientists think occurred with the sudden appearance of anatomically modern humans (Klein & Edgar, 2002). Other scientists think that different aspects of Upper Paleolithic culture appear at different times during the later Middle Stone Age (MSA), thus indicating a more gradual evolution of behaviorally modern humans (McBrearty & Brooks, 2000).

Models of Modern Human Origins

Many scientists have attempted to assemble anatomical, behavioral, and genetic data into comprehensive models of the origins of modern humans. In the past two decades, two basic frameworks have been debated: the replacement and multiregional models. Both agree that there was an initial dispersal of *H. erectus* (or *H. ergaster*) from Africa into the rest of the Old World. However, they disagree as to what happened next.

MULTIREGIONAL AND REPLACEMENT MODELS

The **replacement models** suggest that modern humans had a localized origin—usually thought to be in Africa—and then dispersed into areas already occupied by *H. erectus* and its descendants. Replacement models thus require a second hominid dispersal from Africa. These models often are called "Out of Africa" models or "Out of Africa II," in recognition of the earlier *H. erectus* dispersal. As the word *replacement* implies, these models predict that anatomically modern humans did not interbreed substantially (or at all) with the indigenous hominids whom they ultimately replaced. One implication is that all geographic variation seen in modern humans today evolved recently, after the origin of anatomically modern humans.

Multiregional models propose that our origins cannot be pinned down to a single population or area. Instead, gene flow, via repeated population movements and intermixing, is thought to have been extensive among Old World hominid populations. Thus the appearance of anatomically modern humans throughout the Old World resulted not from replacement of many populations by one but from the transmission of alleles underlying the modern human phenotype between populations that were in genetic contact. Therefore, multiregional models do not suggest the later dispersal of a second hominid species from Africa. Note that the multiregional models do not call for separate and multiple origins for modern humans; rather, they suggest that modern humans originated in the context of gene flow between multiple regions.

It is not entirely true that multiregional and replacement models are irreconcilable. Certainly, any proof of genetic contributions from regionally dispersed populations means that total replacement could not have happened. But population expansion from a single region could have been the dominant event in recent human evolution, with genetic contributions from other populations being trivial. Conversely, it is very likely that over the past 500,000 years, hominid populations in some regions have been replaced by others without interbreeding, but this does not preclude gene flow from having occurred between other populations in the species.

PREDICTIONS OF THE TWO MODELS

Replacement models predict that we should first see modern human fossils in Africa and then at least two anatomically distinct lineages of hominids in each region of the Old World: Neandertals and modern humans in Europe, *Homo heidelbergensis* (archaic *H. sapiens*) and modern humans in mainland Asia, and possibly relict populations of *H. erectus* and modern humans in Southeast Asia. Replacement further predicts that these lineages will overlap for at least a brief period of time in each region. Like the anatomy, the archaeological record would show abrupt changes in technology and behavior (as modern humans brought their technology

Two basic models of human origins make different predictions for the evidence found in the fossil, archaeological, and genetic records.

replacement models
Phylogenetic models that suggest that modern humans evolved in one location and then spread geographically, replacing other earlier hominid populations without or with little admixture.

multiregional models
Phylogenetic models that suggest that modern humans evolved in the context of gene flow between Middle to Late Pleistocene hominid populations from different regions, so there is no single location where modern humans first evolved.

with them to new areas), and the genetic record would indicate little overlap between the gene pools of the two lineages.

In contrast, multiregional models predict only a single evolving lineage that displays slightly different anatomical trends in each region. Across regions, we should see anatomical evidence of this evolution in the form of intermediate fossils with characteristics of the ancestors and the descendants. In addition, we should see regional anatomical characters continue from earlier to later populations. The archaeological record should show evidence of behavioral continuity, and the genetic evidence should show ancient contributions to the modern gene pool, assuming there has not been a strong genetic bottleneck.

In the next section, we will see how these predictions fare against the fossil, archaeological, and genetic records.

Anatomy and Distribution of Early Humans

Early modern human fossils are rare (Figure 14.2). Using archaeological evidence alone to assess the early appearance of modern humans is risky because, as we have seen before, it is unwise to equate a given tool culture only with a specific hominid, especially in periods when significant evolutionary transformations took place. However, where we are certain that earlier hominids did not exist (such as in Australia and the Americas), we can use archaeological sites without human remains to chart the earliest appearance of modern humans.

In many cases, early modern human fossils possess both derived features linking them to us and primitive features they may share with archaic *H. sapiens* or Neandertals (Pearson, 2000). For example, several early humans possess a long pubic ramus, a trait also seen in Neandertals. If this trait is unique to Neandertals it would signal Neandertal ancestry for certain modern human populations, supporting a multiregional model. Alternatively, if it is a primitive feature inherited by both Neandertals and modern humans from their common ancestor (we do not know because the postcranial fossil record of archaic *H. sapiens* is so sparse), then it does not necessarily reflect a Neandertal ancestry for some modern human populations and may support replacement models. In each region, we must assess the combinations of traits seen in modern human fossils, and whether the traits they share with earlier hominids of the region are shared-derived characters that suggest a unique relationship between the two or primitive characters that they share from a deeper common ancestor.

AFRICA

While Neandertals were evolving in Europe, a different kind of hominid was evolving in Africa: anatomically modern *H. sapiens*. As we discussed in Chapter 13, archaic *H. sapiens* fossils such as Bodo and Kabwe have been found in Africa during the period from around 600,000 to about 200,000 years ago. Starting at about 150,000 years ago we begin to see fossils that look more, but not entirely, modern from sites such as Herto in Ethiopia, Ngaloba in Tanzania, and Florisbad in South Africa. Their anatomy typically is intermediate in form, and their ages often are imprecisely known. Slightly later, fully anatomically modern humans appear at sites such as Klasies River Mouth and Border Cave in South Africa and Aduma in Ethiopia. Although some scientists like to distinguish these earlier and later groups by calling them different subspecies, most scholars include both in our species and subspecies, *H. sapiens sapiens*.

Perhaps the most securely dated of the earlier group of fossils are the recent discoveries from the Herto locality in the Middle Awash region of Ethiopia (Figure 14.3). Herto dates to between 160,000 and 154,000 years ago and yielded the crania of two adults and one juvenile (White et al., 2003). Like other African specimens from this period, the Herto crania "sample a population that is on the verge of anatomical modernity but not yet fully modern" (White et al., 2003, p. 745).

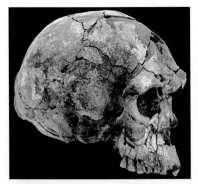

FIGURE 14.3 Hominid remains from Herto, Ethiopia, may be the oldest anatomically modern humans yet discovered.

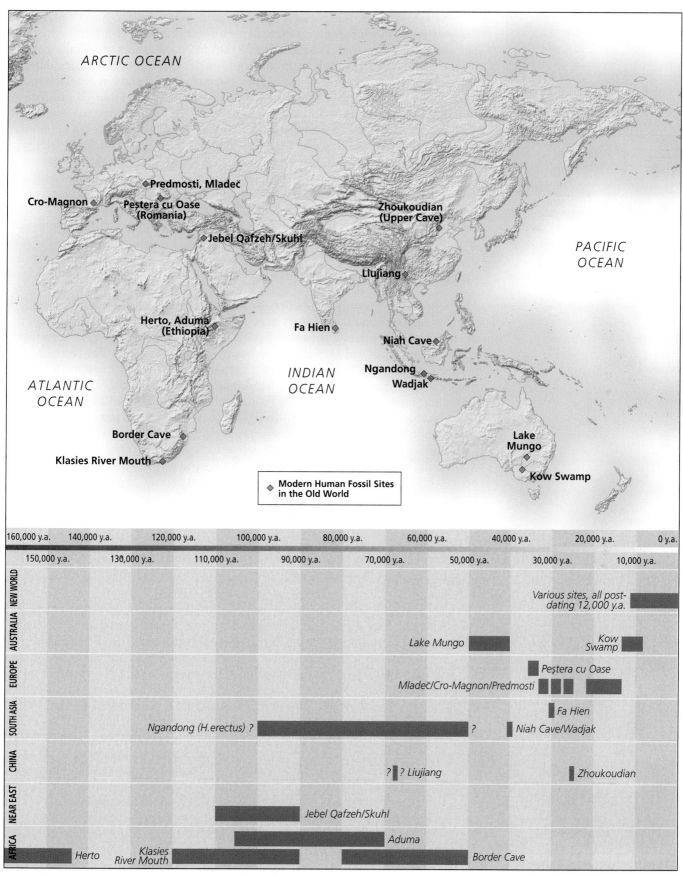

FIGURE 14.2   Modern human fossil sites in the Old World.

FIGURE 14.4 Anatomically modern humans from the Israeli cave sites of Skūhl and Qafzeh may be the earliest found outside of Africa.

The later group, represented by Aduma in Ethiopia and Border Cave and Klasies River Mouth in South Africa, date to about 120,000 to 50,000 years ago. The cranial remains from Aduma are 105,000 to 70,000 years old (Haile-Selassie et al., 2004). A partial adult cranium from Border Cave in South Africa dates to between 80,000 and 50,000 years ago. Fragmentary cranial and postcranial remains from Klasies River are between 120,000 and 90,000 years old (Rightmire & Deacon, 1991). For the most part, these early *H. sapiens sapiens* are found with typical MSA tool assemblages. But at Border Cave, the Howieson's Poort industry may be considered an advanced MSA assemblage because it features a tool type more typical of the Upper Paleolithic.

This sequence of African fossils provides evidence that *H. sapiens sapiens* was well established by 100,000 years ago at least on that continent. Furthermore, a series of specimens dating from 200,000 to 100,000 years ago provides strong evidence of the African transformation of archaic *H. sapiens* into anatomically modern humans.

NEAR EAST

The Near East is the only region outside Africa to yield reliable evidence of modern humans earlier than 60,000 years ago. As discussed in Chapter 13, anatomically modern *H. sapiens* dating between 110,000 and 90,000 years ago have been found at the sites of Skūhl and Qafzeh, located on Mt. Carmel in Israel. The Near East sits between Africa and Asia, so if modern humans (or modern human morphology) first evolved in Africa sometime after 150,000 years ago, then the Skūhl and Qafzeh hominids (Figure 14.4) could be considered the first sign of an expansion out of Africa that would only later (60,000–40,000 years ago) spread into Asia, Australia, and Europe. Neandertals are known to have occupied the Near East for tens of thousands of years, usually during glacial periods. Many scientists have interpreted the correlation of anatomically modern human specimens with warm (interglacial) periods and of later Neandertals with cold (glacial) periods as a sharing of this area by these two groups through time. Both Neandertals and early *H. sapiens sapiens* in the Near East are associated with MSA tool assemblages.

EUROPE

Scores of Neandertal remains have been recovered in Europe that date to between 150,000 and 30,000 years ago. However, modern human skeletal remains do not appear in Europe until relatively late, about 40,000 years ago. An Upper Paleolithic assemblage known as the Aurignacian appears in Europe about 40,000 years ago, and when it is found with hominid fossils, starting around 36,000 years ago, they are always *Homo sapiens sapiens*. A mandible recently discovered in the Carpathian region of Romania, at the site of Peștera cu Oase ("cave with bones"), is so far the oldest modern human in Europe, dating from 36,000 to 34,000 years ago (Trinkaus et al., 2003). Like other early modern human specimens, the Oase 1 mandible is robust and is argued to exhibit a mix of clearly derived features aligning it with anatomically modern *H. sapiens* (such as development of the chin) and features (such as its robustness and anatomy of the mandibular foramen—a small hole in the mandible through which nerves and blood vessels pass) linking it to Neandertals (Figure 14.5). The appearance of the mandibular foramen of Oase 1 may be a derived feature shared with Neandertals and not seen in human populations today. Although it is an insignificant biological feature, this is the kind of diagnostic trait that can become quite important in debates about phylogenetic relationships among late Pleistocene hominids.

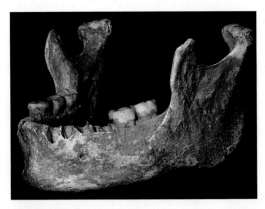

FIGURE 14.5 The Oase 1 mandible, earliest modern human in Europe.

The central European sites of Mladeč and Předmostí, both located in the Czech Republic, have yielded numerous fossils of anatomically modern *H. sapiens,* which also display characters that may align them with Neandertals (Smith, 1984; Frayer et al., 2006). These sites date from between 35,000 and 25,000 years ago, with the Předmostí site being somewhat younger than Mladeč. Both were discovered in the late nineteenth century; unfortunately, the Předmostí remains were destroyed during World War II. At these sites several crania, probably representing males, have an occipital bun or hemi-bun, which is not as fully developed as the Neandertal occipital bun. Some anthropologists have argued that this feature, in combination with the development of browridges, suggests a Neandertal ancestry of these early modern humans.

In contrast, early Upper Paleolithic human postcranial skeletons in Europe appear to be tropically adapted, lacking the cold-adapted proportions we saw in Neandertal skeletons. They have narrower, more linear body proportions of the limbs and thorax, associated with humans living in tropical climates who easily dissipate heat. Some scholars interpret this as evidence that modern humans migrated from tropical Africa to cold Europe more quickly than their skeleton could adapt to the climatic shift. If true, this would support a replacement model.

The best-known early anatomically modern humans from Europe come from the Cro-Magnon rock shelter located in the Dordogne region of France, which includes a number of Neandertal sites as well. Discovered in 1868, the Cro-Magnon remains include at least four adults (with partial crania and mandibles), an infant, and an assortment of other cranial and postcranial remains. The site is about 27,000 years old, much younger than the first appearance of modern humans in Europe (Gambier, 1989). The "Old Man" of Cro-Magnon (or Cro-Magnon 1) has a gracile cranium that combines a very small face with a large and bulbous braincase, in striking anatomical contrast to Neandertals from the same region (Figure 14.6). Because of these anatomical differences, archaeologists developed an evolutionary scenario for western Europe in which the Middle Paleolithic Neandertals were replaced quickly by Upper Paleolithic modern humans, sometime between 40,000 and 30,000 years ago. However, critics argue that the Cro-Magnon 1 specimen is not like other early modern humans in Europe (including those from central Europe and even some of the other Cro-Magnon individuals), who show a more mosaic pattern of archaic and modern features.

Given their late appearance, it is not surprising that European anatomically modern humans are found only with Upper Paleolithic technologies. In fact, in western Europe there appears to be a one-to-one correlation between *H. sapiens sapiens* and the Aurignacian technology. As we saw in Chapter 13, a different Upper Paleolithic technology, the Châtelperronian, is contemporaneous with the Aurignacian but appears to be a Neandertal technology.

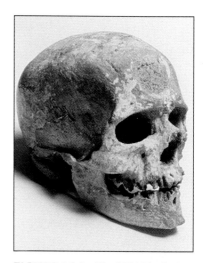

FIGURE 14.6 The "Old Man" of Cro-Magnon, from the Dordogne region of France.

ASIA AND SOUTHEAST ASIA

In Asia there is a gap in the hominid fossil record between about 100,000 and 40,000 years ago. Archaic or premodern *H. sapiens* are known from a number of sites dating from between 250,000 and 100,000 years ago in China (Etler, 1996), but anatomically modern humans do not appear until perhaps 65,000 years ago or later in China and possibly 40,000 years ago in Indonesia.

Dating is a problem for establishing the earliest human remains in Asia. In China, the site of Liujiang has been dated to at least 18,000 years ago, and perhaps as old as 67,000 years, but there is some question as to the provenience of the human remains recovered from that site (Shen et al., 2002). Well-accepted dates of 25,000 years ago have been obtained for the site of Hebei and for the Upper Cave at Zhoukoudian (approximately 42 km southwest of Beijing; Figure 14.7). Although clearly modern humans, the three Upper Cave skulls differ anatomically from one another and are not similar to skulls of recent East Asian peoples. Stringer and Andrews (1988) think that the Upper Cave skulls most closely resemble early modern humans

FIGURE 14.7 The Upper Cave at Zhoukoudian yields ages of about 25,000 years for *Homo sapiens*.

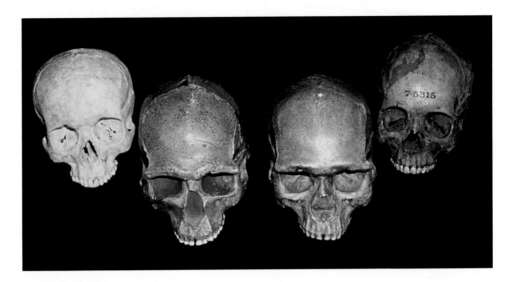

FIGURE 14.8 Fossil remains of anatomically modern humans from the Czech Republic and from China (center crania) are more robust than recent human crania but are otherwise anatomically identical. All four crania are *Homo sapiens sapiens*.

from the European sites of Mladeč and Předmostí (Figure 14.8) which would mean that both European and Asian early modern human populations had a common origin (presumably Africa) and that there is little evidence of regional continuity.

The earliest *H. sapiens sapiens* in Southeast Asia are equally problematic. Specimens such as the "Deep Skull" from the Niah Cave complex in Borneo and Wadjak from Java (one of the first specimens discovered by Eugene Dubois's team) have been assigned dates of about 40,000 years ago. The complex cave stratigraphy and questions of where precisely the fossils were found led many scientists to consider these dates highly provisional. However, recent archaeological and archival work by Graeme Barker and colleagues (2007) lends support to an age of 34,000 to 46,000 years ago for the "Deep Skull" from Niah Cave (Figure 14.9).

The possible evolutionary relationships of these Asian modern humans exemplify contrasting views of the origin of all modern humans: Some researchers argue that they represent the culmination of an unbroken evolutionary trajectory in China and Indonesia that began with variants of *H. erectus* in each area and that extends to contemporary East Asian populations (Wolpoff et al., 1994). Other researchers argue that the Upper Cave individuals do not resemble modern Asians in any meaningful way, nor do the early Indonesians represent modern Indonesians, and that both may represent a migration into the region by individuals of an early, geographically undifferentiated modern human group (e.g., Stringer & Gamble,

FIGURE 14.9 The Niah Cave complex in Borneo.

1993). Filling the Asian fossil gap between 100,000 and 40,000 years ago will be essential in resolving some of these issues.

AUSTRALIA

Although Australia is separated by water from the major Eurasian land mass, evidence suggests that modern humans were in Australia before they were in Europe. To get to Australia, modern humans almost certainly had to go through island Southeast Asia; so the ages of the earliest Australian occupation are also relevant to the peopling of Southeast Asia. During glacial maxima, when sea levels are lowest, Australia and New Guinea form a single land mass known as Sahul. Sahul is always separated by water from the land mass Sunda, which forms from some of the islands of Southeast Asia. Although all kinds of primates, including extinct hominids, occupy or occupied Sunda, only modern humans were able to disperse throughout Sahul. However, a stunning recent discovery from Flores, Indonesia, shows that at least one other hominid was able to make the jump from Sunda (see Insights and Advances: The Little People of Flores on page 418). Some scientists argue that the settlement of Australia, New Guinea, and other islands of Melanesia was a fundamental advance in the behavior of modern humans over earlier hominids (Noble & Davidson, 1996), in part because settlement of these islands could have been accomplished only by using a boat or raft of some kind.

The earliest human remains from Australia come from a site in the southeastern part of the continent known as Lake Mungo. Two incomplete skeletons from burials, along with other fragmentary remains and some cremations, have been found and recently dated to 40,000 years ago (Figure 14.10). Flake tools from Lake Mungo date to 50,000 years ago, which matches the earliest archaeological dates in Australia (Bowler et al., 2003). Mungo I, the buried remains of a young female, shows signs of having been cremated; the other burial, Mungo III, is an old male whose body was covered with red ochre. These are the earliest known examples of such mortuary practices. Both specimens are anatomically modern *H. sapiens*, and they both exhibit a gracile build.

Other Australian sites, such as Kow Swamp and Willandra Lakes, have yielded a number of reasonably complete crania that are substantially more robust than those of the Lake Mungo people. They are also substantially younger, dating between 13,000 and 9,500 years ago. The Kow Swamp individuals are interesting, however, because their thick cranial bones and moderate development of browridges have been argued to demonstrate their close affinities with the latest *H. erectus* found at the site of Ngandong in Indonesia (Wolpoff et al., 1984). As we saw in Chapter 13, Ngandong may be a relict population of *H. erectus* that persisted on Java until less than 100,000 years ago and perhaps as late as 25,000 years ago, although these dates are controversial (Swisher et al., 1996). If true, this finding would support a replacement model of human origins (Figure 14.11). However they

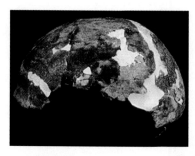

FIGURE 14.10 Partially cremated skull from Lake Mungo, Australia.

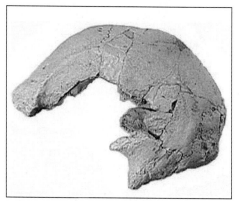

(a)   (b)

FIGURE 14.11 Evidence of regional continuity: (a) The anatomically modern Willandra Lakes Hominid 50 Calvaria from Australia and (b) a later *Homo erectus* cranium from Ngandong, Indonesia.

INSIGHTS AND ADVANCES

The Little People of Flores

Homo sapiens never coexisted with Homo erectus. Or did they? Conventional wisdom has held that H. erectus went extinct in the Middle Pleistocene after giving rise to Homo sapiens. But as we saw in Chapter 12, geochronologists estimate that the Ngandong H. erectus from Java lived somewhere between 50,000 and 25,000 years ago, overlapping in time and space with modern humans who reached the region by as early as 60,000 years ago. Controversial discoveries on the island of Flores suggest to many scientists that another group of hominids survived until 18,000 years ago. At the cave of Liang Bua where Indonesian archaeologists led by R. P. Soejono have been excavating since 1976, the remains of a diminutive hominid were recovered (Brown, P., et al., 2004). Analyses by Peter Brown show that the skull had a cranial capacity of 380 to 420 cc (Figure A) (Falk D., et al., 2005), and the postcranial skeleton suggests a female biped that stood just about a meter tall—the size of the A. afarensis skeleton "Lucy." Stone tools at the site may be associated with the hominid.

Although some scientists call it a new species, H. floresiensis, Brown's description of the skull makes it difficult to distinguish from H. erectus except on the basis of its small size. And the shoulder skeleton is also reminiscent of H. erectus (Larson et al.,

2007). But other aspects of the postcranial skeleton look more primitive (Morwood et al., 2005). The hand skeleton in particular suggests to Matt Tocheri that the hominids from Flores were more primitive than even Homo habilis (Gibbons, 2007; Tocheri et al., 2007). Alternatively, Teuku Jacob and colleagues (2006) argue the Flores remains are just those of a short human with an abnormally small brain. Jacob's initial claim has gained support from studies of the relationship between brain and body size by Bob Martin (Martin et al., 2006) and Tom Schoenemann (Schoenemann & Allen, 2006). The studies suggest that the relationship between brain and body size in the Flores specimen is more similar to humans with a condition known as microcephaly or perhaps to some kind of dwarfism than to fossil hominids. And recent work by Israel Hershkovitz and colleagues (2007) argues the Flores material represents modern individuals with a congenital deficiency in insulin-like growth factor production.

A common phenomenon for large mammals that colonize small islands (Flores is about 1400 km² or 540 square miles) is to become smaller over many generations. In fact the fossil record of Flores yields the remains of a dwarfed elephant as well (Figure B). This size reduction (called "insular dwarfism") is related to two selective

pressures on large island mammals: Fewer resources favor smaller individuals who need less food to survive, and fewer predators mean that having a small body doesn't increase the chance of being eaten. If the Flores hominid is a new species it may represent such a process. Perhaps a few members of H. erectus were washed onto the island on natural rafts during a storm. Stranded there they were isolated from other members of their species. Their isolation may explain not only their small size but also their survival. In their island refuge they did not come into competition for resources with and were not replaced by modern humans until much later than other archaic hominids.

There is so much disagreement over the interpretation of the Flores individual because only a single skull has been found, and the critical characters (such as cranial capacity) for assessing what species a hominid belongs to are found in the skull, although most of the new studies of the postcrania all seem to support the idea that the Flores specimens are not modern humans. If they are not pathological, the remains from Flores almost undoubtedly represent a distinct type of hominid, and remind us that it may have been only a few thousand years since we last shared the earth with another hominid species.

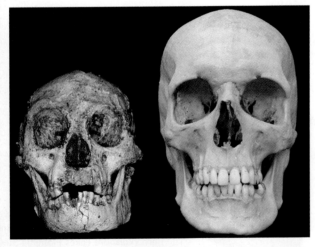

FIGURE A   The skull from Flores is tiny, less than one-third of the capacity of a modern human skull.

FIGURE B   Insular dwarfism commonly affects mammals isolated on islands.

arose, it seems clear that anatomically modern humans had the ability to cross large bodies of open water and colonize Australia by at least 50,000 if not 60,000 years ago.

Archaeology of Modern Human Origins

The archaeological remains of later modern humans reflect cultural and individual behaviors that are substantially more complex than those of earlier hominids or even of the earliest *H. sapiens sapiens*; but just which behaviors allowed us to become the dominant hominid species throughout the world by about 40,000 years ago?

STONE AND OTHER TOOLS

The changes in tool industries associated with the emergence of anatomically modern humans is a tale of two continents: Europe and Africa. For many years, the European archaeological and fossil records formed the basic model for the emergence of modern people. Over the past few decades, however, the archaeology of Africa has provided a new context for understanding human origins.

The very earliest modern humans, those dating to 100,000 years ago or earlier in Africa and the Near East, are found with MSA assemblages that are indistinguishable in most ways from those of earlier hominids (or later Neandertals). Thus modern anatomy appears before the development of modern—Upper Paleolithic—technology.

The European Upper Paleolithic and the African Later Stone Age are distinguished from the MSA by a greater reliance on the standardized production of blades: long flakes that could be used as blanks to produce a variety of different flaked tools. A number of blades could be taken off a prepared stone core in a systematic manner (see Figure 13.22 on page 399). Refinements in tool flaking techniques also distinguish Upper Paleolithic and Later Stone Age tool industries from the MSA. For example, long, exquisitely flaked blades from the Solutrean industry of Europe demonstrate the extraordinary level of skill of Upper Paleolithic toolmakers (Figure 14.12).

Microliths are another common feature of Upper Paleolithic and Later Stone Age tool industries, which appeared after 25,000 years ago in most regions. **Microliths** are small, shaped flakes that probably were once attached to wood or bone to make composite tools. Arrowheads are a late-version microlith that appear for the first time around 13,000 to 10,000 years ago. Unlike the MSA, in which a basic set of tools and techniques emerged early and persisted for the next 250,000 years, tool types change frequently and continuously throughout the Upper Paleolithic and Later Stone Age.

Another striking feature of the Upper Paleolithic and Later Stone Age is the vastly greater use of tools made from bone, ivory, antler, and shell. These were ground, polished, and drilled to form objects such as harpoons, fishhooks, spear-throwers, awls, needles, and buttons. (Such materials were used but at a much cruder level and very rarely in earlier industries.) Upper Paleolithic peoples also produced well-known examples of representational cave art and other artistic or ritual objects.

With one or two exceptions, the appearance of Upper Paleolithic tool industries in Europe coincided with the appearance of anatomically modern humans. In the nineteenth century, the shift from the Mousterian to the Upper Paleolithic was considered to represent a behavioral or cultural revolution that occurred when modern humans replaced Neandertals in Europe. For decades many scientists thought that similar replacements had occurred in other parts of the world as well. However, given the relatively late appearance of modern humans in Europe, it seems unlikely that Europe should be a good model for the original appearance of modern humans.

microliths Small, flaked stone tools probably designed to be hafted to wood or bone; common feature of Upper Paleolithic and Later Stone Age tool industries.

FIGURE 14.12 Upper Paleolithic refinement in stone tool production, a Solutrean blade.

Indeed, many archaeological elements thought to be uniquely associated with the Upper Paleolithic and Later Stone Age actually made their first appearance in the Middle Stone Age of Africa (McBrearty & Brooks, 2000). These innovations did not appear suddenly in a single locality but in different sites at different times. For example, blades are known from several sites, dating from 75,000 years ago to perhaps as early as 280,000 years ago in East Africa. Flake technologies based on the production of points rather than scrapers (a hallmark of the Mousterian in Europe) are also abundant in African MSA sites, some dating to 235,000 years ago.

More surprisingly, microliths (Figure 14.13), which are typically associated with the late Upper Paleolithic, were being made in the African MSA 65,000 years ago. The site of Mumba in Tanzania shows a continuous sequence of the development of microlith technology, starting from larger flake tools. In South Africa, the Howieson's Poort industry (dating to 70,000–60,000 years ago) is also characterized by an abundance of microliths. At Border Cave, the Howieson's Poort industry is found in association with anatomically modern human remains. Tools made from bone have also been found at a variety of African MSA sites. Sally McBrearty and Alison Brooks (2000) suggest that the transition to the kind of cultural assemblage we associate with modern humans developed through the gradual accumulation of different techniques and tool types and that it was more evolutionary than revolutionary. Thus, the rapid replacement of the Middle

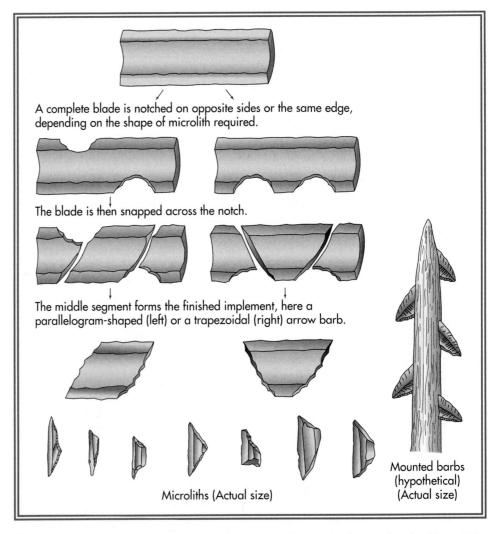

A complete blade is notched on opposite sides or the same edge, depending on the shape of microlith required.

The blade is then snapped across the notch.

The middle segment forms the finished implement, here a parallelogram-shaped (left) or a trapezoidal (right) arrow barb.

Microliths (Actual size)

Mounted barbs (hypothetical) (Actual size)

FIGURE 14.13 Microlith production. Although microliths are typically considered an Upper Paleolithic technology, their origins can be traced to the Middle Stone Age of Africa.

Paleolithic by the Upper Paleolithic in Europe may not be representative of what happened in Africa, the region where modern humans first evolved.

We should pause at this point to reflect on what *modernity* really means. The appearance of such tools as blades often has been the basis for inferring the appearance of modern behavior. However, it is not clear that these archaeological signals are good proxies for modernity. Can modern behavior, like modern anatomy, be signaled by the appearance of a single derived character or the presence of a single tool type, however briefly it appears in the record? Or is it indicated only by the presence of a comprehensive package of behaviors that signifies a different set of interactions with the world?

SUBSISTENCE

Much evidence supports the idea that modern humans exploited a wider variety of foodstuffs than did Neandertals or archaic *H. sapiens*. Ultimately, this ability to exploit natural resources led to the development of agriculture, starting about 12,000 years ago, which allowed a sustained increase in population growth. However, by expanding their subsistence base in other ways, early anatomically modern humans may have established a pattern of increased population growth relative to other hominids even at the very origins of our species, long before the introduction of agriculture.

One example is the use of aquatic resources, such as fish and shellfish. Earlier hominids, including some Neandertal populations, made limited use of marine resources. And some African MSA coastal sites show exploitation of marine mammals, fish, shellfish, and tortoises earlier than 40,000 years ago, perhaps signaling an earlier shift to modern behavior on that continent. However, only in the Upper Paleolithic and Later Stone Age do aquatic resources become a widespread and systematic part of human subsistence.

Besides archaeological remains, other information points to the expansion of subsistence patterns in modern humans. Dental microwear analyses reveal wear patterns on Neandertal teeth that are more similar to those seen in recent human populations who are highly carnivorous (Lalueza et al., 1996). In contrast, Upper Paleolithic wear patterns indicate a diet incorporating a greater amount of vegetable matter. Similarly, stable isotope analyses of Neandertals (dating from 130,000–28,000 years ago) and Upper Paleolithic burials (aged 26,000–20,000 years) indicate that Neandertals ate mostly terrestrial herbivores, like deer, but that the Upper Paleolithic people ate a more varied diet that included fish, mollusks, or possibly shorebirds (Richards et al., 2001; see Chapter 8 for a review of the stable isotope methods).

SYMBOLISM

Perhaps the most striking difference between later modern humans and earlier hominids is the extent to which modern human archaeological assemblages incorporate clear evidence of symbolic behavior. Remember the scant and debatable evidence of Neandertal symbolism reviewed in the last chapter. In contrast, by 50,000 to 40,000 years ago modern humans apparently dedicated large percentages of their time to symbolic acts such as creating and presumably wearing ornamentation, making cave and portable art, and burying their dead. All this suggests that symbolic behavior had a survival value for modern humans and that their relationship to the world and to other hominids may have been ordered by symbols.

Symbolism must have been important for the survival of anatomically modern humans, because they spent so much time making beads, ornaments, and other art.

Burials   The significance and even the existence of Neandertal burials are debated, and their symbolic implications are questioned as well. By about 40,000 years ago these questions became moot because evidence of new mortuary practices, including cremation at Lake Mungo in Australia, appears at modern human sites at this time. In Europe, Upper Paleolithic burials (the earliest of which date to about 28,000 years ago) differ from Mousterian burials in several ways. Whether found

FIGURE 14.14 Anatomically modern humans left archaeological clues, including evidence of burials, which indicate that ritual and symbolic behavior were important parts of their culture.

in caves or open air sites, Upper Paleolithic burials are composed of burial pits. More important perhaps, a number of Upper Paleolithic burials contain an elaborate array of grave goods, and multiple, carefully arranged bodies (Figure 14.14). Obviously, not every Upper Paleolithic burial is an elaborate affair complete with an abundance of finely made grave goods. However, such burials are completely absent in the earlier archaeological records. Interestingly, evidence of deliberate burial of any kind in the later MSA is quite scanty, and Aurignacian burials are also scarce.

Upper Paleolithic European burials often are covered in beads and bear other indications that the dead were buried in decorated garments (Stringer & Gamble, 1993). Thousands of beads, both isolated and associated with bodies, have been found at Upper Paleolithic sites. Pendants of animal teeth—often from animals that Upper Paleolithic people did not eat, such as fox—are also found (Figure 14.15). There are even examples of pendants made from human molars. Experimental work by Randall White suggests that most beads were attached to garments and took a few hours each to make. Thus, the Upper Paleolithic peoples invested a huge amount of time into making these grave items and personal ornaments.

Art and Ornamental Objects   Unlike the equivocal engravings of Neandertals, the artistic expression of Upper Paleolithic humans is astounding (Figure 14.16). Cave art and *petroglyphs* (rock carvings) occur not only in Europe but also in Africa and Australia. The earliest cave art in Europe appeared about 32,000 years ago at Chauvet, France, and is complex in its technique and representation. Rock art appeared in Africa about 26,000 years ago at Apollo 11 cave in Namibia, and somewhat earlier than that in Australia, at places such as Carpenter's Gap, which may be 40,000 years old. The rock art of Australia, which spans thousands of years, provides a particularly rich record of human artistic expression. The animals represented on cave walls such as Chauvet were once interpreted as sympathetic magic to assist in hunting success. But when compared with animal remains at archaeological sites of the same period, these images suggest that, as with their pendants, people were mostly focusing on animals they did not hunt. Perhaps the animals had some other symbolic or ritual importance for them. In addition to cave art, portable art is prevalent in modern human archaeological sites as well (Figure 14.17). The most famous of these pieces are the Venus figurines that represent various female figures, often interpreted as fertility totems. However, other figurines also exist, including many zoomorphic statuettes. All are small enough to be carried around in a pocket—although we do not know if they were.

Red ochre (iron oxide) and the color red were of great significance to modern humans. Evidence from one of the Lake Mungo burials in Australia indicates that the body may have been covered with red ochre. At the Qafzeh site, dating to about 92,000 years ago, seventy-one red ochre pieces, including some that were flaked or marked in some way, were associated with remains of anatomically modern humans, and several stone artifacts were stained with red ochre, although there was no evidence that the bodies themselves were covered in ochre (Hovers et al., 2003). Erella Hovers and her colleagues suggest that the form and distribution of the red ochre pieces indicate they were deliberately mined from a variety of local sources.

These elaborate displays of human symbolic behavior occur late in the archaeological record of modern humans, usually 40,000 years ago or later, not with

FIGURE 14.15 Personal ornamentation, including pendants such as this ivory piece from Arcy-sur-Cure in France, are often found with modern humans but rarely with Neandertals.

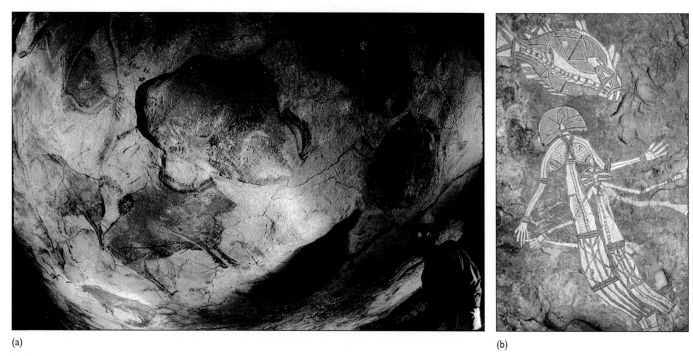

(a)

(b)

FIGURE 14.16 Abundant cave art after about 30,000 years ago is evidence of the importance of symbolic behavior for modern human cultures. (a) European cave art. (b) Australian cave art.

the earliest moderns. However, several examples of perforated shell, bone, and stone have been found at African MSA sites earlier in time, and perforated shell beads have recently been argued to be present at 73,000 years ago at Blombos Cave in South Africa (Henshilwood et al., 2004). If these prove on further inspection to be worked beads, they would represent the earliest known ornamentation and important support for a gradual accumulation of modern human behaviors.

The extensive evidence of artistic abilities of Late Pleistocene modern humans, expressed in a wide range of media over a large number of populations, stands in stark contrast to the paucity of evidence for such activities in Neandertals and

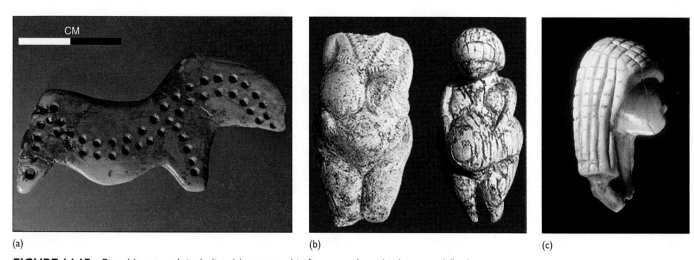

(a)

(b)

(c)

FIGURE 14.17 Portable artwork including (a) zoomorphic figures such as this horse and (b, c) Venus figurines appears frequently in the archaeological sites of anatomically modern humans, suggesting that symbolic behavior played an important role in their lives.

other hominids. Of course, this does not mean that earlier hominids were incapable of symbolic or artistic expression. Indeed, two examples of putative anthropomorphic carvings have been found in Acheulean deposits from Morocco and Israel dated to between about 400,000 and 250,000 years ago (Bednarik, 2003), which may give us a hint of the artistic abilities of archaic *H. sapiens*. Nonetheless, even though modern humans may not have been the only hominid capable of making art, it is clear that symbolic behavior took on a whole new significance with the evolution of our species.

SETTLEMENT OF THE NEW WORLD AND PACIFIC ISLANDS

Using behavioral rather than physical adaptations and perhaps ordering their world symbolically, modern humans also had the ability to dominate environments that were already occupied by other hominids and to settle regions that earlier hominids could not. As we have seen, modern humans were the first to colonize Australia, perhaps 50,000 years ago. Later, they would also settle high-latitude areas (see Insights and Advances: The "Vitamin D Line" on page 427), the Americas, and the remote islands of the Pacific.

The Americas   During ice ages, when sea levels are at their lowest, the Old and New Worlds are connected via the Bering landbridge, a broad swath of land (more than 2,000 km wide at its maximum) linking eastern Siberia with western Alaska (Figure 14.18). This bridge was open and ice free only periodically, most recently between 75,000 and 45,000 years ago and again between 25,000 and 11,000 years ago (Mandryk, 1992). Even when the landbridge was ice free, crossing it was no walk in the park but seems rather to have entailed a level of technological or subsistence development not reached by earlier hominids. Alternatively, we know that at least some modern human populations had watercraft by about 40,000 years ago, as demonstrated by the successful over-water colonization of Australia. Colonization of the New World via the coast of Siberia and Alaska or along the Pacific Rim may have been possible (Dixon, 2001).

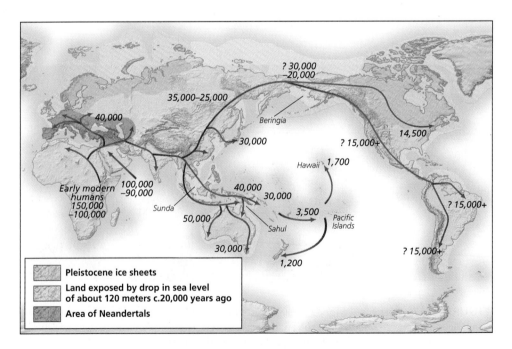

FIGURE 14.18   Routes for the human colonization of the New World and Pacific islands.

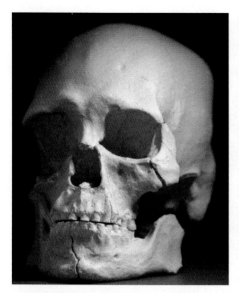

FIGURE 14.19 Paleo-Indian skeletal remains are rare. Kennewick man was discovered eroding from a riverbed and is about 9,000 years old.

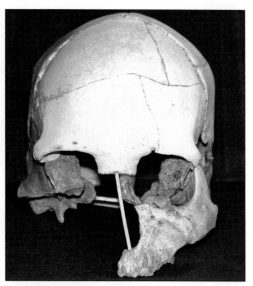

FIGURE 14.20 The Warm Mineral Springs individuals from Florida may be among the earliest Paleo-Indian skeletal remains.

By around 13,000 years ago, Paleo-Indian sites of the Clovis culture, which is distinguished by a characteristic finely flaked point, appeared all over North America. Additional Paleo-Indian sites appear not much later at sites in Central and South America. For many years the Clovis people were considered the first colonizers of the New World. However, scholars continue to argue over whether a pre-Clovis settlement existed.

Archeological sites aside, Paleo-Indian skeletal remains are rare. The earliest of them, such as Kennewick Man from Washington State (8,400 years old; Figure 14.19), the Browns Valley skull from Minnesota (8,700 years old), and the Warm Mineral Springs crania from Florida (perhaps 10,000 years old; Figure 14.20), exhibit features that differentiate them from recent Native American populations. These Paleo-Indian skulls show a great degree of variation and do not typically show a strong resemblance to contemporary Native American populations (Jantz & Owsley, 2001). The settlement history of the Americas is clearly complex and is being addressed by genetic, linguistic, archaeological, and paleontological researchers.

The Pacific   The last regions of the world to be colonized by humans are the Pacific Islands. Although people crossed the ocean between Sunda and Sahul about 50,000 years ago and inhabited islands such as New Britain off the east coast of Papua New Guinea as early as 28,000 years ago, most of the Pacific was not colonized until 3,500 years ago or later. Only the invention of long-distance voyaging technology allowed such crossings, which settlers undertook over vast areas of ocean (Irwin, 1992).

Genetic, archaeological, and linguistic data seem to indicate that the peopling of the Pacific started with populations somewhere in East Asia or island Southeast Asia who moved into New Guinea, fusing with peoples and cultures there, and then moved into Polynesia (Kirch, 2001). The earliest expansion of these peoples in the Pacific often is traced by their archeological sites, characterized by a pottery style called Lapita. The Lapita peoples appeared earliest in Near Oceania (the Bismarck Archipelago) around 3,500 years ago and from there spread to Fiji (around 3,000 years ago) and then further out to Tonga, Samoa, and Far Oceania.

The Pacific was the last part of the world to be settled by anatomically modern humans.

FIGURE 14.21 Far Oceania was the last of the regions of the world to be colonized by humans. Pictured here is an example of the importance of symbolism as shown by an ancient rock carving in the Cook Islands.

Presumably in outrigger canoes, they brought with them pigs, dogs, rats, agricultural crops, and enough food and water to survive their journey. Once on these remote islands, humans did what we do best. They modified the landscape, took advantage of new natural resources, and interacted with the environment in symbolic ways (Figure 14.21). The archaeological records of most islands reveal strong, not necessarily positive, human influences on these island ecosystems, including the extinction of land birds and evidence of deforestation.

These settlements mark the end of the initial colonization of the globe by humans. Although the rest of human history on Earth will be marked by both dispersal and migration, no longer is it into ecosystems never before occupied by humans.

Molecular Genetics and Human Origins

In looking at modern human origins, geneticists have used two types of data. The first considers living human genetic variation with the goal of identifying the **most recent common ancestor (MRCA)** of all people living today. The second set of data attempts to isolate DNA sequences from fossil *H. sapiens* and other hominids such as Neandertals. These ancient DNA analyses then consider the difference between the ancient groups and the extent of relatedness between them (see Innovations: Neandertal Genes in Chapter 13).

In a phylogenetic tree, the MRCA is indicated by the deepest node from which all contemporary variants can be shown to have evolved. Because all living people are genetically related to each other, the deepest node in a phylogenetic tree corresponds to a basic biological reality: All the variation we observe today evolved from a common ancestor. However, identifying the deepest node poses some problems. First, in large, complex datasets we can construct a huge number of possible phylogenetic trees. Thus, any particular tree represents a statistical model, which incorporates our assumptions about population size, the effects of natural selection, and other factors. Second, after identifying the deepest node in a tree, researchers want to know the date of the node. Putting a date to the node

most recent common ancestor (MRCA) In a phylogenetic tree, the MRCA is indicated by the deepest node from which all contemporary variants can be shown to have evolved.

INSIGHTS AND ADVANCES

The "Vitamin D Line"

Hominids began migrating long distances starting nearly 2 million years ago. Despite all the wandering that *Homo erectus* and archaic *H. sapiens* did, no hominids lived at relatively high latitude until the anatomically modern humans of the late Upper Paleolithic. Colonization beyond 50° latitude north or south seems to have been biologically limited until perhaps 15,000 years ago or so, when new behavioral adaptations overcame the problem.

Living humans show a skin color cline that is related to the availability and intensity of UV radiation (see Chapter 5). Darker skin color is prevalent in the tropics, and lighter skin color toward the poles. The cline seems to be selected for by two opposing forces—the tendency of melanin in darker skin to protect against folate degradation in UV-intense environments, such as those near the equator, and for lighter skin to allow sufficient vitamin D synthesis in UV-deprived environments nearer the poles. Such skin color clines do not exist in furred animals—whose skin is protected from UV radiation damage by their fur and who dissipate heat through panting and other mechanisms besides

sweating. Our "naked" skin likely evolved as part of a whole-body mechanism for reducing heat stress as our ancestors grew larger bodies and became more active during the day. The reduction of fur and the increase in numbers of sweat glands substantially increased the efficiency of sweating as a cooling mechanism. Such a cooling mechanism was probably necessary when *Homo erectus* first appeared (around 1.8 million years ago), and larger body size and more human-like body proportions evolved. Given that they lived in the tropics, *H. erectus* populations were probably dark-skinned. Subsequent migrations to higher latitudes eventually led to the evolution of the skin color cline; aDNA evidence suggests that some skin depigmentation occured in the Neandertal lineage.

However, even this skin color cline reaches its biological limit at about 50° latitude north or south. At about this latitude even light-colored skin does not receive enough UV radiation during any part of the year to adequately synthesis vitamin D (Jablonski, 2004). It is not until human popu-

lations are able to routinely acquire vitamin D through their diets, as opposed to synthesizing it from sunlight, that we see permanent archaeological sites beyond this latitude. Dietary sources of vitamin D include marine mammals, fish, lichen, or meat from animals that eat lichen, such as reindeer (Figure A). Human settlement passes this so-called "Vitamin D Line" in the late Paleolithic with populations whose material culture included fish hooks and harpoons and other implements that suggest they routinely ate fish and shellfish.

FIGURE A   Reindeer eat lichen and are therefore good sources of dietary vitamin D.

---

representing the MRCA entails calibration and an accurate determination of rates of genetic change (that is, setting the molecular clock; see Chapter 9). Finally, genetic data provide no insights into what the bodies carrying the genes looked like. In the case of human origins, for example, the MRCA need not have been an anatomically modern human.

At a fundamental level, the biological issue of modern human origins can be addressed only by both genetic and anatomical (paleontological) data. The molecular identification of the MRCA does not give us any idea about the physical or behavioral changes that led to the establishment of our species; the fossil record has no direct information about whether any past species or populations had any descendants.

MITOCHONDRIAL DNA

Mitochondrial DNA is transmitted maternally (only through the mother), has a relatively rapid rate of evolution, and does not undergo recombination. In the 1980s, researchers began using mtDNA to investigate modern human origins. Rebecca Cann and her colleagues (1987) constructed a phylogenetic tree based on sequence differences distributed throughout the human mtDNA genome. To do this they used mtDNA from a large group of people representing several populations. The tree was quite complex, and there was much overlap between individuals from different populations. There was one exception: At the deepest node (representing the MRCA), on one side of the tree there was a cluster of mtDNA lineages represented exclusively in Africa. Although African mtDNA lineages were also found on the other side of the tree, the exclusive African cluster indicated that the MRCA lived in Africa. Cann and her colleagues suggested a tentative date for the MRCA between 90,000 and 180,000 years ago (Figure 14.22). Although an mtDNA phylogeny traces the lineages down to a single mtDNA source, it is important to remember that there was more than one female in the population at the time; we should not think of the mtDNA studies as identifying an African "Eve."

More recently, Max Ingman and his colleagues (2000) confirmed that three of the deepest branches of the tree were exclusively African, with the next deepest being a mixture of Africans and non-Africans (Figure 14.22). All non-African mtDNA branches are of a very similar depth. Ingman and colleagues argue that such a pattern would arise if mtDNA lineages evolved initially for some time in Africa, followed by a migration of a small number of individuals out of Africa. This small gene pool results in a population bottleneck, followed by a population expansion, with all later Eurasian mtDNA lineages derived from this initial

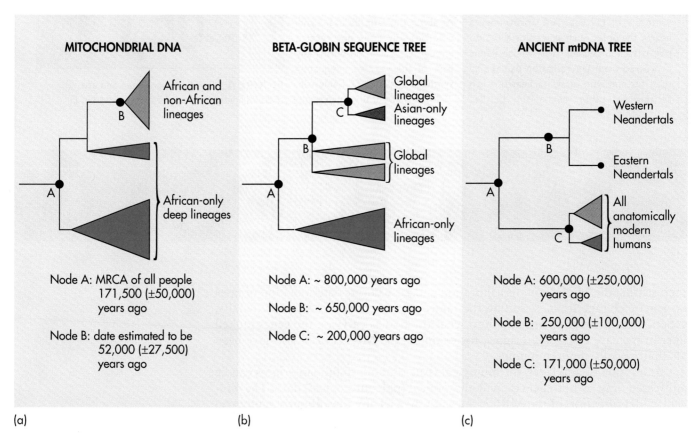

(a)   (b)   (c)

FIGURE 14.22   Three phylogenetic representations of modern human origins: (a) mtDNA, (b) beta-globin gene, and (c) ancient mtDNA.

small population that left Africa. Ingman and colleagues put the date of the MRCA for the whole tree at 171,500 ($\pm$50,000) years ago, somewhat earlier than that found in Cann's study. The date of the earliest clade that included African and non-African mtDNA was 52,000 ($\pm$27,500) years ago.

THE Y CHROMOSOME

The Y chromosome is in some ways the male equivalent of mtDNA. Like mtDNA, it is transmitted across generations in only one sex, in this case, males. Although parts of the Y chromosome undergo recombination, a large portion does not, and studies of this portion have been widely used in evolutionary research (Mitchell & Hammer, 1996; Stumpf & Goldstein, 2001; Jobling & Tyler-Smith, 2003). Phylogenetic analyses of the Y chromosome are based on both sequence and haplotype data. Haplotypes are combinations of mutations found together on a single chromosome; we can analyze them phylogentically or calculate population frequencies for different haplotypes (see Chapter 5). There are at least eighteen major haplotype groups for the Y chromosome. Haplotypes are useful for tracing population movements and demographic events that have occurred across human history (see Chapter 18, Insights and Advances: The Genghis Khan Effect).

The Y chromosome data seem to support the mtDNA story. Several estimates of a date for the Y chromosome MRCA have been suggested; most researchers accept an estimate of 100,000 to 180,000 years ago. Thus, the variation we observe in the Y chromosome and mtDNA of living humans appears to have evolved within similar timeframes. For both, the MRCA is dated with some confidence to less than 200,000 years ago. The Y chromosome and mtDNA data also both place the location of the MRCA in Africa. As was the case for the mtDNA, the deepest Y chromosome lineages are found exclusively in Africa, indicating evolution there first, followed by a population expansion into other parts of the world.

MRCAS FOR NUCLEAR GENES

Although the Y chromosome is part of the nuclear genome, it is a special case because such a large proportion of it is nonrecombining and it has only a small number of genes that are subject to natural selection. The remainder of the nuclear genome affords countless opportunities for reconstructing the evolutionary histories of human populations.

Large-scale compilations of protein allele data (see Chapter 5) are generally consistent with the evolutionary picture provided by mtDNA and the Y chromosome (Cavalli-Sforza et al., 1994; Cavalli-Sforza & Feldman, 2003), especially in locating the MRCA in Africa. In a phylogenetic tree derived from an analysis of allelic variation in 120 protein genes distributed in 1,915 populations, Luca Cavalli-Sforza and his colleagues show that the deepest node in the tree represents a split between African populations and all other populations.

In contrast to mtDNA and Y chromosome analyses, phylogenetic analyses of some nuclear genes (or portions of genes) and noncoding regions of chromosomes indicate MRCAs that are substantially older than 200,000 years. In the case of genes that code for proteins, this is not necessarily surprising because variation in their structures could be strongly constrained or influenced by natural selection (of course, this is also true of the coding regions of mtDNA and the Y chromosome). However, even if natural selection is involved in shaping the patterns of variability we see, the geographic origins of different alleles can provide insights into human evolutionary history.

Rosalind Harding and her colleagues (1997) analyzed a 3,000–base pair region of the beta-globin gene (one of the chains of the hemoglobin protein). They calculated an MRCA for the gene as existing 800,000 years ago, with the oldest sequence coming from Africa (Figure 14.22b). This finding does not contradict the mtDNA and Y chromosome results because the variation in this gene could have arisen and evolved in Africa before a population expansion out of Africa less than 200,000 years ago. However, Harding and her colleagues also found Asia-specific beta-globin sequences that had MRCAs more than 200,000 years ago. This would indicate that Asian populations that existed before 200,000 years ago made unique genetic contributions to the contemporary human genome, a finding that is difficult to reconcile with the mtDNA and Y chromosome results. Harding and her colleagues also found evidence of gene flow between Asian and African populations during the last several hundred thousand years.

Results broadly similar to those for the beta-globin gene have been obtained in other studies of the nuclear genome (Zhao et al., 2000). These findings support the beta-globin results in that an ancient MRCA (>400,000 years old) is identified, with the deepest root of the tree indicating an African origin, and the MRCA for regional variation outside Africa is found to be more than 200,000 years old. Again, these kinds of results indicate a more complex picture of the genetic origins of our species than those suggested by mtDNA and Y chromosome analyses.

ANCIENT DNA

DNA from fossil Neandertals and modern humans differs more than does DNA among living human populations. Some scholars think this is evidence that Neandertals and anatomically modern humans are different species.

Ancient DNA (aDNA) recovered from fossils can provide a direct window into the genetics of past populations. Ancient mtDNA has been isolated from more than a dozen Neandertals and seven fossil *H. sapiens*. Nuclear DNA has now been isolated for a single Neandertal from Vindija (see Chapter 13, Innovations: Neandertal Genes on page 396).

These studies agree that the Neandertal mtDNA samples all fall outside the range of variation that has been observed in modern humans (Figure 14.22c). And, Neandertal samples cluster together as a clade separate from living humans on a phylogenetic tree. Sequence variation in the Neandertal clade is approximately equivalent to that observed in living modern human groups. More importantly, ancient mtDNA from Neandertals falls outside the range of variation found in ancient DNA from fossil modern humans. And all fossil humans fail to show any Neandertal mtDNA or any intermediate sequences and are much closer to living human DNA, despite being closer in age to the Neandertal remains.

Researchers estimate from ancient mtDNA that the MRCA for modern humans and Neandertals lived between 365,000 and 853,000 years ago. The recently extracted nuclear DNA suggests a broadly similar picture. The MRCA is estimated to date to sometime between 460,000 and 700,000 years, with an inferred population split of around 370,000 years ago.

Many researchers think that the Neandertal ancient DNA data strongly support the replacement model of modern human origins. However, some analysts (e.g., Nordborg, 1998; Relethford, 2001) argue that a small number of divergent mtDNA sequences from Neandertals do not rule out the possibility that they may have interbred with anatomically modern humans; it is not that difficult to construct mathematical population models that can account for the mtDNA data in the context of modern human–Neandertal admixture. At this time, the Neandertal genetic data do not support including Neandertals in *H. sapiens,* but they cannot be used to definitely rule out such a possibility.

Interpreting Models of Human Origins

We have looked at three sets of data—paleontology, archaeology, and genetics—that are the basis for understanding the origin of modern human origins. Remember that the two main models for human origins, the Out of Africa and multiregional models, differ in whom they see as the immediate ancestors of modern humans. The Out of Africa model suggests that modern humans evolved in Africa and subsequently replaced more archaic hominids elsewhere in the Old World. Alternatively, the multiregional model suggests that the appearance of anatomically modern humans throughout the Old World resulted not from replacement of many populations by one but from the transmission of alleles underlying the modern human phenotype between archaic populations that were in genetic contact. We now consider how our three datasets are interpreted in light of these models.

PALEONTOLOGY AND ARCHAEOLOGY

As originally developed by Milford Wolpoff, Wu Xin Zhi, and Alan Thorne (1984), the multiregional model proposed that *local regional anatomical continuity* provides strong evidence of the multiregional origins of modern humans (see also Wolpoff et al., 1994; Wolpoff & Caspari, 1997). *Local regional continuity* means we can trace a particular evolutionary trajectory through a suite of anatomical features shared by fossil hominids in a particular region. For example, widely dispersed populations of *H. erectus* exhibited regional anatomical variation (see Chapter 12), and that regional variation may have been retained in later hominid populations living in the same area.

In contrast to the multiregional model, the replacement model suggests that the earliest modern humans should look very different from the local populations they replaced and should exhibit regional continuity in only one source region, Africa (Bräuer, 1984; Stringer & Andrews, 1988). Fossil lineages from archaic *H. sapiens* at Bodo to Herto, Aduma, and Klasies River Mouth provide evidence of an African origin of *H. sapiens sapiens* that predates such a lineage elsewhere in the world. At the same time as anatomically modern humans appear in Africa, archaic *H. sapiens* populations in Europe seem to be evolving into classic Neandertals. From about 40,000 to 30,000 years ago, Neandertals and anatomically modern humans appear to overlap in time and space in Europe, although they are physically and culturally distinct. By about 30,000 years ago modern humans replaced Neandertals in Europe.

Multiregional model proponents argue that the occasional appearance of occipital buns in modern human crania, the appearance of a retro-molar gap in some early human fossils, and the general robustness of early European modern human fossils, especially those from central Europe, are all evidence of regional continuity in Europe (Smith,1984). However, that some of these transitional populations, such as Vindija and Mladeč, reveal no sign of genetic admixture in their ancient DNA (Vindija is entirely Neandertal-like, Mladeč entirely modern human-like), does not support the multiregional position.

Asia and Australia may provide the best evidence of multiregional evolution, although the gap in the fossil record between about 100,000 and 40,000 years ago poses an interpretive challenge. Multiregional proponents argue that regional characters seen in *H. erectus* in China and Indonesia are mirrored in modern humans in China and Australia. For example, the high vertical frontal bone of Chinese *H. erectus* is considered continuous with that seen in Chinese modern humans. The sagittal keel, occipital torus, and supraorbital tori of Indonesian *H. erectus* are suggested to continue through, in lesser degrees, to modern human Australians. Likewise, the Ngandong hominids are thought to represent morphological and temporal intermediates between *H. erectus* and some modern Australians (Frayer et al., 1993). Alternatively, replacement proponents counter that Ngandong is not anatomically intermediate but morphologically *H. erectus* and potentially overlaps in time and space with modern humans of the region (Antón, 2003; Swisher et al., 1996). Replacement proponents also suggest that

Australasia provides the best paleontological and archaeological evidence for multiregional models of human origins.

early modern human fossils from Asia more closely resemble modern humans from other regions of the world than they do earlier Asian *H. erectus* (Stringer & Andrews, 1988).

It is probably safe to say that within the paleoanthropological community, there is more support for some version of the replacement model than for the multiregional model of evolution. However, it is equally safe to say that the field is far from consensus on the issue and that many paleoanthropologists think that the fossil record provides at least some support in some regions for multiregional evolution.

MOLECULAR GENETICS

Genetic data from both living humans and fossil remains provide some clear support for a replacement model of human origins. Although the molecular data can say nothing about the anatomy of the MRCA, the picture presented by mtDNA and the Y chromosome is easy to reconcile with the paleontological replacement model, which places the origins of anatomically modern humans in Africa during roughly the same time period of the MRCA for these molecular phylogenies. The divergent mtDNA and nuclear sequences of the Neandertals provide further support for a replacement event in Europe, especially in light of the fact that early modern humans in Europe have mtDNA that is well within the range of variation seen in contemporary humans. According to estimates from several genetic systems, modern humans may have evolved from a population of about 10,000 breeding individuals that existed about 100,000 years ago (Harpending et al., 1998).

For many years, there were few molecular challenges to replacement models of human origins, but data primarily from nuclear genes of living humans appear to strongly indicate MRCAs that significantly predate the MRCAs suggested by mtDNA and the Y chromosome of living humans. The most ancient lineages of these nuclear genes tend to come from Africa, but not all do, and some of the lineages outside Africa predate 200,000 years ago (Harding et al., 1997; Takahata et al., 2001).

Alan Templeton (2002) has provided a combined analysis of haplotype trees derived from mtDNA, the Y chromosome, two regions of the X chromosome, and six autosomal nuclear sequences. He argues that his analysis indicates the existence of extensive gene flow between populations throughout the Old World, dating to at least 500,000 years ago and probably longer. Several population expansions out of Africa are indicated in the analysis dating back to the original dispersal 1.7 million years ago and including the expansion indicated by mtDNA and the Y chromosome of approximately 100,000 years ago. Templeton suggests that the expansion of cranial capacity that begins to appear about 500,000 to 400,000 years ago in archaic *H. sapiens* also coincides with genetic evidence for another out-of-Africa expansion (in the context of gene flow). Templeton's analysis may be overreaching (Cann, 2002), but it clearly indicates that the molecular data do not unequivocally support a replacement model. Even some models of the differences between Neandertals and modern human ancient nuclear DNA can include as much as a 20% genetic contribution from Neandertals into modern gene pools (Green et al., 2006).

There is no simple answer to the question, Where did modern humans come from? (Table 14.1). Genetic, paleontological, and archaeological data can be woven together to produce several different scenarios to explain our complex origins. Some of the controversy surrounding the issue derives from scientific success as new dating methods, new archaeological and fossil discoveries, and innovative genetic approaches provide an unprecedented amount of information devoted to a single evolutionary event. The controversy over which particular model of human origins is correct should not blind us to the fact that we know far more about the biological and cultural evolution of our own species than ever before.

TABLE 14.1	Comparing Replacement and Multiregional Models of Human Origins		
	Fact	**Replacement Interpretation**	**Multiregional Interpretation**
Paleontological Record, Middle Pleistocene	Between about 200,000 and 500,000 years ago, archaic *H. sapiens* lived in Africa, Europe, and Asia.	Archaic *H. sapiens* in Europe evolved into Neandertals.	Neandertals and modern humans are not separate evolutionary lineages. Neandertals are transitional to European modern humans.
	Fully modern humans and classic Neandertals appeared by 125,000 years ago.	African archaic populations evolved into anatomically modern *Homo sapiens*.	
Paleontological Record, Late Pleistocene	The anatomically modern human phenotype first appeared outside Africa 90,000–100,000 years ago in the Middle East.	Anatomically modern humans replaced preexisting hominids throughout the Old World without or with little genetic mixing.	Anatomically modern humans arose from extensive gene flow between Middle and Late Pleistocene hominid populations throughout the Old World.
		Similarities between early anatomically modern humans from widely dispersed populations are best explained by evolution from a common source population in Africa.	Some fossils show transitional anatomy.
Recent DNA Studies	mtDNA and the Y chromosome phylogenies indicate greatest variability in Africa, suggesting that the most recent common ancestor (MRCA) of modern humans lived in Africa 150,000–200,000 years ago.	mtDNA and the Y chromosome support an African origin for modern humans and indicate a population expansion out of Africa starting about 100,000 years ago.	
	Nuclear gene sequences indicate MRCAs that significantly predate 200,000 years ago. Furthermore, deep lineages of these trees have been traced to variants that appear to have originated outside Africa.	Nuclear gene sequences reflect the age of the first dispersal (*H. erectus*) from Africa and do not preclude another dispersal by modern *H. sapiens* about 100,000 years ago. They are inconsistent with a complete replacement event.	Nuclear gene sequences indicate extensive gene flow between Old World populations over the last 500,000 years and perhaps longer.
			Diverse ancient Old World populations contributed to the modern human gene pool.
Ancient DNA	Ancient DNA from Neandertal and modern human fossils of the same age differ more from one another than does the DNA of living human groups.	Neandertals are a separate species that did not make a substantial genetic contribution to modern humans.	Differences between Neandertals and humans are less than those between chimp species and do not support a separate species for Neandertals.
	Differences between Neandertal and modern human DNA are not as great as those between chimp species.		
	Even some fossils considered transitional in anatomy do not have transitional DNA.	Neandertals were replaced across their range 30,000–40,000 years ago.	

SUMMARY

1. How do modern humans differ anatomically from earlier hominids?

The emergence of modern humans can be seen anatomically in a combination of cranial features that distinguish us from archaic *H. sapiens* and Neandertals. These include a gracile skull and postcranial anatomy, limited development of browridges or other cranial superstructures, a rounded cranium with a high maximum cranial breadth and parallel sides, a prominent mastoid process, a retracted face with a canine fossa, small teeth and jaws, and development of an obvious chin.

2. How do replacement models explain the origin of modern humans?

Replacement models of modern human origins argue that our species evolved initially in one location (Africa) and then spread out from that location, replacing all other hominid populations without interbreeding with them. All regional variation—genetic or anatomical—that we now observe in contemporary human populations has arisen since that replacement event occurred.

3. How do multiregional models explain the origin of modern humans?

Multiregional models suggest that *H. erectus* hominids distributed throughout the Old World have formed one widely distributed species with substantial gene flow between its diverse populations. Genetic innovations that arose in one population of the species were passed by gene flow to other populations in different regions. Regional variation in *H. erectus* and other Middle to Late Pleistocene taxa is considered to have been maintained even as local *H. erectus* populations made the transition to anatomically modern human form.

4. How do Upper Paleolithic and Middle Paleolithic tools differ?

Although they may occur sporadically in the Middle Paleolithic, the main distinguishing feature of Upper Paleolithic stone tools is a reliance on blades and microliths. In addition, Upper Paleolithic industries show a greater reliance on tools made from material other than stone, such as bone, antler, and shell.

5. What is an MRCA?

In a phylogenetic tree, the most recent common ancestor (MRCA) is indicated by the deepest node from which all contemporary variants can be shown to have evolved. Because all living people are genetically related to each other, the deepest node in a phylogenetic tree corresponds to a basic biological reality: All the variation we observe today evolved from a common ancestor.

CRITICAL THINKING QUESTIONS

1. What do you think is the significance of early signals of modern behavior in the archaeological record of Africa? How would you define modern behavior?

2. What might be the importance of modern humans using symbolic behavior to interact with their environment? What advantages and disadvantages would this have for them?

3. Why do you think humans kept expanding into new territories? Do you think we will continue to, and where will those areas be?

KEY TERMS

replacement models
multiregional models
microliths

most recent common
    ancestor (MRCA)

SUGGESTED READINGS

Jablonski, N. G. (2007). *Skin*. University of California Press, San Francisco.

Klein, Richard G., and Edgar, Blake. (2002). *The Dawn of Human Culture*. Wiley, New York.

Wells, Spencer. (2003). *The Journey of Man: A Genetic Odyssey*. Princeton University Press, Princeton, NJ.

Wolpoff, M. H., and Caspari, R. 1998. *Race and Human Evolution*. Simon and Schuster, New York.

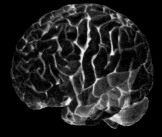

Left

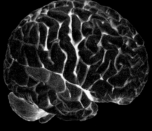

Right

On the morning of April 12, 1861, Professor Paul Broca walked through the surgical ward of the Bicêtre hospital in Paris. An eminent scientist and surgeon and later a member of the French Senate, Broca walked like a man who was used to people getting out of his way. He was there that morning to meet a patient, named Leborgne, who was gravely ill with a gangrenous infection of his entire right leg. Broca was not particularly concerned with Leborgne's infection. Rather, he was interested in Leborgne as a neurological patient with a long history of abnormal behavior.

At the time of Broca's meeting with Leborgne, scientists interested in the human brain were embroiled in a fundamental debate about the nature of brain function. Some argued that the functions of the brain were evenly distributed throughout the brain; they believed that there were no regions of the brain that were specialized for any particular behavior or function. Others, such as Broca, believed that at least some of the functions of the brain were based in, or localized to, certain specific areas. Unfortunately for the advocates of localization, the pseudoscience of phrenology held a similar viewpoint, although the phrenologists believed they could define localized, functional areas of the brain based on the external morphology—of the skull. That the phrenologists' claims were not based on empirical studies did not prevent phrenology from becoming a popular fad, famous throughout the world.

When Broca examined Leborgne, he found a 50-year-old man who was very weak and could no longer walk. His vision was poor, but his hearing was still good. He clearly understood what was being said to him, but he had only one response to any question asked of him: "Tan." As Broca talked to his caregivers (Leborgne had been under care for more than 20 years), his parents, and other patients on the ward, he learned that Leborgne had suffered from seizures as a child but had recovered from them. At age 30, however, Leborgne lost the ability to speak, at which time he was first admitted to the Bicêtre hospital. Starting 10 years after losing his speech, Leborgne had slowly developed a paralysis in his right arm and then his right leg, which eventually confined him to his bed.

Leborgne was not senile or insane, although the other patients generally considered him to be egotistical and rude. Because almost the only word he could say was *tan,* he became known as Tan to the rest of the hospital. The other word he could say was an expletive that he uttered when agitated or angry. Broca inadvertently elicited this expletive while repeating a test that Leborgne found tiresome.

Leborgne died only 5 days after meeting Broca, on the morning of April 17. Within 24 hours, Broca had performed an autopsy on the patient, and on that same day, obviously with some sense of urgency, he discussed Leborgne's case at a meeting of the Society of Anthropology, an organization he had founded in 1859, which was the first anthropological organization in the world. Broca described in careful detail the damage he had found on the outer (lateral) surface of the left hemisphere of Leborgne's brain, a region that he concluded must have a specialized function involving the articulation of speech.

Broca had identified a language area of the brain. Later neuroscientists called this part of the brain "Broca's area" in honor of his demonstration of the localization of function in the human brain.

ALTHOUGH THE HUMAN SPECIES possesses many features that help to make us unique, it is our complex behavior and extraordinary traditional and material cultures that set us apart from all other animals. Our behavior is ultimately the product of an anatomical feature: the human brain. Complex cultural behavior is made possible by a specific behavioral adaptation—**language**—which has evolved since the hominid lineage split from the great apes. The study of the evolution of the brain and language highlights the relationship between our behavior and our biology.

In this chapter, we will review the evolution of the human brain and language. The human brain is a structure of great complexity, and it produces behaviors that are of unparalleled sophistication in the animal world. At some point in hominid evolution, changes in the brain led to the appearance of a species that behaved more like us and less like our ape cousins. Compared with the brains of our closest relatives, the human brain is larger, and it exhibits important differences in its functional organization.

Some of these organizational differences in the human brain reflect the evolution of language. When we consider the fundamental importance of language to human social existence, it is not surprising that it is a behavior that is well represented in the organization of the brain. Language has also helped shape the anatomy of the throat, leading to the development of an organ of speech capable of producing an extraordinary range of sounds.

We will never know exactly when our hominid ancestors started to communicate with one another using a system of communication that was more like language and less like the forms of communication used by other primates. Language, and the soft tissues that produce it, do not fossilize. But with a greater understanding of brain function and of the natural history of language, anthropologists, linguists, psychologists, and other scientists in recent years have turned to the problem of language origins with increasing enthusiasm.

Issues in Hominid Brain Evolution

language   The unique system of communication used by members of the human species.

neurons   The basic cellular units of the nervous system. A neuron consists of a cell body and specialized processes called dendrites (which receive inputs from other neurons) and axons (outgrowths through which neurons send impulses to other neurons).

cerebral cortex   The layer of gray matter that covers the surface of the cerebral hemispheres, divided into functional regions that correspond to local patterns of neuronal organization.

cerebellum   The "little brain" tucked under the cerebrum, and important in the control of balance, posture, and voluntary movement.

cerebrum   The largest part of the human brain, which is split into left and right hemispheres. Seat of all "higher" brain functions.

paleoneurology   The study of the evolution of brain structure and function.

The anatomy of the brain is rather complex. At the microscopic level, the brain is composed of billions of specialized cells called **neurons** (nerve cells), which communicate with one another to form functional networks (see Appendix A). At the visible level, the **cerebral cortex**, the surface of the brain composed of neuron cell bodies, is divided into a complex pattern of grooves and ridges called *sulci* (sing., *sulcus*) and *gyri* (sing., *sulcus*), some of which can be used as landmarks to divide the brain into functional regions. Two of the major parts of the brain are the **cerebellum** and the **cerebrum**. The cerebellum, or "little brain," sits tucked under the cerebrum, and is important in the control of balance, posture, and voluntary movements. It also plays an important role in "higher" cognitive functions that were once thought to be solely under the control of the cerebrum. The cerebrum itself, which is where most complex cognitive functions are located, is the part of the brain that most people recognize as being "the brain." In humans and other primates, the cerebrum forms most of the brain's volume, and it is generally thought that the expansion of the cerebrum in human evolution has occurred as a direct result of selection for more complex forms of behavior.

Recent technological advances have provided us with some extraordinary tools for examining the brain, but the study of the evolution of brain structure and function, or **paleoneurology**, remains for the most part dependent on the study of endocasts. *Endocasts* are impressions of the interior part of the cranium, from which we can make inferences about the size and structure of the brain (Tobias, 1971) (Figure 15.1). Scientists make endocasts from fossil skulls, or in rare cases endocasts form naturally during fossilization (see Chapter 11). Unfortunately, the brain is separated from the inside of the cranium by several protective tissue layers and cerebrospinal fluid, so endocasts are inevitably a poor reflection of the brain's anatomy. Nonetheless, they provide us with the only source of direct information we have about the brain structure of extinct species.

FIGURE 15.1 Endocasts from South African *australopithecines*.

Most of the important questions concerning hominid brain evolution address ways in which the human brain is different from the brains of other primates and mammals. But there are many ways in which our brains are similar to those of other mammals. We use the same neurochemicals, share a basic microscopic and macroscopic architecture, and have some basic sulci and gyri around which functional regions are organized.

BRAIN SIZE AND ENCEPHALIZATION

One of the defining features of the genus *Homo,* and especially of our own species, is large brain size. But what do we mean by "large"? In absolute terms, the human brain weighs in at about 1,300 g, and human cranial capacities usually are reported to be in the region of 1,300 to 1,400 cc. These are average figures, and there is much variation in brain size. However, for purposes of cross-species comparisons, the 1,350-cc estimate for the volume of the typical human brain is good enough.

Look at the cranial capacities of various primates listed in Table 15.1 on page 440. As you can see, humans have the largest brains among primates. The second largest brains belong to the gorillas. Among the Old World monkeys, baboons appear to have relatively large brains. As discussed in Chapter 6, among the New World monkeys, spider monkeys have substantially larger brains than their close relatives, howler monkeys. To put these data in a broader zoological context, cattle have brains of about 486 cc and horses of about 609 cc—somewhat larger than that seen in a great ape (Figure 15.2 on page 441). The bottle-nosed dolphin has a brain volume of about 1,118 cc, which is nearly human-sized (Hofman, 1988).

Encephalization Quotients   Many scientists find absolute brain size values to be of limited usefulness in understanding brain evolution or the relationship between brain size and behavior. After all, it comes as no surprise that bigger animals have bigger brains than smaller animals, but just because a big animal has

The mouse lemur may possess the smallest primate brain—it weighs in at 1.8 grams.

TABLE 15.1	Cranial Capacities, Body Weights, and EQs of Several Primate Species		
Species	Cranial Capacity (cc)	Body Weight (kg)	EQ
APES			
Homo sapiens, male	1,424.5	71.9	4.32
Homo sapiens, female	1,285.2	57.2	4.64
Gorilla gorilla (gorilla), male	537.4	169.5	0.85
Gorilla gorilla (gorilla), female	441.4	71.5	1.34
Pan troglodytes (chimpanzee)	388.6	83.7	1.48
Pongo pygmaeus (orangutan), male	393.1	87.7	1.08
Pongo pygmaeus (orangutan), female	341.2	37.8	1.69
Hylobates lar (gibbon)	98.3	5.5	2.10
OLD WORLD MONKEYS			
Papio anubis (baboon), male	166.4	23.5	1.18
Papio anubis (baboon), female	141.4	11.9	1.69
Cercocebus albigena (gray-cheeked mangabey)	97.3	7.69	1.63
Colobus guerza (black and white colobus)	75.4	9.05	1.11
NEW WORLD MONKEYS			
Ateles geoffroyi (spider monkey)	126.4	6.00	2.55
Alouatta palliata (howler monkey)	62.8	6.55	1.18
Saimiri sciureus (squirrel monkey)	24.4	0.68	2.58

Note: Values from Kappelman (1996), using Martin's (1983) formula for EQ. New World monkey values calculated from Harvey et al. (1987). If male and female values are not shown, midpoint values between male and female averages are shown.

encephalization quotient (EQ) The ratio of the actual brain size of a species to its expected brain size based on a statistical regression of brain-to-body size based on a large number of species.

a big brain does not mean that the animal is more intelligent. For many years, scientists have tried to determine ways to measure brain size relative to body size. Researchers such as Harry Jerison (1991) and Robert Martin (1983) have shown that the relationship between brain size and body size is somewhat more complicated than a simple linear relationship. By looking at large numbers of mammal species, they derived equations that allow us to calculate the expected brain size for a mammal of any size. The **encephalization quotient (EQ)** is a ratio of the actual brain size to the expected size. Thus mammals that have EQs greater than 1.00 have brains that are larger than expected for a mammal of their size; an EQ less than 1.00 means that it is smaller than expected.

Returning to Table 15.1, we see that humans have the largest brains not only in absolute but also in relative terms, as measured by the EQ. In general, anthropoid primates have EQs greater than 1.00, indicating that their brains are larger than would be expected for mammals of their size. So even though cattle and horses have brains that are ape-sized in absolute terms, their EQs are

HORSE: weight, 400 kg; cranial capacity 600 cc
CHIMPANZEE: weight, 80 kg; cranial capacity, 400 cc

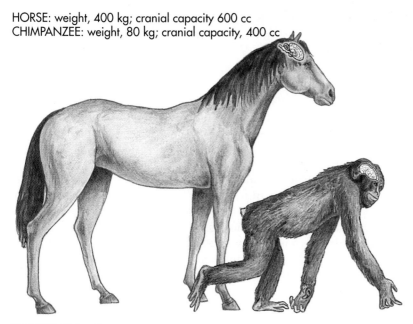

FIGURE 15.2   Chimpanzees and horses have brains that are similar in size.

FIGURE 15.3   Encephalization is a function of both brain size and body size.

smaller than those of apes because of their larger body sizes. It is generally assumed that the larger brain size in anthropoid primates has evolved in conjunction with the evolution of complex social behavior and adaptation to the arboreal environment.

Can we say that mammals with higher EQs are in some sense "smarter" than those with lower EQs? Yes and no. Terrence Deacon (1997) points out that the encephalization quotient is derived from both brain size *and* body size and that there is a tendency to overlook the fact that animals face strong selection pressures that shape body size as well as brain size. Among dog breeds, for example, chihuahuas are more encephalized than German shepherds; artificial selection on chihuahuas has driven body size down at a faster rate than brain size (Figure 15.3) But no one (except chihuahua fanciers) would argue that a chihuahua is smarter than a German shepherd. In anthropoids, small or even dwarfed species, such as the squirrel monkey in the New World or the talapoin monkey in the Old World, have high EQs. Again, rather than interpreting this as a sign of large brain size, we could also see it as an example of selection for small body size, which is probably more correct.

Colobine monkeys tend to have lower EQs than cercopithecine monkeys (see the mangabey versus the colobus in Table 15.1). There is no evidence that colobine behavior is in some sense less sophisticated than cercopithecine behavior (Figure 15.4). As discussed in Chapter 6 colobine monkeys are adapted to a leafy diet; this digestive requirement has driven selection for greater gut and body size, resulting in lower EQs. Colobines are still more encephalized than a typical mammal. Gorillas, who have large brains in absolute size, also have low EQs. Again, their low-quality, leafy diet (as well as other factors, such as protection from predation) may have driven selection for larger body size, leaving them with EQs lower than their closest relatives, the other apes. However, in a comparison of two closely related species sharing a particular environment, such as the spider and howler monkeys, it is reasonable to hypothesize that larger brain size in the spider monkey may have evolved as a result of the greater cognitive demands of a fruit-based diet. In summary, the EQ is a potentially valuable indicator of cognitive ability but we need to remember that it is a function of both brain and body size.

FIGURE 15.4   The proboscis monkey demonstrates that large gut size contributes to a lower EQ.

Sex Differences in Primate Brain Size   In almost all primate species, males have larger brains than do females. In the three highly sexually dimorphic species listed in Table 15.1 (orangutans, gorillas, and baboons), the absolute brain size differences are large, as are the body size differences. In each case, EQs for the females are substantially larger than for males. The EQ for male gorillas is below 1.0, indicating that their brains are smaller than we would expect for a mammal their size. There is strong selection for increased male body size in highly sexually dimorphic primate species, but there is no reason to suppose that there are profound differences in behavioral sophistication between the sexes.

Even in less sexually dimorphic primate species, such as rhesus macaques and humans, males have larger brains than females. This is true after we correct for body size (Holloway, 1980; Falk et al., 1999). Although we could speculate on the selection forces on behavior or other biological processes that might drive such a sex difference, one conclusion is that the sex difference in brain size observed in humans is not a function of recent evolution for higher cognitive function in hominids but seems to reflect a general primate trend (Falk et al., 1999).

BRAIN SIZE AND THE FOSSIL RECORD

In previous chapters, you read that increasing brain size is a characteristic of genus *Homo*. A compilation of average cranial capacities of different hominid fossil taxa is presented in Table 15.2. (Please note that the *H. sapiens* values in Tables 15.1 and 15.2 differ because they are based on different samples.) As you can see, the different groups can be sorted to some extent according to their cranial capacities and EQs. Of course, this comes as no surprise because cranial capacity is one of the morphological features we use to classify specimens into different taxonomic groups. Brain evolution in hominids can be divided into three phases (Holloway et al., 2004).

Phase 1: Early Hominids and Robust *Australopithecus*   Brain size increases from the early australopithecines (*A. afarensis* and *A. africanus*) to the "robust australopithecines," or *Paranthropus*. The early australopithecines have cranial

TABLE 15.2   Average Cranial Capacities for Fossil Hominids (adult specimens only)

Taxon	Number of Specimens	Average Cranial Capacity (cc)	Range (cc)	Estimated EQ
A. afarensis	2	450	400–500	1.87
A. africanus	7	445	405–500	2.16
A. robustus and A. boisei	7	507	475–530	2.50
H. habilis	7	631	509–775	2.73–3.38
H. erectus	22	1,003	650–1,251	3.27
Archaic H. sapiens	18	1,330	1,100–1,586	3.52
H. neanderthalensis	19	1,445	1,200–1,750	4.04
Modern H. sapiens (older than 8,000 years)	11	1,490	1,290–1,600	5.27

Sources: Aiello and Dean (1990), Kappelman (1996), and Holloway (1999).

Note: Estimated EQs are not derived using all the specimens included in the second column.

capacities in the range of 400 to 500 cc, whereas the later *A. robustus* and *A. boisei* are in the 475 to 530 cc range. The early australopithecines have cranial capacities similar in size to those seen in chimpanzees, orangutans, and female gorillas, whereas the cranial capacities of the paranthropines are more similar to those seen in male gorillas.

Are the robust australopithecines species more encephalized than the earlier australopithecines? Are graciles and robusts more encephalized than the contemporary great apes? Answers to these questions depend on estimates of body mass and brain size. As we have already seen, gorillas have large brains, but they also have large bodies, especially male gorillas, so they are not impressively encephalized. (They *are* impressively big.) Estimating body mass of fossilized individuals is very difficult and depends on how well sizes of available parts of the skeleton correlate to overall body size. EQs calculated for any individual fossil specimen therefore should be taken with a grain of salt. Henry McHenry (1992; see also Kappelman, 1996) estimates that *A. afarensis*, *A. africanus*, and *A. robustus* had male body sizes of 40 to 45 kg and female sizes of 30 to 32 kg; *A. boisei* was about 10% larger. These estimates indicate that these hominids were smaller than contemporary great apes; given that their cranial capacities were at least as large, we can conclude that gracile and robust australopithecines were indeed more encephalized than the great apes. In addition, the brain size increase seen in the robust forms relative to the earlier forms is also likely to reflect an increase in encephalization.

Phase 2: Early *Homo* and *Homo erectus*   Hominid fossils assigned to *Homo habilis* or early *Homo* have cranial capacities substantially larger on average (by 25–30%) than those seen in *Australopithecus* or the great apes (see Chapter 11). Although the smallest early *Homo* specimens (for example, KNM-ER 1813, which has a cranial capacity of 509 cc) and the largest gorillas may overlap in cranial size, the relatively small habiline body size, estimated by McHenry (1992) to be 52 kg for males and 32 kg for females, combined with the larger brain size, represents an increase in encephalization over earlier hominids. As you read earlier, the appearance of *H. habilis* roughly coincides with the appearance of stone tools in the archaeological record, providing evidence of at least one kind of cognitive evolution.

The average cranial capacity of fossils assigned to *H. erectus* shows an even more profound jump than *H. habilis* in both relative and absolute size compared with earlier hominid taxa. Although both brain and body size increased in *H. erectus*, brain size may have increased relatively more quickly leading to an increase in encephalization (Kappelman, 1996). As discussed in Chapter 12, *H. erectus* was widely distributed geographically and exhibited gradual change over its more than 1 million years in existence. On average, the earliest *H. erectus* specimens (such as KNM-ER 3883 and KNM-ER 3733) have smaller cranial capacities than do later specimens. Thus the range of cranial capacities seen in *H. erectus* specimens is quite large (from 650–1,250 cc), which is one reason that some investigators have justified splitting the taxon into two or more species. The recently discovered Dmanisi crania from Georgia, dating to 1.75 million years ago, have cranial capacities of between 600 and 780 cc; the smallest of these is a subadult (Vekua et al., 2002). Their cranial capacities are well within the range of *H. habilis* and *H. erectus*, but their cranial anatomy links them with *H. erectus*.

Phase 3: Archaic *Homo sapiens*, Neandertals, and Modern *Homo sapiens*
Cranial capacities in the modern range are found in both archaic *H. sapiens* and Neandertal specimens. Indeed, one of the apparent paradoxes of the later hominid fossil record is that Neandertal cranial capacities often exceed the average cranial capacity of modern humans (see Tables 15.1 and 15.2). Even the archaic *H. sapiens* mean is within the range of modern *H. sapiens*. The increase in average cranial capacity from *H. erectus* to the later *Homo* species is quite profound and undoubtedly

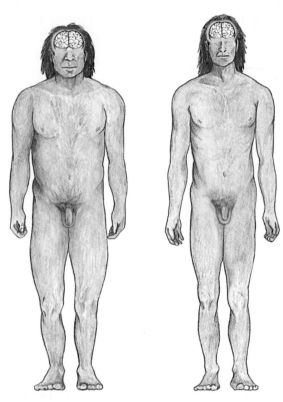

FIGURE 15.5 Although Neandertal brain sizes fall well within (or exceed) the modern human range, their EQ is lower than modern humans because they had larger bodies.

exceeds any increase in body size. Thus the hominid trend for increasing brain size and encephalization continues—and even accelerates—through the appearance of archaic *H. sapiens* and Neandertals.

What about the apparent decline in brain size in modern humans compared with Neandertals and even with earlier modern humans? We should keep in mind that there may be some kind of sampling bias (for example, toward larger males); after all, we have only small numbers of fossils available to compare with large numbers of modern humans. More critically, John Kappelman (1996) points out that the larger body size of archaic *H. sapiens* and Neandertals, relative to modern humans, often is overlooked or underemphasized (see Chapter 13). Thus modern humans are more encephalized than Neandertals because their bodies are much smaller but their brains are almost as large as Neandertal brains (Figure 15.5).

Brain size increase and increased encephalization have characterized hominid evolution over the past 3 to 4 million years (Figure 15.6). These trends have become more marked over the past 2 million years, as absolute brain size has nearly tripled. During the past 2 million years, increases in brain size have outpaced increases in body size, thus leading to increasingly encephalized hominids. Although brain size and encephalization are not everything, expanding brain size in the hominid lineage clearly reflects an adaptation, given how "expensive" brain tissue is (see Insights and Advances: The Ten-Percent Myth: Evolution and Energy).

BRAIN REORGANIZATION

As the brain has expanded, its functional organization has also changed. We know this by comparing our brains with those of our closest relatives, such as the chimpanzee, or of the rhesus macaque, an animal often used as the primate standard

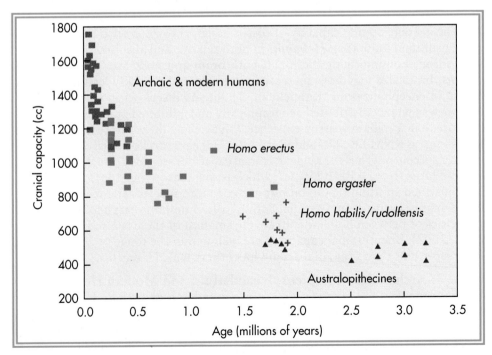

FIGURE 15.6 Cranial capacity has increased approximately fourfold over the last 3.5 million years of hominid evolution.

INSIGHTS AND ADVANCES

The Ten-Percent Myth: Evolution and Energy

We have all heard the myth that we humans use only 10% of our brains. Indeed, it is apparent that not only have many people heard it but they believe it. Psychologist Barry Beyerstein (1999) has spent many years researching the origins of this mistaken idea. Although he cannot pinpoint its origins with precision, he has shown that it has been around for quite some time. One of the first groups that latched onto and spread the myth was the early self-improvement ("positive thinking") industry. For example, a 1929 advertisement states that "scientists and psychologists tell us that we use only about TEN PERCENT of our brain power" and that by enrolling in the course being advertised, a person might tap some of that brain that is not being used. The advertisement uses the 10% figure as though it were common knowledge. This indicates that the origins of the myth must date to significantly earlier than 1929. Although Beyerstein has tried to identify the "scientists and psychologists" who may have said something like this, he has so far failed to find any specific reference to it in the literature.

Even if the 10% figure came from a scientist working at the turn of the twentieth century, the state of the art of neuroscience was not particularly advanced at that time. Most people would agree that any sweeping scientific pronouncement, based on little empirical research, is eventually due for some reconsideration. Indeed, there is plenty of evidence from neurology and psychology that the 10% figure is wholly untenable. Research methods that directly measure the activity of the brain show that even at rest, a large proportion of the brain may be showing metabolic activity. In addition, although certain functions of the brain are localized to small areas of the brain, these regions are connected to other regions via networks of neurons that draw on multiple brain areas.

One of the most compelling arguments against the 10% myth comes from the perspective of energy and evolution. The brain uses a lot of energy. In humans, it accounts for about 2% of the body mass but uses about 16–20% of the total energy and oxygen consumed by the body. It is an "expensive tissue" (Aiello & Wheeler, 1995). The brain cannot store significant energy reserves, and is extremely vulnerable if the oxygen supply is cut off.

From an evolutionary standpoint, maintaining such an expensive organ only to use 10% of it does not make any sense. When you consider that there are other costs associated with large brain size (such as birth difficulties; see Chapter 16), if we used only 10% of the brain, there would have been substantial fitness benefits in reducing the brain to a more efficient and less costly size. This did not happen, of course, as brain expansion has characterized evolution in genus *Homo*.

Leslie Aiello and Peter Wheeler point out that the brain is not the only expensive tissue in the body. The heart, kidneys, liver, and gastrointestinal tract consume at least as much energy as the brain. Human bodies use energy at about the rate that would be expected for a mammal our size. Given that our brains are much larger than would be expected for a mammal our size, how do we maintain the expected energy consumption rate? Aiello and Wheeler argue that a tradeoff with one of the other expensive tissues has occurred. Specifically, at the same time as the brain has increased in size in human evolution, it appears that the stomach and intestines have decreased in size. These size reductions presumably have been accompanied by a reduction in energy use. The smaller gastrointestinal tract also indicates a reliance on higher-quality, easier-to-digest foods (such as meat).

The complex relationship between behavior, brain size, diet, and gut size is one of the most fascinating problems in the study of human evolution. Although it is tempting to see brain size and gut size as engaged in a neat tradeoff, the situation probably was a bit more complex than that. Nonetheless, Aiello and Wheeler make clear that we have to pay for what we have: a large, energy-hungry brain. And a brain that wastes 90% of its volume would never have evolved.

in experimental neurological research. For example, there are parts of the brain that are essential for normal language production. Because other primates do not have language, obviously some reorganization of the brain has accompanied the evolution of language ability. Although scientists debate the relative importance of reorganization and expansion in hominid brain evolution, it is quite reasonable to assume that both processes have been crucial.

Investigators have tried to trace the evolution of other aspects of brain organization via both comparative anatomy and the examination of fossil endocasts. Reorganization can occur in three ways: An anatomical region of the brain associated with a specific function can become larger or smaller compared with the rest of the brain or functional regions of the brain can shift or change position, independently of regional expansion or contraction. Alternately, new behaviors may lead to the evolution of new functional fields, which would supplant or enhance previously existing functional associations in those areas.

We will discuss examples illustrating the first two kinds of reorganization in this section but will save the third for the section on language later in this chapter. Several studies have shown that when we look at large numbers of mammal species, the anatomical organizations of their brains are remarkably uniform in terms of the relative size of one structure compared with another or with the whole brain (Jerison, 1991; Finlay & Darlington, 1995). This is true whether the brains are big or little. As with any statistical generalization, there are exceptions. What we want to know is, What exceptions are present in the human brain and when did they evolve?

Olfactory Bulbs   In the human brain, the **olfactory bulbs**, which control our sense of smell, are small, knoblike structures found on the bottom of the frontal lobes in each hemisphere (Figure 15.7). Compared with other mammals, anthropoids have olfactory bulbs that are small for their overall brain size (Jerison, 1991), measuring only about 0.1 cc in volume (Stephan et al., 1981). In contrast, wolves have olfactory bulbs that are about 6 cc in volume, a 60-fold advantage over the human-sized olfactory bulb. Humans have olfactory bulbs that are about the same size as those found in strepsirhine species whose brains are only 1–2% the size of human brains.

Humans reflect (in more extreme form) a basic trend in olfactory bulb reduction that we can see in all living anthropoids. We presume that this reduction occurred as other sensory domains (such as vision) and higher-level cognition became more important, reducing reliance on the sense of smell. Studies of endocasts of the Oligocene primate *Aegyptopithecus* may indicate that olfactory bulb reduction was already present in this early anthropoid (Radinsky, 1979).

Frontal Lobes   Olfactory bulbs are a good example of reorganization by size reduction in the human brain. At the other end of the spectrum, many brain investigators (such as Deacon, 1997, but see also Holloway, 1968) have argued that one of the largest regions of the brain, the frontal lobe, has expanded over the course of hominid evolution, relative to the rest of the brain (see Appendix A). Scientists believe that the **prefrontal region**—the parts of the frontal lobe that do not include the primary motor regions—has shown a marked relative expansion.

olfactory bulbs   Knoblike structures, located on the underside of the frontal lobes, that form the termination of olfactory nerves running from the nasal region to the brain.

prefrontal region   The association cortex of the frontal lobes, located forward of the primary motor region of the precentral gyrus and the supplemental motor areas.

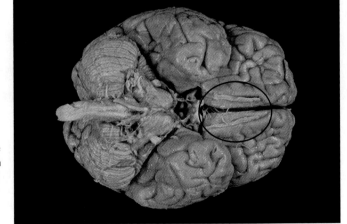

FIGURE 15.7 View of the bottom surface of the human brain. The olfactory bulbs are small structures located on the underside of the frontal lobes.

In other words, we may have a larger prefrontal region (and frontal lobe) than we would expect given the size of the human brain.

Why should we expect that humans have evolved a larger frontal lobe relative to overall brain size? The functions of the frontal lobe seem to coincide with many of the higher functions that we associate with intelligence, specifically with the kind of intelligence that we seem to have more of than any other animal, such as forming goals and devising plans to attain them. It is not unreasonable to predict that given our apparent reliance on these functions, our prefrontal region should be large.

However, recent MRI studies of human, ape, and monkey brains conducted by Katerina Semendeferi and her colleagues (2000, 2002) indicate that the frontal lobe is not proportionally larger in human brains (Figure 15.8). They found that the frontal lobe makes up about 36–37% of the hemisphere in humans, orangutans, chimpanzees, and gorillas. It is proportionally larger in humans and great apes than in gibbons (29%) and in a combined sample of rhesus macaque and cebus monkeys (31%). These results indicate that we and the great apes may share a small increase in relative frontal lobe size.

The high forehead of modern humans compared with the sloping foreheads of close relatives such as Neandertals and archaic *H. sapiens* might seem to be an obvious indication of frontal lobe expansion. As you recall in Chapter 13 Neandertals and archaic *H. sapiens* differ substantially from modern humans in the anatomy of the forehead and eye orbits: In general, their foreheads slope backward from large browridges. Looking at profiles of frontal bones in cross-section, Fred Bookstein and his colleagues (1999) found that despite differences in external morphology of the frontal region, the internal morphology was remarkably similar, indicating that the shape of the frontal lobe probably was also similar in these groups.

Primary Visual Regions   The *primary visual region* is the part of the brain where visual information from the eyes is initially processed. Although it is present in the occipital lobes (at the rear of the cerebrum) in both humans and other primates, in humans the primary visual region is located in a sulcus on the inner surface of the lobe, whereas in primates the primary visual cortex encompasses most

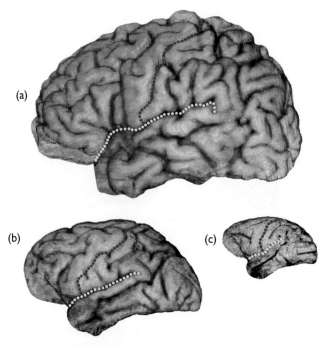

FIGURE 15.8   The frontal lobe (green) bounded by the Sylvian fissure (yellow line) and central sulcus (red line), in a (a) human, (b) chimpanzee, and (c) gibbon.

of the lobe's outer surface. Furthermore, the visual cortex is smaller than we would expect for a primate brain its size: It is only about 1.5 times larger than the visual cortex of a chimpanzee or gorilla, whereas the brain as a whole is about 3 times larger (Stephan et al., 1981). The reduction and shift of the visual region in primates presumably has allowed the expansion of the parietal cortex. The parietal cortex is a region where sensory information from different sources is processed and synthesized; it is also important in tool usage.

Controversy about reorganization of the visual region in hominid brain evolution has been not about whether but about when it occurred. The beginnings of the controversy go back to when Raymond Dart (1925) published his initial description of the Taung child (*A. africanus*) skull and endocast. In nonhuman primates, the primary visual region of the occipital lobe is reliably separated from the rest of the brain by the **lunate sulcus**, a well-defined sulcus that is almost always present. In contrast, in humans the lunate sulcus often is absent or very poorly developed and it does not mark the primary visual region, which is marked by the calcarine sulcus located on the interior surface of the occipital lobe (Figure 15.9).

When Dart analyzed the Taung endocast, he confidently marked the lunate sulcus in a posterior, "human-like" position. He interpreted this to mean that despite the apelike size of the Taung brain, it showed evidence of human-like brain reorganization. This conclusion was accepted for many years, but in the 1980s a vigorous debate about the location of the lunate sulcus in Taung and other australopithecines broke out between Ralph Holloway and Dean Falk, two of the most experienced paleoneurologists working in the field (Falk, 1980, 1983b, 1985a, 1985b, 1989, 1991; Holloway, 1981, 1984, 1988, 1991; Holloway & Kimbel, 1986). Falk argued that Dart's positioning of the lunate was incorrect and that it was in a more apelike position. Holloway, who initially accepted Dart's placement, argued that Falk's positioning of the lunate on the endocast was also anatomically untenable. Currently, the weight of evidence, including new discoveries and further reassessments of older specimens, indicates that the lunate sulcus was located more posteriorly in australopithecines compared to its location in the great apes, and thus the primary visual region was in a more human-like position (Holloway et al., 2004). This change in position marked the beginning of the extensive reorganization of the visual regions of the human brain, compared to great apes and other primates.

lunate sulcus A prominent sulcus on the lateral side of the hemisphere of most nonhuman primates, which divides the primary visual cortex of the occipital lobe from the rest of the cerebrum.

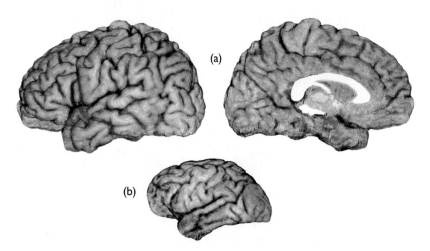

FIGURE 15.9 Primary visual processing areas (blue) in (a) a human (lateral and mesial views) and (b) a chimpanzee. In humans, the primary visual areas surround the calcarine sulcus. In chimpanzees, the lunate sulcus forms the anterior boundary.

Language: Biology and Evolution

Much of what makes human behavior more complex and more sophisticated than the behavior of other animals depends on our possession of spoken language. It is one thing to possess sophisticated cognitive abilities—to make plans; to draw complex cause-and-effect relationships between the things you see in the environment; and to think in terms of the past, present, and future—but without the ability to convey these thoughts to other members of the social group, their usefulness for enhancing survival and reproductive success would be limited.

Language is an adaptation. It is easy to imagine that a social group of hominids who possess language would have an advantage over a social group of hominids who did not. Language ability, however, is as much an anatomical as a behavioral adaptation. Modern humans are designed by natural selection—in the anatomy of their throats and respiratory system and in various aspects of the structure and function of their brains—to produce language.

What is language? Language is the system of communication used by members of the human species. Although linguists differ on which features are most critical in defining language, they all tend to agree on certain critical aspects that make language a unique form of animal communication. Language is *spoken*, and we are anatomically specialized to produce language and to process language-oriented sounds. Language is *semantic*: The words we use when speaking have meanings that represent real-world objects, events, or actions. Language is *phonemic*. Words are made from small sound elements called phonemes; there is no biological limit to the number of words that can be formed from phonemes and there is no intrinsic association between a word and the object or concept it represents. Finally, language is *grammatical*. All languages have a grammar, an implicit set of rules that governs the way word classes are defined and used. Although there may be a limit on the number of words a person can know, there is no limit on the ways the may be grammatically linked together. As a child acquires its first language, he or she assimilates the grammatical rules of language subconsciously.

THE EVOLUTION OF GRAMMAR

The place of grammar in defining language and studying its evolution has been a point of controversy over the years. One school of linguistic thought, led by Noam Chomsky (1967), placed grammar at the center of the linguistic universe. Chomsky and his followers (such as Jackendoff, 1994) argued that by studying the general grammatical rules of language, we can find a "deep structure," which in turn is a reflection of a "mental grammar" found in the brains of all people. Evidence of the existence of mental grammar comes from language acquisition in children. With little effort, children master the rules of grammar of any language to which they are exposed, despite their complexity. Linguist Steven Pinker (1994) has called this ability the *language instinct*: Children appear to be genetically specialized to learn language.

An interesting piece of evidence of the relationship between children and a possible deep structure of language comes from the study of *pidgins* and *creoles*. Pidgins are simplified, nongrammatical communication systems that have arisen in areas where speakers of different languages need to communicate with one another but do not spend enough time around each other to learn each other's languages (new colonial situations, fishers from different countries meeting on the seas). In contrast, creoles are grammatical languages that have arisen and developed, typically in colonial situations (such as in Hawaii or New Guinea), in the context of an ongoing situation of linguistic change or instability (Figure 15.10 on page 450). It has long been noticed that creole languages around the world converge on a similar grammatical structure. Linguist Derek Bickerton (1983, 1990) suggests

English-speakers recognize the phrase "Colorless green ideas sleep furiously" as grammatical, even though it is nonsensical.

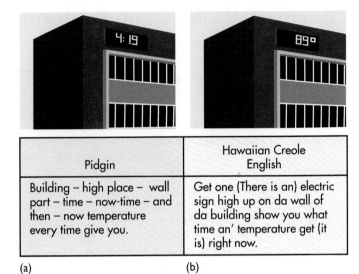

Pidgin	Hawaiian Creole English
Building – high place – wall part – time – now-time – and then – now temperature every time give you.	Get one (There is an) electric sign high up on da wall of da building show you what time an' temperature get (it is) right now.
(a)	(b)

FIGURE 15.10 A comparison of (a) pidgin and (b) Hawaiian creole.

that the source of this convergence is not a common language of origin but the fact that creoles are invented by children who share a common, biologically based, deep structure for language. The first generation of children growing up in these disrupted linguistic environments will not tolerate a nongrammatical system of communication, and they impose a linguistic structure on the language around them, thus leading to the development of creoles.

Many advocates of the deep grammar point of view believe that language represents a cognitive process that is fundamentally different from that underlying any other form of animal communication. However, several recent evolutionary theorists of language have argued against the existence of a universal mental grammar (Savage-Rumbaugh & Rumbaugh, 1993; Hurford, 1991; Schoenemann, 1999). Savage-Rumbaugh and Rumbaugh believe that syntax and grammar must develop once anyone tries to go beyond a two-word utterance; rules have to exist to let the listener know what the speaker is talking about. They write, "Whatever commonalities there are among grammars may well exist because only a limited number of solutions to the same problem are workable, given the constraints placed on the problem itself" (1993, p. 106–107). Thus grammars inevitably emerge, but there is no universal grammar. Such a position is consistent with the view that human language exhibits evolutionary continuity with other forms of animal communication, because it does not posit a zoologically unique cognitive mechanism, such as a deep mental grammar, for the evolution of language (Figure 15.11).

LANGUAGE IN THE BRAIN

We can define a *language area* of the brain as any part of the brain that is activated during the production or comprehension of speech. The classical language regions are found around the left Sylvian fissure, or *perisylvian language area* (Figure 15.12). In the frontal lobe, there is *Broca's area*. As we saw earlier, a lesion in Broca's area causes a disruption in speech production (an *aphasia*), yet comprehension remains intact. At the posterior end of the Sylvian fissure, spanning the top of the temporal lobe and the bottom of the parietal lobe, another language area was identified by German physician Carl Wernicke in 1874. *Wernicke's area* lesions cause a person to have difficulties in speech comprehension. People with Wernicke's area aphasia produce fluent but nonsensical speech, substituting one word for another or producing incomprehensible strings of words. Wernicke predicted that because it is likely that his area and Broca's area are in communication, different lesions in the white matter joining the two should produce aphasias with different symptoms. These *conduction aphasias* have been observed; for example,

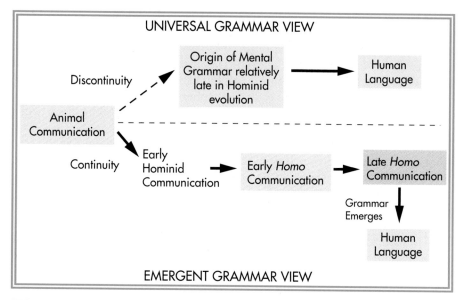

FIGURE 15.11   The universal grammar and emergent grammar viewpoints lead to very different scenarios of the evolution of language.

a lesion in the projection from Wernicke's area to Broca's area causes someone to produce fluent, nonsensical speech while retaining comprehension (Damasio & Damasio, 1989).

Wernicke's insights about conduction aphasias taught us to think about language as the product of interactive networks in the brain rather than of just one or two areas. In addition to Broca's and Wernicke's areas, the perisylvian language areas include several other regions important for speech. In the frontal lobe, Broca's area sits just in front of the motor strip controlling the tongue and mouth, which are obviously involved in speech production. Along the top of the temporal lobe lies the primary auditory cortex, where sound signals from the ear are initially processed, which is essential for speech perception. The angular gyrus in the parietal lobe is important for the comprehension of written language. This is not surprising because projections from the primary visual cortex in the occipital lobe pass through the angular gyrus on the way to Wernicke's area.

Language Lateralization   When a function of the brain typically and consistently occurs in only one of the hemispheres, we say that function is *lateralized*.

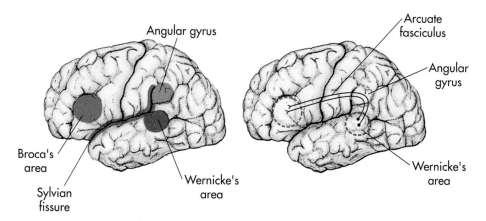

FIGURE 15.12   The major language areas of the left hemisphere of the brain. The connection between Wernicke's and Broca's areas passes through the angular gyrus.

In general, chimpanzees show no strong hand preference at the population level, although individuals may have a preference for certain tasks.

In 95% of people, the perisylvian language area is in the left hemisphere. Most people are also right-handed, and because motor control of one side of the body is housed in the opposite side of the brain, it is very likely that right-handedness and language ability evolved in tandem. The classical view that both language and right-handedness are associated with the left hemisphere has led to the notion of left hemisphere dominance over the right hemisphere (except in about half of the left-handers—who make up about 10% of the population—who have right hemisphere dominance).

Although it is easy to focus on the classical left perisylvian regions as the seat of language, keep in mind that lesions in other parts of the brain also disrupt normal speech. Lesions in the right hemisphere (of people with left hemisphere language dominance) disrupt the musical or *prosodic* elements of speech. Prosody is essential for speech to sound normal; otherwise, it would have the flat sound of computer-synthesized speech. Lesions in the right inferior frontal lobe (opposite Broca's area) lead to deficits in the production of normal prosody in speech, and lesions in the right hemisphere opposite Wernicke's area lead to deficits in the comprehension of prosody in speech (see Innovations: Music, the Brain, and Evolution on page 454). Neuroimaging studies have shown that the numerous parts of the brain dedicated to the control of the lips, tongue, larynx, and voluntary control of the diaphragm are active during speech production (Wise et al., 1999).

LANGUAGE IN THE THROAT

Although there is little evidence that evolving language capabilities has cost us anything in terms of brain function—just the opposite, in fact—it is quite clear that the rearrangement of the anatomy of our throats for language purposes has introduced new risks in everyday life that our ancestors did not have to worry about (Laitman, 1984; Lieberman, 1991). To offset these risks, there must have been a strong selective advantage for the development of language abilities over the course of hominid evolution.

The *supralaryngeal airway* is a more precise way to describe the parts of the throat and head that have undergone changes during hominid evolution (Figure 15.13). As the name suggests, it is that part of the airway that is above the *larynx*, or voice box. The larynx sits at the top of the *trachea* and has vocal folds (vocal cords), which can modulate the passage of air through the trachea to produce different sounds. The cavity above the larynx, at the back of the mouth, is known as the *pharynx*. The posterior part of the tongue, the epiglottis, and the soft palate form the boundaries of the pharynx.

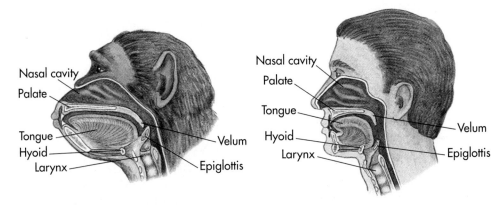

FIGURE 15.13 The supralaryngeal airway in a chimpanzee and a human. Note the relatively low position of the larynx in the human and how the back of the thickened and shortened tongue forms the front part of the pharynx.

When we compare the supralaryngeal airway of a human with that of a more typical mammal, such as a chimpanzee, we can see several differences that have profound functional implications (Figure 15.13). First, the larynx in humans is much lower than in other mammals. The new position of the larynx leads to an expansion of the pharynx. This expanded pharynx, whose anterior wall is formed uniquely in humans by a shortened and rounded tongue, is much more efficient for modifying the stream of air passing through the larynx to generate a greater variety of sounds, leading to fully articulate speech. In other mammals, the small pharynx has very little capacity for modifying the sounds produced by the larynx; supralaryngeal modification of sound can be done only by alteration of the shape of the oral cavity and lips (Laitman, 1984) (see Insights and Advances: Ape Language Studies on page 456).

These changes in anatomy have a profound cost, however: they greatly increase the risk of choking on food or liquid. There is too much distance between the human larynx and nasal cavity for a sealed connection to form between the two, as it does in the typical mammal. The epiglottis and soft palate are separated by the rear part of the tongue. Everything we swallow must pass over the incompletely sealed opening of the larynx, which greatly increases the risk of choking and suffocation. Interestingly, human babies less than 1 year old have a supralaryngeal anatomy that more closely resembles the mammalian norm. This allows them to drink, swallow, and breathe at the same time, which greatly enhances their suckling ability. During the second year, the larynx begins the shift to the adult position, which increases their risk of choking while increasing their ability to produce articulate speech. Darwin noted in *On the Origin of Species* that the position of the trachea in the human throat was an example of natural selection working with what history makes available to it.

LANGUAGE ABILITY AND THE FOSSIL RECORD

The brain and supralaryngeal tract—anatomical structures that demonstrate most clearly our adaptations associated with the production of spoken language—are composed primarily of soft tissues that do not fossilize. However, we do have endocasts, which might preserve information about gross changes in the brain that might be associated with the development of language. In addition the supralaryngeal tract is connected by muscles and ligaments to bony structures at the base of the cranium and in the neck. It is possible some insights into the evolution of the soft tissues of the throat may be gained by examining these bony structures.

Endocasts and the Evolution of Brain Asymmetries   Because language in the brain is associated with a leftward lateralization of function, it is possible that asymmetries in gross brain structure may be pronounced enough that they could be seen in endocasts. In most modern humans, the left occipital lobe protrudes further back than the right occipital, and the right frontal lobe protrudes more forward than the left. Other primates also show this pattern, but Holloway and de Lacoste-Lareymondie (1982) found that the left occipital and right frontal pattern is found most often in contemporary humans and in hominids, including australopithecines and the KNM-ER 1470 *H. habilis* specimen. Although this asymmetry may not be directly related to language or handedness, it does reflect an asymmetric pattern that may be unique to hominids.

Another region of the brain that might also show evidence of asymmetry in an endocast is Broca's area. The endocast of 1470 has a well-preserved left inferior frontal region (the location of Broca's area). Anthropologists interested in hominid endocasts tend to agree that 1470 resembles humans more than pongids in the anatomical complexity of the region corresponding to Broca's area (Holloway, 1976, 1999; Falk, 1983b; Tobias, 1987). A similar claim has been made for a recently discovered Indonesian *H. erectus* specimen, Sambungmacan 3 (Broadfield et al., 2001). Although this specimen has protrusions in the inferior frontal lobe on both

Music, the Brain, and Evolution

Music is a cross-cultural universal. If we survey the world's cultures, we will find that people engage in vocal behaviors that use standardized tones (notes) and rhythmic patterns; these elements form the basis of musical production. The notes and rhythms are not the same in all cultures, just as the phonemes employed in different languages are not all the same, but it is possible to recognize musical behavior as distinct from other kinds of behaviors (e.g., talking versus singing; walking versus dancing). In our culture, a sharp line can be drawn between musicians and nonmusicians, reflecting differences in formal or informal training or professional status. It is important to remember, however, that almost everyone can sing or dance at some level, even if there are great individual differences in competence (Peretz, 2006).

Over the past decade, neuroscientists with their growing arsenal of imaging tools have become increasingly interested in music and the brain. What evidence is there for the biological basis of music? First, there is the existence of people who have great difficulty producing or recognizing music, even with extensive training; this is a condition known as *amusia*, or tone

deafness, and it affects about 4 percent of the population. The congenital absence of this ability suggests that the more typical human brain has structures or networks dedicated to the recognition of tones. Imaging studies indicate that part of the right frontal lobe (the inferior frontal gyrus) is important for processing tone, and that people with amusia may have reduced neuronal connections in this area (Hyde et al., 2006).

At the other extreme, there are people who have *perfect pitch*, an ability to identify musical notes without a reference tone. Only a small proportion of all trained musicians have perfect pitch. Many famous musicians and composers had it (among them Mozart, Beethoven, and Jimi Hendrix), but many others did not. The existence of people with perfect pitch suggests an elaboration of the structures in the more typical brain

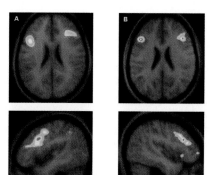

From: Nature Neuroscience 6: 692–697, Fig 2, Dr. Robert J. Zatorre (2003), "Absolute Pitch: A model for understanding the influence of genes and development on natural and cognitive function."

What about the evolution of musical ability? We have seen that there is individual variation in musical ability that is both biologically and genetically based. Such variability is the possible raw material for selection to have acted on, if musical ability was a kind of adaptation. Some researchers, such as the cognitive scientist Steven Pinker, see music as the evolutionary equivalent of cheesecake—we like it, but it simply takes advantage of senses and abilities that are in place for other reasons. For example, spoken language also employs rhythm and tone, so it is possible that musical ability arises from those abilities without being specifically selected for. In terms of selection, many researchers have pointed out that vocal calling, as seen in gibbons, is usually the result of sexual selection (Geissman, 2000). Could singing be a product of sexual selection? It's possible, but if so, it would be competing with sexual selection that is operating in several other potential domains (e.g., body size and shape, provisioning ability, even language ability itself). It has also been sug-

dedicated to musical ability. Anatomical studies suggest that there are differences between musicians, those with and those without perfect pitch, in the regions of the temporal lobe associated with processing sound (Schlaug et al., 1995). In addition, Robert Zatorre has used functional brain imaging to show that when identifying tones, people with perfect pitch use their working memory differently than those without it (Zatorre, 2003).

Both amusia and perfect pitch likely reflect the individual differences in musical ability with which people are born, however, neuroscientists are also interested in looking at the effects of formal musical training on brain structure. Producing music requires integrating mental and physical operations—such as memory, reading, and complicated hand and arm movements—into the production of sound that must be simultaneously self-monitored by listening (Gaser & Schlaug, 2003). One area of the brain that appears to reflect intensive musical training is the anterior part of the corpus callosum. This part of the *corpus callosum* includes the connections between the motor regions of the frontal lobes of the two hemispheres. Gottfried Schlaug (2001) has found that this region is bigger in musicians who began musical training

before the age of 7 years as compared to those who started training at a later age. He suggests that the development of the fibers of the corpus callosum reflects the plasticity of the brain during childhood, and that greater connections between these two regions may be a result of the coordinated bimanual action required in keyboard and string playing.

gested that the rhythmic qualities of music work to enhance group solidarity and it may have been selected for in that context.

There is still much to be learned about the biological basis and origins of music. People sing, dance, and chant for many reasons and in many contexts, ranging from the ridiculous to the sublime. Whatever the evolutionary history of music, it remains a quintessentially human activity.

INSIGHTS AND ADVANCES

Ape Language Studies

Few scientific developments in the twentieth century captured the public's imagination as much as the extraordinary spectacle of great apes communicating with their handlers and others via sign language (see Lieberman [1984] and Ristau [1999] for historical overviews). Although there had been several attempts to teach apes raised in close contact with humans to talk, these all failed miserably. Humans are adapted to produce the sounds of spoken language, and apes are not. In 1965, a husband-and-wife team of psychologists named Allen and Beatrix Gardner had the idea to train a 10-month-old chimpanzee named Washoe to communicate using American Sign Language, thereby by-passing the inherent vocal limitations of chimpanzees. Although Washoe was disadvantaged in starting her language training at an advanced age and her handlers were not expert ASL signers, she still managed to obtain a substantial number of signs (at least 132) in her initial 4 years of training, used them appropriately, and even coined novel two-word combinations, such as *water bird* for swan and *metal hot* for cigarette lighter. Washoe was also observed signing to herself and to other chimpanzees. In overall language skill, Washoe reached the level of a 2- or

3-year-old human child. Using ALS, she had no trouble making her wishes known to her handlers:"You go car gimme orange. Hurry" (quoted from Lieberman, 1984, p. 248).

Other investigators taught sign language to other apes, such as a gorilla and an orangutan. In some "ape language" studies, hand sign language was not used; rather, chimpanzees were taught to communicate via symbols they could point to or via a kind of keyboard. But even as some investigators were initiating and expanding research into the language skills of great apes, a backlash against such research started to grow. Many scientists were critical of the idea that the word *language* could be used in association with the communication skills displayed by Washoe and the other signing apes. Critics claimed that the signing apes were exhibiting nothing more than a "Clever Hans" phenomenon. Clever Hans was a horse who amazed people in Europe around the turn of the twentieth century with his counting and adding abilities until it was discovered that his numerical skills (which he expressed by stomping with one hoof) were actually unintentionally cued by his trainer. Although it was easy to refute the Clever Hans claims about signing apes (by using substitute handlers, setting up situations where cuing

would have been impossible, and so on), the critics made it difficult to obtain funding for ape language studies (Gibbons, 1991).

However, despite the critics, research on signing apes continued throughout the 1970s and 1980s. Roger Fouts and colleagues took over the Washoe project, which had grown to include several other signing chimpanzees, from the Gardners. Among these were Loulis, a young male whom Washoe adopted as a ten-month-old. Loulis was not exposed to signing by humans, and Fouts and his colleagues did a series of careful studies to chart the cultural transmission of sign language from Washoe to her adopted son. They observed Loulis making his first sign 7 days after Washoe adopted him; by age 15 months, Loulis was able to combine signs, and by 73 months of age, he had a vocabulary of 51 signs, all learned without human intervention (Fouts & Waters, 2001). Fouts also initiated a project of remotely video taping the activities of the signing chimpanzee group; this work showed definitively that they used signing during interactions among themselves in the absence of human cuing. Fouts and Waters (p. 790) describe one incident: ". . . chimpanzees often signed emphatically during high-arousal interaction such as fights and

the left and right hemispheres, the total size of the protrusion is larger in the left hemisphere, indicating the possible presence of a Broca's area in that hemisphere.

Base of the Cranium and Hyoid Bone   According to some investigators, the bony remains of fossil hominids yield real clues to the form and position of the supralaryngeal tract, offering insights into the vocal abilities of these earlier hominids. However, most of these claims are somewhat controversial and reflect the inherent difficulty of reconstructing soft tissues from fossil remains.

Jeffrey Laitman (1984; Laitman & Heimbuch, 1982; Laitman & Reidenberg, 1988) has argued that the degree of *flexion* of the *basicranium* is an anatomical marker of larynx position (Figure 15.14 on page 458). His studies show that among living mammals, human adults are unique in that they have a pronounced degree of basicranial flexion; the more flexed the base of the cranium, the lower

active play. For example, after separating Dar and Loulis during a fight and with all the chimpanzees still screaming, Washoe signed *come hug* to Loulis. He signed *no* and continued to move away from her."

In the 1980s Sue Savage-Rumbaugh and Duane Rumbaugh initiated a sign language research project with bonobos, using symbols (lexigrams) that could be pointed to in sequence to generate phrases. One of their subjects, a young male named Kanzi, similarly to Loulis, picked up the language by simply observing his mother as she was being taught by humans (Figure A). He has since

become the most proficient sign language ape yet studied, mastering hundreds of symbols and generating thousands of novel combinations of symbols, often referring to objects and situations not in his immediate vicinity (Savage-Rumbaugh & Rumbaugh, 1993). His ability to comprehend simple and complex sentences in spoken English, even though he had never been explicitly taught to do so, is also striking. At 5 years of age, his grasp of spoken English exceeded that of a 2-year-old child. For a fascinating account of Kanzi's life, training, and personality, see Savage-Rumbaugh, Shanker, and Taylor (1998).

No one would argue that Kanzi and the other signing apes have *human language,* but they do provide us with several insights into the evolution of human language. First, a certain level of linguistic competence is present as part of the general cognitive abilities of great apes and presumably of the common ancestor we shared with them. Second, the research with Kanzi indicates that comprehension exceeds production in the apes. This means that the "speaker–receiver" issue probably was not a problem in the evolution of language: The evolution of speech production skills would not have been limited by the ability of listeners to understand that speech. Third, the learning situation (exposure at a young age to a rich linguistic environment) is critical for language acquisition. We did not know about the language abilities of apes until they were placed in an environment where they could be expressed. Critics of the studies have argued, why would they have such capacity and never use it? But, all reasonably complex, behaviorally sophisticated animals have new skills they can develop given the proper environmental stimuli. Language abilities in hominids did not evolve from nothing, but reflect an enhancement and elaboration of abilities found in their pongid ancestors and cousins.

FIGURE A Kanzi talks using his keyboard language.

the larynx and the wider range of sounds that can be produced. Laitman and Reidenberg suggest that the degree of flexion seen in the base of *H. erectus* crania is greater than that seen in pongids and australopithecines and may signal the beginning of the lowering of the larynx to a more human-like position. These claims are controversial, and other investigators (Arensburg et al., 1990) believe that the basic premise of a correlation between variation in the cranial base and vocal abilities has yet to be proven.

Reconstructions of the Neandertal vocal tract have been equally controversial. Philip Lieberman (1984, 1991) claims that because of their long palate and other factors, the shape of the Neandertal tongue would be different from a modern human's, the pharynx would not be as large, and the larynx would be higher up in the throat. In fact, Lieberman argues that it would be impossible to put a human supralaryngeal

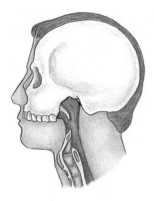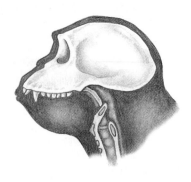

FIGURE 15.14   The base of the human cranium is more flexed than the base of the chimpanzee cranium.

tract into a Neandertal because the larynx would have to be placed in the chest cavity. Lieberman suggests that Neandertals would be missing phonetic elements present in human spoken language. Like claims about the basicranium and language ability, these assertions have also been the subject of much criticism (such as Falk, 1975).

A potentially more direct source of evidence about the speech abilities of Neandertals has come with the discovery of a Neandertal **hyoid bone** from Kebara Cave, Israel, dating to about 60,000 years ago (Arensburg et al., 1990). The hyoid is a small, free-floating bone (that is, it does not articulate with any other bones) that sits in the throat in front of the larynx and in close association (via muscles and ligaments) with the mandible, larynx, and other structures. Arensburg and colleagues argue that the Kebara hyoid is essentially human-like in its size and shape and very distinct from that of a chimpanzee, for example (Figure 15.15). The hyoids of chimpanzees and other apes have a boxlike body with two narrow, flaring horns, whereas the human hyoid has a much more regular horseshoe shape. Because the Kebara hyoid was found with a mandible and neck vertebrae, its location in the living individual could be suggested because these are the bony structures with which the hyoid makes soft tissue connections. According to Arensburg and colleagues, its position was human-like within a neck that was similar in length to human necks. Thus they conclude that the larynx was also in a human-like position and that Neandertals were fully capable of producing speech. In contrast to the Neandertal hyoid, the recently discovered *A afarensis* juvenile from Dikika, Ethiopia (dated to 3.3 MYA) possesses a hyoid bone that is much more similar to those of the great apes than to modern humans (Alemseged et al., 2006). If the hyoid is indeed a marker of speech ability, then this hyoid suggests that *A. afarensis* did not possess human-like speech. However, this is a hypothesis that still remains to be fully tested; at this point, it is reasonable to say that *A. afarensis* retained the primitive condition of the hyoid as seen in the great apes.

SCENARIOS OF LANGUAGE EVOLUTION

The absence of direct evidence concerning the evolution of language ability means that there are many theories or models for how it might have occurred

hyoid bone   A small "floating bone" in the front part of the throat, which is held in place by muscles and ligaments.

FIGURE 15.15   The hyoid bone from a Neandertal and a chimpanzee. The Neandertal hyoid is much more similar to those found in modern humans.

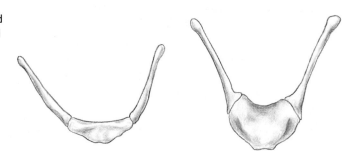

(Hewes, 1999). Most are untestable, although it is possible to assess the plausibility of some of the claims based on contemporary data. Since the 1980s, scenarios about the evolution of language have proliferated as new kinds of information have become available to researchers. We will discuss and assess three of these speculative models.

Throwing and Language Evolution   In the 1980s, neuroscientist William Calvin (1982, 1983) suggested that there was an intimate connection between the evolution of one-armed throwing ability, handedness, and language. Calvin pointed out that language and throwing are both lateralized activities (left hemisphere dominance). The throwing of projectiles is clearly important in hunting by humans, and it is reasonable to assume that expert throwing ability could have been an important adaptation in hominid evolution. Calvin argued that because the motor strip controlling the hands and arms is close to important centers for speech control, the evolution of language could have "piggybacked" on the evolution of throwing ability.

Calvin's hypothesis is fascinating, and it attempts to tie together several different kinds of information. Some problems with it include the fact that regions in the brain controlling throwing and speech are not really that close to each other, and there is no way to determine whether language piggybacked on throwing or vice versa. Nonetheless, the model is useful in that it highlights the potentially profound importance of the evolution of throwing ability, which is indeed a lateralized behavior just like language.

Language as a Replacement for Grooming   As you learned in Chapter 7, one of the main ways in which primate social groups maintain group cohesion is by social grooming (Figure 15.16). Primatologist Robin Dunbar (1993, 1997) points out that although humans may gain comfort from touch, they do not actually engage in very much social grooming. Looking at a wide range of primate species, Dunbar found that there was a positive statistical relationship between time spent grooming, brain size, and social group size. In other words, primates with larger brains lived in larger social groups, which required them to spend more time grooming in order to maintain social cohesiveness.

Humans are an exception to this pattern. Dunbar hypothesized that at some point in human evolution, with selection pressures to increase group size, hominids replaced social grooming with social language. Based on empirical studies, Dunbar argues that most of what people talk about is other people and their relationships (that is, gossip). Through such discussions, language maintains its primary role as a social reinforcer.

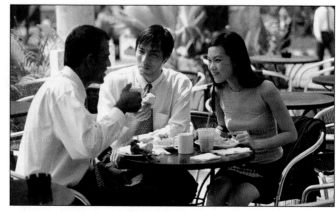

FIGURE 15.16   Language facilitates social interaction among humans. In apes, grooming one another is an essential part of social interaction, while gossiping may have a similar function in human communication.

Like Calvin's throwing model, Dunbar's model weaves the evolution of language into other aspects of hominid evolution. It is also has the basic chicken-and-egg problem: Did we evolve language in order to have larger group sizes, or did larger group sizes (and brain size) evolve because we evolved language? Furthermore, the grooming hypothesis does not say much about language per se but simply about one of the many ways language can be used (although gossip obviously is one of the more important ways). Dunbar's hypothesis brings home a fundamental point, however. At some point during our evolution, hominids stopped living in primate-like social groups of small size and started living in larger, ethnicity- or culture-based societies. Without language, such a transition would have been impossible.

Symbols and Sex   In his model of language origins, anthropologist Terrence Deacon (1997) emphasizes symbols as the key feature of human language. The ordering of words in even a simple sentence constitutes a manipulation and application of symbols that goes beyond that seen in any other animal. Language puts us in a world fully shaped by symbols. Early hominids would have had a verbal and nonverbal communication system similar to those seen in other primates. They would have adopted symbolic communication slowly, in the context of the preexisting communication system. As the use of symbols increased, however, the costs of learning and mastering them would also increase. But because humans have clearly evolved a symbolic system of communication, the benefits must have outweighed the costs.

Deacon suggests that symbolic communication may have first arisen in the context of the maintenance of exclusive sexual and provisioning relationships. His scenario posits that around 2 million years ago, at the onset of genus *Homo*, male hominids began provisioning sexual partners and their offspring in the context of an exclusive relationship. Deacon argues that these hominids were living in multimale, multifemale groups—as you would find with chimpanzees today—in which paternity would be difficult to establish. Because cooperative hunting increases the chances for success, there would be a conflict between selection for paternity certainty and for a social lifestyle.

Nonhunting gibbons solve this problem by being monogamous. Deacon suggests that hominids solved it by evolving symbolic language, which reinforced the pair bond between a male and a female within a social group, ensuring sexual exclusivity for the male and provisioning for the female. Symbols would also be useful in communicating to others in the social group that such an exclusive relationship exists (Figure 15.17).

A weakness of Deacon's model is its emphasis on pair bonds, which is a controversial issue in hominid evolution (see Chapter 10). However, it does not really require that pair bonds exist, only that exclusive and identifiable sexual and provisioning relationships are present within a larger social group. For example, establishing an exclusive relationship between one male and two females would also benefit from symbolic communication. Deacon's theory asserts that the reproductive advantages conferred by a component of language—symbolic communication—at a specific moment in hominid evolution may have initiated the journey down the path to full-blown human language.

Brain Size, Language, and Intelligence

If there is a fundamental issue in understanding the evolution of human behavior, it is interpreting the relationships of brain size, language, and intelligence. We have not been too concerned with defining what intelligence is. People interested in material culture, such as archaeologists, have tended to look for clues of intelligence in stone tool remains, attempting to define the level of technical intelligence our ancestors may have had (Wynn, 1999) while acknowledging that these tools may

FIGURE 15.17 Symbolic language may have helped reinforce exclusive sexual relationships within social groups in later hominid evolution.

represent only a biased sample of the total material culture repertoire of past hominids. But if language ability is closely tied to level of intelligence, tools give us little to go on. As Thomas Wynn (p. 284) has said, "Tools tell us little about language ... [They] are not windows to symbolic behavior." It is also quite clear that the level of sophistication we observe in stone tool production does not correlate very much or at all with changes in brain size over hominid evolution. This does not mean that no insights into human cognition are to be gained from the archaeological record but that stone tools must be considered in a broader investigatory context (Mithen, 1996).

In contrast to archaeologists, scientists more interested in the behavior of living animals and humans have emphasized the importance of social behavior in the lives of past hominids as the driving force behind the increase in intelligence (Byrne & Whiten, 1988a; see Dunbar's grooming model of language evolution described earlier). They argue that technical aspects of intelligence have been emphasized over the social aspects. That may be true, but a reasonable view is that both technical and social intelligences were critical in human evolution. Theorists of intelligence have emphasized the multifaceted nature of intelligence in the real world (Gardner, 1993; Sternberg, 1990), which goes beyond things such as IQ test scores. As we discussed earlier, increases in brain size tend to be distributed throughout the structure rather than localized to specific regions (with some exceptions, of course). Thus selection for one aspect of intelligence that is localized to one part of the brain will lead to size increases in other parts of the brain. This might in turn lead to the appearances of new capabilities that may themselves be selected for (see Calvin's model of throwing and language evolution described earlier).

Although we lack direct information about the evolution of brain functional organization, intelligence, and language, we are developing a clearer and more sophisticated understanding of what happened in human evolution over the past several million years. Increases in knowledge about brain structure and function, the nature of language as an evolving system, the communicatory behavior of humans and other animals, and the hominid fossil and archaeological record means that our speculations are both informed and constrained by a growing scientific database.

SUMMARY

1. **What is paleoneurology?**

   Paleoneurology is the study of the evolution of brain structure and function. It depends on a thorough understanding of the comparative neuroanatomy of living brains in conjunction with information that can be gathered from an examination of fossil endocasts.

2. **What does *encephalization* mean?**

   Encephalization refers to the size of the brain relative to body size. Because larger brain size correlates with larger body size, it is often useful to look at brain size in relation to body size to gain an impression of overall cognitive ability. We can derive an encephalization quotient by looking at many species and determining the typical brain–body size relationship. Species with larger than expected brains given their body sizes have encephalization quotients that are greater than 1.0. Although the term *encephalization* puts the emphasis on the brain size part of the equation, body size is an equal contributor.

3. **How does the cranial capacity of modern humans compare with that seen in Neandertals and some archaic *Homo sapiens*?**

   Cranial capacities in Neandertals tend on average to be larger than those seen in modern *Homo sapiens,* and some archaic specimens have cranial capacities that are well within the human range. The (estimated) lean body mass of Neandertals and archaic *Homo sapiens* probably was substantially greater than that for modern humans; thus encephalization is greater in modern humans than in these recently extinct hominids.

4. **Are primary olfactory and visual areas in modern humans smaller or larger than expected?**

   Compared with that of some other mammals and the prosimians, the olfactory region of the human brain is much smaller than we would expect relative to overall brain size. The primary visual region in the occipital lobe is also smaller than expected compared with that of other primates. Functional reorganization of the primary visual areas of the occipital lobe has occurred in the hominid lineage because its position in modern humans is substantially different from that in our closest ape relatives. When this occurred in hominid evolution is not known, although there has been much debate on the topic, centered on determining the position of the lunate sulcus in fossil endocasts.

5. **What are four hallmarks of human language?**

   First, language is spoken. An evolutionary tradeoff indicates the importance of language as a biological adaptation: Anatomical changes in the throat that allow humans to produce the large variety of sounds in spoken language make us uniquely susceptible to choking. Second, language is semantic. Words have meanings that correspond to real-world objects, events, or actions. Third, language is phonemic. The words used in language are composed of small sound elements known as phonemes. There are no semantic constraints on how these elements can be combined. Finally, language is grammatical. The ways in which words are combined in language are governed by implicit rules relating to word classes and proper word ordering in phrases or sentences. All native speakers of a language can easily detect violations of grammatical rules.

6. **What are two areas of the brain that are part of the network that underlies the production of spoken language?**

   Broca's area is in the frontal lobe; Wernicke's area spans the top of the temporal lobe and bottom of the parietal lobe at the end of the Sylvian fissure. In 95% of people these language areas are located in the left hemisphere. In people who are left hemisphere dominant for language, the right hemisphere region corresponding to Broca's area controls the prosodic (musical) aspects of speech.

7. **Why is the hyoid bone important in debates about the evolution of language?**

   The hyoid is a small bone that sits at the front of the throat. Reconstructions of the soft tissue of the throat—specifically of the supralaryngeal airway—are controversial because they were based on the anatomy of the base of the cranium, mandible, and other structures, without the hyoid, until the discovery of the Kebara Neandertal hyoid. This bone appears to be very human-like and indicates that Neandertals may have been capable of producing all the sounds that modern humans are capable of producing. In contrast, the recently discovered Dikika *afarensis* hyoid is quite apelike, suggesting an absence of human-like spoken language about 3.3 MYA. However, given the inherent uncertainties in soft tissue reconstruction, these claims have not gone unchallenged.

CRITICAL THINKING QUESTIONS

1. Which is more important: increases in brain size over hominid evolution or reorganization of brain function?

2. Chihuahuas are more encephalized than German shepherds. Does that mean that they are smarter than German shepherds? Why is this relevant to brain evolution in primates?

3. Provide your own assessments of the three theories of language evolution presented in this chapter. Do you think such speculative theories are useful for understanding how language may have evolved?

4. From an evolutionary perspective, what is intelligence? Defend or refute the statement "Human beings are smarter than chimpanzees."

KEY TERMS

language	cerebellum	encephalization quotient	prefrontal region
neurons	cerebrum	(EQ)	lunate sulcus
cerebral cortex	paleoneurology	olfactory bulbs	hyoid bone

SUGGESTED READING

Deacon, Terrence W. (1997). *The Symbolic Species*. Norton, New York.

Geary, D. C. (2005). *The Origin of Mind: Evolution of Brain, Cognition, and General Intelligence*. American Psychological Association, Washington, DC.

Lieberman, Philip. (1991). *Uniquely Human*. Harvard University Press, Cambridge, MA.

Pinker, Steven. (1994). *The Language Instinct*. Harper-Perennial, New York.

CHAPTER OUTLINE

Epidemiology: Basic Tools for Biomedical Anthropology

Biocultural and Evolutionary Approaches to Disease

Birth, Growth, and Aging

Infectious Disease and Biocultural Evolution

Diet and Disease

FICVS foliis palmatis
sativa fructu majori violaceo oblongo: cute

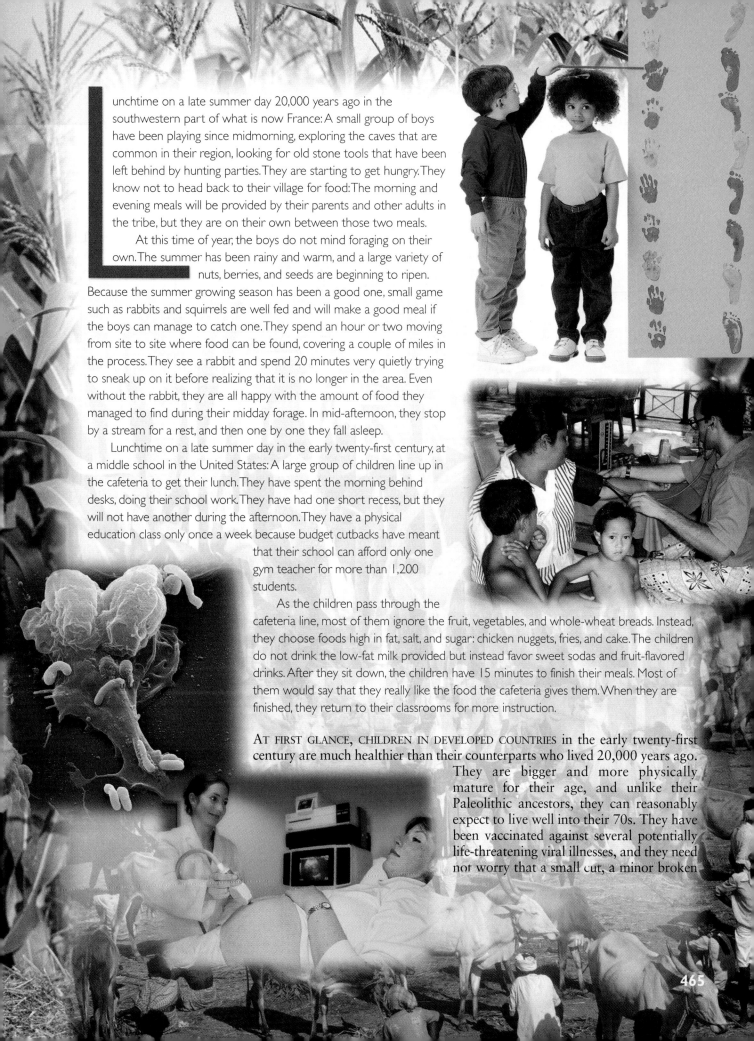

Lunchtime on a late summer day 20,000 years ago in the southwestern part of what is now France: A small group of boys have been playing since midmorning, exploring the caves that are common in their region, looking for old stone tools that have been left behind by hunting parties. They are starting to get hungry. They know not to head back to their village for food: The morning and evening meals will be provided by their parents and other adults in the tribe, but they are on their own between those two meals.

At this time of year, the boys do not mind foraging on their own. The summer has been rainy and warm, and a large variety of nuts, berries, and seeds are beginning to ripen. Because the summer growing season has been a good one, small game such as rabbits and squirrels are well fed and will make a good meal if the boys can manage to catch one. They spend an hour or two moving from site to site where food can be found, covering a couple of miles in the process. They see a rabbit and spend 20 minutes very quietly trying to sneak up on it before realizing that it is no longer in the area. Even without the rabbit, they are all happy with the amount of food they managed to find during their midday forage. In mid-afternoon, they stop by a stream for a rest, and then one by one they fall asleep.

Lunchtime on a late summer day in the early twenty-first century, at a middle school in the United States: A large group of children line up in the cafeteria to get their lunch. They have spent the morning behind desks, doing their school work. They have had one short recess, but they will not have another during the afternoon. They have a physical education class only once a week because budget cutbacks have meant that their school can afford only one gym teacher for more than 1,200 students.

As the children pass through the cafeteria line, most of them ignore the fruit, vegetables, and whole-wheat breads. Instead, they choose foods high in fat, salt, and sugar: chicken nuggets, fries, and cake. The children do not drink the low-fat milk provided but instead favor sweet sodas and fruit-flavored drinks. After they sit down, the children have 15 minutes to finish their meals. Most of them would say that they really like the food the cafeteria gives them. When they are finished, they return to their classrooms for more instruction.

AT FIRST GLANCE, CHILDREN IN DEVELOPED COUNTRIES in the early twenty-first century are much healthier than their counterparts who lived 20,000 years ago. They are bigger and more physically mature for their age, and unlike their Paleolithic ancestors, they can reasonably expect to live well into their 70s. They have been vaccinated against several potentially life-threatening viral illnesses, and they need not worry that a small cut, a minor broken bone, or a toothache will turn into a fatal bacterial infection. They are blissfully free of parasites.

On the other hand, a child from 20,000 years ago might have grown up more slowly than a contemporary child, but upon reaching adulthood he would have had a strong, lean body, with much more muscle than fat. He would not have spent a lifetime consuming more calories than he expended. If he were lucky enough to avoid infectious disease, injury, and famine, in his middle and old age he would have been less likely to suffer from heart disease, high blood pressure, diabetes, and even some kinds of cancer than would an adult living today.

Health and illness are fundamental parts of the human experience. The individual experience of illness is produced by many factors. Illness is a product of our genes and culture, our environment and evolution, the economic and educational systems we live under, and the things we eat. When we compare how people live now to how they lived 20,000 years ago, it is apparent that it is difficult to define a healthful environment. Is it the quantity of life (years lived) or the quality that matters most? Are we healthier living as our ancestors did, even though we cannot re-create those past environments, or should we rejoice in the abundance and comfort that a steady food supply and modern technology provide us?

Biomedical anthropology is the subfield of biological anthropology concerned with issues of health and illness. Biomedical anthropologists bring the traditional interests of biological anthropology—evolution, human variation, genetics—to the study of medically related phenomena. Like medicine, biomedical anthropology is a biological science, which relies on empiricism and hypothesis testing and, when possible, experimental research to further the understanding of human disease and illness. Biomedical anthropology is also like cultural medical anthropology in its comparative outlook and its attempt to understand illness in the context of specific cultural environments.

In this chapter, we will look at many aspects of human health from both biocultural and evolutionary perspectives. We will see how health relates to growth, development, and aging. We will then consider infectious disease and the problems associated with evolving biological solutions to infectious agents that can also evolve. Finally, we will examine the interaction between diet and disease and the enormous changes in diet our species has gone through since the advent of modern agriculture. But before going on to those topics, let us briefly consider some basic concepts from an allied discipline, epidemiology, which provides the quantitative foundations for population-level health research.

biomedical anthropology The subfield of biological anthropology concerned with issues of health and illness.

epidemiology The quantitative study of the occurrence and cause of disease in populations.

Epidemiology: Basic Tools for Biomedical Anthropology

FIGURE 16.1 Epidemiologists look for the causes of disease, such as toxic waste and industrial pollution, at the population level.

Biomedical anthropology is particularly concerned with understanding the expression of disease at the population level. Another health science with a population-level outlook is **epidemiology**. Epidemiology is the quantitative study of the occurrence and cause of disease in populations. Compared with anthropologists, epidemiologists are "number-crunchers," looking for broad-scale statistical associations between ill health and the factors that produce it in specific populations (Figure 16.1). In the same way that understanding the cell is essential for developing a proper understanding of anatomical structure, familiarity with some of the basic statistical tools of epidemiology is essential for the anthropologist's understanding of the distribution of disease in human populations.

RATES: MORTALITY, INCIDENCE, AND PREVALENCE

The most basic epidemiological statistic is the *rate* of disease per 1,000 individuals, or even per 1 million individuals for rare conditions. We define rate as

Rate = Events/Population at risk

The *event* is the disease or condition you are interested in. It is important to specify the population at risk. For instance, we should calculate the ovarian cancer rate for adult women, not for the population as a whole.

Mortality rates are measures of the probability of dying within a population over a given period of time. The *crude death rate* is defined as

Crude death rate = (All deaths during a calendar year/Population at midyear) × 1,000
= Deaths per 1,000

We have to be wary in interpreting crude death rates. For example, in 1997 the death rate in Pennsylvania was 10.6/1,000, whereas in Utah it was only 5.6/1,000. Does this mean that we would all be better off living in Utah rather than Pennsylvania? Not necessarily. The birth rate in Utah for that year was 21.2/1,000, whereas in Pennsylvania it was only 11.8/1,000. What is this telling us? Age is an important variable in determining a person's chance of dying in a given period of time. We can infer from these data that Utah has a much younger population than Pennsylvania. The different *age structures* of the two states undoubtedly explain much of the difference in crude death rate between them.

Two of the most important epidemiological statistics are **incidence rate** and **prevalence rate**. They are defined as follows:

Incidence rate = (Number of new cases of a disease/Total population)/Period of time (usually a year)

Prevalence rate = Total number of cases of a disease at a given time/Total population

Incidence rate is the occurrence of new cases of a disease. The higher the incidence rate, the more new cases are developing over a period of time. A change in incidence rate indicates a change in the balance of ecological factors that influence the expression of a disease, which could result from some naturally occurring factor or the development of an effective intervention program. Incidence rates of diagnosed cases of AIDS peaked in the United States in the early 1990s, with more than 106,000 new cases in 1993 (starting from only a handful of cases in 1981), and then leveled off to a steady 40,000 new cases per year starting in 1997 (Stine, 2003). This decline in incidence rate undoubtedly was caused by changes in behavior brought about by AIDS education programs. If a vaccine for AIDS were developed, the incidence rate would plummet.

The prevalence rate is a function of both incidence and *duration*. Changes in the prevalence rate of a disease do not necessarily tell us anything about the incidence rate. For example, with the introduction of new drugs to treat AIDS, people who develop the condition are now surviving longer than ever. Fifty percent of the people in the United States who were diagnosed with AIDS in 1995 were still alive in 2002 (Stine, 2003). Because the drugs only control the symptoms of AIDS and do not cure it, the prevalence rate may actually *increase* as a result of these new treatments with increased duration of illness, while the incidence rate remains the same. In contrast, a disease that kills quickly—or, looking on the bright side, is quickly cured—could have an incidence rate higher than its prevalence rate.

EPIDEMIOLOGICAL TRANSITIONS

In 1971, Abdel Omran coined the term *epidemiological transition* to describe changes in the patterns of disease and mortality in developed countries. In less developed societies, most deaths are caused by infectious diseases. In developed

In 2003, the incidence rate of lung cancer in men was 78.5/100,000 and in women 51.3/100,000. Ninety percent of people diagnosed with lung cancer smoked at some point in their lives.

incidence rate   The number of new occurrences of a disease over a given period of time divided by the population size.

prevalence rate   The number of existing cases of a disease divided by the population (or the population at risk).

countries that have passed through the epidemiological transition of the twentieth century, the most common causes of death are chronic diseases of old age. Infectious disease rates dropped dramatically in developed countries thanks to better nutrition and hygiene, a better understanding of how infectious agents cause illness, and widespread use of antibiotics and vaccinations.

Table 16.1 lists the top ten causes of death in the United States in 1900 and 2000. The death rate from accidents holds almost the same position in both lists, although the death rate from accidents in 2000 was about half the 1900 rate. The three big causes of death in 2000—heart disease, cancer, and stroke—are all primarily diseases of old age, accounting for 60% of all deaths. In 1900, they accounted for only 16% of deaths. In 1900, people were at risk from a variety of infectious diseases. In 2000, the infectious diseases that made the top ten list— pneumonia, influenza, and septicemia—were all diseases to which older, chronically ill people are particularly vulnerable.

The concept of an epidemiological transition, which is based on an evolutionary and comparative view of diseases in populations, fits in well with much biomedical anthropological research. Anthropologist George Armelagos (1997) and colleagues have argued that Omran's epidemiological transition is in fact the second epidemiological transition. The first occurred with the introduction of

TABLE 16.1	Top 10 Causes of Death in the United States, 1900 and 2000		
Rank	Cause of Death	Deaths Per 100,000	Percentage of All Deaths
		1900	
1	Pneumonia	202	12
2	Tuberculosis	194	11
3	Diarrhea and enteritis	140	8
4	Heart disease	137	8
5	Kidney disease	81	5
6	Accidents	76	4
7	Stroke	73	4
8	Diseases of early infancy	72	4
9	Cancer	64	4
10	Diphtheria	40	2
		2000	
1	Heart disease	258	30
2	Cancer	201	23
3	Stroke	61	7
4	Chronic respiratory disease	44	5
5	Accidents	36	4
6	Diabetes mellitus	25	3
7	Influenza and pneumonia	24	3
8	Alzheimer disease	18	2
9	Kidney disease	14	2
10	Septicemia	11	1

Sources: R. D. Grove and A. M. Hetzel, *Vital Statistics Rates of the United States, 1940–1960* (Washington, DC: U.S. GPO 1988); U.S. National Center for Health Statistics, *National Vital Statistics Report,* 50 (15): 2002.

FIGURE 16.2 Before the advent of vaccinations and antibiotics, infectious diseases such as cholera were the scourge of human populations.

agriculture, which in turn led to the development of large urban populations. These larger populations became the setting for the spread of infectious diseases, many of which still plagued large cities in 1900 (Figure 16.2).

Biocultural and Evolutionary Approaches to Disease

Epidemiology provides the quantitative foundation for biomedical anthropology's mission to understand the evolutionary and cultural factors underlying human disease. Although these factors are interrelated, within biomedical anthropology the biocultural and evolutionary approaches provide insights into the population-level expression of disease from somewhat different perspectives.

THE BIOCULTURAL APPROACH

The *biocultural approach* recognizes that when we are looking at something as complex as human illness, both biological and cultural variables offer important insights. The biocultural view recognizes that human behavior is shaped by both our evolutionary and our cultural histories and that, just as human biology does, our behavior influences the expression of disease at both the individual and population levels (Wiley, 1992, 2004).

An example of an illness that can be understood only in light of both biology and culture is *anorexia nervosa,* a kind of self-starvation in which a person fails to maintain a minimal normal body weight, is intensely afraid of gaining weight, and exhibits disturbances in the perception of his or her body shape or size (Figure 16.3) (American Psychiatric Association, 1994). The anorexic person fights weight gain by not eating, purging (vomiting) after eating, or exercising excessively. The prevalence rate for anorexia is about 0.5 to 1.0%; about 90% of sufferers are female. Anorexia is a serious illness with both long- and short-term increases in mortality. For example, at 6–12 years' follow-up after diagnosis, the mortality rate is 9.6 times the expected rate (Nielsen, 2001).

An ideal of female attractiveness emphasizing thinness often is thought to provide a cultural stress leading to the development of anorexia. Obviously, because not all girls living in this environment become anorexic, there are undoubtedly biological factors that also make some individuals more likely than others to have the illness. Anorexia is also found in non-Western cultures. However, anorexic patients in Hong Kong do not have the "fat phobia" we associate with Western anorexia but rather exhibit a generalized avoidance of eating (Katzman & Lee,

FIGURE 16.3 A teenaged girl with anorexia.

1997). This indicates that even though anorexia is not limited to Western cultures, the focus on fat is shaped by the Western cultural concerns with obesity, thinness, and weight loss.

Most young women maintain their body weight without starving themselves, habitually purging, or even dieting. In a 1-year longitudinal study of the eating and dieting habits of 231 American adolescent girls, medical anthropologist Mimi Nichter and colleagues (1995) showed that most of the subjects maintained their weight by watching what they eat and trying to follow a healthful lifestyle rather than taking more extreme measures. Anthropological studies such as this are important because clinicians are not as interested in what the healthy population is doing, and they help to provide a biocultural context for the expression of disease.

THE EVOLUTIONARY APPROACH

Biological anthropologists have long looked at disease from an evolutionary perspective. In the 1990s, Randolph Nesse and George C. Williams (1994) coined the term *evolutionary medicine* to describe a "Darwinian approach" to understanding disease. Nesse and Williams argued that the evolutionary perspective provides several insights into the expression of disease.

- *Defenses versus defects.* Every disease produces certain signs and symptoms. A *defect* results from the disease process itself, whereas a *defense* is a part of the body's attempt to fight the disease. For example, a fair-skinned person with pneumonia may have a cough and darkening skin color. The darkening skin color is a defect, caused by the fact that the person's hemoglobin is not carrying sufficient oxygen. The cough is a defense—an adaptation—that evolved as a mechanism to eject infectious material from the throat and lungs.

- *Infection and "arms races."* The environment is filled with infectious agents or **pathogens**, such as bacteria and viruses. As our bodies evolve defenses to fight them, they too are evolving to combat our defenses. A familiar example is the evolution of *antibiotic resistance* in bacteria. Antibiotics were first introduced in the 1930s. By 1944, some strains of staphylococcal bacteria were showing signs of resistance to penicillin, and today 95% are penicillin resistant. As a result we have to use other antibiotics to fight them.

- *Environmental mismatch.* Human bodies did not evolve to deal with most aspects of modern life, including fatty diets, low reproductive rates, and noise. Thus certain diseases may be considered to be the result, in whole or part, of the mismatch between our bodies, adapted for life in a hunter–gatherer environment, and contemporary environments. We will discuss examples of these diseases later in the chapter.

- *Pleiotropic gene effects.* We have many genes or alleles that probably did not lead to adaptations in past environments but were simply harmless. However, in modern environments these genes may be expressed in new ways. For example, because we now live longer, we have to deal with genes that cause diseases such as Alzheimer disease and cancer, which are typically expressed only in old age.

- *Design compromises.* A classic example of an evolutionary design compromise leading to human suffering is back pain. The S-shaped spine we evolved in order to walk upright clearly predisposes us to developing back pain (Figure 16.4). This shape, combined with a sedentary lifestyle, causes 50 to 80% of all people in industrialized society to suffer from lower back pain at some point in their lives (Anderson, 1999).

pathogens Organisms and entities that can cause disease.

Biomedical anthropology sits at the intersection of evolutionary and biocultural approaches to health and illness. A central concept of biomedical anthropology is adaptation. As we have discussed in previous chapters, an adaptation is a feature or behavior that serves over the long term to enhance fitness in an evolutionary sense. But we can also look at adaptation in the short term; this is known as *adaptability* (see Chapter 5). A basic question biomedical anthropologists try to answer is, To what extent is adaptability itself an adaptation? The life history stages that all people go through have been shaped by natural selection, but our biology must be flexible enough to cope with the different environmental challenges we will face over a lifetime.

Birth, Growth, and Aging

All animals go through the processes of birth, growth, and aging. Normal growth and development are not medical problems per se, but the process of growth is a sensitive overall indicator of health status (Tanner, 1990). Therefore, studies of growth and development in children provide useful insights into the nutritional or environmental health of populations.

HUMAN CHILDBIRTH

Nothing should be more natural than giving birth. After all, the survival of the species depends on it. However, in industrialized societies birth usually occurs in hospitals. Of the more than 4 million births in the United States in 2000, more than 90% occurred in hospitals; in 2001, 24.4% of all births were Cesarean deliveries (MacDorman et al., 2002). In 1900, only 5% of U.S. births occurred in a hospital (Wertz & Wertz, 1989). At that time, given the high risk of contracting an untreatable infection, hospitals were seen as potentially dangerous places to give birth.

Human females are not that much larger than chimpanzee females, yet they give birth to infants whose brains are nearly as large as the brain of an adult chimpanzee and whose heads are very large compared with the size of the mother's pelvis (Trevathan, 1999). The easiest evolutionary solution to this problem would be for women to have evolved larger pelves, but too large a pelvis would reduce bipedal efficiency. Wenda Trevathan points out that the shape as well as the size of the pelvis is a critical factor in the delivery of a child. Not only is there a tight fit between the size of the newborn's head and the mother's pelves, but the baby's head and body must rotate or twist as they pass through the birth canal, which is a process that introduces other dangers (such as the umbilical cord wrapping around the baby's neck). In contrast to humans, birth is easy in the great apes. Their pelves are substantially larger relative to neonatal brain size, and the shape of their quadrupedal pelves allows a more direct passage of the newborn through the birth canal (Figure 16.5 on page 472).

In traditional cultures, women usually give birth with assistance from a midwife (almost always a woman). Trevathan (1999) observes that although women vary across cultures in their reactions to the onset of labor, in almost all cases, the reaction is emotion-charged and results in the mother seeking assistance from others. She hypothesizes that this behavior is a biocultural adaptation. A human birth is much more likely to be successful if someone is present to assist the mother in delivery. Part of the assistance is in actually supporting the newborn through multiple contractions as it passes through the birth canal, but much recent research has shown that the emotional support of mothers provided by birth assistants is also of critical importance (Klaus & Kennell, 1997). Such emotional support often is lacking in contemporary hospital deliveries, although there has been some effort in recent years to remedy this situation (Figure 16.6 on page 472).

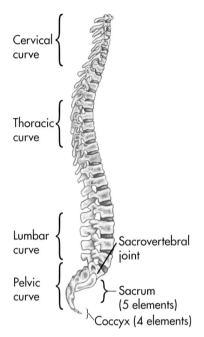

FIGURE 16.4 The S-curve in the human vertebral column—a result of the evolution of bipedality—makes humans highly susceptible to back injury and pain.

The term "medicalization" is used to describe the process whereby a condition, such as pregnancy, once not considered to be of clinical interest, becomes the target of medical treatment.

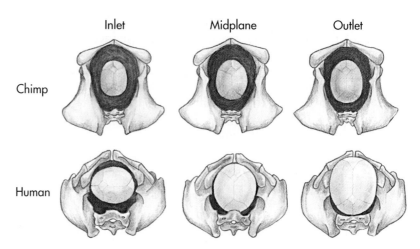

FIGURE 16.5   Compared to a chimpanzee, the human newborn has relatively little room to spare as it passes through the birth canal.

PATTERNS OF HUMAN GROWTH

The study of human growth and development is known as **auxology**. All animals go through stages of growth that are under some degree of genetic control. However, the processes of growth and development can be acutely sensitive to environmental conditions. Thus patterns of growth that emerge under different environmental conditions can provide us with clear examples of *biological plasticity* (Mascie-Taylor & Bogin, 1995) (see Chapter 5).

Looking at human growth, we can imagine an optimal environment in which an individual will reach his or her genetic potential. However, most environments are not optimal. We can view growth responses to nonoptimal environments in two different ways (Schell, 1995). The anthropological model views the way humans grow in high-stress environments (with a lack of food, heavy infectious disease load, and pollution) in the context of nongenetic adaptation, or adaptability. Growth patterns are responses to environmental conditions, which may actually enhance survival. On the other hand, the medical approach assumes that any

auxology   The science of human growth and development.

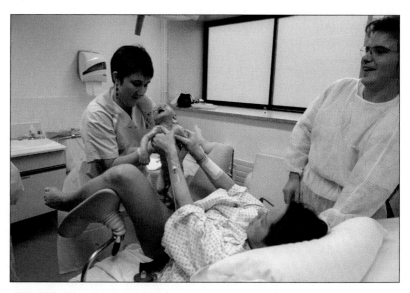

FIGURE 16.6   Women giving birth in traditional cultures usually receive help from other women, or midwives. Midwife-assisted births are also becoming increasingly common in hospital settings.

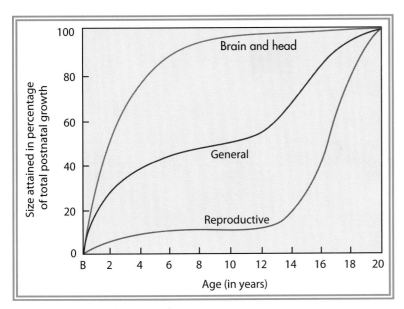

FIGURE 16.7 Different parts of the body mature at different rates. "General" refers to the body as a whole: the major organ systems (nonreproductive), musculature, and blood volume.

deviation from optimal growth patterns is evidence of ill health. The biomedical anthropological approach incorporates both these perspectives.

We chart growth and development using several different measures including height, weight, and head circumference. Cognitive skills, such as those governing the development of language, also appear in a typical sequence as the child matures. We can also assess age by looking at dentition or sexual reproductive capacity. Different parts of the body mature at different rates (Figure 16.7). For example, a nearly adult brain size is achieved very early, whereas physical, and reproductive maturation all come later in childhood and adolescence.

STAGES OF HUMAN GROWTH

In the 1960s, Adolph Schultz (1969) proposed a model of growth in primates that incorporated four stages shared by all primates (Figure 16.8 on page 474). In general, as life span increases across primate species, each stage of growth increases in length as well.

The Prenatal or Gestational Stage   The first stage of growth is the prenatal or gestational stage. This begins with conception and ends with the birth of the newborn. As indicated in Figure 16.8 on page 474, gestational length increases across primates with increasing life span but is not simply a function of larger body size. Gibbons have a 30-week gestation, compared with the approximately 25-week gestation of baboons, even though they are much smaller. Growth during the prenatal period is extraordinarily rapid. In humans, during the *embryonic stage* (first 8 weeks after conception), the fertilized ovum (0.005 mg) increases in size 275,000 times. During the remainder of the pregnancy (the *fetal period*), growth continues at a rate of about 90 times the initial weight (the weight at the end of the embryonic stage) per week, to reach a normal birth weight of about 3,200 g.

Although protected by the mother both physically and by her immune system, the developing embryo and fetus are highly susceptible to the effects of some substances in their environment. Substances that cause birth defects or abnormal development of the fetus are known as **teratogens**. The most common human teratogen is alcohol. *Fetal alcohol syndrome* (FAS) is a condition seen in children that results from "excessive" drinking of alcohol by the mother during pregnancy. At this point, it is not exactly clear what the threshold for excessive drinking is or

teratogens   Substances that cause birth defects or other abnormalities in the developing embryo or fetus during pregnancy.

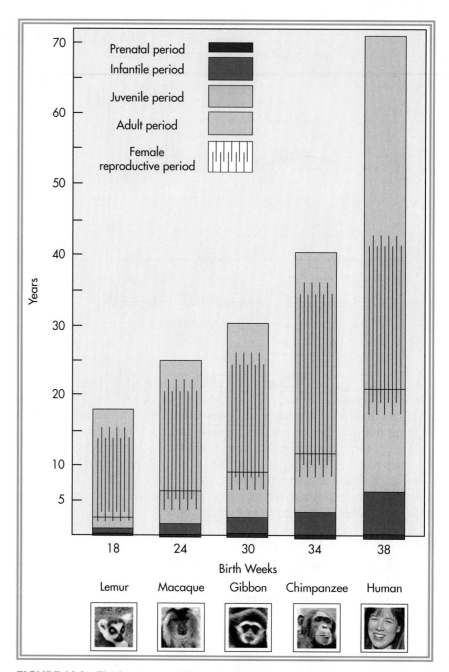

FIGURE 16.8 The four stages of life expressed in five different primates. Note that gestation length increases with increased life span, and the long postreproductive (female) life span observed in humans but not in other primates.

whether binge drinking or a prolonged low level of drinking is worse for the fetus (Thackray & Tifft, 2001). Nonetheless, it is clear that heavy maternal drinking can lead to the development of characteristic facial abnormalities and behavioral problems in children. It is estimated that between 0.5 and 5 in 1,000 children have some form of alcohol-related birth defect.

Although they are not teratogens, other substances in the environment may affect the developing fetus. Pollutants such as lead and polychlorinated biphenyls may cause low birth weight and other abnormalities. Excessive noise in the environment has been conclusively linked to reduced prenatal growth (Schell, 1991).

Infancy, Juvenile Stage, Adolescence, and Adulthood   Schultz defined the three stages of growth following birth—infancy, juvenile stage, and adulthood—with reference to the appearance of permanent teeth. Infancy lasts from birth until the appearance of the first permanent tooth. In humans, this tooth usually is the lower first molar, and it appears around 5 or 6 years of age. The juvenile stage begins at this point and lasts until the eruption of the last permanent tooth, the third premolar, which can occur anywhere between 15 and 25 years of age. Adulthood follows the appearance of the last permanent tooth.

Tooth eruption patterns provide useful landmarks for looking at stages of growth across different species of primates, but they do not tell the whole story. Besides length of stages, there is much variation in the patterns of growth and development in primate species. Barry Bogin (1999) suggests that the four-stage model of primate growth is too simple and does not reflect patterns of growth that may be unique to humans. In particular, he argues that in humans the juvenile stage does not take us all the way to adulthood. Instead we have an additional discrete stage, *adolescence*, when a growth spurt that reflects a species-specific adaptation occurs. The length of the juvenile stage, most of which occurs after brain size has reached adult proportions, varies widely among mammal species. There is a cost to a prolonged juvenile stage because it delays the onset of full sexual maturity and the ability to reproduce. But the juvenile stage is also necessary as a training period during which younger animals can learn their adult roles and the social behaviors necessary to survive and reproduce within their own species. The evolutionary costs of delaying maturation are offset by the benefits of social life. Among mammals, the juvenile stage is longest in highly social animals, such as wolves and primates.

Bogin places the end of the juvenile period, and the beginning of adolescence, at the onset of puberty. The word *puberty* literally refers to the appearance of pubic hair, but as a marker of growth it refers more comprehensively to the period during which there is rapid growth and maturation of the body (Tanner, 1990). The age at which puberty occurs is tremendously variable both within and between populations, and even within an individual, different parts of the body may mature at different rates and times. Puberty tends to occur earlier in girls than it does in boys. In industrialized societies, almost all children go through puberty between the ages of 10 and 14 years (Figure 16.9). During adolescence, maturation of the primary and secondary sexual characteristics continues. In addition, there is an *adolescent growth spurt*. According to Bogin (1993, 1999), the expanding database on primate maturation patterns indicates that the adolescent growth spurt—and therefore adolescence—is most pronounced in humans.

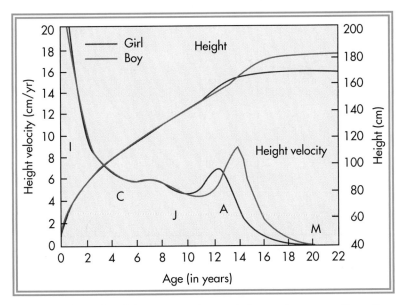

FIGURE 16.9 The adolescent growth spurt in humans is seen as a "bump" in the height curve and a "spike" in the height velocity curve.

Why do we need adolescence? Humans are the ultimate social animal. Bogin argues that the complex social and cultural life of humans, mediated by language, requires an adolescence, which is an extended period of social learning and development. In support of the view that adolescence is a period necessary for social learning, recent research on human brain growth has demonstrated that although approximate adult brain size is reached around 6 or 7 years of age, there is also an adolescent period of growth in the gray matter (neurons) of some parts of the brain, including the frontal and parietal lobes (Giedd et al., 1999; Sowell et al., 1999). These are both areas substantially devoted to higher brain functions (such as decision making). Thus, the uniquely human adolescent growth spurt includes the brain.

THE SECULAR TREND IN GROWTH

One of the most striking changes in patterns of growth identified by auxologists is the *secular trend in growth*. By using data collected as long ago as the eighteenth century, they demonstrated that in industrialized countries, children have been growing larger and maturing more rapidly with each passing decade, starting in the late nineteenth century in Europe and North America (Figure 16.10). The secular trend started in Japan after World War II, and it is just being initiated now in parts of the developing world. In Europe and North America, since 1900, children at 5 to 7 years of age averaged an increase in stature of 1 to 2 cm per decade (Tanner, 1990). In Japan between 1950 and 1970, the increase was 3 cm per decade in 7-year-olds and 5 cm per decade in 12-year-olds.

The secular trend in growth undoubtedly is a result of better nutrition (more calories and protein in the diet) and a reduction in the impact of diseases during infancy and childhood. We find evidence for this over the short term from *migration studies*, which have shown that changes in the environment (from a less healthful to a more healthful environment) can lead to the development of a secular trend in growth. Migration studies look at a cohort of the children of migrants born and raised in their new country and compare their growth with either their parents' growth (if the children have reached adulthood) or that of a cohort of children in the country from which they immigrated. Recent migration studies of Mayan refugees from Guatemala to the United States show evidence of a secular trend in growth (Bogin, 1995). Mayan children raised in California and Florida were on average 5.5 cm taller and 4.7 kg heavier than their counterparts in Guatemala.

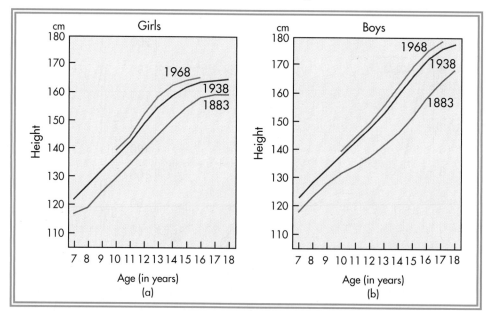

FIGURE 16.10   The secular trend in growth as measured in Swedish (a) girls and (b) boys between 1883 and 1968.

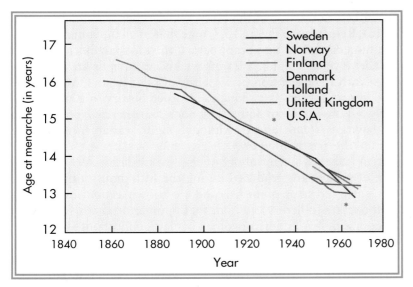

FIGURE 16.11   The declining age of menarche over the past 150 years has been measured in many European countries, and has also been observed more recently in developing countries.

The secular trend in growth in industrialized societies has been so pervasive that it tends to obscure variation within populations caused by socioeconomic factors (Tanner, 1990). However, we can measure the effect of the economy on child growth in some locales. Deborah Crooks (1999) looked at the growth of children in a rural, eastern Kentucky county at the edge of the Appalachian Mountains where 35% of the children live below the poverty level. Crooks found mild but persistent patterns of short stature among the children, with 21.7% of them having a stature below the fifteenth percentile of a broader U.S. sample. Among girls, "stunted growth" was about twice as common in this county as elsewhere in the United States (9.1% versus 5%).

Although the secular trend in growth appears to highlight a straightforward relationship between increased stature and industrialization, the stature each individual achieves is the result of the complex interaction of genetics, economic status, and nutrition.

MENARCHE AND MENOPAUSE

Another hallmark of the secular trend in growth is a decrease in the age of **menarche**—a girl's first menstrual period—seen throughout the industrialized world. From the 1850s until the 1970s, the average age of menarche in European and North American populations dropped from around 16 to 17 years to 12 to 13 years (Figure 16.11) (Tanner, 1990; Coleman & Coleman, 2002). A recent comprehensive study of U.S. girls (sample size of 17,077) found that the age of menarche was 12.9 years for White girls and 12.2 years for Black girls (Herman-Giddens et al., 1997). This does not reflect a substantial drop in age of menarche since the 1960s.

In cultures undergoing rapid modernization, changes in the age of menarche have been measured over short periods of time. Among the Bundi of highland Papua New Guinea, age of menarche dropped from 18.0 years in the mid-1960s to 15.8 years for urban Bundi girls in the mid-1980s (Worthman, 1999). Over the long term, the rate of decrease in age of menarche in most of the population was in the range 0.3 to 0.6 years per decade. For urban Bundi girls, the rate is 1.29 years per decade, which may be a measure of the rapid pace of modernization in their society.

Menarche marks the beginning of the reproductive life of women, whereas **menopause** marks its end. Menopause is the irreversible cessation of fertility that

menarche   The onset of a girl's first menstrual period.

menopause   The postreproductive period in the lives of women, after the cessation of ovulation and menses.

occurs in all women before the rest of the body shows other signs of advanced aging (Peccei, 2001a). Returning to Figure 16.8, note that of all the primate species illustrated, only in humans does a significant part of the life span extend beyond the female reproductive years. In fact, as far as we know, humans are unique in having menopause (with the exception of a species of pilot whale). Menopause has occurred in the human species for as long as recorded history (it is mentioned in the Bible), and there is no reason to doubt that it has characterized older human females since the dawn of *Homo sapiens*. Although highly variable, menopause usually occurs around the age of 50 years.

Menopause occurs when women run out of eggs for ovulation. All the eggs a human female will ever have are produced during the fifth month of gestation. These eggs are in an arrested stage of meiosis and are known as *oocytes*. At birth a girl has 2 million oocytes in her ovaries, but that number drops to 400,000 at puberty. Over the course of her lifetime, a woman ovulates only about 400 mature eggs. The rest of the eggs are lost through programmed cell death or *atresia*. If human females maintained the rate of atresia they have for most of their adult life, they would have enough oocytes to last until they were 70 years old. However, the rate of atresia increases starting at age 40, with menopause resulting by about the age of 50. There is no strong evidence that the secular trend in growth has influenced the age of menopause in any way (Peccei, 2001b).

At first glance, menopause looks to be a well-defined, programmed life history stage. Why does it occur? Jocelyn Peccei (1995) suggests a combination of factors, including adaptation, physiological tradeoff, and an artifact of the extended human life span. Some adaptive models focus on the potential fitness benefits of having older women around to help their daughters raise their children, termed the *grandmothering hypothesis* (Hill & Hurtado, 1991). Kristen Hawkes (2003) proposes that menopause is the most prominent aspect of a unique human pattern of longevity and that this pattern has been shaped largely by the inclusive fitness benefits derived by postmenopausal grandmothers who contribute to the care of their grandchildren. In support of this idea, a recent study of Finnish and Canadian historical records indicates that women who had long postreproductive lives had greater lifetime reproductive success (Lahdenpera et al., 2004). Peccei suggests that an alternative to the grandmothering hypothesis may be more plausible: the mothering hypothesis. She argues that the postreproductive life span of women allows them to devote greater resources to the (slowly maturing) children they already have and that this factor alone could account for the evolution of menopause.

AGING

Compared with almost all other animal species, humans live a long time, at least as measured by maximum life span potential (approximately 120 years). But the human body begins to age, or to undergo **senescence**, starting at a much younger age. Many bodily processes actually start to decline in function starting at age 20, although the decline becomes much steeper starting between the ages of 40 and 50 (Figure 16.12). The physical and mental changes associated with aging are numerous and well known, either directly or indirectly, to most of us (Schulz & Salthouse, 1999).

Why do we age? We can answer from both the physiological and the evolutionary standpoints (Figure 16.13). From a physiological perspective, several hypotheses or models of aging have been offered (Nesse & Williams, 1994; Schulz & Salthouse, 1999). Some have focused on DNA, with the idea that over the lifetime, the accumulated damage to DNA, in the form of mutations caused by radiation and other forces, leads to poor cell function and ultimately cell death. Higher levels of DNA repair enzymes are found in longer-lived species, so there may be some validity to this hypothesis, although in general the DNA molecule is quite stable. Support for the DNA damage theory of aging comes from a rare (1 in 10 million people) autosomal recessive disorder known as *Werner syndrome* (Kirkwood, 2002).

senescence Age-related decline in physiological or behavioral function in adult organisms.

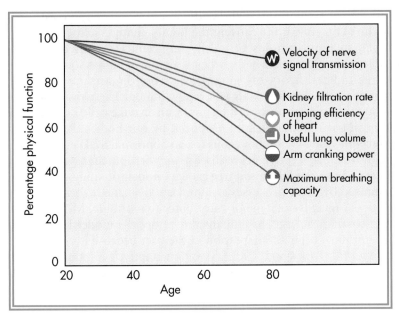

FIGURE 16.12   The effects of aging can be seen in the decline in function of many physiological systems.

When they are young, people with this condition suffer from a variety of ailments that are common in the elderly (such as cataracts and osteoporosis). Werner syndrome is caused by an abnormal form of the enzyme *helicase,* which unwinds DNA during replication, repair, and gene expression. This disease provides evidence that accumulating DNA errors can cause aging.

Another model of aging focuses on the damage that *free radicals* can do to the tissues of the body (Finkel & Holbrook, 2000). Free radicals are molecules that contain at least one unpaired electron. They can link to other molecules in tissues and thereby cause damage to those tissues. Oxygen free radicals, which

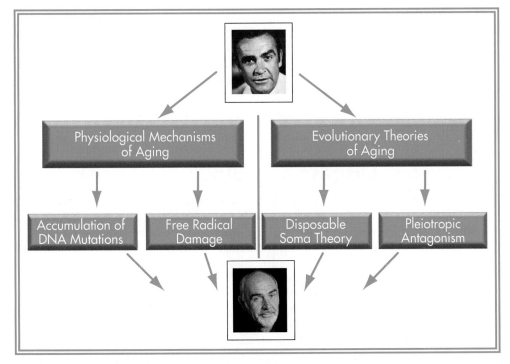

FIGURE 16.13   Physiological and evolutionary theories of aging.

result from the process of oxidation (as the body converts oxygen into energy), are thought to be the main culprit for causing the bodily changes associated with aging. Antioxidants, such as vitamins C and E, may reduce the effects of free radicals, although it is not clear yet whether they slow the aging process. Further evidence for the free radical theory of aging comes from diseases in which the production of the body's own antioxidants is severely limited. These diseases seem to mimic or accelerate the aging process. For example, an enzyme called *superoxide dismutase* (SOD) is an antioxidant usually produced by our bodies. People who do not make this enzyme (they are homozygous for an abnormal SOD gene) develop a familial form of the degenerative nerve disease *amyotrophic lateral sclerosis* (Lou Gehrig's disease). Both the DNA and free radical models of aging emphasize that the damage caused by these processes accumulates over the lifetime.

In wild populations, aging is not a major contributor to mortality: Most animals die of something other than old age, as humans did before the modern age. Thus aging per se could not have been an adaptation in the past because it occurred so rarely in the natural world (Kirkwood, 2002). Two nonadaptive evolutionary models of aging are the *disposable soma hypothesis* (Kirkwood & Austad, 2000) and the *pleiotropic gene hypothesis* (Williams, 1957; Nesse & Williams, 1994). Both take the position that old organisms are not as evolutionarily important as young organisms. The disposable soma theory posits that it is more efficient for an organism to devote resources to reproduction rather than to maintenance of a body. After all, even a body in perfect shape can still be killed by an accident, predator, or disease. Therefore, organisms are better off devoting resources to getting their genes into the next generation rather than fighting the physiological tide of aging.

The pleiotropic gene theory has a similar logic, although it comes at the problem from a different angle. *Pleiotropy* refers to the fact that most genes have multiple phenotypic effects (see Chapter 3). For all organisms, the effects of natural selection are more pronounced based on the phenotypic effects of the genes during the earliest rather than later phases of reproductive life. The simple reason for this is that a much higher proportion of organisms live long enough to reach the early reproductive phase than do the proportion who survive until the late reproductive phase. For example, imagine that a gene for calcium metabolism helps a younger animal heal more quickly from wounds and thus increase its fertility (Nesse & Williams, 1994). A pleiotropic effect of that same gene in an older animal might be the development of calcium deposits and heart disease; this "aged" effect has little influence on the lifetime fitness of the animal. Aging itself may be caused by the cumulative actions of pleiotropic genes that were selected for their phenotypic effects in younger bodies but have negative effects as the body ages. A key point of the pleiotropic model of aging is that you cannot select against senescence because the effects of natural selection are always more pronounced earlier rather than later in the life span.

Research on rats and monkeys shows that a restricted diet with 30% fewer calories slows the aging process and increases longevity.

Infectious Disease and Biocultural Evolution

Our bodies provide the living and reproductive environment for a wide variety of viruses, bacteria, single-celled eukaryotic parasites, and more biologically complex parasites, such as worms. As we evolve defenses to combat these disease-causing organisms, they in turn are evolving ways to get around our defenses. Understanding the nature of this arms race and the environments in which it is played out may be critical to developing more effective treatments in the future.

Infectious diseases are those in which a biological agent, or pathogen, parasitizes or infects a *host*. Human health is affected by a vast array of pathogens. These pathogens usually are classified taxonomically (such as bacteria or viruses), by their *mode of transmission* (such as sexually transmitted, airborne, or waterborne), or by the organ systems they affect (such as respiratory infections, encephalitis, or "food poisoning" for the digestive tract). Pathogens vary tremendously in their survival strategies. Some pathogens can survive only when they are in a host, whereas others can persist for long periods of time outside a host. Some pathogens live exclusively within a single host species, whereas others can infect multiple species or may even depend on different species at different points in their life cycle.

HUMAN BEHAVIOR AND THE SPREAD OF INFECTIOUS DISEASE

Human behavior is one of the critical factors in the spread of infectious disease. Actions we take every day influence our exposure to infectious agents and determine which of them may or may not be able to enter our bodies and cause an illness. Food preparation practices, sanitary habits, sex practices, whether one spends time in proximity to large numbers of adults or children—all these can influence a person's chances of contracting an infectious disease. Another critical factor that influences susceptibility to infectious disease is overall nutritional health and well-being. People weakened by food shortage, starvation, or another disease (such as cancer) are especially vulnerable to infectious illness (Figure 16.14). Of course, it works both ways. Some studies indicate that children in areas where the parasitic worm *Ascaris* is common show improved nutritional status after receiving medication to treat the infection, even without changes in diet (Mascie-Taylor, 1993; Brown & Gilman, 1986).

Just as individual habits play an important role in the spread of infectious disease, so can widespread cultural practices. Sharing a communion cup has been linked to the spread of bacterial infection, as has the sharing of a water source for ritual washing before prayer in poor Muslim countries (Mascie-Taylor, 1993). Cultural biases against homosexuality and the open discussion of sexuality gave shape to the entire AIDS epidemic, from its initial appearance in gay communities to delays by leaders in acknowledging the disease as a serious public health problem. A fascinating example of the influence of cultural practices on the spread of an infectious disease involves a condition known as *kuru* (see Insights and Advances: Kuru, Cannibalism, and Prion Diseases on page 483).

Agriculture   Agricultural populations are not necessarily more vulnerable to infectious disease than hunter–gatherer populations. However, by virtue of their larger population size, agricultural populations are likely to play host to all the diseases that affect hunter–gatherer populations and others that can be maintained only in larger populations. This is the basis of the first epidemiological transition discussed earlier. For example, when a child is exposed to measles, his or her immune system takes about 2 weeks to develop effective antibodies to fight the disease. This means that in order to be maintained in a population, the measles virus needs to find a new host every 2 weeks; in other words, there must be a pool of twenty-six new children available over the course of a year to host the measles virus. This is possible in a large agricultural population but almost impossible in a much smaller hunter–gatherer population (Figure 16.15 on page 482).

Another difference between agricultural and nonagricultural populations is that the former tend to be sedentary, whereas the latter tend to be nomadic. Large, sedentary agricultural populations therefore are more susceptible to diseases that are transmitted by contact with human waste products, which include a variety of bacterial diseases and parasitic worms. In addition, many diseases are carried by water, and agricultural populations are far more dependent on a limited number of water sources than nonagricultural populations. Finally, agricultural populations often have domestic animals and also play host to a variety of commensal animals, such as rats, all of which are potential carriers of diseases that may affect humans.

Specific agricultural practices may change the environment and encourage the spread of such infectious diseases as sickle cell and malaria. Slash-and-burn agriculture leads to more open forests and standing pools of stagnant water. Such pools

FIGURE 16.14 A child suffering from malaria, one of the most common and deadly infectious diseases.

(a)

(b)

FIGURE 16.15 Risks of infectious disease increase in (a) high-density agricultural populations compared to (b) low-density, dispersed hunter–gatherer populations.

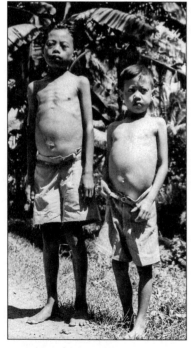

FIGURE 16.16 Two children with schistosomiasis.

are an ideal breeding ground for the mosquitoes that carry the protozoa that cause malaria. Agriculture that makes extensive use of irrigation and water damming brings people into contact with large flatworms of the genus *Schistoma*. These flatworms cause a disease known as *schistosomiasis,* which is often characterized by blood in the urine. *Schistoma* species have an extraordinary life cycle that involves several distinct stages lived both inside and outside its two hosts: humans and a particular snail species. Schistosomiasis can damage the bladder, kidney, liver, spleen, and intestines. The World Health Organization estimates that 200 million people may be infected with the parasite and that 200,000 die annually from its effects (Figure 16.16).

Mobility and Migration   The human species is characterized by its mobility. One price of this mobility has been the transmission of infectious agents from one population to another, leading to uncontrolled outbreaks of disease in the populations that have never been exposed to the newly introduced diseases.

The Black Death in Europe (1348–1350) is one example of just such an outbreak (Figure 16.17 on page 484). The "Black Death" was bubonic plague, a disease caused by the bacterium *Yersinia pestis.* The bacterium is transmitted by the rat flea, which lives on rats. When the fleas run out of rodent hosts, they move to other mammals, such as humans. The bacteria can quickly overwhelm the body, causing swollen lymph nodes (or *buboes,* hence the name) and in more severe cases lead to infection of the respiratory system and blood. It can kill very quickly. An outbreak of bubonic plague was recorded in China in the 1330s, and by the late 1340s it had reached Europe. In a single Italian city, Florence, a contemporary report placed the number dying between March and October 1348 at 96,000. By the end of the epidemic, one-third of Europeans (25–40 million) had been killed, and the economic and cultural life of Europe was forever changed.

Similar devastation awaited the native peoples of the New World after 1492 with the arrival of European explorers and colonists. Measles, smallpox, influenza, whooping cough, and sexually transmitted diseases exacted a huge toll on native populations throughout North and South America, the Island Pacific, and Australia. Some populations were completely wiped out, and others had such severe and rapid population depletion that their cultures were destroyed. In North America, for example, many communities of native peoples lost up to 90% of their population through the introduction of European diseases (Pritzker, 2000). Infectious diseases often reached native communities before the explorers or colonizers did, giving the impression that North America was an open and pristine land waiting to be filled.

INSIGHTS AND ADVANCES

Kuru, Cannibalism, and Prion Diseases

One of the most striking examples of a specific cultural practice contributing to the spread of an infectious disease is the case of *kuru,* a disease that once afflicted members of the Fore tribe in highland New Guinea (Gajdusek & Zigas, 1957; Goldfarb, 2002). Kuru is a progressive neuromuscular disorder that advances from tremors in the arms and legs to total paralysis over the course of a year (Figure A). Behavioral changes, such as dementia, accompany the physical changes.

The kuru epidemic among the Fore started in the early twentieth century, and by the mid-1940s there were more than 200 new cases a year appearing in a population of only about 12,000 individuals. Over the course of the epidemic, approximately 3,000 people were killed by kuru, all of them members of the Fore ethnic group or related in some way. About three-quarters of the victims were women, with children forming the next largest group afflicted.

Because kuru tended to appear in families, it was initially thought to be a genetic disease. Scientific investigation of kuru

FIGURE A   A victim of kuru.

started in the late 1950s, which was about the same time as the sickle cell trait and anemia balanced polymorphism was being worked out. Therefore, it is not surprising that some investigators suggested kuru was also being maintained as a balanced polymorphism of some kind. They were shown to be wrong, however, when Carleton Gajdusek and colleagues (1966) demonstrated that they could transmit kuru to chimpanzees by injecting them with tissue extracts from kuru victims.

We now know that kuru is a *prion disease,* one of a family of diseases that affect the tissues of the brain leading to both muscular degeneration and behavioral abnormalities (Sy et al., 2002). They are also called transmissible spongiform encephalopathy [TSE] diseases, and are almost always fatal. All humans and many other mammals make the prion protein, especially in brain tissue. The exact function of the protein is still unknown.

Prion diseases can be genetic: A mutation in the prion gene can lead to familial versions of TSE diseases (such as fatal familial insomnia), and spontaneous mutations in the prion gene are also a major cause. However, the striking thing about prion diseases is that they are also communicable. If a person with a normal prion protein is exposed to the abnormal, disease-causing prion protein, the abnormal prion protein can "seed" a transformation of the normal protein to the disease-causing form, leading to the development of a TSE disease. Unlike bacteria or viruses, the prion is a transmissible infectious agent that spreads without the use of a nucleic acid.

Kuru in the Fore people probably can be traced back to a mutation that arose in

the prion gene of a person living sometime at the end of the nineteenth century. But it did not spread through the population as a genetic disease would have. Instead, the transmission of kuru in the Fore was caused almost entirely by ritual cannibalism undertaken during funeral rites, usually by relatives of the deceased. Such rites were almost always directed by women, and cannibalism was considered to be in the women's domain. Young children accompanying their mothers and other relatives also consumed human flesh (the youngest kuru victim recorded was 4 years old). Although other groups living near the Fore also practiced ritual cannibalism, the disease was found only among the Fore or those who were related to the Fore in some way.

The Fore stopped practicing cannibalism in the 1950s, and kuru has largely disappeared. No person born after 1960 has had the disease. However, sporadic cases occur from time to time in older individuals. This is an indication of the long latency period that can occur in these prion diseases. TSE diseases are quite rare, and although protein-based infectivity is biologically fascinating, there was no reason to view prion diseases as a public health threat. This all changed in the 1990s, when it was shown that bovine spongiform encephalopathy (BSE), or "mad cow disease," can lead to the development of prion disease in humans who have consumed beef or other products derived from a cow with BSE. Kuru went from being an example of biomedical exotica of historical interest to a model for a disease with potentially major economic and public health ramifications (Lindenbaum, 2001).

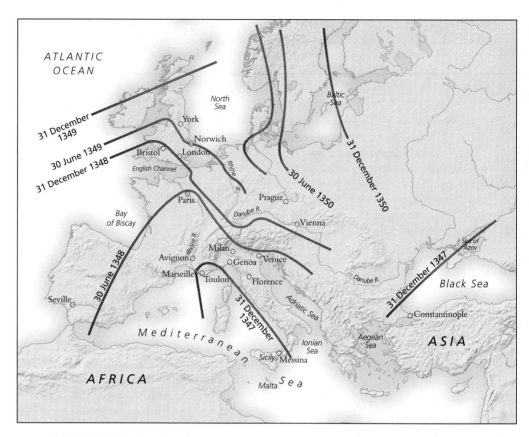

FIGURE 16.17 The Black Death spread over much of Europe in a three-year period in the middle of the fourteenth century.

INFECTIOUS DISEASE AND THE EVOLUTIONARY ARMS RACE

As a species, we fight infectious diseases in many ways. However, no matter what we do, parasites and pathogens continuously evolve to overcome our defenses. Over the last 50 years, it appeared that medical science was gaining the upper hand on infectious disease, at least in developed countries. However, despite real advances, infectious diseases such as the virus that causes AIDS and antibiotic-resistant bacteria remind us that this primeval struggle will continue.

The Immune System   One of the most extraordinary biological systems that has ever evolved is the vertebrate immune system, the main line of defense in the fight against infectious disease. At its heart is the ability to distinguish self from nonself. The immune system identifies foreign substances, or **antigens,** in the body and synthesizes **antibodies,** which comprise a class of proteins known as **immunoglobulins,** which are specifically designed to bind to and destroy specific antigens (Figure 16.18).

Antibodies are produced by white blood cells known as *B lymphocytes.* These originate in the bone marrow and circulate between lymph tissue and the bloodstream. Another class of lymphocytes, *T cells,* is also critical in the immune response. *Helper T cells* lead to the activation of B lymphocytes to produce antibodies and stimulate the production of specialized cells called *phagocytes,* which destroy infectious agents, such as viruses, by engulfing and destroying them. One of the most extraordinary qualities of the immune system is its ability to remember previous exposures to an antigen, thus priming the system in case later exposures to the antigen occur. This is the immunological basis of *vaccination* (discussed in more detail in the next section), whereby exposure to a killed or inactivated form

antigens   Whole or part of an invading organism that prompts a response (such as production of antibodies) from the body's immune system.

antibodies   Proteins (immunoglobulins) formed by the immune system that are specifically structured to bind to and neutralize invading antigens.

immunoglobulins   Proteins produced by B lymphocytes that function as antibodies.

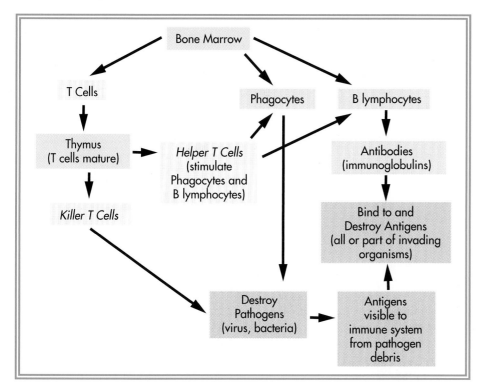

FIGURE 16.18 The immune system has several different components that work in concert.

of an antigen such as a virus protects an individual from developing an illness upon later exposure to the active form of the antigen. The memory function of the immune system is carried out by specialized T and B lymphocytes.

The immune system is a complex mechanism that has evolved to deal with the countless number of potential antigens in the environment. An example of what happens when just one of the components of the immune system is not functioning occurs in AIDS. The *human immunodeficiency virus* (HIV) that causes AIDS attacks the helper T cells. As mentioned earlier, the helper T cells respond to antigens by inducing the B lymphocytes to produce antibodies, leading to the production of phagocytes; when their function is compromised, the function of the entire immune system is also compromised. This leaves a person with HIV infection vulnerable to a host of opportunistic infections, a condition that characterizes the development of full-blown AIDS.

Cultural and Behavioral Interventions   Although the immune system does a remarkable job fighting infectious disease, it is obviously not always enough. Even before the basis of infectious diseases was understood, humans took steps to limit their transmission. Throughout the Old World, people with leprosy were shunned and forced to live apart from the bulk of the population. This isolation amounted to *quarantine,* in recognition of the contagious nature of their condition.

One of the most effective biocultural measures developed to fight infectious diseases is vaccination. The elimination of *smallpox* as a scourge of humanity is one of the great triumphs of widespread vaccination. Smallpox is a viral illness that originated in Africa some 12,000 years ago and subsequently spread throughout the Old World (Barquet & Domingo, 1997). It was a disfiguring illness, causing pustulant lesions on the skin, and it was often fatal. Smallpox killed millions of people upon its introduction to the New World; in the Old World, smallpox epidemics periodically decimated entire populations. In A.D. 180, a smallpox epidemic killed between 3.5 and 7 million people in the Roman Empire, precipitating the first period of its decline.

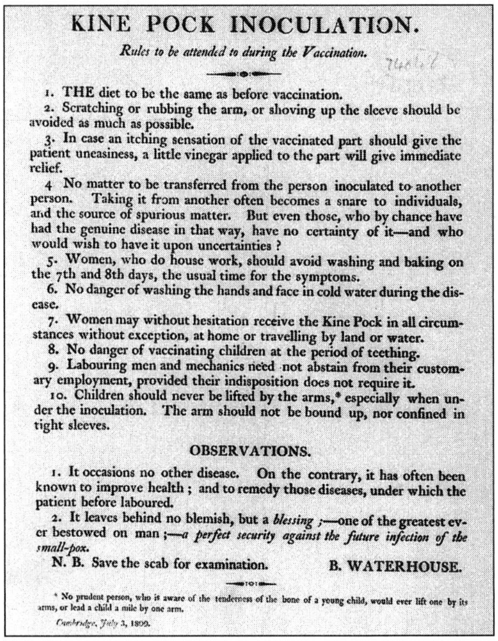
KINE POCK INOCULATION.

Rules to be attended to during the Vaccination.

1. THE diet to be the same as before vaccination.
2. Scratching or rubbing the arm, or shoving up the sleeve should be avoided as much as possible.
3. In case an itching sensation of the vaccinated part should give the patient uneasiness, a little vinegar applied to the part will give immediate relief.
4. No matter to be transferred from the person inoculated to another person. Taking it from another often becomes a snare to individuals, and the source of spurious matter. But even those, who by chance have had the genuine disease in that way, have no certainty of it—and who would wish to have it upon uncertainties?
5. Women, who do house work, should avoid washing and baking on the 7th and 8th days, the usual time for the symptoms.
6. No danger of washing the hands and face in cold water during the disease.
7. Women may without hesitation receive the Kine Pock in all circumstances without exception, at home or travelling by land or water.
8. No danger of vaccinating children at the period of teething.
9. Labouring men and mechanics need not abstain from their customary employment, provided their indisposition does not require it.
10. Children should never be lifted by the arms,* especially when under the inoculation. The arm should not be bound up, nor confined in tight sleeves.

OBSERVATIONS.

1. It occasions no other disease. On the contrary, it has often been known to improve health; and to remedy those diseases, under which the patient before laboured.
2. It leaves behind no blemish, but a *blessing*;—one of the greatest ever bestowed on man;—*a perfect security against the future infection of the small-pox.*

N. B. Save the scab for examination. B. WATERHOUSE.

* No prudent person, who is aware of the tenderness of the bone of a young child, would ever lift one by its arms, or lead a child a mile by one arm.

Cambridge, July 3, 1809.

FIGURE 16.19 Early instructions for administration of the smallpox vaccine. Note in the last lines that the vaccine was considered to be a "blessing."

Only two live stocks of smallpox virus are known to exist, one at the Centers for Disease Control and Prevention in the United States and the other at a virology institute in Russia.

Numerous remedies were used to combat the spread of smallpox. In some cultures, children were exposed to people with mild cases of smallpox in the hopes that it would strengthen their resistance to the disease. In China, powdered scabs of smallpox sores were blown into the nostrils of healthy people. Women in the harems of the Turkish Ottoman Empire were inoculated on parts of their body where the smallpox scars (which result in the area of the vaccination) could not be seen. The Turkish method was to make four or five small scratches on the skin and introduce some pus from an infected person into them. This method was introduced to England (and Western medicine) in the early eighteenth century, and early medical statisticians verified its success at preventing the development of serious forms of the illness (although 23% of the people vaccinated by this method died). We now have much safer forms of vaccination against smallpox, which have led to the total eradication of this horrible disease (Figure 16.19).

The most recently developed forms of intervention against infectious disease are drug based. The long-term success of these drugs will depend on the inability of the infectious agents to evolve resistance to their effects. Overuse of anti-infectious drugs may actually hasten the evolution of resistant forms by intensifying the selection pressures on pathogens.

Evolutionary Adaptations The immune system is the supreme evolutionary adaptation in the fight against infectious disease. However, specific adaptations to disease that do not involve the immune system are also quite common (Jackson, 2000). For example, a class of enzymes known as *lysozymes* attacks the cell wall structure of some bacteria. Lysozymes are found in high concentrations in the tear ducts, salivary glands, and other sites of bacterial invasion.

The sickle-cell allele has spread in some populations because it functions as an adaptation against malaria. Another adaptation to malaria is the Duffy blood group (see Chapter 5). In Duffy-positive individuals, the proteins Fya and Fyb are found on the surface of red blood cells. These proteins facilitate entry of the malaria-causing protozoan *Plasmodium vivax*. Duffy-negative individuals do not have Fya and Fyb on the surface of their red blood cells, so people with this phenotype are resistant to vivax malaria. Many Duffy-negative people are found in parts of Africa where malaria is common; others, who live elsewhere, have African ancestry.

Diet and Disease

It seems that there are always conflicting reports on what particular parts of our diet are good or bad for us. Carbohydrates are good one year and bad the next. Fats go in and out of fashion. From a biocultural anthropological perspective, American attitudes toward diet and health at the turn of the twenty-first century provide a rich source of material for analysis. For example, what do you think when you hear the word *cholesterol?* On one hand, this steroid alcohol is essential for the synthesis of many steroid hormones in the body, and its consumption is normal and necessary. On the other hand, high blood serum levels of cholesterol increase the risk of heart disease. Some people feel as if having high cholesterol is a sign of moral failure or weakness. Thus cholesterol has gone from being just a molecule to being a nutritional boogeyman, to be avoided via the consumption of low-cholesterol and cholesterol-free foods.

Despite all the confusion about diet, we all have the same basic nutritional needs. We need energy (measured in calories or kilojoules) for body maintenance, growth, and metabolism. Carbohydrates, fat, and proteins are all sources of energy. We require protein for tissue growth and repair. In addition to energy, fat provides us with essential fatty acids important for building and supporting nerve tissue. We need vitamins, which basically are organic molecules that our bodies cannot synthesize yet are essential in small quantities for a variety of metabolic processes. We also need a certain quantity of inorganic elements, such as iron and zinc. For example, with insufficient iron, the ability of red blood cells to transport oxygen is compromised, leading to anemia. Finally, we all need water to survive.

Over the past two decades, scientists have tried to reconstruct a typical *Paleolithic diet,* which theoretically reflects the kinds of foods people ate during the pre-agricultural part of human history. Many researchers believe that our bodies are evolved for functioning in this kind of nutritional environment. From the perspective of the human diet, agriculture changed everything. New foods were introduced, but variety was lost, and problems associated with specific dietary deficiencies (other than total calories) became common in some agricultural populations. Ultimately, however, the legacy of modern agriculture is not scarcity but abundance, and, as a species, we are not particularly well adapted to living in an environment of continuous nutritional abundance.

THE PALEOLITHIC DIET

For most of human history, people lived in small groups and subsisted on wild foods that they could collect by hunting or gathering. Obviously, diets varied in different areas: Sub-Saharan Africans were not eating the same thing as Native Americans on the northwest Pacific coast. Nonetheless, S. Boyd Eaton and Melvin Konner (Eaton & Konner, 1985; Eaton et al., 1999) argue that we can reconstruct an *average* Paleolithic diet from a wide range of information derived from paleoanthropology, epidemiology, and nutritional studies. A comparison of the average Paleolithic and contemporary diets is presented in Table 16.2 on page 488 (Eaton et al., 1999).

The contemporary diet is not simply a more abundant version of the hunter–gatherer diet. It differs fundamentally in both composition and quality. Compared with contemporary diets, the hunter–gatherer diet can be characterized as being high in micronutrients, protein, fiber, and potassium and low in fat and sodium. Total caloric and carbohydrate intake is about the same in both diets, but hunter–gatherers typically were more active than contemporary peoples and thus needed more calories, and their carbohydrates came from fruits and vegetables rather than processed cereals and refined sugars.

The comparison between hunter–gatherer and contemporary diets indicates that increasing numbers of people are living in nutritional environments for which their bodies are not necessarily well adapted. With few exceptions (such as the

TABLE 16.2 Comparison of Paleolithic and Contemporary Diets		
Dietary Component	**Paleolithic Diet**	**Contemporary Diet**
Energy (calories)	High caloric intake and expenditure to support active lifestyle and large body size.	More sedentary lifestyle uses fewer calories, yet caloric consumption often exceeds expenditure.
Micronutrients (vitamins, antioxidants, folic acid, iron, zinc)	High consumption (65–70% of diet) of foods rich in micronutrients, such as fruits, roots, nuts, and other noncereals.	Low consumption of foods rich in micronutrients.
Electrolytes (sodium, calcium, and potassium, needed for a variety of physiological processes)	High consumption of potassium relative to sodium (10,500 mg/day vs. 770 mg/day). High blood pressure is rare in contemporary hunter–gatherers with high potassium/sodium ratios.	Low consumption of potassium relative to sodium (3,000 mg/day vs. 4,000 mg/day). High sodium intake from processed foods is associated with high blood pressure.
Carbohydrates	Provide about 45–50% of daily calories, mostly from vegetables and fruits, which are rich in amino acids, fatty acids, and micronutrients.	Provide about 45–50% of daily calories, mostly from processed cereal grains, sugars, and sweeteners, which are low in amino acids, fatty acids, and micronutrients.
Fat	Provides about 20–25% of daily calories, mostly from lean game animals, which have less fat and saturated fat than domestic animals, leading to lower serum cholesterol levels.	Provides about 40% of calories, mostly from meat and dairy products. Some contemporary diets, such as from Japan and the Mediterranean region, are low in total or saturated fat and are associated with lower heart disease rates.
Protein	High consumption, providing about 30% of daily calorie intake, mostly from wild game that is low in fat.	Recommended daily allowance about 12% of total calories. High protein intake has been associated with higher heart disease rates, probably because contemporary high-protein diets also tend to be high in fat.
Fiber	50–100 g/day. High-fiber diets sometimes are considered risky because of loss of micronutrients, but this would be less of a worry in a Paleolithic diet rich in micronutrients.	20 g/day.

evolution of lactose tolerance) there has not been enough time, or strong enough selection pressures, for us to develop adaptations to this new nutritional environment. Indeed, because most of the negative health aspects of contemporary diets (obesity, diabetes, cancer) become critical only later in life, it is likely that health problems associated with the mismatch between our bodies and our nutritional environment will be with us for some time.

AGRICULTURE AND NUTRITIONAL DEFICIENCY

Agriculture allowed the establishment of large population centers, which in turn led to the development of large-scale, stratified civilizations with role specialization. Agriculture also produced an essential paradox: From a nutritional standpoint, most agricultural people led lives that were inferior to the lives of hunter–gatherers. Agricultural peoples often suffered from *nutritional stress* as dependence on a few crops made their large populations vulnerable to both chronic nutritional shortages and occasional famines. The "success" of agricultural peoples relative to hunter–gatherers came about not because agriculturalists lived longer or better lives but because there were more of them.

An example of the decline in health associated with the intensification of agriculture comes from paleopathological research in the Illinois Valley (Cook, 1979; Cook & Buikstra, 1979). Over the period A.D. 600–1200, the people there went from lives that were characterized predominantly by subsistence based on hunting and gathering (with some trade for agricultural products) to an agricultural economy with significant maize production. Population centers increased in size. However, at the same time, signs of malnutrition also increased. Enamel defects in tooth development became more common, and we can associate them with higher death rates during the weaning years (Figure 16.20). Skeletal growth rates slowed. Specific skeletal lesions associated with malnutrition also increased in frequency.

With their dependence on a single staple cereal food, agricultural populations throughout the world have been plagued by diseases associated with specific nutritional deficiencies. As in the Illinois Valley, many populations of the New World were dependent on maize as a staple food crop. Dependence on maize is associated with the development of *pellagra*, a disease caused by a deficiency of the B vitamin *niacin* in the diet. Pellagra causes a distinctive rash, diarrhea, and mental disturbances, including dementia. Ground corn is low in niacin and in the amino acid tryptophan, which the body can use to synthesize niacin. Even into the twentieth century, poor sharecroppers in the southern United States and poor farmers in southern Europe, both groups that consumed large quantities of cornmeal in their diets, were commonly afflicted with pellagra. Some maize-dependent groups in Central and South America were not so strongly affected by pellagra because they processed the corn with an alkali (lye, lime, ash) that released niacin from the hull of the corn.

In Asia, rice has been the staple food crop for at least the last 6,000 years. In China, a disease we now call *beriberi* was first described in 2,697 B.C. Although it was not recognized at that time, beriberi is caused by a deficiency in vitamin B_1 or *thiamine*. Beriberi is characterized by fatigue, drowsiness, and nausea, leading to a variety of more serious complications related to problems with the nervous system (especially tingling, burning, and numbness in the extremities) and ultimately heart failure. Rice is not lacking in vitamins; however, white rice, which has been polished and milled to remove the hull, has been stripped of most of its vitamin content, including thiamine. Recognition of an association between rice overdependence and beriberi began to develop in the late nineteenth century, when the Japanese navy reported that beriberi could be eliminated among its sailors (half of whom contracted the disease) by increasing the meat, vegetables, and fish in their diets.

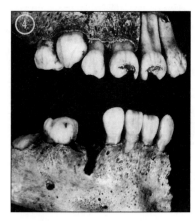

FIGURE 16.20 Enamel defects due to malnutrition in a child from the Illinois Valley (A.D. 600–1200).

AGRICULTURE AND ABUNDANCE: THRIFTY AND NONTHRIFTY GENOTYPES

The advent of agriculture ushered in a long era of nutritional deficiency for most people. However, the recent agricultural period, as exemplified in the developed nations of the early twenty-first century, is one of nutritional excess, especially in terms of the consumption of fat and carbohydrates of little nutritional value other than calories. The amount and variety of foods available to people in contemporary societies are unparalleled in human history.

In 1962, geneticist James Neel introduced the idea of a *thrifty genotype*, a genotype that is very efficient at storing food in the body in the form of fat, after observing that many non-Western populations that had recently adopted a Western or modern diet were much more likely than Western populations to have high rates of obesity, diabetes (especially Type 2 or non-insulin-dependent diabetes), and all the health problems associated with those conditions (see also Neel, 1982). Populations such as the Pima-Papago Indians in the southwest United States have diabetes rates of about 50%, and elevated rates of diabetes have been observed in Pacific Island-, Asian-, and African-derived populations with largely Western diets (Figure 16.21).

FIGURE 16.21 Pima Indian woman receiving an eye exam. Eye problems are a common result of diabetes.

According to Neel, hunter–gatherers needed a thrifty genotype to adapt to their nonabundant nutritional environments; in contrast, the thrifty genotype had been selected against in the supposedly abundant European environment through the negative consequences of diabetes and obesity. The history of agriculture and nutritional availability in Europe makes the evolution of a *non-thrifty genotype* unlikely (Allen & Cheer, 1996); Europe was no more nutritionally favored than other agricultural or hunter–gatherer populations. However, the notion of a thrifty genotype retains validity. At its heart is the idea that we are adapted to a lifestyle and nutritional environment far different from those we find in contemporary populations.

Douglas Crews and Linda Gerber (1994; Gerber & Crews, 1999) have proposed a refinement and expansion of the thrifty genotype model that they call the *thrifty-pleiotropic genotype* model. Whereas Neel concentrated primarily on energy intake, they point out that the thrifty genotype should apply to any nutrient in the environment that is (or was) potentially scarce. Thus we should expect negative health consequences for the overconsumption of a variety of nutrients: Excess cholesterol consumption leads to heart disease, excess salt consumption leads to high blood pressure, and so on. The deficiency syndromes of agriculture are part of this adaptive balance: Too little of a nutrient can also lead to disease. The pleiotropic aspect of Crews and Gerber's model is based on the observation that most of the diseases associated with overconsumption are chronic illnesses that have their effects late in life; they are to some extent a consequence of aging. If the efficiency of the thrifty genotype increases reproductive fitness early in life, the negative pleiotropic consequences in middle and old age will not be selected against, even in an environment of nutritional abundance.

We have seen how growth patterns, infectious disease exposure, nutritional status, and a host of other health-related issues are fundamentally changed by the adoption of new cultural practices and technologies. Conditions such as rickets and diabetes have been called diseases of civilization because they seem to be a direct result of the development of the industrialized urban landscape and food production. But this label is misleading. Rickets could also be called a disease of migration and maladaptation to a specific environment. Diabetes could be characterized as a disease of nutritional abundance, which was certainly *not* a characteristic of civilization for most of human history.

Biomedical anthropology is interested in understanding the patterns of human variation, adaptation, and evolution as they relate to health issues. This entails an investigation of the relationship between our biologies and the environments we live in. Understanding environmental transitions helps us understand not only the development of disease but also the mechanisms of adaptation that have evolved over thousands of years of evolution. Change is the norm in the modern world. In the future, we should expect human health to be affected by these changes. By their training and interests, biological anthropologists will be in an ideal position to make an important contribution to understanding the dynamic biocultural factors that influence human health and illness.

SUMMARY

1. **What is the difference between incidence rate and prevalence rate? How do they relate to each other?**

   The incidence rate is the rate at which new cases of a disease appear in a population over a certain period of time (usually a year). The prevalence rate is the total number of cases of disease divided by the population size at any given time. Prevalence is a function of both incidence and the duration of the disease. For example, a disease with a low incidence rate but a long duration could have a higher prevalence rate than a disease with a high incidence rate that is quickly cured or quickly fatal.

2. **Why are both biocultural and evolutionary approaches important in biomedical anthropology?**

   Biomedical anthropology is concerned with the processes of adaptation and adaptability with reference to health and human variation. In evolutionary terms, this encompasses how human biology adapts to stressful environments by evolving adaptations to overcome them; in addition, understanding the mismatch between biological adaptations and current environments can also provide insights into human health. Humans must also respond to environmental stress in the short term. Human adaptability studies show that biological plasticity and biocultural traditions can have a profound effect on health status.

3. **What are the four stages of growth seen across primates? Why is adolescence possibly a fifth stage of growth unique to humans?**

The four stages of growth are prenatal or gestational, infancy, juvenile stage, and adulthood. Barry Bogin argues that humans have a unique stage of growth, adolescence, which begins with puberty and is marked by a growth spurt not seen in other mammals. Adolescence may also provide an extended time period for human children to better learn their adult behavioral roles.

4. **What is the secular trend in growth?**

It has been demonstrated in several populations at different times that stature and weight increase with the advent of development, industrialization, and improved nutrition. This trend plateaus when the population reaches its genetic potential. Migration studies provide further evidence of the secular trend in growth by comparing growth between migrant populations living in nutrition-rich environments and nonmigrant populations in nutrition-poor environments.

5. **Why are agricultural populations more susceptible to infectious disease than hunter–gatherer populations?**

Agricultural populations are larger than hunter–gatherer populations, providing a larger pool of potential hosts who have not developed antibodies to the pathogen. They are more sedentary, which makes them more susceptible to diseases transmitted in human waste. Agricultural populations are also more dependent on only a few water sources, making them more vulnerable to waterborne diseases. Finally, they live in close proximity to both domestic animals and commensals (such as rats) and therefore are susceptible to diseases these animals carry or transmit.

6. **What are pellagra and beriberi?**

Both are vitamin deficiency diseases. Pellagra is caused by niacin deficiency and is seen in populations that have corn or maize as a staple cereal. Ground corn is low in niacin and the amino acid tryptophan, which the body uses to synthesize niacin. Beriberi is a disease common in populations where polished white rice is a staple cereal. It is caused by a deficiency in thiamine, which is present in the rice hull but is removed during processing to make white rice.

CRITICAL THINKING QUESTIONS

1. Can there be a cure for aging? Should curing aging be a public health priority?

2. What do we mean when we say there is an evolutionary "arms race" between pathogens and hosts?

3. Should everyone adopt the Paleolithic diet? Why or why not?

KEY TERMS

biomedical anthropology
epidemiology
incidence rate
prevalence rate

pathogens
auxology
teratogens
menarche

menopause
senescence
antigens
antibodies

immunoglobulins

SUGGESTED READINGS

Bogin, Barry. (2001). *The Growth of Humanity.* Wiley-Liss, New York.

Nesse, Randolph M., and Williams, George C. (1994). *Why We Get Sick: The New Science of Darwinian Medicine.* Times Books, New York.

Tanner, J. M. (1990). *Fetus into Man* (Revised Edition). Harvard University Press, Cambridge.

Trevathan, Wenda, Smith, E. O., and McKenna, J. J. (Eds.). (1999). *Evolutionary Medicine.* Oxford University Press, New York.

The Evolution of Human Behavior

CHAPTER OUTLINE

Studying the Evolution of Human Behavior

Traditional Lives in Evolutionary Ecological Perspective

Sexual Selection and Human Behavior

Language-Related Cross-Cultural Behaviors

Behavioral Disease

Henri Lhote Collection. Musee de l'Homme, Paris, France. © Photograph by Erich Lessing/Art Resource, NY

Debates about the relevance of biological and evolutionary approaches to understanding human behavior have a long history. One of the liveliest periods in this ongoing intellectual dialogue (to use a polite term) was the mid-1970s. During this period, new evolutionary and ecological approaches to understanding animal behavior were starting to be applied to human behavior. Increasing knowledge about the sophisticated social behavior of other primates further fueled the effort to place human behavior in a broader evolutionary and zoological context.

In early 1978, the American Association for the Advancement of Science held a meeting in Washington, D.C., which attempted to bring together representatives from all sides in the sociobiology "debate." Two of the most prominent scientists to attend the meeting were Edward Wilson, a proponent of the evolutionary study of human behavior (which was then called sociobiology), and Stephen Jay Gould, who cautioned that arguments about the biological basis of human behavior historically had been used to justify racist and sexist ideologies. Many of Wilson's critics accused him of arrogance for suggesting that evolutionary explanations of human behavior would come to dominate thinking in the traditional social sciences. In contrast, proponents of sociobiology felt that Wilson and other workers in the field were being unfairly accused of holding political and ideological views that they themselves found to be repugnant. Advocates on both sides of the debate were fueled by arrogance and righteousness, a volatile combination.

Sociologist of science Ullica Segerstråle attended this landmark meeting. She describes the extraordinary scene when Wilson faced some of his more enthusiastic critics:

"The two-day symposium featured about twenty speakers in all. As a member of the audience, I can say that for those who anticipated a public showdown, it was somewhat disappointing to sit through rather technical talks dealing with animal sociobiology . . . . But there was anticipation in the air, particularly in the session where both Wilson and Gould were to speak. The ballroom was filled to capacity. Would Gould demolish sociobiology? Would Wilson stand up to Gould? By now, the audience wanted some action. The result exceeded anybody's expectation.

"What happens is a total surprise. The session has already featured Gould, among others, and Wilson is one of the later speakers. Just as Wilson is about to begin, about ten people rush up on the speaker podium shouting 'Racist Wilson you can't hide, we charge you with genocide!' While some take over the microphone and denounce sociobiology, a couple of them rush up behind Wilson (who is sitting in his place) and pour a pitcher of ice-water over his head, shouting 'Wilson, you are all wet!' Then they quickly disappear again. Great commotion ensues but things calm down when the session organizer steps up to the microphone and apologizes to Wilson for the incident. The audience gives Wilson a standing ovation. Now Gould steps up to the microphone saying that this kind of activism is not the right way to fight sociobiology—here he has a Lenin quote handy, on 'radicalism, an infantile disorder of socialism.' For his valiant handling of the situation, Gould, too, gets a standing ovation. (The audience does not quite know how to react to any of this but applauding seems somehow right.) Wilson—still wet—gives his talk, in spite of the shock of the physical attack . . . . his calmly delivered talk is something of an anticlimax" (Segerstråle, 2000).

WE ARE FORTUNATE THAT MOST DEBATES about the evolution of human behavior do not end (or begin) with someone being doused with water. But the incident provides an indication of just how heated these debates can become. They reflect a basic conflict over whether human behavior is "in the genes" or is a product of our culture and upbringing: the old *nature versus nurture* debate. The nurture, or cultural, side accuses the nature, or evolutionary, side of being *genetic determinists,* people who believe that all observed behavioral differences between individuals, the sexes, or populations can be ascribed only to differences in genetics. The genetic side accuses the cultural side of embracing the logic of creationism: That once culture evolved, the rules of the game changed, and we were no longer subject (at the behavioral level) to the forces of evolution, which are so readily apparent in the animal world.

As you might expect, neither of these two extreme views reflects the views of most biological anthropologists. Biological anthropologists, with their appreciation for the biology and behavior of our closest primate relatives, understand that human bodies and human behavior evolved. Although behaviors do not fossilize, we can draw inferences about how they may have evolved by examining contemporary human and nonhuman primate behavior and biology. Biological anthropologists also understand the importance of culture and experience in shaping human behavior. Behavioral plasticity is one of the critical adaptations that accompanied the evolution of a large brain. But many behavioral scientists today believe that although a large brain allows humans to adopt a wide range of behaviors, some patterns of behavior we observe across cultures and populations are most directly explained by evolution and natural selection. The behaviors are not genetically determined but reflect the interactions of genes and environments that yield patterns of behavior—observable cross-culturally—we can analyze statistically.

To understand the evolutionary foundations of contemporary human behavior we need to apply the same logic and inferences that we use when studying other evolutionary phenomena. We can use the vast amount of information we have about human behavior and look for patterns that are consistent with evolutionary models. We can also take advantage of "natural experiments" that provide unusual combinations of variables and allow us to gain new perspectives on human behavior. The same principles that we use to make inferences about the phylogenetic relationships of the Old World monkeys, the adaptive value of the trunk of an elephant, the plumage of the male peacock, or the social behavior of prairie dogs can also guide our inferences about the evolution of human behavior. However, human behavior occurs in a cultural context. Like the medical anthropology approach to health and illness (discussed in Chapter 16), a comprehensive understanding of the evolution of human behavior entails a biocultural perspective.

In this chapter, we will address several aspects of human behavior from an evolutionary perspective. These include the ecology and demography of traditional human societies, patterns of human behavior that have been shaped by sexual selection, the interaction between culture and biology in the expression of language, and the emergence of behavioral disease in an evolutionary context. We recognize, of course, that each of these topics can be productively analyzed from a cultural or nonevolutionary perspective; these other perspectives may provide alternative or complementary analyses to those provided here. However, as we have emphasized throughout this text, the biological anthropological approach is defined both by evolutionary theory and by the quest to understand the human species—including human behavior—in a biocultural context. Therefore, this chapter focuses on these evolutionary and biocultural explanations of human behavior.

Studying the Evolution of Human Behavior

Evolutionary approaches to understanding behavior did not make much of an impact through the first half of the twentieth century. A major development in the study of the evolution of behavior was the publication of G. C. Williams's book *Adaptation and Natural Selection* (1966). Williams saw the evolution of social behavior in terms of benefits not to the group as a whole but to the individuals who made up the group (and their genes). Following on this work and others, in 1975 zoologist Edward O. Wilson published a book called *Sociobiology: The New Synthesis*. For a variety of social and political reasons, which are beyond the scope of this text (see Segerstråle, 2000; Alcock, 2001), Wilson's book became a lightning rod for critics of evolutionary interpretations of human behavior. Wilson defined **sociobiology** simply as the science of the biological basis of social behavior. Only a small part of his book was dedicated to humans, with most of it focusing on examples and discussions drawn from the animal world, especially the insects that were the main focus of his research. Although a classic work, *Sociobiology* was not *The Origin of Species:* It emerged from an intellectual climate that was, at least in part, already in tune with the message.

Critics of sociobiology, such as the paleontologist and writer Stephen Jay Gould, claimed that sociobiology in general was not good science and was susceptible to political misapplication. Mindful of these criticisms, the field of the evolution of human behavior has moved away from Wilson's grand vision of human sociobiology (that it would subsume all the social sciences) and embraced several different, sometimes competing approaches to human behavior, which are seen to be complementary to or a part of traditional human behavioral sciences.

From an evolutionary theory perspective, a "fast herd of deer" is not the same as a "herd of fast deer."

THE EVOLUTION OF HUMAN BEHAVIOR: FOUR APPROACHES

Anthropologists and other scientists interested in the evolution of human behavior use quite different approaches to the subject depending on their particular research interests and training (Figure 17.1). Four of the most common approaches are paleontological reconstructions of behavior, biocultural approaches, evolutionary

sociobiology Name popularized by E. O. Wilson for the evolutionary study of animal social behavior.

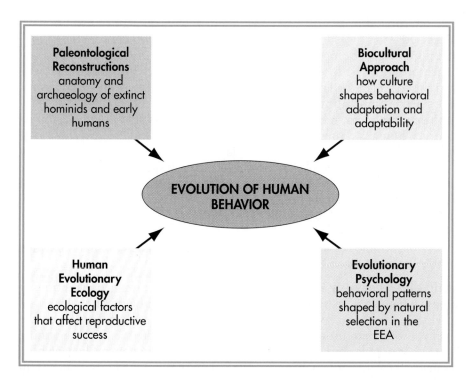

FIGURE 17.1 Four approaches to studying the evolution of human behavior.

psychology, and human evolutionary (or behavioral) ecology. The examples covered in this chapter make use of the latter three approaches.

Paleontological Reconstructions of Behavior   In Chapters 9 through 14 we discussed several reconstructions of the behavior of earlier hominids. These reconstructions were based on the anatomy of extinct hominids and, when present, the archaeological remains with which they were associated. They were also based on correlations among behavior, anatomy, and ecology we have observed in nonhuman primate species and in contemporary humans, especially those living under traditional hunter–gatherer conditions. Any reconstruction of the behavior of our hominid ancestors is a synthesis of both paleontological and contemporary data. Although there are limits to how much we can learn from such reconstructions, they are the only source of information we have to understand the *sequence* of events in human behavioral evolution.

Biocultural Approaches   It is clear that human cultural behavior has influenced human evolution. For example, the adoption of slash-and-burn agriculture had an indirect effect on the evolution of the sickle cell polymorphism, and the development of dairying in some populations was a direct selective factor in the evolution of lactose tolerance (see Chapter 5). Our biological and evolutionary heritage may have shaped several patterns of behavior that are expressed in a cultural context. One aspect of human behavior that we have already discussed in detail— language—is a prime example.

Evolutionary Psychology   An adherence to three main principles characterizes **evolutionary psychology**. First, human and animal behavior is not produced by minds that are general purpose devices. Rather, the mind is composed of *cognitive modules*, which are assumed to have an underlying neuroanatomical basis. These modules express specific behaviors in specific situations. Second, cognitive modules are complex design features of organisms. Because natural selection is the only way to evolve complex design features, evolutionary psychology focuses on understanding behaviors or cognitive modules as adaptations. Third, for most of our history, humans and hominids have lived in small groups as hunter–gatherers. Evolutionary psychologists believe that our evolved behavior may reflect or should be interpreted in terms of this hypothetical **environment of evolutionary adaptedness (EEA)**.

Evolutionary psychologists acknowledge that some behaviors, like some physical features, are the by-products of other evolutionary forces and therefore should not be considered adaptations (musical ability may be such a behavior, for example). Furthermore, although the EEA figures prominently in their interpretation of behavioral data, most evolutionary psychologists study the behavior of contemporary humans living in developed countries, via surveys, psychological experiments, and observations of people in day-to-day settings. This is not simply a matter of convenience: Evolutionary psychologists seek species-wide adaptations, which can be examined in any cultural setting (although data from cross-cultural studies is always helpful). They use such data to uncover the adaptations that characterized life in the EEA, whatever that may have been. Over the past two decades the principles of evolutionary psychology have been elucidated by two of its main proponents, anthropologist John Tooby and psychologist Leda Cosmides (Barkow et al., 1992; Tooby & Cosmides, 2000).

Human Evolutionary (or Behavioral) Ecology   In contrast to evolutionary psychology, which focuses more on psychological experiments and surveys of people living in developed countries, **human evolutionary ecology** focuses on the ecological factors that influence reproductive success in the few remaining hunter–gatherer populations. Among the groups studied most intensely have been the Yanomamö of Amazonia (Chagnon, 1988, 1997), the Aché of Paraguay (Hill & Hurtado, 1996), and the Hadza of Tanzania (Hawkes et al., 2001). Topics of

evolutionary psychology
Approach to understanding the evolution of human behavior that emphasizes the selection of specific behavioral patterns in the context of the environment of evolutionary adaptedness.

environment of evolutionary adaptedness (EEA)   According to evolutionary psychologists, the critical period for understanding the selective forces that shape human behavior; exemplified by hunter–gatherer lifestyles of hominids before the advent of agriculture.

human evolutionary ecology
Approach to understanding the evolution of human behavior that attempts to explore ecological and demographic factors important in determining individual reproductive success and fitness in a cultural context.

interest to human evolutionary ecologists include the relationship between status and reproductive success, demographic effects of tribal warfare and aggression, and the underlying social impact of hunting and food sharing. Researchers use data on contemporary hunter–gatherer groups to refine models that purport to reconstruct the behavior of extinct hominids (Marlowe 2005).

BEHAVIORAL PATTERNS AND EVOLUTION

Human behavior can be observed at the individual, cultural, or even species-wide levels. Biological and evolutionary explanations of different behavioral patterns vary depending on the contexts in which those behaviors are expressed. To understand the natural history of human behavior, it is important to remember the mosaic nature of its evolution. Just as different parts of the human body evolved at different points in our past, different aspects of human behavior may reflect different evolutionary periods.

Cognitive Universals   As a species we share many behaviors by virtue of our shared biology. These **cognitive universals** include behaviors studied by cognitive scientists, such as sensory processing, the basic emotions, consciousness, motor control, memory, and attention (Gazzaniga et al., 1998). Language also is typically included among the cognitive behaviors shared by all people. At a biological level, we share the neurological mechanisms underlying some of these cognitive universals with many other mammalian species. For example, much of what we know about the specifics of visual processing comes from experimental work on cats and monkeys. Other universals, such as language, clearly have emerged fully only in the hominid lineage (although we may study its biological antecedents by looking at other species).

Given the universal, and in many cases cross-species, expression of these cognitive processes, it is reasonable to assume they are biological adaptations that have been shaped by natural selection. Although cognitive universals have a basic common expression in all people, we often see variation in the way they are expressed. It is likely that this variation results from both environmental and genetic factors, in the same way, for example, that variation in stature arises within and between populations.

Cross-Cultural Universals   When we look across the diverse cultures of the world, it is easy to notice that many commonalities emerge, which can be called **cross-cultural universals** (Brown, D. E., 1991). For example, all cultures have a language. We also find that each culture develops rituals and traditions to mark and recognize status. They develop systems for identifying and naming kin. They organize social and occupational roles along sex and gender lines. Standards of sexual attractiveness and beauty may show common patterns across cultures. Many biological anthropologists argue that common cultural practices did not develop independently over and over again but rather reflect underlying genetic factors that are widely distributed in our species. If we cannot find a common cultural origin for a widespread behavioral pattern observed across cultures, then it is reasonable to hypothesize that the pattern may reflect a common biological origin. This is especially true if we find the behavior in a majority of human cultures or if we can show it to be associated with a common ecological variable. One way to look at this is that we are not "hardwired" to develop these behaviors but rather are "prewired" to express them given a proper ecological or cultural environment (Marcus, 2004).

Remember that cross-cultural universals are *not* individual universals. For example, we could say that singing and dancing are cross-cultural universals, but that does not mean that all members of every culture sing and dance. Similar forms of behavioral disease are found in different cultures, so in one sense we can say that

cognitive universals
Cognitive phenomena such as sensory processing, the basic emotions, consciousness, motor control, memory, and attention that are expressed by all normal individuals.

cross-cultural universals
Behavioral phenomena, such as singing, dancing, and mental illness, that are found in almost all human cultures, but are not necessarily exhibited by each member of a cultural group.

mental illnesses are a cross-cultural universal, even if only a small proportion of the population develops these conditions.

Within-Culture Variation   Male and female mammals may adopt different sexual and reproductive strategies because of their differential investment in time and energy in each offspring. How has this mammalian pattern been rendered in a human cultural context? Do we see evidence that humans have evolved away from typical primate patterns? If so, how and why has this *within-culture variation* happened? Variation in behavior correlated with age may also have been shaped by evolutionary pressures. For example, is the young, risk-taking male a Western cultural construct or a cross-cultural phenomenon amenable to evolutionary theorizing? Although age and sex are the primary biological variables that figure into studies of the evolution of within-culture variation, we can study other aspects of within-culture variation from an evolutionary perspective.

Biological Constraints on Human Behavior   People are capable of doing just about anything, and any number of behaviors shaped by culture are not easily explained in a bioevolutionary context. On the other hand, when we look across cultures, there seem to be some *constraints* on what people do, which in turn lead to behavioral convergences across cultures. Unlike cross-cultural universals, behavioral convergences that arise from biological constraints are not the primary result of biological processes. A nonbehavioral example of a behavioral convergence is footwear. Footwear tends to converge on a similar basic shape, which is functionally constrained by the shape and action of the human foot. In a similar fashion, human behavior may be channeled into similar patterns by constraints imposed by our neurobiology. A basic issue in the evolution of behavior is determining whether any given behavior is an adaptation or simply the result of a biological constraint on behavior. Of course, similar debates arise about anatomical features as well.

Traditional Lives in Evolutionary Ecological Perspective

Over the past three decades human evolutionary ecologists have undertaken intensive study of traditional cultures to better understand the interplay between biological and cultural factors in human behavior and human behavioral evolution. Studies of traditional hunter–gatherers and traditional agricultural cultures are important because their lifestyles reflect more closely the selective environments (the EEA) that shaped hominid evolution, until the advent of agriculture and large-scale societies starting about 10,000 years ago.

Evolutionary ecology represents a profound theoretical departure from traditional cultural anthropology. Investigating the complex interplay between behavior, culture, and ecology, evolutionary ecologists typically live for extended periods of time with the groups they are studying (as cultural anthropologists do) (Figure 17.2). However, they differ from other cultural anthropologists in their reliance on quantitative research methods, which are necessary to test evolutionary hypotheses.

QUANTIFICATION IN EVOLUTIONARY ECOLOGY RESEARCH

To rigorously test evolutionary hypotheses and to discover how ecological factors affect human behavior, evolutionary ecologists must collect quantifiable data. These data include birth, death, and marriage statistics (that is, demographic variables); nutritional data; and calculations of daily energy expenditure. Some evolutionary

FIGURE 17.2 Evolutionary ecologists live and do research in contemporary cultures that maintain all or some aspects of their traditional lifeways, such as these tribespeople from New Guinea.

ecologists use sophisticated mathematical models to try to understand human cultural behavior in an evolutionary context (Boyd & Richerson, 1988). Others use data from multiple cultures to look at how ecological and environmental variables interact to potentially influence the behavior of hunter–gatherers (Marlowe, 2005).

Wealth, Reproductive Success, and Survival   One of the basic tenets of human evolutionary ecology is that cultural success should be related to increased fitness (Irons, 1979). William Irons tested this hypothesis in a study of fertility and mortality among the tribal Turkmen of Iran. In this culture, wealth (in terms of money, jewelry, and consumable goods) is a primary measure of cultural success. Irons found that for men, fertility and survivorship were higher for the wealthier half of the population than for the poorer half (Figure 17.3); survivorship was significantly higher for the wealthier women, but there was no difference in fertility. He also found that male reproductive success was more variable among men than among women (that is, the difference between the richer and poorer halves was more pronounced for men than for women), as predicted by sexual selection theory.

Monique Borgerhoff Mulder (1987, 1990) looked at the relationship between wealth and reproductive success in a different population, the Kipsigis of Kenya

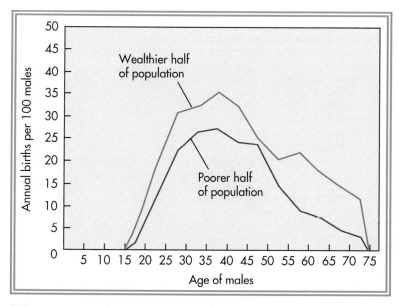

FIGURE 17.3   Male Turkmen in the wealthier half of the population had higher fertility rates than those in the poorer half.

FIGURE 17.4   The Kipsigis of Kenya.

(Figure 17.4). The Kipsigis are a pastoral people who moved into Kenya from northeastern Africa in the late eighteenth century. The wealth of a Kipsigis man is defined in terms of his land holdings, the number of animals he has, and his household possessions. Borgerhoff Mulder found that all these measures correlate strongly to amount of land owned, so she used that as her primary statistic of wealth.

The Kipsigis practice polygyny, which means that a man can have more than one wife at a time. When a man wants to marry a young woman, he approaches her parents with an offer of **bridewealth,** a payment that can equal up to a third of an average man's wealth. Borgerhoff Mulder looked at wealth and reproductive success among Kipsigis men in a series of different age groups and found a strong correlation between wealth and number of offspring. For example, in a group of forty-four men who were circumcised between 1922 and 1930 (circumcision marks coming of age), there was a very high correlation between number of offspring and acres of land owned (Figure 17.5). Ownership of 30 acres correlated to having fifteen to twenty surviving offspring, whereas men with 90 acres had twenty-five to

bridewealth   Payment offered by a man to the parents of a woman he wants to marry.

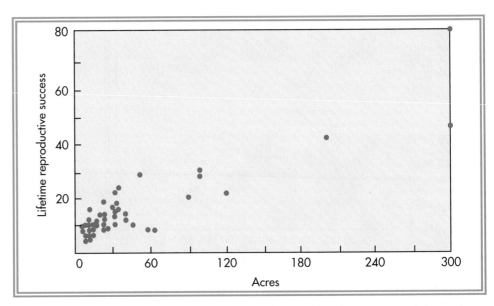

FIGURE 17.5   The relationship between number of acres a Kipsigis man owns and the number of offspring he has during his lifetime.

thirty offspring. In general, the fertility of the wives of richer and poorer men was approximately the same. Wealthier men have more children because they can have more wives, being able to afford more bridewealth payments. And although larger families may lead to increased wealth, Borgerhoff Mulder found no evidence that this was the causal direction: Wealthier men were able to afford large families, not the other way around.

The Turkmen and Kipsigis studies, and others done elsewhere, support the hypothesis that one measure of cultural success—wealth—correlates with reproductive success. However, this correlation does not generally hold for developed, urbanized, capitalist cultures, where higher socioeconomic status typically is not associated with a higher birth rate. This is an important example of the kind of fundamental biocultural change that can occur in a society when it transforms from an undeveloped to a developed economy.

Physiology and Ecology   Another method for quantifying the relationship between cultural and ecological factors in human behavior is to look at the way physiological measures vary across ecological contexts. For example, Peter Ellison (1990, 1994) developed a method of measuring levels of reproductive hormones in saliva as a noninvasive means to assess reproductive function in women living in diverse environments.

Progesterone is a steroid hormone produced by the corpus luteum and the placenta that prepares the uterus for pregnancy and helps maintain pregnancy once fertilization has occurred. Progesterone levels measured in saliva correlate with ovarian function. Ellison and his colleagues found that salivary progesterone levels are strongly correlated with age over the course of a woman's reproductive life (between about ages 15 and 50 years). Progesterone levels increase from a baseline level at the end of puberty, peaking between 25 and 30 years of age and dropping off thereafter. Ellison suggests that ovarian function matures at approximately the same age as the pelvis becomes structurally mature (early to mid-20s).

Studies among two traditional agricultural groups, the Lese of Zaire and the Tamang of Nepal, and women from the Boston area, showed that the basic age-dependent curve of salivary progesterone production was the same in all three populations (Figure 17.6). Ellison believes that this pattern probably represents a fundamental feature of human reproductive physiology. This discovery refines our view of the female reproductive years as an evolved life history stage (beginning at menarche and ending at menopause).

progesterone A steroid hormone produced by the corpus luteum and the placenta, which prepares the uterus for pregnancy and helps maintain pregnancy once fertilization has occurred.

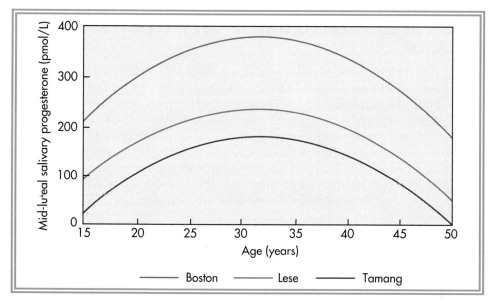

FIGURE 17.6 The age-dependent curve of salivary progesterone levels in three populations.

Although the shapes of the progesterone-versus-age curves were the same in Boston, Lese, and Tamang women, the amount of progesterone produced varied among the groups. Boston women, who presumably had the most nutritionally rich environment with few infectious diseases, had higher progesterone levels at every age than was found in the other two populations. Ellison suggests that chronic stress that delays growth and maturation, such as nutritional deficiencies, could lead to lower levels of ovarian function throughout the lifetime. Such a stress-response relationship could be adaptive because in a stressful environment it may be better to devote more effort and energy to body maintenance and survival rather than reproduction.

Another steroid hormone whose levels can be measured in saliva is **testosterone**. Testosterone is produced primarily in the testes and ovaries; it is known as the "male hormone" since the testes produce about 10 times as much as the ovaries, and testosterone is primarily responsible for the development of the primary male sexual characteristics in the fetus and the secondary characteristics at puberty. It has also been hypothesized that testosterone is an important modulator of behavior, especially in the context of male dominance and reproductive behavior. Much evidence for this hypothesis has been gathered from studies of numerous mammal species, but what is the situation in humans?

One way to test the hypothesis claiming that testosterone influences behaviors related to male–male competition and mate-seeking behavior is to compare testosterone levels in men who are in a committed relationship with those who are single. T. C. Burnham (2003) and his colleagues found that in a sample of 122 American business school students, men who were married or in a committed relationship had 21% lower salivary testosterone levels than those who were single. Peter Gray and his colleagues (2006) looked at testosterone levels in a group of men in Beijing, China, and they found that married non-fathers had slightly lower levels than unmarried men but the difference did not reach statistical significance; however, they did find that married fathers had significantly lower levels than either of the other two groups. These studies demonstrate that testosterone levels vary in human males according to their marital/parental status, and that these patterns can be observed in different biological and cultural groups. They support the hypothesis that testosterone level is a modulator of, or reacts to, an individual male's reproductive situation. Burnham and colleagues (2003) point out that since testosterone may impair immune function and encourage risk-taking, lower levels of testosterone in married men may help explain the fact that married men generally are healthier and have lower mortality than unmarried men.

HUNTING, GATHERING, AND THE SEXUAL DIVISION OF LABOR

Recent research on contemporary hunter–gatherer groups has revolutionized our knowledge of how people without agriculture acquire the food they eat and how hunting and gathering patterns in hominids may have evolved. It has become increasingly clear that earlier speculations (Lee & DeVore, 1968) were based on inadequate understanding of hunter–gatherer lifeways. The concept of "man the hunter, woman the gatherer" reflects a division of labor between the sexes in all human cultures, but it is all too easy to turn it into a simplistic, stereotypical picture of evolved, hardwired gender roles (Bird, 1999; Panter-Brick, 2002). Furthermore, observing sex differences in food acquisition practices is not the same as explaining why they exist.

In almost every traditional foraging culture, both men and women devote a substantial portion of their time and energy to the search for and acquisition of food. And in almost every culture, despite the fact that they live in the same environment, men and women exploit different aspects of that environment when acquiring food, leading to a pronounced sexual division of labor, although not

testosterone   A steroid produced primarily in the testes and ovaries, and at a much higher level in men than in women. Responsible for the development of the male primary and secondary sexual characteristics. Strongly influences dominance and reproductive behavior.

FIGURE 17.7 The evolutionary significance of "Man the Hunter" (or in this instance "Man the Fisher") has been debated for decades.

necessarily along the simplistic division that "men hunt and women gather." For example, among the aboriginal peoples of Mer Island in the Coral Sea, both men and women forage for food on the coral reef. Men concentrate on using large spears to kill large fish swimming around the edges of the reef while women walk the dry part of the reef, collecting shellfish or catching small fish or octopus with small spears (Figure 17.7). Women almost always succeed in bringing home a reasonable amount of food, whereas the men have much more variable success (Bird, 1999). In the Hadza of Tanzania, men concentrate on large game hunting while women focus almost exclusively on foraging for berries, nuts, fruits, and roots (O'Connell et al., 1992; Hawkes et al., 1997).

There are several models for the origins of the sexual division of labor. The *cooperative provisioning model,* based on the study of monogamous birds, predicts that the sexual division of labor occurred as a result of the evolution of monogamous relationships, because it would allow the pair to more fully exploit the environment if they did not compete with each other for resources (see discussion of Lovejoy's model in Chapter 10). An alternative model, the *conflict model,* suggests that hominid males and females were already exploiting the environment in fundamentally different ways before males began contributing energy and resources to females and their young (Bird, 1999). The "sexual division of labor" is not really a division but reflects the fact that males and females have different problems to overcome (conflicts) in the course of mating, reproduction, and parenting.

It is nonsensical to ask whether hunting or gathering is more important. Neither provides more energy than the other on a regular basis. The productivity of hunting and gathering varies by season, environment, and a host of other factors (Kaplan et al., 2000). Women and men do vary in the *package size* of the food they focus on acquiring. Women concentrate on small foodstuffs that tend to be predictable, immobile, and obtainable while caring for infants and young children. Even though she almost always receives assistance from others, including female relatives and the father of her children, an individual woman is responsible primarily for feeding herself and her children.

Men concentrate on obtaining foods in large sizes that they cannot consume at once by themselves and that they redistribute to families or the larger social group. These foods almost always come in the form of dead animals, which may be obtained by hunting, trapping, fishing, or even scavenging. In some Melanesian societies, however, men compete to grow the largest yams, which, although they are too fibrous to eat, can be distributed and used for propagation of new plants (Weiner, 1988). Big yams aside, animals provide protein and fat in quantities not available from any other source, and animal food is almost always highly prized in human cultures. As Hilliard Kaplan and colleagues (2000, p. 174) state, "The primary activity for adult males is hunting to provide nutrients for others . . . . [Hunting] is a fundamental feature of the human life-history adaptation." But why do males provide nutrients for others?

Why Do Men Hunt and Share Meat?   As we discussed in Chapter 10, male co-operative hunting and meat sharing, which we see in chimpanzees, may have a long history in hominid evolution. As hominids became more adept at hunting larger game that could not be butchered, transported, or consumed by a single individual, meat sharing could become a central component of human culture. A fascinating aspect of big game hunting in many cultures is that the hunter or hunters most responsible for the catch may have little to say about how the meat is distributed. Research among the Hadza in Tanzania shows that a successful hunter may not even be able to recoup his losses via reciprocal altruism later (Hawkes et al., 2001).

The *tolerated theft model* of hunting and meat sharing explains meat sharing in part by suggesting that defending a large kill takes more energy than it is worth; in other words, it may pay off in the long run to tolerate the "theft" of meat (that is, sharing) rather than to work hard to defend a kill (which may be too large for a single individual to consume). The reward for hunting would come not from the meat itself but from the increase in social status and prestige, which reflects on family members as well (Figure 17.8). In effect then, large animal hunting becomes a form of *costly signaling* (Bird, 1999), which ultimately increases the opportunities for males to acquire new mates. In the tolerated theft model, large game hunting did not evolve primarily as a means of paternal provisioning, although females and their young definitely benefit from males' hunting activity.

Critics of the tolerated theft or costly signaling model argue that because most of the food that is shared after a hunt goes to close kin or reproductive partners, sharing enhances the fitness of the male hunter and therefore should be considered an adaptation (Hill & Kaplan, 1993); they suggest that the provisioning itself, not the costly signaling, is the fitness-enhancing aspect of the behavior. Kaplan and colleagues (2000) propose that hunting and meat sharing intensified in hominid evolution in the context of a pair bond and paternal investment in the young. Part of their evidence for this hypothesis is that reproductive-age women in hunter–gatherer populations almost always receive nutritional support from men. Because most of that support comes in the form of animals that have been hunted, and such altruistic behavior is much more likely to have evolved in the context of provisioning kin, paternal investment via hunting may be an adaptation, not simply a secondary result of hunting for social prestige.

In the costly signaling model, hunting by men and meat sharing evolved in the context of sexual selection. Hunting itself is not seen as a critical behavior in hominid

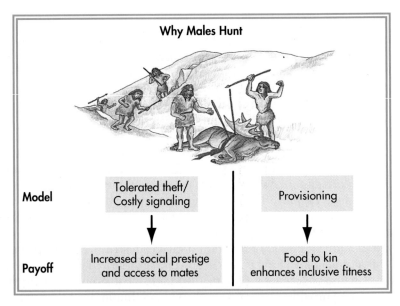

FIGURE 17.8 Models for the evolution of hunting by males.

evolution, and nutritional benefits to children may be an incidental outcome of the process (Bird, 1999). In contrast, advocates of the provisioning model give hunting and meat sharing a central role in hominid evolution: They argue that it was a prime impetus in the evolution of a larger brain and increased longevity (Kaplan et al., 2000). Studies of the Aché in Paraguay show that hunters do not achieve peak hunting proficiency until they are in their 40s (Walker et al., 2002).

Resolution of the debate about why men hunt—for mates and prestige, as Kristen Hawkes, Rebecca Bird, and others argue, or to provision, as Hilliard Kaplan, Kim Hill, and their colleagues suggest—will require further study. Unfortunately, the limited number of cultures that still practice a hunter–gather lifestyle (mostly in marginal environments) may make obtaining new data on the issue difficult. Obviously there is merit to both views, but they cannot both be correct because they posit divergent views on the importance of hunting in hominid evolution.

Sexual Selection and Human Behavior

The study of human sexual behavior has been revolutionized over the past 25 years by the development of an evolutionary perspective on human reproductive strategies, sex and gender differences in behavior, and cross-cultural patterns of attractiveness and mate selection (Symons, 1979; Fisher, 1992; Buss, 2003). This evolutionary perspective is based in large part on the fact that humans are mammals. Male and female mammals vary profoundly in their energetic investment in producing offspring. Female mammals provide not only eggs but also a body in which fetal growth takes place. After birth, they are obligated to provide milk and care for offspring until the age of weaning. Males are obligated to provide sperm at the time of conception, and that is all. Subsequent investment, which can take the form of provisioning a pregnant or lactating female or providing food for the young, is not required, and in many species, including most primate species, males do not directly participate or invest in rearing of young.

Mammalian males and females also vary in their reproductive potential. The energetic costs of gestation and lactation constrain a female mammal's reproductive potential; she can only have a limited number of offspring in her lifetime. On the other hand, sperm production does not impose much of a limit on a male mammal's reproductive potential. Given their energetic investment in reproduction, we would expect mammalian females to be choosier when selecting mates than males would be. Males should also be choosy, but if they are successful in impregnating a large number of females, choosing a specific, high-quality mate is less of an issue. In general, mammalian males compete for access to females, and mammalian females should choose high-quality males, however that is defined. We can also expect males to vary more in their reproductive success than females. For example, there may be a large number of males that never reproduce, whereas almost every female will find a reproductive partner.

Research on human mate selection and standards of attractiveness in different cultures indicates that women tend to value resource-providing ability in their partners, whereas men tend to value youth and appearance (indicators of reproductive potential) in their potential partners (Buss, 2003). These observations are consistent with predictions derived from mammalian evolutionary biology. Of course, these are statistical patterns generated from surveys of large numbers of individuals. Obviously, different cultures define sexual attractiveness differently, and there is much individual variation in sexual preferences. Nonetheless, according to many evolutionary researchers, the statistical patterns of sexual behavior that are observed across cultures are not easily explained by cultural convergence. Instead, they may reflect underlying behavioral trends that have been shaped by natural selection.

"I'm tired of all this nonsense about beauty being only skin-deep. That's deep enough. What do you want, an adorable pancreas?"

–Jean Kerr

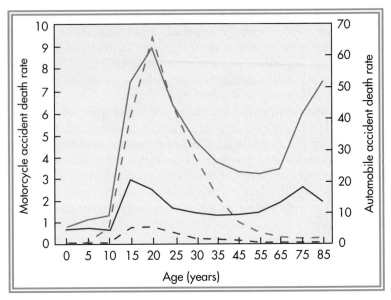

FIGURE 17.9 Risk of death from motorcycle accidents (dashed lines) and passenger car accidents (solid lines) per 100,000 U.S. population during 1980–1986 for males (green lines) and females (maroon lines).

RISK-TAKING BEHAVIOR

When we look across human cultures, we find that as a group young adult males (ages 15–29) have the highest death rates from accidents or violence (Figure 17.9). For example, death rates in motor vehicle accidents for 20-year-old Americans are three to four times higher in men than women (Hill & Chow, 2002). Young males do not die from accidents more often because they are unlucky but because they are more likely to put themselves in risky situations (Figure 17.10). Proclivity toward risk-taking behavior in males may reflect a significant sex difference in human behavior, which may have a long evolutionary history (Low, 2000).

Why should males engage in risk-taking behavior more than females? Bobbi Low (2000) argues that the reason goes back to general sex differences in mammalian biology. For a female mammal, the costs associated with risk-taking behavior are unlikely to outweigh the benefits. She is likely to be able to find mates and fulfill her reproductive potential throughout her lifetime, so she has no particular need to engage in risk-taking behavior to acquire mates. On the other hand, male mammals vary much more in reproductive success. A male mammal may engage in high-risk, potentially very costly (even life-threatening) activities because such behaviors could have a potentially high reproductive benefit. For example, aggressive behavior between male mammals over access to females is very common; it has clearly been selected for in the context of sexual access to mates. Females may also find risk-taking in males to be attractive because they may consider it a manifestation of ambition or "good genes" or a proxy for the ability to provide resources for the female and her offspring.

Elizabeth Hill and Krista Chow (2002) suggest that risky or binge drinking may also be understood in the context of sexual selection for risk-taking behavior. First, among college-age people, risky drinking is about 50% more common in men than women (48% versus 33%, although figures vary depending on criteria for defining a binge), and males are more likely to engage in driving after drinking. The peak age for alcohol abuse in males is 15 to 29 years. College men who were not married were twice as likely to engage in binge drinking as those who were married. These aspects of risky drinking in young men suggest to Hill and Chow that it is another manifestation of the evolved pattern of risk-taking behavior. They argue that risk-taking behaviors are not deviant but that we should recognize them as an evolved response

FIGURE 17.10 Risk-taking behavior by young males.

to environmental instability. With specific reference to risky drinking at the individual level, Hill and Chow suggest that dealing with instability in the person's family or work life may be one avenue of therapy for the treatment for alcohol abuse.

INBREEDING AVOIDANCE AND INCEST TABOOS

Evolutionary factors may have played an important role in shaping not only mate choice preferences but also mate choice aversions. Inbreeding is defined as reproduction between close relatives. Close inbreeding has several major biological costs (Rudan & Campbell, 2004). A highly inbred population or species loses genetic variability over time. This means that when environments or other selective forces change, the population does not have the variability to respond to these changes via natural selection. Populations with reduced variability have fewer opportunities to evolve balanced polymorphisms maintained by heterozygous advantage, which also limits their ability to respond genetically to environmental changes.

When close relatives interbreed, it increases the likelihood that lethal or debilitating recessive alleles will be expressed. Because relatives share a high percentage of their alleles, there is a good chance they will both possess a lethal recessive that may be passed on to their offspring. Studies of a wide range of mammal species have demonstrated that inbred individuals suffer from greater mortality or loss of fitness, a phenomenon known as **inbreeding depression**, relative to less inbred individuals in the same species (Mettler et al., 1988). Studies of inbreeding in humans clearly demonstrate the potentially harmful effects of reproduction between first-degree relatives (such as father and daughter or sister and brother) and between relatives who share 25% of their alleles (such as uncle and niece or grandparent and grandchild). Offspring of first-degree relatives (who share 50% of alleles) are far more likely than other children to be stillborn or to die within the first year of life, and physical and mental abnormalities are much more common among them. Even in situations where inbreeding is less close than among first-degree relatives (such as in the many societies where first-cousin marriage is prescribed), there are costs to inbreeding in the form of higher rates of genetic disorders (Overall et al., 2002) and perhaps an increased accumulation of genetic risk factors for late-onset conditions such as heart disease and diabetes (Rudan & Campbell, 2004).

Up to half of all traditional cultures prescribe some form of *consanguineous* marriage, usually between first or second cousins or in some cases uncle–niece (Bittles et al., 1991). Alan Bittles and his colleagues argue that understanding the effects of inbreeding requires looking at it in a broader social and demographic context. For example, women in consanguineous marriages typically start to reproduce at an earlier age, and thus their longer reproductive lives may compensate to some extent for the loss of fitness due to inbreeding depression. Estimates for increases in mortality of the offspring of first-cousin marriages are between 1.0 and 6.4%. This is a substantial increase, especially in the context of a developed country, but as Bittles and colleagues point out, in a traditional setting with a high load of infectious and nutritional disease, the relative cost would not be as great, at least in the short term.

It is important to remember that only a very small proportion of all human births are the result of matings between first-degree relatives. Sexual contact between close relatives is rare, and the proportion of those contacts in which pregnancy could occur (in which both parties are sexually mature and sexual intercourse takes place) is also very small (Van den Berghe, 1983). Across the world's cultures, 2 to 3% allow matings between first-degree relatives, but this is usually only among elites, and it has the primary goal of consolidating resources or political power.

Inbreeding Avoidance and Incest Rules   All human cultures have rules and traditions that regulate sexual contact and reproductive relationships. **Incest** is any violation of such rules by members of a kin group. *Incest rules* are sometimes explicit (stated in legal or customary form) and sometimes implicit (followed but

inbreeding depression   Lesser fitness of offspring of closely related individuals compared with the fitness of the offspring of less closely related individuals, caused largely by the expression of lethal or debilitating recessive alleles.

incest   A violation of cultural rules regulating mating behavior.

not overtly stated or codified). Definitions of kin vary from culture to culture and do not always closely follow biological patterns of relatedness. For example, in American culture, sexual contact between stepparents and stepchildren is generally regarded as being incestuous, although from a biological standpoint a pregnancy that resulted from such a mating would not constitute inbreeding.

Both cultural and biological scientists agree on the universality of cultural rules governing sexual relations between close kin—the *incest taboo*—but they differ on why it exists. For many years, Freudian ideas dominated cultural explanations of the incest taboo: Incest rules were necessary to prevent people from acting on their "natural" desire to commit incest. The evidence that people innately desire to commit incest is very slight, and the Freudian viewpoint, despite its historical popularity, has little cross-cultural, empirical support (Thornhill, 1991). Biological theories of inbreeding avoidance have focused on the fact that mechanisms that encourage outbreeding should be selected for; the cross-cultural universality of the incest taboo, which is essentially a mechanism for outbreeding, is taken to be evidence that such an adaptive mechanism may be present in the human species as a whole.

A basic social science criticism of the biological evolutionary view of inbreeding avoidance asks, Why do cultures make laws against it? If it is biological, the argument goes, then there should be no need to have cultural laws or institutions to prevent it. Nancy Thornhill's (1991) analysis of incest rules suggests that most of them are more concerned with regulating sexual (and economic and power) relationships between more distantly related kin; incest taboos among close relatives are more likely to be implicit than explicit. Thus the assumption that most cultures regulate inbreeding between close relatives using explicit cultural rules is unfounded.

Brother–Sister Inbreeding and the Westermarck Hypothesis   Finnish anthropologist Edvard Westermarck (1891) long ago suggested, in what became known as the *Westermarck hypothesis,* that siblings raised together develop an aversion to seeing each other as reproductive partners when they are adults. In order for the aversion to develop, siblings must be in proximity to one another during a *critical period,* usually thought to encompass the first 5 years of life. The psychological mechanism governing this aversion may be an adaptation because it was probably selected for as a mechanism to promote outbreeding.

Evidence for the Westermarck hypothesis comes from a variety of sources, including some natural experiments. In the mid-twentieth century, the *kibbutz* movement in Israel led to the establishment of numerous small, independent communities dedicated to socialist and egalitarian principles. Similarly aged boys and girls were raised communally in "children's houses" in some of these kibbutzim (Shepher, 1983) (Figure 17.11). In his groundbreaking study, anthropologist Joseph Shepher found that of 2,769 marriages between children raised in kibbutzim, only 14 united couples who had been reared in the same children's house. Shepher interpreted these results as strong evidence for the Westermarck hypothesis. The child-rearing arrangement in the kibbutz "fooled" biology (and the psychological mechanism leading to sexual aversion) by bringing unrelated children into close proximity with one another during the critical period. In usual circumstances, children raised in close proximity to one another are close relatives, and there should be strong selection pressures against them mating with one another. Thus kibbutz children raised in the same children's house saw each other as siblings and did not see their housemates as potential spouses.

Similar evidence supporting the Westermarck hypothesis has been obtained from the study of *sim-pua* marriages in Taiwan (Wolf, 1966, 1970). Sim-pua is a form of arranged marriage whereby a girl is adopted into a household at a young age and then later expected to marry a biological son of the same family when they are older. These marriages were found to have much higher rates of divorce and lower numbers of offspring than non–sim-pua marriages. Anthropologist

FIGURE 17.11   Children in a kibbutz.

Arthur Wolf, who conducted the research, suggests that these marriages often failed because of a sexual aversion that developed between the adopted sister and her brother/groom who were raised in close proximity during the critical period.

The Westermarck hypothesis is supported by evidence from these diverse natural experiments and is based on a strong theoretical foundation in the context of the biological costs of close inbreeding. It applies only to sibling inbreeding avoidance, of course. Clearly, different biological or cultural mechanisms would have to regulate intergenerational inbreeding avoidance.

Language-Related Cross-Cultural Behaviors

In Chapter 15 we discussed the evolution of language, a behavior (in a very large sense) that almost all scientists agree is a biological universal in our species. It is not surprising that something as pervasive and essential as language has multiple effects on several aspects of human behavior (see Insights and Advances: Reading, Writing, and Evolution on page 511). Many anthropologists believe that language is what makes human culture possible. Indeed, when we look at the central place of language in defining a specific culture, we could argue that cultural diversity is inevitable given that languages themselves evolve and diverge. And yet, even beyond the basic biology and structure of language, cross-cultural patterns emerge that we can best explain from a broader evolutionary perspective.

MOTHERESE OR INFANT-DIRECTED SPEECH

Human infants are remarkably proficient at acquiring language. If they are placed in an environment where language is used, they will pass through a series of stages that, typically by the age of 3 years, result in a fully linguistically competent human being (Pinker, 1994). *Language development* entails training of both the mind and the body: the body to produce sounds and the mind to put them in the correct order to produce language. A critical stage in language development in babies is *babbling*. Starting at about 7 to 8 months of age, babies start to say syllables such as *ba-ba* or *da-da*. This is the beginning of the production of spoken language. Even babies who are born deaf babble with their hands as they learn sign language (Petitto & Marentette, 1991) (Figure 17.12).

The stages of language development that babies go through form a kind of cross-cultural behavioral universal. But language development is so clearly biologically hardwired, and babies have so little cultural exposure, that it does not make much sense to think of it in terms of cross-cultural universals. In contrast, the way adults talk to babies seems to be much more of a culturally influenced behavior.

As we look at how adults talk to babies in different cultures with very different languages, we find striking similarities in their use of **motherese** or **infant-directed speech** (Ferguson, 1964; Fernald et al., 1989). Compared with adult-directed speech, speech directed at infants tends to be slower, higher-pitched, and more repetitive, with shorter utterances and longer pauses. Most of us are familiar with what "baby-talk" sounds like; it tends to sound the same in a wide variety of languages (Figure 17.13 on page 510). In fact, one study has shown that native English-speaking mothers could differentiate between adult- and infant-directed Hindi language song excerpts with much greater success than chance suggests (Trehub et al., 1993).

Although motherese is not universal, it is widespread and found in diverse cultures that do not share a recent common origin. One idea about motherese is that it is not directly related to teaching language but instead strengthens the emotional bond between mother and infant (Fernald, 1992). Compared with adult-directed speech, infant-directed speech is less emotionally inhibited; more emotional forms of adult-directed speech more closely resemble infant-directed

motherese (infant-directed speech) Emotive spoken language used by mothers and other adults when addressing prelinguistic babies and children.

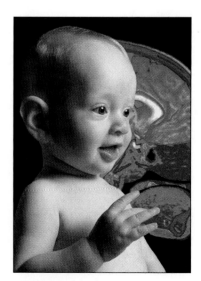

FIGURE 17.12 A deaf baby attempting to sign.

FIGURE 17.13 Motherese may be just one of many ways the emotional bond between mother and child is reinforced.

speech (Trainor et al., 2000). There can be no doubt that babies do not understand the words in baby talk, but it clearly provokes some response or adults would not persist with it. Anne Fernald argues that motherese helps establish emotional communication between the mother and infant before the development of verbal language. As we learned in Chapter 7, the mother–infant relationship is the fundamental relationship in primate societies, and it is based in part on the development of a strong emotional bond between mother and child. Motherese may serve as an adaptation to facilitate the emotional development of the mother–infant bond, which is expressed through the mother's spoken language.

BASIC COLOR TERMS

A trip to the paint store or a glance at a large box of crayons could lead you to believe that there is an almost unlimited number of color names. But if we look beyond the "peach parfaits" and "iceberg whites" of the world, we see that we can limit the number of *basic color terms* to a much smaller number. Anthropological linguists Brent Berlin and Paul Kay published a groundbreaking study in 1969 in which they analyzed color terms used by native informants speaking a wide range of languages and found significant constraints on the ways in which languages identify color. Color term data on more than 100 languages are now available (Kay & Berlin, 1997).

Berlin and Kay defined basic color terms as single words used to describe colors that can be applied to a wide range of objects, that are widely known within a culture, and that are not subsumed into a more inclusive color category (for example, *green* is a basic color term but *lime* is not). Berlin and Kay did not find that the actual words used to describe colors are similar cross-culturally; rather, the naming of colors appears to follow a systematic and perhaps evolved pattern. In cultures that identify only two *focal colors*, or colors that exemplify the basic color categories, these always correspond to black and white (light and dark). In cultures that have three color terms, the named colors are always black, white, and red. In cultures with four terms, the colors are black, white, red, and blue/green/yellow. Above four color terms, patterns are still evident, although they are more variable and complex. The cross-cultural distribution of color terms suggests a cultural evolutionary scenario for developing color terms: The black-versus-white distinction came first, followed by the addition of red and then other colors.

The ancient Greeks believed that the eye emits invisible particles that gives objects their colors. This is not so far off the mark—the colors we perceive are produced by the brain.

INSIGHTS AND ADVANCES

Reading, Writing, and Evolution

Reading and writing are *not* human cross-cultural universals. After all, most traditional cultures do not or did not have writing systems. The invention of writing, which has occurred several times in diverse locations, is recent; even the oldest writing systems are only a few thousand years old. We did not evolve to read and write, although it is quite clear that almost all people, no matter what their particular cultural or biological heritage, are capable of learning these skills.

The ability to learn to read is clearly part of our shared biological heritage, even if it is not a biologically evolved behavior. Neuroscientist Stanislas Dehaene (2003) believes that although our brains have not been shaped by evolution specifically to read, our brains have shaped the writing systems that cultures develop: "I suggest that writing systems themselves were subjected to selective pressure and had to evolve within constraints fixed by our primate visual system" (p. 33).

Dehaene points out that our brains are truly adept at reading. For example, we recognize that EVOLUTION, *evolution,* evolution, eVoLuTiOn, and evolution are all the same word, despite their varied appearances. On the other hand, we also easily recognize that subtle differences, such as that between "but" and "butt," can signal profound differences in meaning. Of course, reading piggybacks on spoken language, whose neural basis has been shaped by natural selection. Neuroimaging research by

Dehaene and his colleagues (Dehaene et al., 1997; Dehaene, 2003) indicates that many parts of our brain are activated by reading. However, a part of the cortex of the left temporal lobe, located near the boundary of the occipital lobe, is invariably activated during reading in all individuals. Furthermore, no matter what the language, whether it uses an alphabet-based writing system, as in English, or a character-based system, such as Japanese Kanji, activation in this region occurs not only during the reading of actual words but also during the recognition of wordlike sequences of letters. As children learn to read, activation in this region increases, whereas adults with *dyslexia* show reduced levels of activation.

In primates, this "reading region" is devoted almost exclusively to visual recognition, especially of complex visual forms. Although part of the temporal lobe, the region is located close to the occipital lobe, which is concerned primarily with visual processing. In humans, the reading region seems to be adapted primarily to identifying objects based on their shape, no matter what their size or orientation (Dehaene, 2003). For example, even without specific training, it is not hard to recognize letters that are upside down (a skill many of us discover while sitting across the desk of a supervisor). Children often have difficulty distinguishing the letters *p, q, d,* and *b.* Given that the reading region may be concerned primarily with shape, this is not too surprising. All these letters have the same

shape, varying only in their orientation in space. The development of reading behavior specifically entails training and refining the shape recognition ability associated with this small part of the temporal lobe. It is interesting that this region is not a classic spoken language area, although the left lateralization of activation follows the spoken language pattern.

Dehaene proposes that our brain biology constrains the cultural expression of human writing systems and that it should be possible to identify features common to all writing systems (Figure A). Although written Chinese and English are profoundly different in some ways, from a neurobiological perspective they obviously share some basic similarities as well.

FIGURE A   Chinese characters.

English has eleven focal colors: black, white, red, yellow, green, blue, brown, purple, pink, orange, and gray. In contrast, the Dani of New Guinea recognize only two colors: *mola* for bright, warm colors and *mili* for dark colors (Figure 17.14 on page 512). Although these are the only two color terms that the Dani use, the color terms themselves do not constrain the Dani perception of the variety of colors in the world. In a series of studies, psychologist Eleanor Rosch (Heider)

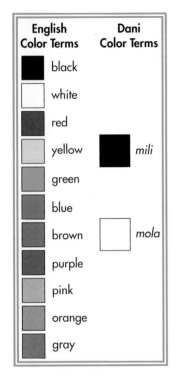

English Color Terms	Dani Color Terms
black	
white	
red	
yellow	*mili*
green	
blue	
brown	*mola*
purple	
pink	
orange	
gray	

FIGURE 17.14 English and Dani basic color terms.

FIGURE 17.15 A Yoruban with a psychotic disorder.

found that Dani people have no trouble remembering or differentiating between colors or hues for which they have no name (Heider, 1972).

Color naming patterns probably are constrained by factors related to the physiology of color vision and perception, although there is much debate about how the physiology of color vision is converted into the psychology of color naming (Dedrick, 1996). Color vision is extremely important to anthropoid primates, including human beings, and our color vision system reflects a long evolutionary history; it comes as no surprise that cultural color naming behaviors might be strongly influenced by this adaptation to the environment. Since 1969, a vast amount of research has been done on color naming, and the cross-cultural sequence of acquiring color terms probably is more complicated than outlined above especially as we get beyond four color terms. Nonetheless, given the infinite number of colors and names that human perception and language could generate, there can be little doubt that this cultural behavior is constrained by some aspect of our perceptual biology.

Behavioral Disease

Anthropologists and psychiatrists once thought mental illnesses and behavioral diseases were limited to "civilized" cultures (Allen, 1997). However, studies of the cross-cultural distribution of mental illness show that many behavioral diseases are expressed in much the same way in different cultures (Murphy, 1976) (Figure 17.15). In modern biological psychiatry, we consider mental illnesses to result primarily from the interaction of genetic predispositions and environmental factors. Because many genetically influenced behavioral disorders are common, and we cannot explain their prevalence by mutation rate or environmental factors alone, it is reasonable to explore the evolutionary factors that may underlie their distribution. Note that this does *not* mean we should necessarily consider the behavioral diseases themselves to be adaptive, but rather that we may better understand them in the context of behavioral phenotypes shaped by natural selection.

DEPRESSION AND NATURAL SELECTION

Psychiatrists define *mood* as a persistent emotional state. Over the course of a lifetime, all people go through periods of high or low mood. Changes in mood in response to the environment or particular events are only natural. For example, low mood, or *minor depression,* is a perfectly reasonable response to an unhappy event, such as the death of a loved one. On the other hand, when depression gets out of hand and strongly affects a person's ability to function or care for himself or herself, then it is clearly not an adaptive behavioral phenotype. Psychiatrists say that a person has *major depression* if he or she suffers from 2 or more weeks of depressed mood or impaired enjoyment, disturbed sleep and appetite, psychomotor changes (such as restlessness or feeling slowed down), reduced concentration, excessive guilt, or suicidal thoughts or actions (American Psychiatric Association, 1994). Major depression is surprisingly common, with about 16.2% of Americans suffering from it at some point in their lives (Kessler et al., 2003).

Why is major depression so common? In its severe form, depression is clearly not adaptive because it not only leads to increased mortality via suicide but also diminishes a person's ability to respond to all kinds of environmental and social stimuli. The genetics underlying mood are undoubtedly complex, but many studies have shown that there is a genetic component to developing major depression, and two specific alleles have been identified

(Caspi et al., 2003; Zubenko et al., 2002). The alleles that cause some people to become clinically depressed have an additive effect, exacerbating a normal tendency toward developing (minor) depression that all people share. It is likely that, as with other phenotypes influenced by multiple genes (such as stature), there is a normal distribution in the expression of mood, with people at one extreme suffering from major depression.

Minor Depression as an Adaptation   Evolutionary psychiatrist Randolph Nesse (2000) suggests that, in general, minor depression, or low mood, is a psychological and physiological mechanism that regulates our behavior when we are placed in any situation that might constitute an adaptive challenge. Minor depression is common because decreased motivation or activity is beneficial in many situations. For example, over the course of hominid evolution, the loss of a loved one probably signaled a number of things: a dangerous situation, loss of information, loss of a contributing member to the community or family, and loss of future contributors to the community (in the case of children)(Figure 17.16). Whatever the particular situation, temporary low mood would encourage the surviving individuals to disengage from activity in the short term, allowing them to establish new goals and directions.

Major depression is increasing in developed countries and becoming a larger health problem. Why? Nesse suggests that another possible adaptive function of low mood is to dissuade people from wasting energy in the pursuit of unreachable goals. Most people living in hierarchical societies (in which resources and power are not distributed equally) face an ongoing conflict between their knowledge of a more prosperous life and their inability to achieve it. According to Nesse, the contemporary media culture exacerbates this conflict by presenting a range of unachievable goals while promoting the pursuit of such goals as a cultural ideal.

In the environments in which it evolved, low mood is a short-term adaptation to a transient challenge; once the challenge or event is over, mood improves. However, in contemporary urbanized societies, people live in an environment in which challenges to status or goal achievement are ongoing, encouraging the development of persistent low mood. This persistent low mood can slip into major depression in genetically susceptible individuals.

Of course, Nesse's hypothesis on the adaptive nature of depression is speculative. However, we know that mood is important in all social primates: Whether or not we want to say they are "happy" or "sad," it is clear that we can see social primates exhibiting high or low mood (see Chapter 7). Mood has been shaped by millions of years of evolution in a social context. Thus sociocultural factors, such as the development of a media culture, may indeed be playing a role in the expression of mood and the increased development of major depression.

 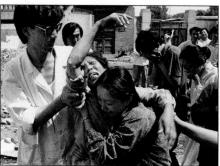 

FIGURE 17.16   Grieving behavior can have common expressions in different cultures.

SCHIZOPHRENIA

Schizophrenia is the chronic brain disease most typically associated with cultural notions of "crazy" behavior or "insanity." It is found in almost all human cultures, with a lifetime prevalence typically estimated to be somewhere between 0.5% and 1.0% (Jablensky et al., 1992). Although that percentage seems low, it translates into nearly 3 million people with schizophrenia in the United States alone. Schizophrenia is characterized by several symptoms, including delusions (often of a paranoid nature), auditory hallucinations, disorganized speech, grossly disorganized or catatonic behavior, and negative symptoms, which are characterized by emotional flattening, not talking, or not moving (American Psychiatric Association, 1994). Age of onset typically is the late teens into the twenties (usually a bit later in females than males), and the course of illness is highly variable.

Schizophrenia is clearly a genetic disease. Evidence of its origin comes from a variety of sources; among them is the fact that a family history of schizophrenia is associated with a much higher risk of developing the disease. However, concordance rates for identical twins tend to be no higher than 50% (Gottesman & Shields, 1982), indicating that some people carry the alleles that predispose development of schizophrenia but do not develop the illness.

Why Is Schizophrenia So Common?

The basic evolutionary question about schizophrenia is, Why is it so common? The estimated prevalence rate of 1% is much higher than can be maintained via mutation rate alone, whether schizophrenia is caused by the effect of a single major allele or of multiple alleles. In addition, numerous studies conducted over the past century have shown that people with schizophrenia, particularly males, have reduced fertility and fitness (Nimgaonkar et al., 1997). This is not surprising because the disease strikes at an age when people are entering their reproductive years.

Because schizophrenia is associated with reduced fertility and is a genetic condition, the alleles underlying the condition eventually should be eliminated from the population by negative selection. This does not seem to be happening. If anything, over the past 200 years schizophrenia seems to be getting more rather than less common, and it may be more common in large, developed societies than in traditional ones (Allen, 1997). The clinical schizophrenia phenotype itself obviously is not adaptive because it leads to demonstrably reduced fitness. Individuals who carry schizophrenia-causing alleles but who do not develop the disease may have some characteristics that help them to reproductively compensate for the loss of alleles in individuals who have full-blown schizophrenia.

The Schizophrenia Genotype as a Balanced Polymorphism

Since the 1960s, numerous theories have been offered to explain the evolution of schizophrenia (see Polimeni & Reiss, 2003, for a review). Given the reduced fitness of individuals who have schizophrenia and the current understanding of the genetics underlying the condition, it is reasonable to suggest that schizophrenia alleles are being maintained in human populations as a balanced polymorphism. Although some argue that schizophrenia is simply a by-product of human brain evolution, several researchers have looked at the alternative phenotypes associated with the schizophrenia genotype to explain how a small reproductive advantage (on the order of 5% [Kidd, 1975]) in the relatives of schizophrenic patients could maintain the alleles in the population.

The earliest exploration of the evolution of schizophrenia modeled it along the lines of sickle-cell anemia (see Chapter 5), describing it as a balanced polymorphism maintained by heterozygous advantage (Huxley et al., 1964). The problem with this view is that genetic studies show that schizophrenia is not an autosomal recessive illness. Allen and Sarich (1988) suggested that if schizophrenia is a balanced polymorphism, it is maintained in a *frequency-dependent* manner (see Chapter 5). Following from the profound social dysfunction associated with clinical schizophrenia, they suggest that the primary advantage of relatives of schizophrenic patients is asociality. Interactive social groups provide benefits to the individuals that live within them, and the individuals within them must devote time and energy to the maintenance of the social group. Asocial individuals (such as those who carry alleles underlying the development of schizophrenia) may receive the benefits of social group living without investing as much in the maintenance of the group as a whole. Because a social group has only so many asocial roles (and there are more of them in more complex societies), there is a frequency-dependent limit to the spread of schizophrenia genotypes; a social group cannot be maintained if there are too many asocial individuals living in it. Other suggested possible reproductive advantages in relatives of people with schizophrenia include creativity, disease resistance, and pain resistance.

PSYCHOACTIVE SUBSTANCE USE AND ABUSE

The consumption of *psychoactive substances* (drugs) seems to be a cross-cultural human universal, and its history dates back tens of thousands of years. The most commonly consumed psychoactive substances are alcohol, tobacco, betel nut (used throughout south and Southeast Asia and Oceania), opium and its derivatives, coca and cocaine (coca leaves are a mild stimulant when chewed; cocaine is a concentrated form of the active ingredient), cannabis (marijuana), caffeine, and khat (chewed in East Africa) (Smith, 1999; Sullivan & Hagen, 2002) (Figure 17.17). Contemporary psychoactive drugs for the most part appeared with the development of agriculture, starting between 10,000 and 15,000 years ago. Pre-agricultural peoples undoubtedly used available psychoactive substances in plants, although large and steady quantities of such substances did not become available until the development of agriculture (Smith, 1999).

Psychoactive drugs generally work by mimicking the effects of neurotransmitters found in the nervous system or by stimulating the production of neurotransmitters that influence behavior or mood. Biological research on *drug addiction,* or *substance dependence,* indicates that both genetic and environmental factors play key roles in the development of drug dependence. A person with a substance dependence problem exhibits the following: tolerance to the effects of a

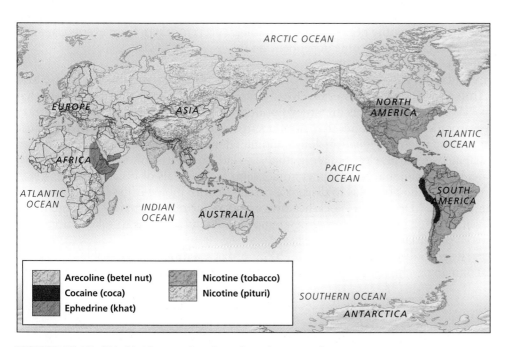

FIGURE 17.17 Worldwide map of traditional psychoactive substance use.

drug, leading to the use of increasing amounts; psychological or physiological withdrawal if the drug is removed, making giving up the drug difficult; and use of the drug despite knowledge of the negative consequences of continued usage.

Genetic Polymorphisms Associated with Psychoactive Substance Dependence

Much biological research on drug dependence has focused on the neurotransmitter *dopamine*. Dopamine is an important component of the pleasure and reward system in the brain. Stimulants, opiates, nicotine, and THC (the active ingredient in marijuana) all affect this neurotransmitter system (Enoch & Goldman, 1999). Kenneth Blum and colleagues (1996) suggest that a whole range of addictive behaviors (including drug addiction, gambling addiction, and so on) may be related to polymorphisms in dopamine receptor genes. Specifically, individuals with severe addiction problems may be much more likely to carry an allele associated with a reduction in the total number of dopamine receptors. These individuals appear to need more of a stimulus (drug or activity) to derive a sense of reward or pleasure. Therefore, they are at higher risk for increased drug usage and ultimately substance dependence. Blum and colleagues call this constellation of behaviors *reward deficiency syndrome*.

In contrast to reward deficiency syndrome, a different polymorphism may make addiction to a specific drug—alcohol—less likely than usual (Enoch & Goldman, 1999). *Ethanol* (the "alcohol" we consume) is metabolized first to acetaldehyde by the enzyme *alcohol dehydrogenase* (ADH) and then to acetate by *aldehyde dehydrogenase* (ALDH). Acetaldehyde is the chemical that produces facial flushing, tachychardia (increased heart rate), and nausea in some people after the consumption of alcohol. In most people acetaldehyde does not accumulate in the body because it is quickly converted to acetate (Figure 17.18). However, alleles found in some East Asian populations lead to a buildup of acetaldehyde in the body, either increasing its rate of synthesis or decreasing its rate of conversion to acetate. For example, an allele *ALDH2*2* (due to a single amino acid substitution in ALDH) is found with a frequency of 35% in the Japanese population. This allele causes a buildup of acetaldehyde in the body, leading to facial flushing and other unpleasant side effects after even modest alcohol consumption. *ALDH2*2* heterozygotes and homozygotes both experience facial flushing; their risk of developing alcoholism is one-tenth to one-fourth that of those who do not possess the allele. No *ALDH2*2* homozygote individual has ever been observed to be an alcoholic, presumably because their physiology prevents them from ever consuming enough alcohol to become dependent on it.

Evolutionary Psychology Theories about Psychoactive Substance Use and Abuse

Randolph Nesse and Kent Berridge (1997) have taken the view that psychoactive substances are an evolutionarily novel feature of the contemporary environment. They argue that psychoactive drug use cannot be adaptive because it so fundamentally disrupts longstanding emotional mechanisms that have been shaped by natural selection. Drugs that simulate positive emotions (heroin, cocaine, alcohol, marijuana, and amphetamine) send false signals of fitness benefit, which in turn has the potential to disrupt a person's entire biological system of "wants" and "likes." Drugs that block negative emotions or reduce anxiety are potentially even more disruptive because they remove the body's signals to take action or to avoid potential threats.

Roger Sullivan and Ed Hagen (2002) provide a different evolutionary analysis of human psychoactive substance use. They argue that hominids have probably had

Both genetic and environmental factors contribute to the development of alcoholism, with children of alcoholics being 4 times more likely than members of the general population to develop the condition.

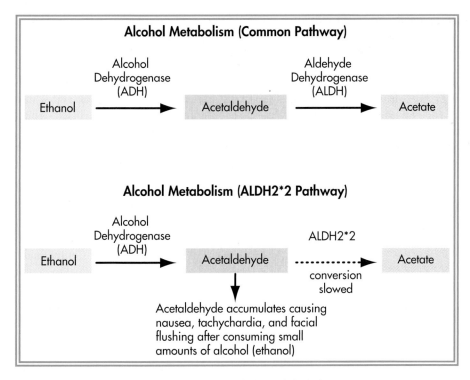

FIGURE 17.18 Genetic variation in the metabolism of alcohol.

a long-term evolutionary relationship with psychoactive substances. With the exception of alcohol, most of the active ingredients of commonly used psychoactive drugs are formed naturally in plants and are similar to neurotransmitters found in the brain. Sullivan and Hagen argue that we benefit from consuming small quantities of these neurotransmitter-like chemicals in the same way that we need to consume small quantities of essential vitamins and minerals. An interesting point raised by Sullivan and Hagen is that in many traditional cultures, no distinction is made between drugs and food. People consume "food" for sustenance and to have more energy; for example, some traditional cultures classify tobacco as a food. Much psychoactive substance use in traditional cultures is associated not with developing a hedonic rush ("getting high") but with gaining increased stamina in a marginal environment (such as the Australian desert or Andean mountains). Even today, nonhedonic substances constitute most drug consumption (caffeine, nicotine, arecoline in betel nuts). Sullivan and Hagen hypothesize that psychoactive drug use in past environments could have been adaptive (providing increased stamina and neurotransmitters), although it may not be so in contemporary environments, which are characterized by easy access to both food and psychoactive substances.

Human behavior is remarkably diverse. An evolutionary perspective is one of many complementary ways to understand why people do what they do. It is not sufficient on its own to serve as a comprehensive explanation for human behavior, but millions of years of evolution have shaped our behavior in ways both subtle and profound. The evolution of human behavior is a relatively new academic field, so there is still much work to be done on this intriguing topic.

SUMMARY

1. **What are four approaches to understanding the evolution of human behavior?**

   The four approaches are palaeontological reconstructions of behavior, evolutionary psychology, biocultural anthropology, and human evolutionary (or behavior) ecology. All approaches are interested in understanding human behavior in an evolutionary context, although they differ in the kinds of data they use and the methods they use to collect those data.

2. **How are human evolutionary ecologists similar and dissimilar to traditional cultural anthropologists?**

   Traditional cultural anthropologists and human evolutionary ecologists both typically engage in intensive fieldwork conducted in traditional and nontraditional communities. Human evolutionary ecologists tend to be more quantitative than cultural anthropologists and focus on collecting data on population structure, reproductive factors, energetic expenditure, and nutrition, which can be used to test evolutionary and ecological hypotheses.

3. **What is the sexual division of labor? In what ways is it manifest in traditional cultures around the world?**

   In the older anthropological literature, the sexual division of labor is characterized by men being hunters and women being gatherers. More recent formulations suggest that men focus on collecting "large package" foodstuffs (such as big game) and women on "small package" items (which include plant material or small game). These differences are manifest in different cultural and ecological environments.

4. **Why are young males deemed risk-takers by researchers interested in the evolution of behavior?**

   Young males (15–30 years of age) have higher accident rates and engage in more apparently antisocial and aggressive behavior than any other sex-age group. This can be understood in terms of sexual selection theory, in which young males who take large risks may ultimately derive from them large reproductive advantages. Although this is not true in contemporary societies, the risk-taking behaviors are still manifest in young males trying to establish themselves in society as a whole.

5. **How does the Westermarck hypothesis explain the rarity of sibling inbreeding in cultures around the world?**

   The Westermarck hypothesis explains the rarity of offspring produced through sibling matings by suggesting that a developmental psychological mechanism exists whereby young children raised in proximity to one another (who would typically be closely related) grow up to not consider each other as potential reproductive partners. The aversion to mating develops only if the children are raised together during a critical period in the first several years of life.

6. **What is the empirical evidence underlying the claim that there are biological constraints on naming color terms?**

   Across a wide range of cultures, if a culture has only two basic color terms, they correspond to black and white. If there are three color terms, then they are black, white, and red. The fourth color term added is blue/green/yellow. The cultural convergence in basic color terms may result from the physiology of color perception in humans.

7. **In what ways might minor depression be considered an adaptation? How are major and minor depression different?**

   Minor depression, or low mood, is a normal response to a variety of events that occur in the lives of individuals. It may be adaptive in that it causes an individual to inhibit his or her actions at a time when low activity may be temporarily beneficial. Low mood prevents individuals from pursuing unrealistic goals and wasting energy. Persistent low mood, or major depression, is not adaptive because it leads not only to increased rates of suicide but also to other behavioral patterns that increase mortality.

8. **Why is it argued that schizophrenia is a phenotype maintained by a balanced polymorphism?**

   Schizophrenia is a genetically influenced brain disease, and as a group, people with schizophrenia have lower fitness than other members of the population. The prevalence of schizophrenia (approximately 1%) remains high compared with the mutation rate. Thus schizophrenia is not being selected out of human populations, despite being a genetic condition with low fitness. This indicates that it is being maintained as a balanced polymorphism through the enhanced fitness of nonschizophrenic carriers of schizophrenia alleles.

9. **Give two examples that illustrate how people vary biologically in their responses to psychoactive substances. How do these relate to the tendency to develop substance dependence?**

   Some individuals have alleles that cause them to have fewer receptors for the neurotransmitter dopamine, which is important in the brain's reward system. These individuals appear to need a greater amount of a stimulant (such as drugs or gambling) before they derive a sense of reward from the substance or activity. This predisposes them to developing addictive behaviors and substance dependence. In contrast, individuals who possess the *ALDH2*2* allele for alcohol metabolism rarely develop alcoholism. The reason is that this allele leads to the buildup of acetaldehyde in the body after the consumption of even limited amounts of alcohol. Acetaldehyde is a toxic substance that can cause facial flushing, rapid heart rate, and nausea. Individuals with the *ALDH2*2* allele do not become alcoholics because they cannot consume enough alcohol to become dependent on it.

CRITICAL THINKING QUESTIONS

1. Why is it necessary to approach the evolution of human behavior from diverse viewpoints?

2. Defend or critique the following statement: Human psychoactive substance use is an adaptive behavior in many environments.

3. Human evolutionary ecologists uncover many cultural patterns of behavior that make sense in light of evolutionary theory. What does this say about the motivations of individuals living in human societies? Should we regard people in general as operating as "fitness maximizers" no matter what they are doing?

4. How should society deal with young male risk-takers? Does the evolutionary perspective help us understand and deal with the antisocial or unduly aggressive behavior of some young adult males? Can increases in the aggressive or antisocial behavior of young females be explained in an evolutionary context?

5. Drawing on what you have learned while reading this textbook, can you think of any areas in which understanding the evolutionary history of our species could directly lead to a betterment of the contemporary human condition?

KEY TERMS

sociobiology
evolutionary psychology
environment of
   evolutionary
   adaptedness (EEA)

human evolutionary
   ecology
cognitive universals
cross-cultural universals
bridewealth

progesterone
testosterone
inbreeding depression
incest

motherese
   (infant-directed
   speech)

SUGGESTED READING

Alcock, J. (2001). *The Triumph of Sociobiology.* Oxford University Press, New York.

Allman, W. F. (1995). *The Stone Age Present.* Touchstone, New York.

Barkow, J. H., Tooby J., and Cosmides, L. (1992). *The Adapted Mind.* Oxford University Press, New York.

Barrett, L., Dunbar, R., and Lycett, J. (2002). *Human Evolutionary Psychology.* Princeton University Press, Princeton, NJ.

Betzig, L. (Editor). (1997). *Human Nature: A Critical Reader.* Oxford University Press, New York.

Fox, R. (1983). *The Red Lamp of Incest.* University of Notre Dame Press, Notre Dame, Indiana.

Low, Bobbi S. (1999). *Why Sex Matters.* Princeton University Press, Princeton, NJ.

CHAPTER 18 Bioarchaeology and Forensic Anthropology

n Ekaterinburg, on the night of July 16–17, 1918, Tsar Nicholas II, the last of the Romanovs, was summoned downstairs with his whole family. . . .

Near midnight a decree of execution was read out to the amazed royal family and their servants: Tsar Nicholas; Alexandra; their frail hemophiliac son Alexei; their four daughters, Olga, Tatiana, Marie, and Anastasia; the family doctor, Sergei Botkin; a cook named Kharitonov; a footman named Trupp; and a maid named Anna Demidova— eleven people in all. . . .

Twenty minutes later the corpses were carried out into the summer night, where they vanished, seemingly forever. . . .

Now, unexpectedly, from a bog on the outskirts of Ekaterinburg nine more or less complete skeletons had come to light in a shallow grave, along with fourteen bullets, bits of rope, and a shattered jar that once contained sulfuric acid. Could these be the remains of the Romanovs? . . .

The nine skeletons were identified only by number. Five were female, four male. Of the five females, three were young women, only recently grown to maturity. All the faces were badly fractured, every single one. This fact made reconstruction of facial features risky or impossible, but also conformed to the accounts of the assassinations: that the faces of the victims were smashed in with rifle butts to render them unrecognizable . . . .

All of the female skeletons had dental work. None of the males did, though we knew from historical records that Dr. Botkin had a denture plate in his upper jaw . . . . Sure enough, one of the males had a few teeth in his lower jaw, no teeth at all in his upper jaw, and probably wore false teeth in life . . . .

There is one skeleton to fit everyone known to be in the party, with the exception of the Tsarevich Alexei and Anastasia, who are missing . . . .

When we compare these ages and the other things we know of the royal family and their entourage with the evidence of the skeletons, everything aligns nicely. Demidova's skeleton is of the right age and sex. Botkin's skeleton has the right forehead, the right age, the right sex, the right dental information.

The three young women's skeletons, as well as that of the oldest woman, have features in common that are often seen in families, suggesting they were related . . . . The oldest woman has the exceptionally rich dental work which is confirmed from numerous mentions in Alexandra's diaries . . . .

DNA tests carried out in Great Britain matched a blood sample from the British royal family with that recovered from the Russian skeletons, with a 98.5 percent degree of certainty . . . .

Taken in conjunction with the compelling physical skeletal evidence, the results are clear and unequivocal . . . . [W]e may say that the mystery of the Romanovs is solved . . . .

—from *Dead Men Do Tell Tales,* by W. R. Maples and M. Browning (pp. 238–267)

OUR SKELETON TELLS A TALE ABOUT THE evolution of our species and of the life (and death) of an individual. So far, we have used the skeleton to understand the evolution of our distant ancestors. But skeletal clues can be used, as they were by Bill Maples in the case of the Romanovs, to identify the age and sex of an individual and to understand recent events in his or her life. More recently, additional bones found near those that Maples examined have been identified as belonging to the Tsar's son Alexei and daughter Maria. Because Alexandra, the wife of Tsar Nicholas, was the granddaughter of Queen Victoria of England, mtDNA matches for her and her children could also be made by comparison with the British royal family. In this chapter we consider how two groups of biological anthropologists, bioarchaeologists and forensic anthropologists, use skeletal remains to understand our more recent evolution. We consider the basic methods used by these two disciplines to recover remains and to construct a biological profile of an individual. We look at the special importance of taphonomy for differentiating between events that occurred around the time of death and those that occurred well after death. Then we examine ancillary techniques, such as DNA technology, that each group employs to better answer the question at hand. Finally, we consider the special applications of these disciplines ranging from understanding the origin of agriculture to helping bring war criminals to justice.

Life, Death, and the Skeleton

Bioarchaeologists and forensic anthropologists are specialists in human osteology who use the theory and method of biological anthropology to answer questions about how recent humans lived and died. Bioarchaeologists study skeletal remains from archaeological sites in the Holocene (the last 10,000 years) to reveal the history of human populations and individual humans. Forensic anthropologists study skeletal remains from crime scenes, war zones, and mass disasters within the very recent past to reveal the life history of the individual, to identify that individual, and to understand something about the context in which death occurred. Both specialists rely on the same fundamental core of expertise, osteological identification and archaeological field methods, to retrieve remains from the field and to develop a profile of the age, sex, and other biological attributes of an individual. Because the morphological form of the skeleton of a human or any other animal is dictated mostly by its function in life and its evolutionary history, the bioarchaeologist and forensic anthropologist can reconstruct the probable age, sex, and ancestry of an individual from his or her skeletal remains. They can observe the influence of certain kinds of diseases on the skeleton, and they can assess some aspects of what happened to an individual just before, around the time of, and after his or her death.

Each specialist then combines this fundamental information with other areas of inquiry to understand, for example, population-level biological changes that occurred when societies shifted from hunting and gathering to farming, or the influence of the number of bodies on the rate of decomposition in a mass grave.

bioarchaeologist A biological anthropologist who uses human osteology to explore the biological component of the archaeological record.

Bioarchaeologists take a population perspective combining the biological profiles of a number of individuals to understand patterns of disease and behavior in the past (Larsen, 1999). They pay particular attention to cultural attributes when trying to understand past behavior from the skeleton, combining osteological inquiry with the evaluation of associated archaeological remains that tell them about past cultures. For example, bioarchaeologists might use the age, sex, and distribution of grave goods found with skeletons in a prehistoric cemetery to consider patterns of social stratification in the past. Or they might use the mechanical properties of bone combined with the archaeological indicators that mark a shift from hunting and gathering to farming in order to understand the influence of these changes in activity on the lifeways of the individual.

Forensic anthropologists, on the other hand, use the principles of skeletal biology in legal or criminal investigations. They reconstruct the circumstances not only of homicides but also of accidental deaths, suicides, mass disasters, war crimes, and combat deaths. They might use information from the skeleton to compare with antemortem medical records to make a positive identification of a serviceman missing in action. Or they may examine the physical traces of a knife wound on a dismembered arm or leg bone to identify the type of weapon used. Their work helps bring closure to grieving relatives and bring criminals to justice. Given the nature of their investigations, forensic anthropologists differ from bioarchaeologists in that they work in a more recent context—usually within the last 50 to 100 years—and with a greater primary focus on the individual. But unlike pathologists and medical examiners, forensic anthropologists bring an anthropological perspective and a hard-tissue focus to investigations of skeletal remains. Both bioarchaeologists and forensic anthropologists bring to their work a broad perspective that encompasses natural human variation, human osteology, and natural selection.

Field Recovery Methods

Results of bioarchaeological and forensic investigations rely on good contextual information (Figure 18.1). Things like body position, relationship to nearby items such as bullets or grave goods, and structures near the individual—such as ancient hearths or recent buildings—require precise and thorough documentation in the field. Without such documentation, we would not know if the bullet recovered at the scene was 10 feet from the individual, or within the victim's chest cavity. We would not be able to reconstruct from the bones alone whether the skeleton clutched a decorated scepter, or whether the artifact lay in a pile of items some distance from the individual. These associations are crucial for inferring the meaning of a burial and the circumstances surrounding the death of an individual. So to ensure full recovery and good contextual information from the field, whether it be a crime

FIGURE 18.1 Biological anthropologists map skeletal remains from a prehistoric site.

FIGURE 18.2 The first step in field recovery involves surveying the site, sometimes with special equipment.

datum point A permanent, fixed point relative to which the location of items of interest are recorded during archaeological mapping and excavation.

FIGURE 18.3 Bioarchaeologists and forensic anthropologists use archaeological excavation techniques to recover remains.

scene or a prehistoric site, both specialists rely on archaeological techniques to find, document, and remove remains from the site.

The site might be found in any number of ways. In forensic anthropology, sites are often accidentally encountered by a passerby, during a walk in the woods, for example, or information from an informant who knows of a crime may lead to a site. Because many body dumps are very recent, cadaver dogs may be useful in finding forensic sites. Bioarchaeologists may also encounter sites accidentally, but often the identification of sites is based on a survey of an area of interest, an evaluation of air or satellite photos, or other directed measures. Once identified, the area of interest is cordoned off to limit disturbance.

By whatever means the area of interest is identified, once on site the anthropologist systematically surveys the area for additional remains to determine the scope of the area to be investigated. Such surveys most commonly include visual surveys in which an individual or team of investigators walk a systematic path over an area searching for remains, associated items, or evidence of burial (Figure 18.2). Other noninvasive technology like ground-penetrating radar (GPR) may also be used to identify subsurface structures. In particular instances, GPR can identify possible burials for future excavation, but this equipment is expensive and requires an expert operator.

In the field, any surface discoveries are mapped and photographed. A permanent **datum point** for the site is established that represents a fixed position from which everything is measured so that the precise "find spot" of each object can be relocated in the future. The feature chosen as the datum point could be a piece of metal pipe cemented into the ground by the scientist, or in urban forensic investigations it is often a particular location on a building. Temporary structures, fence posts, and trees are poor datum choices as they are liable to be gone in the future, thwarting attempts to relocate a site.

If the remains are buried, the anthropologist will excavate using archaeological techniques. Forensic investigations require speedy recovery so teams may also use heavy equipment such as backhoes to skim off overlying soil and rocks. The archaeologist sets up a grid system, usually with 1 × 1-meter squares, and plots these relative to the datum. The excavator begins by skimming off shallow layers of dirt using a hand trowel. Objects are revealed in place and their coordinates, including their depth, are recorded relative to the grid system (Figure 18.3), and photographs are taken. Soil and rock samples may be collected to assist in dating of prehistoric remains (see Chapter 8) or the identification of insects and plants in forensic cases. All the dirt that is removed is sieved through fine mesh to ensure even the smallest pieces of bone are recovered (Figure 18.4). In the field, the anthropologist makes a preliminary determination of whether the remains are human or nonhuman (they could be those of a dog or deer, for instance) and, based on the bones, whether more

FIGURE 18.4 After excavation, recovered remains are screened to ensure that even tiny fragments are retrieved and saved.

than one individual is present. Once exposed and mapped, individual bones are tagged, bagged, and listed on a preliminary catalog for removal to the laboratory.

Laboratory Processing, Curation, and Chain of Custody

In the lab more detailed curation and examination can begin. Both bioarchaeologists and forensic anthropologists will start a detailed catalog in order to retain the important contextual pieces of information gained during the field recovery. However, for the forensic anthropologist this log becomes part of an evidence file, and a strict **chain of custody** must be established to ensure that the remains cannot be tampered with, in case they should become evidence in a court of law. Detailed notes are taken to demonstrate that the remains in question are those from the scene and that they have not been contaminated or modified since their removal from the scene. This chain may consist of catalogs and inventories of remains, signed transfers of evidence, and details concerning those who participated in recovery efforts and who had access to the area where remains are stored.

After the remains are cataloged, they are cleaned of any adhering soft tissue and dirt, and then laid out in anatomical position, the way they would have looked in the skeleton in life (Figure 18.5 on page 526). An inventory is made of each bone present and its condition. Most adult humans have 206 bones, many of which are extremely small (see Appendix B). Because most bones develop as several bony centers that fuse together only later in life, fetuses and children contain many more bones than do adults. Often decay of a long-buried body results in the presence of no more than a few bone fragments. The bioarchaeologist and forensic anthropologist therefore must be skilled osteologists who are very familiar with patterns of human variation. Once the initial inventory has been completed, the scientist sets about evaluating the clues that the skeleton reveals about the life and death of the individual. The first step in this process is constructing the biological profile of the individual—including determining age, sex, height, and disease status.

The Biological Profile

Bioarchaeologists and forensic anthropologists both construct **biological profiles**—but for slightly different reasons. The bioarchaeologist is interested in the life of the individual, of course, but also wants to evaluate population-wide response to natural and cultural selective pressures (Larsen, 1999). And except in rare circumstances, the bioarchaeologist cannot make a positive individual identification. On the other hand, the forensic anthropologist seeks to positively identify the victim and any clues that may assist a medical examiner in discerning the cause and manner of his or her death (Snow, 1982). To meet both their goals, the

chain of custody In forensic cases, the detailed notes that establish what was collected at the scene, the whereabouts of these remains, and the access to them after retrieval from the scene.

biological profile The biological particulars of an individual as estimated from their skeletal remains. These include estimates of sex, age at death, height, ancestry, and disease status.

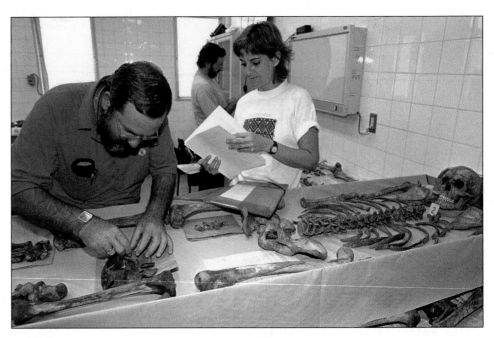

FIGURE 18.5 After skeletal remains are cleaned, they are laid out in anatomical position for inventory.

bioarchaeologist and forensic anthropologist seek information about several features that may be clues to life history and identity.

AGE AT DEATH

As the human body develops, from fetus to old age, dramatic changes occur throughout the skeleton (Figure, 18.6). Scientists use the more systematic of these changes to estimate the age at death of an individual. However, whenever scientists determine age, they always report it as a range (such as 35–45 years) rather than as a single definitive number. This range reflects the variation in growth and aging seen in individuals and across human populations and denotes the person's biological rather than chronological age (age in years). The goal is that the range also encompasses the person's actual age at the time of their death.

Because the skeleton grows rapidly during childhood, assessing the age of a subadult younger than about 18 years of age is easier and often more precise than estimating the age of an adult skeleton. Virtually all skeletal systems except the small bones of the ear (the ear ossicles) change from newborn to adult. For example, in small children the degree of closure of the cranial bones (covering the fontanelles, or "soft spots" of the skull) changes with age, as does the development of the temporal bone, the size and shape of the wrist bones, and virtually every other bone. However, dental eruption and the growth of long bones are the most frequently used means of assessing subadult age.

Humans have two sets of teeth of different sizes that erupt at fairly predictable intervals. Which teeth are present can help distinguish between children of different ages and between older subadults and adults of the same size (Figure 18.7). For more precise ages, the relative development of the tooth roots can also be used. However, once most of the adult teeth have erupted, by about the age of 12 years in humans, the teeth are no longer as good a guide to predicting age.

In these older children, growth of the limb bones can also be used to assess age. The long bones of the arms and legs have characteristic bony growths at each end—the epiphyses—which are present as separate bones while the person is still

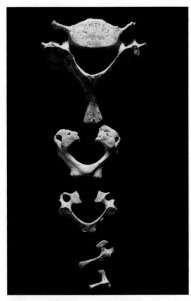

FIGURE 18.6 Bones change radically in size and shape from newborn to adult, as these cervical vertebrae demonstrate.

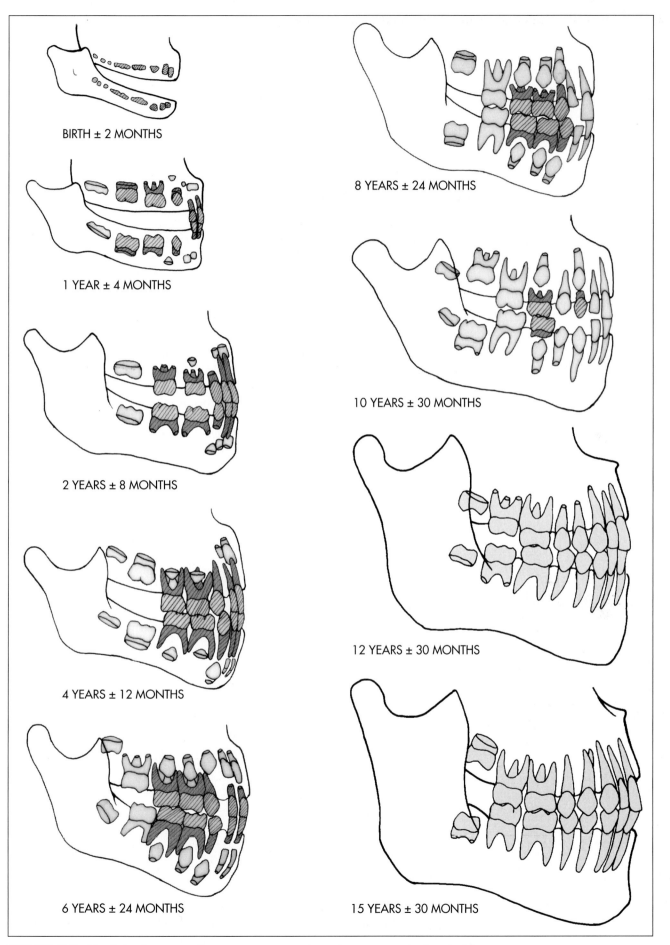

BIRTH ± 2 MONTHS

1 YEAR ± 4 MONTHS

2 YEARS ± 8 MONTHS

4 YEARS ± 12 MONTHS

6 YEARS ± 24 MONTHS

8 YEARS ± 24 MONTHS

10 YEARS ± 30 MONTHS

12 YEARS ± 30 MONTHS

15 YEARS ± 30 MONTHS

FIGURE 18.7 Tooth development and eruption are commonly used to assess age in the subadult skeleton. Deciduous (baby) teeth are indicated by hatching and shades of brown.

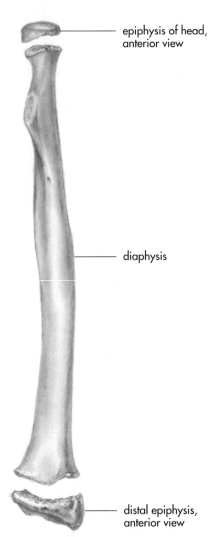

epiphysis of head, anterior view

diaphysis

distal epiphysis, anterior view

FIGURE 18.8 Long bones develop from several bony centers—one for the shaft and at least one for each end. The end caps are known as epiphyses.

growing rapidly (Figure 18.8). Most epiphyses are not present at birth—which helps to separate fetuses from newborns—but appear during infancy and childhood. The lengths and proportions of bones change in predictable ways as children grow and are especially good indicators for assessing fetal age (Sherwood et al., 2000). In older children, the epiphyses start to fuse to the shafts of the limb bones around the age of 10 in some bones, and fusion of most epiphyses is completed in the late teenage years. However, the process of fusion may occur as late as the early 20s in a few bones (such as the clavicle). Depending upon which bones and which parts of those bones are fused, a reasonably good estimate of subadult age can be made.

In adults, age is harder to determine because growth is essentially complete. Some of the last epiphyses to fuse, such as the clavicle and top of the ilium, can be used to estimate age in young adults in their early 20s. But estimating the age of the older adult skeleton relies mostly on degeneration of parts of the skeleton. For example, the pubic symphysis and auricular surface of the innominate, and the end of the fourth rib near the sternum all show predictable changes with age (Todd, 1920, 1921; McKern & Stewart, 1957; Iscan et al., 1984; Lovejoy et al., 1985). Examination of as many of these bones as possible helps to increase age accuracy (Bedford et al., 1993). The pubic symphysis is a particularly useful indicator of adult age, and age standards have been developed separately for males and females (Gilbert & McKern, 1973; Katz & Suchey, 1986; Brooks & Suchey, 1990). The standards show how the symphysis develops from cleanly furrowed to more granular and degenerated over time (Figure 18.9). These changes tend to occur more quickly in females than in males due to the trauma the symphysis experiences during childbirth.

The degree of obliteration of cranial sutures (the junction of the different skull bones) can also give a relative sense of age—obliteration tends to occur in older individuals (Lovejoy & Meindl, 1985). The antero–lateral sutures of the skull are

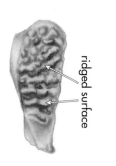

ridged surface

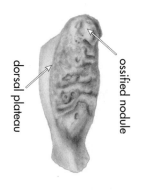

dorsal plateau

ossified nodule

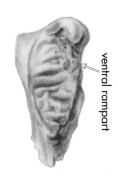

ventral rampart

PHASE 1: 15 to 23 YEARS   PHASE 2: 19 to 35 YEARS   PHASE 3: 22 to 43 YEARS

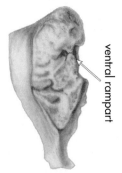

ventral rampart

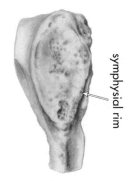

symphysial rim

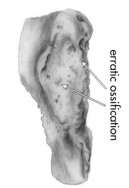

erratic ossification

PHASE 4: 23 to 59 YEARS   PHASE 5: 28 to 78 YEARS   PHASE 6: 36 to 87 YEARS

FIGURE 18.9 The pubic symphysis of the pelvis is useful for estimating age in the adult skeleton.

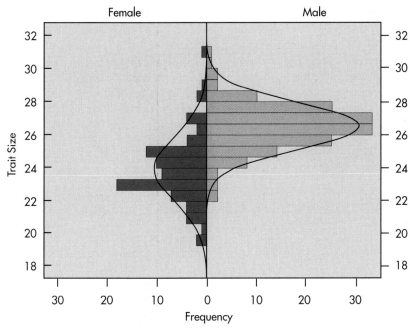

FIGURE 18.10 Although males tend to be larger than females, the two overlap significantly in size. The size of a bone alone cannot be used to assess sex.

the best for these purposes. However, the correlation between degree of obliteration and age is not very close, and the age ranges that can be estimated are wide.

SEX

If certain parts of the skeleton are preserved, identifying biological sex is easier than estimating age at death, at least for adults. The two parts of the skeleton that most readily reveal sex are the pelvis and the skull, and sex characteristics are more prominent in an adult skeleton than in a child. Humans are moderately sexually dimorphic, with males being larger on average than females. But their ranges of variation overlap so that size alone cannot separate male and female humans (Figure 18.10).

The best skeletal indicator of sex is the pelvis. Because of selective pressures for bipedality and childbirth, human females have evolved pelves that provide a relatively large birth canal (see Chapter 10). This affects the shape of the innominate and sacrum in females; the pubis is longer, the sacrum is broader and shorter, and the sciatic notch of the ilium is broader in females than in males (Figure 18.11 on page 530). The method is highly accurate (Rogers & Saunders, 1993) because the pelvis reflects directly the different selective pressures that act on male versus female bipeds. Thus the pelvis is considered a primary indicator of the sex of the individual. And because the femur has to angle inward from this wider female pelvis to the knee (to keep the biped's foot under its center of gravity; see Chapter 10), the size and shape of the femur also differentiate males and females fairly well (Porter, 1995).

The skull is also a useful indicator of sex, at least in adults. Around puberty, circulating hormones lead to so-called secondary sex characters such as distribution of body and facial hair. During this time male and female skulls also diverge in shape. Male skulls are more robust on average than female skulls of the same population. However, these differences are relative and population dependent; some human populations are more gracile than others. The mastoid process of the temporal bone and the muscle markings of the occipital bone tend to be larger in males than in females, and the chin is squarer in males than in females (Figure 18.11). The browridge is less robust and the orbital rim is sharper in females than in males, and the female frontal (forehead) is more vertical. These differences form a

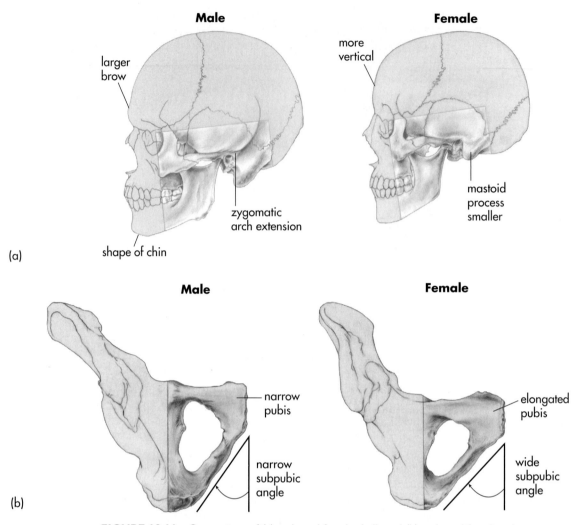

FIGURE 18.11   Comparison of (a) male and female skulls and (b) male and female pelves.

continuum and provide successful sex estimates in perhaps 80 to 85% of cases when the population is known.

ANCESTRY

Knowing the ancestry of an individual skeleton is important for improving the accuracy of sex, age, and stature estimates. There is no biological reality to the idea of fixed biological races in humans (see Chapter 5), but we have learned that the geographic conditions in which our ancestors evolved influence the anatomy of their descendants. The term *ancestry* takes into account the place of geographic origin, which corresponds to biological realities in ways that the term *race* does not.

Bioarchaeologists and forensic anthropologists are interested in ancestry for different reasons. A bioarchaeologist may be interested in determining the extent to which ethnic (cultural) differences in prehistoric Chile, for example, relate to actual biological relationships among groups. To do this the bioarchaeologist might look at skeletal and dental traits known to be under genetic control and compare frequencies among populations of skeletons to consider how closely related the groups are. She might then compare these frequencies with cultural attributions of ethnicity such as the use of particular pottery styles or the practice of artificially deforming the head (Figure 18.12). In this way, she can discern how strong the cultural differences were and whether these also reflect biological difference. However, forensic anthropologists more often need to broadly categorize a single victim's

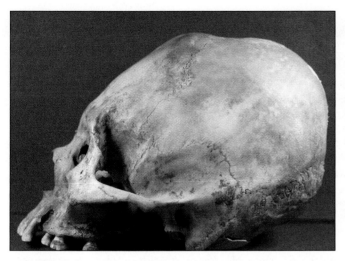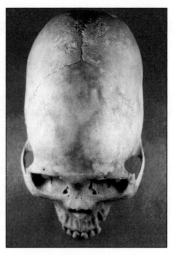

FIGURE 18.12 Head binding, or artificial deformation, was used by some populations as a sign of identity.

remains in order to narrow the scope of possible missing individuals to whom the bones may belong (in much the same way that determining the sex of a skeleton narrows the search focus to only cases of that sex). So the ability to estimate even continent of origin (e.g., European American) may be useful in limiting the scope of the search. Such forensic assessments of ancestry usually are made from the skull but can also include the postcrania.

Forensic anthropologists base ancestry assessments on comparisons with skeletal populations of known ancestry. An isolated skull can be measured and compared using multivariate statistics with the University of Tennessee Forensic Data Bank of measurements from crania of known ancestry. This process provides a likely assignment of ancestry and a range of possible error. However, human variation is such that many people exist in every population whose skulls do not match well with most other skulls of similar geographic origin. Nonetheless, the ability to even partially assign ancestry can be useful in several forensic contexts. Missing person reports often provide an identification of ancestry, and although this is not based directly on the skeleton, a skeletal determination of ancestry may suggest a match that could be confirmed by other more time-consuming means such as dental record comparisons or DNA analysis (see Insights and Advances: Ancestry Genetics). In another context, forensic anthropologists are still working to identify the remains of soldiers killed in the Vietnam War, 30 years after that conflict ended. If a local contact leads a forensic team to a field where an American soldier was reportedly buried, the team will begin to search and excavate. Upon finding human remains, the forensic anthropologist may be able to use the skeleton to assess whether the remains are likely to be those of a Vietnamese or of an American individual. More detailed analyses, including DNA and other means, will later be applied to test the attribution.

HEIGHT AND WEIGHT

Physical stature reflects the length of the bones that contribute to a person's height. Different body shapes have evolved in response to different climatic pressures (see the ecological rules described by Bergmann and Allen in Chapter 5). Thus, height and weight estimates will be more accurate if the population of the individual is known. These differences in proportions relate to differences in bone lengths; as a result, some populations will tend to have more of their stature explained by leg length, and some by torso length, for example.

The best estimates of stature from the skeleton are based on summing the heights of all the bones in the skeleton that contribute to overall height including the cranium, vertebral column, limb, and foot bones (Fully, 1956). This so-called

INSIGHTS AND ADVANCES

Ancestry Genetics

There was a time in the United States when intensive genealogical study was undertaken only by a few particularly enthusiastic individuals and by members of The Church of Jesus Christ of Latter-day Saints (in the context of the baptism of the dead). In recent years, however, genealogy has gone mainstream as the Internet has made all kinds of information, such as census data and birth records, easily available to everyone. The LDS church has long maintained extensive genealogical records, which are now available on their website (FamilySearch.org). Molecular biology has also provided a new tool for the amateur genealogist: the *personalized genetic history* (PGH).

Genetic studies have long been used for tracing the histories of populations (Chapters 5 and 14). As geneticists have discovered an increasing variety of markers that are associated with specific geographical regions and populations, the ability to trace individual genetic histories has increased greatly. In addition, the development of technologies allowing direct sequencing of DNA regions quickly and relatively inexpensively means that anyone can obtain a genetic profile in a matter of a few weeks.

There are two basic approaches to determining PGHs (Shriver and Kittles 2004). The first one is the *lineage-based* approach. These are based on maternally inherited mtDNA genomes and the paternally inherited Y chromosome DNA. The lineage-based approach has been very useful for population studies, and allows individuals to trace their ultimate maternal and paternal origins. For example, African-American individuals can find out what part of Africa their founding American ancestors may have come from (www.africanancestry.com). From the perspective of determining an individual's PGH, however, the lineage-based approach is limited, because it only traces the origins of a very small portion of an individual's genome and does not reflect the vast bulk of a person's genetic history.

In contrast to the lineage based approach, *autosomal marker-based tests* make use of information from throughout the genome. *Ancestry informative markers* (AIMs) are alleles on the autosomal chromosomes that show substantial variation among different populations. The more AIMs that are examined in an individual, the more complete the picture of that individual's *biogeographical ancestry* can be obtained (Shriver and Kittles 2004). Combining the information from all of these AIMs requires some major statistical analysis, which has to take into account the expression of each marker and its population associations. There is going to be some statistical noise in the system due to factors such as the overlapping population distribution of the markers and instances of convergent evolution. In addition, even when a hundred markers are used, the tests sample only a small portion of your genome that is the product of the combined efforts of thousands of ancestors. The biogeographical ancestry of a person, expressed in terms of percentage affiliations with different populations, is a statistical statement, not a direct rendering of a person's ancestry. And both AIMs and lineage-based tests are limited by the comparative samples that form the basis of our knowledge about the distribution of DNA markers. Nonetheless, they provides us with an intriguing snapshot of the geographic origins of a person's ancestors.

Several commercial companies are now in the ancestry genetics business. We contacted one of these companies, DNAPrint Genomics (www.AncestryByDNA.com), and obtained the biogeographical ancestry of two of the authors of this text (CS and JSA). The genetic testing product used is called AncestryByDNA 2.5, which provides a breakdown of an individual's PGH in terms of affiliations with four major geographical groups: European, Native American, Sub-Saharan African, and East Asian. It combines information derived from about 175 AIMs.

John Allen's results were as follows: 46% European, 46% East Asian, 8% Native American, and 0% Sub-Saharan African. These results squared quite well with his known family history: his mother was Japanese and his father an American of English and Scandinavian descent. The 8% Native American could have come from one or more ancestors on his father's side (some of whom arrived in the U.S. in the early colonial period). However, the 95% confidence intervals of the test indicate that for people of predominantly European ancestry, a threshold of 10% Native American needs to be reached before the result is statistically significant. For people of predominantly East Asian descent, the threshold is 12.5%. Therefore in the absence of a family history of Native American ancestry, it is best to consider the 8% as statistical noise.

Craig Stanford's results were: 82% European, 14% Native American, 4% Sub-Saharan African and 0% East Asian. The Native American result, which easily exceeds the statistical threshold, was a real surprise, since CS has no family history of Native American ancestry. Following this result, his father was tested and was found to have 91% European and 9% Sub-Saharan African ancestry. Thus all of CS's Native American ancestry was derived from his mother's side. Although she was not tested, it is reasonable to conclude that her Native American percentage would be greater than 25%—the equivalent of grandparent, although this does not have to represent the contribution of a single individual. CS found this result to be somewhat ironic since earlier generations of women on his mother's side of the family had been proud members of the Daughters of the American Revolution, a lineage-based organization that was once (but is no longer) racially exclusionary. Stanford also requested a more detailed European ancestry genetic test (EuroDNA 1.0). Along with European ancestry, the tests showed 12% Middle Eastern ancestry. One of his paternal grandparents was from Italy, and the ancestry of southern Europeans often reflects population movements around the Mediterranean Sea, including Middle Eastern markers. In addition, there has been a long history of some gene flow from Sub-Saharan Africa into north Africa and the Middle East, which could explain his father's statistically significant Sub-Saharan African ancestry.

Ancestry genetics opens windows to the past, but in some cases, it raises more questions than answers about where you came from. We can attest, however, that for anyone interested in their own biological ancestry, getting a personalized genetic history can be an exciting and enlightening experience. Incidentally, humans are not the only species whose biological past can be explored: genetic ancestry testing for dogs is also becoming

Fully method is fairly accurate, but requires a complete skeleton, a rarity in archaeological or forensic contexts. Biological anthropologists have developed formulas, which vary by population, for estimating stature based on the length of a single or several long bones, so that the femur, tibia, or even humerus can be used to predict stature. These methods use the relationship between the limb bones and the height in skeletal remains of individuals of known stature to predict stature for an unknown individual (e.g., Trotter, 1970). For even more incomplete remains, there are formulas for estimating total length of a long bone from a fragment of that bone (e.g., Steele & McKern, 1969). The estimated length can then be used to estimate height—although the error margin increases with each estimate. Like age, stature is estimated as a range (for example, 5′ 10″ to 6′ 0″) that hopefully captures the person's true height at the time of death.

As you might expect, weight is more difficult to predict since it can vary quite a lot over an individual's life time. Nonetheless, formulas exist for predicting the approximate weight of an individual from his or her weight-bearing joints, such as the head of the femur. Using the entire skeleton, scientists can estimate body weight based on formulas that relate height and body breadth to weight in populations of different build (Ruff, 2000). Some of these estimates also form the basis for inferring body size and weight in earlier hominids (see Chapters 12 and 13).

PREMORTEM INJURY AND DISEASE

Injuries and sickness suffered during life are also an important part of the biological profile and critical for understanding an individual's life and, perhaps, identity. The study of ancient diseases in skeletal remains is called paleopathology. Not all diseases or injuries leave marks on bone. However, we can distinguish the ones that do as having occurred while the person was alive because the bones show evidence of healing and remodeling. Arthritis and infections of bone show up clearly in skeletal remains. Old healed injuries, such as broken limbs and even gunshot wounds that a person survived for several weeks, also leave their mark (Figure 18.13).

Premortem fractures can be key evidence of lifeways. In forensic anthropology, multiple healed fractures—especially of the ribs and those typical of defensive wounds—can establish a series of episodes of violence, as is often the case in child abuse (Walker et al., 1997). Old injuries can also be matched to premortem X-rays

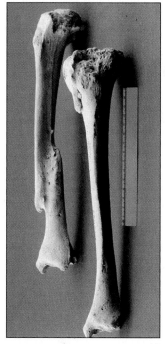

(a)

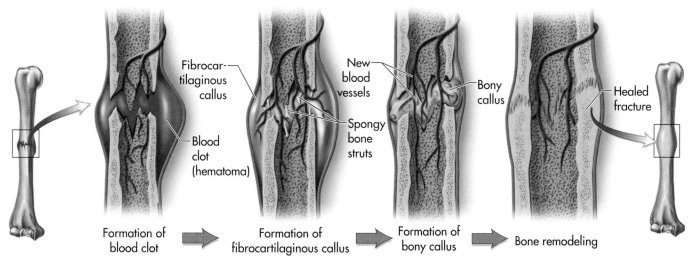

(b)

FIGURE 18.13 Bone fractures that occur before death show signs of healing. (a) Note the foreshortened tibia (left bone) due to a massive healed fracture, and the less severe fracture on one end (top) of the right bone. (b) The process of fracture healing starts with soft callus formation and proceeds to bone fusion.

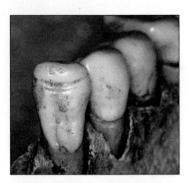

FIGURE 18.14 Linear defects in tooth enamel as seen on this canine are responses to high fevers, disease, or other insults during development.

taken when a victim sought medical attention and thereby help to establish identity (see the section on Identification and Forensic Anthropology, p. 536). Bioarchaeologists also use patterns of trauma in skeletal series to infer behavior. For example, ritualized warfare is suggested by the high incidence of healed nose fractures in a population from the Atacama Desert, Chile (Lessa et al., 2006). Such ritualized warfare is one means by which groups can resolve serious conflicts without the risk of actual deaths, just a few bloody noses.

Bioarchaeologists use the signs of health and disease in many individuals to understand the health status of a past population as well as the evolution of disease. Some infectious diseases, like syphilis and tuberculosis, may leave their mark on the skeleton. In these kinds of systemic diseases a particular distribution of bone abnormalities is often typical of a particular disease—but diseases are also sometimes difficult to tell apart. Bone can only respond to disease or injury in very limited ways. As in health, in disease bone can only be deposited or resorbed—so sometimes diagnosing a particular cause of this bony change is impossible. In the case of syphilis and tuberculosis, skeletal evidence forms the primary argument for whether these diseases are Old World introductions to the New World, or vice versa. DNA and bone evidence suggests that both diseases may have existed in the New World before Columbus and his men arrived, although the case is stronger for tuberculosis (Salo et al., 1994).

The skeleton also offers clues about nutritional stress. Iron deficiency anemias, brought on either from too little dietary iron or from a heavy parasite load that precludes adequate absorption of iron, are recorded in the bone of the eye orbits and occipital as the body attempts to produce additional red blood cells in these regions. Teeth can record disruptions in growth during a high fever or an infection, which appear as linear defects in the tooth crown (Figure 18.14). Limb bones may also show lines resulting from the resumption of growth after either nutritional or disease stress. These lines appear on X-rays and are called Harris lines. And levels of left–right asymmetry in facial bones and other bones of the skeleton are higher in populations under greater stress. Taken together, bioarchaeologists use these signals to understand the nutrition of individuals and populations in the past, and if present in individuals the signals may form the basis of probable or positive identifications, depending on the uniqueness of the feature.

In addition to injury and disease, lifestyle may leave an indelible mark on the skeleton; an athlete who uses one side of the body for intense activity (such as a baseball pitcher or tennis player) will have a more robustly developed arm on that side—especially if he or she began the activity during childhood and continued through adulthood. Other repetitive activities also cause bone deposition to differ systematically between individuals. In either a forensic or archaeological context such hypertrophy suggests several possible types of repetitive activity. When compared in many individuals across populations such differences can tell about increases or decreases in general activity level through time. Other markers provide clues to a sexual division of labor, for example. Repetitive exposure of the ear canal to cold water can stimulate bone growth, and in coastal populations in ancient Peru, such small nodules grow almost exclusively in the ear canals of males. This distribution, along with archaeological clues, helps to establish a sexual division of labor in which males dove into cold water to retrieve marine foods, while females worked onshore.

Injury, disease, and lifestyle all leave clues on the skeleton that tell the story of an individual's life. The skeleton may also be modified by events that occur well after or around the time of death. These changes can be critically important for understanding the context of death, but to be of use the scientist must be able to distinguish premortem bone changes from those that happened later in time.

Taphonomy

Taphonomy is the study of the ways in which various processes affect the skeleton after death (Chapter 8). Both forensic anthropologists and bioarchaeologists use taphonomic analysis to distinguish naturally caused bone damage from damage caused by human activity. And for forensic anthropologists, who are particularly keen to determine the length of time a victim has been dead and what contributed to this death, it is critical to distinguish events that occur well after death, or postmortem events, from perimortem events, those that occur right around the time of death. Neither perimortem nor postmortem trauma shows healing, distinguishing them from premortem injuries and disease. To be of use in understanding the context of death, however, perimortem and postmortem trauma must be differentiated from one another since postmortem events do not suggest cause or manner of death.

PERIMORTEM TRAUMA

Perimortem trauma is the physical evidence of activity that happened slightly before, during, or slightly after the time of death. We can differentiate it from premortem injury because in perimortem trauma no healing is evident. We can distinguish perimortem from postmortem trauma that happened well after death, because bones retain a large percentage of their organic component during the perimortem interval. As a result, they are more pliable and break differently than those that are well dried-out after death; think of the difference between how a small branch that has just been plucked from a tree bends when you try to break it, whereas a long-dead, dried-out stick is brittle and snaps in two.

Bioarchaeologists are less concerned with perimortem trauma than are forensic anthropologists. The older age of archaeological sites means fewer clues remain to distinguish perimortem changes from those that are definitely postmortem changes. So, except in particular instances in which an interpretation hinges on determining whether the individual was recently dead when his or her skeleton was damaged, bioarchaeologists often focus on postmortem trauma. Cases in which bioarchaeologists might focus on perimortem trauma include trying to make a case for ritual sacrifice or cannibalism. At archaeological sites in the southwest United States, some human remains were broken during the perimortem interval, when the bones were fresh. These findings, along with many other lines of evidence, suggest the remains were the result of cannibalism (White, 1992).

Distinguishing perimortem trauma is one of the most routine tasks a forensic anthropologist undertakes. This type of evidence helps investigators understand what happened right around the time of death. This information also helps the medical examiner or coroner determine the cause and manner of death (whether homicide, suicide, or accident) and may help to establish intent in murder cases. For example, the presence of telltale fractures of the hyoid, a small bone in the neck, suggests strangulation. Perimortem trauma may also indicate a perpetrator's intent to hide or dispose of a body, implying that death was not accidental. Circular saws and reciprocating saws are often used to dismember bodies after a murder. These tools leave different marks on bone and sometimes leave traces of metal fragments embedded in bone. Experts can identify types of blades and sometimes make direct matches to tools owned by a suspect. Being able to show, based on anatomical knowledge, that a body was fleshed when dismembered rather than skeletonized has important implications for inferring a crime or interpreting mortuary ritual in past societies.

POSTMORTEM TRAUMA

Definitively postmortem events are not related to establishing cause and manner of death and are often of greater interest to bioarchaeologists than they are to forensic anthropologists. Analyses of postmortem events can be critical for establishing how bones arrived at a site: Were they deliberately placed in a burial cave, or did the individual unceremoniously fall through a chasm in the rock? Despite their greater importance for bioarchaeologists, postmortem events may rule out a crime if they suggest that marks on bone are made by natural causes, rather than knives, guns, or chainsaws, or if they show that the skeleton is of ancient rather than forensic interest. For instance, Willey and Leach (2003) cite a case in which forensic

Fractures that occur around the time of death look different than those that had a chance to heal during life. This perimortem trauma may provide clues as to how an individual died.

anthropologists sought to identify a human skull found in a suburban home. The skull was discolored in a variety of ways that most closely resembled the way in which skulls are sometimes treated when collected as trophies of war. As it turned out, the skull in question was a "souvenir" brought home from the Vietnam War by a man who had since moved away, leaving the skull in his garage. Many clues about both peri- and postmortem events can be gleaned from the visual examination of skeletal remains. This differentiation can have important implications for how burial rituals are reconstructed for past societies, for example. However, bones also yield clues at a molecular level that can help to identify individuals or their relatives.

DNA, Kinship, and Identity

DNA can be used to make a positive identification in forensic cases if a reference sample from the victim or their family is available for comparison. Bioarchaeologists use DNA to look at relationships among groups and at migration patterns.

The rise of technologies able to establish kinship using DNA analysis has given bioarchaeologists and forensic scientists a powerful new tool for investigating relationships among groups, identifying victims, and establishing the presence of an alleged perpetrator at a crime scene. However, there are also limitations to each of these uses. DNA testing can use tiny samples of hair, skin, blood, other body fluids, and even bone. However, the older the bone sample and the more hot and humid the environment in which it was buried, the less likley that DNA can be extracted from bone. Forensic scientists use a variety of tests, including DNA profiling (examining gene sequences that only kin would be likely to share), DNA typing (isolating particular segments of the genetic sequence for analysis), and DNA fingerprinting (the original DNA test, in which the same segments of DNA are lined up to examine the degree of similarity between samples from two people) (Nafte, 2000). Bioarchaeologists use ancient DNA techniques to look at relationships among groups, migration patterns, and so on.

When skeletal material has been fragmented during a disaster (as in the World Trade Center crime scene in 2001), the identification process can be extraordinarily difficult, a biological profile may be impossible, and in such cases forensic scientists may rely heavily on comparisons with DNA reference samples, typically obtained from relatives of the victims, to make positive identifications. To use DNA for identification, the scientist must have some knowledge of who the victim might have been to find living relatives to whom DNA can be matched, or to find personal items such as toothbrushes that might yield remnants of the victim's own DNA. Without such reference samples no identification can be made, although DNA may be able to narrow down the ancestry and identify the sex of the individual.

Unlike forensic anthropologists who are seeking positive identifications, bioarchaeologists are more interetested in general kinship between groups. Ancient DNA techniques, like those used on the Neandertals (see Chapter 13, Innovations: Neandertal Genes), are most frequently used to establish relationships among groups and the origins of groups. For example, population-level considerations of DNA variation have also been used to look at and model the dispersal of historic human groups (see Insights and Advances: The Genghis Khan Effect). And ancient DNA has been used to establish the sex of fragmentary adult and subadult remains as well.

Identification and Forensic Anthropology

Because the forensic anthropologist is concerned with making a positive identification and contributing data for understanding the cause and manner of death, there are a number of methods of inquiry unique to forensic investigations. These include techniques for estimating the time since death, which in a forensic case may be days, weeks, or months—rather than hundreds or thousands of years. They also include specific means for establishing a positive identification—which may entail obtaining antemortem medical or dental records, examining surgical implants or specific unique clothing or tattoos, or undertaking facial reconstruction.

INSIGHTS AND ADVANCES

The Genghis Khan Effect

Y chromosome haplotypes can be an important tool in understanding the genetic histories of human populations. In a survey of more than 2,000 men from Asia using more than thirty-two genetic markers, Tatiana Zerjal and her colleagues (2003) found a Y chromosome lineage that exhibited an unusual pattern. Given the large number of markers used, most men in the survey had a unique haplotype; if two men shared a haplotype, they were always from the same population. However, one group consisted of very similar haplotypes clearly derived from a single Y chromosome ancestral haplotype; Zerjal and colleagues called this haplotype the star cluster (reflecting the emergence of these similar variants from a common source). The interesting thing about the star cluster lineage is that it is found in sixteen different populations, distributed across Asia from the Pacific Ocean to the Caspian Sea. What could explain this wide distribution?

The MRCA (most recent common ancestor) for this cluster was dated to about 1,000 years ago. Zerjal and her colleagues point out that the distribution of populations in which the lineage is found corresponds roughly to the maximum extent of the Mongol Empire, which reached its peak under Genghis Khan (c. 1162–1227) (Figure A). Khan and his close male relatives are known to have fathered many children (thousands, according to some historical sources). The lineage appears to have originated in Mongolia, where populations today have some

of the highest frequencies of star cluster haplotypes.

The Mongols were notoriously brutal and efficient conquerors, and as they expanded their empire across Asia, they killed many thousands of people. In many areas, relatives of Genghis Khan established dynastic lineages that ruled for centuries after the Mongol Empire proper fell apart (as a unified entity, it did not last long after the death of Genghis Khan). One additional population outside the Mongol Empire also has a high frequency of the star cluster Y chromosome: the Hazaras of Pakistan (and Afghanistan). This is puzzling at first glance,

FIGURE A Genghis Khan spread more than fear across Eurasia.

but the Hazaras may have a Mongol origin; in fact, many Hazaras consider themselves to be direct male-line descendants of Genghis Khan. The star cluster pattern is absent from other Pakistani populations.

The star cluster lineage clearly has its roots in Mongolia, and its spread across Asia seems to be linked to the expansion of the Mongol Empire. This distribution could have resulted from the migration of a group of Mongols carrying the haplotype or may even reflect the Y chromosome carried specifically by Genghis Khan and his relatives. Zerjal and her colleagues favor the latter explanation. They point out that there is still a substantial amount of haplotype diversity in Mongolian populations; therefore, it is more likely that the star cluster represents the Y chromosome found in a group of closely related individuals, namely Genghis Khan and his male relatives. Zerjal and colleagues state that the wide distribution of the star cluster lineage is evidence of "a novel form of selection in human populations on the basis of social prestige" (p. 720). With that social prestige and political power, Genghis Khan and his male descendants obviously took advantage of the many reproductive opportunities that came their way. Centuries later, we see the effects of this extraordinary history written in the structure of the Y chromosome, even though the Mongol rulers themselves disappeared long ago, physically and culturally assimilated into the populations they ruled.

TIME SINCE DEATH

One of the more difficult tasks for a forensic anthropologist is determining how long a victim has been dead. Anyone who has ever watched a police show knows that body temperature can be used to estimate time since death if the death is sufficiently recent. But over longer periods of time, other means are necessary. The research program in forensic anthropology at the University of Tennessee has maintained for many years an outdoor morgue in which bodies are left to decompose under a variety of controlled conditions so researchers can learn how natural processes affect the rate of decay (Bass & Jefferson, 2003). Many other such programs are now being developed. All the bodies used in the program are willed to the facility for this purpose, and once they are skeletonized the remains are curated in a research collection for other types of forensic research including the development of comparative databases.

Decomposition is a continuum that includes a typical trajectory from cooling and rigidity, to bloating, skin slippage, liquefaction, deflation, and skeletonization. The rate at which decay proceeds is determined by aspects of the surrounding environment including burial depth, soil type, temperature, humidity, and so on. In general, bodies left on the surface of the ground decompose most quickly and those buried deeply in the ground most slowly. Surface remains decay more quickly because they are more likely to be interfered with by scavengers, such as rodents and carnivores, who destroy and scatter the remains. And insects also have greater access to surface remains, speeding up decomposition. The timing of insect life cycles is well known, and their preferences for certain types of tissues and extent of decay are also well studied. Forensic entomologists therefore are important members of any forensic team. Decomposition is quicker in the summer, averaging just a week or two for surface remains in the summer of the mid-Atlantic states. Although in very dry environments, such as deserts, bodies may mummify rather than skeletonize. The delay in wintertime decomposition is due almost entirely to lower temperatures and humidity, both of which reduce insect activity as well as the natural physiological rates of decay of the body itself. Corpses that are wrapped in impervious containers, like garbage bags, decompose more slowly than surface remains for many of the same reasons that buried bodies decompose more slowly. With all things being equal, single burials tend to decompose more quickly than do the more protected individuals in the middle of a mass grave—although individuals on the periphery decompose at rates similar to those of individual burials. Using all these clues and others, scientists work together to estimate time since death. This can help to narrow the focus of possible identifications and possible perpetrators by suggesting a time frame for the crime.

ANTEMORTEM RECORDS AND POSITIVE IDS

Ideally, forensic anthropologists are trying to establish the positive identity of a victim. To do this they first develop the biological profile to narrow the field of focus of potential identities, and they define the time frame of the event. Once they have several possibilities, they can compare a number of different antemortem records to try to establish an identification. The most common are dental records, surgical implants, and the matching of antemortem and postmortem X-rays.

Your dentist keeps a chart of which teeth you have, which have been extracted, and which have been filled or crowned. All of your X-rays are also kept on file. These records can prove invaluable for making positive identifications because no two mouths are the same. However, comparing dental charts is time consuming, so the biological profile is used to limit the scope of possible identities. Forensic odontologists, specially trained dentists, work with forensic anthropologists to make identifications from dental records. Both dental X-rays and dental charts can be used for positive identifications (Adams, 2003). Exact matches of antemortem and postmortem dental X-rays can establish an identification in ways similar to antemortem medical X-rays (Stinson, 1975). But when X-rays are absent, comparing dental charts is an effective means of identification as well. A dental chart is made for the remains and this chart is compared, sometimes using the computerized program, OdontoSearch, with antemortem charts of missing individuals (Adams, 2003).

Medical X-rays taken before death can also be used for making identifications. An X-ray of a person's head after an accident may reveal the frontal sinus, an

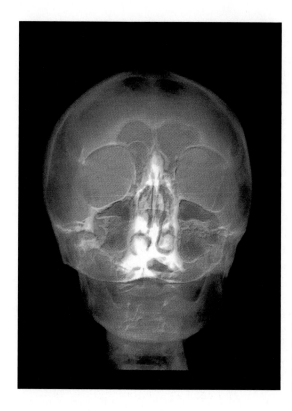

FIGURE 18.15 The frontal sinus, an air-filled space just behind the brow, is a unique size and shape in each of us and can be used to make a positive identification if antemortem X-rays are available.

air-filled space within the frontal bone just behind the brow area (Figure 18.15). The sinus is uniquely developed in each of us, so comparison of an X-ray from a skull with an antemortem film of a known individual may lead to a positive identification. Healed wounds and infections that are caught on antemortem X-rays can also be compared to postmortem X-rays. If the healing is particularly idiosyncratic, this might lead to a positive identification or at least to a possible identification that could be confirmed by other tests.

Orthopedic implants and pins often resolve issues of identity. These implanted items often have either unique or batch serial numbers than can be traced back to an individual patient's medical records. And antemortem X-rays of a pin in place can also be compared to postmortem X-rays to lead to a positive identification. Sometimes, the biological profile doesn't match any possible identities, and so there are no antemortem records to establish a positive ID. In these cases, other more exploratory methods, such as facial reconstructions, may help the general public suggest a possible identity.

FACIAL RECONSTRUCTION

Facial reconstruction—the fleshing out of the skull to an approximation of what the individual looked like in life—is part art and part science. It is based on careful systematic studies of the relationship between skin thickness and bone features—and clay is used to layer on muscle, fat, and skin over a model of a victim's skull (Wilkinson, 2004). Digital technologies are also being developed to render three-dimensional virtual reconstructions. Eyes and ears are placed, although their color and shape can't be known for sure. The size of the nose is based on the height and breadth of the nasal aperture and the bony bridge. But some artistic license is required to estimate the shape of the end of the nose. Skin and hair color can't be known from the bone. Once rendered, the reconstruction may be photographed and shown to the general public in the hopes that someone might recognize something about the individual. When possible identities are proposed, antemortem records can be checked—and perhaps an ID will be made.

Applications of Bioarchaeology

The emerging field of bioarchaeology traces its origins to the 1980s with the recognition of the importance of human remains in archaeological contexts for understanding the biocultural evolution of past populations (Larsen, 1999). The population-level approach sets the field apart from earlier enterprises that focused on individual case studies. A key component to bioarchaeological study of human remains is the emphasis on understanding the cultural context of the uncovered remains. Such information helps researchers understand the biological effects of certain cultural practices. This means comparing skeletal populations across important cultural transitions—such as the transition between hunting and gathering to farming, or the impact of European contact on indigenous peoples in the New World. It also means using biological clues to better understand the biological impact of cultural practices, such as the influence of social stratification on diet and disease. Bioarchaeologists approach a diverse number of evolutionary questions in this interdisciplinary way including looking at mortuary behavior, health and disease, and activity patterns.

MORTUARY ARCHAEOLOGY

Studying where and how individuals are buried helps bioarchaeologists to interpret the social organizations of past societies.

Ancient burial places not only preserve skeletons but are reflections of belief systems, kin structures, and social organization. Grave goods, burial position, and grouping of individuals all provide a window into past society. Using information from headstones, historians have traced cultural shifts in the outlook toward death in early American history, and they can examine the distribution within a cemetery of individuals of certain ages and sexes. In some cultures, families are buried together, but in others males and females may be separated. Both patterns tell you something about how the living society was structured. Deeper in time, archaeologists and bioarchaeologists combine their expertise to make inferences about social stratification and culture change. In the absence of headstones, the biological profiles of the buried skeletons provide critical data for these undertakings.

For example, on Mangaia, the second largest and southernmost of the Cook Islands in the South Pacific, archaeological and bioarchaeological studies document changes in burial practices through time. Prior to European contact, which occurred on Mangaia in 1823 with the arrival of Christian missionaries, individuals were buried under house floors and in burial caves, but after contact, many individuals were buried in church cemeteries (Antón & Steadman, 2003). Using the biological profiles of the skeletal remains we see that even though burial caves continued to be used after contact, the style of the burials changed. Before contact nearly equal numbers of adults and children were placed in burial caves and evidence of secondary burials, in which the skeleton had been rearranged, and of multiple burials in which several individuals were buried simultaneously was frequent (Figure 18.16). After European contact, few adults were found in burial caves and they were buried individually. In addition, secondary burials do not seem to have been present. These changes suggest that indigenous mortuary practices, and likely religion, were influenced by Christian missionaries. Individuals were no longer buried near or among the living, and the more unusual practices (from a Christian perspective), such as secondary processing of skeletal remains, were eliminated. Although burial caves are no longer used on Mangaia today, they remain places of reverence and connection to ancestors. Only through the combined perspective of both archaeological and biological data can we see when this transition began and how it emerged.

BIOCULTURAL EVOLUTION OF HEALTH AND DISEASE

The combination of archaeological and biological information is also used to understand the complex interaction between cultural practices, health, and disease.

(a)

(b)

FIGURE 18.16 Burial caves from Mangaia, Cook Islands, document the changing patterns of mortuary ritual. Secondary burials, seen here in detail (a) and from a distance (b), are rare after contact with Christian missionaries.

Biological profiles and detailed analyses of health indicators in a group of skeletons of known time period, environmental context, and social status can help elucidate the evolution of disease and the role of culture change on the health of a population.

In the Channel Island's populations of prehistoric California (7200 B.C. to A.D. 1780), increased exploitation of marine foods has been linked to increases in population size and density through time. Archaeological evidence of increasing quantities of fish and shellfish, and the tools for catching and processing these fish, have been found in Channel Island sites. These very local marine resources allowed Channel Islanders to lead more sedentary lives and allowed their populations to grow in size and density. With these changes, their social organization became more complex. General health also declined; with increasing population density more individuals show bone infections and stature decreases—both indicators of general stress (Lambert & Walker, 1991). In addition, cranial fractures increased, indicating an increase in interpersonal violence perhaps due to stresses associated with increasing population size (Walker, 1989). Only the combination of these archaeological data with the biological profiles of hundreds of individuals allows the interpretations and understanding of these widespread changes in the Channel Island populations through time.

ACTIVITY PATTERNS AND SUBSISTENCE CHANGE

Comparisons of groups of skeletons of individuals with very different activity patterns offer further insights into the influence of, for example, subsistence change on lifestyles. Activity patterns are often assessed through CT studies of the postcrania that take advantage of the fact that systematic changes in activity influence the development of the human skeleton. The distribution of bone in cross-sections of the leg bones, for example, reflects the predominant direction of force through the limb.

As the activity patterns of Native American populations from the coastal region of Georgia changed, the strength of limb bones changed with time (Ruff et al., 1984; Larsen & Ruff, 1994). Archaeology of the area indicates continuous occupation for thousands of years before European contact up until about A.D. 1550. Around A.D. 1150, the hunter–gatherers incorporated maize agriculture into their economy and became more sedentary. Comparisons of the strength of the femora (thigh bones) of Native Americans from before and after the switch to sedentary agriculture show a decrease in strength in the agricultural population. The results suggest a decrease in activity level and in the types of activities once the shift to agriculture was made. Interestingly, comparison of the leg strength of these agriculturalists with early contact period (A.D. 1565–1680) groups of sedentary Native Americans living in missions in Georgia found the later groups to be stronger. Scientists interpret this to mean that the Native Americans living in missions, although also sedentary, were working harder than their precontact forebears (Larsen & Ruff, 1994). These bioarchaeological studies use the same techniques that forensic anthropologists apply, although in very different settings.

Applications of Forensic Anthropology

Forensic anthropologists work on individual cases, and on cases of mass disasters and war crimes.

The field of forensic anthropology has achieved recent popularity due in part to television shows such as *CSI* and *Bones*. But like most popularizations, the fantasy is more glamorous than the reality. The field traces its professional origins to the 1970s, when the physical anthropology section of the American Academy of Forensic Sciences (AAFS) was formed, although U.S. anatomists and biological anthropologists have been assisting in human skeletal identification since the late 1800s. Each state has medical examiners or coroners who are legally responsible for signing death certificates and determining the cause and manner of death of people not in the care of a doctor. They also have the authority to consult other experts in their investigations, including forensic anthropologists. Usually a forensic anthropologist is involved when soft tissue remains are absent or badly decomposed. Forensic anthropologists must work in accordance with the rules of science but also of the courts. They must be able to convince their colleagues of their findings, and their findings must withstand the scrutiny of lawyers, juries, and judges. Although forensic anthropologists most often work on cases of lone victims of homicide, suicide, or accidental death, they are also called to the scene of mass fatalities, to search for soldiers killed in combat, and to investigate human rights abuses that result in hidden or mass graves.

MASS FATALITIES

In the days after the attack on the World Trade Center in New York on September 11, 2001, forensic anthropologists from around the country were called in to help identify the victims. The Oklahoma City bombing case 7 years earlier had brought in a similar influx of anthropologists as did the later devastation wrought by Hurricane Katrina. Forensic anthropologists play key roles in the attempt to identify victims of earthquakes, plane crashes, floods, and other natural and human-wrought disasters. The United States has regional emergency response teams called Disaster Mortuary Teams (DMORT) that include pathologists, forensic anthropologists, and forensic odontologists who are mobilized in response to national mass disasters such as the World Trade Center fire and collapse. Military forensic experts respond when U.S. citizens or military are involved in mass fatalities abroad.

In 1994 a DMORT team responded to an unusual mass disaster. Flooding of historic proportions caused the remains from a cemetery in Albany, Georgia, to surface. The lids of the concrete vaults in which coffins were placed during burial were removed by the floodwaters, and coffins floated to the surface and into town. Some remains were separated entirely from their coffins. The DMORT team recovered the remains and established a morgue. DMORT scientists, including forensic anthropologists, studied the remains to construct biological profiles. They then worked with antemortem dental and medical records and information collected from relatives to establish positive identifications with the goal of reconnecting the remains to their place of interment (Figure 18.17). No DNA analyses were used in this case. Of the 415 disinterred individuals, the DMORT

FIGURE 18.17 Forensic anthropologists working at a temporary morgue following the recovery of remains from a flooded cemetery in Georgia.

team was able to positively identify 320 people using the various techniques we have discussed.

WAR DEAD

U.S. forensic anthropologists first became involved in the identification of those who died in war when the Central Identification Laboratory (CIL) in Hawaii (CILHI) was formed to aid in the identification of those missing in action during World War II. Since then the skeletal remains of U.S. soldiers and civilians from World War II, the Korean War, the Vietnam War, and other military actions have been recovered and identified by this group of anthropologists. The CIL, now part of the Joint Prisoner of War/Missing in Action Accounting Command (JPAC), sends teams around the world to identify and recover U.S. soldiers lost in the wars of the twentieth century. The remains are brought back to the CIL, thoroughly examined, and identified. In addition to standard forensic anthropological techniques, JPAC teams also extensively use forensic DNA techniques to reach a positive identification so that remains may be returned to the next of kin.

Not only does this group of forensic anthropologists help in identifying missing personnel, but they have also undertaken some of the most important systematic research used in forensic anthropology and bioarchaeology. For example, Dr. Mildred Trotter, an early director of the CIL, developed regression analyses for determining stature from long bone lengths based on the skeletal remains of soldiers who died in the Korean War. This large body of work remains a standard in forensic and bioarchaeological analyses today and would not have been possible without the detailed medical histories of these military personnel.

WAR CRIMES AND GENOCIDE

Finally, forensic anthropologists may play a key role in uncovering mass graves and identifying bodies in them, and these scientists may be important witnesses in the investigation of war crimes. Whether in Cambodia, Rwanda, Argentina, Bosnia, or Iraq, when repressive regimes crack down on their citizens, they often attempt to intimidate the population through mass murder. The mass graves that are left contain the bodies of hundreds or even thousands of victims, whose loved ones spend lifetimes attempting to locate them and determine their fate. Forensic

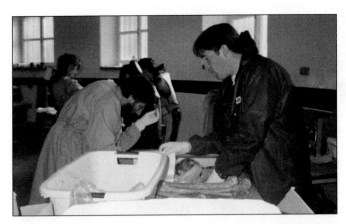

FIGURE 18.18 A team of forensic experts working on remains recovered from Ovcara in the former Yugoslavia.

anthropologists help to identify the victims for the sake of surviving family members and may provide key evidence in reconstructing a mass crime scene in an effort to bring those responsible to justice. Forensic anthropologists in these areas work for both government and private groups such as Physicians for Human Rights, the International Commission for Missing Persons, and the United Nations (UN). Such teams often start work before the conflicts end; for example, U.S. forensic archaeologists and anthropologists are currently at work in Iraq.

One example of such work is the effort to exhume mass graves in the former Yugoslavia that began in 1996 under the auspices of the United Nations, and in particular the International Criminal Tribunal for the former Yugoslavia (ICTY), in partnership with Physicians for Human Rights. Some of these exhumations concentrated in eastern Croatia on a grave site known as Ovcara, which contained victims from a massacre in Vukovar. The Vukovar massacre occurred in November 1991, and the mass grave site was located in 1992 based on information from a survivor. Excavation waited until 1996 because of continuing hostilities in the region (although the site was guarded by the UN for the entire time).

The forensic teams consisted of scientists from around the world and included forensic anthropologists and archaeologists, pathologists, evidence technicians, radiologists, odontologists, autopsy technicians, and computer scientists (Figure 18.18). The teams exhumed about 200 bodies from Ovcara, nearly all of them males. Mapping the grave site took more than a month. The remains were autopsied in Zagreb with the goals of constructing a biological profile that would help in identification and interpreting perimortem trauma to understand the cause of death. Many of the victims had multiple gunshot wounds and other forms of perimortem trauma. Biological profiles were compared with the medical and dental records of missing people, a task hampered by the destruction of hospitals and other medical facilities during the war, and lists of identifying characteristics (including tattoos) provided by family members of missing people. Through these comparisons about half of the 200 were positively identified. This evidence has been used in the prosecution of war crimes by the UN-ICTY, including the case against the region's former leader, Slobodan Milošević.

Bioarchaeologists and forensic anthropologists use the changes wrought in the human skeleton by natural selection and an individual's life experiences to read the clues of recent human history and prehistory. They apply the same principles, theory, and method to recent humans that primate paleoanthropologists applied to understanding our 65-million-year-old fossil ancestors all in a struggle to understand what makes us universally and uniquely human.

Epilogue

The place of humans in the natural world has been the major theme of this book. We have explored this topic from a wide variety of perspectives, including the fossil record, the behavior of living nonhuman primates, the lives of people in traditional societies, the workings of the brain, and the biology of modern people. However, our explorations of these diverse topics have been linked by a single common thread: evolutionary theory.

You've now completed a comprehensive look at your own evolutionary past, and at the place of humankind in the history of the world. As you have seen, the evidence of our past is present in us today. It's visible in our DNA, our hominid anatomy, our physiological adaptations, and even in aspects of our behavior. Many people live in denial or in ignorance of this evolutionary past. In contrast, we feel that embracing and understanding it is critical to being an enlightened citizen of the twenty-first century.

It is important to keep in mind, however, that to embrace an evolutionary perspective of humankind is not to deny the importance of culture in our lives. We have seen that culture may be the most fundamental of human traits. Many aspects of the biology of modern people are influenced in some way by culture, while at the same time our cultural nature is a direct outgrowth of our biology.

This book has been concerned with our evolutionary past, but the most pressing question for humankind in the early twenty-first century is whether our species will survive long enough to experience significant evolutionary change. Environmental degradation, overpopulation, warfare, and a host of other problems plague our species. It is safe to say that no species in Earth's history has contended with so many self-induced problems and survived. But of course, no other species has had the capability to solve problems and change its world for the better the way that we humans have.

SUMMARY

1. **Describe the methods used to recover skeletal remains from a site or crime scene.**

   Once the site is identified and cordoned off, a survey of the area is done, a datum is established, and any surface remains are mapped in. If buried remains are suspected, an archaeological excavation is undertaken and the position of discovered remains, including their depth relative to datum, is recorded. All sediment is screened for small fragments and items. All items are individually cataloged for return to the laboratory.

2. **What is a biological profile and how do bioarchaeologists and forensic anthropologists use these profiles differently?**

   The biological profile includes the estimation of an individual's age, sex, stature, and ancestry in addition to any signs of disease or premortem injury to the skeleton. Bioarchaeologists use biological profiles from multiple individuals to understand the general status of a population as well as biological changes through time. The forensic anthropologist uses the biological profile of an individual to aid in establishing a positive identification of a victim and to assess the circumstances surrounding death.

3. **Why is it possible to tell the sex of an individual from the skeleton?**

   An individual's skeleton reflects both events during his or her lifetime as well as selective pressures that acted on the person's ancestors. It is possible to determine sex so accurately because the selective pressures acting on male and female bipeds are very different and result in a differently shaped pelvis in the female.

4. **What is the difference between perimortem and postmortem damage to bones? How can you distinguish between the two types of damage?**

   Perimortem damage occurs at, during, or shortly after death. Postmortem damage occurs long after death, after the perimortem interval, and once the bone is less pliable. Perimortem and postmortem damage are distinguishable because of the way bone breaks due to this difference in pliability.

5. **What methods do forensic anthropologists use to make a positive identification?**

   Forensic anthropologists use many methods to make positive identifications. These include the comparison of antemortem and postmortem dental and medical records, especially X-rays; the comparison of surgical implants with medical X-rays; the comparison of tattoos; and sometimes facial reconstruction.

CRITICAL THINKING QUESTIONS

1. If you had the skeletal remains of two groups, how would you design a study to look at differences between them in terms of health and nutrition?

2. Why don't bioarchaeologists and forensic anthropologists just skip the skeletons and use only DNA?

3. Do you think television shows like *CSI* and *Bones* are positive or negative reflections on the field of forensic anthropology? How do you think they might positively or negatively impact the field?

KEY TERMS

bioarchaeologists   datum point   chain of custody   biological profile

SUGGESTED READING

Larsen, Clark Spencer. (1999). *Bioarchaeology: Interpreting Behavior from the Human Skeleton.* Cambridge Studies in Biological Anthropology, 21.

Maples, William R., and Browning, Michael. (1994). *Dead Men Do Tell Tales.* Doubleday, NY.

Steadman, Dawnie. (2002) *Hard Evidence: Case Studies in Forensic Anthropology.* Prentice-Hall, NJ.

OVERVIEW OF THE BRAIN

The central nervous system consists of two main parts: the spinal cord and the brain. The spinal cord is a thick bundle of nerve fibers that runs through the bony canal formed by the vertebrae of the spine. It is the structure through which all the nerves of the body connect to the brain. The spinal cord passes through the foramen magnum of the skull where it connects to the brain.

The brain consists of three major parts: the *brain stem*, the *cerebellum*, and the *cerebrum* (Figure A.1). As its name suggests, the brain stem sits at the base of the brain and connects directly to the spinal cord. The brain stem is important in the regulation and control of complex motor patterns, in breathing, and in the regulation of sleep and consciousness. The cerebellum, or "little brain," sits tucked in under the rest of the brain, behind the brain stem. It is densely packed with nerve cells, or *neurons*. The cerebellum is important in the control of balance, posture, and voluntary movements.

The cerebrum is the part of the brain that has undergone the most obvious changes over the course of human evolution. It is divided almost evenly along the sagittal midline into *left* and *right hemispheres*. The hemispheres can differ subtly in morphology and more substantially in function. The outer surface of the cerebrum is crisscrossed by a complex arrangement of grooves known as *sulci* (singular, *sulcus*), which gives the human cerebrum its characteristic wrinkled appearance. The sulci divide the surface of the brain into a series of thick bands or ridges, which are called *gyri* (singular, *gyrus*). Although there is individual variation, several basic sulci divide the brain into functional regions that are common to almost everyone.

If we look at a cross-section through the cerebrum (Figure A.2 on page 548), we notice that its outer surface is actually formed by a rim of tissue (4–6 mm thick) that follows the surface down into the valleys formed by the sulci; this is the *cerebral cortex*. The cerebral cortex is made of *gray matter* (which looks more brown in the living brain). Gray matter consists mostly of the cell bodies of neurons, which have a characteristic structure (Figure A.3 on page 548). From the cell body, there emerge branchlike projections through which neurons communicate with one another: The *dendrites* receive inputs from other neurons, and the *axon* is the outgrowth through which one neuron sends a signal to another neuron. Neurons can have many dendrites but only one axon. The junction where the axon of one cell meets the dendrite of another cell is called a *synapse*. Communication across the synapse is facilitated by chemical agents known as *neurotransmitters*. The human nervous system consists of about 100 billion neurons. Because each neuron may form synapses with thousands or even millions of other neurons, the web of communication that forms among neurons must be of mind-boggling complexity.

Gray matter makes up about 55–60% of the cerebrum. The rest of the cerebrum is composed of *white matter*, which forms the core of the hemisphere. The white matter is made up predominantly of the axons of neurons. Axons are sheathed in a white, fatty substance known as *myelin*, which facilitates the transmission of the electrical impulse along the axon. Diseases such as *multiple sclerosis*, which results from the demyelination of axons in different parts of the nervous system, demonstrate how important myelin is for normal nerve transmission. The *corpus callosum* is a large band of white matter located in the center of the brain. It is composed of axons linking the neurons of the two cerebral hemispheres.

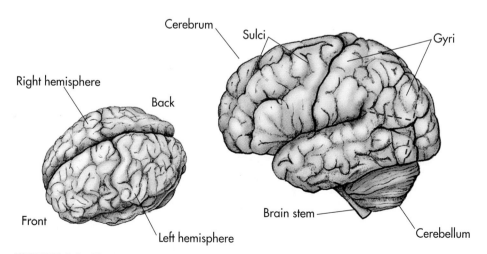

FIGURE A.1 The human cerebrum is divided into two hemispheres, which are themselves divided by sulci into gyri.

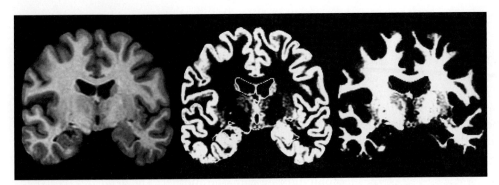

FIGURE A.2 A cross-section through the cerebral cortex, which is then divided into gray and white matter.

Studies of patients who have had their corpus callosum surgically severed to prevent the recurrence of seizures have yielded many insights into how the two hemispheres work together and separately.

Major Divisions of the Cerebrum

Each of the hemispheres is divided into four major sectors, or *lobes* (Figure A.4). Two of the major boundaries of the lobes are formed by the *Sylvian fissure* and the *central sulcus*. The *frontal lobe,* which makes up about 38% of the hemisphere (Allen et al., 2002), is the part of the brain located just behind your forehead. The *parietal lobe* (about 25% of the hemisphere) is just behind the frontal lobe on the other side of the central sulcus. Below the Sylvian fissure, the *temporal lobe* (22%) forms the "thumb" of the hemisphere, as it appears in a side view. The *occipital lobe* (9–10%) forms the "knob" at the back of the hemisphere. In chimpanzees and other primates, the occipital lobe is clearly separated from the other lobes by the *lunate sulcus*, a semicircular sulcus running in an arc along the posterior (back) lateral surface of the hemisphere. In humans, the lunate sulcus often is missing or present only as a minor sulcus that does not indicate a functional boundary for the occipital lobe.

Another major part of the cerebrum—not by size but by function—is the *limbic system*. The limbic system is buried within the hemispheres in the midline region of the brain and is composed of several interrelated structures, and is most notable for being the seat of emotion (Ledoux, 1996).

Primary and Association Areas of the Cerebral Cortex

Different regions of the cerebrum have different functions. The limbic regions encompass regions of the brain important for producing emotions, and some of its regions are critically important for forming new memories. The cerebral cortex is divided into two kinds of functional areas. *Primary cortex* is involved directly with either motor control or input from the senses. *Primary motor* regions are concentrated in the frontal lobe, just in

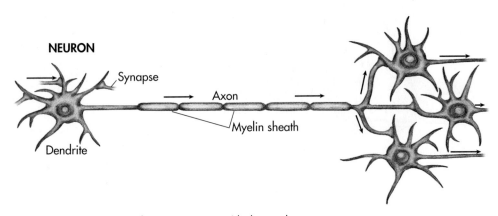

FIGURE A.3 A neuron forming synapses with three other neurons.

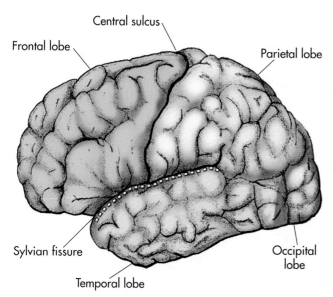

Central sulcus

Frontal lobe

Parietal lobe

Sylvian fissure

Occipital lobe

Temporal lobe

FIGURE A.4 The major lobes of the cerebrum.

Methods for Studying Brain Structure and Function

Several different methods for studying brain structure and function have developed over the past 150 years. The *autopsy* was for many years the only way scientists had of studying brain structure, in which the brain is examined and described after a person's death. The *lesion method* correlates a behavioral abnormality in a living person with a brain abnormality observed at autopsy. The lesion method relies on "natural experiments": observations of people who have sustained a brain injury (for example, via stroke or infection) and who also exhibit a behavioral deficit. It has also been used widely as an experimental tool using animals as subjects; much of what we know about mammalian brain function comes from such studies.

Over the past 20 years, the development of a field called *neuroimaging* has revolutionized the study of the brain. Noninvasive methods allow us to observe the structure and function of the brain in living, healthy people under controlled experimental conditions. *Magnetic resonance imaging (MRI)* is the most commonly used method to study brain structure in living individuals (Figure A.5). A magnetic resonance image of the brain is essentially a high-resolution map of water concentration in the brain. It provides good contrast between gray and white matter and cerebrospinal fluid. For the study of brain function and activity, scientists use techniques such as *positron emission tomography* (PET) scanning and *functional MRI*. These methods show which parts of the brain are activated during a cognitive act (thinking of a word, listening to a sound, remembering an emotion) by identifying areas where metabolism or blood flow has increased.

front of the central sulcus. *Primary sensory* regions are distributed throughout the cerebrum.

Most of the human cerebral cortex is not primary cortex but rather *association cortex*. Association cortex comprises the regions where the processing of primary inputs or information occurs. It is generally believed that in mammals, as brain size increases, the proportion of the brain devoted to association rather than primary regions also increases. Some association areas receive inputs from only one primary area, and other regions receive inputs from multiple primary regions. Anything that we think of as a higher-level function, such as thought, decision making, art, or music, originates in association cortices.

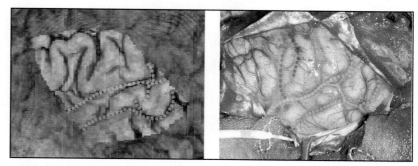

FIGURE A.5 On the left, a portion of the surface of the brain as seen in an MRI. On the right, the same portion of the brain shown during surgery.

PRIMATE AND HUMAN COMPARATIVE ANATOMY

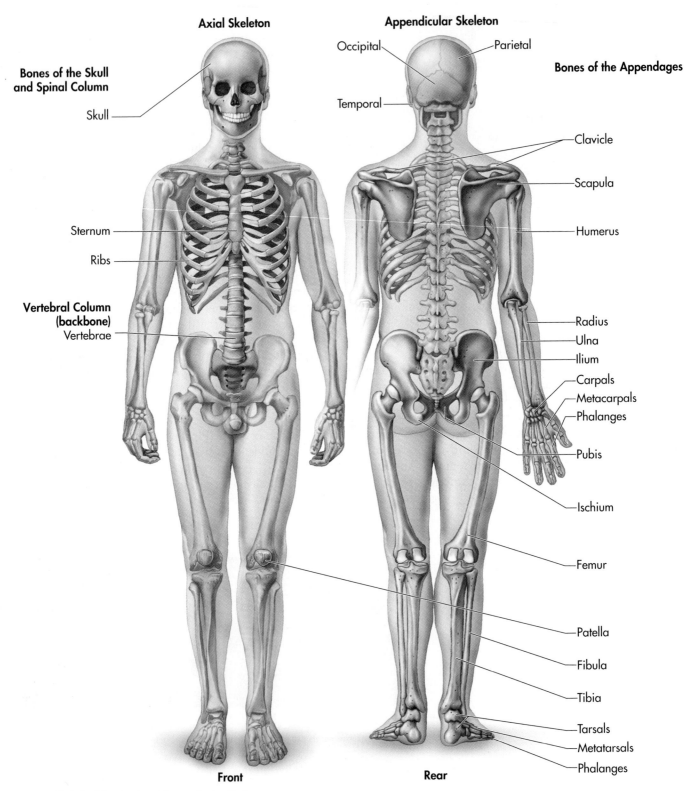

Axial Skeleton

Appendicular Skeleton

Occipital — Parietal

Bones of the Skull and Spinal Column

Bones of the Appendages

Skull

Temporal

Clavicle

Scapula

Sternum

Ribs

Humerus

Vertebral Column (backbone)
Vertebrae

Radius
Ulna
Ilium
Carpals
Metacarpals
Phalanges

Pubis

Ischium

Femur

Patella

Fibula

Tibia

Tarsals
Metatarsals
Phalanges

Front

Rear

FIGURE B.1   The Axial and Appendicular Skeletons.

Gorilla

Homo

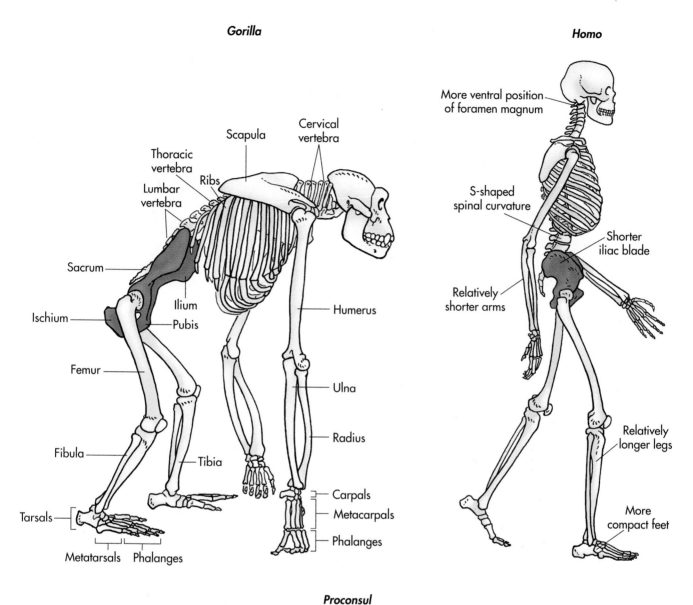

- Thoracic vertebra
- Scapula
- Cervical vertebra
- Lumbar vertebra
- Ribs
- Sacrum
- Ischium
- Ilium
- Pubis
- Femur
- Humerus
- Fibula
- Tibia
- Ulna
- Radius
- Tarsals
- Carpals
- Metacarpals
- Phalanges
- Metatarsals
- Phalanges

- More ventral position of foramen magnum
- S-shaped spinal curvature
- Shorter iliac blade
- Relatively shorter arms
- Relatively longer legs
- More compact feet

Proconsul

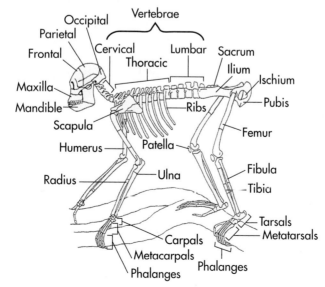

- Occipital
- Parietal
- Frontal
- Maxilla
- Mandible
- Vertebrae
- Cervical
- Thoracic
- Lumbar
- Sacrum
- Ilium
- Ischium
- Pubis
- Ribs
- Scapula
- Humerus
- Patella
- Femur
- Radius
- Ulna
- Fibula
- Tibia
- Tarsals
- Metatarsals
- Carpals
- Metacarpals
- Phalanges
- Phalanges

FIGURE B.2 Comparisons of *Gorilla*, *Homo* and *Proconsul* skeletons.

Human Skull

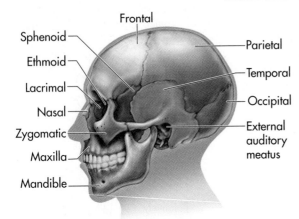

(a) The major bones of the skull and face

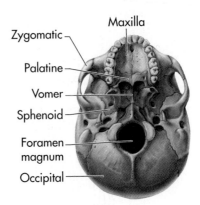

(b) Lower surface of skull

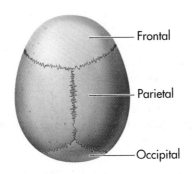

(c) Top view of skull

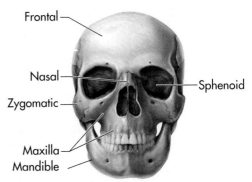

(d) Front view of skull showing facial bones

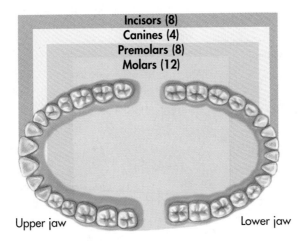

(e) Upper and lower jaws

FIGURE B.3   (a, b, c) The major bones of the skull and face, (d) facial bones and, (e) dentition.

The Vertebral Column

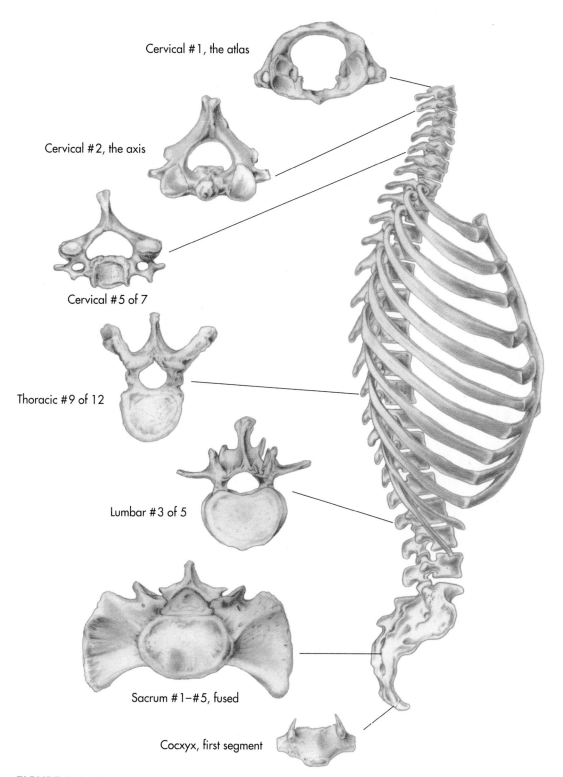

Cervical #1, the atlas

Cervical #2, the axis

Cervical #5 of 7

Thoracic #9 of 12

Lumbar #3 of 5

Sacrum #1–#5, fused

Cocxyx, first segment

FIGURE B.4   The Vertebral Column. The human vertebral column consists of 7 cervical, 12 thoracic, 5 lumbar, 5 fused sacral, and 4 or 5 diminutive coccygeal vertebrae.

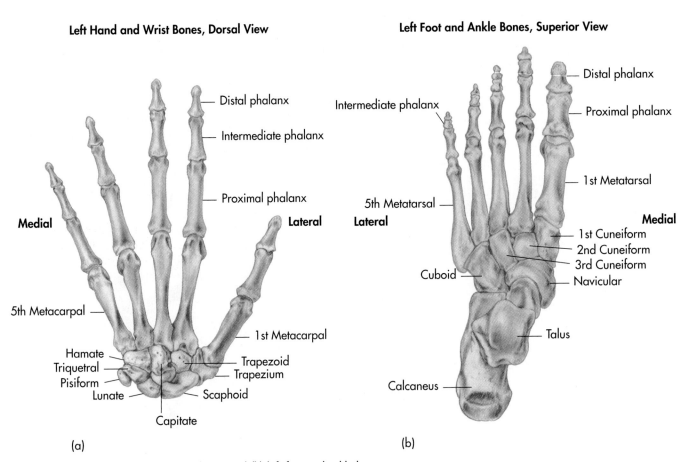

Left Hand and Wrist Bones, Dorsal View

Left Foot and Ankle Bones, Superior View

Distal phalanx

Intermediate phalanx

Proximal phalanx

Medial

Lateral

5th Metacarpal

1st Metacarpal

Hamate

Triquetral

Pisiform

Lunate

Capitate

Trapezoid

Trapezium

Scaphoid

(a)

Intermediate phalanx

Distal phalanx

Proximal phalanx

5th Metatarsal

1st Metatarsal

Lateral

Medial

1st Cuneiform

2nd Cuneiform

3rd Cuneiform

Cuboid

Navicular

Talus

Calcaneus

(b)

FIGURE B.5   (a) Left hand and wrist bones and (b) left foot and ankle bones.

THE HARDY–WEINBERG EQUILIBRIUM

In Chapter 5, we introduced the Hardy–Weinberg equilibrium in the context of our discussion of the forces of evolutionary change. Population genetics provides the mathematical underpinnings of evolutionary theory, and the Hardy–Weinberg equilibrium is at the heart of mathematical and quantitative approaches to understanding evolutionary change in diploid organisms. In this appendix, we will briefly go over a derivation of the Hardy–Weinberg equilibrium and show some applications of the equilibrium in evolutionary research.

Throughout the discussion, we will use the simplest case to illustrate our examples: a single gene (or locus) with two alleles, A and a. The frequency of A in the population is represented by p; the frequency of a is represented by q. By definition, $p + q = 1$.

Derivation of the Hardy–Weinberg Equilibrium

The Hardy–Weinberg equilibrium states that, given known allele frequencies p and q, we can represent the genotype frequencies by $AA = p^2$, $Aa = 2pq$, and $aa = q^2$. Furthermore, these allele frequencies remain constant from generation to generation if the following conditions are met:

- Large population size (or theoretically infinite population size), which minimizes the influence of genetic drift on allele frequencies

- Random mating (no inbreeding or assortative or disassortative mating)

- No mutation

- No gene flow

- No natural selection

Let us begin by considering a specific example, where the allele frequency of A is 0.6 ($p = 0.6$) and that of a is 0.4 ($q = 0.4$). To look at this another way, the probability that any given sperm or egg will carry A is 0.6, and the probability that it will carry a is 0.4. Thus under conditions of totally random mating with, no other evolutionary forces in effect (under equilibrium conditions), the probability of producing a zygote with a homozygous AA genotype is $(0.6)(0.6) = 0.36$. We can represent the probabilities of all the genotypes occurring in a modified Punnett square:

		Sperm	
		freq(A) = p = 0.6	freq(a) = q = 0.4
Eggs	freq(A) = p = 0.6	freq(AA) = p^2 = (0.6)(0.6) = 0.36	freq(Aa) = pq = (0.6)(0.4) = 0.24
	freq(a) = q = 0.4	freq(Aa) = pq = (0.6)(0.4) = 0.24	freq(aa) = q^2 = (0.4)(0.4) = 0.16

This gives us a population with genotype frequencies of 0.36 (for AA), 0.48 (for Aa), and 0.16 (for aa). What are the allele frequencies for this population? For A, it is $0.36 + (0.5)(0.48) = 0.36 + 0.24 = 0.6$, which is what the frequency of A was originally. The allele frequency of a is $0.16 + (0.5)(0.48) = 0.16 + 0.24 = 0.40$, which is the original frequency of a. This demonstrates that allele frequencies are maintained in equilibrium under conditions of random mating and in the absence of other evolutionary forces.

The general equation for the distribution of genotypes for a population in Hardy–Weinberg equilibrium is given by the equation

$$p^2 + 2pq + q^2 = 1$$

We can derive this equation directly from the modified Punnett square.

The constancy of allele frequencies over generations is shown by the following equations. Let p' equal the allele frequency of A in the first generation. From the preceding example we see that

$$p' = (\text{frequency of } AA) + (0.5)(\text{frequency of } Aa)$$

We want to count only half the alleles for A in the heterozygotes. Substituting the allele frequency values from the Hardy–Weinberg equation, we get

$$p' = p^2 + (0.5)(2pq)$$

Because $(0.5)(2pq) = pq$, we now have

$$p' = p^2 + pq$$

Which, factoring out p, is the same thing as

$$p' = p(p + q)$$

As you recall, $p + q = 1$; therefore,

$$p' = p$$

This demonstrates that allele frequencies remain constant in a population in Hardy–Weinberg equilibrium.

One of the main uses of the Hardy–Weinberg equation is to determine if a population is *not* in equilibrium. We do this by comparing observed allele frequencies with observed genotype frequencies. If the observed genotype frequencies are significantly different from those expected based, on the allele frequencies (which we usually check by using a chi-square statistical test), then we can say the population is not in equilibrium. This result indicates that one of the assumptions of the Hardy–Weinberg equilibrium is being violated and that an evolutionary force may be acting on the population or acted on the population in the past to produce the non-equilibrium distribution of alleles.

Another application of the Hardy–Weinberg equation is to estimate the frequency of heterozygotes in a population. As we discussed in Chapter 6, it is particularly useful for estimating the frequency in a popuiation of carriers of a recessive autosomal illnesses, such as Tay–Sachs disease or cystic fibrosis. The recessive allele frequency is simply

$$q = \sqrt{\text{frequency of autosomal recessive condition}}$$

And the dominant allele frequency is

$$p = 1 - q$$

Thus the frequency of heterozygous carriers = $2pq$.

Hardy–Weinberg and Natural Selection

The Hardy–Weinberg equilibrium can help us mathematically model the effects of any of the forces of evolution (mutation, genetic drift, gene flow, and natural selection). Let us consider how to use the Hardy–Weinberg equation to understand how natural selection may affect the distribution of allele frequencies in a population. In these equations, we assume that natural selection is the only force of evolution acting on the population.

In the simple case of one gene with two alleles, we have three possible genotypes that are subject to natural selection. To model the change in allele frequencies, we need to know not the absolute fitness of each genotype (which we could measure as its likelihood of survival) but rather the genotypes' fitness relative to each other. Relative fitness usually is represented by the letter w; thus we have

$$w_{AA} = \text{relative fitness of } AA$$
$$w_{Aa} = \text{relative fitness of } Aa$$
$$w_{aa} = \text{relative fitness of } aa$$

Let's say that the homozygous genotype AA has the highest fitness; its relative fitness w_{AA} therefore would be equal to 1. The relative fitnesses of Aa and aa are lower, such that

$$w_{AA} = 1.0$$
$$w_{Aa} = 0.8$$
$$w_{aa} = 0.4$$

Let's also assume starting allele frequencies of $p = 0.7$ and $q = 0.3$.

If the population were in Hardy–Weinberg equilibrium, the expected genotype frequencies after one generation would be

$$p^2 = (0.7)(0.7) = 0.49 \text{ for } AA$$
$$2pq = 2(0.7)(0.3) = 0.42 \text{ for } Aa$$
$$q^2 = (0.3)(0.3) = 0.09 \text{ for } aa$$

However, natural selection is working on this population and affecting the survival of the different genotypes. So the genotype frequencies after selection are

$$w_{AA}p^2 = 1.0(0.7)(0.7) = 0.49 \text{ for } AA$$
$$w_{Aa}2pq = 0.8(2)(0.7)(0.3) = 0.336 \text{ for } Aa$$
$$w_{aa}q^2 = 0.4(0.3)(0.3) = 0.036 \text{ for } aa$$

The frequency of p after natural selection has acted on the population is

$$p' = [(0.49) + (0.5)(0.336)]/(0.49 + 0.336 + 0.036)$$
$$= 0.658/0.862$$
$$= 0.763$$

The frequency of q is

$$q' = 1 - p' = 1 - 0.763 = 0.237$$

So after only one generation of natural selection operating at these levels, there is a substantial change in allele frequencies, with A going from 0.7 to 0.763 and a decreasing from 0.3 to 0.237. Following this through five generations, the allele frequencies would be

In the case of a lethal autosomal recessive condition (such as Tay–Sachs disease), in which the relative fitness

Generation	I	2	3	4	5
p	0.763	0.813	0.852	0.883	0.907
q	0.237	0.187	0.148	0.117	0.093

of the recessive homozygote is 0 and for the other two genotypes it is 1, we can represent the change in allele frequency of the recessive allele by a simple equation (which is derived from the Hardy–Weinberg equation):

$$q_g = q_0/(1 + gq_0)$$

where g is the number of generations passed, q_G is the frequency of a in generation g, and q_0 is the starting frequency of a. Consider a founding population in which the allele frequency of a lethal recessive is 0.20. Over ten generations, the frequency of this allele will decrease to

$$q_{10} = 0.2/[1 + (10)(0.2)]$$
$$= 0.2/3$$
$$= 0.067$$

Of course, a small founding population violates one of the conditions of the Hardy–Weinberg equilibrium (infinite population size), but we can ignore that for the sake of this example.

METRIC–IMPERIAL CONVERSIONS

METRIC UNIT	IMPERIAL EQUIVALENT
1 centimeter	0.39 inches
1 meter	3.28 feet
1 kilometer	0.62 miles
1 kilogram	2.20 pounds
454 grams	1 pound
1 gram	0.035 ounces
1 liter	1.06 quarts
400 cubic centimeters	24.4 cubic inches
1 square kilometer	0.39 square miles
1 square kilometer	247 acres
0 degrees Celsius	32 degrees Fahrenheit

ABO blood type system   Refers to the genetic system for one of the proteins found on the surface of red blood cells. Consists of one gene with three alleles: A, B, and O.

acclimatization   Short-term changes in physiology that occur in an organism in response to changes in environmental conditions.

acetabulum   The cup-shaped joint formed by the ilium, ischium, and pubis at which the head of the femur attaches to the pelvis.

Acheulean   Stone tool industry of the early and middle Pleistocene characterized by the presence of bifacial hand axes and cleavers. This industry is made by a number of *Homo* species, including *H. erectus* and early *H. sapiens*.

activity budget   The pattern of waking, eating, moving, socializing, and sleeping that all nonhuman primates engage in each day.

adapoids   Family of mostly Eocene primates, probably ancestral to all strepsirhines.

adaptability   The ability of an individual organism to make positive anatomical or physiological changes after short- or long-term exposure to stressful environmental conditions.

adaptation   A trait that increases the reproductive success of an organism, produced by natural selection in the context of a particular environment.

adaptationism   A premise that all aspects of an organism have been molded by natural selection to a form optimal for enhancing reproductive success.

adaptive radiation   The diversification of one founding species into multiple species and niches.

alleles   Alternative versions of a gene. Alleles are distinguished from one another by their differing effects on the phenotypic expression of the same gene.

Allen's rule   Stipulates that in warmer climates, the limbs of the body are longer relative to body size to dissipate body heat.

allopatric speciation   Speciation occurring via geographic isolation.

amino acids   Molecules that form the basic building blocks of protein.

anagenesis   Evolution of a trait or a species into another over a period of time.

analogous   Having similar traits due to similar use, not due to shared ancestry.

angular torus   A thickened ridge of bone at the posterior inferior angle of the parietal bone.

anthropoid   Members of the primate suborder Anthropoidea that includes the monkeys, apes, and hominids.

athropology   The study of humankind in a cross-cultural context. Anthropology includes the subfields cultural anthropology, linguistic anthropology, archaeology, and biological anthropology.

anthropometry   The measurement of different aspects of the body, such as stature or skin color.

antibodies   Proteins (immunoglobulins) formed by the immune system that are specifically structured to bind to and neutralize invading antigens.

antigens   Whole or part of an invading organism that prompts a response (such as production of antibodies) from the body's immune system.

archaeology   The study of the material culture of past peoples.

arboreal hypothesis   Hypothesis for the origin of primate adaptation that focuses on the value of grasping hands and stereoscopic vision for life in the trees.

argon/argon (^{40}Ar/^{39}Ar) dating   Radiometric technique modified from K–Ar that measures ^{40}K by proxy using ^{39}Ar. Allows measurement of smaller samples with less error.

artifacts   The objects, from tools to art, left by earlier generations of people.

australopithecines   The common name for members of the genus *Australopithecus*.

autosomal dominant disease   A disease that is caused by a dominant allele: Only one copy needs to be inherited from either parent for the disease to develop.

autosomal recessive disease   A disease caused by a recessive allele; one copy of the allele must be inherited from each parent for the disease to develop.

autosomes   Any of the chromosomes other than the sex chromosomes.

auxology   The science of human growth and development.

balanced polymorphism   A stable polymorphism in a population in which natural selection prevents any of the alternative phenotypes (or underlying alleles) from becoming fixed or being lost.

base   Variable component of the nucleotides that form the nucleic acids DNA and RNA. In DNA, the bases are adenine, guanine, thymine, and cytosine. In RNA, uracil replaces thymine.

Bergmann's rule   Stipulates that body size is larger in colder climates to conserve body temperature.

bifaces   Stone tools that have been flaked on two faces or opposing sides forming a cutting edge between the two flake scars.

binomial nomenclature   Linnaean naming system for all organisms, consisting of a genus and species label.

bioarchaeologist   A biological anthropologist who uses human osteology to explore the biological component of the archaeological record.

biocultural anthropology   The study of the interaction between biology and culture, which plays a role in most human traits.

biological anthropology   The study of humans as biological organisms, considered in an evolutionary framework; sometimes called physical anthropology.

biological profile   The biological particulars of an individual as estimated from their skeletal remains. These include estimates of sex, age at death, height, ancestry, and disease status.

biological species concept   Defines species as interbreeding populations reproductively isolated from other such populations.

biomedical anthropology   The subfield of biological anthropology concerned with issues of health and illness.

biostratigraphy   Relative dating technique using comparison of fossils from different stratigraphic sequences to estimate which layers are older and which are younger.

blades   Flakes that are twice as long as they are wide.

blending inheritance   Discredited nineteenth-century idea that genetic factors from the parents averaged-out or blended together when they were passed on to offspring.

brachiation   Mode of arm-hanging and arm-swinging that uses a rotating shoulder to suspend the body of an ape or hominid beneath a branch or to travel between branches.

breccia   Cement-like matrix of fossilized rock and bone. Many important South African early humans have been found in breccias.

bridewealth   Payment offered by a man to the parents of a woman he wants to marry.

butchering site   A place where there is archaeological evidence of the butchering of carcasses by hominids.

calibrated relative dating techniques   Techniques that use regular or somewhat regular processes that can be correlated to an absolute chronology to estimate the age of a site.

calotte   The skullcap, or the bones of the cranium, exclusive of those that form of the face and the base of the cranium.

calvaria   The braincase; includes the bones of the calotte and those that form the base of the cranium but excludes the bones of the face.

canine fossa   An indentation on the maxilla above the root of the canine, an anatomical feature usually associated with modern humans that may be present in some archaic *Homo* species in Europe.

captive study   Primate behavior study conducted in a zoo, laboratory, or other enclosed setting.

Catarrhini   Infraorder of the order Primates that includes the Old World monkeys, apes, and hominids.

catastrophism   Theory that there have been multiple creations interspersed by great natural disasters such as Noah's flood.

centromere   Condensed and constricted region of a chromosome. During mitosis and meiosis, location where sister chromatids attach to one another.

cerebellum   The "little brain" tucked under the cerebrum, and important in the control of balance, posture, and voluntary movement.

cerebral cortex   The layer of gray matter that covers the surface of the cerebral hemispheres, divided into functional regions that correspond to local patterns of neuronal organization.

cerebrum   The largest part of the human brain, which is split into left and right hemispheres. Seat of all "higher" brain functions.

cervical vertebrae   The seven neck vertebrae.

chain of custody   In forensic cases, the detailed notes that establish what was collected at the scene, the whereabouts of these remains, and the access to them after retrieval from the scene.

Châtelperronian   An Upper Paleolithic tool industry that has been found in association with later Neandertals.

chromatin   The diffuse form of DNA as it exists during the interphase of the cell cycle.

chromosomes   Discrete structures composed of condensed DNA and supporting proteins.

chronometric dating techniques   Techniques that estimate the age of an object in absolute terms through the use of a natural clock such as radioactive decay or tree ring growth.

cladistics   Method of classification using ancestral and derived traits to distinguish patterns of evolution within lineages.

cladogenesis   Evolution through the branching of a species or a lineage.

cladogram   Branching diagram showing evolved relationships among members of a lineage.

cleaver   Type of Acheulean bifacial tool, usually oblong with a broad cutting edge.

cline   The distribution of a trait or allele across geographical space.

coccyx   The fused tail vertebrae that are very small in humans and apes.

co-dominant   In a diploid organism, two different alleles of a gene that are both expressed in a heterozygous individual.

codon   A triplet of nucleotide bases in mRNA that specifies an amino acid or the initiation or termination of a polypeptide sequence.

cognitive universals   Cognitive phenomena such as sensory processing, the basic emotions, consciousness, motor control, memory, and attention that are expressed by all normal individuals.

compound temporonuchal crest   Bony crest at the back of the skull formed when an enlarged temporalis muscle approaches enlarged neck (nuchal) muscles, present in apes and *A. afarensis*.

convergent evolution   Similar form or function brought about by natural selection under similar environments rather than shared ancestry.

core   The raw material source (a river cobble or a large flake) from which flakes are removed.

core area   The part of a home range that is most intensively used.

CP₃ (sectorial premolar complex)   Combination of canine and first premolar teeth that forms a self-sharpening apparatus.

cranial crests   Bony ridges on the skull to which muscles attach.

creation science   A creationist attempt to refute the evidence of evolution.

cross-cultural universals   Behavioral phenomena, such as singing, dancing, and mental illness, that are found in almost all human cultures, but are not necessarily exhibited by each member of a cultural group.

crossing over   Exchange of genetic material between homologous chromosomes during the first prophase of meiosis; mechanism for genetic recombination.

cultural anthropology   The study of human societies, especially in a cross-cultural context; the subdivision of anthropology that includes ethnology, archaeology, and linguistics.

culture The sum total of learned traditions, values, and beliefs that groups of people, and a few species of highly intelligent animals, possess.

cytoplasm In a eukaryotic cell, the region within the cell membrane that surrounds the nucleus; it contains organelles, which carry out the essential functions of the cell, such as energy production, metabolism, and protein synthesis.

data The scientific evidence produced by an experiment or by observation, from which scientific conclusions are made.

datum point A permanent, fixed point relative to which the location of items of interest are recorded during archaeological mapping and excavation.

daughter isotope (product) The isotope that is produced as the result of radioactive decay of the parent isotope.

deduction A conclusion that follows logically from a set of observations.

deletion mutation A change in the base sequence of a gene that results from the loss of one or more base pairs in the DNA.

deme Local, interbreeding population that is defined in terms of its genetic composition (for example, allele frequencies).

dental apes Early apes exhibiting Y-5 molar patterns but monkey-like postcranial skeletons.

dental arcade The parabolic arc that forms the upper or lower row of teeth.

deoxyribonucleic acid (DNA) A double-stranded molecule that is the carrier of genetic information. Each strand is composed of a linear sequence of nucleotides; the two strands are held together by hydrogen bonds that form between complementary bases.

diastema Gap between anterior teeth.

diploid number Full complement of paired chromosomes in a somatic cell. In humans, the diploid number is 46 (23 pairs of different chromosomes).

directional selection Natural selection that drives evolutionary change by selecting for greater or lesser frequency of a given trait in a population.

diurnal Active during daylight hours.

dominance hierarchy Ranking of individual primates in a group that reflects their ability to displace, intimidate, or defeat group mates in contests.

dominant In a diploid organism, an allele that is expressed when present on only one of a pair of homologous chromosomes.

Duffy blood group Red blood cell system useful for studying admixture between African- and European-derived populations.

Early Stone Age (or Lower Paleolithic) The earliest stone tool industries including the Oldowan and Acheulean industries, called the ESA in Africa and the Lower Paleolithic outside Africa.

ecological intelligence Hominid intelligence and brain size increase theorized as a result of benefits of navigating and foraging in a complex tropical forest ecosystem.

ecological species concept Defines species based on the uniqueness of their ecological niche.

ecology The study of the interrelationships of plants, animals, and the physical environment in which they live.

electron spin resonance (ESR) Electron trap technique that measures the total amount of radioactivity accumulated by a specimen such as tooth or bone since burial.

electron trap techniques Radiometric techniques that measure the accumulation of electrons in traps in the crystal lattice of a specimen.

encephalization quotient (EQ) The ratio of the actual brain size of a species to its expected brain size based on a statistical regression of brain-to-body-size based on a large number of species.

endocast A replica (or cast) of the internal surface of the braincase that reflects the impressions made by the brain on the skull walls. Natural endocasts are formed by the filling of the braincase by sediments.

endoplasmic reticulum (ER) An organelle in the cytoplasm consisting of a folded membrane.

environment of evolutionary adaptedness (EEA) According to evolutionary psychologists, the critical period for understanding the selective forces that shape human behavior; exemplified by hunter–gatherer lifestyles of hominids before the advent of agriculture.

environmentalism The view that the environment has great powers to directly shape the anatomy of individual organisms.

enzyme A complex protein that is a catalyst for chemical processes in the body.

epidemiology The quantitative study of the occurrence and cause of disease in populations.

estrus Hormonally influenced period of sexual receptivity in some female mammals, which corresponds to the timing of ovulation.

ethnic group A human group defined in terms of sociological, cultural, and linguistic traits.

ethnobiology The study of how traditional cultures classify objects and organisms in the natural world.

ethnography The practice of cultural anthropology. Ethnographers study the minute-to-minute workings of human societies, especially non-Western societies.

ethnology The study of human societies, their traditions, rituals, beliefs, and the differences in these traits between societies.

eukaryotes A cell that possesses a well-organized nucleus.

eutheria Mammals that reproduce with a placenta and uterus.

evolution A change in the frequency of a gene or a trait in a population over multiple generations.

evolutionary psychology Approach to understanding the evolution of human behavior that emphasizes the selection of specific behavioral patterns in the context of the environment of evolutionary adaptedness.

evolutionary species concept Defines species as evolutionary lineages with their own unique identity.

experimentation The testing of a hypothesis.

falsifiable Able to be shown to be false.

female philopatry Primate social system in which females remain and breed in the group of their birth, whereas males emigrate.

femoral condyles The enlarged inferior end of the femur that forms the top of the knee joint.

field study   Primate behavior study conducted in the habitat in which the primate naturally occurs.

fission track dating   Radiometric technique for dating non-crystalline materials using the decay of ^{238}Ur and counting the tracks that are produced by this fission. Estimates the age of sediments in which fossils are found.

fission–fusion   Form of mating system seen in chimpanzees, bonobos, and a few other primates in which there are temporary subgroups but no stable, cohesive groups.

fission–fusion (polygyny)   Type of primate polygyny in which animals travel in foraging parties of varying sizes instead of a cohesive group.

fitness   Reproductive success.

flake   The stone fragment struck from a core, thought to have been the primary tools of the Oldowan.

folivores   Animals who eat a diet composed mainly of leaves, or foliage.

foramen magnum   Hole in the occipital bone through which the spinal cord connects to the brain.

forensic anthropology   The study of human remains applied to a legal context.

fossils   The preserved remnants of once-living things, often buried in the ground.

founder effect   A component of genetic drift theory, stating that new populations that become isolated from the parent population carry only the genetic variation of the founders.

frequency-dependent balanced polymorphism   Balanced polymorphism that is maintained because one (or more) of the alternative phenotypes has a selective advantage over the other phenotypes only when it is present in the population below a certain frequency.

frugivorous   An animal that eats a diet composed mainly of fruit.

gametes   The sex cells: sperm in males and eggs (or ova) in females.

gene flow   Movement of genes between populations.

gene   The fundamental unit of heredity. Consists of a sequence of DNA bases that carries the information for synthesizing a protein (or polypeptide) and occupies a specific chromosomal locus.

genetic bottleneck   Temporary dramatic reduction in size of a population or species.

genetic code   The system whereby the nucleotide triplets in DNA and RNA contain the information for synthesizing proteins from the twenty amino acids.

genetic drift   Random changes in gene frequency in a population.

genome   The sum total of all the genes carried by an individual.

genotype   The genetic makeup of an individual. *Genotype* can refer to the entire genetic complement or more narrowly to the alleles present at a specific locus on two homologous chromosomes.

geologic time scale (GTS)   The categories of time into which Earth's history is usually divided by geologists and paleontologists: eras, periods, epochs.

geology   The study of Earth systems.

geomagnetic polarity time scale (GPTS)   Time scale composed of the sequence of paleomagnetic orientations of strata through time.

gluteal muscles   Gluteus maximus, medius, and minimus, the muscles of walking, which have undergone radical re-alignment in habitual bipeds.

gradualism   Darwinian view of slow, incremental evolutionary change.

group selection   Notion, largely discredited by the rise of Darwinian theory, proposing that animals act for the good of their social group or of their species.

half-life   The time it takes for half of the original amount of an unstable isotope of an element to decay into more stable forms.

hammerstone   A stone used for striking cores to produce flakes or bones to expose marrow.

hand axe   Type of Acheulean bifacial tool, usually teardrop-shaped, with a long cutting edge.

haploid number   The number of chromosomes found in a gamete, representing one from each pair found in a diploid somatic cell. In humans, the haploid number is 23

haplorhine (Haplorhini)   Suborder of the order Primates that includes the anthropoids and the tarsier.

haplotypes   Combinations of alleles (or at the sequence level, mutations) that are found together in an individual.

hard object feeding   Chewing tough, hard-to-break food items such as nuts or fibrous vegetation.

Hardy–Weinberg equilibrium   The theoretical distribution of alleles in a given population in the absence of evolution, expressed as a mathematical equation.

hemoglobin   Protein found in red blood cells that transports oxygen.

heritability   The proportion of total phenotypic variability observed for a given trait that can be ascribed to genetic factors.

heterodont   Tooth array in which different teeth have different forms and functions.

heterozygous advantage   With reference to a particular genetic system, the situation in which heterozygotes have a selective advantage over homozygotes (for example, sickle-cell disease); a mechanism for maintaining a balanced polymorphism.

heterozygous   Having two different alleles at the loci for a gene on a pair of homologous chromosomes (or autosomes).

home base   Archaeological term for an area to which early hominids may have brought tools and carcasses and around which their activities were centered.

home range   The spatial area used by a primate group.

hominid   A member of the primate family Hominidae, distinguished by bipedal posture and, in more recently evolved species, a large brain.

homodont   Having teeth that are uniform in form, shape, and function.

homologous chromosomes   Members of the same pair of chromosomes (or autosomes). Homologous chromosomes undergo crossing over during meiosis.

homology   Similarity of traits resulting from shared ancestry.

homozygous   Having the same allele at the loci for a gene on both members of a pair of homologous chromosomes (or autosomes).

hormone   A natural substance (often a protein) produced by specialized cells in one location of the body that influences the activity or physiology of cells in a different location.

human biology   Subfield of biological anthropology dealing with human growth and development, adaptation to environmental extremes, and human genetics.

human evolutionary ecology   Approach to understanding the evolution of human behavior that attempts to explore ecological and demographic factors important in determining individual reproductive success and fitness in a cultural context.

human leukocyte antigen (HLA) system   Class of blood group markers formed by proteins expressed on the surface of white blood cells (leukocytes).

hylobatid (Hylobatidae)   Member of the gibbon, or lesser ape, family.

hyoid bone   A small "floating bone" in the front part of the throat, which is held in place by muscles and ligaments.

hypothesis   A preliminary explanation of a phenomenon. Hypothesis formation is the first step of the scientific method.

ilium   The blade of the innominate to which gluteal muscles attach.

immunoglobulins   Proteins produced by B lymphocytes that function as antibodies.

immutability (or fixity)   Stasis, lack of change.

inbreeding   Mating between close relatives.

inbreeding depression   Lesser fitness of offspring of closely related individuals compared with the fitness of the offspring of less closely related individuals, caused largely by the expression of lethal or debilitating recessive alleles.

incest   A violation of cultural rules regulating mating behavior.

incidence rate   The number of new occurrences of a disease over a given period of time divided by the population size.

inclusive fitness   Reproductive success of an organism plus the fitness of its close kin.

infanticide   The killing of infants, either by members of the infant's group or by a member of a rival group.

innominate bones (os coxae)   The pair of bones that compose the lateral parts of the pelvis; each innominate is made up of three bones that fuse during adolescence.

insertion mutation   A change in the base sequence of a gene that results from the addition of one or more base pairs in the DNA.

intelligent design   A creationist school of thought that proposes that natural selection cannot account for the diversity and complexity of form and function seen in nature.

ischium   Portion of the innominate bone that forms the bony underpinning of the rump.

isotopes   Variant forms of an element that differ based on their atomic weights and numbers of neutrons in the nucleus. Both stable and unstable (radioactive) isotopes exist in nature.

juxtamastoid eminence   A ridge of bone next to the mastoid process; in Neandertals, it is larger than the mastoid process itself.

karyotype   The complete chromosomal complement of an individual; usually based on a photograph of the chromosomes visualized under the microscope.

kin selection   Principle that animals behave preferentially toward their genetic kin; formulated by William Hamilton.

k-selected   Reproductive strategy in which fewer offspring are produced per female, interbirth intervals are long, and maternal investment is high.

lactose intolerant   The inability to digest lactose, the sugar found in milk; most adult mammals (including humans) are lactose intolerant as adults.

language   The unique system of communication used by members of the human species.

Levallois technique   A Middle Paleolithic technique that made use of prepared cores to produce uniform flakes.

linguistic anthropology   The study of language, its origins, and use; also called anthropological linguistics.

linkage   Genes that are found on the same chromosome are said to be linked. The closer together two genes are on a chromosome, the greater the linkage and the less likely they are to be separated during crossing over.

lithostratigraphy   The study of geologic deposits and their formation, stratigraphic relationships, and relative time relationships based on their lithologic (rock) properties.

locus   The location of a gene on a chromosome. The locus for a gene is identified by the number of the chromosome on which it is found and its position on the chromosome.

lumbar vertebrae   The five vertebrae of the lower back.

lunate sulcus   A prominent sulcus on the lateral side of the hemisphere of most nonhuman primates, which divides the primary visual cortex of the occipital lobe from the rest of the cerebrum.

Lysenkoism   Soviet-era research program that tried to apply Lamarckian thinking to agricultural production.

macroevolution   Evolution of major phenotypic changes over relatively short time periods.

male philopatry   Primate social system in which males remain and breed in the group of their birth, whereas females emigrate.

mastoid process   A protrusion from the temporal bone of the skull located behind the ear.

material culture   The objects or artifacts of past human societies.

maternal–fetal incompatibility   Occurs when the mother produces antibodies against an antigen (for example, a red blood cell surface protein) expressed in the fetus that she does not possess.

matrilineal   Pattern of female kinship in a primate social group.

megadontia   Enlarged teeth.

meiosis   Cell division that occurs in the testes and ovaries that leads to the formation of sperm and ova (gametes).

melanin   A dark pigment produced by the melanocytes of the epidermis, which is the most important component of skin color.

melanocytes   Cells in the epidermis that produce melanin.

menarche   The onset of a girl's first menstrual period.

Mendel's law of independent assortment   Genes found on different chromosomes are sorted into sex cells independently of one another.

Mendel's law of segregation   The two alleles of a gene found on each of a pair of chromosomes segregate independently of one another into sex cells.

menopause   The postreproductive period in the lives of women, after the cessation of ovulation and menses.

messenger RNA (mRNA)   Strand of RNA synthesized in the nucleus as a complement to a specific gene (transcription). It carries the information for the sequence of amino acids to make a specific protein into the cytoplasm, where it is read at a ribosome and a protein molecule is synthesized (translation).

metatarsals   Five foot bones that join the tarsals to the toes and form a portion of the longitudinal arch of the foot.

metatheria   Mammals that reproduce without a placenta, including the marsupials.

metopic keel   Longitudinal ridge or thickening of bone along the midline of the frontal bone.

microevolution   The study of evolutionary phenomena that occur within a species.

microliths   Small, flaked stone tools probably designed to be hafted to wood or bone; common feature of Upper Paleolithic and Later Stone Age tool industries.

Middle Paleolithic (Middle Stone Age)   Stone tool industries that used prepared core technologies.

midfacial prognathism   The forward projection of the middle facial region, including the nose.

mitochondria   Organelles in the cytoplasm of the cell where energy production for the cell takes place. Contains its own DNA.

mitochondrial DNA (mtDNA)   Small loop of DNA found in the mitochondria. It is clonally and maternally inherited.

mitosis   Somatic cell division in which a single cell divides to produce two identical daughter cells.

molecular clock   A systematic accumulation of genetic change that can be used to estimate the time of divergence between two groups if relative rates are constant and a calibration point from the fossil record is available.

monogamy   A mating bond; primates can be socially monogamous but still mate occasionally outside the pair bond.

monogenism   Ancient belief that all people are derived from a single creation.

most recent common ancestor (MRCA)   In a phylogenetic tree, the MRCA is indicated by the deepest node from which all contemporary variants can be shown to have evolved.

motherese (infant-directed speech)   Emotive spoken language used by mothers and other adults when addressing prelinguistic babies and children.

Movius line   The separation between areas of the Old World in which Acheulean technology occurs and those in which it does not; named by archaeologist Hallam Movius.

multiregional models   Phylogenetic models that suggest that modern humans evolved in the context of gene flow between Middle to Late Pleistocene hominid populations from different regions, so there is no single location where modern humans first evolved.

muscles of mastication   The chewing muscles: masseter, temporalis, medial and lateral pterygoids.

mutation   An alteration in the DNA, which may or may not alter the function of a cell. If it occurs in a gamete, it may be passed from one generation to the next.

natural selection   Differential reproductive success over multiple generations.

neocortex   The part of the brain that controls higher cognitive function.

neurons   The basic cellular units of the nervous system. A neuron consists of a cell body and specialized processes called dendrites (which receive inputs from other neurons) and axons (outgrowths through which neurons send impulses to other neurons).

nocturnal   Active at night.

nondisjunction error   The failure of homologous chromosomes (chromatids) to separate properly during cell division. When it occurs during meiosis, it may lead to the formation of gametes that are missing a chromosome or have an extra copy of a chromosome.

nuchal plane   Flattened bony area of the occipital posterior to the foramen magnum, to which neck muscles attach.

nucleotide   Molecular building block of nucleic acids DNA and RNA; consists of a phosphate, sugar, and base.

nucleus   In eukaryotic cells, the part of the cell in which the genetic material is separated from the rest of the cell (cytoplasm) by a plasma membrane.

null hypothesis   The starting assumption for scientific inquiry, that one's research results occur by random chance. One's hypothesis must challenge this initial assumption.

observation   The gathering of scientific information by watching a phenomenon.

occipital bun   A backward-projecting bulge on the occipital part of the skull.

occipital torus   A thickened horizontal ridge of bone on the occipital bone at the rear of the cranium.

Oldowan   The tool industry characterized by simple, usually unifacial core and flake tools.

olfactory bulbs   Knoblike structures, located on the underside of the frontal lobes, that form the termination of olfactory nerves running from the nasal region to the brain.

omomyoids   Family of mostly Eocene primates probably ancestral to all haplorhines.

ontogeny   The life cycle of an organism from conception to death.

optically stimulated luminescence (OSL)   Electron trap technique that uses light to measure the amount of radioactivity accumulated by crystals in sediments (such as sand grains) since burial.

osteodontokeratic culture   A bone, tooth, and horn tool kit envisioned by Raymond Dart as made by *Australopithecus*.

osteology   The study of the skeleton.

paleoanthropology　The study of the fossil record of ancestral humans and their primate kin.

paleomagnetism　The magnetic polarity recorded in ancient sediments. Reversed or normal direction is used to correlate with the geomagnetic polarity time scale to infer an age for a site.

paleoneurology　The study of the evolution of brain structure and function.

paleontology　The study of extinct organisms, based on their fossilized remains.

paleopathology　The study of diseases in ancestral human populations.

paleosol　Ancient soil.

paradigm　A conceptual framework useful for understanding a body of evidence.

parapatric speciation　Speciation occurring when two populations have continuous distributions and some phenotypes in that distribution are more favorable than others.

parent isotope　The original radioactive isotope in a sample.

particulate inheritance　The concept of heredity based on the transmission of genes (alleles) according to Mendelian principles.

pathogens　Organisms and entities that can cause disease.

pedigree　A diagram used in the study of human genetics that shows the transmission of a genetic trait over several generations of a family.

phalanges　Bones that form the fingers and toes.

phenology　The leafing and fruiting cycles of a forest.

phenotype　An observable or measurable feature of an organism. Phenotypes can be anatomical, biochemical, or behavioral.

phenylketonuria (PKU)　Autosomal recessive condition that leads to the accumulation of large quantities of the amino acid phenylalanine, which causes mental retardation and other phenotypic abnormalities.

phylogeny　An evolutionary tree indicating relatedness and divergence of taxonomic groups.

physical anthropology　The study of humans as biological organisms, considered in an evolutionary framework.

phytoliths　Silica bodies produced by some plants, especially grasses, that can be used to indicate the presence of certain types of vegetation at a fossil site.

platycnemic　A bone that is flattened from side to side.

platymeric　A bone that is flattened from front to back.

Platyrrhini　Infraorder of the order Primates that is synonymous with the New World monkeys, or ceboids.

pleiotropy　The phenomenon of a single gene having multiple phenotypic effects.

plesiadapiforms　Mammalian order or suborder of mammals that may be ancestral to later Primates, characterized by some but not all of the primate trends.

point mutation　A change in the base sequence of a gene that results from the change of a single base to a different base.

polyandrous　Mating system in which one female mates with multiple males.

polyandry　Mating system in which one female mates with multiple males.

polygenic traits　Phenotypic traits that result from the combined action of more than one gene; most complex traits are polygenic.

polygenism　Ancient belief that people are derived from multiple creations.

polygynandrous　Primate social system consisting of multiple males and multiple females.

polygynous　Mating system in which one man is allowed to take more than one wife.

polygyny　Mating system consisting of at least one male and more than one female.

polymerase chain reaction (PCR)　Method for amplifying DNA sequences using the Taq polymerase enzyme. Can potentially produce millions or billions of copies of a DNA segment starting from a very small number of target DNA.

polymorphic　Two or more distinct phenotypes (at the genetic or anatomical levels) that exist within a population.

polypeptide　A molecule made up of a chain of amino acids.

polytypic species　Species that consist of a number of separate breeding populations, each varying in some genetic trait.

pongid (Pongidae)　One of the four great apes species: gorilla, chimpanzee, bonobo, or orangutan.

population　An interbreeding group of organisms.

population genetics　The study of genetic variation within and between groups of organisms.

postorbital bar　A bony ring encircling the lateral side of the eye but not forming a complete cup around the eye globe.

postorbital constriction　The pinching-in of the cranium just behind the orbits where the temporalis muscle sits. Little constriction indicates a large brain and small muscle; great constriction indicates a large muscle, as in the robust australopithecines.

potassium–argon (K–Ar) dating　Radiometric technique using the decay of ^{40}K to ^{40}Ar in potassium-bearing rocks; estimates the age of sediments in which fossils are found.

prefrontal region　The association cortex of the frontal lobes, located forward of the primary motor region of the precentral gyrus and the supplemental motor areas.

prehensile tail　Grasping tail possessed by some species of the primate families Cebidae and Atelidae.

prevalence rate　The number of existing cases of a disease divided by the population (or the population at risk).

primate　Member of the mammalian order Primates, including prosimians, monkeys, apes, and humans, defined by a suite of anatomical and behavioral traits.

primatology　The study of the nonhuman primates and their anatomy, genetics, behavior, and ecology.

progesterone　A steroid hormone produced by the corpus luteum and the placenta, which prepares the uterus for pregnancy and helps maintain pregnancy once fertilization has occurred.

prognathic face　Projection of the face well in front of the braincase.

prokaryotes　Single-celled organisms, such as bacteria, in which the genetic material is not separated from the rest of the cell by a nucleus.

prosimian   Member of the primate suborder Prosimii that includes the lemurs, lorises, galagos, and tarsiers.

protein synthesis   The assembly of proteins from amino acids, which occurs at ribosomes in the cytoplasm and is based on information carried by mRNA.

proteins   Complex molecules formed from chains of amino acids (polypeptide) or from a complex of polypeptides. They function as structural molecules, transport molecules, antibodies, enzymes, and hormones.

prototheria   Mammals that reproduce by egg-laying, then nurse young from nipples. The Australian platypus and echidna are the only living monotremes.

provenience   The origin or original source (as of a fossil).

pubis   Portion of the innominate that forms the anterior part of the birth canal.

punctuated equilibrium   Model of evolution characterized by rapid bursts of change, followed by long periods of stasis.

qualitative variation   Phenotypic variation that can be characterized as belonging to discrete, observable categories.

quantitative variation   Phenotypic variation that is characterized by the distribution of continuous variation (expressed using a numerical measure) within a population (for example, in a bell curve).

quarrying site   An archaeological site at which there is evidence that early hominids were obtaining the raw material to make stone tools.

race   In biological taxonomy, same thing as a subspecies; when applied to humans, sometimes incorporates both cultural and biological factors.

racism   A prejudicial belief that members of one ethnic group are superior in some way to those of another.

radiocarbon dating   Radiometric technique that uses the decay of ^{14}C in organic remains such as wood and bone to estimate the time since death of the organism.

radiometric dating   Chronometric techniques that use radioactive decay of isotopes to estimate age.

recessive   In a diploid organism, refers to an allele that must be present in two copies (homozygous) in order to be expressed.

recognition species concept   Defines species based on unique traits or behaviors that allow members of one species to identify each other for mating.

recombination   The rearrangement of genes on homologous chromosomes that occurs during crossing over in meiosis. The source of variation arising out of sexual reproduction; important for increasing rates of natural selection.

reductionism   Paradigm that an organism is the sum of many evolved parts and that organisms can best be understood through an adaptationist approach.

regulatory genes   Guide the expression of structural genes, without coding for a protein themselves.

relative dating techniques   Dating techniques that establish the age of a fossil only in comparison to other materials found above and below it.

relative rate test   A means of determining whether molecular evolution has been occurring at a constant rate in two lineages by comparing whether these lineages are equidistant from an outgroup.

replacement models   Phylogenetic models that suggest that modern humans evolved in one location and then spread geographically, replacing other earlier hominid populations without or with little admixture.

reproductive isolating mechanisms (RIMs)   Any factor—behavioral, ecological, or anatomical—that prevents a male and female of two different species from hybridizing.

reproductive potential   The possible output of offspring by one sex.

reproductive variance   A measure of variation from the mean of a population in the reproductive potential of one sex compared with the other.

rhesus (Rh) system   Blood type system that can cause hemolytic anemia of the newborn through maternal–fetal incompatibility if the mother is Rh-negative and the child is Rh-positive.

ribonucleic acid (RNA)   Single-stranded nucleic acid that performs critical functions during protein synthesis and comes in three forms: messenger RNA, transfer RNA, and ribosomal RNA.

ribosomes   Structures composed primarily of RNA, which are found on the endoplasmic reticulum. They are the site of protein synthesis.

r-selected   Reproductive strategy in which females have many offspring, interbirth intervals are short, and maternal investment per offspring is low.

sacrum   The fused vertebrae that form the back of the pelvis.

sagittal crest   Bony crest running lengthwise down the center of the cranium on the parietal bones; for the attachment of the temporalis muscles.

sagittal keel   Longitudinal ridge or thickening of bone on the sagittal suture not associated with any muscle attachment.

scientific method   Standard scientific research procedure in which a hypothesis is stated, data are collected to test it, and the hypothesis is either supported or refuted.

secondary compounds   Toxic chemical compounds found in the leaves of many plants which the plants use as a defense against leaf-eating animals.

semi–free-ranging   Primate behavior study conducted in a large area that is encloed or isolated in some way so the population is captive.

senescence   Age-related decline in physiological or behavioral function in adult organisms.

sex chromosomes   In mammals, chromosomes X and Y, with XX producing females and XY producing males.

sexual dimorphism   Difference in size, shape, or color between the sexes.

sexual receptivity   Willingness and ability of a female to mate, also defined as fertility.

sexual selection   Differential reproductive success within one sex of any species.

shovel-shaped incisors   Anterior teeth which on their lingual (tongue) surface are concave with two raised edges that make them look like tiny shovels.

sickle cell disease An autosomal recessive disease caused by a point mutation in an allele that codes for one of the polypeptide chains of the hemoglobin protein.

social intelligence Hominid intelligence and brain size increase theorized as a result of benefits of being politically or socially clever when living with others; sometimes called Machiavellian intelligence.

social system The grouping pattern in which a primate species lives, including its size and composition evolved in response to natural and sexual selection pressures.

sociality Group living, a fundamental trait of haplorhine primates.

sociobiology Name popularized by E. O. Wilson for the evolutionary study of animal social behavior.

somatic cells The cells of the body that are not sex cells.

speciation Formation of one or more new species via reproductive isolation.

species An interbreeding group of animals or plants that are reproductively isolated through anatomy, ecology, behavior, or geographic distribution from all other such groups.

stabilizing selection Selection that maintains a certain phenotype by selecting against deviations from it.

stem cells Undifferentiated cells found in the developing embryo that can be induced to differentiate into a wide variety of cell types or tissues. Also found in adults, although adult stem cells are not as totipotent as embryonic stem cells.

strata Layers of rock.

stratigraphy The study of the order of rock layers and the sequence of events they reflect.

strepsirhine (Strepsirhini) Suborder of the order Primates that includes the prosimians, excluding the tarsier.

structural genes Genes that contain the information to make a protein.

subspecies Group of local populations that share part of the geographic range of a species, and can be differentiated from other subspecies based on one or more phenotypic traits.

supraorbital torus Thickened ridge of bone above the eye orbits of the skull; a browridge.

sympatric speciation Speciation occurring in the same geographic location.

systematics Branch of biology that describes patterns of organismal variation.

taphonomy The study of what happens to the remains of an animal from the time of death to the time of discovery.

tarsals Foot bones that form the ankle and arches of the foot.

taurodontism Molar teeth with expanded pulp cavities and fused roots.

taxon A group of organisms assigned to a particular category.

taxonomy The science of biological classification.

technical intelligence Hominid intelligence and brain size increase modeled as a result of tool use and extractive foraging.

tephrostratigraphy A form of lithostratigraphy in which the chemical fingerprint of a volcanic ash is used to correlate across regions.

teratogens Substances that cause birth defects or other abnormalities in the developing embryo or fetus during pregnancy.

territory The part of a home range that is defended against other members of the same species.

testosterone A steroid produced primarily in the testes and ovaries, and at a much higher level in men than in women. Responsible for the development of the male primary and secondary sexual characteristics. Strongly influences dominance and reproductive behavior.

theory of inheritance of acquired characteristics Discredited theory of evolutionary change proposing that changes that occur during the lifetime of an individual, through use or disuse, can be passed on to the next generation.

theory of mind Ability to place oneself into the mind of others; necessary for possessing an awareness of the knowledge or cognitive ability of others and for imitating or teaching others.

thermoluminescence (TL) Electron trap technique that uses heat to measure the amount of radioactivity accumulated by a specimen such as a stone tool since its last heating.

thoracic vertebrae The twelve vertebrae of the thorax that hold the ribs.

tool industry A particular style or tradition of making stone tools.

transfer RNA (tRNA) RNA molecules that bind to specific amino acids and transport them to ribosomes to be used during protein synthesis.

trinucleotide repeat diseases A family of autosomal dominant diseases that is caused by the insertion of multiple copies of a three-base pair sequence (CAG) that codes for the amino acid glutamine. Typically, the more copies inserted into the gene, the more serious the disease.

twin method A method for estimating the heritability of a phenotypic trait by comparing the concordance rates of identical and fraternal twins.

type specimen According to the laws of zoological nomenclature, the anatomical reference specimen for the species definition.

uniformitarianism Theory that the same gradual geological process we observe today was operating in the past.

Upper Paleolithic (Later Stone Age) Stone tool industries that are characterized by the development of blade-based technology.

uranium series (U-series) techniques Radiometric techniques using the decay of uranium to estimate an age for calcium carbonates including flowstones, shells, and teeth.

vertebral column The column of bones, and cartilaginous disks, that houses the spinal cord and provides structural support and flexibility to the body.

visual predation hypothesis Hypothesis for the origin of primate adaptation that focuses on the value of grasping hands and stereoscopic vision for catching small prey.

X-linked disorders   Genetic conditions that result from mutations to genes on the X chromosome. They are almost always expressed in males, who have only one copy of the X chromosome; in females, the second X chromosome containing the normally functioning allele protects them from developing X-linked disorders.

zygomatic arch   The bony arch formed by the zygomatic (cheek) bone and the temporal bone of the skull.

zygote   A fertilized egg.

Abbate E, Albianelli A, Azzaroli A, et al. 1998. A one million year old *Homo* cranium from the Danakil (Afar) depression of Eritrea. *Nature* 393:458–460.

Adams B.A. 2003. Establishing personal identification based on specific patterns of missing, filled, and unrestored teeth. *J. Forensic Science* 48:2–10.

Aiello L, Dean C. 1990. *An Introduction to Human Evolutionary Anatomy*. Academic Press, London.

Aiello LC, Wheeler P. 1995. The expensive-tissue hypothesis. *Current Anthropology* 36:199–221.

Akazawa T, Muhesen S. 2002. Neandertal burials: Excavation at Dederiyeh Cave, Afrin, Syria. Kyoto: International Research Center for Japanese Studies.

Albrecht A, Mundlos S. 2005. The other trinucleotide repeat: Polyalanine expansion disorders. *Current Opinion in Genetics and Development* 15:285–293.

Alcock J. 2001. *The Triumph of Sociobiology*. Oxford University Press, New York.

Alemseged Z, Spoor F, Kimbel W, et al. 2006. A juvenile early hominin skeleton from Dikika, Ethiopia. *Nature* 443:296–301.

Alemseged Z, Spoor F, Kimbel WH, Bobe R, Geraads D, Reed D, Wynn JG. 2006. A juvenile early hominin skeleton from Dikika, Ethiopia. *Nature* 443:296–301.

Allen JS. 1989. Franz Boas's physical anthropology: The critique of racial formalism revisited. *Current Anthropology* 30:79–84.

Allen JS. 1997. Are traditional societies schizophrenogenic? *Schizophrenia Bulletin* 23:357–364.

Allen JS, Cheer SM. 1996. The non-thrifty genotype. *Current Anthropology* 37:831–842.

Allen JS, Damasio H, Grabowski TJ. 2002. Normal neuroanatomical variation in the human brain: An MRI-volumetric study. *American Journal of Physical Anthropology* 118:341–358.

Allen JS, Sarich VM. 1988. Schizophrenia in an evolutionary perspective. *Perspectives in Biology and Medicine* 32:132–153.

Allison AC. 1954. Protection afforded by sickle-cell trait against malarial infection. *British Medical Journal* 1:290–294.

Altmann J. 1980. *Baboon Mothers and Infants*. Harvard University Press, Cambridge, MA.

Alvarez LW, Alvarez W, Asaro F, Michel HV. 1980. Extraterrestrial cause for the Cretaceous–Tertiary extinction. *Science* 208:1095–1108.

Alvarez W. 1997. *T. rex and the Crater of Doom*. Princeton University Press, Princeton, NJ.

Ambrose SH. 2001. Paleolithic technology and human evolution. *Science* 291:1748–1753.

American Psychiatric Association. 1994. *Diagnostic and Statistical Manual of Mental Disorders*, 4th ed. American Psychiatric Association, Washington, DC.

Anderson R. 1999. Human evolution, low back pain, and duallevel control. In *Evolutionary Medicine* (WR Trevathan, EO Smith, JJ McKenna, eds.), pp. 333–349. Oxford University Press, Oxford.

Andersson S. 1992. Female preference for long tails in lekking Jackson's widow-birds: Experimental evidence. *Animal Behavior* 43:379–388.

Antón SC. 1996. Tendon-associated bone features of the masticatory system in Neandertals. *Journal of Human Evolution* 31:391–408.

Antón SC. 2002. Evolutionary significance of cranial variation in Asian *Homo erectus*. *American Journal of Physical Anthropology* 118:301–323.

Antón SC. 2003. A natural history of *Homo erectus*. *Yearbook of Physical Anthropology* 46:126–170.

Antón SC, Leonard WR, Robertson M. 2002. An ecomorphological model of the initial hominid dispersal from Africa. *Journal of Human Evolution* 43:773–785.

Antón SC, Spoor F, Fellmann CD, Swisher CC. 2007. Defining *Homo erectus*: Size Considered. In Henke, Rothe and Tattersall (Eds). *Handbook of Paleoanthropology*, Volume 3, Chapter 11. Springer-Verlag.

Antón SC, Steadman DW. 2003. Mortuary patterns in burial caves on Mangaia, Cook Islands. *International J. Osteoarchaeology* 13:132–146.

Antón SC, Swisher CC III. 2001. Evolution and variation of cranial capacity in Asian *Homo erectus*. In *A Scientific Life: Papers in Honor of Professor Dr. Teuku Jacob* (E Indriati, SC Antón, J Kurtz, eds.), pp. 25–39. Bigraf Publishing, Yogyakarta, Indonesia.

Aoki K. 1986. A stochastic model of gene-culture coevolution suggested by the "cultural-historical hypothesis" for the evolution of adult lactose absorption in humans. *Proceedings of the National Academy of Sciences* 83:2929–2933.

Ardrey R. 1966. *The Territorial Imperative*. Atheneum, New York.

Arensburg B, Schepartz LA, Tillier AM, et al. 1990. A reappraisal of the anatomical basis for speech in Middle Paleolithic hominids. *American Journal of Physical Anthropology* 83:137–146.

Armelagos G. 1997. Disease, Darwin, and medicine in the third epidemiological transition. *Evolutionary Anthropology* 5:212–220.

Arsuaga JL. 2002. *The Neanderthal's Necklace*. Four Wall Eight Windows, New York.

Arsuaga JL, Martines A, Garcia A, Lorenzo C. 1997. The Sima de los Huesos crania (Sierra de Atapuerca, Spain). A comparative study. *Journal of Human Evolution* 33:219–281.

Arsuaga JL, Martínez I, Lorenzo C, et al. 1999. The human cranial remains from Gran Dolina Lower Pleistocene site (Sierra de Atapuerca, Spain). *Journal of Human Evolution* 37:431–457.

Asfaw B, Gilbert WH, Beyene Y, et al. 2002. Remains of *Homo erectus* from Bouri, Middle Ethiopia. *Nature* 416:317–320.

Asfaw B, White TD, Lovejoy CO, et al. 1999. *Australopithecus garhi*: A new species of early hominid from Ethiopia. *Science* 284:629–635.

Atran S. 1998. Folk biology and the anthropology of science: Cognitive universals and cultural particulars. *Behavioral and Brain Sciences* 21:547–609.

Bailey SE, Hublin JJ. 2006. Dental remains from the Grotte du Renne, Arcy-sur-Cure (Yonne). *Journal of Human Evolution* 50:485–508.

Barker G, Barton H, Bird M, et al. 2007. The 'human revolution' in lowland tropical Southeast Asia: the antiquity and behavior of anatomically modern humans at Niah Cave (Sarawak, Borneo). *Journal of Human Evolution* 52:243–261.

Barkow JH, Cosmides L, Tooby J, eds. 1992. *The Adapted Mind: Evolutionary Psychology and the Generation of Culture*. Oxford University Press, New York.

Barquet N, Domingo P. 1997. Smallpox: The triumph over the most terrible ministers of death. *Annals of Internal Medicine* 127:635–642.

Bass WA, Jefferson J. 2003. *Death's Acre: Inside the body farm, the legendary forensic laboratory*. Putnam Adult.

Bateson W. 1900–1901. Problems of heredity as a subject for horticultural investigation. *Journal of the Royal Horticultural Society* 25:54–61.

Bateson W. 1902. *Mendel's Principles of Heredity: A Defence*. Cambridge University Press, Cambridge.

Beall CM. 2001. Adaptations to altitude: A current assessment. *Annual Review of Anthropology* 30:423–456.

Beall CM, Decker MJ, Brittenham GM, et al. 2002. An Ethiopian pattern of human adaptation to high-altitude hypoxia. *Proceedings of the National Academy of Sciences* 99:17215–17218.

Beall CM, Steegman AT. 2000. Human adaptation to climate: Temperature, ultraviolet radiation, and altitude. In *Human Biology: An Evolutionary and Biocultural Perspective* (S Stinson, B Bogin, R Huss-Ashmore, D O'Rourke, eds.), pp. 163–224. Wiley-Liss, New York.

Beals KL, Smith CL, Dodd SM. 1984. Brain size, cranial morphology, climate, and time machines. *Current Anthropology* 25:301–330.

Beard CK, Qi T, Dawson MR, Wang B, Li C. 1994. A diverse new primate fauna from middle Eocene fissure fillings in southeastern China. *Nature* 368:604–609.

Bearder SK, Honess PE, Ambrose L. 1995. Species diversity among galagos with special reference to mate recognition. In *Creatures of the Dark: The Nocturnal Prosimians* (L Alterman, GA Doyle, MK Izard, eds.), pp. 1–22. Plenum, New York.

Beauval C, Maureille B, Lacrampe-Cuyaubere F, et al. 2005. A late Neandertal femur from Les Rochers-de-Villeneuve, France, *Proc. Natl. Acad. Sci. USA* 102:7085–7090.

Bedford ME, Russell KF, Lovejoy CO, Meindl RS, Simpson SW, Stuart-Macadam PL. 1993. Test of the multifactorial aging method using skeletons with known ages-at-death from the grant collection. *American Journal of Physical Anthropology* 91: 287–297.

Bednarik RG. 2003. A figurine from the African Acheulian. *Current Anthropology* 44:405–413.

Behe M. 1996. *Darwin's Black Box*. The Free Press, New York.

Behrensmeyer AK, Hill A, eds. 1980. *Fossils in the Making*. University of Chicago Press, Chicago.

Bellomo RV. 1994. Methods of determining early hominid behavioral activities associated with the controlled use of fire at FxJj 20 Main, Koobi Fora, Kenya. *Journal of Human Evolution* 27:173–195.

Benefit BR. 1999. *Victoriapithecus*, the key to Old World monkey and catarrhine origins. *Evolutionary Anthropology* 7:155–174.

Benefit BR, McCrossin ML. 1995. Miocene hominoids and hominid origins. *Annual Review of Anthropology* 24:237–256.

Benefit BR, McCrossin ML. 2002. The Victoriapithecidae, Cercopithecoidea. In *The Primate Fossil Record* (WC Hartwig, ed.), pp. 241–253. Cambridge University Press, Cambridge.

Benit P, Rey F, Blandin-Savoja F, et al. 1999. The mutant genotype is the main determinant of the metabolic phenotype in phenylalanine hydroxylase deficiency. *Molecular Genetics and Metabolism* 68:43–47.

Berger T, Trinkaus E. 1995. Patterns of trauma among the Neandertals. *Journal of Archaeological Science* 22:841–852.

Berlin B. 1992. *Ethnobiological Classification: Principles of Categorization of Plants and Animals in Traditional Societies*. Princeton University Press, Princeton, NJ.

Bermudez de Castro JM, Arsuaga JL, Carbonell E, et al. 1997. A hominid from the lower Pleistocene of Atapuerca, Spain: Possible ancestor to Neandertals and modern humans. *Science* 276:1392–1395.

Beynon AD, Dean M. 1988. Distinct dental development patterns in early fossil hominids. *Nature* 335:509–514.

Bischoff JL, Williams RW, Rosenbauer RJ, Aramburu A, Arsuaga JL, Garcia N, Cuenca-Bescos G. 2007. High-resolution U-series dates from the Sima de los Huesos hominids yields 600 ±66 kyrs: implications for the evolution of the Neanderthal lineage. *Journal of Archaeological Science* 24:763–770.

Bickerton D. 1983. Pidgin and creole languages. *Scientific American* 249:116–122.

Bickerton D. 1990. *Language and Species*. University of Chicago Press, Chicago.

Bird R. 1999. Cooperation and conflict: The behavioral ecology of the sexual division of labor. *Evolutionary Anthropology* 8:65–75.

Bittles AH, Mason WM, Greene JC, Rao NA. 1991. Reproductive behavior and heath in consanguineous marriages. *Science* 252:789–794.

Bix HP. 2000. *Hirohito and the Making of Modern Japan*. HarperCollins, New York.

Bloch JI, Silcox MT. 2001. New basicrania of Paleocene–Eocene *Ignacius*: Re-evaluation of the Plesiadapiform–Dermopteran link. *American Journal of Physical Anthropology* 116:184–198.

Blum K, Cull JG, Braverman ER, Comings DE. 1996. Reward deficiency syndrome. *American Scientist* 84:132–145.

Blumenschine RJ. 1986. Carcass consumption sequences and the archaeological distinction of scavenging and hunting. *Journal of Human Evolution* 15:639–659.

Blumenschine RJ. 1987. Characteristics of an early hominid scavenging niche. *Current Anthropology* 28:383–407.

Boas F. 1912. Changes in the bodily form of descendants of immigrants. *American Anthropologist* 14:530–533.

Boas F. 1938(1911). *The Mind of Primitive Man*, rev. ed. Macmillan, New York.

Boas F. 1940. *Race, Language, and Culture*. University of Chicago Press, Chicago.

Bobe R, Behrensmeyer AK. 2004. The expansion of grassland ecosystems in Africa in relation to mammalian evolution and the origin of the genus *Homo Palaeogeography Palaeoclimatology Palaeoecology* 207:399–420.

Boesch C, Boesch H. 1989. Hunting behavior of wild chimpanzees in the Taï National Park. *American Journal of Physical Anthropology* 78:547–573.

Bogin B. 1993. Why must I be a teenager at all? *New Scientist* 137:34–38.

Bogin B. 1995. Plasticity in the growth of Mayan refugee children living in the United States. In *Human Variability and Plasticity* (CGN Mascie-Taylor, B Bogin, eds.), pp. 46–74. Cambridge University Press, Cambridge.

Bogin B. 1999. Evolutionary perspective on human growth. *Annual Review of Anthropology* 28:109–153.

Boinski S. 1987. Mating patterns in squirrel monkeys (*Saimiri oerstedi*). *Behavioral Ecology & Sociobiology* 21:13–21.

Boinski S. 1994. Affiliation patterns among male Costa Rican squirrel monkeys. *Behaviour* 130:191–209.

Borgerhoff Mulder M. 1987. On cultural and reproductive success: Kipsigis evidence. *American Anthropologist* 89:617–634.

Borgerhoff Mulder M. 1990. Kipsigis women's preferences for wealthy men: Evidence for female choice in mammals. *Behavioral Ecology and Sociobiology* 27:255–264.

Borries C, Launhardt K, Epplen C, et al. 1999. DNA analyses support the hypothesis that infanticide is adaptive in langur monkeys. *Proceedings of the Royal Society of London* B 266:901–904.

Bottini N, Meloni GF, Finocchi A, et al. 2001. Maternal–fetal interaction in the ABO system: A comparative analysis of healthy mothers and couples with recurrent spontaneous abortion suggests a protective effect of B incompatibility. *Human Biology* 73:167–174.

Bowler JM, Johnston H, Olley JM, et al. 2003. New ages for human occupation and climatic change at Lake Mungo, Australia. *Nature* 421:837–840.

Boyd R, Richerson P. 1988. *Culture and the Evolutionary Process.* University of Chicago Press, Chicago.

Boyd WC. 1950. *Genetics and the Races of Man.* Little, Brown, Boston.

Brain CK. 1981. *The Hunters or the Hunted? Introduction to African Cave Taphonomy.* University of Chicago Press, Chicago.

Branda RF, Eaton JW. 1978. Skin color and nutrient photolysis: An evolutionary hypothesis. *Science* 201:625–626.

Bräuer G. 1984. The "Afro-European *sapiens* hypothesis" and hominid evolution in East Asia during the Late Middle and Upper Pleistocene. *Courier Forschunginstitut Senckenberg* 69:145–165.

Britten RJ. 2002. Divergence between samples of chimpanzee and human DNA sequences is 5%, counting indels. *Proceedings of the National Academy of Sciences* 99:13633–13635.

Broadfield DC, Holloway RL, Mowbray K, et al. 2001. Endocast of Sambungmacan 3: A new *Homo erectus* from Indonesia. *The Anatomical Record* 262:369–379.

Brockelman WY, Reichard U, Treesucon U, Raemakers JJ. 1998. Dispersal, pair formation, and social structure in gibbons (*Hylobates lar*). *Behavioral Ecology and Sociobiology* 42:329–339.

Bromage, TG. 1989. Ontogeny of the early hominid face. *J. Hum. Evol.* 18:751–773.

Brooks S, Suchey JM. 1990. Skeletal age determination based on the os pubis: A comparison of the Acsadi–Nemeskeri and Suchey–Brooks methods. *Human Evolution, 5:* 227–238.

Broom R. 1947. Discovery of a new skull of the South African ape-man, *Plesianthropus. Nature* 159:672.

Brown DE. 1991. *Human Universals.* McGraw-Hill, New York.

Brown FH. 1983. Correlation of Tulu Bor Tuff at Koobi Fora with the Sidi Hakoma Tuff at Hadar. *Nature* 306:210.

Brown FH. 1992. Methods of dating. In *The Cambridge Encyclopedia of Human Evolution* (S Jones, R Martin, D Pilbeam, eds.), pp. 179–186. Cambridge University Press, Cambridge.

Brown KH, Gilman R. 1986. Nutritional effects of intestinal helminths with special reference to ascariasis and strongyloidiasis. In *The Interaction of Parasitic Diseases and Nutrition* (C Chagas, GT Keusch, eds.), pp. 213–232. Pontifica Academia Scientarium, Vatican City.

Brown P, Sutikana T, Morwood MJ, et al. Due (2004) A new small-bodied hominid from the Late Pleistocene of Flores, Indonesia. *Nature* 431:1055–1061.

Brues AM. 1977. *People and Races.* Macmillan, New York.

Brunet M, Beauvilain A, Coppens Y, et al. 1995. The first australopithecine 2,500 kilometres west of the Rift Valley (Chad). *Nature* 378:273–275.

Brunet M, Beauvilain A, Coppens Y, et al. 1996. *Australopithecus bahrelghazali,* une nouvelle espece d'hominide ancien de la region de Koro Toro (Tchad). *Comptes Rendus des Seances de l'Academie des Sciences* 322:907–913.

Brunet M, Guy F, Pilbeam D, et al. 2002. A new hominid from the Upper Miocene of Chad, Central Africa. *Nature* 418:145–151.

Bshary R, Noë R. 1997. The formation of red colobus–diana monkey associations under predation pressure from chimpanzees. *Proceedings of the Royal Society of London* B 264:253–259.

Buckley GA. 1997. A new species of *Purgatorius* (Mammalia; Primatomorpha) from the Lower Paleocene Bear Formation, Crazy Mountains Basin, South-Central Montana. *Journal of Palaeontology* 71:149–155.

Bumpus HC. 1899. The elimination of the unfit as illustrated by the introduced sparrow, *Passer domesticus. Biol. Lectures, Marine Biological Laboratory, Woods Hole* 209–226.

Bunn HT, Ezzo JA. 1993. Hunting and scavenging by Plio-Pleistocene hominids: Nutritional constraints, archaeological patterns, and behavioural implications. *Journal of Archaeological Science* 20:365–398.

Burger J, Kirchner M, Bramanti B, Haak W, Thomas MG. 2007. Absence of the lactase-persistence-associated allele in early Neolithic Europeans. *Proceedings of the National Academy of Sciences* 104:3736–3741.

Burnham TC, Chapman JF, Gray PB, McIntyre MH, Lipson SF, Ellison PT. 2003. Men in committed, romantic relationships have lower testosterone. *Hormones and Behavior* 44:119–122.

Buss DM. 2003. *The Evolution of Desire.* Basic Books, New York.

Byrne RW. 1995. *The Thinking Ape.* Oxford University Press, Oxford.

Byrne RW, Whiten A, eds. 1988a. *Machiavellian Intelligence: Social Expertise and the Evolution of Intellect in Monkeys, Apes, and Humans.* Clarendon, Oxford.

Byrne RW, Whiten A. 1988b. Towards the next generation in data quality: A new survey of primate tactical deception. *Behavioral and Brain Sciences* 11:267–273.

Calvin WH. 1982. Did throwing stones shape hominid brain evolution? *Ethology and Sociobiology* 3:115–124.

Cande SC, Kent DV. 1995. Revised calibration of the geomagnetic polarity timescale for the Late Cretaceous and Cenozoic. *Journal of Geophysical Research* 100:6093–6095.

Cann RL. 2001. Genetic clues to dispersal in human populations: Retracing the past from the present. *Science* 291:1742–1748.

Cann RL. 2002. Tangled genetic routes. *Nature* 416:32–33.

Cann RL, Stoneking M, Wilson AC. 1987. Mitochondrial DNA and human evolution. *Nature* 325:31–36.

Caramelli D, Lalueza-Fox C, Vernesi C, et al. 2003. Evidence for a genetic discontinuity between Neandertals and 24,000-year-old anatomically modern Europeans. *Proceedings of the National Academy of Sciences* 100:6593–6597.

Caramelli D, Lalueza-Fox C, Condemi S, et al. 2006. A highly divergent mtDNA sequence in a Neandertal individual from Italy. *Curr. Biol.* 16:R630–R632.

Carroll, SB. 2005. *Endless Forms Most Beautiful. The New Science of Evo Devo.* Norton, New York.

Cartmill M. 1974. Rethinking primate origins. *Science* 184:436–443.

Caspi A, Sugden K, Moffitt TE, et al. 2003. Influence of life stress on depression: Moderation by a polymorphism in the 5-HTT gene. *Science* 301:386–389.

Cavalli-Sforza LL, Bodmer WF. 1999(1971). *The Genetics of Human Populations.* Dover, Mineola, NY.

Cavalli-Sforza LL, Feldman MS. 2003. The application of molecular genetic approaches to the study of human evolution. *Nature Genetics* (suppl.) 33:266–275.

Cavalli-Sforza LL, Menozzi P, Piazza A. 1994. *The History and Geography of Human Genes.* Princeton University Press, Princeton, NJ.

Chagnon NA. 1988. Life histories, blood revenge, and warfare in a tribal population. *Science* 239:985–992.

Chagnon NA. 1997. *Yanomamö: The Fierce People.* Holt, Rinehart, and Winston, New York.

Chakravarti A, Chakraborty R. 1978. Elevated frequency of Tay–Sachs disease among Ashkenazic Jews unlikely by drift alone. *American Journal of Human Genetics* 30:256–261.

Charles-Dominique P. 1977. *Ecology and Behaviour of Nocturnal Prosimians.* Columbia University Press, New York.

Cheney DL, Seyfarth RM. 1991. *How Monkeys See the World.* University of Chicago Press, Chicago.

Cheney D, Seyfarth RM, Andelman SJ, Lee PC. 1988. Reproductive success in vervet monkeys. In *Reproductive Success* (TH Clutton-Brock, ed.), pp. 384–402. University of Chicago Press, Chicago.

Cheng Z, Ventura M, She X, Khaitovich P, Graves T, Osoegawa K, Church D, DeJong P, Wilson RK, Pääbo S, Rocchi M, Eichler EE. 2005. A genome-wide comparison of recent chimpanzee and human segmental duplications. *Nature* 437:88–93.

Chomsky N. 1967. The formal nature of language (Appendix A). In *Biological Foundations of Language* (EH Lenneberg, ed.), pp. 397–442. Wiley, New York.

Clark WEL. 1975. *The Fossil Evidence for Human Evolution.* University of Chicago Press, Chicago.

Coghlan A. 2003. A sad farewell for Dolly the sheep, the world's first cloned mammal. *New Scientist* 177:5.

Copeland SR. 2007. Vegetation and plant food reconstruction of lowermost Bed II, Olduvai Gorge, using modern analogs. *Journal of Human Evolution,* 53:146–175.

Cohen P. 2004. Unlocking the secret power of RNA. *New Scientist* 27 November: 36.

Coleman L, Coleman J. 2002. The measurement of puberty: A review. *Journal of Adolescence* 25:535–550.

Collard M, Wood B. 2000. How reliable are human phylogene hypothesis? *Proceedings of the National Academy of Sciences.* Vol.: 97:5003–5006.

Conroy GC. 1997. *Reconstructing Human Origins.* Norton, New York.

Conroy GC, Jolly CJ, Cramer D, Kalb JE. 1978. Newly discovered fossil hominid skull from the Afar depression, Ethiopia. *Nature* 275:67–70.

Cook D. 1979. Subsistence base and health in the lower Illinois Valley: Evidence from the human skeleton. *Medical Anthropology* 4:109–124.

Cook D, Buikstra JE. 1979. Health and differential survival in prehistoric populations: Prenatal dental defects. *American Journal of Physical Anthropology* 51:649–664.

Cooke GS, Hill AVS. 2001. Genetics of susceptibility to human infectious disease. *Nature Reviews: Genetics* 2:967–977.

Cords M. 1990. Vigilance and mixed-species association of some East African forest monkeys. *Behavioral Ecology and Sociobiology* 26:297–300.

Covert HH. 2002. The earliest fossil primates and the evolution of the prosimians: Introduction. In *The Primate Fossil Record* (WC Hartwig, ed.), pp. 13–20. Cambridge University Press, Cambridge.

Crews DE, Gerber L. 1994. Chronic degenerative diseases and aging. In *Biological Anthropology and Aging* (DE Crews, R Garruto, eds.), pp. 154–181. Oxford University Press, New York.

Crooks D. 1999. Child growth and nutritional status in a high-poverty community in eastern Kentucky. *American Journal of Physical Anthropology* 109:129–142.

Cuatrecasas PD, Lockwood H, Caldwell J. 1965. Lactase deficiency in the adult: A common occurrence. *Lancet* 1:14–18.

Curtin RA, Dolhinow P. 1978. Primate behavior in a changing world. *American Scientist* 66:468–475.

Damasio H, Damasio AR. 1989. *Lesion Analysis in Neuropsychology.* Oxford University Press, New York.

Dart RA. 1925. *Australopithecus africanus:* The man-ape of South Africa. *Nature* 115:195–199.

Darwin C. 1839. *Journal of Researches into the Geology and Natural History of the Various Countries Visited by H.M.S. Beagle.* Colburn, London.

Darwin C. 1859. *On the Origin of Species by Means of Natural Selection; or, The Preservation of Favoured Races in the Struggle for Life.* John Murray, London.

Darwin C. 1871. *The Descent of Man and Selection in Relation to Sex.* J. Murray, London.

Deacon TW. 1990. Fallacies of progression in theories of brainsize evolution. *International Journal of Primatology* 11:193–236.

Deacon TW. 1997. *The Symbolic Species: The Co-Evolution of Language and the Brain.* Norton, New York.

Dean C. 2007. A radiographic and histological study of modern human lower first permanent molar root growth during the supraosseous eruptive phase. *Journal of Human Evolution, Volume* 53:635–646.

Dean F, Hildebolt C, Smith K, Morwood MJ, et al. 2005. The Brain of LB1, *Homo floresiensis.* Science 308: 242–245.

Dean MC, Leakey MG, Reid D, et al. 2001. Growth processes in teeth distinguish modern humans from *Homo erectus* and earlier hominins. *Nature* 414:628–63.

de Bonis L, Koufos G. 1993. The face and mandible of *Ouranopithecus macedoniensis:* Description of new specimens and comparisons. *Journal of Human Evolution* 24:469–491.

Dedrick D. 1996. Color language universality and evolution: On the explanation for basic color terms. *Philosophical Psychology* 9:497–524.

Defleur A, White T, Valensi P, Slimak L, Crégut-Bonnoure E. 1999. Neanderthal cannibalism at Moula-Guercy, Ardèche, France. *Science* 286:128–131.

Dehaene S. 2003. Natural born readers. *New Scientist* 179:30–33.

Dehaene S, Dupoux E, Mehler J, et al. 1997. Anatomical variability in the cortical representation of first and second language. *NeuroReport* 8:3809–3815.

De Heinzelen J, Clark JD, White T, et al. 1999. Environment and behavior of 2.5 million-year-old Bouri hominids. *Science* 284:625–628.

Deino AL, Renne PR, Swisher CC. 1998. ^{40}Ar/^{39}Ar dating in paleoanthropology and archaeology. *Evolutionary Anthropology* 6:63–75.

Delgado RA, van Schaik CP. 2000. The behavioral ecology and conservation of the orangutan (*Pongo pygmaeus*): A tale of two islands. *Evolutionary Anthropology* 9:201–218.

Delson E. 1980. Fossil macaques, phyletic relationships and a scenario of deployment. In *The Macaques: Studies in Ecology, Behavior, and Evolution* (DG Lindburg, ed.), pp. 10–30. Van Nostrand Reinhold, New York.

d'Errico F, Blackwell LR, Berger LR. 2001. Bone tool use in termite foraging by early hominids and its impact on understanding early hominid behaviour. *South African Journal of Science* 97:71–75.

DeSilva J, Shoreman E, MacLatchy L. 2006. A fossil hominoid proximal femur from Kikorongo Crater, southwestern Uganda. *Journal of Human Evolution, Volume 50:* 687–695.

Dettwyler KA. 1991. Can paleopathology provide evidence for "compassion"? *American Journal of Physical Anthropology* 84:375–384.

de Waal FBM. 1982. *Chimpanzee Politics.* Johns Hopkins University Press, Baltimore.

de Waal FBM, Lanting F. 1997. *Bonobo: The Forgotten Ape.* University of California Press, Berkeley.

de Waal Malefijt A. 1968. *Homo monstrosus. Scientific American* 219:112–118.

Di Fiore A, Rendall D. 1994. Evolution of social organization: A reappraisal for primates by using phylogenetic methods. *Proceedings of the National Academy of Sciences* 91:9941–9945.

Digby L. 1995. Infant care, infanticide, and female reproductive strategies in polygynous groups of common marmosets (*Callithrix jacchus*). *Behavioral Ecology and Sociobiology* 37:51–61.

Dunbar RIM. 1983. *Reproductive Decisions: An Economic Analysis of Gelada Baboon Social Strategies*. Princeton. Princeton University Press.

Dunbar, RIM. 1992. Neocortex size as a constraint on group size in primates. *Journal of Human Evolution* 20:469–493.

Dunbar R. 1997. *Grooming, Gossip, and the Evolution of Language*. Harvard University Press, Cambridge, MA.

Durham WH. 1991. *Coevolution: Genes, Culture, and Human Diversity*. Stanford University Press, Stanford, CA.

Eaton SB, Eaton SB III, Konner MJ. 1999. Paleolithic nutrition revisited. In *Evolutionary Medicine* (WR Trevathan, EO Smith, JJ McKenna, eds.), pp. 313–332. Oxford University Press, Oxford.

Eldredge N, Gould SJ. 1972. Punctuated equilibrium: An alternative to phyletic gradualism. In *Models in Paleobiology* (TJM Shopf, ed.), pp. 82–115. Freeman, Cooper, and Co., San Francisco.

Ellison PT. 1990. Human ovarian function and reproductive ecology: New hypotheses. *American Anthropologist* 92:933–952.

Ellison PT. 1994. Advances in human reproductive ecology. *Annual Review in Anthropology* 23:255–275.

Endler J. 1983. Natural and sexual selection on color patterns in poeciliiad fishes. *Environmental Biology of Fishes* 9:173–190.

Endler J. 1986. *Natural Selection in the Wild*. Princeton University Press, Princeton, NJ.

Enoch MA, Goldman D. 1999. Genetics of alcoholism and substance abuse. *Psychiatric Clinics of North America* 22:289–299.

Etler DA. 1996. The fossil evidence for human evolution in Asia. *Annual Review of Anthropology* 25:275–301.

Evernden JF, Curtis GH. 1965. Potassium–argon dating of Late Cenozoic rocks in East Africa and Italy. *Current Anthropology* 6:643–651.

Fairburn HR, Young LE, Hendrich BD. 2002. Epigenetic reprogramming: How now, cloned cow? *Current Biology* 12:R68–R70.

Falk D. 1975. Comparative anatomy of the larynx in man and chimpanzee. *American Journal of Physical Anthropology* 43:123–132.

Falk D. 1980. A reanalysis of South African australopithecine natural endocasts. *American Journal of Physical Anthropology* 53:525–539.

Falk D. 1983b. The Taung endocast: A reply to Holloway. *American Journal of Physical Anthropology* 60:479–489.

Falk D. 1985a. Apples, oranges, and the lunate sulcus. *American Journal of Physical Anthropology* 67:313–315.

Falk D. 1985b. Hadar AL 162-28 endocast as evidence that brain enlargement preceded cortical reorganization in hominid evolution. *Nature* 313:45–47.

Falk D. 1989. Ape-like endocast of "ape-man" Taung. *American Journal of Physical Anthropology* 80:335–339.

Falk D. 1990. Brain evolution in *Homo*: The "radiator" theory. *Behavioral and Brain Sciences* 13:333–381.

Falk D. 1991. Reply to Dr. Holloway: Shifting positions on the lunate sulcus. *American Journal of Physical Anthropology* 84:89–91.

Falk D, Conroy G. 1983. The cranial venous sinus system in early hominids: Phylogenetic and functional implications for *Australopithecus afarensis*. *Nature* 306:779–781.

Falk D, Froese N, Sade DS, Dudek BC. 1999. Sex differences in brain/body relationships of rhesus monkeys and humans. *Journal of Human Evolution* 36:233–238.

Falk D. Hildebolt C, Smith K, et al. 2005. The Brain of LB1, *Homo floresiensis*. *Science* 308:242–245.

Feathers JK. 1996. Luminescence dating and modern human origins. *Evolutionary Anthropology* 5:25–36.

Feibel CS. 1999. Tephrostratigraphy and geological context in paleoanthropology. *Evolutionary Anthropology* 8:87–100.

Feibel CS, Brown FH, McDougall I. 1989. Stratigraphic context of fossil hominids from the Omo Group deposits, northern Turkana Basin, Kenya and Ethiopia. *American Journal of Physical Anthropology* 78:595–622.

Feldman MW, Cavalli-Sforza LL. 1989. On the theory of evolution under genetic and cultural transmission with application to the lactose absorption problem. In *Mathematical Evolutionary Theory* (MW Feldman, ed.), pp. 145–173. Princeton University Press, Princeton, NJ.

Ferguson CA. 1964. Baby talk in six languages. *American Anthropologist* 66:103–114.

Fernald A. 1992. Human maternal vocalizations to infants as biologically relevant signals: An evolutionary perspective. In *The Adapted Mind* (JH Barkow, L Cosmides, J Tooby, eds.), pp. 391–428. Oxford University Press, New York.

Fernald A, Taeschner T, Dunn J, et al. 1989. A cross-language study of prosodic modifications in mothers' and fathers' speech to preverbal infants. *Journal of Child Language* 16:477–501.

Finkel T, Holbrook NJ. 2000. Oxidants, oxidative stress and the biology of ageing. *Nature* 408:239–247.

Fisher H. 1992. *Anatomy of Love*. Fawcett Columbine, New York.

Fisher RA. 1958. *The Genetical Theory of Natural Selection*, 2nd ed. Dover Publications, New York.

Fleagle JG. 1998. *Primate Adaptation and Evolution*, 2nd ed. Academic Press, San Diego, CA.

Fleagle JG, Kay RF. 1987. The phyletic position of the Parapithecidae. *Journal of Human Evolution* 16:483–532.

Fleagle JG, Stern JT, Jungers WL, et al. 1981. Climbing: A biomechanical link with brachiation and with bipedalism. *Symposia of the Zoological Society of London* 48:359–375.

Fleagle JG, Tejedor MF. 2002. Early platyrrhines of southern South America. In *The Primate Fossil Record* (WC Hartwig, ed.), pp. 161–173. Cambridge University Press, Cambridge.

Fossey D. 1983. *Gorillas in the Mist*. Houghton Mifflin, Boston.

Fouts RS, Waters G. 2001. Chimpanzee sign language and Darwinian continuity: Evidence for a neurological continuity of language. *Neurological Research* 23:787–794.

Franciscus RG. 1999. Neandertal nasal structures and upper respiratory tract "specialization." *Proceedings of the National Academy of Sciences* 96:1805–1809.

Franciscus RG. 2003. Internal nasal floor configuration in *Homo* with special reference to the evolution of Neandertal facial form. *Journal of Human Evolution* 44:701–729.

Frayer D, Wolpoff MH, Smith FM, et al. 1993. Theories of modern human origins: The paleontological test. *American Anthropologist* 95:14–50.

Frayer DW, Jelinek J, Oliva M, Wolpoff MH. 2006. Chapter 9 Aurignacian male crania, jaws and teeth from the Mladec Caves, Czech Republic. In: Teschler-Nicola M. (Ed.). *Early Modern Humans at the Moravian Gate The Mladec Caves and their Remains*. Springer, Wien pp. 185–272.

Frisancho AR, Baker PT. 1970. Altitude and growth: A study of the patterns of physical growth of a high altitude Peruvian Quechua population. *American Journal of Physical Anthropology* 32:279–292.

Fully G. 1956. Une nouvelle methode de determination de la taille. *Ann. Med. Legale Criminol.* 35: 266–273.

Furuichi T. 1987. Sexual swelling, receptivity, and grouping of wild pygmy chimpanzee females at Wamba, Zaïre. *Primates* 28:309–318.

Gabunia L, Antón SC, Lordkipanidze D, et al. 2001. Dmanisi and dispersal. *Evolutionary Anthropology* 10:158–170.

Gabunia L, Vekua A, Lordkipanidze D, et al. 2000. Earliest Pleistocene cranial remains from Dmanisi, Republic of Georgia: Taxonomy, geological setting, and age. *Science* 288:1019–1025.

Gagneux P, Wills C, Gerloff U, et al. 1996. Mitochondrial sequences show diverse evolutionary histories of African hominoids. *Proceedings of the National Academy of Sciences* 96:5077–5082.

Gajdusek DC, Gibbs CJ Jr, Alpers M. 1966. Experimental transmission of a kuru-like syndrome to chimpanzees. *Nature* 209:794–796.

Galdikas BMF. 1985. Subadult male sociality and reproductive tactics among orangutans at Tanjung Putting. *American Journal of Primatology* 8:87–99.

Galdikas BMF, Wood JW. 1990. Birth spacing patterns in humans and apes. *American Journal of Physical Anthropology* 83:185–191.

Galik K, Senut B, Pickford M, et al. 2004. External and internal morphology of the BAR 1002'00 *Orrorin tugenensis* femur. *Nature* 305:1450–1453.

Gambier D. 1989. Fossil hominids from the early Upper Paleolithic (Aurignacian) of France. In *The Human Revolution: Behavioral and Biological Perspectives on the Origins of Modern Humans* (P Mellars, C Stringer, eds.), pp. 194–211. Princeton University Press, Princeton, NJ.

Ganzhorn HU, Kappeler PM. 1993. *Lemur Social Systems and Their Ecological Basis.* Plenum, New York.

Garber PA. 1989. Role of spatial memory in primate foraging patterns: *Saguinus mystax* and *Saguinus fuscicollis. American Journal of Primatology* 19:203–216.

Garber P. 1997. One for all and breeding for one: Cooperation and competition as a tamarin reproductive strategy. *Evolutionary Anthropology* 5:187–199.

Gardiner BG. 2003. The Piltdown forgery: a re-statement of the case against. *Hinton Zoological Journal of the Linnean Society,* 139:315–335.

Gardner H. 1993. *Frames of Mind: The Theory of Multiple Intelligences,* 2nd ed. Basic Books, New York.

Gargett RH. 1989. Grave shortcomings: The evidence for Neandertal burial. *Current Anthropology* 30:157–190.

Gargett RH. 1999. Middle Paleolithic burial is not a dead issue: The view from Qafzeh, Saint-Césaire, Amud, and Dederiyeh. *Journal of Human Evolution* 37:27–90.

Garner KJ, Ryder OA. 1996. Mitochondrial DNA diversity in gorillas. *Molecular Phylogenetics and Evolution* 6:39–48.

Gaser C, Schlaug G. 2003. Brain structures differ between musicians and non-musicians. *Journal of Neuroscience* 23:9240–9245.

Gautier-Hion A, Quris R, Gautier JP. 1983. Monospecific vs. polyspecific life: A comparative study of foraging and antipredatory tactics in a community of *Cercopithecus* monkeys. *Behavioral Ecology and Sociobiology* 12:325–335.

Gazzaniga MS, Ivry RB, Mangun GR. 1998. *Cognitive Neuroscience: The Biology of the Mind.* Norton, New York.

Gebo DL. 1996. Climbing, brachiation, and terrestrial quadrupedalism: Historical precursors of hominid bipedalism. *American Journal of Physical Anthropology* 101:55–92.

Gebo DL, MacLatchy L, Kityo R, et al. 1997. A hominoid genus from the early Miocene of Uganda. *Science* 276:401–404.

Geissmann T. 2000. Gibbon song and human music from an evolutionary perspective. In *The Origins of Music* (N Wallin, B Merker, S Brown, eds.), pp. 103-123. The MIT Press, Cambridge, MA.

Gerber LM, Crews DE. 1999. Evolutionary perspectives on chronic degenerative diseases. In *Evolutionary Medicine* (WR Trevathan, EO Smith, JJ McKenna, eds.), pp. 443–469. Oxford University Press, Oxford.

Gibbons A. 1991. Déjà vu all over again: Chimp-language wars. *Science* 251:1561–1562.

Gibbons A. 2007. Paleoanthropology: Hobbit's status as a new species gets a hand up. *Science* 316:34.

Giedd JN, Blumenthal J, Jeffries NO, et al. 1999. Brain development during adolescence: A longitudinal MRI study. *Nature Neuroscience* 2:861–863.

Gilbert BM, McKern TW. 1973. A method for aging the female *Os pubis. American Journal of Physical Anthropology* 38: 31–38.

Gislén A, Dacke M, Kröger RHH, et al. 2003. Superior underwater vision in a human population of sea gypsies. *Current Biology* 13:833–836.

Glander KE, Wright PC, Seigler DS, Randrianasolo VB. 1989. Consumption of cyanogenic bamboo by a newly discovered species of bamboo lemur. *American Journal of Primatology* 19:119–124.

Gleason TM, Norconk MA. 2002. Predation risk and antipredator adaptation in white-faced sakis, *Pithecia pithecia.* In *Eat or Be Eaten: Predation Sensitive Foraging among Primates* (LE Miller, ed.), pp. 169–186. Cambridge University Press, Cambridge.

Godfrey LR, Jungers WL. 2002. Quaternary fossil lemurs. In *The Primate Fossil Record* (WC Hartwig, ed.), pp. 97–121. Cambridge University Press, Cambridge.

Godinot M, Dagosto M. 1983. The astragalus of *Necrolemur* (Primates, Microchoerinae). *Journal of Paleontology* 57:1321–1324.

Goldberg A, Wrangham RW. 1997. Genetic correlates of social behaviour in chimpanzees: Evidence from mitochondrial DNA. *Animal Behaviour* 54:559–570.

Goldberg P, Weiner S, Bar-Yosef O, Xu Q, Liu J. 2001. Site formation processes of Zhoukoudian, China. *Journal of Human Evolution* 41:483–530.

Goldfarb LG. 2002. Kuru: The old epidemic in a new mirror. *Microbes and Infection* 4:875–882.

Goldsmith ML. 1999. Ranging behavior of a lowland gorilla (*Gorilla g. gorilla*) group at Bai Hokou, Central African Republic. *International Journal of Primatology* 20:1–23.

Golovanova LV, Hoffecker JF, Kharitonov VM, Romanova GP. 1999. Mezmaiskaya Cave: A Neanderthal occupation in the northern Caucasus. *Current Anthropology* 40:77–86.

Goodall J. 1963. Feeding behaviour of wild chimpanzees: A preliminary report. *Symposium of the Zoological Society of London* 10:39–48.

Goodall J. 1968. Behaviour of free-living chimpanzees of the Gombe Stream area. *Animal Behaviour Monographs* 1:163–311.

Goodall J. 1968. *In the Shadow of Man.* National Geographic Society, Washington, DC.

Goodall J. 1986. *The Chimpanzees of Gombe: Patterns of Behavior.* Harvard University Press, Cambridge, MA.

Goodman M. 1962. Immunochemistry of the primates and primate evolution. *Annals of the New York Academy of Sciences* 102:219–234.

Goodman M. 1963. Serological analysis of the systematics of recent hominoids. *Human Biology* 35:377–436.

Goodman M. 1999. The genomic record of humankind's evolutionary roots. *American Journal of Human Genetics* 64:31–39.

Goodman M, Porter CA, Czelusniak J, et al. 1998. Toward a phylogenetic classification of primates based on DNA evidence complemented by fossil evidence. *Molecular Phylogenetics and Evolution* 9:585–598.

Goodman SM, O'Connor S, Langrand O. 1993. A review of predation on lemurs: Implications for the evolution of social behavior in small, nocturnal primates. In *Lemur Social Systems and Their Ecological Basis* (PM Kappeler, JU Ganzhorn, eds.), pp. 51–66. Plenum, New York.

Gottesman II, Shields J. 1982. *Schizophrenia: The Epigenetic Puzzle.* Cambridge University Press, Cambridge.

Gould SJ, Lewontin RC. 1979. The spandrels of San Marco and the Panglossian paradigm. *Proceedings of the Royal Society of London* B 205:581–598.

Grant PR. 1986. *Ecology and Evolution of Darwin's Finches.* Princeton University Press, Princeton, NJ.

Gray PB, Yang C-FJ, Pope HG. 2006. Fathers have lower salivary testosterone levels than unmarried men and married non-fathers in Beijing, China. *Proceedings of the Royal Society of London* B 273:333–339.

Gravlee CC, Bernard HR, Leonard WR. 2003. Heredity, environment, and cranial form: A reanalysis of Boas's immigrant data. *American Anthropologist* 105:125–138.

Green RE, Krause J, Ptak SE, et al. 2006. Analysis of one million base pairs of Neanderthal DNA. *Nature* 444:330–336.

Groves C. 2001. *Primate Taxonomy.* Smithsonian Institution Press, Washington, DC.

Grün R, Huang PH, Huang W, et al. 1998. ESR and U-series analyses of teeth from the paleoanthropological site of Hexian, Anhui Province, China. *Journal of Human Evolution* 34:555–564.

Grün R, Huang PH, Wu X, et al. 1997. ESR analysis of teeth from the paleoanthropological site of Zhoukoudian, China. *Journal of Human Evolution* 32:83–91.

Grün R, Stringer CB. 1991. Electron spin resonance dating and the evolution of modern humans. *Archaeometry* 33:153–199.

Grün R, Stringer CB, Schwarcz HP. 1991. ESR dating of teeth from Garrod's Tabun Cave collection. *Journal of Human Evolution* 20:231–248.

Guglielmino CR, Desilvesteri A, Berres J. 2000. Probable ancestors of Hungarian ethnic groups: An admixture analysis. *Annals of Human Genetics* 64:145–159.

Gursky S. 1994. Infant care in the spectral tarsier (*Tarsius spectrum*) Sulawesi, Indonesia. *International Journal of Primatology* 15:843–853.

Gursky S. 1995. Group size and composition in the spectral tarsier, *Tarsius spectrum:* Implications for social organization. *Tropical Biodiversity* 3:57–62.

Haile-Selassie Y, Asfaw B, White TD. 2004. Hominid cranial remains from Upper Pleistocene deposits at Aduma, Middle Awash, Ethiopia. *American Journal of Physical Anthropology* 123:1–10.

Haile-Selassie Y, White T, Suwa G. 2004. Late Miocene teeth from Middle Awash Ethiopia and early hominid dental evolution. *Science* 303:1503–1505.

Haller JS. 1970. The species problem: Nineteenth-century concepts of racial inferiority in the origin of man controversy. *American Anthropologist* 72:1321–1329.

Hamilton WD. 1964. The genetical evolution of social behaviour, I and II. *Journal of Theoretical Biology* 7:1–52.

Hansson GC. 1988. Cystic fibrosis and chloride-secreting diarrhoea. *Nature* 333:711.

Harcourt AH. 1978. Strategies of emigration and transfer by primates, with particular reference to gorillas. *Zeitschrift für Tierpsychologie* 48:401–420.

Harding RM, Fullerton SM, Griffiths RC, et al. 1997. Archaic African and Asian lineages in the genetic ancestry of modern humans. *American Journal of Human Genetics* 60:772–789.

Hardy GH. 1908. Mendelian proportions in a mixed population. *Science* 28:49–50.

Harpending HC, Batzer MA, Gurven M, et al. 1998. Genetic traces of ancient demography. *Proceedings of the National Academy of Sciences* 95:1961–1967.

Harrison GA, Tanner JM, Pilbeam DR, Baker PT. 1988. *Human Biology,* 3rd ed. Oxford University Press, Oxford.

Harrison T, Gu Y. 1999. Taxonomy and phylogenetic relationships of early Miocene catarrhines from Sihong, China. *Journal of Human Evolution* 37:225–277.

Hartwig WC. 1994. Patterns, puzzles and perspectives on platyrrhine origins. In *Integrative Paths to the Past: Paleoanthropological Essays in Honor of F. Clark Howell* (RS Corruccini, RL Ciochon, eds.), pp. 69–94. Prentice Hall, Englewood Cliffs, NJ.

Harvey P, Martin RD, Clutton-Brock TH. 1987. Life histories in comparative perspective. In *Primate Societies* (BB Smuts, DL Cheney, RM Seyfarth, RW Wrangham, TT Struhsaker, eds.), pp. 181–196. University of Chicago Press, Chicago.

Hassold T, Hunt P. 2001. To err (meiotically) is human: The genesis of human aneuploidy. *Nature Reviews: Genetics* 3:280–291.

Hauser MD, Sulkowski GM. 2001. Can rhesus monkeys spontaneously subtract? *Cognition* 79:239–262.

Hausfater G. 1975. Dominance and reproduction in baboons (*Papio cynocephalus*). In *Contributions to Primatology,* vol. 7. Karger, Basel.

Hawkes K. 2003. Grandmothers and the evolution of human longevity. *American Journal of Human Biology* 15:380–400.

Hawkes K, O'Connell JF, Blurton Jones NG. 1997. Hadza women's time allocation, offspring production, and the evolution of long postmenopausal life spans. *Current Anthropology* 38:551–577.

Hawkes K, O'Connell JF, Blurton Jones NG. 2001. Hadza meat sharing. *Evolution and Human Behavior* 22:113–142.

Heider ER. 1972. Universals in color naming and memory. *Journal of Experimental Psychology* 93:10–20.

Henshilwood C, d'Errico F, Vanhaeren M, et al. 2004. Middle Stone Age shell beads from South Africa. *Science* 304:404.

Herman-Giddens ME, Slora E, Wasserman RC, et al. 1997. Secondary sexual characteristics and menses in young girls seen in office practice: A study from the Pediatric Research in Office Settings Network. *Pediatrics* 99:505–512.

Hershkovitz I, Kornreich L, Laron Z. 2007. Comparative skeletal features between *Homo floresiensis* and patients with primary growth hormone insensitivity (Laron syndrome). *American Journal Physical Anthropology* 134:198–208.

Hewes GW. 1999. A history of the study of language origins and the gestural primacy hypothesis. In *Handbook of Human Symbolic Evolution* (A Lock, CR Peters, eds.), pp. 571–595. Blackwell, Oxford.

Hill EM, Chow K. 2002. Life-history theory and risky drinking. *Addiction* 97:401–413.

Hill K, Hurtado AM. 1991. The evolution of premature reproductive senescence and menopause in human females: An evaluation of the "grandmother hypothesis." *Human Nature* 2:313–350.

Hill K, Hurtado AM. 1996. *Aché Life History: The Ecology and Demography of a Foraging People*. Aldine de Gruyter, New York.

Hill K, Kaplan H. 1993. On why male foragers hunt and share food. *Current Anthropology* 34:701–706.

Hirszfeld L, Hirszfeld H. 1919. Essai d'application des methods au problème des races. *Anthropologie* 29:505–537.

Hladik CM. 1975. Ecology, diet and social patterns in Old and New World Primates. In *Socioecology and Psychology of Primates* (RH Tuttle, ed.), pp. 3–35. Mouton, The Hague.

Hodgen MT. 1964. *Early Anthropology in the Sixteenth and Seventeenth Centuries*. University of Pennsylvania Press, Philadelphia.

Hofman M. 1988. Size and shape of the cerebral cortex. II. The cortical volume. *Brain, Behavior and Evolution* 32:17–26.

Hohmann G, Fruth B. 1993. Field observations on meat sharing among bonobos (*Pan paniscus*). *Folia Primatologica* 60:225–229.

Holick MF, MacLaughlin JA, Doppelt SH. 1981. Regulation of cutaneous previtamin D3 photosynthesis in man: Skin pigment is not an essential regulator. *Science* 211:590–593.

Holliday TW. 1995. Body size and proportions in the late Pleistocene western Old World and the origins of modern humans. PhD dissertation, University of New Mexico, Albuquerque.

Holloway RL. 1968. The evolution of the primate brain: Some aspects of quantitative relations. *Brain Research* 7:121–172.

Holloway RL. 1976. Paleoneurological evidence for language origins. *Annals of the New York Academy of Sciences* 280:330–348.

Holloway RL. 1980. Within-species brain–body weight variability: A reexamination of the Danish data and other primate species. *American Journal of Physical Anthropology* 53:109–121.

Holloway RL. 1981. Revisiting the South African Taung australopithecine endocast: The position of the lunate sulcus as determined by stereoplotting technique. *American Journal of Physical Anthropology* 56:43–58.

Holloway RL. 1984a. The poor brain of *Homo sapiens neanderthalensis*: See what you please. In *Ancestors: The Hard Evidence* (E Delson, ed.), pp. 319–324. Alan R. Liss, New York.

Holloway RL. 1984b. The Taung endocast and the lunate sulcus: A rejection of the hypothesis of its anterior position. *American Journal of Physical Anthropology* 64:285–287.

Holloway RL. 1988. Some additional morphological and metrical observations on *Pan* brain casts and their relevance to the Taung endocast. *American Journal of Physical Anthropology* 77:27–33.

Holloway RL. 1991. On Falk's 1989 accusations regarding Holloway's study of the Taung endocast: A reply. *American Journal of Physical Anthropology* 84:87–88.

Holloway RL. 1999. Evolution of the human brain. In *Handbook of Human Symbolic Evolution* (A Lock, CR Peters, eds.), pp. 74–125. Blackwell, Oxford.

Holloway RL, de LaCoste-Lareymondie MC. 1982. Brain endocast asymmetry in pongids and hominids: Some preliminary findings on the paleontology of cerebral dominance. *American Journal of Physical Anthropology* 58:101–110.

Holloway RL, Kimbel WH. 1986. Endocast morphology of Hadar hominid AL 162-28. *Nature* 321:536–537.

Holloway RL, Broadfield DC, Yuan MS. 2004. *The Human Fossil Record Volume Three: Brain Endocasts, The Paleoneurological Record*. Wiley-Liss, Hoboken, NJ.

Hollox EJ, Poulter M, Zvarik M, et al. 2001. Lactase haplotype diversity in the Old World. *American Journal of Human Genetics* 68:160–172.

Hovers E, Ilani S, Bar-Yosef O, Vandermeersch B. 2003. An early case of color symbolism: Ochre use by modern humans in Qafzeh Cave. *Current Anthropology* 44:491–522.

Hovers E, Kimbel WH, Rak Y. 2000. The Amud 7 skeleton: Still a burial. Response to Gargett. *Journal of Human Evolution* 39:253–260.

Howell FC. 1957. The Evolutionary significance of variation and varieties of "Neanderthal' Man. *Quat. Rev. Biol.* 32:330–347.

Howell FC. 1964. Pleistocene glacial ecology and the evolution of "classic Neandertal" man. *Southwestern Journal of Anthropology* 8:377–410.

Howell FC. 1966. Observations on the earlier phases of the European Lower Paleolithic. *American Anthropologist* 68:111–140.

Howell FC. 1994. A chronostratigraphic and taxonomic framework of the origins of modern humans. In *Origins of Anatomically Modern Humans* (MH Nitecki, DV Nitecki, eds.), pp. 253–319. Plenum, New York.

Howell FC, Butzer KW, Freeman LG, Klein RG. 1991. Observations on the Acheulean occupation site of Ambrona (Soria province, Spain). Jahrb. Romish. Germanisch. Zentralmus. Mainz. 38:33–82.

Howells WW. 1973. *Cranial Variation in Man*. Papers of the Peabody Museum, Cambridge, MA.

Hrdy SB. 1977. *The Langurs of Abu*. Harvard University Press, Cambridge, MA.

Hrdy SB, Whitten PL. 1987. Patterning of sexual activity. In *Primate Societies* (BB Smuts, DL Cheney, RM Seyfarth, RW Wrangham, TT Struhsaker, eds.), pp. 370–384. University of Chicago Press, Chicago.

Hublin JJ. 1985. Human fossils from the North African Middle Pleistocene and the origin of *Homo sapiens*. In *Ancestors: The Hard Evidence* (E Delson, ed.), pp. 283–288. Alan R. Liss, New York.

Hublin JJ, Spoor F, Braun M, et al. 1996. A late Neanderthal associated with Upper Paleolithic artefacts. *Nature* 381:224–226.

Hunt KD. 1996. The postural feeding hypothesis: An ecological model for the evolution of bipedalism. *South African Journal of Science* 92:77–90.

Hurford JR. 1991. The evolution of the critical period for language acquisition. *Cognition* 40:159–201.

Huxley J, Mayr E, Osmond H, Hoffer A. 1964. Schizophrenia as a genetic morphism. *Nature* 204:220–221.

Hyde KL, Zatorre RJ, Griffiths TD, Lerch JP, Peretz I. 2006. Morphometry of the amusic brain: A two-site study, *Brain* 129:2562–2570.

Ingman M, Kaessmann H, Pääbo S, Gyllensten U. 2000. Mitochondrial genome variation and the origin of modern humans. *Nature* 408:708–713.

Irons W. 1979. Cultural and biological success. In *Evolutionary Biology and Human Social Behavior* (NA Chagnon, W Irons, eds.), pp. 257–272. Duxbury Press, North Scituate, MA.

Irwin G. 1992. *The Prehistoric Exploration and Colonisation of the Pacific*. Cambridge University Press, New York.

Isaac GL. 1978. The food-sharing behavior of proto-human hominids. *Scientific American* 238:90–108.

Isbell L, Young T. 1996. The evolution of bipedalism in hominids and reduced group size in chimpanzees: Alternative responses to decreasing resource availability. *Journal of Human Evolution* 30:389–397.

Iscan MY, Loth SR, Wright RK. 1984. Metamorphosis at the sternal rib end: a new method to estimate age at death in white males. *American Journal of Physical Anthropology* 65:147–156, 1984.

Ishida H, Pickford M. 1997. A new late Miocene hominoid from Kenya: *Samburupithecus kiptalami* gen et sp. nov. *Comptes Rendus de l'Academie des Sciences de Paris* 325:823–829.

Ivanoff J. 2005. Sea gypsies of Myanmar. *National Geographic* April: 36–55.

Jablensky A, Sartorius N, Ernberg G, et al. 1992. Schizophrenia: Manifestations, incidence and course in different cultures: A World Health Organization Ten-Country Study. *Psychological Medicine* 20(suppl.):1–97.

Jablonski NG, Chaplin G. 1993. Origin of habitual terrestrial bipedalism in the ancestor of the Hominidae. *Journal of Human Evolution* 24:259–280.

Jablonski NG, Chaplin G. 2000. The evolution of human skin coloration. *Journal of Human Evolution* 39:57–106.

Jablonski NG, Chaplin G. 2002. Skin deep. *Scientific American* 287:74–81.

Jackendoff R. 1994. *Patterns in the Mind: Language and Human Nature.* Basic Books, New York.

Jackson FLC. 2000. Human adaptations to infectious disease. In *Human Biology: An Evolutionary and Biocultural Perspective* (S Stinson, B Bogin, R Huss-Ashmore, D O'Rourke, eds.), pp. 273–293. Wiley-Liss, New York.

Jacob T, Indriati E, Soejono RP, et al. 2006. Pygmoid Australomelanesian *Homo sapiens* skeletal remains from Liang Bua, Flores: Population affinities and pathological abnormalities. *Proc. Natl. Acad. Sci,* USA. 103:13421–13426.

Janson CH. 1985. Aggressive competition and individual food consumption in wild brown capuchin monkeys (*Cebus apella*). *Behavioral Ecology and Sociobiology* 18:125–138.

Jantz RL, Owsley DW. 2001. Variation among early North American crania. *American Journal of Physical Anthropology* 114:146–155.

Jarman PJ. 1974. The social organization of antelope in relation to their ecology. *Behaviour* 48:215–267.

Jeffreys AJ, Wilson V, Thein SL. 1985. Hypervariable "minisatellite" regions in human DNA. *Nature* 314:67–73.

Jensen-Seaman M, Kidd KK. 2001. Mitochondrial variation and biogeography of eastern gorillas. *Molecular Ecology* 10:2240–2247.

Jerison HJ. 1991. Brain size and the evolution of mind. In *59th James Arthur Lecture on the Evolution of the Human Brain, 1989.* Columbia University Press, New York.

Jobling MA, Tyler-Smith C. 2003. The human Y chromosome: An evolutionary marker comes of age. *Nature Reviews Genetics* 4:598–612.

Johanson D, Edey M. 1981. *Lucy: The Beginnings of Humankind.* Simon & Schuster, New York.

Johanson DC, Lovejoy CO, Kimbel WH, et al. 1982. Morphology of the Pliocene partial hominid skeleton (AL 288-1) from the Hadar Formation, Ethiopia. *American Journal of Physical Anthropology* 57:403–452.

Johanson DC, Taieb M. 1976. Plio-Pleistocene hominid discoveries in Hadar, Ethiopia. *Nature* 260:293–297.

Johanson DC, White TD. 1979. A systematic assessment of early African hominids. *Science* 202:321–330.

Jolly CJ. 1970. The seed-eaters: A new model of hominid differentiation based on a baboon analogy. *Man* 5:1–26.

Jordan P. 1999. *Neanderthal.* Sutton Publishing, Phoenix Mill, Gloucestershire.

Kandel ER, Schwartz JH, Jessell TM. 2000. *Principles of Neural Science,* 4th ed. McGraw-Hill, New York.

Kano T. 1992. *The Last Ape.* Stanford University Press, Stanford, CA.

Kaplan H, Hill K, Lancaster J, Hurtado AM. 2000. A theory of human life history evolution: Diet, intelligence, and longevity. *Evolutionary Anthropology* 9:156–185.

Kappelman J. 1996. The evolution of body mass and relative brain size in hominids. *Journal of Human Evolution* 30:243–276.

Katz D, Suchey JM. 1986. Age determination of the male Os pubis. *American Journal of Physical Anthropology* 69: 427–435

Katzman MA, Lee S. 1997. Beyond body image: The integration of feminist and transcultural theories in the understanding of self starvation. *International Journal of Eating Disorders* 22:385–394.

Kay P, Berlin B. 1997. Science imperialism: There are nontrivial constraints on color naming. *Behavioral and Brain Science* 20:196–201.

Keith A. 1923. Man's posture: Its evolution and disorders. *British Medical Journal* 1:451–454, 499–502, 545–548, 587–590, 624–626, 669–672.

Keith A. 1940. Blumenbach's centenary. *Man* 40:82–85.

Kennedy KA, Sonakia A, Chiment J, Verma KK. 1991. Is the Narmada hominid an Indian *Homo erectus? American Journal of Physical Anthropology* 86:475–496.

Kessler RC, Berglund P, Demler O, et al. 2003. The epidemiology of major depressive disorder. *Journal of the American Medical Association* 289:3095–3105.

Kevles DJ. 1985. *In the Name of Eugenics.* Alfred A. Knopf, New York.

Kidd K. 1975. On the magnitude of selective forces maintaining schizophrenia in the population. In *Genetic Research in Psychiatry* (R Fieve, D Rosenthal, H Brill, eds.), pp. 135–145. Johns Hopkins University Press, Baltimore.

Kimbel WH, Rak Y, Johanson DC. 2004. *The Skull of* Australopithecus afarensis. Oxford University Press, New York.

Kimbel W, Lockwood C, Ward C, Leakey M, Rak Y, Johanson D. 2006. Was *Australopithecus anamensis* ancestral to *A. afarensis?* A case of anagenesis in the hominin fossil record. *Journal Human Evolution* 51:134–152.

Kirch PV. 2001. *On the Road of the Winds: An Archaeological History of the Pacific Islands before European Contact.* University of California Press, Berkeley.

Kirk CE, Simons EL. 2001. Diets of fossil primates from the Fayum Depression of Egypt: a quantitative analysis of molar shearing. *Journal of Human Evolution* 40:203–229.

Kirkpatrick M. 1982. Sexual selection and the evolution of female choice. *Evolution* 36:1–12.

Kirkpatrick RC. 1998. Ecology and behavior of the snub-nosed and douc langurs. In *The Natural History of the Doucs and Snub-Nosed Langurs* (NG Jablonski, ed.), pp. 155–190. World Scientific, Singapore.

Kirkwood TBL. 2002. Evolution theory and the mechanisms of aging. In *Brocklehursts' Textbook of Geriatric Medicine and Gerontology,* 6th ed. (R Tallis, HM Fillit, eds.), pp. 31–35. Churchhill Livingstone, Edinburgh and New York.

Kirkwood TBL, Austad SN. 2000. Why do we age? *Nature* 408:233–238.

Klein RG, Edgar B. 2002. *The Dawn of Human Culture.* Wiley, New York.

Kloosterman WP, Plasterk RH. 2006. The diverse functions of microRNAs in animal development and disease. *Developmental Cell* 11:441-450.

Klug WS, Cummings MR. 2003. *Concepts of Genetics.* Prentice Hall, Upper Saddle River, NJ.

Knott CD. 1998. Social system dynamics, ranging patterns, and male and female strategies in wild Bornean orangutans (*Pongo pygmaeus*). *American Journal of Physical Anthropology* 26(suppl.):140.

Koda Y, Tachida H, Liu Y, et al. 2001. Contrasting patterns of polymorphisms at the ABO-secretor gene (FUT2) and plasma (1,3)fucosyltransferase gene (FUT6) in human populations. 747–756.

Kondo O, Dodo Y, Akazawa T, Muhesen S. 2000. Estimation of stature from the skeletal reconstruction of an immature Neandertal from Dederiyeh Cave, Syria. *Journal of Human Evolution* 38:457–473.

Kornberg A. 1960. Biological synthesis of DNA. *Science* 131:1503–1508.

Kostianovsky M. 2000. Evolutionary origin of eukaryotic cells. *Ultrastructural Pathology* 24:59–66.

Krings M, Capelli C, Tschentscher F, et al. 2000. A view of Neandertal genetic diversity. *Nature Genetics* 26:144–146.

Krings M, Geisert H, Schmitz RW, et al. 1999. DNA sequence of the mitochondrial hypervariable region II from the Neandertal type specimen. *Proceedings of the National Academy of Sciences* 96:5581–5585.

Krings M, Stone A, Schmitz RW, et al. 1997. Neandertal DNA sequences and the origin of modern humans. *Cell* 90:19–30.

Kummer H. 1968. *Social Organization of Hamadryas Baboons*. University of Chicago Press, Chicago.

Lahdenpera M, Lummaa V, Helle S, et al. 2004. Fitness benefits of prolonged post-reproductive lifespan in women. *Nature* 428:178–181.

Laidlaw SA, Kopple JD. 1987. Newer concepts of the indispensable amino acids. *American Journal of Clinical Nutrition* 46:593–605.

Laitman J. 1984. The anatomy of human speech. *Natural History* 92:20–27.

Laitman JT, Heimbuch RC. 1982. The basicranium of Plio-Pleistocene hominids as an indicator of their upper respiratory systems. *American Journal of Physical Anthropology* 59:323–343.

Laitman JT, Reidenberg JS. 1988. Advances in understanding the elationship between skull base and larynx, with comments on the origins of speech. *Human Evolution* 3:101–111.

Lalueza C, Perez-Perez A, Turbon D. 1996. Dietary inferences through buccal microwear analysis of middle and upper Pleistocene human fossils. *American Journal of Physical Anthropology* 100:367–387.

Lalueza-Fox C, Sampietro ML, Caramelli D, et al. 2005. Neandertal evolutionary genetics; mitochondrial DNA data from the Iberian Peninsula. *Mol. Biol. Evol.* 22:1077–1081.

Lambert PM, Walker PL. 1991. Physical anthropological evidence for the evolution of social complexity in coastal Southern California. *Antiquity* 65(249):963–973.

Larick R, Ciochon RL, Zaim Y, et al. 2001. Early Pleistocene 40Ar/39Ar ages for Bapang Formation hominids, Central Java, Indonesia. *Proceedings of the National Academy of Sciences* 98:4866–4871.

Larsen CS, Ruff, CB. 1994. The stresses of conquest in Spanish Florida: structural adaptation and change before and after contact. In Larsen, CS and Milner, GR (Eds.). *In the Wake of Contact: Biological Responses to Conquest*. New York: Wiley-Liss, pp. 21–34.

Larson E. 2001. *Evolution's Workshop: God and Science on the Galapagos Islands*. Basic Books, New York.

Leakey LSB. 1959. A new fossil skull from Olduvai. *Nature* 184:491–493.

Leakey MG, Feibel CS, McDougall I, Walker A. 1995. New four-million-year-old hominid species from Kanapoi and Allia Bay, Kenya. *Nature* 376:565–571.

Leakey MG, Spoor F, Brown FH, et al. 2001. New hominid genus from eastern Africa shows diverse middle Pliocene lineages. *Nature* 410:433–440.

LeBlanc S, Register K. 2003. *Constant Battles: The Myth of the Peaceful, Noble Savage*. St. Martin's Press, New York.

Ledoux J. 1996. *The Emotional Brain*. Touchstone, New York.

Lee RB, DeVore I, eds. 1968. *Man the Hunter*. Aldine, Chicago.

Lee-Thorp JA, van der Merwe NJ, Brain CK. 1994. Diet of *Australopithecus robustus* at Swartkrans from stable carbon isotope analysis. *Journal of Human Evolution* 27:361–372.

Le Gros Clark WE, Thomas DP. 1952. The Miocene lemuroids of East Africa. *Fossil Mammals of Africa* 5:1–20.

Leigh SR. 1992. Cranial capacity evolution in *Homo erectus* and early *Homo sapiens*. *American Journal of Physical Anthropology* 87:1–13.

Leighton M. 1993. Molding diet selectivity by Bornean orangutans: Evidence for integration of multiple criteria for fruit selection. *International Journal of Primatology* 14:257–313.

Leonard WR, Robertson ML. 1997. Rethinking the energetics of bipedality. *Current Anthropology* 38:304–309.

Lessa A, Mendoca de Souza SMF. 2006. Broken noses for the gods: ritual battles in the Atacama Desert during the Tiwanaku period. *Mem. Inst. Oswaldo Cruz*, 101:133–138.

Li T, Etler DA. 1992. New Middle Pleistocene hominid crania from Yunxian in China. *Nature* 357:484–487.

Lieberman P. 1984. *The Biology and Evolution of Language*. Harvard University Press, Cambridge, MA.

Lieberman P. 1991. *Uniquely Human: The Evolution of Speech, Thought, and Selfless Behavior*. Harvard University Press, Cambridge, MA.

Lindee MS. 2000. Genetic disease since 1945. *Nature Reviews Genetics* 1:236–241.

Lindenbaum S. 2001. Kuru, prions, and human affairs: Thinking about epidemics. *Annual Review in Anthropology* 30:363–385.

Livingstone FB. 1958. Anthropological implications of sickle cell gene distribution in West Africa. *American Anthropologist* 60:533–562.

Loomis WF. 1967. Skin-pigment regulation of vitamin D biosynthesis in man. *Science* 157:501–506.

Lordkipanidze D, Jashashvili T, Vekua A, et al. 2007. Postcranial evidence from early *Homo* from Dmanisi, Georgia. *Nature*.

Lovejoy CO. 1978. A biomechanical review of the locomotor diversity of early hominids. In *Early Hominids of Africa* (CJ Jolly, ed.), pp. 403–429. St. Martin's, New York.

Lovejoy CO. 1988. The evolution of human walking. *Scientific American* 259:118–125.

Lovejoy CO, Meindl RS. 1985. Ectocranial suture closure: A revised method for the determination of skeletal age at death based on the lateral-anterior sutures. *American Journal of Physical Anthropology Volume* 68:57–66.

Lovejoy CO, Meindl RS, Pryzbeck TR, Mensforth RP. 1985. Chronological metamorphosis of the auricular surface of the ilium: a new method for the determination of adult skeletal age at death. *American Journal of Physical Anthropology* 68:15–28.

Lovejoy OW. 1981. The origin of man. *Science* 211:341–350.

Low BS. 2000. *Why Sex Matters*. Princeton University Press, Princeton, NJ.

Lowe JJ, Walker MJC. 1997. *Reconstructing Quaternary Environments*, 2nd ed. Prentice Hall, Essex, England.

MacDorman MF, Minino AM, Strobino DM, Guyer B. 2002. Annual summary of vital statistics: 2001. *Pediatrics* 110:1037–1052.

Mackintosh NJ. 1998. *IQ and Human Intelligence*. Oxford University Press, Oxford.

MacLatchy L, Gebo D, Kityo R, Pilbeam D. 2000. Postcranial functional morphology of *Morotopithecus bishopi*, with implications for the evolution of modern ape locomotion. *Journal of Human Evolution* 39:159–183.

Maggioncalda AN, Sapolsky RM, Czekala NM. 1999. Reproductive hormone profiles in captive male orangutans: Implications for understanding development arrest. *American Journal of Physical Anthropology* 109:19–32.

Malenky RK, Kuroda S, Vineberg EO, Wrangham RW. 1994. The significance of terrestrial herbaceous foods for bonobos, chimpanzees and gorillas. In *Chimpanzee Cultures* (RW Wrangham, WC McGrew, FB de Waal, PG Heltne, eds.), pp. 59–75. Harvard University Press, Cambridge, MA.

Mandryk C. 1992. Paleoecologist finds corridor ice-free but forbidding. *Mammoth Trumpet March* 1992.

Maples WR, Browning M. 1994. *Dead Men Do Tell Tales*. Broadway Books, New York.

Marcus G. 2004. *The Birth of the Mind*. Basic Books, New York.

Marean C. 1989. Sabertooth cats and their relevance for early hominid diet. *Journal of Human Evolution* 18:559–582.

Marean CW, Assefa Z. 1999. Zooarcheological evidence for the faunal exploitation behavior of Neandertals and early modern humans. *Evolutionary Anthropology* 8:22–37.

Marlowe FW. 2005. Hunter-gatherers in human evolution. *Evolutionary Anthropology* 14:54–67.

Marshack A. 1996. A Middle Paleolithic symbolic composition from the Golan Heights: The earliest known depictive image. *Current Anthropology* 37:357–365.

Martin RD. 1983. Human brain evolution in an ecological context. In *52nd James Arthur Lecture on the Evolution of the Human Brain, 1982*. Columbia University Press, New York.

Martin RD, MacLarnon AM, Phillips JL, Dussubieux L, Williams PR, Dobyns WB. 2006. Comment on "The Brain of LB1, *Homo floresiensis*." *Science* 312:999.

Mascie-Taylor CGN. 1993. The biological anthropology of disease. In *The Anthropology of Disease* (CGN Mascie-Taylor, ed.), pp. 1–72. Oxford University Press, Oxford.

Mascie-Taylor CGN, Bogin B, eds. 1995. *Human Variability and Plasticity*. Cambridge University Press, Cambridge.

Matisoo-Smith E, Roberts RM, Allen JS, et al. 1998. Patterns of prehistoric mobility in Polynesia revealed by mitochondrial DNA from the Pacific rat. *Proceedings of the National Academy of Sciences* 95:15145–15150.

Mayr E. 1942. *Systematics and the Origin of Species*. Columbia University Press, New York.

Mayr E. 1963. *Animal Species and Evolution*. Harvard University Press, Cambridge, MA.

Mayr E. 1983. How to carry out the adaptationist program. *American Naturalist* 121:324–334.

Mazurek R. 1999. Back from the dead. *New Scientist* 164:40.

McBrearty S, Brooks AS. 2000. The revolution that wasn't: A new interpretation of the origin of modern human behavior. *Journal of Human Evolution* 39:453–563.

McBrearty S, Jablonski NG. 2005. First fossil chimpanzee. *Nature* 437:105–108.

McCollum MA. 2007/2008. Nasomaxillary remodeling and facial form in robust Australopithecus: a reassessment. *Journal of Human Evolution*, In Press, Corrected Proof, Available online 10 September 2007.

McCracken RD. 1971. Lactase deficiency: An example of dietary evolution. *Current Anthropology* 12:479–517.

McCrossin ML, Benefit BR. 1993. Recently recovered *Kenyapithecus* mandible and its implications for great ape and human origins. *Proceedings of the National Academy of Sciences USA* 90:1962–1966.

McDougall I. 1985. K–Ar and ^{40}Ar/^{39}Ar dating of the hominid-bearing Pliocene–Pleistocene sequence at Koobi Fora, Lake Turkana, northern Kenya. *Geological Society America Bulletin* 96:159–175.

McFadden et al. 1999. Global ecology and biogeography Journal of 8:137–149.

McGrew WC. 1992. *Chimpanzee Material Culture*. Cambridge University Press, Cambridge.

McHenry HM. 1991. Sexual dimorphism in *Australopithecus afarensis*. *Journal of Human Evolution* 20:21–32.

McHenry HM. 1992. Body size and proportions in early hominids. *American Journal of Physical Anthropology* 87:407–431.

McHenry HM. 1994. Behavioral ecological implications of early hominid body size. *Journal of Human Evolution* 27:77–87.

McHenry HM, Coffing K. 2000. *Australopithecus* to *Homo*: Transformations in body and mind. *Annual Review of Anthropology* 29:125–146.

McKern TW, Stewart TD. 1957. Skeletal age changes in young American male. The United States of America Army Quartermaster Research and Development Command, Technical Report EP-45, Natick, Massachusetts.

McKusick VA, Eldridge R, Hostetler JA, Egeland JA. 1964. Dwarfism in the Amish. *Transactions of the Association of American Physicians, Philadelphia* 77:151–168.

Meehan JP. 1955. Individual and racial variations in vascular response to cold stimulus. *Military Medicine* 116:330–334.

Meier B, Albibnac R, Peyrieras A, et al. 1987. A new species of Hapalemur (Primates) from South East Madagascar. *Folia Primatologica* 48:211–215.

Meindl RS. 1987. Hypothesis: A selective advantage for cystic fibrosis heterozygotes. *American Journal of Physical Anthropology* 74:39–45.

Melnick D, Hoelzer GA. 1996. Genetic consequences of macaque social organization and behavior. In *Evolution and Ecology of Macaque Societies* (JE Fa, DG Lindburg, eds.), pp. 412–442. Cambridge University Press, Cambridge.

Mendel G. 1866. Versuche über Pflanzenhybriden [Experiments in plant hybridization]. *Verhandlungen des Naturforschenden Vereines in Brünn, Bd. IV für das Jahr 1865*, 3–47.

Menzel CR. 1991. Cognitive aspects of foraging in Japanese monkeys. *Animal Behaviour* 41:397–402.

Mettler LE, Gregg TG, Schaffer HE. 1988. *Population Genetics and Evolution*. Prentice Hall, Upper Saddle River, NJ.

Meyer D, Thomson G. 2001. How selection shapes variation of the human major histocompatibility complex: A review. *Annals of Human Genetics* 65:1–26.

Milton K. 1980. *The Foraging Strategy of Howler Monkeys: A Study in Primate Economics*. Columbia University Press, New York.

Milton K. 1981. Distribution patterns of tropical food plants as a stimulus to primate mental development. *American Anthropologist* 83:534–548.

Milton K. 1982. Dietary quality and demographic regulation in a howler monkey population. In *The Ecology of a Tropical Forest* (EG Leigh, AS Rand, DM Windsor, eds.), pp. 273–289. Smithsonian Institution Press, Washington, DC.

Milton K. 1999. A hypothesis to explain the role of meat-eating in human evolution. *Evolutionary Anthropology* 8:11–21.

Mitani JC. 1985. Responses of gibbons (*Hylobates muelleri*) to self, neighbor and stranger song duets. *International Journal of Primatology* 6:193–200.

Mitani JC, Gros-Louis J, Manson JH. 1996. Number of males in *American Journal of Primatology* 38:315–332.

Mitchell RJ, Hammer MF. 1996. Human evolution and the Y chromosome. *Current Opinion in Genetics and Development* 6:737–742.

Mithen S. 1996. *The Prehistory of the Mind.* Thames and Hudson, London.

Mittermeier RA, Konstant WR, Rylands AB. 2002. Priorities for primate conservation in the first decade of the 21st century. XIXth Congress of International Primatological Society, Beijing, China (abstract).

Molnar S. 2002. *Human Variation,* 5th ed. Prentice Hall, Upper Saddle River, NJ.

Morwood MJ, Soejono RP, Roberts RG, et al. 2004. Archaeology and age of a new hominin from Flores in eastern Indonesia. *Nature 431*:1087–1091.

Moran EF. 2000. *Human Adaptability,* 2nd ed. Westview Press, Boulder, CO.

Moyà-Solà S, Kohler M. 1996. The first *Dryopithecus* skeleton: Origins of great ape locomotion. *Nature 379*:156–159.

Moyà-Solà S, Kohler M, Alba DM, Cassanovas-vilar I, Galindo J. 2004. *Pierolapithecus catalunicus* a new Middle Miocene great ape from Spain. *Science 306*:1339–1344.

Mullis K. 1990. The unusual origins of the polymerase chain reaction. *Scientific American* April:56–65.

Murphy J. 1976. Psychiatric labeling in cross-cultural perspective. *Science* 191:1019–1028.

Murray FG. 1934. Pigmentation, sunlight, and nutritional disease. *American Anthropologist* 36:438–445.

Myrianthopoulos NC, Aronson SM. 1966. Population dynamics of Tay–Sachs disease. I. Reproductive fitness and selection. *American Journal of Human Genetics* 18:313–327.

Nafte M. 2000) *Flesh and Bone: An Introduction to Forensic Anthropology.* Carolina Academic Press, Durham, NC.

Neel JV. 1962. Diabetes mellitus: A thrifty genotype rendered detrimental by "progress"? *American Journal of Human Genetics* 14:353–362.

Neel JV. 1982. The thrifty genotype revisited. In *The Genetics of Diabetes Mellitus* (J Kobberling, R Tattersall, eds.), pp. 283–293. Academic Press, London.

Nesse RM. 2000. Is depression an adaptation? *Archives of General Psychiatry* 57:14–20.

Nesse RM, Berridge KC. 1997. Psychoactive drug use in evolutionary perspective. *Science* 278:63–66.

Nesse RM, Williams GC. 1994. *Why We Get Sick: The New Science of Darwinian Medicine.* Times Books, New York.

Newman RW, Munroe EH. 1955. The relation of climate and body size in U.S. males. *American Journal of Physical Anthropology* 13:1–17.

Newton PN. 1987. The variable social organization of Hanuman langurs (*Presbytis entellus*), infanticide, and the monopolization of females. *International Journal of Primatology* 9:59–77.

Nichter M, Ritenbaugh C, Nichter M, Vuckovic N, Aickin M. 1995. Dieting and "watching" behaviors among adolescent females: Report of a multimethod study. *Journal of Adolescent Health* 17:153–162.

Nielsen S. 2001. Epidemiology and mortality of eating disorders. *Psychiatric Clinics of North America* 24:201–214.

Nimgaonkar VL, Ward SE, Agarde H, et al. 1997. Fertility in schizophrenia: Results from a contemporary US cohort. *Acta Psychiatrica Scandinavica* 95:364–369.

Nishida T. 1990. *The Chimpanzees of the Mahale Mountains.* University of Tokyo Press, Tokyo.

Njau JK, Blumenschine RJ. 2006. A diagnosis of crocodile feeding traces on larger mammal bone, with fossil examples from the Plio-Pleistocene Olduvai Basin, Tanzania. *Journal of Human Evolution 50*:142–162.

Noble W, Davidson I. 1996. *Human Evolution, Language and Mind.* Cambridge University Press, Cambridge.

Nolte J. 2002. *The Human Brain: An Introduction to Its Functional Anatomy,* 5th ed. Mosby, St. Louis.

Noonan JP, Coop G, Kudaravalli S, et al. 2006. Sequencing and analysis of Neanderthal genomic DNA. *Science* 314:1113–1118.

Nordborg M. 1998. On the probability of Neanderthal ancestry. *American Journal of Human Genetics* 63:1237–1240.

Oakley K. 1963. Analytical methods of dating bones. In *Science in Archaeology* (D Brothwell, E Higgs, eds.). Basic Books, New York.

O'Connor CF, Franciscus RG, Holton NE. 2004. Bite force production capability and efficiency in Neandertals and modern humans. *American J. Physical Anthropology* 127:129–151.

Ogonuki N, Inoue K, Yamamoto Y, et al. 2002. Early death of mice cloned from somatic cells. *Nature Genetics* 30:253–254.

Orlando L, Darlu P, Toussaint M, Bonjean D, Otte M, Hänni C. 2006. Revisiting Neandertal diversity with a 100,000 year old mtDNA sequence. *Curr. Biol. 16*:R400

Ovchinnikov IV, Götherström A, Romanova GP, et al. 2000. Molecular analysis of Neanderthal DNA from the northern Caucasus. *Nature* 404:490–493.

Overall ADJ, Ahmad M, Nichols RA. 2002. The effect of reproductive compensation on recessive disorders within consanguineous human populations. *Heredity* 88:474-479.

Palombit RA. 1994. Extra-pair copulations in a monogamous ape. *Animal Behaviour* 47:721–723.

Panter-Brick C. 2002. Sexual division of labor: Energetic and evolutionary scenarios. *American Journal of Human Biology* 14:627–640.

Parish AR. 1996. Female relationships in bonobos (*Pan paniscus*). *Human Nature* 7:61–96.

Parra EJ, Marcini A, Akey J, et al. 1998. Estimating African American admixture proportions by use of population-specific alleles. *American Journal of Human Genetics* 63:1839–1851.

Paterson HEH. 1986. Environment and species. *South African Journal of Science* 82:62–65.

Paterson JD. 1996. Coming to America: Acclimation in macaque body structures and Bergmann's rule. *International Journal of Primatology* 17:585–611.

Pearson OM. 2000. Postcranial remains and the origin of modern humans. *Evolutionary Anthropology* 9:229–247.

Peccei JS. 2001a. A critique of the grandmother hypothesis: Old and new. *American Journal of Human Biology* 13:434–452.

Peccei JS. 2001b. Menopause: Adaptation or epiphenomenon? *Evolutionary Anthropology* 10:43–57.

Peretz I. 2006. The nature of music from a biological perspective. *Cognition* 100:1–32.

Perusse L, Rankinen T, Zuberi A, Chagnon YC, Weisnagel SJ, Argyropoulos G, Walts B, Snyder EE, Bouchard C. 2005. The human obesity map: The 2004 update. *Obesity Research* 13:381–490.

Petitto LA, Marentette PF. 1991. Babbling in the manual mode: Evidence for the ontogeny of language. *Science* 251:1493–1496.

Pickford M, Senut B. 2001. "Millennium Ancestor," a 6-millionyear-old bipedal hominid from Kenya: Recent discoveries push back human origins by 1.5 million years. *South African Journal of Science* 97:2–22.

Pilbeam D. 1982. New hominoid skull material from the Miocene of Pakistan. *Nature* 295:232–234.

Polimeni J, Reiss JP. 2003. Evolutionary perspectives on schizophrenia. *Canadian Journal of Psychiatry* 48:34–39.

Poole J. 1996. *Coming of Age With Elephants: A Memoir.* New York: Hyperion.

Porter AMW. 1995. Analyses of measurements taken from adult femurs of a British population. *International Journal of Osteoarchaeology* 5:305–323.

Potts R. 1984. Home bases and early hominids. *American Scientist* 72:338–347.

Potts R. 1988. *Early Hominid Activities at Olduvai.* Aldine, Chicago.

Potts R. 1996. *Humanity's Descent: The Consequences of Ecological Instability.* New York: William Morrow.

Potts R, Behrensmeyer AK, Deino A, Ditchfield P, Clark J. 2004. Small mid-Pleistocene hominin associated with East African acheulean technology. *Science 305:*75–78.

Pritzker BM. 2000. *A Native American Encyclopedia.* Oxford University Press, New York.

Pusey A, Williams J, Goodall J. 1997. The influence of dominance rank on the reproductive success of female chimpanzees. *Science* 277:828–831.

Rak Y, Kimbel WH, Hovers E. 1994. A Neandertal infant from Amucd Cave, Israel. *Journal of Human Evolution* 26:313–324.

Rasmussen DT. 2002. The origin of primates. In *The Primate Fossil Record* (WC Hartwig, ed.), pp. 5–9. Cambridge University Press, Cambridge.

Ratjen F, Döring G. 2003. Cystic fibrosis. *Lancet* 361:681–689.

Reed KE. 1997. Early hominid evolution and ecological change through the African Plio-Pleistocene. *Journal of Human Evolution* 32:289–322.

Reed TE. 1969. Caucasian genes in American Negroes. *Science* 165:762–768.

Relethford JH. 2001. Absence of regional affinities of Neandertal DNA with living humans does not reject multiregional evolution. *American Journal of Physical Anthropology* 115:95–98.

Remis MJ. 1997a. Ranging and grouping patterns of a western lowland gorilla group at Bai Hokou, Central African Republic. *American Journal of Primatology* 43:111–133.

Remis MJ. 1997b. Western lowland gorillas (*Gorilla gorilla gorilla*) as seasonal frugivores: Use of variable resources. *American Journal of Primatology* 43:87–109.

Richard A. 1992. Aggressive competition between males, female-controlled polygyny and sexual monomorphism in a Malagasy primate, *Propithecus verreauxi. Journal of Human Evolution* 22:395–406.

Richards MP, Pettitt PB, Stiner MC, Trinkaus E. 2001. Stable isotope evidence for increasing dietary breadth in the European mid–Upper Paleolithic. *Proceedings of the National Academy of Sciences* 98:6528–6532.

Richards MP, Pettitt PB, Trinkaus E, et al. 2000. Neanderthal diet at Vindija and Neanderthal predation: The evidence from stable isotopes. *Proceedings of the National Academy of Sciences* 97:7663–7666.

Richmond BG, Strait DS. 2000. Evidence that humans evolved from a knuckle-walking ancestor. *Nature* 404:382–385.

Rightmire GP. 1990/1993. *The evolution of* Homo crcctus, *comparative anatomical studies of an extinct human species.* New York: Cambridge University Press.

Rightmire GP. 1993. *The Evolution of* Homo erectus, *Comparative Anatomical Studies of an Extinct Human Species.* Cambridge University Press, New York.

Rightmire GP, Deacon HJ. 1991. Comparative studies of Late Pleistocene human remains from Klasies River Mouth, South Africa. *Journal of Human Evolution* 20:131–156.

Rightmire GP, Lordkipanidze D, Vekua A. 2006. Anatomical descriptions, comparative studies and evolutionary significance of the hominin skulls from Dmanisi, Republic of Georgia. *Journal of Human Evolution, 50:* 115–141.

Ristau CA. 1999. Animal language and cognition projects. In *Handbook of Human Symbolic Evolution* (A Lock, CR Peters, eds.), pp. 644–685. Blackwell, Oxford.

Roberts DF. 1978. *Climate and Human Variability.* Cummings, Menlo Park, CA.

Roberts MB, Stringer CB, Parfitt SA. 1994. A hominid tibia from Middle Pleistocene sediments at Boxgrove, U.K. *Nature* 369:311–313.

Robins AH. 1991. *Biological Perspectives on Human Pigmentation.* Cambridge University Press, Cambridge.

Rodman PS, McHenry HM. 1980. Bioenergetics and the origin of hominid bipedalism. *American Journal of Physical Anthropology* 52:103–106.

Rogers T, Saunders S. 1994. Accuracy of sex determination using morphological traits of the human pelvis. *J Forensic Sci.*39:1047–56.

Rollo F, Ermini L, Luciani S, Marota I, Olivieri C, Luisella D. 2006. Fine characterization of the Iceman's mtDNA haplogroup. *American Journal of Physical Anthropology* 130:557–564.

Rosenberg KR, Trevathan WR. 1996. Bipedalism and human birth: The obstetrical dilemma revisited. *Evolutionary Anthropology* 4:161–168.

Rosenberger AL. 2002. Platyrrhine paleontology and systematics: The paradigm shifts. In *The Primate Fossil Record* (WC Hartwig, ed.), pp. 151–159. Cambridge University Press, Cambridge.

Rowe JH. 1965. The Renaissance foundations of anthropology. *American Anthropologist* 67:1–20.

Rowell TE. 1988. Beyond the one-male group. *Behaviour* 104:189–201.

Rudan I, Campbell H. 2004. Five reasons why inbreeding may have considerable effect on post-reproductive human health. *Collegium Antropologicum* 28:943–950.

Ruff CB. 2000. Prediction of body mass from skeletal frame size in elite athletes. *Am. J. Phys. Anthropol.* 113: 507–17

Ruff CB, Larsen CS, Hayes WC. 1984. Structural changes in the femur with the transition to agriculture on the Georgia coast. *American Journal of Physical Anthropology* 64:125–136.

Russell MD. 1987. Bone breakage in the Krapina hominid collection. *American Journal of Physical Anthropology* 72:373–379.

Ruvolo M. 1997. Molecular phylogeny of the hominoids: Inferences from multiple independent DNA sequence data sets. *Molecular Biology and Evolution* 14:248–265.

Ryan MJ. 1990. Sexual selection, sensory systems, and sensory exploitation. *Oxford Surveys in Evolutionary Biology* 7:156–195.

Ryan T, Krovitz G. 2006.Trabecular bone ontogeny in the human proximal femur *Journal of Human Evolution, Volume* 51:591–602.

Salo WL, Aufderheide AC, Buikstra J, Holcomb TA. 1994. Identification of Mycobacterium tuberculosis DNA in a Pre-Columbian Peruvian Mummy. *PNAS 91:* 2091–2094.

Sabater-Pi J, Bermejo M, Ilera G, Vea JJ. 1993. Behavior of bonobos (*Pan paniscus*) following their capture of monkeys in Zaïre. *International Journal of Primatology* 14:797–804.

Sarich VM, Wilson AC. 1967. Immunological time scale for hominid evolution. *Science* 158:1200–1203.

Sauther ML. 2002. Group size effects on predation sensitive foraging in wild ring-tailed lemurs (*Lemur catta*). In *Eat or Be Eaten: Predation Sensitive Foraging among Primates* (LE Miller, ed.), pp. 107–125. Cambridge University Press, Cambridge.

Sauther ML, Sussman RW, Gould L. 1999. The socioecology of the ringtailed lemur: Thirty-five years of research. *Evolutionary Anthropology* 8:120–132.

Savage-Rumbaugh S, Lewin R. 1994. *Kanzi: The Ape at the Brink of the Human Mind*. New York: Wiley.

Savage-Rumbaugh S, Rumbaugh D. 1993. The emergence of language. In *Tools, Language, and Cognition in Human Evolution* (KR Gibson, T Ingold, eds.), pp. 86–108. Cambridge University Press, Cambridge.

Savage-Rumbaugh S, Shanker SG, Taylor TJ. 1998. *Apes, Language, and the Human Mind*. Oxford University Press, New York.

Sawada J, Kondo O, Nara T, Dodo Y, Akazawa T. 2004. Bone histomorphology of the Dederiyeh Neanderthal child. *Anthropological Science* 112:247–256.

Schaaffhausen H. 1858. Zur Kentiss der ältesten Rassenschädel. *Archiv für Anatomie* 5:453–488.

Schell L. 1991. Pollution and human growth: Lead, noise, polychlorobiphenyl compounds and toxic wastes. In *Applications of Biological Anthropology to Human Affairs* (CGN Mascie-Taylor, GW Lasker, eds.), pp. 83–116. Cambridge University Press, Cambridge.

Schell L. 1995. Human biological adaptability with special emphasis on plasticity: History, development and problems for future research. In *Human Variability and Plasticity* (CGN Mascie-Taylor, B Bogin, eds.), pp. 213–237. Cambridge University Press, Cambridge.

Schell LM, Hills EA. 2002. Polluted environments as extreme environments. In *Human Growth from Conception to Maturity* (G Gilli, LM Schell, L Benso, eds.), pp. 249–261. Smith-Gordon, London.

Schick K, Toth N. 1993. *Making Silent Stones Speak: Human Evolution and the Dawn of Technology*. Simon & Schuster, New York.

Schlaug G. 2001. The brain of musicians. A model for functional and structural adaptation. *Annals of the New York Academy of Sciences* 930:281–299.

Schlaug G, Jäncke L, Huang Y, Staiger JF, Steinmetz H. 1995. Increased corpus callosum size in musicians. *Neuropsychologia* 33:1047–1055.

Schoenemann PT. 1999. Syntax as an emergent characteristic of the evolution of semantic complexity. *Mind and Machines* 9:309–346.

Schoenemann T, Allen JS. 2006. Scaling of body and brain weight within modern and fossil hominids: Implications for the Flores specimen. *American Journal of Physical Anthropology* 129 S42:159–160.

Schoetensack O. 1908. *Der unterkiefer des* Homo heidelbergensis *aus den Sanden von Mauer bei Heidelberg*. W. Engelmann, Leipzig.

Schultz AH. 1969. *The Life of Primates*. Universe Books, New York.

Schulz R, Salthouse T. 1999. *Adult Development and Aging: Myths and Emerging Realities*. Prentice Hall, Upper Saddle River, NJ.

Schuman LM. 1953. Epidemiology of frostbite: Korea. In *Cold Injury: Korea 1951–52*, pp. 205–568. Army Medical Research Laboratory Report 113, Ft. Knox.

Segerstråle U. 2000. *Defenders of the Truth: The Battle for Science in the Sociobiology Debate*. Oxford University Press, New York.

Seiffert E, Simons E, Clyde W, Rossie J, Attia Y, Bown T, Chatrath P, Mathison M. 2005. Basal Anthropoids from Egypt and the Antiquity of Africa's Higher Primate Radiation. *Science* 310:300.

Seiffert ER, Simons EL, Attia Y. 2003. Fossil evidence for an ancient divergence of lorises and galagos. *Nature* 422:421–424.

Serre D, Langaney A, Chech M, et al. 2004. No evidence of Neandertal mtDNA contribution to early modern humans. *PLoS Biology* 2:E57.

Seymour RM, Allan MJ, Pomiankowski A, Gustafsson K. 2004. Evolution of the human ABO polymorphism by two complementary selective pressures. *Proceedings of the Royal Society of London B.* 22:1065–1072 Vol. 22: 1065–1072.

Shen G, Wang J. 2000. Chronological studies on Chinese middle–late Pleistocene hominid sites, actualities and prospects. *Acta Anthropologica Sinica* 19(suppl.):279–284.

Shen G, Wang W, Wang Q, et al. 2002. U-series dating of Liujiang hominid site in Guangxi, southern China. *Journal of Human Evolution* 43:817–829.

Shepher J. 1983. *Incest: A Biosocial View*. Academic Press, New York.

Sherman PW. 1977. Nepotism and the evolution of alarm calls. *Science* 197:1246–1253.

Sherwood RJ, Meindl RS, Robinson HB, May RL. 2000. Fetal age: Methods of estimation and effects of pathology. *Am. J. Phys. Anthropol.* 113:305–315.

Shipman P. 1981. *Life History of a Fossil*. Harvard University Press, Cambridge, MA.

Shipman P. 1986. Scavenging or hunting in early hominids. *American Anthropologist* 88:27–43.

Shipman P. 2001. *The Man Who Found the Missing Link*. Harvard University Press, Cambridge, MA.

Shipman P, Rose J. 1983. Evidence of butchery and hominid activities at Torralba and Ambrona. *Journal of Archaeological Science* 10:475–482.

Shipman P, Walker A. 1989. The costs of becoming a predator. *Journal of Human Evolution* 18:373–392.

Shriver MD, Kittles RA. 2004. Genetic ancestry and the search for personalized genetic histories. *Nature Reviews Genetics* 5:611–618.

Sibley CG, Ahlquist JE. 1984. The phylogeny of the hominoid primates, as indicated by DNA–DNA hybridization. *Journal of Molecular Evolution* 20:2–15.

Sillen A. 1988. Elemental and isotopic analyses of mammalian fauna from southern Africa and their implications for paleodietary research. *American Journal of Physical Anthropology* 76:49–60.

Simons EL. 1987. New faces of *Aegyptopithecus* from the Oligocene of Egypt. *Journal of Human Evolution* 16:273–290.

Simons EL. 1995. Egyptian Oligocene primates: A review. *Yearbook of Physical Anthropology* 38:199–238.

Simoons FJ. 1970. Primary adult lactose intolerance and the milking habit: A problem in biological and cultural interrelations. 2. A cultural historical hypothesis. *American Journal of Digestive Diseases* 15:695–710.

Simpson GG. 1961. *Principles of Animal Taxonomy*. Columbia University Press, New York.

Small MF. 1989. Female choice in nonhuman primates. *Yearbook of Physical Anthropology* 32:103–127.

Smith EO. 1999. Evolution, substance abuse, and addiction. In *Evolutionary Medicine* (WR Trevathan, EO Smith, JJ McKenna, eds.), pp. 375–406. Oxford University Press, New York.

Smith FH. 1984. Fossil hominids from the Upper Pleistocene of central Europe and the origin of modern Europeans. In *The Origins of Modern Humans* (FH Smith, F Spencer, eds.), pp. 137–210. Alan R. Liss, New York.

Smith MT. 1998. Genetic adaptation. In *Human Adaptation* (GA Harrison, H Morphy, eds.), pp. 1–54. Berg, Oxford.

Smith SS. 1965(1810). *An Essay on the Causes of the Variety of Complexion and Figure in the Human Species.* Belknap Press-Harvard University Press, Cambridge, MA.

Smuts BB. 1985. *Sex and Friendship in Baboons.* Aldine, New York.

Snow CC. 1982. Forensic anthropology. *Annual Review of Anthropology* 11:97–131.

Solecki R. 1971. *Shanidar: The First Flower People.* Knopf, New York.

Solter D. 2000. Mammalian cloning: Advances and limitations. *Nature Reviews: Genetics* 1:199–207.

Sommer V. 1994. Infanticide among the langurs of Jodhpur: Testing the sexual selection hypothesis with a long-term record. In *Infanticide and Parental Care* (S Parmigiani, F vom Saal, eds.), pp. 155–198. Harwood Academic Publishers, London.

Sommer V, Reichard U. 2000. Rethinking monogamy: the gibbon case. In *Primate Males: Causes and Consequences of Variation in Group Composition* (PM Kappeler, ed.), pp. 159–168. Cambridge University Press, Cambridge.

Sorensen M, Leonard WR. 2001. Neandertal energetics and foraging efficiency. *Journal of Human Evolution* 40:483–495.

Sowell ER, Thompson PM, Holmes CJ, et al. 1999. *In vivo* evidence for post-adolescent brain maturation in frontal and striatal regions. *Nature Neuroscience* 2:859–861.

Sparks CS, Jantz RL. 2002. A reassessment of human cranial plasticity: Boas revisited. *Proceedings of the National Academy of Sciences* 99:14636–14639.

Spencer F. 1990. *Piltdown: A Scientific Forgery.* Oxford University Press.

Spencer F, ed. 1997. *History of Physical Anthropology.* Garland, New York.

Speth JD, Tchernov E. 2001. Neandertal hunting and meat processing in the Near East. In *Meat-Eating and Human Evolution* (CB Stanford, HT Bunn, eds.), pp. 52–72. Oxford University Press, New York.

Spoor F, Hublin JJ, Braun M, Zonneveld F. 2003. The bony labyrinth of Neanderthals. *Journal of Human Evolution* 44:141–165.

Spoor F, Leakey MG, Gathogo PN, et al. 2007. Implications of new early *Homo* fossils from Ileret, East Lake Turkana (Kenya). *Nature* 448:688–691.

Spurdle AB, Jenkins T. 1996. The origins of the Lemba "Black Jews" of southern Africa: Evidence from p12F2 and other Y-chromosome markers. *American Journal of Human Genetics* 59:1126–1133.

Stanford CB. 1998a. *Chimpanzee and Red Colobus: The Ecology of Predator and Prey.* Harvard University Press, Cambridge, MA.

Stanford CB. 1998b. The social behavior of chimpanzees and bonobos: Empirical evidence and shifting assumptions. *Current Anthropology* 39:399–420.

Stanford CB. 1999. *The Hunting Apes.* Princeton University Press, Princeton, NJ.

Stanford CB. 2001. The subspecies concept in primatology: The case of mountain gorillas. *Primates* 42:309–318.

Stanford CB. 2002. Arboreal bipedalism in Bwindi chimpanzees. *American Journal of Physical Anthropology* 119:87–91.

Stanford CB. 2003. *Upright.* Houghton Mifflin, Boston.

Stanford CB, Nkurunungi JB. 2003. Sympatric ecology of chimpanzees and gorillas in Bwindi Impenetrable National Park, Uganda. Diet. *International Journal of Primatology* 24:901–918.

Stanton W. 1960. *The Leopard's Spots: Scientific Attitudes toward Race in America 1815–59.* University of Chicago Press, Chicago.

Steadman DW. 2003. *Hard Evidence: Case Studies in Forensic Anthropology.* Prentice Hall, Upper Saddle River, NJ.

Steegman AT. 2007. Human cold adaptation: An unfinished agenda. *American Journal of Human Biology* 19:218–227.

Steele G, McKern TW. 1969. A method for assessment of maximum long bone length and living stature from fragmentary long bones. *American Journal of Physical Anthropology* 31:215–227.

Steno N. 1669. *De Solido intra Solidum Naturaliter Contento.* Dissertatio Prodromus, Florence.

Stern JT, Susman RL. 1983. The locomotor anatomy of *Australopithecus afarensis. American Journal of Physical Anthropology* 60:279–317.

Sternberg R. 1990. *Metaphors of Mind: Conceptions of the Nature of Intelligence.* Cambridge University Press, Cambridge.

Steudel KL. 1996. Limb morphology, bipedal gait, and the energetics of hominid locomotion. *American Journal of Physical Anthropology* 99:345–355.

Stewart C, Disotell TR. 1998. Primate evolution: in and out of Africa. *Current Biology* 8:R582–R588.

Stewart R, Pryzborski S. 2002. Non-neural adult stem cells: Tools for brain repair? *BioEssays* 24:708–713.

Stine GJ. 2003. *AIDS Update 2003.* Prentice Hall, Upper Saddle River, NJ.

Stinson PG. 1975. Radiology in forensic odontology. *Dent. Radiogr. Photogr.* 48:51–55.

Stocking GW. 1987. *Victorian Anthropology.* The Free Press, New York.

Stringer CB. 1994. Out of Africa: A personal history. In *Origins of Anatomically Modern Humans* (MH Nitecki, DV Nitecki, eds.), pp. 149–172. Plenum, New York.

Stringer CB, Andrews P. 1988. Genetic and fossil evidence for the origin of modern humans. *Science* 239:1263–1268.

Stringer CB, Gamble C. 1993. *In Search of the Neanderthals.* Thames and Hudson, New York.

Stringer CB, Grün R, Schwarcz HP, Goldberg P. 1989. ESR dates for the hominid burial site of Es Skhul in Israel. *Nature* 338:756–758.

Stringer CB, Hublin JJ, Vandermeersch B. 1984. The origin of anatomically modern humans in Western Europe. In *The Origins of Modern Humans* (FH Smith, F Spencer, eds.), pp. 51–136. Alan R. Liss, New York.

Stringer CB, Trinkaus E, Roberts MB, et al. 1998. The Middle Pleistocene human tibia from Boxgrove. *Journal of Human Evolution* 34:509–547.

Strum SC. 1981. Processes and products of change: Baboon predatory behavior at Gilgil, Kenya. In *Omnivorous Primates.* (RSO Harding, G Teleki, eds.), pp. 255–302. Columbia University Press, New York.

Stumpf MPH, Goldstein DB. 2001. Genealogical and evolutionary inference with the human Y chromosome. *Science* 291:1738–1742.

Sullivan RJ, Hagen EH. 2002. Psychotropic substance-seeking: Evolutionary pathology or adaptation? *Addiction* 97:389–400.

Susman R, ed. 1984. *The Pygmy Chimpanzee.* Plenum, New York.

Susman RL, Stern JT, Jungers WL. 1984. Arboreality and bipedality in the Hadar hominids. *Folia Primatologica* 43:113–156.

Sussman RW. 1991. Primate origins and the evolution of angiosperms. *American Journal of Primatology* 23:209–223.

Swisher CC, Curtis GH, Jacob T, et al. 1994. Age of the earliest known hominids in Java, Indonesia. *Science* 263:1118–1121.

Swisher CC III, Rink WJ, Antón SC, et al. 1996. Latest *Homo erectus,* in Java: Potential contemporaneity with *Homo sapiens* in Southeast Asia. *Science* 274:1870–1874.

Sy MS, Gambetti P, Wong BS. 2002. Human prion diseases. *Medical Clinics of North America* 86:551–571.

Symons D. 1979. *The Evolution of Human Sexuality*. Oxford University Press, New York.

Szalay FS. 1975. Where to draw the nonprimate–primate taxonomic boundary. *Folia Primatologia* 23:158–163.

Szalay FS, Delson E. 1979. *Evolutionary History of the Primates*. Academic Press, New York.

Takahata N, Lee SH, Satta Y. 2001. Testing multiregionality of modern human origins. *Molecular Biology and Evolution* 18:172–183.

Tan CL. 1999. Group composition, home range size, and diet of three sympatric bamboo lemur species (genus *Hapalemur*) in Ranomafana National Park, Madagascar. *International Journal of Primatology* 20:547–566.

Tanner JM. 1990. *Fetus into Man* (2nd edition). Harvard University Press, Cambridge, MA.

Tanner NM, Zihlman AL. 1976. Women in evolution part 1: Innovation and selection in human origins. *Signs: Journal of Women, Culture, and Society* 1:585–608.

Tattersall I. 1986. Species recognition in human paleontology. *Journal of Human Evolution* 15:165–175.

Taylor RE. 2000. Fifty years of radiocarbon dating. *American Scientist* 88:60–67.

Taylor A. 2006. Feeding behavior, diet, and the functional consequences of jaw form in orangutans, with implications for the evolution of *Pongo*. *Journal of Human Evolution*, 50: 377–393.

Taylor H, Minger SL. 2005. Regenerative medicine in Parkinson's disease: Generation of mesencephalic dopaminergic cells from embryonic stem cells. *Current Opinion in Biotechnology* 16:487–492.

Templeton AR. 2002. Out of Africa again and again. *Nature* 416:45–51.

Terborgh J. 1983. *Five New World Primates*. Princeton University Press, Princeton, NJ.

Thackray HM, Tifft C. 2001. Fetal alcohol syndrome. *Pediatrics in Review* 22:47–55.

Thieme H. 1997. Lower palaeolithic hunting spears from Germany. *Nature* 385:807–810.

Thornhill NW. 1991. An evolutionary analysis of rules regulating human inbreeding and marriage. *Behavioral and Brain Sciences* 14:247–293.

Thorpe SKS, Holder RL, Crompton RH. 2007. Origin of human bipedalism as an adaptation for locomotion on flexible branches. *Science* 316:1328–1331.

Tobias PV. 1971. *The Brain in Hominid Evolution*. Columbia University Press, New York.

Tocheri M, Orr CM, Larson SG, et al. 2007. The Primitive Wrist of *Homo floresiensis* and Its Implications for Hominin Evolution. *Science* 317:1743–1745.

Todd TW. 1920. Age changes in the pubic bone, 1. The male White pubis. *American Journal of Physical Anthropology*.

Tomasello M, Savage-Rumbaugh S, Kruger A. 1993. Imitative learning of actions on objects by children, chimpanzees and enculturated chimpanzees. *Child Development* 64:1688–1705.

Tooby J, Cosmides L. 2000. Toward mapping the evolved functional organization of mind and brain. In *The New Cognitive Neurosciences*, 2nd ed. (MS Gazzaniga, editor-in-chief), pp. 1167–1178. MIT Press, Cambridge, MA.

Toth N, Schick K, Savage-Rumbaugh S. 1993. *Pan* the tool-maker: Investigations into the stone tool-making and tool using capabilities of a bonobo (*Pan paniscus*). *Journal of Archaeological Science* 20:81–91.

Trainor LJ, Austin CM, Desjardins RN. 2000. Is infant-directed speech prosody a result of the vocal expression of emotion? *Psychological Science* 11:188–195.

Trehub SE, Unyk AM, Trainor LJ. 1993. Maternal singing in cross-cultural perspective. *Infant Behavior and Development* 16:285–295.

Trevathan WR. 1999. Evolutionary obstetrics. In *Evolutionary Medicine* (WR Trevathan, EO Smith, JJ McKenna, eds.), pp. 183–207. Oxford University Press, Oxford.

Trinkaus E. 1983. *The Shanidar Neandertals*. Academic Press, New York.

Trinkaus E. 1995. Neanderthal mortality patterns. *Journal of Archaeological Science* 22:121–142.

Trinkaus E. 2003. Neandertal faces were not long; modern human faces were short. *Proceedings of the National Academy of Sciences* 100:8142–8145.

Trinkaus E, Moldovan O, Milota S, et al. 2003. An early modern human from the Petera cu Oase, Romania. *Proceedings of the National Academy of Sciences* 100:11231–11236.

Trinkaus E, Shipman P. 1992. *The Neandertals*. Vintage Press, New York.

Trotter M. 1970. Estimation of stature from intact long limb bones. In TD Stewart. (Ed.) *Personal Identification in Mass Disasters*. Washington: National Museum Natural History. Pp. 71–83.

Turner CG. 1989. Teeth and prehistory in Asia. *Scientific American* 260:88–91, 94–96.

Turner CG. 1990. Major features of Sundadonty and Sinodonty, including suggestions about East Asian microevolution, population history, and late Pleistocene relationships with Australian aboriginals. *American Journal of Physical Anthropology* 82:295–317.

Tutin CEG. 1996. Ranging and social structure of lowland gorillas in the Lopé Reserve, Gabon. In *Great Ape Societies* (WC McGrew, LF Marchant, T Nishida, eds.), pp. 58–70. Cambridge University Press, Cambridge.

Tuttle RH. 1981. Evolution of hominid bipedalism and prehensile capabilities. *Philosophical Transactions of the Royal Society of London* B 292:89–94.

Ulijaszek SJ, Lofink H. 2006. Obesity in biocultural perspective. *Annual Review in Anthropology* 35:337–360.

Van den Berghe PL. 1983. Human inbreeding avoidance: Culture in nature. *Behavioral and Brain Sciences* 6:91–123.

van Schaik CP, Hörstermann M. 1994. Predation risk and the number of adult males in a primate group: A comparative test. *Behavioral Ecology and Sociobiology* 35:261–272.

van Schaik CP, Monk KR, Yarrow Robertson JM. 2001. Dramatic decline in orang-utan numbers in the Leuser ecosystem, northern Sumatra. *Oryx* 35:14–25.

van Schaik CP, van Hooff JARAM. 1983. On the ultimate causes of primate social systems. *Behaviour* 85:91–117.

Van Valen L. 1976. Ecological species, multispecies, and oaks. *Taxon* 25:233–239.

Vasey N. 1996. Feeding and ranging behavior of red ruffed lemurs (*Varecia variegata rubra*) and white-fronted lemurs (*Lemur fulvus albifrons*). *American Journal of Physical Anthropology* (suppl. 22):234–235.

Venter JC, Adams MD, Myers EW, et al. 2001. The sequence of the human genome. *Science* 291:1304–1351.

Vervaecke H, van Elsacker L, Möhle U, et al. 1999. Inter-menstrual intervals in captive bonobos (*Pan paniscus*). *Primates* 40:283–289.

Videan E, McGrew WC. 2001. Are bonobos (*Pan paniscus*) really more bipedal than chimpanzees (*Pan troglodytes*)? *American Journal of Primatology* 54:233–239.

Von Koenigswald GHR. 1952. *Gigantopithecus blacki* von Koenigswald, a giant fossil hominoid from the Pleistocene of southern China. *Anthropological Papers of the American Museum of Natural History* 43:291–326.

Walker A, Leakey R, eds. 1993. *The Nariokotome* Homo erectus *Skeleton.* Harvard University Press, Cambridge, MA.

Walker AC, Leakey RE, Harris JM, Brown FH. 1986. 2.5-myr *Australopithecus boisei* from west of Lake Turkana, Kenya. *Nature* 322:517–522.

Walker A, Shipman P. 1996. *The Wisdom of the Bones.* Vintage Books, New York.

Walker A, Zimmerman MR, Leakey REF. 1982. A possible case of hypervitaminosis A in *Homo erectus. Nature* 296:248–250.

Walker PL. 1989. Cranial injuries as evidence of violence in prehistoric southern California. *American Journal of Physical Anthropology* 80: 313–323.

Walker PL, Cook DC, Lambert PM. 1997. Skeletal evidence for child abuse: a physical anthropological perspective. *J Forensic Sci.* 42:196–207.

Walker R, Hill K, Kaplan H, McMillan G. 2002. Age-dependency in hunting ability among the Ache of eastern Paraguay. *Journal of Human Evolution* 42:639–657.

Walsh PD, Abernethy KA, Bermejo M, et al. 2003. Catastrophic ape decline in western equatorial Africa. *Nature* 422:611–614.

Walter RC, Aronson JL. 1982. Revisions of K/Ar ages for the Hadar hominid site, Ethiopia. *Nature* 296:122–127.

Ward CV. 1997. Functional anatomy and phylogenetic implications of the hominoid trunk and hindlimb. In *Function, Phylogeny and Fossils: Miocene Hominoid Evolution and Adaptation* (DR Begun, CV Ward, MD Rose, eds.), pp. 101–130. Plenum, New York.

Watts DP. 1989. Infanticide in mountain gorillas: New cases and a reconsideration of the evidence. *Ethology* 81:1–18.

Wayne RK, Leonard JA, Cooper A. 1999. Full of sound and fury: The recent history of ancient DNA. *Annual Review in Ecology and Systematics* 30:457–477.

Weidenreich F. 1943. The skull of *Sinanthropus pekinensis:* A comparative study of a primitive hominid skull. *Palaeontologica Sinica* D10:1–485.

Weiner A. 1988. *The Trobrianders of Papua New Guinea.* Holt, Rinehart, and Winston, New York.

Weiner J. 1994. *The Beak of the Finch.* Vintage Books, New York.

Weiss KM. 2002. Goings on in Mendel's garden. *Evolutionary Anthropology* 11:40–44.

Wertz RC, Wertz DC. 1989. *Lying-In: A History of Childbirth in America.* Yale University Press, New Haven, CT.

Westermarck EA. 1891. *The History of Human Marriage.* Macmillan, New York.

Wheeler PE. 1991. The thermoregulatory advantages of hominid bipedalism in open equatorial environments: The contribution of increased convective heat loss and cutaneous evaporative cooling. *Journal of Human Evolution* 21:107–115.

White R. 2001. Personal ornaments from Grotte du Renne at Arcy-sur-Cure. *Athena Review* 2:41–46.

White TD. 1986. Cut marks on the Bodo cranium: A case of prehistoric defleshing. *American Journal of Physical Anthropology* 69:503–509.

White TD. 1992. *Prehistoric Cannibalism at Mancos 5MTUMR02346.* Princeton: Princeton University Press.

White TD, Asfaw B, DeGusta D, et al. 2003. Pleistocene *Homo sapiens* from Middle Awash, Ethiopia. *Nature* 423:742–747.

White TD, Harris JM. 1977. Suid evolution and correlation of African hominid localities. *Science* 198:13–21.

White TD, Moore RV and Suwa G. 1984. Hadar biostratigraphy. *Journal of Vertebrate Paleontology* 4:575–581.

White TD, Suwa G, Asfaw B. 1994. *Australopithecus ramidus,* a new species of early hominid from Aramis, Ethiopia. *Nature* 371:306–312.

Whiten A, Goodall J, McGrew WC, et al. 1999. Cultures in chimpanzees. *Nature* 399:682–685.

Wiens JJ. 2001. Widespread loss of sexually selected traits: How the peacock lost its spots. *Trends in Ecology and Evolution* 16:517–523.

Wiley A. 1992. Adaptation and the biocultural paradigm in medical anthropology: A critical review. *Medical Anthropology Quarterly* 6:216–236.

Wiley AS. 2004. *An Ecology of High-Altitude Infancy: A Biocultural Perspective.* Cambridge University Press, Cambridge.

Wilkinson C. 2004. *Forensic Facial Reconstruction.* Cambridge: Cambridge University Press.

Willey P, Leach P. 2003. The skull on the lawn: trophies, taphonomy and forensic anthropology. In *Hard Evidence: Case Studies in Forensic Anthropology* (DW Steadman, ed.), pp. 176–188. Prentice Hall, Upper Saddle River, NJ.

Williams DR. 2003. The biomedical challenges of space flight. *Annual Review in Medicine* 54:245–256.

Williams GC. 1957. Pleiotropy, natural selection, and the evolution of senescence. *Evolution* 11:398–411.

Williams GC. 1966. *Adaptation and Natural Selection.* Princeton University Press, Princeton, NJ.

Wilson EO. 1975. *Sociobiology: The New Synthesis.* Harvard University Press, Cambridge, MA.

Wise RJ, Greene J, Buchel C, Scott SK. 1999. Brain regions involved in articulation. *Lancet* 353:1057–1061.

WoldeGabriel G, White TD, Suwa G, et al. 1994. Ecological and temporal placement of early Pliocene hominids at Aramis, Ethiopia. *Nature* 371:330–333.

Wolf AP. 1966. Childhood association, sexual attraction, and the incest taboo: A Chinese case. *American Anthropologist* 68:883–898.

Wolf AP. 1970. Childhood association and sexual attraction: A further test of the Westermarck hypothesis. *American Anthropologist* 72:503–515.

Wolff G, Wienker T, Sander H. 1993. On the genetics of mandibular prognathism: Analysis of large European noble families. *Journal of Medical Genetics* 30:12–16.

Wolpoff MH. 1999. *Paleoanthropology,* 2nd ed. McGraw-Hill, New York.

Wolpoff M, Caspari R. 1997. *Race and Human Evolution.* Westview Press, Boulder, CO.

Wolpoff MH, Senut B, Pickford M, Hawks J. 2002. Paleoanthropology: *Sahelanthropus* or *"Sahelpithecus"? Nature* 419:581–582.

Wolpoff MH, Thorne AG, Smith FH, et al. 1994. Multiregional evolution: A world-wide source for modern human populations. In *Origins of Anatomically Modern Humans* (MH Nitecki, DV Nitecki, eds.), pp. 175–199. Plenum, New York.

Wolpoff MH, Zhi WX, Thorne AG. 1984. Modern *Homo sapiens* origins: A general theory of hominid evolution involving the fossil evidence from east Asia. In *The Origins of Modern Humans* (FH Smith, F Spencer, eds.), pp. 411–484. Alan R. Liss, New York.

Wood B, Collard M. 1999. The changing face of genus *Homo. Evolutionary Anthropology* 8:195–207.

Worthman CM. 1999. Evolutionary perspectives on the onset of puberty. In *Evolutionary Medicine* (WR Trevathan, EO Smith, JJ McKenna, eds.), pp. 135–163. Oxford University Press, Oxford.

Wrangham RW. 1980. An ecological model of female-bonded primate groups. *Behaviour* 75:262–292.

Wrangham RW, Jones JH, Laden G, et al. 1999. Cooking and human origins. *Current Anthropology* 40:567–594.

Wu R, Dong X. 1985. *Homo erectus* in China. In *Palaeoanthropology and Palaeolithic Archaeology in the People's Republic of China* (R Wu, JW Olsen, Eds.), pp. 79–89. Academic Press, New York.

Wu X, Poirer FE. 1995. *Human Evolution in China: A Metric Description of the Fossils and a Review of the Sites.* Oxford University Press, New York.

Wynn TG. 1999. The evolution of tools and symbolic behaviour. In *Handbook of Human Symbolic Evolution* (A Lock, CR Peters, Eds.), pp. 263–287. Blackwell, Oxford.

Wynne-Edwards VC. 1962. *Animal Dispersion in Relation to SocialBehaviour.* Oliver & Boyd, Edinburgh.

Yamashita N. 2002. Diets of two lemur species in different microhabitats in Beza Mahafaly Special Reserve, Madagascar. *InternationalJournal of Primatology* 23:1025–1051.

Yellen JE. 1991. Small mammals: !Kung San utilization and the production of faunal assemblages. *Journal of Anthropological-Research* 10:1–26.

Yule GU. 1902. Mendel's laws and their probable relations to intra-racial heredity. *New Phytologist* 1:193–207, 222–238.

Zahavi A. 1975. Mate selection: A selection for a handicap. *Journal of Theoretical Biology* 53:205–214.

Zatorre RJ. 2003. Absolute pitch: A model for understanding the influence of genes and development on neural and cognitive function. *Nature Neuroscience* 6:692–695.

Zerjal T, Xue Y, Bertorelle G, et al. 2003. The genetic legacy of the Mongols. *American Journal of Human Genetics* 72:717–721.

Zhao Z, Jin L, Fu YX, et al. 2000. Worldwide DNA sequence variation in a 10-kilobase noncoding region on human chromosome 22. *Proceedings of the National Academy of Sciences* 97:11354–11358.

Zhu RX, Potts R, Xie F, et al. 2004. New evidence on the earliest human presence at high northern latitudes in northeast Asia. *Nature* 431:559–562.

Zubenko GS, Hughes HB, Maher BS, et al. 2002. Genetic linkage of region containing the *CREB1* gene to depressive disorders in women from families with recurrent, early-onset, major depression. *American Journal of Medical Genetics* 114:980–987.

Chapter 15: **436**, Susan Kuklin/Science Source /Photo Researchers, Inc.; Zephyr/Photo Researchers, Inc.; **437**, © John Reader/Science Photo Library/Photo Researchers, Inc.; John Karapelou, CMI/Phototake NYC; **439**, Fig. 15.1, John Reader/SPL/Photo Researchers, Inc.; **441**, Fig. 15.3, Jorg & Petra Wegner/Animals Animals/Earth Scenes; Fig. 15. 4, Peter Weinmann/Animals Animals/Earth Scenes; **442**, Table 15.2, Aiello & Dean (1990), Kappelman (1996), and Holloway (1999); **446**, Fig. 15.7, Visuals Unlimited; **447**, Fig. 15.8, Hanna Damasio, M.D.; **448**, Fig. 15.9, Hanna Damasio, M.D.; **452**, Fig. 15.13, Philip Lieberman, *Uniquely Human: The Evolution of Speech, Thought, and Selfless Behavior*, Cambridge, MA: Harvard University Press, 1991. Copyright © 1991 by the President and Fellows of Harvard University. Reprinted by permission of the publisher; **454**, © Cha Young-Jin/ EPA/ CORBIS- NY; Ben Mangor/SuperStock, Inc.; SuperStock; © The Art Archive/ CORBIS- NY; Pictorial Press Ltd./Alamy; **455**, Dr. Robert J. Zatorre, "Absolute Pitch: A Model for Understanding the Influence of Genes and Development on Natural and Cognitive Function," *Nature Neuroscience* 6: 692-697 (2003), Fig. 2; Toby Wales/Lebrecht Music & Arts Photo Library; © 2002-2007 Nature Picture Library; **457**, Fig. A, Yerkes National Primate Research Center; **459**, Fig. 15.16a, EyeWire Collection/Getty Images – Photodisc; Fig. 15.16b, Yang Liu/Corbis/Bettmann.

Chapter 16: **464**, Phillip de Bay/Corbis/Bettmann; CDC/PHIL/Corbis/Bettmann; Geri Engberg/Geri Engberg Photography; **465**, SPL/Photo Researchers, Inc.; Alexandra Brewis, Prof. of Medical Anthropology; Sam Ashfield/Photo Researchers, Inc.; Sheldon Collins/Corbis/Bettmann; Medford Taylor/National Geographic Image Collection; Paul Bricknell © Dorling Kindersley; **466**, Fig. 16.1, Gabe Palmer/Corbis/Bettmann; **469**, Fig. 16.2, National Library of Medicine; Fig. 16.3, Barrett Stinson/The Grand Island Independent/AP Wide World Photos; **472**, Fig. 16.6, Vo Trung Dung/Corbis/Bettmann; **474**, Fig. 16.8, A. H. Schultz, *The Life of Primates*, 1969, © Weidenfeld & Nicholson, a division of the Orion Publishing Group; **475**, Fig. 16.9, B. Bogin, *The Growth of Humanity*, 2001, p.4. This material is used by permission of Wiley-Liss, Inc., a subsidiary of John Wiley & Sons, Inc.; **476**, Fig. 16.10, B. O. Ljung, A. Bergsten-Brucefors, and G. Lindgren, "The Secular Trend in Physical Growth in Sweden," *Annals of Human Biology 1*: 245–246; **477**, Fig. 16.11, sources of data and methods of plotting from J. M. Tanner, "Fetus into Many," and R. J. Rona, A. V. Swan, and D. G. Altman, "Social Factors and Height of Primary Schoolchildren in England and Wales," *Journal of*

Epidemiology and Community Health 32:147–154; **479**, Fig. 16.13a, Corbis/Bettmann; **480**, Fig. 16.13b, Fafael Roa/Corbis/Bettmann; **481**, Fig. 16.14, WHO/National Library of Medicine; **482**, Fig. 16.15a, Sheldon Collins/Corbis/Bettmann; Fig. 16.15b, Martin Harvey/Corbis/Bettmann; Fig. 16.16, WHO/National Library of Medicine; **483**, Fig. A, National Institute of Health; **486**, Fig. 16.19, National Library of Medicine; **489**, Fig. 16.20, Courtesy of Della Collins Cook; Fig. 16.21, National Library of Medicine.

Chapter 17: **492**, Henri Lhote Collection. Musée de l'Homme, Paris, France. © Photograph by Erich Lessing/Art Resource, NY; Guy Sauvage/Photo Researchers, Inc.; Robert Knopes/Omni-Photo Communications, Inc.; **493**, © Angus Beare; Jack Fields/Corbis/Bettmann; **499**, Fig. 17.02, Jack Fields/Corbis/Bettmann; **500**, Fig. 17.4, Corbis/Bettmann; **503**, Fig. 17.7, Cary Wolinsky/Aurora & Quanta Productions Inc.; **506**, Fig. 17.10, William Sallaz/Duomo/Corbis/Bettmann; **508**, Fig. 17.11, Tom Spiegel/Corbis/Bettmann; **509**, Fig. 17.12, Courtesy of Laura-Ann Petitto/Photo by Jeff DeBelle; **510**, Fig. 17.13, Owen Franken/Corbis/Bettmann; **511**, Fig. A, Getty Images/Digital Vision; **512**, Fig. 17.15, Reproduced with permission from Dr. Jane M. Murphy, *Science*: 1976. Copyright © 2006 American Association for the Advancement of Science; **513**, Fig. 17.16a, Peter Turnley/Corbis/ Bettmann; Fig. 17.16b, David Turnley/Corbis/Bettmann; Fig. 17.16c, Shaul Schwarz/Corbis/Bettmann.

Chapter 18: **520**, Dr. Christian Crowder; © Reuters / Diario El Pais / Corbis; Reuters/Rickey Rogers/Corbis/Reuters America LLC; **521**, Dr. Christian Crowder; AP Wide World Photos; Susan C. Antón; **523**, Fig. 18.1, Jeannette Fridie; **524**, Fig. 18.2, Dr. Christian Crowder; Fig. 18.3, Paul Sledzik/National Transportation Safety Board; **525–526**, Fig. 18.4 Dr. Christian Crowder; Fig. 18.6, Susan C. Antón; **527–529**, Figs. 18.7, 18.8, 18.9, 18.11, Karen Ramey Burns, *Forensic Anthropology Training Manual*, 1st edition, Upper Saddle River, NJ: Prentice Hall, p. 89. Reprinted by permission; **531**, Figs. 18.12a and 18.12b, Susan C. Antón; **533**, Fig. 18.13a, Paul Sledzik/National Transportation Safety Board; Fig. 18.13b, Goodenough, *Biology of Humans*, 1st edition, Upper Saddle River, NJ: Prentice Hall, p. 93, Fig. 5.5. Reprinted by permission; **534**, Fig. 18.14, Susan C. Antón; **537**, Fig. A, The Granger Collection, New York; **539**, Fig. 18.15, Alfred Pasieka/Photo Researchers, Inc.; **541**, Figs. 18.16a and 18.16b, Susan C. Antón; **543**, Fig. 18.17, Paul Sledzik/National Transportation Safety Board; **544**, Fig. 18.18, Courtesy Dr. J. Josh Snodgrass.

Note: page numbers followed by *f* denote figures; *t*, tables.